# THE APOCALYPTIC IMAGINATION

# The Apocalyptic Imagination

*An Introduction to Jewish Apocalyptic Literature*

• •

THIRD EDITION

John J. Collins

WILLIAM B. EERDMANS PUBLISHING COMPANY

GRAND RAPIDS, MICHIGAN

First edition published 1984 by Crossroad
Third edition published 2016 by

Wm. B. Eerdmans Publishing Co.
2140 Oak Industrial Drive N.E., Grand Rapids, Michigan 49505

Printed in the United States of America

22  21  20  19  18  17  16       7  6  5  4  3  2  1

**Library of Congress Cataloging-in-Publication Data**
Names: Collins, John J. (John Joseph), 1946- author.
Title: The apocalyptic imagination :
an introduction to Jewish apocalyptic literature / John J. Collins.
Description: THIRD EDITION. |
Grand Rapids, Michigan : Eerdmans Publishing Company, 2016. |
Includes bibliographical references and index.
Identifiers: LCCN 2015033151 | ISBN 9780802872791 (pbk. : alk. paper)
Subjects: LCSH: Apocalyptic literature — History and criticism.
Classification: LCC BS646 .C65 2016 | DDC 229/.913 — dc23
LC record available at http://lccn.loc.gov/2015033151

www.eerdmans.com

*For*
*Jesse Yarbro*
*Sean Ryan*
*and*
*Aidan Michael*

# Contents

vii

# Preface to the Third Edition

More than thirty years have gone by since the first edition of *The Apocalyptic Imagination*, and seventeen since the second edition. In that time there has been a profusion of studies relevant to ancient Jewish apocalypticism. The years around the turn of the millennium saw several major publications, including the three volume *Encyclopedia of Apocalypticism*. The Enoch Seminar, founded by Gabriele Boccaccini, has stimulated discussion of apocalyptic texts, not only those ascribed to Enoch. The Dead Sea Scrolls have now been fully published, and their relevance to apocalypticism has undergone significant revision. There has been a renaissance in the study of the Slavonic apocalypses. The interest in "Empire Studies," especially in New Testament scholarship has brought the political aspect of apocalyptic literature to the fore.

The third edition of *The Apocalyptic Imagination* attempts to take account of these developments. Most obviously, the bibliography has been expanded, but there are also minor changes in every chapter. The main lines of interpretation, however, remain unchanged. The apocalyptic literature is viewed through the lens provided by the discussion of the genre apocalypse in *Semeia* 14, published in 1979.

I am grateful to Michael Thomson of Eerdmans. Without his initiative, this revision and updating would not have taken place.

# *Preface to the Second Edition*

*The Apocalyptic Imagination* was originally published by Crossroad in 1984. For the second edition, notes and bibliography have been updated to 1997, and the text itself has been revised at numerous points along the way. The chapter on Qumran has been completely rewritten, because of the explosion of scholarship on the Dead Sea Scrolls since the full corpus became available in 1991. Early Christianity, which was only discussed in the Epilogue in the first edition, is now the subject of a separate chapter. While this chapter does not pretend to be an adequate treatment of the subject, it is hoped that it at least introduces the reader to the major issues in that area.

I should like to express my gratitude to Daniel Harlow and Michael Thomson and the staff at Eerdmans, for facilitating this edition, and to my graduate assistant Brenda Shaver for her checking the manuscript and preparing the indexes.

*Chicago, Illinois*
*August 1997*

# *Preface to the First Edition*

This volume is the product of more than a decade of study, begun when I was a graduate student at Harvard University. Along the way numerous mentors and friends have informed and corrected my work. Three groups deserve special mention: my teachers at Harvard (Frank M. Cross, Paul D. Hanson, and John Strugnell), the task-force on Forms and Genres of Religious Literature in Late Antiquity, and my colleagues in the Pseudepigrapha Group of the Society of Biblical Literature. Above all my thanks are due to my most constant collaborator, Adela Yarbro Collins. The book is dedicated to our children, who show us how fantastic imagination can be.

I also wish to thank the editors of: *Catholic Biblical Quarterly* for permission to adapt my article "The Apocalyptic Technique: Setting and Function in the Book of the Watchers" (*CBQ* 44 [1982] 91-111); *Journal for the Study of the Old Testament* for permission to adapt my article "Apocalyptic Genre and Mythic Allusions in Daniel" (*JSOT* 21 [1981] 83-100); Eisenbrauns for permission to adapt my article "Patterns of Eschatology at Qumran" (*Traditions in Transformation,* edited by B. Halpern and J. D. Levenson); Scholars Press for permission to adapt my article "The Heavenly Representative: The 'Son of Man' in the Similitudes of Enoch" (from *Ideal Figures in Ancient Judaism,* edited by G. W. E. Nickelsburg and J. J. Collins) and to use material from *Semeia* 14; J. C. B. Mohr, Tübingen, for permission to adapt my article "The Genre Apocalypse in Hellenistic Judaism" (from *Apocalypticism in the Mediterranean World and the Near East,* edited by D. Hellholm).

# Abbreviations

| | |
|---|---|
| AB | Anchor Bible |
| *AJP* | *American Journal of Philology* |
| *ANET* | *Ancient Near Eastern Texts Relating to the Old Testament*, edited by J. B. Pritchard. 3d ed. Princeton: Princeton University Press, 1969. |
| *ANRW* | *Aufstieg und Niedergang der römischen Welt*, edited by W. Haase and H. Temporini. Berlin: de Gruyter. |
| ANTZ | Arbeiten zur neutestamentlichen Theologie und Zeitgeschichte |
| AOAT | Alter Orient und Altes Testament |
| *APOT* | *The Apocrypha and Pseudepigrapha of the Old Testament*, edited by R. H. Charles. 2 vols. Oxford: Clarendon, 1913. |
| *AUSS* | *Andrews University Seminary Studies* |
| AYB | Anchor Yale Bible |
| AYBRL | Anchor Yale Bible Reference Library |
| *BA* | *Biblical Archaeologist* |
| *BASOR* | *Bulletin of the American Schools of Oriental Research* |
| BETL | Bibliotheca ephemeridum theologicarum lovaniensium |
| *Bib* | *Biblica* |
| *BJRL* | *Bulletin of the John Rylands University Library of Manchester* |
| BJS | Brown Judaic Studies |
| BKAT | Biblische Kommentar: Altes Testament |
| *BR* | *Biblical Research* |
| *BSOAS* | *Bulletin of the School of Oriental and African Studies* |
| *BZ* | *Biblische Zeitschrift* |
| BZNW | Beihefte zur *ZNW* |
| *CBQ* | *Catholic Biblical Quarterly* |

xi

| | |
|---|---|
| CBQMS | Catholic Biblical Quarterly Monograph Series |
| CRINT | Compendia rerum iudaicarum ad novum testamentum |
| DJD | Discoveries in the Judaean Desert |
| *DSD* | *Dead Sea Discoveries* |
| *EDSS* | *Encyclopedia of the Dead Sea Scrolls* |
| *EJ* | *Encyclopedia Judaica* |
| FAT | Forschungen zum Alten Testament |
| FOTL | The Forms of Old Testament Literature |
| FRLANT | Forschungen zur Religion und Literatur des Alten und Neuen Testaments |
| HDR | Harvard Dissertations in Religion |
| *HR* | *History of Religions* |
| HSM | Harvard Semitic Monographs |
| *HTR* | *Harvard Theological Review* |
| HTS | Harvard Theological Studies |
| *HUCA* | *Hebrew Union College Annual* |
| *IDBSup* | *The Interpreter's Dictionary of the Bible: Supplementary Volume,* edited by Keith Crim et al. Nashville: Abingdon, 1976. |
| *IEJ* | *Israel Exploration Journal* |
| *Int* | *Interpretation* |
| *JAAR* | *Journal of the American Academy of Religion* |
| *JAJSup* | *Journal of Ancient Judaism Supplements* |
| *JBL* | *Journal of Biblical Literature* |
| *JCS* | *Journal of Cuneiform Studies* |
| *JETS* | *Journal of the Evangelical Theological Society* |
| *JJS* | *Journal of Jewish Studies* |
| *JNES* | *Journal of Near Eastern Studies* |
| *JQR* | *Jewish Quarterly Review* |
| *JRS* | *Journal of Roman Studies* |
| JSHRZ | Jüdische Schriften aus hellenistisch-römischer Zeit |
| *JSJ* | *Journal for the Study of Judaism* |
| *JSJSup* | *Journal for the Study of Judaism Supplements* |
| *JSNT* | *Journal for the Study of the New Testament* |
| JSNTSup | Journal for the Study of the New Testament — Supplement Series |
| *JSOT* | *Journal for the Study of the Old Testament* |
| JSOTSup | Journal for the Study of the Old Testament — Supplement Series |
| *JSP* | *Journal for the Study of the Pseudepigrapha* |

# Abbreviations

| | |
|---|---|
| JSPSup | Journal for the Study of the Pseudepigrapha — Supplement Series |
| *JSS* | *Journal of Semitic Studies* |
| *JTC* | *Journal for Theology and the Church* |
| *JTS* | *Journal of Theological Studies* |
| LCL | Loeb Classical Library |
| LXX | Septuagint |
| MT | Masoretic Text |
| *NTS* | *New Testament Studies* |
| OBO | Orbis Biblicus et Orientalis |
| OTL | Old Testament Library |
| OTM | Old Testament Message |
| *OTP* | *The Old Testament Pseudepigrapha,* ed. J. H. Charlesworth |
| *OTS* | *Oudtestamentische Studien* |
| PVTG | Pseudepigrapha Veteris Testamenti Graece |
| *RB* | *Revue biblique* |
| *RelStudRev* | *Religious Studies Review* |
| *RevQ* | *Revue de Qumrân* |
| *RHR* | *Revue de l'histoire des religions* |
| *RSR* | *Recherches des science religieuse* |
| SBLDS | Society of Biblical Literature Dissertation Series |
| SBLEJL | Society of Biblical Literature Early Judaism and Its Literature |
| SBLMS | Society of Biblical Literature Monograph Series |
| SBLSCS | Society of Biblical Literature Septuagint and Cognate Studies |
| SBT | Studies in Biblical Theology |
| SJLA | Studies in Judaism in Late Antiquity |
| SNTSMS | Society for New Testament Studies Monograph Series |
| STDJ | Studies on the Texts of the Desert of Judah |
| SVTP | Studia in Veteris Testamenti Pseudepigrapha |
| *TDNT* | *Theological Dictionary of the New Testament.* 10 vols. Grand Rapids: Eerdmans, 1964-76. |
| *TLZ* | *Theologische Literaturzeitung* |
| TSAJ | Texte und Studien zum antiken Judentum |
| *USQR* | *Union Seminary Quarterly Review* |
| *VT* | *Vetus Testamentum* |
| VTSup | Vetus Testamentum Supplements |
| WBC | Word Biblical Commentary |
| WMANT | Wissenschaftliche Monographien zum Alten und Neuen Testament |

| WUNT | Wissenschaftliche Untersuchungen zum Neuen Testament |
| ZA | *Zeitschrift für Assyriologie* |
| ZAW | *Zeitschrift für die alttestamentliche Wissenschaft* |
| ZNW | *Zeitschrift für die neutestamentliche Wissenschaft* |
| ZThK | *Zeitschrift für Theologie und Kirche* |

CHAPTER ONE

# The Apocalyptic Genre

Two famous slogans coined by German scholars may serve to illustrate the ambivalent attitudes of modern scholarship toward the apocalyptic literature. The first is Ernst Käsemann's dictum that "apocalyptic was the mother of all Christian theology."[1] The other is the title of Klaus Koch's polemical review of scholarly attitudes, *Ratlos vor der Apokalyptik,* "perplexed" or "embarrassed" by apocalyptic.[2] Both slogans are, of course, deliberately provocative and exaggerated, but each has nonetheless a substantial measure of truth. Apocalyptic ideas undeniably played an important role in the early stages of Christianity and, more broadly, in the Judaism of the time. Yet, as Koch demonstrated, the primary apocalyptic texts have received only sporadic attention and are often avoided or ignored by biblical scholarship.

The perplexity and embarrassment that Koch detected in modern scholarship has in part a theological source. The word "apocalyptic" is popularly associated with fanatical millenarian expectation, and indeed the canonical apocalypses of Daniel and especially John have very often been used by millenarian groups.[3] Theologians of a more rational bent are often reluctant to admit that such material played a formative role in early Christianity. There is consequently a prejudice against the apocalyp-

1. E. Käsemann, "The Beginnings of Christian Theology," *JTC* 6 (1969) 40.
2. K. Koch, *Ratlos vor der Apokalyptik* (Gütersloh: Mohn, 1970); English trans., *The Rediscovery of Apocalyptic* (Naperville, IL: Allenson, 1972).
3. See Amy Johnson Frykholm, "Apocalypticism in Contemporary Christianity," in John J. Collins, ed., *The Oxford Handbook of Apocalyptic Literature* (New York: Oxford, 2014) 441-56; Lorenzo DiTommaso, "Apocalypticism and Popular Culture," ibid., 473-509; Catherine Wessinger, "Apocalypse and Violence," ibid., 422-40.

tic literature which is deeply ingrained in biblical scholarship. The great authorities of the nineteenth century, Julius Wellhausen and Emil Schürer, slighted its value, considering it to be a product of "Late Judaism" which was greatly inferior to the prophets, and this attitude is still widespread today. In his reply to Käsemann, Gerhard Ebeling could say that "according to the prevailing ecclesiastical and theological tradition, supremely also of the Reformation, apocalyptic — I recall only the evaluation of the Revelation of John — is to say the least a suspicious symptom of tendencies towards heresy."[4] Whatever we may decide about the theological value of these writings, it is obvious that a strong theological prejudice can impede the task of historical reconstruction and make it difficult to pay enough attention to the literature to enable us even to understand it at all. It will be well to reserve theological judgment until we have mastered the literature.

Not all the perplexity is theological in origin. In some part it also springs from the semantic confusion engendered by the use of the word "apocalyptic" as a noun. The word has habitually been used to suggest a worldview or a theology which is only vaguely defined but which has often been treated as an entity independent of specific texts.[5] Scholars have gradually come to realize that this "apocalyptic myth" does not always correspond to what we find in actual apocalypses. Koch already distinguished between "apocalypse" as a literary type and "apocalyptic" as a historical movement. More recent scholarship, with some unfortunate exceptions, has abandoned the use of "apocalyptic" as a noun and distinguishes between apocalypse as a literary genre, apocalypticism as a social ideology, and apocalyptic eschatology as a set of ideas and motifs that may also be found in other literary genres and social settings.[6]

---

4. G. Ebeling, "The Ground of Christian Theology," *JTC* 6 (1969) 51.

5. See the comments of R. E. Strum, "Defining the Word 'Apocalyptic': A Problem in Biblical Criticism," in J. Marcus and M. L. Soards, eds., *Apocalyptic and the New Testament* (JSNTSup 24; Sheffield: JSOT, 1989) 37.

6. M. E. Stone, "Lists of Revealed Things in the Apocalyptic Literature," in F. M. Cross et al., eds., *Magnalia Dei: The Mighty Acts of God* (Garden City: Doubleday, 1976) 439-43; idem, "Apocalyptic Literature," in M. E. Stone, ed., *Jewish Writings of the Second Temple Period* (CRINT 2/2; Philadelphia: Fortress, 1984) 392-94; P. D. Hanson, "Apocalypse, Genre," "Apocalypticism," *IDBSup*, 27-34. See the comments of M. A. Knibb, "Prophecy and the Emergence of the Jewish Apocalypses," in R. Coggins et al., eds., *Israel's Prophetic Tradition: Essays in Honour of Peter Ackroyd* (Cambridge: Cambridge University Press, 1982) 160-61. Knibb and Stone prefer a twofold distinction between the apocalypses and apocalyptic eschatology. For the persistent use of "apocalyptic" as a noun see Lester L. Grabbe, "Prophetic and Apocalyptic: Time for New Definitions – and New Thinking," in

These distinctions are helpful in drawing attention to the different things traditionally covered by the term "apocalyptic." The question remains whether or how they are related to each other: Does the use of the literary genre imply a social movement? Or does an apocalypse always contain apocalyptic eschatology? Before we can attempt to answer these questions we must clarify what is meant by each of the terms involved.

## The Genre Apocalypse

The notion that there is a class of writings that may be labeled "apocalyptic" has been generally accepted since Friedrich Lücke published the first comprehensive study of the subject in 1832.[7] Lücke's synthesis was prompted in part by the recent edition of *1 Enoch* by Richard Laurence (who also edited the *Ascension of Isaiah,* which Lücke discussed as a Christian apocalypse). The list of Jewish apocalyptic works included Daniel, *1 Enoch,* 4 Ezra, and the *Sibylline Oracles,* and he adduced this literature as background for the book of Revelation. Subsequent discoveries have enlarged the corpus and modified the profile of the genre: *2* and *3 Baruch, 2 Enoch,* the *Apocalypse of Abraham,* and the *Testament of Abraham* were all published in the later part of the nineteenth century. While there has been inevitable scholarly dispute about the precise relation of this or that work to the genre, there has been general agreement on the corpus of literature that is relevant to the discussion and can be called "apocalyptic" at least in an extended sense.

Most of the works that figure in discussions of the Jewish apocalyptic literature were not explicitly designated as apocalypses in antiquity. The use of the Greek title *apokalypsis* (revelation) as a genre label is not attested in the period before Christianity. The first work introduced as an *apoka-*

---

Lester L. Grabbe and Robert D. Haak, eds., *Knowing the End from Beginning: The Prophetic, the Apocalyptic and their Relationships* (JSPSup 46; London: T & T Clark, 2003) 107-33, and my rejoinder, "Prophecy, Apocalypse and Eschatology: Reflections on the Proposals of Lester Grabbe," ibid., 44-52.

7. F. Lücke, *Versuch einer vollständigen Einleitung in die Offenbarung Johannis und in die gesamte apokalyptische Literatur* (Bonn: Weber, 1832). For the early discussions of apocalyptic literature see J. M. Schmidt, *Die jüdische Apokalyptik* (Neukirchen–Vluyn: Neukirchener Verlag, 1969), and P. D. Hanson, "Prolegomena to the Study of Jewish Apocalyptic," in *Magnalia Dei,* 389-413. A sampling of the older literature can be found in K. Koch and J. M. Schmidt, eds., *Apokalyptik* (Darmstadt: Wissenschaftliche Buchgesellschaft, 1982). Further essays are collected in P. D. Hanson, ed., *Visionaries and Their Apocalypses* (Philadelphia: Fortress, 1983).

*lypsis* is the New Testament book of Revelation, and even there it is not clear whether the word denotes a special class of literature or is used more generally for revelation. Both 2 and 3 *Baruch*, which are usually dated about the end of the first century CE, are introduced as apocalypses in the manuscripts, but the antiquity of the title is open to question. Morton Smith concludes from his review of the subject that "the literary form we call an apocalypse carries that title for the first time in the very late first or early second century A.D. From then on both the title and form were fashionable, at least to the end of the classical period."[8] The subsequent popularity of the title has recently been illustrated by the Cologne Mani Codex, where we read that each one of the forefathers showed his own *apokalypsis* to his elect, and specific mention is made of apocalypses of Adam, Sethel, Enosh, Shem, and Enoch.[9] These apocalypses tell of heavenly ascents. The series concludes with the rapture of Paul to the third heaven.

The ancient usage of the title *apokalypsis* shows that the genre apocalypse is not a purely modern construct, but it also raises a question about the status of early works (including most of the Jewish apocalypses) that do not bear the title. The question is complicated by the fact that some of these works are composite in character and have affinities with more than one genre. The book of Daniel, which juxtaposes tales in chaps. 1–6 and visions in chaps. 7–12, is an obvious example. This problem may be viewed in the light of what Alastair Fowler has called the life and death of literary forms.[10] Fowler distinguishes three phases of generic development. During the first phase "the genre complex assembles, until a formal type emerges." In the second phase the form is used, developed, and adapted consciously. A third phase involves the secondary use of the form — for

8. M. Smith, "On the History of *Apokalyptō* and *Apokalypsis*," in D. Hellholm, ed., *Apocalypticism in the Mediterranean World and the Near East: Proceedings of the International Colloquium on Apocalypticism, Uppsala, August 12-17, 1979* (Tübingen: Mohr Siebeck, 1983) 9-20.

9. R. Cameron and A. J. Dewey, trans., *The Cologne Mani Codex: "Concerning the Origin of His Body"* (Missoula, MT: Scholars Press, 1979) pars. 47-62 (pp. 36-48). The codex dates from the late fourth or early fifth century CE. See the comments of W. Adler, "Introduction," in J. C. VanderKam and W. Adler, eds., *The Jewish Apocalyptic Heritage in Early Christianity* (CRINT 3/4; Assen: Van Gorcum; Minneapolis: Fortress, 1996) 11-12, and D. Frankfurter, "Apocalypses Real and Alleged in the Mani Codex," *Numen* 44 (1997) 60-73, who doubts the existence of these apocalypses.

10. A. Fowler, "The Life and Death of Literary Forms," *New Literary History* 2 (1971) 199-216. The metaphor of life and death suggests too organic a view of forms and genres, but the insight into phases of development remains valid.

example, by ironic inversion or by subordinating it to a new context. In historical reality these phases inevitably overlap, and the lines between them are often blurred. It would seem that the Jewish apocalyptic writings that lack a common title and are often combined with other forms had not yet attained the generic self-consciousness of Fowler's second phase, although the genre complex had already been assembled. We should bear in mind that the production of apocalypses continued long into the Christian era.[11]

The presence or absence of a title cannot, in any case, be regarded as a decisive criterion for identifying a genre. Rather, what is at issue is whether a group of texts share a significant cluster of traits that distinguish them from other works. A systematic analysis of all the literature that has been regarded as "apocalyptic," either in the ancient texts or in modern scholarship, was undertaken by the Society of Biblical Literature Genres Project, and the results were published in *Semeia* 14 (1979).[12] That analysis will serve as our point of departure. The purpose of *Semeia* 14 was to give precision to the traditional category of "apocalyptic literature" by showing the extent and limits of the conformity among the allegedly apocalyptic texts.

The thesis presented in *Semeia* 14 is that a corpus of texts that has been traditionally called "apocalyptic" does indeed share a significant cluster of traits that distinguish it from other works. Specifically, an apocalypse is defined as: *"a genre of revelatory literature with a narrative framework, in which a revelation is mediated by an otherworldly being to a human recipient, disclosing a transcendent reality which is both temporal, insofar as it envisages eschatological salvation, and spatial insofar as it involves another, supernatural world."*

This definition can be shown to apply to various sections of *1 Enoch*, Daniel, 4 Ezra, *2 Baruch, Apocalypse of Abraham, 3 Baruch, 2 Enoch, Testament of Levi* 2–5, the fragmentary *Apocalypse of Zephaniah,* and with some qualification to *Jubilees* and the *Testament of Abraham* (both of which also have strong affinities with other genres). It also applies to a fairly wide body of Christian and Gnostic literature and to some Persian and Greco-Roman material.[13] It is obviously not intended as an adequate

11. VanderKam and Adler, eds., *The Jewish Apocalyptic Heritage;* P. J. Alexander, *The Byzantine Apocalyptic Tradition* (Berkeley: University of California Press, 1989); B. McGinn, *Apocalyptic Spirituality* (New York: Paulist, 1979).

12. J. J. Collins, ed., *Apocalypse: The Morphology of a Genre* (*Semeia* 14; Missoula, MT: Scholars Press, 1979).

13. Analysis of the Christian material in *Semeia* 14 was contributed by Adela Yarbro

description of any one work, but rather indicates what Klaus Koch has called the *Rahmengattung* or generic framework.[14] The analysis in *Semeia* 14 differs, however, from Koch's "preliminary demonstration of the apocalypse as a literary type." Koch listed six typical features: discourse cycles, spiritual turmoils, paraenetic discourses, pseudonymity, mythical imagery, and composite character.[15] He did not claim that these are necessary elements in all apocalypses. In contrast, the definition above is constitutive of all apocalypses and indicates the common core of the genre.[16] More importantly, it constitutes a coherent structure, based on the systematic analysis of form and content.

The form of the apocalypses involves a narrative framework that describes the manner of revelation. The main means of revelation are visions and otherworldly journeys, supplemented by discourse or dialogue and occasionally by a heavenly book. The constant element is the presence of an angel who interprets the vision or serves as guide on the otherworldly journey. This figure indicates that the revelation is not intelligible without supernatural aid. It is out of this world. In all the Jewish apocalypses the human recipient is a venerable figure from the distant past, whose name is used pseudonymously.[17] This device adds to the remoteness and mystery of the revelation. The disposition of the seer before the revelation and his reaction to it typically emphasize human helplessness in the face of the supernatural.

---

Collins, the Gnostic material by F. T. Fallon, the Greco-Roman material by H. W. Attridge, and the rabbinic material by A. J. Saldarini.

14. G. von Rad argued that "apocalyptic" is not a single genre but a "mixtum compositum" of smaller forms; *Theologie des Alten Testaments* (2 vols.; 4th ed.; Munich: Kaiser, 1965) 2:330. It is true that any apocalypse contains several subsidiary forms — visions, prayers, exhortations, etc. This fact cannot preclude the presence of a generic framework that holds these elements together. In the case of a composite work like Daniel we can still claim that the apocalypse is the dominant form of the book. For discussion of the subsidiary forms, see J. J. Collins, *Daniel, with an Introduction to Apocalyptic Literature* (FOTL 20; Grand Rapids: Eerdmans, 1984).

15. This list may be regarded as a refinement of the more diverse characteristics of the apocalyptic writings presented and discussed by D. S. Russell, *The Method and Message of Jewish Apocalyptic* (Philadelphia: Westminster, 1964) 104-39.

16. In this respect it also differs from the "family resemblance" approach advocated by J. G. Gammie, "The Classification, Stages of Growth, and Changing Intentions in the Book of Daniel," *JBL* 95 (1976) 192-93. Gammie is correct that a broader corpus of related literature is relevant to the discussion.

17. A few Christian apocalypses, most notably Revelation and *Hermas,* are not pseudonymous.

The content of the apocalypses, as noted, involves both a temporal and a spatial dimension, and the emphasis is distributed differently in different works. Some, such as Daniel, contain an elaborate review of history, presented in the form of a prophecy and culminating in a time of crisis and eschatological upheaval.[18] Others, such as *2 Enoch,* devote most of their text to accounts of the regions traversed in the otherworldly journey. The revelation of a supernatural world and the activity of supernatural beings are essential to all the apocalypses. In all there are also a final judgment and a destruction of the wicked. The eschatology of the apocalypses differs from that of the earlier prophetic books by clearly envisaging retribution beyond death. Paraenesis occupies a prominent place in a few apocalypses (e.g., *2 Enoch, 2 Baruch*), but all the apocalypses have a hortatory aspect, whether or not it is spelled out in explicit exhortations and admonitions.

Within the common framework of the definition, different types of apocalypses may be distinguished. The most obvious distinction is between the "historical" apocalypses such as Daniel and 4 Ezra and the otherworldly journeys. Only one Jewish apocalypse, the *Apocalypse of Abraham,* combines an otherworldly journey with a review of history, and it is relatively late (end of the first century CE). It would seem that there are two strands of tradition in the Jewish apocalypses, one of which is characterized by visions, with an interest in the development of history, while the other is marked by otherworldly journeys with a stronger interest in cosmological speculation.[19] These two strands are interwoven in the Enoch literature. Two of the earliest "historical" apocalypses, the Animal Apocalypse and the Apocalypse of Weeks, are found in *1 Enoch.* These books presuppose the Enoch tradition attested in the Book of the Watchers (*1 Enoch* 1–36) and may in fact presuppose Enoch's otherworldly journey, although they do not describe it. The

---

18. On the apocalyptic treatment of history, see R. G. Hall, *Revealed Histories: Techniques for Ancient Jewish and Christian Historiography* (JSPSup 6; Sheffield: Sheffield Academic Press, 1991) 61-121.

19. M. Himmelfarb, *Tours of Hell: An Apocalyptic Form in Jewish and Christian Literature* (Philadelphia: University of Pennsylvania Press, 1983) 61, takes these as two distinct genres. On the broader Hellenistic and Near Eastern context of the otherworldly journeys, see Jan N. Bremmer, "Descents to Hell and Ascents to Heaven in Apocalyptic Literature," in Collins, ed., *The Oxford Handbook of Apocalyptic Literature,* 340-57, and Richard Bauckham, *The Fate of the Dead: Studies on the Jewish and Christian Apocalypses* (NTSup 93; Leiden: Brill, 1998) 9-48.

Similitudes of Enoch also shows the influence of both strands, although it does not present an overview of history. *1 Enoch* as we now have it is a composite apocalypse embracing different types. Yet we can find an apocalypse such as *4 Ezra* (late first century), which sharply rejects the tradition of heavenly ascent and cosmological speculation, whereas *2 Enoch* and *3 Baruch,* from about the same time, show no interest in the development of history.

Within the otherworldly journeys it is possible to distinguish sub-types according to their eschatology: (a) only the *Apocalypse of Abraham* includes a review of history; (b) several (Book of the Watchers, Astronomical Book, and Similitudes in *1 Enoch; 2 Enoch; Testament of Levi 2–5*) contain some form of public, cosmic, or political eschatology; (c) a number, *3 Baruch, Testament of Abraham,* and *Apocalypse of Zephaniah,* are concerned only with the individual judgment of the dead. No apocalypse of this third subtype is likely to be earlier than the first century CE. The distribution of the temporal and eschatological elements is illustrated in Table 1:

|  | otherworldly journeys | | | | | | | "historical" apocalypses | | | | | | | |
|---|---|---|---|---|---|---|---|---|---|---|---|---|---|---|---|
|  | Apoc. Zephaniah | T. Abraham | 3 Baruch | T. Levi 2–5 | 2 Enoch | Similitudes | Astonomical Book | 1 Enoch 1–36 | Apoc. Abraham | 2 Baruch | 4 Ezra | Jubilees | Apoc. of Weeks | Animal Apocalypse | Daniel |
| Cosmogony |  |  |  |  | • |  |  |  |  | • | • |  |  |  |  |
| Primordial events |  | • |  |  | • |  |  | • | • | • | • |  |  |  |  |
| Recollection of past |  |  |  |  |  |  |  | • | • | • |  |  |  |  | • |
| *Ex eventu* prophecy |  |  |  |  |  |  |  | • | • | • | • |  | • | • | • |
| Persecution |  |  |  |  |  | • |  | • |  | • | • |  |  | • | • |
| Other eschatological upheavals |  |  |  | • |  | • | • | • | • | • | • | • | • | • | • |
| Judgment/destruction of wicked | • | • | • | • | • | • | • | • | • | • | • | • | • | • | • |
| Judgment/destruction of world | ? |  |  |  |  | • |  | ? | • |  | ? | • |  | • |  |
| Judgment/destruction of otherworldly beings |  |  |  |  |  |  | • | • | ? | • |  |  | • | • | • |
| Cosmic transformation |  |  |  | • | • | • | • | • | • | • | • | ? | • | • | • |
| Resurrection |  |  |  |  |  | • |  |  |  | • | • |  | ? | • | • |
| Other forms of afterlife | • | • | ? | • | • | • | • | • | • |  |  |  | • | ? | ? |

[This grid is adapted from *Semeia* 14, p. 28, where a more complete form may be found.]

The study of the genre is designed to clarify particular works by showing both their typical traits and their distinctive elements. It is not intended to construct a metaphysical entity, "apocalyptic" or *Apokalyptik* in any sense independent of the actual texts. The importance of genres, forms, and types for interpretation has been axiomatic in biblical studies since the work of Hermann Gunkel and the rise of form criticism. It is also well established in literary and linguistic theory and in philosophy and hermeneutics.[20] E. D. Hirsch, Jr., a literary critic, has expressed the essential point well.[21] Understanding depends on the listener's or reader's expectations. These expectations are of a type of meaning rather than of a unique meaning "because otherwise the interpreter would have no way of expecting them." Consequently, utterances must conform to typical usages if they are to be intelligible at all. Even the unique aspects of a text (and every text is unique in some respect) can only be understood if they are located relative to conventional signals. As Hirsch has lucidly shown, "the central role of genre concepts in interpretation is most easily grasped when the process of interpretation is going badly, or when it has to undergo revision." An interpreter always begins with an assumption about the genre of a text. If our expectations are fulfilled, the assumptions will need no revision. If they are not fulfilled, we must revise our idea of the genre or relinquish the attempt to understand. There can be no understanding without at least an implicit notion of genre.

The generic framework or *Rahmengattung* indicated in the definition of apocalypse above is important because it involves a conceptual structure or view of the world. It indicates some basic presuppositions about the way the world works, which are shared by all the apocalypses. Specifically, the world is mysterious and revelation must be transmitted from a supernatural source, through the mediation of angels; there is a hidden world of angels and demons that is directly relevant to human destiny; and this destiny is finally determined by a definitive eschatological judgment. In short, human life is bounded in the present by the supernatural world of angels and demons and in the future by the inevitability of a final judgment.[22]

20. L. Hartman, "Survey of the Problem of Apocalyptic Genre," in Hellholm, ed., *Apocalypticism,* 329-43; D. Hellholm, *Das Visionenbuch des Hermas als Apokalypse* (Lund: Gleerup, 1980) 14-95; J. Barton, *Reading the Old Testament: Method in Biblical Study* (2d ed.; Louisville: Westminster, 1996) 8-19; M. Gerhart, "Genre Studies: Their Renewed Importance in Religious and Literary Interpretation," *JAAR* 45 (1977) 309-25.

21. E. D. Hirsch, Jr., *Validity in Interpretation* (New Haven: Yale University Press, 1967) 68-102.

22. For a fuller treatment of the apocalyptic worldview see Stefan Beyerle, *Die*

This conceptual structure already carries some implications for the function of the genre, since it provides a framework for viewing the problems of life. The appeal to supernatural revelation provides a basis for assurance and guidance, and establishes the authority of the text. The prospect of a final judgment creates a context for the clarification of values. The specific problems may vary from one apocalypse to another, and so may the specific guidance and demands. Two apocalypses such as 4 Ezra and 2 Baruch may disagree on particular issues, but their differences are articulated within the framework of shared presuppositions. If we say that a work is apocalyptic we encourage the reader to expect that it frames its message within the view of the world that is characteristic of the genre.

The literary genre apocalypse is not a self-contained isolated entity. The conceptual structure indicated by the genre, which emphasizes the supernatural world and the judgment to come, can also be found in works that are not revelation accounts, and so are not technically apocalypses. So, for example, the Qumran War Scroll is widely and rightly regarded as "apocalyptic" in the extended sense, although it is not presented as a revelation.[23] Furthermore, the generic framework is never the only factor that shapes a text. The visions of Daniel, for example, must be seen in the context not only of the genre but also of the tales in Daniel 1–6 and of the other literature inspired by the persecution of Antiochus Epiphanes. Consequently there is always a corpus of related literature that is relevant in varying degrees to the understanding of a particular text. Any discussion of apocalyptic literature must also take account of oracles and testaments, which parallel the apocalypses (especially the "historical" ones) at many points. In short, the genre, like all genres, has fuzzy edges, and some works may participate in more than one genre.[24] (The Book of Jubilees is a good

---

Gottesvorstellungen in der antik-jüdischen Apokalyptik ( JSJSup 103; Leiden: Brill, 2005); idem, "The Imagined World of the Apocalypses," in Lim and Collins, eds., The Oxford Handbook of the Dead Sea Scrolls, 373-87.

23. See further J. J. Collins, "Genre, Ideology, and Social Movements in Jewish Apocalypticism," in J. J. Collins and J. H. Charlesworth, eds., Mysteries and Revelations: Apocalyptic Studies Since the Uppsala Colloquium ( JSPSup 9; Sheffield: JSOT, 1991) 23-24 (= Collins, Seers, Sibyls, and Sages in Hellenistic-Roman Judaism [Leiden: Brill, 1997] 25-38).

24. See the excellent discussion of genre, with an eye to the genre apocalypse, by Carol A. Newsom, "Spying Out the Land: A Report from Genology," in R. L. Troxel, K. G. Friebel and D. R. Magary, eds., Seeking Out the Wisdom of the Ancients (Winona Lake, IN: Eisenbrauns, 2005) 437-50, and my own comments in "The Genre Apocalypse Reconsidered," in my book, Apocalypse, Prophecy and Pseudepigraphy (Grand Rapids: Eerdmans, 2015) chapter 1.

example, to which we will return in chapter 2.) Yet the definition is important for providing a focus for the discussion and indicating a core to which other literary types may be related.

## Other Views of the Genre

It may be useful to contrast the view of the genre presented here and in *Semeia* 14 with other views that have been recently advocated.[25] At one extreme of the spectrum, Richard Horsley, probably the most prolific writer on the subject of Empire in relation to ancient Judaism and early Christianity, does not recognize a distinct apocalyptic genre, or a distinctive apocalyptic worldview, at all, and finds "no defined boundaries between texts and other cultural expressions previously categorized as either apocalyptic or sapiential."[26] For Horsley, the (only?) important feature of these texts is that they are struggling with oppressive violence by foreign imperial powers, and their religious ideas are to be understood in "down-to-earth" political-economic terms.[27] In a less extreme way, E. P. Sanders has proposed a return to an "essentialist" definition of Jewish apocalypses as a combination of the themes of *revelation* and *reversal* (of the fortunes of a group, either Israel or the righteous).[28] The attractiveness of this proposal lies in the simplicity with which Sanders can then view the social function of the genre as literature of the oppressed. However, the proposal suffers from two crucial disadvantages. First, the combined themes of revelation and reversal are characteristic of the whole tradition of biblical prophecy, as well as of the political oracles of the ancient Near East. Second, it takes no account at all of the cosmological and mystical tendencies in the apocalypses, which have been repeatedly emphasized in a number of studies.[29] It

25. For a wide-ranging review of recent scholarship, see Lorenzo DiTommaso, "Apocalypses and Apocalypticism in Antiquity, Part 1," *Currents in Biblical Research* 5/2 (2007) 235-86.

26. Richard A. Horsley, *Scribes, Visionaries and the Politics of Second Temple Judea* (Louisville: Westminster John Knox, 2007) 4. Compare ibid., 193-206; *Revolt of the Scribes: Resistance and Apocalyptic Origins* (Minneapolis: Fortress, 2010) 193-207; R. A. Horsley and P. A. Tiller, *After Apocalyptic and Wisdom: Rethinking Texts in Context* (Eugene, OR: Cascade, 2012) 10-13.

27. E.g. *Scribes, Visionaries*, 5.

28. E. P. Sanders, "The Genre of Palestinian Jewish Apocalypses," in Hellholm, ed., *Apocalypticism*, 447-59.

29. M. E. Stone, "Lists of Revealed Things"; idem, *Scriptures, Sects, and Visions*

may also be that Sanders's view of the social function is too simple. While several major Jewish apocalypses (especially those of the historical type) can be viewed as literature of the oppressed, this is seldom evident in otherworldly journeys, although the latter type frequently bore the label "apocalypse" in antiquity. In the Middle Ages, we also find apocalypses of the historical type used in support of the empire and the papacy.[30]

In a related vein, some scholars see no difference between apocalypticism and prophecy.[31] Lester Grabbe has argued that apocalypticism should be considered a subdivision of prophecy, and that the differences between, say, Amos and Daniel are no greater than those between Amos and Nahum (or between Daniel and *1 Enoch*).[32] He argues that both prophecy and apocalypticism present themselves as delivering a divine message, presuppose a mythical worldview in which the heavenly world determines what will happen on earth and look forward to an ideal age. He subsumes both, and also "mantic wisdom," under the label of divination. In part, the issue here is the level of abstraction one finds helpful. Both prophecy and apocalypticism are certainly forms of revelation. The question is whether there are still significant differences between the apocalypses of the Hellenistic and early Roman periods and the canonical prophetic writings. I submit that there are.

On the formal level, we seldom find direct inspired speech, which is typical of prophetic oracles, in the apocalypses. There is certainly continuity between the symbolic visions of the prophets and those of the apocalypses, although the latter are more elaborate. But the heavenly journey, which provides the framework for a major subset of apocalypses, has only faint precedents in the prophets. Isaiah describes his vision in the heavenly throne room, but he does not describe how he got there, or what he saw along the way. The greater interest in cosmology in the apocalypses reflects

---

(Philadelphia: Fortress, 1980); I. Gruenwald, *Apocalyptic and Merkavah Mysticism* (Leiden: Brill, 1980); C. Rowland, *The Open Heaven: A Study of Apocalyptic in Judaism and Early Christianity* (New York: Crossroad, 1982); M. Himmelfarb, *Ascent to Heaven in Jewish and Christian Apocalypses* (New York: Oxford University Press, 1993).

30. B. McGinn, *Visions of the End* (New York: Columbia University Press, 1979) 33-36.

31. John Barton famously wrote that "the 'transition from prophecy to apocalyptic' is the title of a process that never occurred" (*Oracles of God: Perceptions of Ancient Prophecy in Israel after the Exile* (Oxford and New York: Oxford University Press, 1986) 200.

32. Lester L. Grabbe, "Introduction and Overview," in Grabbe and Haak, ed., *Knowing the End from the Beginning*, 2-43, especially 22-24; "Prophetic and Apocalyptic: Time for New Definitions and New Thinking," ibid., 107-33.

a shift in emphasis from the auditory reception of the message to a quest for broader understanding that is more akin to wisdom than to classical prophecy. This is not to say that there is no formal continuity at all: there obviously is continuity in the case of symbolic visions. But the differences are considerable, and nothing is gained by overlooking them.

At the other extreme, a number of scholars have argued that definitions of "apocalypse" or "apocalyptic" should make no mention of eschatology.[33] So an apocalypse might be defined simply as a revelation of heavenly mysteries.[34] Such a definition is unobjectionable as far as it goes. It would of course cover a much wider corpus than the definition given above, but it is certainly accurate for all apocalypses. If one wishes to give a more descriptive definition of the literature that has been traditionally regarded as apocalyptic, then the question arises whether some revelations of heavenly mysteries are distinguished from others by their content. The issue here has usually centered on eschatology. It is true that the scholarly literature has been preoccupied with eschatology to a disproportionate degree and that it is by no means the only concern of the apocalypses. Yet an approach that denies the essential role of eschatology is an overreaction and no less one-sided.[35]

Yet another, highly original approach to the apocalyptic genre has been pioneered by Paolo Sacchi, and has been very influential in European scholarship.[36] Sacchi's approach is distinguished by its diachronic

33. Rowland, *The Open Heaven*; J. Carmignac, "Qu'est-ce que l'Apocalyptique? Son emploi à Qumrân," *RevQ* 10 (1979) 3-33; H. Stegemann, "Die Bedeutung der Qumranfunde für die Erforschung der Apokalyptik," in Hellholm, ed., *Apocalypticism,* 495-530; C. H. T. Fletcher-Louis, "Jewish Apocalyptic and Apocalypticism," in S. E. Porter and T. Holmén, eds., *The Handbook of the Study of the Historical Jesus* (4 vols.; Leiden: Brill, 2011), 1569-1607.

34. Compare Rowland, *The Open Heaven,* 14: "To speak of apocalyptic, therefore, is to concentrate on the theme of the direct communication of the heavenly mysteries in all their diversity." Rowland later (p. 50) posits a threefold structure of legends, visions, and admonitions, but neither the legends nor the admonitions are consistent features of the genre.

35. C. H. T. Fletcher-Louis, "2 Enoch and the New Perspective on Apocalyptic," in Andrei Orlov and Gabriele Boccaccini, eds., *New Perspectives on 2 Enoch: No Longer Slavonic Only* (Studia Judaeoslavica 4; Leiden: Brill, 2012) 127-28, proposes a "new perspective" on "apocalyptic" that has two conceptual foci. Humanity is made in the image of God, and the structure of the cosmos, and access to its secrets, is defined by the Jewish temple cult. Neither of these foci is consistent in the extant apocalyptic texts.

36. P. Sacchi, *L'apocalittica giudaica e la sua storia* (Brescia: Paideia, 1990); English translation: *Jewish Apocalyptic and Its History* (Sheffield: Sheffield Academic Press, 1997). See G. Boccaccini, "Jewish Apocalyptic Tradition: The Contribution of Italian Scholarship," in Collins and Charlesworth, eds., *Mysteries and Revelations,* 33-50, with bibliography up to 1990.

character. Rather than look for essential characteristics of the corpus as a whole, Sacchi identifies the underlying problem of the oldest apocalypse, which he takes to be the Book of the Watchers, and traces its influence on a developing tradition. The underlying problem is the origin of evil, and the distinctively apocalyptic solution lies in the idea that evil is prior to human will and is the result of an original sin that has irremediably corrupted creation. This motif can be traced clearly in the Enoch corpus and identified in a somewhat different form in 4 Ezra and 2 *Baruch*. F. García Martínez has effectively shown the influence of this trajectory in the Dead Sea Scrolls.[37]

It is to Sacchi's credit that he has highlighted an important motif in apocalyptic literature, especially in the Enochic corpus. But the genre cannot be identified with a single motif or theme, and the early Enoch literature, important though it is, cannot be regarded as normative for all apocalypses. Gabriele Boccaccini has pointed out that by Sacchi's definition, the book of Daniel should not be classified as apocalyptic.[38] Other themes and motifs, including eschatology, are no less important than the origin of evil. Nonetheless, Sacchi has had a salutary impact on the discussion by directing attention to the diachronic development of apocalyptic traditions.

## Apocalyptic Eschatology

The debate over the definition of the genre leads us back to the question of apocalyptic eschatology. The touchstone here must be the kind of eschatology that is found in the apocalypses. Two problems have been raised. First, some have questioned whether the apocalypses exhibit a consistent eschatology.[39] We must bear in mind that as there are different types of apocalypses, there are correspondingly different types of apocalyptic eschatology. The common equation of "apocalyptic" with the scenario of the end of history is based only on the "historical" type like Daniel, and scholars have rightly objected that this is not typical of

37. F. García Martínez, "Les traditions apocalyptiques à Qumrân," in C. Kappler, ed., *Apocalypses et voyages dans l'au-delà* (Paris: Cerf, 1987) 201-35.

38. G. Boccaccini, *Middle Judaism: Jewish Thought 300 BCE to 200 CE* (Minneapolis: Fortress, 1991) 126-60.

39. Rowland, *The Open Heaven*, 29, 71. Fletcher-Louis, "Jewish Apocalyptic and Apocalypticism," 1578-9. J. Carmignac argues that the term "eschatology" is too diffuse to be of any service ("Les Dangers de l'Eschatologie," *NTS* 17 [1971] 365-90).

all apocalypses. All the apocalypses, however, involve a transcendent eschatology that looks for retribution beyond the bounds of history. In some cases *(3 Baruch, Apocalypse of Zephaniah)* this takes the form of the judgment of individuals after death, without reference to the end of history. We should bear in mind that retribution after death is also a crucial component in a "historical" apocalypse like Daniel and constitutes a major difference from the eschatology of the prophets.[40] The fact that apocalyptic eschatology has often been erroneously identified with the "historical" type in the past does not justify the denial that there is any apocalyptic eschatology at all.

Second, neither the judgment of the dead nor even the scenario of the end of history is peculiar to apocalypses: hence the objection that there is no *distinctive* apocalyptic eschatology.[41] Insofar as this objection bears on the definition of the genre, we must note that visions and heavenly journeys are not distinctive either. The genre is not constituted by one or more distinctive themes but by a distinctive combination of elements, all of which are also found elsewhere. A more significant problem arises if we wish to speak of apocalyptic eschatology outside of the apocalypses, for example, in the Gospels or Paul. What is at issue here is the affinity between the eschatological allusions and the scenarios which are found in more elaborate form in the apocalypses. Affinities vary in degree, and, although the label "apocalyptic eschatology" may be helpful in pointing up the implications of some texts, we should always be aware that the adjective is used in an extended sense.

## Apocalypticism

We may now return to the relation between the apocalypses and apocalypticism. Koch's "preliminary demonstration of apocalyptic as a historical movement" singled out eight clusters of motifs: (1) urgent expectation of the end of earthly conditions in the immediate future; (2) the end as a cosmic catastrophe; (3) periodization and determinism; (4) activity of angels and demons; (5) new salvation, paradisal in character; (6) manifestation of the kingdom of God; (7) a mediator with royal functions; (8) the

---

40. J. J. Collins, "Apocalyptic Eschatology as the Transcendence of Death," *CBQ* 36 (1974) 21-43 (= *Seers, Sibyls, and Sages,* 75-98).

41. Rowland, *The Open Heaven,* 29-37, 71.

catchword "glory."[42] Koch does not claim that all these elements are found in every apocalypse, even in his rather limited list, which essentially corresponds to the "historical" apocalypses of *Semeia* 14. It is apparent, however, that these characteristics do not correspond at all to an apocalypse like 2 *Enoch* and that they ignore much of the speculative material that is prominent even in the earliest works of the Enoch tradition. So Michael Stone has argued that "there are some of the books which are conventionally regarded as apocalypses which are for all practical purposes devoid of apocalypticism" and that "truly apocalyptic apocalypses are the exception rather than the rule."[43] Hence he concludes that a clear distinction must be maintained between apocalypses and apocalypticism.

It is obvious that there are indeed distinctions to be made, but to speak of apocalypses that are not apocalyptic can only compound the semantic confusion. We may begin by clarifying the valid distinctions and then try to sort out the terminology. Insofar as apocalypticism is a historical movement or "refers to the symbolic universe in which an apocalyptic movement codifies its identity and interpretation of reality,"[44] it is not simply identical with the content of apocalypses. There are apocalypses that are not the product of a movement in any meaningful sense. Equally, there are movements, such as the sect of the Dead Sea Scrolls and early (pre–70 CE) Christianity, that did not produce apocalypses but are nonetheless commonly regarded as apocalyptic. The question remains, however, when a movement can appropriately be called apocalyptic. Since the adjective "apocalyptic" and the noun "apocalypticism" are derived from "apocalypse," it is only reasonable to expect that they indicate some analogy with the apocalypses. A movement might reasonably be called apocalyptic if it shared the conceptual framework of the genre, endorsing a worldview in which supernatural revelation, the heavenly world, and eschatological judgment played essential parts. Arguably, both the sectarian Scrolls and early Christianity are apocalyptic in this sense, quite apart from the production of apocalypses. We should remember, however, that the argument depends on analogy with the apocalypses and that the affinity is always a matter of degree.

If the word "apocalypticism" is taken to mean the ideology of a movement that shares the conceptual structure of the apocalypses, then we must

---

42. Koch, *The Rediscovery of Apocalyptic*, 28-33.
43. Stone, "Lists of Revealed Things," 440, 443.
44. Hanson, *IDB Sup,* 30.

recognize that there may be different types of apocalyptic movements, just as there are different types of apocalypses. Koch's list of features corresponds well enough to the "historical" type. We must also allow for mystically oriented movements which are "apocalyptic" insofar as they correspond to the "heavenly journey" type of apocalypse. We are only beginning to explore the historical setting in which Jewish mysticism developed.[45]

The debate over the relation between apocalypses and apocalypticism arises from the fact that previous scholarship has been preoccupied with the "historical" apocalypses and neglected those that incline to mysticism and cosmic speculation. One of the more significant developments of recent years has been the rediscovery of the mystical side of apocalyptic literature. The mystical component cannot be neatly isolated from the historical, but is an integral factor in all apocalyptic literature. A comprehensive understanding of the genre apocalypse in its different types also calls for a more complex view of the social phenomenon of apocalypticism.

## Apocalyptic Language

Up to this point we have been concerned with the generic framework that enables us to identify the apocalypses as a distinct class of writings. We must now turn to two other aspects of the genre that were not examined in *Semeia* 14: the nature of apocalyptic language and the question of setting and function.

The literary conventions that determine the manner of composition and the nature of the literature are no less important than the generic framework.[46] On this issue we may distinguish two fundamentally different approaches, one of which is associated with the name of R. H. Charles and the other with that of Hermann Gunkel. This is not, of course, to suggest that the approaches of these scholars were always incompatible with each other or that every subsequent scholar can be neatly aligned with one

---

45. For a critical study of the relevance of apocalyptic literature to early Jewish mysticism see Ra'anan Boustan and Patrick G. McCullough, "Apocalyptic Literature and the Study of Early Jewish Mysticism," in Collins, ed., *The Oxford Handbook of Apocalypticism*, 85-103.

46. See Carol A. Newsom, "The Rhetoric of Jewish Apocalyptic Literature," in Collins, ed., *The Oxford Handbook of Apocalypticism*, 201-17; Greg Carey, "Early Christian Apocalyptic Rhetoric," ibid., 218-34. See also the essays in Greg Carey and L. Gregory Bloomquist, eds., *Vision and Apocalypse: Rhetorical Dimensions of Apocalyptic Discourse* (St. Louis: Chalice, 1999).

or the other. They do, however, represent two divergent tendencies in the study of apocalyptic literature.[47]

## The Influence of R. H. Charles

The study of apocalyptic literature in the English-speaking world has to a great extent been influenced by R. H. Charles. His textual editions, translations, and notes remained standard reference works for most of the twentieth century, and his knowledge of the material was undeniably vast.[48] Yet such a sober critic as T. W. Manson wrote that "there was a sense in which the language of Apocalyptic remained a foreign language to him. He could never be completely at home in the world of the Apocalyptists. And this made it impossible for him to achieve that perfect understanding which demands sympathy as well as knowledge."[49] Charles's lack of empathy with the material is apparent in two characteristics of his work. First, he tended to treat the texts as compendia of information and paid great attention to identifying historical allusions and extracting theological doctrines. In contrast, he gave little attention to such matters as literary structure or mythological symbolism. The second characteristic is related to this. Since he assumed that the original documents presupposed a doctrinal consistency similar to his own and that the canons of style that governed them were similar to those of his own day, he posited interpolations and proposed emendations rather freely. So F. C. Burkitt wrote in his obituary of Charles: "If he came to have any respect for an ancient author he was unwilling to believe that such a person could have entertained conceptions which to Charles's trained and logical western mind were 'mutually exclusive,' and his favorite explanation was to posit interpolations and a multiplicity of sources, each of which may be supposed to have been written from a single and consistent point of view."[50]

47. See my essay, "Apocalyptic Literature," in R. A. Kraft and G. W. E. Nickelsburg, eds., *Early Judaism and Its Modern Interpreters* (Atlanta: Scholars Press, 1986) 345-70.

48. In addition to his monumental *Apocrypha and Pseudepigrapha of the Old Testament*, Charles published editions of *1 Enoch, Ascension of Isaiah, 2 Baruch, Jubilees, Testaments of the Twelve Patriarchs, Assumption of Moses,* and (with W. R. Morfill) *2 Enoch.*

49. Cited by J. Barr, "Jewish Apocalyptic in Recent Scholarly Study," *BJRL* 58 (1975) 32 (from the *Dictionary of National Biography* [1931-40] 170).

50. Cited by Barr, "Jewish Apocalyptic," 31.

Of course Charles was a child of his age. The principles of literary/ source criticism typified by J. Wellhausen were dominant in biblical studies when he wrote. It is to Charles's credit that he did not share Wellhausen's negative evaluation of apocalypticism. The underlying assumptions of this type of approach have continued to play a prominent part in the study of apocalyptic literature. In large part this has been due to the persistence of a tradition that "has tended towards clarity and simplicity, and . . . has tended to lose from sight the essential problem of understanding the apocalyptic books as literary texts with their own strange form and language."[51] This tendency has been especially, though not exclusively, evident in British scholarship. The two most comprehensive and widely read books on "apocalyptic" in the mid-twentieth century were by British authors — H. H. Rowley and D. S. Russell.[52] Both books contain much that is still valuable, but as James Barr has pointed out, they are characterized by the "reduction of the very enigmatic material to essentially simple questions."[53] It is also significant that Charles, Rowley, and Russell all sought the sources of apocalyptic language primarily in Old Testament prophecy. While prophecy may indeed be the single most important source on which the apocalyptists drew, the tendency to assimilate apocalyptic literature to the more familiar world of the prophets risks losing sight of its stranger mythological and cosmological components.

The problem with the source-critical method is obviously one of degree. No one will deny that it is sometimes possible and necessary to distinguish sources and identify interpolations. We have learned, however, that the apocalyptic writings are far more tolerant of inconsistency and repetition than Charles and his collaborators realized. Consequently, we must learn the conventions that are actually employed in the text rather than assume that our own criteria of consistency are applicable. In short, our working assumptions should favor the unity of a document, unless there is cogent evidence to the contrary. The burden of proof falls on the scholar who would divide a text into multiple sources.

The methodological assumptions that posit sources and interpolations to maintain an ideal of consistency are frequently coupled with a lack of appreciation of symbolic narratives. The tendency of much

51. Ibid.

52. H. H. Rowley, *The Relevance of Apocalyptic* (London: Athlone, 1944; reprint, Greenwood, SC: Attic, 1980); D. S. Russell, *Method and Message*.

53. Barr, "Jewish Apocalyptic," 32.

historical scholarship has been to specify the referents of apocalyptic imagery in as unambiguous a manner as possible. This enterprise has indeed contributed much to our understanding of passages like Daniel 11. Yet Paul Ricoeur has rightly protested against the tendency to identify apocalyptic symbols in too univocal a way.[54] This tendency misses the element of mystery and indeterminacy that constitutes much of the "atmosphere" of apocalyptic literature. In short, Ricoeur suggests that we should sometimes "allow several concurrent identifications *play*" and that the text may on occasion achieve its effect precisely through the element of uncertainty. It has been common to assume that apocalyptic symbols are mere codes whose meaning is exhausted by single referents. So Norman Perrin contrasted the rich and multidimensional use of the "kingdom of God" in the teaching of Jesus (a "tensive" symbol) with what he conceived to be the one-dimensional usage of the apocalypses ("steno-symbols").[55] Such a contrast shows little appreciation for the allusive and evocative power of apocalyptic symbolism, but we must admit that Perrin's approach was consistent with much English-language scholarship.[56]

## *The Influence of Hermann Gunkel*

Hermann Gunkel, who pioneered so many creative developments in biblical study, also pointed the way to a more satisfactory appreciation of the apocalypses.[57] Much of Gunkel's work on apocalyptic literature was directed to the recovery of traditional, and especially mythological, materials embedded in the apocalypses. On the one hand, this work suggested that the various seams detected by the so-called literary critics

54. P. Ricoeur, preface to A. Lacocque, *The Book of Daniel* (Atlanta: John Knox, 1979) xxii-xxiii.

55. N. Perrin, "Eschatology and Hermeneutics: Reflections on Method in the Interpretation of the New Testament," *JBL* 93 (1974) 3-14. See my critique, "The Symbolism of Transcendence in Jewish Apocalyptic," *BR* 19 (1974) 5-22.

56. See the fine study of apocalyptic symbolism by Bennie H. Reynolds, *Between Symbolism and Realism: The Use of Symbolic and Non-Symbolic Language in Ancient Jewish Apocalypses 333-63 BCE* (JAJSup 8; Göttingen: Vandenhoeck & Ruprecht, 2011).

57. H. Gunkel, *Schöpfung und Chaos in Urzeit und Endzeit* (Göttingen: Vandenhoeck & Ruprecht, 1895); idem, "Das vierte Buch Esra," in E. Kautzsch, ed., *Die Apokryphen und Pseudepigraphen des Alten Testaments* (Tübingen: Mohr Siebeck, 1900) 2:331-401. See J. M. Schmidt, *Die jüdische Apokalyptik*, 195-204; Hanson, "Prolegomena," 393-96.

(e.g., when an interpretation ignores some elements in a vision) need not point to multiple authorship but only to the use of traditional material by a single author. In short, authors who work with traditional material do not conform to the standards of consistency and coherence presupposed by Charles and Wellhausen but may well allow loose ends and even contradictions to stand in their work. On the other hand, by pointing to the mythological roots of much apocalyptic imagery, Gunkel showed its symbolic and allusive character. Apocalyptic literature was not governed by the principles of Aristotelian logic but was closer to the poetic nature of myth.

Gunkel's critique of the principles of "literary" criticism was long neglected by students of apocalyptic literature but has been repeatedly vindicated in recent study. The insight that the apocalypses did not aspire to conceptual consistency but could allow diverse formulations to complement each other is especially important. The juxtaposition of visions and oracles, which cover essentially the same material, with varying imagery is a feature of a great number of apocalypses and related writings — Daniel, *Sibylline Oracles,* Similitudes of Enoch, 4 Ezra, 2 *Baruch,* Revelation. This phenomenon cannot be adequately explained by positing multiple sources, since we should still have to explain why sources are consistently combined in this way. In fact, repetition is a common literary (and oral) convention in ancient and modern times. A significant parallel to the apocalypses is found in the repetition of dream reports — for example, the multiple dreams of Joseph or of Gilgamesh. The recognition that such repetition is an intrinsic feature of apocalyptic writings provides a key to a new understanding of the genre.

Biblical scholarship in general has suffered from a preoccupation with the referential aspects of language and with the factual information that can be extracted from a text. Such an attitude is especially detrimental to the study of poetic and mythological material, which is expressive language, articulating feelings and attitudes rather than describing reality in an objective way. The apocalyptic literature provides a rather clear example of language that is expressive rather than referential, symbolic rather than factual.[58]

---

58. On the various nonreferential aspects of biblical language see G. B. Caird, *The Language and Imagery of the Bible* (Philadelphia: Westminster, 1981; reprint, Grand Rapids: Eerdmans, 1997).

## Traditional Imagery

The symbolic character of apocalyptic language is shown especially by its pervasive use of allusions to traditional imagery. Like much of the Jewish and early Christian literature, the apocalypses constantly echo biblical phrases. This point has been demonstrated especially by the Swedish scholar Lars Hartman. The title of Hartman's basic book, *Prophecy Interpreted,* may be somewhat misleading, if it is taken to suggest that the use of the biblical material is primarily exegetical. To be sure, the direct interpretation of older prophecies is a significant factor in apocalyptic writings; the interpretation of Jeremiah's prophecy in Daniel 9 is an obvious example. In many cases, however, the use of older texts consists only in the use of a phrase that brings a biblical passage to mind without claiming to interpret it in a definitive way. So the opening chapter of *1 Enoch* is a patchwork of biblical phrases, alluding *inter alia* to Balaam's oracle in Numbers 23–24.[59] This allusiveness enriches the language by building associations and analogies between the biblical contexts and the new context in which the phrase is used. It also means that this language lends itself to different levels of meaning and becomes harder to pin down in a univocal, unambiguous way.

The importance of biblical allusions in apocalyptic literature is generally admitted. Far more controversial is the use of mythological allusions. In part, the controversy arises from the notorious diversity of ways in which the word "myth" is used: sometimes as a genre label, sometimes as a mode of thought, sometimes implying an association with ritual, and sometimes even as a derogatory term for what is false or "pagan."[60] A case can be made, I believe, for using "myth" as a genre label (on a broader level than apocalypse) in any of a number of senses — for example, as a paradigmatic narrative (à la M. Eliade) or as a story that obscures or mediates the contradictions of experience (à la C. Lévi-Strauss). In view of the ambiguity of the word, however, such a generic use of "myth" is scarcely helpful. The word is used in biblical studies primarily to refer to the religious stories of the ancient Near East and the Greco-Roman world. When we speak of mythological allusions in the apocalyptic literature we are referring to motifs and patterns that are ultimately derived from these stories.

The importance of Near Eastern mythology for understanding the

---

59. L. Hartman, *Asking for a Meaning: A Study of 1 Enoch 1–5* (Lund: Gleerup, 1979) 22.

60. J. W. Rogerson, *Myth in Old Testament Interpretation* (Berlin: de Gruyter, 1974).

apocalyptic literature was forcefully suggested by Gunkel in his famous book *Schöpfung und Chaos in Urzeit und Endzeit* in 1895. The insight was kept alive by writers of the "myth and ritual" school such as S. H. Hooke and especially by A. Bentzen and S. Mowinckel.[61] In English-language scholarship it has been revived especially by Paul D. Hanson, building on the work of Frank M. Cross.[62] Whereas Gunkel sought his mythological parallels in the Babylonian material then available and subsequent scholars posited vast Persian influence, more recent scholarship has looked to the Canaanite-Ugaritic myths — especially in the case of Daniel.

There is still widespread resistance to the idea that Jewish apocalypses use mythological motifs.[63] In large part this resistance is theological, when the myths are viewed as "false" or "pagan." In fact, however, Canaanite motifs had been domesticated in the religion of Israel from very early times.[64] In some measure, the resistance arises from misconceptions. The Ugaritic texts come from the middle of the second millennium BCE, more than a thousand years before the earliest apocalypses. However, no one would claim that the authors of Daniel or Enoch had before them the exact texts we now have. We have very little documentation of the Canaanite religious tradition. The Ugaritic myths provide examples of a tradition that is largely lost. They are not the immediate sources of the apocalyptic imagery, but they illustrate the traditional usage that provides the context for the allusions. Before the Ugaritic texts were discovered, Gunkel appealed primarily to the Babylonian myths. The Ugaritic parallels now appear more adequate at some points. Future discoveries may yield even better comparative material. Gunkel was not wrong to appeal to the Babylonian material, since the issue is not the exact derivation but the kinds of allusions involved.

It should also be clear that a mythological allusion does not carry the same meaning and reference in an apocalyptic context as it did in the

---

61. S. H. Hooke, "The Myth and Ritual Pattern in Jewish and Christian Apocalyptic," in idem, *The Labyrinth* (London: SPCK, 1935) 213-33; A. Bentzen, *Daniel* (2d ed.; Tübingen: Mohr Siebeck, 1952); S. Mowinckel, *He That Cometh* (Nashville: Abingdon, 1955).

62. Hanson, "Jewish Apocalyptic Against Its Near Eastern Environment," *RB* 78 (1971) 31-58; Cross, "New Directions in the Study of Apocalyptic," *JTC* 6 (1969) 157-65.

63. For elaboration of the following see my essay, "Apocalyptic Genre and Mythic Allusions in Daniel," *JSOT* 21 (1981) 83-100. I will return to the debate about mythic allusions in Daniel in chapter 3 below.

64. F. M. Cross, *Canaanite Myth and Hebrew Epic* (Cambridge, MA: Harvard University Press, 1973).

original myth. If the "one like a son of man" who comes on the clouds in Daniel 7 alludes to the Canaanite figure of Baal, this is not to say that he is identified as Baal, or that the full story of Baal is implied. Rather, it suggests that there is some analogy between this figure and the traditional conception of Baal. In the same way, the "Son of Man" passage in Mark 13:26 alludes to Daniel, but the figure in Mark does not have the same reference as it had in Daniel, and the full narrative of Daniel 7 is not implied. Mythological allusions, like biblical allusions, are not simple copies of the original source. Rather they transfer motifs from one context to another. By so doing they build associations and analogies and so enrich the communicative power of the language.

## The Quest for Traditional Sources of Apocalypticism

The recognition of allusions, and of the sources from which they derive, is an important factor in the study of apocalyptic literature. Yet it is important to distinguish the *generic* approach advocated here from the *genetic* approach which has long been dominant in this field of study.

An extraordinary amount of the scholarly literature has been devoted to the quest for the "origins of apocalyptic." For much of this century opinion was divided between those who viewed "apocalyptic" as the child of prophecy (e.g., Rowley) and those who regarded it as a "foreign" adaptation of Persian dualism.[65] More recently Gerhard von Rad suggested that it was derived from wisdom.[66] The renewed interest in mythological, especially Canaanite, sources is usually combined with the derivation from prophecy.

Much of this quest must be considered misdirected and counterproductive. Any given apocalypse combines allusions to a wide range of sources. The book of Daniel has obvious continuity with the prophets in the vision form and the use of Jeremiah's prophecy among other things. Yet we will argue that Canaanite imagery plays a crucial role in Daniel 7, and the schema of the four kingdoms is borrowed from the political propaganda of the Hellenistic Near East. While the importance of Persian

---

65. For example, W. Bousset, *Die Religion des Judentums im späthellenistischen Zeitalter* (3d ed.; ed. H. Gressmann; Tübingen: Mohr Siebeck, 1926).

66. G. von Rad, *Theologie*, 2:315-30. A connection between wisdom and apocalyptic literature was proposed as early as 1857 by L. Noack.

dualism was greatly exaggerated in the past, it cannot be dismissed entirely. It is widely admitted in the Qumran scrolls and is quite compatible with the extensive use of Israelite traditions. Ultimately the meaning of any given work is constituted not by the sources from which it draws but by the way in which they are combined.

The quest for sources has often led scholars to view apocalypticism as a derivative phenomenon, a product of something other than itself. This tendency reflects a theological prejudice, inherited from the Wellhausen era, which views the apocalyptic writers (and postexilic Judaism in general) as inherently inferior to the prophets. In fact, the designation of sources has often been used as a covert way of making theological judgments. If "apocalyptic" is the child of prophecy it is legitimate; if it is a Persian import it is not authentically biblical. This logic is patently defective. The sources from which ideas are developed do not determine the inherent value of those ideas. Many of the central biblical ideas were in any case adapted from the mythology of the Canaanites and other Near Eastern peoples.[67]

The designation of sources also sometimes serves as an indirect way of expressing the character of the phenomenon. Scholars who relate the apocalyptic literature exclusively to prophecy tend to concentrate on the eschatology and neglect the cosmological and speculative concerns that are also found in the apocalypses. Von Rad's theory that apocalypticism is derived from wisdom sought to correct that emphasis, but the issues have been confused by the genetic formulation of his thesis.[68] The apocalypses do indeed present a kind of wisdom insofar as they, first, offer an understanding of the structure of the universe and of history and, second, see right understanding as the precondition of right action. This wisdom, however, is not the inductive kind that we find in Proverbs or Sirach, but is acquired through revelation. The wisdom of Daniel and Enoch has close affinities with the *mantic* wisdom

67. See the classic work of Frank Moore Cross, *Canaanite Myth and Hebrew Epic* (Cambridge, MA: Harvard University Press, 1973) and my essay "The Legacy of Canaan in Ancient Israel and Early Christianity," in C. Frechette, C. Matthews, and T. Stegeman, eds., *Opportunity for No Little Instruction: Studies in Honor of Richard J. Clifford, S.J. and Daniel J. Harrington, S.J.* (New York, Paulist Press,2014) 71-84.

68. See Matthew J. Goff, "Wisdom and Apocalypticism," in Collins, ed., *The Oxford Handbook of Apocalypticism*, 52-68. See also the review of scholarship in DiTommaso, "Apocalypses and Apocalypticism in Antiquity," Part 2: *Currents in Biblical Research* 5.3 (2007) 374-81.

of the Babylonians.[69] The quest for higher wisdom by revelation is well attested in the Hellenistic age,[70] and it is significant that the biblical wisdom book that shows most correspondence with the apocalypses is the Hellenistic (deuterocanonical) Wisdom of Solomon.[71] There is also an analogy between the wisdom literature and some apocalypses on the level of the underlying questions, insofar as both are often concerned with theodicy or the problem of divine justice. The use of the dialogue form in 4 Ezra recalls the book of Job in this regard, although the culminating revelations in the two books are very different.[72] The relation to wisdom is seldom a matter of derivation but concerns the way we perceive the nature of the apocalypses. The most fruitful effect of von Rad's proposal has been to redirect attention to those aspects of the apocalypses which are cosmological and speculative rather than eschatological.

## The Settings of the Genre

The study of the apocalyptic genre rejects the genetic orientation of previous scholarship and places its primary emphasis on the internal coherence of the apocalyptic texts themselves. It is apparent that the apocalypses drew on various strands of tradition and that the new product is more than the sum of its sources. There is, however, a different genetic question that must be considered, concerning the historical and social matrix of the genre. In 1970 Klaus Koch could still assume that "if there was really a community of ideas and spirit between the different books which we now call apocalypses, these books must go back to a common sociological starting point; they must have a comparable *Sitz-im-Leben*."[73] Koch went on to

---

69. H.-P. Müller, "Mantische Weisheit und Apokalyptik," in *Congress Volume: Uppsala 1971* (VTSup 22; Leiden: Brill, 1972) 268-93; J. J. Collins, *The Apocalyptic Vision of the Book of Daniel* (HSM 16; Missoula, MT: Scholars Press, 1977) 67-88; J. C. VanderKam, *Enoch and the Growth of an Apocalyptic Tradition* (CBQMS 16; Washington, DC: Catholic Biblical Association of America, 1984) chapter 3. Note also the critique of von Rad by P. von der Osten-Sacken, *Die Apokalyptik in ihrem Verhältnis zu Prophetie und Weisheit* (Munich: Kaiser, 1969).

70. M. Hengel, *Judaism and Hellenism* (2 vols.; Philadelphia: Fortress, 1974) 1.210-18.

71. J. J. Collins, "Cosmos and Salvation: Jewish Wisdom and Apocalyptic in the Hellenistic Age," *HR* 17 (1977) 121-42 (= *Seers, Sibyls, and Sages*, 317-38).

72. Rowland, *The Open Heaven*, 205-8.

73. Koch, *The Rediscovery of Apocalyptic*, 21.

complain that "the secondary literature shows an unsurpassed jumble of opinions" and concluded that apocalypse is a genre whose *Sitz im Leben* we do not yet know.

More recent study has shown that this formulation of the problem is inadequate. In an important critique of Old Testament form criticism in 1973, Rolf Knierim argued that "the conclusion seems unavoidable that 'setting' in the sense biblical form criticism has understood it, cannot be regarded indispensably as one of the factors that constitute genres."[74] The reason is not only the obvious practical one that we often do not have the necessary information to establish the setting of a text. More fundamental is the realization that settings are of different sorts, and so there is need of a typology of settings. The "jumble of opinions" about which Koch complains is due in large part to the lack of such a typology.

It is generally agreed that apocalypse is not simply "a conceptual genre of the mind"[75] but is generated by social and historical circumstances. On the broadest level "the style of an epoch can be understood as a matrix insofar as it furnishes the codes or raw materials — the typical categories of communication — employed by a certain society."[76] Much of the traditional debate about the sources of apocalypticism is relevant here insofar as the "codes and raw materials" are thought to be provided by late prophecy, Persian dualism, etc. On another level we may consider Philip Vielhauer's thesis that "the home of Apocalyptic is in those eschatologically excited circles which were forced more and more by the theocracy into a kind of conventicle existence."[77] A more specific variant of this type of setting would assign the apocalypses to a particular party, such as the Hasidim or the Essenes. A different type of setting is reflected in Vielhauer's further claim that the apocalypses "were frequently written out of actual distresses and for the strengthening of the community in them."[78] There is no necessary assertion about the existence of apocalyptic groups on this level. Yet another type of setting concerns the manner of composition. Do apocalypses reflect authentic visionary experience? Are they products of learned scribes? Or do they articulate popular beliefs?

---

74. R. Knierim, "Old Testament Form Criticism Reconsidered," *Int* 27 (1973) 441.

75. Ibid., 438. Knierim suggests that "myth" may be considered such a genre.

76. Ibid., 464.

77. P. Vielhauer, "Apocalypses and Related Subjects," in E. Hennecke and W. Schneemelcher, eds., *New Testament Apocrypha* (2 vols.; Philadelphia: Westminster, 1965) 2:598.

78. Ibid.

Finally, one may discuss the function of a text without specifying a social or historical setting at all. Recently Lars Hartman and David Hellholm have focused on the *illocution* of a text, or that which it does *in* saying what it says.[79] Hartman suggests that exhortation and consolation are typical illocutions of apocalypses. Even on this level, the function of a text may be more or less specific. Exhortation to pacifism is distinctly different from exhortation to violence, and either may be the function of a given text. We should also note that a text remains in existence and may be reused in various settings at different times.

## The General Matrix

### Postexilic Prophecy

We may begin with the question of the matrix of the genre on the most general level. In an influential study published in 1975, Paul Hanson argued that "the dawn of apocalyptic" should be located in postexilic prophecy in the late sixth century BCE.[80] Hanson was well aware that the main corpus of apocalyptic literature comes from a much later time. His point was that the basic configuration of apocalyptic thought can already be found in the late prophetic texts.

Hanson distinguishes two parties in the postexilic community: the hierocratic party represented by Haggai, the early chapters of Zechariah, and Ezekiel 40–48 and the visionary heirs of Second Isaiah, represented by Isaiah 56–66, Zechariah 9–14, and a number of other passages, most notably Isaiah 24–27.[81] The closest formal analogies to the apocalypses are found in the "hierocratic" literature, especially in the visions of Zechariah that are interpreted by an angel.[82] On the other hand, Hanson sees in the visionary

---

79. Hartman, "Survey"; Hellholm, *Das Visionenbuch*, 1.52-58. The term is taken from J. L. Austin, *How to Do Things with Words* (2d ed.; Cambridge, MA: Harvard University Press, 1975) 98-108.

80. P. D. Hanson, *The Dawn of Apocalyptic* (Philadelphia: Fortress, 1975). On the significance of the Persian period for the development of apocalypticism, see further J. J. Collins, "From Prophecy to Apocalypticism: The Expectation of the End," in J. J. Collins, B. McGinn, and S. Stein, eds., *The Encyclopedia of Apocalypticism* (New York: Continuum, 1998) 1:129-61.

81. Hanson, *IDBSup*, 33.

82. H. Gese, "Anfang und Ende der Apokalyptik dargestellt am Sacharjabuch," *ZThK*

literature the dawn of apocalyptic eschatology, which he associates with the eclipse of human instrumentality in the divine intervention in history. The oracles of Isaiah 56–66 are written out of a growing sense of alienation from the hierocracy. The prophet calls on God to "rend the heavens and come down" (64:1). Divine intervention is necessary to set the situation right. The vision of the future is a new creation, new heavens and a new earth. In addition to the hope for a transcendent future, these oracles anticipate the use of mythological language in the apocalypses. The most striking illustrations are found in Isaiah 24–27. God will swallow up Death forever (25:8, an allusion to the figure of Mot or Death in Canaanite mythology) and will punish Leviathan and slay the dragon that is in the sea (27:1). Further, the social and historical matrix of these oracles has significant affinities with that of at least some later apocalypses. The sense of alienation from the present order is fundamental to many apocalypses, especially the historical type.

Hanson's sociological model was criticized by Stephen Cook, who points out that millennialism can also be found among groups that enjoy power.[83] Power and deprivation are notoriously relative terms. Zechariah was close to power in the province of Judah, because of his support for Joshua and Zerubbabel, but the whole province was marginal in the Persian empire. Cook's understanding of the phenomenon of apocalypticism, however, is still close to that of Hanson, emphasizing especially the use of mythological language.[84] A more fundamental critique, emphasizing the distinction between postexilic prophecy and apocalypticism and considering the visions of Zechariah in their specific social context has been provided by Antonios Finitsis.[85]

There is significant continuity between the apocalypses and the prophetic tradition, and especially that the apocalyptic use of mythological imagery has ample biblical antecedents. Yet some major defining characteristics of apocalyptic thought are lacking in these oracles. One is the

---

70 (1973) 20-49; R. North, "Prophecy to Apocalyptic via Zechariah," in *Congress Volume: Uppsala 1971* (VTSup 22) 47-71. See more recently E. J. C. Tigchelaar, *Prophets of Old and the Day of the End: Zechariah, the Book of the Watchers, and Apocalyptic* (OTS 35; Leiden: Brill, 1996), and S. L. Cook, *Prophecy and Apocalypticism: The Postexilic Social Setting* (Minneapolis: Fortress, 1995) 123-65.

83. Cook, *Prophecy and Apocalypticism*, 55-84.

84. See Cook, "Apocalyptic Prophecy," in Collins, ed., *The Oxford Handbook of Apocalyptic Literature*, 19-35.

85. Antonios Finitsis, *Visions and Eschatology: A Socio-Historical Analysis of Zechariah 1-6* (Library of Second Temple Studies 79; London: T & T Clark, 2011).

interest in the heavenly world. Angels play some part in Zechariah, but scarcely any in the so-called visionary literature. Nothing in these books prepares for the mystical and speculative aspects of the Enoch literature.[86] The eschatology too is rather different from the later apocalypses. In the "new earth" of Isaiah 65 "the child shall die a hundred years old and the sinner a hundred years old shall be accursed" and "like the days of a tree shall the days of my people be." Life will be transformed, but it will still be distinctly this-worldly ("they shall plant vineyards and eat their fruit"). It will also be finite, however lengthened it may be. This conception is quite different from the expectation of resurrection or of the judgment of the dead as we find it in Daniel and *Enoch*. When the goal of life is located beyond death, then there is evidently a greater impulse also to speculation about the world beyond and to the mystical elements in the apocalyptic literature.

While postexilic prophecy shares some significant features of the apocalypses, it still lacks the generic framework of apocalyptic thought.[87] The so-called Apocalypse of Isaiah in Isaiah 24–27 comes closer to the later literature than the other oracles.[88] Isaiah 25 speaks of the destruction of Death, and Isa 26:19 of the resurrection of the dead. From the context it would seem that this language is metaphorical for the restoration of Israel, as is explicitly the case in Ezekiel's vision of the dry bones (Ezekiel 37). The dead who shall live are contrasted with the lords who ruled over Israel, who are gone without remembrance.[89] Yet the use of such language is a significant factor in the development of apocalyptic thought. An intriguing pas-

---

86. See my essay, "The Place of Apocalypticism in the Religion of Israel," in P. D. Miller, P. D. Hanson, and S. D. McBride, eds., *Ancient Israelite Religion: Essays in Honor of Frank Moore Cross* (Philadelphia: Fortress, 1987) 539-58 (= *Seers, Sibyls, and Sages,* 39-58). See, however, the interesting attempt of Tigchelaar, *Prophets of Old,* to trace connections between Zechariah and the Book of the Watchers.

87. M. A. Knibb regards Zechariah 1–8 as an apocalypse but admits that its form is inchoate ("Prophecy and the Emergence of the Jewish Apocalypses," 175). His claim that the visions express an eschatology, however, requires a very broad definition of that term. See my essay, "The Eschatology of Zechariah," in Grabbe and Haak, ed., *Knowing the End from the Beginning,* 74-84.

88. See my essay, "The Beginning of the End of the World in the Hebrew Bible," in John J. Ahn and Stephen L. Cook, eds., *Thus Says the Lord: Essays on the Former and Latter Prophets in Honor of Robert R. Wilson* (London: T & T Clark, 2009) 137-55.

89. See, however, E. Puech, *La Croyance des Esséniens en la Vie Future: Immortalité, Résurrection, Vie Éternelle?* (Paris: Gabalda, 1993) 66-73, who argues for a belief in individual resurrection here. So also Cook, "Apocalyptic Prophecy," 29.

sage in Isa 24:21-22 speaks of a day when God will punish "the host of heaven in heaven and the kings of the earth on the earth" and they will be shut up in prison for many days until they are punished. This passage, like all of Isaiah 24–27, remains enigmatic, but it suggests an underlying mythology that is more elaborate than anything expressed in the texts, and which may well have been significant for the development of apocalyptic eschatology.[90]

## *The Earliest Apocalypses*

Postexilic prophecy undoubtedly supplied some of the codes and raw materials utilized by the later apocalypses. However, if we wish to examine the matrix in which the configuration of the genre emerged, we must surely begin with the earliest actual apocalypses, rather than with their partial antecedents.

The earliest apocalypses, by the definition given above, are found in *1 Enoch*. Substantial fragments of the Book of the Watchers and the Astronomical Book have been found at Qumran in manuscripts from the early second or even late third century BCE, and the antiquity of these works is also corroborated by allusions in the book of *Jubilees*.[91] The early date of this Enoch material is significant for our perception of the genre, since the contrast with the prophetic literature is much greater than in the case of Daniel. The noncanonical apocalypses can no longer be dismissed as "second-rate imitators" of Daniel. Both the Book of the Watchers and the Astronomical Book involve otherworldly journeys and a good deal of cosmological speculation.

The place of composition of these documents is far from certain. There has been a general tendency to assign them to Palestinian Judaism. There are indeed some references to Palestinian geography: Enoch is located in "Dan which is southwest of Hermon" (13:7) and the description of

---

90. For contrasting assessments of Isaiah 24–27, see W. R. Millar, *Isaiah 24–27 and the Origin of Apocalyptic* (HSM 11; Missoula, MT: Scholars Press, 1976); J. Vermeylen, *Du prophète Isaïe à l'Apocalyptique* (Paris: Gabalda, 1977) 1.349-91; D. Johnson, *From Chaos to Restoration: An Integrative Reading of Isaiah 24–27* (JSOTSup 61; Sheffield: JSOT, 1988) and Donald C. Polaski, *Authorizing an End: The Isaiah Apocalypse and Intertextuality* (Leiden: Brill, 2001).

91. J. T. Milik, *The Books of Enoch: Aramaic Fragments from Qumrân Cave 4* (Oxford: Clarendon, 1976) 5-7. Milik (p. 31) argues that these Enochic books are presupposed in Genesis, but his arguments have been widely rejected.

the "middle of the earth" in *1 Enoch* 26 is in fact a description of Jerusalem and its surroundings.[92] Yet it is doubtful whether this evidence necessarily requires that the author lived in the homeland. Several scholars have noted the prominence of Babylonian lore in both the Book of the Watchers and the Astronomical Book.[93] The possibility that this literature originated in the eastern Diaspora cannot be discounted. It is noteworthy that the tales in Daniel 1–6 are set in Babylon. There again a Diaspora origin is possible, although the visions in Daniel 7–12 were certainly composed in Judea. In no case can we point to an apocalyptic writing that was definitely composed in Babylon or the eastern Diaspora, nor can we assume that all were definitely composed in Judea. Later we will find that some apocalyptic writings also originated in the Hellenistic Diaspora.

## A Babylonian Matrix?

In view of the manifest associations of the earliest Enoch and Daniel literature with Babylon, we must consider whether the apocalyptic genre owes its distinctive shape to a Babylonian matrix. Our question here is not whether the earliest apocalypses were written in the eastern Diaspora, since this possibility cannot be decisively verified at present. Rather the question is to what extent the "codes and raw materials" of the apocalypses were Babylonian in origin.

Several scholars have noted affinities between apocalyptic revelation and the "mantic wisdom" of the Chaldeans. Daniel in the tales (Daniel

---

92. Ibid., 36-37. On Enoch's association with Galilee, see G. W. E. Nickelsburg, "Enoch, Levi, and Peter: Recipients of Revelation in Upper Galilee," *JBL* 100 (1981) 575-600.

93. Milik, *Books of Enoch*, 13-18, 29-30; P. Grelot, "La géographie mythique d'Hénoch et ses sources orientales," *RB* 65 (1958) 33-69; Stone, *Scriptures, Sects, and Visions*, 39; VanderKam, *Enoch and the Growth of an Apocalyptic Tradition*, 33-71; H. S. Kvanvig, *Roots of Apocalyptic: The Mesopotamian Background of the Enoch Figure and of the Son of Man* (WMANT 61; Neukirchen–Vluyn: Neukirchener Verlag, 1988) 160-342; Amar Annus, "On the Origin of Watchers: A Comparative Study of the Antediluvian Wisdom in Mesopotamian and Jewish traditions," *JSP* 19 (2010) 277-320; Ida Fröhlich, "Mesopotamian Elements in the Watchers Tradition," in Angela Kim Harkins, Kelley Coblentz Bautch and John C. Endres, S. J., eds., *The Watchers in Jewish and Christian Traditions* (Minneapolis: Fortress, 2014) 11-24; Mladen Popović, "Networks of Scholars: The Transmission of Astronomical and Astrological Learning between Babylonians, Greeks and Jews," in Jonathan Ben-Dov and Seth L. Sanders, eds., *Ancient Jewish Sciences and the History of Knowledge in Second Temple Literature* (New York: New York University Press, 2014) 153-93.

1–6) operates as a Babylonian wise man, skilled in the interpretation of dreams. The figure of Enoch is to some degree modeled on Enmeduranki, founder of the guild of *bārûs,* or Babylonian diviners. There is also a general similarity between the methods of apocalyptic revelation and of divination, insofar as both involve the interpretation of mysterious signs and symbols, and both carry overtones of determinism. Yet it must also be said that the apocalyptic visions of Daniel 7–12 and the actual revelations of Enoch are quite different from the literature of divination and omen collections.[94] Some scholars have tried to find a mediating link in the Akkadian prophecies, which have only come to light in recent years.[95] This genre has been described as follows by A. K. Grayson: "An Akkadian prophecy is a prose composition consisting in the main of a number of 'predictions' of past events. It then concludes either with a 'prediction' of phenomena in the writer's day or with a genuine attempt to forecast future events. The author, in other words, uses *vaticinia ex eventu* to establish his credibility and then proceeds to his real purpose, which might be to justify a current idea or institution, or, as it appears in the *Dynastic Prophecy,* to forecast doom for a hated enemy."[96] Five exemplars of the genre have been recognized, ranging in date from the twelfth century to the Seleucid era: the Marduk and Shulgi prophetic speeches, Text A, the Uruk prophecy, and the *Dynastic Prophecy.* The Marduk and Shulgi speeches provide early examples of pseudonymity. The affinity of these prophecies with the Jewish apocalypses lies primarily in their "predictions" of past events, or *vaticinia ex eventu.* The cryptic manner in which these predictions are presented ("A prince will arise . . . another man who is unknown will arise")

94. VanderKam, *Enoch and the Growth of an Apocalyptic Tradition,* 62: "However similar Mesopotamian divination and Jewish apocalypticism may be in some respects, they certainly have not produced comparable literature."

95. A. K. Grayson and W. G. Lambert, "Akkadian Prophecies," *JCS* 18 (1964) 7-30; W. W. Hallo, "Akkadian Apocalypses," *IEJ* 16 (1966) 231-42. Hallo's designation "apocalypses" has been generally rejected. For sober evaluations see W. G. Lambert, *The Background of Jewish Apocalyptic* (London: Athlone, 1978); S. A. Kaufman, "Prediction, Prophecy, and Apocalypse in the Light of New Akkadian Texts," in A. Shinan, ed., *Proceedings of the Sixth World Congress of Jewish Studies, 1973* (Jerusalem: World Union of Jewish Studies, 1977) 221-28. For the definitive presentation of these prophecies, see A. K. Grayson, *Babylonian Historical-Literary Texts* (Toronto: University of Toronto Press, 1975). See also Matthew Neujahr, *Predicting the Past in the Ancient Near East: Mantic Historiography in Ancient Mesopotamia, Judah, and the Mediterranean World* (BJS 354; Providence, RI: Brown Judaic Studies, 2012) 13-118.

96. Grayson, *Babylonian Historical-Literary Texts,* 6.

has rightly been compared to Daniel 11, or Daniel 8:23-25.[97] More extensive parallels can be found in the *Sibylline Oracles*. In this respect at least the Akkadian prophecies provide noteworthy precedents for a prominent characteristic of the historical apocalypses. Yet the Babylonian prophecies fall far short of providing a comprehensive model for the apocalypses, even for the historical type. The extant examples provide no parallel for the apocalyptic reception of revelation in a vision or heavenly tour and have no suggestion of an eschatology involving the judgment of the dead. In all, they seem closer to such political prophecies as the *Sibylline Oracles* than to the apocalypses.[98] We will have occasion to discuss them further in connection with Daniel.

There are, however, also Babylonian antecedents for the apocalyptic manner of revelation. The tradition of Akkadian dream visions has been brilliantly outlined by Helge Kvanvig, in a major contribution to the study of apocalypticism in the Near East.[99] Kvanvig focused special attention on *The Vision of the Netherworld*, a text first published by E. Ebeling in 1931,[100] and translated into English by E. Speiser in *ANET*.[101] In this text, one Kummaya has a vision in the night, in which he sees Nergal, the god of the netherworld, seated on a throne. He is attended by the vizier of the netherworld, fifteen gods in hybrid form, and "one man" whose body is black like pitch and his face like the Anzu bird. He wears a red robe and is armed with a bow and sword. The terrified Kummaya is brought before Nergal, but a counselor successfully intercedes for his life. Nergal then asks Kummaya why he has dishonored the queen of the netherworld. He identifies the figure he has seen (presumably the "one man") as "the exalted shepherd to whom my father, the king of the gods, gives full responsibility," and also refers to "your begetter," who "ate the taboo and stamped on the abomination." The dreamer awakes, shaken, and proceeds to give praise to Nergal and his queen. Kvanvig proposes that Kummaya should be identified as a son of the seventh century BCE Assyrian king Esarhaddon, most likely Ashurbanipal.[102]

---

97. Ibid., 21; Lambert, *The Background of Jewish Apocalyptic*, 13.

98. Neujahr, *Predicting the Past*, 202-22.

99. Kvanvig, *Roots of Apocalyptic*, 355-441.

100. E. Ebeling, *Tod und Leben nach den Vorstellungen der Babylonier* (Berlin: de Gruyter, 1931) 1-19. See also W. von Soden, "Die Unterweltsvision eines assyrischen Kronprinzen," *ZA* 9 (1936) 1-31 = *Aus Sprache, Geschichte und Religion Babyloniens: Gesammelte Aufsätze* (Naples: Istituto universitario orientale, 1989) 29-67.

101. *ANET*, 109-10.

102. Kvanvig, *Roots of Apocalyptic*, 433-34.

Kvanvig goes on to argue for a specific relationship between this Akkadian text and the vision in Daniel 7. In my judgment, this argument is not persuasive.[103] But Kvanvig is surely right that there is a relationship between these Akkadian dream visions and the genre apocalypse, especially the apocalypses that describe the ascent of a visionary to the divine throne. The Akkadian text is not yet an apocalypse, since it lacks the eschatological dimension, but the dream vision is one of the main media of revelation in the Jewish apocalypses.[104]

In addition to the divinatory and revelatory material, it is increasingly apparent that Jewish apocalyptic writings often exhibit an interest in natural phenomena that may be considered scientific, or quasi-scientific.[105] The Astronomical Book in *1 Enoch* is the prime example, but there are many other examples in the Enoch literature and Dead Sea Scrolls. This material too is most plausibly traced to a Babylonian background.[106]

No one would argue that the Babylonian material provides a complete or sufficient matrix for the apocalyptic genre. It must, however, be seen as a significant contributing factor, especially insofar as apocalyptic revelation resembles divination in the decoding of mysterious signs. To be sure, divination and dream interpretation were not exclusively Babylonian

103. See my article "Stirring Up the Great Sea: The Religio-Historical Background of Daniel 7," in A. S. van der Woude, ed., *The Book of Daniel in the Light of New Findings* (BETL 106; Leuven: Leuven University Press, 1993) 121-36 (= *Seers, Sibyls, and Sages*, 139-56).

104. VanderKam notes that dream reports about otherworldly travel also fall within the province of divination, but he adds that these are generally of consequence only to the dreamer himself (*Enoch and the Growth of an Apocalyptic Tradition*, 60).

105. Jonathan Ben-Dov, "Scientific Writings in Aramaic and Hebrew at Qumran: Translation and Concealment," in Katell Berthelot and Daniel Stökl Ben Ezra, ed., *Aramaica Qumranica: Proceedings of the Conference on the Aramaic Texts from Qumran in Aix-en-Provence 30 June – 2 July 2008* (STDJ 94; Leiden: Brill, 2010) 379-40; Philip S. Alexander, "Enoch and the Beginnings of Jewish Interest in Natural Science," in Charlotte Hempel et al., eds., *The Wisdom Texts from Qumran and the Development of Sapiential Thought* (BETL 149; Leuven: Peeters, 2002) 223-43; Ben-Dov and Sanders, ed., *Ancient Jewish Sciences*. See already M. E. Stone, "Lists of Revealed Things in the Apocalyptic Literature," in F. M. Cross, W. E. Lemke, and P. D. Miller, eds., *Magnalia Dei: The Mighty Acts of God* (Garden City, NY: Doubleday, 1976) 414-54.

106. Ben-Dov, "Scientific Writings," 398; Henryk Drawnel, "Some Notes on the Aramaic Manuscripts from Qumran and Late Mesopotamian Culture," *RevQ* 26 (2013) 145-68. On the Babylonian traditions see Francesca Rochberg, *The Heavenly Writing: Divination, Horoscopy, and Astronomy in Mesopotamian Culture* (Cambridge: Cambridge University Press, 2004).

phenomena. There are obvious parallels between Daniel and Joseph, while Enoch is implicitly compared with Balaam in *1 Enoch* 1. In view of the Babylonian associations of both Enoch and Daniel, however, it is reasonable to assume that the affinities between apocalyptic revelation and mantic wisdom are due in some part to Babylonian influence.

## Persian Apocalypticism

For much of the twentieth century Jewish apocalypticism was widely assumed to have been heavily influenced by Persian thought.[107] There is a strong case for such influence in the case of the Qumran scrolls, at least in the dualism of light and darkness.[108] In general, however, scholars have become reticent on this subject because of the notorious difficulty of dating the Persian material.[109] The Zoroastrian scripture, the Avesta, consists of writings from diverse periods which were collected in the Sassanian period (221–642 CE). The Gathas are believed to derive from Zoroaster himself, but the other components of the Avesta (the Younger Avesta) cannot be dated with precision. Moreover, only about one quarter of the original Avesta has survived. Much old material is preserved in the Pahlavi books,

107. For a review of the subject, with extensive bibliography, see G. Widengren, "Leitende Ideen und Quellen der iranischen Apokalyptik," in Hellholm, ed., *Apocalypticism,* 77-162; A. Hultgård, "Das Judentum in der hellenistisch-römischen Zeit und die iranische Religion — ein religionsgeschichtliche Problem," in W. Haase and H. Temporini, eds., *ANRW,* II.19.1 (1979) 512-90; idem, "Persian Apocalypticism," in J. J. Collins, B. McGinn, and S. Stein, eds., *The Encyclopedia of Apocalypticism* (New York: Continuum, 1998), 1.39-83; and with a different interpretation, H. G. Kippenberg, "Die Geschichte der Mittelpersischen Apokalyptischen Traditionen," *Studia Iranica* 7 (1978) 49-80. A recent review of the entire subject can be found in Jason M. Silverman, *Persepolis and Jerusalem: Iranian Influence on the Apocalyptic Hermeneutic* (London: T & T Clark, 2012).

108. S. Shaked, "Iranian Influence on Judaism: First Century BCE to Second Century CE," in W. D. Davies and L. Finkelstein, eds., *The Cambridge History of Judaism* (Cambridge: Cambridge University Press, 1984) 1.308-25; M. Philonenko, "La Doctrine Qoumrânienne des deux Esprits," in G. Widengren, A. Hultgård, and M. Philonenko, eds., *Apocalyptique Iranienne et Dualisme Qoumrânien* (Paris: Maisonneuve, 1995) 163-211.

109. See, however, N. Cohen, *Cosmos, Chaos, and the World to Come: The Ancient Roots of Apocalyptic Faith* (New Haven: Yale University Press, 1993) 77-104, 220-26, who argues that the apocalyptic worldview was first developed by Zoroaster, whom he dates to the second millennium BCE (1500–1200 BCE). Cf. M. Boyce, "Persian Religion in the Achaemenid Age," in Davies and Finkelstein, eds., *The Cambridge History of Judaism,* 1.279-81; G. Gnoli, *Zoroaster's Time and Homeland* (Naples: Istituto universitario orientale, 1980).

but these, in their present form, date chiefly from the ninth century CE.[110] The most important documents of Persian apocalypticism and eschatology belong to this Pahlavi literature. The difficulty lies in determining how far this Pahlavi literature preserves material from the pre-Christian era.[111]

The potential significance of Persian apocalypticism can be seen from a consideration of one of these Pahlavi works, the *Zand-ī Vohuman Yasn*, or *Bahman Yasht*.[112] This work is allegedly a "zand" or interpretation of a lost book of the Avesta, the *Vohuman Yašt*. The lost Yašt is also widely thought to have influenced other Persian apocalyptic writings and, perhaps, some non-Persian oracles, such as the Egyptian *Potter's Oracle*. The Zand also claims (1:1) to depend on the lost *Stûtkar Nask* of the Avesta.

According to the Zand, chapter 1, Zarathustra asked for immortality from Ahura Mazdā but was granted instead "wisdom of all-knowledge." He then saw a tree with four branches, one of gold, one of silver, one of steel, and one of mixed iron. Ahura Mazdā explained the vision, saying that the four branches were four kingdoms of which the last is ruled by the "dīvs who have disheveled hair." The fourth kingdom is said to come when the

---

110. See J. Tavadia, *Die Mittelpersische Sprache und Literatur der Zarathustrier* (Leipzig: Harrassowitz, 1956); M. Boyce, "Middle Persian Literature," in *Handbuch der Orientalistik*, vol. 4/1 (Leiden: Brill, 1968) 31-61; Prods Oktor Skjaervø, "Zoroastrian Dualism" with an appendix on "The Sources of Zoroastrianism," in Armin Lange, Eric M. Meyers, Bennie H. Reynolds III and Randall Styers, eds., *Light against Darkness: Dualism in Ancient Mediterranean Religion and the Contemporary World* (JAJSup 2; Göttingen: Vandenhoeck & Ruprecht, 2011) 55-91. Silverman, *Persepolis and Jerusalem*, 39-75, provides a broad review of sources for the study of Iranian religion, including Greek authors.

111. The antiquity of Persian apocalypticism is defended by M. Boyce, "On the Antiquity of Zoroastrian Apocalyptic," *BSOAS* 47 (1984) 57-75, and A. Hultgård, "Bahman Yasht: A Persian Apocalypse," in Collins and Charlesworth, eds., *Mysteries and Revelations*, 114-34; idem, "Mythe et histoire dans l'Iran ancien," in Widengren, Hultgård, and Philonenko, *Apocalyptique Iranienne et Dualisme Qoumrânien*, 63-162. It is denied by P. Gignoux, "Apocalypses et voyages extra-terrestres dans l'Iran mazdéen," in C. Kappler, ed., *Apocalypses et voyages dans l'au-delà*, 351-74; idem, "L'apocalyptique iranienne est-elle vraiment la source d'autres apocalypses?" *Acta Antiqua Academiae Scientiarum Hungaricae* 31 (1988) 67-78; I. P. Culianu, *Psychanodia I: A Survey of the Evidence concerning the Ascension of the Soul and Its Relevance* (Leiden: Brill, 1983); "Ascension," in M. Eliade, ed., *The Encyclopedia of Religion* (New York: Macmillan, 1987) 435-41.

112. B. T. Anklesaria, *Zand-ī Vohuman Yasn* (Bombay: Camay Oriental Institute, 1967); C. G. Cereti, *The Zand Ī Wahman Yasn: A Zoroastrian Apocalypse* (Rome Oriental Series 75; Rome: Istituto italiano per il medio ed estremo oriente, 1995). See A. Hultgård, "Bahman Yasht: A Persian Apocalypse"; idem, "Mythe et histoire." For a contrary assessment see P. Gignoux, "Sur l'inexistence d'un Bahman Yasht avestique," *Journal of Asian and African Studies* 32 (1986) 53-64.

tenth century, or millennium, of Zarathustra is at an end. Chapter 3 of the Zand contains an extended version of this incident, in which Zarathustra sees seven branches which are again interpreted as kingdoms, and concludes with the "dīvs" of disheveled hair and the end of the millennium of Zarathustra. In chapter 4 Zarathustra inquires about the signs of the tenth century and end of the millennium, and Ahura Mazdā replies by describing a long series of upheavals and disturbances, both political and cosmic. Chapters 7–9 prophesy what will happen when Zarathustra's millennium will end and Aûsîtar's will begin (8:8). Near the end of the second millennium Pêsyôtan son of Vistâsp will appear as a savior figure who will destroy the dīvs. The millennium of Aûsîtarmāh follows, when men will not even die because they "will be so versed in medicine" (9:12). Then at the end of this millennium "Sôsîyôs will make the creatures pure again" and the resurrection will follow (9:23).

The *Bahman Yasht* contains all the key features of an apocalypse of the historical type. It has the appearance of a compilation of sources, but in the words of Anders Hultgård: "the intention of the compiler seems to have been to create a coherent apocalypse, since he orders his materials so as to form a consistent narrative, starting with an account of the manner in which divine revelation comes to Zarathustra, and ending with the description of the final renewal of the world."[113] This is in fact the only extant Persian work that combines the apocalyptic manner of revelation with the elaborate periodization of history and eschatology. There is no doubt that periodization and the succession of millennia, with the attendant sense of determinism, is an integral feature of Persian theology. The classic expression of this view of cosmic history is found in the *Bundahišn*, a late (twelfth-century) compendium of traditional teaching. There the course of history is divided into twelve thousand years. The last nine thousand involve a conflict between Ahura Mazdā and Ahriman. Three thousand years pass according to the will of Ahura Mazdā, three thousand according to the will of both, and in the final three thousand Ahura Mazdā triumphs. The *Bundahišn* contains also an account of the resurrection and the purification of the world by fire (chapter 34).

It is by no means certain that the full schema of history and eschatology that we find in the *Bundahišn* was already developed in the Hellenistic period.[114] We do have a brief early account of Persian religion in Plutarch's

113. Hultgård, "Bahman Yasht," 121.
114. Kippenberg, "Die Geschichte," 53, argues that the schema of twelve thou-

treatise *On Isis and Osiris* (47).[115] There we are told that Ahura Mazdā (Horomazes) and Ahriman (Areimanus) have an ongoing struggle: "for three thousand years alternately the one god will dominate the other and be dominated, and for another three thousand years they will fight and make war, until one smashes up the domain of the other. In the end Hades will perish and men shall be happy." It is not clear whether this schema should be understood as corresponding to the last nine thousand years of the *Bundahišn* or whether it represents a different, earlier system. It is also not certain how far Plutarch's account was representative of Persian theology. Plutarch ascribes this account to Theopompus, who flourished in the fourth century BCE. Although much is uncertain, the passage in Plutarch corroborates the idea that the dualistic struggle of Ahura Mazdā and Ahriman and the division of world history into set periods were at home in Persian thought at the beginning of the Hellenistic age. We know from Theopompus that the belief in resurrection was also developed by this time.[116]

Another witness to Persian apocalyptic thought that can be dated to pre-Christian times is found in the *Oracle of Hystaspes*.[117] References to this oracle are found in Justin, Clement, and Aristokritos, but our main source is the *Divine Institutions* of Lactantius. The nature of the oracle can be seen from *Div. Inst.* 7.15: "A wonderful dream, upon the interpretation of a boy who uttered divinations, announcing long before the Trojan nation that the Roman name would be taken from the world." The manner of revelation is reminiscent of Daniel 2. The content is political upheaval, but there is also a reference to the destruction of the world by fire (Justin, *Apol.* 1.20). Other

---

sand years was derived from the Babylonian zodiac and cannot be earlier than the fourth century BCE.

115. J. G. Griffiths, *Plutarch's De Iside et Osiride* (Cambridge: University of Wales Press, 1970) 193. See M. V. Cerutti, *Antropologia e Apocalittica* (Rome: Bretschneider, 1990) 19-62; A. de Jong, *Traditions of the Magi: Zoroastrianism in Greek and Latin Literature* (Leiden: Brill, 1997). 157-204.

116. Diogenes Laertius, *Proem* 6-9; Hultgård, "Das Judentum," 543.

117. J. R. Hinnells, "The Zoroastrian Doctrine of Salvation in the Roman World: A Study of the Oracle of Hystaspes," in E. J. Sharpe and J. R. Hinnells, eds., *Man and His Salvation: Studies in Memory of S. G. F. Brandon* (Manchester: Manchester University Press, 1973) 125-48. D. Flusser, "Hystaspes and John of Patmos," in S. Shaked, ed., *Irano-Judaica* (Jerusalem: Magnes, 1982) 12-75, argues that Hystaspes is a Jewish pseudepigraph. See the discussion by Frantz Grenet, "Y a-t-il une Composante Iranienne dans l'Apocalyptique Judéo-Chrétienne? Retour sur un vieux Problème," in David Hamidovic, ed., *Aux Origines des Messianismes Juifs* (VTSup 158; Leiden: Brill, 2013) 121-44. See also C. Colpe, "Hystaspes," *Reallexikon für Antike und Christentum* 16 (1991) cols. 1057-82.

features of the oracle may be gathered from passages in Lactantius where Hystaspes is not explicitly mentioned but appears to be used. In *Div. Inst.* 7.16 there is a description of the signs of the end that shows several parallels with the *Bahman Yasht,* and to a lesser extent with the *Bundahišn.* In *Div. Inst.* 7.17 there is a reference to a "great king" who has been variously identified as Mithras, Sošiyans, or a national king.[118] Further, Aristokritos, in the passage that refers to Hystaspes, indicates that "the fulfillment would take place after the fulfillment of 6,000 years." Lactantius (*Div. Inst.* 7.14) says that six *saecula* would elapse before the reign of Christ. Presumably, then, Hystaspes had a schema of six thousand (or seven thousand) years, in contrast to the twelve thousand of the *Bundahišn.* The *Oracle of Hystaspes* has been dated to the first, or possibly the second, century BCE.[119] It is not an apocalypse in form, but it throws important light on Persian eschatology, in a pre-Christian form.

It appears then that several key features of the historical apocalypses were paralleled in Persian writings already in the Hellenistic age, notably the periodization of history, eschatological woes, resurrection, and the supernatural forces of good and evil. Further, the *Bahman Yasht* presents its overview of history in a revelation that is interpreted by a divine being, and in the form of an *ex eventu* prophecy. If this accurately represents the Avestan Yasht, then it may well be that the generic framework or *Rahmengattung* had already been developed by the Persians and was adapted by the Jews. In view of the problems of dating, this can be no more than a possibility. Even if it were true, we should still have to allow for considerable freedom in the Jewish adaptations, since the Persian conception of a sequence of millennia is quite different from what we find in the Jewish apocalypses. The *Bahman Yasht* itself cannot be regarded as the prototype of any Jewish apocalypse, although it is certainly relevant to the discussion of Daniel.[120]

Persian analogues can also be found for the second type of apocalypse, which involves a heavenly journey.[121] There is a full-blown apoc-

118. Kippenberg, "Die Geschichte," 74.

119. Hinnells, "The Zoroastrian Doctrine of Salvation," 145-46. The Persian character of the oracle was established by H. Windisch, *Die Orakel des Hystaspes* (Amsterdam: Akademie, 1929). See also C. Colpe, "Der Begriff 'Menschenson' und die Methode der Erforschung messianischer Prototypen," *Kairos* 12 (1970) 81-112.

120. J. J. Collins, *Daniel: A Commentary on the Book of Daniel* (Hermeneia; Minneapolis: Fortress, 1993) 163-64.

121. See P. Gignoux, "Apocalypses et voyages extra-terrestres dans l'Iran Mazdéen," in C. Kappler, ed., *Apocalypses et voyages dans l'au-delà,* 351-74, especially 364-70.

alypse of this type in the *Book of Arda Viraf*, but it dates from the ninth century.[122] Viraf was a priest who drugged himself to release his spirit to explore the fate of the dead. The book describes his visions of heaven and hell, attended by interpreting angels. The name Viraf occurs in the Avesta, and the book has been thought to have an old kernel; but, of course, any earlier form is hypothetical. The motif of the ascent of the soul is certainly old in Persian tradition.[123] Here again the general outline of this type of apocalypse may have had Persian precedents, but we cannot be certain, because of the dating problem.

The Persian parallels to the apocalyptic genre are more comprehensive in nature than what we find in either postexilic prophecy or the Babylonian prophecies. Yet even if the Persian apocalypses could be dated securely to the Hellenistic age, the Jewish genre cannot be regarded as a simple borrowing, since it is adapted to the needs of Jewish monotheism. Some features of the apocalypses, such as the periodization of history, do indeed seem to be Persian in origin, but the actual motifs in which the Jewish revelations are expressed are drawn predominantly from Jewish tradition. In short, whatever was taken over from Persian apocalypticism was thoroughly reconceived and integrated with other strands of thought.

## The Hellenistic Milieu

Neither the Babylonian nor the Persian material can be conceived as an exclusive matrix for Jewish apocalypticism. There was some interpenetration of Persian and Babylonian ideas in any case, and both circulated widely in the Hellenistic world.[124] The division of history into a set number of periods is attributed to the pagan sibyl of Cumae in Italy, and the famous schema of four kingdoms, which may also be Persian in origin, is attested in several Roman sources.[125] Chaldean astronomy and astrology

122. M. Haug and E. W. West, *The Book of Arda Viraf* (London: Trübner, 1872); P. Gignoux, *Le Livre d'Ardâ Vîrâz* (Paris: Editions Recherches sur les civilisations, 1984); F. Wahman, *Ardā Wirāz Nāmag: The Iranian "Divina Commedia"* (Copenhagen: Curzon, 1986).

123. Hultgård, "Das Judentum," 527-28; Widengren, "Iran and Israel," 126-27.

124. See the classic study of J. Bidez and F. Cumont, *Les Mages Hellénisés* (2 vols.; Paris: Les Belles Lettres, 1938) and de Jong, *Traditions of the Magi*.

125. D. Flusser, "The Four Empires in the Fourth Sibyl and in the Book of Daniel," *Israel Oriental Studies* 2 (1972) 148-75.

enjoyed widespread currency in the Hellenistic age.[126] Analogous material is found in the astrological oracles of Nechepso and Petosiris from Egypt in the second century BCE. In the broadest sense the matrix of the Jewish apocalypses is not any single tradition but the Hellenistic milieu, where motifs from various traditions circulated freely.[127]

The affinities of the apocalypses with widespread Hellenistic conceptions can be seen by considering two clusters of texts, the first involving otherworldly journeys, the second, eschatological prophecy. The motif of the otherworldly journey, both ascent to heaven and descent to the netherworld, was widespread in antiquity and is found already in Homer's *Odyssey*, Book 11.[128] The motif was sufficiently widespread in the early third century BCE to inspire the satire of Menippus of Gadara (in Palestine). In Plato's Myth of Er (*Republic,* Book 10) the journey motif is used to convey a revelation about the judgment of the dead, and Plato's work served as a model for Cicero in the *Somnium Scipionis* and for Plutarch (*De genio Socratis* 21–22 and *De sera numinis vindicta* 22–31).[129] This classical tradition is marked by strong philosophical interests, which are quite different from what we find in the Jewish apocalypses, but the similarities in the conceptual structure are nonetheless noteworthy. Another, less philosophical kind of otherworldly journey is found in Virgil's *Aeneid,* Book 6, where Aeneas is accompanied to Hades by the sibyl.[130]

---

126. F. Cumont, *Astrology and Religion among the Greeks and Romans* (1912; reprint: New York: Dover, 1960) 3-21. On the Chaldeans see Diodorus Siculus 2.29-31; Philo, *Mig. Abr.* 32 (178–81); *Quis Heres* 20 (96–99).

127. For elaboration of the following see my articles "Cosmos and Salvation" and "Jewish Apocalyptic against Its Hellenistic Near Eastern Environment," *BASOR* 220 (1975) 27-36 (= *Seers, Sibyls, and Sages,* 59-74).

128. Attridge, "Greek and Latin Apocalypses," *Semeia* 14 (1979) 162-67; Hengel, *Judaism and Hellenism,* 1.210-17. For the motif in general see C. Colpe, "Die Himmelsreise der Seele ausserhalb und innerhalb der Gnosis," in U. Bianchi, ed., *Le Origini dello Gnosticismo* (Leiden: Brill, 1967) 429-47; A. F. Segal, "Heavenly Ascent in Hellenistic Judaism, Early Christianity and Their Environment," in W. Haase and H. Temporini, eds., *ANRW,* II.23.2 (1980) 1333-94; Jan N. Bremmer, "Descents to Hell and Ascents to Heaven in Apocalyptic Literature," in Collins, ed., *The Oxford Handbook of Apocalyptic Literature,* 340-57. For Greek parallels on the afterlife, heaven, and the netherworld, see T. F. Glasson, *Greek Influence on Jewish Eschatology* (London: SPCK, 1961).

129. On this material see H. D. Betz, "The Problem of Apocalyptic Genre in Greek and Hellenistic Literature: The Case of the Oracle of Trophonius," in Hellholm, ed., *Apocalypticism,* 577-97.

130. See H. Cancik, "Der Eingang in die Unterwelt: Ein religionswissenschaftlicher Versuch zu Vergil, Aeneis 6, 236-72," in *Der altsprachliche Unterricht* (1983) 55-66.

In this case there is also a "prophecy" of the future greatness of Rome. The parodies of Lucian, based on those of Menippus, would suggest that the motif of the otherworldly journey must have been well known in the Greco-Roman world. In the *Nekyomanteia*, Menippus is said to go to Babylon to find a magus to accompany him on his descent. The parody requires that such meddling in the supernatural was associated with magi or with the exotic East. It is possible that the Greek use of this motif was influenced by Eastern prototypes to some extent, although it was developed in a thoroughly Hellenistic way.

These otherworldly journeys provide parallels for the apocalypses that deal primarily with personal eschatology or life after death. The most noteworthy similarities are found in the Diaspora apocalypses, such as *2 Enoch* and the *Testament of Abraham,* which probably date from the first century CE. There are, of course, significant differences in detail — for example, the belief in reincarnation. Plato's Myth of Er is quite alien to the Jewish tradition. Yet the interest in the judgment of the dead is one of the motifs that clearly distinguish the Jewish apocalypses from the earlier biblical tradition. It is noteworthy that belief in the afterlife was widespread in the Hellenistic age in many forms, from Plato's adaptation of the Orphic myths to popular notions of astral immortality.[131]

The second cluster of relevant texts consists of eschatological prophecies.[132] We have already noted the use of *ex eventu* prophecy in the Babylonian tradition. An early Hellenistic example of this phenomenon is found in the *Alexandra* of Lycophron, an obscure learned poem that purports to be the prophecy of Cassandra or Alexandra.[133] Its purpose is apparently to glorify the Trojans and their descendants, the Romans. The four-kingdom schema apparently originated in the context of Near Eastern resistance to Greek and Roman rule, but it was then adapted by the Romans for their purpose. The most significant parallels to the Jewish apocalypses are found in the anti-Hellenistic oracles of various Near Eastern traditions. Here mention should be made of the Babylonian *Dynastic Prophecy* and the

---

131. Jan N. Bremmer, *The Rise and Fall of the Afterlife* (London: Routledge, 2001); Fritz Graf and Sarah Iles Johnston, *Ritual Texts for the Afterlife: Orpheus and the Bacchic Gold Tablets* (London: Routledge, 2007).

132. Attridge, "Greek and Latin Apocalypses," 168-70; Hengel, *Judaism and Hellenism,* 1.181-202.

133. A. W. Mair, *Callimachus, Lycophron, and Aratus* (LCL; Cambridge, MA: Harvard University Press, 1921, 1955). The poem is Alexandrian and dates to either the third or the early second century BCE.

Persian *Oracle of Hystaspes* (and possibly *Bahman Yasht*). In Egypt there was an ongoing tradition of such prophecy, which had its native antecedents in ancient works such as the *Admonitions of Ipuwer* and the *Vision of Neferrohu*.[134] From the Hellenistic period we have the *Demotic Chronicle,* which is written as a "pesher"-like commentary on ancient oracles. The commentary provides *ex eventu* prophecies of the oppression of Egypt by Persians and Greeks and prophesies a future king who will set things right.[135] Another Demotic text, the *Oracle of the Lamb to Bocchoris,* predicts an invasion of Egypt from Syria, followed by nine hundred years of oppression, but ending with a restoration. The most famous example of Hellenistic Egyptian prophecy is the *Potter's Oracle,* which is preserved in, and was probably composed in, Greek.[136] It contains a "prophecy" of Greek domination, followed by cosmic and social chaos and a war with a king from Syria. Finally, Alexandria will be laid waste and a king will come from the sun, sent by the great goddess Isis, to restore Egypt. It has been argued that a later redaction of this text speaks of cosmic renewal rather than national restoration.[137]

These political prophecies typically claim to have been issued in an ancient time — the *Demotic Chronicle* under Pharaoh Tachos, the *Potter's Oracle* under King Amenhotep, etc. They also draw on ancient traditions. The *Potter's Oracle* draws on the structure of Egyptian creation myths and echoes the prophecy of Neferty from the twentieth century BCE. Naturally, an Egyptian oracle draws on primarily Egyptian traditions, but the implication is that even when the Jewish apocalypses draw on biblical or

---

134. C. C. McCown, "Hebrew and Egyptian Apocalyptic Literature," *HTR* 18 (1925) 357-411; J. G. Griffiths, "Apocalyptic in the Hellenistic Era," in Hellholm, ed., *Apocalypticism,* 273-93; A. Blasius and B. U. Schipper, eds., *Apokalyptik und Ägypten: eine kritische Analyse der relevanten Texte aus dem griechisch-römischen Ägypten* (Leuven: Peeters, 2002). On the earlier material see J. Assmann, "Königsdogma und Heilserwartung: Politische und kultische Kaosbeschreibungen in altägyptischen Texten," in Hellholm, ed., *Apocalypticism,* 345-77. For other apocalyptic motifs in Egyptian tradition, see J. G. Griffiths, *The Divine Verdict* (Leiden: Brill, 1991) 201-42.

135. F. Daumas, "Littérature prophétique égyptienne et commentaires esséniens," in A. Barucq, ed., *À la Rencontre de Dieu: Mémorial Albert Gelin* (Le Puy: Mappus, 1961) 203-21.

136. On Bocchoris and the Potter's Oracle see L. Koenen, "The Prophecies of a Potter: A Prophecy of World Renewal Becomes an Apocalypse," in D. H. Samuel, ed., *Proceedings of the Twelfth International Congress of Papyrology* (Toronto: Hakkert, 1970) 249-54; F. Dunand, "L'Oracle du Potier et la formation de l'apocalyptique en Égypte," in *L'Apocalyptique,* 39-67.

137. So Koenen, "The Prophecies of a Potter."

Canaanite traditions, such retrieval of ancient imagery is a common phenomenon of the Hellenistic age.[138]

These Hellenistic parallels do not argue that the apocalyptic genre is derived from Hellenistic culture or that the Jewish apocalypses lack their own originality and integrity. In Rolf Knierim's terms, the Hellenistic world furnishes some of the codes that are used in the apocalypses. It remains true that the apocalypses draw heavily on biblical tradition and that common Hellenistic motifs take on a distinctive appearance in a Jewish context. The pseudonymous authors of the apocalypses are, predominantly, patriarchs and leaders from biblical history, and the ancient traditions to which the Jewish writers looked were predominantly their own. It is equally true, however, that Jewish tradition is adapted in ways that are broadly typical of the Hellenistic age. It is important that several of the most prominent aspects of the apocalypses involve modifications of biblical tradition that are in accord with widespread ideas of the Hellenistic age: pseudepigraphy, periodization, *ex eventu* prophecy, heavenly journeys, interest in the heavenly world, judgment of the dead. In the earliest Jewish apocalypses these motifs are woven together with considerable originality, and indeed variety, into a composite structure that was distinctively Jewish but was also strikingly new, as over against the earlier biblical tradition.

The Hellenistic parallels may be explained by two factors. First, the conquests of Alexander brought changes that were common to the entire Near East. The network of Hellenistic cities facilitated the spread of ideas. Hence we get the sense of a *Zeitgeist,* of a common atmosphere of ideas and attitudes, even when they are not clearly articulated and when we cannot document specific borrowings. Second, the spread of Hellenism changed the political and social circumstances of the Near East. The Jews had lost their native kingship at the time of the Babylonian exile. Now the Egyptians and Babylonians had lost theirs too. When the *Potter's Oracle* anticipates the coming of an ideal king, we need not suppose that it has been influenced by Jewish messianism or vice versa. Similar circumstances could produce similar effects in traditions that had considerable similarity to begin with.[139] The Hellenistic age was marked by widespread nostalgia for the past and alienation from the present. In a

---

138. See further J. Z. Smith, "Wisdom and Apocalyptic," in B. Pearson, ed., *Religious Syncretism in Antiquity* (Missoula, MT: Scholars Press, 1975) 136-37.

139. J. Z. Smith, "Native Cults in the Hellenistic Period," *HR* 11 (1971) 236-49.

broad sense this "Hellenistic mood" may be considered a matrix for the apocalyptic literature.

## The Social Settings

The more specific social and historical matrices of the apocalyptic literature will be discussed in relation to the specific texts. Older scholarship in this area has suffered from excessive hastiness because of the tendency to assume that the setting of one or two well-known apocalypses is representative of the whole genre. We will refrain deliberately from applying a sociological or anthropological model.[140] Such models may well prove to be illuminating, but if they are to be used validly they must presuppose an adequate literary understanding of the apocalypses. We cannot assume a priori that the Enoch literature attests the same phenomenon that anthropologists, on the basis of very different evidence, call a millenarian movement or "apocalyptic religion."

When we approach the question of social setting inductively, it is apparent that some commonplace assumptions are in need of qualification. There is no basis for the assumption that all the apocalyptic literature was produced by a single movement.[141] We may speak of apocalyptic movements in specific cases such as Qumran and early Christianity. There are also clusters of texts, such as the early Enoch books, which belong to a common tradition. In those cases we may assume some social and historical continuity on the part of the authors. It is not apparent, however, that the authors of Daniel belonged to the same circles as those of *1 Enoch*. The apocalypses 4 Ezra and 2 *Baruch* represent a very different theological tradition from the Enoch literature. It is misleading, then, to

---

140. For exploratory studies see R. R. Wilson, "This World — and the World to Come," *Encounter* 38 (1977) 117-24; J. G. Gager, *Kingdom and Community: The Social World of Early Christianity* (Englewood Cliffs, NJ: Prentice-Hall, 1975); P. R. Davies, "The Social World of the Apocalyptic Writings," in R. E. Clements, ed., *The World of Ancient Israel* (Cambridge: Cambridge University Press, 1989) 251-71; L. L. Grabbe, "The Social World of Early Jewish Apocalypticism," *JSP* 4 (1989) 27-47; S. L. Cook, *Prophecy and Apocalypticism: The Postexilic Social Setting* (Minneapolis: Fortress, 1995) 1-84; Philip F. Esler, "Social-Scientific Approaches to Apocalyptic Literature," in Collins, ed. *The Oxford Handbook of Apocalyptic Literature*, 123-44.

141. Compare R. R. Wilson, "From Prophecy to Apocalyptic: Reflections on the Shape of Israelite Religion," *Semeia* 21 (1981) 79-95.

speak of "the apocalyptic movement"[142] as though it were a single unified social phenomenon.

P. Vielhauer's thesis that the apocalypses were conventicle litera-ture[143] finds some support in the case of Qumran (where the sectarian literature is "apocalyptic" in a broader sense, though not in the form of apocalypses). It is possible, but only hypothetical, that the Enoch liter-ature originated in conventicles. The thesis would have to be modified somewhat for a work like Daniel and has no apparent justification in the case of 4 Ezra or 2 *Baruch*. The "conventicle" theory of apocalypticism is at best an unwarranted generalization.

Vielhauer's broader thesis, that the apocalypses were "written out of actual distresses," holds true, if we allow that the distresses may be of var-ious kinds.[144] Daniel 7–12 was written in the heat of persecution, but this seems to be rather exceptional. The apocalypses 4 Ezra and 2 and 3 *Baruch* reflect the aftermath of the destruction of Jerusalem after a considerable interval. The kind of division within the community which Paul Hanson posits as the matrix of postexilic prophecy may have been generative in the case of the Qumran community, but it is by no means a constant factor.[145] In some cases, such as the Book of the Watchers, we cannot specify the underlying crisis with any confidence. We must also reckon with the fact that what is perceived as a crisis by an apocalyptic author may not have been universally so perceived.[146]

## The Compositional Setting

The apocalyptic literature is a "scribal phenomenon,"[147] a product of learned activity rather than popular folklore. The pseudonymous authors

---

142. W. Schmithals, *The Apocalyptic Movement* (Nashville: Abingdon, 1975). The orig-inal German title was *Die Apokalyptik: Einführung und Deutung*.

143. P. Vielhauer and G. Strecker, "Apocalypses and Related Subjects," in E. Hen-necke, W. Schneemelcher, and R. McL. Wilson, eds., *New Testament Apocrypha* (2 vols.; Louisville: Westminster, 1991) 2:558.

144. Ibid.

145. See Adler, "Introduction," in VanderKam and Adler, eds., *The Jewish Apocalyptic Heritage*, 19-20.

146. G. W. E. Nickelsburg, "Social Aspects of Palestinian Jewish Apocalypticism," in Hellholm, ed., *Apocalypticism*, 639-42.

147. J. Z. Smith, "Wisdom and Apocalyptic," 140.

are frequently identified as wise men or scribes — Enoch, Daniel, Ezra, Baruch.[148] The pervasive allusions to biblical and other traditional lore most probably reflect systematic study. Our clearest illustrations of the use of scripture in this period are found in the Qumran writings, which reflect the constant study of the sacred writings that was practiced by the members of the community. This literature was esoteric insofar as it was produced by the learned few, but it was not necessarily designed to be kept secret. The wise in Daniel were to instruct the masses, presumably by divulging their revelations. Even in 4 Ezra 14, where we are told that seventy books are reserved for the wise among the people, it would seem that the time has come to make this material available to the larger public.

A more difficult question concerns the authenticity of the visionary experiences recorded in the apocalypses. On the one hand there are manifold resemblances between the vision accounts and the experience of visionaries and shamans elsewhere (e.g., the visionaries often fast or make other preparations for reception of visions).[149] On the other hand the phenomenon of pseudonymity complicates the issue, since we do not hear elsewhere of pseudonymous shamans.

Pseudonymity was very widespread in the Hellenistic age.[150] It is attested in Babylonian, Persian, and Egyptian prophecy, and in various Greek and Latin genres. It cannot be explained simply as a consequence of the decline of Israelite prophecy,[151] although it does imply a height-

---

148. von Rad, *Theologie*, 2:316.

149. M. Stone, "Apocalyptic — Vision or Hallucination?" *Milla wa-Milla* 14 (1974) 47-56; "A Reconsideration of Apocalyptic Visions," *HTR* 96 (2003) 167-80; *Ancient Judaism. New Visions and Views* (Grand Rapids: Eerdmans, 2011) 90-109; Rowland, *The Open Heaven*, 214-47; S. Niditch, "The Visionary," in G. W. E. Nickelsburg and J. J. Collins, eds., *Ideal Figures in Ancient Judaism* (Missoula, MT: Scholars Press, 1980) 153-79; D. Merkur, "The Visionary Practices of Jewish Apocalyptists," in L. Bryce Boyer and S. A. Grolnick, eds., *The Psychoanalytic Study of Society* 14 (Hillsdale, NJ: The Analytic Press, 1989) 119-48.

150. B. Metzger, "Literary Forgeries and Canonical Pseudepigrapha," *JBL* 91 (1972) 3-24; W. Speyer, "Religiöse Pseudepigraphie und literarische Fälschung im Altertum," in idem, *Frühes Christentum im antiken Strahlungsfeld* (Tübingen: Mohr Siebeck, 1989) 21-58; "Fälschung, pseudepigraphische freie Erfindung und 'echte religiöse Pseudepigraphie,' " ibid., 100-33; Jörg Frey, Jens Herzer, Martina Janssen, and Clare K. Rothschild, eds., *Pseudepigraphie und Verfasserfiktion in frühchristlichen Briefen* (WUNT 246; Tübingen: Mohr Siebeck, 2009) especially 105-330.

151. R. H. Charles, *The Apocrypha and Pseudepigrapha of the Old Testament* (2 vols.; Oxford: Clarendon, 1913) 2:ix.

ened veneration of the past. The theory that it was intended to shelter the real authors from persecution is also unsatisfactory:[152] not all the apocalypses would have provoked persecution, and some apocalyptic writers would in any case have welcomed martyrdom (see, e.g., Daniel 11). While the reasons for pseudonymity may have varied from case to case,[153] the most fundamental reason would seem to be bound up with a claim to authority. There is no doubt that a pseudonym such as Enoch or Abraham enhanced the authority of a writing. It also augmented a sense of determinism, especially in the "historical" apocalypses, by affirming that the course of history or the structure of the cosmos was determined long ago. In many cases, the presumed analogy between the situations of the ancient sage and the real author helped to provide perspective on the present. In view of the extent of the phenomenon, we must assume that the authors of this literature were conscious of its conventional character. At the same time, the effectiveness of the device presupposes the credulity of the masses.[154]

To say that pseudonymity was a device is not to say that it was used arbitrarily. The pseudonym had to be appropriate for the subject matter. So heavenly revelations could aptly be ascribed to Enoch, but a wisdom book was more appropriate to Solomon. Hindy Najman proposes that we think of pseudepigraphic compositions as "discourse tied to a founder." So, for example, the book of *Jubilees* is "Mosaic discourse," and the writings of Enoch are "Enochic discourse."[155] She writes that "by extending a discourse attached to a founder of an earlier period, writers in the late Second Temple period and even after the destruction of the Second Temple are able to authorize and link their new texts to old established traditions and founders."[156] This is an illuminating suggestion in some instances, but not necessarily in all.[157]

152. Hanson, *The Dawn of Apocalyptic*, 252.

153. See the broad-ranging discussions of pseudepigraphy by Stone, *Ancient Judaism*, 109-21, and Vicente Dobroruka, *Second Temple Pseudepigraphy: A Cross-cultural Comparison of Apocalyptic Texts and Related Jewish Literature* (Ekstasis 3; Berlin: de Gruyter, 2014).

154. See further my discussion in *The Apocalyptic Vision of the Book of Daniel*, 67-74.

155. Hindy Najman, "How Should We Contextualize Pseudepigrapha? Imitation and Emulation in 4 Ezra," in eadem, *Past Renewals: Interpretative Authority, Renewed Revelation and the Quest for Perfection in Jewish Antiquity* (JSJSup 53; Leiden: Brill, 2010) 235-43 (here 238).

156. Ibid.

157. See my essay "Enoch and Ezra," in Matthias Henze and Gabriele Boccaccini, eds., *Fourth Ezra and Second Baruch: Reconstruction after the Fall* (Leiden: Brill, 2013) 83-97.

How far the real author can be said to have identified with his pseudonymous counterpart is more difficult to say. Christopher Rowland appeals to Johannes Lindblom's discussion of visionary psychology for the view that "frequently the visionary distinguishes between two persons representing himself; the one being his everyday *ego,* the other the extraordinary *ego,*"[158] but he admits that this phenomenon is still some distance from the pseudonymity of the apocalypses. The psychology of pseudonymity is closely related to the question of the authenticity of the visions. Rowland suggests that many (not necessarily all) apocalyptic visions were experienced in the context of reflection on scripture. In general, though, it would seem that the underlying problems addressed in the visions were not exegetical but concerned historical and existential matters. The scriptures provided at most the occasion of the revelation, and the authority of the apocalypses was not derived from scripture but from new revelation.[159] The contrast between "authentic religious experience" and literary activity may be overdrawn. The composition of highly symbolic literature involves a vivid use of the imagination, which may be difficult to distinguish from visionary experience in any case. Similarly, the apocalyptists may have felt an intense and emotional kinship with their pseudonymous counterparts, while still being aware of the fiction involved. It is worth bearing in mind that even shamans have to learn the cosmology and mythology of their ascents before they can "experience" them in ecstasy.[160]

## The Literary Function

From the preceding discussion it is apparent that the settings of the apocalyptic genre present complex problems and that generalizations are of limited value. It is possible, however, to speak of the illocution or literary function of a text apart from the social setting. David Hellholm has pro-

---

158. Rowland, *The Open Heaven,* 243; J. Lindblom, *Prophecy in Ancient Israel* (Oxford: Blackwell, 1962) 44. D. S. Russell appealed to the supposedly Hebrew notions of corporate personality and contemporaneity to suggest a quasi-mystical identification with the pseudonymous hero (*Method and Message,* 132-39).

159. Stone, "Apocalyptic Literature," 429.

160. M. Eliade, *Shamanism: Archaic Techniques of Ecstasy* (Princeton: Princeton University Press, 1964) 266; R. R. Wilson, *Prophecy and Society in Ancient Israel* (Philadelphia: Fortress, 1980) 54-56.

posed that the definition of apocalypse in *Semeia* 14 be emended by the following addition: *"intended for a group in crisis with the purpose of exhortation and/or consolation by means of divine authority."*[161]

The reference to a "group in crisis" is appropriate for many apocalypses, though scarcely for all; but it is perhaps too suggestive of the conventicle theory of apocalypticism. It is true, however, that all apocalypses address some underlying problem. It is obvious enough that the manner of revelation is designed to lend supernatural authority to the message (the divinity is not always directly invoked).[162] The main problem with specifying the function in the definition is that even on this general level the purpose of a text may be a matter of dispute. Is the function of 4 Ezra to console or to instruct and refute? Even if we concluded that its purpose was refutation (of a heretical party represented by Ezra, as some have claimed), 4 Ezra would surely be still an apocalypse.

In fact, however, the illocutionary functions of exhortation and consolation can generally be maintained for the Jewish apocalypses.[163] Two qualifications must be kept in mind. First, the nature of the exhortations may vary. The Animal Apocalypse in *1 Enoch* encourages support for the Maccabean revolt. The message of Daniel, in the same setting, is quite different. Second, the literary function must be seen to be integrally related to form and content in what may be called the "apocalyptic technique." Whatever the underlying problem, it is viewed from a distinctive apocalyptic perspective. This perspective is framed spatially by the supernatural world and temporally by the eschatological judgment. The problem is not viewed simply in terms of the historical factors available to any observer. Rather it is viewed in the light of a transcendent reality disclosed by the apocalypse, or, to put it differently, an apocalyptic vision facilitates an alternative experience of reality.[164] The transcendent world may be expressed through

---

161. D. Hellholm, "The Problem of Apocalyptic Genre and the Apocalypse of John," in A. Yarbro Collins, ed., *Early Christian Apocalypticism: Genre and Social Setting* (*Semeia* 36; Decatur, GA: Scholars Press, 1986) 27. Hellholm would accept the emended version as a "paradigmatic" definition. He is primarily concerned with developing a "syntagmatic" approach; see his *Das Visionenbuch des Hermas als Apokalypse*.

162. Cf. Adler, "Introduction," in VanderKam and Adler, eds., *The Jewish Apocalyptic Heritage*, 19-21.

163. Compare *Semeia* 14 (1979) 9, 12. On the hortatory function of the apocalypses, see further C. Münchow, *Ethik und Eschatologie* (Göttingen: Vandenhoeck & Ruprecht, 1982).

164. Jin Hee Han, *Daniel's Spiel: Apocalyptic Literacy in the Book of Daniel* (Lanham, MD: University Press of America, 2008) 29.

mythological symbolism or celestial geography or both. It puts the problem in perspective and projects a definitive resolution to come. This apocalyptic technique does not, of course, have a publicly discernible effect on a historical crisis, but it provides a resolution in the imagination by instilling conviction in the revealed "knowledge" that it imparts. The function of the apocalyptic literature is to shape one's imaginative perception of a situation and so lay the basis for whatever course of action it exhorts.[165]

165. Compare the emendation of the definition of the genre by A. Yarbro Collins, "Introduction: Early Christian Apocalypticism," in *Semeia* 36 (1986) 7: an apocalypse is "intended to interpret present, earthly circumstances in light of the supernatural world and of the future, and to influence both the understanding and the behavior of the audience by means of divine authority." Cf. also D. Aune, "The Apocalypse of John and the Problem of Genre," ibid., 87.

# CHAPTER TWO

# The Early Enoch Literature

The publication of the Ethiopic *Book of Enoch* in the early nineteenth century was a major stimulus to the modern study of apocalyptic literature. In recent years the publication of the Aramaic fragments of *Enoch* from Qumran has intensified interest in the subject and changed our conception of its history. In fact, *1 Enoch* is not just one work, but is a major collection of apocalyptic writings. Five separate compositions have long been distinguished: the Book of the Watchers (chaps. 1–36), the Similitudes (chaps. 37–71), the Astronomical Book (chaps. 72–82), the Book of Dreams (chaps. 83–90), and the Epistle of Enoch (chaps. 91–108). Within the Epistle, the Apocalypse of Weeks (93:1-10; 91:11-17) stands out as a distinct unit.[1] The full corpus of *1 Enoch* is only extant in Ethiopic.[2] Substantial portions of the first and fifth parts and a passage from the fourth have been discovered in Greek.[3] In recent years Aramaic fragments of all parts except the Similitudes have been found at Qumran, and also fragments of a related composition, the Book of Giants. The editor of the Aramaic fragments,

---

1. R. H. Charles, *APOT*, 2:168-70; idem, *The Book of Enoch* (Oxford: Clarendon, 1893). This is one of the few instances in which Charles's division of an apocalyptic book has stood the test of time. See George W. E. Nickelsburg, *1 Enoch 1* (Hermeneia; Minneapolis: Fortress, 2001) 7-8.

2. Text and translation: M. A. Knibb, *The Ethiopic Book of Enoch* (2 vols.; Oxford: Clarendon, 1978). See also the textual information provided by E. Isaac, "1 Enoch," in J. H. Charlesworth, ed., *OTP*, 1:6, 10-12; and M. Black, *The Book of Enoch or 1 Enoch* (SVTP 7; Leiden: Brill, 1985). For a convenient translation see George W. E. Nickelsburg and James C. VanderKam, *1 Enoch: A New Translation* (Minneapolis: Fortress, 2004).

3. M. Black, *Apocalypsis Henochi Graece* (PVTG 3; Leiden: Brill, 1970). Extracts from the Greek and Latin literature were known before the discovery of the Ethiopic text.

J. T. Milik, argued that the five books, counting the Book of Giants, found at Qumran constituted an Enochic pentateuch, which was a counterpart of the Mosaic pentateuch.[4] The Astronomical Book, however, was copied on a separate scroll. There is no textual evidence that the Enochic corpus was conceived as a pentateuch or was correlated with the Mosaic Torah. A more plausible suggestion is that the order of the collection reflects the sequence of Enoch's supposed career.[5]

R. H. Charles was already aware that the earliest sections of *1 Enoch* were written before the Maccabean revolt. The discoveries at Qumran considerably strengthened the evidence. The earliest manuscript of the Astronomical Book is dated by Milik to "the end of the third or the beginning of the second century."[6] The oldest fragments of the Book of the Watchers are ascribed to the first half of the second century. Since the compositions are presumably somewhat older than the earliest fragments, and since the Book of the Watchers shows evidence of multiple stages of composition, it is probable that both these works were extant in some form already in the third century BCE.[7] Indeed Milik has argued that both the Astronomical Book and the Book of the Watchers are presupposed in Genesis 5–6. It seems clear enough that Genesis is alluding to some more extensive traditions, but the correspondences between the biblical text and *1 Enoch* can be more satisfactorily explained on the assumption that Genesis is prior.[8] The link between Enoch and the fallen angels is neither

4. J. T. Milik, *The Books of Enoch: Aramaic Fragments from Qumrân Cave 4* (Oxford: Clarendon, 1976) 4. On the Book of the Giants that was preserved and adapted in Manichaeism, see Milik, *Books of Enoch,* 298-339; J. C. Reeves, *Jewish Lore in Manichaean Cosmogony: Studies in the Book of Giants Traditions* (Cincinnati: Hebrew Union College, 1992); L. T. Stuckenbruck, *The Book of Giants from Qumran* (Tübingen: Mohr Siebeck, 1997). Milik's conclusions on the late date of the Similitudes will be discussed in a later chapter.

5. So D. Dimant, "The Biography of Enoch and the Books of Enoch," *VT* 33 (1983) 14-29.

6. Milik, *Books of Enoch,* 7. On the identification of the fragments, see J. C. VanderKam, *Enoch and the Growth of an Apocalyptic Tradition* (CBQMS 16; Washington, DC: Catholic Biblical Association of America, 1984) 80-83; Nickelsburg, *1 Enoch 1,* 9-10; Michael A. Knibb, "The Book of Enoch or Books of Enoch? The Textual Evidence for 1 Enoch," in Gabriele Boccaccini and John J. Collins, eds., *The Early Enoch Literature* (JSJSup 121; Leiden: Brill, 2007) 21-40.

7. See M. E. Stone, "The Book of Enoch and Judaism in the Third Century BCE," *CBQ* 40 (1978) 479-92; idem, *Scriptures, Sects, and Visions: A Profile of Judaism from Ezra to the Jewish Revolts* (Philadelphia: Fortress, 1980) 31.

8. Note however the ingenious argument of Helge Kvanvig, *Primeval History: Babylo-*

made nor presumed in Genesis, but rather seems to have been suggested by the juxtaposition of these episodes in the biblical story. No section of *1 Enoch* as we have it can be dated prior to the Hellenistic age, although it undoubtedly draws on older traditions.

## The Figure of Enoch

The figure of Enoch is a highly enigmatic one in the biblical text. In Gen 4:17, Enoch is the son of Cain, but in Gen 5:18-24 we read that Enoch was the son of Jared and the father of Methuselah. "Thus, all the days of Enoch were three hundred and sixty-five years. Enoch walked with God; and he was not, for God took him."[9] Evidently this brief notice does not imply the full account of Enoch's otherworldly journeys which we find in *1 Enoch,* but is rather the seed from which later speculation grew. We do not know how elaborate a story is presupposed in Genesis. The biblical allusion does, however, contain some intriguing indications of the context in which Enoch speculation developed.[10]

Enoch is listed in Genesis as seventh in line from Adam. In the *Sumerian King List,* the seventh king is Enmeduranki or Enmenduranna. Sippar, the city ruled by this king, was a center of the cult of Shamash, the sun god. Enoch is associated with the solar calendar: his age is given as 365 years in Genesis and the Astronomical Book presupposes a calendar of 364 days. Enmeduranki was also the founder of a guild of diviners and a recipient of revelations. His enthronement is described as follows:[11]

---

nian, Biblical, and Enochic: An Intertextual Reading ( JSJSup 149; Leiden: Brill, 2011) 373-95, that one strand of the Book of the Watchers is prior to Genesis.

9. So NRSV, but see VanderKam, who argues that 'elohîm ("God") should be translated "angels" (*Enoch and the Growth of an Apocalyptic Tradition,* 31). Compare Dimant, "Biography of Enoch," 21.

10. For the following, compare VanderKam, *Enoch and the Growth of an Apocalyptic Tradition,* 33-51; idem, *Enoch: A Man for All Generations* (Columbia, SC: University of South Carolina Press, 1995) 6-8; P. Grelot, "La légende d'Hénoch dans les apocryphes et dans la Bible: Son origine et signification," *RSR* 46 (1958) 5-26, 181-210; H. S. Kvanvig, *Roots of Apocalyptic: The Mesopotamian Background of the Enoch Figure and of the Son of Man* (WMANT 61; Neukirchen–Vluyn: Neukirchener Verlag, 1988) 160-213. Less reliable is H. Ludin Jansen, *Die Henochgestalt* (Oslo: Dybwad, 1939).

11. G. Widengren, *The Ascension of the Apostle and the Heavenly Book* (Uppsala: Almqvist & Wiksell, 1950) 7-8; W. G. Lambert, "Enmeduranki and Related Matters," *JCS* 21 (1967) 126-38; VanderKam, *Enoch and the Growth of an Apocalyptic Tradition,* 39-41.

Šamaš in Ebabbarra [appointed]
Enmeduranki, [king of Sippar]
the beloved of Anu, Enlil [and Ea].
Šamaš and Adad [brought him in] to their assembly.
Šamaš and Adad set him on a large throne of gold;
they showed him how to observe oil on water,
a mystery of Anu, they gave him
the tablet of the gods, the liver,
a secret of heaven [and the underworld],
they put in his hand the cedar (rod), beloved of the great gods.

This text is of interest in view of the elevation of Enoch, and especially in view of his identification with the "Son of Man" figure in *1 Enoch* 71. Enoch's wisdom is derived from "the heavenly vision . . . the words of the holy angels and . . . the tablets of heaven" (93:2). Evidently the biblical seventh man emulates the Mesopotamian seventh king.

Other Mesopotamian analogies can be found for the figure of Enoch. Utuabzu, the seventh sage, a contemporary of Enmeduranki, was said to have been taken up to heaven.[12] A noteworthy parallel to the translation of Enoch (by which "God took him") is found in the epic of Gilgamesh. There, after the flood had subsided, the god Enlil declared to Utnapishtim/Atrahasis, the flood hero:

"Hitherto Utnapishtim has been but human.
Henceforth Utnapishtim and his wife shall be like us gods.
Utnapishtim shall reside far away, at the mouth of the rivers!"
Then they took me and made me reside far away,
At the mouth of the rivers.[13]

The biblical equivalent of Utnapishtim is Noah, but it is Enoch, not Noah, who is "taken" by God. It is also noteworthy that Ea "let Atrahasis see a dream and he perceived the secret of the gods"[14] — specifically, the imminent flood. We might compare Enoch's dream-vision of the destruction

---

12. R. Borger, "Die Beschwörungsserie Bīt Mēseri und die Himmelfahrt Henochs," *JNES* 33 (1974) 183-96.

13. *ANET*, 95.

14. Ibid.

of the earth in *1 Enoch* 83. Enoch had also acquired some features of the Mesopotamian flood hero.

We should not attempt to identify one Mesopotamian figure as the sole, sufficient prototype of Enoch. Rather, the Jewish figure picks up and combines elements associated with various mythical heroes. The purpose of the development of this Enoch legend vis-à-vis Mesopotamian legend is clear enough. The peoples of the ancient Near East engaged in what might be called "competitive historiography" to show how their national heroes outshone the heroes of other peoples or were the true and most ancient founders of culture.[15] The Babylonian Berossus and the Egyptian Manetho produced national histories in Greek in the third century which stressed the antiquity of their own peoples. A fragment of a Samaritan work that Eusebius incorrectly ascribed to Eupolemus claims that Enoch, not the Egyptians, invented astrology and that he was really identical with Atlas, to whom the Greeks ascribe the invention.[16] The parallels between Enoch and the legendary Mesopotamian figures suggest that Enoch was developed as a Jewish counterpart of such heroes as Enmeduranki — no less than them in antiquity, status, or access to divine knowledge. Insofar as he combined traits of various heroes, he might be said to be superior to any of them. The most natural setting for the development of the figure of Enoch, with its strong Babylonian associations, was surely the eastern Diaspora, although the extant Enoch books may still have been composed in Judea, and some of them certainly were.

The figure of Enoch, then, might be viewed from one aspect as an answer to the heroes for whom the Babylonians claimed great wisdom and revelatory power. The figure was also of significance within the Jewish tradition. Since Enoch was mysteriously "taken" by God, he was well qualified to be the revealer of heavenly mysteries. Further, he was more ancient than Moses and was associated with primordial history. There is no necessary opposition between Enoch and Moses, but Enoch could serve as the authority for a revelation over and above that of Moses. We should also note that Enoch is not associated with the distinctive history of Israel but with the primordial history of all humanity.

---

15. M. Braun, *History and Romance* (Oxford: Oxford University Press, 1938); J. J. Collins, *Between Athens and Jerusalem: Jewish Identity in the Hellenistic Diaspora* (New York: Crossroad, 1983; revised ed., Grand Rapids: Eerdmans, 2000) chap. 1.

16. Ps.-Eupolemus *PE* 9.17.2-9; VanderKam, *Enoch: A Man for All Generations*, 108-10.

## The Book of the Watchers

The Book of the Watchers may serve as our introduction to the Enoch literature, since it is one of the oldest, pre-Maccabean Enochic works and gives the most explicit elaboration of the story of Enoch. It has received extensive attention in recent years.[17] Much of the discussion has focused on smaller units within *1 Enoch* 1–36: chaps. 6–11, 6–16, or 6–19. There is no doubt that the book is composite in origin, although it is questionable whether we can separate the strands exactly or profitably discuss the date and provenance of the components. It is also clear that the various sources have been woven together into a unified whole. The earliest fragments, 4QEn[a], extend from 1:1-6 to 12:4-6. The apparently distinct unit of chaps. 6–11 was already integrated into a larger whole. The full book of chaps. 1–36 is fragmentarily represented in manuscripts from the first century CE but seems to be presupposed already in the book of *Jubilees* in the mid-second century BCE.[18] Milik maintained that the Qumran manuscripts "allow us to establish that from the first half of the second century onwards the *Book of the Watchers* had essentially the same form as that in which it is known through the Greek and Ethiopic versions."[19]

The book may be divided into three main sections: chaps. 1–5, 6–16, and 17–36.[20]

17. For bibliography and much of the following discussion, see my article "The Apocalyptic Technique: Setting and Function in the Book of the Watchers," *CBQ* 44 (1982) 91-111; also G. W. E. Nickelsburg, "The Books of Enoch in Recent Research," *RelStudRev* 7 (1981) 210-17; *1 Enoch 1*, 109-25; also P. Sacchi, *Jewish Apocalyptic and Its History* (Sheffield: Sheffield Academic Press, 1997) 32-71. More recent discussions can be found in Gabriele Boccaccini, ed., *The Origins of Enochic Judaism* = Henoch 24.1-2 (Turon: Zamporani, 2002).

18. J. C. VanderKam, "Enoch Traditions in Jubilees and Other Second-Century Sources," in P. J. Achtemeier, ed., *Society of Biblical Literature 1978 Seminar Papers* (2 vols.; Missoula, MT: Scholars Press, 1978) 1:235, despite the demurral of Dimant, "Biography of Enoch," 23. See also John S. Bergsma, "The Relationship between Jubilees and the Early Enochic Books," in Gabriele Boccaccini and Giovanni Ibba, eds., *Enoch and the Mosaic Torah: The Evidence of Jubilees* (Grand Rapids: Eerdmans, 2009) 36-51.

19. Milik, *Books of Enoch*, 25.

20. Annette Yoshiko Reed, *Fallen Angels and the History of Judaism and Christianity: The Reception of Enochic Literature* (Cambridge: Cambridge University Press, 2005) 24-25, distinguishes five units, 1-5; 6-11; 12-16; 17-19 and 20-32.

## *The Introduction*

Chapters 1–5 constitute an introduction. The book is characterized as "the words of the blessing of Enoch according to which he blessed the chosen and righteous who must be present on the day of distress (which is appointed) for the removal of all the wicked and impious" (1:1). The "chosen" and "righteous" are stereotyped designations in the Enoch literature. We will return below to the question whether they indicate a distinct group or movement. The term "blessing" recalls the Blessing of Moses in Deuteronomy 33. It evidently refers to the destiny of the righteous on "the day of distress." Already from the opening verse, the book has an eschatological horizon: it is ultimately concerned with the final judgment of righteous and wicked. The second verse adds a second characterization which is more obviously appropriate: "a holy vision in the heavens which the angels showed to me." Although Enoch is described in terms reminiscent of Balaam's oracle ("whose eyes were opened"), the manner of revelation goes beyond the conventions of the prophets and is typically apocalyptic. Since Enoch is supposed to have lived in primordial times, his revelation is inevitably "for a distant generation."

The initial characterization of the book is followed by a prophecy of God's coming in judgment, reminiscent of the theophanies in Deuteronomy 33, Judges 5, Habakkuk 3, Micah 1, etc.[21] In Deuteronomy 33, God comes *from* Sinai. Here he comes from "his dwelling" and will tread from there upon Mount Sinai. The slight change is significant. Sinai has a place in Enoch's revelation, but it is not the ultimate source.[22] The Watchers, whose story is told in *1 Enoch* 6–16, are said to shake at the revelation of God. The story of the Watchers, then, is clearly oriented toward this eschatological horizon. Finally, we note that "he comes with ten thousand holy ones." A similar, even greater, angelic entourage will surround the Ancient of Days in Daniel, and also in the Book of Giants.[23] This angelic world forms the backdrop for the human action in both books.

---

21. On the theophanic tradition and its mythical allusions, see F. M. Cross, *Canaanite Myth and Hebrew Epic* (Cambridge, MA: Harvard University Press, 1973) 100-105. On theophany in *1 Enoch*, see Beyerle, *Die Gottesvorstellungen*, 51-117.

22. Andreas Bedenbender, *Der Gott der Welt tritt auf den Sinai. Entstehung, Entwicklung und Funktionsweise der frühjüdischen Apokalyptik* (ANTZ 8; Berlin: Institut Kirche und Judentum, 2000) 215, claims that chaps. 1-5 constitute a *Mosaisierung* of the Book of the Watchers, but this is not necessarily so.

23. Loren T. Stuckenbruck, "Daniel and Early Enoch Traditions in the Dead Sea

The remainder of the introduction, chaps. 2–5, sets the scene for the judgment in a different manner. Here the idiom is closer to the wisdom literature.[24] The reader is invited to contemplate and consider all the works of nature, how "they do not transgress their law." In contrast "you have not persevered, nor observed the law of the Lord." As a result, Enoch pronounces curses on the wicked but predicts a blessed state for the "chosen."

The reference to "the law of the Lord" is of some importance for understanding the Book of the Watchers. Lars Hartman has argued at length that the "referential background" of *1 Enoch* 1–5 is the Mosaic covenant.[25] This is indicated, for Hartman, by the allusion to Mount Sinai, the terminology of the denouncement speech, the echoes of the last chapters of Deuteronomy, and the constellation of blessing and curse motifs. These motifs are indeed present, but they are placed in a new context here. The most obvious "law of the Lord" in chaps. 2–5 is not the law of Moses, which was unknown in the fictive time of Enoch, but the law of nature. The sinfulness of the wicked is demonstrated in contrast to the orderliness of nature, not by the special revelation of Sinai. To be sure, there is no suggestion that Sinai is at variance with the laws of nature, but the ultimate authority is older than Moses and applies not only to Israel but to all humanity. The contrast between the order of nature and the disorder of sinful humanity forms the backdrop for the eschatological judgment.

*1 Enoch* 1–5 is not very explicit about the eschatological rewards of the chosen: "for the chosen there will be light and joy and peace, and they will inherit the earth" (5:7). The impression given is of a utopian life on earth "in eternal peace all the days of their life" (5:9). We might compare the "new creation" in Isa 65:17-25, where "the child shall die a hundred years old." This picture will be complemented in the later chapters. Constitutive of the blessed state is the gift of wisdom: "when wisdom is given to the chosen, they will all live, and will not again do wrong" (5:8). Wis-

---

Scrolls," in Collins and Flint, eds., *The Book of Daniel: Composition and Reception*, 2. 368-86, especially 380.

24. Cf. R. A. Argall, *1 Enoch and Sirach: A Comparative Literary and Conceptual Analysis of the Themes of Revelation, Creation, and Judgment* (Atlanta: Scholars Press, 1995) 101-7.

25. L. Hartman, *Asking for a Meaning: A Study of 1 Enoch 1–5* (Lund: Gleerup, 1979). So also, with nuance, Bedenbender, *Der Gott der Welt*, 228-29. Compare the thesis of E. P. Sanders that *1 Enoch* shares the pattern of "covenantal nomism"; see his *Paul and Palestinian Judaism* (Philadelphia: Fortress, 1977). C. Münchow recognizes that the law is placed in a wider context in *1 Enoch, Ethik und Eschatologie* (Göttingen: Vandenhoeck & Ruprecht, 1982) 39-40.

dom here is a gift that is given only through supernatural revelation. The attainment of such wisdom is a recurring goal of apocalyptic literature.

## The Story of the Watchers

The second section, chaps. 6–16, is an elaboration of the story of the "sons of God" in Genesis 6.[26] The main story is in chaps. 6–11; chaps. 12–16 are transitional chapters that introduce Enoch and provide the point of departure for his revelatory journey. As transitional chapters, they provide a key to the way in which the parts of the book are connected. Enoch is introduced specifically in response to the crisis caused by the Watchers, and he acts as an intermediary between them and heaven.

The story of the Watchers is itself complicated by the interweaving of distinct traditions.[27] In one tradition the leader of the Watchers is Šemiḥazah, and the primary sin is marriage with humans and procreation of giants; in another tradition the leader is ʿAśaʾel, and the primary sin is improper revelation.[28] Both the professional skills of ʿAśaʾel and the manner of his punishment have been explained against a Mesopotamian background,[29] but there are also numerous Hellenistic traditions about

26. See my essay, "The Sons of God and the Daughters of Men," in Martti Nissinen and Risto Uro, eds., *Sacred Marriages: The Divine-Human Sexual Metaphor from Sumer to Early Christianity* (Winona Lake, IN: Eisenbrauns, 2008) 259-74; James C. VanderKam, "Genesis 6:1-4 and the Angel Stories in the Book of the Watchers (1 Enoch 1-36)," in Angela Kim Harkins, Kelley Coblentz Bautch, and John C. Endres, S. J., eds., *The Fallen Angels Traditions: Second Temple Developments and Reception History* (CBQMS 53; Washington, DC: Catholic Biblical Association, 2014) 1-7. On the original story see Ronald Hendel, "The Nephilim Were on the Earth: Genesis 6:1-4 and Its Ancient Near Eastern Context," in Christoph Auffarth and Loren T. Stuckenbruck, eds., *The Fall of the Angels* (Leiden: Brill, 2004) 11-34.

27. See Nickelsburg, *1 Enoch 1*, 165-201; Reed, *Fallen Angels*, 27-29.

28. G. W. E. Nickelsburg, "Apocalyptic and Myth in 1 Enoch 6–11," *JBL* 96 (1977) 383-405; P. D. Hanson, "Rebellion in Heaven: Azazel and Euhemeristic Heroes in 1 Enoch 6–11," *JBL* 96 (1977) 195-233; Archie T. Wright, *The Origin of Evil Spirits* (WUNT 2/198; Tübingen: Mohr Siebeck, 2005) 96-137. The name Aśael is original in the Aramaic and presupposed by the Greek. The Ethiopic has Asael in 6:7 but Azazel elsewhere. The name Azazel is found in the fragmentary *Pesher on Azazel and the Angels* (4Q180) at Qumran. See Milik, *Books of Enoch*, 248-52. Kvanvig, *Primeval History*, 373-95, argues that the Šemiḥazah story is presupposed in Genesis.

29. Henryk Drawnel, "Professional Skills of Asael (1 Enoch 8:1 and Their Mesopotamian Background," *RB* 119 (2012) 518-542; idem, "The Punishment of Asael (1 En. 10:4-8) and Mesopotamian Anti-Witchcraft Literature," *RevQ* 25 (2012) 518-42.

the supernatural origins of metallurgy and magic, notably those about Prometheus.[30] Annette Reed is probably correct to caution against taking any specific parallels to explain the origin of the instruction motif in the Book of the Watchers.[31]

The story of the Watchers recounts the spread of evil on earth, if not necessarily its origin. James VanderKam has suggested that these authors "perceived a deficiency in the text of Genesis" since it had not recounted evils of sufficient magnitude to warrant the Flood as a punishment.[32] It is doubtful, however, whether this text was inspired by exegesis. Rather than explaining the deficiencies of Genesis, the authors may have been trying to explain the rampant violence and sinfulness that they saw around them in the Hellenistic age. This wickedness seemed to them to require a supernatural origin.

It is readily obvious that both the Šemiḥazah and the 'Aśa'el stories have allegorical potential. Yet, unlike some other apocalyptic allegories, such as those in Daniel, the story of the Watchers does not have a clearly identifiable referent. The situation is confused to a considerable degree by the tension between the 'Aśa'el and the Šemiḥazah material, but even the separate traditions are quite evasive. George Nickelsburg emphasizes the violence that pollutes the earth and ingeniously detects in the Šemiḥazah material a reflection of the wars of the Diadochi, the Hellenistic princes who succeeded Alexander the Great. The suggestion is attractive in view of the pretensions to divinity on the part of the Hellenistic princes and their irruption into the Near East as aliens from outside. The instruction motif in the 'Aśa'el tradition could also be easily applied to Hellenistic culture. An alternative view emphasizes the sexual sin in the Šemiḥazah material and adduces passages from the *Testament of Levi* and the *Damascus Document* from Qumran (CD) in support of an application to the Jerusalem priesthood.[33] These proposals need not be seen as mutually ex-

30. Fritz Graf, "Mythical Production: Aspects of Myth and Technology in Antiquity," in R. Buxton, ed., *From Myth to Reason? Studies in the Development of Greek Thought* (Oxford: Oxford University Press, 1999) 317-28.

31. Reed, *Fallen Angels*, 39.

32. James C. VanderKam, "The Interpretation of Genesis in 1 Enoch," in Peter W. Flint, ed., *The Bible at Qumran: Text, Shape, and Interpretation* (Grand Rapids: Eerdmans, 2001) 139.

33. D. W. Suter, "Fallen Angel, Fallen Priest: The Problem of Family Purity in 1 Enoch 6–16," *HUCA* 50 (1979) 115-35. Siam Bhayro, *The Shemihaza and Asael Narrative of 1 Enoch 6-11: Introduction, Text, Translation and Commentary with Reference to Ancient Near Eastern*

clusive, and indeed Nickelsburg also sees polemic against the priesthood in chaps. 12–16, which he regards as a separate redactional stage.[34] At least the citations from *T. Levi* 14:1-8 and 4QTLevi[a] show that this myth could indeed be applied to the Jerusalem priesthood in the second century BCE whether it was originally composed for that purpose or not.[35] Even if Nickelsburg is right that the Watchers originally referred to Hellenistic princes, we cannot confine the application of the myth to the period of conquest. It could apply to the general conditions of Hellenistic rule in the East at any point in the third century.[36] In any case the myth as it now stands, in combination with the 'Aśa'el story, must have been reapplied to other situations after the wars of the Diadochi. The story mainly suggests a situation of cultural change. When 'Aśa'el spread his instruction on earth, "the world was changed" (8:2). The fallen angels induced culture shock in the pre-diluvian generation. Similar culture shock in Israel in the Hellenistic period gave rise to the apocalyptic visions ascribed to Enoch.

## Apocalyptic Multivalence

What we touch on here is the essential multivalence of apocalyptic symbolism. We may reasonably claim that the myth of the Watchers, both in the separate Šemiḥazah and 'Aśa'el traditions and in their combined form, reflects

---

*and Biblical Antecedents* (AOAT 322; Münster: Ugarit Verlag, 2005) 21-39, argues that the Šemiḥazah narrative is a polemic against divination, and that the 'Aśa'el story introduces the motif of human sin. Bhayro takes the Watchers as "not angels, but part of the Babylonian mantic system" (27).

34. G. W. E. Nickelsburg, *Jewish Literature between the Bible and the Mishnah* (2d ed.; Minneapolis: Fortress, 2005) 51; idem, "Enoch, Levi, and Peter: Recipients of Revelation in Upper Galilee," *JBL* 100 (1981) 586-87.

35. 4QTLevi[a] 8.3.6-7 is cited by Milik as the earliest allusion to the Book of the Watchers (*Books of Enoch*, 23-24). The context of the fragment is *Testament of Levi* 14. It refers to an accusation by Enoch, which presumably corresponds to his accusation against the Watchers and which is applied to the sons of Levi. The manuscript dates from the second century. In *Testament of Levi* 14:1 (Greek), Levi tells his sons that he has "learnt from the writing of Enoch that in the end ye will transgress against the Lord" and emphasizes sexual sins and marriage with Gentiles. The reference to the Watchers in CD 2:16 is not explicitly applied to the priesthood.

36. Anathea Portier-Young, "Symbolic Resistance in the Book of the Watchers," in Angela Kim Harkins, Kelley Coblentz Bautch, and John C. Endres, S. J., eds., *The Watchers in Jewish and Christian Traditions* (Minneapolis: Fortress, 2014) 39-49, reads the story as anti-Hellenistic resistance.

some kind of crisis. The pollution of the earth is a figurative expression in any case, but the story suggests violence and lawlessness. Even here we should beware of drawing too firm a conclusion about social reality from symbolic description. *1 Enoch* 6–11 records *perceived* crises, whether the perception was generally shared or peculiar to a small group. We have no hard evidence about the historical specificity of the crises. The author chose not to refer explicitly to the wars of the Diadochi or to the Jerusalem priesthood. Instead, the problem — whatever it was — is transposed to a mythological plane. By telling the story of the Watchers rather than of the Diadochi or the priesthood, *1 Enoch* 1–36 becomes a paradigm which is not restricted to one historical situation but can be applied whenever an analogous situation arises.

In the Book of the Watchers, as in all the Jewish apocalypses, the situation of the historical author is concealed. This is effected in part through the use of the pseudonym Enoch, which imposes the setting of the fictive author on the historical situation. A typological view of history is thereby implied. The crises of the Hellenistic age are presumed to bear some analogy to the story of Enoch and the Watchers. In other Jewish apocalypses the Babylonian crisis of the sixth century often provides the filter through which later crises are viewed. The emphasis is not on the uniqueness of historical events but on recurring patterns, which assimilate the particular crisis to some event of the past whether historical or mythical.

The transposition of situations involved in apocalyptic symbolism is in itself part of the solution for the problem generating the text. By concealing the historical specificity of the immediate situation beneath the primeval archetype, the apocalyptic symbolism relieves anxiety. The resolution of the ancient conflict generated by the Watchers emerges with an inevitability that guarantees a similar resolution to the conflicts of the Hellenistic age. The superhuman status of the actors takes the action out of the sphere of human control and places the immediate situation in a deterministic perspective which also serves to relieve anxiety. This transposition of situations has been aptly illuminated by application of C. Lévi-Strauss's discussion of the effectiveness of symbols by analogy with psychotherapy.[37] The apocalyptic "cure" is effected by reexperiencing and working through the past. We might also compare Lévi-Strauss's

---

37. So, independently, J.-C. Picard, "Observations sur L'Apocalypse grecque de Baruch I," *Semitica* 20 (1970) 87-90; J. G. Gager, *Kingdom and Community: The Social World of Early Christianity* (Englewood Cliffs, NJ: Prentice-Hall, 1975) 54-55. See C. Lévi-Strauss, *Structural Anthropology* (New York: Basic Books, 1963) 186-205.

theory on the function of myth. The perplexing problems of the present are "mediated" or obscured and so are overcome by the superimposition of the myth.[38] We should note, however, that the fear and anxiety caused by violence and lawlessness are not merely avoided. They are aroused on a grander scale by the story of the Watchers and giants, but then they are all the more effectively allayed.

The story of the Watchers, then, cannot be tied too closely to any one historical situation. It provides a paradigm for the origin of sin and evil. The distinctive aspect of this paradigm lies in the role of supernatural agents, in this case the fallen angels.[39] While other paradigms for the origin of evil can be found in the apocalyptic literature (the two spirits in the Qumran *Community Rule;* the Adamic myth in *4 Ezra* and *2 Baruch*), the tendency to explain the human situation in mythic terms is characteristic of apocalyptic literature.

### The Mission of Enoch

The allegorization of the crisis is not the only way in which the apocalypse provides a therapy. The more obvious and elaborate response is found in the mission of Enoch and his heavenly journey. Whatever the stages of composition of the Book of the Watchers, the heavenly revelation is now presented in the context of Enoch's address to the Watchers. Only a brief part of that address is concerned with the divine response to their petition. The journeys of Enoch are related to the story of the Watchers insofar as they present a proper revelation, in contrast to the improper revelation of the Watchers.

To appreciate the coherence of the heavenly revelation with the story of the Watchers, we must observe that the two strands of tradition associated with Šemiḥazah and ʿAśaʾel are not merely juxtaposed but are carefully intertwined. Thus, we read in chap. 7, after the Watchers had chosen wives, "And they began to go in to them and were promiscuous with them. And they taught them charms and spells, and showed to them the cutting of roots and trees. And they became pregnant and bore large

---

38. For a succinct formulation of Lévi-Strauss's theory, see E. Leach, "Lévi-Strauss in the Garden of Eden: An Examination of Some Recent Developments in the Analysis of Myth," in E. Nelson Hayes and Tanya Hayes, eds., *Claude Lévi-Strauss: The Anthropologist as Hero* (Cambridge, MA: MIT Press, 1970) 51.

39. This point is emphasized especially by Sacchi, *Jewish Apocalyptic,* 72-87.

giants. . . ." It is true that the instruction here breaks the sequence between the sexual union and the pregnancy, but we should not too easily assume editorial carelessness. The sexual sin of the giants is immediately associated with the improper revelation. Further, chap. 7 concludes with the violence caused by the giants, which evokes the complaint of the earth. In chap. 8, violence and fornication result from the revelations of the Watchers, and again the earth cries out. The complaint of the angels in chap. 9 puts the sin of 'Aśa'el first and says that Šemiḥazah revealed spells before mentioning the illicit union with women. Moreover, the sexual sin appears in chap. 9 as the occasion of the revelation: the Watchers "lay with these women, and became unclean, and revealed to them these sins" (9:8). The divine judgment in chap. 10 gives first and longest attention to Šemiḥazah's revelation of a mystery. In chap. 15 the main indictment is directed against the sexual sin of the Watchers, but the conclusion of chap. 16 returns to the "worthless mystery" that they made known to the women.[40]

The cry of the earth is caused by pollution[41] — mainly through violence but also through fornication. Two accounts of the source of that violence are interwoven side by side. If recent critics are correct in holding that the 'Aśa'el revelation material was added latest we must consider whether the redactor wished to offer a reinterpretation of the sexual myth in terms of inappropriate revelation. Given the long traditional usage in the Hebrew prophets of fornication as a metaphor for religious infidelity, it is even possible to take the story of the descent of the Watchers as a metaphorical expression of illicit revelation. The understanding of the sin of the Watchers as improper revelation provides the obvious counterpart of the proper revelation of Enoch in the rest of the book. In view of these considerations, it would seem that the 'Aśa'el tradition was not merely added but significantly influenced the final shape of the book.

## The Throne Vision

The heavenly revelation of Enoch occupies more than half the entire Book of the Watchers. The revelation begins with Enoch's ascent to heaven in

---

40. *1 Enoch* 16:3. The Greek is corrupt here and reads "a mystery which was from God." See Nickelsburg, *1 Enoch 1*, 269.

41. H. D. Betz, "On the Problem of the Religio-Historical Understanding of Apocalypticism," *JTC* 6 (1969) 146-54. Betz discusses parallels from the *Kore Kosmu* and the Pseudo-Clementine homilies.

14:8.[42] He then proceeds through a house that was "hot as fire and cold as snow" and then another, larger house that was built of a tongue of fire. Here he sees a high throne, beneath which flow rivers of burning fire. On it sat "He who is great in glory" whose "raiment is brighter than the sun and whiter than any snow." Ten thousand times ten thousand stood before him, and the Holy Ones who were near him did not depart from him. This divine figure then gives Enoch his response for the Watchers: "You ought to petition on behalf of men, not men on behalf of you . . . (15:2). You were in heaven, but (its) secrets had not yet been revealed to you and a worthless mystery you knew." Say to them therefore "you have no peace" (16:4).

This throne vision has recently attracted attention as "the oldest Merkavah vision we know of from the literature outside of the canonical Scriptures."[43] The vision raises intriguing questions about the development of Jewish mysticism. Heaven is understood as a temple, through which Enoch proceeds to the inner sanctum.[44] For this reason, his role is often understood as priestly, but *1 Enoch* 12:6, where Enoch writes out their petition, suggests rather the role of a scribe.[45] In this passage, at least, it is plausible to see the fallen angels as fallen priests. Enoch undertakes the role that should normally be filled by priest-angels. So he is instructed to tell them: "You ought to petition on behalf of men, not men on behalf of you" (15:2). The allegorical implication would seem to be that the official cult is not operating properly, but mystical ascent offers an alternative access to the divine throne, at least for a chosen individual such as Enoch.[46] The Dead Sea Scrolls will provide further

42. Beate Ego, "Henochs Reise vor den Thron Gottes (1 Hen 14,8-16,4). Zur Funktion des Motivs der Himmelsreise im 'Wächterbuch' (1 Hen 1-36)," in Jörg Frey and Michael Becker, eds., *Apokalyptik und Qumran* (Paderborn: Bonifatius, 2007) 105-21.

43. I. Gruenwald, *Apocalyptic and Merkavah Mysticism* (Leiden: Brill, 1980) 36; C. Rowland, "The Visions of God in Apocalyptic Literature," *JSJ* 10 (1979) 137-54.

44. M. Himmelfarb, "From Prophecy to Apocalypse: The *Book of the Watchers* and Tours of Heaven," in A. Green, ed., *Jewish Spirituality: From the Bible through the Middle Ages* (New York: Crossroad, 1986) 149-51; followed by Andrei A. Orlov, *The Enoch Metatron Tradition* (TSAJ 107; Tübingen: Mohr Siebeck, 2005) 70-71.

45. J. J. Collins, "A Throne in the Heavens: Apotheosis in Pre-Christian Judaism," in J. J. Collins and M. Fishbane, eds., *Death, Ecstasy, and Other Worldly Journeys* (Albany: State University of New York, 1995) 46. Martha Himmelfarb, "The Book of the Watchers and the Priests of Jerusalem," in Boccaccini, ed., *The Origins of Enochic Judaism*, 131-5, suggests that the book "shares Ben Sira's ideal of the wise priest despite a different set of images for conflating priest and scribe" (134).

46. Orlov, *The Enoch Metatron Tradition*, 51, notes that early portrayals of Enoch depict him as both celestial and terrestrial scribe.

evidence that the mystical participation in the heavenly world could function as an alternative to the temple cult, when that was deemed unsatisfactory.

The detailed observations on the heavenly "house," its effect on Enoch, and the throne itself go beyond the biblical prototypes and surely presuppose mystical speculation.[47] The vision also illustrates the mystical component in apocalyptic literature. The correspondences to Daniel 7 in the appearance of the divinity, the rivers of fire beneath the throne, and the entourage of Holy Ones (ten thousand times ten thousand) suggest that even the more historically oriented apocalypses drew on mystical traditions.[48] The context of the vision here must also be noted. While the scene is not specifically a court scene, as in Daniel, it is the setting for the divine condemnation of the Watchers. The numinous elements in the vision such as the repeated fire imagery and the careful observation of Enoch's terrified reaction ("fear covered me and trembling took hold of me," 14:13) acquire added significance in this context. If the vision is so awesome that even the righteous Enoch shakes and trembles, how much more should those who face condemnation be terrified? The primary purpose of the vision, however, is surely to establish Enoch's authority. Enoch's acceptance into the presence of God inevitably enhances the status of his entire revelation.[49]

## The Commission of Enoch

Enoch is given a message to take back to the Watchers: "you should petition on behalf of humans, not humans on behalf of you" (15:1). The Most High goes on to spell out the problem with the Watchers. They were holy

---

47. For the biblical precedents and later elaborations, see Gruenwald, *Apocalyptic and Merkavah Mysticism,* 29-72. See however the cautionary remarks of Ra'anan Boustan and Patrick G. McCullough, "Apocalyptic Literature and the Study of Early Jewish Mysticism," in Collins, ed., *The Oxford Handbook of Apocalyptic Literature,* 85-103.

48. C. Rowland, *The Open Heaven: A Study of Apocalyptic in Judaism and Early Christianity* (New York: Crossroad, 1982) 255. Another parallel is found in the Book of Giants. See Loren T. Stuckenbruck, "Daniel and the Early Enoch Traditions," 382-84; Ryan E. Stokes, "The Throne Visions of Daniel 7, *1 Enoch* 14, and the Qumran *Book of Giants* (4Q530): An Analysis of Their Literary Relationship," *DSD* 15 (2008) 340-58; Jonathan R. Trotter, "The Tradition of the Throne Vision in the Second Temple Period. Daniel 7:9-10; 1 Enoch 14:18-23 and the Book of Giants (4Q530)" *RevQ* 25 (2012) 451-66.

49. J. D. Tabor, *Things Unutterable: Paul's Ascent to Paradise in Its Greco-Roman, Judaic, and Early Christian Contexts* (Lanham, MD: University Press of America, 1986) 75, classifies Enoch's ascent as "ascent to receive revelation."

ones living in heaven as spirits, who were immortal and had no need of women to procreate, but they have traded their immortal spiritual existence for a mortal life, defiled by blood. Implicitly, Enoch is the reverse: a human being who ascends to live with the angels. This may be the earliest passage in Jewish or Christian tradition that presents the heavenly, angelic life as the ideal to which human beings should aspire.[50]

This passage also gives us the earliest reference to the origin of evil spirits in a Jewish text:

> But now the giants who were begotten by the spirits and flesh – they will call them evil spirits on the earth, for their dwelling will be on the earth. The spirits that have gone forth from the body of their flesh are evil spirits, for from humans they came into being, and from the holy watchers was the origin of their creation. Evil spirits they will be on the earth, and evil spirits they will be called.[51]

This theme will be more fully developed in the Book of Jubilees.

## The Otherworldly Journey

In chap. 17 Enoch begins his tour, guided by the angels. The places he visits are mostly located at the extremities of this world, but they are accessible to no other human.[52] What he sees are the foundations of the universe, from the water of life to the mouth of the deep.[53] This material surely draws on a learned tradition of cosmological speculation, which is shared by wisdom writers such as Ben Sira.[54] In the context in *1 Enoch* 1–36, however,

50. See my essay, "Ethos and Identity in Jewish Apocalyptic Literature," in Matthias Konradt and Ulrike Steinert, eds., *Ethos und Identität. Einheit und Vielfalt des Judentums im hellenistisch-römischer Zeit* (Munich: Schöningh, 2002) 51-65.

51. Loren T. Stuckenbruck, "The Origins of Evil in Jewish Apocalyptic Tradition: The Interpretation of Genesis 6:1-4 in the Second and Third Centuries BCE," in Christoph Auffarth and Loren T. Stuckenbruck, eds., *The Fall of the Angels* (Leiden: Brill, 2004) 99-104; Wright, *The Origin of Evil Spirits*, 152-57; Kevin Sullivan, "The Watchers Traditions in 1 Enoch 6-16. The Fall of Angels and the Rise of Demons," in Harkins, Bautch and Endres, ed., *The Watchers*, 91-103.

52. Rowland, *The Open Heaven*, 124-26.

53. Kelley Coblentz Bautch, *A Study of the Geography of 1 Enoch 17–19: 'No One Has Seen What I Have Seen'* (JSJSup 81; Leiden: Brill, 2003).

54. See especially Randal A. Argall, *1 Enoch and Sirach: A Comparative Literary and*

the speculation is by no means disinterested. The first stage of the tour culminates with "the prison for the stars of heaven and the host of heaven" (18:14), where they are kept until the great judgment day. If the book at one time ended at 19:3,[55] the point of the tour in chaps. 17–19 would seem to be to reinforce the certainty of the judgment by showing that the place of judgment is "really" there, thereby amplifying the fear of God.

As it now stands, however, the tour is prolonged in chap. 21. The extension in chaps. 21–23 is primarily eschatological. Chapter 22 describes the places where the "spirits of the souls of the dead" will be kept until the day of judgment. These are in three compartments: the righteous, the wicked who were not punished on earth, and sinners who were killed.[56] This scenario is quite exceptional in apocalyptic literature, and is quite different from what we find in later apocalypses. The eschatological interest persists in chap. 25 with a discourse about a fragrant tree that will be given to the righteous when God "comes down to visit the earth for good." The effect of this tree is that those who eat of it "will live a long life on earth as your fathers lived also in their days" (25:6). This promise of earthly fulfillment is atypical of the Enoch literature, and suggests that these chapters draw on old traditions. Chaps. 26–27 provide the counterpoint to this with a description of Gehenna, where those who are cursed forever will be gathered. Only in chaps. 28–36 is explicit eschatological material lacking. These chapters fill out the comprehensive tour of the ends of the earth and include the Garden of Eden in chap. 32. There Enoch sees the tree of wisdom "from which your father of old and your mother of old, who were before you, ate and learned wisdom. And their eyes were opened, and they knew they were naked, and they were driven from the garden" (32:6). The author was evidently familiar with the biblical story of Adam and Eve, but there is no suggestion that their sin determined the fate of all humanity.[57]

Even if the eschatological material of chaps. 21–23 is an extension

---

*Conceptual Analysis of the Themes of Revelation, Creation and Judgment* (SBLEJL 8; Atlanta: Scholars Press, 1995) 101-64.

55. Milik, *Books of Enoch*, 25. This contention is supported by the apparent finality of 19:3: "And I Enoch alone saw the sight, the ends of everything; and no man has seen what I have seen."

56. Originally four compartments were envisaged. See the detailed treatment by M.-T. Wacker, *Weltordnung und Gericht: Studien zu 1 Henoch 22* (Würzburg: Echter, 1982); Nickelsburg, *1 Enoch 1*, 300-9.

57. Reed, *Fallen Angels*, 49, says that this passage takes a dismissive approach to the story of Adam and Eve.

of the original book, it is only making explicit what was implied all along. The judgment of the Watchers is paradigmatic for human sinners. These chapters do, however, add a dimension to the eschatology of the book by addressing the judgment of the dead. Chapter 5 had spoken of the life of the righteous in a rather this-worldly manner reminiscent of the prophets. In chaps. 10–11 the resolution of the crisis with the Watchers provides a prototype for the eschatological judgment. On the one hand, the angel Raphael is told to "bind Azazel by his hands and his feet, and throw him into the darkness. And split open the desert which is in Dudael and throw him there. And throw on him jagged and sharp stones, and cover him with darkness; and let him stay there forever, and cover his face, that he may not see light and that on the great day of judgment he may be hurled into the fire" (10:4-6, trans. Knibb). Correspondingly, Šemiḥazah and his followers are bound "under the hills of the earth until the day of their judgment and of their consummation, until the judgment which is for all eternity is accomplished. And in those days they will lead them to the abyss of fire; in torment and in prison they will be shut up for all eternity" (10:12-13). On the other hand, Raphael is also told to "restore the earth which the angels have ruined" (10:7). This is further explicated in 10:16-22: "And let the plant of righteousness and truth appear . . . and now all the righteous will be humble, and will live until they beget thousands; and all the days of their youth and their Sabbaths they will fulfil in peace." The resolution of the crisis with the Watchers, then, has two aspects: the confinement of the sinners until the final judgment, and the present healing of the earth. In view of chaps. 21–22 it appears that the final judgment is not only for the Watchers. The spirits of the dead, both righteous and wicked, are also kept for a day of judgment. This judgment of the dead is not clearly correlated with the hope that the earth will be healed. In chaps. 10–11 the earthly restoration is "for all the generations of eternity," but then in 10:10 "eternal life" is synonymous with "five hundred years." In short, it is not clear whether the earthly restoration is terminated or at all affected by the final judgment. The author of the Book of the Watchers is not attempting to give a precise account of eschatological developments. It is apparent that he looks for a restoration on earth, which will be definitively satisfying, whether it lasts forever or not. It is also clear from chap. 22 that he looks for a judgment of the dead beyond this life, where the destiny of righteous and wicked is ultimately decided.

Enoch's journey has no close parallel in the Hebrew scriptures, and it does not appear to be closely modeled on a nonbiblical source either.

Partial analogies abound. We have noted Enoch's affinities with the Mesopotamian heroes Enmeduranki and Utuabzu, both of whom were said to ascend to heaven. Enoch's journeys are in a limited way reminiscent of the journeys of Gilgamesh. Both Babylonian and Greek motifs are used in the description of the abodes of the dead in chap. 22.[58] The widespread motif of heavenly ascent provides a general backdrop, but Enoch's development of the motif is distinctive. The Book of the Watchers is even significantly different from the ascents we find in later Jewish apocalypses, which describe a more orderly ascent through a set number of heavens. We must acknowledge, then, a considerable degree of originality here in the way that various traditional motifs are combined. The possibility that the author had a mystical experience cannot be discounted, but we can more profitably discuss the work as a literary product, and consider its function and effect.

One model for understanding Enoch's journey has been derived from ancient Near Eastern diplomacy as illustrated in 2 Kings 20, where Hezekiah displays his treasures to the Babylonian envoys.[59] The function of the display is to impress and intimidate. This proposal is helpful up to a point in clarifying the rationale for the tour. The heavenly realm is often modeled on the conventions of royalty in Near Eastern mythology — hence such conceptions as the divine council, the celestial guardians, and perhaps also the treasuries. Yet the analogy with royal diplomacy does not adequately account for some fundamental aspects of the Enoch story. It is of crucial importance that Enoch's journey takes him outside the world that is normally accessible to humanity. His successful and appropriate elevation to the heavenly world provides the counterpart of the disastrous descent of the Watchers. It is because of the supernatural location of his journey that his revelation qualifies as a "mystery" surpassing the worthless mystery of the giants. The elements of mystery and mysticism in the ascent and journey are not clarified by the diplomatic practice reflected in 2 Kings 20. Again, the story in 2 Kings provides no explicit analogy for the correlation of cosmology and judgment, which not only is essential to *1 Enoch* but also is typical of other apocalypses. Even the details of the tour are necessarily concerned with cosmological marvels of a different order from the splendors of an earthly kingdom.

---

58. Ibid., 132-233. The entry into the base of a mountain is a Babylonian motif. The spring of water and light in the abode of the righteous are Greek, Orphic, motifs.

59. C. A. Newsom, "The Development of 1 Enoch 6–19: Cosmology and Judgment," *CBQ* 42 (1980) 310-29.

Yet the tour does indeed display God's wisdom and power. It also establishes the wisdom of Enoch, but this wisdom depends on divine revelation and so on the power and wisdom of God. This dependence is made very explicit also in Daniel and is indeed typical of apocalyptic literature. The intimate connection of power and wisdom is shown also in the equivalence of the "tablets of wisdom" and the "tablets of destiny" in Mesopotamian texts.[60]

The demonstration of power has a clear enough purpose. On the level of communication internal to the text, it invites the Watchers to look on the mighty works of God and despair. On the external level, the readers too must share Enoch's awe before the mysteries of creation and judgment. The emotion aroused by Enoch's journey is primarily awe — including a strong component of fear but also of hope and reassurance.

The demonstration of wisdom is no less important. On one level it convinces the Watchers of the reality of the judgment, since the place of judgment is already prepared. On the other level it enables the human beings who are submerged by the violence and corruption expressed in the story of the Watchers to believe that there is another dimension to the world. The sufferings of the present can be viewed from the perspective of ultimate transcendence. What is offered is not only hope but also knowledge, guaranteed by supernatural revelation. Its certainty is established by the wealth of cosmological detail. The comprehensive tour of the cosmos is designed to show that the destiny of humanity is not left to chance but is built into the structure of the universe. The eschatological focus is shown by the climactic location of the prison of the Watchers in chaps. 18–19 and by the amount of space devoted to eschatology in chaps. 21–27. It is true that eschatology is only one component in the comprehensive view of the cosmos, but it is an essential component and is fully integrated with the cosmological speculations.[61]

More definitively than the narrative in chaps. 6–16, the otherworldly journey provides the response to the crisis evoked by the Watchers.

---

60. Widengren, *Ascension of the Apostle*, 10. The association of power and wisdom in the biblical tradition is especially conspicuous in Second Isaiah and Daniel 2–6, both of which have a Babylonian setting. On the heavenly tablets see further S. Paul, "Heavenly Tablets and the Book of Life," *Journal of the Ancient Near Eastern Society of Columbia University* 5 (1973) 345-53.

61. See further G. W. E. Nickelsburg, "The Apocalyptic Construction of Reality in *1 Enoch,*" in J. J. Collins and J. H. Charlesworth, eds., *Mysteries and Revelations: Apocalyptic Studies Since the Uppsala Colloquium* ( JSPSup 9; Sheffield: JSOT Press, 1991) 51-64.

Enoch's tour of the hidden regions of the cosmos provides a frame within which human problems are seen in a new perspective. Whatever crisis pollutes the earth, the foundations of the cosmos, its outer regions and the places of judgment remain intact, as of course does the heavenly court. The frame is both spatial and temporal: it refers both to the hidden regions traversed by Enoch and to the coming judgment. The Book of the Watchers does not convey the sense of an imminent ending that is characteristic of some apocalypses. It is sufficient that there is an eventual judgment. It is also important that the places of judgment are there in the present and can be contemplated through the revelation of Enoch.

## The Setting

Our interpretation of the Book of the Watchers has proceeded on the assumption that the crisis of the fallen angels is an allegory for some crisis of the Hellenistic age. This assumption is well founded by analogy with other apocalypses. We cannot determine precisely what crisis it was that generated the Book of the Watchers, and in any case the allegory could be reapplied in several different situations. We should note that there is no indication that religious persecution is envisaged here. The original crisis may have been of a rather general nature, such as the spread of Hellenistic culture in the East.

The Book of the Watchers in itself gives us little clear indication of its specific setting. It is evidently the work of scribes,[62] but to say that a piece of literature is the work of scribes is almost tautological, and tells us nothing of the setting in which these particular scribes worked. There is no evidence that the authors were priests, or presented Enoch as a model priest.[63] The authors were familiar with various learned traditions, but this does not require that they were "in the orbit of the Jerusalem temple."[64] Neither is there any indication that the authors were subject to persecution. The stark difference in worldview over against the traditions known from the Hebrew Bible suggests that the tradents of this material were not in the orbit of the Jerusalem temple but stood apart from other

---

62. As emphasized by Horsley and Tiller, "The Social Settings of the Components of 1 Enoch," in their *After Apocalyptic and Wisdom*, 96.

63. *Pace* Martha Himmelfarb, *A Kingdom of Priests: Ancestry and Merit in Ancient Judaism* (Philadelphia: University of Pennsylvania Press, 2006) 28.

64. *Pace* Reed, *Fallen Angels*, 69.

strands of Jewish tradition, whether in upper Galilee, as Nickelsburg has tentatively suggested,[65] or in the eastern Diaspora. We will return below to the question of the relation of the Book of the Watchers to the early Enoch tradition.

But while its social and political provenance remain obscure, the Book of the Watchers casts considerable light on the literary technique of an apocalypse. Whatever crisis generated this text, it is viewed from a distinctive apocalyptic perspective. The situation is transposed to the mythical time of Enoch by the device of pseudonymity. It is not described directly but is covered by the allegory of the Watchers. In this way the outcome of the crisis is already known and so is guaranteed. At the same time, the human situation is placed in perspective by the otherworldly geography, where the places of judgment are already prepared. The Book of the Watchers, then, does not explicitly address any crisis of the Hellenistic age or advocate specific conduct. Rather, it provides a lens through which any crisis can be viewed. By evoking a sense of awe and instilling conviction in its revelation of the transcendent world and the coming judgment, the apocalypse enables the faithful to cope with the crises of the present and so creates the preconditions for righteous action in the face of adversity.

## The Astronomical Book

The Astronomical Book, *1 Enoch* 72–82, is attested in fragments of four manuscripts from Qumran.[66] The earliest of these dates from the end of the third or the beginning of the second century and so is the earliest of the Enoch manuscripts. The Aramaic work represented in these fragments was much longer than the text that survived in Ethiopic. Milik surmises that those who translated the Aramaic into Greek (on which the Ethiopic was based) "were at pains to shorten the voluminous, prolix and terribly monotonous original."[67] VanderKam is more cautious: "There is no doubt that something drastic happened between the Aramaic and the Ethiopic forms of the Enochic astronomical work," but we cannot be sure how much the

---

65. Nickelsburg, *1 Enoch 1*, 65.

66. Milik, *The Books of Enoch*, 273; Eibert J. Tigchelaar and Florentino García Martínez, "4QAstronomical Enoch[a-b] ar: Introduction," in *Qumran Cave 4 XXVI: Cryptic Texts and Miscellanea*, Part 1 (DJD 36; Oxford Clarendon, 2000) 95-172; Henryk Drawnel, *The Aramaic Astronomical Book from Qumran* (Oxford: Oxford University Press, 2011).

67. Milik, *Books of Enoch*, 19.

original Aramaic work contained.[68] So for example there is no proof that the material in 1 Enoch 72 was included in the Aramaic work, although it may well have been.

The beginning of the book has not been preserved in Aramaic. In the Ethiopic it is introduced as:

> The book of the revolutions of the lights of heaven, each as it is, according to their classes, according to their (period of) rule and their times, according to their names and their places of origin and according to their months, which Uriel, the holy angel who was with me and is their leader showed to me; and he showed me all their regulations, exactly as they are, for each year of the world and forever, until the new creation shall be made which will last for ever. (72:1)

There is no account of the actual process of revelation, such as we usually find in an apocalypse, through the description of a vision or of a heavenly journey. We are given the content of a revelation rather than a report of the revelation itself. (This is also true of the Apocalypse of Weeks.) Yet a heavenly tour would seem to be implied. Uriel is the accompanying angel or tour guide. Enoch ranges all over the heavens to the ends of the earth (76:1).[69] In 81:5 he is brought back to earth by "three holy ones," who set him before the door of his house. This passage appears to be a secondary addition to the Astronomical Book, but the presumption of a heavenly journey is consistent with the preceding chapters.

The content of the revelation is primarily cosmological and concerned with the movements of the sun, moon, and stars.[70] The astronomical observations are primitive in relation to Babylonian and Hellenistic knowledge, although the conception of the world definitely shows Babylonian influence.[71] The descriptions are highly mythological. The heavens

---

68. James C. VanderKam, "1 Enoch 72-82. The Book of the Luminaries," in George W. E. Nickelsburg and James C. VanderKam, *1 Enoch 2: A Commentary on the Book of 1 Enoch Chapters 37-82* (Hermeneia; Minneapolis: Fortress, 2012) 357.

69. VanderKam, in Nickelsburg and VanderKam, *1 Enoch 2*, 368, thinks it more likely that Enoch sees the ends of the earth on the horizon, without actually being there.

70. M. Albani, *Astronomie und Schöpfungsglaube: Untersuchungen zum astronomischen Henochbuch* (WMANT 68; Neukirchen–Vluyn: Neukirchener Verlag, 1994).

71. O. Neugebauer, *The Astronomical Chapters of the Ethiopic Book of Enoch (72–82): With Additional Notes on the Aramaic Fragments by M. Black* (Copenhagen: Munksgaard, 1981); VanderKam, *Enoch and the Growth of an Apocalyptic Tradition*, 91-104; and Jonathan

are peopled with angels: "the leaders of the heads of thousands who are in charge of the whole creation and in charge of all the stars" (75:1). Uriel is the leader of the lights of heaven.

The lengthy descriptions of the heavenly bodies are in part a celebration of the order of the universe. They also have an immediate purpose. They support the contention that "the year amounts to exactly three hundred and sixty-four days" (72:32). The solar calendar of 364 days is also a subject of interest in the book of *Jubilees* and in the Qumran scrolls. It is at variance with the 354-day luni-solar calendar of the rabbinic period and has usually been taken as a sign of sectarian provenance, since the calendar determined the proper observance of the festivals.[72] The Astronomical Book, however, does not make an issue of the festivals and does not polemicize against the 354-day calendar. Instead it attacks a 360-day calendar that fails to include the four additional days (75:1-2; 82:4-6), although we do not know that such a calendar was ever used in Judaism.[73] We will return below to the possible implications of the 364-day calendar for the social setting of the Enoch literature.

Although most of the Astronomical Book is devoted to cosmological speculation, the eschatological horizon is also present. At the outset the heavenly regulations are said to hold "until the new creation" (72:1). Eschatological concerns emerge more clearly in chap. 80: "In the days of the sinners the years will become shorter. . . . And many heads of the stars in command will go astray . . . and the entire law of the stars will be closed to the sinners, and the thoughts of those who dwell upon the earth will go astray over them . . . and will think them gods. And many evils will overtake them, and punishment will come upon them to destroy them all." These disruptions are in marked contrast to the order of the heavens in the preceding chapters. VanderKam argues strongly that chap. 80, like chap. 81, is a secondary addition, since the disruptions come before the new creation and so contradict 72:1.[74] This is possible, but scarcely necessary. We are

---

Ben-Dov, *Head of All Years: Astronomy and Calendars at Qumran in Their Ancient Context* (STDJ 78; Leiden: Brill, 2008).

72. For example, R. T. Beckwith, "The Earliest Enoch Literature and Its Calendar: Marks of Their Origin, Date and Motivation," *RevQ* 10 (1981) 365-403.

73. J. VanderKam, "The 364-Day Calendar in the Enochic Literature," in K. H. Richards, ed., *Society of Biblical Literature 1983 Seminar Papers* (Chico, CA: Scholars Press, 1983) 157-65. See VanderKam, *Calendars in the Dead Sea Scrolls: Measuring Time* (London: Routledge, 1998); Ben-Dov, *Head of All Years*, 21-67.

74. VanderKam, *Enoch and the Growth of an Apocalyptic Tradition*, 76-79; in Nickelsburg and VanderKam, *1 Enoch 2*, 364.

reminded of the contrast between orderly nature and sinful humanity in *1 Enoch* 1–5. The original unchanging order of creation is the foil against which the later transgressions appear heinous. Here the transgressions originate with the heads of the stars. Earthly sinfulness has a supernatural cause, just as it has in the story of the Watchers. The correlation of stars and angelic beings was old in Israel (see Judg 5:19-20; Job 38:7) and was ultimately derived from the belief in astral divinities that is condemned here. It should be noted, however, that Chapter 80 is not attested in Aramaic, and so there is no guarantee that it was part of the original book.

Chapter 81 stands apart from the rest of the work because of its lack of cosmological interest. Here Enoch derives his explanation from "the tablets of heaven" and the book where the deeds of men are recorded. Enoch's response, "Blessed is the man who dies righteous and good . . . ," implies some form of afterlife. Milik points out that the reference to "three holy ones" who bring Enoch back to earth in 81:5 presupposes the reference to three angels in 87:3 in the Animal Apocalypse; 81:9 ("and those who practice righteousness will die because of the deeds of men") suggests a time of persecution. Chapter 81 then was probably an addition to the Astronomical Book. It serves a twofold purpose in its present context. It explains how Enoch is given one year after his heavenly journeys to impart his wisdom to Methuselah before he is finally taken up, and it gives Enoch's revelation an ethical orientation.

Chapter 82 is in the form of a parting address to Methuselah. Accordingly it illustrates the overlap between apocalypse and testament, although the dominant form in this case is clearly the revelation. The exhortation in chap. 82 is more specific than that in 81 and is integrally related to the revelations about the sun and moon: "Blessed are all those who walk in the way of righteousness and do not sin like the sinners in the numbering of all their days." The chapter goes on to elaborate the law of the stars and the names of the angels who lead them.

The address to Methuselah underlines the primary purpose of the Astronomical Book: to prevent sin by calendrical error. The purpose here is far more specific than in the Book of the Watchers, but the technique is rather similar. Right observance is determined by an understanding of the heavenly world. What Enoch conveys is wisdom, but a "wisdom which is beyond their thoughts" (82:2), which must be obtained through revelation. The alleged experience of Enoch evokes a sense of awe at the workings of the heavenly bodies, under their angelic leaders, and instills conviction in the understanding he imparts. The revelation provides assurance "in the days of the sinners" and this assurance is confirmed, in the present form of the book, by the eschatological revelation in chap. 81.

Nonetheless, the Astronomical Book is at best a marginal apocalypse.[75] It is supposedly a revelation mediated by an angel, but the manner of revelation is not described. The content is primarily astronomical and calendrical lore. If chapters 80 and 81 were not part of the original composition, it would lack the eschatological focus that is constitutive of an apocalypse.[76] The author or authors of the original work seem to have been primarily concerned with "scientific" knowledge of the natural world, and to have been learned in somewhat outdated Babylonian lore.[77] This is significant for the provenance of the Enoch tradition, but the Astronomical Book is exceptional in that tradition as it unfolded, and indeed in Jewish tradition as a whole.

## The Apocalypse of Weeks

The Apocalypse of Weeks in *1 Enoch* 93 has long been recognized as a distinct apocalypse.[78] It is also well known that its conclusion is found in *1 Enoch* 91. The Aramaic fragments from Qumran have provided confirmation that the verses in chap. 91 are displaced in the Ethiopic tradition. In one fragment (En[g]) 91:11-17 follows directly on 93:9-10. Accordingly, the Apocalypse may be confidently delineated as 93:1-10 + 91:11-17. The Apocalypse of Weeks is a self-contained unit, but opinion is divided on whether it actually circulated separately. Milik sees no evidence that it was ever independent of the Epistle of Enoch (chaps. 92–105). Matthew Black finds signs of redaction in the Apocalypse and infers that it is older than its context.[79] Like the Book of the Watchers, both the Apocalypse of Weeks

75. Bedenbender, *Der Gott der Welt*, 151-74, assigns it to the *Vorgeschichte* of Enochic apocalypticism.

76. VanderKam, in Nickelsburg and VanderKam, *1 Enoch 2*, 367-68.

77. Philip Alexander, "Enoch and the Beginnings of Jewish Interest in Natural Science," in Charlotte Hempel et al., ed., *The Wisdom Texts from Qumran and the Development of Sapiential Thought* (BETL 149; Leuven: Peeters, 2002) 223-43; Ben-Dov, *Head of All Years*. See also Ben-Dov and Sanders, ed., *Ancient Jewish Sciences*.

78. Charles, *APOT*, 2:171; F. Dexinger, *Henochs Zehnwochenapokalypse and offene Probleme der Apokalyptikforschung* (Leiden: Brill, 1977) 102. For full commentaries see Nickelsburg, *1 Enoch 1*, 434-50; Loren T. Stuckenbruck, *1 Enoch 91-108: Commentaries on Early Jewish Literature* (Berlin: de Gruyter, 2007) 49-152.

79. M. Black, "The Apocalypse of Weeks in the Light of 4QEn[g]," *VT* 28 (1978) 464-69; idem, *The Book of Enoch*, 288.

and the Epistle avoid explicit reference to historical figures and events, and so frustrate the desire to date them precisely. Charles tentatively dated the Apocalypse of Weeks before the Maccabean revolt because "there is in it no reference to the persecution of Antiochus," but he located the Epistle under the Hasmoneans in the early first century.[80] A major factor in dating these books is the fact that the book of *Jubilees* apparently alludes to both the Apocalypse of Weeks and the Epistle. According to *Jub.* 4:18 "he was the first to write a testimony, and he testified to the sons of men among the generations of the earth and recounted the weeks of the jubilees. . . ." The theme of testifying is more prominent in the Epistle than in any other Enochic writing (see also 105:1). While the date of *Jubilees* is also in dispute, several copies at Qumran date from the late Hasmonean period.[81] Consequently, if *Jubilees* indeed refers to the Epistle, a first-century date for the Enochic document can be excluded.

## The Schematization of History

Although Enoch's ascent is presupposed in the Apocalypse of Weeks, it is not described, and there is no allusion to a heavenly tour. Enoch's revelation is imparted as an address to his children, but he claims to have received this revelation in typical apocalyptic fashion: "that which appeared to me in the heavenly vision, and (which) I know from the words of the holy angels and understand from the tablets of heaven." Again, he imparts understanding or wisdom — but a wisdom that is accessible only through revelation. It is also a *mediated* revelation, given in "the books" and tablets of heaven and conveyed to Enoch by angels.

The substance of this apocalypse is made up not of heavenly cosmology but of an overview of history. The history is highly schematized and organized into periods of "weeks." Ultimately there are ten periods specified, but the crucial transition occurs in the seventh week with the election of the "chosen righteous." The division of history into ten periods is most probably derived from the Persian idea of the millennium.[82] It is common

80. *APOT*, 2:171. On the date of the Apocalypse of Weeks see Nickelsburg, *1 Enoch 1*, 440-41; Stuckenbruck, *1 Enoch 91-108*, 60-62.

81. J. C. VanderKam and J. T. Milik, "Jubilees," in H. Attridge et al., eds., *Qumran Cave 4–VIII: Parabiblical Texts* (DJD 13; Oxford: Clarendon, 1994) 1-185.

82. D. Flusser, "The Four Empires in the Fourth Sibyl and in the Book of Daniel," *Israel Oriental Studies* 2 (1972) 148-75.

in the *Sibylline Oracles* and is a major structuring element in *Sib. Or.* 1 and 2 and *Sib. Or.* 4. It is found in the Melchizedek scroll from Qumran, and Milik cites two fragments of a "commentary on the (book of) periods created by God" (4Q180 and 181), where there are ten weeks from Noah to Abraham.[83] Multiples of seven also figure prominently in eschatological texts. Already in *1 Enoch* 10:12 the Watchers are bound under the earth for seventy generations. *T. Levi* 16:1 says that the descendants of Levi will err for seventy weeks, but claims to have learned this from the book of *Enoch*. In Daniel 9 the seventy weeks of years are tied to the prophecy of Jeremiah (Jer 25:11-12 and 29:10). In the Animal Apocalypse in *1 Enoch* 85–90, the "sheep" (Israel) are subjected to seventy shepherds in the period after the exile. The ten jubilees of 11QMelchizedek are also equivalent to seventy weeks of years. In the "pesher on the periods" (4Q180 and 181) 'Aśa'el and the angels lead Israel astray for seventy weeks. Underlying all of this is the notion of the Sabbath and of sabbatical and jubilee years, expounded in the priestly laws of the Torah (Leviticus 25). Moreover, Enoch was said to be seventh from Adam while the flood, which terminated the first epoch of history, was in the tenth generation.

The division of history into a set number of periods is a common feature of the "historical" type of apocalypse. One effect of this periodization is the impression of an ordered universe where everything proceeds in a predetermined manner. There is an analogy between the set number of periods here and the set number of heavens that will be seen in later apocalypses. Periodization also makes it possible to locate the present in an overall schema of history. In the case of the Apocalypse of Weeks, the time of the real author is evidently to be situated in the seventh week, before the "root of iniquity" is cut off in the eighth. The schematization of history then shows that the greater number of periods has already elapsed and that the turning point is at hand. The use of an ancient pseudonym like Enoch permits a *vaticinium ex eventu*, a review of past history as if it were future, and so adds to the impression that all is determined in advance, and under divine control.

The treatment of history in the Apocalypse of Weeks is not exhausted

---

83. Milik, *Books of Enoch*, 248-51. See further P. J. Kobelski, *Melchizedek and Melchireša'* (CBQMS 10; Washington, DC: Catholic Biblical Association of America, 1981) 49-51; A. Yarbro Collins, "Numerical Symbolism in Jewish and Early Christian Apocalyptic Literature," in eadem, *Cosmology and Eschatology in Jewish and Early Christian Apocalypticism* (Leiden: Brill, 1996) 80-83.

by the division into periods. There is also a pattern of sin and salvation.[84] In the first week "justice and righteousness still lasted." In the second, "great wickedness will arise" but "in it a man will be saved." The reference is to Noah. After this God "will make a law for sinners," presumably the covenant with Noah. The third week is marked by the election of Abraham: "a man will be chosen as the plant of righteousness forever." The fourth includes the giving of the law "for all generations" and the gift of the land. In the fifth "a house of glory and sovereignty will be built forever." In the sixth week all will be blinded, but a man will ascend, presumably Elijah. This week concludes with the destruction of the temple and the exile. The seventh week is dominated by an apostate generation, but at its end "the chosen righteous from the eternal plant of righteousness" will be chosen. The pattern that emerges is that periods of wickedness culminate in the separation of the elect. At the end of the second generation Noah is saved; in the sixth, Elijah is taken up. After the flood, Abraham is chosen as the plant of righteous judgment. After the corrupt seventh generation, the "chosen righteous from the eternal plant of righteousness" are elected. The election of this group thus becomes a focal point of the whole schema. It is prefigured in the case of Abraham, and to some extent in Noah and Elijah. The eighth, ninth, and tenth weeks provide the eschatological finale. The eighth week is "that of righteousness" when sinners are destroyed by the sword. In the ninth the righteous judgment will be revealed to the whole world, and "the world is written down for destruction." Then in the tenth week "the eternal judgment will be executed on the Watchers." Then the first heaven will pass away and a new heaven will appear. After this "there will be many weeks without number forever in goodness and righteousness."[85]

In view of the reference to the Watchers, it would seem that the whole schema of history here is an elaboration of the seventy generations of *1 Enoch* 10. The culmination is reminiscent of Isaiah 65, where the new heaven and new earth are interpreted as a transformed state where successive generations live in peace. The Enochic text is more explicit that this world is written down for destruction. Matthew Black argues that

---

84. G. W. E. Nickelsburg, "The Apocalyptic Message of 1 Enoch 92–105," *CBQ* 39 (1977) 313-15; idem, *1 Enoch* 1, 439.

85. On the basis of this passage VanderKam (*Enoch and the Growth of an Apocalyptic Tradition,* 141-60) questions the appropriateness of the usual designation "Ten-Week Apocalypse," but the significant course of history is concentrated in the ten weeks.

some of the original ending has been lost in the Ethiopic.[86] The Qumran text, En$^g$, has a passage before 91:18 of which only one or two words are decipherable, but which occupied roughly four lines. Milik identifies this verse with 91:10. Black reconstructs it on the basis of 92:3. In either case it would contain a reference to resurrection. This reference would bring the eschatology of the apocalypse more explicitly into line with the full Book of the Watchers and the expectations of other apocalypses. It is not certain, however, that this verse was actually part of the Apocalypse of Weeks.

The emphasis in the Apocalypse of Weeks is primarily on the historical axis: the assurance that time is measured out and under control. Even here the heavenly world is not lacking. Enoch's revelation is received through the angels, and at the end angels (and the Watchers) figure in the new creation. The control of history is in the hands of supernatural agents. The overview of history and the cosmic judgment provide encouragement for the "chosen righteous" and, more basically, confirm their special status in the design of God.

## The Epistle of Enoch

The Apocalypse of Weeks is embedded in a longer composition generally known as the Epistle of Enoch.[87] This is said to be "written by Enoch the scribe" for "all my sons who dwell upon the earth and for the last generations who will practice uprightness and peace." It bears some resemblance to a testament, although it lacks the usual third-person narrative of a deathbed scene. Enoch asserts his authority by such formulas as "I say to you" or "I swear to you," but he also appeals to his knowledge of the heavenly realm: "I swear to you that I understand this mystery. And I have read the tablets of heaven and seen the writing of the holy ones . . ." (103:1-2). Enoch's heavenly revelation is presupposed throughout, but the dominant form is paraenesis.

The bulk of the Epistle is taken up with woes against the sinners and exhortations for the righteous. The accusations against the wicked are of two types. On the one hand, the sinners are accused of blasphemy (94:9; 96:7) and idolatry (99:7). On the other hand, the majority of the

---

86. Black, "The Apocalypse of Weeks in the Light of 4QEn$^g$," *VT* 28 (1978) 464-69; idem, *The Book of Enoch*, 295.

87. Nickelsburg, *1 Enoch 1*, 416-33; Stuckenbruck, *1 Enoch 91-108*, 185-216.

accusations are social in character: "Woe to those who build their houses with sin, for from their whole foundation they will be thrown down, and by the sword they will fall; and those who acquire gold and silver will quickly be destroyed in the judgment" (94:8). "Woe to you who devour the finest in the wheat and drink the best of the water and trample upon the humble through your power" (96:5). Such explicit concern with social issues is exceptional in the early Enoch literature. The class divisions reflected in the woes were not peculiar to any one period, but they are thoroughly intelligible against the background of the Hellenization of Palestine in the period before the Maccabean revolt, as illustrated by the story of the Tobiads in Josephus.[88] Nickelsburg also leans towards a pre-Maccabean date but allows that a Hasmonean, or even Herodian, date is also possible.[89] Stuckenbruck argues that the *terminus ante quem* must be set in the mid-first century BCE because of the earliest Qumran manuscript (4QEn^g) but regards a date in the second half of the second century BCE as most plausible.[90]

We have noted that Charles saw in the Epistle a reflection of disputes between Pharisees and Sadducees. Milik points out that the accusation of idolatry could scarcely be applied to the Sadducees.[91] The woes could be applied more appropriately to Hellenizing Jews in the period before the revolt. Twice Enoch denounces those who "alter and distort the words of truth" and "write books in their (own words)" (104:10; 98:15). This could be read as a rejection of those authors who attempted to present the Jewish tradition in Greek dress. The concern with the sea in 101:4-9 has been taken to suggest provenance in a maritime town.[92] All of this is, of course, extremely tentative. The highly general language in which the Epistle is couched lent itself to application in several different settings.

Although the Epistle preserves major motifs of Enoch's revelation, there is at least one striking discrepancy with the earlier Enoch books. In 98:4 Enoch declares that as "a mountain has not, and will not, become a slave, nor a hill a woman's maid, so sin was not sent on the earth, but man of himself created it." This pronouncement would seem to contradict

---

88. On the social message of the Epistle, see Nickelsburg, *Jewish Literature*, 145-51; idem, "Riches, the Rich and God's Judgment in 1 Enoch 92–105 and the Gospel According to Luke," *NTS* 25 (1979) 324-44. On the background of the period, see M. Hengel, *Judaism and Hellenism* (2 vols.; Philadelphia: Fortress, 1974) 1:6-57.

89. Nickelsburg, *1 Enoch 1*, 427.

90. Stuckenbruck, *1 Enoch 91-108*, 156.

91. Milik, *Books of Enoch*, 49.

92. Ibid., 49-51.

the explanation of the origin of evil in the story of the Watchers.[93] This discrepancy may reflect a revision within a unified tradition, or it may be indicative of a different provenance for the Epistle. In the absence of some more specific evidence, we cannot be certain.

The exhortations in the Epistle resemble the apocalypses in their argumentation. At the outset the righteous are assured that "the Holy Great One has appointed days for all things, and the righteous man will rise from sleep, will rise and will walk in the path of righteousness" (92:3). In 104:2-6 they will shine like the lights of heaven and be associates of the host of heaven. The angels will gather the sinners for judgment (100:4). The wicked "will be given into the hand of the righteous, and they will cut your throats and kill you and not have mercy on you" (98:12). The wisdom imparted in the Epistle, which is derived from the heavenly tablets, is primarily concerned with the eschatological judgment.[94] In short, Enoch appeals to the authority of heaven to show that the righteous who are oppressed in this world can hope for salvation outside it and that the present world order will eventually be reversed. An apocalyptic view of the world provides consolation and the basis for perseverance in the seemingly unprofitable ways of righteousness.

## The Animal Apocalypse

One other apocalypse of Enoch, the Animal Apocalypse, is attested at Qumran. It can be dated on internal grounds to the Maccabean revolt.[95] This apocalypse is itself part of the Book of Dreams (chaps. 83–91). Enoch recounts to Methuselah "two visions I saw before I took a wife." The first was a simple vision of cosmic destruction, how the earth "is about to sink into the abyss and be utterly destroyed." We are reminded of Jer 4:23-26: "I looked on the earth, and lo, it was waste and void, and to the heavens and they had no light." This brief vision is a paradigm of judgment, a

---

93. Ibid., 53. Note, however, that *Jubilees* combines a version of the Watchers story with a doctrine of the earthly origin of sin. See also Sacchi, *Jewish Apocalyptic,* 146.

94. Nickelsburg, *Resurrection, Immortality, and Eternal Life in Intertestamental Judaism* (2d ed.; Cambridge, MA: Harvard University Press, 2006) 141-62; L. Ruppert, *Der leidende Gerechte* (Würzburg: Echter, 1972) 70-105.

95. Charles, *APOT,* 2:170-71; Milik, *Books of Enoch,* 44; P. A. Tiller, *A Commentary on the Animal Apocalypse of 1 Enoch* (Atlanta: Scholars Press, 1993) 61-82. Nickelsburg, *1 Enoch 1,* 361.

reminder that the whole world could be destroyed. It implies the contingency of the world, its dependence on its Maker. It need not refer to any particular crisis.

The second vision in chaps. 85–91 is a complex allegory. The figures of biblical history are represented by animals. Adam is a white bull. Cain and Abel are black and red bullocks. Seth and his descendants are white bulls. The descent of the Watchers is expressed in chap. 86 as the descent or fall of stars from heaven, in accordance with the common identification of stars with angels or heavenly beings. The giants begotten by them are "elephants, camels, and asses." Then "there came from heaven beings who were like white men." These are the angels who bind the Watchers and imprison them.[96] Three angels also lift Enoch up to a high place from which he can view the course of history. Enoch does not undertake a heavenly tour, but his vision is assisted by the angels.

Noah, like Adam, is a white bull. The key to his salvation is that he is taught a mystery by the angels. He then "became a man." This development does not contradict the general symbolism by which humans are represented as animals and angels as humans. Noah is transformed to an angel-like state.[97] The sons of Noah "began to beget wild animals and birds, so that there arose from them every kind of species" (89:10). As in Ezekiel 34, the nations are represented by the wild creatures. From these Abraham emerges as a white bull. Isaac is also a bull, but Jacob is a sheep — which marks the transition from the patriarchal period to the history of Israel. The imagery for the nations is also nuanced. The Ishmaelites to whom Joseph is sold are asses, but the Egyptians are wolves. The exodus is narrated at some length. Moses is a sheep at first, but he, like Noah, "became a man" (89:36, 38). The kings are represented as rams.

The account of the kingdoms is similar to the sixth week in the Apocalypse of Weeks. The sheep are blinded and go astray. The ascension of Elijah is noted. God delivers the sheep into the hands of the wild animals.

---

96. See further Karina Martin Hogan, "The Watchers Traditions in the Book of the Watchers and the Animal Apocalypse," in Harkins, Bautch and Endres, eds., *The Watchers in Jewish and Christian Traditions*, 107-20.

97. For other examples of such transformation, see J. H. Charlesworth, "The Portrayal of the Righteous as an Angel," in G. W. E. Nickelsburg and J. J. Collins, eds., *Ideal Figures in Ancient Judaism: Profiles and Paradigms* (SBLSCS 12; Chico, CA: Scholars Press, 1980) 135-47. Cf. M. Himmelfarb, "Revelation and Rapture: The Transformation of the Visionary in the Ascent Apocalypses," in Collins and Charlesworth, eds., *Mysteries and Revelations,* 79-90.

Then seventy shepherds are appointed to watch over the sheep and destroy some of them while "another" is told to record what the shepherds do.

Charles regarded the seventy shepherds as "the most vexed question in Enoch," but he showed conclusively that they are the angelic patrons of the nations.[98] They are later grouped with the fallen angels at the judgment, while "another" who records their deeds is clearly an angel in chap. 90. The background of this conception is found in Deuteronomy 32, where God divided the nations according to the number of the sons of God.[99] The conception figures prominently in Daniel 10. The number seventy corresponds to Daniel's seventy weeks of years and the common division of history into seventy generations, which we have noted above. Both the number seventy and the "shepherd" imagery are found in Jeremiah 25.[100]

The reign of the seventy shepherds is divided into four periods, which are allotted 12, 23, 23, and 12 shepherds respectively. This division roughly corresponds to the periods of Babylonian, Persian, Ptolemaic, and Seleucid rule, but the correlations are not explicit. Neither does Enoch correlate it with a four-kingdom schema such as we find in Daniel. The division conveys a sense of order and providential control. The first period culminates in the rebuilding of the temple. Here we are told that all the bread offered in the new temple was unclean and not pure. This verdict on the Jewish restoration is quite compatible with the Apocalypse of Weeks, which simply refers to an "apostate generation." We need not infer that the Second Temple was rejected in principle, but that the actual cult of the early restoration period was regarded as impure.

At the end of the third period (90:6) "small lambs were born from these white sheep, and they began to open their eyes." This development corresponds to the emergence of the "chosen righteous" in the Apocalypse of Weeks. *1 Enoch* 90:8 describes how "one of these lambs" was killed. This has been taken as a reference to the murder of the high priest Onias III.[101]

---

98. *APOT*, 2:255; Tiller, *A Commentary*, 325.

99. So LXX, supported by evidence from Qumran. The MT reads "sons of Israel." See P. W. Skehan, "A Fragment of the 'Song of Moses' (Deut 32) from Qumran," *BASOR* 136 (1954) 12-15.

100. See further VanderKam, *Enoch and the Growth of an Apocalyptic Tradition*, 166. For the parallels between the Animal Apocalypse and Daniel, see P. A. Porter, *Metaphors and Monsters: A Literary-Critical Study of Daniel 7 and 8* (Lund: Gleerup, 1983) 43-60.

101. Charles, *APOT*, 2:257; Milik, *Books of Enoch*, 43. See 2 Macc 4:33-35 and Dan 9:26. See, however, Tiller, *A Commentary*, 349, who reads "seized those lambs" in the plural. See his comments on the more usual reading on pp. 353-54.

No other plausible referent is known. If this is correct, the rejection of the Second Temple must be modified. There is no doubt that the great horn that grew on one of those sheep in 90:9 is Judas Maccabee. Eventually the recording angel goes down to help Judas, a probable reference to the tradition that an angel appeared at the battle of Beth-Zur.[102] Beyond this point the apocalypse is no longer describing history but rather is describing its anticipated conclusion. God himself comes down and sets up his throne for judgment. A sword is given to the "sheep" as it was given to the righteous in the Apocalypse of Weeks. Then the Watchers and the seventy shepherds are destroyed but also the "blind sheep" or apostate Jews. Then the "old house" is replaced and all the nations bow down to the Jews. Those that had been destroyed are brought back, presumably by resurrection, and all are transformed into "white bulls" — the condition of Adam and the early patriarchs. The "wild animals" are also gathered in the new "house," but it is not clear that they are transformed. In view of 90:30 they are clearly subject to the Jews. The final transformation then is located in the land of Israel, but since God has come down and lives among them we may speak of heaven on earth, just as the new Jerusalem comes down from heaven in Revelation 21. The "house" here may indeed refer to Jerusalem, since the temple is represented as a "tower."[103]

The technique of the Animal Apocalypse is similar to the other Enoch writings we have considered. The work is addressed to the crisis that led to the Maccabean revolt. This crisis is put in perspective by being located in an overview of all history. The history is treated allegorically, so the emphasis is on the typical rather than the particular. It is also measured out and said to be under supernatural control. The eschatological finale is integrated into the sequence of history and so gains credibility from the accurate detail of the preceding "prophecy." The message is ultimately that the judgment is at hand and that the heavenly angels will dispose of the Gentile rulers as they originally disposed of the Watchers. Unlike what we will find in Daniel, this apocalypse affirms a militant role for the righteous.[104] Yet the victory is in the hands of God and his angels, and the resolution involves a resurrection beyond this life, even if it is located on

---

102. Milik, *Books of Enoch*, 44; 2 Macc 11:6-12.

103. Tiller, *A Commentary*, 376.

104. This is disputed by Daniel Assefa, *L'Apocalypse des animaux (1 Hen 85-90): une propagande militaire. Approches narrative, historico-critique, perspectives théologiques* (JSJSup 120; Leiden: Brill, 2007) 332, who argues that the reference to Judas Maccabee is a late interpolation.

earth. The Animal Apocalypse then provides the "elect" with an understanding of their situation which not only can relieve anxiety but also can be an effective support for their action.

## An Apocalyptic Movement?

The four apocalypses of Enoch that we have considered show literary continuity in the reuse of the legend of Enoch's ascent and, in the Apocalypse of Weeks and the Animal Apocalypse, the allusions to the Watchers. It is reasonable to suppose that there was also some historical and social continuity and to ask whether these books are the product of a single movement or group.

Evidence that the Enoch literature articulates the ideology of a movement can be found in the Apocalypse of Weeks and in the Animal Apocalypse. We have noted above that a major focus of the Apocalypse of Weeks is the emergence of "the chosen righteous from the eternal plant of righteousness."[105] The apocalypse is introduced (93:2) as "concerning the sons of righteousness and concerning the chosen of the world and concerning the plant of righteousness and uprightness." The plant of righteousness appears in the third generation as the descendants of Abraham. The "chosen righteous from the eternal plant of righteousness," which is chosen in the seventh generation, is then an offshoot of the people of Abraham. This special elect group will be given "sevenfold teaching concerning his whole creation." The movement is not entirely pietistic, however. It evidently endorses the use of the sword against the wicked: "And after this the roots of iniquity will be cut off, and the sinners will be destroyed by the sword" and, in the eighth generation, "the sinners will be handed over into the hands of the righteous." These statements can be read as purely future expectation, since the author's own time is most probably located in the climactic seventh week. Yet the ideology they reflect is obviously compatible with that of the Maccabean revolt.

A few other items in the Apocalypse of Weeks may be indicative of group identity. The "chosen righteous" will be given "sevenfold teaching concerning his whole creation" (93:10). They are possessors of some special wisdom. Then, at the end of the eighth week "they will acquire houses

---

105. For a study of the terminology, with special attention to parallels from Qumran, see Dexinger, *Henochs Zehnwochenapokalypse,* 164-77.

because of their righteousness." Both of these points relate the apocalypse to the Epistle of Enoch. There we are told "that books will be given to the righteous and wise" (104:12). We might infer that the "righteous" are a scribal class, and the inference may be corroborated by the description of Enoch as a "scribe of righteousness" in the Book of the Watchers (12:4). The Epistle complains more than once about those who "build their houses with sin" (94:7) or "with the toil of others" (99:13) and consoles the righteous with the hope of an angelic afterlife. The apocalypse provides for some material compensation, within the context of cosmic transformation.[106] The Epistle shares the militant tone of the apocalypse (95:3; 96:1; 98:12) but lacks the reference to the "chosen" as a group designation. The righteous are still to testify to the sons of the earth about the wisdom in them (105:1). They are not, then, closed off from the society around them.[107] There would seem to be some progression between the Epistle and the Apocalypse of Weeks toward clearer definition of a group, but the evidence is very slight.[108]

Both the Epistle and the Apocalypse of Weeks draw sharp contrasts between the righteous and the wicked. The sinners in the Epistle are accused of idolatry and oppression. They are evidently a wealthy class, but the extent of their role in Jewish society is unclear. The Apocalypse of Weeks, in contrast, dismisses the whole postexilic period as "an apostate generation." There is no mention of the rebuilding of the temple until the eighth week in the eschatological period. It is unclear whether the sweeping characterization of the postexilic period expresses a total rejection of the restoration or should be regarded as a hyperbolic reaction to the circumstances at the time of composition.

The emergence of the "chosen righteous" can be correlated with the "small lambs" which "began to open their eyes" in the Animal Apocalypse. Here there is clear support for the Maccabean revolt, but Judas is not said to be one of the lambs, but one of the sheep. We may infer from this that he was not part of the original movement. The Animal Apocalypse also

---

106. This point is emphasized by S. B. Reid, *Enoch and Daniel: A Form-Critical and Sociological Study of the Historical Apocalypses* (Berkeley: Bibal, 1989).

107. G. W. E. Nickelsburg, "The Epistle of Enoch and the Qumran Literature," *JJS* 33 (1982) 333-48.

108. Horsley and Tiller, *After Apocalyptic and Wisdom*, 131, say that "we should not think that 1 Enoch 91-104 is the product of a movement or group any more than we would understand the text of Sirach as evidence of Ben Sira heading a social movement," but they ignore the links between the Epistle and the other parts of the Enochic corpus.

implies that the lambs had taken up arms and been defeated (by the "ravens," 90:9) before the rise of Judas.

In this apocalypse the foreign rulers of Israel are the primary enemies. We have noted the apparent rejection of the worship of the Second Temple in 89:73, which must be modified if the high priest Onias III is regarded as "one of the lambs" in 90:8.

Neither the Book of the Watchers nor the Astronomical Book, which appear to be the oldest Enochic writings, attests a particular group identity in its terminology. In *1 Enoch* 10:16 the plant of righteousness and truth is apparently Israel, and we are not told of any other offshoot. The story of the Watchers may have reflected a division within the people, by criticism of the priesthood, but party lines are not clearly drawn. It has been suggested that the punishment of 'Aśa'el/Azazel in *1 Enoch* 10 is an adaptation of the scapegoat ritual in Leviticus 16 and constitutes an implicit rejection of the official ritual of atonement.[109] In the Aramaic fragments from Qumran, however, the name of the Watcher is 'Aśa'el, not Azazel, and so it is doubtful whether there was any allusion to Leviticus 16.[110] Even if the association with Leviticus 16 were established, the cult would not necessarily be devalued. The scapegoat ritual might simply be given a new level of reference.

The Astronomical Book makes the usual Enochic distinction between righteous and sinners in chap. 81. The main indicator of group identity in this writing, however, is the allegiance to the 364-day calendar. This has often been taken as a sign of sectarian provenance. The issue is clouded, however, by a number of factors.

First, there is no direct evidence concerning what calendar was officially in use in Judaism in the third or the early second century. It is generally assumed that the luni-solar calendar of later Judaism was already in force,[111] but some have argued that the solar calendar was official, even

109. Hanson, "Rebellion in Heaven," 226.

110. The identification with Azazel is already made in a fragmentary Hebrew text from Qumran that speaks of Azazel and the angels (Milik, *Books of Enoch*, 251).

111. For example, M. D. Herr, "The Calendar," in S. Safrai and M. Stern, eds., *The Jewish People in the First Century* (CRINT 1/2; Philadelphia: Fortress, 1976) 834-64; Sacha Stern, "Qumran Calendars and Sectarianism," in Timothy H. Lim and John J. Collins, eds., *The Oxford Handbook of the Dead Sea Scrolls* (Oxford: Oxford University Press, 2010) 234, claims that this calendar had been observed in Judah since the Achaemenid period. See also Stern, "The 'Sectarian' Calendar of Qumran," in idem, ed., *Sects and Sectarianism in Jewish History* (Leiden: Brill, 2011) 39-62.

down to the time of Antiochus Epiphanes.[112] The latter position is open to some objection: Antiochus is known to have disrupted the Jewish festivals, but it is doubtful whether a change in the calendar regulating the traditional festivals could have resulted from his actions.[113] Yet the fact remains that we are ill-informed about the official calendar in pre-Maccabean times.[114]

Second, as already noted, the Astronomical Book does not polemicize against a lunar or soli-lunar calendar, but only against a 360-day calendar, which was never official in Judaism.[115] In the light of this, the Astronomical Book does not seem to have been generated by a conflict with the Jerusalem temple. It is difficult to see how the authors of this book could have functioned in a temple regulated by a lunar calendar. This problem would be avoided if the Astronomical Book was composed in the eastern Diaspora, where actual use of the temple was not an immediate issue. It is also possible that the 364-day calendar was a theoretical, academic, construct, and not observed in practice.[116] There is no provision for intercalation. The 364-day calendar is explicit only in the Astronomical Book in the Enochic corpus, but the Book of the Watchers lists the path

112. J. C. VanderKam, "The Origin, Character, and Early History of the 364-Day Calendar: A Reassessment of Jaubert's Hypotheses," *CBQ* 41 (1979) 390-411; idem, "2 Maccabees 6, 7a and Calendrical Change in Jerusalem," *JSJ* 12 (1981) 1-23; idem, *Calendars in the Dead Sea Scrolls*, 113-14. A. Jaubert held that the solar calendar was official in the postexilic period but that lunar modifications had been introduced by the time of Ben Sira (*The Date of the Last Supper* [Staten Island, NY: Alba House, 1965]).

113. P. R. Davies argues that the decrees of Antiochus suppressed the Jewish festivals and introduced pagan ones, which had no bearing on the Jewish cultic calendar (cf. 2 Macc 6:6) ("Calendrical Change and Qumran Origins: An Assessment of VanderKam's Theory," *CBQ* 45 [1983] 80-89).

114. Jaubert's argument for the official use of the solar calendar depends on implications in the priestly writings of the Old Testament, but this evidence does not necessarily bear on the official calendar of the third or second century. It has been disputed, moreover, by J. Baumgarten, "The Calendar in the Book of Jubilees and the Bible," in *Studies in Qumran Law* (Leiden: Brill, 1977) 101-14. On the other hand, the apparent evidence for a lunar calendar in the Hebrew text of Sir 43:6-7 is not decisive either. The ancient versions say only that the sign for a festival is derived from the moon — possibly referring to the new moon. See further VanderKam, "The Origin, Character, and Early History of the 364-Day Calendar," 409.

115. VanderKam, "The 364-Day Calendar in the Enochic Literature," 157-65.

116. Sacha Stern, *Calendar and Community: A History of the Jewish Calendar Second Century BCE – Tenth Century CE* (Oxford: Oxford University Press, 2001) 8, and "Qumran Calendars and Sectarianism," 249, questions whether the 364-day calendar was ever observed in practice.

of the moon among the harmful teachings of the Watchers (*1 Enoch* 8:3). The solar calendar is not contradicted in the other early Enoch books and is probably presupposed, but the evidence is lacking.

The internal evidence for an apocalyptic movement in *1 Enoch,* then, is less than complete. If we may assume that all these works come from an ongoing tradition (which is plausible though not certain), then we have a movement that had its roots in the third century. In the earliest writings, the group identity is not prominent. The authors were presumably scribes, like Enoch, who had a mission to their fellow Jews and to humanity at large. While its calendar may have differed from that of the Jerusalem temple, it was not involved in explicit polemics against mainline Judaism. The Apocalypse of Weeks and the Animal Apocalypse show a heightened group identity, apparently reflecting the recent emergence of a stronger group formation. They are also more militant and more directly critical of the temple and of the Jewish leadership. It is of interest that in these apocalypses, written in a time of conflict, the cosmological interests of the apocalyptic genre recede, and the historical interests come to the fore.

The movement or group that is clearly attested in the Apocalypse of Weeks and the Animal Apocalypse must be correlated with some analogous developments in *Jubilees* and the *Damascus Document* (CD).[117] In *Jubilees* 23, after a period of suffering at the hands of the Gentiles, "the children shall begin to study the laws and to seek the commandments and to return to the paths of righteousness" (23:26). Life will then be transformed, so that their days will be close to a thousand years and "there shall be no Satan or any evil destroyer." At that time the servants of the Lord will "rise up and see great peace and drive out their adversaries." *Jubilees* does not use a specific group designation such as "chosen righteous." A relationship with Enochic circles is suggested, however, by *Jubilees'* defense of the solar calendar, which in this case is directly opposed to a lunar system (*Jub.* 6:32-38). *Jubilees* still insists on the use of the temple (e.g., the Passover must be celebrated there, 49:16). How this relates to the actual temple cult at the time when *Jubilees* was written is unclear.

The opening column of the so-called *Damascus Document* (CD) also

---

117. Hengel, *Judaism and Hellenism,* 1:175-80; D. Dimant, "Qumran Sectarian Literature," in M. E. Stone, ed., *Jewish Writings of the Second Temple Period* (CRINT 2/2; Assen: Van Gorcum; Philadelphia: Fortress, 1984) 542-47; F. García Martínez, "Qumran Origins and Early History: A Groningen Hypothesis," *Folia Orientalia* 25 (1989) 119; P. R. Davies, *Behind the Essenes* (Atlanta: Scholars Press, 1987) 107-34.

describes the rise of a movement and, like *1 Enoch,* uses the metaphor of "plant" to describe it:

> For when they were unfaithful and forsook Him, He hid His face from Israel and His Sanctuary and delivered them up to the sword. But remembering the Covenant of the forefathers, He left a remnant to Israel and did not deliver it up to be destroyed. And in the age of wrath, three hundred and ninety years after He had given them into the hand of king Nebuchadnezzar of Babylon, He visited them, and He caused a plant root to spring from Israel and Aaron to inherit His Land and to prosper on the good things of His earth. And they perceived their iniquity and recognized that they were guilty men, yet for twenty years they were like blind men groping for the way. And God observed their deeds, that they sought Him with a whole heart, and He raised for them a Teacher of Righteousness to guide them in the way of His heart. (CD 1:3-11)[118]

The figure of 390 years is presumably derived from Ezek 4:5 and cannot be taken as chronologically exact, but it requires a lapse of several hundred years after the exile.[119] CD 1 then distinguishes three developments in the postexilic period: first, the "remnant," which apparently refers to all Jews who survived the destruction of Jerusalem; second, the "plant root," an offshoot that arose several hundred years later and was a penitential movement; and, third, the arrival of the Teacher of Righteousness, who is generally regarded as the founder of the Qumran settlement, although this is never explicit in the texts. The latter development is usually placed in the mid-second century BCE, but in fact the archaeological data (primarily the coins) would seem to point to a somewhat later date, in the first half of the first century BCE.[120]

Neither CD nor the Apocalypse of Weeks, nor *Jubilees* 1, acknowledges the restoration from the Babylonian exile in the sixth century BCE. Daniel 9 still looks for the fulfillment of Jeremiah's prophecy, even though it acknowledges the return in the Persian period. The Animal Apocalypse

---

118. Trans. G. Vermes, *The Dead Sea Scrolls in English* (4th ed.; London: Penguin, 1995) 97.

119. See further J. J. Collins, "The Origin of the Qumran Community," in M. P. Horgan and P. J. Kobelski, eds., *To Touch the Text: Biblical and Related Studies in Honor of Joseph A. Fitzmyer, S.J.* (New York: Crossroad, 1989) 167-70 (= *Seers, Sibyls, and Sages,* 239-60).

120. Jodi Magness, *The Archaeology of Qumran and the Dead Sea Scrolls* (Grand Rapids: Eerdmans, 2002) 65.

disputes the validity of the Second Temple.[121] The statements of CD on developments after the destruction of Jerusalem must be read in this light.[122] A reference to an "exilic generation" provides no chronological information if the exile is thought to persist for several hundred years.

CD is written from the perspective of the Teacher's community, which is usually identified with the Essene sect. We will consider it further in the context of the Qumran scrolls. Its relevance to the Enoch literature lies in the information that the "plant root" preceded the arrival of the Teacher by some twenty years and at this time was not so clearly organized as the later Qumran community. The relevance to the Enoch literature is strengthened by the fact that the revelations associated with the new covenant in 3:14 concern "His holy Sabbaths and His glorious festivals" — in short, the calendar.

Martin Hengel suggested that the Apocalypse of Weeks, the Animal Apocalypse, and the *Damascus Document* refer to the formation of a group that is mentioned in 1 Maccabees 2 as the "assembly of the pious" or Hasidim *(synagōgē asidaiōn)*.[123] Hengel also attributed the book of Daniel to this group. He then takes the Hasidim as the forerunners of the Qumran community. This hypothesis is attractive in drawing together diverse pieces of evidence from the early second century, but it also presents some problems.[124]

The Hasidim are mentioned three times in the books of Maccabees.[125] In 1 Macc 2:42 they are "mighty warriors of Israel" who join the Maccabees after the slaughter of a group of pious Jews on the Sabbath. In 1 Macc 7:12-13 they seem to be identified with a group of scribes who sought peace with the high priest Alcimus but who were taken by surprise, so that 60 of them were killed. In 2 Macc 14:6 Alcimus reports to the Syrian king Demetrius that "those of the Jews who are called Hasideans, whose leader is Judas Maccabeus, are keeping up the war and stirring up sedition

---

121. Compare also *Testament of Moses* 4:8, but the interpretation is disputed.

122. See further M. A. Knibb, "The Exile in the Literature of the Intertestamental Period," *Heythrop Journal* 17 (1976) 253-72.

123. Hengel, *Judaism and Hellenism,* 1:97.

124. J. J. Collins, *The Apocalyptic Vision of the Book of Daniel* (HSM 16; Missoula, MT: Scholars Press, 1977) 201-5; G. W. E. Nickelsburg, "Social Aspects of Palestinian Jewish Apocalypticism," in D. Hellholm, ed., *Apocalypticism,* 639-52; P. R. Davies, "Hasidim in the Maccabean Period," *JJS* 28 (1977) 127-40.

125. The most thorough discussion is by J. Kampen, *The Hasideans and the Origin of Pharisaism* (Atlanta: Scholars Press, 1988).

and will not let the kingdom attain tranquility." While Judas Maccabee's relation to the Hasidim may be overstated in the latter passage, it is clear that they did support him, at least for a time, and that they participated actively in the military campaign. These three references are the only evidence for an organized party of Hasidim in Maccabean times. References to the "assembly of the pious" or Hasidim in Psalm 149, the Qumran *Psalm Scroll* (11QPs$^a$ 154, 155), and in the *Psalms of Solomon* (4:1; 17:16) cannot be taken as evidence for such a party.

Our evidence for the Hasidim, then, is extremely scanty. One of the few things we can say of them with confidence is that they participated in the revolt in support of Judas Maccabee. They were not quietists or pacifists. This point should enable us to correct at least one element in Hengel's reconstruction. The book of Daniel reflects a quietistic ideology and cannot be ascribed to the militant Hasidim. Victor Tcherikover argued that the Hasidim were the initiators of the revolt.[126] According to his reconstruction, they had rebelled against Jason, the Hellenizing high priest, and ousted him from Jerusalem. This disturbance led to the intervention of Antiochus Epiphanes and then to the persecution. The martyrs in the wilderness in 1 Maccabees 2, who let themselves be slaughtered rather than break the Sabbath, were not pacifists, but militants who were strict observers of the law. Tcherikover identified the Hasidim as "the chief scribes."[127] 1 Macc 7:12-13 does indeed support the view that they were scribes, but there is no evidence for their status among the people.

The Apocalypse of Weeks, the Animal Apocalypse, and *Jubilees* are all compatible with what we know of the Hasidim, although the allusions in 1 and 2 Maccabees give no hint of the range of concerns in those books. The Animal Apocalypse is especially intriguing in the light of Tcherikover's reconstruction, since it implies that the "lambs" took up arms before the rise of Judas. The Apocalypse of Weeks and *Jubilees* are not so clearly tied to the Maccabean revolt but still make good sense in that context. The relation of the *Damascus Document* to the other texts is less clear. It contains no reference to militant action and refers rather to a reform movement. Yet the metaphor of planting forms a link with the Enoch literature. Moreover, the 364-day solar calendar of *1 Enoch* and *Jubilees* was also observed

---

126. V. Tcherikover, *Hellenistic Civilization and the Jews* (New York: Atheneum, 1970) 197-203.

127. Ibid., 197; J. Sievers, *The Hasmoneans and Their Supporters* (Atlanta: Scholars Press, 1990) 39-40.

at Qumran. CD has much in common with *Jubilees* in their adherence to priestly traditions. The Enoch books and *Jubilees* were preserved at Qumran. Yet it would be too simple to suppose that all these books attest a single movement that later settled at Qumran.[128]

The claim of continuity between "Enochic Judaism" and the sectarian movement of the Dead Sea Scrolls has been made especially by Gabriele Boccaccini.[129] Philip Davies had already equated the group in CD 1 that was like blind men for 20 years before the coming of the Teacher, with the Essenes,[130] and claimed that it seemed "unnecessarily pedantic" not to call the Apocalypse of Weeks or *Jubilees* "Essene."[131] Boccaccini builds on this suggestion and claims that "what ancient historians called Essenism encompasses not only the Qumran community but also what modern scholars have identified, on the basis of its extant documents, as Enochic Judaism."[132]

Boccaccini's thesis has been widely criticized.[133] The identification of the sect known from the Scrolls as "Essene" is based to a great degree on the similarities between the community organization described in the Community Rule (*Serek ha-Yahad*) and the accounts of the Essenes in Philo and Josephus.[134] There is no description of community structures in the Enochic books or *Jubilees*, and no basis for calling those texts Essene.

There are significant differences between the eschatology of the scrolls, which show little evidence for a belief in resurrection and which

128. J. P. Thorndike ("The Apocalypse of Weeks and the Qumran Sect," *RevQ* 3 [1961] 163-84) argues that the Apocalypse of Weeks is a veiled history of the Qumran sect. Dimant, "Qumran Sectarian Literature," 544, makes a similar claim for the Animal Apocalypse.

129. Gabriele Boccaccini, *Beyond the Essene Hypothesis: The Parting of the Ways between Qumran and Enochic Judaism* (Grand Rapids: Eerdmans, 1998); idem, *Roots of Rabbinic Judaism: An Intellectual History from Ezekiel to Daniel* (Grand Rapids: Eerdmans, 2002); "Enochians, Urban Essenes, Qumranites," in Boccaccini and Collins, eds. *The Early Enoch Literature*, 301-27.

130. P. R. Davies, *Behind the Essenes* (Atlanta: Scholars Press, 1987) 30.

131. Ibid., 109, 129.

132. Boccaccini, *Beyond the Essene Hypothesis*, 11.

133. John J. Collins, "'Enochic Judaism' and the Sect of the Dead Sea Scrolls," in Boccaccini and Collins, *The Early Enoch Literature*, 283-99; James C. VanderKam, "The Book of Enoch and the Qumran Scrolls," in Lim and Collins, eds., *The Oxford Handbook of the Dead Sea Scrolls*, 254-77.

134. Todd S. Beall, *Josephus' Description of the Essenes Illustrated by the Dead Sea Scrolls* (Cambridge: Cambridge University Press, 1988); John J. Collins, *Beyond the Qumran Community: The Sectarian Movement of the Dead Sea Scrolls* (Grand Rapids: Eerdmans, 2010) 122-65.

emphasize messianic expectation, and that of the Enoch literature. Even in the case of the "plant root" of CD before the arrival of the Teacher we should probably speak rather of pre-Essenes. Most obviously, the sectarian scrolls do not look to Enoch as the mediator of revelation, but rather to Moses.

The lack of engagement with the Mosaic covenant is one of the most striking aspects of the earliest Enoch literature, the Astronomical Book and the Book of the Watchers.[135] This lack cannot be explained by the fact that it would be anachronistic in materials relating to Enoch. The Book of Jubilees has no qualms about reading halakhic concerns back into primeval history. The very choice of Enoch as mediator bespeaks a different attitude to revelation and tradition than what we find in Mosaic literature such as the Scrolls. There is more engagement with specifically Israelite traditions in the Apocalypse of Weeks and the Animal Apocalypse,[136] but even then the engagement with the Law, as distinct from the narratives, is not extensive. The Apocalypse of Weeks refers briefly to "a covenant for all generations," apparently in reference to the revelation at Sinai (1 Enoch 93:6). The Animal Apocalypse refers to the ascent of Mount Sinai, but surprisingly does not mention the giving of the Law (1 Enoch 89:28-35). There appears to be some movement towards integrating Enochic and Mosaic revelation in the Enochic corpus, and this integration will be taken much further in *Jubilees*, but the early Enoch literature still attests to a form of Judaism in Second Temple times that was not primarily oriented towards the Torah of Moses. Consequently, it is at best misleading to characterize the early Enochic writings as "covenantal nomism."[137]

Our reconstruction of the social matrix of the Enoch tradition must remain very tentative. Fundamental matters, such as the status of the 364-

---

135. George W. E. Nickelsburg, "Enochic Wisdom and Relationship to the Mosaic Torah," in Boccaccini and Collins, *The Early Enoch Literature*, 81-94; John J. Collins, "Enochic Judaism: An Assessment," in Adolfo D. Roitman, Lawrence H. Schiffman and Shani Tzoref, eds., *The Dead Sea Scrolls and Contemporary Culture: Proceedings of the International Conference held at the Israel Museum, Jerusalem* (July 6-8, 2008) (STDJ 93; Leiden: Brill, 2011) 219-34, *pace* Himmelfarb, *A Kingdom of Priests*, 39.

136. Andreas Bedenbender, "The Place of the Torah in the Early Enoch Literature," in Boccaccini and Collins, eds., *The Early Enoch Literature*, 65-79.

137. Contra Sanders, *Paul and Palestinian Judaism*, 346-62; Richard Bauckham, "Apocalypses," in D. A. Carson, P. T. O'Brien, and M. A. Seifrid, eds., *Justification and Variegated Nomism. Volume 1. The Complexities of Second Temple Judaism* (WUNT 2.140; Tübingen: Mohr Siebeck, 2001) 139-49; Mark Elliott, *The Survivors of Israel: A Reconsideration of the Theology of Pre-Christian Judaism* (Grand Rapids: Eerdmans, 2000) 424-34.

day calendar in the third century, remain quite uncertain. We may say with some confidence that this literature was produced by scribes who were distressed by the encroachments of Hellenism and the consequent erosion of traditional customs and aggravation of class divisions. We may also say that the tradition involved distinctive tendencies from the start, by its appeal to the higher revelation of Enoch, over and above the Mosaic Torah. It does not appear, however, that the bearers of the Enoch tradition before the Maccabean revolt were separated from the rest of Judaism in the manner of the later sect known from the Scrolls. They could at least make common cause with other strands of Judaism at the time of the revolt.

## Appendix: The Book of Jubilees

The book of *Jubilees* is preserved in full in Ethiopic but was originally composed in Hebrew.[138] Fifteen fragmentary Hebrew manuscripts have been found among the Dead Sea Scrolls.[139] The oldest, 4Q216 is dated by paleography to the last quarter of the second century BCE.

The book is introduced as "the history of the division of the days of the law and of the testimony, of the events of the years, of their (year) weeks, of their Jubilees throughout all the years of the world, as the Lord spoke to Moses on Mount Sinai when he went up to receive the tables of the law and of the commandment." In fact it is an expansionistic paraphrase of the book of Genesis and, more briefly, of Exodus down to the revelation of Sinai. The focus of the work is on halakhic matters that regulate the Jewish way of life. So the account of creation highlights the Sabbath in chap. 2, and the book concludes with instructions for the Sabbath in chap. 50. Great attention is paid to the festivals and to rituals such as circumcision. A major concern of the work is to defend the 364-day calendar and to warn against "the feast of the Gentiles" and the aberration of the moon (6:32-38). The biblical narrative is expanded to show how the patriarchs observed the Torah. The practical concerns of the book may be illustrated from the deathbed speech of Abraham in chaps. 20-22. Abraham warns his sons to practice circumcision, renounce fornication

---

138. For the Ethiopic text of *Jubilees*, see VanderKam, *The Book of Jubilees: A Critical Text* (Leuven: Peeters, 1989).

139. James C. VanderKam and J. T. Milik, "Jubilees," in H. Attridge et al., eds., *Qumran Cave 4–VIII: Parabiblical Texts* (DJD 13; Oxford: Clarendon, 1994), 1-185.

and uncleanness, refrain from marriage with Canaanite women, avoid idolatry, eat no blood, and perform washings before and after sacrificing. Marriage with Gentiles is emphatically forbidden in the story of the destruction of Shechem (*Jubilees* 30).[140] Michael Segal has argued that the halakhic passages, together with passages that pertain to the division of times and chronology, pertain to the redactional layer that ties together the various sources used in the book.[141]

Detailed discussion of the halakhic positions and exegetical techniques of *Jubilees* falls outside the scope of our present study.[142] Rather, our concern is with the apocalyptic dimension of the book. The content of the book is evidently quite different from what we usually find in an apocalypse. Yet the work as a whole is presented as a revelation communicated to Moses by the angel of the presence.[143] The laws are often said to be written "on the heavenly tablets" (3:10, 31; 4:5, 32; etc.).[144] James Kugel has argued that the references to the heavenly tablets belong to a layer of interpolated material that constituted a revision of the book.[145] In contrast, VanderKam defends the unity of the composition.[146]

140. See further M. Testuz, *Les Idées Religieuses du Livre des Jubilés* (Paris: Menard, 1960) 101-19; Nickelsburg, *Jewish Literature,* 69-73.

141. Michael Segal, *Rewritten Bible, Redaction, Ideology and Theology* (JSJSup 117; Leiden: Brill, 2007) 317-19.

142. See J. C. Endres, S.J., *Biblical Interpretation in the Book of Jubilees* (CBQMS 18; Washington, DC: Catholic Biblical Association of America, 1987).

143. In the Ethiopic text Moses is sometimes said to write the book, sometimes the angel, but the confusion may be a problem of translation. VanderKam argues that in the original Hebrew Moses alone wrote down what the angel dictated ("The Putative Author of the Book of Jubilees," *JSS* 26 [1981] 209-17); idem, "the Angel of the Presence in the Book of *Jubilees,*" *DSD* 7 (2000) 378-93.

144. Hindy Najman, "Interpretation as Primordial Writing: *Jubilees* and Its Authority Conferring Strategies," in eadem, *Past Renewals: Interpretive Authority, Renewed Revelation and the Quest for Perfection in Jewish Antiquity* (JSJSup 53; Leiden: Brill, 2010) 39-71. This article was originally published in *JSJ* 30 (1999) 379-410. See also Martha Himmelfarb, "Torah, Testimony, and Heavenly Tablets: The Claim to Authority in the Book of Jubilees," in Benjamin G. Wright, ed., *A Multiform Heritage: Studies on Early Judaism and Christianity in Honor of Robert A. Kraft* (Atlanta: Scholars Press, 1999) 22-28. On the heavenly tablets see Florentino García Martínez, "The Heavenly Tablets in the Book of Jubilees," in Matthias Albani, Jörg Frey, and Armin Lange, eds., *Studies in the Book of Jubilees* (Tübingen: Mohr Siebeck, 1997) 243-60.

145. James L. Kugel, "The Interpolations in the Book of Jubilees," *RevQ* 24 (2009) 215-72; idem, *A Walk through Jubilees: Studies in the Book of Jubilees and the World of Its Creation* (JSJSup 156; Leiden: Brill, 2012) 11-16.

146. James C. VanderKam, "Moses Trumping Moses: Making the Book of Jubilees,"

Moses, rather than Enoch, is the recipient of revelation here. More clearly than the Enoch books, *Jubilees* works within Mosaic tradition. Yet the choice of Moses as the recipient should not obscure the fact that *Jubilees* is rewriting the Mosaic law and modifying it at several points. It is significant that the speaker — and ultimately the authoritative figure here — is not Moses, but the angel.[147] Accordingly, it is not "Mosaic discourse,"[148] but "angelic discourse." *Jubilees* can correct the traditional law by appealing to the words of the angel and the heavenly tablets. That which is written in the heavenly tablets is the "testimony," which complements the Torah, and which, as VanderKam argues persuasively, should be identified with the contents of the book of *Jubilees* itself.[149]

The angel's revelation is presented as an account of the jubilees of history. We may compare the role of jubilees in the Apocalypse of Weeks, Daniel 9, and 11QMelchizedek. In *Jubilees,* the account extends only as far as the Sinai revelation. Yet in the introduction the account is said to cover "all the years of the world, and until God descends to dwell among them for all eternity" (1:26). We have no reason to believe that the account was ever completed,[150] but *Jubilees* does envisage history as a whole, with an eschatological conclusion. There are a few anticipatory glances toward the end of history, which may satisfy the claim of the introduction.

The eschatological finale of history is developed especially in two places. *Jubilees* 1:23-29 anticipates a time when the Jews will turn to God and he will live among them for all eternity. There will be a new creation, and heaven and earth shall be renewed "and all the luminaries (will) be

---

in Sarianna Metso, Hindy Najman, and Eileen Schuller, eds., *The Dead Sea Scrolls: Transmission of Traditions and Production of Texts* (STDJ 92; Leiden: Brill, 2010) 25-44.

147. The tradition that the law was given by angels is found in the New Testament (Acts 7:53; Gal 3:19; Heb 2:2).

148. So Najman, *Seconding Sinai*, 41-69. VanderKam, "Moses Trumping Moses," 31, comments: "he was not seconding Sinai; he was initiating Sinai."

149. VanderKam, "Moses Trumping Moses, 42: "it appears that those scholars who identify Jubilees itself, less the introductory material in the Prologue and ch. 1, as the testimony are correct, though the book may not exhaust all that is present in the written testimony on the heavenly tablets." Cana Werman, "The *Torah* and the *Teudah* Engraved on the Tablets," *DSD* 9 (2002) 75-103, thinks that the "testimony" is "the preordained march of history."

150. It is interesting to note that the *Testament (Assumption) of Moses* picks up where *Jubilees* leaves off. The title "Testament of Moses" precedes a quotation from *Jubilees* in the Catena of Nicephorus (Charles, *APOT*, 2:2). A connection between the two works is possible, but very hypothetical.

renewed for healing and for peace and for blessing for all the elect of Israel." The other passage in *Jubilees* 23 is more explicit. Here we get a rapid over-view of all generations from the time of Abraham. There is an extended account of the decline of humanity and the abuses of "an evil generation" (23:14) of the Hellenistic age. One of the charges against this generation is that it has forgotten "feasts and months and sabbaths and jubilees," a possible reference to a change of calendar. But then (23:26) "the children shall begin to study the laws" and the transformation will begin. They will drive out their adversaries and live in peace. Finally, "their bones shall rest in the earth and their spirits will have much joy," an apparent reference to afterlife without resurrection.[151]

Although *Jubilees* does not conclude with eschatological prediction, the prospect of a final judgment is of crucial importance throughout: "the judgment of all is ordained and written on the heavenly tablets in righ-teousness" (5:13). This formulation highlights another typically apocalyptic aspect of *Jubilees* — its determinism. Already in 1:29 we hear of "the tables of the divisions of the years," an indication that the course of the future is inscribed in advance. In 32:21 Jacob is allowed to read from heavenly tablets all that would befall him and his sons through the ages. Yet it is apparent that the deterministic framework functions as a hortatory device. If "the judgment of all is ordained and written in the heavenly tablets in righteous-ness," this is especially a warning for "all who depart from the path" that "if they walk not therein, judgment is written down for every creature and for every kind" (5:13). The inevitability of judgment is the ultimate sanction for the laws of *Jubilees*.

The eschatological horizon is, then, crucial for *Jubilees,* as it is for any apocalypse. The heavenly world is no less important. *Jubilees* does not pur-sue the speculative interest of the early Enoch books, but it is nonetheless interested in the order of nature. The account of creation (2:2) lists the angels of the spirits of the elements. The world of *Jubilees* is as thoroughly supervised by angelic beings as that of the Astronomical Book of Enoch. In addition to the angels of the elements there are angels of the presence and of sanctification. These interact with humanity by transmitting messages and by protecting the elect from their demonic adversaries. The latter are constituted by the descendants of the Watchers and are led by Mastema or Beliar (1:20). As a result, humanity is torn between two ways, each

151. Nickelsburg, *Resurrection,* 47-49; G. L. Davenport, *The Eschatology of the Book of Jubilees* (Leiden: Brill, 1971) 32-46.

controlled by supernatural powers, in a manner similar to what we will find at Qumran.[152]

We have already had occasion to note some of the affinities of the book of *Jubilees* with the early Enoch literature, of which the most notable is the calendar. *Jubilees* clearly presupposes the Book of the Watchers and the Astronomical Book and possibly alludes to the Book of Dreams, the Apocalypse of Weeks, and the Epistle.[153] Even in the use of material derived from Enoch, significant variations occur.[154] According to *Jubilees* the initial descent of the angels was so "that they should instruct the children of men, and that they should do judgment and justice on earth" (4:15). In short, there was no rebellion in heaven. Their initial sin was with the daughters of men. Later, after the flood, one-tenth of their offspring are allowed to remain with Mastema (Satan) to afflict mankind (10:11). In *1 Enoch* 15:9-12 the spirits of the giants will rise against humanity, without limitation. The eschatology of *Jubilees* is less elaborate than that of the Enoch books, and of course *Jubilees* has extensive areas of interest that are not paralleled in Enoch at all. In short, the conformity between *Jubilees* and the Enoch literature is not complete. One of the most important differences between them is that the Mosaic covenant has a far more prominent and central place in *Jubilees* than in the books of Enoch.[155]

152. Testuz, *Les Idées Religieuses,* 75-92; VanderKam, *Textual and Historical Studies in the Book of Jubilees* (HSM 14; Missoula, MT: Scholars Press, 1977) 265-67. Segal, *The Book of Jubilees,* 268-69, associates the dualistic material with the redactional layer, and argues that it is related to the dualism of the sectarian scrolls.

153. VanderKam, "Enoch Traditions," 229-45; idem, "The Book of Enoch and the Qumran Scrolls," in Lim and Collins, eds., *The Oxford Handbook of the Dead Sea Scrolls,* 254-77; John S. Bergsma, "The Relationship between *Jubilees* and the Early Enochic Books," in Gabriele Boccaccini and Giovanni Ibba, eds., *Enoch and the Mosaic Torah* (Grand Rapids: Eerdmans, 2009) 36-51.

154. James C. VanderKam, "The Angel Story in the Book of Jubilees," in E. G. Chazon and M. E. Stone, eds., *Pseudepigraphic Perspectives: The Apocrypha and Pseudepigrapha in Light of the Dead Sea Scrolls* (STDJ 31; Leiden: Brill, 1999) 151-70; J. T. A. G. M. van Ruiten, *Primaeval History Interpreted: The Rewriting of Genesis 1-11 in the Book of Jubilees* (JSJSup 66; Leiden: Brill, 2000) 195-97; Reed, *Fallen Angels,* 87-95; Stuckenbruck, "The Origins of Evil," 111-15; idem, "The Book of Jubilees and the Origin of Evil," in Boccaccini and Ibba, eds., *Enoch and the Mosaic Torah,* 294-308; Segal, *The Book of Jubilees,* 103-43; John C. Endres, S.J., "The Watchers Traditions in the Book of Jubilees," in Harkins, Bautch, and Endres, eds., *The Watchers,* 121-35.

155. Annette Yoshiko Reed, "Enochic and Mosaic Traditions in Jubilees: The Evidence of Angelology and Demonology," in Boccaccini and Ibba, eds., *Enoch and the Mosaic Torah,* 353-68.

*Jubilees* represents a borderline case for the apocalyptic genre, or, alternatively, may be considered a work of hybrid genre.[156] Confusion about its genre is reflected in the various titles used for the book: *Jubilees,* which suggests a treatment of history; the *Little Genesis,* which suggests a biblical paraphrase (sometimes loosely called midrash); but also the *Apocalypse of Moses.*[157] Testuz regarded the work as of composite genre, combining historical, legal, chronological, apocalyptic, and testamentary aspects.[158] Most often it is categorized as "rewritten Bible," a designation that has its own problems.[159] *Jubilees* differs from other apocalypses in its close reliance on the biblical narrative and its halakhic interests, and these factors should be given due weight in a full description of its genre. It remains true, however, that the *Rahmengattung* or generic framework of *Jubilees* is an apocalypse.[160] It is a revelation mediated by an angel to a venerable figure of the past. The laws it presents are reinforced by the inevitability of the predetermined judgment and are guidelines for the conflict between the angels and the demons. The apocalyptic ideas of revelation, eschatology, and the good and evil spirits constitute the view of the world within which the laws of *Jubilees* are vitally important. We may compare the role of the apocalyptic framework here with the Astronomical Book of Enoch. The specific message of the Astronomical Book concerns the observance of the 364-day calendar, which is not in itself distinctively apocalyptic. In both *Enoch* and *Jubilees,* however, the calendrical and halakhic ideas are given a supporting structure, in a view of the cosmos and of history, which is distinctively apocalyptic.[161]

156. John J. Collins, "The Genre of the Book of Jubilees," in Eric F. Mason, Kelley Coblentz Bautch, Angela Kim Harkins, and Daniel A. Machiela, eds., *A Teacher for All Generations: Essays in Honor of James C. VanderKam* (JSJSup 153/2; Leiden: Brill, 2012) 737-55. Armin Lange, "Divinatorische Träume und Apokalyptik im Jubiläenbuch," in M. Albani, J. Frey, and A. Lange eds., *Studies in the Book of Jubilees* (Tübingen: Mohr Siebeck, 1997) 25-38, has argued against the classification of *Jubilees* as an apocalyptic writing, because of its avoidance of symbolic dreams, even in its re-telling of the Joseph story. Lange's observation is certainly significant for our understanding of *Jubilees,* but it alone cannot determine the literary genre of the work.

157. Charles, *APOT,* 2:2. The title "Apocalypse of Moses" is more commonly applied to a variant of the *Life of Adam and Eve.*

158. Testuz, *Les Idées Religieuses,* 12.

159. Segal, *The Book of Jubilees,* 4.

160. Compare Rowland, *The Open Heaven,* 51-52.

161. Todd R. Hanneken, *The Subversion of the Apocalypses in the Book of Jubilees* (SBLEJL 34; Atlanta: SBL, 2012) argues that Jubilees imitates the apocalypses on the sur-

Some special emphases of *Jubilees* acquire added significance with reference to the period of the Maccabean revolt. The story of Adam and Eve is taken as showing that "they should cover their shame and not uncover themselves as the Gentiles uncover themselves" (3:31). Nudity in the gymnasium had been a major scandal in Jerusalem on the eve of the revolt (1 Macc 1:14-15). Making war on the Sabbath is explicitly forbidden in 50:12. In 1 Maccabees 2 we read of those who were slaughtered because they refused to defend themselves on the Sabbath. Thereafter the Hasidim joined Mattathias, who had decided to make an exception to this law. *Jubilees* would seem to represent a purist position on the issue.

*Jubilees* is not related to an historical crisis in as obvious a manner as the Animal Apocalypse or Daniel. Many scholars have sought to date the book by reference to the eschatological section of chap. 23. The "children" who begin to study the laws and rise up and drive out their adversaries can be plausibly associated with the Hasidim or a wing of that party, and the prohibitions against nudity, marriage with Gentiles, and fighting on the Sabbath make good sense in that context. It has been argued that "possibly in one instance, *Jub.* 34:2-9, and almost certainly in another, 37:1–38:14, *Jub.*'s author has composed accounts of battles whose inspiration was the victories of Judas Maccabeus."[162] Even if we grant the inspiration, however, this only provides a *terminus a quo*.[163] A further indication of date is found in the relation of *Jubilees* to the Qumran scrolls.[164] It is well known that *Jubilees* shares key doctrines and observances with Qumran: the calendar, determinism, dualism (ethical and angelic), and an eschatology that lacks, or at least minimizes, the idea of resurrection. Yet *Jubilees* lacks any indication of organization in a separate community and is concerned with the full nation of Israel, although the "children" who study the laws are a distinct group within it. In view of these considerations, *Jubilees* has been thought to come from the general milieu in which the sectarian movement developed, probably in the second half of the second century BCE. Doron

---

face level but subverts and caricatures the ideas that apocalypses typically convey. While the content of Jubilees is atypical of the Jewish apocalypses, I regard its use of the apocalyptic framework as positive and constructive.

162. VanderKam, *Textual and Historical Studies*, 217-24.

163. See the cautionary comments of Robert Doran, "The Non-dating of Jubilees: Jub 34–38; 23:14-32 in Narrative Context," *JSJ* 20 (1989) 1-11.

164. VanderKam, *Textual and Historical Studies*, 258-80; Testuz, *Les Idées Religieuses*, 179-95; K. Berger, *Das Buch der Jubiläen* (JSHRZ 2/3; Gütersloh: Mohn, 1981) 295-98; Segal, *The Book of Jubilees*, 320-22.

Mendels has argued that the territorial references in *Jubilees* require a date no earlier than the 120s: *Jubilees* 38 "must refer to the final conquest of Idumea . . . in 125 BCE."[165] The Qumran fragments require a date no later than 100 BCE.[166] *Jubilees*, then, is a product of the early Hasmonean period, and indirectly of the Maccabean crisis. The crisis perceived in *Jubilees*, however, is not the political crisis or the persecution which dominates the book of Daniel. It is rather the crisis of piety, occasioned by the neglect of the solar calendar and disregard for the laws. The crisis is primarily within the Jewish community: hence the appeal to the authority of Moses and the attempt to rewrite the law to incorporate *Jubilees'* special interests. *Jubilees* responds to the crisis not only by reaffirming the law of Moses and ascribing its own disputed laws to him (or rather, beyond Moses, to the angel and the heavenly tablets). It also provides a view of the cosmos and of history where the good angels and their followers will prevail and the sinners will be doomed to an inevitable judgment.

---

165. D. Mendels, *The Land of Israel as a Political Concept in Hasmonean Literature* (Tübingen: Mohr Siebeck, 1987) 80. Cf. *Jub.* 38:14: "And the Edomites have not got quit of the yoke of servitude that Jacob's twelve sons imposed on them to this day."

166. VanderKam and Milik, "Jubilees," in H. Attridge et al., eds., *Qumran Cave 4–VIII: Parabiblical Texts* (DJD 13). Nickelsburg prefers a date about 168 since *Jubilees* 23 contains no allusion to Antiochus Epiphanes (*Jewish Literature*, 77; compare J. A. Goldstein, "Jewish Acceptance and Rejection of Hellenism," in E. P. Sanders, A. I. Baumgarten, and A. Mendelson, eds., *Jewish and Christian Self-Definition* [3 vols.; Philadelphia: Fortress, 1981] 2:64-87). B. Z. Wacholder also argues for a date before the revolt (*The Dawn of Qumran* [New York: Ktav, 1983] 41-42). Berger argues for a date between 145 and 140 (*Das Buch der Jubiläen*, 300). Davenport distinguishes three stages: the body of the work is dated prior to the Maccabean revolt; 1:4b-26, part of 1:29, 23:14-31, and 50:5 are dated to 166-160; 1:27-28 and a few other verses were added later (*Eschatology*). The reasons for this division are not compelling.

# CHAPTER THREE

# *Daniel*

The book of Daniel contains the only full-blown example of apocalyptic literature in the Hebrew Bible. Consequently it has received far more attention than any other Jewish apocalypse,[1] but its special status has not always been beneficial. On the one hand, there has been a tendency to treat Daniel as the paradigmatic apocalypse, although in fact it is representative of only one type. On the other hand, there is even now the agonized attempt to disassociate the canonical book from the rest of the (disreputable) genre.[2] Attempts to dismiss the noncanonical apocalypses as Daniel's "second-rate imitators" should by now be discredited. There are, however, differences between Daniel and the Enoch tradition, some apparent and some real, which require consideration.

## The Figure of Daniel

The most obvious difference between Daniel and *1 Enoch* is that the visions of Daniel are prefaced by a collection of tales that purport to describe his career. Unlike the prediluvian Enoch, Daniel is presented as a figure from the relatively recent past. Details of the stories could, in principle,

---

1. For a bibliographic survey see K. Koch, *Das Buch Daniel* (Darmstadt: Wissenschaftliche Buchgesellschaft, 1980); J. E. Goldingay, *Daniel* (WBC 30; Dallas: Word, 1989) xxi-xl; J. J. Collins, *Daniel: A Commentary on the Book of Daniel* (Hermeneia; Minneapolis: Fortress, 1993) 72-123; Carol A. Newsom, with Brennan Breed, *Daniel: A Commentary* (OTL; Louisville, 2014) xxiii - liv.

2. E.g., F. D. Mazzaferri, *The Genre of the Book of Revelation from a Source-Critical Perspective* (BZNW 54; Berlin: de Gruyter, 1989) 190-94.

be verified from historical sources, and conservative scholars have labored unceasingly, and in vain, to do so.[3] The tales in Daniel bristle with historical problems.[4] The famous case of Darius the Mede may serve as an illustration. The conqueror of Babylon was Gobryas, governor of Gutium, a general of Cyrus, king of Persia. No such person as Darius the Mede is known in history. The successor of Cyrus as king of Persia was named Darius. The author of Daniel inherited a schema of four kingdoms in which Media preceded Persia, and it seems highly probable that he created the figure of Darius the Mede to fit this schema. Similarly, there is a wide consensus that the tale of Nebuchadnezzar's madness was developed from a tradition that originally concerned the later Babylonian king Nabonidus.[5] What is at issue in all this is not the veracity of "the word of God," as literalists usually construe it, but a question of genre. An assumption that the "word of God" must be factual historical reporting, and cannot be literary fiction, is theologically unwarranted. Whether or not a given passage is historically accurate is a question of relative probability in view of our total evidence. Nothing is gained by straining credibility in the hope of saving the historical appearances.[6]

The fact that Daniel is located in the historical setting of the exile rather than in primordial antiquity is no indication of historical reliability. Other apocalypses are ascribed to Ezra and Baruch, whose historical existence is beyond doubt, but the books attributed to them in the first century CE are nonetheless fictions. We should also expect the tales in

3. For the conservative arguments, see G. F. Hasel, "The Book of Daniel: Evidences Relating to Persons and Chronology," *AUSS* 19 (1981) 37-49; idem, "The Book of Daniel and Matters of Language: Evidences Relating to Names, Words, and the Aramaic Language," *AUSS* 19 (1981) 211-25.

4. See the classic discussion by H. H. Rowley, *Darius the Mede and the Four World Empires* (Cardiff: University of Wales Press, 1935); also L. F. Hartman and A. A. DiLella, *The Book of Daniel* (AB 23; Garden City, NY: Doubleday, 1978) 46-54; Collins, *Daniel*, 29-33.

5. Collins, *Daniel*, 217-19; A. Lacocque, *The Book of Daniel* (Atlanta: John Knox, 1979) 74-75; Hartman and DiLella, *The Book of Daniel*, 178-80. See J. J. Collins, "Prayer of Nabonidus," in G. Brooke et al., eds., *Qumran Cave 4–XVII: Parabiblical Texts, Part 3* (DJD 22; Oxford: Clarendon, 1996) 83-93; Carol A. Newsom, "Why Nabonidus? Excavating Traditions from Qumran, the Hebrew Bible, and Neo-Babylonian Sources," in Sarianna Metso, Hindy Najman, and Eileen Schuller, eds., *The Dead Sea Scrolls: Transmission of Traditions and Production of Texts* (STDJ 92; Leiden: Brill, 2010) 57-79.

6. For example, Hasel argues that since Cyrus did not assume the title "King of Babylon" for about nine months, this is evidence for Darius as a historical person. In fact, it provides no evidence whatever for Darius. Hasel also construes a fragmentary Babylonian text to imply a lapse into madness by Nebuchadnezzar.

Daniel to contain historical reminiscences and local color of the Persian and even the Babylonian period, but these are only the building blocks of the stories. Even if one were to prove the historical existence of both Daniel and Darius the Mede, one would not thereby verify the story of the lions' den.

In fact, the figure of Daniel may be more akin to Enoch than to Ezra or Baruch. The Bible contains no reference to a prophet by this name outside the actual book of Daniel. In the book of Ezekiel (an actual prophet of the exile) we do, however, have two references to Daniel. Ezek 14:14 says that when a land sins against God "even if these three men, Noah, Daniel and Job, were in it, they would deliver only their own lives." Ezekiel 28:3 taunts the king of Tyre: "Are you wiser than Daniel?" It would appear from these references that Daniel was the name of a legendary wise and righteous man. Further, the name *(Dnil)* appears in the Ugaritic story of Aqhat. Daniel is the father of Aqhat and is conspicuous for offering oblations to the gods and judging the case of the widow and the fatherless. The motif of judging is implied in the name Daniel and is found again in the story of Susanna. At the other end of the biblical period, we read in *Jub.* 4:20 that Enoch married "Edni, the daughter of Dânêl, the daughter of his father's brother." We are given no further information about this Dânêl, but the association with Enoch of a name so similar to Daniel, and possibly identical with it, is intriguing.

It is distinctly possible that the same traditional figure underlies the Daniel of Ugarit and Ezekiel, and the Dânêl of *Jubilees*.[7] It is in any case clear from Ezekiel that the name carried traditional associations that could only enhance the authority of the biblical book. The tales in Daniel 1–6, however, give this hero a new identity. The differences with Enoch become more significant at this point. Enoch's wisdom was derived primarily from his ascent. Daniel is at first an interpreter of dreams. Later, in Daniel 7–12, he is the dreamer himself. Obviously the difference here is not absolute. Enoch too has dream visions and in some apocalypses is, like Daniel, preoccupied with the course of history. The difference emerges mainly in contrast to the Book of the Watchers and the Astronomical Book. Daniel lacks the interest in cosmological speculation that is characteristic of much of the Enoch tradition.

---

7. J. Day, "The Daniel of Ugarit and Ezekiel and the Hero of the Book of Daniel," *VT* 30 (1980) 174-84. The name Dânêl is given to an angelic figure in *1 Enoch* 6:7 and 69:2.

## The Date and Unity of Daniel

The crucial argument on the date of Daniel was already formulated by the Neo-Platonic philosopher Porphyry in the third century.[8] Porphyry argued that Daniel was not written in the course of the Babylonian exile but in the time of Antiochus Epiphanes. His basic point was that Daniel "predicted" accurately the course of events down to the time of Antiochus Epiphanes but not beyond it.[9] This argument has stood the test of time. The issue is not "a dogmatic rejection of predictive prophecy" as conservatives like to assert, but a calculation of probability. Everyone recognizes that the predictions of Enoch are after the fact. The same logic holds in the case of Daniel.

The second-century date for the visions of Daniel (chaps. 7–12) is accepted as beyond reasonable doubt by critical scholarship.[10] The dating of the tales in chaps. 1–6 is less evident and is keenly debated. Doubts about the unity of the book arise from several factors. To begin with, the book is written in two languages: Hebrew (1:1–2:4a; chaps. 8–12) and Aramaic (2:4b–7:28). Second, there is the formal distinction between the tales in chaps. 1–6, in which Daniel appears in the third person, and the first-person accounts of revelations in chaps. 7–12. Third, there is the fact that further additions were made to Daniel, which are not found in the Hebrew Bible. The Prayer of Azariah and the Song of the Three Young Men are inserted in Daniel 3 in the Greek translations. The stories of Susanna and of Bel and the Dragon are added on in the Greek versions. These additions attest the ongoing accumulation of Danielic material, although they do not necessarily tell us anything about the composition of the Hebrew/Aramaic book. The so-called Prayer of Nabonidus (4QPrNab), discovered at Qumran, throws more light on the manner in which the tales developed.[11] This

8. P. M. Casey, "Porphyry and the Origin of the Book of Daniel," *JTS* 27 (1976) 15-33.

9. Porphyry's work is known to us only through Jerome's *Commentary on Daniel*. According to Jerome, Porphyry believed that the account of the death of Epiphanes in Dan 11:45 was written after the fact and accurate, whereas we now know that it was not. He understood the resurrection of the dead in Daniel 12 as a metaphor for the success of the Maccabean revolt.

10. There is, however, a tradition of conservative scholarship that holds to the exilic date; for example, J. G. Baldwin, *Daniel: An Introduction and Commentary* (Tyndale Old Testament Commentaries; Downers Grove, IL: InterVarsity, 1978).

11. Collins, "Prayer of Nabonidus"; Klaus Koch, "Gottes Herrschaft über das Reich des Menschen. Daniel 4 im Licht neuer Funde," in A. S. van der Woude, ed., *The Book of Daniel* (Leuven: Peeters, 1993), 77-119.

document is obviously related to the story of Nebuchadnezzar's madness in Daniel 4, although the relationship is not one of literary dependence in either direction. 4QPrNab suggests that Daniel 4 drew on an old tradition that was preserved and adapted in various ways.

The existence of these related documents may suggest that the book of Daniel was in part a compilation of traditional materials. The crucial argument, however, against the original unity of Daniel comes from the indications of date. The visions in Daniel 7–12 clearly refer to the persecution of Antiochus Epiphanes. There is no clear allusion to this period in the tales. To be sure, these stories were found relevant to the time of persecution, and many elements (such as Nebuchadnezzar's madness) could be applied very well in that setting.[12] Nothing in these chapters, however, requires a Maccabean date, and it does not appear that they were composed in the time of Antiochus. However arrogant the kings may be in the tales, they are not without hope of reform. In contrast, in chaps. 7–12 the Gentile kings have acquired a near demonic status. In chaps. 3 and 6 the faithful Jews are rescued alive. In chap. 12 they must look beyond death to a resurrection. The aggravated sense of crisis and negative attitude toward the Gentile kings coincide with the formal transition from tales to visions. One of the puzzles of the book of Daniel is the fact that the formal division does not coincide with the transition between the two languages.

Various explanations have been put forward for the problem of the two languages. There is a consensus that chaps. 2–6 were composed in Aramaic. Some scholars hold that an earlier form of chap. 7 completed the Aramaic Daniel. Some also hold that chaps. 8–12 were composed in Aramaic and then translated into Hebrew.[13] The evidence for the latter point is not compelling, nor is it apparent why only these chapters should have been translated. Chapter 1 may have been composed as an introduction either to the tales, in Aramaic, or to the whole book, in Hebrew.[14]

The key to this problem seems to lie in the fact that an author of the Maccabean period wished to incorporate the collection of Aramaic tales,

12. The main defender of a Maccabean date for the whole book was H. H. Rowley, "The Unity of the Book of Daniel," in *The Servant of the Lord and Other Essays on the Old Testament* (London: Lutterworth, 1952) 237-68.

13. So Hartman and DiLella, *The Book of Daniel*, 14-15.

14. See K. Koch, *Daniel 1,1-21* (BKAT 22; Neukirchen–Vluyn: Neukirchener Verlag, 1986) 16-18; A. S. van der Woude, "Die Doppelsprachigkeit des Buches Daniel," in idem, ed., *The Book of Daniel* (Leuven: Peeters, 1993) 3-12.

but himself preferred to write in Hebrew.[15] Although the tales were not composed with the Maccabean situation in mind, the author now wished to integrate them into a new unity. This was accomplished not by rewriting the tales but by binding them to the visions through editorial devices.[16] Daniel 7 was composed in Aramaic (perhaps at a slightly earlier time than chaps. 8–12). Since this vision was thematically related to Daniel 2, it completed a symmetrical arrangement in which chaps. 3 and 6 and chaps. 4 and 5 were closely related pairs.[17] In this way, chap. 7 was associated with the foregoing tales. However, the chronological dating of the chapters associates 7 rather with 8–12. Chapters 2, 3, and 4 are set in the time of Nebuchadnezzar. Chapter 5 refers to the transition from Belshazzar to Darius the Mede. Chapter 6 is set under Darius but ends with a reference to Cyrus of Persia. The sequence of Nebuchadnezzar, Belshazzar, Darius, and Cyrus is not, of course, historical, but it corresponds to the traditional schema of the four kingdoms, in which Persia was preceded by Media. Chapter 7, however, does not continue this sequence but reverts to the reign of Belshazzar. The sequence is then repeated with Darius (chap. 9) and Cyrus (chap. 10) and a reference to the coming "prince" of Greece (10:20). In short, the book of Daniel presents two sequences of dates, and chap. 7 is linked with chaps. 8–12. In this way chap. 7 is associated with both halves of the book and forms a bridge between them. The Hebrew chap. 1 serves to form an enclosure with the later Hebrew chapters. Whether it was specially composed for this purpose is uncertain. The rejection of the king's food in this chapter is not repeated in the tales. Yet chap. 1 sets the scene for chaps. 2–6 but does not anticipate the concerns of chaps. 7–12. It seems somewhat more probable that it was originally an introduction to the tales, presumably in Aramaic.

The unity of Daniel, then, is a secondary unity, achieved through the integration of older tales. We should not think, however, that the connection between tales and visions is purely external. Rather, they represent the continuity of a tradition. The characterization of Daniel and his friends is significant for the author of the visions and his circle. The continuity is indicated by the fact that Daniel and his friends are said to be *maśkîlîm*

15. Anathea Portier-Young, *Apocalypse Against Empire: Theologies of Resistance in Early Judaism* (Grand Rapids: Eerdmans), 228, goes farther, claiming that the switch to Aramaic is intended to "call an end to cooperation and accommodation." See also her article, "Languages of Identity and Obligation: Daniel as Bilingual Book," *VT* 60 (2010) 98-115.

16. See further, Collins, *Daniel*, 33-37.

17. A. Lenglet, "La structure littéraire de Daniel 2–7," *Bib* 53 (1972) 169-90.

*bĕkol ḥokmāh* (1:4) ("skillful in all wisdom"), whereas the heroes of the Antiochan persecution in chap. 11 are called *maśkîlîm* ("wise teachers"). The
theme of Jewish relations to Gentile kings runs through both tales and visions. The tales anticipate the crisis of persecution in the stories of the fiery
furnace and the lions' den. Most important, however, is the understanding
of wisdom and revelation developed in the tales, since it shows the background of one strand of tradition that led into the apocalyptic literature.

We cannot attempt a full discussion of the tales of Daniel here.[18]
We will take Daniel 2 as our illustration because it is the most complex
of the tales and the one which has the most obvious affinities with the
apocalyptic visions.

## Daniel 2

On one level, the story in Daniel 2 can be read as an adaptation of a traditional folktale, in which a person of lower status is called on by a superior
to solve an apparently insoluble problem, succeeds in doing so, and is
rewarded.[19] This type of tale is widely known. Important Near Eastern
precedents include the tale of Ahikar and the biblical story of Joseph.[20] In
this case, Daniel is a Jewish exile at the Babylonian court, and his challenge
is to tell the king not only the meaning of his dream but also the dream
itself, when all the Babylonian wise men have failed. This formulation of
the story rings some changes on the traditional folktale. On the one hand,
a prominent theological element is introduced. Daniel does not solve the
problem by his own wits but by praying to his God for a revelation. The
recourse to God is necessitated by the sheer impossibility of the king's
demand. The contrast between Daniel and the unsuccessful Chaldeans
is a consequence of the contrast between their respective gods. Even the
Babylonian king attests the theological implications of the story: "Truly
your God is God of gods and Lord of kings, and a revealer of mysteries,

18. For fuller treatment see Collins, *Daniel*, 38-52, 127-273. See also L. M. Wills, *The
Jew in the Court of the Foreign King* (HDR 26; Minneapolis: Fortress, 1990); Tawny Holm,
*Of Courtiers and Kings: The Biblical Daniel Narratives and Ancient Story Collections* (Winona
Lake, IN: Eisenbrauns, 2013); Newsom, *Daniel*, 15-18.

19. S. Niditch and R. Doran, "The Success Story of the Wise Courtier: A Formal
Approach," *JBL* 96 (1977) 179-93.

20. See especially Wills, *The Jew in the Court of the Foreign King*, 39-74, who draws
several examples of the genre from Herodotus.

for you have been able to reveal this mystery" (2:47).[21] On the other hand, the story has obvious political and ideological implications. Daniel has been said, justifiably, to be a model for "a life-style for the Diaspora." He illustrates how strict Jewish piety is not only compatible with success at a foreign court, but is precisely the key to such success.[22] At the same time, the actual interpretation has obvious subversive implications, since it predicts that all Gentile kingdoms will ultimately crumble.[23]

The portrayal of Daniel is significant not only as a model for the Diaspora but also as background for the understanding of the apocalyptic visionary in chaps. 7–12. Daniel is presented as a colleague of the Chaldean wise men whose functions include, conspicuously, the interpretation of dreams.[24] Throughout the ancient world dreams were regarded as an important means of communication between the gods and humanity.[25] They are regarded ambivalently in the Hebrew Bible.[26] Their validity is assumed in Genesis, but questioned by Jeremiah (cf. Jer 23:27-28) and Ben Sira (Sir 34:1-8). They are a positive means of revelation here. Daniel does not use the traditional Babylonian devices of divination; he has a superior means of access to revelation, by prayer to his God. Yet it is noteworthy that revelation is given in the veiled symbolism of dreams and so is a mystery

21. Compare Deutero-Isaiah, which carries on a recurring polemic against Chaldean wise men. See J. J. Collins, *The Apocalyptic Vision of the Book of Daniel* (HSM 16; Missoula, MT: Scholars Press, 1977) 44-45; P. von der Osten-Sacken, *Die Apokalyptik in ihrem Verhältnis zu Prophetie and Weisheit* (Munich: Kaiser, 1969) 18-27; J. G. Gammie, "On the Intention and Sources of Daniel I–VI," *VT* 31 (1981) 282-92.

22. W. Lee Humphreys nuances his conclusion differently ("A Life-Style for the Diaspora: A Study of the Tales of Esther and Daniel," *JBL* 92 [1973] 211-23).

23. The subversive aspect of this and the other tales in Daniel 1-6 is emphasized by Daniel Smith-Christopher, "The Book of Daniel," *The New Interpreter's Bible* (Nashville: Abingdon, 1996) 7.30-33; Portier-Young, *Apocalypse against Empire*, 223-27.

24. A. L. Oppenheim, *The Interpretation of Dreams in the Ancient Near East* (Philadelphia: American Philosophical Society, 1956); Frances Flannery, "Dreams and Visions in Early Jewish and Early Christian Apocalypses and Apocalypticism," in Collins, ed., *The Oxford Handbook of Apocalyptic Literature*, 105-8; Frances Flannery-Dailey, *Dreamers, Scribes and Priests: Jewish Dreams in the Hellenistic and Greco-Roman Eras* (JSJSup 90; Leiden: Brill, 2004) 17-56.

25. F. Bovon, "Ces chrétiens qui rêvent: L'autorité du rêve dans les premiers siècles du christianisme," in H. Cancik, H. Lichtenberger, and P. Schäfer, eds., *Geschichte — Tradition — Reflexion: Festschrift für Martin Hengel* (Tübingen: Mohr Siebeck, 1996) 3:631-53, gives extensive bibliography.

26. E. L. Ehrlich, *Der Traum im Alten Testament* (Berlin: de Gruyter, 1953); A. Resch, *Der Traum im Heilsplan Gottes* (Freiburg: Herder, 1964).

*(raz)*, which is in need of interpretation *(pesher)*. Both these terms, *raz* and *pesher*, are prominent in the Qumran scrolls. In the apocalypses, as already in Daniel 7, the mystery is heightened by the fact that the interpretation is given by an angel but the structure of mystery and interpretation persists. Related to this is a sense of determinism. The course of events is already decided. All one can do is understand and take one's position accordingly. In view of this emphasis on understanding, G. von Rad made his famous proposal that the apocalyptic understanding of revelation is more closely akin to wisdom than to prophecy. It is important, however, that the wisdom of Daniel is mantic wisdom, concerned with dreams and mysteries, not proverbial wisdom, which sets little store by such obscure phenomena.[27] There was a biblical precedent for mantic wisdom in the story of Joseph, but the context in Daniel is the Babylonian interest in dream interpretation, which confronted the Jews in the eastern Diaspora. It is significant that the Joseph story is also set in a place of exile, in Egypt.

The test of Daniel's wisdom, and that of his God, is the revelation of Nebuchadnezzar's dream. Because of its famous prophecy of the four kingdoms, the dream has been more intensively studied than any other part of the tales. Yet, as the chapter now stands, the emphasis is not on the content of the dream but on the fact that Daniel is able to reveal it. Nebuchadnezzar is apparently oblivious to the implied demise of the Babylonian kingdom and even does homage to Daniel. The king's apparent disregard for the future of his kingdom has been explained as an illustration of the staying power of the old motifs of the folktale, which requires that the hero, Daniel, be rewarded at the end.[28] Yet it is clear that the content of the interpretation carries political implications that strain the conventions of the folktale.

### The Four Kingdoms

The actual dream and the interpretation are of considerable interest for the background of the apocalyptic view of history. Two complexes of traditional ideas are involved. The statue is made of metals of declining value: the head of gold, breast and arms of silver, belly and thighs of bronze, legs

27. H.-P. Müller, "Mantische Weisheit und Apokalyptik," in *Congress Volume: Uppsala 1971* (VTSup 22; Leiden: Brill, 1972) 268-93.

28. So Niditch and Doran, "Success Story," 192.

of iron, feet partly iron and partly clay. This succession is strikingly reminiscent of Hesiod's *Works and Days*, 106–201, which speaks of the declining ages of men — first golden, then silver, third bronze, and finally iron.[29] It is probable that Hesiod was already adapting a traditional source, which may have originated in the East, possibly in Persia.[30] It is unlikely that Daniel depended directly on Hesiod. More probably they drew on a common tradition. The significance of Hesiod for our present purpose is that he makes quite explicit the logic of the sequence, which is one of gradual decline. Hesiod also implies that there is something better to follow the generation of iron.

The second complex of traditional ideas involves a schema of four kingdoms followed by a fifth of definitive character. This schema is attested in a fragment of the Roman chronicler Aemilius Sura, who wrote in the early second century BCE: "The Assyrians were the first of all races to hold power, then the Medes, after them the Persians and then the Macedonians. Then, when the two kings Philip and Antiochus, of Macedonian origin, had been completely conquered, soon after the overthrow of Carthage, the supreme command passed to the Roman people."[31] The schema is evidently of Eastern origin, since the Assyrians and Medes never ruled over the West. The inclusion of the Medes suggests an origin in Media or Persia. Before the Greek, Macedonian, kingdom was added to the list, the sequence of Assyria, Media, and Persia was already attested in Herodotus and Ctesias. Aemilius Sura adapted the sequence to support the definitive status of Roman rule.

The schema is also found in the fourth *Sibylline Oracle* (*Sib. Or.* 4:49-101). Here again the kingdoms are identified as Assyria, Media, Persia, and Macedonia. The schema of the four kingdoms is combined with a division of world history into ten generations. Six generations are attributed to the Assyrians, two to the Medes, and one each to the Persians and the Macedonians. The Macedonian kingdom is the last of the sequence and

---

29. In Hesiod the iron generation is the fifth. The fourth generation is not associated with a metal.

30. D. Flusser, "The Four Empires in the Fourth Sibyl and in the Book of Daniel," *Israel Oriental Studies* 2 (1972) 167. Flusser's article provides the fullest treatment of the four kingdoms.

31. J. W. Swain, "The Theory of the Four Monarchies: Opposition History under the Roman Empire," *Classical Philology* 35 (1940) 1-21. See also D. Mendels, "The Five Empires: A Note on a Hellenistic Topos," *AJP* 102 (1981) 330-37; Klaus Koch, *Daniel 1–4* (BKAT 22/1; Neukirchen–Vluyn: Neukirchener Verlag, 2005) 200-8; Newsom, *Daniel*, 80-81.

coincides with the last generation. In the present form of the fourth Sibyl there follows an oracle on Rome, but this is not integrated into the numerical sequence and is apparently added to update the oracle. Rome is not envisaged as a definitive or lasting empire. The oracle concludes with cosmic destruction and resurrection of the dead.

The present form of *Sib. Or.* 4 is a Jewish oracle from the late first century CE. The original four-kingdom oracle must have been written before the rise of Rome, possibly before the battle of Magnesia in 190 BCE, in which the Romans defeated Antiochus the Great of Syria, but at least before the definitive Roman conquest of the East at Actium.[32] We cannot be sure how the original oracle concluded, whether with the expectation of a fifth kingdom, as in Daniel 2, or with cosmic destruction. We cannot even be sure whether it was Jewish. In any case, the Sibyl has no pro-Roman sympathies, but it is clear that the fourth kingdom, that of the Greeks, would be destroyed. Accordingly, the four-kingdom oracle could represent the hopes of any Near Eastern people for an end to Hellenistic rule.[33]

An intriguing instance of a four-kingdom schema is provided by the Persian *Zand-ī Vohuman Yasn* or *Bahman Yasht,* which combines the four kingdoms with a sequence of metals in a manner similar to Daniel.[34] The opening chapter of the Zand describes a dream in which Ahura Mazdā showed Zarathustra a tree with four branches, one of gold, one of silver, one of steel, and one of mixed iron. These branches are explained as four periods: the first is the time of Zarathustra and king Hystaspes, the second and third are the reigns of later, Sassanian kings, and the fourth is the sovereignty of the "divs" with disheveled hair, when the tenth century of Zarathustra will be at an end. Despite the inclusion of later kings, many scholars have held that the original schema dates from Hellenistic times and that the "divs" were originally identified with the Greeks, the first conquerors of Persia.[35] The schema of four periods illustrated by metals

32. J. J. Collins, "The Place of the Fourth Sibyl in the Development of the Jewish Sibyllina," *JJS* 25 (1974) 365-80.

33. On Near Eastern resistance to Hellenism, see the colorful, but not always reliable, account of S. K. Eddy, *The King Is Dead: Studies in Near Eastern Resistance to Hellenism, 334-31 B.C.* (Lincoln: University of Nebraska Press, 1961).

34. See the discussion by Silverman, *Persepolis and Jerusalem*, 149-69.

35. Anders Hultgård, "Bahman Yasht: A Persian Apocalypse," in J. J. Collins and J. H. Charlesworth, eds., *Mysteries and Revelations: Apocalyptic Studies Since the Uppsala Colloquium* (JSPSup 9; Sheffield: JSOT Press, 1991) 114-34. Chapter 3 of the *Bahman Yasht* has a variant of this vision with seven branches instead of four. M. Boyce suggests that the

(gold, silver, steel, and mixed iron) is also found in *Dēnkard* 9.8. Both the *Dēnkard* and the *Bahman Yasht* draw on old Avestan tradition.[36]

It is evident, then, that the dream and interpretation in Daniel 2 draw on traditional motifs but use them in a distinctive way. In a Jewish context the final kingdom set up by the God of heaven must inevitably be read as a Jewish kingdom. Since this point receives no emphasis in the conclusion of the story, there is reason to question whether the dream was composed for its present context. Various suggestions have been made concerning the extent and meaning of the original dream. One suggestion is that the interpretation in Daniel 2, which specifies that the dream refers to four kingdoms, is secondary.[37] The original statue in the dream would have symbolized Nebuchadnezzar and his successors, Amel-Marduk, Neriglissar, and Nabonidus. The iron mixed with clay might refer to the coregency of Belshazzar with Nabonidus. The declining value of the metals would then symbolize fading power. The point of the dream would be the imminent collapse of the Babylonian empire, symbolized by the whole statue, and the dream would have an anti-Babylonian character. The stone that became a great mountain could then be understood as a messianic Jewish kingdom or conceivably, in a non-Jewish context, the Persian empire. The extant interpretation would have been added in the Hellenistic age to update the oracle.

Alternatively, the interpretation in terms of four kingdoms may have been originally attached to the dream.[38] The first kingdom is the Babylonian kingdom of Nebuchadnezzar. The combination of the sequence of metals with the four-kingdom schema implies a gradual decline in the political situation. The oracle was presumably written under the fourth kingdom, which it regarded as the nadir of history. The reign of Nebuchadnezzar is looked on as a golden age. We may compare the contrast between

---

sevenfold schema developed under Babylonian influence and that chap. 1 is more purely Iranian ("Middle Persian Literature," in *Handbuch der Orientalistik*, vol. 4/1 [Leiden: Brill, 1968] 49).

36. See further Collins, *Daniel*, 163-64.

37. E. Bickermann, *Four Strange Books of the Bible* (New York: Schocken, 1967) 62-63; P. R. Davies, "Daniel Chapter Two," *JTS* 27 (1976) 392-401. Cf. the interpretation of R. G. Kratz, *Translatio Imperii: Untersuchungen zu den aramäischen Danielerzählungen und ihrem theologiegeschichtlichen Umfeld* (WMANT 63; Neukirchen–Vluyn: Neukirchener Verlag, 1991) 55-62, who argues that the eschatological references in Daniel 2 are secondary, and that the vision originally referred to the overthrow of the Babylonian kingdom by the Medo-Persian empire.

38. So Collins, *Apocalyptic Vision*, 36-43.

the golden age of Hystaspes and the evil sovereignty of the "divs" in the *Bahman Yasht*. It seems unlikely that this prophecy was Jewish in origin. Nebuchadnezzar was not so fondly remembered in Jewish tradition.[39] In contrast, Babylonians of the Hellenistic age looked back nostalgically to the age of Nebuchadnezzar and developed his exploits to surpass those of Alexander the Great and Seleucus.[40] The identification of Nebuchadnezzar with the head of gold appears more appropriate for a Hellenistic Babylonian than for a Jew of any period.

Daniel 2 does not specify the identities of the other kingdoms. The fourth, which is "strong as iron" and breaks and shatters all, is surely the Hellenistic kingdom. Since the first is Babylon, the second and third must then be the Median and Persian empires. This sequence of kingdoms is in fact presupposed throughout Daniel (hence the introduction of Darius the Mede). It is not an historical sequence but is adapted from the traditional schema of Assyria, Media, Persia, and Greece by substituting Babylon for Assyria. The inclusion of Media can be explained only by reference to the schema. According to this interpretation the stone that shatters the entire statue must be viewed as part of the Jewish redaction. The original dream might have ended with the description of the statue, as the dream in *Bahman Yasht* chap. 1 simply describes the tree. The anticipated final kingdom would be a Babylonian restoration.

Our knowledge of Babylonian prophecy is still very fragmentary, although it has increased substantially in recent years.[41] A. K. Grayson identifies five main compositions in the genre, ranging in date from the twelfth century BCE to the Hellenistic era.[42] These are all predictions after the event. They are concerned with the succession of reigns. No names are mentioned, but the references can often be identified, much in the manner of what we will find below in Daniel 11. The latest of these, the *Dynastic*

---

39. Dan 2:38, which is certainly Jewish, echoes Jer 27:6, where God declares that he has given Nebuchadnezzar the beasts of the field to serve him, but this is far from presenting his reign as a golden age. Jewish perceptions of Nebuchadnezzar in the Hellenistic period are reflected in the book of Judith.

40. Collins, *Apocalyptic Vision,* 41; Eddy, *The King Is Dead,* 125-27.

41. Maria de Jong Ellis, "Observations on Mesopotamian Oracles and Prophetic Texts: Literary and Historiographic Considerations," *JCS* 41 (1989) 127-86; Martti Nissinen, "Neither Prophecies nor Apocalypses: The Akkadian Literary Predictive Texts," in Grabbe and Haak, eds., *Knowing the End from the Beginning,* 134-48; Neujahr, *Predicting the Past,* 13-118.

42. A. K. Grayson, *Babylonian Historical-Literary Texts* (Toronto: University of Toronto Press, 1975) 14-15; Neujahr, *Predicting the Past,* 13-73.

*Prophecy,* has been adduced in the discussion of Daniel 2, since it apparently describes a sequence of four kingdoms.[43] According to Grayson, "Each of the first three columns contains a description of a change or fall of a dynasty (column i: fall of Assyria, rise of Babylonia; column ii: fall of Babylonia, rise of Persia; column iii: fall of Persia, rise of Macedonia."[44] Column iv is badly preserved. Grayson suggests that it may refer to the capture of Babylon by Seleucus I. These reigns are alternatively good and bad: those at the ends of columns i and iii are good, those in ii and iv (presumably) bad. The text is fragmentary and many details are uncertain.

The *Dynastic Prophecy* is of some, though limited, relevance to Daniel 2. It provides an instance of Babylonian political prophecy from the Hellenistic age. If Grayson is correct in his interpretation, the prophecy ends with a prediction of the downfall of the Seleucids.[45] It is, then, a rare illustration of the use of prophecy for political propaganda in Hellenistic Babylonia.[46] It is doubtful, however, whether the prophecy can be said to attest a four-kingdom schema. Given the fragmentary character of the text, we cannot be sure that the number four is regarded as definitive. It cannot be regarded as a prototype for Daniel, since it omits Media.[47]

Unfortunately the conclusion of the *Dynastic Prophecy* is fragmentary, and so its significance remains ambiguous. We should note, however, that the idea of an everlasting kingdom is attested in Babylonian prophecy. The Uruk prophecy, which apparently refers to the time of Nebuchadnezzar II, says, "After him, his son will arise as king in Uruk and rule the entire

43. G. F. Hasel, "The Four World Empires of Daniel 2 Against Its Near Eastern Environment," *JSOT* 12 (1979) 17-30.

44. Grayson, *Babylonian Historical-Literary Texts,* 17. For the problems and subsequent discussion, see Neujahr, *Predicting the Past,* 63-64.

45. See, however, Susan Sherwin-White, "Seleucid Babylonia: A Case Study for the Installation and Development of Greek Rule," in A. Kuhrt and S. Sherwin-White, eds., *Hellenism in the East: The Interaction of Greek and non-Greek Civilizations from Syria to Central Asia after Alexander* (Berkeley: University of California, 1987) 11, 14, who thinks the text ends with a negative assessment of Antigonus, and is pro-Seleucid.

46. Grayson cites *Sib. Or.* 3:381-87 as another possible Babylonian oracle, but this is doubtful (*Babylonian Historical-Literary Texts,* 18).

47. Hasel argues that there was no fixed schema and that Daniel 2 is in some respects closer to the *Dynastic Prophecy* than to the other four-kingdom passages ("Four World Empires"). However, while the schema Assyria–Media–Persia was not universal, it was widespread; and it can explain the inclusion of Media in Daniel, whereas the Babylonian prophecy cannot. Grayson sees the closest parallels in Daniel not in Daniel 2 but in 8:23-25 and 11:3-45 (*Babylonian Historical-Literary Texts,* 21). So also W. G. Lambert, *The Background of Jewish Apocalyptic* (London: Athlone, 1978).

world. He will exercise authority and kingship in Uruk and his dynasty will last forever. The kings of Uruk will exercise authority like the gods."[48] This Babylonian hope is ironically subverted in the Jewish redaction of the oracle in Daniel 2. The kingdom which will be set up by the God of heaven and which will never pass to another people is surely Jewish, but its identity is not made explicit for Nebuchadnezzar.

The interpretation in Daniel 2 clearly requires a date in the Seleucid period since it refers to the unsuccessful intermarriage of the Ptolemaic and Seleucid houses (2:43). It is, of course, difficult to be sure at what point particular verses were added.[49] In any case, the use of the four-kingdom schema points to a date after the conquest of Alexander.

Any reconstruction of the original oracle that has been used in Daniel 2 must be tentative and hypothetical. It is, nevertheless, apparent that the dream in Daniel 2 is drawn from the world of political prophecy, and the interpretation in terms of four kingdoms reflects the Near Eastern resistance to Hellenism in the era after Alexander. This interest in political prophecy is obviously an important strand in the traditions that nourished the apocalyptic literature.

Taken in itself, Nebuchadnezzar's dream and its interpretation imply a theology of history. The context in Daniel 2, however, highlights not the development of history or the prediction of a messianic kingdom but the superior wisdom of Daniel's God. The image of the stone that crushes the statue ignores the element of chronological sequence. The destruction of the statue here must be viewed in the light of the references to statues and metals elsewhere in the tales. In Daniel 3 Nebuchadnezzar sets up an image of gold. The Jewish youths are prepared to die rather than worship it. In Daniel 5 Belshazzar comes to grief because "you have praised the gods of silver and gold, of bronze, iron, wood and stone" (5:23). In this light, the destruction of the statue in Daniel 2 is primarily an affirmation of the transcendent power of God to destroy all idols and the kingdoms that worship them. This power goes hand in hand with the divine ability to

---

48. S. A. Kaufman, "Prediction, Prophecy, and Apocalypse in the Light of New Akkadian Texts," in A. Shinan, ed., *Proceedings of the Sixth World Congress of Jewish Studies, 1973* (Jerusalem: World Union of Jewish Studies, 1977) 224; Neujahr, *Predicting the Past*, 53. The "prophecy" is *ex eventu* down to this point. The "son" in question is apparently Nebuchadnezzar's son Amel-Marduk. His dynasty was in fact short-lived. See further P. Höffken, "Heilszeitherrscherwartung im babylonischen Raum," *Die Welt des Orients* 9 (1977) 57-71.

49. Kratz, *Translatio Imperii*, 61, argues that verses 40-44 are an addition by the author of Daniel 7.

reveal all mysteries. As in the Book of the Watchers, the themes of wisdom and power are closely related.

Despite the destructive conclusion of the dream, Daniel 2 does not reject pagan rule. Rather, this too is viewed as part of God's providential design.[50] The message of the chapter is summed up succinctly in 2:20-23. God has wisdom and might. He removes kings and sets up kings, and he gives wisdom to the wise. The orderly sequence of four kingdoms suggests that this is, after all, a managed universe. The fall of the pagan empires will come at its appointed time.[51] For the present, Daniel's fidelity to his own God is in no way incompatible with his service to the king. Rather, his God-given wisdom makes him preeminent among the sages of Babylon. Throughout the tales we find a strikingly optimistic attitude. Good Gentile kings will come to acknowledge the God of the Jews. The arrogant will be chastened. Despite the political supremacy of the Gentiles, God's in his heaven and all's well with the world.

## The Apocalyptic Visions: Daniel 7

When we turn to the second half of the book of Daniel, we find ourselves in a very different atmosphere. To be sure, there is continuity. These chapters, too, are concerned with God's control of the destinies of all peoples. His sovereignty is not publicly evident; it is seen through special revelations by the wise and through exceptional acts of deliverance.[52] These are themes that run through the whole book. Even these themes, however, take on a new coloring in the face of the persecution by Antiochus Epiphanes in 167 BCE.[53] The Gentile kingdoms were no longer seen as potential

50. For a quite different reading of the court tales as resistance, see D. Smith-Christopher, "The Book of Daniel," in *The New Interpreter's Bible* (Nashville: Abingdon, 1996) 19-96; Portier-Young, *Apocalypse Against Empire*, 223-27.

51. Cf. John J. Collins, "Nebuchadnezzar and the Kingdom of God: Deferred Eschatology in the Jewish Diaspora," in C. Elsas and H. G. Kippenberg, eds., *Loyalitätskonflikte in der Religionsgeschichte* (Würzburg: Königshausen und Neumann, 1990) 252-57 (= *Seers, Sibyls, and Sages*, 131-38).

52. Jin Hee Han, *Daniel's Spiel: Apocalyptic Literacy in the Book of Daniel* (Lanham, MD: University Press of America, 2008) 29, speaks of "an alternative experience of reality." On the theme of divine sovereignty in the Book of Daniel see Amy C. Merrill Willis, *Dissonance and the Drama of Divine Sovereignty in the Book of Daniel* (London: T & T Clark, 2010).

53. For contrasting interpretations of the conflict see, on the one hand, V. Tcherikover (*Hellenistic Civilization and the Jews* [New York: Atheneum, 1970] 191-203) and M. Hengel

servants of God. Instead they were rebellious monsters that could only be destroyed. The aspiration of the faithful Jews was no longer to rise to high position in the Gentile court but to shine like the host of heaven in the afterlife.

## The Beasts from the Sea

Daniel 7, like Daniel 2, presents a dream-vision that concerns a schema of four kingdoms, but the context and the specific imagery are quite different. The contest of wisdom between Chaldean and Jew is no longer a factor in chap. 7, nor is there any question of winning the approval of a Gentile king. Now Daniel himself is the dreamer and he has need of an interpreter, in the person of an angel. The dream-vision has become an apocalypse, where the mysterious revelation must be explained by a supernatural being. Daniel's vision has older formal precedents, most notably in the early chapters of Zechariah, where the interpreting angel is introduced.[54] We might also compare the *Bahman Yasht* chap. 1, where Zarathustra's dream vision about four kingdoms is explained by Ahura Mazdā.[55] The change from the human

---

(*Judaism and Hellenism* [2 vols.; Philadelphia: Fortress, 1974] 1:267-314), who argue that the fighting first broke out among the Jews, and on the other hand F. Millar ("The Background to the Maccabean Revolution: Reflections on Martin Hengel's 'Judaism and Hellenism,' " *JJS* 29 [1978] 1-21) and J. A. Goldstein (*1 Maccabees* [AB 41; Garden City, NY: Doubleday, 1976] 104-60), who argue that Antiochus initiated it. For a clear presentation of the evidence, see D. J. Harrington, *The Maccabean Revolt: Anatomy of a Biblical Revolution* (Wilmington: Glazier, 1988). See John J. Collins, "Cult and Culture: The Limits of Hellenization in Judea," in idem, *Jewish Cult and Hellenistic Culture* ( JSJSup 100; Leiden: Brill, 2005) 21-43; Robert Doran, "The Persecution of Judeans by Antiochus IV: The Significance of Ancestral Laws," in Daniel C. Harlow et al., eds., *The "Other" in Second Temple Judaism: Essays in Honor of John J. Collins* (Grand Rapids: Eerdmans, 2011) 423-33; Portier-Young, *Apocalypse Against Empire*, 78-114, 176-216. Sylvie Honigman, *Tales of High Priests and Taxes: The Books of the Maccabees and the Judean Rebellion against Antiochus IV* (Oakland, CA: University of California Press, 2014) 386, endorses Tcherikover's view that the Jewish revolt came first.

54. On the development of the apocalyptic vision, see K. Koch, "Vom prophetischen zum apokalyptischen Visionsbericht," in D. Hellholm, ed., *Apocalypticism in the Mediterranean World and the Near East: Proceedings of the International Colloquium on Apocalypticism, Uppsala, August 12-17, 1979* (Tübingen: Mohr Siebeck, 1983) 413-46; S. Niditch, *The Symbolic Vision in Biblical Tradition* (HSM 30; Chico: Scholars Press, 1983).

55. Persian influence is chronologically possible but remains uncertain in both Zechariah and Daniel. H. S. Kvanvig (*Roots of Apocalyptic: The Mesopotamian Background of the Enoch Figure and of the Son of Man* [WMANT 61; Neukirchen–Vluyn: Neukirchener

interpreter of Daniel 2 to the angel of chap. 7 expresses a deeper sense of mysteriousness in the later vision.

Like Nebuchadnezzar's dream in chap. 2, Daniel 7 draws freely on traditional motifs. In this case the schema of the four kingdoms is combined with the imagery of beasts coming up out of the sea. The Hebrew Bible contains several scattered allusions to sea monsters, which are defeated or slain by Yahweh, although there is no explicit account of such a battle. Sometimes this mythic conflict is linked with creation, as in Job 26:7, 12-13:

> He stretches out the north over the void
> and hangs the earth upon nothing . . .
> By his power he stilled the sea,
> by his understanding he smote Rahab.
> By his wind the heavens were made fair,
> his hand pierced the fleeing serpent.

At other times it is linked with the Exodus, as in Isa 51:9-10:

> Was it not thou that didst cut Rahab in pieces,
> that didst pierce the dragon?
> Was it not thou that didst dry up the sea,
> the waters of the great deep;
> that didst make the depths of the sea a way
> for the redeemed to pass over?

Yet again, in late prophecy the struggle could be projected into the future: "In that day the Lord with his hard and great and strong sword will punish Leviathan, the fleeing serpent, Leviathan, the twisting serpent and he will slay the dragon that is in the sea" (Isa 27:1). From all this it is clear that the biblical writers were familiar with mythological traditions, which are much more extensive than what we now find in the Bible and which are highly relevant for Daniel 7.[56] Much light has been thrown on these traditions by the discovery of the Ugaritic myths.

---

Verlag, 1988] 536-602) claims to have identified an Akkadian background for Daniel 7, in the *Vision of the Netherworld,* but the parallels are very tenuous. See the critique in Collins, *Daniel,* 283-86.

56. See further J. J. Collins, "Stirring Up the Great Sea: The Religio-Historical Background of Daniel 7," in van der Woude, ed., *The Book of Daniel,* 121-36 (= *Seers, Sibyls, and Sages,* 139-56).

In the Ugaritic myths, the Sea, Yamm, appears as a god who challenges the sovereignty of Baal.[57] They fight, and Baal destroys him. Elsewhere we read that Baal "smote Lotan, the ancient dragon, destroyed the crooked serpent, Shilyat with the seven heads." In a variant of the myth we read that Anat smote "the beloved of El, Sea," destroyed El's river Rabbim, muzzled the dragon and smote the crooked serpent, Shilyat of the seven heads. In this conflict between Baal and the Sea we evidently have a prototype of Yahweh's battle with the sea monsters in biblical poetry.

Against this background we can appreciate the evocative power of Daniel's vision. The reference to the winds of heaven stirring up the great sea may be said to echo the primordial scene in Gen 1:2,[58] but here the winds serve to arouse chaos rather than subdue it. Daniel sees a world engulfed by disorder. The beasts of the sea, the traditional "dragons on the waters" (Ps 74:13) and the "dragon that is in the sea" (Isa 27:1), are let loose upon the world. Specifically, chaos takes the form of Gentile rule, expressed by the traditional schema of four kingdoms. Subsequently we are told that "these four great beasts are four kings that will arise out of the earth" and again that the fourth beast represents a "kingdom." It should be apparent that this interpretation does not exhaust the significance of the vision. It gives the reference of the four beasts. It does not give their expressive value.[59] The vision of terrible beasts rising out of the sea does not merely give factual information that four kings or kingdoms will arise. It paints a picture of these kingdoms as monstrous eruptions of chaos, in order to convey a sense of terror far beyond anything suggested by the flat statement of the interpretation. The impact is more profound when we recognize the mythological overtones of the imagery. The kings are not merely human but are manifestations of the primordial force of chaos. As St. Paul might say, "our struggle is not against flesh and blood but against principalities and powers."

---

57. F. M. Cross, *Canaanite Myth and Hebrew Epic* (Cambridge, MA: Harvard University Press, 1973) 112-20; J. Day, *God's Conflict with the Dragon and the Sea: Echoes of a Canaanite Myth in the Old Testament* (Cambridge: Cambridge University Press, 1985) 151-78. For the texts, see M. D. Coogan and M. S. Smith, *Stories from Ancient Canaan* (Louisville: Westminster John Knox, 2012).

58. So Hartman and DiLella, *The Book of Daniel*, 211.

59. A. J. Ferch objects that "the sea and beasts are interpreted as the earth and four kings or kingdoms, not as chaos symbols" ("Daniel 7 and Ugarit: A Reconsideration," *JBL* 99 [1980] 75-86). This is to confuse different levels of meaning, as if one were to say that an object is not red but a box. See my critique of Ferch in "Apocalyptic Genre and Mythic Allusions in Daniel," *JSOT* 21 (1981) 91-94.

The terror of the beasts is aroused only to be allayed. In 7:9 the scene changes to one of divine majesty. Thrones are placed and the Ancient of Days takes his seat. The divine throne, surrounded by myriad angels and a stream of fire, recalls Enoch's vision in *1 Enoch* 14:22, and the throne vision in 4Q530, the Book of Giants, and suggests that the apocalyptic visionaries drew on common traditions. A judgment follows in accordance with the heavenly books (also a common motif in Enoch). The fourth beast is slain and burned in the fire, while the others lose their power. Then follows the famous apparition of "one like a son of man" coming with the clouds of heaven, and dominion, glory, and kingdom are conferred on him.[60]

## One Like a Son of Man

The meaning or identity of the "one like a son of man" is perhaps the most celebrated question in all the apocalyptic literature. We must distinguish two levels of the problem: the traditional associations of the imagery and its reference in its present context.

Many scholars have noted that in traditional biblical usage the rider of the clouds is Yahweh.[61] Indeed, Michael Segal has argued that the one like a son of man must be identified with Yahweh even in Daniel 7.[62] Yet here the one who comes with clouds is clearly subordinate to the Ancient of Days.[63] This imagery is not readily explicable from the Hebrew Bible.[64]

60. On the appearance of the "one like a son of man" as a theophany, see Beyerle, *Die Gottesvorstellungen*, 123-37.

61. J. A. Emerton, "The Origin of the Son of Man Imagery," *JTS* 9 (1958) 225-42: "The act of coming with clouds suggests a theophany of Yahweh himself. If Dan vii 13 does not refer to a divine being, then it is the only exception out of about seventy passages in the OT" (231-32). Newsom, *Daniel*, 219, regards this imagery as another case of the tendency to describe angels in language otherwise used for God (cf. Dan 10:5-6) but provides no parallel for the specific imagery, or for the kingdom conferred on this figure.

62. Michael Segal, "Reconsidering the Theological Background of Daniel 7," in idem, *Dreams, Riddles, and Visions: Textual, Intertextual, and Exegetical Studies of the Book of Daniel* (Berlin: de Gruyter, 2016); idem, "Who Is the 'Son of God' in 4Q246? An Overlooked Example of Early Biblical Interpretation," *DSD* 21 (2014) 289-312.

63. Segal explains this not as a radical theological perspective, but as due to literary dependence on sources. This would imply that the author either did not notice the hierarchical implications of the vision or that he expected his readers to recognize a literary allusion and distinguish between the view of the source and the view intended in the text. Either scenario is highly problematic.

64. Segal explains it in part from Deuteronomy 32 and Psalm 82, both of which seem

However, the Hebrew depiction of Yahweh as rider of the clouds is it-self adapted from the older Canaanite storm imagery of the theophanies of Baal.[65] Baal is repeatedly called "rider of the clouds" in the Ugaritic texts. He is, of course, a divine figure, but in the Canaanite pantheon he is subordinate to El, the father of gods and human beings. El is called *abu shanima* in a Ugaritic text, a phrase that is most plausibly interpreted as "father of years" and suggests that El is indeed the prototype for the Ancient of Days.[66]

Since the visions of the Ancient of Days and one like a son of man stand out from their present context, some have regarded them as frag-ments of ancient sources.[67] This is possible, but they cannot be divorced from the earlier vision of beasts rising from the sea. The exaltation of the Baal-like rider of the clouds over the sea monsters must be related to Baal's triumph over Yamm in the Canaanite myths. The parallel lies in the pattern, not just in the individual motifs.[68] Of course, Daniel does not give an exact reproduction of the Ugaritic myth.[69] To begin with, the Ug-aritic myths are more than a thousand years older than Daniel, and the traditions must inevitably have undergone some change.[70] Besides, the

---

to distinguish between El and Yahweh, but this is at most a partial explanation. Paul Mosca, "Ugarit and Daniel 7: A Missing Link," *Biblica* 67 (1986) 496-517, argues that Psalm 89 pro-vides a link between Canaanite mythology and Daniel 7, but it does not refer to anyone other than Daniel riding on the clouds.

65. For the following see Cross, *Canaanite Myth and Hebrew Epic,* 112-20 (on Baal); 13-43 (on El). For a review of possible mythological backgrounds and defense of the Canaanite hypothesis, see C. Colpe, "Ho huios tou anthrōpou," *TDNT,* 8:408-20.

66. Cross, *Canaanite Myth and Hebrew Epic,* 16; M. Pope, *El in the Ugaritic Texts* (VTSup 2; Leiden: Brill, 1955) 32.

67. For references and critique, see Collins, *Daniel,* 277-80.

68. Contra Newsom, *Daniel,* 219; eadem, "The Reuse of Ugaritic Mythology in Daniel 7: an Optical Illusion?" in C. Frechette, C. Matthews, and T. Stegeman, ed., *Opportunity for No Little Instruction: Studies in Honor of Richard J. Clifford, S.J. and Daniel J. Harrington, S.J.* (New York: Paulist, 2014) 85-100. See my article, "Stirring Up the Great Sea: The Religio-Historical Background of Daniel 7," in A. S. van der Woude, ed., *The Book of Daniel in the Light of New Findings* (BETL 106; Leuven: Leuven University Press, 1993) 121-36 (= *Seers, Sibyls, and Sages,* 139-56).

69. The arguments of Ferch against the relevance of the Ugaritic parallels depend heavily on a demand for complete reproduction (despite a disclaimer, "Daniel 7 and Ugarit," 86). So he repeatedly emphasizes that Daniel has no parallel to Mot, although no scholar has claimed otherwise.

70. Daniel Boyarin, *The Jewish Gospels: The Story of the Jewish Christ* (New York: The New Press, 2012) 45, has argued that what we find in Daniel 7 is an "unreconstructed relic of

tradition provides the building blocks for Daniel's vision, and he adapts it for his own purpose. So the judicial scene replaces the violent conflict of the myth. Yet the juxtaposition of the sea and its monsters with the rider of the clouds shows that we have here more than a borrowing of isolated motifs. Daniel is adapting the structure, or pattern of relationships, of the Canaanite myth.

The use of traditional imagery here should not be confused with the reference of the vision. Daniel is not talking about Baal or Yamm but is characterizing the situation of the Jews under Antiochus Epiphanes. The purpose of the traditional imagery is to bring out the meaning of that situation by analogy. There is some fundamental similarity between the arrogance of the Gentile kings, especially the "little horn" Antiochus, and the raging of Yamm (Sea). The use of this imagery obscures the historical particularity of the present crisis and assimilates it to a cosmic pattern. For this reason Daniel's vision could be reinterpreted and reapplied in subsequent situations (as we find in 4 Ezra 12 and in the New Testament). No names are named. There would be other arrogant beasts after the demise of Antiochus. The effect of the imagery is twofold. On the one hand, it articulates the terror and revulsion evoked by Gentile rule in the light of the persecution.[71] On the other hand, the use of a traditional pattern carries the assurance that the outcome is inevitable. The monsters of chaos will be overcome not, of course, by Baal but by the one like a son of man, who takes his place.

As we have noted, there is no doubt that Daniel 7 is describing the persecution of the Jews under Antiochus Epiphanes. The exaltation of the one like a son of man represents the triumph of the Jews. What is at issue in the scholarly debate over the one like a son of man is the manner in which that triumph is conceived and symbolized. The corporate interpretation holds that the one like a son of man is merely or purely a symbol, whose meaning is exhausted by the identification of its referent.[72] Other views

---

Israel's religious past (if not her present as well)." It calls up "a very ancient strand in Israel's religion, one in which, it would seem, the El-like sky god of justice and the younger rider of the clouds, storm god of war, have not really been merged as they are for most of the Bible."

71. On Seleucid state terror see Portier-Young, *Apocalypse Against Empire*, 140-75.

72. Defenders of this position include Hartman and DiLella, *The Book of Daniel*, 85-102; P. M. Casey, *Son of Man: The Interpretation and Influence of Daniel 7* (London: SPCK, 1979) 7-50; N. W. Porteous, *Daniel* (2d ed.; London: SCM Press, 1979) 192; O. Keel, "Die Tiere und der Mensch in Daniel 7," in O. Keel and U. Staub, *Hellenismus und Judentum: Vier Studien zu Daniel 7 und zur Religionsnot unter Antiochus IV*. (OBO 178; Freiburg: Universi-

see a more complex relation between this figure and the Jewish people. The traditional view, that the one like a son of man is the messiah, is still occasionally defended.[73] This view draws support from the fact that the beasts in the vision are said to be kings and that there is a fluid relationship between the king and the kingdom that he represents. However, it suffers from the fact that there is no clear reference to the messiah elsewhere in Daniel. The main alternative to the corporate interpretation is the view that this figure is the angelic leader of the heavenly host.[74]

Several considerations support the view that the one like a son of man is an angelic being. There is an obvious contrast between this human-like figure and the beasts. The beasts are not mere steno-symbols for corporate entities. They represent kings as well as kingdoms, but in addition they symbolize the chaotic power that these kingdoms embodied. The exalted appearance of the figure who comes with clouds suggests that the righteous Israelites too have supernatural support. The supernatural backdrop of the struggle is made fully explicit in Daniel 10–12. There we are told that behind the human conflicts of the Hellenistic age there is an ongoing battle in heaven between Michael, the patron angel of Israel (assisted by Gabriel), and the angelic "princes" of Persia and Greece. At the end of the conflict Michael will "arise" in victory. In view of the parallelism between Daniel 7 and 10–12 it is apparent that the conflict is not envisaged in purely human terms. It is unlikely that the one like a son of man is merely a corporate symbol for the Jews. Rather we should expect him to represent their angelic or supernatural counterpart. In fact, similar expressions are used elsewhere in Daniel to refer to angels. Gabriel is "like the appearance of a man" (8:15; 10:18), has the voice of a man (8:16), is "like the resemblance of the sons of man" (10:16). Angels are simply "men" at 9:21; 10:5; 12:6, 7. (Compare the symbolism of the Animal Apocalypse, where men represent angels or humans transformed to an angelic state.) Furthermore, the

---

tätsverlag, 2000) 22. These scholars also deny the mythological allusions in Daniel 7. For the term "steno-symbol" applied to Daniel, see N. Perrin, "Eschatology and Hermeneutics: Reflections on Method in the Interpretation of the New Testament," *JBL* 93 (1974) 11.

73. For example, G. R. Beasley-Murray, "The Interpretation of Daniel 7," *CBQ* 45 (1983) 44-58.

74. Collins, *Daniel,* 304-10 (with older bibliography). Other supporters of the angelic interpretation include Lacocque, *The Book of Daniel,* 133; R. Hammer, *The Book of Daniel* (Cambridge: Cambridge University Press, 1976) 79; C. Rowland, *The Open Heaven: A Study of Apocalyptic in Judaism and Early Christianity* (New York: Crossroad, 1982) 178-82; Day, *God's Conflict,* 172; Newsom, *Daniel,* 235-6.

adaptation and reinterpretation of the "Son of Man" figure through the New Testament period is invariably in the individual sense.[75] In *1 Enoch* 46:1 the "Son of Man" has the appearance of a man, and his face is full of graciousness like one of the holy angels. In the New Testament the Son of Man is repeatedly associated with the angels (Matt 13:41; 16:27; 24:31; 25:31; Mark 8:38; 13:27; Luke 9:26). In Rev 14:14 "one like a son of man" appears, seated on a cloud, who is evidently an angel and is not identified with Christ. This development of the tradition is most readily intelligible if the expression was originally understood to refer to an angel.

## The Holy Ones of the Most High

In 7:18 the interpreting angel informs Daniel that "the holy ones of the Most High shall receive the kingdom and possess the kingdom for ever, for ever and ever." Since the kingdom was given to the "one like a son of man" in the vision, this figure and the holy ones are obviously correlative — although they are not necessarily identical without remainder. The expression "holy ones," used substantively, in the Hebrew Bible refers to angels or supernatural beings in the great majority of cases.[76] The evidence is not entirely conclusive, since the term "his holy ones" in Ps 34:10 presumably refers to the Israelites. Again, in the Qumran scrolls "holy ones" usually refers to angels. In 1QM 10:10 "the people of the holy ones" is clearly Israel, but this phrase may be equivalent to "the people of the angels" (analogous to "the people of God"). A number of occurrences in the Qumran scrolls are ambiguous, including the closest parallel to Daniel's "holy ones of the Most High" in CD 20:8: "Let no man agree with him in property or work for all the holy ones of the Most High have cursed him." It may be argued, however, that the extension of the term "holy ones" to human beings at Qumran is mediated by the belief that the community enjoyed fellowship with the angels.

---

75. Casey (*Son of Man,* 51-70) argues that the corporate interpretation was the original one in the Syriac tradition, but his earliest witness is Porphyry. Evidence for the corporate interpretation in rabbinic literature is rare and late.

76. The evidence has been laid out several times: C. W. Brekelmans, "The Saints of the Most High and Their Kingdom," *OTS* 14 (1965) 305-29; L. Dequeker, "The 'Saints of the Most High' in Qumran and Daniel," *OTS* 18 (1973) 133-62; G. F. Hasel, "The Identity of the 'Saints of the Most High' in Daniel 7," *Bib* 56 (1975) 173-92. The judgments of these scholars on the interpretation of the evidence differ and must be evaluated with caution. See Collins, *Daniel,* 313-17; Newsom, *Daniel,* 237.

Although the philological evidence is not conclusive, it must be held to create a balance of probability. The probability is strengthened by the fact that the unambiguous occurrences in the book of Daniel itself (4:13, 17, 23; 8:13)[77] refer to angels, and the "holy ones" in *1 Enoch* 14:22-23, a passage closely related to Daniel 7, are also clearly angelic.

Objections to taking the holy ones as angels have been raised mainly on the basis of Dan 7:21 ("the horn made war on the holy ones and prevailed over them") and 7:25 ("He shall speak words against the Most High, and shall wear out the holy ones of the Most High").[78] It is not, of course, disputed that the experiential datum that gives rise to these assertions is the persecution of the Jews by Antiochus. The issue, again, is how that conflict is conceptualized and symbolized. We have seen that the battle between angelic forces is explicit in Daniel 10–12. In 11:36 we read that Antiochus will exalt and magnify himself above every god and "speak astonishing things against the God of gods." In a parallel passage in 8:10, the little horn "grew great, even to the host of heaven; and some of the host of the stars it cast down to the ground and trampled upon them." Here the horn quite explicitly fights with the heavenly host.[79] The stars, which are cast to the ground, were commonly identified with angels or gods both in Israel and elsewhere in the ancient Near East.[80] In the light of this passage the objection to the angelic interpretation in 7:21 and 25 cannot be sustained.

We should emphasize that the interpretation of the holy ones as the angelic host does not in any case exclude reference to the persecuted Jews. Scholars who reject this interpretation have failed to grasp the nature of the homology between the heavenly and earthly worlds in ancient Near Eastern thought.[81] In modern thinking we assume the priority of human

---

77. The expression "holy people" (*'am qōdeš* 12:7) cannot be regarded as an equivalent linguistic expression to "holy ones" (contra Casey, *Son of Man*, 44-45).

78. Some proponents of the angelic interpretation, such as M. Noth ("The Holy Ones of the Most High," in idem, *The Laws in the Pentateuch and Other Essays* [Philadelphia: Fortress, 1967] 215-28) and Dequeker ("The 'Saints of the Most High' "), resort to interpolation theories to explain these verses. This procedure is neither justified nor necessary.

79. The parallel passage in the interpretation of the dream is textually corrupt, but it may also be read as an assault on the angelic host; see Collins, *Daniel*, 325-26.

80. P. D. Miller, *The Divine Warrior in Early Israel* (HSM 5; Cambridge, MA: Harvard University Press, 1973) 21-23, 66-69.

81. So DiLella objects that "Daniel 7 would then have virtually no meaning or relevance for the addressees of the book" (Hartman and DiLella, *The Book of Daniel*, 91; compare Casey, *Son of Man*, 44). If so, the explicit triumph of Michael in Daniel 12 would be equally meaningless.

experience and see the mythological world of the gods as a projection.[82] In the ancient world, in contrast, the priority of the world of the gods is assumed, and earthly affairs are regarded as reflections of the greater reality. This homology is quite explicit in Daniel 10, where the struggle between Jews and Greeks is viewed as a battle between their angelic patrons. The link between the holy ones and the Jewish people is clarified in Dan 7:27, which says that "the kingdom and the dominion and the greatness of the kingdoms under the whole heaven shall be given to the people of the holy ones of the Most High." The genitival relationship of the people to the holy ones is analogous to that of the holy ones to the Most High.[83] Dan 7:27 complements 7:18, where the holy ones receive the kingdom. In view of the homology between the people and the holy ones, a kingdom that is given to one is given to both.

The interpretation of the holy ones as angels fits naturally with the identification of the one like a son of man as Michael, leader of the heavenly host. The relation between this figure and the holy ones, then, is not identity, but representation. The three formulations of Dan 7:14, 18, and 27, in which the one like a son of man, the holy ones of the Most High, and the people of the holy ones are said in turn to receive the kingdom, represent three levels of a multidimensional reality. A closely similar conception is found in the Qumran *War Scroll*, where God "will raise up the kingdom of Michael in the midst of the gods, and the realm of Israel in the midst of all flesh" (1QM 17:6-8).[84]

Daniel 7 does not mention Michael by name, as indeed it does not mention any proper names. The suppression of proper names lends an air of mystery to the whole vision. The specific identification of the one like a son of man is not of ultimate importance. What matters is that there is a heavenly savior figure who represents the righteous community on the supernatural level. This figure is specified in various ways in different texts. Michael is named explicitly in Daniel 10–12 and 1QM. Melchizedek in 11QMelch, "that son of man" in the Similitudes of Enoch, the man from the sea in 4 Ezra 13, and the Son of Man in the New Testament all fill this function with varying nuances. Apocalyptic thought allows for consider-

---

82. Lacocque, *The Book of Daniel*, 131: "It is a question of men before it is a question of angels."

83. Contra Casey, who takes it as "the people consisting of the holy ones" (*Son of Man*, 41). Note, however, the interpretation of Goldingay, *Daniel*, 143, 146, who takes the phrase as "the holy ones on high."

84. So also U. B. Müller, *Messias und Menschensohn in jüdischen Apokalypsen und in der Offenbarung des Johannes* (Gütersloh: Mohn, 1972) 28; Rowland, *The Open Heaven*, 181.

able fluidity in its mythological conceptions. Although there is now general agreement that Son of Man was not a title in pre-Christian Judaism, the mysterious figure in Daniel represents a type that is widespread in the apocalyptic literature.[85]

The "kingdom" that is conferred in Daniel 7 is also characterized by indeterminacy. There is no attempt to specify a manner of administration. We are not told the extent to which it will be continuous with previous history or how great a transformation it will entail. In the light of our interpretation of the "holy ones," we should expect it to have both a heavenly and an earthly dimension. Daniel is not concerned with giving us information about this future kingdom. He is, however, quite definite that the kingdoms of the Gentiles will come to an end. As in Daniel 2 this judgment is pronounced on all at once, without regard for chronological sequence. Daniel is less concerned with the sequential development of history than with the confrontation with Gentile power in the critical moment of the present.

## The Parallel Visions

Daniel 7 does not stand alone. Its picture of the Antiochan crisis is complemented by three parallel revelations that go over the same events in slightly different ways. Some scholars have argued that these chapters are the work of different authors.[86] Even if this were so, we should have to assume that the additional authors belonged to the same circle and wrote within a very short time of each other.[87] We should also have to assume that a member of this circle imposed an editorial unity on the book by

85. See further B. Lindars, "Re-enter the Apocalyptic Son of Man," *NTS* 22 (1975-76) 52-72.

86. For example, Hartman and DiLella, *The Book of Daniel,* 11-14; Casey, *Son of Man,* 9-10; also B. Hasslberger, *Hoffnung in der Bedrängnis* (St. Ottilien: Eos, 1977) 411.

87. Newsom, *Daniel,* 10-11, argues that Daniel 7 is pre-Maccabean, and has different eschatological interests from chapters 8-12. The argument depends on seeing the admitted references to Antiochus Epiphanes in Daniel 7 as secondary insertions, and leaves the occasion of the original composition uncertain. While the imagery of chapters 9-12 is quite different from that of chapter 7 ( and 8) it can be seen as complementary, rather than as a sign of different authorship. On the symbolism of the different chapters in Daniel 7-12 see now Bennie H. Reynolds III, *Between Symbolism and Realism: The Use of Symbolic and Non-Symbolic Language in Ancient Jewish Apocalypses 333-63 BCE* (JAJSup 8; Göttingen: Vandenhoeck & Ruprecht, 2011) 120-57 (chaps. 7 and 8) and 225-62 (chaps. 10-12).

repeating the sequence of Babylonian, Median, and Persian empires in chaps. 7–12, to parallel that of chaps. 1–6. The authors' circle must in any case have been bilingual, since Hebrew and Aramaic are allowed to stand in juxtaposition. It is surely simpler to suppose that these chapters, which are woven so closely together, are the work of a single author.

In fact, the juxtaposition of complementary revelations is a typical feature of apocalyptic literature. It can be seen in the Similitudes of Enoch, 4 Ezra, and 2 Baruch. An elaborate example is found in the book of Revelation. In none of these cases can the multiplicity of revelatory units be taken as evidence of multiple authorship. Repetition of a structural pattern with variations of specific detail is a basic means of communication, well attested in myth and folklore as well as in modern communication theory. The English anthropologist Edmund Leach has explained this phenomenon by the analogy of electronic communications.[88] If a message has to be communicated in the face of distractions or "noise," the communicator must use "redundance" by repeating the message several times in slightly different ways. In this way the basic structure of the message gets through. No one formulation exhausts the total message. This use of redundance is crucially important for our understanding of apocalyptic language. It implies that the apocalypses are not conveying a "literal" or univocal truth that can be expressed precisely in one exclusive way. Rather, they share the poetic nature of myth and allude symbolically to a fullness of meaning that can never be reduced to literalness.

## Daniel 9

The parallel revelations in Daniel 8–12 consist of a vision in chap. 8, which closely resembles chap. 7,[89] the interpretation of Jeremiah's prophecy of seventy weeks in Daniel 9, and an angelic discourse in Daniel 10–12. Daniel 9 stands out from the rest insofar as it is explicitly formulated as an interpretation of older biblical texts.[90] The passages in question are found in Jer

88. E. Leach, "Genesis as Myth," in J. Middleton, ed., *Myth and Cosmos* (Garden City, NY: Natural History Press, 1967) 1-13.

89. For discussion see Collins, *Daniel*, 328-43; Lacocque, *The Book of Daniel*, 167-73; Goldingay, *Daniel*, 194-222; Newsom, *Daniel*, 252-73.

90. See M. Fishbane, *Biblical Interpretation in Ancient Israel* (Oxford: Clarendon, 1985) 479-89. Reinhard G. Kratz, "The Visions of Daniel," in Collins and Flint, ed., *The Book of Daniel*, 105-6, thinks Daniel 9 was inserted secondarily. So also Christoph Berner, *Jahre, Jahrwochen und Jubiläen: Heptadische Geschichtskonzeption im antiken Judentum* (BZAW

25:11-12; 29:10 and say that the dominion of Babylon will last for seventy years, after which time the Jews will be restored. Historically, this prophecy was not accurate. Less than seventy years elapsed before the Jewish restoration. More seriously, the "desolations of Jerusalem" were not then brought to an end, as was painfully obvious in the Maccabean era. Accordingly, the biblical text is treated as a mystery, just as the symbolic visions were. The interpretation must be provided by an angel, in apocalyptic fashion.

Before proceeding to the interpretation, Daniel 9 places a lengthy prayer on the lips of Daniel. In many ways this prayer seems incongruous in its present context. It is not a prayer for illumination, by an individual, as we might expect. It is rather a communal prayer of confession, of a type widely used in the postexilic period.[91] The fluency of its Hebrew is in marked contrast to the rest of Daniel 8–12. Most importantly, the theology of the prayer contrasts sharply with the apocalyptic framework of Daniel. The logic of the prayer is that the affliction of Jerusalem is a punishment for sin and will be removed if the people repent and pray. Yet when the angel arrives he tells Daniel that the response was sent forth at the beginning of his supplication (in effect without waiting to hear it) and he emphasizes that the end is decreed. In short, events will follow their predetermined course, irrespective of prayer and repentance. Whether this prayer was deliberately placed here by the author to show this contrast[92] or was inserted by a later redactor, it neatly highlights a fundamental difference between the apocalyptic view of history and the traditional Deuteronomic theology. In the apocalyptic view, the course of events is predetermined. This does not mean that there is no room for human freedom. People can determine their own destiny by their reactions, but they cannot change the course of events.

The angel explains that the seventy weeks of Jeremiah are really seventy weeks of years. It is assumed that the biblical number can be regarded as a symbol and interpreted allegorically. The seventy weeks of years, 490 years, are not the product of any chronological calculation. Rather they reflect a traditional schema, ultimately inspired by the idea of the jubilee year (Leviticus 25) and may be taken as an instance of "sabbatical

---

363; Berlin: de Gruyter, 2006) 22. See the comment of Newsom, *Daniel*, 287, on the links between chapters 8 and 9.

91. A. Lacocque, "The Liturgical Prayer in Daniel 9," *HUCA* 47 (1976) 119-42; O. H. Steck, *Israel und das gewaltsame Geschick der Propheten* (Neukirchen–Vluyn: Erziehungsverein, 1967) 110-36; Newsom, *Daniel*, 288.

92. B. W. Jones, "The Prayer in Daniel IX," *VT* 18 (1968) 488-93.

eschatology."[93] We have seen similar schemata in connection with the Apocalypse of Weeks, the seventy generations in *1 Enoch* 10, and the seventy shepherds in the Animal Apocalypse. At least some of the Enochic passages are older than Daniel and show that Daniel drew on traditions that were shared by other apocalyptic writings.

The first seven weeks represent the period "from the going forth of the word to restore and build Jerusalem" (at the time of Daniel's prayer, 9:23) to the coming of an anointed one, a prince (either Zerubbabel or, more probably, Joshua, the first postexilic high priest). Then 62 weeks pass virtually without comment. The focus of the prophecy is on the last week, the real time of the author. This is marked by the murder of an anointed one (Onias III, see 2 Macc 4:34-35) and the profanation of the temple. The point of the prophecy is that all this is determined in advance, and an end is decreed. What follows this "end" is primarily concerned with the restoration of the cult: transgression will be ended, everlasting righteousness established, and the holy place anointed (9:24).[94] His main concern is not in speculating on the future but in providing an assurance that the predetermined period of Gentile sovereignty is coming to an end.[95]

## Daniel 10–12

The most elaborate revelation in the book of Daniel extends from 10:1 to 12:4.[96] The introductory verse alludes to a vision but does not describe it. The apparition of the interpreting angel, presumably Gabriel, is described in detail, so as to emphasize its overpowering effect.[97] The revelation itself has two dimensions. First, the angel explains the supernatural backdrop of the Hellenistic wars. There is an ongoing battle between Michael, "one of the chief

---

93. For the term see G. W. Buchanan, *The Consequences of the Covenant* (Leiden: Brill, 1970) 9-17.

94. See Winfried Vogel, *The Cultic Motif in the Book of Daniel* (New York: Lang, 2010) 194-97.

95. For different nuances as to whether Daniel thinks in terms of an "end" or "goal" of history, contrast M. Noth ("The Understanding of History in Old Testament Apocalyptic," in *The Laws in the Pentateuch*, 194-214) with K. Koch, "Spätisraelitisches Geschichtsdenken am Beispiel des Buches Daniel," *Historische Zeitschrift* 193 (1961) 1-32 (= K. Koch and J. M. Schmidt, eds., *Apokalyptik* [Darmstadt: Wissenschaftliche Buchgesellschaft, 1982] 276-310).

96. See Regina Wildgruber, *Daniel 10-12 als Schlüssel zum Buch* (FAT 2/58; Tübingen: Mohr Siebeck, 2013).

97. See Rowland, *The Open Heaven*, 98-101.

princes," and the princes of Persia and Greece. Second, in chap. 11, he outlines the course of the Hellenistic wars in terms of human actions. The supernatural backdrop is of crucial importance for Daniel's conception of history, as we have already seen in connection with Daniel 7. It is rooted in a common mythological assumption that whatever happens on earth is a reflection of a celestial archetype.[98] A battle between two earthly powers is a reflection of a battle between their respective gods. This conception is vividly illustrated in Isa 36:18-20 (2 Kgs 18:32-35) in the words attributed to the commander of the Assyrian army: "Beware lest Hezekiah mislead you by saying 'The Lord will deliver us.' Has any of the gods of the nations delivered his land out of the hand of the king of Assyria? Where are the gods of Hamath and Arpad? Where are the gods of Sepharvaim? Have they delivered Samaria out of my hand? Who among all the gods of these countries have delivered their countries out of my hand, that the Lord should deliver Jerusalem out of my hand?" Behind every nation stands a god who does battle on behalf of his people. The "princes" of Daniel 10 are clearly an adaptation of this idea. Their significance is that they add a dimension of depth to the record of events. The course of history is not in human hands but is determined by forces beyond our control.

The "prophecy" of Hellenistic history mentions no names, but the people and events can be readily identified.[99] The struggles of the kings of the south (Ptolemies) with the kings of the north (Seleucids) are swiftly reviewed, reaching a preliminary crescendo with the career of Antiochus III (the Great).[100] The main focus of attention is Antiochus IV Epiphanes, to whose reign more than half the chapter is devoted. The preceding review of Hellenistic history bridges the gap between the supposed time of Daniel and the actual composition of the book. It is presented as a prediction and follows the cryptic style of prophecy. In this way it suggests that the course of history has been determined in advance. It also lends credibility to the real prophecy with which the passage concludes. If the "predictions" are known to have been accurate down to the present, then they are likely to be reliable for the future too. In fact, the concluding prophecy of the death of the king was not fulfilled, and so Daniel 11 provides a clear indication of the time when the book was composed.

The technique of Daniel 11 presupposes a willingness to believe that

---

98. M. Eliade, *The Myth of the Eternal Return* (New York: Pantheon, 1954) 3-4.

99. See, for example, Hartman and DiLella, *The Book of Daniel*, 286-305; Collins, *Daniel*, 377-88. For Babylonian parallels to this kind of prophecy, see Lambert, *The Background of Jewish Apocalyptic*; Neujahr, *Predicting the Past*, 13-73.

100. R. J. Clifford, "History and Myth in Daniel 10–12," *BASOR* 220 (1975) 23-26.

this prophecy had been written by Daniel, some hundreds of years before. We must assume that the immediate circles of the apocalyptic writers were aware of the fiction of pseudonymity, but, although this literature was produced by scribes of considerable learning, it was addressed to the masses at large. Its general effectiveness was undoubtedly enhanced by the willingness of common people to accept the ancient authorship of newly promulgated books.

Daniel 11 provides a rare insight into the nature and goals of the author and his circle. In 11:32 we are told that Antiochus will "seduce with flattery those who violate the covenant," a reference to the Hellenizing Jews who supported his policies. In contrast to these, "the people who know their God" will stand firm and take action, and the wise teachers of the people (literally "those who make the people wise") will make the masses understand. Some of these teachers will be killed. They will receive "a little help," although many will join them insincerely. Their deaths are said to refine and purify them until the appointed end.

There is no doubt that the author of Daniel belonged to these wise teachers (the *maśkîlîm*), who are portrayed here as the true heroes of the persecution and in chap. 12 are singled out for special honor at the resurrection. They are portrayed as activists, but they are not said to fight. Their activism lies in making the masses understand. The understanding they convey is presumably the revelation contained in the book of Daniel. The thesis of the visions is that the true meaning of events is not publicly evident but is known to the wise, through revelations. The real struggle is being fought between the angelic princes. Its course and eventual outcome are already predetermined. This knowledge provides a perspective that enables the faithful Jews to bear up under persecution. Further, it gives them a rationale for laying down their lives, since by so doing they will be purified and will be assured of their reward at the resurrection. We are reminded of the story in 1 Maccabees 2 of the martyrs who let themselves be massacred rather than violate the Sabbath. We will find a similar stance in the *Testament of Moses*.

This passage throws an interesting light on the alleged esotericism of apocalyptic literature.[101] It is true that the perspective conveyed in the visions is not publicly accessible but requires special, apocalyptic revelation. Yet the whole purpose of this revelation, in the case of Daniel, is to

---

101. Cf. M. E. Stone, "Apocalyptic Literature," in idem, ed., *Jewish Writings of the Second Temple Period* (CRINT 2/2; Assen: Van Gorcum; Philadelphia: Fortress, 1984) 431-33.

make the masses understand. The command of the angel in Dan 12:4 to "shut up the words and seal the book" must be regarded as a consequence of pseudonymity — it explains why the revelations of Daniel had not been circulated before the Maccabean era. It is possible that some other apocalyptic writings were intended for a restricted group, but at least Daniel is addressed to the *rabbîm* or populace at large.

In this light we can also see the location of Daniel within the Jewish community. There is a division within Israel between "those who violate the covenant" and "those who know their God." The commitment of the masses appears uncertain. The *maśkîlîm,* then, constitute a distinct group. Yet they are oriented outward, and they function within the larger community. There is no evidence of separate organization, such as we find at Qumran. The temple and central institutions of the religion are evidently not rejected, although for the present they are defiled.

Many scholars have held that the *maśkîlîm* of Daniel are identical with the Hasidim.[102] This theory does not warrant the consensus it has received. One of the few things we know about the Hasidim is that they were militant supporters of Judas Maccabee. There is no evidence that Daniel supports such a stance. The reference to "a little help" in Dan 11:34 has traditionally been taken as a slighting reference to the Maccabees. In fact it is doubtful whether the author of Daniel would have considered the militant Maccabees to be a help at all. For him, the objective of the wise was to make others understand and to purify themselves. The battle could be left to Michael and his angels.

It is apparent that Daniel lacks the enthusiasm for the Maccabean revolt that characterizes the Animal Apocalypse of Enoch. We must conclude that the group from which Daniel emerged was different from that which developed the Enoch literature, although they occasionally drew on common traditions. The apocalyptic literature was not the product of a single unified movement.

### The Resurrection

The angel's revelation reaches its climax in 12:1-3. There we read that when Michael will arise all the people whose names are inscribed in the book

---

102. Hengel, *Judaism and Hellenism,* 1:175-80; O. Plöger, *Theocracy and Eschatology* (Richmond: John Knox, 1968) 22-25; A. Lacocque, "The Socio-Spiritual Formative Milieu of the Daniel Apocalypse," in van der Woude, ed., *The Book of Daniel,* 315-43.

will be delivered. Then "many of those who sleep in the land of dust will awake, some to eternal life and some to shame and everlasting contempt. The wise teachers will shine like the glory of the firmament and those who make the masses righteous will be like the stars for ever and ever." Daniel does not envisage a general resurrection.[103] Many, not all, will arise, presumably the very good and very bad. The *maśkîlîm* are singled out for special honor. Shining like the stars should not be dismissed as a mere metaphor. We have noted above that the stars often represent the heavenly host and are used in that sense in Dan 8:10. The significance of the reference in Daniel 12 can be seen clearly in the light of a parallel in *1 Enoch* 104. There the righteous are promised that they "will shine as the lights of heaven and the portals of heaven will be opened to you" (vs. 2) and a few verses later that they will "become companions to the host of heaven" (vs. 6). In this case it is quite clear that to "shine like the stars" is to join the angelic host. This conception is found also in other apocalyptic texts. In the Similitudes of Enoch (39:5) "the dwelling places of the righteous are with the holy angels." In Mark 12:25 (and parallels) Jesus tells the Sadducees that when men rise from the dead they are like the angels in heaven. In the Qumran scrolls the members of the community mingle with the angels even before death. In Daniel 12, too, the identification of stars and angels is implied. The wise teachers, who derive their wisdom from angelic revelations throughout the book, hope to mingle with the angels after their death. In view of this hope we can appreciate the full significance of the triumph of the holy ones in Daniel 7.

The most obvious function of the resurrection in Daniel 12 is to lend support to those who had to lay down their lives if they refused to betray their religion. In the perspective of Daniel, martyrdom makes sense. Belief in vindication beyond death undercuts the greatest threat at the disposal of the tyrant. Yet the function of the resurrection should not be understood exclusively with reference to the persecution. Daniel 12:3 does not say that only the martyred *maśkîlîm* will shine like stars. Presumably this is the destiny of all the wise teachers. Fellowship with the angels is the fulfillment of a life of wisdom and purity.

Daniel 12 says nothing of a kingdom.[104] It does not exclude the continu-

---

103. Nickelsburg, *Resurrection, Immortality, and Eternal Life*, 23-42; E. Puech, *La Croyance des Esséniens en la Vie Future: Immortalité, Résurrection, Vie Éternelle?* (Paris: Gabalda, 1993) 79-85.

104. Rainer Albertz, "The Social Setting of the Aramaic and Hebrew Book of Daniel," in Collins and Flint, eds., *The Book of Daniel*, 191, argues that the Tendenz of chapters 10-12

ation of life on earth, and, in the light of Daniel 7 and 9, we must assume that it is implied. However, the earthly fulfillment is not the goal of the *maśkîlîm,* and Daniel gives no indication that resurrection of a fleshly body is implied.[105] Rather, their attention is focused on the higher world from which the affairs of this life are directed. While Daniel is directly concerned with political affairs, and not with cosmological speculation such as we found in parts of *1 Enoch,* the mystical side of apocalyptic thought is important here too.

## Setting and Function

The book of Daniel is related to a specific historical crisis to a degree that is unusual in an apocalyptic book. The sharp reduction in speculative material relative to *1 Enoch* can probably be attributed to the urgency of that crisis. In fact there is little speculative material in the Enochic Apocalypse of Weeks and Animal Apocalypse, which may have been written about the same time. The heat of persecution also underlies the attempts in Daniel to specify the number of days until the end. Such attempts are rare in the apocalypses. In the case of Daniel, contradictory numbers were allowed to stand side by side (Dan 12:11: 1,290 days; 12:12: 1,335 days). This shows that they were not taken with absolute literalness.[106] The final figure was presumably the result of a revised calculation when the first date passed.[107] It should be noted that these figures point to a date later than the actual reconsecration of the temple by Judas Maccabee, which occurred just three years after the desecration.[108]

The visions of Daniel are not, of course, mere reflections of the historical crisis. They are highly imaginative constructions of it, shaped as much by mythic paradigms as by the actual events. Fundamental to the

---

differs completely from that of chapter 7. Cf. also Newsom, *Daniel,* 8. I see these chapters as rather complementary.

105. *Pace* Newsom, *Daniel,* 364.

106. L. Hartman, "The Function of Some So-Called Apocalyptic Timetables," *NTS* 22 (1976) 1-14. It is noteworthy that despite the passage of time Josephus could still affirm that Daniel not only prophesied future things but also fixed the time at which they would come to pass (*Antiquities* 10.11.7 §267).

107. Gabriele Boccaccini, "The Solar Calendars of Daniel and Enoch," in Collins and Flint, eds., *The Book of Daniel,* 311-28, tries to explain the dates on the basis of a solar calendar, but this does not explain why the different numbers are juxtaposed.

108. 1 Macc 1:54; 4:52-54. See further Collins, *Daniel,* 401.

perspective of Daniel is the belief that events are guided by higher powers, expressed through the mythological symbolism of the beasts and the rider of the clouds in chap. 7 and, more directly, as angelic princes in chap. 10. A concomitant belief is the idea that the course of history is predetermined and that its end is assured. The destiny of the wise lies beyond this life in a resurrection and pertains to the world of the angels. Since life is thus bounded by a supernatural world, the revelation mediated by the angels acquires crucial importance.

This imaginative construction enables the persecuted Jews to cope with the crisis of the persecution, first by bringing its enormity to expression so that it can be clearly recognized, second by providing assurance that the forces of evil will inevitably be overcome by a higher power, and ultimately by providing a framework for action since it furnishes an explanation of the world that supports those who have to lay down their lives if they remain faithful to their religion. It provides a basis for nonviolent resistance to Hellenistic rule, even in the throes of the Maccabean rebellion.[109]

It is apparent that some elements of the worldview of the visions are derived from the tales about Daniel preserved in Daniel 1–6. There too the sovereignty of the God of the Jews is hidden in the present but revealed to the wise. The tales show how Jews could work in the service of Gentile kings and still maintain the purity of their religion. They posit compatibility between the kingdom of God and the Gentile kingdoms. That compatibility was shattered by the persecution of Antiochus Epiphanes. In the light of that crisis, the tradents of the Daniel stories sought a new genre that could symbolize more fully the forces behind events — which seemed beyond human control — and could also articulate a hope that transcended what is possible in this life. Daniel 7–12 adapts various traditional patterns and forms in a distinctive and original way, but its basic structure conforms to the apocalyptic genre, which we have already seen exemplified in various ways in *1 Enoch*.[110]

---

109. Cf. J. J. Collins, "Apocalyptic Eschatology as the Transcendence of Death," *CBQ* 36 (1974) 21-43 (= *Seers, Sibyls, and Sages,* 75-98).

110. This is not to suggest that Daniel depends directly on *1 Enoch,* but only to note that Daniel did not invent the genre.

# CHAPTER FOUR

# Related Genres: Oracles and Testaments

## I. ORACLES

The "historical" apocalypses, which view the course of history from the perspective of supernatural forces and the coming judgment, first emerge clearly in the period of the Maccabean revolt. There is obvious continuity with biblical prophecy, especially in the case of Daniel, in the use of the vision form and the expectation of decisive divine intervention. We have seen, however, that there were also important lines of continuity with the political oracles of the Hellenistic age. This Hellenistic background is more immediately obvious in another genre, that of sibylline oracles, which is closely related to the historical apocalypses and appears in Judaism about the same time.

## Sibylline Oracles

The genre of sibylline oracles had a long tradition behind it before it was taken over by the Jews.[1] Heraclitus, in the fifth century BCE, was already

---

1. See especially H. W. Parke, *Sibyls and Sibylline Prophecy in Classical Antiquity* (ed. B. C. McGing; London: Routledge, 1988); A. Momigliano, "From the Pagan to the Christian Sibyl," in *Nono Contributo* (Rome: Edizioni di Storia e Letteratura, 1992) 725-44. Also J. J. Collins, "The Jewish Adaptation of Sibylline Oracles," in idem, *Seers, Sibyls, and Sages in Hellenistic-Roman Judaism* (Leiden: Brill, 1997) 181-98; idem, *The Sibylline Oracles of Egyptian Judaism* (SBLDS 13; Missoula, MT: Scholars Press, 1974) 1-19; J. L. Lightfoot, *The Sibylline Oracles: With Introduction, Translation, and Commentary on the First and Second Books* (Oxford: Oxford University Press, 2007).

familiar with the figure of the sibyl as an ecstatic woman who uttered prophecies of a predominantly gloomy nature. In the Hellenistic period several sibyls were known, of whom the best known were those of Erythrea (in Asia Minor) and Cumae (in Italy). The most famous collection of sibylline oracles was the official one at Rome.[2] Only fragments of the pagan sibylline oracles have survived.[3] We know that they were often concerned with prodigies but also that they were interpreted with reference to historical and political occurrences. So Plutarch argues that "the prophecies have witnesses to testify for them in the numerous desolations and migrations of Grecian cities, the numerous descents of barbarian hordes and the overthrow of empires. And these recent and unusual occurrences near Cumae and Dicaearcheia, were they not recited long ago in the songs of the Sibyl?" (*De Pythiae Oraculis* 9 [398]). One of the surviving sibylline fragments prophesies that the land of Italy and the Latins will always be subject to Rome. The Cumean sibyl, according to Virgil's *Fourth Eclogue,* foretold a final age, or *ultima aetas,* and a later commentary on the *Eclogue* by Servius says that the sibyl divided the ages according to metals and foretold who would rule over each.[4] It is not at all certain, however, whether Virgil is referring to an actual sibylline oracle. The division of history into *saecula* or ages had a native Italian background in Etruscan lore, and there was some speculation in the first century BCE that the final *saeculum* was at hand.[5] The value of Virgil's poem as a witness to pagan sibylline oracles remains uncertain.

The Roman sibylline oracles were not regarded as different in kind from those associated with other locations. When the temple of Jupiter was burned down in 83 BCE and the sibylline books were destroyed, oracles were gathered from various places, especially Erythrea.[6] Such oracles played a serious role in the political propaganda of

---

2. See H. Cancik, "Libri Fatales, Römische Offenbarungsliteratur und Geschichtstheologie," in D. Hellholm, ed., *Apocalypticism in the Mediterranean World and the Near East: Proceedings of the International Colloquium on Apocalypticism, Uppsala, August 12-17, 1979* (Tübingen: Mohr Siebeck, 1983) 549-76; Parke, *Sibyls and Sibylline Prophecy,* 190-215.

3. One of the surviving Roman sibylline oracles deals with the birth of an androgyne. See further Livy 42.2-6; Tibullus 2.5.67-74.

4. D. Flusser, "The Four Empires in the Fourth Sibyl and in the Book of Daniel," *Israel Oriental Studies* 2 (1972) 163-65.

5. Cancik, "Libri Fatales," 557-58; B. Gladigow, "Aetas, aevum und saeclorum ordo: Zur Struktur zeitlicher Deutungssysteme," in Hellholm, ed., *Apocalypticism,* 262-65.

6. Dionysius of Halicarnassus 4.62.6.

the Hellenistic age.[7] Their importance is reflected in the fact that Augustus had two thousand oracles destroyed and even edited the Roman sibylline books.[8]

The sibylline oracles must be viewed in the wider context of the oracles of the Hellenistic age and especially the political oracles. There was a tradition of prophecy in Egypt which looked for the restoration of native Egyptian rule and the demise of the Greeks.[9] The most important examples are the *Demotic Chronicle* and the *Potter's Oracle*. We have already had occasion to refer to the Persian *Bahman Yasht* because of its affinities with Daniel. From a slightly later period, the *Oracle of Hystaspes* also exhibits the interest in periodization of history and eschatological upheaval that is characteristic of both the historical apocalypses and the Jewish *Sibylline Oracles*.[10] It is against this general background that we must understand the Jewish adaptation of the sibylline form. Unlike the apocalypses of Enoch and Daniel, which are ascribed to figures of the Israelite tradition, the oracles are attributed to the pagan sibyl, and so enter explicitly into the world of Hellenistic propaganda.[11]

The Jewish and Christian *Sibylline Oracles* are preserved in a standard collection of twelve books (conventionally numbered 1–8 and 11–14).[12]

---

7. See Strabo 17.1.43 (814) for a flurry of oracular activity in connection with Alexander the Great. In general, see S. K. Eddy, *The King Is Dead: Studies in Near Eastern Resistance to Hellenism, 334-31 B.C.* (Lincoln: University of Nebraska Press, 1961); H. Fuchs, *Der geistige Widerstand gegen Rom in der antiken Welt* (Berlin: de Gruyter, 1938).

8. Suetonius, *Augustus* 31.1.

9. F. Dunand, "L'Oracle du Potier et la formation de l'apocalyptique en Egypte," in F. Raphael, ed., *L'Apocalyptique* (Paris: Geuthner, 1977) 39-67; J. G. Griffiths, "Apocalyptic in the Hellenistic Era," in Hellholm, ed., *Apocalypticism,* 273-93; A. Blasius and B. U. Schipper, eds., *Apokalyptik und Ägypten: Eine kritische Analyse der relevanten Texte aus dem griechisch-römischen Ägypten* (Orientalia Lovaniensia Analecta 107; Leuven: Peeters, 2002).

10. J. R. Hinnells, "The Zoroastrian Doctrine of Salvation in the Roman World: A Study of the Oracle of Hystaspes," in E. J. Sharpe and J. R. Hinnells, eds., *Man and His Salvation: Studies in Memory of S. G. F. Brandon* (Manchester: Manchester University Press, 1973) 125-48. See the comments of Grenet, "Y a-t-il une Composante Iranienne dans l'Apocalyptique Judéo-Chrétienne?" 131-44.

11. See my article "Sibylline Discourse," in Eibert Tigchelaar, ed., *Old Testament Pseudepigrapha and the Scriptures* (BETL 270; Leuven: Peeters, 2014) 195-210.

12. The anomalous numbering arises from the nature of the manuscript tradition. The two main collections are numbered 1–8 and 9–14, but books 9 and 10 merely repeat material from the first collection, and so they are omitted in the standard editions. See my introductions to, translations of, and notes for all twelve books in J. H. Charlesworth, ed., *OTP,* 1:317-472 and my article, "The Development of the Sibylline Tradition," in W. Haase

Of these, books 3–5 and 11–14 are entirely Jewish (except for minor interpolations), whereas books 1–2 and 8 contain a Jewish substratum. Only books 6 and 7 are original Christian compositions. The latest material, in book 14, extends down to the Arab conquest of Egypt. Books 3–5, however, date from the period between the Maccabees and Bar Kokhba. *Sib. Or.* 3 is generally recognized as the oldest of the Jewish books, and it will be the subject of our attention here. Books 4 and 5 will be considered in a later chapter.

## The Third Sibyl

*Sib. Or.* 3 is itself a complex composition that collects material from a span of two centuries.[13] In the words of Erich Gruen, "it seems clear that the third Book of the Sibylline Oracles constitutes a conglomerate, a gathering of various prophecies that stem from different periods ranging from the second century BCE through the early Roman empire."[14] Rieuwerd Buitenwerf divides the book into six sections.[15] Verses 1-92 are left out of account as constituting the end of a different book. He identifies the first section with Fragment i, and the second with Fragment iii plus *Sib. Or.* 3:93-161. The remaining sections are marked by introductory formulae in which the Sibyl exclaims that God inspires her to prophesy. These formulae are found in 3:162-65; 3:196-98; 3:295-300 and 3:489-91. The last section, 3:489-829 is

---

and H. Temporini, eds., *ANRW* II.20.1 (Berlin: de Gruyter, 1987) 421-59; also M. Goodman, "The Sibylline Oracles," in E. Schürer, *The History of the Jewish People in the Age of Jesus Christ* III.1 (rev. and ed. G. Vermes, F. Millar, and M. Goodman; Edinburgh: T & T Clark, 1986) 618-54.

13. For details see Collins, *Sibylline Oracles,* 21-33; "The Third Sibyl Revisited," in idem, *Jewish Cult and Hellenistic Culture,* 82-98. The classic treatment is that of J. Geffcken, *Komposition and Entstehungszeit der Oracula Sibyllina* (Leipzig: Hinrichs, 1902). V. Nikiprowetzky defends the unity of the book with only minor exceptions in *La Troisième Sibylle* (Paris: Mouton, 1970). On the figure of the sibyl in *Sib. Or.* 3 see R. Buitenwerf, "The Identity of the Prophetess Sibyl in *Sibylline Oracles* III," in Joseph Verheyden, Korinna Zamfir, and Tobias Nicklas, eds., *Prophets and Prophecy in Jewish and Early Christian Literature* (WUNT 286; Tübingen: Mohr Siebeck, 2010) 41-55.

14. Erich S. Gruen, *Heritage and Hellenism: The Reinvention of Jewish Tradition* (Berkeley, CA: University of California Press, 1998) 272.

15. Rieuwerd Buitenwerf, *Book III of the Sibylline Oracles and Its Social Setting, with an Introduction, Translation, and Commentary* (SVTP 17; Leiden: Brill, 2003) 137-43.

disproportionately long. Buitenwerf distinguishes four admonitions within it, in 545-623, 624-731, 732-61, and 762-829.

Even a cursory reading of Buitenwerf's structure shows that his section 5 (3:295-488) consists of a different kind of material from the other sections. It is essentially a string of very brief pronouncements of doom against a wide range of peoples and places, many of them in Asia. The only reference to Jewish history in this section is in an oracle against Babylon at the beginning. There is also a mention of Gog and Magog in verse 319. After that, there is no mention of anything Jewish for 170 verses. Verses 350 to 488 could as easily have been written by a Gentile as by a Jew. Within this section, the oracle against Rome in verses 350-80 stands out because of its length, coherence and passion. Verses 400-88 have sometimes been attributed to the Erythrean Sibyl, who is said to have sung of the Trojan war (cf. 3:414-16) and to have said that Homer would write falsehoods (3:419).[16] All the undisputed references to the first century BCE in *Sib. Or.* 3:93-829 fall in this section, as do the great bulk of the references to Asia. It seems likely that verses 350-488 are pagan oracles that were included to establish the Sibylline credentials of the book.[17]

If we bracket out these apparently pagan oracles, we are left with a main corpus of Jewish oracles in vss. 97-349 and 489-829.[18] This material can be traced to Egypt in the middle of the second century BCE because of the references to the "seventh king," which we will discuss below.[19] The oracles against various nations in vss. 350-488 are diverse in origin, and at least some of them derive from the first century BCE. The oracles in vss. 1-96 are also diverse in origin. These have been thought to be displaced here and to have been originally the conclusion of a different book.[20]

The initial oracle of the main corpus, vss. 97-161, stands apart from the rest of the book. It describes the fall of the tower of Babylon (vss. 97-104) and the war of the Titans against Cronos and his sons (vss. 105-55). It then concludes with a list of world kingdoms (vss. 156-61). The account

---

16. Varro in Lactantius, *Div Inst* 1.6; Pausanias 10.2.2; Collins, *The Sibylline Oracles*, 27.

17. Collins, "Sibylline Discourse," 201-2.

18. This is disputed by Gruen, *Heritage and Hellenism*, 271, but he fails to consider the character of the material in verses 350-88.

19. Buitenwerf, *Book III*, 130-33, is exceptional in arguing for a provenance in Asia Minor for the whole book, mainly on the basis of the references to Asia in vss. 295-488. Since he does not distinguish layers in the book, he dates it all to the first century BCE.

20. A. Kurfess, "Christian Sibyllines," in E. Hennecke and W. Schneemelcher, eds., *New Testament Apocrypha* (2 vols.; Philadelphia: Westminster, 1965) 2:707.

of Cronos and the Titans is euhemeristic — it "demythologizes" the gods and treats them as figures of ancient history.[21] Such concern with pagan mythology is exceptional in the Jewish sibyllines. Here it establishes a major theme of the sibyl: the struggle for kingship and sovereignty, a struggle that had gone on from the dawn of history. The list of world kingdoms in vss. 156-61 specifies eight, but we should supply the initial kingdom of Cronos and probably also a final kingdom to come. A list of ten kingdoms is a common feature of sibylline oracles.[22]

Four other oracles in *Sib. Or.* 3 may be said to display a common pattern, in which sin (usually idolatry) leads to disasters and tribulations, which are ended by the advent of a king or kingdom:[23] vss. 162-95, 196-294, 545-656, and 657-808. The second of these sections (vss. 196-294) describes the Babylonian exile and restoration. In the other sections, the king or kingdom is expected in the future. In vss. 162-95 the king who brings the disasters to an end is identified as the seventh king of Egypt from the Greek dynasty. In vss. 545-656 he is a "king from the sun." In the final oracle the reference is to a kingdom that will be raised up by God.

### The Seventh King

The interpretation of *Sib. Or.* 3 depends heavily on our understanding of this future king or kingdom, and this in turn is closely bound up with the date and setting of the book. The "seventh king of Egypt" is mentioned not only in vs. 193 but also in vss. 318 and 608. According to vs. 318 Egypt will be torn by strife in the seventh generation of kings, but then war will cease. In vss. 606-8, men will throw away idols when "the young seventh king of Egypt rules his own land, numbered from the dynasty of the Greeks." While seven is admittedly an ideal number, these passages could scarcely have been written after the death of the seventh Ptolemy.[24] Some confu-

---

21. The term is derived from Euhemerus of Messene, who published an anthropological theory of the gods about 300 BCE. He held that the gods were originally great kings and benefactors of humanity.

22. The fourth and combined first and second books of the *Sibylline Oracles* are structured around a sequence of ten kingdoms. Compare the tenfold schematization of history in the Apocalypse of Weeks. On *Sib. Or.* 1-2 see now Lightfoot, *The Sibylline Oracles*, 257-534; Olaf Wassmuth, *Sibyllinische Orakel 1-2. Studien und Kommentar* (Leiden: Brill, 2011).

23. Collins, *Sibylline Oracles*, 37.

24. Gruen, *Heritage and Hellenism*, 272-77, and "Jews, Greeks and Romans in the

sion was possible on the enumeration of the Ptolemies, since Ptolemy VI Philometor and Ptolemy VIII Euergetes II (Physcon) were coregents in the years 170-164. Philometor also shared the throne with his son, Ptolemy VII (Neos Philopator) in the last year of his reign, and the youth reigned very briefly after his father's death. On any reckoning, the date of composition cannot be later than the end of Physcon's reign (117 BCE). Since the seventh king is still anticipated as future, a date in the reign of Philometor is more likely, especially in view of the good favor of that Ptolemy toward the Jews.[25] Such a date fits well with the other indications in the book. Vss. 175-93 contain a vigorous attack on Rome, which is said to cause evils in many places, but especially in Macedonia. This can only refer to the Roman conquest of Greece in the mid-second century BCE.[26] The sibyl's negative attitude toward Rome probably reflects the attitude of Philometor, who lost the support of Rome from 161 BCE onward.[27] It stands in marked contrast to the good relations between Rome and the Maccabees in this period.

The statement in vss. 315-18 that Egypt would be torn by civil strife has been usually taken as a reference to the civil war between Philometor and Physcon (Euergetes II).[28] In vs. 611, in a passage that follows immediately on

---

Third Sibylline Oracle," in M. Goodman, ed., *Jews in a Graeco-Roman World* (Oxford: Clarendon, 1998) 15-36, followed by Buitenwerf, *Book III*, 126-30, argues that the adjective "seventh" should not be accorded any numerical significance, but numbers are typically used to specify points in history in apocalyptic writings. See Adela Yarbro Collins, "Numerical symbolism in Jewish and Early Christian Apocalyptic Literature," in eadem, *Cosmology and Eschatology in Jewish and Christian Apocalypticism* (Leiden: Brill, 1996), and my comments in "The Third Sibyl Revisited," 89-90. Nikiprowetzky identified the seventh king somewhat paradoxically as Cleopatra VII (*La Troisième Sibylle*, 215).

25. P. Fraser, *Ptolemaic Alexandria* (2 vols.; Oxford: Clarendon, 1972) 1:709-13; 2:989-99. The Jewish temple at Leontopolis was built in Philometor's reign. Josephus claims that Philometor's entire army was under the command of two Jews, Onias and Dositheus (*Against Apion* 2.49). The Jewish philosopher Aristobulus allegedly dedicated his book to Philometor (Clement, *Stromateis* 1.150.1).

26. Macedonia was divided after the battle of Pydna in 168 BCE and was made a Roman province in 147 BCE.

27. Polybius 31.20 and 18; Fraser, *Ptolemaic Alexandria*, 1:120; 2:214. Gruen, *Heritage and Hellenism*, 273 objects that "no *ex eventu* forecast could have set the fall of Roman power to that period," but the passage does not say that Rome will fall, only that "the people of the great God will again be strong," and that part of the oracle is not *ex eventu*.

28. Gruen, *Heritage and Hellenism*, 274, says that "nothing in the passage gives any reason to evoke the era of Philometor and Euergetes," but the reference to the seventh generation of kings points precisely to this era.

an allusion to the seventh king, we read that a king will come from Asia and destroy Egypt. This destruction becomes the occasion of the conversion of the Egyptians. Many scholars have identified the king from Asia as Antiochus Epiphanes who invaded Egypt in 170 and again in 169.[29] In fact the king from Asia was a traditional enemy of Egypt, a tradition that went back to the time of the Hyksos.[30] In vs. 611, the invasion would seem to be a future, eschatological event. However, if this allusion was triggered by the recent experience of the invasion of Epiphanes, we have a further indication of a date in the time of Philometor. The "young" seventh king could be Philometor himself[31] or, more plausibly, his anticipated successor, Neos Philopator.

## The King from the Sun

The passages that refer to the seventh king do not depict him as an active savior figure, but they say that a crucial turning point will come in his reign. In vss. 652-56 the expected king is portrayed in more active terms: "Then God will send a king from the sun, who will stop the whole earth from evil war, killing some, imposing oaths of fidelity on others. He will not do all these things by his own plans, but in obedience to the noble teachings of the great God." This "king from the sun" has been the subject of much controversy. The phrase has been commonly rendered "king from the east" and has been presumed to refer to a Jewish messiah,[32] but there is no precedent either for a simple equation of "sun" with "east" or for a messiah from the east. The closest parallel for the expression is found not in a Jewish work at all but in the Egyptian *Potter's Oracle.*[33] There we read "and then Egypt

29. For example, H. C. Lanchester, "The Sibylline Oracles," in Charles, ed., *APOT,* 2:389.

30. Collins, *Sibylline Oracles,* 29. Other notorious invaders were Cambyses and Artaxerxes Ochus.

31. Philometor was only three or four years old when he came to the throne, and he was still a youth when Antiochus invaded.

32. So A. Momigliano, "La Portata Storica dei Vaticini sul Settimo Re nel Terzo Libro degli Oracoli Sibillini," in *Forma Futuri: Studi in Onore del Cardinale Pellegrino* (Turin: Bottega d'Erasmo, 1975) 1077-84; J. M. G. Barclay, *Jews in the Mediterranean Diaspora from Alexander to Trajan (323 BCE – 117 CE)* (Edinburgh: T & T Clark, 1996) 223; Gruen, *Heritage and Hellenism,* 277-78; Isa 41:2, 25 is often invoked in this connection, but there the connotation "east" is quite explicit (from the sunrise).

33. J. J. Collins, "The Sibyl and the Potter," in L. Bormann, K. del Tredici, and A. Standhartinger, eds., *Religious Propaganda and Missionary Competition in the New Tes-*

will increase, when the king from the sun, who is benevolent for fifty-five years, becomes present, appointed by the greatest goddess Isis." Here "king from the sun" is an old pharaonic title. The *Potter's Oracle* is predicting a native Egyptian king who would overthrow the Ptolemies. However, the Ptolemies could also adopt the pharaonic titles for their own purposes. Ptolemaic kings are elsewhere said to be "chosen by the sun" and "son of the sun, to whom the sun has given victory."[34] In *Sib. Or.* 3, the "king from the sun" cannot be divorced from "the seventh king of Egypt from the line of the Greeks." The king who will stop the earth from war must be presumed to be the same as the one in whose reign war will cease, pending arguments to the contrary.[35] The "king from the sun," then, must be identified with the seventh Ptolemy, either Philometor or his anticipated successor.

If this interpretation is correct, it follows that *Sib. Or.* 3 hails a Ptolemaic king as a virtual messiah. Precedent for such a positive attitude to a Gentile king can be found in Isa 45:1, where Cyrus is hailed as "my messiah" or "my anointed one."[36] Precisely this analogy is brought to mind by *Sib. Or.* 3:286-94. There we read:

> And then the heavenly God will send a king and will judge each man in blood and the gleam of fire. There is a certain royal tribe whose race will never stumble. This too, as time pursues its cyclic course, will reign, and it will begin to raise up a new temple of God. All the kings of the Persians will bring to their aid gold and bronze and much-wrought iron. For God himself will give a holy dream by night and then indeed the temple will again be as it was before.

---

*tament World* (Leiden: Brill, 1994) 57-69 (= *Seers, Sibyls, and Sages*, 199-210). On the Potter's Oracle see L. Koenen, "Die Apologie des Töpfers an König Amenophis, oder das Töpferorakel," in Blasius and Schipper, ed., *Apokalyptik und Ägypten*, 139-87.

34. Collins, *Sibylline Oracles*, 40-43. See also Collins, *Between Athens and Jerusalem: Jewish Identity in the Hellenistic Diaspora* (2d ed.; Grand Rapids: Eerdmans, 2000) 94, for a critique of Momigliano's position.

35. *Pace* Barclay, *Jews in the Mediterranean Diaspora*, 223.

36. Barclay, *Jews in the Mediterranean World*, 222, objects that the sibylline author could not have endorsed "Ptolemaic ideology" in light of the persistent criticism of Greek and Egyptian religion. But the endorsement does not extend to the religious practices of the Ptolemies any more than Second Isaiah endorsed Zoroastrianism when he hailed Cyrus as messiah. The Jewish author in each case hails the pagan king as a potential deliverer of the Jewish people. The assertion that these kings are sent by God may be sincere, but it also smacks of political flattery.

The mention of the "kings of the Persians" makes clear that the reference is to the restoration from the exile in the fifth century. The "king" who is sent is not an eschatological messiah, but Cyrus, who released the Jews from Babylon. The passage might, however, be said to provide a typology for the eschatological time. The typology would suggest that the well-being of the Jews depends on the power of a benevolent Gentile king.[37] In fact, the Jews had been loyal subjects of Gentile rulers throughout the postexilic period. Before the Maccabean revolt there was a significant division between those who supported the Seleucids of Syria and those who favored the Ptolemies.[38] At a time when Judea was locked in deadly combat with the Seleucids, it was natural that some Jews, especially those in Egypt, should look to the Ptolemies for deliverance.

## The Judaism of the Sibyl

*Sib. Or.* 3 is not simply propaganda for a Ptolemaic king. The eschatological sections, including the predictions of the seventh king, serve as a frame for the religious and ethical message of the book.[39] In several passages the sibyl specifies the kinds of conduct that lead to destruction and those that lead to deliverance. The religious stance might be characterized as "covenantal nomism."[40] The Jews are praised for "fulfilling the word of the great God, the hymn of the law" (vs. 246) and "sharing in the righteousness of the law of the Most High" (vs. 580). They can fail, on occasion, and be punished, as is shown by the example of the Babylonian exile, but they are restored if they keep their trust in the laws (vss. 283-84). Yet the sibyl treats the law in practice as if it were natural law. Other nations can be condemned for failing to observe it (vss. 599-600). The main requirements that are emphasized are not the

---

37. J. Nolland ("Sib Or 3.265-94, An Early Maccabean Messianic Oracle," *JTS* 30 [1979] 158-67) argues that the typology points to a Davidic messiah, but the king who played the crucial role in the restoration in the sixth century was the pagan king Cyrus.

38. See especially V. Tcherikover, *Hellenistic Civilization and the Jews* (New York: Atheneum, 1970) 39-89.

39. See Stewart Moore, *Jewish Ethnic Identity and Relations in Hellenistic Egypt: With Walls of Iron?* (JSJSup 171; Leiden: Brill, 2015).

40. This is the phrase of E. P. Sanders, *Paul and Palestinian Judaism* (Philadelphia: Fortress, 1977) 70.

distinctive Jewish laws, such as circumcision or dietary restrictions, but the common ethic, which the Diaspora Jews hoped to share with enlightened Gentiles.[41] Idolatry is the chief sin. Sexual abuses, especially homosexuality, are repeatedly denounced. There are warnings against arrogance and greed. A more distinctive position is taken in the unequivocal condemnation of astrology, augury, and divination. The central points of the ethical teaching are summed up in vss. 762-66: "Urge on your minds in your breasts and shun unlawful worship. Worship the Living One. Avoid adultery and indiscriminate intercourse with males. Rear your own offspring and do not kill it, for the Immortal is angry at whoever commits these sins."

There is, however, another important aspect of the sibyl's teaching. In an address to the Greeks in vss. 545-72 she specifies that the rejection of idolatry entails offering sacrifices in "the temple of the great God." The future ideal is the restoration of pious men who not only keep the law but fully honor the temple of the great God with all kinds of sacrifices (vs. 575). In the final utopian state the Jews will all live peacefully around the temple, and the Gentiles will be moved to "send to the temple" and ponder the law of God (vss. 702-31). The Jerusalem temple is of vital importance for the true religion and should become a place of worship for all nations. Apart from sending gifts there, the Gentiles are warned to keep their hands off Jerusalem: "But wretched Greece, desist from proud thoughts. Do not send against this city your planless people which is not from the holy land of the Great One" (vss. 732-35). The Greeks who in fact sent armies against Jerusalem in this period were the Seleucids, and the admonition is addressed to them. It is apparent, however, that it would also apply if a Ptolemy were to attack Jerusalem. The sibyl includes a fantasy, reminiscent of Psalms 2 and 48, in which the kings of the Gentiles assemble to attack Jerusalem but are judged by God (vss. 657-68).[42]

The Ptolemaic king is not exalted for his own sake. Rather, his role is to facilitate and pave the way for a utopian Jewish state centered on Jerusalem. This was also the role of the "messiah" Cyrus in Deutero-Isaiah. The fact that a Ptolemaic king has a role in this scenario is a significant indication of the political perspective from which the sibyl wrote.

41. See Collins, *Between Athens and Jerusalem*, 160-5.

42. Barclay, *Jews in the Mediterranean World*, 216-25, reads these oracles as alienated from the Gentile world and antagonistic to it. The alienation, however, is by no means complete. The sibyl repeatedly appeals for the conversion of the Gentiles, and the use of a pagan pseudonym and literary form shows an acceptance of some aspects of Hellenistic culture.

## The Provenance of Sib. Or. 3

We may now inquire which circles in Judaism in the mid-second century BCE would have produced a document such as this. The combination of Jewish law and temple cult, on the one hand, and enthusiasm for a Ptolemaic king, on the other, could plausibly be attributed to Onias III, the last legitimate high priest before the Maccabean revolt. 2 Maccabees presents Onias as a man of great piety, especially devoted to the temple cult. His father, Simon the Just, was pro-Seleucid, but Onias himself seems to have inclined toward the Ptolemies. This may be inferred from the fact that the pro-Ptolemaic Hyrcanus, son of Tobias, deposited funds in the Jerusalem temple, and also from the readiness of Antiochus Epiphanes to displace Onias. After the Maccabean revolt, Onias's son, Onias IV, sought refuge in Egypt. There he attained distinction in the service of Philometor and was allowed to build a temple at Leontopolis. The hypothesis that *Sib. Or.* 3 was composed in circles close to the younger Onias accounts satisfactorily for all aspects of the work. The enthusiasm for the Ptolemaic house is more readily intelligible among the supporters of the warrior priest than in any academic circles in Alexandria. Such a provenance would also explain the strange silence of *Sib. Or.* 3 on the Maccabean revolt.[43] Onias was no supporter of the Maccabees. Yet he never actively opposed them either.

*Sib. Or.* 3 is definitely oriented toward the Jerusalem temple. This fact should not militate against the view that its author was associated with Leontopolis. The Leontopolis temple was probably not founded until several years after Onias arrived in Egypt.[44] The oracles may have come from the earlier period. It is improbable that Leontopolis was ever intended as a rival of Jerusalem. Its remote location makes such a role unlikely.[45] Although the Jews of the land of Onias continued to play a

43. Momigliano ("La Portata Storica," 1081) finds an allusion to the rebellion in lines 194-95 ("and then the race of the great God will again be strong"), but the reference here is to a future revival. Barclay, *Jews in the Mediterranean World,* 223, endorses Momigliano's suggestion but admits that "the oracles make no reference to the Maccabees or their revolt (beyond a possible echo in 194-95)."

44. M. Delcor, "Le Temple d'Onias en Egypte," *RB* 75 (1968) 188-205; Gideon Bohak, *Joseph and Aseneth and the Jewish Temple in Heliopolis* (SBLEJL 10; Atlanta: SBL, 1996) 20-22; Livia Capponi, *Il tempio di Leontopoli in Egitto: Identità politica e religiosa dei Giudei di Onia (c. 150 a.c.-73 d.c.)* (Florence: ETS, 2007) 58-59.

45. Tcherikover, *Hellenistic Civilization,* 280.

prominent part in Egyptian Judaism, their temple was never a bone of contention. We know from the example of Qumran that rejection of the current priesthood did not necessarily exclude the hope for an ultimate restoration of Jerusalem.

*Sib. Or.* 3, then, is a highly propagandistic document. It presents Judaism to the Hellenistic world in terms that are primarily ethical: avoidance of idolatry, superstition, and sexual misconduct. This view of Judaism is integrated into a political vision where the Ptolemaic kingship would continue to play a role. The use of the sibyl's name was intended to lend the weight of a venerable pagan authority to this view. The suggestion of determinism in the oracular form, enhanced by the frequent use of *ex eventu* prophecy, lent an air of inevitability to the sibyl's message. In all, then, this was a medium well suited for Jewish propaganda in the Hellenistic world.

## The Sibyllines and the Apocalypses

Philip Vielhauer wrote that "the Sibyllines represent the Apocalyptic of Hellenistic Diaspora Judaism (from which only one real Apocalypse is known, slav. Enoch)."[46] He went on to elaborate on the ambivalence of this remark. The oracles do indeed share some prominent features with the historical apocalypses: pseudonymity, historical reviews, periodization of history, expectation of a definitive kingdom.[47]

Vielhauer distinguished the two genres primarily in terms of their function. He regarded the apocalypses as "conventicle literature," whereas the sibyllines were outward-directed "missionary propaganda." We have seen already that Vielhauer's understanding of the function of the apocalypses requires some modification. The function of the sibyllines is also less clear-cut when we consider *Sib. Or.* 5 in a later chapter. It is true, however, that no Jewish apocalypse serves the function of propaganda to the Gentile world in the way we have found in *Sib. Or.* 3. It is not apparent that an apocalypse could not be used in that way, but in fact it does not seem to have been. The function of these documents

46. P. Vielhauer, "Apocalypses and Related Subjects," in Hennecke and Schneemelcher, eds., *New Testament Apocrypha*, 2:600.

47. See Lightfoot, *The Sibylline Oracles*, 111-13, on some parallels in the periodization of history, and Neujahr, *Predicting the Past*, 195-242, on the use of *ex eventu* prophecy.

is variable, however, on the level of social function which Vielhauer has in mind.

Other differences are more deeply rooted in the structure of the genres themselves. We have seen that the sibyl, like the apocalypses, uses the eschatological horizon as a frame to lend urgency to an ethical and political message. In the sibyllines, however, the supporting framework is all on the horizontal axis — the authority of the sibyl, the allusions to historical events, the expectation of a kingdom. The vertical axis of the apocalypses is missing. There is no interest in angels and demons or in the cosmology of the heavenly world. Consequently, the oracles lack the mystical dimension of the apocalypses, and this difference is reflected in the eschatology. *Sib. Or.* 3 contains no hint of a judgment of the dead; all is on a political, earthly level. Some later sibyllines, notably Books 1-2 and 4, acquired an interest in the judgment of the dead, but this interest was not an intrinsic part of the sibylline genre.[48]

## Oracles from the First Century BCE

*Sib. Or.* 3 inaugurated a tradition of sibylline prophecy in Egyptian Judaism. In its present form the book contains a number of oracles from the first century BCE. The most notable of these is found in vss. 350-80. It predicts the vengeance of Asia on Rome, which will be exacted by a lady, a *despoina*. The lady in question should be identified as Cleopatra, who also represented Egypt, as its queen, and the goddess Isis, whom she claimed to incarnate.[49] The oracle must have been written shortly before the battle of Actium and the decisive fall of Cleopatra. This oracle lacks the ethical and religious convictions characteristic of the earlier oracles of *Sib. Or.* 3, but the enthusiasm for the Ptolemaic house is carried on. Such enthusiasm might well be expected in the military colony of the land of Onias. The oracle continues a vein of anti-Roman polemic that was already

---

48. See further my essay, "The Sibyl and the Apocalypses," in David E. Aune and Frederick E. Brenk, eds., *Greco-Roman Culture and the New Testament* (Leiden: Brill, 2012) 185-202.

49. Collins, *Sibylline Oracles,* 57-64; W. W. Tarn, "Alexander Helios and the Golden Age," *JRS* 22 (1932) 135-48. See, however, H. Kippenberg, "Dann wird der Orient herrschen und der Okzident dienen," in N. W. Bolz and W. Hübner, eds., *Spiegel und Gleichnis* (Würzburg: Königshausen & Neumann, 1983) 40-48, who relates this oracle to the campaign of Mithridates.

present in *Sib. Or.* 3:175-90 and came to play an increasing part in the later Jewish sibyllina.

A quite different attitude to Cleopatra is found in two brief oracles in vss. 46-62 and 75-92, both of which were written in the aftermath of Actium. Both reflect the disillusionment of Cleopatra's supporters after her defeat. The hope for a glorious kingdom is replaced by the expectation of a day of destruction. This is marked by brimstone from heaven in vss. 60-61, and by the collapse of the heavens and a stream of fire in vss. 80-85. The "lady" Cleopatra, of whom so much is expected, is now the "widow" (vs. 77) who brings desolation to the world. It is significant that the decline of the confident hopes in the Ptolemaic house is accompanied by an increasing use of the imagery of cosmic destruction, familiar from the historical apocalypses. This tendency is even more strongly evident in *Sib. Or.* 3:63-74, which says that "Beliar will come from the Sebasteni." This should be read as an allusion to Nero, from the house of the Augusti. Nero becomes a central figure in several later sibylline books. The mythic portrayal of the emperor as Beliar marks a further rapprochement with apocalyptic imagery.

Not all the sibylline oracles are devoted to political upheavals. *Sib. Or.* 11 is an early oracle, possibly written in the early first century CE.[50] It shares the political interests of the other sibyllines, but is pro-Roman in stance and predicts no political upheaval. This dispassionate attitude is also in evidence in the later Jewish books 12–14. These books show that the oracles, like the apocalypses, could be used in more than one way, in the service of more than one ideology. In fact there are a few oracles in *Sib. Or.* 3:1-45 and the *Sibylline Fragments* that are not concerned with history or politics at all, but with a highly spiritual philosophy.

We will return in a later chapter to examine *Sib. Or.* 4 and 5, books written in the disastrous period between 70 and 132 CE. In these works the affinities with the historical apocalypses are closer than in *Sib. Or.* 3. The entire sibylline tradition remains, however, important background for the apocalypses, since it illustrates a strand of political prophecy that had a considerable impact on one aspect of apocalyptic thought.[51]

---

50. See my introduction to *Sib. Or.* 11 in Charlesworth, ed., *OTP*, 1:430-33; A. Kurfess, *Sibyllinische Weissagungen* (Berlin: Heimeran, 1951) 333-41.

51. See especially B. McGinn, *Visions of the End: Apocalyptic Traditions in the Middle Ages* (New York: Columbia University Press, 1979).

## II. THE TESTAMENTARY LITERATURE

Another literary genre that is closely related to the apocalypses and appears in the Hellenistic age is the testament. A testament is a discourse delivered in anticipation of imminent death. The speaker is typically a father addressing his sons or a leader addressing his people or his successor. The narrative framework describes, in the third person, the situation in which the discourse is delivered and ends with an account of the speaker's death. The actual discourse is delivered in the first person.[52]

Biblical prototypes can be found in the "blessings" of Jacob (Genesis 49) and Moses (Deuteronomy 33–34).[53] The genre was also known, though poorly attested, in the Hellenistic world.[54] The Jewish and Christian pseudepigrapha include testaments of the twelve patriarchs, Isaac, Jacob, Moses, and Job, and the so-called *Visions of Amram* from Qumran cave 4 and the *Testament of Adam* (in part) are close to the testamentary form.[55] Only the testaments of Moses and Job and the *Visions of Amram* can be regarded as Jewish in their present form, but all the others contain substantial Jewish material.[56] In addition, testaments occur as subsidiary forms in several Jewish works: Tobit 14; 1 Macc 2:49-70; *Jubilees* 21, 36; Pseudo-Philo's *Biblical Antiquities* 19, 23–24, 33; *2 Enoch* 39–55; *2 Baruch* 43–47.

52. J. J. Collins, "Testaments," in M. E. Stone, ed., *Jewish Writings of the Second Temple Period* (CRINT 2/2; Assen: Van Gorcum; Philadelphia: Fortress, 1984) 325. E. von Nordheim argues for a more complex definition, including a pattern of historical retrospective, ethical exhortation, and prediction of the future, a pattern typical of the *Testaments of the Twelve Patriarchs;* see von Nordheim, *Die Lehre der Alten,* vol. 1 (Leiden: Brill, 1980).

53. Compare also the last words of Joshua (Joshua 23–24), Samuel (1 Samuel 12), David (1 Kgs 2:1-9; 1 Chronicles 28–29). E. Cortés, *Los discursos de adiós de Gen 49a a Jn 13–17: Pistas para la historia de un género literario en la antigua literatura judía* (Barcelona: Herder, 1976).

54. M. Küchler, *Frühjüdische Weisheitstraditionen* (Göttingen: Vandenhoeck & Ruprecht, 1979) 415-19; E. Lohmeyer, *Diatheke* (Leipzig: Hinrichs, 1913) 32-35.

55. The so-called *Testament of Abraham* is not a testament at all (see Chapter 8). The *Testament of Solomon* is Christian in its present form and bears only a superficial resemblance to the testamentary form. See the overview of the corpus in von Nordheim, *Die Lehre der Alten,* vol. 1.

56. For a review of alleged but dubious fragments of Testaments in the Dead Sea Scrolls see Jörg Frey, "On the Origins of the Genre of the 'Literary Testament': Farewell Discourses in the Qumran Library and Their Relevance for the History of the Genre," in Berthelot and Stökl Ben Ezra, eds., *Aramaica Qumranica,* 345-70.

## The Testament of Moses

The affinities of testaments with apocalypses are most readily obvious in the *Testament of Moses*. This work is known from a single Latin manuscript, published by A. Ceriani in 1861 and identified as the *Assumption of Moses*.[57] In fact, however, this document does not refer to the assumption of Moses but is a prophecy delivered before his death. Accordingly, the dominant opinion of scholars is now that this text corresponds to the work known in antiquity as the *Testament of Moses,* not the *Assumption*.[58] Since the conclusion of the text is missing, it is possible that it originally contained an assumption of Moses too. We should expect that it at least referred to his death.

The *Testament* begins by having Moses summon Joshua and commission him as his successor, since his own death is at hand. Chapters 2–9 then give an extensive prophecy of the history of Israel. Chapter 2 very rapidly surveys the period from the conquest to the exile; chap. 3 deals with the exile as a punishment for sin. Then in chap. 4 "one who is over them" enters to intercede, and the restoration follows. Chapter 5 refers to the rise of kings "who share in their guilt and punish them," and chap. 6 to "kings bearing rule" who will call themselves high priests of God and work iniquity in the holy of holies, followed by "an insolent king," who is evidently Herod. Chapter 7 describes a time of impious and treacherous men, followed in chap. 8 by a persecution. Then a man named Taxo and his seven sons resolve to purify themselves and die rather than break the laws. Chapter 10 prophesies how God's kingdom will then appear. The book concludes with an interchange between Moses and Joshua.

---

57. The basic edition, translation, and commentary are still those of R. H. Charles, *The Assumption of Moses* (London: Black, 1897). See also his treatment in *APOT*, 2:407-24. The identification was based on 1:14, which corresponds to a quotation from the *Assumption of Moses* by Gelasius (*Hist. Eccl.* 2.17.17).

58. See, however, J. Tromp, *The Assumption of Moses: A Critical Edition with Commentary* (SVTP 10; Leiden: Brill, 1992) 115, who warns that the ancient title cannot be inferred from the modern generic label, and defends the title "Assumption of Moses." Both a *Testament* and an *Assumption* are mentioned in the *Stichometry* of Nicephorus and other lists. The *Assumption* referred to a dispute between Michael and the devil, which is alluded to already in the New Testament in Jude, verse 9. The allusion is not identified in Jude but is specified in Clement, Origen, and Gelasius. The traditional title is also retained by N. J. Hofmann, *Die Assumptio Mosis. Studien zur Rezeption massgültiger Überlieferung* (JSJSup 67; Leiden: Brill, 2000).

## Date

In its present form the *Testament of Moses* dates from the early years of the first century CE.[59] Chapter 6 clearly refers to the Hasmoneans (the kings who will call themselves priests), Herod, and the campaign of Varus in 4 BCE (6:8-9, "cohorts and a powerful king of the west will come, who will conquer them, and he will take captives, and burn a part of their temple with fire, and crucify some around their colony").[60] Yet the account that follows in chap. 8 is reminiscent of the persecution of Antiochus Epiphanes: Jews are persecuted because of their circumcision and are forced to participate in idolatry and blasphemy; circumcision is disguised by medical means. Although the correspondence with other accounts of the persecution is not exact, it is more specific than we should expect if this passage were intended as a prophecy of purely future events.[61] Accordingly, R. H. Charles proposed that chaps. 8 and 9 originally stood before chap. 6 and so fitted into the chronological sequence of the book.[62] This proposal is now universally rejected. Not only has it no textual basis, but it also violates the logic of the book, which requires that chap. 10 follow as a response to chaps. 8 and 9.[63] Most probably we should reckon with two stages in the composition of *T. Moses*. The first culminated in the crisis under Antiochus Epiphanes. The second updated the historical review by inserting the references to the Hasmoneans and Herod in chap. 6 and culminated in the partial destruction of the temple by Varus.[64]

59. Tromp, *The Assumption of Moses*, 116-17; J. J. Collins, "The Date and Provenance of the Testament of Moses," in G. W. E. Nickelsburg, ed., *Studies on the Testament of Moses* (Missoula, MT: Scholars Press, 1973) 19-20; J. Priest, "The Testament of Moses," in Charlesworth, ed., *OTP*, 1:920-21; Hofmann, *Die Assumptio Mosis*, 27-30.

60. Tromp, *The Assumption of Moses*, 117, rejects the allusion to Varus.

61. G. W. E. Nickelsburg, "An Antiochan Date for the Testament of Moses," in Nickelsburg, ed., *Studies on the Testament of Moses*, 33-37.

62. Charles, *Assumption of Moses*, 28-30.

63. J. Licht, "Taxo, or the Apocalyptic Doctrine of Vengeance," *JJS* 12 (1961) 95-103.

64. So Nickelsburg, *Jewish Literature between the Bible and the Mishnah*, 74-77. For the arguments see Nickelsburg, ed., *Studies on the Testament of Moses*, 15-43. For literary evidence of the redaction, see A. Yarbro Collins, "Composition and Redaction of the Testament of Moses 10," *HTR* 69 (1976) 179-86. A number of scholars date the whole document to the first century CE, for example, E. Brandenburger, *Himmelfahrt Moses* (JSHRZ 5/2; Gütersloh: Mohn, 1976) 59-60, Hofmann, *Die Assumptio Mosis*, 329; and Tromp, *The Assumption of Moses*, 120-23, who offers a detailed critique of Nickelsburg's arguments.

## Theology

The basic theology of the book is consistent throughout. God created the world on behalf of his people but did not manifest his purpose, in order to confound the Gentiles (1:12-13). The work may be viewed somewhat loosely as a rewriting of Deuteronomy 31–34.[65] The announcement of Moses' death, the commissioning of Joshua, and instructions to preserve the books are all paralleled in Deuteronomy 31. Deuteronomy 32 has a schematic review of history, although it is much less extensive than what we find in *T. Moses* and is not presented as a prediction. Deuteronomy 33, the blessing of Moses, may be said to have eschatological implications for the destiny of Israel, and the account of Moses' death in Deuteronomy 34 was presumably adapted in the lost conclusion of the *Testament.* It is true in any case that history in *T. Moses* is governed by a Deuteronomic pattern of sin and punishment. History falls into two cycles. The first, in chaps. 2–4, extends from the conquest to the Babylonian exile. Although some southern kings broke the covenant, the main sin of this period was the apostasy of the northern tribes, which broke with the Jerusalem temple. Accordingly, the southern tribes complain "inasmuch as you have sinned we too are led away with you." The restoration follows from the intercession of "one who is over them."[66] The second cycle then concerns the postexilic period. Again there is a period of sin (chaps. 5, 7), followed by punishment in the form of persecution. This time Taxo intervenes as mediator, and the eschatological kingdom of God is ushered in.[67] This theology might also be aptly described as covenantal nomism. Salvation comes through

---

65. D. J. Harrington, "Interpreting Israel's History: The Testament of Moses as a Rewriting of Deut 31–34," in Nickelsburg, ed., *Studies on the Testament of Moses,* 59-68; B. Halpern-Amaru, *Rewriting the Bible: Land and Covenant in Postbiblical Jewish Literature* (Valley Forge, PA: Trinity Press International, 1994) 55-68; Hofmann, *Die Assumptio Mosis,* 123-89.

66. Charles (*Assumption of Moses,* 14) identifies this figure as Daniel, but for no good reason. If the figure can be specified at all, he was presumably a leader of the postexilic community, possibly the high priest. Tromp, *The Assumption of Moses,* 174-76, identifies him as Ezra, on the grounds that "Ezra's priestly office and Mosaic character qualify him as an intercessor."

67. The name Taxo (Greek *taxōn*) has been correlated with the Hebrew *měḥōqēq* (S. Mowinckel, "The Hebrew Equivalent of Taxo in Ass. Mos. IX," in *Congress Volume: Copenhagen 1953* [VTSup 1; Leiden: Brill, 1953] 88-96). It means "orderer" and may be roughly equivalent to "one who is over them." For other proposed explanations, see Tromp, *Assumption of Moses,* 124-28.

membership of the Jewish people and requires observance of the law. The pattern of sin and punishment is affirmed even in the face of persecution where the righteous are killed.

## Taxo

The story of Taxo and his sons plays a crucial role in the *Testament of Moses,* since it marks the transition from the persecution to the revelation of God's kingdom. Taxo resolves, "Let us fast for the space of three days and on the fourth let us go into a cave which is in the field, and let us die rather than transgress the commands of the Lord . . . for if we do this and die, our blood will be avenged before the Lord" (9:6-7). The logic of this resolution is supplied by Deut 32:35-43: "Vengeance is mine, and recompense . . . for the Lord will vindicate his people . . . for he avenges the blood of his servants and takes vengeance on his adversaries." The way to bring about a change in the course of history is not by violent rebellion but by moving God to action — specifically by letting oneself be killed rather than break the law. Then God will consecrate an angel to take vengeance on the enemy and will himself rise from his throne and punish the Gentiles.[68] Nature will be thrown into upheavals. Satan will be no more, and Israel will be exalted to the heaven of stars and look down on its enemies in Gehenna. This astral exaltation recalls the destiny of the *maśkîlîm* in Daniel and clarifies the willingness of Taxo to submit to death. The pious Jew can afford to lose his life, if by so doing he ensures his future happiness with the heavenly host.

The attitude represented by Taxo is reminiscent of the story in 1 Macc 2:29-38 of the martyrs who refused to defend themselves on the Sabbath but resolved, "Let us all die in our innocence; heaven and earth testify for us that you are killing us unjustly." (The allusion to heaven and earth again recalls Deuteronomy 32.) We have seen in Chapter 3 that this attitude is close to the stance of Daniel, where the *maśkîlîm* are prepared to lay down their lives in the hope of future glory. It stands in sharp contrast to the model of Phinehas the zealot (Num 25:6-15), which is invoked to justify the action of Mattathias in 1 Maccabees 2. *T. Moses* evidently advocates a policy of nonviolence which emphasizes purity and fidelity to the law, even at the price of death.

---

68. Compare the theophany in *1 Enoch* 1.

## Relation to the Apocalypses

The affinity of *T. Moses* with the apocalypses is most obvious in comparison with Daniel. A major purpose of the *Testament* is to assure the faithful Jews that the world is created for them, despite the contrary appearances in the present. In Daniel too the course of history is mysterious and is only revealed through special revelation. In both documents, the culmination of history is the revelation of a heavenly kingdom, and in both an angel plays a key role in bringing it about. In both books the overview of history is designed to support a stance of martyrdom. The outcome of history will be achieved on the supernatural level. The task of the Jew is one of piety, not militance.

The literary form of the *Testament* is different from that of an apocalypse: it is prophecy uttered by Moses, not an angelic revelation received by him. Even here there are also similarities. One is the use of pseudonymity. The *Testament*, like the apocalypses, is given a weight of authority by its association with a venerable figure of the past. The schematic review of history is also a typical feature of the "historical" apocalypses and conveys the sense that there is indeed a divine design. Yet there is also a significant theological difference between *T. Moses* and either Daniel or *1 Enoch*. The choice of Moses as pseudonym is significant. *T. Moses* is deeply rooted in the covenantal theology of Deuteronomy, and in this respect it is closer to the apocalypses of the late first century CE, *4 Ezra* and *2 Baruch*.[69] Consequently, it is less deterministic than the apocalypses. In both Daniel and the Enochic apocalypses the course of history is set. Humanity can only understand and react. In *T. Moses* the course of history can be changed by human intervention, in the case of the mediator in chap. 4 and of Taxo in chap. 9. True, humanity does not change the course of events directly, but can only persuade God to do so. Yet the *Testament* preserves the interaction of human and divine initiative, which is at the heart of the Deuteronomic theology. This theological difference is not entailed by the literary genres of apocalypse and testament in themselves. Testaments are not necessarily bound to covenantal theology. Rather, the difference reflects the ways in which these genres were actually used in the second century BCE.

---

69. As noted by Hofmann, *Die Assumptio Mosis*, 329.

## The Redaction of the Testament of Moses

The theology of the *Testament of Moses* is not modified by the updating insertion of chap. 6, which denounces the Hasmoneans and Herod.[70] The pacifistic tendency of the work is probably more evident in the later edition. The figure of Taxo suggests a contrast with the portrayal of Mattathias in 1 Maccabees 2.[71] Both are from priestly families. Both are loyal to the law and their fathers and deplore the impiety of the Gentiles. Both exhort their sons to die rather than be guilty of apostasy. However, Mattathias advocates militant resistance. His sons number five; Taxo has the perfect number seven. Mattathias looks to Judas for vengeance; Taxo looks to God. It is not clear how far this contrast would have been evident at the actual time of the revolt, although the basic contrast between militance and martyrdom was inevitable. At the turn of the era, when 1 Maccabees had long been in circulation, the full contrast was surely apparent. We know that the Maccabees served as prototypes for Jewish revolutionaries in the later period.[72] Taxo could now serve as an antitype. The stance of nonviolent resistance flourished in Judaism side by side with the impulse to zealotry throughout the period leading up to the war with Rome.[73]

## The Location in Judaism

The *Testament of Moses* evidently presupposes a division within Israel between those who observe the law and those who do not (12:10-11). It is not apparent that the righteous are organized in a distinct community.[74] In 4:8 we read that after the restoration "the two tribes will continue in their prescribed faith, sad and lamenting because they will not be able to offer sacrifices to the Lord of their fathers." This statement has usually been read as a rejection of the worship of the Second Temple, an attitude that finds possible parallels in the Apocalypse of Weeks, the Animal Apocalypse

---

70. On the revised *Testament of Moses* see Nickelsburg, *Jewish Literature*, 247-48.

71. Collins, "Date and Provenance," 28-29.

72. W. R. Farmer, *Maccabees, Zealots, and Josephus* (New York: Columbia University Press, 1956) 125-58.

73. J. J. Collins, *The Apocalyptic Vision of the Book of Daniel* (HSM 16; Missoula, MT: Scholars Press, 1977) 215-18.

74. Several scholars have ascribed the *Testament* to the Qumran sect. For a defense of this view, see E.-M. Laperrousaz, "Le Testament de Moïse," *Semitica* 19 (1970).

(*1 Enoch* 89:73), and *T. Levi* 16:1.[75] It is possible that the passage refers to those of the two tribes who remain in exile and so are prevented by distance from offering sacrifices.[76] In view of the elliptic nature of the text, it is not possible to be certain.


## The Testaments of the Twelve Patriarchs

The most extensive corpus of testamentary literature from the ancient world is the *Testaments of the Twelve Patriarchs*. This work is certainly Christian in its present form,[77] but there is also no doubt that it incorporates Jewish material.[78] The history of composition is one of the most controversial issues in the current study of the Pseudepigrapha. The traditional view that the *Testaments* were Christian gave way in the nineteenth century to a theory of Jewish composition with Christian interpolations.[79] The dissertation of M. de Jonge in 1953 revived the theory of Christian authorship.[80] De Jonge and his students have strenuously defended this position in recent years.[81] Many scholars, however, continue to reconstruct a Jewish *Grundschrift*, in a Semitic language, which was then expanded in a Greek edition and finally underwent a Christian redaction.[82] In the wake of the discovery of the Qumran scrolls, a number

75. For example, Charles, *Assumption of Moses*, 15.

76. D. R. Schwartz, "The Tribes of As. Mos. 4:7-9," *JBL* 99 (1980) 217-23.

77. Robert A. Kugler, *The Testaments of the Twelve Patriarchs* (Sheffield: Sheffield Academic Press, 2001) 31-38.

78. See James L. Kugel, "Some Translation and Copying Mistakes from the Original Hebrew of the Testaments of the Twelve Patriarchs," in S. Metso, H. Najman, and E. Schuller, ed., *The Dead Sea Scrolls, Transmission of Traditions and Production of Texts* (STDJ 92; Leiden: Brill, 2010) 45-56.

79. H. D. Slingerland, *The Testaments of the Twelve Patriarchs: A Critical History of Research* (SBLMS 21; Missoula, MT: Scholars Press, 1977).

80. M. de Jonge, *The Testaments of the Twelve Patriarchs: A Study of Their Text, Composition and Origin* (Assen: van Gorcum, 1953).

81. M. de Jonge, ed., *Studies on the Testaments of the Twelve Patriarchs: Text and Interpretation* (SVTP 3; Leiden: Brill, 1975); H. W. Hollander and M. de Jonge, *The Testaments of the Twelve Patriarchs: A Commentary* (SVTP 8; Leiden: Brill, 1985).

82. J. Becker, *Die Testamente der zwölf Patriarchen* (JSHRZ 3/1; Gütersloh: Mohn, 1980); idem, *Untersuchungen zur Entstehungsgeschichte der Testamente der zwölf Patriarchen* (Leiden: Brill, 1970); A. Hultgård, *L'Eschatologie des Testaments des Douze Patriarches* (2 vols.; Uppsala: Almqvist & Wiksell, 1977, 1981); H. C. Kee, "The Testaments of the Twelve Patriarchs," in Charlesworth, ed., *OTP*, 1:775-828; J. H. Ulrichsen, *Die Grundschrift der Tes-*

of scholars proposed that the *Testaments* were Essene documents.[83] This proposal has won little acceptance, but we are still far from a consensus on the history of composition.[84]

## Jewish Traditions

The use of Jewish traditions in the *Testaments* is shown by the existence of parallel materials. The exploits of Judah in *T. Judah* 3–7 are paralleled in *Jub.* 34:1-9 and *Midrash Wayissaʿu,* but the similarities appear to derive from a common tradition rather than from direct dependence.[85] A Hebrew *Testament of Naphtali* has been known since the end of the last century. This is definitely not the source of the Greek testament but is a much later document. It is possible that both Greek and Hebrew testaments of Naphtali depend on a common source.[86] A further parallel to *T. Naphtali* 1:6-12, in Hebrew, has been found at Qumran.[87] Aramaic parallels to *T. Levi* from the Cairo Geniza were discovered at the beginning of the century.[88] These

---

*tamente der Zwölf Patriarchen: Eine Untersuchung zu Umfang, Inhalt, und Eigenart der ursprünglichen Schrift* (Stockholm: Almqvist & Wiksell, 1991); James L. Kugel, "Testaments of the Twelve Patriarchs," in Louis H. Feldman, James L. Kugel, and Lawrence H. Schiffman, eds., *Outside the Bible: Ancient Jewish Writings Related to Scripture* (Lincoln: University of Nebraska, 2013) 1697-1700.

83. The main proponents of this view are A. Dupont-Sommer, *Nouveaux aperçus sur les manuscrits de la Mer Morte* (Paris: Maisonneuve, 1953); M. Philonenko, *Les Interpolations chrétiennes des Testaments des Douze Patriarches et les manuscrits de Qoumrân* (Paris: Presses universitaires de France, 1960). Note also the view of D. Flusser, who finds here a fusion of the Essene and Pharisaic outlooks ("The Testaments of the Twelve Patriarchs," *EJ* 13 [1971] 184-86).

84. The issues have been complicated by uncertainties about the text of the *Testaments.* At least there is now a consensus that the Christian elements cannot be removed by textual criticism. For the Greek text, see M. de Jonge, *The Testaments of the Twelve Patriarchs: A Critical Edition of the Greek Text* (Leiden: Brill, 1978).

85. De Jonge, *The Testaments: A Study of Their Text,* 71.

86. This document was published by M. Gaster, "The Hebrew Text of One of the Testaments of the Twelve Patriarchs," in *Proceedings of the Society of Biblical Archeology* (1893-94) 33-49, 109-17. For a recent study, see T. Korteweg, "The Meaning of Naphtali's Visions," in M. de Jonge, ed., *Studies on the Testaments,* 261-90.

87. M. E. Stone, "Testament of Naphtali," in G. Brooke et al., eds., *Qumran Cave 4– XVII: Parabiblical Texts, Part 3* (DJD 22; Oxford: Clarendon, 1996) 73-82.

88. A translation of these fragments and the Hebrew *Testament of Naphtali* can be found in Charles, *APOT,* 2:361-67.

fragments provide a partial parallel to *T. Levi* 8–13 and a remote parallel to *T. Levi* 6. There are also two Greek additions that are inserted into a Mount Athos manuscript of *T. Levi* of the *Testaments of the Twelve Patriarchs* at 2:3 and 18:2. The Greek insert at 18:2 shows extensive agreement with the Aramaic Geniza fragments. An Aramaic fragment from Qumran has been found which corresponds to the Greek addition at 2:3.[89] The Qumran fragments have been held to represent "essentially the same document"[90] as the Aramaic fragments from the Geniza and also show other points of contact with the Greek text of the *Testaments of the Twelve Patriarchs*.[91] From all this it appears that there was an original Aramaic Levi apocryphon which served as a source for the *Testament of Levi*. It is not certain, however, whether the Aramaic Levi material or the Hebrew Naphtali material was in the form of a testament. The *Aramaic Levi Document* is now recognized as an interesting document in its own right, apart from its relation to the *Testament*.[92] If the Qumran Naphtali material represents a *Testament of Naphtali,* then we should suppose that there was a Hebrew *Testaments of the Twelve Patriarchs* in the second century BCE, since Naphtali was such an obscure patriarch.[93] But in fact the extant evidence does not show the literary form of the Qumran fragments. Even if they represent an original *Testaments of the Twelve Patriarchs,* it is apparent that this original document did not correspond exactly to the Greek text that has come down to us. The Aramaic Levi apocryphon contains material that is not found in the Greek testament. On the other hand, no Semitic parallels for the extensive

89. J. T. Milik, "Le Testament de Lévi en araméen: fragment de la grotte 4 de Qumrân," *RB* 62 (1955) 398-406. For the Qumran Levi fragments, see M. E. Stone and J. C. Greenfield, "Aramaic Levi Document," in Brooke et al., eds., *Qumran Cave 4–XVII,* 1-72; M. E. Stone, J. C. Greenfield and E. Eshel, eds., *The Aramaic Levi Document: Edition, Translation, Commentary* (SVTP 19; Leiden: Brill, 2004).

90. M. de Jonge, "Notes on Testament of Levi II–VII," in de Jonge, ed., *Studies on the Testaments,* 256.

91. Ibid., 251-58; Greenfield and Stone, "Aramaic Levi Document," 3. See R. A. Kugler, *From Patriarch to Priest: The Levi-Priestly Tradition from Aramaic Levi to Testament of Levi* (SBLEJL 9; Atlanta: Scholars Press, 1996) 45-53, who cautions against reconstructing the Qumran apocryphon on the basis of the Greek testament.

92. See especially Henryk Drawnel, *An Aramaic Wisdom Text from Qumran: A New Interpretation of the Levi Document* (JSJSup 86; Leiden: Brill, 2004).

93. Fragments of the testaments of Judah, Joseph, and Benjamin have also been identified from Qumran, but they are very scanty and less than certain. See J. T. Milik, "Ecrits préesséniens de Qumrân: d'Henoch à Amram," in M. Delcor, ed., *Qumrân: Sa piété, sa théologie et son milieu* (Leuven: Leuven University Press, 1978) 91-106.

homiletic material in the *Testaments* have been found. Many scholars hold that this material was originally composed in Greek, possibly in the Hellenistic Diaspora.[94] So, while it is clear that the *Testaments* incorporate pre-Christian Jewish material, it is also apparent that the Jewish elements can only be identified tentatively and with caution.

## The Content of the Testaments

The *Testaments of the Twelve Patriarchs* display a consistent pattern which involves three basic elements:[95] (1) historical retrospective, in the form of a narrative about the patriarch's life (*T. Asher* is the only exception); (2) ethical exhortation; and (3) prediction of the future (these predictions often display the so-called sin–exile–return pattern,[96] which is typical of Deuteronomic theology). These elements are logically related. The ethical exhortation is supported by the example of the patriarch's life (which can be a negative example) and by the threats and promises of the future predictions. This logic of persuasion has often been compared with the traditional, Deuteronomic covenant form, where the stipulations of the covenant are given motivation by the recollection of the mighty acts of Yahweh and by the blessings and curses.[97] In the *Testaments,* however, the "historical" segment is replaced by the individual example of the patriarchs, and the ethical sections are oriented toward individual virtues (e.g., chastity, simplicity) rather than the societal emphases of the Pentateuchal laws. The covenantal nomism of the *Testaments* is most obvious in the so-called sin–exile–return passages, which posit a strict correlation between obedience to the law and prosperity in the land.[98] This pattern, too, has an evident hortatory purpose. The *Testaments of the Twelve Patriarchs* are vehicles for paraenesis in a much more explicit way than is the *Testament*

---

94. Becker, *Die Testamente,* 23-27; H. W. Hollander, *Joseph as an Ethical Model in the Testaments of the Twelve Patriarchs* (SVTP 6; Leiden: Brill, 1981) 92. See also K.-W. Niebuhr, *Gesetz und Paränese* (WUNT 28; Tübingen: Mohr Siebeck, 1987) 84-86, who emphasizes the uncertainty of provenance, but discusses the parenetic material largely in the context of Diaspora traditions.

95. For a detailed analysis, see von Nordheim, *Die Lehre der Alten,* vol. 1, 89-107.

96. M. de Jonge, *The Testaments: A Study of Their Text,* 83-86.

97. See especially K. Baltzer, *The Covenant Formulary* (Philadelphia: Fortress, 1971).

98. *T. Issachar* 6; *T. Levi* 10, 14–15, 16; *T. Judah* 23; *T. Zebulun* 9:5-7; *T. Dan* 5:4, 8-9; *T. Naphtali* 4; *T. Asher* 7; *T. Benjamin* 9:1-2.

*of Moses,* where the exhortation is conveyed indirectly through the review of history and the story of Taxo. In the *Testaments of the Twelve Patriarchs* the ethical message is made fully explicit, and at great length. Hence some scholars have argued that the *Testaments* can be viewed as an offshoot of the wisdom literature.[99]

## The Apocalyptic Elements

The *Testaments* are clearly not apocalypses in form. Their framework is the address of a father to his sons, not the transmission of supernatural revelation by an angel. The covenantal theology of the *Testaments of the Twelve Patriarchs* is rather different from what we have found in *1 Enoch* and Daniel, although the theological difference is not necessarily required by the genres. In *1 Enoch* and Daniel the course of events is set and cannot be changed. In the *Testaments* the course of events is determined by human actions. The extent of the explicit hortatory material in the *Testaments* is also without parallel in the apocalypses. Yet there are also noteworthy similarities, beginning with the obvious use of pseudonymity, by which a name from venerable antiquity is used to lend authority to the message.

Although the instruction of the patriarch is usually based on his own experience, there are occasional appeals to higher authority. Prophecies of the future, especially of the sins of the Israelites, are often said to be derived from the writings of Enoch. Allusions to Enoch are found in approximately half the *Testaments.*[100] Correspondence with the actual book of *Enoch* is never precise,[101] but there are enough prophecies of wickedness in all the

---

99. So Küchler, *Frühjüdische Weisheitstraditionen,* 415-545; von Nordheim, *Die Lehre der Alten,* vol. 1, 11. On the role of the sapiential elements in the *Testaments,* see also J. J. Collins, "Wisdom, Apocalyptic, and Generic Compatibility," in L. G. Perdue, B. B. Scott, and W. J. Wiseman, eds., *In Search of Wisdom: Essays in Memory of John G. Gammie* (Louisville: Westminster John Knox, 1993) 178-79 (= *Seers, Sibyls, and Sages,* 385-408).

100. *T. Simeon* 5:4; *T. Levi* 10:5; 14:1; 16:1; *T. Judah* 18:1; *T. Zebulun* 3:4; *T. Dan* 5:6; *T. Naphtali* 4:1; *T. Benjamin* 9:1; 10:6. The reference in *T. Zebulun* is to the "law of Enoch." This is surely an error. A number of manuscripts more plausibly read the "law of Moses."

101. For example, in *Testament of Levi* 16:1 Levi claims to have read in the book of *Enoch* that his descendants will err for seventy weeks. The clearest allusion to seventy weeks (of years) is in Daniel's reinterpretation of Jeremiah, but compare the seventy shepherds in the Animal Apocalypse and the schema of weeks in the Apocalypse of Weeks. In *Testament of Levi* 17 the seventy weeks are understood as seven jubilees, thereby corresponding to the first seven weeks in the Apocalypse of Weeks.

early Enoch writings to provide a general context for the allusions. It is noteworthy that what is attributed to the Enoch literature is primarily historical and eschatological prediction.

## The Ascent of Levi

The patriarchs can also claim on occasion to be recipients of revelation themselves. So Asher claims to know what is written in the tablets of heaven (2:10; 7:5) and Naphtali has two visions in which he learns about the future. The main instances of apocalyptic revelation are found in *T. Levi*. In chapters 2–5 we find a full-blown apocalypse. The heavens were opened and an angel of God called on Levi to enter. This ascent-vision has been thought to be based on the ascent of Enoch in *1 Enoch* 14–16.[102] It differs from that vision markedly by enumerating the heavens. The cosmology has evidently undergone a process of growth. In chap. 2 Levi sees three heavens and is promised that he will see four more. Chap. 3 speaks of seven heavens, but the highest heaven, where God resides, is mentioned fourth in the sequence.[103] Chapter 3, in particular, is close to the orderly sequence of heavens that we will later find in *2 Enoch* and *3 Baruch*. There is little evidence of Christian influence in these chapters.[104] The Aramaic Levi apocryphon from Qumran is relevant to the context in chap. 2, but does not contain the enumeration of the heavens. Consequently, we cannot be sure how much of this material was derived from the Aramaic source. Our other Jewish attestations of a numbered sequence of heavens are thought to come from the Diaspora in the first century CE. It is quite possible that Levi's ascent also attained its final form in the Diaspora or in the Christian redaction of the *Testaments*.[105]

*T. Levi* 3 is atypical of the *Testaments* in its interest in cosmological speculation and the angelic world. Even here an eschatological focus is

---

102. Nickelsburg, *Jewish Literature*, 236; idem, "Enoch, Levi, and Peter: Recipients of Revelation in Upper Galilee," *JBL* 100 (1981) 575-600.

103. The textual tradition on these chapters is confused. See Charles, *APOT*, 2:304-6; de Jonge, *The Testaments: A Critical Edition*, 24-29.

104. A possible Christian reference is found in 2:11: "through you and Judah, the Lord will be seen among men, saving among them the whole race of men."

105. See especially A. Yarbro Collins, "The Seven Heavens in Jewish and Christian Apocalypses," in eadem, *Cosmology and Eschatology in Jewish and Christian Apocalypticism* (Leiden: Brill, 1996) 25-30.

also present. In the third heaven are the heavenly armies, drawn up for the day of judgment to do vengeance on Beliar and the spirits of deception. Chapter 4 describes the cosmic upheaval of the day of judgment. Levi is separated from injustice and made a son and servant of God. In chap. 5 he is commissioned as priest in a supplementary vision, "until I come and dwell in the midst of Israel." Then he is given a sword to punish Shechem for the rape of Dinah.

It would appear that the primary purpose of this little apocalypse is to legitimate Levi as priest and one chosen by God. The legitimation presumably extends to his successors, and so elevates the office of the priesthood. Another vision that describes the investiture of Levi as priest by seven angelic "men" follows in *T. Levi* 8. In view of the complex history of the development of the *Testaments,* it is difficult to determine the historical setting for which these visions were designed, especially since, as we have seen, there is evidence of multiple layers in chap. 3. A clue to one possible setting is provided in 5:3, when the angel brings Levi back to earth, gives him a sword, and tells him to take vengeance on Shechem. We are further told that the destruction of the sons of Hamor had been written on the heavenly tablets. This heavenly justification of the destruction of Shechem must be seen in the context of Jewish-Samaritan hostility, which culminated in the destruction of Shechem and Mount Gerizim by John Hyrcanus. R. H. Charles regarded this passage as evidence of a pro-Hasmonean ideology and as a clue to the date of the *Testaments.*[106] This view now seems less likely, because of the links of the Levi tradition with the Qumran sect. The sectarians would hardly have been receptive to Hasmonean propaganda. In fact hostility to the Samaritans was not peculiarly Hasmonean. Ben Sira 50:26 already refers to "the foolish people that lives in Shechem," a phrase that is echoed in *T. Levi* 7:2. The biblical story of the sack of Shechem is retold in several Jewish sources, from *Jubilees* 30 to Josephus (*Antiquities* 1.21.1-2 [§§337–41), and is always justified.[107] The *Testaments* show many points of contact with *Jubilees,* where the sack of Shechem is also associated with the priesthood of Levi.[108] Much light

---

106. Charles, *APOT,* 2:289-90. For criticism of some of Charles's arguments, see J. J. Collins, *The Scepter and the Star: Messianism in Light of the Dead Sea Scrolls* (2d ed.; Grand Rapids: Eerdmans, 2010) 102-3.

107. See J. J. Collins, "The Epic of Theodotus and the Hellenism of the Hasmoneans," *HTR* 73 (1980) 91-104.

108. In *Jub.* 30:18 Levi is chosen as priest after his zealous action against Shechem, after the manner of Phinehas in Numbers 25. In *Testament of Levi* 6 the appointment to

would be thrown on the setting of this apocalypse if we knew the full extent of the Levi apocryphon from Qumran. Whatever the original setting of *T. Levi* 2–5 may have been, the text evidently lends itself to legitimating the institution of the priesthood and the use of violence — against Shechem in particular or, by analogy, against unbelievers. It is noteworthy that an apocalyptic vision can thus be used to support the use of power, just as well as to express rebellion or dissent.

## *The Eschatological Sections*

Significant analogies with the historical apocalypses are also found in the passages in the *Testaments* which involve future predictions. As we have noted, the sin–exile–return passages are firmly rooted in the Deuteronomic tradition. However, they typically culminate in an eschatological scenario that involves Beliar, messianic expectation, and the resurrection of the dead.

Beliar is mentioned in every testament except *T. Gad,* and Satan is mentioned there. Over against Beliar stands the angel of peace. In *T. Judah* 20:1 two spirits lie in wait for man, that of truth and that of error. These spirits are primarily the agents of an ongoing ethical dualism, but they also have eschatological roles: "The ends of men show their righteousness when they encounter the angels of the Lord and of Satan. For if the soul departs troubled, it is tortured by the evil spirit, which it also served, . . . but if it is peacefully and joyfully greeted by the angel of peace, he will summon it to life" (*T. Asher* 6:4-6). In *T. Levi* 18:12 Beliar will be bound by the eschatological priest. In *T. Judah* 25:3 he will be cast into fire forever.

The resemblance to the apocalypses in all of this lies in the idea that supernatural forces direct and influence human actions. In Daniel, this role was filled by the patron angels of the nations and by the contrasting symbols of the beasts and "one like a son of man." In *1 Enoch,* the Watchers and the angels were such supernatural powers. In the *Testaments* the forces of evil come to a focus in the single figure of Beliar, who attains a greater universality than the historically specific beasts of Daniel. The closest parallels

---

priesthood comes first. In *Jubilees* the main point of the story is a polemic against intermarriage with the Gentiles. On the complex relationship between *Jubilees* and the Aramaic Levi apocryphon, see J. Kugel, "Levi's Elevation to the Priesthood in Second Temple Writings," *HTR* 86 (1993) 1-64; Kugler, *From Patriarch to Priest,* 139-69.

to the *Testaments* are found in the Qumran scrolls, where the *Community Rule* (1QS) contrasts the Spirit of Light and the Spirit of Darkness and the *War Scroll* prepares for an eschatological battle between Belial, leading the Sons of Darkness, and Michael, leading the Sons of Light. The *Testaments* lack the strong deterministic note that we will find in the scrolls. *T. Asher* emphasizes that men are free to choose between the two ways. The Qumran *Community Rule* suggests that humanity is already divided into two lots, although in practice a choice would still seem to be required.

We cannot be sure at what point this metaphysical dualism was introduced into the *Testaments*. Similar conceptions are found in early Christianity, notably in *Barnabas* 18–21, where the angels of God and the angels of Satan preside over the ways of Light and Darkness.[109] The role of Beliar does not tie the *Testaments* directly to the Qumran sect but illustrates how such ideas were diffused in ancient Judaism and early Christianity. The dualistic contrast of supernatural forces can indeed be viewed as a development of the mythological symbolism of the early apocalypses. It was given a distinctive expression at Qumran, where, as we shall see, Persian influence was also possible. In the case of Qumran this dualism carried deterministic overtones. The *Testaments* show that it could also be used to undergird a vigorous ethic of free choice.

## Messianic Expectation

The most striking characteristic of the expectation of the *Testaments* is the association of the messiah with both Levi and Judah.[110] These two patriarchs have a leading role throughout.[111] They are ranked first and second in the resurrection (*T. Judah* 25:1) and elsewhere (e.g., *T. Reuben* 6:7; *T. Gad* 8:2; *T. Issachar* 5:7). Not all passages that speak of the leadership of Levi and Judah are messianic. Some affirm Levi's priesthood and Judah's kingship. Others speak of salvation which is to come from Levi and Judah (*T. Dan* 5:10; *T. Naphtali* 8:2). Others refer more explicitly to messianic expectation. In *T. Simeon* 7:2 the Lord "will raise up from Levi as it were a

---

109. Compare also Hermas, *Mandates.* See J.-P. Audet, "Affinités littéraires et doctrinales du 'Manuel de Discipline,'" *RB* 59 (1952) 219-38; 60 (1953) 41-82.

110. The term "messiah" is not actually used in the *Testaments*. I use it to refer to an eschatological savior figure who is human rather than angelic. On the terminological issue, see further Collins, *The Scepter and the Star*, 16-18.

111. De Jonge, *The Testaments: A Study of Their Text*, 86-89.

chief priest and from Judah as it were a king, god and man. He will save all the nations and the race of Israel." Similarly in *T. Joseph* 19:6 the children of Joseph are to honor Levi and Judah because from them will arise the Lamb of God who will save all the nations and Israel by grace. *T. Levi* 18 focuses on the priestly figure. He will be a "new priest," but his star will rise in heaven like a king. He will open the gates of paradise and bind Belial. *T. Judah* 24 speaks of a man from the seed of Judah. The heavens will be opened for him and no sin will be found in him. He will save all who call upon the Lord among the Gentiles. Christian influence is obvious in these messianic passages.

In their final form the *Testaments* envisage one messiah, who is associated with both Levi and Judah and is evidently identified as Christ.[112] Since the messiah is associated with both these tribes and they are both singled out for leadership, it is probable that the *Testaments* adapt an earlier Jewish expectation of two messiahs. The main parallel for such a conception is found in the Qumran scrolls, which speak of messiahs from Aaron and Israel. Precedent for such dual leadership is found in the organization of the early postexilic community, as attested by the two "sons of oil" in Zechariah 4. Already in Zechariah, and throughout the postexilic period, the chief priest played the predominant role, and this is also the case in the *Testaments*.[113] Levi always takes precedence. *T. Judah* 21:2 explicitly says that God made the kingship subordinate to the priesthood. Both Levi and Judah are also singled out for special prominence in the blessing of Jacob in *Jubilees* 31.[114] It would seem then that the theme of dual leadership had emerged in Judaism in the second century BCE, before the rise of the Dead Sea sect. It should be emphasized, however, that the messianic passages in the Greek *Testaments of the Twelve Patriarchs* have clear Christian traits, and so the reconstruction of the underlying Jewish tradition must be very tentative.

Messianic expectation plays scarcely any role in the early apocalypses, which rely rather on angelic deliverance. (Only in the Animal Apocalypse does a human leader have a prominent role.) The primary expectation of a priestly messiah in the *Testaments* would seem to have

---

112. M. de Jonge, "Two Messiahs in the Testaments of the Twelve Patriarchs?" in idem, *Jewish Eschatology, Early Christian Christology, and the Testaments of the Twelve Patriarchs* (Leiden: Brill, 1991) 191-203.

113. Hultgård, *L'Eschatologie*, 1:64-68.

114. J. C. VanderKam, "Jubilees and the Priestly Messiah of Qumran," *RevQ* 13 (1988) 363-64; Collins, *The Scepter and the Star*, 95-96.

arisen in reaction to the corruption of the priesthood in the Maccabean era. The great prophecy of the "new priest" in *T. Levi* 18 comes at the end of a prophecy that divides history into seventy weeks, or seven jubilees, a schema that corresponds to the first seven weeks in the Apocalypse of Weeks. The seventh jubilee is marked by the sins of the priests: idolatry, violence, greed, licentiousness. It is not clear from *T. Levi* whether the entire postexilic period is corrupt, but at least the final jubilee stands out from the rest. At its end the old priesthood will lapse and God will send the new priest. He will also be the recipient of revelation and have attributes of judge and king,[115] but the motif of kingship may well have been introduced by the Christian redactor. It has been suggested that the dual leadership of Levi and Judah was developed in protest against the combination of priestly and political power by the Hasmonean priest kings.[116] This rationale may also have inspired the distinction of the messiahs of Aaron and Israel at Qumran.

A number of the *Testaments* conclude with a prediction of resurrection.[117] Although the earliest clear attestations of afterlife and resurrection in Judaism are found in the apocalypses of Enoch and Daniel, the belief became widespread and does not necessarily imply the full apocalyptic worldview. Nonetheless, these passages constitute another point of similarity between the *Testaments* and the apocalypses.

Our discussion of the *Testaments of the Twelve Patriarchs* is necessarily inconclusive in view of the uncertainty of the history of composition. The final, Christian *Testaments* evidently incorporated material from various sources. Some of this material might be designated "apocalyptic" because of its similarity to what we find in the apocalypses, and *T. Levi* even includes an apocalypse in the account of Levi's ascent. Moreover, some sources of the *Testaments,* including the Aramaic Levi apocryphon, were closely related to the Enoch literature and *Jubilees* and to the Qumran scrolls. The *Testaments,* then, are witnesses to apocalypticism in the broader sense, although they are not in the form of apocalypses.

---

115. Hultgård, *L'Eschatologie,* 1:268-90. Also his "The Ideal 'Levite,' the Davidic Messiah, and the Saviour Priest in the Testaments of the Twelve Patriarchs," in G. W. E. Nickelsburg and J. J. Collins, eds., *Ideal Figures in Ancient Judaism: Profiles and Paradigms* (SBLSCS 12; Chico, CA: Scholars Press, 1980) 93-110.

116. Hultgård, *L'Eschatologie,* 1:68; Collins, *The Scepter and the Star,* 107-8.

117. *T. Judah* 25; *T. Benjamin* 10:6-10; *T. Zebulun* 10:1-4; *T. Simeon* 6:7. Afterlife is also implied in *T. Levi* 18:10-14.

## Messianism in the Psalms of Solomon

The "new priest" is complemented in the *Testaments* by the man from Judah, the star that will arise from Jacob according to Balaam's oracle in Numbers 24. This figure has rightly been identified as the Davidic messiah.[118] Clear messianic references are rare in the Jewish Pseudepigrapha. Apart from the complex evidence of the *Testaments,* the only passage dealing with the Davidic messiah in the Pseudepigrapha that can be dated before the turn of the era is found in the *Psalms of Solomon* 17–18.[119] The evidence of the Dead Sea Scrolls, however, shows that messianic expectation became widespread from the first century BCE, and that it was often expressed by allusion to such texts as Balaam's oracle and Isaiah 11.[120]

The *Psalms of Solomon* are only remotely related to the apocalyptic literature, and so are of marginal interest in this study. They contain nothing of the apocalyptic manner of revelation and show no interest in the angelic or heavenly world. They attest a belief in afterlife (3:12; 13:11; 14:3; 15:13; 16:1-3), but the primary focus of the eschatology is on the restoration of Jerusalem, which will be brought about by the Davidic messiah.[121] The *Psalms* were written in the wake of Pompey's conquest of Jerusalem in 63 BCE. In part the figure of the messiah is a counter to the Roman general (who is given a mythical connotation by being called a dragon in 2:25). However, the *Psalms* also insist that Jerusalem was punished because of the sins of the Jews: "From the chief of them to the least of them the people were in complete sinfulness. The king was in transgression, the judge in disobedience, and the people in sin" (17:20). Those that "loved the synagogues of the pious" (presumably the circles that produced the *Psalms*) had to flee from this wickedness. The *Psalms* repeatedly castigate the arrogance of the rich. Not least among their crimes was the fact that they set up a king who was not from the Davidic line (17:6-7). It appears that

---

118. Hultgård, *L'Eschatologie,* 1:69.

119. J. H. Charlesworth, "The Concept of the Messiah in the Pseudepigrapha," in W. Haase and H. Temporini, eds., *ANRW* II.19.1 (1979) 188-218.

120. Collins, *The Scepter and the Star,* 52-78.

121. Kenneth Atkinson, *I Cried to the Lord: A Study of the Psalms of Solomon's Historical Background and Social Setting* (JSJSup 84; Leiden: Brill, 2004); Antti Laato, *A Star Is Rising: The Historical Development of the Old Testament Royal Ideology and the Rise of the Jewish Messianic Expectations* (Atlanta: Scholars Press, 1997); Loren Stuckenbruck, "Messianic Ideas in the Apocalyptic and Related Literature of Early Judaism," in Stanley Porter, ed., *The Messiah in the Old and New Testaments* (Grand Rapids: Eerdmans, 2007) 93-97.

the hope for a Davidic messiah was inspired in large part by opposition to the Hasmonean monarchy (as may also be true in the *Testaments* and at Qumran). Because of their general theology, the *Psalms* are often ascribed to Pharisaic circles.[122]

The portrait of the messiah echoes the language of the canonical Psalms (especially Psalm 2) and Isaiah.[123] He will at once subdue and save the nations. The traditions embodied in this picture are largely independent of the apocalyptic literature. In the first century CE, however, this traditional picture of the messiah was increasingly integrated into the apocalyptic scenario, as we will find in the Similitudes of Enoch, 4 Ezra, and *2 Baruch*.[124]

---

122. G. B. Gray, "The Psalms of Solomon," in Charles, *APOT*, 2:630; Nickelsburg, *Jewish Literature*, 212; J. Schüpphaus, *Die Psalmen Salomos* (Leiden: Brill, 1977) 127-37; M. Winninge, *Sinners and the Righteous: A Comparative Study of the Psalms of Solomon and Paul's Letters* (Stockholm: Almqvist & Wiksell, 1995) 158-80.

123. Kenneth Atkinson, *An Intertextual Study of the Psalms of Solomon* (Lewiston, NY: Mellen, 2001) 336-41. On the portrait of the messiah, see further G. L. Davenport, "The 'Anointed of the Lord' in Psalms of Solomon 17," in Nickelsburg and Collins, eds., *Ideal Figures*, 67-92. See further Collins, *The Scepter and the Star*, 57-60; K. E. Pomykala, *The Davidic Dynasty Tradition in Early Judaism: Its History and Significance for Messianism* (SBLEJL 7; Atlanta: Scholars Press, 1995) 159-70; Winninge, *Sinners and the Righteous*, 89-109.

124. On the integration of messianism into apocalyptic literature, see U. B. Müller, *Messias und Menschensohn in jüdischen Apokalypsen und in der Offenbarung des Johannes* (Gütersloh: Mohn, 1972).

# CHAPTER FIVE

# The Dead Sea Scrolls

The discovery of the Dead Sea Scrolls has shed new light on several aspects of postbiblical Judaism, not least on the area of Jewish apocalypticism.[1] This new light has been twofold. On the one hand, the early Enoch manuscripts have revised our understanding of the origin and early development of apocalyptic literature. On the other hand, there are obvious similarities between the newly discovered sectarian documents and what we find in the apocalypses, especially in their interest in the angelic world and in their eschatology. So Qumran has been dubbed "an apocalyptic community" and held to offer a unique opportunity to study the institutional setting of apocalyptic thought.[2]

Now that the full corpus of the scrolls is in the public domain, it is clear that not all the documents found at Qumran were products of a single community or of the Essene sect. Apart from biblical texts, some apocryphal and pseudepigraphic works are older than the Qumran settlement and were also transmitted independently of the scrolls. These include the oldest Enoch apocalypses (all the major sections of *1 Enoch* except

---

1. A fuller treatment of the themes of this chapter can be found in J. J. Collins, *Apocalypticism in the Dead Sea Scrolls* (London: Routledge, 1997). See also Michael A. Knibb, "Apocalypticism and Messianism," in Lim and Collins, eds., *The Oxford Handbook of the Dead Sea Scrolls*, 403-32, and the essays in Jörg Frey and Michael Becker, eds., *Apokalyptik und Qumran* (Paderborn: Bonifatius, 2007).

2. F. M. Cross, *The Ancient Library of Qumran* (3d ed.; Sheffield: Sheffield Academic Press, 1995) 68-70. See J. J. Collins, "Was the Dead Sea Sect an Apocalyptic Community?" in L. H. Schiffman, ed., *Archaeology and History in the Dead Sea Scrolls: The New York University Conference in Memory of Yigael Yadin* (Sheffield: JSOT Press, 1990) 25-51 (= *Seers, Sibyls, and Sages*, 261-86).

for the Similitudes) and *Jubilees*. Even works that were not known before the discovery of the scrolls are not necessarily sectarian in origin. The *Genesis Apocryphon* and the *Words of the Heavenly Luminaries* are cases in point. Nonetheless, there remains a core of major sectarian writings which can be identified as the products of one movement (but not necessarily of a single community).[3] These include the *Community Rule,* the *Damascus Document,* the *War Rule,* the *pesharim* or biblical commentaries, and the *Hôdāyôt* or *Thanksgiving Hymns.* The movement that produced these writings is still most plausibly identified as the Essene sect, described by Josephus and Philo, although the correspondence between the scrolls and these accounts is by no means complete.[4] Philo and Josephus most probably drew on second-hand sources,[5] and either they or their sources tailored their accounts of the Jewish texts to Hellenistic tastes.[6] In fact, most of the apocalyptic elements that we find in the scrolls are absent from the Greek accounts.[7] The only point at which these accounts enter into our discussion here concerns the belief in life after death and the disputed question of resurrection.

The fact that the books of Daniel, *Enoch,* and *Jubilees* are all found in multiple copies at Qumran, and seem to be regarded as authoritative writings, already bespeaks an interest in apocalyptic revelations. There is surely some continuity between the sect and the movements attested in *Enoch,* and there are marked similarities between *Jubilees* and the scrolls. Gabriele Boccaccini has gone so far as to claim that "Enochic Judaism

3. For an attempt to establish criteria for distinguishing sectarian works, see C. A. Newsom, " 'Sectually Explicit' Literature from Qumran," in W. H. Propp, B. Halpern, and D. N. Freedman, eds., *The Hebrew Bible and Its Interpreters* (Winona Lake, IN: Eisenbrauns, 1990) 167-87.

4. J. J. Collins, *Beyond the Qumran Community: The Sectarian Movement of the Dead Sea Scrolls* (Grand Rapids: Eerdmans, 2010) 122-65; J. C. VanderKam, *The Dead Sea Scrolls Today* (2d ed.; Grand Rapids: Eerdmans, 2010) 97-119.

5. See R. Bergmeier, *Die Essener-Berichte des Flavius Josephus* (Kampen: Kok Pharos, 1993); Collins, *Beyond the Qumran Community,* 133-38.

6. The main accounts are found in Josephus, *Jewish War* 2.8.2–13 §§119–61; Philo, *Quod omnis probus liber sit* 75-91. See G. Vermes and M. D. Goodman, eds., *The Essenes according to the Classical Sources* (Sheffield: JSOT Press, 1989); T. S. Beall, *Josephus' Description of the Essenes Illustrated by the Dead Sea Scrolls* (Cambridge: Cambridge University Press, 1988).

7. This is true of Josephus' account of Judaism as a whole. See Arnaldo Momigliano, "What Josephus Did Not See," in idem, *Essays on Ancient and Modern Judaism* (Chicago: University of Chicago Press, 1994) 67-78.

is the modern name for the mainstream body of the Essene party, from which the Qumran community parted as a radical, dissident, and marginal offspring."[8] But there are also significant points of continuity with Daniel.[9] Consequently, many scholars have subscribed to the view that the Dead Sea sect (= the Essenes) originated as a faction within the Hasidim of the Maccabean period, and that the Pharisees originated as another faction.[10] It is by no means certain, however, that all the apocalyptic literature of the early second century BCE pertains to a single movement or that its relation to the scrolls is necessarily genetic. Besides, the scrolls show many other sources of influence (including sapiential and priestly traditions) besides the apocalypses. The apocalypticism of Qumran brings together traditions derived from the books of *Enoch* and Daniel with a fundamental interest in the Torah, especially in its halakhic or legal aspects.[11] Consequently, the people of the scrolls should not be identified too closely with any one party of the Maccabean period, such as the Hasidim, or the Enoch tradition.

The books of Daniel and Enoch were not the only apocalyptic writings preserved among the Scrolls. Two other Aramaic texts mention Daniel (4Q243-44; 4Q245).[12] Both contain extended prophecies of history, written

8. Boccaccini, *Beyond the Essene Hypothesis*, 16. See also Boccaccini, "Enochians, Urban Essenes, Qumranites," in Boccaccini and Collins, eds., *The Early Enoch Literature*, 301-27. See my critique of Boccaccini's theses: "'Enochic Judaism' and the Sect of the Dead Sea Scrolls," in Boccaccini and Collins, eds., *The Early Enoch Literature*, 283-99; reprinted in Collins, *Scriptures and Sectarianism, Essays on the Dead Sea Scrolls* (WUNT 332; Tübingen: Mohr Siebeck, 2014) 150-63. D. Dimant, "Qumran Sectarian Literature," in M. E. Stone, ed., *Jewish Writings of the Second Temple Period* (CRINT 2/2; Assen: Van Gorcum; Philadelphia: Fortress, 1984) 483-550, would identify the movement in the Animal Apocalypse of *1 Enoch* with the early Essenes.

9. See especially F. García Martínez, "Qumran Origins and Early History: A Groningen Hypothesis," *Folia Orientalia* 25 (1988) 113-36; John J. Collins, "The Book of Daniel and the Dead Sea Scrolls," in Nóra Dávid et al., eds., *The Hebrew Bible in Light of the Dead Sea Scrolls* (FRLANT 239; Göttingen: Vandenhoeck & Ruprecht, 2012) 203-17, reprinted in *Scriptures and Sectarianism*, 102-15.

10. Scholars who subscribe to this view, with minor variations, include F. M. Cross, M. Hengel, and G. Vermes. See especially H. Stegemann, *Die Entstehung der Qumrangemeinde* (Bonn: printed privately, 1971). For a survey, see P. Callaway, *The History of the Qumran Community: An Investigation* (Sheffield: JSOT Press, 1988).

11. On the fundamental halakhic interests of the Dead Sea Scrolls, see especially L. H. Schiffman, *Reclaiming the Dead Sea Scrolls: The History of Judaism, the Background of Christianity, the Lost Library of Qumran* (Philadelphia: Jewish Publication Society, 1994).

12. John J. Collins and Peter W. Flint, "243-245. 4QpsDaniel[a-c]," in George J. Brooke et al., eds., *Qumran Cave IV. XVII* (DJD XXII; Oxford: Oxford University Press, 1996) 95-164.

after the fact (*ex eventu*). It is not apparent that either depends directly on the canonical Book of Daniel, and their view of history seems somewhat different.[13] Another Aramaic text predicts the advent of a figure who will be called the Son of God, and who should be identified with the Davidic messiah.[14] In this case several phrases recall the biblical Book of Daniel (e.g. "his kingdom will be an everlasting kingdom"), and it is possible that the text is an interpretation of the vision in Daniel 7, but this cannot be shown conclusively. All these texts are fragmentary, and crucial elements are missing at the beginnings and ends, so that it is difficult to determine their genre with any precision, although they obviously bear some affinity to the Daniel tradition.[15]

Also fragmentary are compositions related to Jeremiah (*Apocryphon of Jeremiah C*) and Ezekiel (*4QPseudo-Ezekiel*), preserved in 4Q383-91.[16] There is controversy as to just how many texts should be distinguished in this lot. At one time the editor, Devorah Dimant, distinguished a third text, which she called Pseudo-Moses, exemplified in 4Q390, but she changed her mind in the official edition. 4Q390 resembles apocalypses of the historical type insofar as it divides history into jubilees.[17] Bennie Reynolds has argued that 4Q390 is part of the Jeremianic text, but not integrated with the other fragments (compare Daniel 7-12 where the different textual units are formally distinct).[18] Kipp Davis argues that 4Q390 represents a later reinterpretation of the Apocryphon.[19] Eibert Tigchelaar concludes that "a construction of Apocryphon of Jeremiah C which contains both

---

13. Lorenzo DiTommaso, "4QPseudo-Daniel[a-b] (4Q243-244) and the Book of Daniel," *DSD* 12 (2005) 101-33.

14. Émile Puech, "246. 4QApocryphe de Daniel ar," in Brooke et al., DJD 22, 165-84; Adela Y. Collins and John J. Collins, *King and Messiah as Son of God* (Grand Rapids: Eerdmans, 2008) 65-74.

15. On the Aramaic apocalyptic writings from Qumran see now Andrew Perrin, *The Dynamics of Dream-Vision Revelation in the Aramaic Dead Sea Scrolls* (JAJSup 19; Göttingen: Vandenhoeck & Ruprecht, 2015).

16. Devorah Dimant, *Qumran Cave 4. XXI. Parabiblical Texts, Part 4: Pseudo-Prophetic Texts* (DJD 30; Oxford: Oxford University Press, 2000); Neujahr, *Predicting the Past,* 163-80.

17. Lorenzo DiTommaso refers to this kind of historical overview as "apocalyptic historiography." DiTommaso, "The Development of Apocalyptic Historiography in Light of the Dead Sea Scrolls," in P. W. Flint, J. Duhaime, and K. S. Baek, eds., *Celebrating the Dead Sea Scrolls: A Canadian Collection* (Leiden: Brill, 2012), 497-522.

18. Reynolds, *Between Symbolism and Realism,* 268.

19. C. J. Patrick Davis, "Torah-Performance and History in the *Golah*: Rewritten Bible or 'Re-Presentational' Authority in the *Apocryphon of Jeremiah C*," in Flint, Duhaime, and Baek, eds., *Celebrating the Dead Sea Scrolls: A Canadian Collection,* 467-95, esp. 468-72.

4Q390 and the other Apocryphon manuscripts should be rejected."[20] Here again it is difficult to determine whether the text should be regarded as an apocalypse because of the fragmentary condition of the text. The Ezekielian fragment (4Q385-86) appears to understand Ezekiel 37 as referring to the resurrection of individuals rather than to the communal restoration of Israel as envisioned in the biblical text.[21]

Related to the Enoch tradition are nine fragmentary manuscripts of the Book of Giants, one of which (4Q530) contains a vision of the divine throne that has close parallels in Daniel 7 and 1 Enoch 14.[22]

Also of note is a fragmentary Aramaic text called *4QFour Kingdoms*[a-b] *ar* (4Q552-53) in which four kingdoms are symbolized as four trees.[23] The motif of four kingdoms is familiar from the book of Daniel, where they are identified as Babylon, Media, Persia, and Greece. In *4QFour Kingdoms*, only the first kingdom is clearly identified, as Babylon, which is then said to rule over Persia. Émile Puech, in the DJD edition, restored Media as the second kingdom, but this is unlikely, since Persia has already been subsumed under Babylon. Moreover, the second tree appears in the west. Bennie Reynolds has argued persuasively that it should be identified as Greece.[24] The third and fourth kingdoms are not preserved. They may have been identified with the Ptolemies and the Seleucids, or perhaps with the Seleucids and Rome, but in any case they do not simply reproduce the four kingdoms of Daniel.

Yet another fragmentary text, preserved in seven Aramaic fragments found in various caves, describes a visionary tour of the new Jerusalem and restored temple. Accordingly, it is known as the "New Jerusalem" text. It is conceived on the model of Ezekiel 40-48, and it also includes an eschatological passage about a sequence of kingdoms, including Babylon, Media, and the Kittim, and a final conflict with Edom, Moab and Ammon (cf. the

20. Eibert Tigchelaar, "Classifications of the Collection of Dead Sea Scrolls and the Case of Apocryphon of Jeremiah C," *JSJ* 43 (2012) 449-50.

21. John Strugnell and Devorah Dimant, "4Q Second Ezekiel," *Revue de Qumrân* 13 (1988) 45-56.

22. Stuckenbruck, "Daniel and Early Enoch Traditions in the Dead Sea Scrolls," 368-86, especially 378-85; Stokes, "The Throne Visions of Daniel 7, *1 Enoch* 14, and the Qumran Book of Giants (4Q530)," 340-58; Trotter, "The Tradition of the Throne Vision in the Second Temple Period: Daniel 7:9-10, 1 Enoch 14:18-23, and the Book of Giants (4Q530)," 451-66. On the Book of Giants in general see Stuckenbruck, *The Book of Giants from Qumran*.

23. Émile Puech, *Qumrân Grotte 4.XXVII: Textes araméens, deuxième partie (4Q550-4Q575a, 4Q580-4Q587)* (DJD 37; Oxford: Oxford University Press, 2009) 57-90.

24. Reynolds, *Between Symbolism and Realism*, 200.

War Scroll, col. 1). Despite its fragmentary state, Lorenzo DiTommaso declares that it is "almost certainly an apocalypse."[25]

The significance of these fragmentary apocalyptic texts has yet to be fully explored. They suggest that there was a good deal more apocalyptic literature in circulation in the last centuries before the turn of the era than was known before the discovery of the Scrolls. The fact that most of these texts are in Aramaic (except for the Jeremianic and Ezekielan fragments) suggests that they were not composed within the community of the new covenant.[26] This does not necessarily mean that they are all older than the sectarian texts. The sectarian communities were not sealed so effectively that they could not have acquired texts that were composed outside their bounds. But the sectarians do not appear to have composed literature in Aramaic. It remains true that there is no undisputed case where an apocalyptic text, ascribed pseudonymously to an ancient figure, was composed within the sectarian community. A few scholars have argued for the sectarian provenance of 4Q390.[27] It does not refer to sectarian structures, but has many motifs that are paralleled in the sectarian Scrolls, especially the Damascus Document.[28] Even if 4Q390 is deemed to be sectarian, however, such compositions were evidently atypical of the sect.[29]

Nonetheless, the worldview of the sectarian scrolls is typically apocalyptic: human destiny is ruled by superhuman forces of light and darkness,

25. Lorenzo DiTommaso, *The Dead Sea New Jerusalem Text* (TSAJ 110; Tübingen: Mohr Siebeck, 2005) 110. Compare Florentino García Martínez, "New Jerusalem," *EDSS* 606-10. See also Adela Yarbro Collins, "The Dream of a New Jerusalem at Qumran," in James H. Charlesworth, ed., *The Bible and the Dead Sea Scrolls* (3 vols.; Waco, TX: Baylor University Press, 2006) 3:231-54.

26. Devorah Dimant, "The Qumran Aramaic Texts and the Qumran Community," in eadem, *History, Ideology and Bible Interpretation in the Dead Sea Scrolls: Collected Studies* (FAT 90; Tübingen: Mohr Siebeck, 2014) 185-92; eadem, "Themes and Genres in the Aramaic Texts from Qumran," ibid, 195-218.

27. Christoph Berner, *Jahre, Jahrwochen und Jubiläen: Heptadische Geschichtskonzeptionen im Antiken Judentum* (BZAW 363; Berlin: de Gruyter, 2006) 429; Cana Werman, "Epochs and End-Time: The 490-Year Scheme in Second Temple Literature," *DSD* 13 (2006): 229-55. See the reflections of Tigchelaar, "Classifications of the Collection of Dead Sea Scrolls and the Case of Apocryphon of Jeremiah C," 519-50.

28. Tigchelaar, "Classifications of the Collection," 547. The parallels relate to specific sins and punishment, and the dominion of Belial.

29. 4Q521, dubbed "a messianic apocalypse" (E. Puech, "Une Apocalypse Messianique [4Q521]," *RevQ* 15 [1992] 475-519), is a hymnic text. See K.-W. Niebuhr, "4Q521,2 II — Ein Eschatologischer Psalm," in Z. J. Kapera, ed., *Mogilany 1995* (Kraków: Enigma, 1996).

history is deemed to be moving inexorably to an end, and people await reward or punishment after death. But these beliefs are not expressed in the form of heavenly revelations to an ancient seer. Two reasons suggest themselves for this phenomenon. First, the movement had found a new authority in the person of the Teacher of Righteousness, an enigmatic figure who played a crucial role in the development of the sect. Second, much of the Teacher's revelation took the form of interpretation of the Torah and the Prophets. Consequently, the Qumran writings are oriented to the Torah of Moses in a way that the apocalypses of Enoch and Daniel were not. This provided an established source of authority, and obviated the need to compose revelations in the name of ancient visionaries.

## The History of the Sect

The history of the Qumran community involves complex questions that cannot be fully treated here.[30] The settlement at Qumran is often dated as early as 150 BCE, but the most authoritative recent overview of the archeology, by Jodi Magness, puts the date between 100 and 50 BCE.[31] This is suggested by the evidence of the coins. One coin was recovered from the reign of John Hyrcanus (134-104 BCE) and 143 from the reign of Alexander Jannaeus (103-76 BCE). Five silver coins of Antiochus Sidetes (138-129 BCE) were also found.[32] Since coins remain in use for some time, the few exemplars from the reigns of Sidetes and Hyrcanus do not necessarily require that the settlement was established in their reigns, and so a date in the first half of the first century BCE is plausible. The dates suggested for most of the sectarian scrolls on the basis of paleography fall in the first century BCE, and the few historical allusions relate to the later Hasmonean period.[33] Individuals mentioned in the scrolls include Alexander Jannaeus, who is mentioned as "Jonathan the King" in 4Q448 and "the lion of wrath who hangs men alive" in the *pesher* on Nahum; Queen Salome Alexandra, "Shelamzion" (76-67 BCE) in

30. See Collins, *Beyond the Qumran Community*, 88-121.

31. Jodi Magness, *The Archaeology of Qumran and the Dead Sea Scrolls* (Grand Rapids: Eerdmans, 2002) 65.

32. Cross, *The Ancient Library of Qumran*, 59. R. de Vaux, *Archaeology and the Dead Sea Scrolls* (London: Oxford University Press, 1973) 18-19.

33. Michael O. Wise, "Dating the Teacher of Righteousness and the Floruit of His Movement," *JBL* 122 (2003) 53-87.

4Q322-24; and Demetrius king of Greece (= Demetrius III, 95-88 BCE) in the *pesher* on Nahum. Remarkably, there is no clear case of a sectarian work that was composed later than the middle of the first century BCE.[34] The site of Qumran was abandoned for a period toward the end of the first century BCE. This is explained either as a result of an earthquake in 31 BCE or of a violent destruction and fire about 9 or 8 BCE.[35] Thereafter, it was reinhabited, and occupied until it was destroyed by the Romans in 68 CE.[36]

The main narrative about the origin of the Dead Sea sect is found in the opening column of the *Damascus Document*:

> And at the moment of wrath, three hundred and ninety years after having delivered them up into the hands of Nebuchadnezzar, king of Babylon, he visited them and caused to sprout from Israel and from Aaron a shoot of planting, in order to possess his land and to become fat with the good things of his soil. And they realized their sin and knew that they were guilty men; but they were like blind persons and like those who grope for the path over twenty years. And God appraised their deeds, because they sought him with a perfect heart and raised up for them a Teacher of Righteousness, in order to direct them in the path of his heart.

Taken literally, the 390 years would point to a date at the beginning of the second century BCE. But the number is symbolic (cf. Ezek 4:5), and it is very doubtful whether any chronological information can be derived from it.[37] It is probably safe to assume that this passage requires a date centuries after the Exile for the rise of the "shoot of planting." It is also clear that the sect began as a reform movement and that some time (half a generation) passed before the arrival of the Teacher who gave it its definitive character. The *pesharim* often refer to disputes between this Teacher and a figure called "the Wicked Priest."[38] The latter figure was clearly a

---

34. H. Stegemann, *Die Essener, Qumran, Johannes der Täufer, und Jesus* (Freiburg im Breisgau: Herder, 1993) 192; English translation, *The Library of Qumran: On the Essenes, Qumran, John the Baptist, and Jesus* (Grand Rapids: Eerdmans, 1998).

35. J. Magness, "The Chronology of the Settlement at Qumran in the Herodian Period," *Dead Sea Discoveries* 2 (1995) 58-65.

36. Magness, *The Archaeology of Qumran*, 47-72.

37. Collins, *Beyond the Qumran Community*, 92-94.

38. See especially 1QpHab 8:9-13; 9:8-12; 11:13-14; 4QpPss[a] 4:8-10.

high priest (the Hebrew *hakkōhēn hārāšaʿ,* "the wicked priest," involves a pun on *hakkōhēn hārōʾš,* "the high priest"). He is most often identified as Jonathan Maccabee,[39] sometimes as Simon,[40] on the assumption that the dispute concerned the usurpation of the high priesthood by the Hasmoneans. But the various references to the Wicked Priest do not all easily fit any one Hasmonean high priest.[41] Moreover, the reasons why the sect split off from the rest of Judaism are addressed in the *Damascus Document* column 3 and especially in the so-called *Halakic Letter,* 4QMMT.[42] These reasons concern a disagreement about the liturgical calendar and the interpretation of purity laws. The legitimacy of the Hasmonean high priests is never raised explicitly as an issue.[43] It seems clear that the separation of the sect took place in the Hasmonean era, and primarily concerned rival interpretations of the Torah. A plausible occasion is the death of Alexander Jannaeus in 76 BCE and the succession of his widow Salome Alexandra, with Hyrcanus II as High Priest. Alexander, who had fought the Pharisees all his life, advised his widow to yield power to them where religious law was concerned. She did so, and according to Josephus, "while she had the title of sovereign, the Pharisees had the power" (*Ant* 13. 408-9). The sectarians were notoriously anti-Pharisaic, and so this is the most likely occasion for the composition of 4QMMT and a definitive breach with the Hasmonean rulers.[44]

Proposals that the community was composed of returnees from Babylon or that the Teacher of Righteousness was high priest in the period

---

39. G. Vermes, *The Dead Sea Scrolls: Qumran in Perspective* (Philadelphia: Fortress, 1981) 151; J. C. VanderKam, "The Wicked Priest Revisited," in Daniel C. Harlow, et al., eds., *The "Other" in Second Temple Judaism: Essays in Honor of John J. Collins* (Grand Rapids: Eerdmans, 2011) 350-67; Hanan Eshel, *The Dead Sea Scrolls and the Hasmonean State* (Grand Rapids: Eerdmans, 2008) 29-61. The identification was proposed by J. T. Milik.

40. Cross, *The Ancient Library,* 111-16.

41. A. S. van der Woude, "Wicked Priest or Wicked Priests? Reflections on the Identification of the Wicked Priest in the Habakkuk Commentary," *JJS* 33 (1982) 349-59, attempts to apply each reference to a different high priest.

42. E. Qimron and J. Strugnell, *Qumran Cave 4–V: Miqṣat Maʿaśê Ha-Torah* (DJD 10; Oxford: Clarendon, 1994).

43. This is acknowledged by Dimant, "The History of the Qumran Community in Light of New Developments," in eadem, *History, Ideology and Biblical Interpretation,* 241. She dates the beginning of the sectarian movement about 200 BCE.

44. Collins, *Beyond the Qumran Community,* 116. See also Michael O. Wise, "The Origin and History of the Teacher's Movement," in Lim and Collins, eds., *The Oxford Handbook of the Dead Sea Scrolls,* 92-122.

between 162 and 152[45] are extremely hypothetical, and no weight can be placed on them.

We cannot attempt here to discuss all aspects of the sect's theology but only those that bear on its apocalyptic character — the idea of revelation, eschatology, and the angelic world. It should be noted, however, that these are by no means incidental areas but provide a conceptual framework for the halakah or prescriptive rules of the community.

We can say little of the evolution of apocalyptic ideas within the Essene movement. The issue here is not the *a priori* likelihood of such evolution but the limitation of our actual evidence. The major documents of the sect were composed early on and continued to circulate throughout the history of Qumran. The oldest copies of 1QS date to the first quarter of the first century BCE and those of CD to the first half of that century. None of these copies is an autograph. Some of the *Hôdāyôt* or *Thanksgiving Hymns* are widely thought to be in part the work of the Teacher himself, although the scroll dates from the first century CE.[46] The *pesharim* date from the mid-first century BCE. The middle of that century seems to have been the heyday of literary productivity in the Dead Sea sect.

## Revelation

Fundamental to the idea of revelation at Qumran is the belief that all things are regulated according to "the mysteries of God."[47] The term for "mystery" *(raz)* is found also in Daniel 2 and 4. The idea is closely bound with the belief in providential control, despite the evidence of evil in the world. All

---

45. J. Murphy-O'Connor, "The Essenes and Their History," *RB* 81 (1974) 215-44; idem, "The Essenes in Palestine," *BA* 40 (1977) 100-24.

46. Michael C. Douglas, "The Teacher Hymn Hypothesis Revisited: New Data for an Old Crux," *DSD* 6 (1999) 239-66.

47. R. E. Brown, *The Semitic Background of the Term "Mystery" in the New Testament* (Philadelphia: Fortress, 1968); Samuel I. Thomas, *The "Mysteries" of Qumran: Mystery, Secrecy, and Esotericism in the Dead Sea Scrolls* (SBLEJL 25; Leiden: Brill, 2009); Valérie Triplet-Hitoto, *Mystères et connaissances cachés à Qumrân* (Paris: Cerf, 2011) 81-180.

The expression *raz nihyeh*, "the mystery that is to be," also figures prominently in 4QInstruction, a wisdom text that may be older than the Qumran community. See D. J. Harrington, *Wisdom Texts from Qumran* (London: Routledge, 1996) 40-59; A. Lange, *Weisheit und Prädestination: Weisheitliche Urordnung und Prädestination in den Textfunden von Qumran* (Leiden: Brill, 1995); Matthew J. Goff, *The Worldly and Heavenly Wisdom of 4QInstruction* (STDJ 50; Leiden: Brill, 2003) 30-79.

that is and is to be comes from the God of knowledge. Before ever they existed he established their design, and they accomplish their task without change. Even the sins caused by the Angel of Darkness are in accordance with the mysteries of God, but also "in the mysteries of his understanding and in his glorious wisdom" God has appointed an end to falsehood (1QS 3–4). These mysteries concern not only the course of history and human affairs. They involve angels as well as men: "for great is your majestic plan and your marvelous mysteries on high, for raising up to you from the dust and casting down angels" (1QM 14:14). They can also involve the workings of the cosmos: "the heavenly lights according to their mysteries, the stars to their paths . . . and the perfect treasuries (of snow and hail) according to their purposes . . ." (1QH 9:11-12, formerly 1:11-12). All is graven before God with the graving tool of the reminder (1QH 9:21-25) as surely as all was inscribed for Enoch on the heavenly tablets.

What is crucially important here is the manner in which these mysteries are revealed.[48] From 1QS 3–4 one might expect that the Spirits of Truth and Falsehood play the roles of revealers, but this is not specified. The speaker in the *Hôdāyôt* claims to be the recipient of direct revelation: "These things I know by the wisdom which comes from Thee, for Thou hast unstopped my ears to marvelous mysteries" (1QH 9:21). The idea that the speaker here is the Teacher of Righteousness is supported by the *pesher* on Habakkuk 7:3-4: "And when it says, 'So that he can run who reads it,' the interpretation of it concerns the Teacher of Righteousness to whom God made known all the mysteries of the words of his servants the prophets." Again in 1QS 11:3 the hymnist says, "from the source of his knowledge he has disclosed his light, and my eyes have observed his wonders, and the light of my heart the mystery that is to be and of what is for always."

It appears that the Teacher of Righteousness was the official mediator of revelation for the community, and we are not told that he needed the services of an interpreting angel.[49] In this regard, the scrolls depart from the conventions of the apocalypses, although the concept of mystery is very similar. The rules and hymns attest a more direct form of communication, where the author appears to have more confidence in his own authority than was the case with the authors of the pseudonymous apocalypses. This

---

48. Alex P. Jassen, *Mediating the Divine: Prophecy and Revelation in the Dead Sea Scrolls and Second Temple Judaism* (STDJ 68; Leiden: Brill, 2007).

49. P. Schulz, *Der Autoritätsanspruch des Lehrers der Gerechtigkeit in Qumran* (Meisenheim am Glan: Hain, 1974); D. Patte, *Early Jewish Hermeneutic in Palestine* (SBLDS 22; Missoula, MT: Scholars Press, 1975) 211-31.

phenomenon may arise from the structure of authority within the community and may be analogous to the revival of prophecy in early Christianity.

The *pesharim* are perhaps the category of literature in the sectarian scrolls that comes closest to the apocalyptic manner of revelation.[50] There is obvious similarity between their interpretation of prophecy and the interpretation of Jeremiah in Daniel 9. The affinity with Daniel's dream interpretation is underlined by the common use of the word *pesher*. In the Qumran *pesharim* the words of scripture are treated as mysteries that refer not to the time of their author but to the end time, which is now being fulfilled in the history of the community. So the statement "for the wicked surround the righteous" (Hab 1:4) is taken as a reference to the Wicked Priest and the Teacher of Righteousness. "Where the lion went to enter" (Nah 2:11) is interpreted as "Demetrius, king of Greece, who sought to enter Jerusalem." This style of interpretation has its roots in the mantic wisdom and divination of the ancient Near East but also has analogues in the Hellenistic world, notably in the Egyptian *Demotic Chronicle*.[51] Presumably the task of interpretation was handed on to others in the community after the death of the original Teacher.

*Pesharim* are not apocalypses. Not only do they differ in their manner of revelation, but their content is not properly eschatological. It refers rather to the historical experience of the community. They also pursue the biblical texts in a manner far more systematic than anything we find in the apocalypses.[52] Yet they bear some resemblance to apocalyptic revelation. The sources of revelation, including scripture, are mysterious. There is need of a special interpretation, which was itself revealed to the Teacher of Righteousness. The scriptural text requires a higher revelation. This is true of the Qumran texts in general. These texts are more directly interested in

50. M. P. Horgan, *Pesharim: Qumran Interpretations of Biblical Books* (CBQMS 8; Washington, DC: Catholic Biblical Association of America, 1979); O. Betz, *Offenbarung und Schriftforschung in der Qumransekte* (Tübingen: Mohr Siebeck, 1960); Jassen, *Mediating the Divine,* 343-62.

51. On mantological exegesis, see M. Fishbane, *Biblical Interpretation in Ancient Israel* (Oxford: Clarendon, 1985) 443-99. On the exegetical method of the *pesharim,* see J. J. Collins, "Prophecy and Fulfillment in the Dead Sea Scrolls," *JETS* 30 (1987) 267-78 (=*Seers, Sibyls and Sages,* 301-14).

52. On the analogy with midrashim, compare W. H. Brownlee, *The Midrash Pesher of Habakkuk* (SBLMS 24; Missoula, MT: Scholars Press, 1979). G. J. Brooke ("Qumran Pesher: Towards the Redefinition of a Genre," *RevQ* 10 [1979-81] 483-503) regards *pesher* as a subtype of midrash. See also Brooke, *Exegesis at Qumran: 4QFlorilegium in Its Jewish Context* (Sheffield: JSOT Press, 1985).

the Torah and the scripture than is usual in the apocalypses. Yet they too rely on a higher revelation. In the *Community Rule* the ceremony of the renewal of the covenant takes on a new character in view of the Instruction on the Two Spirits, which is in effect an exposition of the underlying mystery. This reliance on a higher revelation is an important modification of the Torah-centered piety of Qumran.[53]

## Creation and Dualism

The most systematic exposition of what might be called an apocalyptic theology in the scrolls is found in the Instruction on the Two Spirits in the *Community Rule,* columns 3 and 4.[54] There we read: "From the God of knowledge comes all that is and is to be. Before ever they existed He established their whole design and when, as ordained for them, they come into being, it is in accord with His glorious design that they accomplish their task without change. . . . He has created man to govern the world, and has appointed for him two spirits in which to walk until the time of His visitation: the spirits of truth and wickedness" (1QS 3:15-19). The passage goes on to associate these two spirits with light and darkness. There is a "Prince of Light" who helps all "the Sons of Light" and an "Angel of Darkness" who rules over the wicked. People have a share in both spirits, and they fight "within the heart of man" (1QS 4:23).[55] This conflict persists through all the periods of history, but "God, in the mysteries of His knowledge and in the wisdom of His glory, has determined an end to the existence of injustice and on the occasion of His visitation He will obliterate it forever" (1QS 4:18-19). After death the wicked will be punished at the hand of angels of destruction, for eternal damnation in the fire of the dark regions (4:12-14), while the righteous will enjoy everlasting blessings in eternal life, and a crown of glory in eternal light (4:7-8).

---

53. John J. Collins, "Covenant and Dualism in the Dead Sea Scrolls," in idem, *Scriptures and Sectarianism,* 179-94. On the covenantal theology of Qumran, see E. P. Sanders, *Paul and Palestinian Judaism* (Philadelphia: Fortress, 1977) 233-328.

54. Collins, *Apocalypticism in the Dead Sea Scrolls,* 30-51.

55. There is some tension within the Instruction on this issue. The beginning of the passage gives the impression that people are ruled entirely by one spirit or the other. It is possible that the text was revised on this point to modify its theology. P. von der Osten-Sacken, *Gott und Belial* (Göttingen: Vandenhoeck & Ruprecht, 1969) 11-27, posits three redactional strata: 1QS 3:13–4:14; 4:15-23a; and 4:23b-26.

The dualistic theology of the Instruction on the Two Spirits owes something to the incipient dualism of *1 Enoch* and *Jubilees*. In *Jubilees* the Satanic figure was called Mastema. In 1QS 3:23-24 the dominion of the Prince of Darkness is called *memšelet maśtēmātô*.[56] It also owes something to the wisdom tradition. There are numerous parallels between the Instruction on the Two Spirits and 4QInstruction.[57] The distinctive teaching on two Spirits of Light and Darkness, however, is clearly derived from Zoroastrian dualism, although it is inevitably modified in its Jewish context.[58] The Gathas, the oldest part of the Avesta, say that humanity has to choose between two spirits, one of whom is holy and the other a destroyer. "In the beginning those two Spirits who are the well-endowed twins were known as the one good and the other evil, in thought, word, and deed. Between them the wise chose rightly, not so the fools."[59] These two spirits were associated with light and darkness from an early time, as can be seen from a citation of Theopompus (about 300 BCE) in Plutarch's *Isis and Osiris, 46-47*.[60] In the Jewish text, God creates rather than begets the two spirits and is transcendent above both light and darkness.[61] One consequence of this, however, is that God is ultimately responsible for the creation of evil. There is some tension within the Instruction as to whether human beings are simply allotted to one spirit or the other, or whether they are free to

---

56. Cf. 1QM 13:10-12, where Belial is called "the angel of Mastema." On the relation and differences between Belial and Mastema, see Dimant, "Between Qumran Sectarian and Qumran Nonsectarian Texts: The Case of Belial and Mastema," in eadem, *History, Ideology, and Biblical Interpretation*, 135-51.

57. See especially Lange, *Weisheit und Prädestination*, 128-29. The parallels include the expressions "God of knowledge" and "to know good and evil," and the word *nihyeh*, *niphal* participle of the verb "to be."

58. M. Philonenko, "La Doctrine Qoumrânienne des Deux Ésprits," in G. Widengren, A. Hultgård, and M. Philonenko, eds., *Apocalyptique Iranienne et Dualisme Qoumrânien* (Paris: Maisonneuve, 1995) 163-211; J. J. Collins, "The Origin of Evil in Apocalyptic Literature and the Dead Sea Scrolls," in J. A. Emerton, ed., *Congress Volume, Paris 1992* (Leiden: Brill, 1995) 25-38 (= *Seers, Sibyls, and Sages*, 287-300); Collins, "Covenant and Dualism,"186-88. *Pace* Paul Heger, "Another Look at Dualism in Qumran Writings," in Géza G. Xeravits, ed., *Dualism in Qumran* (London: T & T Clark, 2010) 39-101, reprinted in idem, *Challenges to Conventional Opinions on Qumran and Enoch Issues* (STDJ 100; Leiden: Brill, 2012) 227-310.

59. *Yasna* 30; trans. R. C. Zaehner, *The Dawn and Twilight of Zoroastrianism* (London: Weidenfeld & Nicolson, 1961) 42.

60. J. Gwyn Griffiths, *Plutarch's De Iside et Osiride* (Cambridge: University of Wales Press, 1970) 471.

61. Cf. Isa 45:7: "I form light and create darkness, I make weal and create woe; I the Lord do all these things."

choose. The Instruction certainly conveys a strong sense of determinism, but freedom of choice and responsibility are not completely eliminated. The determinism was not inherited from the Zoroastrian texts, which assume freedom of choice.[62] In this respect, the *Testament of Amram*, which is dated by J. T. Milik to the second century BCE, is closer to the Persian model.[63] It tells of two angelic figures quarreling over the patriarch.[64] Each has three names, and their opposition is formulated in terms of light and darkness.

How far the Instruction on the Two Spirits can be taken as typical of the theology of the Dead Sea sect is a matter of dispute.[65] On the one hand, aspects of this theology can be found in several texts.[66] The *War Rule* describes the final conflict as a battle between the Sons of Light and the Sons of Darkness, with their respective angelic patrons, identified as Michael and Belial. Belial is also linked with the forces of darkness in other texts, such as 4Q177, 4Q280, and 4Q286.[67] This dualism informs the covenant renewal ceremony in 1QS 1–3, and the very fact that the Instruction is embedded in the *Community Rule* gives it a measure of official status. On the other hand, it is not found consistently in the sectarian scrolls. The Instruction on the Two Spirits is lacking in some manuscripts of the *Community Rule,* and this suggests that it may have been a secondary addition.[68] While Belial has an integral role in the *Damascus Document,* the most explicit

62. Albert de Jong, "Iranian Connections in the Dead Sea Scrolls," in Lim and Collins, eds., *The Oxford Handbook of the Dead Sea Scrolls,* 492.

63. Liora Goldman, "Dualism in the Visions of Amram," *RevQ* 95 (2010) 421-32.

64. J. T. Milik, "4Q Visions de 'Amram et une citation d'Origène," *RB* 79 (1972) 77-97; idem, "*Milkî-ṣedeq* et *Milkî-reša*' dans les anciens écrits juifs et chrétiens," *JJS* 23 (1972) 95-144; P. J. Kobelski, *Melchizedek and Melchireša*' (CBQMS 10; Washington, DC: Catholic Biblical Association of America, 1981) 24-36.

65. Charlotte Hempel, "The Treatise on the Two Spirits and the Literary History of the Rule of the Community," in Xeravits, ed., *Dualism in Qumran,* 102-20.

66. Philip Alexander, "Predestination and Free Will in the Theology of the Dead Sea Scrolls," in John M. G. Barclay and Simon Gathercole, eds., *Divine and Human Agency in Paul and His Cultural Environment* (Library of New Testament Studies 335; London: T & T Clark, 2006) 39-47. He points to 4Q502, the Songs of the Sabbath Sacrifice, and the physiognomic text, 4Q186.

67. See Collins, *Apocalypticism in the Dead Sea Scrolls,* 45-47; Kobelski, *Melchizedek and Melchireša*', 49-74.

68. J. H. Charlesworth, ed., *The Dead Sea Scrolls: Hebrew, Aramaic, and Greek Texts with English Translations.* Volume 1: *Rule of the Community and Related Documents* (Tübingen: Mohr Siebeck; Louisville: Westminster John Knox, 1994) 53-103; P. S. Alexander, "The Redaction History of *Serekh ha Yaḥad:* A Proposal," *RevQ* 17 (1996) 437-56.

dualistic statement in that text appears as a parenthetic example in CD 5:18-19. There is no mention of Belial or the Angel of Darkness in CD 2:2-13, a passage that has many parallels with the Instruction on the Two Spirits.[69]

The inconsistency of the scrolls in this regard has been explained in various ways. Some scholars see the Instruction as an independent text that was incorporated into the *Community Rule* and "certainly pre-Essene."[70] Others argue that dualism is a relatively late development, and that progression towards dualism can be seen in the redactional history of several texts.[71] Both extremes are problematic. Dualism can scarcely be a late development in view of the early manuscript date of *Testament of Amram*, and even 1QS dates to the first half of the first century BCE. Yet the failure of the *Damascus Document* to refer to the doctrine of the Two Spirits can be explained most satisfactorily if the author either did not know or did not accept the doctrine. We should probably see the Instruction on the Two Spirits as the culmination of a development, but one that was already complete by the early first century BCE. It is not apparent that all members of the sect must have embraced that doctrine or that there was any requirement of orthodoxy in this regard, but the dualism of the Two Spirits was certainly an important and influential aspect of sectarian theology.[72]

## The Periods of History

According to the Instruction on the Two Spirits, humanity is divided between the powers of Light and Darkness "for all the periods of ages" until the final period or end *(qēṣ 'aḥărôn)*.[73] The division of history into periods was developed in the Apocalypse of Weeks and Daniel 9, among other

---

69. P. R. Davies, *The Damascus Covenant: An Interpretation of the "Damascus Document"* (JSOTSup 25; Sheffield: JSOT Press, 1983) 72-73; Lange, *Weisheit und Prädestination*, 242.

70. Stegemann, *Die Essener*, 154; Lange, *Weisheit und Prädestination*, 126-28.

71. P. R. Davies, "Eschatology at Qumran," *JBL* 104 (1985) 39-55; J. Duhaime, "Dualistic Reworking in the Scrolls from Qumran," *CBQ* 49 (1987) 32-56.

72. On the complexity of dualism in the Scrolls see Jörg Frey, "Different Patterns of Dualistic Thought in the Qumran Library," in Moshe Bernstein, Florentino García Martínez and John Kampen, eds., *Legal Texts and Legal Issues* (Leiden: Brill, 1997) 275-335 and Loren T. Stuckenbruck, "The Interiorization of Dualism within the Human Being in Second Temple Judaism: The Treatise of the Two Spirits (1QS III:13 – IV:26 in its tradition-historical context," in Lange et al., eds., *Light Against Darkness*, 145-68.

73. Collins, *Apocalypticism in the Dead Sea Scrolls*, 52-70.

apocalyptic passages.[74] At Qumran, we find a work entitled "Pesher concerning the periods made by God . . ." (4Q180).[75] Unfortunately this work is very fragmentary, but a developed exposition based on periodization is found in 11QMelchizedek.[76] History is divided into ten jubilees, like the ten weeks of the Apocalypse of Weeks. The duration is 490 years, or the seventy weeks of years of Daniel 9 (which is cited explicitly in 11QMelch 2:18). The focus of the text is on the events of the tenth jubilee. The Day of Expiation is at the end of the tenth jubilee, when "expiation (will be made) for . . . the men of the lot of Melchizedek" (2:8). Melchizedek is envisioned as a heavenly figure, and is even called "god" (*'elōhîm*).[77] He is taken to be the figure to whom Psalm 82 refers when it says "God has taken His place in the divine council; in the midst of the gods He judges." He appears to be the equivalent of Michael or the Prince of Light, and he is pitted against Belial at the end of days. Since the evil angel or Watcher in the *Testament of Amram* is called Melchireša' ("king of wickedness" in contrast to Melchizedek, "king of righteousness"), it is reasonable to assume that Melchizedek is one of the three names of the Angel of Light in that document.

A chronology based on seventy weeks of years or 490 years is also implied in the *Damascus Document*. The time from the Exile to the emergence of the sect is 390 years (column 1). In CD 20:14 we are told that the time "from the day of the ingathering of the unique teacher until the destruction of all the men of war who turned back with the man of lies there shall be about 40 years." If we allow the standard number of 40 years for the career of the Teacher, we arrive at a period of 490 years from the Exile to the day of judgment. It seems likely that the sectarians attempted to calculate the end in the first century BCE. The *pesher* on Habakkuk comments as follows on Hab 2:3:

> For there is yet a vision concerning the appointed time. It testifies to the end time (*qēṣ*) and it will not deceive. The interpretation of it is that the last end time (*haqqēṣ hā 'aḥărôn*) will be prolonged, and it will be greater than anything of which the prophets spoke, for the

---

74. Berner, *Jahre, Jahrwochen und Jubiläen.*

75. D. Dimant, "The 'Pesher on the Periods' (4Q180 and 4Q181)," *Israel Oriental Studies* 9 (1979) 77-102 (= *History, Ideology and Bible Interpretation*, 385-404).

76. Kobelski, *Melchizedek and Melchireša',* 3-23. Eric F. Mason, *"You Are a Priest Forever": Second Temple Jewish Messianism and the Priestly Christology of the Epistle to the Hebrews* (STDJ 74; Leiden: Brill, 2008) 168-90.

77. Mason, *"You Are a Priest Forever,"* 168-90; Joseph L. Angel, *Otherworldly and Eschatological Priesthood in the Dead Sea Scrolls* (STDJ 86; Leiden: Brill, 2010) 146-64.

mysteries of God are awesome. If it tarries, wait for it, for it will surely come, and it will not be late. The interpretation of it concerns the men of truth, those who observe the Law, whose hands do not grow slack in the service of truth, when the last end time is drawn out for them, for all of God's end times will come according to their fixed order. (1QpHab 7:6-13)

This passage implies that the end is delayed, and had not come when initially expected, about forty years after the death of the Teacher.[78] The sect does not, however, appear to have set its hopes on a specific day or year, and perhaps for this reason the disappointment did not have too great an effect.

The scrolls speak frequently (more than 30 times) of *'aḥarît hayyāmîm*, "the end of days." Most of the references are found in exegetical texts, such as 11QMelchizedek and the so-called *Eschatological Midrash* (4Q174, the *Florilegium*, + 4Q177, the *Catena*).[79] The reference is not to a specific point in time, but to an eschatological period, the last period before the time of salvation.[80] This period will be a time of testing and distress, but it is also the time of the coming of the messiahs.[81] It is generally assumed that the sectarians believed that they were living in the end of days, and one text, 4QMMT (C 13-15) actually says "this is the end of days," but it is clear that the coming of the messiahs remains in the future. The so-called *Messianic Rule* (1QSa) legislates for the "end of days."[82] It would seem that the conditions of human existence would not be greatly altered. Provision is still made for the education of children and for community meals and regulations. A *pesher* on Isaiah, 4QpIs[a], includes the eschatological war against the Gentiles in this period, but no text extends the "end of days" to the time of salvation after the final war.

---

78. Stegemann, *Die Essener,* 174, and A. Steudel, "*'aḥarît hayyāmîm* in the Texts from Qumran," *RevQ* 16 (1993) 236-39, calculate this date as 70 BCE and 72 BCE, respectively, but these calculations presuppose the reliability of the 390 years in CD 1, which is doubtful.

79. A. Steudel, *Der Midrasch zur Eschatologie aus der Qumrangemeinde (4QMidr-Eschat[a,b])* (Leiden: Brill, 1994).

80. Steudel, "*'aḥarît hayyāmîm,*" 231.

81. The *Temple Scroll* (11QTemple) is often thought to be a Torah for the end of days (M. O. Wise, "The Eschatological Vision of the Temple Scroll," *JNES* 49 [1990] 155-72), but the king in the *Temple Scroll* is clearly not a messiah.

82. L. H. Schiffman, *The Eschatological Community of the Dead Sea Scrolls* (Atlanta: Scholars Press, 1989).

The texts are less explicit than we might expect as to what would happen at the time of the end, and indeed there may have been some variation on this subject. It is clear, however, that there would be a day of judgment, when God would put an end to wickedness and destroy the enemies of the sect. This judgment would be executed in the context of a final war against the Gentiles. Before that time, however, it was expected that God would fulfill the promises by restoring the legitimate temple cult and the Davidic kingdom through the agency of the messiahs of Aaron and Israel.

## Messianic Expectation

Messianic expectation in ancient Judaism is usually focused on the restoration of the Davidic kingship. This expectation had a clear basis in 2 Samuel 7, where God promised David that his house and his kingdom would be made sure forever before him. But in fact the Davidic line was broken by the Babylonian Exile. Some prophetic texts, notably Jer 23:5-6 and 33:17-22, promise that God would raise up for David a righteous branch or shoot, to restore the kingdom. But messianic expectation is strikingly absent from the literature of the Maccabean period and appears to have been in abeyance. It reappears in the first century BCE, in the *Psalms of Solomon* and the Dead Sea Scrolls. It seems likely that the revival of messianic expectation was related to dissatisfaction with the kingship of the Hasmoneans, the heirs of the Maccabees. The *Psalms* denounce the Hasmoneans as "those to whom you did not make the promise," who took away by force and despoiled the throne of David (*Pss Sol* 17:5-6). It is likely that opposition to the Hasmoneans also played a part in the messianic expectations of the scrolls.[83]

The expectation of a Davidic messiah was closely associated with a

83. For a full account of the messianism of the Dead Sea Scrolls, see Collins, *The Scepter and the Star*; Johannes Zimmermann, *Messianische Texte aus Qumran* (WUNT 2/104; Tübingen: Mohr Siebeck, 1998); James H. Charlesworth, Hermann Lichtenberger and Gerbern S. Oegema, eds., *Qumran-Messianism: Studies on the Messianic Expectations in the Dead Sea Scrolls* (Tübingen: Mohr Siebeck, 1998); Gerbern S. Oegema, *The Anointed and His People: Messianic Expectations from the Maccabees to Bar Kochba* (Sheffield: Sheffield Academic Press, 1998); Joseph A. Fitzmyer, *The One Who Is to Come* (Grand Rapids: Eerdmans, 2007). On the expectations centered on the house of David, see K. E. Pomykala, *The Davidic Dynasty Tradition in Early Judaism: Its History and Significance for Messianism* (SBLEJL 7; Atlanta: Scholars Press, 1995).

few biblical texts, chiefly Isaiah 11, Balaam's Oracle in Numbers 24, Psalm 2, Genesis 49, and Jeremiah 23 and 33. These passages were typically read to yield a picture of a warrior messiah, who would liberate Israel and drive out the Gentiles. His role is spelled out clearly in *Psalms of Solomon* 17:

> See, Lord, and raise up for them their king, the son of David, to rule over Israel in the time known to you, O God. Undergird him with the strength to destroy the unrighteous rulers, to purge Jerusalem from Gentiles who trample her to destruction; in wisdom and righteousness (cf. Isaiah 11) to drive out the sinners from the inheritance; to smash the arrogance of sinners like a potter's jar; to shatter all their substance with an iron rod (cf. Psalm 2), to destroy the warring nations with the word of his mouth . . .[84]

Similarly, the blessing of the Prince of the Congregation, "to establish the kingdom of his people forever," in the *Scroll of Blessings* (1QSb), is replete with allusions to Isaiah 11: "(May you smite the peoples) with the might of your hand and ravage the earth with your scepter; may you bring death to the ungodly with the breath of your lips! (Isa 11:4b) . . . and everlasting might, the spirit of knowledge and of the fear of God (Isa 11:2); may righteousness be the girdle (of your loins) and may your reins be girded (with faithfulness) (Isa 11:5)." The blessing goes on to compare the Prince to a young bull with horns of iron and hooves of bronze, and (probably) to a lion (cf. Gen 49:9). The phrase "for God has established you as the scepter" (1QSb 5:27) is an allusion to the scepter of Balaam's Oracle in Num 24:17. The warrior messiah also appears in a *pesher* on Isaiah 10 and 11 (4QpIsaᵃ) and 4Q285, a fragment of the *War Rule*.[85] Both of these texts refer to the messianic figure as "Prince of the Congregation" and "Branch of David." Again, the *Damascus Document,* manuscript A, interprets the scepter of Balaam's Oracle as "the Prince of the whole congregation, and when he comes he shall smite all the children of Sheth" (CD 7:19). The association of Balaam's Oracle with a warrior messiah continues into the Christian era. The most famous application of the oracle is attributed to

---

84. The "word of his mouth" reflects the Greek translation of Isa 11:4, where the Hebrew has "the rod of his mouth." Cf. *Pss Sol* 17:35 and also the use of Isaiah 11 in *Pss Sol* 18:6-8.

85. Collins, *The Scepter and the Star*, 64-67. On the interpretation of 4Q285, see especially M. Abegg, "Messianic Hope and 4Q285: A Reassessment," *JBL* 113 (1994) 81-91.

Rabbi Akiba, who identified the star as the rebel leader Simon bar Kosiba, in the second Jewish revolt against Rome in 132 CE.[86]

The much disputed "Son of God" text, 4Q246, should also be interpreted in terms of a warrior messiah. This Aramaic text survives in two columns. The first is torn vertically, so that only the latter part of each line is preserved. Someone falls before a throne and proceeds to address a king with reference to "your vision." The text goes on to refer to affliction and carnage and kings of Asshur and Egypt. The second column is fully preserved:

> "Son of God" he shall be called, and they will name him "Son of the Most High." Like sparks which you saw (or: of the vision), so will be their kingdom. For years they will rule on earth, and they will trample all. People will trample on people and city on city, [VACAT] until the people of God arises, (or: until he raises up the people of God) and all rest from the sword. His (or: its) kingdom is an everlasting kingdom and all his (or: its) ways truth. He (or: it) will judge the earth with truth, and all will make peace. The sword will cease from the earth, and all cities will pay him (or: it) homage. The great God will be his (or: its) strength. He will make war on his (or: its) behalf; give nations into his (or: its) hand and cast them all down before him (or: it). His (or: its) sovereignty is everlasting sovereignty and all the depths. . . .[87]

Because there is a blank space (VACAT) immediately before "until the people of God arises," some scholars take this as the turning point of the text and argue that everything before that point, including the figure who is called "Son of God," must be negative, and identify him as a Syrian king.[88] This reasoning is not compelling. Apocalyptic texts do not proceed in such a simple linear fashion. In several texts, the appearance of a savior figure is followed initially by further woes and distress (cf. Daniel

86. *y. Ta'anit* 68d. G. Vermes, *Jesus the Jew* (Philadelphia: Fortress, 1981) 134. The popular name of the leader, Bar Kochba, means "son of the star," and is a pun on Bar Kosiba.

87. For the text, see E. Puech, "246. 4QApocryphe de Daniel ar," in Brooke et al., DJD XXII, 165-84. See Collins, *The Scepter and the Star*, 171-90.

88. This interpretation was first proposed by J. T. Milik in a lecture at Harvard in December 1972, which remains unpublished. Puech allows it as a possible interpretation. The most thorough argument for the identification as a Syrian king is provided by E. Cook, "4Q246," *Bulletin for Biblical Research* 5 (1995) 43-66. See my rejoinder to Cook in J. J. Collins, "The Background of the 'Son of God' Text," *Bulletin for Biblical Research* 7 (1997) 51-62.

12; 4 Ezra 13). There are plenty of precedents for Gentile kings who claim divine honors (Isaiah 14; Ezekiel 28; Dan 11:36-39); the Jewish texts never leave any doubt that their claims are unjustified and that the pretenders are eventually cast down. No judgment is passed on the "Son of God" in the extant Aramaic text. Moreover, there is ample support for a messianic interpretation of the phrase "Son of God." The closest parallel to the language of 4Q246 is found in Luke 1:32-33, where the angel Gabriel tells Mary that her child "will be great, and will be called the Son of the Most High, and the Lord God will give to him the throne of his ancestor David. He will reign over the house of Jacob forever, and of his kingdom there will be no end." Luke 1:35 adds, "he will be called the Son of God." The messianic connotations of the phrase derive from two biblical texts, 2 Sam 7:14 ("I will be a father to him, and he shall be a son to me") and Ps 2:7 ("you are my son; today I have begotten you"). Psalm 2 also refers to the king as the Lord's anointed, or *māšîaḥ*. 2 Sam 7:14 is interpreted as follows in the *Florilegium* from Qumran (4Q174): "[I will be] his father and he shall be my son. He is the Branch of David who shall arise with the Interpreter of the Law [to rule] in Zion (at the end) of days."

If the Son of God text is read as messianic, it fits perfectly with what we have otherwise seen of the Davidic messiah.[89] He will make war by the power of God, conquer the Gentiles, and restore the kingdom of Israel. The text has several parallels with Daniel 7, but the savior figure is a human king, rather than a heavenly "Son of Man." It is possible that the Qumran text is reinterpreting Daniel's vision, but the evidence on this point is not decisive.

## Two Messiahs

The expectation of a warrior Davidic messiah in the scrolls is not distinctive, but was widely shared in Judaism around the turn of the era. It reappears in the apocalypses of 4 Ezra and *2 Baruch* towards the end of the first century CE, and again in the Bar Kokhba revolt in the second century. The messianism of Qumran was distinctive, however, insofar

89. The messianic interpretation was originally proposed by F. M. Cross. See *The Ancient Library of Qumran*, 189-91. See Cross, "Notes on the Two Messiahs at Qumran and the Extracanonical Daniel Apocalypse," in D. W. Parry and S. D. Ricks, eds., *Current Research and Technological Developments on the Dead Sea Scrolls* (Leiden: Brill, 1996) 1-13. See also Zimmermann, *Messianische Texte*, 128-70.

as this royal messiah is often paired with, and subordinated to, a priestly messiah.[90]

When the *Damascus Document* (CD) was first discovered in the Cairo Geniza at the beginning of the twentieth century, it was found to refer in several places to "the messiah of Aaron and Israel."[91] Louis Ginzberg argued that it implied two messiahs rather than one.[92] This interpretation was supported by the reference in 1QS 9:11 to the coming of a prophet and the messiahs of Aaron and Israel, which has generally been taken to represent the standard messianic expectations of the sect.[93] It is true that this is the only passage that uses the plural "messiahs of Aaron and Israel,"[94] and that the passage in question is lacking in a fragmentary manuscript from Cave 4 (4QS^e).[95] But the argument for dual messianism at Qumran does not rest only on the use of these phrases.

The scriptural basis for this expectation is laid out in 4QTestimonia, where we find juxtaposed the prediction of a prophet like Moses (Exod 20:21, Samaritan text = Deut 5:28-29 + Deut 18:18-19), Balaam's Oracle in Num 24:15-17 ("a star shall come out of Jacob and a scepter shall rise out of Israel"), and the blessing of Levi in Deut 33:8-11 ("Give thy Thummim to Levi"). The texts suggest, respectively, the coming of an ideal prophet, king, and priest. Finally, in 1QSa, the rule for the community "at the end of days," we read that "the priest" will take precedence over "the messiah of Israel." Here again the priest is clearly the messiah of Aaron, and a dual messiahship is envisaged. Although the terminology of CD could, gram-

---

90. Collins, *The Scepter and the Star*, 79-109; S. Talmon, "Waiting for the Messiah at Qumran," in idem, *The World of Qumran from Within* (Leiden: Brill, 1989) 273-300. On the tradition of priestly messianism see Angel, *Otherworldly and Eschatological Priesthood*, 171-310; Mason, *"You Are a Priest Forever,"* 64-133.

91. CD 12:23–13:1; 14:19; 19:11. CD 20:1 refers to a messiah from Aaron and from Israel.

92. L. Ginzberg, *An Unknown Jewish Sect* (New York: Jewish Theological Seminary, 1976, translation of 1922 German edition) 209-56.

93. See, e.g., G. Vermes, "The Qumran Messiahs and Messianism," in E. Schürer, *The History of the Jewish People in the Age of Jesus Christ,* II (rev. and ed. G. Vermes, F. Millar, and M. Goodman; Edinburgh: T & T Clark, 1986) 2:550-54; J. C. VanderKam, "Messianism in the Scrolls," in E. Ulrich and J. VanderKam, eds., *The Community of the Renewed Covenant: The Notre Dame Symposium on the Dead Sea Scrolls* (Notre Dame, IN: University of Notre Dame Press, 1994) 211-34.

94. M. O. Wise and J. Tabor, "The Messiah at Qumran," *Biblical Archaeology Review* (Nov.–Dec. 1992) 60-65; See the discussion by M. Abegg, "The Messiah at Qumran: Are We Still Seeing Double?" *Dead Sea Discoveries* 2 (1995) 125-44.

95. Charlesworth, ed., *The Rule of the Community and Related Documents*, 41.

matically, refer to either one or two messiahs, there is no reason why a single messiah should be said to come from both Aaron and Israel unless a dual messiahship had been envisaged at an earlier stage.[96] There is no evidence that CD is later than the texts that explicitly refer to two messiahs. Accordingly, the references in CD must be understood in the dual sense.

The expectation of two messiahs is not such an anomaly as it first appeared. We have seen that the *Testaments of the Twelve Patriarchs* imply belief in some Jewish circles in a messiah from Levi and a messiah from Judah. The biblical precedent for such dual messiahship is found in Zech 4:14, which speaks of two "sons of oil," the governor Zerubbabel and the high priest Joshua. Already in Zechariah, the priest is the more prominent figure, and the priestly messiah takes precedence both in the *Testaments* and in the scrolls. The idea of dual leadership would seem to have been revived in the second century BCE, the ideal priest in reaction to abuses of the priesthood, the duality of leadership in reaction to the Hasmonean combination of priestly and political power. Yet insofar as it had a biblical precedent it may be called "restorative" eschatology.[97] It is modeled on a situation of the past, looks for an idealized fulfillment of that situation, but is not entirely different from it. There is nothing to suggest that the messiahs are other than human. They will fill institutional roles within the community. They are eschatological figures, in the sense that they imply a definitive change in the course of history, but they do not imply an end of the historical process. S. Talmon has perceptively noted that the difference between the dual messiahship of Qumran and the single messiahship of Christianity is qualitative as well as quantitative.[98] What is involved at Qumran is an ideal community structure. There is no emphasis on the personalities of the messiahs as savior figures. In fact, the scrolls are tantalizingly reticent on the activities of the messiahs and in most cases merely assert that they will arise. The activity of the messiahs in 1QSa takes place within the eschatological age and is not envisaged as saving action that brings that age into being. The focus is on the community of which the messiahs are a part, rather than on the exaltation of the messiahs themselves.

96. Cf. F. M. Cross, "Some Notes on a Generation of Qumran Studies," in J. Trebolle Barrera, and L. Vegas Montaner, eds., *The Madrid Qumran Congress: Proceedings of the International Congress on the Dead Sea Scrolls, Madrid 18-21 March, 1991* (2 vols.; Leiden: Brill, 1992) 1:14.

97. Talmon, "Waiting for the Messiah," 293.

98. Ibid. See also J. J. Collins, " 'He Shall Not Judge by What His Eyes See': Messianic Authority in the Dead Sea Scrolls," *Dead Sea Discoveries* 2 (1995) 145-64.

The institutional focus of Qumran messianism is evident in the so-called *Messianic Rule*, 1QSa.[99] This brief document is introduced as "the rule for all the congregation of Israel in the last days." It is largely concerned with the different stages of initiation and authority in the community and with restrictions on membership of the assembly. Then in 1QSa 2:11-22 we find instructions for a time "when [God] begets the messiah to be with them."[100] The passage first describes the entry of the congregation in which the priest enters at the head of the Aaronids and then the messiah of Israel and the rest of the congregation. At the common table, the priest is the first to bless the bread and wine, then the messiah of Israel "shall stretch out his hand to the bread and then all the congregation shall give thanks and partake." The passage concludes: "And they shall act according to this prescription whenever (the meal) [is arr]anged when as many as ten solemnly meet together." There is a close parallel between the messianic meal of 1QSa and the community meal in 1QS 6:4: "and when they prepare the table to eat or the wine to drink, the priest will first stretch out his hand to bless the bread and the wine." The messianic age is expected to continue the current practices of the sect; or to put the matter another way, the sect is already anticipating the practices of the messianic age.[101]

The correspondences between the institutions of the sect and the messianic age sometimes lead to ambiguities. CD 6:2-11 applies Num 21:18 to the history of the community and concludes: "And the Staff (*měhôqeq*) is the Interpreter of the Law (*dôrēš hattôrāh*) . . . and the nobles of the people are those that have come to dig the well with precepts (*měhôqěqôt*) which the Staff laid down, that they might walk in them during the whole epoch of wickedness. Except for them they cannot grasp (the Law) until he who shall teach righteousness arises in the end of days." The "Righteous Teacher" is well known from other passages as the key figure in the founding of the sect.[102] Here, however, he is preceded by an "Interpreter of the Law," who sets out the precepts which are apparently still in force. There are two possible interpretations of this figure. Either he is a precur-

99. L. H. Schiffman, *The Eschatological Community of the Dead Sea Scrolls*.

100. The reading is disputed. For conflicting recent assessments, see G. Vermes, *The Dead Sea Scrolls in English* (rev. ed.; London: Penguin, 2004) 161, who reads *yôlîd*, "begets," and E. Puech, "Préséance sacerdotale et messie-roi dans la règle de la congregation (1QSa ii 11-22)," *RevQ* 63 (1994) 351-65, who reads *ytglh*, "is revealed."

101. Cf. Cross, *The Ancient Library*, 75-77.

102. G. Jeremias, *Der Lehrer der Gerechtigkeit* (Göttingen: Vandenhoeck & Ruprecht, 1963).

sor of the Teacher at the earliest beginnings of the sect,[103] or he is the one elsewhere called the "Righteous Teacher"; and the one who shall teach righteousness here is a messianic figure.[104] It is important that the one who shall teach righteousness here appears to be expected in the future. Elsewhere in CD the Righteous Teacher is always a figure in the past. In CD 20:1, 14 the "unique teacher" is already dead, and in 20:32 the voice of the Righteous Teacher is the normative way to salvation. CD 20 has been thought to be part of a separate, later source, but the Righteous Teacher (*môrēh haṣedeq*) is also mentioned in CD 1:11 in the account of the origin of the sect. One attempt to resolve the anomaly of the future reference in CD 6:11 has proposed that the document was composed before the rise of the Teacher. The phrase in CD 6:11, then, would refer to a messianic figure, with whom the historical Teacher was subsequently identified. This theory, however, fails to explain the present form of CD, where the "one who teaches righteousness" is still in the future, although the historical Teacher is clearly in the past. The conclusion that CD 6:11 refers to a messianic figure, presumably the messiah of Aaron, is inevitable. There is no warrant for the conclusion that such a figure was expected before the rise of the historical Teacher, or that the Teacher claimed to be a messiah.[105] Rather, the point is that the future messiah will fill the same role in the community as the historical Teacher. Most scholars have correctly seen that the "Interpreter of the Law" in this passage is none other than the historical Teacher. The complexity of the passage is compounded by the ambiguity of the expression "Interpreter of the Law," which clearly refers to a figure of the past in CD 6. In CD 7:18-20, however, the Interpreter is identified with the star of Balaam's Oracle, the scepter is the "Prince of the Whole Congregation," and the allusion is most probably messianic. In 4QFlor 1:11-12 the Interpreter is clearly messianic: the "Branch of David" will arise with the Interpreter of the Law in Zion at the end of days. "Interpreter of the Law," then, can refer to a figure of the past or to a messiah, or even in 1QS 6 to a present figure in the community. This ambiguous usage becomes intelligible if we bear in mind that the scrolls are concerned with functions and institutions rather than with personalities.

103. So P. R. Davies, *The Damascus Covenant*, 124; idem, "The Teacher of Righteousness at the End of Days," *RevQ* 13 (1988) 313-17.

104. Collins, *The Scepter and the Star*, 102-4.

105. See M. Knibb, "The Teacher of Righteousness — A Messianic Title?" in P. R. Davies and R. T. White, eds., *A Tribute to Geza Vermes: Essays on Jewish and Christian Literature and History* (Sheffield: JSOT Press, 1990) 51-65.

There have been various attempts to trace a development in the messianic expectation of the scrolls, but they have not been successful. J. Starcky proposed a four-stage theory of development, corresponding to four stages in the history of the community.[106] According to this theory, there was no messianism in the first stage, but the second, Hasmonean, phase was marked by dual messianism, with the priest taking precedence. The third stage is represented by the *Damascus Document*, which is understood to refer to only one messiah, of Aaron and Israel. The fourth stage is marked by the revival of expectation of a Davidic messiah. This theory has been widely criticized. It depends heavily on the paleographic dating of the manuscripts and assigns a later date to the *Damascus Document* than is now generally accepted. An alternative theory has been proposed by G. Brooke.[107] On his account, the original, "pre-Qumran," expectation was for a single "messiah of Aaron and Israel," as reflected in CD 19:7-13 (MS B). This expectation was revised at Qumran, and the revision is reflected in MS B of the same document, in CD 7:14-21. A third stage reverts to a single, priestly messiah.

Both of these theories require that the *Damascus Document* be understood to refer to one messiah, and therefore be at variance with 1QS 9:11. But CD 7:14-21 (MS A) clearly interprets Balaam's Oracle in terms of two figures, the Interpreter of the Law and the Prince of the Whole Congregation, and these are plausibly understood as the messiahs of Aaron and Israel. This passage is attested in the fragments of CD found at Qumran, whereas the corresponding passage from MS B is not. Moreover, a strong case has been made that both the readings of MS A and of MS B are part of the original document,[108] and in that case the dual messianism was inherent in CD from the beginning. This in turn strongly favors the dual interpretation of the phrase "messiah of Aaron and Israel." There is no clear evidence that this phrase ever carried a singular meaning.[109]

106. J. Starcky, "Les quatres étapes du messianisme à Qumrân," *RB* 70 (1963) 481-505. See the critique by R. Brown, "J. Starcky's Theory of Qumran Messianic Development," *CBQ* 28 (1966) 51-57.

107. G. J. Brooke, "The Messiah of Aaron in the Damascus Document," *RevQ* 15 (1991) 215-30.

108. S. A. White, "A Comparison of the 'A' and 'B' Manuscripts of the Damascus Document," *RevQ* 12 (1987) 537-53.

109. In CD 14:19 Rabin translates, "until there shall arise the Messiah of Aaron and Israel and he will make conciliation for their trespass . . ." (C. Rabin, *The Zadokite Document* [Oxford: Clarendon, 1958] 70). However, the verb for "make conciliation," *ykpr*, could also be read as a *pual*, with "their trespass" as subject: "their trespass will be covered over."

Consequently, theories of messianic development in the scrolls have no firm foundation.[110]

The prophet who is mentioned in connection with the messiahs in 1QS 9:11 remains a shadowy figure. The biblical basis for this figure in Deuteronomy 18 is cited in the *Testimonia*. There is also some evidence for the expectation of a prophet like Elijah, or Elijah *redivivus,* in accordance with Mal 3:1; 4:5, and Sir 48:10. One very fragmentary text mentions Elijah explicitly.[111] The most interesting text in this regard, however, is the subject of dispute. The text in question, 4Q521 2 ii, speaks of a messiah whom heaven and earth will obey. The text goes on to weave together allusions to Psalm 146, Isaiah 61, and other biblical passages. God will "glorify the pious on the throne of an eternal kingdom, releasing captives, giving sight to the blind and raising up those who are bo[wed down]." Finally, "the glorious things that have not taken place the Lord will do as he s[aid], for he will heal the wounded, give life to the dead, and preach good news to the poor, and he will [sat]isfy the [weak] ones and lead those who have been cast out and enrich the hungry. . . ."[112] It is surprising to find God as the subject of preaching good news. That is normally the work of a herald or messenger.[113] The phrase in question is taken from Isa 61:1-2: "The spirit of the Lord God is upon me, because the Lord has anointed me; he has sent me to preach good news to the poor, to bind up the brokenhearted, to proclaim liberty to the captives and release to the prisoners; to proclaim the year of the Lord's favor, and the day of vengeance of our God." In Isaiah 61, the speaker is a prophet, who speaks in the name of the Lord. There is little evidence for the anointing of prophets in the Hebrew Bible,[114] but prophets are called "anointed ones" in CD 2:12; 6:1; and 1QM 11:7.

110. H. Stegemann, "Some Remarks to 1QSa, to 1QSb and to Qumran Messianism," *RevQ* 17 (1996) 479-506, has proposed a new theory in which the *War Rule* represents the earliest stage, 1QSa and 1QSb represent the second stage, and CD and the *Testimonia* represent the third stage, but the dating of these documents is very problematic.

111. 4Q558 (= 4QarP). See Puech, *La Croyance des Esséniens en la Vie Future: Immortalité, Résurrection, Vie Éternelle?* (Paris: Gabalda, 1993) 676-77.

112. For the text, see Puech, "Une Apocalypse Messianique." On the interpretation, see Collins, *The Scepter and the Star,* 131-41.

113. Simon J. Joseph, *Jesus, Q, and the Dead Sea Scrolls* (WUNT 2.333; Tübingen: Mohr Siebeck, 2012) 174, fails to grasp or deal with this point. He nonetheless maintains that "there is an implicit relationship between the deeds performed and the appearance of an 'anointed' figure" (183). He maintains, without any positive argumentation, that the "messiah" in this text is a royal figure.

114. In 1 Kgs 19:16 Elijah is told to anoint Elisha, but he is not actually said to do so.

THE APOCALYPTIC IMAGINATION

Isaiah 61 is also cited in 11QMelchizedek, which also refers to a messenger, who is called "the anointed of the spirit" (11QMelch 2:18). The suspicion arises, then, that the works of the Lord in 4Q521 are performed through the agency of a prophet. The works of healing and especially the raising of the dead were associated with Elijah and Elisha. Elijah also had power to command the heavens, and so could easily be identified with the anointed one whom heaven and earth obey.[115] This figure then may be identified as Elijah *redivivus* or a prophet like Elijah. Since the identification is not made explicitly, however, it is likely to remain in dispute.

## The War of Light and Darkness

The "end of days" would be marked not only by the coming of the messiahs but also by the definitive war against the forces of evil. Several Qumran documents allude to this war. A *pesher* on Isaiah (4Q161) refers to "the war of the Kittim" and mentions Magog in a fragment that also speaks of the Branch of David. The *Hôdāyôt* refer to "the war of the heavenly warriors" that fills the earth in the time of the wrath of Belial (1QH 11:35, formerly 3:35).[116] The most elaborate account of this war, however, is found in the *War Rule,* which survives in a substantially complete manuscript from Cave 1 (1QM) and in several fragmentary copies from Cave 4.[117]

Even before the publication of the Cave 4 fragments, it was clear that the *War Scroll* was not a unified document. The first column of 1QM outlines a war in seven lots between the Sons of Light and the Sons of Darkness. Column 2, however, envisages a war of forty years and pays great attention to the temple service in a sabbatical year. Columns 2–9 deal with various aspects of mobilization for battle. Columns 10–14 provide prayers related to the battle. Finally, columns 15–19 provide a more detailed review of the seven-stage war envisaged in column 1. While a few scholars

---

115. Cf. Sir 48:3; Rev 11:6.

116. Cf. the militant role of the Prince of the Congregation in CD 7:20-21 and the time of trial in the *Florilegium.*

117. J. Duhaime, "War Scroll," in J. H. Charlesworth, ed., *The Dead Sea Scrolls: Hebrew, Aramaic and Greek Texts with English Translations.* Volume 2: *Damascus Document, War Scroll, and Related Documents* (Tübingen: Mohr Siebeck; Louisville: Westminster John Knox, 1995) 80-203.

have defended the unity of the composition,[118] most have recognized a fundamental difference between the conception of the war in columns 1 and 15–19 and that of columns 2–9.[119] The framing columns provide the metaphysical context of the war, while columns 2–9 are concerned more with human participation.

The picture is complicated by the fragments from Cave 4, which contain numerous variants and readings that have no parallel in 1QM. The most important additional text is found in 4Q285, which gives the Davidic messiah a significant role in the conflict, which was not apparent in 1QM.[120] These fragments show that the *War Rule* had a complicated redactional history. 1QM is dated on paleographical grounds to the second half of the first century BCE. 4Q496, which is somewhat older, already contains parallels to both column 1 and column 2, and so the essential structure of the *War Rule* had probably taken shape by the middle of the first century BCE.

The material in 1QM columns 2–9 bears a general similarity to Hellenistic military manuals,[121] and shows some acquaintance with Hellenistic and Roman military strategy.[122] The most distinctive aspect of these columns, however, is their ritualistic character. The *War Rule* draws heavily on the organization of the Israelite tribes in the wilderness, as depicted in the book of Numbers. (The forty-year duration of the war is also an allusion to the wilderness period.) The army is divided into organizational units: camp, tribe, myriad, thousand, hundred, fifty, ten (cf. Exodus 18). Banners are used to distinguish the different units (cf. Num 2:2; 17:2-3). The use of trumpets is mandated by Num 10:1-10. Several of these features are also attested in the Maccabean wars, and the Romans also made use of standards and trumpets.[123] The ritualistic character of the *War Rule* is shown most clearly in the provision for the purity of the camp in 1QM

118. Most notably Y. Yadin, *The Scroll of the War of the Sons of Light against the Sons of Darkness* (Oxford: Oxford University Press, 1962).

119. J. van der Ploeg, *Le Rouleau de la Guerre* (Leiden: Brill, 1959); P. von der Osten-Sacken, *Gott und Belial*; P. R. Davies, *1QM: The War Scroll from Qumran* (Rome: Biblical Institute Press, 1977).

120. M. Abegg, "Messianic Hope and 4Q285."

121. J. Duhaime, "The War Scroll from Qumran and the Greco-Roman Tactical Treatises," *RevQ* 13 (1988) 133-51.

122. Yadin, *The Scroll of the War*, 147, 174-75, argues that the use of "gates of war," spaces within and between the lines from which skirmishers issued forth, reflects the Roman *intervalla*.

123. Cf. 1QpHab 6:4, which notes the Roman custom of worshipping their standards.

7:3-7.[124] Women and young boys are barred from the camp, as are the halt, blind, and lame. Moreover, "any man who is not pure with regard to his sexual organs on the day of battle shall not join them in battle, for holy angels are in communion with their hosts."[125] Moreover, the ages assigned for military functions suggest that theological considerations took precedence. The youngest group is aged 25-30, and these are assigned to despoil the slain, collect the booty, and cleanse the land, not to military tasks that required physical agility. (In the book of Numbers, the age of mobilization was 20.) Further ritualistic characteristics are the emphasis on the temple service, in 1QM 2, and the string of prayers collected in columns 10-14. The prayers in columns 10-12 are highly traditional. Dualistic elements appear more strongly in columns 13 and 14. The prayers in column 12 sum up a crucial aspect of the view of warfare that permeates this document:

> Thou wilt muster the [hosts of] Thine [el]ect, in their Thousands and Myriads, with Thy Holy Ones [and with all] Thine Angels, that they may be mighty in battle, [and may smite] the rebels of the earth by Thy great judgments. . . . For Thou art [terrible], O God, in the glory of Thy kingdom, and the congregation of Thy Holy Ones is among us for everlasting succor . . . the King of Glory is with us together with the Holy Ones. Valiant [warriors] of the angelic host are among our numbered men, and the Hero of war is with our congregation; the host of his spirits is with our foot-soldiers and horsemen. (1QM 12:4-9)

All parts of the *War Rule* are permeated with a sense of the presence of angelic forces. While the regulations in columns 2-9 have some parallels with Maccabean practice, the overall picture that we get from the *Rule* is very different from the pragmatic approach presented by 1 Maccabees.[126]

The metaphysical backdrop of the war is more clearly in evidence in columns 1 and 15-19. The opening column identifies the antagonists as "the Sons of Light" and "the Sons of Darkness, the army of Belial." The Sons of Darkness are assisted by Edom, Moab, and the sons of Ammon (cf.

124. A different recension of this material can be found in 4Q491, fragments 1-3, lines 6-8.

125. Cf. the provisions for the purity of the eschatological community in 1QSa 2:4-10. The parallel makes clear that the problem with the blind and the lame was not a matter of military fitness.

126. The analogy with Maccabean warfare is pressed by Davies, *1QM*.

Dan 11:41), the dwellers of Philistia (Isa 11:14), and the Kittim. The name "Kittim" is derived from Citium in Cyprus and was applied, according to Josephus (*Antiquities* 1.3.1 §128), to all islands and most maritime countries. In Daniel 11 the Kittim are the Romans, but 1 Maccabees says that Alexander the Great came from the land of Kittim, and calls Perseus, king of Macedonia, "king of the Kittim" (8:5). In the Qumran *pesharim* the Kittim are clearly the Romans, and in the first century CE the reference in the *War Rule* would certainly have been applied to the Romans too. Yet it is clear that "Kittim" could refer to either Romans or Greeks, and the "Kittim of Asshur" may well have been originally the Seleucids (compare the "chief of the kings of Greece," CD 8).[127] The "king of the Kittim" (15:3) would then be a Greek king, not necessarily a historical individual but whoever happened to be king at the time of the final conflict. In the first century CE the phrase would have been applied to the Roman emperor. In any case, it would appear that the "Kittim" function here like "the nations" in Psalm 2, as the consummation of Gentile hostility in the end time.

1QM column 1 has numerous allusions to Daniel.[128] The opening column of the *Scroll* has various terminological echoes of Daniel 11-12. These include "violators of the covenant" (1QM 1:2), Kittim passim, one who will "go forth in great wrath . . . to destroy" (1QM 1:4), no helper for Assyria (1QM 1:6, cf. Dan 11:42, 45). The time of the battle is a time of distress (1QM 1:11-12; Dan 12:1). The archangel Michael, prince of Israel, who arises in victory in Dan 12:1, is also exalted in 1QM 17:7. The *War Scroll* takes these terms and applies them in a new context. For example, the Kittim in Daniel are clearly the Romans, and they have only an incidental role in the drama of the end-time. In the *War Scroll*, they are the primary enemy, and it is arguable that "the Kittim of Assyria" are the Seleucids.[129] David Flusser, followed now by Brian Schultz, has argued that the dependence on Daniel is not only terminological: "the eschatological vision of the *War Scroll* is predicated on an actualizing interpretation of Daniel's unfulfilled

---

127. Brian Schultz, *Conquering the World: The War Scroll (1QM) Reconsidered* (STDJ 76; Leiden: Brill, 2009) 127-58.

128. von der Osten-Sacken, *Gott und Belial,* 30-34; Collins, "The Book of Daniel in the Dead Sea Scrolls."

129. D. Flusser, "Apocalyptic Elements in the *War Scroll*," in idem, *Judaism of the Second Temple Period.* Vol. 1. *Qumran and Apocalypticism* (Grand Rapids: Eerdmans, 2007) 149. Schultz, *Conquering the World*, 393; D. J. Harrington, "Holy War Texts Among the Qumran Scrolls," in P. W. Flint, E. Tov, and J. C. VanderKam, eds., *Studies in the Hebrew Bible, Qumran, and the Septuagint presented to Eugene Ulrich* (VTSup 101; Leiden: Brill, 2006) 178.

prophecy."[130] The wicked king must yet be destroyed. Schultz argues that while the new scenario offered by the *War Scroll* is less dependent than Daniel on precise historical events, yet it reflects the same socio-political dynamics: "there is still conflict between Egypt in the south and Syria in the north; within Judea, those who violate the covenant do so by their alliance with Syria."[131] He argues that this supports an early (Seleucid period) date at least for this section of the *War Scroll*:

> From the perspective of realism, the sooner it is composed after the people have realized that that portion of Daniel's prophecy did not come to fruition, the easier it is to reflect the same socio-political environment and the more plausible the scenario will seem to its readers.[132]

The Seleucid context in itself does not require a date before the first century BCE. Schultz argues that the apparent independence of Edom, Moab, Ammon, and Philistia, argues for a date before the time of Alexander Jannaeus.[133] In any case, the dependence of the opening column of the *War Scroll* on Daniel is clear.

The overall structure of the war in the *War Rule,* however, departs from Daniel at several significant points.[134] The course of the war is now measured out in seven phases, with the forces of light and darkness dominating in turn, until God intervenes decisively in the final period. This balanced division, the imagery of light and darkness, and the opposing roles of Michael and Belial as well-matched adversaries under God all suggest that the Qumran *War Rule* has been influenced by Persian dualism.

The following account of Persian dualism is found in Plutarch's treatise *On Isis and Osiris* 47, but Plutarch claims to derive it from Theopompus, who wrote about 300 BCE:

> But they (the Persians) also relate many mythical details about the gods, and the following are instances. Horomazes is born from the purest light and Areimanius from darkness, and they are at war with

130. Flusser, "Apocalyptic Elements," 156. Compare Schultz, *Conquering the World*, 93-99.

131. Schultz, *Conquering the World*, 101.

132. Ibid., 102.

133. Schultz, *Conquering the World*, 101-2.

134. See J. J. Collins, "The Mythology of Holy War in Daniel and the Qumran War Scroll," *VT* 25 (1975) 596-612.

one another. . . . Theopompus says that, according to the Magians, for three thousand years alternately the one god will dominate the other and be dominated, and that for another three thousand years they will fight and make war, until one smashes up the domain of the other. In the end Hades shall perish and men shall be happy . . . while the god who will have brought this about shall have quiet and rest.[135]

Plutarch's account is problematic in some respects. It is not clear what branch of Zoroastrianism it represents, and there is debate as to precisely how the periodization of history should be understood.[136] Yet, the division of history into periods and the dualism of light and darkness are well attested in Persian tradition. Most significant for our purpose is the motif of a balanced conflict between light and darkness, which has no part in traditional Israelite religion. It is not suggested that the *War Rule* reproduces any Persian source accurately, but only that these motifs, which are new in a Jewish context, were suggested by an acquaintance, however superficial, with Zoroastrianism.[137]

Various attempts have been made to trace a process of development within the *War Rule*. Several scholars, primarily German, have argued that the *Rule* is at least in part older than the Qumran community. It lacks distinctive sectarian terminology.[138] The word *yahad* is used as an adjective ("together with") rather than as a noun ("commune"). The designation "God of Israel" is rare in the other scrolls. The *War Rule* addresses all Israel and endorses the temple cult. The analogy of the camp in the wilderness might have originated in the military setting and been taken over subsequently for other aspects of sectarian organization. But the pan-Israelite perspective may be due to the fact that the *Rule* is intended for the "end of days." The *Messianic Rule*, 1QSa, is likewise addressed to "all the congregation of Israel in the last days." P. von der Osten-Sacken argued for an early Maccabean date for the dualistic frame of the *War Rule*, because of

---

135. Griffiths, *Plutarch's De Iside et Osiride*, 46-47.

136. The rival gods may each dominate for three thousand years, or may dominate in turn within the three-thousand-year periods. The total period involved could be either nine thousand or seven thousand years. See Kobelski, *Melchizedek and Melchireša'*, 86-87; Collins, *Apocalypticism in the Dead Sea Scrolls*, 102.

137. See further Collins, *Apocalypticism in the Dead Sea Scrolls*, 101-3.

138. L. Rost, "Zum Buch der Kriege der Söhne des Lichtes gegen die Söhne der Finsternis," *TLZ* 80 (1955) 205-8; von der Osten-Sacken, *Gott und Belial*; Stegemann, *Die Essener*, 145-48.

parallels with Daniel.[139] But while the *Rule* uses Daniel, its conception of the war is quite different. All we may conclude is that it is later than Daniel, but it could be considerably later. Conversely, Philip Davies has argued for the priority of columns 2–9, which he associates with the Maccabean wars. Davies argues that the dualistic frame was only introduced in the final stage, which he dates to the first century CE.[140] The latter date is shown to be impossible by the Cave 4 fragments, which had not been published when Davies wrote, and the *Rule* has more distinctive parallels with Roman military practice than it has with the Maccabees. While the *War Rule* evidently incorporates diverse traditions, it is not possible to establish a chronological sequence between its constituent parts. The dualistic frame and the traditions about the forty-year war seem to have been combined by the middle of the first century BCE.

The militancy of the *War Rule* is often thought to contrast with the quietism of the Qumran community as a whole. The hymn appended to 1QS proclaims, "I will pay to no man the reward of evil; I will pursue him with goodness. For judgment of all the living is with God, and it is He who will render to man his reward. . . . I will not grapple with the men of perdition until the Day of Revenge" (1QS 10:17-19). But this position is not one of absolute pacifism. The author has no qualms about exacting vengeance on the Day of Revenge. We know that the Qumran settlement was destroyed by the Roman army in 68 CE. We do not know whether it was defended by the community that had lived there, or whether it had been taken over by Jewish rebels. It is quite possible, however, that the community believed that the Day of Revenge had come, and took up arms in expectation that the drama of the eschatological war would be acted out.[141] If so, it was cruelly disappointed.

## The Afterlife

The extant text of the *War Rule* does not clearly describe the state of salvation that follows the eschatological war. It will extend "unto all appointed times of [eternity] for peace and blessing, glory and joy, and long life for all Sons

139. von der Osten-Sacken, *Gott und Belial,* 85.

140. Davies, *1QM,* 124.

141. Josephus, *Jewish War* 2.8.10 §§152–53, claims that the Essenes exhibited great bravery under torture by the Romans.

of Light" (1:9). The hymnic passage in 1QM 12:11-15 uses a string of biblical phrases to paint a picture of this-worldly glory in Zion. These passages are at least compatible with a this-worldly view of salvation. 1QM envisages the "eternal annihilation of all the lot of Belial" (1QM 1:5), but there is no reference to the destruction of the world, and the historical process is not necessarily brought to an end. All of this corresponds to what we find in the Instruction on the Two Spirits in the *Community Rule*. God "has put down a limited time for the existence of deceit. At the time fixed for visitation He will destroy it for ever, and then the truth of the earth will appear forever" (1QS 4:18-19). The outcome for the Sons of Light involves "healing and great peace in a long life, multiplication of progeny, together with all everlasting blessings, endless joy in everlasting life, and a crown of glory together with a resplendent attire in eternal light" (1QS 4:7-8), and for the Sons of Darkness "eternal perdition by the fury of God's vengeful wrath, everlasting terror and endless shame, together with disgrace of annihilation in the fire of dark regions" (1QS 4:12-13). Neither the *War Rule* nor the *Community Rule* uses the language of resurrection or speaks clearly of an end of this world.

The kind of afterlife envisioned in the scrolls has been the subject of a debate that has been framed in large part by the conflicting accounts of the eschatology of the Essenes. According to Josephus:

> It is a firm belief among them that although bodies are corruptible, and their matter unstable, souls are immortal and endure for ever; that, come from subtlest ether, they are entwined with the bodies which serve them as prisons . . . but that when they are freed from the bonds of the flesh, liberated, so to speak, from long slavery, then they re-joice and rise up to the heavenly world. Agreeing with the sons of the Greeks, they declare that an abode is reserved beyond the Ocean for the souls of the just; a place oppressed neither by rain nor snow nor torrid heat, but always refreshed by the gentle breeze blowing from the Ocean. But they relegate evil souls to a dark pit shaken by storms, full of unending chastisement. (*Jewish War* 2.8.11 §§154–56)[142]

While this account is obviously tailored to Greek tastes, it corresponds quite well to what we have cited above from the *Community Rule*.

---

142. Trans. Vermes and Goodman, *The Essenes*, 47. For Josephus's broader treatment of immortality in Judaism of the time, see C. D. Elledge, *Life after Death in Early Judaism* (WUNT 28; Tübingen: Mohr Siebeck, 2006) 53-145.

The Hebrew texts do not speak of immortality of the soul, but they agree with Josephus in describing reward and punishment after death in a way that does not require the resurrection of the body.[143]

A very different account of Essene eschatology, however, is found in the writings of Hippolytus, bishop of Rome, who flourished about 200 CE:

> The doctrine of the resurrection has also derived support among them, for they acknowledge both that the flesh will rise again and that it will be immortal, in the same manner as the soul is already imperishable. They maintain that when the soul has been separated from the body it is now borne into one place, which is well ventilated and full of light, and there it rests until judgment. This locality the Greeks were acquainted with by hearsay, calling it Isles of the Blessed. But there are many tenets of these men which the wise of the Greeks have appropriated . . . for they affirm that there will be both a judgment and a conflagration of the universe, and that the wicked will be eternally punished. (*Refutation of All Heresies* 27)

Hippolytus almost certainly knew Josephus's account.[144] The differences between them can be attributed to confusion or distortion on the part of Hippolytus. He confused the Essenes with the Zealots, and he suppressed a reference to sun worship on the part of the Essenes. His account of Essene eschatology corresponds almost exactly to what he says about the beliefs of the Pharisees (*Ref* 9.28.5) and to his accounts of both Jewish and Christian eschatology in general (*Ref* 9.30.8; *Ref* 10.34). His reference to a conflagration of the universe, however, finds striking confirmation in the *Hôdāyôt* from Qumran. 1QH 11:29-36 (formerly 1QH 3) says that "the torrents of Belial will overflow their high

---

143. See further John J. Collins, "Conceptions of Afterlife in the Dead Sea Scrolls," in Michael Labahn and Manfred Lang, eds., *Lebendige Hoffnung – ewiger Tod?! Jenseitsvorstellungen im Hellenismus, Judentum und Christentum* (Leipzig: Evangelische Verlagsanstalt, 2007) 103-25.

144. M. Smith, "The Description of the Essenes in Josephus and the Philosophoumena," *HUCA* 29 (1958) 273-313, argued that Hippolytus was independent of Josephus, but later changed his mind. See Smith, "Helios in Palestine," *Eretz Israel* 16 (1982) 212*-13*. See further Christoph Burchard, "Die Essener bei Hippolyt. Hippolyt, Ref. IX 18,2-28 und Josephus, Bell. 2.119-161," *JSJ* 8 (1977) 1-42, and Collins, *Scriptures and Sectarianism*, 222-26. A synopsis of the accounts of the Essenes in Josephus and Hippolytus can be found in Elledge, *Life after Death*, 163-67.

banks like a fire that devours . . . the bases of the mountains shall burn and the roots of flint rock become streams of lava. It consumes right to the great deep." Some scholars also accept the account of Hippolytus that the Essenes believed in resurrection,[145] but this remains highly controversial.

Belief in resurrection was certainly known at Qumran, since it is found in the books of Daniel and Enoch, which were preserved in multiple copies. Among the previously unknown texts found at Qumran, however, explicit references to resurrection are rare. Resurrection figures prominently in 4Q521, the text that speaks of a messiah whom heaven and earth obey. The wonderful works of the Lord in the eschatological time include raising the dead (fragment 2 ii 12), and another fragment refers to God as the one who gives life to the dead ones of his people (fragment 7 + 5 ii).[146] The Pseudo-Ezekiel text, 4Q385, recounts Ezekiel's vision of the valley full of dry bones in response to a question about the recompense of Israelites who walk in righteousness.[147] The logic of the question would seem to require individual recompense, and so the vision is probably understood as referring to the resurrection of individuals, rather than to the corporate resurrection of Israel. Neither of these texts, however, is clearly sectarian in origin. They may be part of the literary heritage of the sect, like the books of Enoch and Daniel.

We have seen already that the *Community Rule* and the *War Rule* refer to reward and punishment after death, but not to resurrection. This is also true of the *Damascus Document,* which threatens the wicked with "great flaming wrath by the hand of all the Angels of Destruction" (CD 2:5-6), while the righteous "are destined to live forever, and all the glory of Adam shall be theirs" (CD 3:20). In these cases, we have immortality without resurrection, a concept that seems to be in substantial agreement with the admittedly Hellenized account of Josephus. We have found such a belief already in *Jubilees* 23. The issue is complicated, however, by the evidence of the *Hôdāyôt.*

On the one hand, these hymns use the eschatological language of resurrection and exaltation to express the present experience of the members of the community. So we read in 1QH 11:19-22 (formerly 1QH 3):

145. So especially Puech, *La Croyance,* 703-69.
146. Puech, "Une Apocalypse Messianique," 500-501.
147. D. Dimant and J. Strugnell, "The Merkabah Vision in Second Ezekiel (4Q385 4)," *RevQ* 14 (1990) 331-48.

I thank Thee, O Lord, for Thou hast released my life from the pit, and from the abyss of Sheol Thou hast raised me up to an eternal height so that I can wander in the plain without limit, and so that I know that there is hope for him whom Thou hast formed out of clay unto an eternal fellowship. And the perverted spirit Thou hast cleansed from the great transgression to stand in the assembly with the hosts of the saints and to come into communion with the congregation of the sons of heaven.

Again in 1QH 19:10-14 (formerly 1QH 11):

For your glory, you have purified man from sin so that he can make himself holy for you from every impure abomination and blameworthy iniquity, to become united with the sons of your truth and in a lot with your holy ones, to raise from the dust the worm of the dead to an [everlasting] community, and from a depraved spirit, to your knowledge, so that he can take his place in your presence with the perpetual host and the [everlasting] spirits, to renew him with everything that will exist, and with those who know in a community of jubilation.

In these passages, the hymnist claims to enjoy in the present the fellowship with the angels that was promised to the righteous after death in the apocalypses of Daniel and Enoch. This claim may reasonably be described as realized eschatology.[148] Fellowship with the angels is a frequent theme in the Dead Sea Scrolls.[149] Angels mingle with the community in the *Messianic Rule* (1QSa) and again in the *War Rule*. The *Community Rule* (1QS 11:5-8) claims that God has caused his chosen ones "to inherit the lot of the holy ones. He has joined their assembly to the sons of heaven to be a council of the community. . . ." Fellowship with the angels, then,

---

148. H.-W. Kuhn, *Enderwartung und Gegenwärtiges Heil* (Göttingen: Vandenhoeck & Ruprecht, 1966); G. W. E. Nickelsburg, *Resurrection, Immortality, and Eternal Life*, 181-93. For an attempt to explain the Hodayot in terms of visionary experience, see Angela Kim Harkins, *Reading with an 'I' to the Heavens: Looking at the Qumran Hodayot Through the Lens of Visionary Traditions* (Ekstasis 3; Berlin: de Gruyter, 2012).

149. D. Dimant, "Men as Angels: The Self-Image of the Qumran Community," in eadem, *History, Ideology and Bible Interpretation*, 465-72; Collins, "The Angelic Life," in idem, *Scriptures and Sectarianism*, 195-211. C. T. H. Fletcher-Louis, *All the Glory of Adam: Liturgical Anthropology in the Dead Sea Scrolls* (STDJ 42; Leiden: Brill, 2002) 88-135 pushes the "angelomorphic" character of the community to an extreme.

is not a peculiarity of the *Hôdāyôt,* but is well attested at Qumran. An extreme form of this claim can be found in the so-called self-exaltation hymn, 4Q491, fragment 11, where the author refers to "a throne of strength in the congregation of the gods" and claims to be "counted among the gods, and my dwelling is in the holy congregation."[150]

The belief that the community enjoyed present fellowship with the angels is perhaps the most distinctive aspect of the eschatology of the Dead Sea Scrolls. Nonetheless, there are also passages in the *Hôdāyôt* that can be interpreted in terms of a belief in resurrection. The passage just cited from 1QH 11 is a case in point. God is said to "raise the worm of the dead from the dust." The same phrase *(twl't mtym)* occurs in 1QH 14:34 (formerly 1QH 6:34): "Hoist a banner, you who lie in the dust; raise a standard, worm of dead ones." This passage alludes to Isa 26:19, which refers to those who dwell in the dust, and to Isa 41:14, "do not fear, worm of Jacob, men of Israel." The Hebrew word for "men" in Isa 41:14 is the rare word *mty,* which occurs only in the construct plural and has the same consonants as the more familiar word for "dead ones." In Isaiah 41, the addressees are downcast but not dead. Consequently the possibility arises that the language is also metaphorical in the *Hôdāyôt.* It is also possible that these passages attest a belief in resurrection, as Emile Puech argues. But even if they do, resurrection was not the primary focus of the eschatology of the community. Since the members believed that they were already living the risen life with the angels, resurrection was relatively unimportant.

## Conclusion

The Dead Sea Scrolls are best viewed as a corpus of writings that do not necessarily all represent the views of the community that collected them. Within this corpus, however, there is a core group of writings, including the rule books, *pesharim,* and *Hôdāyôt,* that exhibits a basic coherence and that may be taken to represent the beliefs of the sect. While none of these core writings is in the form of an apocalypse, they share some fundamental aspects of the apocalyptic worldview, and they also adapt it in significant ways. The world is mysterious, and the most important truths require special revelation. In the scrolls, however, this revelation is tied to

---

150. Collins, *The Scepter and the Star,* 149-70; Philip Alexander, *The Mystical Texts: Songs of the Sabbath Sacrifice and Related Manuscripts* (London: T & T Clark, 2006) 85-92.

the interpretation of the traditional scriptures to a far greater degree than was the case in the apocalypses of *Enoch* and Daniel. The scrolls share with the apocalypses the idea that history is divided into periods and that the time of the end is predetermined. Unlike the books of *Enoch* and Daniel, but like some later apocalypses, they envision a messianic age, when the promises to Israel will be fulfilled in this world. The restoration of the temple cult, under a messiah of Aaron, is an important feature of this age. The scrolls also envisage a war for the extermination of wickedness, and the notion of a final conflagration is attested in the *Hôdāyôt,* but only in one passage. Whether the community expected a final, public resurrection remains questionable. They believed that they already enjoyed the fellowship with the angels that was promised to the righteous after death in the apocalypses, and they believed that this blessed life would last forever, despite the obvious fact of human mortality. They also believed in the everlasting punishment of the damned. These beliefs and ideas appear to be typical of the Dead Sea sect. It is not suggested, however, that there was any fixed creed. Even the properly sectarian writings are not systematically consistent, and there seems to have been considerable flexibility in the formulation of beliefs. Orthopraxy in the observance of the Law is emphasized more than orthodoxy of belief, although beliefs also played an integral part in the constitution of the community.

The Dead Sea Scrolls, along with the writings of early Christianity, provide our main evidence from antiquity for a community in which apocalyptic beliefs played an important part. It is clear that these beliefs were not the only factor that was constitutive of the sect. There was also a strong priestly theology and a particular, strict, tradition of interpretation of the Law. The apocalyptic ideas put the theology of the sect in a cosmic context. The claim of divine revelation underpins that theology with supernatural certainty. The community's interpretation of the Law now becomes the criterion for judgment, which will determine eternal blessedness or damnation. The claim that "this is the end of days" lends urgency to the message of the sect. It is quite conceivable, however, that a rival sect with a different interpretation of the Law, or a quite different theological tradition, could have framed its teachings with similar apocalyptic beliefs. The claim of revelation and the expectation of imminent judgment do not in themselves determine the content of what is revealed or the values on which the judgment will be based. Apocalypticism is compatible with various theological traditions, but is likely to intensify whatever beliefs a group may hold.

Nonetheless, the apocalyptic frame of the teaching of the sect has some implications for the nature of its theology. Even though the scrolls look for an earthly fulfillment in the messianic age, the belief that this world is passing away lends an otherworldly orientation to their world-view. The goal of the Qumran community, even more clearly than was the case in Daniel and *Enoch,* was an angelic form of life. In the worldview of the scrolls, this required a high degree of purity, which was demanded already by Levitical laws but was intensified by the eschatological beliefs of the sect. The accounts of the Essenes by Philo, Josephus, and Pliny make much of their practice of celibacy,[151] even though Josephus admits that some Essenes married.[152] Whether these accounts are compatible with the evidence of the scrolls is much disputed.[153] While several major scrolls (CD, 1QSa, the *War Rule*) clearly provide for marriage, it is true that the scrolls have restrictive rulings on sexual activity, and some passages have been taken to imply some practice of celibacy.[154] Abstention from marriage, whether temporary or permanent, would certainly be compatible with the desire to live an angelic life. Not all members of the sect withdrew from society to the same degree. The *Community Rule* provides for an elite group that "shall separate from the habitation of unjust men and shall go into the wilderness to prepare there the way of Him" (1QS 8:13). This group may correspond to "those who walk in perfect holiness," who are contrasted with those who live in camps and marry in CD 7:5-6, and are often thought be the nucleus of the *yaḥad,* including the actual Qumran settlement, as distinct from other sectarian communities. In this case, the priestly theology of the sect and its apocalyptic conviction of imminent change fitted well together to produce a community that withdrew from society to seek heaven on earth in the wilderness of Judea.

151. Philo, *Hypothetica* 11.14; Josephus, *Jewish War* 2.8.2 §§120–21; Pliny, *Natural History* 5.17.4 §73.

152. Josephus, *Jewish War* 2.8.13 §§160–61.

153. See, e.g., E. Qimron, "Celibacy in the Dead Sea Scrolls and the Two Kinds of Sectarians," in J. Trebolle Barrera and L. Vegas Montaner, eds., *The Madrid Qumran Congress,* 1:287-94; H. Stegemann, "The Qumran Essenes — Local Members of the Main Jewish Union of Late Second Temple Times," ibid., 1:83-175.

154. See especially J. Baumgarten, "Qumran-Essene Restraints on Marriage," in Schiffman, ed., *Archaeology and History in the Dead Sea Scrolls,* 13-24.

# CHAPTER SIX

# The Similitudes of Enoch

The Aramaic fragments discovered at Qumran have thrown new light on much of the book of *Enoch*. In the case of the Similitudes (*1 Enoch* 37–71), however, no fragments have been found. J. T. Milik was thus led to conclude that the Similitudes are not a Jewish work at all but rather a late, third-century Christian composition.[1] This thesis has attracted considerable attention, since it involves a matter of central importance for New Testament studies as well as ancient Judaism: the figure of the "Son of Man," which plays a major role in the Similitudes. This document has been regarded as the principal evidence for Jewish speculation on a "Son of Man" figure in New Testament times. Its historical significance would be greatly altered if it were shown to be a later Christian product.

Milik's argument rests not only on the absence from Qumran but also on his theory that the Similitudes displaced the Book of Giants in an original Enochic pentateuch and on alleged parallels with Christian sections of the *Sibylline Oracles*. No aspect of this argument has withstood the test of criticism.[2] Absence from Qumran cannot prove that the Similitudes did not exist in this period. The Essene library did not include all the literature of the day, and the Similitudes may have been unacceptable in any case because of the near equality of the sun and moon in chap. 41, as opposed to the special treatment of the sun elsewhere in the scrolls.[3] There is no tex-

---

1. J. T. Milik, *The Books of Enoch: Aramaic Fragments from Qumrân Cave 4* (Oxford: Clarendon, 1976) 89-98.

2. For an early review of the literature, see D. W. Suter, "Weighed in the Balance: The Similitudes of Enoch in Recent Discussion," *RelStudRev* 7 (1981) 217-21.

3. See J. C. Greenfield and M. E. Stone, "The Enochic Pentateuch and the Date of the Similitudes," *HTR* 70 (1977) 51-65, who attribute this insight to David Flusser.

tual evidence that the Enochic books were ever regarded as a pentateuch. The parallels with the *Sibylline Oracles* are quite superficial. The overall genre is different, since the oracles lack the visionary aspect. The present form of the Similitudes, which explicitly identifies Enoch as the "Son of Man," must be Jewish. It is unlikely that a Jewish author would have accorded such a central role to a "Son of Man" figure after that expression had become established as a christological title. Indeed, the "Son of Man" passages in the Gospel of Matthew (Matt 19:28 and 25:31), which refer to the "glorious throne," seem to depend on the Similitudes.[4] Consequently, a date prior to 70 CE is likely, and there is nothing in the Similitudes incompatible with this. The most specific historical allusions are the mention of the Parthians and Medes in 56:5-7 and a reference to hot springs in 67:5-13. The allusion to the Parthians is eschatological but is most plausibly dated after the invasion of Palestine by the Parthians in 40 BCE. The springs are said to serve the kings and the mighty but will change to become instruments of judgment. This passage is probably inspired by Herod's attempt to cure himself in the waters of Callirhoe, which is recorded by Josephus (*Antiquities* 17.6.5 §§171-73; *Jewish War* 1.33.5 §§657-58). The Similitudes, then, should be dated to the early or mid-first century CE, prior to the Jewish revolt of 66-70 CE, to which it makes no reference.[5] Although the Ethiopic is the only extant text, it is probable that it derives from an Aramaic original.[6] The Similitudes fully belong in the discussion of ancient Jewish apocalypticism.

---

4. J. Theisohn, *Der auserwählte Richter* (Göttingen: Vandenhoeck & Ruprecht, 1975) 149-82.

5. So also Greenfield and Stone on different grounds; Nickelsburg, in Nickelsburg and VanderKam, *1 Enoch 2*, 58-63, argues for a date at the end of the first century BCE or the beginning of the first century CE. D. W. Suter, *Tradition and Composition in the Parables of Enoch* (SBLDS 47; Missoula, MT: Scholars Press, 1979) 32, argues for a date between the last quarter of the first century BCE and 70 CE. M. A. Knibb ("The Date of the Parables of Enoch: A Critical Review," *NTS* 25 [1979] 345-59) prefers a date in the period 70-135 CE (after the destruction of Qumran). M. Black, who formerly shared Milik's views, finally came around to the view that they are basically Jewish, composed around the turn of the millennium. See M. Black, "The Messianism of the Parables of Enoch," in J. H. Charlesworth, ed., *The Messiah: Developments in Earliest Judaism and Christianity* (Minneapolis: Fortress, 1992) 162.

6. N. Schmidt, "The Original Language of the Parables of Enoch," in *Old Testament and Semitic Studies in Memory of W. R. Harper* (Chicago: University of Chicago Press, 1908) 2:329-49; E. Ullendorff, "An Aramaic 'Vorlage' of the Ethiopic Text of Enoch?" in *Ethiopia and the Bible* (Oxford: Oxford University Press, 1968) 31-62.

## The Genre of the Similitudes

The Similitudes of Enoch consist of three "parables" (chaps. 38–44, 45–57, and 58–69) and a double epilogue in chaps. 70 and 71.[7] Chapter 37 introduces the entire composition as a "vision of wisdom." The eschatological import of this wisdom is indicated by the observation that "the lot of eternal life has been given to me" (37:4).

Each parable is introduced by a chapter presenting the subject of the revelation proper. Chapter 38 begins with a question:

> When the community of the righteous appears, and the sinners are judged for their sins and are driven from the face of the dry ground, and when the Righteous One appears before the chosen righteous whose works are weighed by the Lord of Spirits, and (when) light appears to the righteous and chosen who dwell on the dry ground, where (will be) the dwelling of the sinners, and where the resting place of those who have denied the Lord of Spirits? It would have been better for them if they had not been born.[8]

What is at issue, then, is the eschatological resting place on the day of judgment. The judgment is also the occasion when "the secrets of righteousness" are revealed. These secrets evidently concern the final destiny of both righteous and wicked. The chapter sounds another characteristic note of the Similitudes when it adds that "the mighty kings" will be destroyed and those who inhabit the earth will not be mighty and exalted.

The revelation proper begins with the ascent of Enoch to "the end of heaven." There he sees "the dwelling of the righteous and the resting places of the holy" with the angels and the holy ones. He then sees "a thousand thousands and ten thousand times ten thousand" who stand before the Lord of Spirits (40:1) and the four archangels, who are identified by

---

7. On the structure of the Similitudes see George W. E. Nickelsburg, "Discerning the Structure(s) of the Enochic Book of Parables," in Gabriele Boccaccini, ed., *Enoch and the Messiah Son of Man: Revisiting the Book of Parables* (Grand Rapids: Eerdmans, 2007) 23-47; idem, *1 Enoch 2*, 10-20; Michael A. Knibb, "The Structure and Composition of the Parables of Enoch," in Boccaccini, ed., *Enoch and the Messiah Son of Man*, 48-64. See also the older treatment by M. D. Hooker, *The Son of Man in Mark* (Montreal: McGill University Press, 1967) 36-37.

8. Quotations follow the translation of M. A. Knibb, *The Ethiopic Book of Enoch* (2 vols.; Oxford: Clarendon, 1978).

Enoch's angelic guide. In chap. 41 he is shown all the secrets of heaven. Once again, the resting places of the holy are first on the list, but the secrets include also the cosmological mysteries of lightning and thunder, sun and moon, etc. When Enoch inquires about the flashes of lightning and the stars of heaven, he is told that "Their likeness has the Lord of Spirits shown to you; these are the names of the righteous who dwell on the dry ground and believe in the name of the Lord of Spirits for ever and ever" (43:4). Although the exact nature of the correspondence is less than clear, it is evident that there is some analogy between the order of the heavens and the righteous on earth.

The first parable is interrupted by a brief wisdom poem, which is an inversion of the great hymn in Sirach 24. In Sirach, wisdom sought a resting place and found it in Jerusalem, and was identified with "the book of the law of the Lord." In *1 Enoch* 41 wisdom found no place where she could dwell, so she returned to heaven and took her seat with the angels. The earth was given over to iniquity. Although this poem seems intrusive in its present context, it fits quite well with the thought of the Similitudes. Wisdom is not to be found on earth but is with the angels in heaven. It can only be obtained by special revelation such as is given to Enoch by his angelic guide in the course of his ascent. This passage illustrates nicely the fundamental difference between the wisdom tradition and the apocalypses. Both find wisdom in the order of the universe, but for the apocalyptist this wisdom is hidden and is obscured by iniquity on earth.[9]

The second parable is "about those who deny the name of the dwelling of the holy ones and the Lord of Spirits." These, we are told, will neither ascend to heaven nor come on earth. More specifically, this parable concerns the judgment day when the Chosen One will sit on his throne of glory.

The parable proper presupposes Enoch's ascent and begins directly with his vision of "one who had a head of days" and another "whose face had the appearance of a man." Enoch's dialogue with the angelic guide here mainly concerns that "Son of Man" and the day of judgment. It is significant that "wisdom has been poured out like water" before him and is no longer withdrawn as in chap. 41. Enoch learns the future destiny of righteous and wicked (chaps. 50 and 51) and also sees cosmological secrets (chap. 52) that "serve the authority of his messiah" and the places and

---

9. J. J. Collins, "Cosmos and Salvation: Jewish Wisdom and Apocalyptic in the Hellenistic Age," *HR* 17 (1977) 140 (= *Seers, Sibyls, and Sages,* 317-38).

instruments of judgment (chaps. 53–57). The places of judgment are built into the structure of the universe and are already prepared. They are not presented as a matter of future hope, but of present knowledge.

The third parable is said in chap. 58 to be about the righteous and the chosen, and their destiny. The revelation begins with the cosmological secrets of thunder, lightning, etc. Chapter 60 has a brief vision of the Head of Days, which is introduced as a separate vision, and then reverts to the cosmological mysteries. This chapter has been thought to be a fragment of the Book of Noah.[10] Chapters 61–64 are devoted to the "Son of Man" figure and the judgment. Chapters 65–67 appear to be a fragment of the Book of Noah dealing with the flood and may have been part of a larger corpus of Enoch literature, since Enoch figures as Noah's grandfather.[11] It is related to its present context by the theme of judgment insofar as the flood provides an analogy for the final destruction. Chapters 68–69 deal with the judgment of the fallen angels.

The book concludes with not one but two, arguably three epilogues.[12] The first of these, in 70:1-2, is written in the third person, and says that after his visions, while he was still living, Enoch, or his name, was lifted up to the presence of "that Son of Man" and to the presence of the Lord of Spirits. This passage is extended by a first person account in 70:3-4. Finally, there is an extended first-person account of the ascension of Enoch in chap. 71. In this case, Enoch is greeted by the Head of Days and told "you are that Son of Man who was born for righteousness" (71:14).

The three parables of Enoch are evidently complementary, in the manner of the visions of Daniel. The main themes of the day of judgment and the destiny of the righteous are prominent from the start. The revelations are parables or similitudes insofar as they involve a complex set of analogies: between the fate of the righteous and that of the wicked, the holy on earth and the holy ones in heaven, the mysterious order of the cosmos and the lot of the righteous.[13] The macrogenre is clearly apocalypse. Enoch receives his revelations by visions in the course of an as-

---

10. Charles, *APOT,* 2:168.

11. Another Noachic passage can be found in 54:7–55:2; also sometimes assigned to this source is 67:1–69:25. See Nickelsburg, *1 Enoch 2,* 20, on "the Noachic Redaction of the Book of Parables." A major Noachic passage is found in *1 Enoch* 106–8. On the Noachic materials in *1 Enoch,* see F. García Martínez, *Qumran and Apocalyptic* (Leiden: Brill, 1992) 26-36.

12. Nickelsburg, "Discerning the Structure(s)," 42-43.

13. D. W. Suter, "Māšāl in the Similitudes of Enoch," *JBL* 100 (1981) 193-212. Enoch is also said to utter a parable in *1 Enoch* 1:3.

cent, and they are explained by his angelic guide. The revelations concern the transcendent world of the heavens and the impending judgment of humanity. Although the frequent allusions to "the kings and the mighty" indicate a political interest, there is no review of history such as we find in the "historical" apocalypses. As in all the Jewish apocalypses that describe heavenly ascents, there is a mystical tendency in the emphasis on revealed wisdom.

## The Righteous in the Similitudes

It is clear from the introductory chapters — 38, 45, and 58 — that the major focus of the Similitudes is on the destiny of "the righteous and the chosen" and their wicked counterparts. The final destiny of both parties is emphatically clear. The righteous will enjoy their heavenly resting places with the holy angels (41:2; 51:4) and will also dwell on a transformed earth (45:5). The wicked will be punished and swallowed up in Sheol.

In contrast, statements about the earthly career of the righteous are frustratingly vague.[14] The term "righteous," which is used interchangeably with "chosen" and "holy," is used as a quasi-technical term or even title for a community.[15] There are, however, a few specific references. In 43:4 we read of "the names of the righteous who dwell on the dry ground and believe in the name of the Lord of Spirits for ever and ever." Chapter 47 refers to the "blood of the righteous," thereby implying that they are persecuted. In 48:6 the righteous "have hated and rejected this world of iniquity, and all its works and its ways they have hated in the name of the Lord of Spirits, for in his name they are saved." The picture of the righteous ones can be filled out from the more frequent descriptions of their opponents, "those who commit sin and evil" (45:5). They are "the kings and the powerful" (46:4; cf. 38:4; 48:8; 53:5; 54:2; 62:9; 63:1). They are also the ones "who have denied the name of the Lord of Spirits" (38:2; cf. 41:2; 45:1). These two characteristics are related. They deny the name of the Lord of Spirits because "their power rests on their riches, and their faith is in the gods which they have made with their hands" (46:7) and

14. For the following see J. J. Collins, "The Heavenly Representative: The 'Son of Man' in the Similitudes of Enoch," in G. W. E. Nickelsburg and J. J. Collins, eds., *Ideal Figures in Ancient Judaism: Profiles and Paradigms* (SBLSCS 12; Missoula, MT: Scholars Press, 1980) 111-33.

15. D. Hill, "Dikaioi as a Quasi-Technical Term," *NTS* 11 (1965) 296-302.

their "hope has been on *the scepter of* our kingdom and of our glory" (63:7).

The issue that divides the righteous and the wicked is belief in the heavenly world of the Lord of Spirits and the Son of Man, and in the judgment where they will prevail. Those who lack such a belief put their trust in such power as is available in the present. Those who enjoy power in the present, the kings and the mighty, are especially prone to such an attitude. Conversely, those who are powerless are more likely to "hate and reject this world of iniquity." Yet powerlessness in itself is no virtue and does not constitute righteousness. Righteousness is rather an attitude of rejecting this world and having faith in the Lord of Spirits and the Son of Man. Faith here involves both belief in the existence of the Lord of Spirits and the Son of Man, and trust and dependence on them for salvation. We should note that the Similitudes do not explicitly refer to keeping the law or distinguish between Jew and Gentile. It may be true that the law is presupposed, and that the "kings and the powerful" who trust in the gods they themselves have made are Gentile rulers, but the opposition is not formulated in terms of Jew and Gentile. It is probable that "righteous" refers to a much narrower group than the Jewish people.

The faith of the righteous entails wisdom and knowledge. This in itself is not surprising, since righteousness and wisdom go hand in hand not only in Old Testament wisdom but also in the mythology of the ancient Near East. In the Jewish tradition wisdom had come to be identified with the law of Moses (Sir 24:23) and was said to have made its dwelling in Israel (Sir 24:8). This identification is not apparent in the Similitudes. Indeed, the wisdom poem in *1 Enoch* 42 is in direct contradiction to Sirach 24. Instead, wisdom is only accessible by special revelation. It is said to abound in the presence of God (48:1; 49:1). The spirit of wisdom dwells in the Chosen One who stands before the Lord of Spirits (49:3). This wisdom is not readily available. Righteousness and faith involve secrets that are known only by revelation. This revelation is never related to the Mosaic covenant. Most obviously it is given to and through Enoch himself ("until now there has not been given by the Lord of Spirits such wisdom as I have received in accordance with my insight" [37:4]). The Similitudes themselves are the revelation of the wisdom disclosed to Enoch in his heavenly journey, in which he sees "all the secrets of heaven" including the judgment (41:1). Yet the revelation of the Similitudes presupposes an antecedent revelation of the "name" of the Son of Man and expects a further definitive revelation in the future. In 48:7 we are told that the wisdom of the Lord of Spirits has revealed the Son of Man to the holy and righteous (cf. 62:7), and in 69:26 the righteous rejoice "because the name of that Son of Man had been revealed to them." The Son of Man or his name is then a fundamental object of revelation, but he in turn "will reveal all the treasures of that which is secret" (46:3) and "judge the things that are secret" (49:4). The final and definitive revelation of the Son of Man is still in the future, on the day of judgment, and that is when he will judge the things that are secret. For the present, faith in "that Son of Man" provides assurance that there will indeed be a judgment over which he will preside. This faith presumably undergirds righteous actions, but it also seems to be constitutive of righteousness in itself, since it involves not only belief but also the attitude of trust, in contrast to the self-sufficiency of the wicked.

## "That Son of Man"

The Similitudes, then, are exceptional among the Jewish apocalypses in focusing attention on a single figure, who is designated as the "Chosen One" or "that Son of Man," or even "messiah" (48:10; 52:4). Since early Christianity also focuses on a single figure who is often called "Son of Man," this individual in the Similitudes acquires considerable historical interest and has given rise to an enormous literature.[16]

The "Son of Man" figure first appears in chap. 46 in the second parable. Enoch sees "one who had a head of days," whose head was white like wool, and with him "another, whose face had the appearance of a man, and his face (was) full of grace, like one of the holy angels." The accompanying angel explains, "This is the Son of Man who has righteousness, and with whom righteousness dwells; he will reveal all the treasures of that which is secret."

The manner in which he is introduced does not presuppose that "Son

---

16. For bibliography, see C. Colpe, "Ho huios tou anthrōpou," *TDNT* 8:423-27; U. B. Müller, *Messias und Menschensohn in jüdischen Apokalypsen und in der Offenbarung des Johannes* (Gütersloh: Mohn, 1972) 36-60; P. M. Casey, "The Use of the Term 'Son of Man' in the Similitudes of Enoch," *JSJ* 7 (1976) 11-29; idem, *Son of Man: The Interpretation and Influence of Daniel 7* (London: SPCK, 1979) 99-112; J. C. VanderKam, "Righteous One, Messiah, Chosen One, and Son of Man in 1 Enoch 37–71," in Charlesworth, ed., *The Messiah*, 169-91; Collins and Yarbro Collins, *King and Messiah as Son of God*, 75-94, Nickelsburg, *1 Enoch 2*, 113-20, and the essays in Boccaccini, ed., *Enoch and the Messiah Son of Man*, especially 153-259.

of Man" is a well-known title: Enoch sees a figure who had "the appearance of a man," and this figure is subsequently referred to as "that Son of Man."[17] The expression "Son of Man," then, is a periphrastic way of referring to the figure with "the appearance of a man" in 46:3. The inference that "Son of Man" "would naturally be read as the equivalent of 'man' "[18] is not warranted, however, since it neglects some important considerations. First, in apocalyptic literature a figure with the appearance of a man is quite commonly found to be an angel.[19] Whether the figure is in fact a man depends on whether he should be identified as Enoch throughout the Similitudes, a problem to which we shall return below. Second, the expression "Son of Man" is an allusion to Daniel 7 (especially in the context of the vision of the head of days in chap. 46). Therefore, whenever the expression "that Son of Man" is repeated, it is not simply equivalent to "the figure you saw" but also implies that this figure carries the eschatological associations of Daniel 7. Although the Similitudes do not assume that "Son of Man" is a well-known title, the expression serves to establish an identity that is more than just "a human figure."

The identity of this "Son of Man" figure does not depend entirely on its association with Daniel. The "Son of Man who has righteousness" cannot be distinguished from the "Righteous One" of 38:2 and 53:6.[20] It is also generally agreed that "the Chosen One," who appears in all three parables, is the same being, since he exercises the same functions as the "Son of Man," and the two expressions are interchanged in such a way that the identification is not in doubt.[21] Both the Righteous One and the Chosen One are used in association with the broader categories of "the righteous" and "the chosen," and these are also described as "the holy" (e.g., 48:1, 4). These terms have several layers of reference. Besides the holy on earth there are "the holy ones who dwell in the heavens" (47:2) — primarily the angelic host but also transformed human righteous ones after their death, since we are told that they "all will become angels in heaven" (51:4) and that they have their "dwellings with the angels and their resting places

17. On the Ethiopic terminology, see Casey, "The Use of the Term 'Son of Man,' " 14-18; idem, *Son of Man*, 100-102.

18. Casey, "The Use of the Term 'Son of Man,' " 23.

19. For example, Dan 8:15; 9:21; 10:5; 12:6.

20. Some manuscripts read "righteousness" instead of "Righteous One" at 38:2. See the comments of VanderKam, "Righteous One," 170, who prefers "righteousness" in this passage.

21. Hooker, *The Son of Man in Mark*, 38-40.

with the holy ones" (39:5). When "the chosen will begin to dwell with the chosen" (61:4), the human, earthly, chosen ones will begin to dwell with the heavenly. In short, the human community of the elect and the righteous stands in very close association with the angelic world and will ultimately be merged with it. The righteous, elect "Son of Man" figure is directly related to both the human and the heavenly righteous.[22] The association does not lie only in "the fact that the son of man figure and the elect and righteous have in common certain basic qualities, those of election and righteousness."[23] His entire function is defined in relation to the human righteous ones: "He will be a staff to the righteous and the holy, that they may lean on him and not fall" (48:4); "the wisdom of the Lord of Spirits has revealed him to the holy and the righteous, for he has kept safe the lot of the righteous" (48:5), and after the judgment "with that Son of Man will they dwell and eat and lie down and rise up for ever and ever" (62:14). His function as eschatological revealer and judge is to vindicate the righteous and condemn their enemies.

This close connection between the individual Son of Man and the community of the righteous has led some scholars to invoke the allegedly Hebrew conception of corporate personality.[24] This idea has rightly been criticized insofar as it implies "psychical unity" and rests on outdated anthropological theories that have been widely discredited.[25] There is no room for doubt that the Similitudes present the "Son of Man" as an individual figure distinct from the community. However, the communal dimension of the figure does not stand or fall with corporate personality. Mowinckel put the matter well: "Representative unity and a corporate conception of the leader as the bearer of the whole, and of the individual as a type of the race, is not the same as literal and actual identity. The fact that in the cult a person represents the whole, or in a symbolic sense is the whole, means that there is an intimate community of destiny between them."[26] The relation of the king to his people illustrates the point. The

22. Müller, *Messias und Menschensohn*, 45.

23. So Casey, "The Use of the Term 'Son of Man,' " 13.

24. For example, T. W. Manson, "The Son of Man in Daniel, Enoch, and the Gospels," in *Studies in the Gospels and Epistles* (Manchester: Manchester University Press, 1962) 123-45; D. S. Russell, *The Method and Message of Jewish Apocalyptic* (Philadelphia: Westminster, 1964) 350-52.

25. J. W. Rogerson, "The Hebrew Conception of Corporate Personality — A Re-examination," *JTS* 21 (1970) 1-16.

26. S. Mowinckel, *He That Cometh* (Nashville: Abingdon, 1955) 381. Mowinckel's

unity involved in the Similitudes is evidently closer to Mowinckel's "representative unity" than to corporate personality. Yet the relation of the king to his people is not the closest analogy we can find. Throughout the parables the Son of Man or Chosen One is located in the heavenly sphere in the presence of the Lord of Spirits: "For from the beginning the Son of Man was hidden and the Most High kept him in the presence of his power and revealed him (only) to the chosen" (62:7; cf. 48:6). As E. Sjöberg has remarked, he is not a man, at least not in the usual sense of the word, but is rather a heavenly being.[27] A closer analogy is found with the patron deities of nations in Near Eastern mythology. These deities have a representative unity with their peoples, although they are definitely distinguished from them. While "the gods of Hamath and Arpad" (Isa 36:19) cannot be conceived of apart from the nations they represent, there is no doubt that any divinity was assumed to have greater power than its people and to be able to act independently over against them. The heavenly counterparts of nations played an important part in apocalyptic literature, most notably in Daniel 10, where the angelic "princes" of Persia and Greece do battle with Michael, "the prince of your people." We have argued above that the "one like a son of man" in Daniel 7 should be understood in this sense, as the heavenly counterpart of the faithful Jews. The Similitudes differ from Daniel insofar as the human community is not identified in national terms but as the "righteous" or the "chosen." Correspondingly, its heavenly counterpart is not identified as Michael, the patron of Israel (who appears independently as one of the archangels), but as "the Son of Man who has righteousness" or the "Chosen One." The difference in terminology is at least potentially significant and may suggest that the community which produced the Similitudes did not find its basic identity in membership of the Jewish people but was sectarian in character. Yet the correspondence between "the Chosen One" and the community of the chosen is analogous to that between Michael and Israel or any other mythological counterpart of a group or nation.

There is a parallelism of action, or "structural homologue"[28] between

---

discussion is flawed by his reliance on a theory of primordial man and *anima generalis* which cannot be maintained.

27. E. Sjöberg, *Der Menschensohn im Äthiopischen Henochbuch* (Lund: Gleerup, 1946) 50. This remains true despite the use of Old Testament motifs and passages associated with the royal, Davidic messiah (Theisohn, *Der auserwählte Richter*, 53-59) and the fact that he is called messiah (48:10).

28. For the phrase, see G. Theissen (*Sociology of Early Palestinian Christianity*

the earthly and heavenly counterparts. The Similitudes resemble Daniel in this respect. In Daniel the one like a son of man stands parallel to the (people of) the saints (of the Most High). His exaltation means their exaltation. Similarly in *1 Enoch* the manifestation of the "Son of Man" figure entails the triumph of the righteous. Nickelsburg has further argued that both the Similitudes and Wisdom 1–5 reflect a common exegetical tradition based on Isaiah 52–53.[29] In Isaiah and Wisdom a single figure, the servant and the righteous man, suffers, dies (at least in Wisdom; the interpretation of Isaiah is disputed), and is exalted. In the Similitudes the Son of Man stands parallel to the persecuted community and is finally exalted, but there is no suggestion that he suffers or dies. Yet the parallels with Isaiah 53 are significant. In Isaiah and Wisdom the true nature and destiny of the servant and the righteous man are hidden until the time of the judgment and cause consternation when they are revealed. In *1 Enoch* the Son of Man is hidden until the judgment and also causes panic on his appearance. The hiddenness of the Son of Man corresponds to the sufferings of the righteous community and the hidden character of their destiny. The structural homologue between the Son of Man and the community is thus complete. Although he does not share their suffering, the pattern of hiddenness and revelation is common to both. The fact that he is preserved from their sufferings makes him a figure of pure power and glory and an ideal embodiment of the hopes of the persecuted righteous. The efficaciousness of the "Son of Man" figure requires that he be conceived as other than the community, since he must possess the power and exaltation which they lack.

In short, the Son of Man is not a personification of the righteous community, but is conceived, in mythological fashion, as its heavenly *Doppelgänger*. Now it is characteristic of mythological thinking that such a *Doppelgänger* is conceived to be *more* real and permanent than its earthly counterpart and prior to it in the order of being.[30] From a modern critical perspective, the reverse is true. It "is a question of men before it is a ques-

---

[Philadelphia: Fortress, 1978] 121), who uses it with reference to the Son of Man in the New Testament.

29. Nickelsburg, *Resurrection, Immortality, and Eternal Life*, 93-97. The influence of the Isaianic servant songs has also been noted by J. Jeremias, "Pais theou," *TDNT*, 5:687-88; Müller, *Messias und Menschensohn*, 38-39; and Theisohn, *Der auserwählte Richter*, 114-26. Cf. VanderKam, "Righteous One," 189-90.

30. See M. Eliade, *The Myth of the Eternal Return* (New York: Pantheon, 1954) 3-6.

tion of angels."[31] The human community is the datum of our experience and knowledge. The heavenly counterpart is posited on the basis of this datum. While the Son of Man is conceived as a real being, he symbolizes the destiny of the righteous community both in its present hiddenness and future manifestation.[32]

## The Identification with Enoch

Up to this point we have not considered the disputed question of the precise identification of the Son of Man. The question arises because of two passages in the epilogues. The first, 70:1, is a disputed reading. The editions of Charles and Knibb read that Enoch's name was lifted up "to the presence of that Son of Man *and* to the presence of the Lord of Spirits." However, one important manuscript, Abbadianus 55 (U), omits the Ethiopic word for "to the presence of" before "that Son of Man," and so reads, "the name of that Son of Man was raised aloft . . . to the Lord of Spirits."[33] This reading is supported by four, possibly five, other manuscripts.[34] The second passage is 71:14, where an angel tells Enoch: "You are the Son of Man who was born to righteousness." The problem, then, is that throughout the Similitudes Enoch has observed "that Son of Man" with no indication that he is seeing himself. Then in 71:14 (and possibly in 70:1) he is identified with the figure in his visions. The solution of Charles was to emend 71:14 to read "this is the Son of Man . . ." and change "you" to "him" in the following verses.[35] This procedure has no basis in the text and is clearly unacceptable. Three possible solutions deserve serious consideration.

The first possible solution might seem at first glance to be the most straightforward: the identification with Enoch may be intended through-

---

31. A. Lacocque, *The Book of Daniel* (Atlanta: John Knox, 1979) 131.

32. Compare the remarks of Theissen (*Sociology*, 101) on the function of the Son of Man in the New Testament.

33. Casey, "The Use of the Term 'Son of Man,' " 25-26.

34. Daniel C. Olson, "Enoch and the Son of Man in the Epilogue of the Parables?" *JSP* 18 (1998) 30-31. Olson argues for an early date for the short reading. See the critique by Michael A. Knibb, "The Translation of 1 Enoch 70:1: Some Methodological Issues," in Ada Rapoport-Albert and Gillian Greenberg, eds., *Biblical Hebrew, Biblical Texts: Essays in Memory of Michael P. Weitzman* (JSOTSup 333; Sheffield: Sheffield Academic Press, 2001) 340-54, and the comments of Nickelsburg, *1 Enoch 2*, 315.

35. Charles, *APOT*, 2:237.

out.[36] Chapter 71 might then be viewed as the climax of the revelation, disclosing that the "name revealed to the elect" (69:26) is the name of Enoch himself.[37] However, the "name" is not necessarily a title or a proper name, but the person himself — as is clearly shown in 70:1, where Enoch's name is lifted up to heaven.[38] Moreover, there are serious problems with the view that the identification with Enoch was intended throughout. First, there is the disputed reading in 70:1, where most manuscripts show a clear distinction between Enoch and the Son of Man. On purely textual grounds this reading is better than that of the manuscripts which imply an identification. If the disagreement of the manuscripts is attributed to a deliberate scribal change in one of them, it is easier to see why a scribe would have harmonized 70:1 with 71:14 than the reverse. If the variation is accidental, the easiest explanation is that a scribe omitted one word *baxabehu* (= "in the presence of") in the Ethiopic text of manuscript 55. Accordingly, it seems more plausible that the majority reading is original.[39] But if this is so, the conclusion that Enoch was distinguished from the "Son of Man" in 70:1 is unavoidable.[40] Second, there is no parallel in the apocalyptic literature for a visionary who fails to recognize himself in his visions.[41] Yet Enoch does not identify himself with "that Son of Man" in the "parables." Third, there is a problem connected with the alleged preexistence of the Son of

36. So Hooker, Casey, VanderKam, and A. Caquot ("Remarques sur les chap. 70 et 71 du livre éthiopien d'Hénoch," in H. Monloubou, ed., *Apocalypses et Théologie de l'Espérance* [Paris: Cerf, 1977] 111-12).

37. Hooker, *The Son of Man in Mark*, 41-42.

38. Müller, *Messias und Menschensohn*, 59. So also Manson, "The Son of Man," 136.

39. Contra Casey, who prefers the reading of ms. U for "considerations of intrinsic probability" (*Son of Man*, 105).

40. VanderKam, "Righteous One," 184, accepts the majority reading, but argues that "what the author appears to have intended in 70:1 was that Enoch's name was elevated to the place where those characters whom he had seen in his visions were to be found, namely in the throne room of the celestial palace. That is, he does not see the son of man here but begins his ascent to the place where he himself will perform that eschatological role." It is difficult, however, to see how this interpretation can be reconciled with what the text says.

41. Caquot ("Remarques," 121) points to the vision of Levi in the *Testament of Levi*, but Levi recognizes himself throughout. Helge Kvanvig, "The Son of Man in the Parables of Enoch," in Boccaccini, ed., *Enoch and the Messiah Son of Man*, 182, argues that in *1 Enoch* 13-14, "Enoch sees himself as a visionary counterpart in heaven." But in chaps. 13-14 Enoch clearly recognizes himself. This is not the case in the Similitudes. Kvanvig is followed by James A. Waddell, *The Messiah: A Comparative Study of the Enochic Son of Man and the Pauline Kyrios* (London: T & T Clark, 2011) 55-60.

Man in *1 Enoch* 48.[42] In 48:2 his name was named even before the sun and the constellations were created, in 48:6 he was chosen and hidden before the world was created, and in 62:7 he was hidden and preserved from the beginning. He is known only by special revelation to the chosen ones and is revealed to others only in the eschatological judgment. There is no suggestion that he was in any sense revealed in the "historical" life of Enoch.

James VanderKam has suggested that some light may be shed on the problem by the idea of a heavenly double or counterpart.[43] The *Prayer of Joseph,* a lost pseudepigraphon that is cited in Origen's *Commentary on John* and in the *Philocalia,* speaks of such a heavenly double in the case of Jacob: "I, Jacob, who is speaking to you, am also Israel, an angel of God and a ruling spirit."[44] We have already argued that the Son of Man was a heavenly double or counterpart for the community of the righteous. Insofar as Enoch was a prototypical righteous man, the Son of Man was his heavenly counterpart too. VanderKam suggests that Enoch becomes one with his heavenly double in chapter 71. This is an intriguing possibility. There is no doubt that Enoch was eventually identified with the "Son of Man," and this tradition is later developed in the figure of Metatron in *3 Enoch,* a mystical text also known as *Sefer Hekalot,* from the fifth or sixth century CE.[45] Metatron is the Prince of the Divine Presence. He is enthroned on a throne of glory, and even called "the lesser YHWH" (*3 Enoch* 12:5). Yet he is also identified with Enoch, son of Jared, who was taken up to heaven before the Flood (*3 Enoch* 4:1-5). It should be noted, however, that the titles applied to the Son of Man in the Similitudes (Son of Man, Messiah, Righteous One, Chosen One) are almost entirely absent from the later text. Only the title "Chosen" is applied to Metatron.[46]

A second possibility is that the phrase "Son of Man" in 71:14 may not

---

42. Sjöberg, *Der Menschensohn,* 83-101; Mowinckel, *He That Cometh,* 370-73. Manson questions whether preexistence is really implied except as a project in the mind of God ("The Son of Man," 136). Similarly, VanderKam, "Righteous One," 181-82.

43. VanderKam, "Righteous One," 182-83. So also Andrew Chester, *Messiah and Exaltation* (WUNT 207; Tübingen: Mohr Siebeck, 2007) 64.

44. J. Z. Smith, "Prayer of Joseph," in Charlesworth, ed., *OTP* 2:699-714.

45. On Metatron see I. Gruenwald, *Apocalyptic and Merkavah Mysticism* (Leiden: Brill, 1980), 181-208; P. S. Alexander, "3 (Hebrew Apocalypse of) Enoch," in Charlesworth, ed., *OTP* 1:243-44; A. A. Orlov, *The Enoch-Metatron Tradition* (TSAJ 107; Tübingen: Mohr Siebeck, 2005) 86-147.

46. Orlov, *The Enoch-Metatron Tradition,* 85; James R. Davila, "Melchizedek, the 'Youth', and Jesus," in idem, ed., *The Dead Sea Scrolls as Background to Postbiblical Judaism and Early Christianity* (STDJ 46; Leiden: Brill, 2003) 284-74.

have the technical reference ("that Son of Man") but may be used as a common noun ("that man who").[47] According to this interpretation, Enoch is not identified with "that Son of Man" and there is no contradiction between chaps. 70 and 71. *1 Enoch* 71:14 is one of two passages in the Similitudes where the phrase "son of man" is used in direct address. The other instance is found in *1 Enoch* 60:10, where Enoch is directly called "son of man" "after the manner of Ezekiel,"[48] with no eschatological implications. It is arguable that the phrase is also used in this sense in 71:14. In this case, Enoch would not actually be identified with the Son of Man, but would be singled out as the human being most closely associated with the heavenly counterpart. Other righteous human beings would eventually share his destiny ("all . . . will walk according to your way . . . with you will be their dwelling and with you their lot," 71:16). On this interpretation, the Son of Man is Enoch's heavenly double, but the two figures are not merged.[49]

The third possible solution is that chap. 71 is a redactional addition to the Similitudes.[50] This view is not an *ad hoc* solution to the "Son of Man" problem but arises independently from literary considerations. Chapters 70 and 71 constitute a double epilogue to the Similitudes. Each tells how Enoch was carried up to the heavens.[51] Redundancy and duplication are not in themselves surprising in a work such as the Similitudes, but we usually find such redundancy in the visions, not in the narrative framework. Accordingly, the repetition here strongly suggests the hand of a redactor. Of course this argument is strengthened if we follow the majority reading at 70:1, which makes a clear distinction between Enoch and the Son of Man in contradiction to 71:14.

47. Mowinckel, *He That Cometh,* 443. See further J. J. Collins, "The Son of Man in First Century Judaism," *NTS* 38 (1992) 451-59.

48. R. H. Charles, *The Book of Enoch* (Oxford: Clarendon, 1893) 156. Nickelsburg, *1 Enoch 2,* 328, dismisses this precedent on the grounds that it is part of a Noahic interpolation.

49. Note, however, the demurral of M. A. Knibb, "Messianism in the Pseudepigrapha in the Light of the Scrolls," *Dead Sea Discoveries* 2 (1995) 179.

50. Müller, *Messias und Menschensohn,* 54-59; Colpe, "Ho huios tou anthrōpou," *TDNT,* 8:426; Nickelsburg, *1 Enoch 2,* 330-33.

51. In fact, there are three statements of the translation of Enoch: 70:1-2; 71:1; and 71:5. Müller defines the addition as 71:5-17. VanderKam, "Righteous One," 177-79, argues strongly for the unity of chapters 70–71, on the grounds that Enoch is carried off to paradise in chapter 70, then to the lower heavens, and finally to the highest heaven in chapter 71. In *1 Enoch* 70:1, however, Enoch is already said to be carried to the presence of the Lord of Spirits.

The view that chap. 71 is redactional explains why other passages stand in tension with that chapter and allows us to recover the original sense of the Similitudes.[52] The question remains why the identification was eventually made. In fact, the identification could claim some basis in the original text. Enoch was in any case preeminent among the righteous ones and shared to some degree the Son of Man's role as revealer. The figure of Enoch was widely used as a paradigm of righteousness. It was the destiny of all the righteous to be with "that Son of Man" in the heavenly resting places (62:14). Enoch had already attained that destiny and so was distinguished from other humans. Accordingly, his identification with the "Son of Man" was not as drastic an innovation as it might at first seem.

We can only hypothesize what stimulus may have occasioned the identification of Enoch with "that Son of Man." One obvious possibility is that the identification was made in response to the Christian appropriation of "Son of Man" as a title for Jesus. The identification would then deny the christological use of the title and affirm that Enoch, sage of the heavenly mysteries, was the model to be followed, rather than Christ. Enoch was believed to have made the transition from earth to heaven, just as Christians believed Jesus had, and Enoch could accordingly be used as a Jewish answer to Christianity. This suggestion, however, remains hypothetical. There is no explicit anti-Christian polemic in *1 Enoch* 71.

## The Function of the Similitudes

The Similitudes of Enoch are designed to reassure the righteous that their destiny is secure in the hands of "that Son of Man." Their representative lives in heaven, and their dwelling places are prepared. What they must do is believe and trust. The authority of Enoch and of his visions provides a basis for belief. The Similitudes do not appear to envisage any acute historical crisis. They can apply to any situation where the righteous feel oppressed by the kings and the mighty. In the first century CE, they could apply to any Jews who resented the rule of the pagan Romans or the impious Herods. The Similitudes offered to the powerless the assurance of a special destiny

52. M. Black recognized the tension between chap. 71 and the main body of the Similitudes but suggested that chap. 71 is the older stratum, because of its similarity to the elevation of Enoch in *1 Enoch* 14 ("The Eschatology of the Similitudes of Enoch," *JTS* 3 [1952] 8). Against this theory is the fact that the Similitudes do not otherwise betray the identification of the "Son of Man" with Enoch.

guaranteed by a heavenly patron. The heavenly world would furnish the respect and dignity denied them in the present.

We may suspect that the matrix of the Similitudes was somewhat more specific than this. The quasi-technical terminology of "righteous" and "chosen" suggests that "the community of the righteous" (38:1) was an actual community and not just a general reference to righteous people. The terminology of "righteous" and "chosen" is drawn from the earlier Enoch books (e.g., the Apocalypse of Weeks). Jonas Greenfield and Michael Stone have noted some terminological resemblances to the Qumran scrolls — for example, "spirits" for angels and the term "lot" (*1 Enoch* 48:2).[53] In view of the absence of the Similitudes from Qumran, we may safely conclude that they were not composed there. In view of the popularity of the other sections of *1 Enoch* at Qumran, and of the near equality of sun and moon in chap. 41, we should hesitate to ascribe them to the group that composed the earlier Enoch writings. In any case, there is no independent evidence that an "Enoch group" remained in existence from the third century down to the first century CE. It is sufficient that the authors of the Similitudes were well versed in the earlier Enoch books and adapted some of their conceptions and terminology. Nonetheless it is quite possible that the Similitudes originated in a closed circle somewhat analogous to Qumran. The quasi-technical terminology and the distinctive faith in "that Son of Man" support the idea that the authors of the Similitudes belonged to a group apart.[54]

## Relation to the New Testament

The historical significance of the Similitudes lies primarily in their attestation of speculation on a "Son of Man" figure outside of Christianity. The

---

53. Greenfield and Stone, "The Enochic Pentateuch," 56-57. See further P. Sacchi, *Jewish Apocalyptic and Its History* (Sheffield: Sheffield Academic Press, 1997) 116, who points to the Essene overtones of *1 Enoch* 41:8, which says that the Lord "has created (a division) between light and darkness and has divided the spirits of men."

54. Pierluigi Piovanelli, "'A Testimony for the Kings and the Mighty Who Possess the Earth': The Thirst for Justice and Peace in the Parables of Enoch," in Boccaccini, ed., *Enoch and the Messiah Son of Man*, 363-79, argues that the Similitudes are addressed to the ensemble of the Jewish people. So also Daniel Boyarin, "Was the Book of Parables a Sectarian Document? A Brief in support of Pierluigi Piovanelli," ibid., 380-85. Lester L. Grabbe, "The Parables of Enoch in Second Temple Jewish Society," ibid., 386-402, suggests that the Similitudes reflect "a messianic group with its own identity but that has not necessarily withdrawn from Jewish society" (402).

Similitudes did not significantly influence the New Testament in this matter. The belief that Jesus would come as Son of Man on the clouds of heaven can be adequately explained as an adaptation of Daniel 7 in conjunction with other Old Testament texts without reference to the Similitudes. Only in two Matthean passages, 19:28 and 25:31, where the Son of Man sits on his glorious throne (cf. *1 Enoch* 61–62), is Enochic influence probable, and this is distinctly a secondary development in the Jesus tradition.[55] The Similitudes do, however, show that an interpretation and application of Daniel 7 similar to what we find in the New Testament could be found independently in Judaism in this period.[56] Scholarly debate has focused too narrowly on the question whether "Son of Man" was a title in Judaism. As we have seen in the Qumran scrolls, titular usage for supernatural figures was quite fluid. More important is the fact that several documents accord a preeminent place to an angelic figure — Michael in Daniel and 1QM, Melchizedek in 11QMelch, the Angel of Truth in the *Community Rule*.[57] "That Son of Man" in the Similitudes must be ranked with these figures although he is distinct from, and above, the archangels. It is also noteworthy that the "Son of Man" figure in the Similitudes is identified with the messiah.[58] The Similitudes thus pave the way for understanding the messiah

---

55. Nickelsburg, *1 Enoch 2*, 72; Theisohn, *Der auserwählte Richter*, 173-200. Leslie W. Walck, "The Son of Man in the Parables of Enoch and the Gospels," in Boccaccini, ed., *Enoch and the Messiah Son of Man*, 299-337, argues for broader influence of the Similitudes on Matthew. Simon J. Joseph, *The Nonviolent Messiah: Jesus, Q, and the Enochic Tradition* (Minneapolis: Fortress, 2014) 148, writes, "We need not appeal to direct literary dependence to posit the Parables' influence on the Jesus tradition; it seems far more difficult to conclude that these are entirely independent developments in first-century Palestinian Judaism."

56. See Collins, "The Son of Man in First Century Judaism," and T. B. Slater, "One Like a Son of Man in First-Century CE Judaism," *NTS* 41 (1995) 183-98.

57. B. Lindars, "Re-Enter the Apocalyptic Son of Man," *NTS* 22 (1975-76) 52-72; P. J. Kobelski, *Melchizedek and Melchireša'* (CBQMS 10; Washington, DC: Catholic Biblical Association of America, 1981) 130-37. On the idea of an exalted angel, see C. Rowland, *The Open Heaven: A Study of Apocalyptic in Judaism and Early Christianity* (New York: Crossroad, 1982) 94-113, and L. W. Hurtado, *One God, One Lord: Early Christian Devotion and Ancient Jewish Monotheism* (Philadelphia: Fortress, 1988) 71-92. On incipient binitarianism in ancient Judaism, see the seminal study of A. F. Segal, *Two Powers in Heaven: Early Rabbinic Reports about Christianity and Gnosticism* (SJLA 25; Leiden: Brill, 1977) and the essays in C. C. Newman, J. R. Davila, and G. S. Lewis, eds., *The Jewish Roots of Christological Monotheism* (JSJSup 63; Leiden: Brill, 1999).

58. *1 Enoch* 48:10. See Theisohn, *Der auserwählte Richter*, 53-59; Sacchi, *Jewish Apocalyptic*, 165-66; W. Horbury, "The Messianic Associations of 'The Son of Man'," *JTS* 36 (1985) 34-55.

as a supernatural figure, as we will find in the later Jewish apocalypses. It is apparent that Jewish conceptions of savior figures in this period were variable, but the Similitudes illustrate the *kind* of speculation that was also at work in the New Testament development of christological titles.

It is also significant that the Similitudes place primary emphasis on faith in this heavenly Son of Man, and in the heavenly realities in general, rather than on practice of the law as the means to salvation. We should not, of course, exaggerate the analogy with Paul. There is no polemic here against the law, and the implications of faith are certainly altered when focused on the death and resurrection of Jesus. Yet there is a limited analogy that should not be ignored. Not all of Judaism can be classified as "covenantal nomism." Faith in apocalyptic mysteries, which has a central role here, was also an important factor in early Christianity.

# CHAPTER SEVEN

# *After the Fall: 4 Ezra, 2 Baruch, and the Apocalypse of Abraham*

No extant Jewish apocalypse can be associated with the Jewish revolt against Rome which broke out in 66 CE. Josephus claims that some alleged revelations contributed to Jewish unrest. After his account of the Sicarii, he refers to

> another body of villains, with purer hands but more impious intentions, who no less than the assassins ruined the peace of the city. Deceivers and impostors, under the pretense of divine inspiration fostering revolutionary changes, they persuaded the multitude to act like madmen and led them out into the desert under the belief that God would there give them tokens of deliverance. Against them Felix, regarding this as but the preliminary to insurrection, sent a body of cavalry and heavy-armed infantry, and put a large number to the sword. (*War* 2.13.4 §§258–60)

This episode recalls the story of Taxo in the *Testament of Moses,* the martyrs in 1 Macc 2:29-38, and even the general attitude of the book of Daniel. There is no evidence, however, that the "impostors" to whom Josephus refers in this passage gave literary expression to their hopes, and we do not know how far these hopes were apocalyptic in nature. Again, Josephus claims that "what more than all else incited them to the war was an ambiguous oracle, likewise found in their sacred scriptures, to the effect that at that time one from their country would become ruler of the world" (*War* 6.5.4 §312). Josephus claimed that the oracle referred not to a Jewish leader but to Vespasian. We do not know what scriptural passage Josephus had in mind. The "sacred scriptures" may be conceived broadly here to include such documents as the *Sibylline Oracles*.[1] The oracle in question was evidently understood as messianic. Some of the leaders of the revolt apparently entertained messianic, or at least royal, pretensions,[2] but we are poorly informed about the actual hopes and expectations of the rebels.[3] The popular movements briefly documented by Josephus belong to the history of Jewish apocalypticism broadly conceived, but it does not appear that their members wrote apocalypses or expressed their ideas in literary form at all.

In contrast, we have several major apocalypses from the period after the revolt: *4 Ezra, 2 Baruch,* and the *Apocalypse of Abraham,* all of which are likely to have been composed in the land of Israel, and *3 Baruch,* which is more probably a product of the Diaspora. Unlike Daniel or the Animal Apocalypse, these works were not composed in the throes of the conflict. In all cases some time is likely to have elapsed after the fall of the temple. The underlying questions of all these works, however, are shaped in large part by the catastrophe of 70 CE. They may, accordingly, be viewed as one cluster of Jewish responses to that national tragedy.[4] The most engaging, profound, and problematic of these works is surely *4 Ezra*, which ranks as one of the greatest of the apocalypses.

---

1. Variants of this oracle are found in Tacitus, *Histories* 2.13 and Suetonius, *Vespasian* 4. In Tacitus, the oracle says that "the east would become strong," a motif that recalls *Sib. Or.* 3:350-80, or even the *Oracle of Hystaspes* (Lactantius, *Divine Institutions* 7.15.11). See Anthony J. Tomasino, "Oracles of Insurrection: The Prophetic Catalyst of the Great Revolt," *JJS* 5 (2008) 86-111.

2. Menahem, son of Judas the Galilean, "returned to Jerusalem as king" (Josephus, *Jewish War* 2.17.8 §§433-34). Simon bar Giora, who was executed in Rome as leader of the revolt, acted in a royal manner (e.g., *Jewish War* 7.2.2 §29). See especially R. A. Horsley and J. S. Hanson, *Bandits, Prophets, and Messiahs: Popular Movements at the Time of Jesus* (Minneapolis: Winston, 1985) 88-134; also Collins, *The Scepter and the Star*, 219-22.

3. Whether any of these figures claimed to be messiahs is uncertain. See Tessa Rajak, "Jewish Millenarian Expectations," in Andrea M. Berlin and J. Andrew Overman, eds., *The First Jewish Revolt: Archaeology, History, and Ideology* (London: Routledge, 2002) 164-88; Martin Goodman, "Messianism and Politics in the Land of Israel, 66-135 CE," in Markus Bockmuehl and James Carleton Paget, eds., *Redemption and Resistance: The Messianic Hopes of Jews and Christians in Antiquity* (London: T & T Clark, 2007) 149-57.

4. Another range of responses is preserved in the rabbinic literature. See A. J. Saldarini, "Varieties of Rabbinic Responses to the Destruction of the Temple," in K. H. Richards, ed., *Society of Biblical Literature 1982 Seminar Papers* (Chico, CA: Scholars Press, 1982) 437-58; J. Neusner, "Judaism in a Time of Crisis: Four Responses to the Destruction of the Second Temple," *Judaism* 21 (1972) 313-27.

## 4 Ezra

4 Ezra (2 Esdras 3–14)[5] is preserved in Latin and various other ancient versions including Armenian, Syrian, and Georgian.[6] There is general agreement that the original language was Hebrew.[7] There is also a consensus that the book was written in Palestine about the end of the first century CE. The apocalypse begins with the statement, "In the thirtieth year after the overthrow of the city I was in Babylon" (3:1), but neither the date nor the place can be taken as evidence of the actual provenance. The figure thirty years is taken from Ezek 1:1. The location in Babylon is prompted by the fictive association with the fall of the first temple, and also by Ezekiel (although it has on occasion been thought to imply that the book was composed in Rome). Most attempts to date 4 Ezra have been based on the vision in chaps. 11–12 of an eagle with twelve wings and three heads. The eagle is the Roman Empire. It is probable that the three heads represent the Flavians — Vespasian, Titus, and Domitian — and possible that the twelve wings are the emperors from Caesar to Domitian.[8] This interpretation points to a date in the last decade of the first century, and the rounded figure of thirty years in the superscription is compatible with this. In view of the content of the book, there is no doubt that 4 Ezra was written in the period after the fall of Jerusalem, whatever the precise date.[9]

5. The nomenclature of the Ezra books is confusing: 1 Ezra = the canonical book of Ezra; 2 Ezra = the book of Nehemiah; 3 Ezra = 1 Esdras (Jewish apocryphon); 4 Ezra = 2 Esdras 3-14; 5 Ezra = 2 Esdras 1-2 (Christian); 6 Ezra = 2 Esdras 15-16 (Christian). There is also a Christian *Apocalypse of Ezra* in Greek.

6. M. E. Stone, *Fourth Ezra: A Commentary on the Book of Fourth Ezra* (Hermeneia; Minneapolis: Fortress, 1990) 1-9. See also T. A. Bergren, "Christian Influence on the Transmission History of 4, 5, and 6 Ezra," in J. C. VanderKam and W. Adler, eds., *The Jewish Apocalyptic Heritage in Early Christianity* (CRINT 3/4; Assen: Van Gorcum; Minneapolis: Fortress, 1996) 102-27.

7. On the questions of date, provenance, and language see J. M. Myers, *I and II Esdras* (AB 42; Garden City, NY: Doubleday, 1974) 113-19, 129-31; J. Schreiner, *Das 4. Buch Esra* (JSHRZ 5/4; Gütersloh: Mohn, 1981) 291-306; Stone, *Fourth Ezra*, 9-10.

8. Myers, *I and II Esdras*, 299-302; Stone, *Fourth Ezra*, 10. See, however, Lorenzo Di Tommaso, "Dating the Eagle Vision of 4 Ezra: A New Look at an Old Theory," *JSP* 20 (1999) 1-26, who argues that the references better fit the Severan empires and point to a date for the vision about 218 CE. He supposes that the vision has been redacted and updated from an earlier composition.

9. On the social and historical setting, see Lester L. Grabbe, "4 Ezra and 2 Baruch in Social and Historical Perspective," in Matthias Henze and Gabriele Boccaccini, eds.,

## Unity and Structure

The literary unity of 4 Ezra was the subject of a classic debate at the end of the nineteenth century between R. Kabisch and H. Gunkel.[10] Kabisch, writing in 1889 and using the source-critical methods then in vogue, argued that the book contained five separate sources from five separate authors, which were then combined by a redactor. Gunkel, writing in 1900, recognized that there are indeed inconsistencies in the text but argued that these may reflect diverse traditions on which the author drew rather than distinct documentary sources. Gunkel's view has prevailed in subsequent research,[11] although the source-critical approach has been perpetuated in the English-speaking world through the work of G. H. Box and R. H. Charles.[12] Box distinguished (1) S, a Salathiel apocalypse that contained the bulk of chaps. 3–10; (2) E, an Ezra apocalypse from which the signs of the end in 4:52–5:13 and 6:13-29 are extracts; (3) the eagle vision; (4) the Son of Man vision; (5) E2, containing the bulk of chap. 14; and, finally, a redactor who connected the whole and made minor insertions. Box found strong evidence for the use of an independent source in the very first verse, where the visionary is identified as "I Salathiel, who am also Ezra." Salathiel (Hebrew: Shealtiel) was the father of Zerubbabel (according to Ezra 3:2; 5:2; Neh 12:1). Why his name should be used here is a mystery. Box held that "the only adequate explanation is that an editor or compiler is using an independent writing in which the seer who is the recipient of the revelations that follow spoke in the name of Salathiel."[13] The revelation would here be transferred to

---

*Fourth Ezra and Second Baruch: Reconstruction after the Fall* (JSJSup 164; Leiden: Brill, 2013) 221-35.

10. R. Kabisch, *Das vierte Buch Esra auf seine Quellen untersucht* (Göttingen: Vandenhoeck & Ruprecht, 1889); H. Gunkel, "Das vierte Buch Esra," in E. Kautzsch, ed., *Die Apokryphen und Pseudepigraphen des Alten Testaments* (2 vols.; Tübingen: Mohr Siebeck, 1900) 2:331-401.

11. For the history of scholarship, see A. L. Thompson, *Responsibility for Evil in the Theodicy of IV Ezra* (SBLDS 29; Missoula, MT: Scholars Press, 1977) 85-120; E. Brandenburger, *Die Verborgenheit Gottes im Weltgeschehen* (Zurich: Theologischer Verlag, 1981) 22-57; B. Longenecker, *Eschatology and the Covenant: A Comparison of 4 Ezra and Romans 1–11* (Sheffield: JSOT Press, 1991) 40-49; Stone, *Fourth Ezra*, 11-21.

12. G. H. Box, *The Ezra Apocalypse* (London: Pitman, 1912); idem, "IV Ezra," in Charles, ed., *APOT*, 2:542-624; R. H. Charles, *A Critical History of the Doctrine of a Future Life* (London: Black, 1899) 283-97.

13. Box, "IV Ezra," 549. This problem must be seen in the wider context of other iden-

the more authoritative figure of Ezra. However, it is odd that no other mention of Salathiel survived, if he was the recipient of the revelations in chaps. 3–10. Some other explanations may be suggested. Ezra was a highly authoritative figure in Judaism, but in this book he is the spokesman for a very skeptical position. It is possible that an editor wished to suggest that the visionary was not *the* Ezra but rather the lesser figure Salathiel, whose name was chosen because he did live during the exile. It is also possible that an editor was aware of the chronological difficulty of placing Ezra thirty years after the fall of Jerusalem and sought to resolve the problem by identifying the visionary with Salathiel. In either case, the identification could result from editorial intervention and need not reflect an independent documentary source.

Even source critics like Kabisch and Box recognized that 4 Ezra, in its present form, consists of seven units, which are commonly called "visions" although that label is not appropriate in all cases.[14] These units are (1) 3:1–5:19; (2) 5:20–6:34; (3) 6:35–9:25; (4) 9:26–10:59; (5) 10:60–12:51; (6) 13:1-58; (7) 14:1-48. The first three are dialogues between Ezra and the angel Uriel. At the end of the first and second, Ezra fasts for seven days in accordance with the angel's command. After the third he is bidden to wait seven days without fasting, but eating the flower of the field. The fourth unit consists of the vision of Zion, at first as a woman, then transformed as a city. The vision is explained by the angel, who then tells Ezra to "remain here tomorrow night." On the second night Ezra has the vision of the eagle, which is followed by an interpretation. At the end of this unit Ezra remains in the field for seven days eating the flowers. The dream vision of the "man from the sea" follows with its interpretation. After this he waits three days, and then he encounters the voice from the bush.

Within the final, seventh unit there is another intermission of a day (14:27-36), when Ezra addresses the people and engages the scribes. Then he withdraws again to the field and is inspired to dictate 94 books. In this case, however, the intermission is not simply a void. Ezra's activity during the day is recorded, and the entire chapter is a continuous narrative. Accordingly, most scholars have recognized that the intermission does not indicate a new unit.[15] Its main purpose is to allow Ezra a summary parting

---

tifications of Ezra that were current in Jewish tradition. See R. A. Kraft, " 'Ezra' Materials in Judaism and Christianity," *ANRW*, II.19.2, 119-36.

14. So already G. Volkmar, *Das vierte Buch Esra* (Tübingen: Fues, 1863).

15. The general consensus on this point has been challenged by W. Harnisch, who argues that chap. 14 should be viewed as two distinct units ("Der Prophet als Widerpart und

message to the people while leaving the reception of the inspired books in the climactic final position.

A sevenfold structure is also found in the New Testament book of Revelation.[16] The main objections to the originality of this structure in 4 Ezra have concerned the eagle vision (10:60–12:51) and the so-called Son of Man vision (more properly the "man from the sea," chap. 13). These chapters have often been regarded as redundant, and this impression has been bolstered by formal considerations.[17] The interlude before the eagle vision is only one night, not seven days, and the visions are introduced directly, without any introductory prayer by Ezra. Yet we have seen from Daniel and the Similitudes of Enoch that redundancy is a well-attested compositional device in apocalypses. Minor variations, such as the interval of one day instead of seven, do not necessarily indicate separate sources either. Such variations occur throughout the book — for example, Enoch fasts after the first two episodes but eats flowers after the third.[18] More importantly, all critics agree that chap. 10 is a turning point in the book. We should expect some formal variations in the following chapters. The omission of Ezra's complaints in chaps. 11–13 is not due to a different hand but to the shifting emphasis of the book. The inclusion of these visions is necessary to fill out the sevenfold structure but also to provide balance over against the skeptical probings of Ezra in the earlier chapters.[19] The final unit in chap. 14 provides an epilogue to the entire composition. While chaps. 11–13 undoubtedly contain traditional material, there is no good reason to deny their authenticity in 4 Ezra.

The macrostructure of 4 Ezra is clearly an apocalypse.[20] Ezra is the

---

Zeuge der Offenbarung: Erwägungen zur Interdependenz von Form und Sache im IV Buch Esra," in D. Hellholm, ed., *Apocalypticism in the Mediterranean World and the Near East: Proceedings of the International Colloquium on Apocalypticism, Uppsala, August 12-17, 1979* [Tübingen: Mohr Siebeck, 1983] 461-93).

16. A. Yarbro Collins, *The Combat Myth in the Book of Revelation* (HDR 9; Missoula, MT: Scholars Press, 1976) 5-55.

17. So Harnisch, "Der Prophet als Widerpart"; W. Harrelson, "Ezra among the Wicked in 2 Esdras 3–10," in J. L. Crenshaw and S. Sandmel, eds., *The Divine Helmsman: Studies on God's Control of Human Events, Presented to Lou H. Silberman* (New York: Ktav, 1980) 21-39.

18. Brandenburger, *Die Verborgenheit Gottes,* 107.

19. See further E. Breech, "These Fragments I Have Shored against My Ruins: The Form and Function of 4 Ezra," *JBL* 92 (1973) 267-74.

20. Hindy Najman, *Losing the Temple and Recovering the Future: An Analysis of 4 Ezra* (Cambridge: Cambridge University Press, 2014) 21, grants that "a generic approach is well-suited to the study of distinct parts of the text" but uses instead the notion of a constellation

pseudonymous seer, who receives revelation through the mediation of the angel Uriel, about the transcendent world, which is to come. Yet within this framework the author fashions a highly original and distinctive work. The first three units, 3:1–5:19; 5:20–6:34; and 6:35–9:25, are not properly visions, but dialogues between Ezra and the angel. The dialogue was used as a medium of revelation in Daniel 10–12. The originality of 4 Ezra lies in the extent of the dialogue, but also in its skeptical character. In a manner reminiscent of Job, 4 Ezra presses the question of the justice of God and at first is hesitant to accept apocalyptic revelations of a transcendent world. Then, in the fourth unit, 9:26–10:59, there is a sudden reversal, and Ezra comes to share the angel's point of view. This acceptance is consolidated in the eagle and "man from the sea" visions. At the end Ezra himself becomes mediator of revelation for the rest of the people.

The book as a whole, then, has the character of a debate.[21] The dialogues are heavily indebted to the wisdom tradition.[22] More specifically, Ezra, as represented here, stands in the tradition of the covenantalized wisdom of Ben Sira, who famously declared that all wisdom is the book of the covenant of the Most High (Sir 24:23), and is preoccupied with God's election of, and covenant with Israel.[23] The angel Uriel, in contrast, expounds a kind of wisdom that makes frequent analogies with nature, but ignores the covenant, and focuses instead on individual salvation.[24] In the end, both kinds of wisdom are overruled by the emotional power of the

---

of features expressing the idea of revelation inflected by destruction. This, in effect, is a thematic approach to 4 Ezra, which yields insights but does not deal adequately with the configuration of the work as a whole.

21. See especially Karina Martin Hogan, *Theologies in Conflict in 4 Ezra: Wisdom Debate and Apocalyptic Solution* ( JSJSup 130; Leiden: Brill, 2008). Najman, *Losing the Temple*, 131, seeks to soften the differences between Ezra and Uriel, but the text certainly portrays them as strongly at variance with each other. Najman insists that on such matters as the origin of sin and human freedom "the text is quite simply indeterminate," and there is no principled way to assign any sharply defined positions — let alone conflicting ones — to the two speakers. But if so, why do the dialogues continue for six and a half chapters?

22. M. A. Knibb, "Apocalyptic and Wisdom in 4 Ezra." *JSJ* 13 (1983) 56-74.

23. Hogan. *Theologies in Conflict in 4 Ezra*, 126-34.

24. Ibid., 140. Hogan finds a precedent for this kind of wisdom in 4QInstruction, a wisdom text found in the Dead Sea Scrolls. Stefan Beyerle, "'Du bist kein Richter über dem Herrn': Zur Konzeption von Gesetz und Gericht im 4.Esrabuch," in S. Beyerle, G. Mayer and H. Strauss, eds., *Recht und Ethos im Alten Testament* (Neukirchen: Neukirchener Verlag, 1999) 315-37, relates Uriel's view to natural theology. See the comments of Hogan, *Theologies in Conflict*, 141.

apocalyptic visions.[25] To be sure, the position of Uriel is also apocalyptic, since it is based on belief in a judgment after death, but it is not true that "the worldview of Uriel and that of the visions are identical."[26] At the least, there is a significant difference in emphasis. Uriel's view of salvation is much more individualistic than that of the visions, but also the rhetorical force of the visions is greater because of the manner in which they are presented.

The central problem of interpretation in 4 Ezra undoubtedly concerns the transition of Ezra from skeptic to believer. This problem is basic to our understanding of the purpose and the coherence of the book. Scholars have held widely different opinions on this issue. On the one hand, some have held that the skeptical questions of Ezra in the dialogues are put forward only so that they can be definitively refuted by the angel. Ezra, then, is the mouthpiece for an erroneous line of thought. He possibly represents some group or movement that the author opposes, perhaps a point of view that had not found clear social expression.[27] On the other hand, some have held that Ezra articulates the author's position and that his complaints are never really answered. Ezra's role reversal in chap. 10 is seen as ironic,[28] or the author is said to have "produced a masterful presentation of his doubts behind a respectable curtain of concern for Israel."[29] Still others, following the pioneering work of Gunkel, have seen the tensions of the book as evidence of an inner struggle[30] or sought an interpretation in which the authenticity of the questions and the acceptance of the final

25. See my essay, "The Idea of Election in 4 Ezra," *Jewish Studies Quarterly* 16 (2009) 83-96.

26. As claimed by Lorenzo DiTommaso, "Who is the 'I' of 4 Ezra?" in Henze and Boccaccini, eds., *Fourth Ezra and Second Baruch*, 127. Di Tommaso rightly insists that the views of Uriel are also apocalyptic, but apocalypticism admits of internal differences.

27. E. Brandenburger, *Adam and Christus* (Neukirchen–Vluyn: Neukirchener Verlag, 1962) 27-36; idem, *Die Verborgenheit Gottes,* 42-51; W. Harnisch, *Verhängnis und Verheissung der Geschichte: Untersuchungen zum Zeit- und Geschichtsverständnis im 4. Buch Esra und in der syr. Baruchapokalypse* (Göttingen: Vandenhoeck & Ruprecht, 1969) 60-67 and passim. Harnisch goes further than Brandenburger in identifying the skeptical viewpoint with a group.

28. So Harrelson, "Ezra among the Wicked."

29. Thompson, *Responsibility for Evil,* 269.

30. Gunkel saw the book as a record of the author's inner struggle ("Das vierte Buch Esra," 340). So also C. G. Montefiore, *IV Ezra: A Study in the Development of Universalism* (London: Allen & Unwin, 1929); M. Knibb, *The Second Book of Esdras* (Cambridge: Cambridge University Press, 1979) 109.

revelation are held together in a conversion experience of Ezra.[31] Since the skeptical probings are attributed to the same Ezra who is authenticated as mediator of revelation in the final chapter, his doubts can scarcely be attributed to an opposition party.[32] The kind of interpretation associated with Gunkel and Stone has the advantage of respecting the unity of the central figure throughout. The apocalyptic revelations of chaps. 11–13 must be seen as the culmination of a movement that begins with the probings of chap. 3.

## The Dialogues

4 Ezra is more explicit than most apocalypses about the problem besetting the visionary: "I was perturbed . . . because I visualized the ruin of Zion and the affluence of those who lived in Babylon." These reflections are not an immediate response to the catastrophe of 70 CE, but rather contemplate the enduring state of affairs that resulted from it.[33] In comparing the fate of Zion with that of Babylon, Ezra moves beyond the specific historical crisis to the general problem of theodicy or the justice of God. The events of 70 CE are the catalyst for the broader question. Of course the standard apocalyptic device of pseudonymity already serves to put the problem in a wider perspective. Ostensibly, the occasion of Ezra's perplexity is the catastrophe of 586 BCE and the resulting exile. The defeat by Rome is only a reenactment of one of the major paradigms of Jewish history.

The opening prayer of Ezra also serves to relate the present dilemma to the universal human situation. Ezra recites the outline of history, beginning with Adam. This passage is quite different from the reviews of history that are presented in other apocalypses in the guise of prophecy. It

---

31. So M. E. Stone, "Reactions to Destructions of the Second Temple: Theology, Perception, and Conversion," *JSJ* 12 (1981) 195-204; idem, "On Reading an Apocalypse," in J. J. Collins and J. H. Charlesworth, eds., *Mysteries and Revelations: Apocalyptic Studies Since the Uppsala Colloquium* (JSPSup 9; Sheffield: JSOT Press, 1991) 65-78; idem, *Fourth Ezra*, 31-32. Longenecker, *Eschatology and Covenant*, 149, concludes that 4 Ezra is "nothing other than a conversion story." P. Hayman concludes that "overwhelming religious experience can dissolve any kind of intellectual doubt" ("The Problem of Pseudonymity in the Ezra Apocalypse," *JSJ* 6 [1975] 47-56).

32. Compare Hayman, "The Problem of Pseudonymity," 50.

33. On 4 Ezra as mourning for the destruction see Dereck Daschke, *City of Ruins: Mourning the Destruction of Jerusalem through Jewish Apocalypse* (Biblical Interpretation Series 99; Leiden: Brill, 2010) 103-39.

is also different from the traditional Deuteronomic recitation of salvation history.[34] The emphasis is not on salvation but on failure. Ezra recognizes that in each generation some remnant was spared. This theme had been used in Enoch's Apocalypse of Weeks to build the expectation of a final deliverance for the chosen few. Ezra, in contrast, emphasizes that even the remnants attain no lasting salvation: "For the first Adam, laden with an evil inclination, transgressed and was overcome; so did all those who issued from him" (3:21). If the law was in the heart of the people, so was the "root of evil," and so the chosen people eventually came to ruin. Two fundamental problems emerge already in this opening prayer. One is the "evil inclination," which is present in human nature from the beginning and poses the question of God's justice toward humanity at large.[35] The second is the relative justice of Israel's fate: "Does Babylon really act any better than Zion?" (3:31). This question is not a new one, but it is pursued in 4 Ezra with unusual intensity. The fate of Israel puts the whole system of the Mosaic covenant in doubt: "When did the inhabitants of the earth not sin before you? Or what nation has so well executed your commandments? You will find exceptional individuals who have kept your commandments, but nations you will not find" (3:35-36). If only "exceptional individuals" can keep the commandments, then membership of a covenant people becomes irrelevant. This pessimistic conclusion is borne out by the actual destruction of Zion.

The angel's reply is reminiscent of God's reply to Job from the whirlwind.[36] It consists of a list of impossible questions that emphasize how little Ezra understands: "Weigh for me the weight of fire, measure for me the measure of the wind, or recover for me the day that is past" (4:5). Yet these are said to be things of this world with which Ezra has been associated. The angel pointedly remarks that he is not asking about the exits

---

34. See P. G. R. de Villiers, "Understanding the Way of God: Form, Function, and Message of the Historical Review in 4 Ezra 3:4-27," in K. H. Richards, ed., *Society of Biblical Literature 1981 Seminar Papers* (Chico, CA: Scholars Press, 1981) 357-78.

35. The importance of the "evil heart" is emphasized by Jason M. Zurawski, "The Two Worlds and Adam's Sin: The Problem of 4 Ezra 7:10-14," in Gabriele Boccaccini and Jason M. Zurawski, eds., *Interpreting 4 Ezra and 2 Baruch* (International Studies. London: Bloomsbury/T & T Clark, 2014) 97-106. On the evil inclination in ancient Judaism see Ishay Rosen-Zvi, *Demonic Desires: yetzer hara and the Problem of Evil in Late Antiquity* (Philadelphia: University of Pennsylvania, 2011).

36. The dialogues are indebted to the Jewish wisdom tradition at many points. See Knibb, "Apocalyptic and Wisdom in 4 Ezra," 56-74.

out of hell or the ways of paradise, since Ezra might have answered that he has neither descended into the abyss nor ascended to heaven. These, of course, are precisely the accomplishments of apocalyptic visionaries such as Enoch. The point here is that Ezra cannot hope to make sense of the world by ordinary human wisdom, even on the premises of the Deuteronomic covenant. Apocalyptic revelation is necessary, and that is what the angel will eventually provide.

Ezra reformulates his question, with a tenacity surpassing that of Job:

> Pray tell me, O Lord, why has the faculty of perception been given to me? For I did not mean to inquire about the ways above, but rather about those things we experience daily:
>> Why Israel is subjected to abuse by the nations . . .
>> The law of our fathers rendered ineffective . . .
>> For we leave this world like grasshoppers . . .
>> Our life is like a vapor
>> And we are unworthy of receiving mercy. (4:22-24)

The angel's reply is indirect. No answer is given to the question, Why? Instead Ezra is told: "If you continue, you will see, and if you go on living, you will often marvel — because the age is speedily coming to an end; for it cannot bear the things promised to the righteous." The mystery persists as to why this age is as it is. We are not told why the grain of evil was sown in the heart of Adam. We cannot proceed faster than the Most High; and, although we are assured that God knows best, we cannot ultimately comprehend his ways. At this point Ezra is distracted from probing the question of justice by curiosity about the end that is to come. He is assured that the time which has passed is greater than that which is left, and he is told some signs that will precede the end. He is also promised the revelation of "things greater than these" after seven days. The effect is bewilderment and amazement. Ezra's initial questions have not been answered, but his attention has been diverted from the distress of the present to the prospect of the world to come.

The main substance of the angel's reply is that this age is passing away. This point will be elaborated much more explicitly, in the third dialogue. The way of the Lord still encompasses both ages.[37] There is no question

---

37. K. Koch, "Esras erste Vision: Weltzeiten und Weg des Höchsten," *BZ* 22 (1978) 46-75.

here of an ultimate dualism. Yet the emphasis is on the discontinuity between this age and the world to come. There is no smooth evolution from this age to the next.

Ezra's problem has been suppressed at the end of the first dialogue, but it has not gone away. The second dialogue does little more than recapitulate the first. Ezra's prayer provides a shorter historical review than his earlier one and focuses more directly on the problem of Zion: "Why have you dispersed your only one among the many?" (5:28). Again the angel begins by contrasting Ezra's limited comprehension with the unlimited, if unfathomable, understanding of the creator. Does Ezra love Israel more than God does? Again there is a brief bombardment with impossible questions: "Count for me those not yet come, collect for me the spattered drops" (5:36). Ezra is told flatly that he will not be able to discover the judgment of God or the purpose of his love for his people.

The angel not only frustrates Ezra's initial question; he also diverts his attention to the future. The creation is already old and in decline (5:48-55). Moreover, the demise of this world had been planned from the beginning. All is securely under divine control. Again, the dialogue concludes with the recitation of signs of the end and a promise of further revelations. This time the angel's purpose is explicit: "Believe, do not fear, and do not be overanxious to speculate uselessly about former times, that you may not be taken by surprise in the last times" (6:33-34).

We can begin at this point to appreciate the purpose of the repetition. The angel is not engaged in rational argumentation but in the psychological process of calming fear and building trust. For this purpose the repetition is crucial, as the fears are gradually eroded by expression and the trust accumulates through multiple reassurances.

The third dialogue not only recapitulates the other two but enlarges and deepens the discussion. Ezra begins by rehearsing the works of creation. The point of this recital is made explicit in 6:55-56: "I have spoken about all these things before you, Lord, because you said that you created the firstborn world for us. As for the rest of the nations sprung from Adam, you declared them to be as nothing, like spittle, and you have likened their profusion to drippings from a bucket. . . . So if the world was created for us, why do we not enjoy possession of the heritage of our world?" Ezra here gives voice to the basic dilemma of the covenantal tradition.

The angel's reply affirms that "I did make the world for their sakes" but subtly changes the presuppositions of the traditional theology. The heir can only claim his inheritance if he traverses the danger set before him. The basis of salvation is individual merit, not membership of a covenant people. Accordingly, the focus shifts from the specific destiny of Israel to the more general problem of human inability to satisfy the law. The angel's insistence that Ezra should "think about what is to come, rather than what now is" (7:16) is disregarded for the moment so that this question may be pursued.

Ezra complains about the fate of the wicked, since indeed the bulk of humanity seems to fall into this category (7:48). The angel's reply is harsh: "You are not a judge superior to God, nor more discriminating than the Most High. Let the many who exist perish rather than that the law of God . . . be slighted" (7:19-20). This pronouncement is buttressed not with a rationale or explanation but with an extended eschatological scenario. That which God will bring about requires no further justification.

The scenario is of considerable interest, since it is the most explicit formulation of the eschatology presumed throughout 4 Ezra.[38] First, the signs will come, then "the hidden city" (presumably the heavenly Jerusalem) and the messiah will be revealed.[39] The messiah will reign for four hundred years but will then die. After seven days of primordial silence the resurrection will follow. The reign of the messiah is included at the end of this age, as a transitional phase, but the age to come is separated from this one by a gulf of seven days "just as it was at the very beginning." 4 Ezra is heir to a longer tradition of eschatological speculation than were Daniel or the Enoch apocalypses. Here the expectation of national restoration under a messiah is integrated with the more typical apocalyptic hope of retribution beyond death in a far more thorough manner than was the case in any earlier document. The three-stage scenario, which distinguishes the reign of the messiah from the world to come, is compatible with all the formulations of 4 Ezra, although it is often difficult to be sure which stage the author has in mind when he speaks of the "end."[40] The fundamental point,

38. On the eschatology of 4 Ezra, see M. E. Stone, *Features of the Eschatology of 4 Ezra* (Atlanta: Scholars Press, 1989).

39. The Latin "filius meus Jesus" is obviously a Christian emendation. There is general agreement that the original read "my messiah." It is also apparent, in the light of the versions, that "filius" translates the Greek *pais*, which in turn reflects the Hebrew *'abdi*, "my servant." See Stone, *Fourth Ezra*, 207-8.

40. M. E. Stone argues that "the end" refers to "the crucial turning point of the eschatological process" and refers in some cases to the advent of the messiah, in other cases to the transition from this world to the next ("Coherence and Inconsistency in the Apocalypses: The Case of 'The End' in 4 Ezra," *JBL* 102 [1983] 229-43). Against this view, P. Schäfer argues that the three-stage schema is presupposed throughout and that the messiah belongs to this age, before the end ("Die Lehre von den zwei Welten im 4. Buch Esra und in der

however, is that "the Most High made not one world, but two" (7:50). The other world is that beyond the resurrection and the judgment, although the reign of the messiah might be regarded as a limited anticipation of it. The belief in another world, beyond this one, is fundamental to all the apocalypses in some form. Both worlds are, of course, within the design of the same God, but they are sharply separated from each other, nonetheless.

The judgment that follows the resurrection is severe: "Then the end will come, and compassion will vanish, pity will cease, and forbearance will be withdrawn. Only judgment will remain . . ." (7:33). There will be no intercession for others thereafter (7:102-15). The severity results from 4 Ezra's generally grim view of the world, where pity is not much in evidence at any stage.[41] It is not required by the apocalyptic expectation of a final judgment, which could accommodate a far more merciful God, as we will find in the *Testament of Abraham*. Yet this severity is in itself the most persistent problem that besets Ezra, for "the world to come will bring joy to the few, but torment to the many" (7:47). The angel counters that just as gold is precious because it is rare, so the value of the righteous is also enhanced by their scarcity. Moreover, he suggests that Ezra "must not get entangled with scorners nor reckon yourself with those who are tormented. For indeed you have a treasure of works stored up with the Most High" (7:77). Once more Ezra is distracted from his questioning by a detailed account of what happens after death (7:78-101).

Ezra, however, is reluctant to distinguish himself from sinful humanity: "O Adam, what have you done? Although you (alone) sinned, the fall was not yours alone but ours too, who descended from you" (7:117-18).[42] When he concedes that God knows best about the totality of mankind, he still appeals for mercy on Israel. The angel commends him for his humility in not reckoning himself with the just (8:49), but is still uncompromising.

---

tannaitischen Literatur," in *Studien zur Geschichte und Theologie des Rabbinischen Judentums* [Leiden: Brill, 1978] 244-91).

41. Richard Bauckham, "Apocalypses," in D. A. Carson, P. T. O'Brien, and M. A. Seifrid, eds., *Justification and Variegated Nomism*. Volume 1: *The Complexities of Second Temple Judaism* (WUNT 2.140; Tübingen: Mohr Siebeck, 2001) 173: "What God does not do, according to 4 Ezra, is exercise mercy to Israelite sinners by withholding judgment from them."

42. Najman, *Losing the Temple*, 82, insists that "4 Ezra does not state that others are punished for the sins of Adam," and suggests that it may only mean that death was decreed as the appropriate punishment, not that all would in fact die. This reading seems strained. If Ezra escapes death, as he does in the Syriac version (14:48), he is exceptional. It is true, however, that 4 Ezra does not have a doctrine of original sin as it later developed in Christianity, whereby people are born in a sinful state.

Ezra is bidden to ask no further questions about the multitude of those who are lost, who have only themselves to blame. Instead he is to concern himself with the salvation of the just and is again instructed in the signs of the end. He is scarcely persuaded as yet. His last statement in the dialogues is a simple assertion: "I said before, say now, and will say hereafter: more numerous are the lost than the saved as the tide is greater than a drop" (9:15-16). This statement does not quite reject the angel's consolation, but it is a rueful reminder of the real limitations of the salvation to come.

The dialogues conclude with a forward pointer. Ezra is to wait seven days without fasting but go into a field of flowers and eat only the flowers. The double change, in diet and location, marks the transition to the visions of chaps. 10–14.

## The Visions

The fourth section of 4 Ezra, or first vision, is generally recognized as the turning point of the book. Ezra begins, in a manner similar to the other dialogues, to complain about the destruction of Israel. In this case, however, he is distracted by a vision of a woman who is grieving for the death of her only son. Ezra suddenly assumes the role of comforter, although his tone is rather severe. He scolds the woman for being obsessed with her individual problem, while "Zion the mother of us all" has suffered a much greater bereavement, and the earth has the greatest grief of all. He concludes with the advice, "Therefore keep your grief to yourself and bear gallantly your calamities, for if you accept as right the verdict of God, you will get back your son in his time and be highly extolled among women" (10:16-17). When she refuses, Ezra insists, "Permit yourself to be persuaded because of the calamity of Zion," but while he is speaking she is transformed into a city with massive foundations.[43] Then Uriel, the angel, appears and explains to Ezra that the woman was Zion and that God had shown him the glory of (the future, restored) Jerusalem because of his wholehearted grief over her ruin.

This encounter marks the end of Ezra's complaints against God. From

---

43. This passage is studied in the context of other transformations of female figures by E. M. Humphrey, *The Ladies and the Cities: Transformation and Apocalyptic Identity in Joseph and Aseneth, 4 Ezra, the Apocalypse, and the Shepherd of Hermas* (JSPSup; Sheffield: Sheffield Academic Press, 1995) 57-83.

this point on his transformation is complete. He readily acquiesces in the remaining revelations and at the end becomes himself a mediator of revelation to others. The fact of this transformation is obvious enough.[44] The reason for it is less immediately apparent. We cannot agree with the view that Ezra's advice is "an ironic answer to the woman, an answer that Ezra cannot accept for himself."[45] Ezra's acceptance of the answer is confirmed in all the remaining sections of the book. Those who speak of a "conversion" or "experiential solution" are on the right track, but how does this conversion come about? The crucial element is the reversal of Ezra's role when he meets the woman.[46] Now that he is cast in the role of comforter he gets a new perspective on the grief of an individual. We might compare the technique of Nathan in his famous parable. There David is induced to pass judgment before he knows that he is judging himself. The allegorical presentation of the case obscures the king's personal interest and allows him to view it with detachment. Similarly, the allegorical dress of Zion deceives Ezra so that he does not at first realize that the advice he gives applies to himself too. He tells the woman to let herself be persuaded because of the calamity of Zion, but the logic of his argument is that we cannot see our problems in perspective and so must resign ourselves before the providence of God. This, of course, is what the angel has been telling Ezra all along. He is able to see the justification of this argument when it is applied to another more readily than when it was addressed to himself.

Ezra's conversion is now consolidated by two dream visions, which clearly show the influence of Daniel 7, and which also qualify the eschatology that Uriel has expounded by emphasizing the nation rather than the individual. In the first, he sees "an eagle coming up out of the sea; it had twelve feathered wings and three heads" (11:1). The vision continues with a complex allegory of wings and wingless that defies precise identification, but the eagle is obviously Rome, and the three heads, as noted above,

---

44. Despite the hesitation of Loren Stuckenbruck, "Ezra's Vision of the Lady. The Form and Function of a Turning Point," in Henze and Boccaccini, eds., *Fourth Ezra and Second Baruch*, 137-50, who questions the degree to which Ezra is transformed and emphasizes the continuity of his grief.

45. Harrelson, "Ezra among the Wicked," 36. Harrelson argues that the vision of Zion transformed shows that the narrow logic of sin and punishment is revoked, but nothing else in 4 Ezra substantiates this optimism.

46. See especially W. Harnisch, "Die Ironie der Offenbarung: Exegetische Erwägungen zur Zionsvision im 4. Buch Esra," in K. H. Richards, ed., *Society of Biblical Literature 1981 Seminar Papers*, 79-104.

should most probably be identified with Vespasian, Titus, and Domitian. Then a raging lion comes out of the forest to denounce the eagle: "The Most High declares to you: Are you not the only one of the four beasts left that I appointed to hold sway over my world that through them the end of my times might come?" (11:39). The accusations are primarily concerned with injustice and oppression and conclude with the promise, "Thus the whole earth will be relieved and delivered from your power; then it can hope for justice and the compassion of him who made it" (11:46).[47]

The dependence on Daniel is explicit in the interpretation: "The eagle you observed coming up out of the sea is the fourth kingdom that appeared in a vision to Daniel your brother, but it was not interpreted to him in the same way I now interpret to you" (12:11-12). Besides the clear application to Rome, Ezra diverges from Daniel in the major role assigned to the lion, "the anointed one whom the Most High has reserved till the end of days, who will arise from the seed of David" (12:32). The interpretation informs us that the messiah's role is not only to accuse but also to destroy. Then "the remnant of my people he will set free with compassion and grant them joy until the end, the day of judgment about which I spoke to you at the beginning" (12:34).

The eagle vision may be understood as a reinterpretation of the fourth beast of Daniel 7, and the vision that follows in 4 Ezra relates to the "one like a son of man" in that chapter.[48] In 4 Ezra 13 the wind "brought up out of the depths of the sea something resembling a man and that man was flying with the clouds of heaven." In Daniel, and in the eagle vision, the sea was the source from which the beasts arose. Here the sea connotes the depths of mystery ("Just as no one can search out or perceive what may be in the depths of the sea, so no one on earth will be able to see my son or those who are with him except in the time of his day" [13:51]).[49] The description of this figure departs radically from Daniel. There is no reference here to the "holy

---

47. On the critique of Rome in this vision, see J. H. Charlesworth, "The Triumphant Majority as Seen by a Dwindled Minority: The Outsider according to the Insider of the Jewish Apocalypses," in J. Neusner and E. Frerichs, eds., *"To See Ourselves as Others See Us": Christians, Jews, "Others" in Late Antiquity* (Chico, CA: Scholars Press, 1985) 625-37.

48. Yarbro Collins and Collins, *King and Messiah*, 94-97; *The Scepter and the Star*, 205-10. See, however, H. S. Kvanvig, *Roots of Apocalyptic: The Mesopotamian Background of the Enoch Figure and of the Son of Man* (WMANT 61; Neukirchen–Vluyn: Neukirchener Verlag, 1988), 514-35, who argues that 4 Ezra 13 is independent of Daniel 7.

49. Kvanvig, *Roots of Apocalyptic*, 531-32, relates the sea to the Mesopotamian netherworld, abode of the dead as well as of demons.

ones of the Most High." In part, his appearance is modeled on old theophanic traditions of the divine warrior: all who hear his voice melt like wax before the fire.[50] The mountain he carves out for himself recalls the stone hewn from the mountain in Daniel 2. The assault of the multitude recalls the traditional motif of the attack of the nations on Mount Zion (cf. Psalm 2). The manner in which he slays his enemies with the breath of his mouth is a standard messianic motif, based on Isa 11:4, and paralleled in Revelation 19 ("the sword of his mouth"). The Latin and Syriac text refers to this figure as "my son" (13:32). Stone prefers the reading "servant," found in some other versions, since both son and servant could be derived from the Greek *pais*. But the Greek *pais* could still reflect Hebrew "son" rather than "servant" (compare Wisdom of Solomon, where the righteous man calls himself *pais theou* ["child of God" or "servant of God," 2:13] and boasts that God is his father [2:16]). The motif of the assault on the mountain recalls Psalm 2, where God tells the anointed king, "You are my son, this day I have begotten you."[51] It is very likely, then, that the man is here called "son (of God)" as a messianic title.[52] He will gather the ten lost tribes. His functions are the same as those of the messiah in the eagle vision: he will berate the peoples for their impiety and destroy their host but protect the people who survive.

The technique of these visions is familiar from our earlier discussion of Daniel 7.[53] The allegorical dreams provide perspective on the state of the Jews under Roman rule at the end of the first century. The allusions to Daniel suggest that Rome is acting out an ancient, mythic paradigm — in this case, the paradigm articulated in Daniel 7. In fact the details of both visions diverge widely from that of Daniel, whose vision serves as a point of departure in both cases but is never interpreted systematically. In part the divergence results from new historical data — hence the introduction of the eagle, the symbol of Rome. In greater part it results from the fusion of different eschatological traditions, specifically from the introduction of the motifs associated with the Davidic messiah, who played no part in Daniel.[54]

50. Compare Pss 46:6; 68:2; 97:5; Mic 1:4; *1 Enoch* 1:6.

51. G. W. E. Nickelsburg, "Son of Man," in *The Anchor Bible Dictionary* (6 vols.; New York: Doubleday, 1992) 6:141.

52. Collins, *Scriptures and Sectarianism*, 97-99.

53. See also A. Lacocque, "The Vision of the Eagle in 4 Esdras, A Rereading of Daniel 7 in the First Century CE," in K. H. Richards, ed., *Society of Biblical Literature 1981 Seminar Papers*, 237-58.

54. U. B. Müller, *Messias und Menschensohn in jüdischen Apokalypsen und in der Offenbarung des Johannes* (Gütersloh: Mohn, 1972) 83-134.

In both visions there are indications that the author is working with traditional material, for which he has supplied new interpretations. Since both have a point of departure in Daniel 7, we should expect that the author would have combined them in a single vision if he were working *de novo*. There is also some unevenness in the way in which the interpretation follows the vision, especially in chap. 13 — for example, the sea, which figures at the beginning of the vision, is not explained until the end.[55] More important than the question of sources, however, is the manner in which the material has been put together by the author. The visions form a complementary pair. The eagle vision is very obviously rooted in the traditional hope for a Davidic messiah. Its culmination is the removal of the most specific enemy of Judaism at the time, the Roman Empire. Only here does 4 Ezra show deep concern over oppression and social injustice.[56] The vision of the "man from the sea" draws on a different complex of traditions, which is associated in modern scholarship with the "Son of Man." Here the enemy is universal, "all the peoples." In the earlier tradition there was a clear-cut distinction between the hope for salvation by an angel (e.g., Michael in Daniel) and by a human messiah, although we have seen that both conceptions were maintained at Qumran, and the "Son of Man" figure in the Similitudes of Enoch was also called messiah. In 4 Ezra the "one like a man" is definitely the messiah, and we know from chap. 7 that he is human and will die. Yet he also embodies many of the traits of the heavenly savior. He rises mysteriously from the sea and is apparently preexistent ("whom the Most High has kept for many ages through whom to deliver his creation" [13:26; compare 7:28]). His appearance is accompanied by the traditional signs of a theophany. His powers are supernatural, and he represents far more than a restoration of the Davidic kingdom. In short, the messiah has not simply displaced the expectation of a heavenly savior. The two strands of tradition have been fused so that both have been transformed.

How far do these visions respond to the original complaints of Ezra? They promise that the humiliation of Israel will not last forever and that the balance over against the other nations will be set right. The emphasis on the coming of the messiah tends to highlight the aspect of national

55. See Stone, *Features of the Eschatology of 4 Ezra*, 123-25; idem, "The Concept of the Messiah in IV Ezra," in J. Neusner, ed., *Religions in Antiquity: Essays in Memory of E. R. Goodenough* (Leiden: Brill, 1968) 305-6.

56. For the denunciation of Rome, compare especially Revelation 17–18 and *Sib. Or.* 8:1-216.

fulfillment and to obscure the problem raised by Ezra, that so few even of the Jews will be saved. Yet the visions do not strictly contradict the severe stance of the angel in the dialogues. Even here only a remnant of the people will be saved (12:34). The interpretations do not address the question whether any non-Jews will be saved. The legend of the lost tribes in chap. 13 promises that the messiah will collect a "peaceful host," but even this legend offers only limited hope for the Jews with whom Ezra was acquainted. The visions qualify rather than refute the position of the angel, by placing more emphasis on national fulfillment. By ignoring the difficulties raised earlier by Ezra, they urge us to think positively about what is to come, rather than about what now is.

## The Epilogue

The final chapter constitutes an epilogue to the revelations, which presupposes that conviction has already been attained. Ezra is cast as the new Moses, summoned by God from the bush. This is the only clear instance where God speaks directly to Ezra.[57] The purpose of the divine speech is not to add to the revelation that has been given (the status of world history is briefly summarized in 14:9-12) but to commission Ezra to "caution your people, console their humble ones, teach their wise ones" (14:13). The analogy with Moses becomes more explicit when Ezra is inspired to dictate to his scribes for forty days. This is necessary because the Torah has been burned (14:21). Yet Ezra's task is not simply to restore the books of Moses, and he cannot be understood as a prophet of the Mosaic law.[58] First, he is directly inspired (after drinking a firelike liquid). His authority, then, is not subject to that of Moses. In fact since the law of Moses is presumed to be burned, Ezra now becomes an ultimate authority on divine revelation. Second, he dictates a total of 94 books. Twenty-four of these are released to the people and presumably correspond to the Hebrew Bible. There are seventy more, however, which are reserved for the wise men. The secret revelations given to Ezra throughout 4 Ezra are representative of this further wisdom. Hence the brunt of Ezra's exhortation to the people is to

57. In the eagle and "man from the sea" visions, Uriel is not mentioned but is probably the implied speaker. Ezra's prayers are addressed to God, but that was also the case in the opening dialogues, where the angel is clearly the respondent. Some manuscripts add a reference to the angel at 12:10 (see Myers, *I and II Esdras*, 292).

58. Contra Harnisch, "Der Prophet als Widerpart."

renounce mortal life and hasten to get out of these times, and look to the judgment after death (14:14, 35). As in Daniel and Enoch, the wisdom of the wise consists not in their knowledge of the Mosaic law but in the apocalyptic wisdom that comes from additional revelation.[59] The final chapter then claims the highest authority for Ezra. His revelation endorses the Mosaic law, but its main purpose is to provide the further revelation which is necessary to make sense of human experience.[60] We can appreciate why the author had to violate chronology to place his meditation on the fall of Jerusalem on the lips of a figure who could bear such weighty authority.

The choice of Ezra as pseudonymous visionary represents a more direct engagement with the Mosaic covenant than what we found in Enoch or Daniel. The profile of Ezra, as it was known from the biblical books of Ezra and Nehemiah, was that of a mediator of the Torah. The biblical Ezra unquestioningly affirms the justice of God's punishments: "You have been just in all that has come upon us, for you have dealt faithfully and we have acted wickedly; our kings, our officials, our priests, and our ancestors have not kept your law or heeded the commandments and the warnings that you gave them" (Neh 9:33-34). In 4 Ezra, however, Ezra has quite a different profile, one that is reminiscent of the biblical Job rather than the biblical Ezra. By the end of the book, he has again become a mediator of the Law, but also of apocalyptic wisdom. The seventy additional, esoteric, books, which are reserved for the wise among the people, contain "the springs of understanding, the fountains of wisdom, and the river of knowledge" (14:47).

Various scholars have suggested reasons for the choice of Ezra as the pseudonymous visionary. Ted Bergren has pointed to his traditional role as the restorer of Jewish worship and legal observance, his piety, and his status as scribe.[61] Pierluigi Piovanelli argues that Ezra qualified for the role as "herald of the end of the exile."[62] But the author of 4 Ezra was not

---

59. Compare U. Luck, "Das Weltverständnis in der jüdischen Apokalyptik: Dargestellt am Äthiopischen Henochbuch und am 4 Esra," *ZThK* 73 (1976) 283-305.

60. Cf. Longenecker, *Eschatology and the Covenant*, 152-53: "He still maintains such traditional concepts as 'law' and 'Israel' in his new pattern of religion, but redefines them in a way which gives them radicalized import."

61. Theodore A. Bergren, "Ezra and Nehemiah Square Off in the Apocrypha and Pseudepigrapha," in Michael E. Stone and Theodore A. Bergren, eds., *Biblical Figures Outside the Bible* (Harrisburg, PA: Trinity Press International, 1998) 340-63.

62. Pierluigi Piovanelli, "Why Ezra and not Enoch? Rewriting the Script of the First Exile with the Hope for a Prompt Restoration of Zion's Fortunes," in Henze and Boccaccini, eds., *Fourth Ezra and Second Baruch*, 242.

unaware of the discrepancy between the theological stance of the biblical Ezra and the stance attributed to him in this book. On the contrary, he uses the famous devotee of the Law in order to critique the traditional covenantal theology. Like his biblical counterpart, Ezra starts out from a position that has reasonably been called "ethnocentric covenantalism."[63] In 4 Ezra, however, that theological position is no longer satisfactory.[64]

Hindy Najman has argued that "pseudonymous attribution should be seen as a metaphorical device, operating at the level of the text as a whole, whereby the actual author emulates and self-identifies as an exemplar."[65] This works well in the case of pseudonyms such as Enoch and Daniel. The case of Ezra is more complicated. At the end of the book, he is indeed a figure to be emulated. In the Syriac and other versions except the Latin, Ezra is caught up and taken to the place of those who are like him, a destiny that had already been foretold in 14:9. Before that, however, he has to undergo a transformation in which he effectively sheds the persona of the biblical Ezra, and recognizes that the covenantal law must be supplemented by apocalyptic revelation.[66] No other pseudonymous apocalyptic mediator undergoes such a transformation.

## The Technique of 4 Ezra

The commissioning of Ezra in the final chapter sets the seal on his acceptance of the ultimate justice of God's judgment. His final message to the people ("control your inclination . . . for judgment comes after death") may be regarded as a summary of his message. This summary, however, by no means adequately represents the impact of the book. Approximately half the work has been devoted to the skeptical questions of the dialogue.

---

63. Longenecker, *Eschatology and the Covenant*, 34.

64. See further my essay, "Enoch and Ezra," in Henze and Boccaccini, eds., *Fourth Ezra and Second Baruch*, 83-97.

65. Hindy Najman, "How Should We Contextualize Pseudepigrapha? Imitation and Emulation in 4 Ezra," in eadem, *Past Renewals: Interpretative Authority, Renewed Revelation and the Quest for Perfection in Jewish Antiquity* (JSJSup 53; Leiden: Brill, 2010) 235-43, here 238.

66. Najman, "Traditionary Process and Textual Unity in 4 Ezra," in Henze and Boccaccini, *Fourth Ezra and Second Baruch*, 99-117, recognizes that in 4 Ezra "the figure of Ezra is transformed into a personality that is a very different figure from that of Ezra-Nehemiah" (p.111).

As in the Book of the Watchers and Daniel 7, the apocalypse deepens our perception of the problem before we can proceed to the solution. The probing questions of Ezra have a cathartic effect. They bring to expression the fears and frustrations of a sensitive and perceptive Jew in the wake of the catastrophe of 70 CE. The fact that no real answer to these questions is forthcoming ("you will be unable to discover my judgment" [5:40]) sets the stage for the eschatological revelation. When Ezra finally acquiesces in this revelation, it is not because he has been given a persuasive argument but because of pastoral necessity. Ezra realizes when he is cast in the role of comforter that we must let ourselves be persuaded (10:20). We believe because we need to believe. The belief is consolidated not by new arguments but by repetition of traditional symbols. If our problems cannot be solved, we must look away from them and contemplate what is positive. It is probable that the story of Ezra represents the author's own spiritual journey. As a literary work, the book stands as a guide to the perplexed. By identifying with Ezra, the reader can acknowledge the dilemmas of history, but come to experience the "apocalyptic cure"[67] by turning his attention to the transcendent perspective provided by the angel and the dream visions.

Ezra is a reluctant apocalyptist. He accepts the apocalyptic revelation only because of necessity. His initial disposition is far from Enochic speculation ("I did not mean to inquire about the ways above" [4:23]). His (frustrated) expectations are focused rather on the Deuteronomic covenant and the election of Israel. 4 Ezra does not deny that covenant but can only salvage it by buttressing it with further revelations and by reconceiving the judgment on a strict basis of individual merits, after death.

Because of the Deuteronomic presuppositions of the early questions, 4 Ezra has often been regarded as a Pharisaic apocalypse.[68] This characterization receives some support from analogies with the rabbinic writings in such matters as the "evil inclination," the distinction between this world and the world to come, and the signs of the end.[69] Yet 4 Ezra's conceptions are generally atypical of rabbinic literature. The difference is apparent in the sharpness of the break between this world and the world to come.[70] It is also apparent in the pessimistic attitude to the judgment, which sees most

67. The phrase of J.-C. Picard, à propos of 3 *Baruch*.
68. For example, Harnisch, *Verhängnis und Verheissung*, 327.
69. G. F. Moore, *Judaism in the First Centuries of the Christian Era* (2 vols.; New York: Schocken, 1971) 1:479-93 (on the evil inclination); 2:321-95 (on messianism and eschatology).
70. Schäfer, "Die Lehre von den zwei Welten," in *Studien zur Geschichte and Theologie des Rabbinischen Judentums,* 290-91.

of humanity as helpless before the evil inclination and allows little if any place for atonement or divine mercy.[71] The perception of human inability to satisfy the law is closer to Paul's teaching in Romans than to the typical attitudes of the Rabbis. This is not to deny that 4 Ezra falls within the spectrum of Jewish opinion at the end of the first century CE. Parallels can be found for such pessimism,[72] and the Judaism of Jamnia was remarkably tolerant of diversity.[73] There is no reason to regard 4 Ezra as sectarian in any sense.[74]

If 4 Ezra is exceptional in its pessimism about human performance, its attitude cannot fairly be described as "legalistic perfectionism."[75] We do not know what level of legalistic performance was regarded as necessary; at least a few, such as Ezra, could meet the standard. The pessimism of the book springs not so much from its lofty standards as from historical experience. If the destruction of Jerusalem represented the judgment of God, that judgment is indeed severe. Moreover, most of the Gentiles could not be said to fulfill the law — even on a lenient interpretation. The anguish of the author comes in part from a concern for those outside the covenant. Even within his own people, Ezra is reluctant to distinguish himself from the wicked. If God, as portrayed in this book, seems to lack compassion, the same cannot be said of the author. His sympathy with fallen human

---

71. See especially E. P. Sanders, *Paul and Palestinian Judaism* (Philadelphia: Fortress, 1977) 409-18; also Longenecker, *Eschatology and the Covenant,* 152; Shannon L. Burkes, *God, Self, and Death: The Shape of Religious Transformation in the Second Temple Period* (JSJSup 79; Leiden: Brill, 2003) 191-233; eadem, " 'Life' Redefined: Wisdom and Law in Fourth Ezra and Second Baruch," *CBQ* 63 (2001) 56-63.

72. F. Rosenthal (*Vier Apokryphische Bücher aus der Zeit und Schule R. Akibas* [Leipzig: Schulze, 1885] 39-71) argued for a special affinity between 4 Ezra and the teaching of Eliezer ben Hyrcanus in such matters as the severity of the judgment (*'Arakin* 17a) and the exclusion of the Gentiles from salvation (*Tosefta Sanhedrin* 13).

73. S. J. D. Cohen, "The Significance of Yavneh: Pharisees, Rabbis, and the End of Jewish Sectarianism," *HUCA* 55 (1984) 27-53.

74. Contra H. C. Kee, " 'The Man' in Fourth Ezra: Growth of a Tradition," in K. H. Richards, ed., *Society of Biblical Literature 1981 Seminar Papers,* 199-208. In this connection it should be noted that the sharp antithesis between rabbinic and apocalyptic religion posited by D. Rössler, *Gesetz und Geschichte* (Neukirchen–Vluyn: Neukirchener Verlag, 1960) has been widely discredited.

75. Sanders, *Paul and Palestinian Judaism,* 409. See the criticisms of Bauckham, "Apocalypses," 173; Jonathan A. Moo, "The Few Who Obtain Mercy: Soteriology in 4 Ezra," in Daniel M. Gurtner, ed., *This World and the World to Come: Soteriology in Early Judaism* (LSTS 74; London, 2011) 98-113. Moo, *Creation, Nature and Hope in 4 Ezra* (FRLANT 237; Göttingen: Vandenhoeck & Ruprecht, 2011) 164, grants an overwhelmingly negative assessment of humankind, but contrasts this with a less negative assessment of nature.

nature and perception of the real limitations of any hope for salvation give this book a humane spirit, which sets it apart from most other apocalypses.

## 2 Baruch

*2 Baruch* is closely related to 4 Ezra to such a degree that some form of interdependence must be posited. The text is preserved in a Syriac manuscript that was translated from Greek but most probably derived from a Hebrew original.[76] There can be little doubt that it was composed in the period between the two Jewish revolts.[77] As in 4 Ezra, the destruction at the hands of the Babylonians serves as an allegory for the fall of 70 CE. (Unlike the biblical Ezra, Baruch actually lived at the time of the Babylonian destruction.)[78] More precise indications of date are difficult to find. B. Violet argued that the earthquake in 70:8 must be that which ravaged Antioch in 115 CE, but in fact it may be merely a stereotypical eschatological sign and not an historical reference at all.[79] The opening verse of the

---

76. A. F. J. Klijn, "2 (Syriac Apocalypse of) Baruch," in Charlesworth, ed., *OTP*, 1:615-16. The letter in chaps. 78–87 is more extensively attested than the rest of the apocalypse. A few verses from chaps. 12–14 are also preserved in Greek. On reception history of *2 Baruch* see Liv Ingeborg Lied, "*Nachleben* and Textual Identity: Variants and Variance in the Reception History of *2 Baruch*," in Henze and Boccaccini, ed., *Fourth Ezra and Second Baruch*, 403-28. For the text see Daniel M. Gurtner, *Second Baruch: A Critical Edition of the Syriac Text. With Greek and Latin Fragments, English Translation, Introduction, and Concordances* (London: T & T Clark, 2009).

77. Matthias Henze, *Jewish Apocalypticism in Late First Century Israel* (TSAJ 142; Tübingen: Mohr Siebeck, 2011) 23-32; Adam H. Becker, "2 Baruch," in Feldman, Kugel, and Schiffman, eds., *Outside the Bible*, 1656. Martin Goodman, "The Date of 2 Baruch," in John Ashton, ed., *Revealed Wisdom: Studies in Apocalyptic in Honour of Christopher Rowland* (Leiden: Brill, 2014) 116-21, claims that we should allow for composition before 70, but provides no positive arguments for the earlier date. Rivka Nir, *The Destruction of Jerusalem and the Idea of Redemption in the Syriac Apocalypse of Baruch* (SBLEJL 20; Atlanta: SBL, 2003) is exceptional in regarding *2 Baruch* as a Christian composition. See the comments of James R. Davila, *The Provenance of the Pseudepigrapha: Jewish, Christian, or Other?* (JSJSup 105; Leiden: Brill, 2005) 130-31. See also Nir, " 'Good Tidings' of Baruch to the Christian Faithful (The Epistle of 2 Baruch 78-87)," in Boccaccini and Zurawski, eds., *Interpreting 4 Ezra and 2 Baruch*, 72-93.

78. On the figure of Baruch, see J. Edward Wright, *Baruch Ben Neriah: From Biblical Scribe to Apocalyptic Seer* (Columbia, SC: University of South Carolina, 2003).

79. B. Violet, *Die Apokalypsen des Esra und des Baruch in deutscher Gestalt* (Leipzig: Hinrichs, 1924) XCII.

apocalypse refers to the 25th year of Jeconiah (Jehoiakin) as the occasion of the destruction. This date makes no historical sense. Jehoiakin was taken into exile in the first year of his reign in 597, when he was 18 years old. The temple was destroyed in 587/86. The figure 25 is apparently taken from Ezek 40:1 ("in the twenty-fifth year of our exile"). It may also be an approximate indication of the actual date of composition (i.e., about 95 CE).[80] However, the figure of 25 years obviously bears some relation to the 30 years given at the beginning of 4 Ezra and must be understood in the context of the overall relations between the two apocalypses. For the present, we may take it that *2 Baruch* was roughly contemporary with 4 Ezra. We will return to the question of priority after we have considered *2 Baruch* in some detail.

### Structure and Unity

Like 4 Ezra, *2 Baruch* is usually divided into seven sections, although there is far less consensus about their precise delimitation.[81] The structure proposed in previous editions of this book relied on two indicators as especially important.[82] On four occasions Baruch is said to fast for seven days (9:1-2; 12:5; 21:1; 47:1-2).[83] On three occasions he addresses the people (31:1–34:1; 44:1–46:7; 77:1-26). If we allow that each of these indicators marks the end of a unit (the address in 44:1–46:7 is reinforced by the fast in 47:1-2) and that the final letter (78:1 to the end) is a further unit, we arrive at a sevenfold division: (1) 1:1–9:1; (2) 10:1–12:5; (3) 13:1–20:6; (4) 21:1–34:1; (5) 35:1–47:2; (6) 48:1–77:26; (7) 78:1 to the end. This structure is by no means a simple replica of 4 Ezra, but there are some similarities. The first three units are devoted to developing the problem addressed by the

---

80. P. Bogaert, *Apocalypse de Baruch* (2 vols.; Paris: Cerf, 1969) 287-95; Daniel M. Gurtner, "The 'Twenty-Fifth Year of Jeconiah' and the Date of 2 Baruch," *JSP* 18 (2008) 23-32. Bogaert's suggestion that the apocalypse was prompted by persecution under Domitian is gratuitous. The earliest citation is in the *Epistle of Barnabas*.

81. Bogaert, *Apocalypse de Baruch*, 58-67; F. J. Murphy, *The Structure and Meaning of Second Baruch* (Atlanta: Scholars Press, 1985) 11-29. Murphy provides a convenient synopsis of different schemata on p. 12, as does Henze, *Jewish Apocalypticism*, 18.

82. Compare A. F. J. Klijn, "The Sources and the Redaction of the Syriac Apocalypse of Baruch," *JSJ* 1 (1970) 68.

83. In 5:7 Baruch fasts "until the evening," but the fast does not disrupt the continuity of the narrative.

apocalypse. Each is terminated by a seven-day fast. These are followed by an extensive eschatological prophecy in the fourth section and then by two allegorical visions in the fifth and sixth units. The final section has the character of an epilogue. Unlike 4 Ezra, Baruch never presses skeptical questions, and so this apocalypse has neither the tension nor the dramatic conversion process of 4 Ezra. It does, however, have a clear movement, from the distress of the early chapters to the consolation of the visions.[84] The contrast between the brevity of the first three units and the length of the subsequent revelations is significant for the emphasis of the book. In this regard the lengthy cloud and water vision (sixth unit), which with its attendant dialogue occupies more than one-third of the work, must be regarded as the climactic revelation.[85]

This structure, however, is by no means a matter of consensus. Henze comments that "the transitions from one text unit to the next are clearly indicated by various means in the text. The problem is that there are more than seven smaller units. As a consequence dissension persists."[86] He insists that 2 Baruch lacks a single organizing principle, and he recognizes several transition markers besides those mentioned above (e.g. change of place). He distinguishes 15 subunits in 2 Baruch, and dismisses all attempts to find a heptadic structure as unwarranted.

As in the case of 4 Ezra, there has been extensive debate over the unity of 2 Baruch. R. H. Charles distinguished no fewer than six separate sources.[87] Three passages that deal with the messiah (27:1–30:1; 36–40; and 53–74) were designated $A^1$, $A^2$, and $A^3$. Chapter 85 constituted $B^3$, and the remaining narrative sections were divided between the "optimistic" $B^1$ and "pessimistic" $B^2$. No subsequent scholars have endorsed this dissection in full, but the quest for sources has not been abandoned.

There is no doubt that 2 Baruch draws on diverse traditional material.[88]

---

84. G. B. Sayler, *Have the Promises Failed? A Literary Analysis of 2 Baruch* (Chico, CA: Scholars Press, 1984) 38.

85. Bogaert (*Apocalypse*, 61), following Violet and Schürer, feels obliged to cut this unit after chap. 52, although he admits the lack of a formal indicator. So also Murphy and Sayler.

86. Henze, *Apocalypticism*, 38.

87. R. H. Charles, *The Apocalypse of Baruch* (London: Black, 1896); idem, "II Baruch," in Charles, ed., *APOT*, 2:470-526. Before Charles, similar analyses were proposed by R. Kabisch and E. de Faye.

88. The affinities between Pseudo-Philo, 4 Ezra, and 2 Baruch are significant in this regard. See Bogaert, *Apocalypse*, 242-58.

There are some apparent contradictions in detail,[89] but they are not beyond dispute. So 32:2-3 ("after a little time the building of Zion will be shaken in order that it may be built again") has usually been taken to imply a date before the destruction of the temple and therefore before the situation described in chap. 1. It is possible, however, that the shaking is not destructive but results in the rebuilding of Zion — compare Hag 2:6-7, where God will shake the nations to fill the temple treasury. (This passage in *2 Baruch,* like the passage in Haggai, deals with the rebuilding of the temple in the Persian period.) Statements that only those who are in the land will be protected (29:2; cf. 71:1) appear to contradict the promise of the return of the exiles (78:7), but the return could be envisaged before the final crisis so that the exiles are by then in the land. According to 13:3 and 25:1, Baruch will be preserved until the end of times, but several other passages refer to his impending death (43:2; 44:2; 46:7; 78:5; 84:1). Here again the contradiction may be only apparent, since Baruch could be preserved after death, and indeed this is the only way in which he could be thought to have been preserved at the time *2 Baruch* was written. These examples may suffice to illustrate the slippery nature of the supposed contradictions.

The basic argument for distinguishing sources in *2 Baruch* does not rest on these matters of detail but on the alleged tension between two kinds of eschatology, one optimistic and oriented toward national restoration and the other pessimistic, looking for the end of this world and a judgment beyond. These two strands of tradition were indeed distinct in origin, but we have seen that they were woven together in the dream-visions of 4 Ezra. The issue in *2 Baruch* is whether the diverse traditions were successfully assimilated or whether the author felt obliged to contradict some of the traditions that he incorporated.

The tension in eschatological conceptions has been alleged in the treatment of the temple and the messiah. In chap. 4 God tells Baruch that there is a heavenly temple that will be revealed in the end time. In chap. 6, however, the temple vessels are hidden, so that they may be restored when Jerusalem is delivered. The final letter gives a different reason for hiding the temple vessels, which does not imply restoration. Should we conclude that the author is not interested in the rebuilding of the temple? Perhaps, but this is not to say that he is contradicting his sources. We must bear in mind that there are two destructions of the temple involved. The first, by

89. A. F. J. Klijn, *Die syrische Baruch-Apokalypse* (JSHRZ 5/2; Gütersloh: Mohn, 1976) 111.

the Babylonians, was a matter of history. It was followed by a restoration. *2 Baruch* acknowledges this fact by the use of traditional legends about the temple vessels,[90] and the restoration has some typological implications for the eschatological time. The destruction that more immediately concerned the author, although it is veiled behind the typology, was that of 70 CE. The most explicit statement about the future of the temple is found in chapter 32. There we are told that when "the building of Zion will be shaken in order that it will be rebuilt, that building will not remain; but it will again be uprooted after some time and will remain desolate for a time. And after that it is necessary that it will be renewed in glory and that it will be perfected into eternity." In short, the temple built after the Exile would be destroyed and remain desolate for a time. The author affirms an eschatological restoration, but it is not imminent. Therefore the heavenly Jerusalem and temple are ultimately more important for the author's own time. Strictly speaking, there is no contradiction in the expectation of *2 Baruch*. We should bear in mind, however, that an apocalypse does not aspire to formulate doctrine in a consistent way, but to suggest the future hope by means of symbols. Both the legends pertaining to the temple vessels and the traditional idea of a heavenly Jerusalem could play a part in suggesting that the temple would endure in some form, and thereby console the Jewish people over its destruction.[91]

In the case of the messiah, there is not even an apparent contradiction. The objection here is that the messiah receives no attention in Baruch's addresses to the people. We should not conclude, however, that "the author is not interested in the Anointed One. He happens to be present in his sources." Still less is the author "correcting" the traditional hope of national restoration.[92] The message of the work cannot be extracted only

90. This material is paralleled in *Pesiqta Rabbati* (Bogaert, *Apocalypse*, 222-41) and also in the *Paraleipomena of Jeremiah* (Bogaert, *Apocalypse*, 177-221; G. W. E. Nickelsburg, "Narrative Traditions in the Paraleipomena of Jeremiah and 2 Baruch," *CBQ* 35 [1973] 60-68).

91. See further F. J. Murphy, "The Temple in the Syriac Apocalypse of Baruch," *JBL* 106 (1987) 671-83. Murphy argues that while *2 Baruch* does not deny the possibility that the temple may be rebuilt, it attaches little importance to it. There is no mention of the temple in passages that deal with the messianic age. Liv Ingeborg Lied, *The Other Lands of Israel: Imaginations of the Land in 2 Baruch* (JSJSup 129; Leiden: Brill, 2008) 243-305, argues for continuity between the heavenly and the earthly land. The heavenly land (and temple) "provides a perfected and comprehensive version of what already existed for Israel on earth" (305).

92. Klijn, "The Sources and the Redaction," 69-76. See also his introduction, "2 Baruch," in Charlesworth, ed., *OTP*, 1:615-20.

from the direct addresses without regard to the revelations, which form the underpinning of those speeches. The correlation between the apocalyptic framework and the specific message of the book is a crucial issue in the interpretation of *2 Baruch,* which throws much light on the relation of this work to 4 Ezra and indeed on the entire apocalyptic genre.

### The Opening Narrative

The opening scene of *2 Baruch* (1:1–9:2) is not set in the exile, as in 4 Ezra, but before the destruction. Baruch is given advance warning of what is to happen and is also given an explanation for it. The southern tribes are to be punished for their sins, just as the northern ones were, but they will only be removed from God's favor *for a time.* Baruch is also assured that the efficacy of himself and those who are like him is in no way impaired. They must retire from Jerusalem before it can fall. When Baruch protests that he would rather die than see the destruction of Zion, the Lord assures him that the destruction is temporary, and moreover reveals that the present edifice is not the temple that was prepared before creation. There is a heavenly temple preserved with God, just as paradise is. The destruction of the earthly temple, then, is not as great a catastrophe as it might seem. When Baruch complains of the humiliation involved in destruction at the hands of Gentiles, he is assured that "the enemy will not overthrow Zion." He is then allowed to witness four angels who burn down the walls of Jerusalem. Before they do this, however, the temple vessels are hidden in the earth "so that strangers may not get possession of them," for Jerusalem will again be delivered.

This narrative opening precludes from the start the kind of anguished questioning we find in 4 Ezra. The destruction of Jerusalem is still a calamity, and the humiliation at the hands of the Gentiles is real. The brief second section of *2 Baruch* (10:1–12:5) is taken up completely with a powerful lament, which shows that the grief is profound and that the destruction is taken very seriously. Yet even at the end of his lament Baruch can tell Babylon that this state of affairs will not last and that the divine wrath will be aroused against her.[93] God's ultimate providential care for Israel is not

---

93. There is no urgency about this punishment, however. Cf. F. J. Murphy, "2 Baruch and the Romans," *JBL* 104 (1985) 663: "he was careful to assure his readers that those who had destroyed the Temple and the city of Jerusalem in 70 CE would be punished,

in doubt. The righteous are spared, the vessels protected; and even the city walls escape the indignity of violation by the Gentiles. Baruch is allowed insight into the heavenly world and into God's plan, which puts the problem in perspective from the outset. This perspective will be enlarged and confirmed by the eschatological revelations.

## The Dialogue in 13:1–20:6

The opening unit includes dialogue between Baruch and the Lord within the narrative. In 13:1–20:6, the dialogue predominates.[94] This is the section in which Baruch comes closest to the probing questions of 4 Ezra, but there are some characteristic differences. The dialogue begins with God's reply to Baruch's lamentation. Baruch is appointed as an eschatological witness against the nations. Israel is chastised so that it may ultimately be saved, whereas the Gentiles, who are allowed to run their course, are headed for final destruction. This argument was widespread in Judaism in the Hellenistic and Roman periods (e.g., Wis 12:20-22; 2 Macc 7:18-19).

Baruch raises two objections. First, a judgment on the nations at some future time does not provide retribution for the preceding generations. Second, Zion should have been pardoned for the deeds of the righteous, not condemned for the offenses of the sinners. Even here Baruch readily admits his inability to comprehend the way of God, in terms reminiscent of the angel's replies to Ezra. He also points to the nucleus of the solution: "The righteous justly hope for the end, and without fear depart from this habitation, because they have with thee a store of works preserved in treasuries" (14:12). He adds, "Woe to us who are now shamefully treated and at that time look forward to evils." He includes himself with the wicked, presumably because of the judgment on his generation, although he has already been clearly set apart in the opening narrative.

God's reply underlines the importance of the world to come. Since the righteous can hope for salvation beyond death, the retribution does not only apply to the last generation. Years in this world are of little account (compare Wis 3:1-19). In effect, the Most High has made not one world but two (4 Ezra 7:50). Baruch, however, does not emphasize the discon-

---

but at the same time he conveyed the idea that that punishment was entirely the business of God."

94. Henze, *Jewish Apocalypticism*, 133-35, calls this "the first dialogue section."

tinuity.[95] The judgment after death is the fulfillment of the Deuteronomic law, and sinners are guilty because they know the law (compare Rom 7:7-12). If many have sinned, while only a few kept the law, this is a matter of human responsibility. We must infer that the true Israel, which is heir to the promises, consists of those who keep the law.

The problem of Zion is more apparent than real, as might have been inferred from the passage on the heavenly temple in chap. 4. Here we are told that God has taken away Zion so that he may "more speedily visit the world in its season." Presumably, that visitation will entail the revelation of the true Zion. Again, the promises of the covenant will be fulfilled but on a different level from what we might have expected. Like Ezra, Baruch is told not to worry about the past and to look to the future, but in this case the future may be said to offer a satisfactory fulfillment to a much greater degree.

## The Visions

The apocalypse 2 *Baruch* involves no great reversal of roles or sudden conversion such as we found in 4 Ezra 10. Yet there is a transition in 21:1–34:1. Up to this point, there had been no extensive eschatological revelation. It is introduced here as a vision (22:1), but the vision is not described. Instead we have a dialogue between Baruch and a heavenly voice, which is presumably the voice of God. The episode concludes not with a fast, as in the first three units, but with an address to the people.

The unit begins with a prayer of Baruch, which does not question the justice of God but asks that its manifestation be hastened. The voice replies that the number of those to be born must be completed, although in fact the time of redemption is near. This assurance leads naturally to the signs of the judgment. The time of tribulation will be divided into twelve woes. These are of a highly general nature, the "wars, famine and pestilence" typical of the prophecies of doom in the Hebrew Bible and the *Sibylline Oracles*. Then the messiah will begin to be revealed. As Henze has noted, "the language implies that the Messiah is a transcendental figure and that he is preexistent."[96] The apocalypse 2 *Baruch* presupposes an eschatological scenario similar to 4 Ezra. After a period of time (unspecified here)

95. Compare Lied, *The Other Lands*, 303.
96. Henze, *Jewish Apocalypticism*, 295.

the messiah will "return in glory." Henze argues that the return is from heaven to earth, since it is followed by the resurrection, which can only take place on earth. He infers that the messiah was absent for a time and now returns.[97] Whether this implies the death of the messiah, as in 4 Ezra 7, is not clear. The passage is elliptic on any interpretation.[98] The resurrection and judgment follow. Baruch draws the moral of the revelation for the people: "We should not be distressed so much over the evil that has now come as over that which is still to be" (32:5). Revelation of the future puts the present in perspective. Yet the law will protect those who practice it. Observance of the law gains greater urgency in view of the coming judgment.

The first allegorical vision, in 36:1–37:1, follows a very brief lamentation by Baruch. The vision itself parallels the more elaborate eagle vision in 4 Ezra. In this case, the cedar is the last remnant of the forest of wickedness. Over against the cedar stands the vine. A fountain from under the vine submerges the forest, and the vine rebukes the cedar. The vision itself has no allusion to Daniel 7, but the interpretation claims that the forest symbolizes a sequence of four kingdoms. Since this symbolism is not apparent, we may suspect that the vision was not composed for its present context. Both the vine and the fountain are referred to the reign of the messiah. The analogy with the eagle vision lies in the prominence of the messiah and his role in rebuking the Gentile power. The reign of the messiah clearly belongs to this age rather than to the world to come: "His principate will stand for ever, until the world of corruption is at an end . . ." (40:3).

The apocalypse 2 Baruch goes beyond 4 Ezra in clarifying the composition of the people who will benefit from the messiah. The criterion is not ethnicity but observance of the law. Proselytes are included; apostates are not.[99] 2 Baruch envisages fulfillment of the covenantal promises, but in the process the covenantal people must be redefined. Conversion to Judaism is still a prerequisite for salvation, but the promises do not apply to all Jews. In view of this insistence on individual performance, it is only natural that Baruch should warn the people: "If ye endure and persevere in His fear and do not forget His law, the times shall change over you for good, and ye shall see the consolation of Zion" (44:7).

97. Ibid., 296.

98. Müller sees a Christian interpolation here (*Messias und Menschensohn,* 142-44).

99. This is the most probable interpretation of an unclear text; see Bogaert, *Apocalypse,* 75-78.

Beginning with Baruch's prayer in chapter 48, the text builds to a climactic revelation. Baruch begins with a long prayer for mercy, concluding with an affirmation: "In Thee do we trust, for lo Thy law is with us, and we know that we shall not fail so long as we keep Thy statutes" (48:22). God responds ("from thy words I will answer thee") by affirming that judgment is in accordance with the law. Mercy, then, only applies to those who convert and obey. Baruch laments, "O Adam, what hast thou done to all those who are born from thee" (48:42), in a rare expression of sympathy for sinful humanity, but even here he does not dispute the justice of God. Instead he goes on to ask about the form of the afterlife. He is told that the earth will restore the dead as it received them, but both just and wicked will then be transformed. The righteous will be made like unto the angels and equal to the stars (51:10).[100] This coming judgment puts human values in perspective: "For what then have those who were on earth exchanged their soul?" (51:15).

This dialogue addresses the question of individual retribution. It is complemented by a vision that explains the order of history by an allegory of a cloud that rains alternately black and white waters. Even before this vision is explained, Baruch praises God "who revealest to those who fear Thee what is prepared for them" (54:4). He goes on to assert that "justly do they perish who have not loved Thy law" (54:14) and that "Adam is therefore not the cause, save only of his own soul, but each of us has been the Adam of his own soul" (54:19). This passage is significant in two respects. On the one hand the lament in 48:43 ("O Adam, what hast thou done . . .") rings hollow in retrospect. On the other hand, the affirmation of individual responsibility is an important modifier for the cloud and waters vision. Although the sequence of history is predetermined, the choice of the individual is not.[101]

The interpretation of the vision, by the angel Ramiel, serves a number of functions. Like historical reviews in other apocalypses, it shows

---

100. On the resurrection in *2 Baruch*, see Henze, *Jewish Apocalypticism*, 305-17; Liv Ingeborg Lied, "Recognizing the Righteous Remnant? Resurrection, Recognition and Eschatological Reversals in 2 Baruch 47-52," in Turid Karlsen Seim and Jorunn Økland, eds., *Metamorphoses: Resurrection, Body and Transformative Practices in Early Christianity* (Ekstasis 1; Berlin: de Gruyter, 2009) 311-35. More generally, Daniel M. Gurtner, "Eschatological Rewards for the Righteous in 2 Baruch," in Boccaccini and Zurawski, eds., *Interpreting 4 Ezra and 2 Baruch*, 107-15; Jared Ludlow, "Death and the Afterlife in 2 Baruch," ibid., 116-23.

101. On determinism in *2 Baruch* and *4 Ezra*, see Harnisch, *Verhängnis und Verheissung*, 249-67.

that the course of history is measured out, even from the beginning. History is an aspect of the cosmos. It also shows that the greater number of periods has passed. The end is relatively near. Baruch himself is located under the eleventh (black) waters. The twelfth period is characterized by bright waters. The people will fall into distress, but will be saved. After a short interval, Zion will again be built. After this, there is in chapter 69 an obscure reference to "the last waters" which were darker than all that went before, and were after the twelfth. This is the time of a final conflict. Finally, the messianic age, symbolized by the lightning of the vision, will come. The messiah will summon the nations, kill all who have ruled over Israel and make the others subject to it (chap. 72).[102]

The vision not only addresses the duration of history. It also discerns a pattern in which light and darkness alternate. This pattern is reminiscent of the Deuteronomic history, but the transition from one period to the next is not ascribed to human agency in any way. Instead, it is determined from above. The pattern, however, places the darkness of the present in perspective. This period must eventually yield to brighter times, even to the lightning of the messiah. The interpretation ends with a description of the transformed world in the messianic age, but this must be understood as the prelude to the resurrection.

Baruch's final address to the people repeats a familiar message. If you observe the law, you will be protected. The catastrophe that has happened is a punishment for transgression. God is merciful, but his mercy is evidently contingent on obedience. This remains true in the final letter. If God "judge us not according to the multitude of His mercies, woe unto all of us who are born" (84:11). Even here there is no forgiveness for unreformed sinners, but 2 Baruch evidently envisages a greater role for mercy than does 4 Ezra.

## The Letter

The final section (78:1 to the end) consists of Baruch's letter to the nine and one-half tribes.[103] Baruch recapitulates the fall of Jerusalem, noting that the enemy was not allowed to destroy the walls. He states that God "showed

---

102. Henze, *Jewish Apocalypticism*, 270, finds echoes of Daniel 7 in this vision.

103. Henze, *Jewish Apocalypticism*, 350-71; Mark F. Whitters, *The Epistle of Second Baruch: A Study in Form and Message* (JSPSup 42; Sheffield: Sheffield Academic Press, 2003).

me visions, that I should not again endure anguish, and He made known to me the mystery of the times" (81:4). These revelations are not repeated here, but they are nonetheless important. They are the basis for Baruch's confidence that the power of the Gentiles will pass like vapor and that this age is coming to an end. In the meantime "we have nothing now save the Mighty One and His law" (85:3). The main emphasis of the letter falls on the need for observance. "If therefore we direct and dispose our hearts we shall receive everything that we lost, and much better things than we lost by many times" (85:4). The urgency of this advice derives from the fact that

> the youth of the world is past,
> and the strength of the creation already exhausted
> and the advent of the times is very short. (85:10)

History, in short, is the limited time of decision.

### Covenantal Theology

The central message of *2 Baruch* is quite clearly the need to observe the law.[104] The eschatological revelations are clearly subordinated to this end. The religion of the book has been described as "covenantal nomism," since salvation depends on the mercy of God in forgiving those within the covenant people who are basically obedient.[105] The law is correlated with wisdom, in the tradition of Deuteronomy and Ben Sira.[106] The dependence on Deuteronomy is explicit at several points (e.g., 19:1; 84:1-6). As Henze notes, the prominence of the law in *2 Baruch* is in sharp contrast to the Enoch tradition. *2 Baruch* "breaks down any potential conflict that might exist between apocalyptic and Mosaic authority and instead incorporates the latter into the former, fully endorsing the single authoritative status of the Torah and turning it into the centerpiece of his apocalyptic program."[107]

---

104. Daniel M. Gurtner, "On the Other Side of Disaster: Soteriology in 2 Baruch," in Gurtner, ed., *This World and the World to Come*, 114-26.

105. E. P. Sanders, "The Covenant as a Soteriological Category and the Nature of Salvation in Palestinian and Hellenistic Judaism," in R. Hamerton-Kelly and R. Scroggs, eds., *Jews, Greeks, and Christians: Studies in Honor of W. D. Davies* (Leiden: Brill, 1976) 11-44. See also Bauckham, "Apocalypses," 175-82.

106. Burkes, "'Life' Redefined," 63-68.

107. Henze, *Jewish Apocalypticism*, 103. See also ibid., 206-27.

We should note, however, that the traditional Deuteronomic covenant undergoes some revision here. First, it must be buttressed by the apocalyptic revelations that Baruch receives. Second, the covenantal people is not constituted simply by the Jewish people, but by those who observe the law, with the inclusion of proselytes and the exclusion of apostates. Finally, the promised salvation finds its fulfillment not in this world but in the world to come.[108] Salvation lies not only in the future of the covenant people but also in the destiny of the individual. As in all the apocalypses, salvation is salvation *out of* this world. 2 *Baruch* can say, like Paul, that "if there were this life only, which belongs to all men, nothing could be more bitter than this" (21:13; cf. 1 Cor 15:19). Yet even in an age of dark waters Baruch is never deprived of "the Mighty One and his law."[109] Accordingly, there is significant continuity from this world to the next.[110]

Even more obviously than 4 Ezra, 2 *Baruch* is related to the rabbinic Judaism of the day.[111] In chap. 2, Baruch and Jeremiah are bidden to withdraw from Jerusalem before its fall. There is an obvious analogy with the escape of Yoḥanan ben Zakkai during the siege by the Romans. Like the sages, 2 *Baruch* attempts to reconstitute Jewish life around the Torah, when the temple is no more. The ideas of the book have been compared with the teachings of Joshua ben Ḥananiah (especially in its positive attitude toward proselytes)[112] and Akiba.[113] The messianic expectation of the book fits well with the ideas of these sages: speculation is discouraged, but the expectation still plays a significant part.[114] The ideas of 2 *Baruch* fall well within the mainstream of rabbinic Judaism, and there is no reason

108. Compare Murphy, *The Structure and Meaning,* 117-33; Lied, *The Other Lands of Israel,* 303.

109. Accordingly, Klijn ("The Sources and Redaction," 72) disputes Harnisch's assertion that this is a time of the absence of God. Yet Harnisch's view has some basis too, since there is at least an absence of salvation in the present.

110. Lied, *The Other Lands of Israel,* 313.

111. F. J. Murphy, "Sapiential Elements in the Syriac Apocalypse of Baruch," *JQR* 76 (1986) 311-27, notes the dependence on the wisdom tradition. He concludes that "There is simply not enough evidence available in 2 *Apoc. Baruch* to call the author a Rabbi. On the other hand, we do not know in what other form 'the wise' existed in that period" (p. 326).

112. Bogaert, *Apocalypse,* 443-44.

113. Rosenthal, *Vier Apokryphische Bücher,* 72-103. Akiba was said to have comforted his colleagues after the destruction by emphasizing that restoration as well as destruction had been prophesied (*Sifre Deut* 4:3).

114. For the views of the sages, see E. E. Urbach, *The Sages* (2 vols.; Jerusalem: Magnes, 1975) 1:667-92. Akiba eventually endorsed Bar Kokhba as messiah.

whatever to ascribe the work to a sect or conventicle.[115] The book shows a strong concern for the welfare of the community at large, which extends also to the Diaspora. Unlike 4 Ezra it does not suggest that special revelations should be reserved for the wise among the people. The theme of leadership plays a prominent role.[116] The fear of the people in the face of Baruch's impending death is similar to Baruch's own distress regarding the destruction of Jerusalem.[117] He assures them that "there shall not be wanting to Israel a wise man, nor a son of the law to the race of Jacob" (46:4). The sage plays a crucial role as mediator between God and the community.

The most striking affinities of *2 Baruch* are undoubtedly those with 4 Ezra. Charles listed some 66 passages that show correspondences.[118] The affinities involve the total conception of the two works. Both are apocalypses of the "historical" type, which make extensive use of dialogue as a revelatory form. Both use seven-day fasts as one of the division markers. In both cases the problem is articulated in the earlier units, and there are allegorical visions in the later part of the works. The final section involves a writing, in each book. Both books take the destruction of Jerusalem as their point of departure and use the Babylonian crisis as an allegory for 70 CE. Both consider questions of theodicy and ultimately appeal to very similar eschatological scenarios, which distinguish this age from the world to come and locate the reign of the messiah in the conclusion of this age.

Within the framework of these affinities there are also significant differences. Ezra converses with an angel, until the final chapter. Baruch usually converses with God; the angel Ramiel is only introduced to interpret the cloud and waters vision. *2 Baruch* has no real equivalent of the impassioned dialogue between Ezra and Uriel in 4 Ezra 3–9 or of the reversal of Ezra's role in chap. 10. On the other hand, 4 Ezra has nothing to correspond to the narrative about the fall of the temple in *2 Baruch*. The revelation given to Ezra in chap. 14, which is in large part reserved for the wise among the people, is very different from Baruch's letter to the exiled tribes.

---

115. So, rightly, Henze, *Jewish Apocalypticism*, 232-35.

116. Sayler, *Have the Promises Failed?* 79.

117. Compare the distress over the loss of teachers in Mishnah Sotah 9.15. Henze, *Jewish Apocalypticism*, 248-49.

118. Charles, *The Apocalypse of Baruch*, 170-71. See also A. B. Kolenkow, "The Fall of the Temple and the Coming of the End," in K. H. Richards, ed., *Society of Biblical Literature 1982 Seminar Papers*, 243-50. In contrast, Sayler, *Have the Promises Failed?* 130-34, emphasizes the differences between the two works.

The most significant differences, however, lie in the respective attitudes of Ezra and Baruch. Ezra is driven by skeptical questioning and never acknowledges that his questions have been adequately answered. Baruch has special knowledge of what really happened to Jerusalem, from the very outset. Although the lament in 2 Baruch 10–11 displays real grief, Baruch's distress is not nearly so profound as that of Ezra, and he shows little resistance to the explanations he is given. Underlying the different degrees of distress are different theological presuppositions. Baruch's concern is focused much more narrowly on the people of Israel than is the case in 4 Ezra. He also shows far less sympathy for sinners. In 2 Baruch the lament "O Adam, what hast thou done" (48:42), which directly echoes 4 Ezra 7:118, is canceled by an assertion that each of us is the Adam of his own soul (54:19).[119] Baruch affirms in a way that Ezra never does that "justly do they perish who have not loved Thy law" (54:14). On the other hand, 2 Baruch is generally the more optimistic book. While 4 Ezra gives the impression that scarcely anyone can fulfill the law, 2 Baruch says that of "others not a few have been righteous" (20:11), emphasizes free will rather than the evil inclination, and leaves some room for divine mercy toward those who repent, including proselytes. Although the sharpest differences are apparent between Baruch's and Ezra's speeches in the dialogues, even the revelations of Uriel do not correspond exactly to the theology of 2 Baruch, since they endorse Ezra's pessimistic view of the judgment. Besides, we have seen that Ezra's complaints in the dialogues must be viewed as an integral part of the work.[120]

In view of the numerous points of contact between the two apocalypses, it is difficult to avoid the impression that one is deliberately taking issue with the other, although it need not have been written exclusively as a response. Scholars have differed on the question of priority. Bogaert has suggested that the figures given in the superscriptions (25 years in 2 Baruch and 30 in 4 Ezra) reflect the approximate number of years after the fall of Jerusalem in each case.[121] It is possible, however, that 2 Baruch used the lower figure deliberately to claim greater antiquity than 4 Ezra. Most critics have been impressed by 4 Ezra's greater "spontaneity."[122] Indeed it is easier

119. Zurawski, "The Two Worlds," 106, notes that "2 Baruch's Adam became the model, the paradigm for sin; 4 Ezra's Adam was simply the first to fall victim."

120. Harnisch tends to exaggerate the similarity between the two books, since he identifies the viewpoint of 4 Ezra with that of the angel (Verhängnis und Verheissung).

121. Bogaert, Apocalypse, 287-88.

122. Violet, Die Apokalypsen des Esra und des Baruch, lxxxi-xc.

to see why *2 Baruch* should have responded to *4 Ezra* than vice versa. Ezra might well be thought to have given too much weight to skepticism and not to have been sufficiently decisive in affirming divine justice. *2 Baruch* then provides its own account of what happened in the fall of Jerusalem and leaves no doubt about the adequacy of the law.

But it may be too simple to see one work as a rejoinder to the other. Henze argues plausibly that both works underwent a process of composition and redaction, oral as well as written, and that "their resemblances are components of a larger literary web that connects them to one another and, at the same time, to their wider literary context."[123] In any case, the primary purpose of *2 Baruch* is not to engage in polemics but to lay a sure foundation for trust in God and obedience to the law. The apocalyptic revelations are combined with the assertions and exhortations of Baruch to this end. The apocalypse works primarily by positive thinking and by repeated assertions of the efficacy of the law. It gives little scope to the expression of fears and doubts. For this reason it lacks the emotional power of *4 Ezra*, but it was surely more acceptable to the scribal leaders, and probably to most of the people.

Taken together, *4 Ezra* and *2 Baruch* throw some interesting light on the nature of the apocalyptic genre. Both share a common framework, which posits a need for special supernatural revelation, over and above what was given in the Torah, and both base their hope of salvation on the belief that there is another world, and life, beyond this one. In both books this framework serves not only to console but also to add urgency to present decisions. Within this framework, however, there is room for substantial disagreement on significant theological issues, such as the degree of human responsibility and the extent of those who will be saved. The genre, in short, does not entail a consistent doctrine. Rather, it provides an imaginative view of the world, usually expressed in traditional symbols, within which there is room for a variety of theological doctrines, even in apocalypses that address a common problem, like the fall of the temple. Both *2 Baruch* and *4 Ezra* draw heavily on theological traditions that are far closer to the rabbinic material than was the case in the books of Enoch. Perhaps for this reason they show little interest in speculation about the heavenly world. They are also averse to calculations about the time of the

---

123. Matthias Henze, "*4 Ezra* and *2 Baruch*: Literary Composition and Oral Performance in the First-Century Apocalyptic Literature," *JBL* 131 (2012) 197. See also his extended treatment in *Jewish Apocalypticism*, 148-86.

end. They illustrate well the way in which the genre could be brought to bear on existential and historical problems, and the flexibility with which it could incorporate diverse theological traditions.

## The Apocalypse of Abraham

A very different theological tradition is represented in the third apocalypse from this period, the *Apocalypse of Abraham*.[124] The work is preserved in Slavonic, which was most probably translated from Greek, but there are clear signs that the original was in Hebrew or Aramaic.[125] The land of Israel is accordingly the most probable place of composition. The approximate date is indicated by the fact that the destruction of the temple is the main event to which reference is made. The book belongs to the same general period as 4 Ezra and 2 *Baruch* and shares some of their concerns about theodicy.[126] In place of the Deuteronomic tradition, which informs these books, however, the mystical tendency of the early Enoch books is taken up here.[127] The book also has a strong cultic focus. The *Apocalypse of Abraham* is exceptional among the Jewish apocalypses in combining the

124. N. Bonwetsch, *Apokalypse Abrahams* (Leipzig: Deichert, 1897); G. H. Box, with J. I. Landsman, *The Apocalypse of Abraham* (London: SPCK, 1918); B. Philonenko-Sayer and M. Philonenko, *L'Apocalypse d' Abraham: Introduction, texte slave, traduction et notes* (*Semitica* 31; Paris: Maisonneuve, 1981); R. Rubinkiewicz, *L'Apocalypse d' Abraham en vieux slave: Introduction, texte critique, traduction et commentaire* (Lublin: Société des Lettres et des sciences de l'Université de l'Université Catholique de Lublin, 1987); A. Pennington, "The Apocalypse of Abraham," in H. F. D. Sparks, ed., *The Apocryphal Old Testament* (Oxford: Clarendon, 1984); Alexander Kulik, *Retroverting Slavonic Pseudepigrapha: Toward the Original of the Apocalypse of Abraham* (Atlanta: SBL, 2004). This apocalypse was not included in the collections of Charles and Kautzech but is included in P. Riessler, *Altjüdisches Schrifttum ausserhalb der Bibel* (1928; reprint, Darmstadt: Wissenschaftliche Buchgesellschaft, 1966) 13-39; and in Charlesworth, ed., *OTP*, 1:681-705, where the treatment is by R. Rubinkiewicz and H. G. Lunt.

125. For example, the names of the idols Merumath and Barisat. See Box, *The Apocalypse*, xv; Rubinkiewicz and Lunt, "Apocalypse of Abraham," in Charlesworth, ed., OTP 1.682; Kulik, *Retroverting*. On the text, see E. Turdeanu, "L'Apocalypse d'Abraham en Slave," in *Apocryphes Slaves et Roumains de l'Ancien Testament* (Leiden: Brill, 1981) 173-200.

126. Alexander Kulik, "Apocalypse of Abraham," in Feldman, Kugel, and Schiffman, eds., *Outside the Bible*, 1453, claims that a date in the late Second Temple period is equally plausible, but it is not clear why.

127. Peter Schäfer, *The Origins of Jewish Mysticism* (Princeton: Princeton University Press, 2009) 86-93.

motif of the heavenly journey with the review and periodization of history, characteristic of the "historical" apocalypses.[128]

The book falls naturally into two parts. Chapters 1-8 recount the story of Abraham's conversion from idolatry. Chapters 9–32 constitute the apocalypse proper. The apocalypse, however, clearly presupposes the legend and refers back to it at several points (e.g., Jaoel is identified as the one who destroyed Terah's house, in chap. 10; God cites the example of Terah as an illustration of free will in chap. 26). In addition, the voice that calls to Abraham in chap. 8 anticipates the heavenly voice in chap. 9. Both parts have clear points of departure in the biblical text. The legend explains why Abraham was told to go forth from his father's house (Genesis 12, read in light of a passing reference in Joshua 24:2-3, which says that Terah and his sons served other gods).[129] The apocalypse is woven around the story of Abraham's sacrifice in Genesis 15 (with an allusion to Genesis 22 insofar as the sacrifice is located on a high mountain).[130]

The theme of Abraham's conversion was a popular one in postbiblical Jewish literature. It was treated already in *Jubilees* 11 and in Josephus (*Antiquities* 1.7.1 §154) and Philo (*De Abrahamo* 15). Closer parallels to the *Apocalypse of Abraham* are found in the midrashim.[131] Here the story provides the occasion for a parody of idol worship, which was also a popular theme.[132] In its present context the story serves two purposes. It defines the religion of Abraham as the rejection of idolatry, and it suggests that idolaters are ultimately doomed to destruction as Terah is in chap. 8.

The apocalypse proper is developed through several well-defined stages.[133]

---

128. Pennington, "The Apocalypse of Abraham," 366, is exceptional among modern commentators in entertaining the possibility that this apocalypse is a Christian composition.

129. James Kugel, *Traditions of the Bible: A Guide to the Bible As It Was at the Beginning of the Common Era* (Cambridge, MA: Harvard University Press, 1998) 247; Daniel C. Harlow, "Idolatry and Alterity: Israel and the Nations in the *Apocalypse of Abraham*," in Harlow et al., *The "Other" in Second Temple Judaism*, 304.

130. The tradition of Abraham's ascent is found in 4 Ezra 3:13-14; 2 Baruch 4:5; Pseudo-Philo's *Biblical Antiquities* 18:5; and *Testament of Abraham*.

131. *Bereshith Rabba* 38:19 (on Gen 11:28); *Tanna debê Eliyahu* 2:25. See Box, *The Apocalypse*, 88-94.

132. Compare the story of Bel and the Dragon. The biblical prototype of idol parodies is Isa 44:9-20.

133. A detailed analysis of the structure is provided by R. Rubinkiewicz, "La vision de l'histoire dans l'Apocalypse d'Abraham," in W. Haase and H. Temporini, eds., *ANRW*, II.19.2 (1979) 137-51.

Chapters 9–12 state the command to sacrifice, with the promise that "I will show thee the ages which have been created . . . and what shall come to pass in them" (chap. 9). They also introduce Jaoel as Abraham's angelic guide.

Chapters 13–14 recount the actual sacrifice and the attempt of Azazel to divert Abraham.

Then in chap. 15 the angel takes Abraham up to heaven on the wing of a pigeon. There he assists Abraham in uttering the celestial song (chap. 17). This is followed by a vision of the divine throne (chap. 18). Abraham is bidden to count the stars which are beneath him in the fifth heaven, and the promise of innumerable descendants follows (chap. 20).

In chap. 21 Abraham is shown a "picture" in which all creation is reflected and humanity is divided into two parties, on the right side and on the left. God explains that those on the right are the chosen people, those on the left, the Gentiles.

In chap. 23 he is told to look again at the picture and consider the story of the fall so that he may know how it will be for his seed at the end of the age. Here the focus is on the role of Azazel, who is said to have power over those that will do evil.

In chap. 24 Abraham is bidden to look again at the picture. This time he is shown the sequence of history, beginning with Adam. This is in effect a catalogue of sins: impurity, theft, unlawful desire. The culminating sin is idolatry: "I saw there the likeness of the idol of jealousy, having the likeness of woodwork such as my father was wont to make." The "idol of jealousy" recalls Ezekiel 8, where the practice of idolatry in the temple is given as the reason for its destruction. Here too the idol is associated with the temple. God's idea of the temple and the priesthood is contrasted with the way in which the people anger him by idolatry and slaughter. When Abraham asks why this is so, he is referred to the example of Terah, to show that it is a matter of human free will.

In chap. 27 Abraham looks again at the picture and sees how the Gentiles, from the left side, run through four entrances and plunder the temple. He is told that this will happen "on account of thy seed who anger me by reason of the statue which thou sawest, and on account of the human slaughter in the picture." The righteous, in contrast, are rewarded with "righteous-dealing rulers." The four "entrances" represent periods of one hundred years or an hour of the age. This ungodly age is divided into twelve hours, but "before the Age of the righteous begins to grow, my judgment shall come upon the lawless heathen through the people of thy seed." Ten plagues will come upon the heathen, but the "righteous men of thy seed" will be restored in the temple. They "shall destroy those who have destroyed them and shall insult those who have insulted them."

In chap. 30 Abraham is returned to earth but complains that "what my soul longed to understand in my heart I do not understand." God interprets this as the ten plagues, which he then outlines, in a manner similar to the signs of the end in *2 Baruch* 27. Chapter 31 completes the eschatological scenario. The Elect One will come to gather the Jews from the nations. Those who have insulted them will not only be burned but also will be food for the fire of Hades. The apocalypse concludes with the biblical prediction of the exile in Egypt (Gen 15:14).

## The Underlying Questions

Although both parts of the *Apocalypse of Abraham* are attached to elements in the biblical story, the text is not generated by exegetical concerns. The problem addressed is not that of the meaning of the texts in Genesis but that of the prominence of evil in the world, especially in the form of idolatry.[134] A corollary of this question is the special role of Abraham and his descendants, the people who reject idolatry. These questions are ultimately brought into focus by the destruction of the temple. The *Apocalypse of Abraham*, like 4 Ezra, may be said to contain a response to the destruction of the temple, but its primary concern is with broader issues of universal significance.

The questions of evil and the special role of the chosen people are not formulated by Abraham at the outset, as they were by Ezra. They emerge in the course of a narrative that gives a comprehensive account of the world and its history. This account is given through supernatural revelation. The voice of God in chap. 9 bases the revelation of the ages and "what is reserved" on the knowledge of the God who was before the ages and created the light of the world.

Abraham is not brought immediately into the presence of God. Instead, the angel Jaoel is sent "in the likeness of a man" (compare the angelophany in Daniel 10). The name is evidently a substitute for Yahweh, or Yahweh El, and Jaoel is said to be "a power in virtue of the ineffable Name that is dwelling in me."[135] His heavenly functions include restrain-

---

134. The focus on idolatry is emphasized by Harlow, "Idolatry and Alterity," 306-10.
135. See further M. Himmelfarb, *Ascent to Heaven in Jewish and Christian Apocalypses*

ing both the Cherubim and Leviathan, and teaching the celestial song. He and Michael are appointed to be with the descendants of Abraham. His appearance suggests that he has a priestly character.[136] In all, Jaoel bears striking resemblance to Metatron in Hekalot literature. Metatron is "the little Yahweh" (*3 Enoch* 12), whose name is like the name of God himself (*b. Sanhedrin* 38b).[137] The *Apocalypse of Abraham* is evidently heir to a tradition of mystical speculation that goes beyond that associated with the archangel Michael or with the "Son of Man" in the Similitudes of Enoch.

A second major supernatural figure is introduced in the figure of Azazel, in chap. 13.[138] Azazel is depicted as a fallen angel, whose heavenly garments are given to Abraham. He is associated with the fires of the netherworld in chap. 14 and again in chap. 31. We have already seen how Azazel was identified as the leader of the fallen angels in the Book of the Watchers (where the name was originally *'Aśa'el*). He plays a more obvious role in human history than does Jaoel.

Unlike the visionaries in other contemporary apocalypses such as *2 Enoch* or *3 Baruch,* Abraham is not said to ascend through the heavens one by one but is placed directly in the seventh heaven.[139] There he joins

---

(New York: Oxford University Press, 1993) 61-62. J. E. Fossum, *The Name of God and the Angel of the Lord: Samaritan and Jewish Concepts of Intermediation and the Origin of Gnosticism* (Tübingen: Mohr Siebeck, 1985) 318-20, argues that Jaoel is the glory of God. See the criticism of this position by L. W. Hurtado, *One God, One Lord: Early Christian Devotion and Ancient Jewish Monotheism* (Philadelphia: Fortress, 1988) 88-89. Andrei A. Orlov, "Praxis of the Voice: The Divine Name Traditions in the *Apocalypse of Abraham,*" *JBL* 127 (2008) 53-70, argues that the *Apocalypse of Abraham* offers a complex blend of the traditions of the divine glory and the divine name. See also Orlov, *Divine Manifestations in the Slavonic Pseudepigrapha* (Piscataway, NJ: Gorgias, 2009) 155-75.

136. Himmelfarb, *Ascent to Heaven,* 62; Orlov, "Eschatological Yom Kippur in the *Apocalypse of Abraham.* The Scapegoat Ritual," in idem, *Dark Mirrors: Azazel and Satanail in Early Jewish Demonology* (Albany: State University of New York, 2011), 27.

137. See further G. Scholem, *Major Trends in Jewish Mysticism* (New York: Schocken, 1961) 67-70; I. Gruenwald, *Apocalyptic and Merkavah Mysticism* (Leiden: Brill, 1980) 54-55; C. Rowland, *The Open Heaven: A Study of Apocalyptic in Judaism and Early Christianity* (New York: Crossroad, 1982) 101-3, and especially Orlov, *The Enoch-Metatron Tradition,* 86-147.

138. Andrei A. Orlov, *Dark Mirrors,* 11-81; idem, *Heavenly Priesthood in the Apocalypse of Abraham* (Cambridge: Cambridge University Press, 2013) 73-92.

139. *Apoc. Abraham* 19:6 actually refers to an eighth heaven, but this would seem to be a mistake for "sixth." See Rubinkiewicz, "Apocalypse of Abraham," 698. John C. Poirier, "The Ouranology of the Apocalypse of Abraham," *JSJ* 35 (2004) 391-409, tries to defend the authenticity of the eighth heaven.

with Jaoel in reciting a song that the angel taught him.[140] The *Apocalypse of Abraham* is exceptional among the apocalypses in providing the words of the heavenly song in chapter 17.[141] Abraham's vision of the divine throne draws heavily on Ezekiel and stands directly in the tradition of Merkavah speculation.[142] It also stands in the tradition of *1 Enoch* 14, conveying a sense of the visionary's experience of awe and terror. From his vantage point in the seventh heaven, Abraham is allowed to view the expanses that are under the firmament and to verify the first principle of cosmology, which is made explicit in chap. 19: there is no other God but the one he has sought. Unlike Enoch in *2 Enoch*, which we will meet in the next chapter, Abraham is not said to be transformed into an angel, although Schäfer argues that such a transformation is implied by his joint song with Jaoel.[143]

The picture of the world which is introduced in chap. 21 exemplifies in an exceptionally clear way the combination of cosmology and history that is always implied in the apocalyptic worldview. The course of history and its consummation are built into the structure of creation from the beginning. Both the heavens and the ages of the world are displayed in orderly numbers that reflect the providential control of God. On the spatial axis, Abraham notes both the paradise of the righteous (the Garden of Eden) and the abyss and its torments. The historical axis is divided into twelve hours, a form of periodization that is also found in *2 Baruch*'s vision of the cloud and waters and probably derives ultimately from Persian sources.[144] The period of oppression by the Gentiles is specified as four "hours" of a hundred years each — a reflection of the four kingdoms of Daniel, which were also reflected in *2 Baruch* and *4 Ezra*. The destruction of the temple must be presumed to take place at the end of the four hours, and so at the end of the age. The periodization of history serves its usual

---

140. Steven Weitzman, "The Song of Abraham," *HUCA* 65 (1994) 21-33, finds the exegetical stimulus for the song in Gen 14:22.

141. See Himmelfarb, *Ascent to Heaven,* 61, who emphasizes the cultic overtones of the ascent.

142. Gruenwald, *Apocalyptic and Merkavah Mysticism,* 55-57; Rowland, *The Open Heaven,* 86-87. Scholem claimed that the *Apocalypse of Abraham* more closely resembled a Merkabah text than any other apocalypse (*Jewish Gnosticism, Merkabah Mysticism, and Talmudic Tradition* [2d ed.; New York: Jewish Theological Seminary, 1965] 23). See also D. Halperin, *The Faces of the Chariot: Early Jewish Responses to Ezekiel's Vision* (Tübingen: Mohr Siebeck, 1988) 103-14; Schäfer, *The Origins of Jewish Mysticism,* 92; Orlov, *Heavenly Priesthood,* 154-89..

143. Schäfer, *The Origins of Jewish Mysticism,* 91.

144. Compare the division of history into twelve thousand years in the *Bundahišn.*

purpose of showing that the course of events is predetermined and that the end is near.

Not only are cosmos and history divided in an orderly way; so also is humanity. The picture reveals a great multitude, half on the right and half on the left, representing the chosen people and the Gentiles respectively. Abraham is the chosen one, and his descendants are the chosen people.[145] The symmetrical division suggests a dualistic view of the world.[146] The nature and extent of this dualism constitute the most controversial problem in the *Apocalypse of Abraham*. In two passages, in chaps. 20 and 22, Azazel appears to be in partnership with God, specifically sharing the heritage of the chosen people. In the case of chap. 22, the reference to Azazel is omitted in one manuscript and seems to be added as a gloss in another. Rubinkiewicz concludes that both this passage and that in chap. 20 have been interpolated by a Bogomil scribe.[147] This suggestion finds support in chap. 29, where the disputed expression "with Azazel" occurs in a passage that is definitely interpolated. An explicit statement that Azazel shares in the heritage of the chosen people would be extraordinary in a Jewish text but has some basis in the original apocalypse. Indeed Abraham's question about the status of Azazel at the end of chap. 20 provides an admirable occasion for the exposition of the world that follows. Some part of the chosen people is, in any case, supposed to be sinful and so to be under the dominion of Azazel. The entire conception may be compared with the doctrine of the two spirits at Qumran.[148] The ultimate supremacy of God is not in doubt. The role of Azazel is carefully delimited in the discussion of the fall in chap. 23: "They who will to do evil . . . over them I gave him power." Abraham's further question about why God "willed to effect that evil should be desired in the hearts of men" is never directly answered. The review of history that follows establishes the undeniable fact of human sinfulness, and the example of Terah affirms that it is a matter of free choice.

The *Apocalypse of Abraham* does not provide a satisfactory expla-

---

145. John C. Poirier, "On a Wing and a Prayer. The Soteriology of the *Apocalypse of Abraham*," in Gurtner, ed., *This World and the World to Come*, 93.

146. Orlov, *Dark Mirrors*, 1-6.

147. Rubinkiewicz, "La vision de l'histoire," 139-41. Rubinkiewicz also identifies other possible glosses. The Bogomils were a heretical sect in the Balkan peninsula between the tenth and the fourteenth century. See Turdeanu, *Apocryphes Slaves*, 1-17. Rubinkiewicz's view is rejected by B. Philonenko-Sayer and M. Philonenko (*L'Apocalypse d'Abraham*, 24), who admit interpolations only in 29:2b-11 and in 17:8-10, which was composed in Greek.

148. Compare Philonenko-Sayer and Philonenko, *L'Apocalypse d'Abraham*, 32.

nation of the origin of evil, any more than 4 Ezra did. The solution lies in the future, in the promise of retribution. Some retribution is provided already in this age, in the punishment of Israelite sin by the destruction of the temple. At this point, however, the second underlying problem of the book emerges: What is the ultimate role of the chosen people descended from Abraham? The answer to this question can be given only in eschatological terms. We must presume that the chastisement involved in the destruction of the temple leaves a purified remnant, although this is not explicitly stated.

The eschatological expectations of this apocalypse are confused by a strange insertion in chap. 29 about a man "from the left side of the heathen" who is insulted and beaten by those on the right side but is worshiped "by the heathen with Azazel." This passage must be taken as a reference to Christ, although the suggestion that he is worshiped by Azazel is unorthodox and reflects a sectarian, Bogomil viewpoint.[149] The eschatology of the Jewish work can be seen in chap. 31, where the Elect One comes to gather the exiles. A passage at the end of chap. 29 says that the righteous will be gathered to the place "which thou sawest devastated" and will be established through sacrifices. This passage is obviously Jewish and envisages a restoration of the temple. There is no reference to resurrection, but the mockers will be food for the fire of Hades, and the righteous had been seen in the Garden of Eden in chap. 21. The eschatological scenario remains elliptic, but it is apparent that both individual retribution after death and the future restoration of the nation are envisaged. The hope of humanity lies beyond the present world, or beyond the present age.

The *Apocalypse of Abraham* resolves its underlying problems by placing them in the context of a construction of the world that embraces both cosmology and history. The origin of evil is only partially explained by the role of Azazel. Ultimately, sin is attributed to free human choice. The election of Abraham is not finally explained either. The problem here is not the cause of the election (which lies in the free choice of God) but how it can be maintained, given the prevalence of idolatry even within the chosen people. This problem, like the problem of evil itself, can be resolved only

149. J. Licht, "Abraham, Apocalypse of," *EJ*, 2:126-27. On the problematic nature of this passage, even in a Christian context, see M. E. Stone, "Apocalyptic Literature," in *Jewish Writings of the Second Temple Period* (CRINT 2/2; Assen: Van Gorcum; Philadelphia: Fortress, 1984) 415-16. For a different view, see R. G. Hall, "The 'Christian Interpolation' in the Apocalypse of Abraham," *JBL* 107/1 (1988) 107-12, who takes the man as the Roman emperor and the passage as thoroughly Jewish.

by the eschatological finale. The book can scarcely be said to provide a rational argument to show that this solution is satisfactory, but that is not its purpose. It proposes a view of the world on the authority of Abraham and his heavenly visions and acquires force from its use of biblical and traditional allusions. The imaginative achievement of such a synthesis of history and cosmology is considerable. The frank recognition of human sinfulness and affirmation of free will enhance its credibility. The total effect enables the reader to set the problems of the present in perspective against the grand design of creation, and thereby be reassured and acquire a basis for action.

The more specific messages of the *Apocalypse of Abraham* are difficult to discern. The focal point of history is the destruction of the temple. The *Apocalypse of Abraham* attributes this calamity to the sins of the Jews, without the misgivings of 4 Ezra over the disproportion of the punishment. The *Apocalypse* has a cultic focus that is lacking in 4 Ezra and 2 *Baruch*,[150] but it lacks the concern of those works for the Law. In chaps. 25 and 27 the sins are discussed with greater specificity, but both passages are enigmatic. In chap. 25, God's ideal of the temple is used as a foil against which his anger with the people should be understood. Cultic defilement would seem to be implied,[151] and this is corroborated by an allusion to Ezekiel 8 ("the idol of jealousy"). There is also a cryptic reference to a man slaughtering. In chap. 27 God's anger is caused by the "statue" (which apparently signifies idolatry) and murder in the temple. The temple has evidently been defiled, and some criticism of the priesthood may be inferred. The slaughter and murder most probably refer to the murders and assassinations in the inner-Jewish struggles at the time of the revolt against Rome (compare *Sib. Or.* 4:118). The blame for the defilement may fall on the Zealots no less than on the priesthood. Unfortunately, the text is too unclear to permit firm conclusions. The great concern of the work with idolatry may reflect the proliferation of idols in Judea because of an increasing Gentile population after the destruction of Jerusalem.[152]

Although the violence of 66–70 CE is apparently condemned, the

---

150. Orlov, *Heavenly Priesthood*, 95-118; "Eschatological Yom Kippur." Orlov sees a reflection of the Day of Atonement in the encounter between Jaoel and Azazel. Jaoel is the senior priest instructing Abraham on how to deal with Azazel.

151. Harlow, "Idolatry and Alterity," 321.

152. So Harlow, ibid., 330, building on Ephraim E. Urbach, "The Rabbinical Law of Idolatry in the Second and Third Centuries in the Light of Archaeological and Historical Facts," *IEJ* 9 (1959) 156-58, 229-33.

apocalypse is not ultimately pacifistic. In the eschatological age the righteous "shall destroy those who have destroyed them and shall insult those who have insulted them" (chap. 29), and God will burn with fire those who have insulted them and ruled them in this age (chap. 31). Can we discern here an attitude that "may have contributed to the atmosphere which precipitated the revolt of Bar Kokhba"?[153] Perhaps, but a qualification is in order. The violence is envisaged as eschatological. The apocalypse does not advocate rebellion against Rome until the end of the age. Whether it could be used to sanction recourse to arms would depend on whether the messianic age was thought to have arrived — as indeed Akiba thought in the case of Bar Kokhba. The attitude of the *Apocalypse of Abraham* may be somewhat similar to the Qumran *War Scroll* in this respect.

The main clues to the provenance of the apocalypse lie in its references to the temple. On the one hand, there is concern over cultic defilement and the hope for restoration of righteous sacrifices. On the other hand, the defilement of the temple may imply a critique of the priesthood. The author *may* have belonged to a group that was priestly in character but alienated from the priesthood of the first century. Both the mystical tendencies and the dualism of the apocalypse find some parallels in the Qumran scrolls, but the *Apocalypse of Abraham* takes a clearer stand on the question of free will. The evidence is scarcely sufficient to warrant the proposal of Box that the author was an Essene.[154] It is, in any case, uncertain how far the Essenes maintained a separate identity after 70 CE. It is true, however, that the *Apocalypse of Abraham* represents a different strand of Judaism from what we found in 4 Ezra and in 2 *Baruch*.

153. So J. R. Mueller, "The Apocalypse of Abraham and the Destruction of the Second Jewish Temple," in K. H. Richards, ed., *Society of Biblical Literature 1982 Seminar Papers*, 342-49.

154. Box, *The Apocalypse*, xxi-xxiv. So also Philonenko-Sayer and Philonenko, *L'Apocalypse d'Abraham*, 34.

# CHAPTER EIGHT

# Apocalyptic Literature from the Diaspora in the Roman Period

Two clusters of texts from the Hellenistic Diaspora are relevant to the discussion of apocalypticism. On the one hand, the *Sibylline Oracles* bear obvious resemblances to the "historical" apocalypses. On the other hand, the actual apocalypses of the Diaspora all involve heavenly journeys and incline to the mystical end of the apocalyptic spectrum.

## The Sibyllines

We have already seen some of the affinities between the *Sibyllines* and the historical apocalypses in the case of *Sib. Or.* 3. These affinities became more pronounced in the Roman period when additions to *Sib. Or.* 3 reflect in their predictions of catastrophe and their heightened mythological imagery the growing alienation of Egyptian Judaism. This tradition is carried further in *Sib. Or.* 5. A different Sibylline tradition is represented in *Sib. Or.* 1 and 2 and *Sib. Or.* 4. In these books the analogy with apocalyptic eschatology (of the historical type) is more complete. They attest an elaborate periodization of history, culminating in the resurrection and the judgment of the dead.[1] The *Sibyllines* are, of course, always presented as oracles, the direct inspired speech of the sibyl. The manner of revelation remains clearly distinct from that of the apocalypses.

---

1. See J. J. Collins, "The Growth of the Sibylline Tradition," in W. Haase and H. Temporini, eds., *ANRW*, II.20.1 (1987) 421-59.

## Sib. Or. 5

The tradition of anti-Roman polemic developed in the additions to *Sib. Or. 3* is continued in *Sib. Or. 5*. This is a composite work, consisting of six substantial oracles. The four central oracles (52-110; 111-78; 179-285; 286-434) show a common pattern:[2] (1) oracles against various nations (mainly Egypt in the first and third oracles, various Asiatic countries in the second and fourth); (2) the return of Nero as an eschatological adversary; (3) the advent of a savior figure; (4) a destruction, usually by fire (the manner is not specified in 52-110). These four oracles were composed after the destruction of Jerusalem in 70 CE but before the great Diaspora revolt in 115-17 CE. The concluding oracle of the book (435-531) was most probably written after the Diaspora revolt. The latest oracle in the book is found in vss. 1-51, a survey of history from Alexander to Hadrian (or, if vs. 51 is original, to Marcus Aurelius), which refers to the emperors by the numbers represented by their initials. This oracle is very different in spirit from the rest of the book and is closer to the pro-Roman sibylline tradition that is found in *Sib. Or.* 11-14.

The bulk of *Sib. Or. 5* is taken up with prophecies of doom against various nations. Egypt is the main subject in two of the oracles, and is denounced for idolatry (81-85) and for persecution of the Jews (68-69). These oracles arise naturally enough from the Jewish experience in Egypt. There are also prophecies of doom against the Gauls (200-205) and Ethiopians (206-13), with whom the Jews had no significant contact. The principal enemy, however, is Rome, which is denounced as an "effeminate and unjust, evil city, ill-fated above all" (162-78). Like Babylon, Rome has said "I alone am" (compare Isa 47:8; Rev 18:7). Accordingly, she will be cast down to the nether regions of Hades. Rome is condemned for immorality (adultery and homosexuality, 5:166, 386-93) and for arrogance, but the wrath of the sibyl is aroused for more immediate reasons. In 5:155-61 it is said that a great star will burn "the deep sea and Babylon itself and the land of Italy, because of which many holy faithful Hebrews and a true people perished." "Babylon" here is a code name for Rome, as in the book of Revelation, and presupposes the analogy between the destructions of 586 BCE and 70 CE. The great sin of Rome is the destruction of the temple. In 5:398-413 the sibyl utters what is perhaps the most powerful lament for the second temple: "When I saw

---

2. J. J. Collins, *The Sibylline Oracles of Egyptian Judaism* (SBLDS 13; Missoula, MT: Scholars Press, 1974) 57-64.

the second temple cast headlong, soaked in fire by an impious hand, the ever-flourishing, watchful temple of God, made by holy people and hoped by their soul and body to be always imperishable. . . . But now a certain insignificant and impious king has gone up, cast it down and left it in ruins. . . ." *Sib. Or.* 5 reacts to the fall of the temple not by pondering divine justice (like 4 Ezra) or seeking to fill the gap it left in religious life (like *2 Baruch*) but by venting its outrage against the heathen power that was responsible.

The sibyl's hatred of Rome also finds expression in the role of Nero as eschatological adversary. At the time of his death there was a widespread belief that Nero had escaped to the Parthians, with whom he had long had friendly relations, and would return leading a Parthian host.[3] This belief was fueled by the appearance of an impostor shortly after Nero's death, and another some twenty years later. The popular belief was given an eschatological cast in *Sib. Or.* 4 and 5 and also in *Sib. Or.* 3:63-74, which refers to Nero as "Beliar" who would come from the line of Augustus.[4] Originally Nero was not thought to have died. Subsequently the belief arose that he would return from the dead — *Nero redivivus*.[5] This belief is reflected in the book of Revelation in the beast who had "a mortal wound" on one of its heads but was healed (chap. 13) and who "was and is not and is to ascend from the bottomless pit" (chap. 17). In Revelation this figure is representative of Roman power and is deliberately fashioned as an Antichrist.[6] *Nero redivivus* continued to play a part in the later sibyllina (*Sib. Or.* 8:68-72, 139-69) and in the Antichrist legend of the Middle Ages.[7]

3. Ibid., 80-87; Tacitus, *Histories* 2.8; Suetonius, *Nero* 57; Dio Chrysostom, *Orations* 21.10.

4. Belial is also said to come in the likeness of Nero ("a lawless king, the slayer of his mother") in *Ascension of Isaiah* 4:1. See the discussion by Hans-Josef Klauck, "Do They Never Come Back? *Nero Redivivus* and the Apocalypse of John," *CBQ* 63 (2001) 683-98.

5. Jan Willem van Henten, "*Nero Redivivus* Demolished: The Coherence of the Nero Traditions in the *Sibylline Oracles*," *JSP* 21 (2000) 3-17, correctly notes that Nero is not supposed to return from the dead in *Sib. Or.* 3-5, and therefore is not strictly *Nero redivivus*.

6. A. Yarbro Collins, *The Combat Myth in the Book of Revelation* (HDR 9; Missoula, MT: Scholars Press, 1976) 174-90.

7. B. McGinn, *Antichrist: Two Thousand Years of the Human Fascination with Evil* (San Francisco: HarperSanFrancisco, 1994) 45-54, 65-67. The classic treatment of W. Bousset, *The Antichrist Legend* (London: Hutchinson, 1896), is outdated but remains invaluable for its collection of references. On the early development of traditions related to the Antichrist, see G. C. Jenks, *The Origin and Early Development of the Antichrist Myth* (BZNW 59; Berlin: de Gruyter, 1991), and L. C. L. Peerbolte, *The Antecedents of Antichrist* (Leiden: Brill, 1996). Chapter 17 of Peerbolte's book is devoted to the *Sibylline Oracles*.

*Sib. Or.* 5 makes extensive use of the Nero legend. *Sib. Or.* 5:137-54 describes "a great king of great Rome" who is clearly identified as Nero by his theatrical ambitions and the murder of his mother. He is said to flee from "Babylon" (Rome) and take refuge with the Persians, or Parthians. The destruction of the temple is still attributed to him. In *Sib. Or.* 5:214-27 he is clearly identified by a reference to the cutting of the isthmus of Corinth. In 5:361-70 he is identified as a "matricide" who will come in the last time to destroy every land and conquer all, including "the one because of whom he himself perished" (presumably Rome).[8] In view of his association with the Persians and his eschatological role, he must also be identified with the "Persian" who will come "like hail" in vss. 93-97.[9] The charges against Nero are the same as the charges against Rome: he is morally evil, he claimed to be God (vss. 34, 140), and he is responsible for the destruction of the temple.

The four central oracles of the book look beyond the evils of the present order and beyond the return of Nero to the advent of a savior figure. In 108-9 he is "a certain king sent from God" to defeat "the Persian" when the latter attempts to destroy the city of the blessed ones. This formulation is compatible with traditional messianic expectations but also recalls a similar expectation in the *Oracle of Hystaspes*.[10] In vss. 414 and 256 the savior appears as a heavenly figure who comes from the expanses of heaven, or "from the sky." In the oracle in 111-78 the function of the savior is exercised by "a great star," which burns the sea and Babylon (158-59). Stars were frequently associated with the advent of savior figures in the Hellenistic world.[11] In the Jewish tradition stars were identified with angels.[12] Moreover, astral imagery had messianic connotations because of Balaam's oracle.[13] Hence the leader of the revolt against Rome in 132 CE was called Bar Kokhba, son of the star. *Sib. Or.* 5 reflects the merging of traditions. Whether the savior figure is expected to be a Davidic king is

---

8. The notion that Nero would return to conquer Rome is common in the later tradition.

9. Nero had been hailed as an emanation of Mithras by the Parthian Tiridates, whom he enthroned as king of Armenia.

10. Lactantius, *Divine Institutions* 7.17: God will "send from heaven a great king."

11. Collins, *Sibylline Oracles*, 90. Comets marked the births of Alexander, Augustus, Mithridates, and of course Jesus.

12. Judg 5:20; Job 38:7. Compare *1 Enoch* 104:2-6. In Rev 22:16 Jesus is referred to as the morning star.

13. Num 24:17. Compare CD 7:18-20; 4QTestimonia and *Testament of Judah* 24:1.

not clear; this is never said of him. It is apparent, however, that he has a strongly supernatural character, as indeed the messiah also has in 4 Ezra. Unlike *Sib. Or.* 3, which based its hopes on the Ptolemaic house, *Sib. Or.* 5 has to look for a savior from beyond this world.[14]

The oracles in 179-285 and 286-434 conclude with prophecies of the restoration of Jerusalem. In 247-85 the focus is a broad one, on "delightful Judea," but Jerusalem will be surrounded by a great wall as far as Joppa. The Gentiles will be converted to revere the law (265), and the earth will be transformed. In 420-27 "the city which God desired" is made more brilliant than the stars, equipped with a holy temple and an immense tower touching the clouds and visible to all. In both cases the restoration is this-worldly and conforms to the messianic oracles of Isaiah rather than to apocalyptic eschatology. The focus of eschatological hope on Jerusalem is remarkable in a document of the Diaspora. For most of the history of the Diaspora, the exiled Jews had been content to seek their future in the land of their residence. In the great revolt of 115-17 CE, however, there are indications that the rebels aspired to bring about the end of the Diaspora and to return to Jerusalem.[15] It is also noteworthy that *Sib. Or.* 5:484-88 exultingly prophesies the destruction of Isis and Sarapis. The temple of Sarapis in Alexandria was one of the most conspicuous casualties of the revolt, and the rebel Jews were noted for their hostility to the pagan cults. *Sib. Or.* 5, more than any other document we have, is likely to reflect the attitude of those who joined in the great and tragic uprising.

Despite its hopes for a savior figure and for the restoration of Jerusalem, *Sib. Or.* 5 is predominantly a pessimistic book. The motif of destruction by fire is found in three of the central oracles. In 155-61 the great star will destroy the whole earth and burn the deep sea and "Babylon." The sea here may echo the ancient mythological tradition in which Yamm or Sea is the embodiment of chaos, the enemy of life and fertility. The advent of the savior figure in vs. 256 is followed by a shower of blazing fire from

14. William Horbury, *Messianism among Jews and Christians. Biblical and Historical Studies* (London: T & T Clark, 2003) 125-55, argues that the "man from heaven" in *Sib. Or.* 5 is a veiled allusion to the Danielic "one like a son of man."

15. J. J. Collins, *Between Athens and Jerusalem: Jewish Identity in the Hellenistic Diaspora* (rev. ed.; Grand Rapids: Eerdmans, 2000) 140-51. See also M. Hengel, "Messianische Hoffnung und politischer 'Radikalismus' in der 'jüdisch-hellenistischen Diaspora,'" in D. Hellholm, ed., *Apocalypticism in the Mediterranean World and the Near East: Proceedings of the International Colloquium on Apocalypticism, Uppsala, August 12-17, 1979* (Tübingen: Mohr Siebeck, 1983) 653-84.

heaven. Again in 414-33 the savior destroys every city with fire and burns the nations of evildoers. This motif has biblical roots and also has parallels in Persian eschatology.[16] It marks a negative conclusion to the present age and stresses the discontinuity with the state of salvation that is to come.

The pessimism of *Sib. Or.* 5 is most readily obvious in the final oracle. The sibyl prophesies the destruction of Isis and Sarapis (484-88) and then goes on to envisage the conversion of Egypt and the building of a temple to the true God. Even this eschatological temple will not last, however, but will be destroyed by the "Ethiopians." The Ethiopians were traditional enemies of Egypt. Ethiopia was also associated with Gog and Magog in *Sib. Or.* 3:319-20 and may serve here as a general reference for eschatological adversaries. It is indicative of the general xenophobia of *Sib. Or.* 5 that such a remote people is accorded a key destructive role in the final scenario.

The book concludes with a battle of the stars, which ends when heaven casts them all to earth.[17] The earth is set ablaze and the sky remains starless. The closing note of the book, then, is a bleak one of cosmic desolation. It is an apt expression of the worldview of Egyptian Judaism after the failure of the great revolt.

The eschatological oracles of *Sib. Or.* 5 frame an ethical message, which is found in the condemnations of the nations for idolatry (vss. 75-85, 278-80, 353-56, 403-5, 495-96) and sexual immorality, especially homosexuality (386-93, 495-96).[18] The dominant emphasis of the book, however, is not ethical but political. The main function of the sibyl is to articulate Jewish anger against the nations in general and Rome in particular. This anger is generated in part by social oppression[19] but chiefly by the humiliation of the destruction of the temple and the arrogance of Rome in posturing as God. *Sib. Or.* 5 is quite probably representative of the feelings of Jews who joined in the revolt in the time of Trajan. We should note that apocalyptic literature was not usually inclined to foment rebellion, but *Sib. Or.* 5 differs from the apocalypses in significant respects, over and beyond the manner of revelation. Despite the propensity for mythological imagery and the supernatural character of the savior figure, *Sib. Or.* 5 does not envisage salvation beyond

---

16. R. Meyer, *Die biblische Vorstellung vom Weltbrand* (Bonn: Bonn University Press, 1956).

17. This motif is found also in *Sib. Or.* 2:200-201; 5:207-13; 2 Pet 3:12. Compare Seneca, *Consolatio ad Marciam* 26.6; *Thyestes* 844-74; *Nat. Quaest.* 3.29.1; and Nonnus, *Dionysiaca* 38.347-409. The idea is related to the Stoic concept of *ekpyrōsis*.

18. On the ethics of the sibyl, see Collins, *Between Athens and Jerusalem*, 165.

19. *Sib. Or.* 5:416-17: the savior figure will restore the wealth to the good.

this world. There is no judgment of the dead, either of the individual soul or of a resurrected humanity in the end time. Consequently, the outcome of political struggles such as the revolt against Rome is far more crucial for the sibyl than for an apocalyptist like the author of 2 *Baruch*.

The tradition of sibylline protest against Rome survived the revolt and was taken up again in a collection of oracles now preserved in *Sib. Or.* 8 and composed in the time of Marcus Aurelius. These later oracles indict Rome on grounds that are predominantly social. The later development of Jewish sibyllines in Egypt, however, was mainly pro-Roman. Books 12–14 continue a tradition initiated in *Sib. Or.* 11, which was probably composed in the first century in Alexandria. These oracles string together brief comments on the reigns of the successive emperors. They have minimal eschatological interest and show little analogy to the apocalypses.[20]

## Sib. Or. 1 and 2

Two sibylline books from the first century CE were not composed in Egypt. These are the Jewish substratum of *Sib. Or.* 1 and 2, and *Sib. Or.* 4. These oracles share an elaborate periodization of history and an expectation of resurrection and judgment of the dead.

It is generally recognized that the first two books of the standard Sibylline collection constitute an original unit, structured by a division of history into ten generations.[21] The first seven generations are preserved without interpolation in *Sib. Or.* 1:1-323. At this point the sequence is disrupted by an interpolation concerning the career of Christ. When the sequence is resumed in 2:15 we are confronted already with the tenth generation, so the eighth and ninth have been lost. The remainder of *Sib. Or.* 2 (vss. 34-347) deals with eschatological crises and the judgment of the dead. There are some clear Christian passages, but the full extent of the Christian redaction is uncertain.[22] Verses 154-76, which culminate in the universal rule of the He-

20. See my introductions to the later Sibylline books in Charlesworth, ed., *OTP*, 1.430-68; also D. S. Potter, *Prophecy and History in the Crisis of the Roman Empire* (Oxford: Oxford University Press, 1990).

21. J. Geffcken, *Komposition und Entstehungszeit der Oracula Sibyllina* (Leipzig: Hinrichs, 1902) 47-53; Olaf Wassmuth, *Sibyllinische Orakel 1-2. Studien und Kommentar* (Leiden: Brill, 2011) 56-59; Lightfoot, *The Sibylline Oracles*, 97.

22. Lightfoot, *The Sibylline Oracles*, 131-43, argues that *Sib. Or.* 2 from verse 194 onward is a sustained adaptation of the Christian *Apocalypse of Peter*.

brews, "as of old," are definitely Jewish. The resurrection in 2:214-37, which is strongly physical in character and recalls Ezekiel 37, is also probably Jewish.

Because of the complications introduced by the Christian redaction, little can be said about the provenance and purpose of the Jewish oracle.[23] There are indications that the place of composition was Phrygia, the first land to emerge after the flood, where Ararat is located. Since the destruction of Jerusalem is mentioned only in a Christian redactional passage (1:393-96), Kurfess inferred that the Jewish oracle was probably composed before then.[24] In view of the loss of the eighth and ninth generations, any conclusions on the date and purpose of the Jewish oracle can only be tentative.

The most interesting analogy with the apocalyptic literature lies in the division of history into ten generations followed by a resurrection.[25] The tenfold periodization was found in the Apocalypse of Weeks and in 11QMelchizedek, but it is unlikely that the sibyl derived it from other Jewish sources.[26] Such a schematization is presupposed in several sibylline oracles. Virgil's *Fourth Eclogue* speaks of the "final age" of the Cumean sibyl, and this was taken as the tenth age by the grammarian Servius (about 400 CE). The roots of the conception most probably lie in the Persian division of world history into millennia, which also involved a belief in resurrection.[27] In *Sib. Or.* 1 and 2 the periodization is found in a particularly

---

23. Lightfoot, *The Sibylline Oracles*, 148, is critical of attempts to separate the Jewish and Christian components, blithely claiming that "the discontinuities do not matter" for a Christian author of the second century or later (149). But they matter for anyone interested in the history of apocalypticism. In contrast, Gordon Watley, "Sibylline Identities: The Jewish and Christian Editions of Sibylline Oracles 1-2," diss. University of Virginia, 2010, mounts a defense of distinguishing a Jewish edition.

24. A. Kurfess, "Oracula Sibyllina I/II," *ZNW* 40 (1941) 151-65. Geffcken maintained a later, third-century date.

25. Lightfoot, *The Sibylline Oracles*, 106-25; Wassmuth, *Sibyllinische Orakel 1-2*, 118-47; Neujahr, *Predicting the Past*, 227-35.

26. Lightfoot, *The Sibylline Oracles*, 149, suggests that the author "assembled it all in imitation of the structure of the Apocalypse of Weeks but wadded with all sort of other material, Enochic, Petrine, Sibylline." There is no explicit reference to resurrection in the Apocalypse of Weeks. See the comments of Neujahr, *Predicting the Past*, 231-32. Neujahr concludes that "the influence of Greek authors . . . is a far more significant influence on the work."

27. D. Flusser, "The Four Empires in the Fourth Sibyl and in the Book of Daniel," *Israel Oriental Studies* 2 (1972) 148-75. On periodization, see further A. Yarbro Collins, "Numerical Symbolism in Jewish and Early Christian Apocalyptic Literature," in *Cosmology and Eschatology in Jewish and Christian Apocalypticism* (Leiden: Brill, 1996) 55-138.

elaborate form. It embraces all of history from creation to the final judgment. The first five generations end with the flood, the second five with destruction by fire, in accordance with the notion of the Great Year.[28] We have seen that the motif of destruction by fire was prominent in *Sib. Or.* 5 even when the full periodization of history was not developed.

In the present form of *Sib. Or.* 1 and 2 the overview of history provides a framework for ethical teaching.[29] The schematization of history builds the impression that the impending destruction is inevitable. The imminence of the judgment provides an occasion for presenting crucial ethical values. So Noah is presented as preaching to his contemporaries before the flood (1:150-70, 174-98). The sins mentioned are commonplace — violence, deceit, adultery, etc. Because of the Christian redaction it is not clear whether humanity is given a similar warning in the tenth generation. It is also possible that the Jewish oracle had a stronger political thrust than is now apparent.

## Sib. Or. 4

*Sib. Or.* 4 also shows evidence of redactional layers. In this case the final product is still distinctly Jewish. The original oracle is structured by a division of history into ten generations and four kingdoms (vss. 49-101).[30] The overview begins after the flood. The Assyrians rule for six generations, the Medes for two, and the Persians for one. The tenth generation and the fourth kingdom coincide in the Macedonian empire. We should expect this climactic kingdom to be followed by the eschatological finale, but instead the account is prolonged to refer to the Romans (102-51). Rome is not integrated into the numerical sequence, but neither is it a final, definitive kingdom. We must assume that the passage on Rome was added to update the oracle. The original oracle may have included the final section on the conflagration, resurrection, and judgment (173-92), in a manner analogous to *Sib. Or.* 1 and 2. Since Macedonia is the last kingdom in the sequence, that oracle was presumably written before the rise of Rome. There is no

---

28. Collins, *Sibylline Oracles,* 101-2. The doctrine of two world cycles is implicit in Hesiod and explicit in Heraclitus and Plato (*Politicus* 273 b-c). See also Josephus, *Antiquities* 1.2.3 §§70-71; *Life of Adam and Eve* 49; I. Chaine, "Cosmogonie aquatique et conflagration finale d'après la secunda Petri," *RB* 46 (1937) 207-16. These parallels are also noted by Lightfoot, *The Sibylline Oracles,* 116-17.

29. Lightfoot, *The Sibylline Oracles,* 144-48.

30. Neujahr, *Predicting the Past,* 235-37.

clear evidence to show whether the original author was Jewish. He was evidently not drawing on the four kingdom schema in Daniel, since Assyria, not Babylon, is the first kingdom. The decline of history explicit in the schema implies that Macedonia is the nadir of history and that its demise is imminent (compare the use of the four-kingdom schema in Daniel 2). The original oracle, then, may be considered a document of Near Eastern resistance to Hellenism.[31]

The passage on Rome in vss. 102-51 extends the view of history through the destruction of the Jerusalem temple. Unlike *Sib. Or.* 5, this oracle expresses no outrage but suggests that it is a punishment for the folly and impiety of the Jews. The legend of Nero's return, which plays such a prominent part in *Sib. Or.* 5, serves here to introduce the eschatological time. The sibyl sounds the familiar sibylline theme that Rome will pay back its plunder to Asia. The oracle, then, has an aspect of anti-Roman polemic.

The major emphasis of the Jewish oracle, however, falls not on the political element but on the plea for conversion, and specifically on the demand that "wretched mortals" should "wash your whole bodies in perennial rivers" (165). If this and the more general ethical demands are not obeyed, "there will be fire throughout the whole world" (173). The oracle is exceptional in making the destruction conditional on human obedience or disobedience. Both the periodization of history and the concluding prophecy of resurrection seem to imply that the course of events is set, and this may well have been the view of the original oracle. In any case, *Sib. Or.* 4 provides a good illustration of the use of periodization and eschatological expectation to throw ethical demands into high relief and add urgency to the demand for obedience.

The demand for baptism in the face of the impending judgment is perhaps the most striking aspect of *Sib. Or.* 4. The most obvious analogies are found in the New Testament account of John the Baptist and again in early Christianity in Acts 2.[32] *Sib. Or.* 4 shows no sign of Christian authorship and has been thought to derive from a Jewish baptist movement in the Jordan valley.[33] Its date is indicated by a reference to

---

31. J. J. Collins, "The Place of the Fourth Sibyl in the Development of the Jewish Sibyllina," *JJS* 25 (1974) 365-80.

32. See further A. Yarbro Collins, "The Origin of Christian Baptism," in *Cosmology and Eschatology,* 218-38.

33. J. Thomas, *Le Mouvement Baptiste en Palestine et Syrie* (Gembloux: Duculot, 1935) 46-60. Although *Sib. Or.* 4 is clearly Jewish, it bears noteworthy resemblances to Ebionite and Elkesaite Christian sectarian teachings.

the eruption of Vesuvius (79 CE), which is taken as an eschatological sign in vs. 130.

The theology of *Sib. Or.* 4 can be filled out from the opening passage in vss. 6-39. These verses stress the transcendence of the invisible God. In addition to the usual polemic against idolatry and immorality, the sibyl insists that God does not have a temple of stone but an invisible one in heaven. She goes on to praise those who reject all temples, altars, and animal sacrifices. In the light of this passage, the sibyl's lack of outrage over the destruction of the temple is intelligible. Like Stephen and the Hellenists in Acts, this sibyl attached little value to the earthly temple. We find here another position in the spectrum of Jewish responses to the fall of the temple, different at once from the apocalypses of 4 Ezra and 2 *Baruch* and from the Egyptian sibylline tradition of *Sib. Or.* 5.

## The Apocalypses

The *Sibylline Oracles* can be called "apocalyptic" only in an extended sense of the term. The actual apocalypses that have survived from the Diaspora are quite different in character. None of them contains a review of history, but all involve heavenly ascents. Three major Diaspora apocalypses have survived, 2 (Slavonic) *Enoch, 3 Baruch,* and the *Testament of Abraham.*[34]

The *Apocalypse of Zephaniah* may well derive from Egyptian Judaism, too, but it has survived only in a quotation in Clement (*Stromateis* 5.11.77) and in a brief fragment in Sahidic.[35] A more extensive apocalyptic fragment in Akhmimic has also been thought to belong to the *Apocalypse of Zephaniah,* but the visionary's name is never mentioned.[36] The quotation in Clement tells how Zephaniah was lifted up to the fifth heaven and saw

---

34. J. J. Collins, "The Genre Apocalypse in Hellenistic Judaism," in Hellholm, ed., *Apocalypticism,* 531-48. See also M. Dean-Otting, *Heavenly Journeys: A Study of the Motif in Hellenistic Jewish Literature* (Frankfurt: Peter Lang, 1984) 98-238.

35. G. Steindorff, *Die Apokalypse des Elias, eine unbekannte Apokalypse und Bruchstücke der Sophonias-Apokalypse* (Leipzig: Hinrichs, 1899).

36. The fragments are combined in P. Riessler, *Altjüdisches Schrifttum ausserhalb der Bibel* (Heidelberg: Kerle, 1927; reprint, Darmstadt: Wissenschaftliche Buchgesellschaft, 1966) 168-77. See K. G. Kuhn, "The Apocalypse of Zephaniah and an Anonymous Apocalypse," in H. F. D. Sparks, ed., *The Apocryphal Old Testament* (Oxford: Clarendon, 1984) 915-25; O. S. Wintermute, "Apocalypse of Zephaniah," in Charlesworth, ed., *OTP,* 1:497-515.

there angels who were called "lords."[37] The Sahidic fragment describes a vision of the underworld and the torments of sinners. The Akhmimic fragment begins with a tour over the visionary's city. The greater part of the apocalypse is concerned with the netherworld and the punishment of the damned. The visionary prays to be delivered but is shown the catalogue of his sins before he is told that he is written in the book of life. Throughout he is in dialogue with an angel. He witnesses the recording angels of good and evil, and when he prays the angel Eremiel comes to deliver him. He is also allowed to witness the angels at prayer. At the end he is told of the coming "Day of the Lord" when heaven and earth will be destroyed. None of the fragments shows any elements that are indisputably Christian, although the visions of the netherworld find their closest analogies in the Christian apocalypses of Peter and Paul.[38] In the Coptic fragments, the dominant concern for individual salvation is reflected in the visionary's anxiety for deliverance from the netherworld. The Akhmimic text spells out its ethical message in the sins attributed to the visionary — mainly neglect of social obligations to the sick, widows, etc. It is apparent, however, that both fragments do not merely exhort but achieve a considerable emotional effect through the tour of otherworldly regions. Because of the fragmentary state of the apocalypse, basic questions of date, provenance, and interpretation remain uncertain. We cannot even be sure that the quotation in Clement and the Coptic fragments belong to the same work.

## 2 Enoch

The apocalypse 2 (Slavonic) *Enoch* is the most elaborate of the Diaspora apocalypses. Despite the contention of J. T. Milik that it is a late, Christian work of the ninth or tenth century,[39] there is a general consensus

---

37. J. Edward Wright, *The Early History of Heaven* (New York: Oxford, 2000) 155-58, suggests that the multi-heaven cosmology represents a secondary revision.

38. The motif also had a background in Greek and Roman literature. See the classic discussion of A. Dieterich, *Nekyia: Beiträge zur Erklärung der neuentdeckten Petrusapokalypse* (3d ed.; Darmstadt: Wissenschaftliche Buchgesellschaft, 1969). M. Himmelfarb, *Tours of Hell: An Apocalyptic Form in Jewish and Christian Literature* (Philadelphia: University of Pennsylvania, 1983) 41-67, emphasizes the affinities with Jewish apocalypses such as the Book of the Watchers. See also her discussion in *Ascent to Heaven in Jewish and Christian Apocalypses* (Oxford: Oxford University Press, 1993) 51-55.

39. J. T. Milik, *The Books of Enoch: Aramaic Fragments of Qumrân Cave 4* (Oxford:

that it is Jewish and no later than the first century, mainly because of the importance attached to animal sacrifice.[40] Andrei Orlov argues that "the affirmations of the value of the animal sacrificial practices and Enoch's ha-lakhic instructions also appear to be fashioned not in the 'preservationist,' mishnaic-like mode of expression, but rather as if they reflected sacrificial practices that still existed when the author was writing his book."[41] The arguments are not necessarily conclusive, but there are no strong arguments for a later date.

The work has survived in two Slavonic recensions, whose relationship is disputed,[42] and in four recently discovered Coptic fragments that agree with the shorter recension.[43] The Coptic fragments date to the eighth to tenth centuries, several centuries earlier than the Slavonic texts. Both

Clarendon, 1976) 107-16. His main argument concerns the use of a late Greek word *syr-maiographa,* but this word could have been introduced secondarily in the course of transmission. Milik's dating is now proven wrong by the Coptic fragments (see n. 43 in this chapter).

40. For the arguments, see J. C. Greenfield, Prolegomenon to H. Odeberg, *3 Enoch or the Hebrew Book of Enoch* (New York: Ktav, 1973) xviii-xx; U. Fischer, *Eschatologie und Jenseitserwartung im Hellenistischen Diasporajudentum* (BZNW 44; Berlin: de Gruyter, 1978) 38-41; E. Schürer, *The History of the Jewish People in the Age of Jesus Christ (175 B.C.-A.D. 135)* 3/2 (rev. and ed. G. Vermes, F. Millar, and M. Goodman; Edinburgh: T & T Clark, 1987) 746-50; Christfried Böttrich, "The 'Book of the Secrets of Enoch' (2 En): Between Jewish Origin and Christian Transmission. An Overview," in Andrei Orlov and Gabriele Boccaccini, eds., *New Perspectives on 2 Enoch. No Longer Slavonic Only* (Studia Judaeoslavica 4; Leiden: Brill, 2012) 37-68, especially 52-57. There is a probable reference to *2 Enoch* in Origen, *De Principiis* 1.3.2.

41. Orlov, "The Sacerdotal Traditions of 2 Enoch and the Date of the Text," in Orlov and Boccaccini, eds., *New Perspectives on 2 Enoch,* 107. Orlov buttresses his argument by appeal to supposed, but questionable, priestly polemics.

42. A. Vaillant, *Le Livre des Secrets d'Hénoch: Texte Slave et Traduction Française* (Paris: Institut d'Etudes Slaves, 1952), argued for the priority of the short recension. He is followed by A. Pennington, "2 Enoch," in Sparks, ed., *The Apocryphal Old Testament,* 321-62, and Liudmila Navtanovich, "The Provenance of 2 Enoch: A Philological Perspective," in Orlov and Boccaccini, eds., *New Perspectives on 2 Enoch,* 69-82. R. H. Charles and W. R. Morfill presuppose the priority of the longer recension (*The Book of the Secrets of Enoch* [Oxford: Clarendon, 1896]). F. Andersen argues that neither recension can be simply accepted as the original ("2 Enoch," in Charlesworth, ed., *OTP,* 1:92-94). So also C. Böttrich, *Weltweisheit, Menschheitsethik, Urkult: Studien zum slavischen Henochbuch* (WUNT 2/50; Tübingen: Mohr Siebeck, 1992) 59-144, who presents an extensive discussion. See also Grant Macaskill, *The Slavonic Texts of 2 Enoch* (Studia Judaeoslavica 5; Leiden: Brill, 2013).

43. Joost L. Hagen, "No Longer 'Slavonic' Only: 2 Enoch Attested in Coptic from Nubia," in Orlov and Boccaccini, eds., *New Perspectives on 2 Enoch,* 7-34. Hagen provides a translation of three of the Coptic fragments, corresponding to *2 Enoch* 36-42.

recensions evidently underwent some scribal changes in the process of transmission. The original language was most probably Greek.[44] Egypt is the most likely place of composition in view of allusions to Egyptian mythology and affinities with Philo and other Diaspora writings.[45] There remains, however, considerable uncertainty about the basic questions of date and provenance, since the work is only extant in Slavonic and Coptic manuscripts, no earlier than the eighth century, and some features are difficult to reconcile with any known context, Jewish or Christian.[46]

The structure of *2 Enoch* has been said to correspond to major blocks of material in *1 Enoch*.[47] Enoch's ascent and commission (chaps. 3–37)[48] would be the counterpart of *1 Enoch* 12–36; his return to earth and instructions (chaps. 38–66), of *1 Enoch* 81, 91–105; and the story of Melchizedek's birth, of *1 Enoch* 106–7 (the birth of Noah). The correspondences, however, are quite loose. The Book of the Watchers was certainly a foundational document in the tradition of apocalyptic ascents. There is a brief account of an ascent in the Aramaic Levi apocryphon, and an ascent is implied but not described in the Similitudes of Enoch. At some point in the first century CE, however, we begin to get accounts of ascents through a numbered series of heaven, typically seven.[49] *2 Enoch* may well be the earliest apocalypse of this type, and it is significantly different from the older, less structured ascent of the Book of the Watchers.

44. A. Rubinstein, "Observations on the Slavonic Book of Enoch," *JJS* 13 (1962) 1-21; Pennington, "2 Enoch," 324. Andersen, "2 Enoch," 94, suspects an original Semitic composition. See also Grant Macaskill, "2 Enoch: Manuscripts, Recensions, and Original Language," in Orlov and Boccaccini, eds., *New Perspectives on 2 Enoch*, 83-101, especially 101, who notes an abundance of Semitisms.

45. R. H. Charles, "The Book of the Secrets of Enoch," in Charles, ed., *APOT*, 2:426; M. Philonenko, "La cosmologie du 'livre des secrets d'Hénoch,' " in *Religions en Egypte Hellénistique et Romaine* (Paris: Presses universitaires de France, 1969) 109-16; Fischer, *Eschatologie und Jenseitserwartung*, 40. Böttrich, *Weltweisheit, Menschheitsethik, Urkult*, 192, argues for composition among the well-off, educated Jews of Alexandria in the first century CE.

46. See the discussion by Andersen, "2 Enoch," 94-97.

47. Nickelsburg, *Jewish Literature*, 221.

48. The chapter divisions given here are those of Charles in *APOT* and Andersen in *OTP*. Vaillant, followed by Pennington, has only 23 chapters. In Vaillant's numbering the ascent is described in chaps. 3-9.

49. See A. Yarbro Collins, "The Seven Heavens in Jewish and Christian Apocalypses," in *Cosmology and Eschatology*, 21-54; Bauckham, *The Fate of the Dead*, 84-6; Wright, *The Early History of Heaven*, 164-81. The motif is generally thought to be of Babylonian origin. Whether it is related to the planets or spheres is disputed.

The instructions in 2 *Enoch* are divided into three distinct exhortations: the first summarizes the revelation and draws the morals (39–55); the second is Enoch's parting testament to Methusalem and his brothers (58–63); the third is a farewell address to the multitude assembled to see him (65–66). The story of Melchizedek is a formally distinct unit.[50] It has sometimes been thought to be of different origin,[51] but is now generally regarded as integral to 2 *Enoch*.[52]

The debt of 2 *Enoch* to 1 *Enoch* lies mainly in the tradition that Enoch had ascended to the heavens and returned to instruct his sons.[53] Although occasional details (e.g., the reference to the Watchers in chap. 18)[54] reflect the earlier books, both the cosmology and the ethical message of 2 *Enoch* are largely independent of 1 *Enoch*. One intriguing point of continuity concerns the 364-day calendar, but more than one calendar is reflected in 2 *Enoch*, and the significance of calendrical considerations is less than clear.[55]

At the beginning of the book Enoch is "in great trouble, weeping with my eyes" and asleep on his couch, when "two very big men," obviously angels, come to escort him to the heavens. In the course of the ascent, two kinds of material are emphasized: cosmological and eschatological.[56] The

50. Orlov, "Melchizedek Legend of 2 *(Slavonic) Enoch*," in idem, *From Apocalypticism to Merkabah Mysticism*, 423-39.

51. Fischer, *Eschatologie und Jenseitserwartung*, 40.

52. H. W. Attridge, "Melchizedek in Some Early Christian Texts and 2 Enoch," in Orlov and Boccaccini, eds., *New Perspectives on 2 Enoch*, 394. Charles A. Gieschen, "Enoch and Melchizedek: The Concern for Supra-Human Priestly Mediators in 2 Enoch," ibid., 369-85, argues for ideological continuity between Enoch and Melchizedek in 2 *Enoch* in a concern for a supra-human priestly mediator. Attridge distinguishes different strands in the Melchizedek tradition, in dialogue with the Christian appropriation of Melchizedek in the Epistle to the Hebrews.

53. For various nuances see Kelley Coblentz Bautch and Daniel Assefa, "Patriarch, Prophet, Author, Angelic Rival: Exploring the Relationship of 1 Enoch to 2 Enoch in Light of the Figure of Enoch," in Orlov and Boccaccini, eds., *New Perspectives on 2 Enoch*, 181-89.

54. Andrei A. Orlov, "The Watchers of Satanail: The Fallen Angels Traditions in 2 Enoch," in Orlov and Boccaccini, eds., *New Perspectives on 2 Enoch*, 149-80.

55. Basil Lourié, "Calendrical Elements in 2 Enoch," in Orlov and Boccaccini, eds., *New Perspectives on 2 Enoch*, 191-219. Daniel Stökl Ben Ezra, "Halakha, Calendars, and the Provenances of 2 Enoch," ibid., 229-42, associates the 364-day calendar with the oldest stratum of 2 Enoch, and argues that it points to a Jewish group with allegiance to one of the groups behind 1 Enoch, Jubilees, or the Essenes.

56. For a summary of the contents of the various heavens, see Böttrich, *Weltweisheit, Menschheitsethik, Urkult*, 150.

cosmological emphasis is dominant in the first, fourth, and sixth heavens.[57] In the first, Enoch sees the angels who govern the stars and the elements; in the fourth, the movements of the sun and moon and regulation of time; and in the sixth, the seven angels who supervise the order of the world. The second, third, and fifth heavens reveal eschatological rewards and punishments. The second heaven contains the place of punishment of the rebellious angels. The third contains paradise, which is both the original Garden of Eden and the place prepared for the just.[58] This heaven also contains, in the north, the place of punishment for sinners. In the fifth heaven Enoch meets the Watchers, who are mourning the fall of their fellow angels. He tells how he has seen their place of punishment and urges the Watchers to persevere in the service of God. Finally, in the seventh heaven Enoch enters the heavenly court, is anointed with sweet oil, given new garments, and transformed to an angel-like state.[59] The exaltation of Enoch is already recounted in the epilogues to the Similitudes of Enoch, but it is described more fully here. It would be taken further again in the later mystical text, *3 Enoch* or *Sefer Hekalot*, where Enoch is enthroned in heaven and called "the lesser YHWH."[60] In the words of Philip Alexander, "what is involved is little short of the deification of man."[61]

The transformed Enoch is reminiscent of postbiblical traditions about the glorious state of the primeval Adam.[62] For example, the Slavonic text can be interpreted to mean that he is venerated by angels (although the angels may be doing obeisance to God rather than to Enoch). Andrei Orlov

57. Orlov, "Secrets of Creation in 2 (Slavonic) Enoch," in Orlov and Boccaccini, eds., *New Perspectives on 2 Enoch*, 175-95.

58. Enoch does not actually see the righteous dead. Bauckham, *The Fate of the Dead*, 88.

59. M. Himmelfarb, "Revelation and Rapture: The Transformation of the Visionary in the Ascent Apocalypses," in J. J. Collins and J. H. Charlesworth, eds., *Mysteries and Revelations: Apocalyptic Studies since the Uppsala Colloquium* (JSPSup 9; Sheffield: JSOT Press, 1991) 83, notes that this process suggests priestly investiture. On the motif of oil, see Orlov, *The Enoch-Metatron Tradition*, 229-31.

60. *3 Enoch* 12:5. See P. S Alexander, "3 (Hebrew Apocalypse of) Enoch," *OTP* 1. 265.

61. P. S. Alexander, "From Son of Adam to Second God. Transformations of the Biblical Enoch," in M. E. Stone and T. E. Bergren, eds., *Biblical Figures Outside the Bible* (Harrisburg, PA: Trinity Press International, 1998) 111. Compare Fletcher-Louis, "2 Enoch and the New Perspective on Apocalyptic,"136-37.

62. Orlov, *The Enoch Metatron Tradition*, 211-53; Compare M. E. Stone, "The Fall of Satan and Adam's Penance: Three Notes on the Books of Adam and Eve," *JTS* 44 (1993) 143-56.

sees here a polemic against the Adamic tradition. What he demonstrates, however, is at most an assimilation of Enoch and Adam. Different groups may have looked to Enoch or Adam as the prototypical man, but if there is polemic here it is subtle and implicit.[63]

Martha Himmelfarb has noted that "the combination of clothing and anointing suggests that the process by which Enoch becomes an angel is a heavenly version of priestly investiture," and that elsewhere in 2 *Enoch* he is regarded as a priest.[64] Most striking in this regard is the statement in 2 *Enoch* 64:5 that Enoch is the one who carried away the sin of mankind. Orlov takes this as anti-Adamic polemic: the sin that is taken away is the sin of Adam.[65] Thereby he recovers the glory of Adam. Fletcher-Louis goes farther and declares this to be the hermeneutical key to the entire work.[66] The passage, however, is exceptional in 2 *Enoch*, and the textual formulations vary. As Grant Macaskil has noted, "Enoch's salvific role is fundamentally that of a revealer, and it is his revelation that deals with the problem of sin."[67]

The angel Vreveil (Uriel?) dictates to Enoch "all things in heaven and earth and sea, the courses and dwellings of all the elements, the seasons of the years, the courses and mutations of the days, and the commandments and teachings" (chap. 23). Enoch writes them all down in 360 books. Then God himself tells him how he created the world. The account is very different from that of Genesis. "All creation" that God wished to create is contained in a stone in the belly of "the very great Adoil," and the foundation of creation is brought forth by another mythical monster Arouchaz. Enoch is then given thirty days to transmit what he has learned to his children.

The purpose of Enoch's revelation is stated by God in chaps. 33–35 (Vaillant, chap. 12). His writings are to survive the impending flood, which will come upon humanity because of idolatry, injustice, and fornication. They will be the means of salvation for humanity after the flood. The instructions of Enoch to his sons and the assembled multitude have their basis in the cosmology and eschatology revealed in the course of his ascent.

---

63. Böttrich, "The Book of the Secrets of Enoch," in Orlov and Boccaccini, eds., *New Perspectives on 2 Enoch*, 61-63, opposes the view that 2 *Enoch* is engaging in polemics.

64. Himmelfarb, *Ascent to Heaven,* 40. Enoch is one of the great priests in 2 *Enoch* 71:32.

65. Orlov, *The Enoch-Metatron Tradition*, 232-34.

66. Fletcher-Louis, "2 Enoch and the New Perspective on Apocalyptic," 141.

67. Macaskill, *Revealed Wisdom and Inaugurated Eschatology in Ancient Judaism and Early Christianity* (JSJSup 115; Leiden: Brill, 2007) 225.

In content, they are remarkably humanistic: they are mainly concerned with such matters as clothing the naked and feeding the hungry.[68] There are warnings against idolatry, but the most striking theme is the insistence that whoever offends "the face of a man" offends the face of God (44:1; compare 52:6; 60:1). This ethic is grounded in creation: God made man in his own likeness (44:1).[69] Likewise Enoch reminds Methusalem and his brothers of the relation between man and beast established at creation, but this in turn is linked directly to the judgment, when even the souls of the animals will accuse humankind (chap. 58). The sin of idolatry is shown by Enoch's experience of the sole authority of God in the heavens and the fact that all the heavenly hosts acknowledge his supremacy (33:7). Yet the appeal to the order of creation is balanced throughout by an appeal to the coming judgment.[70] When Enoch returns to earth he begins by summarizing the mysteries he has learned (39–55). The account of the secrets of nature culminates in the assertion that "before man was, a judgment place was prepared for him" (49:2), and the moral instructions, complete with blessings and curses, are given in the light of that assertion, for "all this will be laid bare in the weighing scales and on the books on the day of the great judgment" (52:15). Similarly, in the course of the ascent, the places of reward and punishment in the third heaven provide the occasion for lists of virtues and vices. Cosmology and eschatology, then, are complementary factors that support the ethical message of the book. Indeed, eschatology is built into the cosmology of *2 Enoch*, since provision for the judgment is an integral part of creation from the beginning.

Unlike many of the apocalypses we have reviewed, *2 Enoch* does not appear to have been written in the context of any great historical crisis. We are not told why Enoch is weeping and grieving in the opening chapter. We may infer from the words attributed to God in chaps. 33–35 that the underlying problem is the sinful conduct of humanity, which will provoke the flood.[71] The threat of the flood, of course, pertains to the time of the pseudepigraphical visionary Enoch, but it carries the implication of another judgment now to come. The problem, however, is no more specific

68. Grant Macaskill, *Revealed Wisdom*, 204-7, notes the similarity of *2 Enoch* to the Gospel of Matthew in this respect.

69. Katell Berthelot, *'L'humanité de l'autre homme' dans la pensée juive ancienne* (JSJSup 87; Leiden: Brill, 2004) 183-89. Macaskill, *Revealed Wisdom*, 212-14.

70. On the interplay of eschatology and ethics in *2 Enoch* see Macaskill, *Revealed Wisdom*, 217.

71. Vaillant, *Le Livre des Secrets*, 3. Compare *1 Enoch* 83.

than human sinfulness, the prevalence of idolatry and injustice. *2 Enoch,* then, has the character of a reflection on the human situation in general. As such it constitutes a kind of wisdom book.[72]

The wisdom of Enoch is apocalyptic wisdom, which posits a supernatural revelation not normally accessible to humanity. It shares with the Jewish wisdom tradition the conviction that right conduct depends on right understanding. For right understanding, however, it is necessary to go beyond the bounds of normal human experience to discover the order of creation, the geography of the heavens, and the nature of the final judgment. This revelation not only transcends the scope of traditional, proverbial wisdom. It also bypasses the Mosaic covenant.[73] Enoch goes to the source of creation. No account is taken of a special history of Israel. It is noteworthy too that the moral exhortations do not mention the peculiarly Jewish laws such as circumcision or dietary regulations. In the words of Lawrence Schiffman, "the phenomenon we call halakhah is completely absent in the book of 2 Enoch."[74] Schiffman concludes, "we do not find evidence that this text emerges from a community of practicing Jews who would have been united with other Jews in the exegesis of biblical law and tradition."[75] But Schiffman assumes a normative view of Judaism, to which halakhah is central. Such a view was typical of Judaism in the Second Temple period, but not without exceptions. We have seen that the Mosaic covenant played little if any role in the tradition

72. The sapiential character of *2 Enoch* is emphasized by Böttrich, *Weltweisheit, Menschheitsethik, Urkult,* 162. See also J. J. Collins, "Wisdom, Apocalypticism, and Generic Compatibility," in L. G. Perdue, B. B. Scott, and W. J. Wiseman, eds., *In Search of Wisdom: Essays in Memory of John G. Gammie* (Louisville: Westminster John Knox, 1993) 177-78 (= *Seers, Sibyls, and Sages,* 385-408).

73. See especially Grant Macaskill, "Personal Salvation and Rigorous Obedience: The Soteriology of 2 Enoch," in Gurtner, ed., *This World and the World to Come,* 127-42. Some scholars have tried to insist that *2 Enoch* has an implicit interpretation of the Mosaic law. So K.-W. Niebuhr, *Gesetz und Paränese: Katechismusartige Weisungsreihen in der frühjüdischen Literatur* (WUNT 2/28; Tübingen: Mohr Siebeck, 1987) 192-94; Böttrich, *Weltweisheit, Menschheitsethik, Urkult,* 178-80. Böttrich concludes correctly, however, that *2 Enoch* envisions a kind of natural law.

74. Lawrence H. Schiffman, "2 Enoch and Halakhah," in Orlov and Boccaccini, eds., *New Perspectives on 2 Enoch,* 227. Stökl Ben Ezra, "Halakha, Calendars, and the Provenances of 2 Enoch," ibid., 229-42, in contrast, finds "enough halakhic reminiscences to firmly place the first stratum of 2 Enoch, which coincides approximately with the short version minus the Melkizedek appendix, in Second Temple Judaism" (241), but argues that material added later was unfamiliar with, or opposed to, basic concepts of Jewish halakha.

75. Ibid.

that makes up *1 Enoch*. Richard Bauckham draws an analogy with Ben Sira, and notes that Sirach's teaching was not meant as an alternative to the law.[76] But unlike Ben Sira, *2 Enoch* does not mention the law at all. Bauckham explains this by the fact that *2 Enoch* is supposed to come from the ante-diluvian period, but we have seen in the case of *Jubilees* that Torah-focused Jewish authors were not troubled by anachronism. The broadly humanistic insistence on justice and dignity conforms rather to the common ethic of Diaspora Judaism and is distinguished as Jewish only by its prohibition of idolatry and its reliance on the authority of the Jewish sage Enoch.[77]

In the case of Moses, even more than that of Adam, some scholars have detected polemics in *2 Enoch*.[78] Orlov assumes that such polemics can already be inferred in the earlier Enochic books, and that the exaltation of Moses by such authors as Philo was a counter-attack. This view of widespread polemics is surely dubious. In the case of *2 Enoch*, however, he can point to Enoch's claim that he has seen the face of God (*2 En* 39: 3-6, short version), whereas Moses was denied the vision of God's face in Exod 33:18-23. Philip Alexander comments that "Moses and Enoch are being set up in some sense as rivals, as representing competing paradigms of Judaism. The circles that looked primarily to *Moshe rabbenu* had a different outlook from those that looked primarily to *Hanokh rabbenu*."[79] Even in the late first century CE, the Mosaic paradigm was not the only model of Judaism available.

In view of the general nature of the instructions of Enoch, it seems very unlikely that this work is the product of a conventicle or closed circle. The only element that suggests the practice of a special group is the peculiar requirement that the four legs of a sacrificial animal be tied together. Since this practice is contrary to the usage in the Mishnah, it has been thought to be "the accepted rite of a sect, which repudiated the sacrificial customs prevailing in Jerusalem."[80] The practice was common in Egypt, however, and the author of *2 Enoch* may have assumed it in

---

76. Bauckham, "Apocalypses," 152.

77. On the common ethic of Diaspora Judaism see Collins, *Between Athens and Jerusalem*, 155-85.

78. Orlov, *The Enoch-Metatron Tradition*, 254-303.

79. Alexander, "From Son of Adam to Second God," 110.

80. S. Pines, "Eschatology and the Concept of Time in the Slavonic Book of Enoch," in R. J. Z. Werblowski and J. C. Bleeker, eds., *Types of Redemption* (Leiden: Brill, 1970) 75. Compare *m. Tamid* 4:1.

ignorance rather than repudiation of the custom in Jerusalem.[81] In any case, 2 *Enoch* makes no attempt to promote membership in a distinct group. The purpose of 2 *Enoch* is primarily hortatory. The illocutionary function of consolation, which is prominent in 4 Ezra and 2 *Baruch*, recedes here. Yet the impact of the book cannot be adequately appreciated if it is reduced to the ethical teaching. The ethics of 2 *Enoch* acquire their authority ultimately "from the mouth of the Lord" (39:2). The persuasive force of the apocalypse does not rely, as prophecy often does, on "the word of the Lord." It derives from the total view of the universe, guaranteed by the experience of Enoch — "this have my eyes seen from the beginning even to the end" (40:8). It is important that the places of judgment, reward, and punishment are already prepared and in existence, and are the potential objects of mystical experience such as Enoch's.[82] The eschatology is primarily concerned with the fate of the individual after death. In this respect, the transformation of Enoch into an angel-like state is paradigmatic. But the apocalypse also provides for a general judgment with cosmic effects. The individual cannot be divorced from society or from the cosmos. The synoptic view of cosmic order and of the place of the individual within it provides the basis for persuasion and also for consolation in the face of whatever distress may be encountered in the present time.[83]

As in all the apocalypses, the conception of cosmic order in 2 *Enoch* involves a sharp division between the present world of normal human experience and the "other" transcendent world revealed to Enoch. Here the division is primarily in spatial terms, although the temporal dimension is also present in the expectation of the coming judgment. The persuasiveness of the book depends on the acceptance of, or belief in, the reality of the transcendent world. Faith, in the sense of insight into the heavenly world, is the underpinning of present action.

---

81. Cf. Böttrich, *Weltweisheit, Menschheitsethik, Urkult*, 201-2.

82. On the mysticism of 2 *Enoch*, see I. Gruenwald, *Apocalyptic and Merkavah Mysticism* (Leiden: Brill, 1980) 47-51; C. Rowland, *The Open Heaven: A Study of Apocalyptic in Judaism and Early Christianity* (New York: Crossroad, 1982) 85, and especially Schäfer, *The Origins of Jewish Mysticism*, 77-85.

83. Böttrich, *Weltweisheit, Menschheitsethik, Urkult*, 209-11, sees 2 *Enoch* as a collection of smaller *Gattungen*, held together primarily by their midrashic grounding in Genesis. But this is to miss the coherence of the work, which is constituted by the interplay of heavenly revelation, ethical teaching, and eschatological horizon.

## 3 Baruch

Unlike *2 Enoch*, *3 Baruch* takes its point of departure from a specific problem: Baruch is weeping over the captivity of Jerusalem. The analogy of situations strongly suggests that the real date of composition was after 70 CE. Egyptian provenance is suggested primarily by the affinities with other products of Diaspora Judaism.[84] Some verses in chaps. 4 and 11–15 are clearly Christian, but the secondary character of the Christian redaction is obvious in chap. 4. The inserted verses give the vine a positive connotation, but the chapter still concludes by asserting that nothing good comes through it. Christian authorship of the whole book was advocated by M. R. James at the end of the nineteenth century[85] and is still occasionally entertained.[86] The Christian redaction goes beyond mere insertions and constitutes a rereading of the book, but the core composition is rightly recognized as Jewish.[87] The Slavonic version is claimed to represent a pre-Christianized stage, which does not contain the Greek additions.[88]

As in *2 Enoch,* an angel comes to escort Baruch through the heavens. In this case only five heavens are mentioned. Whether this number is original, or is an abbreviation of the more usual seven, has been much disputed.[89] Origen, *De Principiis,* 2.3.6, refers to a book of Baruch that treats of seven heavens, and this is usually assumed to be *3 Baruch,* but this is not certain, and besides Origen may not have known the work to which he referred first-hand. It is apparent that the dwelling of God is above the fifth heaven, but unlike other apocalyptic visionaries, Baruch does not ascend to the divine throne room. Several recent studies have argued that the five-heaven ascent is original.[90] The most persuasive argument in this

84. J.-C. Picard, *Apocalypsis Baruchi Graece* (PVTG 2; Leiden: Brill, 1967) 77-78; Fischer, *Eschatologie und Jenseitserwartung,* 75. The main affinities are with *2 Enoch* and the *Testament of Abraham.*

85. M. R. James, "The Apocalypse of Baruch," in *Apocrypha Anecdota II* (Texts and Studies 5/1; Cambridge: Cambridge University Press, 1897) li-lxxi.

86. Himmelfarb, *Ascent to Heaven,* 87.

87. For a sophisticated treatment of both Jewish and Christian editions of the work, see D. C. Harlow, *The Greek Apocalypse of Baruch (3 Baruch) in Hellenistic Judaism and Early Christianity* (SVTP 12; Leiden: Brill, 1996).

88. Alexander Kulik, *3 Baruch. Greek-Slavonic Apocalypse of Baruch* (CEJL; Berlin: de Gruyter, 2010) 14. Kulik lists the Greek interpretations on pp. 20-21. Bauckham, "Apocalypses," 182-83, claims that 16:4-8 in the Slavonic is Christian, but it is not clear why.

89. See Harlow, *The Greek Apocalypse of Baruch,* 34-76.

90. J. C. Picard, "Observations sur l'Apocalypse grecque de Baruch I: Cadre his-

regard has been offered by Daniel Harlow, who holds that the apocalypse presupposes the usual schema of seven heavens, but that Baruch's ascent is aborted, to make the point that a human visionary cannot attain full unmediated access to the divine.[91] This apocalypse is also exceptional in rejecting the transformation of the visionary to angelic status.[92]

The first two heavens are occupied respectively by those who built the tower of strife against God and those who gave counsel to build the tower. Both now have hybrid animal forms ("faces of oxen, horns of stags, feet of goats," etc.). The third heaven is the most complex. There Baruch sees a dragon that devours the bodies of the wicked, and Hades in the form of a monster that drinks from the sea. (In 5:1-3, Hades is simply the belly of the dragon.)[93] He also sees the vine, "the plant that led Adam astray," and hears of its sinful effects. He sees how the phoenix shields the world from the rays of the sun, and how the sun is defiled by witnessing the sins of humanity and must be purified every day. Finally, he sees the movements of the moon. The fourth heaven is occupied by a multitude of birds that sing the praise of the Lord. These are generally thought to represent the souls of the righteous.[94] The gate to the fifth heaven is closed, until Michael opens it. In the Greek version, Michael takes the merits of humanity in baskets up to God in a higher heaven; in the Slavonic, he takes their prayers. He returns with rewards for the meritorious and a stern insistence that those who have no merits fail through their own fault.[95] Baruch is then returned to earth.

*3 Baruch* contains no testament or farewell address to serve as the vehicle for its hortatory message. That message is conveyed in the course

---

torique et efficacité symbolique," *Semitica* 20 (1970) 77-103; idem, " 'Je te montrerai d'autres mystères plus grandes que ceux-ci . . .': Notes sur 3 Bar et quelques écrits apparentés," in *Histoire et Anthropologie des Communautés Juives et Chrétiennes dans les Sociétes Anciennes* (Canal 8; Paris: Centre de Recherches de l'École Pratique des Hautes Études, 1991) 17-40; J. E. Wright, "The Cosmography of the Greek Apocalypse of Baruch and Its Affinities," diss., Brandeis University, 1992.

91. Harlow, *The Greek Apocalypse of Baruch*, 34-76. Wright, *The Early History of Heaven*, 173, supposes that the heavenly temple where God resides is in the fifth heaven, but unapproachable to all except Michael. See the discussion by Kulik, *3 Baruch*, 306-22.

92. Himmelfarb, *Ascent to Heaven*, 87.

93. On the relation between Hades and the dragon, see Fischer, *Eschatologie und Jenseitserwartung*, 80-82.

94. H. M. Hughes, "3 Baruch or The Greek Apocalypse of Baruch," in Charles, ed., *APOT*, 2:539. Compare *b. Sanhedrin* 92b.

95. This is clearer in the Greek than in the Slavonic. In the latter, he brings a response to the prayers of humanity.

of the revelations especially by the lists of vices: those associated with the vine and those which defile the sun in chap. 4, and those reported by the angels in chap. 13. Most of the sins are commonplace — murder, adultery, etc. — but the special blame attached to the vine gives the book an ascetic accent. The hortatory aspect of the book derives from the fact that those who sin "are surrendering themselves to eternal fire" (4:16). The moral, that one should do otherwise, is clearly implied.

In *3 Baruch*, however, the illocutionary function of consolation has a clearer role than in *2 Enoch* and predominates over the exhortation. Baruch is initially grieving over the fall of Jerusalem at the hands of the Gentiles: "Lord, why did you set your vineyard on fire, and lay it waste?" The angel's response to his distress is remarkable: "Understand, O man greatly beloved, and do not trouble yourself so greatly over the salvation of Jerusalem. . . . Come and I will show you the mysteries of God."[96] The mysteries of God are the five heavens through which Baruch is then guided. The heavenly tour does not so much answer Baruch's questions as distract from them by placing the problems in the broader perspective of the structure of the entire universe. This process has been described as an "apocalyptic cure."[97] The grief of Judeans after the destruction of 70 CE is given fictional expression in the story of Baruch. Both author and reader can then imaginatively identify with Baruch in his ascent through the heavens. The wonders of "the mysteries of God" allay the original grief and fear, and so at the end we are caught up with Baruch in glorifying God. The problem is resolved in a manner similar to what we have seen in *4 Ezra*, not by rational argument but by concentration on wonderful revelations.

Three elements in the revelations respond directly to Baruch's original grief. First, he witnesses the punishment of the builders of the tower — that is, the Babylonians. Presumably these find their counterparts in the Romans, the latter-day destroyers of Jerusalem. It is noteworthy, however, that they are not said to be punished for destroying Jerusalem but for cruelty in imposing the labor of brick-making, even on a woman in the hour of childbirth,[98] and for attempting to discover the nature of heaven. We may see here an indictment of Rome for arrogance and oppression, but this is not in itself the cause of the fall of Jerusalem.

96. The Slavonic reads: "It came to Jerusalem to accept this." Kulik, *3 Baruch*. 103.
97. Picard, "Observations sur l'Apocalypse grecque de Baruch," with reference to Lévi-Strauss's discussion of the "shamanistic cure." For a discussion of the therapeutic effect of *3 Baruch* from a psychological perspective, see Daschke, *City of Ruins*, 174-86.
98. The brick making recalls the labors of the Israelites in Egypt.

Second, the vine is singled out as the tree that led Adam astray. In chap. 1, however, Israel, or Jerusalem, is the vineyard of God. If the symbolism is used consistently, the implications are stunning.[99] If no good comes through the vine, no good can come through the vineyard either. This would amount to a definitive rejection of Jerusalem, unparalleled in Jewish literature, which might, however, be seen as the culmination of a tendency in Diaspora Judaism towards independence from the homeland. There is no explicit allusion to Jerusalem (or the vineyard) in the discussion of the vine in chap. 4, and so we cannot be certain of the implication, but this interpretation of the symbolism would throw much light on the angel's advice not to trouble oneself about the salvation of Jerusalem. There is certainly no hint of a restoration of Jerusalem in *3 Baruch,* and in this regard it differs sharply from 4 Ezra and 2 *Baruch.*

The third passage that bears on Baruch's opening question is found in chap. 16. Michael reports the pronouncement of God on those who had no merits: "Be not sad of countenance and weep not, nor let the sons of men alone. But since they angered me in their works, go and make them envious and angry and provoked against *a people that is* no people, a people that has no understanding. Further, besides these, send for the caterpillar and the unwinged locust, and the mildew. . . . For they did not hearken to my voice, nor did they observe my commandments. . . ."[100] The covenantal overtones of this passage are obvious; 16:2 is a paraphrase, verging on a quotation of the LXX of Deut 32:21. The people of whom the Jews are now envious and against whom they are angry — chiefly the Romans — are a people that is no people and has no understanding. Yet this slighting of the Gentiles involves no absolution for Jerusalem. The Jews are provoked in this way because they as a people had no merits to present to God (although the righteousness of individuals like Baruch is surely presumed). The covenant has been broken, and there is no hint that it will be restored. Instead it is replaced with a system of individual rewards and punishments. This position might be seen as the logical culmination of the kind of analysis advanced by Ezra in 4 Ezra 3–9. In this context the salvation of Jerusalem is of little significance.

The resolution of Baruch's distress depends on the reality of the heavenly world disclosed in the visions. *3 Baruch* does not even seem to envisage a public general judgment as 2 *Enoch* did. The individualized judgment

---

99. Picard, "Observations sur l'Apocalypse grecque de Baruch," 101-2.

100. Trans. H. M. Hughes, in Charles, ed., *APOT,* 2:541. This passage is not found in the Slavonic. Kulik, *3 Baruch,* 373.

of the dead is presented as the solution to the public historical crisis of the fall of Jerusalem.[101] The eschatology, in turn, is integrated into a total view of the universe, the credibility of which is enhanced by the wealth of cosmological detail. The system of judgment is not merely future but is already in operation. Human conduct and historical crises must be related to an understanding of the cosmic order, but this understanding in turn depends on supernatural revelations and so in effect becomes a matter of belief or of imagination about a transcendent world.

## The Testament of Abraham

The final apocalypse of the Hellenistic Diaspora is the *Testament of Abraham*.[102] In this case the generic classification is ambiguous.[103] Abraham's heavenly journey is only one episode in the story of his death and is narrated in the third person (so the work is not strictly pseudepigraphical). Yet the apocalypse proper is not merely a subordinate element but provides the crucial revelation on which the story turns. What is important here is not so much to decide whether the *Testament of Abraham* should be labeled an "apocalypse" as to understand how Abraham's ascent and vision of the judgment function in the context of the whole narrative. In no case can the work be said to be a "testament." Indeed, Abraham conspicuously fails to make a testament.[104]

---

101. This is disputed by Bauckham, "Apocalypses," 182-85, but his reasoning is incoherent. On the one hand he denies that there is any explicit eschatology in *3 Baruch* (183). On the other, he admits that the text refers to the judgment of the dead in the case of the builders of the tower. He claims that since Deut 32 goes on to declare that God will have mercy on his people, this must be implicit in *3 Baruch* too, although 3 Baruch conspicuously says nothing to this effect.

102. For text and translation, see M. E. Stone, *The Testament of Abraham* (Missoula, MT: Society of Biblical Literature, 1972); F. Schmidt, *Le Testament grec d'Abraham* (Tübingen: Mohr Siebeck, 1986). See the full commentary by Dale Allison, *Testament of Abraham* (CEJL; Berlin: de Gruyter, 2003).

103. See the full discussion by Allison, *Testament of Abraham*, 12-27; Jared W. Ludlow, *Abraham Meets Death. Narrative Humor in the Testament of Abraham* (JSPSup 41; Sheffield: Sheffield Academic Press, 2002) 152-80. Also E. Janssen, *Testament Abrahams* (JSHRZ 3/2; Gütersloh: Mohn, 1975) 196; cf. Dean-Otting, *Heavenly Journeys*, 175.

104. A. B. Kolenkow, "The Genre Testament and the Testament of Abraham," in G. W. E. Nickelsburg, ed., *Studies on the Testament of Abraham* (Missoula, MT: Scholars Press, 1976) 139-52.

The *Testament of Abraham* is preserved in two recensions. While both may go back to a common original, the longer form (Recension A) provides the more coherent outline of the story.[105] The original language was most probably Greek.[106] Egyptian provenance is supported by parallels in Egyptian mythology (e.g., the weighing of the souls) and in Egyptian Jewish literature (e.g., the *Testament of Job*).[107] While the book was transmitted by Christians, most scholars assume that the original was Jewish. For Dale Allison, the telling point is not the overwhelming number of verses whose language or thought has Jewish parallels but rather the places that have no Christian parallels and indeed clash with what we otherwise know of Christian beliefs.[108] It is inconceivable that a Christian author would have made Abel the judge in the judgment scene and not mentioned the exalted Christ.[109] The date is usually put in the first century CE on the basis of parallels to other Hellenistic Jewish writings, but clear evidence is lacking.[110] If it is indeed the work of an Egyptian Jew, it is very unlikely to be later than the Diaspora Revolt of 115-18 CE, especially in light of its irenic spirit.[111]

The *Testament of Abraham* takes as its point of departure the end of Abraham's life, when the archangel Michael is sent to announce his death. The opening chapters illustrate the virtue of Abraham, so that Michael "cannot pronounce the mention of death to that righteous man, for I have

105. G. W. E. Nickelsburg, "Structure and Message in the Testament of Abraham," in *Studies on the Testament of Abraham*, 92. F. Schmidt, however, has argued for the priority of the short recension, "The Two Recensions of the Testament of Abraham: In Which Way Did the Transformation Take Place?" ibid., 65-83.

106. M. Delcor, *Le Testament d'Abraham* (Leiden: Brill, 1973) 34; Janssen, *Testament Abrahams,* 198-99. N. Turner, who once defended a Hebrew original of recension B ("The Testament of Abraham: A Study of the Original Language, Place of Origin, Authorship and Relevance," diss., University of London, 1953), has now abandoned this view. See E. P. Sanders, "The Testaments of the Three Patriarchs," in Charlesworth, ed., *OTP* 1:873-74.

107. Delcor, *Le Testament,* 67-68; Janssen, *Testament Abrahams,* 199-201; Allison, *Testament of Abraham,* 32-33.

108. Allison, *Testament of Abraham,* 29. He notes especially the "soteriological optimism" regarding the salvation of sinners. Davila, *The Provenance of the Pseudepigrapha,* 205-7, allows that it could have been composed by a Jew, a gentile Christian, or a God-fearer.

109. Nickelsburg, *Jewish Literature,* 327.

110. Annette Yoshiko Reed, "Testament of Abraham," in Feldman, Kugel, and Schiffman, eds., *Outside the Bible,* 1672, finds the resonances of rabbinic Judaism most striking, specifically traditions about the death of Moses in *Sifre Deuteronomy* and *Devarim Rabbah.*

111. Allison, *Testament of Abraham,* 38-39.

not seen his like upon the earth — merciful, hospitable, just, truthful, pious, refraining from any evil action" (chap. 4). Yet when Abraham learns Michael's identity and mission, he refuses to go with him but requests to see "the whole of the inhabited world and all the creations" while still in the body (chap. 9). He is then taken in the cherubim chariot and shown the whole world, and he is then brought to the gate of heaven to witness the judgment. Yet when he is returned to earth in chap. 15, he still refuses to go. Then Death is sent to him in disguise (chap. 16). Abraham still refuses to go and asks for further revelations — this time the true nature of Death and all his metamorphoses. Finally Death has to take Abraham by deceit, by inducing him to kiss his hand. The angels convey his soul to heaven. There is evident parallelism between the mission of Michael and the heavenly tour, on the one hand, and the mission of Death and his revelations, on the other.[112]

The most striking feature of the *Testament of Abraham* is the patriarch's reluctance to die. His refusal to obey the divine command in this regard, despite protestations of his loyalty (e.g., chap. 9), not only constitutes a veritable parody of the biblical Abraham, but also is highly ironic in view of Michael's admiration of his righteousness. The point of this irony is related to the underlying problem of the work, which is that "the common inexorable bitter cup of death" (chap. 1) comes upon all, including Abraham. If Abraham stands apart from the rest of humankind by his righteousness, he at least shares the instinctive human denial of death. He becomes, then, a figure with whom we can identify, so that by following through his (fictional) experience we can experience an "apocalyptic cure" for the fear of death.

For those who believe in a judgment of the dead, the fear of death is often bound up with fear of the judgment, as Epicurus already knew. Consequently, the revelations to Abraham in the course of his ascent bear directly on the judgment. This motif is introduced already in the overview of the earth. When Abraham sees thieves and fornicators, he prays that they be destroyed on the spot, and so they are. God is moved to bid Michael turn the chariot back: "For behold, Abraham has not sinned, and he has no mercy upon the sinners. I, in contrast, made the world, and I do not wish to destroy any one of them, but I await the death of the sinner, until he turns and lives" (chap. 10). Then at the first gate of heaven Abraham

---

112. Nickelsburg, *Jewish Literature*, 323-24. On the characterization of Death, see Ludlow, *Abraham Meets Death*, 95-118.

sees the grief of Adam "mourning over the destruction of the wicked, for the lost are many but the saved are few" (chap. 11). The judgment itself is a fearsome spectacle.[113] Angels with fiery whips drive hordes of souls to destruction. Abel, son of Adam, presides over the judgment[114] "looking like the sun, like a son of God," with recording angels on the right and on the left. Other angels weigh the souls in the balance and test them in fire. Abraham is told that this is only the first judgment. A second by the twelve tribes of Israel and a third by God himself will follow.

The catalysis in this revelation comes when a soul is found whose sins and righteous deeds are equally balanced. Abraham is moved to ask what it needs to be saved. He asks the angel to join him in prayer, and the soul is saved. Abraham now repents of having had sinners destroyed during his tour. Most importantly, he recognizes that his previous zeal was sinful and prays for forgiveness.[115] He is forgiven, and the sinners are restored to life. Abraham is informed that God does not requite in death those whom he destroyed living on the earth.

The tour on the chariot, then, is not a mere diversion, even though it does not persuade Abraham to yield up his soul. It puts the judgment of the dead in a new perspective. The number of the saved is still slight in proportion to the damned, as in 4 Ezra. The severity of the judgment is modified, however, by a number of considerations. First, intercession is possible. Abraham's prayer can supply the deficiency of a soul. (This was explicitly denied in 4 Ezra.) Second, God, as creator, has mercy on sinners and is less severe than a righteous human being like Abraham. He does not further punish those who have been destroyed on earth. We may add that Abraham is found to be a sinner after all, since his excessive zeal is offensive to God.

The revelations of the judgment scene also put the revelation of Death in perspective. Abraham sinned by destruction of life. Death boasts that he is "the destroyer of the world" and devastates the world for seven ages (symbolized by seven dragons' heads).[116] In all, there are 72 deaths, only

---

113. For Jewish Greek and Egyptian parallels to various motifs in the judgment scene, see G. W. E. Nickelsburg, "Eschatology in the Testament of Abraham: A Study of the Judgment Scenes in the Two Recensions," in *Studies on the Testament of Abraham*, 23-64.

114. It should be noted that "Son of Adam" would be equivalent to "son of man" in Hebrew. On this judgment scene, see Rowland, *The Open Heaven*, 107-9.

115. Kolenkow, "The Genre Testament," 142.

116. This is the only hint of a periodization of history in the *Testament of Abraham*. Compare the beast with seven heads in Revelation 17, but the idea of a seven-headed beast is ancient (e.g., the Ugaritic Shilyat of seven heads).

one of which is the just death in its fitting hour. Yet, if God has mercy on those who die prematurely, the victory of Death is hollow. Consequently, Death, for all his hideous appearance, is no longer so terrible.

Of course, the human fear of death persists. Some seven thousand servants die at the very sight of Death (they are later revived), and Abraham faints. Abraham continues to the end in his refusal to die. Yet the understanding provided by the revelation should mitigate the fear of death. Finally, the peaceful removal of Abraham's soul by the angels provides the concluding paradigm for those who follow in his footsteps.

The illocutionary function of the *Testament of Abraham* is primarily consolation. Ordinary mortals who fear death are reassured that this is only human — even Abraham was reluctant to go. Yet, if the fear is based on the judgment, there is more hope than we may have thought; and even Abraham was not without sin. The book also has a hortatory message, which is implied in the experience of Abraham. Mercy, rather than severity, is pleasing to God. The apocalyptic ascent of Abraham to the place of judgment provides the crucial underpinning for both the consolation and the exhortation.

The *Testament of Abraham* differs from 2 *Enoch* and 3 *Baruch* in its lack of attention to cosmological detail. There is no sequence of numbered heavens here. Yet the scene of the judgment at the first gate of heaven is extremely important. The *Testament of Abraham* speaks only of the judgment of individuals, not of a general judgment to come. Belief in the judgment after death and in its present ongoing reality is a presupposition of the book that provides the context for the consolation and exhortation conveyed.

It is apparent that the technique of the *Testament of Abraham* is very similar to that of 3 *Baruch*. In both cases we can speak of an "apocalyptic cure" although the underlying problems are different — in 3 *Baruch* the fate of Jerusalem, in the *Testament of Abraham* the fear of death. Like 3 *Baruch* and 2 *Enoch*, the *Testament of Abraham* is remarkably tolerant and humane in its ethics, and there is no evidence whatever that it was produced by a sect or conventicle.[117] The open and tolerant atmosphere, coupled with irony and even humor, is quite different from the stereotypes of apocalypticism and indeed marks an extreme on the spectrum of apocalyptic writings. The lack of dualism and imminent expectation or eschatological fervor should not be taken to deny that the *Testament of Abraham* is apocalyptic in any sense. The importance of this work for the genre is

---

117. Delcor ascribes the *Testament of Abraham* to the Therapeutae (*Le Testament*, 73).

that it shows how the common apocalyptic motifs of the heavenly journey and judgment scene can be used in the service of diverse viewpoints. The apocalyptic framework is not itself tied to a particular ideology. It rather constitutes the premises of argument, within which disagreement is still possible on specific matters, such as the possibility of intercession or the severity of the judgment. Belief in a transcendent world and judgment of the dead most often served to separate the sheep from the goats or sons of light from sons of darkness, but it was not necessarily so. The *Testament of Abraham* shows that these beliefs could also serve to enhance the sense of human solidarity, so that even the righteous Abraham is in need of mercy and has to submit to the common fate of death. The judgment scene in *Testament of Abraham* remains an apocalypse, although the genre of the work as a whole is mixed and ambiguous, and is arguably a parody of various genres.[118]

118. Allison, *Testament of Abraham*, 41-42.

# CHAPTER NINE

# Apocalypticism in Early Christianity

The review of Jewish apocalyptic literature in the preceding chapters has skipped over one major development in the first century CE. This was the movement associated with Jesus of Nazareth, which developed into early Christianity after his death. Originally, this was a movement within Judaism, and it pertains to the history of Jewish apocalypticism in the decades preceding and following the first Jewish revolt against Rome. Jesus preached that the kingdom of God was at hand, and he was executed by the Romans as a royal pretender. *Prima facie*, he invites comparison with the various prophets and messianic pretenders, such as Theudas and the Egyptian, described by Josephus.[1] In the case of these figures, we are entirely dependent on the brief and unsympathetic accounts of Josephus and know very little about their ideas and ambitions. In the case of Jesus, we have the opposite problem. The extended narratives of the Gospels are problematic both because of their diversity and because they are written from a perspective of faith that Jesus was the messiah, exalted as Lord.[2] These

---

1. R. A. Horsley with J. S. Hanson, *Bandits, Prophets, and Messiahs: Popular Movements at the Time of Jesus* (Harrisburg, PA: Trinity Press International, 1999); Collins, *The Scepter and the Star*, 215-28.

2. The literature on these problems is enormous. See the ongoing series of volumes by J. P. Meier, *A Marginal Jew: Rethinking the Historical Jesus*, in the Anchor Bible Reference Library, initiated with Doubleday in 1991 and continuing with Yale. As of Fall 2014, 4 volumes have appeared and a fifth is in press. See also B. D. Chilton and C. A. Evans, eds., *Studying the Historical Jesus: Evaluations of the State of Current Research* (Leiden: Brill, 1994); M. J. Borg, *Jesus in Contemporary Scholarship* (Valley Forge, PA: Trinity, 1994) and the wide-ranging essays in Tom Holmén and Stanley E. Porter, eds., *Handbook for the Study of the Historical Jesus* (4 vols.; Leiden: Brill, 2011).

problems bear directly on the role of apocalypticism in early Christianity. The New Testament only includes one example of the genre apocalypse, the book of Revelation. Both the Synoptic Gospels and the writings of Paul, however, are colored by an apocalyptic worldview to a significant degree.[3] Whether Jesus himself already shared that worldview is one of the most keenly debated issues in New Testament scholarship.

## Jesus and Eschatology

For much of the twentieth century, discussion of the historical Jesus was dominated by the work of Johannes Weiss and Albert Schweitzer.[4] Against the liberal scholarship of the nineteenth century, Weiss argued that when Jesus spoke of the kingdom he was not referring to God's rule in the human heart, but to a coming eschatological event. Schweitzer agreed, but felt that Weiss did not go far enough. All the teaching of Jesus should be seen in an eschatological perspective, for which Schweitzer coined the phrase "thoroughgoing eschatology." In the following decades the most influential New Testament scholars accepted the essential point that Weiss and Schweitzer had made. Rudolf Bultmann stated the position in classic form: "Jesus' message is connected with the hope . . . primarily documented by the *apocalyptic* literature, a hope which awaits salvation not from a miraculous change in historical (i.e., political and social) conditions, but from a cosmic catastrophe which will do away with all conditions of the present world as it is."[5] Joachim Jeremias, whose theological perspective was very different from Bultmann's, followed Schweitzer in interpreting the teaching of Jesus consistently from an eschatological point of view.[6]

---

3. See Adela Yarbro Collins, "Apocalypticism and Christian Origins," in Collins, ed., *The Oxford Handbook of Apocalyptic Literature*, 326-39.

4. J. Weiss, *Jesus' Proclamation of the Kingdom of God* (Philadelphia: Fortress, 1971; German original, 1892); A. Schweitzer, *The Quest of the Historical Jesus* (New York: Macmillan, 1968; German original, 1906). For a concise summary of scholarship, see D. C. Allison, "The Eschatology of Jesus," in J. J. Collins, ed., *The Encyclopedia of Apocalypticism*. Volume 1: *The Origins of Apocalypticism in Judaism and Early Christianity* (New York: Continuum, 1998) 267-302.

5. R. Bultmann, *Theology of the New Testament* (2 vols.; New York: Scribners, 1951–55) 1:4.

6. J. Jeremias, *New Testament Theology* (New York: Scribners, 1971).

In the late twentieth century, however, this consensus was called into question.[7] Several scholars have argued that Jesus was primarily a wisdom teacher, for whom the kingdom was not something coming with signs to be observed but was a state attainable in the present (cf. Luke 20–21). On this view, overtly apocalyptic passages like Mark 13 are creations of the early church. In part this revision was prompted by the discovery of the Gospel of Thomas among the Gnostic writings from Nag Hammadi and by the realization that it may in some cases contain sayings of Jesus in a primitive form. This document "proposes an interpretation of the sayings of Jesus which has no futuristic eschatological component, but instead proclaims the presence of divine wisdom as the true destiny of human existence."[8] Many scholars suspect that the absence of eschatology reflects the Gnostic circles in which the document was transmitted,[9] but some take it as an authentic witness to the teaching of the historical Jesus.[10] In part the reaction against Schweitzer has been bolstered by the study of the source Q, which is reconstructed from the common material in the Gospels of Matthew and Luke. John Kloppenborg has argued that the apocalyptic elements in Q are a secondary stage in the composition of the document.[11] While Kloppenborg is careful to avoid the conclusion that the older stratum of Q represents the original teaching of Jesus, that implication is sometimes drawn from his work.[12] It should be noted, moreover, that the stratigraphy proposed by Kloppenborg is of necessity hypothetical, and not all scholars are persuaded that the apocalyptic elements in Q are secondary.[13] Most

7. E.g., M. Borg, "A Temperate Case for a Non-Eschatological Jesus," *Forum* 2/3 (1986) 81-102; B. L. Mack, *A Myth of Innocence: Mark and Christian Origins* (Philadelphia: Fortress, 1988); J. D. Crossan, *The Historical Jesus: The Life of a Mediterranean Jewish Peasant* (San Francisco: HarperSanFrancisco, 1991).

8. H. Koester, *Introduction to the New Testament* (2 vols.; Philadelphia: Fortress, 1982) 2:153.

9. Meier, *A Marginal Jew*, 1:112-41.

10. J. D. Crossan, *Four Other Gospels: Shadows on the Contours of Canon* (New York: Winston, 1985) 15-62.

11. J. S. Kloppenborg, *The Formation of Q: Trajectories in Ancient Wisdom Collections* (Philadelphia: Fortress, 1987); idem, *Q, the Earliest Gospel: An Introduction to the Original Stories and Sayings of Jesus* (Louisville: Westminster John Knox Press, 2008).

12. See J. S. Kloppenborg, "The Sayings Gospel Q and the Quest of the Historical Jesus," *HTR* 89 (1996) 307-44.

13. A. Yarbro Collins, "The Son of Man Sayings in the Sayings Source," in M. P. Horgan and P. J. Kobelski, eds., *To Touch the Text: Biblical and Related Studies in Honor of Joseph A. Fitzmyer, S.J.* (New York: Crossroad, 1989) 369-89.

fundamentally, however, the revisionist view arises from the observation that the literary forms in which the Jesus tradition is preserved consist to a great degree of sayings and parables. While apocalyptic writings can certainly include hortatory sayings (cf. the Epistle of Enoch, 2 *Enoch*), the overall form and style of the Gospels are very different from those of the apocalypses. The Gospels lack many of the typical apocalyptic forms and motifs, such as visions, heavenly ascents, or extended prophecies of the periods of history.

Nonetheless, the view that Jesus was an apocalyptic prophet was not without basis, and has been vigorously defended by several scholars.[14] One of the best-attested facts about Jesus is that he preached that the kingdom of God was at hand. While the symbol of "kingdom" was used in various ways in antiquity, it lent itself to an eschatological interpretation in the context of Jewish literature from around the turn of the era, especially in literature deriving from the land of Israel that was originally composed in a Semitic language.[15] Advocates of a noneschatological Jesus argue that the phrase "kingdom of God" could just as easily have been heard as a sapiential expression.[16] John Dominic Crossan acknowledges the apocalyptic connotation, citing the *Psalms of Solomon, Testament of Moses,* and Similitudes of Enoch, all of which are likely to derive from Judea around the turn of the era. This corpus could be greatly expanded by drawing on the Dead Sea Scrolls. For the sapiential understanding, however, he has to look to the Greek-speaking Diaspora, citing Philo and the Wisdom of Solomon from Alexandrian Judaism, and the *Sentences of Sextus,* a work

---

14. Dale C. Allison, *Jesus of Nazareth. Millenarian Prophet* (Minneapolis: Fortress, 1998); Bart D. Ehrman, *Jesus. Apocalyptic Prophet of the New Millennium* (Oxford: Oxford University Press, 1999); Frederick J. Murphy, *Apocalypticism in the Bible and Its World. A Comprehensive Introduction* (Grand Rapids: Baker, 2012) 281-305; Benedict T. Viviano, "Eschatology and the Quest for the Historical Jesus," in Jerry L. Walls, ed., *The Oxford Handbook of Eschatology* (Oxford: Oxford University Press, 2008) 73-90. See also Robert J. Miller, ed., *The Apocalyptic Jesus. A Debate* (Santa Rosa, CA: Polebridge, 2001), with contributions by Allison, Borg, Crossan, and Stephen J. Patterson. The view of Crispin Fletcher-Louis, "Jesus and Apocalypticism," in Holmén and Porter, eds., *The Handbook of the Study of the Historical Jesus,* 3:2877-2909, is based on his eccentric view of apocalypticism as revelations primarily concerned with temple symbolism.

15. See D. C. Allison, "A Plea for Thorough-Going Eschatology," *JBL* 113 (1994) 659-60. O. Camponovo, *Königtum, Königsherrschaft und Reich Gottes in frühjüdischen Schriften* (Göttingen: Vandenhoeck & Ruprecht, 1984); W. Willis, ed., *The Kingdom of God in Twentieth-Century Interpretation* (Peabody, MA: Hendrickson, 1987).

16. Crossan, *The Historical Jesus,* 287.

of uncertain origin found at Nag Hammadi. These texts are far removed from the cultural context in which Jesus lived. Burton Mack has argued that "discourse about kings and kingdoms was not limited to Jewish sectarians during the Greco-Roman period. It was much more prevalent, as a matter of fact, in Hellenistic traditions of popular and school philosophy."[17] The issue here is whether Jesus should be understood in the context of Hellenistic philosophy or in the context of the Judaism of the land of Israel, where that philosophy has left only modest traces.

Jesus was crucified as "King of the Jews," and this suggests that he was viewed as a messianic pretender and that the kingdom he proclaimed was understood, at least by some of his followers, as a messianic kingdom. The teaching attributed to Jesus in the Synoptic Gospels often has apocalyptic overtones. Consider, for example, the following description of Q, taken as a whole, by John Kloppenborg:

> Q's perspective is framed both spatially by transcendent realities — heaven (6:23; 12:33), hell or Hades (10:5; 12:5), Sophia (7:35; 11:49), the Son of Man (12:8-9, 10, 40 etc.), angels (12:8-9), demons (11:14-26), and the devil (4:1-13) — and temporally by the coming judgment (3:7-9; 10:13-15; 11:31-32; 22:28-30), the destruction of the impenitent at the Parousia (3:17; 17:26-30), and the eschatological meal in the Kingdom (13:28-29; cf. 14:16-24). Consistent with apocalyptic idiom, the Parousia marks an abrupt termination of the present age. However for Q, as for some other expressions of Christian apocalypticism, the present already partakes of eschatological realities.[18]

Kloppenborg resists the conclusion that Q represents "apocalyptic Christianity," but it is not difficult to see why others have thought that it does.[19] Moreover, Jesus began his career as a disciple of John the Baptist, who preached that an apocalyptic judgment was at hand.[20] After the death of Jesus, the movement of his followers had a strong eschatological orientation

---

17. Mack, *A Myth of Innocence*, 72.

18. J. S. Kloppenborg, "Symbolic Eschatology and the Apocalypticism of Q," *HTR* 80 (1987) 296.

19. Ibid., 306. Contrast N. Perrin and D. C. Duling, *The New Testament: An Introduction* (2d ed.; New York: Harcourt Brace Jovanovich, 1982) 100-107.

20. R. L. Webb, *John the Baptizer and Prophet: A Socio-Historical Study* (Sheffield: JSOT, 1991); J. E. Taylor, *The Immerser: John the Baptist within Second Temple Judaism* (Grand Rapids: Eerdmans, 1997).

in most of its forms.[21] It would be surprising indeed if there were no continuity between Jesus and his followers in this respect.

These considerations do not obliterate the differences between the Gospel traditions and apocalyptic literature, but they make the hypothesis of a completely uneschatological Jesus rather unlikely. The differences in literary form may reflect different social locations. The apocalyptic literature surveyed in this book was primarily the work of scribes. The numerical patterns in historical predictions and heavenly enumeration reflect the interest of the scribe in learned detail. Precisely this kind of detail is lacking in the Gospels. But there was also a popular eschatology, manifested in the activities of the prophets and messiahs described by Josephus.[22] These movements did not, to our knowledge, articulate their worldview in literary compositions, and they lacked the more speculative interests of the apocalypses. Their eschatological focus was none the less for that. Just as the apocalypticism of the Dead Sea Scrolls reflects the priestly ideology of the sect, the eschatological hopes of the Gospels are couched in forms and language that reflect their origin in a popular movement in Galilee.[23]

To say that the Jesus movement had an eschatological orientation does not necessarily mean that it should be described as apocalyptic. E. P. Sanders argues that the eschatological goal of Jesus was the restoration of Israel, but he regards restoration eschatology as typical of the apocalypses.[24] Somewhat similarly, Richard Horsley writes, "Jesus' proclamation and practice of the kingdom of God indeed belonged in the milieu of Jewish apocalypticism. But far from being an expectation of an imminent cosmic catastrophe, it was the conviction that God was now driving Satan from control over personal and historical life, making possible the renewal

---

21. The argument for continuity is made by E. P. Sanders, *Jesus and Judaism* (Philadelphia: Fortress, 1985) 323-24.

22. Horsley and Hanson, *Bandits, Prophets, and Messiahs*; Crossan, *The Historical Jesus,* 158-59, 292. Crossan categorizes Jesus under popular wisdom rather than under popular apocalypticism.

23. Sean Freyne, *Jesus. A Jewish Galilean: A New Reading of the Jesus-story* (London: T & T Clark, 2004); *The Jesus Movement and Its Expansion: Meaning and Mission* (Grand Rapids: Eerdmans, 2014).

24. Sanders, *Jesus and Judaism.* Cf. Sanders, "The Genre of Palestinian Jewish Apocalypses," in D. Hellholm, ed., *Apocalypticism in the Mediterranean World and the Near East: Proceedings of the International Colloquium on Apocalypticism, Uppsala, August 12-17, 1979* (Tübingen: Mohr Siebeck, 1983) 456: "What is peculiar to the works which have traditionally been considered Palestinian Jewish apocalypses is the combination of revelation with the promise of restoration and reversal."

of the people Israel. The presence of the kingdom of God meant the termination of the old order."[25] In his more recent work, Horsley has argued that Jesus, Paul, and all the apocalyptic writers were single-mindedly obsessed with opposition to empire, as embodied by Rome.[26] While resistance to empire is certainly an important element in apocalyptic literature, apocalypticism cannot be so simplistically reduced to a single theme.[27]

We have seen repeatedly that there is no necessary opposition between hopes for the restoration of Israel, which were often, from the Hasmonean period onward, associated with the Davidic messiah, and the belief in imminent cosmic catastrophe. In the apocalypses of the historical type (Daniel, the Animal Apocalypse, Apocalypse of Weeks, etc.) and in the Dead Sea Scrolls, the restoration of Israel is set in a context of cosmic upheaval, which typically includes the judgment of the dead, in some form. It is precisely this cosmic perspective that distinguishes the eschatology of these apocalypses from the older prophetic eschatology.

## Son of Man and Messiah

Whether the teaching of Jesus entailed apocalyptic eschatology in this cosmic sense is closely bound up with the interpretation of the "Son of Man" sayings in the Synoptic Gospels. Not all these sayings are prophetic or apocalyptic, or entail an allusion to Dan 7:13.[28] When we read, for example, that "foxes have holes and birds of the air have nests, but the son of man has nowhere to lay his head" (Matt 8:20//Luke 9:58), it is not necessary to see an allusion to Daniel or any apocalyptic overtones. In this case the phrase can be taken satisfactorily as a generic reference to "a man" or "a human being," in a way

---

25. R. A. Horsley, *Jesus and the Spiral of Violence: Popular Jewish Resistance in Roman Palestine* (San Francisco: Harper & Row, 1987) 160; Compare his article, "The Kingdom of God and the Renewal of Israel: Synoptic Gospels, Jesus Movements, and Apocalypticism," in Collins, ed., *The Encyclopedia of Apocalypticism*, 1. 303-44.

26. Horsley, *Jesus and Empire. The Kingdom of God and the New World Disorder* (Minneapolis: Fortress, 2003); "Jesus and Empire," *USQR* 59 (2005) 44-74; *The Prophet Jesus and the Renewal of Israel: Moving Beyond Diversionary Debate* (Grand Rapids: Eerdmans, 2012).

27. See my critique of Horsley in my essay, "Apocalypse and Empire," *Svensk Exegetisk Årsbok* 76 (2011) 1-19 (=*Apocalypse, Prophecy, and Pseudepigraphy*, chapter 17).

28. P. M. Casey, *Son of Man: The Interpretation and Influence of Daniel 7* (London: SPCK, 1979) 157-223. For a more nuanced categorization, see A. Yarbro Collins, "The Origin of the Designation of Jesus as 'Son of Man,' " in *Cosmology and Eschatology in Jewish and Christian Apocalypticism* (Leiden: Brill, 1996) 139-58.

that includes the speaker.[29] In contrast, Mark 13:24-26 describes a coming cosmic upheaval and predicts that "then they will see the Son of Man coming with the clouds with great power and glory," and in Mark 14:61-62 Jesus affirms that he is the messiah and adds, "you will see the Son of Man seated at the right hand of the power and coming with the clouds of heaven." In both cases, the association with the clouds of heaven constitutes a clear allusion to Daniel 7 and implies a context of cosmic judgment. Moreover, several sayings that have no overt allusion to Daniel 7 nonetheless entail a claim of specific authority that cannot be derived from the generic sense of the phrase. So the statements that "the Son of Man has authority on earth to forgive sins" (Mark 2:10) or "the Son of Man is lord even of the sabbath" (Mark 2:27-28) probably presuppose that "Son of Man" is a messianic title, unless they are taken to mean that the authority in question is given to humanity at large.[30]

In the context of the Gospels, the Son of Man must be identified with Jesus. It is difficult to see, however, how Jesus could have been identified with the Son of Man prior to his crucifixion. Why should anyone expect him to come on the clouds when he was already present on earth? That identification would seem to presuppose the resurrection and ascension. When Mark 14 refers to the Son of Man seated at the right hand of the power, there is a further allusion to Psalm 110, which is used as a prooftext for the ascension in Acts 2:34-35. The same combination of references is found in Stephen's speech in Acts 7:56.[31] The identification of Jesus with the Danielic Son of Man makes excellent sense in the context of the post-Easter early church. Jesus had been expected, at least by some, to restore the kingdom of Israel, but he had ignominiously failed to do so. The identification with the figure in Daniel 7 permitted his followers to believe that he was nonetheless the messiah and that he would come again to complete the work of deliverance. This belief was later elaborated in the book of Revelation.

---

29. G. Vermes has argued repeatedly that the phrase should be understood as a circumlocution for the first person, and so as a form of self-reference. See his *Jesus the Jew: A Historian's Reading of the Gospels* (Philadelphia: Fortress, 1973) 160-91. In each of the examples he cites, however, the speaker is included in a general statement about human beings. See A. Yarbro Collins, "The Origin of the Designation of Jesus as 'Son of Man'," in *Cosmology and Eschatology*, 146-47, and the literature cited there. See also her discussion in "The Influence of Daniel on the New Testament," in J. J. Collins, *Daniel: A Commentary on the Book of Daniel* (Hermeneia; Minneapolis: Fortress, 1993) 94-95.

30. Yarbro Collins, "The Origin of the Designation," 146-51.

31. N. Perrin, *A Modern Pilgrimage in New Testament Christology* (Philadelphia: Fortress, 1974) 10-22.

It is possible, however, that Jesus referred to the figure in Daniel's vision but did not identify himself with that figure. This was the position of Rudolf Bultmann,[32] and although it has often been criticized,[33] it is still defended in contemporary scholarship.[34] Several of the Son of Man sayings in the Gospels do not explicitly identify him with Jesus (e.g., Mark 13:26; Matt 24:27 and parallels; Matt 24:37-39 and parallels; Matt 24:44 and parallels).[35] Some scholars object that "Son of Man" was not an established title in the first century, but it did not have to be. Daniel 7 was well established as sacred scripture, and we know that it was taken to refer to an eschatological agent in the Similitudes of Enoch and 4 Ezra.[36] There is no reason in principle why Jesus should not have made similar use of Daniel 7.[37] Such usage would make the subsequent prominence of this figure in early Christianity and his identification with Jesus all the more intelligible. In this case, the nonapocalyptic sayings should not be read in the generic sense, but taken as secondary uses of "Son of Man" as a title for Jesus.[38] In view of the notorious difficulty of establishing the authenticity of particular sayings, the Son of Man sayings in the Gospels are likely to remain extremely controversial.

32. R. Bultmann, *The History of the Synoptic Tradition* (New York: Harper & Row, 1968) 112, 122, 128, 151-52. Bultmann identified such sayings in Mark 8:38; Luke 12:8-9; 17:23-24; Matt 24:37-39; 24:43-44.

33. P. Vielhauer, "Gottesreich und Menschensohn in der Verkündigung Jesu," in *Festschrift für Günther Dehn* (Neukirchen: Kreis Moers, 1957) 51-79; N. Perrin, *Rediscovering the Teaching of Jesus* (New York: Harper & Row, 1967) 154-206.

34. Yarbro Collins, "The Origin of the Designation"; eadem, "The Influence of Daniel on the New Testament," 93; B. Chilton, "The Son of Man — Who Was He?" *Bible Review* 12 (1996) 34-39, 45. Yarbro Collins agrees that Vielhauer showed that Luke 12:8-9 does not go back to Jesus, but she argues for the authenticity of other passages that do not explicitly identify Jesus with the Son of Man. See also Ehrman, *Jesus. Apocalyptic Prophet*, 146-48.

35. Luke 12:8-9 ("everyone who acknowledges me before others, the Son of Man also will acknowledge before the angels of God") is often taken as the clearest case where a distinction is implied, but Vielhauer showed that this saying has its setting in the early church. See Yarbro Collins, "The Origin of the Designation," 152.

36. J. J. Collins, "The Son of Man in First-Century Judaism," *NTS* 38 (1992) 448-66.

37. Compare Ehrman, *Jesus. Apocalyptic Prophet*, 146. Simon J. Joseph, *The Nonviolent Messiah. Jesus, Q, and the Enochic Tradition* (Minneapolis: Fortress, 2014) 159-60, is unusual in arguing for broad influence of the Similitudes of Enoch on the Jesus tradition. He takes the Similitudes as offering a precedent for the heavenly exaltation of a human being. See the more restrained assessment of Leslie W. Walck, "The Son of Man in the Parables of Enoch and the Gospels," in Boccaccini, ed., *Enoch and the Messiah Son of Man*, 299-337.

38. Chilton, however, argues that "Jesus was smart enough to use the phrase in both ways (as generic and as angelic)" ("The Son of Man," 45).

There should be less doubt, however, about the eschatological character of the kingdom. The word "Christ," Greek equivalent of "messiah," became a virtual name for Jesus within a short time of his death. It is unlikely that this would have happened if messianic claims had not been made on his behalf before the crucifixion.[39] How Jesus came to be viewed as the Davidic messiah remains something of a mystery. The messiah was primarily expected to be a warrior king who would drive out the Gentiles, and little in the traditions about Jesus fits this mold. It is possible that Jesus was initially identified as a messianic prophet, one anointed by the Spirit after the model of Isaiah 61.[40] The works identified as "the works of the messiah" in Matt 11:2 correspond remarkably to the eschatological works of God in 4Q521, in the passage that begins "heaven and earth will obey his messiah."[41] The messiah in question is likely to be a prophetic, Elijah-like figure rather than a Davidic king.[42] Ultimately, the hope that Jesus might be the messianic king arose from the fact that he preached the coming of the kingdom. The Gospels represent Jesus as being very reticent about any messianic claim, but the expectation nonetheless arose that he would bring about what he preached. But while some of his followers hoped that he would restore the kingdom of David when he went up to Jerusalem, these hopes were disappointed. Consequently, after his death the disciples searched the scriptures for an explanation of this surprising turn of events. Daniel's prophecy provided them with a different model of messiah, and they concluded that Jesus would come again, not as an earthly king but as the Danielic Son of Man on the clouds of heaven.

## The Resurrection

The identification of Jesus as the Son of Man who would come on the clouds of heaven presupposed the belief that he was risen and ascended. This belief became the cornerstone of early Christian apocalypticism.

39. M. Hengel, "Jesus, der Messias Israels," in I. Gruenwald, S. Shaked, and G. Stroumsa, eds., *Messias und Christos* (Tübingen: Mohr Siebeck, 1992) 155-76.

40. J. J. Collins, "Jesus and the Messiahs of Israel," in H. Cancik, H. Lichtenberger, and P. Schäfer, eds., *Geschichte — Tradition — Reflexion: Festschrift für Martin Hengel* (Tübingen: Mohr Siebeck, 1996) 1:287-302.

41. J. J. Collins, "The Works of the Messiah," *Dead Sea Discoveries* 1 (1994) 98-112.

42. *Pace* Joseph, *Jesus, Q, and the Dead Sea Scrolls*, 175. Joseph argues that the author of the NT text borrowed from 4Q521.

The resurrection is the premise on which all hope of the second coming is based. But the resurrection cannot be understood in isolation. It was viewed as part of an eschatological sequence similar to what we find in the apocalypses of the historical type.

The earliest discussion we have of the resurrection is provided by Paul in 1 Corinthians 15.[43] His argument is striking, since he makes no mention of an empty tomb. Rather, he mentions the apparitions of Jesus to the apostles, to more than five hundred brethren at one time, and to Paul himself. Yet even the visions are not regarded as conclusive proof, for "if there is no resurrection of the dead, then Christ has not been raised" (1 Cor 15:13). An empty tomb or visions can be explained in various ways and cannot convince anyone who denies *a priori* that resurrection is possible. For Paul, the resurrection of Jesus is not an isolated event. It is not enough to believe that God could raise a privileged individual, as he had taken Elijah up to heaven according to the Old Testament. Rather, Christ is the firstfruits of those who have fallen asleep, and his resurrection is as fateful for humanity as the sin of Adam had been. In short, Paul argues that the resurrection of Jesus must be understood in the context of a general resurrection and presupposes a full scenario such as we find in the historical apocalypses. Since one person has already been raised, the rest cannot be far behind. The end is at hand. The urgency of this belief is apparent in 1 Cor 15:51-52: "Lo! I tell you a mystery. We shall not all sleep but we shall all be changed, in a moment, in the twinkling of an eye, at the last trumpet. For the trumpet will sound, and the dead will be raised imperishable, and we shall be changed."

## Paul's Apocalyptic Perspective

Paul's eschatological revelation is not given in the form of an apocalypse, but it is declared to be a *mystery*.[44] The terminology is reminiscent of

---

43. M. C. de Boer, *The Defeat of Death: Apocalyptic Eschatology in 1 Corinthians 15 and Romans 5* (Sheffield: JSOT Press, 1988); J. Holleman, *Resurrection and Parousia: A Traditio-Historical Study of Paul's Eschatology in 1 Cor 15:20-23* (Leiden: Brill, 1995). On the nature of the resurrected body, see the discussion in Dale B. Martin, *The Corinthian Body* (New Haven: Yale, 1995) 104-36.

44. For recent discussions of Pauline apocalypticism. see J. C. Beker, *Paul the Apostle: The Triumph of God in Life and Thought* (Philadelphia: Fortress, 1980); W. A. Meeks, "Social Functions of Apocalyptic Language in Pauline Christianity," in Hellholm, ed.,

Qumran. Paul presents himself as a "steward of the mysteries" (1 Cor 4:1). The mysteries are not only eschatological; they embrace the full plan of God which has hitherto been hidden:

> Yet among the mature we do impart wisdom, although it is not a wisdom of this age or of the rulers of this age who are doomed to pass away. But we impart a secret and hidden wisdom of God, which God decreed before the ages for our glorification. None of the rulers of this age understood this; for if they had, they would not have crucified the Lord of glory. (1 Cor 2:6-8)

This wisdom is imparted not by men but by the spirit. The precise manner of revelation is not described in 1 Corinthians, but in 2 Corinthians 12 Paul can boast of visions and revelations of the Lord:

> I know a man in Christ who fourteen years ago was caught up to the third heaven — whether in the body or out of the body I do not know, God knows. And I know that this man was caught up into Paradise . . . and he heard things that cannot be told, which man may not utter. (2 Cor 12:2-4)

It would seem that Paul's revelatory experience embraced some of the media that we have found to be typical of the apocalypses.[45]

The crucial element in Paul's revelation is the affirmation of another world and life, beyond this one: "If for this life only we have hoped in Christ, we are of all men most to be pitied" (1 Cor 15:19). Undoubtedly

*Apocalypticism*, 685-703; M. C. de Boer, "Paul and Jewish Apocalyptic Eschatology," in J. Marcus and M. L. Soards, eds., *Apocalyptic and the New Testament* (Sheffield: JSOT Press, 1989) 169-90; idem, "Paul and Apocalyptic Eschatology," in Collins, ed., *The Encyclopedia of Apocalypticism* 1.345-83; Greg Carey, *Ultimate Things. An Introduction to Jewish and Christian Apocalyptic Literature* (St. Louis: Chalice, 2005) 125-46; Murphy, *Apocalypticism in the Bible and Its World*, 310-54; Emma Wasserman, *Apocalypse as Holy War: Religious Polemic and Violence in the World of Paul* (AYBRL; New Haven: Yale University Press, forthcoming).

45. On Paul's visionary experience, see J. D. Tabor, *Things Unutterable: Paul's Ascent to Paradise in Its Greco-Roman, Judaic, and Early Christian Contexts* (Lanham, MD: University Press of America, 1986); A. F. Segal, *Paul the Convert: The Apostolate and Apostasy of Saul the Pharisee* (New Haven: Yale University Press, 1990) 34-71; C. R. Morray-Jones, "Paradise Revisited (2 Cor 12:1-12): The Jewish Mystical Background of Paul's Apostolate. Part 1: The Jewish Sources," *HTR* 86/2 (1993) 177-217; Part 2: "Paul's Heavenly Ascent and Its Significance," *HTR* 86/3 (1993) 265-92.

Paul felt, at least in the earlier part of his career, that this world would pass *soon,* even in his own lifetime. The most explicit assertion is found in 1 Thess 4:15-17:

> For this we declare to you by the word of the Lord, that we who are alive, who are left until the coming of the Lord, shall not precede those who have fallen asleep. For the Lord himself will descend from heaven with a cry of command, with the archangel's call, and with the sound of the trumpet of God. And the dead in Christ will rise first; then we who are alive, who are left, shall be caught up together with them in the clouds to meet the Lord in the air; and so we shall always be with the Lord.[46]

1 Thessalonians was written about 50 CE. It is the oldest of Paul's letters and indeed the oldest book of the New Testament.[47] This is significant, as our first window into the early church shows a high level of eschatological anticipation.[48] "You know very well," Paul tells the Thessalonians, "that the day of the Lord will come like a thief in the night" (1 Thess 5:2). It is also noteworthy that the Lord is expected to come on the clouds, even though the expression "Son of Man" is not used. The intensity of expectation eventually came to be a problem for the Thessalonian church. 2 Thessalonians was probably written after Paul's death,[49] possibly around the time of the Jewish war against Rome, when eschatological expectations were high.[50] The author warns the readers, "Now concerning the coming of our Lord Jesus Christ and our assembling to meet him, we beg you brothers not to be quickly shaken in mind or alarmed, either by spirit or by word or by letter, as though from us, to the effect that the day of the Lord is already

---

46. On the rhetorical function of such claims, see Duane F. Watson, "Paul's Appropriation of Apocalyptic Discourse. The Rhetorical Strategy of 1 Thessalonians," in Greg Carey and L. Gregory Bloomquist, eds., *Rhetorical Dimensions of Apocalyptic Discourse* (St. Louis: Chalice, 1999) 61-80.

47. Koester, *Introduction to the New Testament,* 2:112.

48. See R. Jewett, *The Thessalonian Correspondence* (Philadelphia: Fortress, 1986) 159-78, on millenarianism as the context of this epistle.

49. Koester, *Introduction to the New Testament,* 2:242. Many scholars, however, accept it as a genuine letter of Paul; e.g., Jewett, *The Thessalonian Correspondence,* 17, regards it as "probably Pauline."

50. See A. Yarbro Collins, "Christian Messianism and the First Jewish War with Rome," in Charlotte Hempel and Judith M. Lieu, eds., *Biblical Traditions in Transmission: Essays in Honour of Michael A. Knibb* (JSJSup 111; Leiden: Brill, 2006) 333-43.

here" (2 Thess 2:1-2). The author reminds his readers that the lawless one must come first and take his seat in the temple. The reference is enigmatic and has been the subject of endless speculation.[51] It should probably be understood in the context of the conquest of Jerusalem by the Romans. In Mark 13 one of the signs of the end is "when you see the desolating sacrilege set up where it ought not to be" (Mark 13:14), presumably a reference to the Roman occupation of the holy place. Mark 13 similarly warns against premature expectation: "And if anyone say to you at that time, 'Look! Here is the messiah!' or 'Look! there he is!' — do not believe it. False messiahs and false prophets will appear and produce signs and omens to lead astray if possible the elect" (Mark 13:21-22). Here again the most probable setting is the Jewish war, when there was a proliferation of messianic pretenders.[52] Both Mark and 2 Thessalonians appeal for calm in the present, but both authors still maintain a thoroughly apocalyptic expectation. The coming of the Son of Man and the day of the Lord are not yet, but they are imminent, and the readers are urged to be alert and watchful.

In the interim, life was to be lived, but lived in the consciousness that this world was passing away.[53] Paul writes to the Corinthians:

I mean, brethren, the appointed time has grown very short; from now on let those who have wives live as though they had none, and those who mourn as though they were not mourning, and those who rejoice as though they were not rejoicing, and those who buy as though they had no goods, and those who deal with the world as though they had no dealings with it. For the form of this world is passing away. (1 Cor 7:29-31)

Paul's advice on such matters as marriage and slavery is largely determined by this perspective.[54]

---

51. See L. J. L. Peerbolte, *The Antecedents of Antichrist* (Leiden: Brill, 1996) 75-79. On the eschatology of 2 Corinthians, see further G. S. Holland, *The Tradition That You Received from Us: 2 Thessalonians in the Pauline Tradition* (Tübingen: Mohr Siebeck, 1988) 91-127.

52. J. Marcus, "The Jewish War and the Sitz im Leben of Mark," *JBL* 111 (1992) 441-62; A. Yarbro Collins, "Mark 13: An Apocalyptic Discourse," in *The Beginning of the Gospel: Probings of Mark in Context* (Minneapolis: Fortress, 1992) 73-91.

53. Gail Corrington Streete, "Paul's Apocalyptic Asceticism in 1 Corinthians," in Carey and Bloomquist, eds., *Vision and Persuasion*, 81-94.

54. On the correlation between eschatology and community, see further Meeks, "Social Functions."

Even more basically, the apocalyptic perspective determined Paul's understanding of salvation. The death of Jesus showed that salvation must be sought beyond this life in resurrection. The way to salvation was henceforth to be like Christ:

> Do you not know that all of us who have been baptized into Christ Jesus were baptized into his death? We were buried therefore with him by baptism into death, so that as Christ was raised from the dead by the glory of the Father, we too might walk in newness of life. For if we have been united with him in a death like his, we shall certainly be united with him in a resurrection like his. (Rom 6:3-5)

In Daniel, the martyrs who lose their lives in this world are precisely those who shine like the stars in resurrection. The example of Jesus has evidently far greater force for Paul and becomes a normative example for Christians, so that the death and resurrection of Jesus become an allegory for the pattern of Christian life. The new event of Jesus' death holds a central place in Paul's theology, but its significance is viewed in an apocalyptic context, insofar as it points the way to the resurrection.

In the Gospels and Acts, too, eschatological expectation shapes behavior in the present. According to Acts 2, the first Christians sold their possessions and had all things in common. As Paul would say, those who had goods behaved as though they had not. The reason, as Paul also recognized, was that they believed that the time was short. There was no reason to plan for the future. Eventually this eschatological ethic would be eroded by the need to cope with the world on an ongoing basis.

In the late twentieth and early twenty-first centuries there has been a trend to emphasize the political implications of Paul's thought and to construe his view of the Lordship of Jesus as a challenge to the ideology of the Roman empire.[55] It is indubitably true that Paul's claim

---

55. Neil Elliott, *Liberating Paul. The Justice of God and the Politics of the Apostle* (Sheffield: Sheffield Academic Press, 1995); Richard A. Horsley, ed., *Paul and Empire. Religion and Power in Roman Imperial Society* (Harrisburg, PA: Trinity Press International, 1997); idem, ed., *Paul and Politics: Ekklesia, Israel, Imperium, Interpretation: Essays in Honor of Krister Stendahl* (Harrisburg, PA: Trinity Press International, 2000); N. T. Wright, "Paul and Caesar: A New Reading of Romans," in C. Bartholomew, ed., *Royal Priesthood: The Use of the Bible Ethically and Politically* (Carlisle: Paternoster, 2002) 173-93; John Dominic Crossan and Jonathan L. Reed, *In Search of Paul: How Jesus' Apostle Opposed Rome's Empire with God's Kingdom* (New York: HarperCollins, 2004).

of absolute sovereignty for Jesus was incompatible with Roman imperial ideology. It is also true that he unambiguously identifies Jesus as the Jewish messiah, a title that normally had political implications.[56] But Paul does not point up the political implications of his message. Rather, as Paula Fredriksen, has argued, he "denationalizes Christ" and "shrinks the significance of contemporary politics."[57] Paul did not need to foster rebellion. Divine intervention was at hand, and the form of this world was passing away. Most telling is the statement in Rom 13:1-2: "Let every person be subject to the governing authorities; for there is no authority except from God, and those authorities that exist have been instituted by God. Therefore whoever resists authority resists what God has appointed, and those who resist will incur judgment."[58] An apocalyptic perspective could lead to fierce criticism of earthly empires, as we shall see in the Book of Revelation, but it is not deployed in that way in the Pauline epistles.

## Christian Apocalypticism

The idea of an eschatological judgment, however, would always remain foundational to Christianity. The Gospel of Matthew reflects the delay of the Parousia in the parables of the unfaithful servant, who begins to beat his fellow slaves when the master is delayed (Matt 24:45-51; Luke 12:41-48), and the ten bridesmaids, some of whom have enough oil while some have not. But Matthew insists on the coming of the Son of Man,

---

56. Matthew V. Novenson, *Christ among the Messiahs. Christ Language in Paul and Messiah Language in Ancient Judaism* (Oxford: Oxford University Press, 2012). See however the argument of Magnus Zetterholm, "Paul and the Missing Messiah," in idem, ed., *The Messiah in Early Judaism and Christianity* (Minneapolis: Fortress, 2007) 33-55, who argues that Paul deliberately downplayed the messianic character of Jesus for Gentile readers.

57. Paula Fredriksen, *From Jesus to Christ. The Origins of New Testament Images of Jesus* (New Haven: Yale, 1988) 173. Waddell, *The Messiah*, 202-3, argues that Paul was familiar with traditions found in the *Similitudes of Enoch*, which portray a heavenly, pre-existent messiah, but he admits "that we cannot say with any certainty that Paul knew the text" of the *Similitudes*. The *Similitudes of Enoch* are much more outspoken about "the kings and the mighty" than are the letters of Paul.

58. On the authenticity of this passage see Robert Jewett, *Romans* (Hermeneia; Minneapolis: Fortress, 2007) 783-84, who comments that "distaste for a passage has no bearing on its authenticity."

even though one know not the day nor the hour.[59] He envisions the Son of Man as judge, in a manner that may be indebted to the Similitudes of Enoch. (In both texts, the Son of Man is said to "sit on his throne of glory.") The criteria for the judgment are humanistic: they are concerned with feeding the hungry, giving drink to the thirsty, and clothing the naked. No attention is paid to ritual. We are reminded of the insistence of 2 *Enoch* that whoever offends the face of a man offends the face of God. According to Matthew, whatever one does to the least of the brethren is done to the Lord (Matt 25:31-46). The prospect of a final judgment, then, leads to no evasion of responsibility in this world, but rather lends urgency to ethical behavior in the present. In all of this, the Christian use of apocalypticism is fully in accordance with its Jewish precedents.

The primary difference between Christian and Jewish apocalypticism in the first century CE was that the Christians believed that the messiah had already come and that the firstfruits of the resurrection had taken place. Consequently, there is an element of realized eschatology in the Christian texts.[60] It is more pronounced in some texts (Colossians, Ephesians, the Johannine writings) than in others. According to John, the believer has already passed from death to life, even though there is still a judgment to come. According to Ephesians, God has already "made us alive with Christ" and "raised us up with him and seated us with him in the heavenly places in Christ Jesus" (Eph 2:5-6). In contrast, the authentic letters of Paul insist that creation is still groaning in travail, waiting for the sons of God to be revealed (Rom 8). But the "realized eschatology" of early Christianity was not without precedent in Judaism; the members of the Dead Sea sect believed that a turning point of history had come with the rise of their movement and that they were already living with the angels.[61] One major difference, however, was that the life and death of Jesus took on a paradigmatic character for the early Christians. Jewish apocalyptic movements were never colored to this extent by an exemplary life. Even the Righteous Teacher of Qumran remains a shadowy figure.

---

59. David C. Sim, *Apocalyptic Eschatology in the Gospel of Matthew* (SNTSMS 88; Cambridge: Cambridge University Press, 1996) especially 93-174.

60. See D. C. Allison, *The End of the Ages Has Come* (Philadelphia: Fortress, 1985).

61. See further J. J. Collins, *Apocalypticism in the Dead Sea Scrolls* (London: Routledge, 1997) 159-63.

## The Book of Revelation

The genre of literature that we call apocalyptic takes its name from the Apocalypse of John, one of the later books of the New Testament, written towards the end of the first century CE.[62] As far we now know, it was the first book in Jewish and Christian tradition that was explicitly presented as an *apokalypsis* (1:1). Whether or not this term was intended as a genre label, the revelation is characterized in a way that underlines its affinity with the Jewish apocalypses: it is mediated to John by an angel and concerns "what must soon take place." The content of Revelation is, in fact, focused on the eschatological scenario that culminates in the end of this world and the judgment of the dead. It also includes visions of the divine throne and elaborate mythological imagery reminiscent of Daniel. It is, in short, a full-blown apocalypse by the definition accepted in this study.[63]

One still encounters occasional attempts to dispute "whether the Apocalypse is an apocalypse"[64] or at least to minimize its apocalyptic character and present it instead as a work of Christian prophecy. The designation as Christian prophecy is not wrong. Revelation is presented not only as *apokalypsis,* but also as a prophecy (1:3; 22:6-7), and its author is properly regarded as an early Christian prophet.[65] Prophecy was a broad

62. On the date and setting of Revelation, see A. Yarbro Collins, *Crisis and Catharsis: The Power of the Apocalypse* (Philadelphia: Westminster, 1984); L. L. Thompson, *The Book of Revelation: Apocalypse and Empire* (Oxford: Oxford University Press, 1990); Steven J. Friesen, *Imperial Cults and the Apocalypse of John. Reading Revelation in the Ruins* (Oxford: Oxford University Press, 2001) 135-51; Craig R. Koester, *Revelation* (AYB 38A; New Haven: Yale, 2014) 71-79. Thomas Witulski, *Die Johannesoffenbarung und Kaiser Hadrian. Studien zur Datierung der neutestamentlichen Apokalypse* (FRLANT 221; Göttingen: Vandenhoeck & Ruprecht, 2007) argues implausibly for a later date, under the emperor Hadrian (117-38 CE). Stefan Witetschek, "Ein weit geöffnetes Zeitfenster? Überlegungen zur Datierung der Johannesapokalypse," in Jörg Frey, James A. Kelhoffer, and Franz Tóth, eds., *Die Johannesapokalypse. Kontexte – Konzepte – Rezeption* (WUNT 287; Tübingen: Mohr Siebeck, 2012) 117-48, and James A. Kelhoffer, "The Relevance of Revelation's Date and the Imperial Cult for John's Appraisal of the Value of Christians' Suffering," ibid., 564-65, argue for a date around 100-110 CE. John W. Marshall, *Parables of War. Reading John's Jewish Apocalypse* (Waterloo, ON: Wilfrid Laurier, 2001) 88-97, is exceptional among recent scholars in arguing for a date between 68 and 70 CE.

63. For a succinct presentation see Adela Yarbro Collins, "The Book of Revelation," in Collins, ed., *The Encyclopedia of Apocalypticism*, 1:384-414.

64. For example, J. Kallas, "The Apocalypse — An Apocalyptic Book?" *JBL* 86 (1967) 69-80.

65. M. E. Boring, "The Apocalypse as Christian Prophecy," in G. W. MacRae, ed.,

category in the Hellenistic and Roman worlds; it could encompass various kinds of revelation including what we call apocalyptic.[66] Daniel was often regarded as a prophet, both in ancient Judaism (Josephus; 4QFlorilegium) and in early Christianity (Matt 24:15), although his book is not grouped with the Prophets in the Hebrew Bible.[67] Apocalyptic literature may be regarded as a form of prophecy, but it is nonetheless distinctive.

Two aspects of Revelation have been especially controversial with respect to its genre: first, the book is presented as a circular letter to the seven churches; and, second, it is not pseudonymous.

In addition to its self-characterization as apocalypse and prophecy, the whole book of Revelation is presented as a circular letter to the seven churches of Asia Minor.[68] The use of the letter form reflects the practice of other Christian teachers, most notably Paul, and says something about the situation in which John wrote. But letters are of many kinds, and the fact that something is sent as a circular letter does not determine the message it contains, the form in which that message is cast, or the kind of authority it claims. The specific letters to the seven churches at the beginning of

---

*SBL Seminar Papers, 1974* (2 vols.; Missoula, MT: Scholars Press, 1974) 2:43-62. D. E. Aune, *Prophecy in Early Christianity and the Ancient Mediterranean World* (Grand Rapids: Eerdmans, 1983) 274-88; E. Schüssler Fiorenza, "Apokalypsis and Propheteia: Revelation in the Context of Early Christian Prophecy," in *The Book of Revelation: Justice and Judgment* (Philadelphia: Fortress, 1985) 133-56; Edmondo Lupieri, *A Commentary on the Apocalypse of John* (Grand Rapids: Eerdmans, 2006) 35. Beate Kowalski, "Prophetie und die Offenbarung des Johannes? Offb 22,6-21 als Testfall," in Joseph Verheyden, Korinna Zamfir, and Tobias Nicklas, eds., *Prophets and Prophecy in Jewish and Early Christian Literature* (WUNT 286; Tübingen: Mohr Siebeck, 2010) 292, insists that Revelation is a prophetic writing, but does not engage the relation between prophecy and apocalypticism.

66. J. Barton, *Oracles of God: Perceptions of Ancient Prophecy in Israel after the Exile* (Oxford: Oxford University Press, 1986). For a balanced appreciation of Revelation as both prophetic and apocalyptic, see R. Bauckham, *The Theology of the Book of Revelation* (Cambridge: Cambridge University Press, 1993) 2-9. See also Bauckham, *The Climax of Prophecy. Studies on the Book of Revelation* (Edinburgh: T & T Clark, 1993), e.g., xi: "Revelation is an apocalypse, whose primary literary context is the tradition of Jewish and Christian apocalypses." Koester, *Revelation*, 104, says that Revelation has features of three genres: apocalypse, prophecy, and circular letter.

67. K. Koch, "Is Daniel Also Among the Prophets?" *Interpretation* 39 (1985) 117-30; Collins, *Daniel: A Commentary*, 52.

68. See the extensive discussion by M. Karrer, *Die Johannesoffenbarung als Brief* (Göttingen: Vandenhoeck & Ruprecht, 1986), but also the more balanced discussion of Bauckham, *The Theology of the Book of Revelation*, 12-17. For the epistolary features of Revelation, see Koester, *Revelation*, 109-10.

Revelation have an obvious parallel in the letter at the end of 2 *Baruch*.[69] Revelation is exceptional insofar as the whole book is presented as a letter, presumably because John was not able to visit the seven churches in person. The letter was evidently read to the assembled congregations to which it was sent. Jewish apocalypses were also circulated, but we do not know how. A difference in the manner of circulation, however, is extrinsic to the nature of the work itself; it points to the distinctiveness of early Christian assemblies rather than to that of Revelation. The body of Revelation, in chaps. 4–22, is unlike anything that we find in any other New Testament epistle.[70] While Revelation is, among other things, a circular letter, this designation is of very limited help in appreciating the content of the book.

Pseudonymity was a constant feature of the Jewish apocalypses. Since John is presumably the author's real name, Revelation is anomalous in this respect. The significance of this deviation is proportional to the importance of pseudepigraphy within the genre. Some scholars have tried to make pseudepigraphy into the *sine qua non* of apocalyptic writing,[71] but this is surely to overrate it. Pseudepigraphy is only one of several formal markers of the apocalypses and is by no means peculiar to the genre. It was basically a way of lending authority to a text, although it had other ramifications besides. It was not the sole basis for authority. A book like 4 Ezra claimed its authority primarily on the basis of the revelation given by the angel — and even, to a lesser degree, on the words of God himself. That the supposed recipient of this revelation was the venerable Ezra added to the authority. The need for such a pseudonym in a Jewish context has often been related to the decline of prophecy, at least to the diminished respect for prophecy in the postexilic period.[72] There was undoubtedly a renewal of prophecy in the eschatological fervor of early Christianity. Yet John does not speak directly in the name of the Lord. In all but the matter

---

69. P. M. Bogaert, "Les Apocalypses contemporaines de Baruch, d'Esdras et de Jean," in J. Lambrecht, ed., *L'Apocalypse johannique et l'Apocalyptique dans le Nouveau Testament* (Leuven: Leuven University Press, 1980) 55, argues that Revelation was influenced by 2 *Baruch* in its use of the epistolary form, but this must be considered dubious. Karrer, in contrast, tries to minimize the relevance of the parallel (*Die Johannesoffenbarung als Brief*, 49-52).

70. Karrer, *Die Johannesoffenbarung als Brief*, 282, argues that there is an implicit dialogue with the reader throughout the book, but such an orientation is not peculiarly epistolary and can be argued equally well for the visions of Daniel.

71. So especially F. D. Mazzaferri, *The Genre of the Book of Revelation from a Source-Critical Perspective* (BZNW 54; Berlin: de Gruyter, 1989) 181-84.

72. For example, R. H. Charles, *APOT*, 2:ix.

of pseudonymity, he adheres to the apocalyptic manner of revelation — mediation by an angel, visions, even a brief suggestion of a heavenly ascent in 4:1. The absence of pseudonymity is a very limited departure from the conventions of the apocalyptic genre and has little bearing on the conceptual structure of the work.

Related to the absence of pseudonymity is the fact that Revelation does not offer an *ex eventu* review of history. By attributing his revelation to a great figure of the past, such as Daniel or Enoch, an author was able to have that figure "prophesy" the course of intervening history after the fact, and thereby enhance both the authority and the credibility of his message.[73] Historical reviews are clearly not a *sine qua non* of the genre, even in historically oriented apocalypses. (They are equally lacking in the Similitudes of Enoch.) Nevertheless, the absence of both these features in Revelation is noteworthy.

The absence of pseudepigraphy and *ex eventu* prophecy points to one fundamental difference between Revelation and all Jewish apocalypses. This concerns its location on the historical and eschatological timetable. One of the purposes of historical reviews was to enable the readers to see where they stood in the course of predetermined events. Typically, they stood near the end. In Daniel, 69 and a half weeks of years have passed; only half a week remains until the time of deliverance. In Revelation, however, as in all the early Christian writings, a crucial act of deliverance has already taken place with the death and resurrection of Jesus. For this reason, Revelation shows no interest in history prior to Jesus. Presumably, it has become irrelevant. The conviction that the eschatological age has begun gave rise in early Christianity to a new outpouring of prophecy and lent new authority to prophetic utterances. For that reason, John did not need to enhance his authority by presenting his work as the revelation of Enoch or Baruch, but could claim authority in his own name. We should note, however, that these changes did not prove to be essential to the Christian adaptation of the apocalyptic genre. Subsequent Christian apocalypses dispense with the epistolary framework, and only the *Shepherd of Hermas* refuses the device of pseudonymity.[74]

Underlying the scholarly disputes about the genre of Revelation is the

---

73. J. J. Collins, "Pseudonymity, Historical Reviews, and the Genre of the Revelation of John," *CBQ* 39 (1977) 329-43.

74. For an overview of the Christian apocalypses, see A. Yarbro Collins, "The Early Christian Apocalypses," *Semeia* 14 (1979) 61-121; Carey, *Ultimate Things*, 179-227.

theological question whether Christian faith entailed a significant transformation of the genre as it had developed in Judaism. The answer to this question does not depend on a specific issue like pseudonymity but on the overall structure of Revelation.

After the prefatory letters to the seven churches, the revelations are associated with two heavenly scrolls.[75] The first is the scroll with seven seals which is opened by the Lamb. The opening of the seven seals is accompanied by a series of seven visions. The seven seals are followed by seven trumpets, accompanied by plagues and catastrophes. Then in chap. 10 the second scroll is introduced — a little scroll open in the hand of the angel. This scroll heralds a series of revelations that reflect more clearly the social and political context of the apocalypse. First there is an unnumbered series of visions, then the sequence of seven bowls, and finally another series of unnumbered visions, culminating in the new heaven and new earth of chap. 21. The successive series of visions, both those associated with the seals, trumpets, and bowls and the unnumbered series, display an eschatological pattern of crisis, including persecution, judgment, and salvation. The concluding chapters provide by far the most elaborate account of the judgment and salvation and constitute a grand finale for the eschatological drama. Revelation envisages a complex scenario that weaves together different strands of Jewish eschatological tradition. First Satan is confined for a thousand years, while the martyrs return to life and reign with Christ. Then Satan is released for a final assault on the saints, but he, Death, Hades, and all the damned are thrown into the lake of fire. The general resurrection and judgment are followed by the revelation of the new heaven and new earth.[76]

Throughout these revelations the heavenly backdrop of the earthly actions is kept constantly in view. The scroll with the seven seals is introduced in a vision of the divine throne and heavenly court. The supernatural dimension is perhaps most obvious in chap. 12, where the Dragon, or Satan, is thrown from heaven by the Archangel Michael. The force of evil on earth, which for John is embodied in the Roman Empire, is

---

75. For the literary structure of Revelation, see A. Yarbro Collins, *The Combat Myth in the Book of Revelation* (HDR 9; Missoula, MT: Scholars Press, 1976) 5-55; eadem, *The Apocalypse* (Wilmington, DE: Glazier, 1979) xii-xiv; Frederick J. Murphy, *Fallen Is Babylon: The Revelation to John* (Harrisburg, PA: Trinity Press International, 1998) 47-56; Koester, *Revelation*, 112-15.

76. See Jörg Frey, "Was erwartet die Johannesapokalypse? Zur Eschatologie des letzten Buches der Bibel," in Frey, Kelhoffer, and Tóth, eds., *Die Johannesapokalypse*, 473-551.

represented by mythological allusions to beasts in chap. 13 that draw on the imagery of Daniel. It is clear that the beasts derive their power from the Dragon. Angels play a prominent role throughout. Before the resurrection, the souls of the martyrs are kept "under the altar" in heaven, waiting for the Lord to "judge and avenge our blood on those who dwell upon the earth" (6:10).

Revelation, then, shares the typical apocalyptic view of the world as the arena of angels and demonic powers in the present and subject to a definitive eschatological judgment. The problem addressed by Revelation, the present sovereignty of Rome, is put in perspective by this view of the world. Christ is the firstborn of the dead, and his death and resurrection are held to inaugurate the eschatological era. Consequently, history is foreshortened in Revelation. Interest is focused on the period between the death of Jesus and the end. Yet the contrast with an apocalypse such as Daniel should not be exaggerated. The eschatological age that has begun is the age of eschatological woes, as can be seen clearly in chap. 12. It is not a period of proleptic fulfillment but corresponds rather to the reign of the fourth beast in Daniel. The tension between present and future results from the contrast between the *vision* of the future and the experience of the present. In this respect Revelation is no different from Daniel or the Similitudes of Enoch (which also lacks the extended "prophecies" of past history).[77] It is not apparent, however, that Revelation was written in a time of intense persecution, as was the case with Daniel, although Christians were subject to sporadic repression in this period.[78] The crisis addressed in Revelation is primarily an ideological conflict, arising from the author's utter rejection of the claims of the Roman Empire to power and authority.

The distinctively Christian character of Revelation derives not from its view of history but from the central role of Jesus Christ. Even here the transformation of the genre is not as great as we might expect. Christ combines the roles of revealer (in part) and of heavenly warrior and judge, but these roles are conceived in accordance with Jewish tradition.[79]

---

77. The manner of revelation in the Similitudes is rather similar to Revelation: predominantly visions, but with a brief reference to an ascent.

78. Yarbro Collins, *Crisis and Catharsis,* 73.

79. See J. J. Collins, "The Christian Adaptation of the Apocalyptic Genre," in *Seers, Sibyls, and Sages in Hellenistic-Roman Judaism* (Leiden: Brill, 1997) 115-30.

## The Son of Man and the Lamb That Was Slain

Twice in the opening chapters of Revelation traditional imagery is applied to Jesus in strikingly new ways. First, in 1:12-16, John sees "one like a Son of Man, clothed in a long robe. . . . His head and his hair were white as white wool, white as snow." What is remarkable about this picture is that two figures from Daniel 7, the white-headed Ancient of Days and the one like a Son of Man, are fused into one.[80] While there is some fluidity in Jewish texts between descriptions of angels and those of the deity, the fusion here must be seen as purposeful. Significantly, the Son of Man does not refuse John's obeisance, as the angels elsewhere do (Rev 19:10; 22:8-9). In Revelation, the Messiah/Son of Man is one who may be worshipped, and this point is reiterated in chap. 5.[81] There were Jewish precedents for referring to the messiah as Son of God, and much of the imagery associated with the Son of Man was also associated with the deity, but worship of any figure other than the Most High God is highly exceptional in a Jewish context.[82] The worship of Jesus, and the way in which divine imagery is applied to him, marks perhaps the most fundamental point at which Revelation departs from Jewish precedent.

Another striking image is offered in chap. 5. John is told that "the Lion of the tribe of Judah, the Root of David, has conquered"; what he sees, though, is not a lion but "a lamb standing as if it had been slaughtered" (5:6). The lion is a traditional messianic symbol (Gen 49:9). The lamb only acquired messianic significance in a Christian context because of its sacrificial connotations and the death of Jesus. The image of the lamb evidently entails a significant modification of the Jewish concept of the messiah.[83] It is important, however, to see that the two symbols are held

---

80. See Yarbro Collins, "The 'Son of Man' Tradition and the Book of Revelation," in *Cosmology and Eschatology*, 159-97. The two figures are also identified in the Old Greek translation of Daniel, but this is most probably due to textual corruption.

81. R. Bauckham, *The Climax of Prophecy: Studies on the Book of Revelation* (Edinburgh: T & T Clark, 1993) 133-40 ("The Worship of Jesus").

82. L. W. Hurtado, *One God, One Lord: Early Christian Devotion and Ancient Jewish Monotheism* (Philadelphia: Fortress, 1988); idem, *How on Earth did Jesus Become a God?* (Grand Rapids: Eerdmans, 2005) 31-55. See also L. T. Stuckenbruck, *Angel Veneration and Christology: A Study in Early Judaism and in the Christology of the Apocalypse of John* (WUNT 2/70; Tübingen: Mohr Siebeck, 1995). It is possible that the Son of Man is the recipient of worship in *1 Enoch* 48:5 (Similitudes), but it is also possible that the worship is directed to the Lord of Spirits in that passage.

83. D. L. Barr, "The Apocalypse as a Symbolic Transformation of the World: A Literary Analysis," *Interpretation* 38 (1984) 41.

in tension. The Lion is not simply replaced by the Lamb, as will become evident later in Revelation chap. 19.[84] Rather, the point is that the Lamb, who died a shameful death on the cross, is now enthroned in power and glory as the Lion. A somewhat similar tension can be found in the Similitudes of Enoch. There the Son of Man, or Righteous One, is the heavenly champion of the poor and the lowly, who are the righteous ones on earth. The heavenly Righteous One is hidden, but when he will be revealed he will cast down the kings and the mighty and exalt the lowly righteous ones. Revelation differs from the Similitudes, however, in one important respect. In the Christian context, the Son of Man is not only the champion of the lowly; he has himself experienced their lot. The persecuted Christians can identify with the Lamb that was slain more fully than with a figure who is only revealed in glory.

## The War with the Dragon

Revelation 12 provides an exceptionally clear example of the use of Jewish source material, in the account of the battle between Michael and the Dragon in vss. 7-9.[85] This passage is surrounded by three other units to make up the chapter.[86] First we read of the woman giving birth in heaven, under the hostile watch of the Dragon. Her child is clearly identifiable as the messiah, the one who is to rule the nations with a rod of iron (cf. Ps 2:9). He is immediately snatched away to God and his throne. This passage is usually understood as a reference to the ascension of Jesus,[87] but the fact that there is no reference to his death has given rise to the suspicion that here too we may have a Jewish source.[88] In the present context, the passage must be read as a highly condensed synopsis of the career of the

---

84. See A. Yarbro Collins, "Eschatology in the Book of Revelation," *Ex Auditu* 6 (1990) 69-70.

85. For the history of interpretation, see Koester, *Revelation*, 527-30. Marshall, *Parables of War*, reads the entire book as Jewish, on the grounds that Christianity had not yet separated from Judaism. Nonetheless, the veneration of Jesus is distinctive in a Jewish context.

86. See the discussion of the literary context by Jan Dochhorn, *Schriftgelehrte Prophetie* (WUNT 268; Tübingen: Mohr Siebeck, 2010) 79-139; Michael Koch, *Drachenkampf und Sonnenfrau. Zur Funktion des Mythischen in der Johannesapokalypse am Beispiel von Apk 12* (WUNT 184; Tübingen: Mohr Siebeck, 2004) 96-124.

87. P. Prigent, *Apocalypse 12: Histoire de l'exégèse* (Tübingen: Mohr Siebeck, 1959) 8, 136.

88. A. Yarbro Collins, *The Combat Myth in the Book of Revelation*, 105.

messiah. There is no interest here in history before the birth of the messiah, not even in the history of Israel. The focus falls on the short interval between the time of Christ and the author's present.

The second section, vss. 7-9, tells of the battle in heaven between Michael and the Dragon. This is a new episode, linked to the preceding verses by the figure of the Dragon. The abrupt transition, and the fact that Michael rather than Christ is the protagonist, constitutes strong evidence that we have here a Jewish source. The casting down of Satan had its biblical source in Isaiah 14 and was developed in an apocalyptic context, possibly as early as the first century CE, in 2 *Enoch* 29 and the *Life of Adam and Eve* 12–17.[89] The role of Michael as heavenly warrior is adumbrated in Daniel 10 in his battle with the Prince of Greece and again in the *War Scroll* from Qumran where his adversary is Belial. The Dragon of Revelation 12 resembles Belial as a cosmic, Satanic, figure. It seems likely, then, that we have here a fragment of a Jewish myth. The placement of this fragment in Revelation is remarkable, however, since it marks neither the beginning nor the end of history but follows the birth and exaltation of the messiah. In short, the birth and snatching up of the messiah only mark the beginning of the eschatological woes. In the context of Revelation as a whole, the messiah will come again. The double coming of the messiah is, of course, a specifically Christian concept, necessitated by the abrupt termination of the earthly career of Jesus.

The third section of Revelation 12 is, for all practical purposes, a reinterpretation of the second. The "loud voice" proclaims "the kingdom of our God" and the authority of the messiah. But here the defeat of Satan is not attributed to Michael, but to the Christian brethren who have defeated him by "the blood of the Lamb" and by their testimony, "for they did not cling to life in the face of death." The martyrs share in the victory of Michael by their willingness to die. Finally, the last section of the chapter describes how the dragon sets off to make war on earth "in great wrath because his time is short."

The third section, in particular, gives a clear picture of the ethical implications of the vision. It is an ethic for martyrdom.[90] Christians can

---

89. Ibid., 82. On the various interpretations of the fall of Satan, see Koester, *Revelation*, 550; Dochhorn, *Schriftgelehrte Prophetie*, 256-60.

90. A. Yarbro Collins, "The Political Perspective of the Revelation to John," in *Cosmology and Eschatology*, 198-217; Jan Willem van Henten, "The Concept of Martyrdom in Revelation," in Frey, Kelhoffer, and Tóth, *Die Johannesapokalypse*, 587-618; Roland Bergmeier, "Zeugnis und Martyrium," ibid., 619-47.

defeat Satan by refusing to cling to life in the face of death. In this they are inspired by the powerful example of Christ; hence the "blood of the Lamb." But while this ethic of martyrdom has a distinctively Christian nuance here, it is not without precedent in Judaism.[91] In Daniel 10–12 the heroes in the time of persecution are the wise teachers who fall by sword and flame "so that they may be refined, purified, and cleansed" (Dan 11:35) but who subsequently shine like the stars in the resurrection. They are not said explicitly to defeat the "Prince of Greece," but they share in the victory at the resurrection. In both texts, the key to victory and exaltation is willingness to renounce life in this world. The primary difference between the two passages is that in Revelation the ethic is reinforced by the example of Jesus, and the ultimate victory is guaranteed by his exaltation. The central Christian event of the death and resurrection of Jesus, then, leads to a modification of the structure of eschatology, insofar as the career of the messiah is both past and future. This modification, however, does not lead to a different ethic from that of a Jewish apocalypse like Daniel, but reinforces it by the example of Christ and strengthens the certainty of the outcome.

Here again it is important to note that the role of Michael is supplemented, not negated. The victory of the martyrs is not just a moral victory. Revelation, like Daniel, emphatically asserts that evil is overthrown in an objective sense. In Daniel and the Qumran *War Scroll,* Michael plays a key role in the final phase of the battle. In Revelation, he is relegated to the first phase. The final phase is ushered in by the theophany of Christ as divine warrior in chap. 19.

### The Sword of His Mouth

A third illustration of the transformation of Jewish tradition in the portrayal of Jesus is provided by Revelation 19. Here John sees the heavens opened and a rider on a white horse, who is identified as the Word of God and is clearly the messiah. He leads the armies of heaven. From his mouth comes a sharp sword with which to strike down the nations. Subsequently, the beast and the false prophet are thrown alive into the lake of fire, and their followers are slain by the rider on the horse.

The image of the sword of the mouth is derived from Isaiah 11:4 and

91. Cf. Bauckham, *The Climax of Prophecy,* 237.

is a staple of messianic prophecy around the turn of the era.[92] The Hebrew text of Isaiah speaks of "the rod of his mouth," with which he shall strike the earth, while with the breath of his lips he shall slay the wicked. The Septuagint rendered the phrase in question as "the word of his mouth," and it is quoted in this form in the *Psalms of Solomon* 17:24-25. The effect is equally destructive: the messiah is "to smash the arrogance of sinners like a potter's jar; to shatter all their substance with an iron rod; to destroy the unlawful nations with the word of his mouth." The apocalypse of 4 Ezra, roughly contemporary with Revelation, envisages the messiah as a man who rises from the sea and wages war against a hostile multitude:

> And behold when he saw the onrush of the approaching multitude, he neither lifted his hand nor held a spear or any weapon of war; but I saw only how he sent forth from his mouth as it were a stream of fire and from his lips a flaming breath and from his tongue he shot forth a storm of sparks. All these were mingled together, the stream of fire and the flaming breath and the great storm, and fell on the onrushing multitude which was prepared to fight and burned them all up, so that suddenly nothing was seen of the innumerable multitude but only the dust and ashes and the smell of smoke. (4 Ezra 13:9-11)

It should be noted that the violence of the messiah typically has a fantastic character. He was not expected to prevail by normal military means, but by divine power. The implications of this imagery for human action might vary. Apocalyptic visions could sometimes be used to encourage militant action, as in the Animal Apocalypse in *1 Enoch,* but more typically they supported a quietistic attitude. Daniel dismissed the Maccabees as at most "a little help" (Dan 11:34). 4 Ezra most probably meant to discourage revolutionary initiatives by promising a greater miraculous deliverance in the future. But if the violence of the judgment had a fantastic, miraculous character, it was nonetheless real. It is essential to the logic of both 4 Ezra and of Revelation that the wicked will actually be destroyed. The activity of Christ as divine warrior in chap. 19 cannot be equated with his death, which has already taken place. It is of the essence of the apocalyptic vision in both Judaism and Christianity that the defeat of evil and the wicked is a real, public event that only takes place at the end of history. The death of Jesus marks a veritable D-day in the eschatological timetable, but the final judgment is yet to come.

92. Collins, *The Scepter and the Star,* 52-78.

Rather than a transvaluation of apocalyptic imagery, what we find in Revelation 19 is a transvaluation of the figure of Jesus of Nazareth. There is nothing in the Gospels to suggest that Jesus wielded a sword against anyone, either by hand or mouth. Precisely for that reason, the idea that he was the messiah, son of David, must have seemed extremely paradoxical to most Jews of the time. The expectations associated with the messiah are set forth quite clearly in such texts as the *Psalms of Solomon* and the *Scroll of Benedictions* (1QSb) from Qumran, which we have cited above. He was to drive the Gentiles from Jerusalem, slay them with the breath of his mouth, and rule them with an iron rod. The historical career of Jesus hardly fulfilled these expectations. What we find in Revelation, and to a lesser extent in other apocalyptic passages such as Mark 13, is the projection into the future of what was unfulfilled in the past. Jesus did not destroy the wicked in his earthly life, but he would return with supernatural power to complete the task. The picture of Christ that we get in Revelation 19 is at variance with any account of the historical Jesus, but it conforms perfectly to the expectations of the apocalyptic genre.

Here again we find that the ethics of Revelation are shaped by apocalyptic tradition rather than by Christian innovation. Nowhere does John of Patmos tell us to love our enemies, and neither does he preach forgiveness. Rather, his themes are justice and judgment,[93] and in this respect he stands fully in the tradition of Jewish apocalypticism.

Revelation is the most clearly anti-imperial book in the New Testament.[94] In this respect it has much in common with contemporary Jewish works such as 4 Ezra, *2 Baruch,* and *Sib Or. 5.* Steven Friesen has demonstrated the antithetical relation of Revelation to the imperial cult.[95]

93. Cf. Fiorenza, *The Book of Revelation: Justice and Judgment.*

94. For a somewhat simplified presentation: Elaine Pagels, *Revelations. Visions, Prophecy, and Politics in the Book of Revelation* (New York: Viking, 2012) 1-35 ("John's Revelation: Challenging the Evil Empire, Rome"). In contrast, Paul Duff, *Who Rides the Beast? Prophetic Rivalry and the Rhetoric of Crisis in the Churches of the Apocalypse* (New York: Oxford, 2001) focuses on conflicts within the churches and argues that opposition to empire is not the central focus of Revelation. He does not deny that John vilifies Rome, but he argues that John "tried to engineer a crisis in the minds of his readers" (129).

95. Steven J. Friesen, *Imperial Cults and the Apocalypse of John,* and "Apocalypse and Empire," in Collins, ed., *The Oxford Handbook of Apocalyptic Literature,* 163-79, The latter work includes an excellent history of scholarship on the subject. On the economic critique, see also Richard Bauckham, "The Economic Critique of Rome in Revelation 18," in Loveday Alexander, ed., *Images of Empire* (JSOTSup 122; Sheffield: Sheffield Academic Press, 1991) 47-90.

Moreover, "John's robust critique of Rome included what we would call economy, politics, trade, religion, popular opinion, and ethics, making his opposition to imperial power systematic enough to be seen as opposed to any empire."[96] Stephen Moore has challenged this view of Revelation, arguing instead for "a symbiotic relationship between Revelation's apocalyptic eschatology and Roman imperial ideology, one that, for all Revelation's ostensible antipathy toward Rome, reduces Revelation to representing the divine sphere as a kind of über-Rome or Roman Empire writ large."[97] The final empire of Christ mimics the earthly empire of Caesar, and this, in Moore's view, "compromises its endeavor to shatter the relentless cycle of empire once and for all."[98] There is some validity in this critique, but the idea of a final everlasting divine kingdom, replacing the sequence of earthly kingdoms, was not an invention of the Roman era. Revelation here was echoing Daniel, and ancient Near Eastern mythologies dating back to the dawn of history. Moore is right, however, that apocalyptic eschatology does not abolish empire, but replaces transitory human empires with an everlasting divine one.[99]

## Conclusion

The new situation of Christianity led to some modifications in the apocalyptic genre, intensifying the focus on the present and imminent future and expanding the role of the messiah. The Christian apocalypticist writes

96. Friesen, "Apocalypse and Empire," 169.

97. Stephen D. Moore, *Empire and Apocalypse. Postcolonialism and the New Testament* (Sheffield: Sheffield Phoenix, 2006) 123.

98. Ibid.

99. Moore was not the first to suggest that Revelation may have been more like the Roman empire than unlike it. See the discussion by Friesen, "Apocalypse and Empire," 168-69. Robert Royalty, *The Streets of Heaven: The Ideology of Wealth in the Apocalypse of John* (Macon, GA: Macon University Press, 1998) 246, argues that Revelation confers the wealth of Rome on the new Jerusalem: "Opposition to the dominant culture in the Apocalypse is not an attempt to redeem that culture but rather an attempt to replace it with a Christianized version of the same thing." Christopher A. Frilingos, *Spectacles of Empire. Monsters, Martyrs, and the Book of Revelation* (Philadelphia: University of Pennsylvania, 2004) argues that Revelation adopts the Roman fascination with spectacle: "the New Jerusalem invites the audience into an imperial arena" (115). Harry Maier, *Apocalypse Recalled: The Book of Revelation after Christendom* (Minneapolis: Fortress, 2001) recognizes mimicry of the Roman empire in Revelation, but sees it as sarcastic mockery.

at a different point on the eschatological timetable from his Jewish counterpart. The messiah has already come. The life of the messiah, and especially his suffering and death, are available to the Christian visionary as a source of inspiration and example. Moreover, the role of the messiah in Revelation is more exalted than in any Jewish apocalypse, since he is the recipient of worship. But Christianity did not simply bend the apocalyptic genre to its purpose. The transformations worked both ways. The impact of apocalyptic conventions is most obvious in the portrayal of Jesus as divine warrior in Revelation 19, a portrayal that draws little from the Gospels and that is strikingly similar to the contemporary portrayal of the messiah in 4 Ezra. Moreover, the ethical values of Revelation are not conspicuously different from those of Jewish apocalypses such as Daniel and 4 Ezra, and lack the most distinctive notes of the teaching of Jesus. This fact has been a source of scandal for some Christian theologians, from Martin Luther, who denied that it either taught or recognized Christ,[100] to Rudolf Bultmann, who regarded it as "a weakly Christianized Judaism."[101] Be that as it may, Christians in every century down to the present have turned to the book for symbols to express their fundamental hopes and fears.[102]

100. M. Luther, "Vorrede auf die Offenbarung des Johannes," in *Das Neue Testament Deutsch* (Wittenberg, 1522); E. Lohse, "Wie Christlich ist die Offenbarung des Johannes?" *NTS* 34 (1988) 322.

101. Bultmann, *Theology of the New Testament*, 2:175.

102. On the reception history of Revelation see Judith Kovacs and Christopher Rowland, *Revelation* (Blackwell Bible Commentaries; Oxford: Blackwell, 2004), especially 1-38. Koester, *Revelation*, also contains rich discussions of the history of interpretation in the course of his commentary.

# Epilogue

The Jewish apocalypses were not produced by a single "apocalyptic move-ment" but constituted a genre that could be utilized by different groups in various situations. This genre was characterized by a conventional manner of revelation, through heavenly journeys or visions, mediated by an angel to a pseudonymous seer. It also involved a conceptual framework which assumed that this life was bounded by the heavenly world of the angels and by the prospect of eschatological judgment. This conceptual frame-work is a symbolic structure that can be given expression through different theological traditions and with varying emphases on the pattern of history or the cosmology of the heavenly regions. The apocalyptic revelation pro-vides a comprehensive view of the world, which then provides the basis for exhortation or consolation. The problems to which these revelations are addressed vary in kind. An apocalypse can provide support in the face of persecution (e.g., Daniel); reassurance in the face of culture shock (pos-sibly the Book of the Watchers) or social powerlessness (the Similitudes of Enoch); reorientation in the wake of historical trauma *(2 Baruch, 3 Ba-ruch);* consolation for the dismal fate of humanity (4 Ezra); or comfort for the inevitability of death (the *Testament of Abraham*). The constant factor is that the problem is put in perspective by the otherworldly revelation of a transcendent world and eschatological judgment.

The apocalyptic worldview described here overlaps with, but is not identical with, the phenomenon that anthropologists call millenarianism (a term which is itself derived from the thousand-year reign in the book of Revelation).[1] Millenarianism usually refers to movements that hope for

---

1. See, e.g., K. Burridge, *New Heaven, New Earth: A Study of Millenarian Activities*

the overthrow or reversal of the present social order. The goals of such movements are often quite this-worldly, the attainment of heaven on earth, and they are often led by a charismatic prophet.[2] These features can all be found in the apocalyptic literature. Daniel and Revelation certainly hoped for the overthrow of the present world order. The messianic age would approximate to heaven on earth. The career of Jesus of Nazareth can be viewed as that of a charismatic prophet who inspired a millenarian movement. But the correspondences are far from complete.

To begin with, we have very little information of a sociological nature about the movements that produced the Jewish apocalyptic literature. There most probably was a movement behind the Enoch literature, but only in the cases of the Dead Sea Scrolls and early Christianity do we have sufficient information to attempt a sociological description.[3] We should not assume that every apocalypse represents a movement in any meaningful sense of the word. We simply do not know whether the author of 4 Ezra had any followers; in any case, he scarcely had a program that could inspire a movement. Many apocalypses, including 4 Ezra, are reflective compositions on the meaning of life and history that look back on a crisis such as the destruction of Jerusalem and try to make sense of it in retrospect. The goal they envision often includes the transformation of the earth, at least for a period. But the most distinctive features of apocalyptic hope are otherworldly; they concern life with the angels or the resurrection of the dead. The great apocalypses from the end of the first century CE, 4 Ezra, 2 *Baruch,* and Revelation, contain compendia of eschatological traditions that include the hope for a messianic reign on earth but also look beyond it to a new creation and the judgment of the dead. Charismatic leaders play a very limited role in the literature we have surveyed. Much remains to be explored about the relation of this literature to millenarian movements. It should be emphasized, however, that these

(New York: Schocken, 1969); Y. Talmon, "Millenarianism," in D. L. Sills, ed., *International Encyclopedia of the Social Sciences* (New York: Free Press, 1968) 10:349-62; B. R. Wilson, *Magic and the Millennium* (New York: Harper and Row, 1973).

2. J. G. Gager, *Kingdom and Community: The Social World of Early Christianity* (Englewood Cliffs, NJ: Prentice-Hall, 1975) 21.

3. P. F. Esler, "Social-Scientific Approaches," in Collins, ed., *The Oxford Handbook of Apocalyptic Literature,* 123-24. For a pioneering sociological study in this area, see A. I. Baumgarten, *The Flourishing of Jewish Sectarianism in the Maccabean Era: An Interpretation* (Leiden: Brill, 1997). On the Dead Sea Scrolls, see Eyal Regev, *Sectarianism in Qumran: A Cross-Cultural Perspective* (Berlin: de Gruyter, 2007); Jutta Jokiranta, "Sociological Approaches to Qumran Sectarianism," in Lim and Collins, eds., *The Oxford Handbook of the Dead Sea Scrolls,* 200-31.

movements are very diverse, and anthropological models derived from one set of data can never be expected to fit another set exactly.

Despite frequent assertions to the contrary, the genre did not die out at the end of the first century CE.[4] After the failure of the Jewish revolts against Rome, the rabbis turned away from eschatological expectation,[5] but various aspects of the tradition flourished in the Hekalot literature and in messianic and eschatological expectation.[6] Messianic and apocalyptic movements have continued to flourish in modern Israel.[7] In Christianity, the genre proliferated from the second century onward.[8] Here again we may distinguish the "horizontal" eschatological concerns associated with the "pursuit of the millennium" in the Middle Ages, and the "vertical" visionary literature that attained a literary afterlife through its adaptation in Dante's *Divine Comedy*.[9]

## Modern Apocalypticism

Perhaps the most obvious way in which apocalypticism persists in the modern world is the recurring expectation of an imminent end of history or of the world itself. Calculation of the end, whether of an immediate

---

4. L. DiTommaso, "Apocalypses and Apocalypticism in Antiquity: Part II," *Currents in Biblical Research* 5 (2007) 398-407.

5. See J. Neusner, *Messiah in Context* (Philadelphia: Fortress, 1984).

6. A. J. Saldarini, "Apocalypses and 'Apocalyptic' in Rabbinic Literature and Mysticism," *Semeia* 14 (1979) 187-205. On the later tradition, see G. Scholem, *The Messianic Idea in Judaism and Other Essays on Jewish Spirituality* (New York: Schocken, 1971); Moshe Idel, "Jewish Apocalypticism: 670-1670," in Bernard McGinn, ed., *The Encyclopedia of Apocalypticism.* Vol. 2: *Apocalypticism in Western History and Culture* (New York: Continuum, 1998) 204-37. For a critical assessment of the continuity between apocalypticism and Jewish mysticism see Boustan and McCullough, "Apocalyptic Literature and the Study of Early Jewish Mysticism," in Collins, ed., *The Oxford Handbook of Apocalypticism*, 85-103.

7. A. Ravitzky, *Messianism, Zionism, and Jewish Religious Radicalism* (Chicago: University of Chicago Press, 1996); J. Marcus, "Modern and Ancient Jewish Apocalypticism," *Journal of Religion* 76 (1996) 1-27; Motti Inbari, "Messianism as a Political Power in Contemporary Judaism," in Collins, ed., *The Oxford Handbook of Apocalyptic Literature*, 407-21.

8. A. Yarbro Collins, "The Early Christian Apocalypses," *Semeia* 14 (1979) 61-121; eadem, "Early Christian Apocalyptic Literature," *ANRW,* II.25.4665-4711.

9. B. McGinn, *Apocalyptic Spirituality* (New York: Paulist, 1979); idem, *Visions of the End: Apocalyptic Traditions in the Middle Ages* (New York: Columbia University Press, 1979); idem, ed., *The Encyclopedia of Apocalypticism.* Vol. 2: *Apocalypticism in Western History and Culture* (New York: Continuum, 1998).

crisis or of history as a whole, is at most a minor motif in the ancient apocalypses, but there is a fateful precedent in the book of Daniel, which calculates the time remaining as a specific number of days. In the context of Daniel, the "end" in question is the end of the profanation of the temple and persecution of the Judeans by Antiochus Epiphanes. Moreover, Daniel offers not one but several calculations of the remaining time, even juxtaposing contradictory numbers. Daniel also offered a broader schema for calculating the duration of history, in the form of a prediction that the time from the destruction of Jerusalem by the Babylonians to the "end" would be 70 weeks of years, or 490 years. Daniel's calculation was already an allegorical reinterpretation of the prophecy of Jeremiah that Jerusalem would be desolate for 70 years. Later interpreters applied a similar method to Daniel's predictions, often reinterpreting days as years. By such a calculation the upstate New York farmer, William Miller, calculated that the world would end about the year 1843. (He interpreted Dan 8:14, "two thousand three hundred evenings and mornings" as 2,300 years, and, somewhat arbitrarily, took 458 BCE, the mission of Ezra, as his point of departure.) When 1843 came and went, some of his followers settled on a new, more specific date, October 22, 1844. The failure of this prediction became known as "The Great Disappointment." His followers eventually gave rise to the Seventh-day Adventist movement. Paul Boyer has argued that Miller's calculation was an archaism in its time, and that he became an example of the perils of date-setting.[10] Nonetheless there have been several high-profile calculations in recent years, notably Harold Camping's prediction that the world would end on May 21, 2011, and the much publicized end of the Mayan calendar on December 21, 2012.

The main "apocalyptic" tradition in modern America is premillennial dispensationalism, which is based on a system formulated by John Nelson Darby, the founder of the Plymouth Brethren. It is based not so much on the classic apocalyptic texts as on all of scripture construed as prophecy about the end-time, and the continual attempt to identify and decode biblical proof-texts. Hal Lindsey's best-selling book, the *Late Great Planet Earth* is a classic formulation, which has been revised through multiple editions without any apparent loss in credibility among its readers.[11]

10. Paul Boyer, *When Time Shall Be No More. Prophecy Belief in Modern American Culture* (Cambridge, MA: Harvard University Press, 1992) 82.

11. Hal Lindsay, with C. C. Carlson, *The Late Great Planet Earth* (Grand Rapids: Zondervan, 1970).

The mind-set was popularized in the *Left Behind* series of novels. The main tenets of dispensationalism are characterized as follows by Paul Boyer: "According to this scheme, as history nears its climax, probably very soon, a series of 'signs' will alert the faithful that the end is near. Wickedness and natural disasters will increase. The founding of the state of Israel in 1948 and Israel's recapture of the Old City of Jerusalem in 1967 are considered prophetic signs of the first importance. These signs will culminate in the Rapture, a doctrine drawn from 1 Thessalonians 4:16. In this event of cosmic import, set to occur at some unknown future time . . . all true believers will join Christ in the air."[12] In the eyes of the secular world and of liberal Christians and Jews, and indeed of anyone who accepts a modern scientific view of the world, dispensationalism, which is often accompanied by political and social conservatism, appears as irrational superstition. Many people tend to equate it with apocalypticism at large. Is this equation fair to the ancient texts?

Dispensational "prophecy-belief" is in some crucial respects a highly reductive variant of apocalypticism. While Hal Lindsey and the *Left Behind* series look forward to life in heaven and so may be said to affirm the apocalyptic hope for transcendence of death, they are mainly preoccupied with the signs of the end. Their writings lack the allusive depth of mythic symbolism, or the imaginative range of the ascent apocalypses. The literalistic decoding of biblical passages seems simplistic. Where the ancient apocalypses often arose out of crisis and persecution, their modern counterparts often seem smugly self-congratulatory on the part of a presumed elect. They lack the sense of anomie and existential *Angst* that characterizes the classic apocalyptic texts.

That said, there are points of continuity too. From the dispensationalist perspective, the world is in crisis, although that perspective may seem paranoid to outsiders. Decoding interpretation, which "involves presenting the meaning of the text in another, less allusive form, showing what the text really means, with great attention to the details,"[13] has a long history, dating back to the *pesharim* in the Dead Sea Scrolls and even to the book of Daniel. It has proven impervious to falsification over the centuries. The ancient apocalypses, too, are prone to dualism, to the division of the world

12. Paul Boyer, "The Apocalyptic in the Twentieth Century," in C. Kleinhenz and F. J. LeMoine, eds., *Waiting in Fearful Hope. Approaching the New Millennium* (Madison: University of Wisconsin, 1999) 151.

13. Kovacs and Rowland, *Revelation*, 8.

between the elect and the damned, and are often gleeful in their anticipation of eschatological vindication. Undeniably, the ancient writers too
pinned their hopes on divine intervention which did not materialize when
they expected that it would.

Consequently, some modern commentators see apocalypticism as
a tradition beyond redemption. Rejecting Amos Wilder's affirmation of
"the healthy function of genuine transcendental apocalyptic,"[14] Lorenzo
DiTommaso writes that "apocalypticism is an *unhealthy* worldview, particularly in its biblical form. It is inimical to a mature vision of human
destiny, or any social order founded on humanistic ideals. It is hostile to
life on Earth, especially in light of the nature and needs of contemporary society."[15] Critics are especially troubled by the violence of apocalyptic rhetoric, which does not directly incite violent action but is widely
perceived as promoting polarization and intolerance. David Frankfurter
dismisses arguments that the violence in Revelation was "directed either
to spark revolutionary justice for the subaltern or to rail against a tyranni-
cal Roman empire — reading the text in either case as advocating justice,
equality, and hope rather than brutality, misogyny and vengeance" — as
attempts to "rationalize" it, and as "canonical special pleading for a very
problematic text."[16]

Critics like Frankfurter are right to object to the revisionist exegesis
that tries to salvage canonical apocalypticism by denying or minimizing its
potential for violence. This is indeed problematic literature. But it is also
reductive to see only "brutality, misogyny and vengeance" in apocalyptic literature. This is a complex tradition that has contributed to western
culture in manifold ways. The argument that texts like Revelation advocate justice and hope (not always equality!) is not without substance. As
Elisabeth Fiorenza has argued, the author of Revelation was "clearly on
the side of the poor and oppressed."[17] In many cases, apocalyptic visions

14. Amos Wilder, "The Rhetoric of Ancient and Modern Apocalyptic," *Int* 25 (1971)
436-53.

15. Lorenzo DiTommaso, "The Apocalyptic Other," in Daniel C. Harlow et al., eds.,
*The "Other" in Second Temple Judaism: Essays in Honor of John J. Collins* (Grand Rapids:
Eerdmans, 2011) 236.

16. David Frankfurter, "The Legacy of Sectarian Rage: Vengeance Fantasies in the
New Testament," in David A. Bernat and Jonathan Klawans, eds., *Religion and Violence. The
Biblical Heritage* (Sheffield: Sheffield Phoenix, 2007) 114-28.

17. Elisabeth Schüssler Fiorenza, *Invitation to the Book of Revelation* (New York:
Doubleday, 1981) 173.

that affirm a radical reversal of the present order give hope to people who otherwise would have no hope at all. If these visions are violent, they are at least honest in bringing to expression feelings that are almost inevitable for people who have suffered at the hands of a conquering power. Anger and fantasies of violence may be life-giving for the powerless. This is not to deny that they may also be brutally violent. In the postmodern world we should have learned that human actions are seldom entirely pure, and that justice and brutality all too often go hand in hand.

Perhaps the most far-reaching legacy of apocalypticism, however, is in the store of images and motifs that it bequeaths to the imagination both in art and in literature. Images of beasts rising from the sea persist from the ancient myths to modern times because they articulate the sense of a world beyond human control. Modern "apocalyptic" novels, such as Cormac McCarthy's *The Road,* often focus on desolation and destruction. But as Amos Wilder noted, "the full apocalyptic scenario should include salvation as well as judgment, the new age as well as the old. The persistence of apocalyptic themes, however, even in secular writings, should warn us against any dismissal of this tradition as something humanity has outgrown. Apocalypticism is born of fears and hopes that are endemic to the human condition.

It is perhaps unfortunate that apocalyptic literature is so often invested with theological authority, with an eye to coded messages and instructions, rather than being read as an exuberant product of the human imagination. Even more unfortunate is the modern proclivity to reduce the symbolic to propositional truths. In the hands of literalists, apocalyptic literature distorts human experience and may be ethically dangerous. But the tradition is too rich and multiform to be left to the literalists. It is a resilient tradition that continues to haunt our imaginations and remains an indispensable resource for making sense of human experience.

# Bibliography

Abegg, M. "The Messiah at Qumran: Are We Still Seeing Double?" *Dead Sea Discoveries* 2 (1995) 125-44.

———. "Messianic Hope and 4Q285: A Reassessment." *JBL* 113 (1994) 81-91.

Adam, A., and C. Burchard. *Antike Berichte über die Essener.* 2d ed. Berlin: de Gruyter, 1972.

Albani, M. *Astronomie und Schöpfungsglaube: Untersuchungen zum astronomischen Henochbuch.* WMANT 68. Neukirchen–Vluyn: Neukirchener Verlag, 1994.

Albani, M., J. Frey, and A. Lange, eds. *Studies in the Book of Jubilees.* TSAJ 65. Tübingen: Mohr Siebeck, 1997.

Albertz, Rainer. "The Social Setting of the Aramaic and Hebrew Book of Daniel." In *The Book of Daniel,* edited by J. J. Collins and P. Flint, 171-204.

Alexander, P. J. *The Byzantine Apocalyptic Tradition.* Berkeley: University of California Press, 1989.

Alexander, P. S. "3 (Hebrew Apocalypse of) Enoch." In *The Old Testament Pseudepigrapha.* Volume 1: *Apocalyptic Literature and Testaments,* edited by J. H. Charlesworth, 223-313. Garden City, NY: Doubleday, 1983.

———. "Enoch and the Beginnings of Jewish Interest in Natural Science." In *The Wisdom Texts from Qumran and the Development of Sapiential Thought,* edited by Charlotte Hempel et al., 223-43. BETL 149. Leuven: Peeters, 2002.

———. "From Son of Adam to Second God. Transformations of the Biblical Enoch." In *Biblical Figures Outside the Bible,* edited by M. E. Stone and T. E. Bergren, 87-122. Harrisburg, PA: Trinity Press International, 1998.

———. *The Mystical Texts: Songs of the Sabbath Sacrifice and Related Manuscripts.* London: T & T Clark, 2006.

———. "Predestination and Free Will in the Theology of the Dead Sea Scrolls." In *Divine and Human Agency in Paul and His Cultural Environment,* edited by J. M. G. Barclay and Simon Gathercole, 39-47. Library of New Testament Studies 335. London: Continuum, 2006.

———. "The Redaction History of *Serekh ha Yaḥad:* A Proposal." *RevQ* 17 (1996) 437-56.

Alexandre, C. *Excursus ad Sibyllina.* Paris: Didot, 1856.

Allison, D. C. *The End of the Ages Has Come.* Philadelphia: Fortress, 1985.

————. "The Eschatology of Jesus." In *The Encyclopedia of Apocalypticism.* Volume 1: *The Origins of Apocalypticism in Judaism and Early Christianity,* edited by J. J. Collins, 267-302. New York: Continuum, 1998.

————. *Jesus of Nazareth: Millenarian Prophet.* Minneapolis: Fortress, 1998.

————. "A Plea for Thorough-Going Eschatology." *JBL* 113 (1994) 651-68.

————. *Testament of Abraham.* CEJL. Berlin: de Gruyter, 2003.

Andersen, F. "2 Enoch." In *The Old Testament Pseudepigrapha.* Volume 1: *Apocalyptic Literature and Testaments,* edited by J. H. Charlesworth, 91-221. Garden City, NY: Doubleday, 1983.

Angel, Joseph L. *Otherworldly and Eschatological Priesthood in the Dead Sea Scrolls.* STDJ 86. Leiden: Brill, 2010.

Anklesaria, B. T. *Zand-ī Vohuman Yasn.* Bombay: Camay Oriental Institute, 1967.

Annus, Amar. "On the Origin of Watchers: A Comparative Study of the Antediluvian Wisdom in Mesopotamian and Jewish Traditions." *JSP* 19 (2010) 277-320.

Argall, R. A. *1 Enoch and Sirach: A Comparative Literary and Conceptual Analysis of the Themes of Revelation, Creation, and Judgment.* Atlanta: Scholars Press, 1995.

Assefa, Daniel. *L'Apocalypse des animaux (1 Hen 85-90): une propagande militaire. Approches narrative, historico-critique, perspectives théologiques.* JSJSup 120. Leiden: Brill, 2007.

Assmann, Jan. "Königsdogma und Heilserwartung: Politische und kultische Kaosbeschreibungen in altägyptischen Texten." In *Apocalypticism in the Mediterranean World and the Near East: Proceedings of the International Colloquium on Apocalypticism, Uppsala, August 12-17, 1979,* edited by D. Hellholm, 345-77. Tübingen: Mohr Siebeck, 1983.

Atkinson, Kenneth. *An Intertextual Study of the Psalms of Solomon.* Lewiston, NY: Mellen, 2001.

————. *I Cried to the Lord: A Study of the Psalms of Solomon's Historical Background and Social Setting.* JSJSup 84. Leiden: Brill, 2004.

Attridge, H. W. "Greek and Latin Apocalypses." *Semeia* 14 (1979) 159-86.

————. "Melchizedek in Some Early Christian Texts and 2 Enoch." In *New Perspectives on 2 Enoch,* edited by Orlov and Boccaccini, 387-410.

Audet, J.-P. "Affinités littéraires et doctrinales du 'Manuel de Discipline.'" *RB* 59 (1952) 219-38; 60 (1953) 41-82.

Aune, D. E. "The Apocalypse of John and the Problem of Genre." In *Early Christian Apocalypticism: Genre and Social Setting. Semeia* 36 (1986), edited by A. Yarbro Collins, 65-96.

————. *Prophecy in Early Christianity and the Ancient Mediterranean World.* Grand Rapids: Eerdmans, 1983.

Austin, J. L. *How to Do Things with Words.* 2d ed. Cambridge, MA: Harvard University Press, 1975.

Baldwin, J. G. *Daniel: An Introduction and Commentary.* Tyndale Old Testament Commentaries. Downers Grove, IL: InterVarsity, 1978.

Baltzer, K. *The Covenant Formulary.* Philadelphia: Fortress, 1971.

Barclay, J. M. G. *Jews in the Mediterranean Diaspora from Alexander to Trajan (323 BCE–117 CE).* Edinburgh: T & T Clark, 1996.

# Bibliography

Barr, D. L. "The Apocalypse as a Symbolic Transformation of the World: A Literary Analysis." *Interpretation* 38 (1984) 39-50.

Barr, J. "Jewish Apocalyptic in Recent Scholarly Study." *BJRL* 58 (1975) 9-35.

Barth, C. *Die Errettung vom Tode in den individuellen Klage- und Dankliedern des Alten Testaments*. Zollikon: Evangelisches Verlag, 1947.

Barton, J. *Oracles of God: Perceptions of Ancient Prophecy in Israel after the Exile*. Oxford: Oxford University Press, 1986.

————. *Reading the Old Testament: Method in Biblical Study*. 2d ed. Louisville: Westminster, 1996.

Bauckham, R. "Apocalypses." In *Justification and Variegated Nomism*. Volume 1: *The Complexities of Second Temple Judaism*, edited by D. A. Carson, P. T. O'Brien, and M. A. Seifrid, 135-87. WUNT 2/140. Tübingen: Mohr Siebeck, 2001.

————. *The Climax of Prophecy: Studies on the Book of Revelation*. Edinburgh: T & T Clark, 1993.

————. "The Economic Critique of Rome in Revelation 18." In *Images of Empire*, edited by Loveday Alexander, 47-90. JSOTSup 122. Sheffield: Sheffield Academic Press, 1991.

————. *The Fate of the Dead: Studies on the Jewish and Christian Apocalypses*. NTSup 93. Leiden: Brill, 1998.

————. *The Theology of the Book of Revelation*. Cambridge: Cambridge University Press, 1993.

Baumgarten, A. I. *The Flourishing of Jewish Sectarianism in the Maccabean Era: An Interpretation*. Leiden: Brill, 1997.

Baumgarten, J. M. "The Calendar in the Book of Jubilees and the Bible." In *Studies in Qumran Law*, 101-14. Leiden: Brill, 1977.

————. "Qumran-Essene Restraints on Marriage." In *Archaeology and History in the Dead Sea Scrolls: The New York University Conference in Memory of Yigael Yadin*, edited by L. H. Schiffman, 13-24. Sheffield: JSOT Press, 1990.

Baynes, Leslie. *The Heavenly Book Motif in Judeo-Christian Apocalypses, 200 BCE to 200 CE*. JSJSup 152. Leiden: Brill, 2012.

Beall, T. S. *Josephus' Description of the Essenes Illustrated by the Dead Sea Scrolls*. Cambridge: Cambridge University Press, 1988.

Beasley-Murray, G. R. "The Interpretation of Daniel 7." *CBQ* 45 (1983) 44-58.

Becker, Adam H. "2 Baruch." In *Outside the Bible*, edited by Feldman, Kugel, and Schiffman, 1565-85.

Becker, J. *Die Testamente der zwölf Patriarchen*. JSHRZ 3/1. Gütersloh: Mohn, 1980.

————. *Untersuchungen zur Entstehungsgeschichte der Testamente der zwölf Patriarchen*. Leiden: Brill, 1970.

Beckwith, R. T. "The Earliest Enoch Literature and Its Calendar: Marks of Their Origin, Date and Motivation." *RevQ* 10 (1981) 365-403.

Bedenbender, Andreas. *Der Gott der Welt tritt auf den Sinai. Entstehung, Entwicklung und Funktionsweise der frühjüdischen Apokalyptik*. ANTZ 8. Berlin: Institut Kirche und Judentum, 2000.

————. "The Place of the Torah in the Early Enoch Literature." In *The Early Enoch Literature*, edited by Boccaccini and Collins, 65-79.

Beker, J. C. *Paul the Apostle: The Triumph of God in Life and Thought.* Philadelphia: Fortress, 1980.

Ben-Dov, Jonathan. *Head of All Years: Astronomy and Calendars at Qumran in Their Ancient Context.* STDJ 78. Leiden: Brill, 2008.

———. "Scientific Writings in Aramaic and Hebrew at Qumran: Translation and Concealment." In *Aramaica Qumranica: Proceedings of the Conference on the Aramaic Texts from Qumran in Aix-en-Provence 30 June – 2 July 2008*, edited by Katell Berthelot and Daniel Stökl Ben Ezra, 379-402. STDJ 94. Leiden: Brill, 2010.

Ben-Dov, Jonathan, and Seth L. Sanders, eds. *Ancient Jewish Sciences and the History of Knowledge in Second Temple Literature.* New York: New York University Press, 2014.

Bentzen, A. *Daniel.* 2d ed. Tübingen: Mohr Siebeck, 1952.

Berger, K. *Das Buch der Jubiläen.* JSHRZ 2/3. Gütersloh: Mohn, 1981.

Bergmeier, R. *Die Essener-Berichte des Flavius Josephus.* Kampen: Kok Pharos, 1993.

———. "Zeugnis und Martyrium." In *Die Johannesapokalypse*, edited by Frey, Kelhoffer and Tóth, 619-47.

Bergren, T. A. "Christian Influence on the Transmission History of 4, 5, and 6 Ezra." In *The Jewish Apocalyptic Heritage in Early Christianity*, edited by J. C. VanderKam and W. Adler, 102-27. CRINT 3/4. Assen: Van Gorcum; Minneapolis: Fortress, 1996.

———. "Ezra and Nehemiah Square Off in the Apocrypha and Pseudepigrapha." In *Biblical Figures Outside the Bible*, edited by Michael E. Stone and Theodore A. Bergren, 340-63. Harrisburg, PA: Trinity Press International, 1998.

Bergsma, John S. "The Relationship between Jubilees and the Early Enochic Books." In *Enoch and the Mosaic Torah*, edited by Boccaccini and Ibba, 36-51.

Berner, Christoph. *Jahre, Jahrwochen und Jubiläen: Heptadische Geschichtskonzeptionen im Antiken Judentum.* BZAW 363. Berlin: de Gruyter, 2006.

Berthelot, Katell. *'L'humanité de l'autre homme' dans la pensée juive ancienne.* JSJSup 87. Leiden: Brill, 2004.

Berthelot, Katell, and Daniel Stökl Ben Ezra, eds. *Qumranica Aramaica: Proceedings of the Conference on the Aramaic Texts from Qumran in Aix-en-Provence 30 June – 2 July 2008.* STDJ 94. Leiden Brill, 2010.

Betz, H. D. "On the Problem of the Religio-Historical Understanding of Apocalypticism." *JTC* 6 (1969) 146-54.

———. "The Problem of Apocalyptic Genre in Greek and Hellenistic Literature: The Case of the Oracle of Trophonius." In *Apocalypticism in the Mediterranean World and the Near East: Proceedings of the International Colloquium on Apocalypticism, Uppsala, August 12-17, 1979*, edited by D. Hellholm, 577-97. Tübingen: Mohr Siebeck, 1983.

Betz, O. *Offenbarung und Schriftforschung in der Qumransekte.* Tübingen: Mohr Siebeck, 1960.

Beyerle, Stefan. *Die Gottesvorstellungen in der antik-jüdischen Apokalyptik.* JSJSup 103. Leiden: Brill, 2005.

———. "'Du bist kein Richter über dem Herrn': Zur Konzeption von Gesetz und Gericht im 4.Esrabuch." In *Recht und Ethos im Alten Testament,* edited by

S. Beyerle, G. Mayer, and H. Strauss, 315-37. Neukirchen: Neukirchener Verlag, 1999.

————. "The Imagined World of the Apocalypses." In *The Oxford Handbook of the Dead Sea Scrolls*, edited by J. J. Collins, 373-87.

Bhayro, Siam. *The Shemihaza and Asael Narrative of 1 Enoch 6-11: Introduction, Text, Translation and Commentary with Reference to Ancient Near Eastern and Biblical Antecedents*. AOAT 322. Münster: Ugarit Verlag, 2005.

Bickermann, E. *Four Strange Books of the Bible*. New York: Schocken, 1967.

Bidez, J., and F. Cumont. *Les Mages Hellénisés*. 2 vols. Paris: Les Belles Lettres, 1938.

Black, M. "The Apocalypse of Weeks in the Light of 4QEn^g." *VT* 28 (1978) 464-69.

————. *Apocalypsis Henochi Graece*. PVTG 3. Leiden: Brill, 1970.

————. *The Book of Enoch or 1 Enoch*. SVTP 7. Leiden: Brill, 1985.

————. "The Eschatology of the Similitudes of Enoch." *JTS* 3 (1952) 1-10.

————. "The Messianism of the Parables of Enoch." In *The Messiah: Developments in Earliest Judaism and Christianity*, edited by J. H. Charlesworth, 145-68. Minneapolis: Fortress, 1992.

————. *The Scrolls and Christian Origins*. New York: Scribners, 1961.

Blasius, A., and B. U. Schipper, eds. *Apokalyptik und Ägypten: eine kritische Analyse der relevanten Texte aus dem griechisch-römischen Ägypten*. Leuven: Peeters, 2002.

Boccaccini, G. *Beyond the Essene Hypothesis: The Parting of the Ways between Qumran and Enochic Judaism*. Grand Rapids: Eerdmans, 1998.

————. "Enochians, Urban Essenes, Qumranites." In *The Early Enoch Literature*, edited by Boccaccini and Collins, 301-27.

————. "Jewish Apocalyptic Tradition: The Contribution of Italian Scholarship." In *Mysteries and Revelations: Apocalyptic Studies since the Uppsala Colloquium*, edited by J. J. Collins and J. H. Charlesworth, 33-50. JSPSup 9. Sheffield: JSOT Press, 1991.

————. *Middle Judaism: Jewish Thought 300 BCE to 200 CE*. Minneapolis: Fortress, 1991.

————. *Roots of Rabbinic Judaism: An Intellectual History from Ezekiel to Daniel*. Grand Rapids: Eerdmans, 2002.

————. "The Solar Calendars of Daniel and Enoch" in *The Book of Daniel*, edited by Collins and Flint, 311-28.

Boccaccini, Gabriele, ed. *Enoch and the Messiah Son of Man: Revisiting the Book of Parables*. Grand Rapids: Eerdmans, 2007.

————, ed. *The Origins of Enochic Judaism = Henoch* 24. 1-2 (2002).

Boccaccini, Gabriele, and John J. Collins, eds. *The Early Enoch Literature*. JSJSup 121. Leiden: Brill, 2007.

Boccaccini, Gabriele, and Giovanni Ibba, eds. *Enoch and the Mosaic Torah: The Evidence of Jubilees*. Grand Rapids: Eerdmans, 2009.

Boccaccini, Gabriele, and Jason M. Zurawski. *Interpreting 4 Ezra and 2 Baruch: International Studies*. LSTS 87. London: Bloomsbury/T & T Clark, 2014.

Boer, M. C. de. *The Defeat of Death: Apocalyptic Eschatology in 1 Corinthians 15 and Romans 5*. Sheffield: JSOT Press, 1988.

————. "Paul and Apocalyptic Eschatology." In *The Encyclopedia of Apocalypticism*, edited by Collins, 345-83.

————. "Paul and Jewish Apocalyptic Eschatology." In *Apocalyptic and the New Testament,* edited by J. Marcus and M. L. Soards, 169-90. Sheffield: JSOT Press, 1989.

Bogaert, P. M. *Apocalypse de Baruch.* 2 vols. Paris: Cerf, 1969.

————. "Les Apocalypses contemporaines de Baruch, d'Esdras et de Jean." In *L'Apocalypse johannique et l'Apocalyptique dans le Nouveau Testament,* edited by J. Lambrecht, 47-68. Leuven: Leuven University Press, 1980.

Bohak, Gideon. *Joseph and Aseneth and the Jewish Temple in Heliopolis.* SBLEJL 10. Atlanta: SBL, 1996.

Bonwetsch, N. *Apokalypse Abrahams.* Leipzig: Deichert, 1897.

Borg, M. J. *Jesus in Contemporary Scholarship.* Valley Forge, PA: Trinity, 1994.

————. "A Temperate Case for a Non-Eschatological Jesus." *Forum* 2/3 (1986) 81-102.

Borger, R. "Die Beschwörungsserie Bīt Mēseri und die Himmelfahrt Henochs." *JNES* 33 (1974) 183-96.

Boring, M. E. "The Apocalypse as Christian Prophecy." In *SBL Seminar Papers, 1974,* edited by G. W. MacRae, 2:43-62. 2 vols. Missoula, MT: Scholars Press, 1974.

Böttrich, C. "The 'Book of the Secrets of Enoch' (2 En): Between Jewish Origin and Christian Transmission. An Overview." In *New Perspectives on 2 Enoch,* edited by Orlov and Boccaccini, 37-68.

————. *Weltweisheit, Menschheitsethik, Urkult: Studien zum slavischen Henochbuch.* WUNT 2/50. Tübingen: Mohr Siebeck, 1992.

Bousset, W. *The Antichrist Legend.* London: Hutchinson, 1896.

————. *Die Religion des Judentums im späthellenistischen Zeitalter.* 3d ed. Edited by H. Gressmann. Tübingen: Mohr Siebeck, 1926.

Boustan, Ra'anan, and Patrick G. McCullough, "Apocalyptic Literature and the Study of Early Jewish Mysticism." *The Oxford Handbook of Apocalyptic Literature,* edited by Collins, 85-103.

Bovon, F. "Ces chrétiens qui rêvent: L'autorité du rêve dans les premiers siècles du christianisme." In *Geschichte — Tradition — Reflexion: Festschrift für Martin Hengel,* edited by H. Cancik, H. Lichtenberger, and P. Schäfer, 3:631-53. Tübingen: Mohr Siebeck, 1996.

Box, G. H. *The Ezra Apocalypse.* London: Pitman, 1912.

————. "IV Ezra." In *The Apocrypha and Pseudepigrapha of the Old Testament.* Volume II: *Pseudepigrapha,* edited by R. H. Charles, 542-624. Oxford: Clarendon, 1913.

Box, G. H., and J. I. Landsman. *The Apocalypse of Abraham.* London: SPCK, 1918.

Boyarin, Daniel. *The Jewish Gospels: The Story of the Jewish Christ.* New York: The New Press, 2012.

————. "Was the Book of Parables a Sectarian Document? A Brief in support of Pierluigi Piovanelli." In *Enoch and the Messiah Son of Man,* edited by Boccaccini, 380-85.

Boyce, M. "Middle Persian Literature." In *Handbuch der Orientalistik,* 4/1:31-61. Leiden: Brill, 1968.

————. "On the Antiquity of Zoroastrian Apocalyptic." *BSOAS* 47 (1984) 57-75.

————. "Persian Religion in the Achaemenid Age." In *The Cambridge History of Judaism.* Volume One: *Introduction; The Persian Period,* edited by W. D. Davies and L. Finkelstein, 279-307. Cambridge: Cambridge University Press, 1984.

Boyer, Paul. "The Apocalyptic in the Twentieth Century." In *Waiting in Fearful Hope: Approaching the New Millennium,* edited by C. Kleinhenz and F. J. LeMoine, 149-69. Madison: University of Wisconsin, 1999.

―――. *When Time Shall Be No More: Prophecy Belief in Modern American Culture.* Cambridge, MA: Harvard University Press, 1992.

Brandenburger, E. *Adam und Christus.* Neukirchen–Vluyn: Neukirchener Verlag, 1962.

―――. *Himmelfahrt Moses.* JSHRZ 5/2. Gütersloh: Mohn, 1976.

―――. *Die Verborgenheit Gottes im Weltgeschehen.* Zurich: Theologischer Verlag, 1981.

Braun, M. *History and Romance.* Oxford: Oxford University Press, 1938.

Breech, E. "'These Fragments I Have Shored against My Ruins: The Form and Function of 4 Ezra.' *JBL* 92 (1973) 267-74.

Brekelmans, C. W. "The Saints of the Most High and Their Kingdom." *OTS* 14 (1965) 305-29.

Bremmer, Jan N. "Descents to Hell and Ascents to Heaven in Apocalyptic Literature." In *The Oxford Handbook of Apocalyptic Literature,* edited by Collins, 340-57.

―――. *The Rise and Fall of the Afterlife.* London: Routledge, 2001.

Brooke, G. J. *Exegesis at Qumran: 4QFlorilegium in Its Jewish Context.* Sheffield: JSOT Press, 1985.

―――. "The Messiah of Aaron in the Damascus Document." *RevQ* 15 (1991) 215-30.

―――. "Qumran Pesher: Towards the Redefinition of a Genre." *RevQ* 10 (1979-81) 483-503.

Brooke, G. J., et al. *Qumran Cave 4–XVII: Parabiblical Texts, Part 3.* DJD 22. Oxford: Clarendon, 1996.

Brown, R. E. "J. Starcky's Theory of Qumran Messianic Development." *CBQ* 28 (1966) 51-57.

―――. *The Semitic Background of the Term "Mystery" in the New Testament.* Philadelphia: Fortress, 1968.

Brownlee, W. H. *The Midrash Pesher of Habakkuk.* SBLMS 24. Missoula, MT: Scholars Press, 1979.

Buchanan, G. W. *The Consequences of the Covenant.* Leiden: Brill, 1970.

―――. *Revelation and Redemption.* Dillsboro, NC: Western North Carolina Press, 1978.

Buitenwerf, Rieuwerd. *Book III of the Sibylline Oracles and Its Social Setting, with an Introduction, Translation, and Commentary.* SVTP 17. Leiden: Brill, 2003.

―――. "The Identity of the Prophetess Sibyl in *Sibylline Oracles* III." In *Prophets and Prophecy in Jewish and Early Christian Literature,* edited by Joseph Verheyden, Korinna Zamfir and Tobias Nicklas, 41-77. WUNT 286. Tübingen: Mohr Siebeck, 2010.

Bultmann, R. *The History of the Synoptic Tradition.* New York: Harper & Row, 1968.

―――. *Theology of the New Testament.* 2 vols. New York: Scribners, 1951-55.

Burchard, Christoph. "Die Essener bei Hippolyt. Hippolyt, Ref. IX 18,2-28 und Josephus, Bell. 2.119-161." *JSJ* 8 (1977) 1-42.

Burkes, Shannon L. *God, Self, and Death: The Shape of Religious Transformation in the Second Temple Period.* JSJSup 79. Leiden: Brill, 2003.

―――. "'Life' Redefined: Wisdom and Law in Fourth Ezra and Second Baruch," *CBQ* 63 (2001) 55-71.

Burridge, K. *New Heaven, New Earth: A Study of Millenarian Activities.* New York: Schocken, 1969.

Caird, G. B. *The Language and Imagery of the Bible.* Philadelphia: Westminster, 1981. Reprint, Grand Rapids: Eerdmans, 1997.

Callaway, P. *The History of the Qumran Community: An Investigation.* Sheffield: JSOT Press, 1988.

Cameron, R., and A. J. Dewey. *The Cologne Mani Codex: "Concerning the Origin of His Body."* Missoula, MT: Scholars Press, 1979.

Camponovo, O. *Königtum, Königsherrschaft und Reich Gottes in frühjüdischen Schriften.* Göttingen: Vandenhoeck & Ruprecht, 1984.

Cancik, H. "Der Eingang in die Unterwelt: Ein religionswissenschaftlicher Versuch zu Vergil, Aeneis 6, 236-72." In *Der altsprachliche Unterricht,* 55-66. Stuttgart, 1983.

———. "Libri Fatales: Römische Offenbarungsliteratur und Geschichtstheologie." In *Apocalypticism in the Mediterranean World and the Near East: Proceedings of the International Colloquium on Apocalypticism, Uppsala, August 12-17, 1979,* edited by D. Hellholm, 549-76. Tübingen: Mohr Siebeck, 1983.

Capponi, Livia. *Il tempio di Leontopoli in Egitto. Identità politica e religiosa dei Giudei di Onia* (c. 150 a.c.-73 d.c.). Florence: ETS, 2007.

Caquot, A. "Le messianisme qumrânien." In *Qumrân,* edited by M. Delcor, 231-47. Leuven: Leuven University Press, 1978.

———. "Remarques sur les chap. 70 et 71 du livre éthiopien d'Hénoch." In *Apocalypses et Théologie de l'Espérance,* edited by H. Monloubou, 111-22. Paris: Cerf, 1977.

Carey, Greg. "Early Christian Apocalyptic Rhetoric." In *The Oxford Handbook of Apocalyptic Literature,* edited by Collins, 218-34.

———. *Ultimate Things: An Introduction to Jewish and Christian Apocalyptic Literature.* St. Louis: Chalice, 2005.

Carey, Greg, and L. Gregory Bloomquist, eds. *Vision and Persuasion: Rhetorical Dimensions of Apocalyptic Discourse.* St. Louis: Chalice, 1999.

Carmignac, J. "Les Dangers de l'Eschatologie." *NTS* 17 (1971) 365-90.

———. "La future intervention de Dieu selon la pensée de Qumrân." In *Apocalypses et Théologie de l'Espérance,* edited by H. Monloubou, 219-29. Paris: Cerf, 1977.

———. "Qu'est-ce que l'Apocalyptique? Son emploi à Qumrân." *RevQ* 10 (1979) 3-33.

Casey, P. M. "Porphyry and the Origin of the Book of Daniel." *JTS* 27 (1976) 15-33.

———. *Son of Man: The Interpretation and Influence of Daniel 7.* London: SPCK, 1979.

———. "The Use of the Term 'Son of Man' in the Similitudes of Enoch." *JSJ* 7 (1976) 11-29.

Cereti, C. G. *The Zand-ī Wahman Yasn: A Zoroastrian Apocalypse.* Rome Oriental Series 75. Rome: Istituto italiano per il medio ed estremo oriente, 1995.

Cerutti, M. V. *Antropologia e Apocalittica.* Rome: Bretschneider, 1990.

Chaine, I. "Cosmogonie aquatique et conflagration finale d'après la secunda Petri." *RB* 46 (1937) 207-16.

Charles, R. H. *The Apocalypse of Baruch.* London: Black, 1896.

———. *The Assumption of Moses.* London: Black, 1897.

———. "II Baruch." In *The Apocrypha and Pseudepigrapha of the Old Testament.* Volume II: *Pseudepigrapha,* edited by R. H. Charles, 470-526. Oxford: Clarendon, 1913.

————. *The Book of Enoch.* Oxford: Clarendon, 1893.

————. *The Book of Jubilees or the Little Genesis.* London: Black, 1902.

————. *A Critical History of the Doctrine of a Future Life.* London: Black, 1899.

Charles, R. H., ed. *The Apocrypha and Pseudepigrapha of the Old Testament.* 2 vols. Oxford: Clarendon, 1913.

Charles, R. H., and N. Forbes. "The Book of the Secrets of Enoch." In *The Apocrypha and Pseudepigrapha of the Old Testament.* Volume II: *Pseudepigrapha,* edited by R. H. Charles, 425-69. Oxford: Clarendon, 1913.

Charles, R. H., and W. R. Morfill. *The Book of the Secrets of Enoch.* Oxford: Clarendon, 1896.

Charlesworth, J. H. "The Concept of the Messiah in the Pseudepigrapha." In *Aufstieg und Niedergang der römischen Welt,* II.19.1, edited by W. Haase and H. Temporini, 188-218. Berlin: de Gruyter, 1979.

————. "The Origin and Subsequent History of the Authors of the Dead Sea Scrolls: Four Transitional Phases among the Qumran Essenes." *RevQ* 10 (1980) 213-33.

————. "The Portrayal of the Righteous as an Angel." In *Ideal Figures in Ancient Judaism: Profiles and Paradigms,* edited by G. W. E. Nickelsburg and J. J. Collins, 135-47. SBLSCS 12. Chico, CA: Scholars Press, 1980.

————. "The SNTS Pseudepigrapha Seminars at Tübingen and Paris on the Books of Enoch." *NTS* 25 (1979) 315-23.

————. "The Triumphant Majority as Seen by a Dwindled Minority: The Outsider according to the Insider of the Jewish Apocalypses." In *"To See Ourselves as Others See Us": Christians, Jews, "Others" in Late Antiquity,* edited by J. Neusner and E. Frerichs, 625-37. Chico, CA: Scholars Press, 1985.

Charlesworth, J. H., ed. *The Dead Sea Scrolls: Hebrew, Aramaic and Greek Texts with English Translations.* Volume 1: *Rule of the Community and Related Documents.* Tübingen: Mohr Siebeck; Louisville: Westminster John Knox, 1994.

————, ed. *The Dead Sea Scrolls: Hebrew, Aramaic and Greek Texts with English Translations.* Volume 2: *Damascus Document, War Scroll, and Related Documents.* Tübingen: Mohr Siebeck; Louisville: Westminster John Knox, 1995.

————, ed. *The Old Testament Pseudepigrapha.* 2 vols. Garden City, NY: Doubleday, 1983-85.

Charlesworth, James H., Hermann Lichtenberger, and Gerbern S. Oegema, eds. *Qumran-Messianism: Studies on the Messianic Expectations in the Dead Sea Scrolls.* Tübingen: Mohr Siebeck, 1998.

Chester, Andrew. *Messiah and Exaltation.* WUNT 207. Tübingen: Mohr Siebeck, 2007.

Chilton, B. D. "The Son of Man — Who Was He?" *Bible Review* 12 (1996) 34-39, 45.

Chilton, B. D., and C. A. Evans, eds. *Studying the Historical Jesus: Evaluations of the State of Current Research.* Leiden: Brill, 1994.

Clifford, R. J. "History and Myth in Daniel 10–12." *BASOR* 220 (1975) 23-26.

Coblentz Bautch, Kelley. *A Study of the Geography of 1 Enoch 17-19: 'No One Has Seen What I Have Seen'.* JSJSup 81. Leiden: Brill, 2003.

Coblentz Bautch, Kelley, and Daniel Assefa. "Patriarch, Prophet, Author, Angelic Rival: Exploring the Relationship of 1 Enoch to 2 Enoch in Light of the Figure of Enoch." In *New Perspectives on 2 Enoch,* edited by Orlov and Boccaccini, 181-89.

Cohen, N. *Cosmos, Chaos, and the World to Come: The Ancient Roots of Apocalyptic Faith*. New Haven: Yale University Press, 1993.

Cohen, S. J. D. "The Significance of Yavneh: Pharisees, Rabbis, and the End of Jewish Sectarianism." *HUCA* 55 (1984) 27-53.

Collins, J. J. "The Angelic Life." In J. J. Collins, *Scriptures and Sectarianism*, 195-211.

―――. "Apocalypse and Empire." *Svensk Exegetisk Årsbok* 76 (2011) 1-19 (=*Apocalypse, Prophecy, and Pseudepigraphy*, chapter 17).

―――. *Apocalypse, Prophecy, and Pseudepigraphy*. Grand Rapids: Eerdmans, 2015.

―――. "Apocalyptic Eschatology as the Transcendence of Death." *CBQ* 36 (1974) 21-43 (= *Seers, Sibyls, and Sages*, 75-98).

―――. "Apocalyptic Genre and Mythic Allusions in Daniel." *JSOT* 21 (1981) 83-100.

―――. "The Apocalyptic Literature." In *Early Judaism and Its Modern Interpreters*, edited by R. A. Kraft and G. W. E. Nickelsburg, 345-70. Atlanta: Scholars Press, 1986.

―――. "The Apocalyptic Technique: Setting and Function in the Book of the Watchers." *CBQ* 44 (1982) 91-111.

―――. *The Apocalyptic Vision of the Book of Daniel*. HSM 16. Missoula, MT: Scholars Press, 1977.

―――. *Apocalypticism in the Dead Sea Scrolls*. London: Routledge, 1997.

―――. "The Background of the 'Son of God' Text." *Bulletin for Biblical Research* 7 (1997) 51-62.

―――. "The Beginning of the End of the World in the Hebrew Bible." In *Thus Says the Lord: Essays on the Former and Latter Prophets in Honor of Robert R. Wilson*, edited by John Ahn and Steven L. Cook, 137-55. London: T & T Clark, 2009.

―――. *Between Athens and Jerusalem: Jewish Identity in the Hellenistic Diaspora*. 2d ed. Grand Rapids: Eerdmans, 2000.

―――. *Beyond the Qumran Community: The Sectarian Movement of the Dead Sea Scrolls*. Grand Rapids: Eerdmans, 2010.

―――. "The Book of Daniel and the Dead Sea Scrolls." In *The Hebrew Bible in Light of the Dead Sea Scrolls*, edited by Nóra Dávid, Armin Lange, Kristin De Troyer, and Shani Tzoref, 203-17. FRLANT 239. Göttingen: Vandenhoeck & Ruprecht, 2012. Reprinted in *Scriptures and Sectarianism*, 102-15.

―――. "The Christian Adaptation of the Apocalyptic Genre." In *Seers, Sibyls, and Sages in Hellenistic-Roman Judaism*, 115-30. Leiden: Brill, 1997.

―――. "Conceptions of Afterlife in the Dead Sea Scrolls." In *Lebendige Hoffnung – ewiger Tod?! Jenseitsvorstellungen im Hellenismus, Judentum und Christentum*, edited by Michael Labahn and Manfred Lang, 103-25. Leipzig: Evangelische Verlagsanstalt, 2007.

―――. "Cosmos and Salvation: Jewish Wisdom and Apocalyptic in the Hellenistic Age." *HR* 17 (1977) 121-42 (= *Seers, Sibyls, and Sages*, 317-38).

―――. "Covenant and Dualism in the Dead Sea Scrolls." In *Scriptures and Sectarianism*, edited by Collins, 179-94.

―――. "Cult and Culture: The Limits of Hellenization in Judea." In idem, *Jewish Cult and Hellenistic Culture*. JSJSup 100. Leiden: Brill, 2005, 21-43.

―――. *Daniel: A Commentary on the Book of Daniel*. Hermeneia. Minneapolis: Fortress, 1993.

# Bibliography

————. *Daniel, with an Introduction to Apocalyptic Literature*. FOTL 20. Grand Rapids: Eerdmans, 1984.

————. "The Date and Provenance of the Testament of Moses." In *Studies on the Testament of Moses,* edited by G. W. E. Nickelsburg, 15-32. Missoula, MT: Scholars Press, 1973.

————. "The Development of the Sibylline Tradition." In *Aufstieg und Niedergang der römischen Welt,* II.20.1, edited by W. Haase and H. Temporini, 422-59. Berlin: de Gruyter, 1987.

————. "Enoch and Ezra." In *Fourth Ezra and Second Baruch,* edited by Henze and Boccaccini, 83-97.

————. "'Enochic Judaism' and the Sect of the Dead Sea Scrolls." In *The Early Enoch Literature,* edited by Boccaccini and Collins, 283-299. Reprinted in Collins, *Scriptures and Sectarianism,* 150-63.

————. "Enochic Judaism: An Assessment." In *The Dead Sea Scrolls and Contemporary Culture: Proceedings of the International Conference held at the Israel Museum, Jerusalem ( July 6-8, 2008),* edited by Adolfo D. Roitman, Lawrence H. Schiffman and Shani Tzoref, 219-34. STDJ 93. Leiden: Brill, 2011.

————. "The Epic of Theodotus and the Hellenism of the Hasmoneans." *HTR* 73 (1980) 91-104.

————. "The Eschatology of Zechariah." In *Knowing the End from the Beginning,* edited by Grabbe and Haack, 74-84.

————. "Ethos and Identity in Jewish Apocalyptic Literature." In *Ethos und Identität. Einheit und Vielfalt des Judentums im hellenistisch-römischer Zeit.* edited by Matthias Konradt and Ulrike Steinert, 51-65. Munich: Schöningh, 2002.

————. "From Prophecy to Apocalypticism: The Expectation of the End." In *The Encyclopedia of Apocalypticism,* edited by B. McGinn, J. J. Collins and S. Stein. New York: Continuum, 1998.

————. "The Genre Apocalypse in Hellenistic Judaism." In *Apocalypticism in the Mediterranean World and the Near East: Proceedings of the International Colloquium on Apocalypticism, Uppsala, August 12-17, 1979,* edited by D. Hellholm, 531-48. Tübingen: Mohr Siebeck, 1983.

————. "Genre, Ideology, and Social Movements in Jewish Apocalypticism." In *Mysteries and Revelations: Apocalyptic Studies Since the Uppsala Colloquium,* edited by J. J. Collins and J. H. Charlesworth, 11-32. JSPSup 9. Sheffield: JSOT Press, 1991 (= *Seers, Sibyls, and Sages,* 25-38).

————. "The Genre of the Book of Jubilees." In *A Teacher for All Generations: Essays in Honor of James C. VanderKam,* edited by Eric F. Mason, Kelley Coblentz Bautch, Angela Kim Harkins, and Daniel A. Machiela, 737-55. JSJSup 153/2. Leiden: Brill, 2012.

————. " 'He Shall Not Judge by What His Eyes See': Messianic Authority in the Dead Sea Scrolls." *Dead Sea Discoveries* 2 (1995) 145-64.

————. "The Heavenly Representative: The 'Son of Man' in the Similitudes of Enoch." In *Ideal Figures in Ancient Judaism: Profiles and Paradigms,* edited by G. W. E. Nickelsburg and J. J. Collins, 111-33. SBLSCS 12. Missoula, MT: Scholars Press, 1980.

————. "The Idea of Election in 4 Ezra." *Jewish Studies Quarterly* 16 (2909) 83-96.

————. "Jesus and the Messiahs of Israel." In *Geschichte — Tradition — Reflexion: Festschrift für Martin Hengel,* edited by H. Cancik, H. Lichtenberger, and P. Schäfer, 1:287-302. Tübingen: Mohr Siebeck, 1996.

————. "The Jewish Adaptation of Sibylline Oracles." In *Seers, Sibyls, and Sages in Hellenistic-Roman Judaism,* 181-98. Leiden: Brill, 1997.

————. "The Jewish Apocalypses." *Semeia* 14 (1979) 21-59.

————. "Jewish Apocalyptic against Its Hellenistic Near Eastern Environment." *BASOR* 220 (1975) 27-36 (= *Seers, Sibyls, and Sages,* 59-74).

————. *Jewish Cult and Hellenistic Culture.* JSJSup 100. Leiden: Brill, 2005.

————. "The Legacy of Canaan in Ancient Israel and Early Christianity." In *Opportunity for No Little Instruction: Studies in Honor of Richard J. Clifford, S.J. and Daniel J. Harrington, S.J.,* edited by C. Frechette, C. Matthews, and T. Stegeman, 71-84. New York: Paulist, 2014.

————. "The Mythology of Holy War in Daniel and the Qumran War Scroll." *VT* 25 (1975) 596-612.

————. "Nebuchadnezzar and the Kingdom of God: Deferred Eschatology in the Jewish Diaspora." In *Loyalitätskonflikte in der Religionsgeschichte,* edited by C. Elsas and H. G. Kippenberg, 252-57. Würzburg: Königshausen und Neumann, 1990 (= *Seers, Sibyls, and Sages,* 131-38).

————. "The Origin of Evil in Apocalyptic Literature and the Dead Sea Scrolls." In *Congress Volume, Paris 1992,* edited by J. A. Emerton, 25-38. Leiden: Brill, 1995 (= *Seers, Sibyls, and Sages,* 287-300).

————. "Patterns of Eschatology at Qumran." In *Traditions in Transformation: Turning Points in Biblical Theology,* edited by B. Halpern and J. D. Levenson, 351-75. Winona Lake, IN: Eisenbrauns, 1981.

————. "The Persian Apocalypses." *Semeia* 14 (1979) 207-17.

————. "The Place of Apocalypticism in the Religion of Israel." In *Ancient Israelite Religion: Essays in Honor of Frank Moore Cross,* edited by P. D. Miller, P. D. Hanson, and S. D. McBride, 539-58. Philadelphia: Fortress, 1987 (= *Seers, Sibyls, and Sages,* 39-58).

————. "The Place of the Fourth Sibyl in the Development of the Jewish Sibyllina." *JJS* 25 (1974) 365-80.

————. "Prayer of Nabonidus." In *Qumran Cave 4–XVII: Parabiblical Texts, Part 3,* edited by G. Brooke et al., 83-93. DJD 22. Oxford: Clarendon, 1996.

————. "Prophecy and Fulfillment in the Dead Sea Scrolls." *JETS* 30 (1987) 267-78 (= *Seers, Sibyls, and Sages,* 301-14).

————. "Prophecy, Apocalypse and Eschatology: Reflections on the Proposals of Lester Grabbe." In *Knowing the End from Beginning: The Prophetic, the Apocalyptic and Their Relationships,* edited by Lester L. Grabbe and Robert D. Haak, 44-52. JSPSup 46. London: T & T Clark, 2003.

————. "Pseudonymity, Historical Reviews, and the Genre of the Revelation of John." *CBQ* 39 (1977) 329-43.

————. *The Scepter and the Star: Messianism in Light of the Dead Sea Scrolls.* 2d ed. Grand Rapids: Eerdmans, 2010.

————. *Scriptures and Sectarianism, Essays on the Dead Sea Scrolls.* WUNT 332. Tübingen: Mohr Siebeck, 2014.

————. *Seers, Sibyls, and Sages in Hellenistic-Roman Judaism.* Leiden: Brill, 1997.

————. "The Sibyl and the Apocalypses." In *Greco-Roman Culture and the New Testament,* edited by David E. Aune and Frederick E. Brenk, 185-202. Leiden: Brill, 2012.

————. "The Sibyl and the Potter." In *Religious Propaganda and Missionary Competition in the New Testament World,* edited by L. Bormann, K. del Tredici, and A. Standhartinger, 57-69. Leiden: Brill, 1994 (= *Seers, Sibyls, and Sages,* 199-210).

————. "Sibylline Discourse." In *Old Testament Pseudepigrapha and the Scriptures,* edited by Eibert Tigchelaar, 195-210. BETL 270. Leuven: Peeters, 2014.

————. "The Sibylline Oracles." In *The Old Testament Pseudepigrapha.* Volume 1: *Apocalyptic Literature and Testaments,* edited by J. H. Charlesworth, 317-472. Garden City, NY: Doubleday, 1983.

————. *The Sibylline Oracles of Egyptian Judaism.* SBLDS 13. Missoula, MT: Scholars Press, 1974.

————. "The Son of Man in First Century Judaism." *NTS* 38 (1992) 448-66.

————. "The Sons of God and the Daughters of Men." In *Sacred Marriages: The Divine-Human Sexual Metaphor from Sumer to Early Christianity,* edited by Martti Nissinen and Risto Uro, 259-74. Winona Lake, IN: Eisenbrauns, 2008.

————. "Stirring Up the Great Sea: The Religio-Historical Background of Daniel 7." In *The Book of Daniel in the Light of New Findings,* edited by A. S. van der Woude, 121-36. BETL 106. Leuven: Leuven University Press, 1993 (= *Seers, Sibyls, and Sages,* 139-56).

————. "The Symbolism of Transcendence in Jewish Apocalyptic." *BR* 19 (1974) 5-22.

————. "Testaments." In *Jewish Writings of the Second Temple Period,* edited by M. E. Stone, 325-55. CRINT 2/2. Philadelphia: Fortress, 1984.

————. "The Third Sibyl Revisited." In idem, *Jewish Cult and Hellenistic Culture,* 82-98.

————. "A Throne in the Heavens: Apotheosis in Pre-Christian Judaism." In *Death, Ecstasy, and Other Worldly Journeys,* edited by J. J. Collins and M. Fishbane, 41-56. Albany: State University of New York, 1995.

————. "Was the Dead Sea Sect an Apocalyptic Community?" In *Archaeology and History in the Dead Sea Scrolls: The New York University Conference in Memory of Yigael Yadin,* edited by L. H. Schiffman, 25-51. Sheffield: JSOT Press, 1990 (= *Seers, Sibyls, and Sages,* 261-86).

————. "Wisdom, Apocalypticism, and Generic Compatibility." In *In Search of Wisdom: Essays in Memory of John G. Gammie,* edited by L. G. Perdue, B. B. Scott, and W. J. Wiseman, 165-86. Louisville: Westminster John Knox, 1993 (= *Seers, Sibyls, and Sages,* 385-408).

————. "The Works of the Messiah." *Dead Sea Discoveries* 1 (1994) 98-112.

Collins, J. J., ed. *Apocalypse: The Morphology of a Genre.* Semeia 14. Missoula, MT: Scholars Press, 1979.

————, ed. *The Encyclopedia of Apocalypticism.* Volume 1: *The Origins of Apocalypticism in Judaism and Early Christianity.* New York: Continuum, 1998.

————, ed. *The Oxford Handbook of Apocalyptic Literature.* New York: Oxford, 2014.

Collins, J. J., and J. H. Charlesworth, eds. *Mysteries and Revelations: Apocalyptic Studies Since the Uppsala Colloquium.* JSPSup 9. Sheffield: JSOT Press, 1991.

Collins, J. J., and P. W. Flint. "243-245. 4QpsDaniel$^{a-c}$." In George J. Brooke et al., *Qumran Cave IV. XVII*, 95-164. DJD XXII. Oxford: Oxford University Press, 1996.

———. *The Book of Daniel: Composition and Reception*. 2 vols. VTSup 83. Leiden: Brill, 2001.

Colpe, C. "Der Begriff 'Menschensohn' und die Methode der Erforschung messianischer Prototypen." *Kairos* 12 (1970) 81-112.

———. "Die Himmelsreise der Seele ausserhalb und innerhalb der Gnosis." In *Le Origini dello Gnosticismo*, edited by U. Bianchi, 429-47. Leiden: Brill, 1967.

———. "Ho huios tou anthrōpou." In *Theological Dictionary of the New Testament*, edited by G. Kittel and G. Friedrich, translated by G. W. Bromiley, 8:400-430. 10 vols. Grand Rapids: Eerdmans, 1972.

———. "Hystaspes." *Reallexikon für Antike und Christentum* 16 (1991) cols. 1057-82.

Coogan, M. D., and M. S. Smith. *Stories from Ancient Canaan* (Louisville: Westminster John Knox, 2012).

Cook, E. "4Q246." *Bulletin for Biblical Research* 5 (1995) 43-66.

Cook, S. L. "Apocalyptic Prophecy." In *The Oxford Handbook of Apocalyptic Literature*, edited by Collins, 19-35.

———. *Prophecy and Apocalypticism: The Postexilic Social Setting*. Minneapolis: Fortress, 1995.

Coppens, J. *La Relève Apocalyptique du Messianisme Royal*. II: *Le Fils d'Homme Vétéro- et Intertestamentaire*. Louvain: Louvain University Press, 1983.

Cortés, E. *Los discursos de adiós de Gen 49a a Jn 13–17: Pistas para la historia de un género literario en la antigua literatura judía*. Barcelona: Herder, 1976.

Cross, F. M. *The Ancient Library of Qumran*. 3d ed. Sheffield: Sheffield Academic Press, 1995.

———. *Canaanite Myth and Hebrew Epic*. Cambridge, MA: Harvard University Press, 1973.

———. "New Directions in the Study of Apocalyptic." *JTC* 6 (1969) 157-65.

———. "Notes on the Two Messiahs at Qumran and the Extracanonical Daniel Apocalypse." In *Current Research and Technological Developments on the Dead Sea Scrolls*, edited by D. W. Parry and S. D. Ricks, 1-13. Leiden: Brill, 1996.

———. "Some Notes on a Generation of Qumran Studies." In *The Madrid Qumran Congress: Proceedings of the International Congress on the Dead Sea Scrolls, Madrid 18-21 March, 1991*, edited by J. Trebolle Barrera and L. Vegas Montaner, 1:1-14. 2 vols. Leiden: Brill, 1992.

Crossan, J. D. *Four Other Gospels: Shadows on the Contours of Canon*. New York: Winston, 1985.

———. *The Historical Jesus: The Life of a Mediterranean Jewish Peasant*. San Francisco: HarperSanFrancisco, 1991.

Crossan, J. D., and Jonathan L. Reed. *In Search of Paul: How Jesus' Apostle Opposed Rome's Empire with God's Kingdom*. New York: HarperCollins, 2004.

Culianu, I. P. "Ascension." In *The Encyclopedia of Religion*, edited by M. Eliade, 435-41. New York: Macmillan, 1987.

———. *Psychanodia I: A Survey of the Evidence concerning the Ascension of the Soul and Its Relevance*. Leiden: Brill, 1983.

Cumont, F. *Astrology and Religion among the Greeks and Romans.* New York: Dover, 1960.

Daschke, Dereck. *City of Ruins: Mourning the Destruction of Jerusalem through Jewish Apocalypse.* Biblical Interpretation Series 99. Leiden: Brill, 2010.

Daumas, F. "Littérature prophétique et exégétique égyptienne et commentaires esséniens." In *À la rencontre de Dieu: Mémorial Albert Gelin,* edited by A. Barucq, 203-21. Le Puy: Mappus, 1961.

Davenport, G. L. "The 'Anointed of the Lord' in the Psalms of Solomon 17." In *Ideal Figures in Ancient Judaism: Profiles and Paradigms,* edited by G. W. E. Nickelsburg and J. J. Collins, 67-92. SBLSCS 12. Missoula, MT: Scholars Press, 1980.

―――. *The Eschatology of the Book of Jubilees.* Leiden: Brill, 1971.

Davies, P. R. *1QM: The War Scroll from Qumran.* Rome: Biblical Institute Press, 1977.

―――. *Behind the Essenes.* Atlanta: Scholars Press, 1987.

―――. "Calendrical Change and Qumran Origins: An Assessment of VanderKam's Theory." *CBQ* 45 (1983) 80-89.

―――. *The Damascus Covenant: An Interpretation of the "Damascus Document."* JSOT Sup 25. Sheffield: JSOT Press, 1983.

―――. "Daniel Chapter Two." *JTS* 27 (1976) 392-401.

―――. "Eschatology at Qumran." *JBL* 104 (1985) 39-55.

―――. "Eschatology in the Book of Daniel." *JSOT* 17 (1980) 33-53.

―――. "Hasidim in the Maccabean Period." *JJS* 28 (1977) 127-40.

―――. "The Social World of the Apocalyptic Writings." In *The World of Ancient Israel,* edited by R. E. Clements, 251-71. Cambridge: Cambridge University Press, 1989.

―――. "The Teacher of Righteousness at the End of Days." *RevQ* 13 (1988) 313-17.

Davies, W. D., and L. Finkelstein, eds. *The Cambridge History of Judaism.* Cambridge: Cambridge University Press, 1984.

Davila, James R. "Melchizedek, the 'Youth', and Jesus." In *The Dead Sea Scrolls as Background to Postbiblical Judaism and Early Christianity,* edited by idem, 248-74. STDJ 46. Leiden: Brill, 2003.

―――. The *Provenance of the Pseudepigrapha: Jewish, Christian, or Other?* JSJSup 105. Leiden: Brill, 2005.

Day, J. "The Daniel of Ugarit and Ezekiel and the Hero of the Book of Daniel." *VT* 30 (1980) 174-84.

―――. *God's Conflict with the Dragon and the Sea: Echoes of a Canaanite Myth in the Old Testament.* Cambridge: Cambridge University Press, 1985.

Dean-Otting, M. *Heavenly Journeys: A Study of the Motif in Hellenistic Jewish Literature.* Frankfurt: Peter Lang, 1984.

Delcor, M. *Les Hymnes de Qumrân.* Paris: Letouzey et Ané, 1962.

―――. *Le Livre de Daniel.* Paris: Gabalda, 1971.

―――. "Le Temple d'Onias en Egypte." *RB* 75 (1968) 188-205.

―――. *Le Testament d'Abraham.* Leiden: Brill, 1973.

Delcor, M., ed. *Qumrân: Sa piété, sa théologie et son milieu.* Leuven: Leuven University Press, 1978.

Dequeker, L. "The 'Saints of the Most High' in Qumran and Daniel." *OTS* 18 (1973) 133-62.

Dexinger, F. *Henochs Zehnwochenapokalypse und offene Probleme der Apokalyptikforschung*. Leiden: Brill, 1977.

Dieterich, A. *Nekyia: Beiträge zur Erklärung der neuentdeckten Petrusapokalypse*. 3d ed. Darmstadt: Wissenschaftliche Buchgesellschaft, 1969.

Dimant, D. "The Biography of Enoch and the Books of Enoch." *VT* 33 (1983) 14-29.

―――. "History according to the Vision of the Animals (Ethiopic Enoch 85–90)." *Mhqry yrwšlym bmhšbt yśr'l* 2 (1982) 18-37 (in Hebrew).

―――. *History, Ideology and Bible Interpretation in the Dead Sea Scrolls*. Collected Studies. FAT 90. Tübingen: Mohr Siebeck, 2014.

―――. "Men as Angels: The Self-Image of the Qumran Community." In eadem, *History, Ideology and Bible Interpretation*, 465-72.

―――. *Qumran Cave 4. XXI. Parabiblical Texts, Part 4: Pseudo-Prophetic Texts*. DJD XXX. Oxford: Oxford University Press, 2000.

―――. "Qumran Sectarian Literature." In *Jewish Writings of the Second Temple Period*, edited by M. E. Stone, 483-550. CRINT 2/2. Assen: Van Gorcum; Philadelphia: Fortress, 1984.

Dimant, D., and J. Strugnell. "The Merkabah Vision in Second Ezekiel (4Q385 4)." *RevQ* 14 (1990) 331-48.

DiTommaso, Lorenzo. "4QPseudo-Daniel^a-b (4Q243-244) and the Book of Daniel." *DSD* 12 (2005) 101-33.

―――. "Apocalypses and Apocalypticism in Antiquity: Parts I and II." *Currents in Biblical Research* 5 (2007) 235-86, 367-432.

―――. "The Apocalyptic Other." In *The "Other" in Second Temple Judaism: Essays in Honor of John J. Collins*, edited by Daniel C. Harlow et al., 221-46. Grand Rapids: Eerdmans, 2011.

―――. "Apocalypticism and Popular Culture." In *The Oxford Handbook of Apocalyptic Literature*, edited by Collins, 473-509.

―――. "Dating the Eagle Vision of 4 Ezra: A New Look at an Old Theory." *JSP* 20 (1999) 1-26.

―――. *The Dead Sea New Jerusalem Text*. TSAJ 110. Tübingen: Mohr Siebeck, 2005.

―――. "The Development of Apocalyptic Historiography in Light of the Dead Sea Scrolls." In *Celebrating the Dead Sea Scrolls: A Canadian Collection*, edited by P. W. Flint, J. Duhaime, and K. S. Baek, 497-522. Leiden: Brill, 2012.

―――. "Who is the 'I' of 4 Ezra?" in Henze and Boccaccini, *Fourth Ezra and Second Baruch*, 119-33.

Dobroruka, Vicente. *Second Temple Pseudepigraphy: A Cross-cultural Comparison of Apocalyptic Texts and Related Jewish Literature*. Ekstasis 3. Berlin: de Gruyter, 2014.

Dochhorn, Jan. *Schriftgelehrte Prophetie*. WUNT 268. Tübingen: Mohr Siebeck, 2010.

Doran, R. "The Non-dating of Jubilees: Jub 34–38; 23:14-32 in Narrative Context." *JSJ* 20 (1989) 1-11.

―――. "The Persecution of Judeans by Antiochus IV: The Significance of Ancestral Laws." In *The "Other" in Second Temple Judaism*. Edited by Harlow et al., 423-33.

Douglas, Michael C. "The Teacher Hymn Hypothesis Revisited: New Data for an Old Crux." *DSD* 6 (1999) 239-66.

Drawnel, Henryk. *The Aramaic Astronomical Book from Qumran*. Oxford: Oxford University Press, 2011.

———. *An Aramaic Wisdom Text from Qumran: A New Interpretation of the Levi Document*. JSJSup 86. Leiden: Brill, 2004.

———. "Professional Skills of Asael (1 Enoch 8:1) and Their Mesopotamian Background." *RB* 119 (2012) 518-42.

———. "The Punishment of Asael (1 En. 10:4-8) and Mesopotamian Anti-Witchcraft Literature." *RevQ* 25 (2012) 518-42.

———. "Some Notes on the Aramaic Manuscripts from Qumran and Late Mesopotamian Culture." *RevQ* 26 (2013) 145-68.

Duff, Paul B. *Who Rides the Beast? Prophetic Rivalry and the Rhetoric of Crisis in the Churches of the Apocalypse*. Oxford: Oxford University Press, 2001.

Duhaime, J. "Dualistic Reworking in the Scrolls from Qumran." *CBQ* 49 (1987) 32-56.

———. "War Scroll." In *The Dead Sea Scrolls: Hebrew, Aramaic, and Greek Texts with English Translations*. Volume 2: *Damascus Document, War Scroll, and Related Documents,* edited by J. H. Charlesworth, 80-203. Tübingen: Mohr Siebeck; Louisville: Westminster John Knox, 1995.

———. "The War Scroll from Qumran and the Greco-Roman Tactical Treatises." *RevQ* 13 (1988) 133-51.

Dunand, F. "L'Oracle du Potier et la formation de l'apocalyptique en Egypte." In *L'Apocalyptique,* edited by F. Raphael, 39-67. Paris: Geuthner, 1977.

Dupont-Sommer, A. "La mère de l'Aspic dans un hymne de Qoumrân." *RHR* 147 (1955) 174-88.

———. *Nouveaux aperçus sur les manuscrits de la Mer Morte*. Paris: Maisonneuve, 1953.

Ebeling, E. *Tod und Leben nach der Vorstellungen der Babylonier*. Berlin: de Gruyter, 1931.

Ebeling, G. "The Ground of Christian Theology." *JTC* 6 (1969) 47-68.

Eddy, S. K. *The King Is Dead: Studies in Near Eastern Resistance to Hellenism 334-31 B.C.* Lincoln: University of Nebraska Press, 1961.

Ego, Beate. "Henochs Reise vor den Thron Gottes (1 Hen 14,8-16,4). Zur Funktion des Motivs der Himmelsreise im 'Wächterbuch' (1 Hen 1-36)." In *Apokalyptik und Qumran,* edited by Jörg Frey and Michael Becker, 105-21. Paderborn: Bonifatius, 2007.

Ehrlich, E. L. *Der Traum im Alten Testament*. Berlin: de Gruyter, 1953.

Ehrman, Bart D. *Jesus: Apocalyptic Prophet of the New Millennium*. Oxford: Oxford University Press, 1999.

Eliade, M. *Shamanism: Archaic Techniques of Ecstasy*. Princeton: Princeton University Press, 1964.

———. *The Myth of the Eternal Return*. New York: Pantheon, 1954.

Elledge, C. D. *Life after Death in Early Judaism*. WUNT 28. Tübingen: Mohr Siebeck, 2006.

Elliott, Neil. *Liberating Paul: The Justice of God and the Politics of the Apostle*. Sheffield: Sheffield Academic Press, 1995.

Ellis, Maria de Jong. "Observations on Mesopotamian Oracles and Prophetic Texts: Literary and Historiographic Considerations." *JCS* 41 (1989) 127-86.

Ellul, J. *Apocalypse: The Book of Revelation*. New York: Seabury, 1977.

Emerton, J. A. "The Origin of the Son of Man Imagery." *JTS* 9 (1958) 225-42.

Endres, J. C., S.J. *Biblical Interpretation in the Book of Jubilees.* CBQMS 18. Washington, DC: Catholic Biblical Association, 1987.

———. "The Watchers Traditions in the Book of Jubilees." In *The Watchers,* edited by Harkins, Bautch, and Endres, 121-35.

Eshel, Hanan. *The Dead Sea Scrolls and the Hasmonean State.* Grand Rapids: Eerdmans, 2008.

Esler, Philip F. "Social-Scientific Approaches to Apocalyptic Literature." In *The Oxford Handbook of Apocalyptic Literature,* edited by Collins, 123-44.

Fallon, F. T. "The Gnostic Apocalypses." *Semeia* 14 (1979) 123-58.

Farmer, W. R. *Maccabees, Zealots, and Josephus.* New York: Columbia University Press, 1956.

Feldman, L. H., James L. Kugel, and Lawrence H. Schiffman, eds. *Outside the Bible: Ancient Jewish Writings Related to Scripture.* Lincoln, Nebraska: University of Nebraska, 2013.

Ferch, A. J. "Daniel 7 and Ugarit: A Reconsideration." *JBL* 99 (1980) 75-86.

Finitsis, Antonios. *Visions and Eschatology: A Socio-Historical Analysis of Zechariah 1-6.* Library of Second Temple Studies 79. London: T & T Clark, 2011.

Fiorenza, E. S. "Apokalypsis and Propheteia: Revelation in the Context of Early Christian Prophecy." In *The Book of Revelation: Justice and Judgment,* 133-56. Philadelphia: Fortress, 1985.

———. *Invitation to the Book of Revelation.* New York: Doubleday, 1981.

———. "The Phenomenon of Early Christian Apocalyptic." In *Apocalypticism in the Mediterranean World and the Near East: Proceedings of the International Colloquium on Apocalypticism, Uppsala, August 12-17, 1979,* edited by D. Hellholm, 295-316. Tübingen: Mohr Siebeck, 1983.

Fischer, U. *Eschatologie und Jenseitserwartung im Hellenistischen Diasporajudentum.* BZNW 44. Berlin: de Gruyter, 1978.

Fishbane, M. *Biblical Interpretation in Ancient Israel.* Oxford: Clarendon, 1985.

Fitzmyer, J. A. "Another View of the 'Son of Man' Debate." *JSNT* 4 (1979) 58-68.

———. *The One Who Is to Come.* Grand Rapids: Eerdmans, 2007.

Flannery, Frances. "Dreams and Visions in Early Jewish and Early Christian Apocalypses and Apocalypticism." In *The Oxford Handbook of Apocalyptic Literature,* edited by Collins, 104-20.

Flannery-Dailey, Frances. *Dreamers, Scribes and Priests: Jewish Dreams in the Hellenistic and Greco-Roman Eras.* JSJSup 90. Leiden: Brill, 2004.

Fletcher-Louis, C. H. T. "2 Enoch and the New Perspective on Apocalyptic." In *New Perspectives on 2 Enoch,* edited by Orlov and Boccaccini, 127-48.

———. *All the Glory of Adam: Liturgical Anthropology in the Dead Sea Scrolls.* STDJ 42. Leiden: Brill, 2002.

———. "Jesus and Apocalypticism." In *The Handbook of the Study of the Historical Jesus,* edited by Holmén and Porter, 3:2877-2909.

———. "Jewish Apocalyptic and Apocalypticism." In *The Handbook of the Study of the Historical Jesus,* ed. T. Holmén and S. E. Porter, 1560-1607. 4 vols. Leiden: Brill, 2011.

Flusser, D. "Apocalyptic Elements in the *War Scroll.*" In idem, *Judaism of the Second*

*Temple Period.* Vol. 1: *Qumran and Apocalypticism*, 91-102. Grand Rapids: Eerdmans, 2007.

———. "The Four Empires in the Fourth Sibyl and in the Book of Daniel." *Israel Oriental Studies* 2 (1972) 148-75.

———. "Hystaspes and John of Patmos." In *Irano-Judaica*, edited by S. Shaked, 12-75. Jerusalem: Magnes, 1982.

———. "The Testaments of the Twelve Patriarchs." *EJ* (1971) 13:184-86.

Fossum, J. E. *The Name of God and the Angel of the Lord: Samaritan and Jewish Concepts of Intermediation and the Origin of Gnosticism.* Tübingen: Mohr Siebeck, 1985.

Fowler, A. "The Life and Death of Literary Forms." *New Literary History* 2 (1971) 199-216.

Frankfurter, D. "Apocalypses Real and Alleged in the Mani Codex." *Numen* 44 (1997) 60-73.

———. "The Legacy of Sectarian Rage: Vengeance Fantasies in the New Testament." In *Religion and Violence: The Biblical Heritage,* edited by David A. Bernat and Jonathan Klawans, 114-28. Sheffield: Sheffield Phoenix, 2007.

Fraser, P. *Ptolemaic Alexandria.* 2 vols. Oxford: Clarendon, 1972.

Frey, Jörg. "Different Patterns of Dualistic Thought in the Qumran Library." In *Legal Texts and Legal Issues,* edited by Moshe Bernstein, Florentino García Martínez, and John Kampen, 275-335. Leiden: Brill, 1997.

———. "On the Origins of the Genre of the 'Literary Testament': Farewell Discourses in the Qumran Library and Their Relevance for the History of the Genre." In *Aramaica Qumranica,* edited by Berthelot and Stökl Ben Ezra, 345-70.

———. "Was erwartet die Johannesapokalypse? Zur Eschatologie des letzten Buches der Bibel." In *Die Johannesapokalypse,* edited by Frey, Kelhoffer, and Tóth, 473-551.

Frey, Jörg, and Michael Becker, eds. *Apokalyptik und Qumran.* Paderborn: Bonifatius, 2007.

Frey, Jörg, et al., eds. *Pseudepigraphie und Verfasserfiktion in frühchristlichen Briefen.* WUNT 246. Tübingen: Mohr Siebeck, 2009.

Frey, Jörg, James A. Kelhoffer, and Franz Tóth, eds. *Die Johannesapokalypse. Kontexte – Konzepte – Rezeption.* WUNT 287. Tübingen: Mohr Siebeck, 2012.

Freyne, Sean. *The Jesus Movement and Its Expansion: Meaning and Mission.* Grand Rapids: Eerdmans, 2014.

———. *A Jewish Galilean: A New Reading of the Jesus-story.* London: T & T Clark, 2004.

Friesen, Steven J. "Apocalypse and Empire." In *The Oxford Handbook of Apocalyptic Literature,* edited by Collins, 163-79.

———. *Imperial Cults and the Apocalypse of John: Reading Revelation in the Ruins.* Oxford: Oxford University Press, 2001.

Frilingos, Christopher A. *Spectacles of Empire: Monsters, Martyrs, and the Book of Revelation.* Philadelphia: University of Pennsylvania, 2004.

Fröhlich, Ida. "Mesopotamian Elements and the Watchers Traditions." In *The Watchers,* edited by Harkins, Bautch, and Endres, 11-24.

Frye, R. N. "Qumran and Iran." In *Christianity, Judaism, and Other Greco-Roman Cults: Studies for Morton Smith at Sixty,* edited by J. Neusner, 3:167-74. Leiden: Brill, 1975.

Frykholm, Amy Johnson. "Apocalypticism in Contemporary Christianity." In *The Oxford Handbook of Apocalyptic Literature,* edited by Collins, 441-56.

Fuchs, H. *Der geistige Widerstand gegen Rom in der antiken Welt.* Berlin: de Gruyter, 1938.

Gager, J. G. *Kingdom and Community: The Social World of Early Christianity.* Englewood Cliffs, NJ: Prentice-Hall, 1975.

Gammie, J. G. "The Classification, Stages of Growth, and Changing Intentions in the Book of Daniel." *JBL* 95 (1976) 191-204.

———. "On the Intention and Sources of Daniel I–VI." *VT* 31 (1981) 282-92.

García Martínez, F. "The Heavenly Tablets in the Book of Jubilees." In *Studies in the Book of Jubilees,* edited by Matthias Albani, Jörg Frey, and Armin Lange, 243-60. Tübingen: Mohr Siebeck, 1997.

———. "New Jerusalem." *EDSS* 606-10.

———. *Qumran and Apocalyptic.* Leiden: Brill, 1992.

———. "Qumran Origins and Early History: A Groningen Hypothesis." *Folia Orientalia* 25 (1988) 113-36.

———. "Les traditions apocalyptiques à Qumrân." In *Apocalypses et voyages dans l'au-delà,* edited by C. Kappler, 201-35. Paris: Cerf, 1987.

Gaster, M. "The Hebrew Text of One of the Testaments of the Twelve Patriarchs." *Proceedings of the Society of Biblical Archeology* (1893-94) 33-49, 109-17.

Gaylord, H. E., Jr. "3 Baruch." In *The Old Testament Pseudepigrapha.* Volume 1: *Apocalyptic Literature and Testaments,* edited by J. H. Charlesworth, 653-79. Garden City, NY: Doubleday, 1983.

Geffcken, J. *Komposition and Entstehungszeit der Oracula Sibyllina.* Leipzig: Hinrichs, 1902.

Gerhart, M. "Genre Studies: Their Renewed Importance in Religious and Literary Interpretation." *JAAR* 45 (1977) 309-25.

Gese, H. "Anfang und Ende der Apokalyptik dargestellt am Sacharjabuch." *ZThK* 70 (1973) 20-49.

Gieschen, Charles A. "Enoch and Melchizedek: The Concern for Supra-Human Priestly Mediators in 2 Enoch." In *New Perspectives on 2 Enoch,* edited by Orlov and Boccaccini, 369-85.

Gignoux, P. "Apocalypses et voyages extra-terrestres dans l'Iran mazdéen." In *Apocalypses et voyages dans l'au-delà,* edited by C. Kappler, 351-74. Paris: Cerf, 1987.

———. "L'apocalyptique iranienne est-elle vraiment la source d'autres apocalypses?" *Acta Antiqua Academiae Scientiarum Hungaricae* 31 (1988) 67-78.

———. *Le Livre d'Ardâ Vîrâz.* Paris: Editions Recherches sur les civilisations, 1984.

———. "Sur l'inexistence d'un Bahman Yasht avestique." *Journal of Asian and African Studies* 32 (1986) 53-64.

Ginzberg, L. *An Unknown Jewish Sect.* New York: Jewish Theological Seminary, 1976.

Gladigow, B. "Aetas, aevum und saeclorum ordo: Zur Struktur zeitlicher Deutungssysteme." In *Apocalypticism in the Mediterranean World and the Near East: Proceedings of the International Colloquium on Apocalypticism, Uppsala, August 12-17, 1979,* edited by D. Hellholm, 255-72. Tübingen: Mohr Siebeck, 1983.

Glasson, T. F. *Greek Influence on Jewish Eschatology.* London: SPCK, 1961.

Gnoli, G. *Zoroaster's Time and Homeland.* Naples: Istituto universitario orientale, 1980.

Goff, Matthew J. "Wisdom and Apocalypticism." In *The Oxford Handbook of Apocalyptic Literature*, edited by Collins, 52-68.

―――. *The Worldly and Heavenly Wisdom of 4QInstruction*. STDJ 50. Leiden: Brill, 2003.

Goldingay, J. E. *Daniel*. WBC 30. Dallas: Word, 1989.

Goldman, Liora. "Dualism in the Visions of Amram." *RevQ* 95 (2010) 421-32.

Goldstein, J. A. *1 Maccabees*. AB 41. Garden City, NY: Doubleday, 1976.

―――. "Jewish Acceptance and Rejection of Hellenism." In *Jewish and Christian Self-Definition*. Volume Two: *Aspects of Judaism in the Greco-Roman Period*, edited by E. P. Sanders, A. I. Baumgarten, and A. Mendelson, 64-87, 318-26. Philadelphia: Fortress, 1981.

Goodman, M. "The Date of 2 Baruch." In *Revealed Wisdom: Studies in Apocalyptic in Honour of Christopher Rowland*, edited by John Ashton, 116-21. Leiden: Brill, 2014.

―――. "Messianism and Politics in the Land of Israel, 66-135 CE." In *Redemption and Resistance: The Messianic Hopes of Jews and Christians in Antiquity*, edited by Markus Bockmuehl and James Carleton Paget, 149-57. London: T & T Clark, 2007.

―――. "The Sibylline Oracles." In E. Schürer, *The History of the Jewish People in the Age of Jesus Christ (175 B.C.–A.D. 135)*, revised and edited by G. Vermes, F. Millar, and M. Goodman, 3.1:618-54. Edinburgh: Clark, 1986.

Grabbe, L. L. "4 Ezra and 2 Baruch in Social and Historical Perspective." In *Fourth Ezra and Second Baruch*, edited by Matthias Henze and Gabriele Boccaccini, 221-35.

―――. "The Parables of Enoch in Second Temple Jewish Society." In *Enoch and the Messiah Son of Man*, edited by Boccaccini, 386-402.

―――. "The Social World of Early Jewish Apocalypticism." *JSP* 4 (1989) 27-47.

Grabbe, L. L., and Robert D. Haak, eds. *Knowing the End from the Beginning: The Prophetic, the Apocalyptic and Their Relationships*. JSPSup 46. London: T & T Clark, 2003.

Graf, Fritz. "Mythical Production: Aspects of Myth and Technology in Antiquity." In *From Myth to Reason? Studies in the Development of Greek Thought*, edited by R. Buxton, 317-28. Oxford: Oxford University Press, 1999.

Graf, Fritz, and Sarah Iles Johnston. *Ritual Texts for the Afterlife: Orpheus and the Bacchic Gold Tablets*. London: Routledge, 2007.

Gray, G. B. "The Psalms of Solomon." In *The Apocrypha and Pseudepigrapha of the Old Testament*. Volume II: *Pseudepigrapha*, edited by R. H. Charles, 625-52. Oxford: Clarendon, 1913.

Grayson, A. K. *Babylonian Historical-Literary Texts*. Toronto: University of Toronto Press, 1975.

Grayson, A. K., and W. G. Lambert. "Akkadian Prophecies." *JCS* 18 (1964) 7-30.

Greenfield, J. C. "Aramaic Levi Document." In *Qumran Cave 4–XVII: Parabiblical Texts, Part 3*, edited by G. Brooke et al., 1-72. DJD 22. Oxford: Clarendon, 1996.

―――. Prolegomenon to *3 Enoch or the Hebrew Book of Enoch*, by H. Odeberg. New York: Ktav, 1973.

―――. "Remarks on the Aramaic Testament of Levi from the Cairo Geniza (Planches XIII–XIV)." *RB* 86 (1979) 214-30.

Greenfield, J. C., and M. E. Stone. "The Enochic Pentateuch and the Date of the Similitudes." *HTR* 70 (1977) 51-65.

Greenspoon, L. "The Origin of the Idea of Resurrection." In *Traditions in Transformation: Turning Points in Biblical Theology,* edited by B. Halpern and J. D. Levenson, 247-321. Winona Lake, IN: Eisenbrauns, 1981.

Grelot, P. "La géographie mythique d'Hénoch et ses sources orientales." *RB* 65 (1958) 33-69.

———. "La legende d'Hénoch dans les apocryphes et dans la Bible: Son origine et signification." *RSR* 46 (1958) 5-26, 181-210.

Grenet, Frantz. "Y a-t-il une Composante Iranienne dans l'Apocalyptique Judéo-Chrétienne? Retour sur un vieux Problème." In *Aux Origines des Messianismes Juifs,* edited by David Hamidovic, 121-44. VTSup 158. Leiden: Brill, 2013.

Griffiths, J. G. "Apocalyptic in the Hellenistic Era." In *Apocalypticism in the Mediterranean World and the Near East: Proceedings of the International Colloquium on Apocalypticism, Uppsala, August 12-17, 1979,* edited by D. Hellholm, 273-93. Tübingen: Mohr Siebeck, 1983.

———. *The Divine Verdict: A Study of Divine Judgment in the Ancient Religions.* Leiden: Brill, 1991.

———. *Plutarch's De Iside et Osiride.* Cambridge: University of Wales Press, 1970.

Gruen, Erich S. *Heritage and Hellenism: The Reinvention of Jewish Tradition.* Berkeley, CA: University of California, 1998.

———. "Jews, Greeks, and Romans in the Third Sibylline Oracle." In *Jews in a Graeco-Roman World,* edited by Martin Goodman, 15-36. Oxford: Clarendon, 1998.

Gruenwald, I. *Apocalyptic and Merkavah Mysticism.* Leiden: Brill, 1980.

Gunkel, H. *Schöpfung und Chaos in Urzeit und Endzeit.* Göttingen: Vandenhoeck & Ruprecht, 1895.

———. "Das vierte Buch Esra." In *Die Apokryphen und Pseudepigraphen des Alten Testaments,* edited by E. Kautzsch, 2:331-401. Tübingen: Mohr Siebeck, 1900.

Gurtner, Daniel M. "Eschatological Rewards for the Righteous in *2 Baruch.*" In *Interpreting 4 Ezra and 2 Baruch*, edited by Boccaccini and Zurawski, 107-15.

———. "On the Other Side of Disaster: Soteriology in 2 Baruch." In *This World and the World to Come,* edited by Gurtner, 114-26.

———. *Second Baruch: A Critical Edition of the Syriac Text. With Greek and Latin Fragments, English Translation, Introduction, and Concordances.* London: T & T Clark, 2009.

———. "The 'Twenty-Fifth Year of Jeconiah' and the Date of 2 Baruch." *JSP* 18 (2008) 23-32.

Gurtner, Daniel M., ed. *This World and the World to Come: Soteriology in Early Judaism.* LSTS 74. London: T & T Clark, 2011.

Hagen, Joost L. "No Longer 'Slavonic' Only: 2 Enoch Attested in Coptic from Nubia." In *New Perspectives on 2 Enoch,* edited by Orlov and Boccaccini, 69-82.

Hall, R. G. "The 'Christian Interpolation' in the Apocalypse of Abraham." *JBL* 107/1 (1988) 107-12.

———. *Revealed Histories: Techniques for Ancient Jewish and Christian Historiography.* JSPSup 6. Sheffield: Sheffield Academic Press, 1992.

Hallo, W. W. "Akkadian Apocalypses." *IEJ* 16 (1966) 231-42.

Halperin, D. *The Faces of the Chariot: Early Jewish Responses to Ezekiel's Vision*. Tübingen: Mohr Siebeck, 1988.

Halpern-Amaru, B. *Rewriting the Bible: Land and Covenant in Postbiblical Jewish Literature*. Valley Forge, PA: Trinity Press International, 1994.

Hammer, R. *The Book of Daniel*. Cambridge: Cambridge University Press, 1976.

Han, Jin Hee. *Daniel's Spiel: Apocalyptic Literacy in the Book of Daniel*. Lanham, MD: University Press of America, 2008.

Hanson, P. D. "Apocalypse, Genre" and "Apocalypticism." In *The Interpreter's Dictionary of the Bible: Supplementary Volume,* edited by K. Crim, 27-34. Nashville: Abingdon, 1976.

———. *The Dawn of Apocalyptic*. Philadelphia: Fortress, 1975.

———. "Jewish Apocalyptic against Its Near Eastern Environment." *RB* 78 (1971) 31-58.

———. "Prolegomena to the Study of Jewish Apocalyptic." In *Magnalia Dei: The Mighty Acts of God,* edited by F. M. Cross, W. E. Lemke, and P. D. Miller, 389-413. Garden City, NY: Doubleday, 1976.

———. "Rebellion in Heaven: Azazel and Euhemeristic Heroes in 1 Enoch 6-11." *JBL* 96 (1977) 195-233.

Hanson, P. D., ed. *Visionaries and Their Apocalypses*. Philadelphia: Fortress, 1983.

Harkins, Angela Kim. *Reading with an "I" to the Heavens: Looking at the Qumran Hodayot Through the Lens of Visionary Traditions*. Ekstasis 3. Berlin: de Gruyter, 2012.

Harkins, Angela Kim, Kelley Coblentz Bautch, and John C. Endres, S.J. *The Fallen Angels Traditions: Second Temple Developments and Reception History*. CBQMS 53; Washington: Catholic Biblical Association, 2014.

———. *The Watchers in Jewish and Christian Traditions*. Minneapolis: Fortress, 2014.

Harlow, D. C. *The Greek Apocalypse of Baruch (3 Baruch) in Hellenistic Judaism and Early Christianity*. SVTP 12. Leiden: Brill, 1996.

———. "Idolatry and Alterity: Israel and the Nations in the *Apocalypse of Abraham*." In *The "Other" in Second Temple Judaism,* edited by Harlow et al., 302-30.

Harlow, Daniel C., Karina Martin Hogan, Matthew Goff, and Joel S. Kaminsky, eds. *The "Other" in Second Temple Judaism: Essays in Honor of John J. Collins*. Grand Rapids: Eerdmans, 2011.

Harnisch, W. "Die Ironie der Offenbarung: Exegetische Erwägungen zur Zionsvision im 4. Buch Esra." In *Society of Biblical Literature 1981 Seminar Papers,* edited by K. H. Richards, 79-104. Chico, CA: Scholars Press, 1981.

———. "Der Prophet als Widerpart und Zeuge der Offenbarung: Erwägungen zur Interdependenz vom Form und Sache im IV Buch Esra." In *Apocalypticism in the Mediterranean World and the Near East: Proceedings of the International Colloquium on Apocalypticism, Uppsala, August 12-17, 1979,* edited by D. Hellholm, 461-93. Tübingen: Mohr Siebeck, 1983.

———. *Verhängnis und Verheissung der Geschichte: Untersuchungen zum Zeit- und Geschichtsverständnis im 4. Buch Esra und in der syr. Baruchapokalypse*. Göttingen: Vandenhoeck & Ruprecht, 1969.

Harrelson, W. "Ezra among the Wicked in 2 Esdras 3-10." In *The Divine Helmsman: Studies on God's Control of Human Events, Presented to Lou H. Silberman,* edited by J. L. Crenshaw and S. Sandmel, 21-39. New York: Ktav, 1980.

Harrington, D. J. "Holy War Texts Among the Qumran Scrolls." In *Studies in the Hebrew Bible, Qumran, and the Septuagint presented to Eugene Ulrich*, edited by P. W. Flint, E. Tov, and J. C. VanderKam, 175-83. VTSup 101. Leiden: Brill, 2006.

―――. "Interpreting Israel's History: The Testament of Moses as a Rewriting of Deut 31-34." In *Studies on the Testament of Moses*, edited by G. W. E. Nickelsburg, 59-68. Missoula, MT: Scholars Press, 1973.

―――. *The Maccabean Revolt: Anatomy of a Biblical Revolution*. Wilmington: Glazier, 1988.

―――. *Wisdom Texts from Qumran*. London: Routledge, 1996.

Hartman, L. *Asking for a Meaning: A Study of 1 Enoch 1–5*. Lund: Gleerup, 1979.

―――. "The Function of Some So-Called Apocalyptic Timetables." *NTS* 22 (1976) 1-14.

―――. *Prophecy Interpreted: The Formation of Some Jewish Apocalyptic Texts and of the Eschatological Discourse Mark 13 par*. Lund: Gleerup, 1966.

―――. "Survey of the Problem of Apocalyptic Genre." In *Apocalypticism in the Mediterranean World and the Near East: Proceedings of the International Colloquium on Apocalypticism, Uppsala, August 12-17, 1979*, edited by D. Hellholm, 329-44. Tübingen: Mohr Siebeck, 1983.

Hartman, L. F., and A. A. DiLella. *The Book of Daniel*. AB 23. Garden City, NY: Doubleday, 1978.

Hasel, G. F. "The Book of Daniel and Matters of Language: Evidences Relating to Names, Words, and the Aramaic Language." *AUSS* 19 (1981) 211-25.

―――. "The Book of Daniel: Evidences Relating to Persons and Chronology." *AUSS* 19 (1981) 37-49.

―――. "The Four World Empires of Daniel 2 Against Its Near Eastern Environment." *JSOT* 12 (1979) 17-30.

―――. "The Identity of the 'Saints of the Most High' in Daniel 7." *Bib* 56 (1975) 173-92.

Hasslberger, B. *Hoffnung in der Bedrängnis*. St. Ottilien: Eos, 1977.

Haug, M., and E. W. West. *The Book of Arda Viraf*. London: Trübner, 1872.

Hayman, P. "The Problem of Pseudonymity in the Ezra Apocalypse." *JSJ* 6 (1975) 47-56.

Heger, Paul. "Another Look at Dualism in Qumran Writings." In *Dualism in Qumran*, edited by Xeravits, 39-101.

―――. *Challenges to Conventional Opinions on Qumran and Enoch Issues*. STDJ 100. Leiden: Brill, 2012.

Hellholm, D. "The Problem of Apocalyptic Genre and the Apocalypse of John." In *Early Christian Apocalypticism: Genre and Social Setting, Semeia* 36, edited by A. Yarbro Collins, 13-64. Decatur, GA: Scholars Press, 1986.

―――. *Das Visionenbuch des Hermas als Apokalypse*. Lund: Gleerup, 1980.

Hellholm, D., ed. *Apocalypticism in the Mediterranean World and the Near East: Proceedings of the International Colloquium on Apocalypticism, Uppsala, August 12-17, 1979*. Tübingen: Mohr Siebeck, 1983.

Hempel, Charlotte. "The Treatise on the Two Spirits and the Literary History of the Rule of the Community." In *Dualism in Qumran*, edited by Xeravits, 102-20.

Hendel, Ronald. "The Nephilim were on the Earth: Genesis 6:1-4 and Its Ancient Near Eastern Context." In *The Fall of the Angels*, edited by Christoph Auffarth and Loren T. Stuckenbruck, 11-34. Leiden: Brill, 2004.

Hengel, M. "Jesus, der Messias Israels." In *Messias und Christos,* edited by I. Gruenwald, S. Shaked, and G. Stroumsa, 155-76. Tübingen: Mohr Siebeck, 1992.

———. *Judaism and Hellenism.* 2 vols. Philadelphia: Fortress, 1974.

———. "Messianische Hoffnung und politischer 'Radikalismus' in der jüdisch-hellenistischen Diaspora." In *Apocalypticism in the Mediterranean World and the Near East: Proceedings of the International Colloquium on Apocalypticism, Uppsala, August 12-17, 1979,* edited by D. Hellholm, 653-84. Tübingen: Mohr Siebeck, 1983.

Henten, Jan Willem van. "The Concept of Martyrdom in Revelation." In *Die Johannesapokalypse,* edited by Frey, Kelhoffer and Tóth, 587-618.

———. "*Nero Redivivus* Demolished: The Coherence of the Nero Traditions in the *Sibylline Oracles.*" *JSP* 21 (2000) 3-17.

Henze, Matthias. *Jewish Apocalypticism in Late First Century Israel.* TSAJ 142. Tübingen: Mohr Siebeck, 2011.

———. "*4 Ezra* and *2 Baruch*: Literary Composition and Oral Performance in the First-Century Apocalyptic Literature." *JBL* 131 (2012) 181-200.

Henze, Matthias, and Gabriele Boccaccini, eds. *Fourth Ezra and Second Baruch: Reconstruction after the Fall.* JSJSup 134. Leiden: Brill, 2013.

Herr, M. D. "The Calendar." In *The Jewish People in the First Century,* edited by S. Safrai and M. Stern, 2:834-64. CRINT 1/2. Philadelphia: Fortress, 1976.

Hill, D. "Dikaioi as a Quasi-Technical Term." *NTS* 11 (1965) 296-302.

Himmelfarb, M. *Ascent to Heaven in Jewish and Christian Apocalypses.* New York: Oxford University Press, 1993.

———. "The Book of the Watchers and the Priests of Jerusalem." In *The Origins of Enochic Judaism,* edited by Boccaccini, 131-35.

———. "From Prophecy to Apocalypse: The *Book of the Watchers* and Tours of Heaven." In *Jewish Spirituality: From the Bible through the Middle Ages,* edited by A. Green, 145-65. New York: Crossroad, 1986.

———. *A Kingdom of Priests: Ancestry and Merit in Ancient Judaism.* Philadelphia: University of Pennsylvania, 2006.

———. "Revelation and Rapture: The Transformation of the Visionary in the Ascent Apocalypses." In *Mysteries and Revelations: Apocalyptic Studies since the Uppsala Colloquium,* edited by J. J. Collins and J. H. Charlesworth, 79-90. JSPSup 9. Sheffield: JSOT Press, 1991.

———. "Torah, Testimony, and Heavenly Tablets: The Claim to Authority in the Book of Jubilees." In *A Multiform Heritage: Studies on Early Judaism and Christianity in Honor of Robert A. Kraft,* edited by Benjamin G. Wright, 22-28. Atlanta: Scholars Press, 1999.

———. *Tours of Hell: An Apocalyptic Form in Jewish and Christian Literature.* Philadelphia: University of Pennsylvania, 1983.

Hinnells, J. R. "The Zoroastrian Doctrine of Salvation in the Roman World: A Study of the Oracle of Hystaspes." In *Man and His Salvation: Studies in Memory of S. G. F. Brandon,* edited by E. J. Sharpe and J. R. Hinnells, 125-48. Manchester: Manchester University Press, 1973.

Hirsch, E. D., Jr. *Validity in Interpretation.* New Haven: Yale University Press, 1967.

Höffken, P. "Heilszeitherrschererwartung im babylonischen Raum." *Die Welt des Orients* 9 (1977) 57-71.

Hofmann, N. J. *Die Assumptio Mosis. Studien zur Rezeption massgültiger Überlieferung.* JSJSup 67. Leiden: Brill, 2000.

Hogan, Karina Martin. *Theologies in Conflict in 4 Ezra: Wisdom Debate and Apocalyptic Solution.* JSJSup 130. Leiden: Brill, 2008.

———. "The Watchers Traditions in the Book of the Watchers and the Animal Apocalypse." In *The Watchers in Jewish and Christian Traditions*, edited by Harkins, Bautch and Endres, 107-20.

Holland, G. S. *The Tradition That You Received from Us: 2 Thessalonians in the Pauline Tradition.* Tübingen: Mohr Siebeck, 1988.

Hollander, H. W. *Joseph as an Ethical Model in the Testaments of the Twelve Patriarchs.* SVTP 6. Leiden: Brill, 1981.

Hollander, H. W., and M. de Jonge. *The Testaments of the Twelve Patriarchs: A Commentary.* SVTP 8. Leiden: Brill, 1985.

Holleman, J. *Resurrection and Parousia: A Traditio-Historical Study of Paul's Eschatology in 1 Cor 15:20-23.* Leiden: Brill, 1995.

Holm, Tawny. *Of Courtiers and Kings: The Biblical Daniel Narratives and Ancient Story Collections.* Winona Lake, IN: Eisenbrauns, 2013.

Holm-Nielsen, S. *Hodayot: Psalms from Qumran.* Aarhus: Universitetsvorlaget, 1960.

Holmén, Tom, and Stanley E. Porter. *Handbook for the Study of the Historical Jesus.* 4 vols. Leiden: Brill, 2011.

Honigman, Sylvie. *Tales of High Priests and Taxes: The Books of the Maccabees and the Judean Rebellion against Antiochus IV.* Oakland, CA: University of California Press, 2014.

Hooke, S. H. "The Myth and Ritual Pattern in Jewish and Christian Apocalyptic." In *The Labyrinth*, 213-33. London: SPCK, 1935.

Hooker, M. D. *The Son of Man in Mark.* Montreal: McGill University Press, 1967.

Horbury, W. "The Messianic Associations of 'The Son of Man'." *JTS* 36 (1985) 34-55.

———. *Messianism among Jews and Christians: Biblical and Historical Studies.* London: T & T Clark, 2003.

Horgan, M. P. *Pesharim: Qumran Interpretations of Biblical Books.* CBQMS 8. Washington, DC: Catholic Biblical Association of America, 1979.

Horsley, R. A. "Jesus and Empire." *USQR* 59 (2005) 44-74.

———. *Jesus and Empire: The Kingdom of God and the New World Disorder.* Minneapolis: Fortress, 2003.

———. *Jesus and the Spiral of Violence: Popular Jewish Resistance in Roman Palestine.* San Francisco: Harper & Row, 1987.

———. "The Kingdom of God and the Renewal of Israel: Synoptic Gospels, Jesus Movements, and Apocalypticism." In *The Encyclopedia of Apocalypticism*, edited by Collins, 1:303-44.

———. *The Prophet Jesus and the Renewal of Israel: Moving Beyond Diversionary Debate.* Grand Rapids: Eerdmans, 2012.

———. *Revolt of the Scribes: Resistance and Apocalyptic Origins.* Minneapolis: Fortress, 2010.

————. *Scribes, Visionaries, and the Politics of Second Temple Judaism*. Louisville: Westminster John Knox, 2007.

Horsley, R. A., ed. *Paul and Empire. Religion and Power in Roman Imperial Society*. Harrisburg, PA: Trinity Press International, 1997.

————, ed. *Paul and Politics: Ekklesia, Israel, Imperium, Interpretation: Essays in Honor of Krister Stendahl*. Harrisburg, PA: Trinity Press International, 2000.

Horsley, R. A., with J. S. Hanson. *Bandits, Prophets, and Messiahs: Popular Movements at the Time of Jesus*. Harrisburg, PA: Trinity Press International, 1999.

Horsley, R. A., and P. A. Tiller. *After Apocalyptic and Wisdom: Rethinking Texts in Context*. Eugene, OR: Cascade, 2012.

Hughes, H. M. "3 Baruch or The Greek Apocalypse of Baruch." In *The Apocrypha and Pseudepigrapha of the Old Testament*. Volume II: *Pseudepigrapha*, edited by R. H. Charles, 527-41. Oxford: Clarendon, 1913.

Hultgård, A. "Bahman Yasht: A Persian Apocalypse." In *Mysteries and Revelations: Apocalyptic Studies since the Uppsala Colloquium*, edited by J. J. Collins and J. H. Charlesworth, 114-34. JSPSup 9. Sheffield: JSOT Press, 1991.

————. *L'Eschatologie des Testaments des Douze Patriarches*. 2 vols. Uppsala: Almqvist & Wiksell, 1977, 1981.

————. "The Ideal 'Levite,' the Davidic Messiah, and the Saviour Priest in the Testaments of the Twelve Patriarchs." In *Ideal Figures in Ancient Judaism: Profiles and Paradigms,* edited by G. W. E. Nickelsburg and J. J. Collins, 93-110. SBLSCS 12. Chico, CA: Scholars Press, 1980.

————. "Das Judentum in der hellenistisch-römischen Zeit und die iranische Religion — ein religionsgeschichtliche Problem." In *Aufstieg und Niedergang der römischen Welt*, II.19.1, edited by W. Haase and H. Temporini, 512-90. Berlin: de Gruyter, 1979.

————. "Mythe et histoire dans l'Iran ancien." In *Apocalyptique Iranienne et Dualisme Qoumrânien*, edited by G. Widengren, A. Hultgård, and M. Philonenko, 63-162. Paris: Maisonneuve, 1995.

————. "Persian Apocalypticism." In *The Encyclopedia of Apocalypticism*, edited by Collins, 1:39-83.

Humphrey, E. M. *The Ladies and the Cities: Transformation and Apocalyptic Identity in Joseph and Aseneth, 4 Ezra, the Apocalypse, and the Shepherd of Hermas*. JSPSup 17. Sheffield: Sheffield Academic Press, 1995.

Humphreys, W. L. "A Life-Style for the Diaspora: A Study of the Tales of Esther and Daniel." *JBL* 92 (1973) 211-23.

Hunzinger, C. H. "Fragmente einer älteren Fassung des Buches Milḥāmā aus Höhle 4 von Qumran." *ZAW* 69 (1957) 131-57.

Huppenbauer, H. W. *Der Mensch zwischen zwei Welten*. Zurich: Zwingli, 1959.

Hurtado, L. W. *How on Earth did Jesus Become a God?* Grand Rapids: Eerdmans, 2005.

————. *One God, One Lord: Early Christian Devotion and Ancient Jewish Monotheism*. Philadelphia: Fortress, 1988.

Idel, Moshe. "Jewish Apocalypticism: 670-1670." In *The Encyclopedia of Apocalypticism*, edited by McGinn, 2:204-37.

Inbari, Motti. "Messianism as a Political Power in Contemporary Judaism." In *The Oxford Handbook of Apocalyptic Literature*, edited by Collins, 407-21.

Isaac, E. "1 Enoch." In *The Old Testament Pseudepigrapha.* Volume 1: *Apocalyptic Literature and Testaments,* edited by J. H. Charlesworth, 5-89. Garden City, NY: Doubleday, 1983.

Isenberg, S. R., and D. E. Owen. "Bodies, Natural and Contrived: The Work of Mary Douglas." *RelStudRev* 3 (1977) 1-16.

James, M. R. "The Apocalypse of Baruch." In *Apocrypha Anecdota II,* li-lxxi. Texts and Studies 5/1. Cambridge: Cambridge University Press, 1897.

Jansen, H. Ludin. *Die Henochgestalt.* Oslo: Dybwad, 1939.

Janssen, E. *Testament Abrahams.* JSHRZ 3/2. Gütersloh: Mohn, 1975.

Jarvie, I. C. *The Revolution in Anthropology.* Chicago: Regnery, 1967.

Jassen, Alex P. *Mediating the Divine: Prophecy and Revelation in the Dead Sea Scrolls and Second Temple Judaism.* STDJ 68. Leiden: Brill, 2007.

Jaubert, A. *The Date of the Last Supper.* Staten Island, NY: Alba House, 1965.

————. *La notion d'alliance dans le Judaisme.* Paris: Seuil, 1963.

Jenks, G. C. *The Origin and Early Development of the Antichrist Myth.* BZNW 59. Berlin: de Gruyter, 1991.

Jeremias, G. *Der Lehrer der Gerechtigkeit.* Göttingen: Vandenhoeck & Ruprecht, 1963.

Jeremias, J. *New Testament Theology.* New York: Scribners, 1971.

————. "*Pais theou.*" In *Theological Dictionary of the New Testament,* edited by G. Kittel and G. Friedrich, translated by G. W. Bromiley, 5:687-88. 10 vols. Grand Rapids: Eerdmans, 1967.

Jewett, R. *Romans.* Hermeneia. Minneapolis: Fortress, 2007.

————. *The Thessalonian Correspondence.* Philadelphia: Fortress, 1986.

Johnson, D. *From Chaos to Restoration: An Integrative Reading of Isaiah 24–27.* JSOTSup 61. Sheffield: JSOT Press, 1988.

Jokiranta, Jutta. "Sociological Approaches to Qumran Sectarianism." In *The Oxford Handbook of the Dead Sea Scrolls,* edited by Lim and Collins, 200-31.

Jones, B. W. "The Prayer in Daniel IX." *VT* 18 (1968) 488-93.

Jong, A. de. "Iranian Connections in the Dead Sea Scrolls." In *The Oxford Handbook of the Dead Sea Scrolls,* edited by Lim and Collins, 479-50.

————. *Traditions of the Magi: Zoroastrianism in Greek and Latin Literature.* Leiden: Brill, 1997.

Jonge, M. de. "Notes on Testament of Levi II–VII." In *Studies on the Testaments of the Twelve Patriarchs,* edited by idem, 247-60. SVTP 3. Leiden: Brill, 1975.

————. *The Testaments of the Twelve Patriarchs: A Critical Edition of the Greek Text.* Leiden: Brill, 1978.

————. *The Testaments of the Twelve Patriarchs: A Study of their Text, Composition and Origin.* Assen: van Gorcum, 1953.

————. "Two Messiahs in the Testaments of the Twelve Patriarchs?" In *Jewish Eschatology, Early Christian Christology, and the Testaments of the Twelve Patriarchs,* 191-203. Leiden: Brill, 1991.

Jonge, M. de, ed. *Studies on the Testaments of the Twelve Patriarchs: Text and Interpretation.* SVTP 3. Leiden: Brill, 1975.

Jonge, M. de, and A. S. van der Woude. "11QMelchizedek and the New Testament." *NTS* 12 (1965-66) 301-26.

Joseph, Simon J. *Jesus, Q, and the Dead Sea Scrolls.* WUNT 2/333. Tübingen: Mohr Siebeck, 2012.

———. *The Nonviolent Messiah: Jesus, Q, and the Enochic Tradition.* Minneapolis: Fortress, 2014.

Kabisch, R. *Das vierte Buch Esra auf seine Quellen untersucht.* Göttingen: Vandenhoeck & Ruprecht, 1889.

Kallas, J. "The Apocalypse — An Apocalyptic Book?" *JBL* 86 (1967) 69-80.

Kampen, J. *The Hasideans and the Origin of Pharisaism.* Atlanta: Scholars Press, 1988.

Kappler, C., ed. *Apocalypses et voyages dans l'au-delà.* Paris: Cerf, 1987.

Karrer, M. *Die Johannesoffenbarung als Brief.* Göttingen: Vandenhoeck & Ruprecht, 1986.

Käsemann, E. "The Beginnings of Christian Theology." *JTC* 6 (1969) 17-46.

Kaufman, S. A. "Prediction, Prophecy, and Apocalypse in the Light of New Akkadian Texts." In *Proceedings of the Sixth World Congress of Jewish Studies, 1973,* edited by A. Shinan, 221-28. Jerusalem: World Union of Jewish Studies, 1977.

Kearns, R. *Vorfragen zur Christologie II. Überlieferungsgeschichtliche und Rezeptionsgeschichtliche Studie zur Vorgeschichte eines christologischen Hoheitstitels.* Tübingen: Mohr Siebeck, 1980.

Kee, H. C. "'The Man' in Fourth Ezra: Growth of a Tradition." In *Society of Biblical Literature 1981 Seminar Papers,* edited by K. H. Richards, 199-208. Chico, CA: Scholars Press, 1981.

———. "The Testaments of the Twelve Patriarchs." In *The Old Testament Pseudepigrapha.* Volume 1: *Apocalyptic Literature and Testaments,* edited by J. H. Charlesworth, 775-828. Garden City, NY: Doubleday, 1983.

Keel, Othmar. "Die Tiere und der Mensch in Daniel 7." In *Hellenismus und Judentum,* edited by Keel and Staub, 1-35.

Keel, Othmar, and Urs Staub, eds. *Hellenismus und Judentum: Vier Studien zu Daniel 7 und zur Religionsnot unter Antiochus IV.* OBO 178. Freiburg: Universitätsverlag, 2000.

Kelhoffer, James A. "The Relevance of Revelation's Date and the Imperial Cult for John's Appraisal of the Value of Christians' Suffering." In *Die Johannesapokalypse,* edited by Frey, Kelhoffer and Tóth, 553-85.

Kippenberg, H. "Dann wird der Orient herrschen und der Okzident dienen." In *Spiegel und Gleichnis,* edited by N. W. Bolz and W. Hübner, 40-48. Würzburg: Königshausen & Neumann, 1983.

———. "Die Geschichte der Mittelpersischen Apokalyptischen Traditionen." *Studia Iranica* 7 (1978) 49-80.

Kittel, B. P. *The Hymns of Qumran.* SBLDS 50. Chico, CA: Scholars Press, 1981.

Klauck, Hans-Josef. "Do They Never Come Back? *Nero Redivivus* and the Apocalypse of John." *CBQ* 63 (2001) 683-98.

Klijn, A. F. J. "2 (Syriac Apocalypse of) Baruch." In *The Old Testament Pseudepigrapha.* Volume 1: *Apocalyptic Literature and Testaments,* edited by J. H. Charlesworth, 615-52. Garden City, NY: Doubleday, 1983.

———. "The Sources and the Redaction of the Syriac Apocalypse of Baruch." *JSJ* 1 (1970) 65-76.

———. *Die syrische Baruch-Apokalypse.* JSHRZ 5/2. Gütersloh: Mohn, 1976.

Kloppenborg, J. S. *The Formation of Q: Trajectories in Ancient Wisdom Collections*. Philadelphia: Fortress, 1987.

———. *Q, the Earliest Gospel: An Introduction to the Original Stories and Sayings of Jesus*. Louisville: Westminster John Knox Press, 2008.

———. "The Sayings Gospel Q and the Quest of the Historical Jesus." *HTR* 89 (1996) 307-44.

———. "Symbolic Eschatology and the Apocalypticism of Q." *HTR* 80 (1987) 287-306.

Knibb, M. A. "Apocalyptic and Wisdom in 4 Ezra." *JSJ* 13 (1983) 56-74.

———. "Apocalypticism and Messianism." In *The Oxford Handbook of the Dead Sea Scrolls*, edited by Lim and Collins, 403-32.

———. "The Book of Enoch or Books of Enoch." In *The Early Enoch Literature*, edited by Boccaccini and Collins, 21-40.

———. "The Date of the Parables of Enoch: A Critical Review." *NTS* 25 (1979) 345-59.

———. *The Ethiopic Book of Enoch*. 2 vols. Oxford: Clarendon, 1978.

———. "Exile in the Damascus Document." *JSOT* 25 (1983) 99-117.

———. "The Exile in the Literature of the Intertestamental Period." *Heythrop Journal* 17 (1976) 253-72.

———. "Messianism in the Pseudepigrapha in the Light of the Scrolls." *Dead Sea Discoveries* 2 (1995) 165-84.

———. "Prophecy and the Emergence of the Jewish Apocalypses." In *Israel's Prophetic Tradition: Essays in Honour of Peter Ackroyd,* edited by R. Coggins, A. Phillips, and M. Knibb, 155-80. Cambridge: Cambridge University Press, 1982.

———. *The Second Book of Esdras*. Cambridge: Cambridge University Press, 1979.

———. "The Structure and Composition of the Parables of Enoch." In *Enoch and the Messiah Son of Man*, edited by Boccaccini, 48-64.

———. "The Teacher of Righteousness — A Messianic Title?" In *A Tribute to Geza Vermes: Essays on Jewish and Christian Literature and History,* edited by P. R. Davies and R. T. White, 51-65. Sheffield: JSOT Press, 1990.

———. "The Translation of 1 Enoch 70:1: Some Methodological Issues." In *Biblical Hebrew, Biblical Texts: Essays in Memory of Michael P. Weitzman*, edited by Ada Rapoport-Albert and Gillian Greenberg, 340-54. JSOTSup 333. Sheffield: Sheffield Academic Press, 2001.

Knierim, R. "Old Testament Form Criticism Reconsidered." *Interpretation* 27 (1973) 435-68.

Kobelski, P. J. *Melchizedek and Melchireša'*. CBQMS 10. Washington, DC: Catholic Biblical Association of America, 1981.

Koch, K. *Das Buch Daniel*. Darmstadt: Wissenschaftliche Buchgesellschaft, 1980.

———. *Daniel 1-4*. BKAT 22/1. Neukirchen–Vluyn: Neukirchener Verlag, 2005.

———. "Esras erste Vision: Weltzeiten und Weg des Höchsten." *BZ* 22 (1978) 46-75.

———. "Gottes Herrschaft über das Reich des Menschen. Daniel 4 im Licht neuer Funde." In *The Book of Daniel*, edited by van der Woude, 77-119.

———. "Is Daniel Also Among the Prophets?" *Interpretation* 39 (1985) 117-30.

———. *Ratlos vor der Apokalyptik*. Gütersloh: Mohn, 1970. English translation, *The Rediscovery of Apocalyptic*. SBT 2/22. Naperville, IL: Allenson, 1972.

———. "Spätisraelitisches Geschichtsdenken am Beispiel des Buches Daniel." *Historische Zeitschrift* 193 (1961) 1-32.

————. "Vom profetischen zum apokalyptischen Visionsbericht." In *Apocalypticism in the Mediterranean World and the Near East: Proceedings of the International Colloquium on Apocalypticism, Uppsala, August 12-17, 1979,* edited by D. Hellholm, 413-46. Tübingen: Mohr Siebeck, 1983.

Koch, K., and J. M. Schmidt, eds. *Apokalyptik.* Darmstadt: Wissenschaftliche Buchgesellschaft, 1982.

Koch, M. *Drachenkampf und Sonnenfrau. Zur Funktion des Mythischen in der Johannesapokalypse am Beispiel von Apk 12.* WUNT 184. Tübingen: Mohr Siebeck, 2004.

Koenen, L. "Die Apologie des Töpfers an König Amenophis, oder das Töpferorakel." In *Apokalyptik und Ägypten,* edited by Blasius and Schipper, 139-87.

————. "The Prophecies of a Potter: A Prophecy of World Renewal Becomes an Apocalypse." In *Proceedings of the Twelfth International Congress of Papyrology,* edited by D. H. Samuel, 249-54. Toronto: Hakkert, 1970.

Koester, Craig R. *Revelation.* AYB 38A. New Haven: Yale University Press, 2014.

Koester, H. *Introduction to the New Testament.* 2 vols. Philadelphia: Fortress, 1982.

Kolenkow, A. B. "The Fall of the Temple and the Coming of the End." In *Society of Biblical Literature 1982 Seminar Papers,* edited by K. H. Richards, 243-50. Chico, CA: Scholars Press, 1982.

————. "The Genre Testament and the Testament of Abraham." In *Studies on the Testament of Abraham,* edited by G. W. E. Nickelsburg, 139-52. Missoula, MT: Scholars Press, 1976.

Korteweg, T. "The Meaning of Naphtali's Visions." In *Studies on the Testaments of the Twelve Patriarchs,* edited by M. de Jonge, 261-90. SVTP 3. Leiden: Brill, 1975.

Kovacs, Judith, and Christopher Rowland. *Revelation.* Oxford: Blackwell, 2004.

Kowalski, Beate. "Prophetie und die Offenbarung des Johannes? Offb 22,6-21 als Testfall." In *Prophets and Prophecy in Jewish and Early Christian Literature,* edited by Joseph Verheyden, Korinna Zamfir and Tobias Nicklas, 253-93. WUNT 286. Tübingen: Mohr Siebeck, 2010.

Kraft, R. A. " 'Ezra' Materials in Judaism and Christianity." In *Aufstieg und Niedergang der römischen Welt,* II.19.2, edited by W. Haase and H. Temporini, 119-36. Berlin: de Gruyter, 1979.

Kraft, R. A., and G. W. E. Nickelsburg, eds. *Early Judaism and Its Modern Interpreters.* Atlanta: Scholars Press, 1986.

Kratz, R. G. *Translatio Imperii: Untersuchungen zu den aramäischen Danielerzählungen und ihrem theologiegeschichtlichen Umfeld.* WMANT 63. Neukirchen–Vluyn: Neukirchener Verlag, 1991.

————. "The Visions of Daniel." In *The Book of Daniel,* edited by Collins and Flint, 91-113.

Küchler, M. *Frühjüdische Weisheitstraditionen.* Göttingen: Vandenhoeck & Ruprecht, 1979.

Kugel, J. "The Interpolations in the Book of Jubilees." *RevQ* 24 (2009) 215-72.

————. "Levi's Elevation to the Priesthood in Second Temple Writings." *HTR* 86 (1993) 1-64.

————. "Some Translation and Copying Mistakes from the Original Hebrew of the Testaments of the Twelve Patriarchs." In *The Dead Sea Scrolls, Transmission of Traditions and Production of Texts*, edited by Metso, Najman, and Schuller, 45-56.

————. "Testaments of the Twelve Patriarchs." In *Outside the Bible*, edited by Feldman, Kugel, and Schiffman, 1697-1855.

————. *Traditions of the Bible: A Guide to the Bible As It Was at the Beginning of the Common Era*. Cambridge, MA: Harvard University Press, 1998.

————. *A Walk through Jubilees: Studies in the Book of Jubilees and the World of Its Creation*. JSJSup 156. Leiden: Brill, 2012.

Kugler, R. A. *From Patriarch to Priest: The Levi-Priestly Tradition from Aramaic Levi to Testament of Levi*. SBLEJL 9. Atlanta: Scholars Press, 1996.

————. *The Testaments of the Twelve Patriarchs*. Sheffield: Sheffield Academic Press, 2001.

Kuhn, H.-W. *Enderwartung und gegenwärtiges Heil*. Göttingen: Vandenhoeck & Ruprecht, 1966.

Kuhn, K. G. "The Apocalypse of Zephaniah and an Anonymous Apocalypse." In *The Apocryphal Old Testament*, edited by H. F. D. Sparks, 915-25. Oxford: Clarendon, 1984.

————. "Die Sektenschrift und die iranische Religion." *ZThK* 49 (1952) 293-316.

————. "The Two Messiahs of Aaron and Israel." In *The Scrolls and the New Testament*, edited by K. Stendahl, 54-64. New York: Harper, 1957.

Kulik, Alexander. *3 Baruch: Greek-Slavonic Apocalypse of Baruch*. CEJL. Berlin: de Gruyter, 2010.

————. "Apocalypse of Abraham." In *Outside the Bible*, edited by Feldman, Kugel, and Schiffman, 1453-81.

————. *Retroverting Slavonic Pseudepigrapha: Toward the Original of the Apocalypse of Abraham*. Atlanta: SBL, 2004.

Kurfess, A. "Christian Sibyllines." In *New Testament Apocrypha*, edited by E. Hennecke and W. Schneemelcher, 2:703-45. 2 vols. Philadelphia: Westminster, 1965.

————. "Oracula Sibyllina I/II." *ZNW* 40 (1941) 151-65.

————. *Sibyllinische Weissagungen*. Berlin: Heimeran, 1951.

Kvanvig, H. S. "An Akkadian Vision as Background for Daniel 7." *Studia Theologica* 35 (1981) 85-89.

————. *Primeval History: Babylonian, Biblical, and Enochic: An Intertextual Reading*. JSJSup 149. Leiden: Brill, 2011.

————. *Roots of Apocalyptic: The Mesopotamian Background of the Enoch Figure and of the Son of Man*. WMANT 61. Neukirchen–Vluyn: Neukirchener Verlag, 1988.

————. "The Son of Man in the Parables of Enoch." In *Enoch and the Messiah Son of Man*, edited by Boccaccini, 179-215.

Laato, Antti. *A Star Is Rising: The Historical Development of the Old Testament Royal Ideology and the Rise of the Jewish Messianic Expectations*. Atlanta: Scholars Press, 1997.

Labahn, Michael, and Manfred Lang, eds. *Lebendige Hoffnung – ewiger Tod?! Jenseitsvorstellungen im Hellenismus, Judentum und Christentum*. Leipzig: Evangelische Verlagsanstalt, 2007.

Lacocque, A. "Apocalyptic Symbolism: A Ricoeurian Hermeneutical Approach." *BR* 26 (1981) 6-15.

————. *The Book of Daniel*. Atlanta: John Knox, 1979.

————. *Daniel et son Temps*. Geneva: Labor et Fides, 1983.

————. "The Liturgical Prayer in Daniel 9." *HUCA* 47 (1976) 119-42.

————. "The Socio-Spiritual Formative Milieu of the Daniel Apocalypse." In *The Book of Daniel*, edited by A. S. van der Woude, 315-43. Leuven: Peeters, 1993.

————. "The Vision of the Eagle in 4 Esdras: A Rereading of Daniel 7 in the First Century CE." In *Society of Biblical Literature 1981 Seminar Papers*, edited by K. H. Richards, 237-58. Chico, CA: Scholars Press, 1981.

Lambert, W. G. *The Background of Jewish Apocalyptic*. London: Athlone, 1978.

————. "Enmeduranki and Related Matters." *JCS* 21 (1967) 126-38.

Lanchester, H. C. "The Sibylline Oracles." In *The Apocrypha and Pseudepigrapha of the Old Testament*. Volume II: *Pseudepigrapha*, edited by R. H. Charles, 368-406. Oxford: Clarendon, 1913.

Lange, A. "Divinatorische Träume und Apokalyptik im Jubiläenbuch." In *Studies in the Book of Jubilees*, edited by Albani, Frey, and Lange, 25-38.

————. *Weisheit und Prädestination: Weisheitliche Urordnung und Prädestination in den Textfunden von Qumran*. Leiden: Brill, 1995.

Lange, A., E. M. Meyers, Bennie H. Reynolds III, and Randall Styers, eds. *Light Against Darkness: Dualism in Ancient Mediterranean Religion and the Contemporary World*. JAJSup 2. Göttingen: Vandenhoeck & Ruprecht, 2011.

Laperrousaz, E.-M. "Le Testament de Moïse." *Semitica* 19 (1970).

Leach, E. "Genesis as Myth." In *Myth and Cosmos*, edited by J. Middleton, 1-13. Garden City, NY: Natural History Press, 1967.

————. "Lévi-Strauss in the Garden of Eden: An Examination of Some Recent Developments in the Analysis of Myth." In *Claude Lévi Strauss: The Anthropologist as Hero*, edited by E. N. Hayes and T. Hayes, 47-60. Cambridge, MA: MIT Press, 1970.

Lenglet, A. "La structure littéraire de Daniel 2-7." *Bib* 53 (1972) 169-90.

Lévi-Strauss, C. *Structural Anthropology*. New York: Basic Books, 1963.

Levine, B. A. "The Temple Scroll: Aspects of Its Historical Provenance and Literary Character." *BASOR* 233 (1978) 5-23.

Licht, J. "Abraham, Apocalypse of." *EJ*, 2:126-27.

————. "Taxo, or the Apocalyptic Doctrine of Vengeance." *JJS* 12 (1961) 95-103.

Lied, Liv Ingeborg. "*Nachleben* and Textual Identity: Variants and Variance in the Reception History of *2 Baruch*." In *Fourth Ezra and Second Baruch*, edited by Henze and Boccaccini, 403-28.

————. *The Other Lands of Israel: Imaginations of the Land in 2 Baruch*. JSJSup 129. Leiden: Brill, 2008.

————. "Recognizing the Righteous Remnant? Resurrection, Recognition and Eschatological Reversals in 2 Baruch 47-52." In *Metamorphoses: Resurrection, Body and Transformative Practices in Early Christianity*, edited by Turid Karlsen Seim and Jorunn Økland, 311-35. Ekstasis 1. Berlin: de Gruyter.

Lightfoot, Jane L. *The Sibylline Oracles: With Introduction, Translation, and Commentary on the First and Second Books*. Oxford: Oxford University Press, 2007.

Lim, Timothy H., and John J. Collins, eds. *The Oxford Handbook of the Dead Sea Scrolls*. Oxford: Oxford University Press, 2010.

Lindars, B. "Re-enter the Apocalyptic Son of Man." *NTS* 22 (1975-76) 52-72.

Lindblom, J. *Prophecy in Ancient Israel*. Oxford: Blackwell, 1962.

Lindsay, Hal, with C. C. Carlson. *The Late Great Planet Earth*. Grand Rapids: Zondervan, 1970.

Lohmeyer, E. *Diatheke*. Leipzig: Hinrichs, 1913.

Lohse, E. "Wie Christlich ist die Offenbarung des Johannes?" *NTS* 34 (1988) 321-38.

Longenecker, B. *Eschatology and the Covenant: A Comparison of 4 Ezra and Romans 1–11*. Sheffield: JSOT Press, 1991.

Lourié, Basil. "Calendrical Elements in 2 Enoch." In *New Perspectives on 2 Enoch*, edited by Orlov and Boccaccini, 191-219.

Luck, U. "Das Weltverständnis in der jüdischen Apokalyptik: Dargestellt am Äthiopischen Henochbuch und am 4 Esra." *ZThK* 73 (1976) 283-305.

Lücke, F. *Versuch einer vollständigen Einleitung in die Offenbarung Johannis und in die gesamte apokalyptische Literatur*. Bonn: Weber, 1832.

Ludlow, Jared. *Abraham Meets Death: Narrative Humor in the Testament of Abraham*. JSPSup 41. Sheffield: Sheffield Academic Press, 2002.

———. "Death and the Afterlife in 2 Baruch." In *Interpreting 4 Ezra and 2 Baruch*, edited by Boccaccini and Zurawski, 116-23.

Lupieri, Edmondo. *A Commentary on the Apocalypse of John*. Grand Rapids: Eerdmans, 2006.

Luther, M. "Vorrede auf die Offenbarung des Johannes." In *Das Neue Testament Deutsch*. Wittenberg, 1522.

Macaskill, Grant. "2 Enoch: Manuscripts, Recensions, and Original Language." In *New Perspectives on 2 Enoch*, edited by Orlov and Boccaccini, 83-101.

———. "Personal Salvation and Rigorous Obedience: The Soteriology of 2 Enoch." In *This World and the World to Come*, edited by Gurtner, 127-42.

———. *Revealed Wisdom and Inaugurated Eschatology in Ancient Judaism and Early Christianity*. JSJSup 115. Leiden: Brill, 2007.

———. *The Slavonic Texts of 2 Enoch*. Studia Judaeoslavica 5. Leiden: Brill, 2013.

Mack, B. L. *A Myth of Innocence: Mark and Christian Origins*. Philadelphia: Fortress, 1988.

Magness, J. *The Archaeology of Qumran and the Dead Sea Scrolls*. Grand Rapids: Eerdmans, 2002.

———. "The Chronology of the Settlement at Qumran in the Herodian Period." *Dead Sea Discoveries* 2 (1995) 58-65.

Maier, Harry O. *Apocalypse Recalled: The Book of Revelation after Christendom*. Minneapolis: Fortress, 2001.

Mair, A. W. *Callimachus, Lycophron, and Aratus*. LCL. Cambridge, MA: Harvard University Press, 1921, 1955.

Manson, T. W. "The Son of Man in Daniel, Enoch, and the Gospels." In *Studies in the Gospels and Epistles*. Manchester: Manchester University Press, 1962.

Mansoor, M. *The Thanksgiving Hymns*. Grand Rapids: Eerdmans, 1961.

Marcus, J. "The Jewish War and the Sitz im Leben of Mark." *JBL* 111 (1992) 441-62.

———. "Modern and Ancient Jewish Apocalypticism." *Journal of Religion* 76 (1996) 1-27.

Marshall, John W. *Parables of War: Reading John's Jewish Apocalypse*. Waterloo, ON: Wilfrid Laurier, 2001.

Martin, Dale B. *The Corinthian Body*. New Haven: Yale University Press, 1995.

Mason, Eric F. *"You Are a Priest Forever": Second Temple Jewish Messianism and the Priestly Christology of the Epistle to the Hebrews*. STDJ 74. Leiden: Brill, 2008.

Mazzaferri, F. D. *The Genre of the Book of Revelation from a Source-Critical Perspective*. BZNW 54. Berlin: de Gruyter, 1989.

McCown, C. C. "Hebrew and Egyptian Apocalyptic Literature." *HTR* 18 (1925) 357-411.

McGinn, B. *Antichrist: Two Thousand Years of the Human Fascination with Evil*. San Francisco: HarperSanFrancisco, 1994.

————. *Apocalyptic Spirituality*. New York: Paulist, 1979.

————. *Visions of the End: Apocalyptic Traditions in the Middle Ages*. New York: Columbia University Press, 1979.

McGinn B., ed. *The Encyclopedia of Apocalypticism*. Vol. 2: *Apocalypticism in Western History and Culture*. New York: Continuum, 1998.

Meeks, W. A. "Social Functions of Apocalyptic Language in Pauline Christianity." In *Apocalypticism in the Mediterranean World and the Near East: Proceedings of the International Colloquium on Apocalypticism, Uppsala, August 12-17, 1979*, edited by D. Hellholm, 685-703. Tübingen: Mohr Siebeck, 1983.

Meier, J. P. *A Marginal Jew: Rethinking the Historical Jesus*. 5 vols. AYBRL. New Haven: Yale University Press, 1991-2015.

Mendels, D. "The Five Empires: A Note on a Hellenistic Topos." *AJP* 102 (1981) 330-37.

————. *The Land of Israel as a Political Concept in Hasmonean Literature*. Tübingen: Mohr Siebeck, 1987.

Merkur, D. "The Visionary Practices of Jewish Apocalyptists." In *The Psychoanalytic Study of Society* 14, edited by L. Bryce Boyer and S. A. Grolnick, 119-48. Hillsdale, NJ: Analytic Press, 1989.

Mertens, A. *Das Buch Daniel im Lichte der Texte vom Toten Meer*. Stuttgart: Katholisches Bibelwerk, 1971.

Metso, Sarianna, Hindy Najman, and Eileen Schuller, eds. *The Dead Sea Scrolls, Transmission of Traditions and Production of Texts*. STDJ 92. Leiden: Brill, 2010.

Metzger, B. M. "Literary Forgeries and Canonical Pseudepigrapha." *JBL* 91 (1972) 3-24.

Meyer, R. *Die biblische Vorstellung vom Weltbrand*. Bonn: Bonn University Press, 1956.

Milgrom, J. "The Temple Scroll." *BA* 41 (1978) 105-20.

Milik, J. T. "4QVisions de 'Amram et une citation d'Origène." *RB* 79 (1972) 77-97.

————. *The Books of Enoch: Aramaic Fragments from Qumrân Cave 4*. Oxford: Clarendon, 1976.

————. "Écrits préesséniens de Qumrân: d'Hénoch à Amram." In *Qumrân: Sa piété, sa théologie et son milieu*, edited by M. Delcor, 91-106. Leuven: Leuven University Press, 1978.

————. "*Melkî-ṣedeq* et *Milkî-reša'* dans les anciens écrits juifs et chrétiens." *JJS* 23 (1972) 95-144.

————. "'Prière de Nabonide' et autres écrits d'un cycle de Daniel." *RB* 63 (1956) 407-15.

————. *Ten Years of Discovery in the Wilderness of Judaea*. London: SCM, 1959.

————. "Le Testament de Lévi en araméen: fragment de la grotte 4 de Qumrân." *RB* 62 (1955) 398-406.

Millar, F. "The Background to the Maccabean Revolution: Reflections on Martin Hengel's 'Judaism and Hellenism.'" *JJS* 29 (1978) 1-21.

Millar, W. R. *Isaiah 24–27 and the Origin of Apocalyptic.* HSM 11. Missoula, MT: Scholars Press, 1976.

Miller, P. D. *The Divine Warrior in Early Israel.* HSM 5. Cambridge, MA: Harvard University Press, 1973.

Miller, Robert J., ed. *The Apocalyptic Jesus: A Debate.* Santa Rosa, CA: Polebridge, 2001.

Momigliano, A. "From the Pagan to the Christian Sibyl." In *Nono Contributo,* 725-44. Rome: Edizioni di Storia e Letteratura, 1992.

————. "La Portata Storica dei Vaticini sul Settimo Re nel Terzo Libro degli Oracoli Sibillini." In *Forma Futuri: Studi in Onore del Cardinale Pellegrino,* 1077-84. Turin: Bottega d'Erasmo, 1975.

————. "What Josephus Did Not See." In idem, *Essays on Ancient and Modern Judaism,* 67-78. Chicago: University of Chicago Press, 1994.

Montefiore, C. G. *IV Ezra: A Study in the Development of Universalism.* London: Allen & Unwin, 1929.

Montgomery, J. A. *The Book of Daniel.* New York: Scribners, 1927.

Moo, Jonathan. *Creation, Nature and Hope in 4 Ezra.* FRLANT 237. Göttingen: Vandenhoeck & Ruprecht, 2011.

————. "The Few Who Obtain Mercy: Soteriology in 4 Ezra." In *This World and the World to Come,* edited by Gurtner, 98-113.

Moore, G. F. *Judaism in the First Centuries of the Christian Era.* 2 vols. New York: Schocken, 1971.

Moore, Stewart. *Jewish Ethnic Identity and Relations in Hellenistic Egypt: With Walls of Iron?* JSJSup 171. Leiden: Brill, 2015.

Morray-Jones, C. R. "Paradise Revisited (2 Cor 12:1-12): The Jewish Mystical Background of Paul's Apostolate. Part 1: The Jewish Sources." *HTR* 86/2 (1993) 177-217.

————. "Paradise Revisited (2 Cor 12:1-12): The Jewish Mystical Background of Paul's Apostolate. Part 2: "Paul's Heavenly Ascent and Its Significance." *HTR* 86/3 (1993) 265-92.

Mosca, Paul. "Ugarit and Daniel 7: A Missing Link." *Biblica* 67 (1986) 496-517.

Mowinckel, S. *He That Cometh.* Nashville: Abingdon, 1955.

————. "The Hebrew Equivalent of Taxo in Ass. Mos. IX." In *Congress Volume: Copenhagen 1953,* 88-96. VTSup 1. Leiden: Brill, 1953.

————. "Some Remarks on Hodayoth 39:5-20." *JBL* 75 (1956) 265-76.

Mueller, J. R. "The Apocalypse of Abraham and the Destruction of the Second Jewish Temple." In *Society of Biblical Literature 1982 Seminar Papers,* edited by K. H. Richards, 341-49. Chico, CA: Scholars Press, 1982.

Müller, H.-P. "Mantische Weisheit und Apokalyptik." In *Congress Volume: Uppsala 1971,* 268-93. VTSup 22. Leiden: Brill, 1972.

Müller, U. B. *Messias und Menschensohn in jüdischen Apokalypsen und in der Offenbarung des Johannes.* Gütersloh: Mohn, 1972.

Münchow, C. *Ethik und Eschatologie: Ein Beitrag zum Verständnis der frühjüdischen Apokalyptik.* Göttingen: Vandenhoeck & Ruprecht, 1982.

Murphy, F. J. "2 Baruch and the Romans." *JBL* 104 (1985) 663-69.

———. *Apocalypticism in the Bible and Its World: A Comprehensive Introduction.* Grand Rapids: Baker, 2012.

———. *Fallen Is Babylon: The Revelation to John.* Harrisburg, PA: Trinity Press International, 1998.

———. "Sapiential Elements in the Syriac Apocalypse of Baruch." *JQR* 76 (1986) 311-27.

———. *The Structure and Meaning of Second Baruch.* Atlanta: Scholars Press, 1985.

———. "The Temple in the Syriac Apocalypse of Baruch." *JBL* 106 (1987) 671-83.

Murphy-O'Connor, J. "The Essenes and Their History." *RB* 81 (1974) 215-44.

———. "The Essenes in Palestine." *BA* 40 (1977) 100-124.

Myers, J. M. *I and II Esdras.* AB 42. Garden City, NY: Doubleday, 1974.

Najman, Hindy. *Past Renewals: Interpretative Authority, Renewed Revelation and the Quest for Perfection in Jewish Antiquity.* JSJSup 53. Leiden: Brill, 2010.

———. *Seconding Sinai: The Development of Mosaic Discourse in Second Temple Judaism.* JSJSup 77. Leiden: Brill, 2003.

———. "Traditionary Process and Textual Unity in 4 Ezra." In *Fourth Ezra and Second Baruch*, edited by Henze and Boccaccini, 99-117.

Navtanovich, Liudmila. "The Provenance of 2 Enoch: A Philological Perspective." In *New Perspectives on 2 Enoch*, edited by Orlov and Boccaccini, 69-82.

Neugebauer, O. *The Astronomical Chapters of the Ethiopic Book of Enoch (72–82): With Additional Notes on the Aramaic Fragments by M. Black.* Copenhagen: Munksgaard, 1981.

Neujahr, Matthew. *Predicting the Past in the Ancient Near East: Mantic Historiography in Ancient Mesopotamia, Judah, and the Mediterranean World.* BJS 354. Providence, RI: Brown Judaic Studies, 2012.

Neusner, J. *Messiah in Context.* Philadelphia: Fortress, 1984.

Newman, C. C., J. R. Davila, and G. S. Lewis, eds. *The Jewish Roots of Christological Monotheism.* JSJSup 63. Leiden: Brill, 1999.

Newsom, C. A. "The Development of 1 Enoch 6–19: Cosmology and Judgment." *CBQ* 42 (1980) 310-29.

———. "The Reuse of Ugaritic Mythology in Daniel 7: an Optical Illusion?" In *Opportunity for No Little Instruction: Studies in Honor of Richard J. Clifford, S.J. and Daniel J. Harrington, S.J.*, edited by C. Frechette, C. Matthews, and T. Stegeman, 85-100. New York, Paulist, 2014.

———. "The Rhetoric of Jewish Apocalyptic Literature." In *The Oxford Handbook of Apocalypticism*, edited by Collins, 201-17.

———. "'Sectually Explicit' Literature from Qumran." In *The Hebrew Bible and Its Interpreters,* edited by W. H. Propp, B. Halpern, and D. N. Freedman, 167-87. Winona Lake, IN: Eisenbrauns, 1990.

———. "Spying Out the Land: A Report from Genology." In *Seeking Out the Wisdom of the Ancients*, edited by R. L. Troxel, K. G. Friebel and D. R. Magary, 437-50. Winona Lake, IN: Eisenbrauns, 2005.

———. "Why Nabonidus? Excavating Traditions from Qumran, the Hebrew Bible, and

Neo-Babylonian Sources." In *The Dead Sea Scrolls: Transmission of Traditions and Production of Texts,* edited by Metso, Najman and Schuller, 57-79.

Newsom, C. A., with Brennan Breed. *Daniel: A Commentary.* OTL. Louisville, 2014.

Nickelsburg, G. W. E. *1 Enoch 1.* Hermeneia. Minneapolis: Fortress, 2001.

—————. "An Antiochan Date for the Testament of Moses." In *Studies on the Testament of Moses,* edited by G. W. E. Nickelsburg, 33-37. Missoula, MT: Scholars Press, 1973.

—————. "Apocalyptic and Myth in 1 Enoch 6–11." *JBL* 96 (1977) 383-405.

—————. "The Apocalyptic Construction of Reality in *1 Enoch.*" In *Mysteries and Revelations: Apocalyptic Studies since the Uppsala Colloquium,* edited by J. J. Collins and J. H. Charlesworth, 51-64. JSPSup 9. Sheffield: JSOT Press, 1991.

—————. "The Apocalyptic Message of 1 Enoch 92–105." *CBQ* 39 (1977) 309-28.

—————. "The Books of Enoch in Recent Research." *RelStudRev* 7 (1981) 210-17.

—————. "Discerning the Structure(s) of the Enochic Book of Parables." In *Enoch and the Messiah Son of Man,* edited by Boccaccini, 23-47.

—————. "Enoch, Levi, and Peter: Recipients of Revelation in Upper Galilee." *JBL* 100 (1981) 575-600.

—————. "The Epistle of Enoch and the Qumran Literature." *JJS* 33 (1982) 333-48.

—————. "Eschatology in the Testament of Abraham: A Study of the Judgment Scenes in the Two Recensions." In *Studies on the Testament of Abraham,* edited by G. W. E. Nickelsburg, 23-64. Missoula, MT: Scholars Press, 1976.

—————. *Jewish Literature between the Bible and the Mishnah.* 2d ed. Minneapolis: Fortress, 2005.

—————. "Narrative Traditions in the Paraleipomena of Jeremiah and 2 Baruch." *CBQ* 35 (1973) 60-68.

—————. *Resurrection, Immortality, and Eternal Life in Intertestamental Judaism.* 2d ed. Cambridge, MA: Harvard University Press, 2006.

—————. "Riches, the Rich, and God's Judgment in 1 Enoch 92–105 and the Gospel According to Luke." *NTS* 25 (1979) 324-44.

—————. "Social Aspects of Palestinian Jewish Apocalypticism." In *Apocalypticism in the Mediterranean World and the Near East: Proceedings of the International Colloquium on Apocalypticism, Uppsala, August 12-17, 1979,* edited by D. Hellholm, 639-52. Tübingen: Mohr Siebeck, 1983.

—————. "Structure and Message in the Testament of Abraham." In *Studies on the Testament of Abraham,* edited by G. W. E. Nickelsburg, 85-93. Missoula, MT: Scholars Press, 1976.

Nickelsburg, G. W. E., ed. *Studies on the Testament of Abraham.* Missoula, MT: Scholars Press, 1976.

—————, ed. *Studies on the Testament of Moses.* Missoula, MT: Scholars Press, 1973.

Nickelsburg, G. W. E., and J. J. Collins, eds. *Ideal Figures in Ancient Judaism: Profiles and Paradigms.* SBLSCS 12. Missoula, MT: Scholars Press, 1980.

Nickelsburg, G. W. E., and James C. VanderKam. *1 Enoch: A New Translation.* Minneapolis: Fortress, 2004.

Nickelsburg, G. W. E., and James C. VanderKam. *1 Enoch 2: A Commentary on the Book of 1 Enoch Chapters 37-82.* Hermeneia. Minneapolis: Fortress, 2012.

Niditch, S. *The Symbolic Vision in Biblical Tradition.* HSM 30. Chico: Scholars Press, 1983.

———. "The Visionary." In *Ideal Figures in Ancient Judaism: Profiles and Paradigms,* edited by G. W. E. Nickelsburg and J. J. Collins, 153-79. SBLSCS 12. Missoula, MT: Scholars Press, 1980.

Niditch, S., and R. Doran. "The Success Story of the Wise Courtier: A Formal Approach." *JBL* 96 (1977) 179-93.

Niebuhr, K.-W. "4Q521,2 II — Ein Eschatologischer Psalm." In *Mogilany 1995,* edited by Z. J. Kapera. Kraków: Enigma, 1996.

———. *Gesetz und Paränese: Katechismusartige Weisungsreihen in der frühjüdischen Literatur.* WUNT 2/28. Tübingen: Mohr Siebeck, 1987.

Nikiprowetzky, V. *La Troisième Sibylle.* Paris: Mouton, 1970.

Nir, Rivka. *The Destruction of Jerusalem and the Idea of Redemption in the Syriac Apocalypse of Baruch.* SBLEJL 20. Atlanta: SBL, 2003.

Nissinen, Martti. "Neither Prophecies nor Apocalypses: The Akkadian Literary Predictive Texts." In *Knowing the End from the Beginning,* edited by Grabbe and Haak, 134-48.

Nolland, J. "Sib Or 3.265-94: An Early Maccabean Messianic Oracle." *JTS* 30 (1979) 158-67.

Nordheim, E. von. *Die Lehre der Alten.* Vol. 1. Leiden: Brill, 1980.

North, R. "Prophecy to Apocalyptic via Zechariah." In *Congress Volume: Uppsala 1971,* 47-71. VTSup 22. Leiden: Brill, 1972.

Noth, M. "The Holy Ones of the Most High." In idem, *The Laws in the Pentateuch and Other Essays,* 215-28. Philadelphia: Fortress, 1967.

———. "The Understanding of History in Old Testament Apocalyptic." In idem, *The Laws in the Pentateuch and Other Essays,* 194-214. Philadelphia: Fortress, 1967.

Novenson, Matthew V. *Christ among the Messiahs: Christ Language in Paul and Messiah Language in Ancient Judaism.* Oxford: Oxford University Press, 2012.

Oegema, Gerbern S. *The Anointed and His People: Messianic Expectations from the Maccabees to Bar Kochba.* Sheffield: Sheffield Academic Press, 1998.

Olson, Daniel C. "Enoch and the Son of Man in the Epilogue of the Parables?" *JSP* 18 (1998) 27-38.

Oppenheim, A. L. *The Interpretation of Dreams in the Ancient Near East.* Philadelphia: American Philosophical Society, 1956.

Orlov, Andrei A. *Dark Mirrors: Azazel and Satanail in Early Jewish Demonology.* Albany: State University of New York, 2011.

———. *Divine Manifestations in the Slavonic Pseudepigrapha.* Piscataway, NJ: Gorgias, 2009.

———. *The Enoch Metatron Tradition.* TSAJ 107. Tübingen: Mohr Siebeck, 2005.

———. "Eschatological Yom Kippur in the Apocalypse of Abraham. The Scapegoat Ritual." In idem, *Dark Mirrors,* 27-46.

———. *From Apocalypticism to Merkabah Mysticism: Studies in the Slavonic Pseudepigrapha.* JSJSup 114. Leiden: Brill, 2007.

———. *Heavenly Priesthood in the Apocalypse of Abraham.* Cambridge: Cambridge University Press, 2013.

———. "Melchizedek Legend of 2 *(Slavonic) Enoch*." In idem, *From Apocalypticism to Merkabah Mysticism*, 423-39.

———. "Praxis of the Voice: The Divine Name Traditions in the Apocalypse of Abraham." *JBL* 127 (2008) 53-70.

———. "The Sacerdotal Traditions of 2 Enoch and the Date of the Text." In *New Perspectives on 2 Enoch*, edited by Orlov and Boccaccini, 103-24.

Orlov, Andrei A., and Gabriele Boccaccini. *New Perspectives on 2 Enoch: No Longer Slavonic Only*. Studia Judaeoslavica 4. Leiden: Brill, 2012.

Osten-Sacken, P. von der. *Die Apokalyptik in ihrem Verhältnis zu Prophetie and Weisheit*. Munich: Kaiser, 1969.

———. *Gott und Belial*. Göttingen: Vandenhoeck & Ruprecht, 1969.

Pagels, Elaine. *Revelations: Visions, Prophecy, and Politics in the Book of Revelation*. New York: Viking, 2012.

Parke, H. W. *Sibyls and Sibylline Prophecy in Classical Antiquity*. Ed. B. C. McGing. London: Routledge, 1988.

Patte, D. *Early Jewish Hermeneutic in Palestine*. SBLDS 22. Missoula, MT: Scholars Press, 1975.

Paul, S. "Heavenly Tablets and the Book of Life." *Journal of the Ancient Near Eastern Society of Columbia University* 5 (1973) 345-53.

Peerbolte, L. J. L. *The Antecedents of Antichrist*. Leiden: Brill, 1996.

Pennington, A. "2 Enoch." In *The Apocryphal Old Testament*, edited by H. F. D. Sparks, 321-62. Oxford: Clarendon, 1984.

———. "The Apocalypse of Abraham." In *The Apocryphal Old Testament*, edited by H. F. D. Sparks, 363-92. Oxford: Clarendon, 1984.

Perrin, Andrew. *The Dynamics of Dream-Vision Revelation in the Aramaic Dead Sea Scrolls*. JAJSup 19. Göttingen: Vandenhoeck & Ruprecht, 2015.

Perrin, N. "Eschatology and Hermeneutics: Reflections on Method in the Interpretation of the New Testament." *JBL* 93 (1974) 3-14.

———. *A Modern Pilgrimage in New Testament Christology*. Philadelphia: Fortress, 1974.

———. *Rediscovering the Teaching of Jesus*. New York: Harper & Row, 1967.

Perrin, N., and D. C. Duling. *The New Testament: An Introduction*. 2d ed. New York: Harcourt Brace Jovanovich, 1982.

Philonenko, M. "La cosmologie du livre des secrets d'Hénoch." In *Religions en Egypte Hellénistique et Romaine*, 109-16. Paris: Presses universitaires de France, 1969.

———. "La Doctrine Qoumrânienne des Deux Ésprits." In *Apocalyptique Iranienne et Dualisme Qoumrânien*, edited by G. Widengren, A. Hultgård, and M. Philonenko, 163-211. Paris: Maisonneuve, 1995.

———. *Les Interpolations chrétiennes des Testaments des Douze Patriarches et les manuscrits de Qoumrân*. Paris: Presses universitaires de France, 1960.

Philonenko-Sayer, B., and M. Philonenko. *L'Apocalypse d'Abraham: Introduction, texte slave, traduction et notes*. Semitica 31. Paris: Maisonneuve, 1981.

Picard, J.-C. *Apocalypsis Baruchi Graece*. PVTG 2. Leiden: Brill, 1967.

———. " 'Je te montrerai d'autres mystères plus grandes que ceux-ci . . .': Notes sur 3 Bar et quelques écrits apparentés." In *Histoire et Anthropologie des Commu-*

*nautés Juives et Chrétiennes dans les Sociétes Anciennes,* 17-40. Canal 8. Paris: Centre de Recherches de l'École Pratique des Hautes Études, 1991.

———. "Observations sur l'Apocalypse grecque de Baruch I: Cadre historique et efficacité symbolique." *Semitica* 20 (1970) 77-103.

Pines, S. "Eschatology and the Concept of Time in the Slavonic Book of Enoch." In *Types of Redemption,* edited by R. J. Z. Werblowski and J. C. Bleeker, 72-87. Leiden: Brill, 1970.

Piovanelli, Pierluigi. " 'A Testimony for the Kings and the Mighty Who Possess the Earth': The Thirst for Justice and Peace in the Parables of Enoch." In *Enoch and the Messiah Son of Man,* edited by Boccaccini, 363-79.

———. "Why Ezra and not Enoch? Rewriting the Script of the First Exile with the Hope for a Prompt Restoration of Zion's Fortunes." In *Fourth Ezra and Second Baruch,* edited by Henze and Boccaccini, 237-49.

Plöger, O. *Theocracy and Eschatology.* Richmond: John Knox, 1968.

Poirier, John C. "On a Wing and a Prayer. The Soteriology of the *Apocalypse of Abraham.*" In *This World and the World to Come,* edited by Gurtner, 87-97.

———. "The Ouranology of the Apocalypse of Abraham." *JSJ* 35 (2004) 391-409.

Polaski, Donald C. *Authorizing an End: The Isaiah Apocalypse and Intertextuality.* Leiden: Brill, 2001.

Pomykala, K. E. *The Davidic Dynasty Tradition in Early Judaism: Its History and Significance for Messianism.* SBLEJL 7. Atlanta: Scholars Press, 1995.

Pope, M. *El in the Ugaritic Texts.* VTSup 2. Leiden: Brill, 1955.

Porteous, N. W. *Daniel.* 2d ed. London: SCM, 1979.

Porter, P. A. *Metaphors and Monsters: A Literary-Critical Study of Daniel 7 and 8.* Lund: Gleerup, 1983.

Porter, Stanley, ed. *The Messiah in the Old and New Testaments.* Grand Rapids: Eerdmans, 2007.

Portier-Young, Anathea. *Apocalypse against Empire: Theologies of Resistance in Early Judaism.* Grand Rapids: Eerdmans, 2011.

———. "Languages of Identity and Obligation: Daniel as Bilingual Book." *VT* 60 (2010) 98-115.

———. "Symbolic Resistance in the Book of the Watchers." In *The Watchers in Jewish and Christian Traditions,* edited by Harkins, Bautch, and Endres, 39-49.

Potter, D. S. *Prophecy and History in the Crisis of the Roman Empire.* Oxford: Oxford University Press, 1990.

Pouilly, J. *La Règle de la Communauté de Qumrân: Son Evolution Littéraire.* Paris: Gabalda, 1976.

Priest, J. "The Testament of Moses." In *The Old Testament Pseudepigrapha.* Volume 1: *Apocalyptic Literature and Testaments,* edited by J. H. Charlesworth, 919-34. Garden City, NY: Doubleday, 1983.

Prigent, P. *Apocalypse 12: Histoire de l'exégèse.* Tübingen: Mohr Siebeck, 1959.

Puech, E. "246. 4QApocryphe de Daniel ar." In Brooke et al., DJD XXII, 165-84.

———. "Une Apocalypse Messianique [4Q521]." *RevQ* 15 (1992) 475-519.

———. *La Croyance des Esséniens en la Vie Future: Immortalité, Résurrection, Vie Éternelle?* Paris: Gabalda, 1993.

————. "Fragment d'une Apocalypse en Araméen (4Q246 = pseudo-Da$^{nd}$) et le 'Royaume de Dieu.'" *RB* 99 (1992) 98-131.

————. "Préséance sacerdotale et messie-roi dans la règle de la congregation (1QSa ii 11-22)." *RevQ* 63 (1994) 351-65.

————. *Qumrân Grotte 4.XXVII: Textes araméens, deuxième partie (4Q550-4Q575a, 4Q580-4Q587)*. DJD 37. Oxford: Oxford University Press, 2009.

Qimron, E. "Celibacy in the Dead Sea Scrolls and the Two Kinds of Sectarians." In *The Madrid Qumran Congress: Proceedings of the International Congress on the Dead Sea Scrolls, Madrid 18-21 March, 1991*, edited by J. Trebolle Barrera and L. Vegas Montaner, 1:287-94. 2 vols. Leiden: Brill, 1992.

Qimron, E., and J. Strugnell. *Qumran Cave 4–V: Miqṣat Maʿaśê Ha-Torah*. DJD 10. Oxford: Clarendon, 1994.

Rabin, C. *The Zadokite Document*. Oxford: Clarendon, 1958.

Rad, G. von. *Theologie des Alten Testaments*. 2 vols. 4th ed. Munich: Kaiser, 1965.

Rajak, Tessa. "Jewish Millenarian Expectations." In *The First Jewish Revolt: Archaeology, History, and Ideology*, edited by Andrea M. Berlin and J. Andrew Overman, 164-88. London: Routledge, 2002.

Ramsey, I. T. *Models and Mystery*. London: Oxford University Press, 1964.

Ravitsky, A. *Messianism, Zionism, and Jewish Religious Radicalism*. Chicago: University of Chicago Press, 1996.

Reed, Annette Yoshiko. "Enochic and Mosaic Traditions in Jubilees: The Evidence of Angelology and Demonology." In *Enoch and the Mosaic Torah*, edited by Boccaccini and Ibba, 353-68.

————. *Fallen Angels and the History of Judaism and Christianity*. The Reception of Enochic Literature. Cambridge: Cambridge University Press, 2005.

————. "Testament of Abraham." In *Outside the Bible*, edited by Feldman, Kugel, and Schiffman, 1671-96.

Reeves, J. C. *Jewish Lore in Manichaean Cosmogony: Studies in the Book of Giants Traditions*. Cincinnati: Hebrew Union College, 1992.

Regev, Eyal. *Sectarianism in Qumran: A Cross-Cultural Perspective*. Berlin: de Gruyter, 2007.

Reid, S. B. "1 Enoch: The Rising Elite of the Apocalyptic Movement." In *Society of Biblical Literature 1983 Seminar Papers*, edited by K. H. Richards, 147-56. Chico, CA: Scholars Press, 1983.

————. *Enoch and Daniel: A Form-Critical and Sociological Study of the Historical Apocalypses*. Berkeley: Bibal, 1989.

Resch, A. *Der Traum im Heilsplan Gottes*. Freiburg: Herder, 1964.

Reynolds, Bennie H. *Between Symbolism and Realism: The Use of Symbolic and Non-Symbolic Language in Ancient Jewish Apocalypses 333-63 BCE*. JAJSup 8. Göttingen: Vandenhoeck & Ruprecht, 2011.

Riessler, P. *Altjüdisches Schrifttum ausserhalb der Bibel*. Heidelberg: Kerle, 1927. Reprint, Darmstadt: Wissenschaftliche Buchgesellschaft, 1966.

Ringgren, H. "Der Weltbrand in den Hodajot." In *Bibel und Qumran: Beiträge zur Erforschung der Beziehungen zwischen Bibel- und Qumranwissenschaft. Hans Bardtke zum 22.9.1966*, edited by S. Wagner, 177-82. Berlin: Evangelische Haupt-Bibelgesellschaft, 1968.

Rochberg, Francesca. *The Heavenly Writing: Divination, Horoscopy, and Astronomy in Mesopotamian Culture.* Cambridge: Cambridge University Press, 2004.

Rogerson, J. W. "The Hebrew Conception of Corporate Personality: A Reexamination." *JTS* 21 (1970) 1-16.

———. *Myth in Old Testament Interpretation.* Berlin: de Gruyter, 1974.

Rosenthal, F. *Vier Apokryphische Bücher aus der Zeit und Schule R. Akibas.* Leipzig: Schulze, 1885.

Rosen-Zvi, Ishai. *Demonic Desires: yetzer hara and the Problem of Evil in Late Antiquity.* Philadelphia: University of Pennsylvania, 2011.

Rössler, D. *Gesetz und Geschichte.* Neukirchen–Vluyn: Neukirchener Verlag, 1960.

Rost, L. "Zum Buch der Kriege der Söhne des Lichts gegen die Söhne der Finsternis." *TLZ* 80 (1955) 205-8.

Rowland, C. *The Open Heaven: A Study of Apocalyptic in Judaism and Early Christianity.* New York: Crossroad, 1982.

———. "The Visions of God in Apocalyptic Literature." *JSJ* 10 (1979) 137-54.

Rowland, C., and M. Corner. *Liberating Exegesis: The Challenge of Liberation Theology to Biblical Studies.* Louisville: Westminster, 1989.

Rowley, H. H. *Darius the Mede and the Four World Empires.* Cardiff: University of Wales, 1935.

———. *The Relevance of Apocalyptic.* London: Athlone, 1944. Reprint, Greenwood, SC: Attic, 1980.

———. "The Unity of the Book of Daniel." In *The Servant of the Lord and Other Essays on the Old Testament,* 237-68. London: Lutterworth, 1952.

Royalty, Robert M. *The Streets of Heaven: The Ideology of Wealth in the Apocalypse of John.* Macon, GA: Macon University Press, 1998.

Rubinkiewicz, R. *L'Apocalypse d' Abraham en vieux slave: Introduction, texte critique, traduction et commentaire.* Lublin: Société des Lettres et des sciences de l'Université de l'Université Catholique de Lublin, 1987.

———. "La vision de l'histoire dans l'Apocalypse d'Abraham." In *Aufstieg und Niedergang der römischen Welt,* II.19.2, edited by W. Haase and H. Temporini, 137-51. Berlin: de Gruyter, 1979.

Rubinkiewicz, R., and H. G. Lunt. "The Apocalypse of Abraham." In *The Old Testament Pseudepigrapha.* Volume 1: *Apocalyptic Literature and Testaments,* edited by J. H. Charlesworth, 681-705. Garden City, NY: Doubleday, 1983.

Rubinstein, A. "Observations on the Slavonic Book of Enoch." *JJS* 13 (1962) 1-21.

Ruiten, J. T. A. G. M. van. *Primaeval History Interpreted: The Rewriting of Genesis 1-11 in the Book of Jubilees.* JSJSup 66. Leiden: Brill, 2000.

Ruppert, L. *Der leidende Gerechte.* Würzburg: Echter, 1972.

Russell, D. S. *The Method and Message of Jewish Apocalyptic.* Philadelphia: Westminster, 1964.

Sacchi, P. *L'apocalittica giudaica e la sua storia.* Brescia: Paideia, 1990. English translation, *Jewish Apocalyptic and Its History.* Sheffield: Sheffield Academic Press, 1997.

Saldarini, A. J. "Apocalypses and 'Apocalyptic' in Rabbinic Literature and Mysticism." *Semeia* 14 (1979) 187-205.

———. "Varieties of Rabbinic Responses to the Destruction of the Temple." In *Society of Biblical Literature 1982 Seminar Papers,* edited by K. H. Richards, 437-58. Chico, CA: Scholars Press, 1982.

Sanders, E. P. "The Covenant as a Soteriological Category and the Nature of Salvation in Palestinian and Hellenistic Judaism." In *Jews, Greeks, and Christians: Studies in Honor of W. D. Davies,* edited by R. Hamerton-Kelly and R. Scroggs, 11-44. Leiden: Brill, 1976.

————. "The Genre of Palestinian Jewish Apocalypses." In *Apocalypticism in the Mediterranean World and the Near East: Proceedings of the International Colloquium on Apocalypticism, Uppsala, August 12-17, 1979,* edited by D. Hellholm, 447-59. Tübingen: Mohr Siebeck, 1983.

————. *Jesus and Judaism.* Philadelphia: Fortress, 1985.

————. *Paul and Palestinian Judaism.* Philadelphia: Fortress, 1977.

————. "The Testaments of the Three Patriarchs." In *The Old Testament Pseudepigrapha.* Volume 1: *Apocalyptic Literature and Testaments,* edited by J. H. Charlesworth, 869-918. Garden City, NY: Doubleday, 1983.

Sayler, G. "2 Baruch: A Story of Grief and Consolation." In *Society of Biblical Literature 1982 Seminar Papers,* edited by K. H. Richards, 485-500. Chico, CA: Scholars Press, 1982.

————. *Have the Promises Failed? A Literary Analysis of 2 Baruch.* Chico, CA: Scholars Press, 1984.

Schade, H.-H. *Apokalyptische Christologie bei Paulus.* Göttingen: Vandenhoeck & Ruprecht, 1981.

Schäfer, P. *The Origins of Jewish Mysticism.* Princeton: Princeton University Press, 2009.

————. *Studien zur Geschichte und Theologie des Rabbinischen Judentums.* Leiden: Brill, 1978.

Schiffman, L. H. "2 Enoch and Halakhah." In *New Perspectives on 2 Enoch,* edited by Orlov and Boccaccini, 221-28.

————. *The Eschatological Community of the Dead Sea Scrolls.* Atlanta: Scholars Press, 1989.

————. *Halakhah at Qumran.* Leiden: Brill, 1975.

————. *Reclaiming the Dead Sea Scrolls: The History of Judaism, the Background of Christianity, the Lost Library of Qumran.* Philadelphia: The Jewish Publication Society, 1994.

Schmidt, F. "Le Testament d'Abraham: Introduction, édition de la recension courte, traduction et notes." Diss., University of Strasbourg, 1971.

————. *Le Testament grec d'Abraham.* Tübingen: Mohr Siebeck, 1986.

————. "The Two Recensions of the Testament of Abraham: In Which Way Did the Transformation Take Place?" In *Studies on the Testament of Abraham,* edited by G. W. E. Nickelsburg, 65-83. Missoula, MT: Scholars Press, 1976.

Schmidt, J. M. *Die jüdische Apokalyptik.* Neukirchen–Vluyn: Neukirchener Verlag, 1969.

Schmidt, N. "The Original Language of the Parables of Enoch." In *Old Testament and Semitic Studies in Memory of W. R. Harper,* 2:329-49. Chicago: University of Chicago Press, 1908.

Schmithals, W. *The Apocalyptic Movement.* Nashville: Abingdon, 1975.

Scholem, G. *Jewish Gnosticism, Merkabah Mysticism, and Talmudic Tradition.* 2d ed. New York: Jewish Theological Seminary, 1965.

————. *Major Trends in Jewish Mysticism.* New York: Schocken, 1961.

————. *The Messianic Idea in Judaism and Other Essays on Jewish Spirituality.* New York: Schocken, 1971.

Schreiner, J. *Das 4. Buch Esra.* JSHRZ 5/4. Gütersloh: Mohn, 1981.

Schultz, Brian. *Conquering the World: The War Scroll (1QM) Reconsidered.* STDJ 76. Leiden: Brill, 2009.

Schulz, P. *Der Autoritätsanspruch des Lehrers der Gerechtigkeit in Qumran.* Meisenheim am Glan: Hain, 1974.

Schüpphaus, J. *Die Psalmen Salomos.* Leiden: Brill, 1977.

Schürer, E. *The History of the Jewish People in the Age of Jesus Christ (175 B.C.–A.D. 135),* revised and edited by G. Vermes, F. Millar, and M. Black. 3 vols., vol. 3 in two parts. Edinburgh: T & T Clark, 1973-87.

Schwartz, D. R. "The Tribes of As. Mos. 4:7-9." *JBL* 99 (1980) 217-23.

Schweitzer, A. *The Quest of the Historical Jesus.* Reprint, New York: Macmillan, 1968; German original, 1906.

Segal, A. F. "Heavenly Ascent in Hellenistic Judaism, Early Christianity and Their Environment." In *Aufstieg und Niedergang der römischen Welt,* II.23.2, edited by W. Haase and H. Temporini, 1333-94. Berlin: de Gruyter, 1980.

————. *Paul the Convert: The Apostolate and Apostasy of Saul the Pharisee.* New Haven: Yale University Press, 1990.

Segal, Michael. *The Book of Jubilees: Rewritten Bible, Redaction, Ideology and Theology.* JSJSup 117. Leiden: Brill, 2007.

————. "Reconsidering the Theological Background of Daniel 7." In idem, *Dreams, Riddles, and Visions: Textual, Intertextual, and Exegetical Studies of the Book of Daniel.* Berlin: de Gruyter, 2016.

————. "Who is the 'Son of God' in 4Q246? An Overlooked Example of Early Biblical Interpretation." *DSD* 21 (2014) 289-312.

Shaked, S. "Iranian Influence on Judaism: First Century BCE to Second Century CE." In *The Cambridge History of Judaism.* Volume One: *Introduction; The Persian Period,* edited by W. D. Davies and L. Finkelstein, 308-25. Cambridge: Cambridge University Press, 1984.

————. "Qumran and Iran: Further Considerations." *Israel Oriental Studies* 2 (1972) 433-46.

Sherwin-White, Susan. "Seleucid Babylonia: A Case Study for the Installation and Development of Greek Rule." In *Hellenism in the East: The Interaction of Greek and Non-Greek Civilizations from Syria to Central Asia after Alexander,* edited by A. Kuhrt and S. Sherwin-White, 1-31. Berkeley: University of California, 1987, 1-31.

Sievers, J. *The Hasmoneans and Their Supporters.* Atlanta: Scholars Press, 1990.

Silverman, Jason M. *Persepolis and Jerusalem: Iranian Influence on the Apocalyptic Hermeneutic.* London: T & T Clark, 2012.

Sim, David C. *Apocalyptic Eschatology in the Gospel of Matthew.* SNTSMS 88. Cambridge: Cambridge University Press, 1996.

Sjöberg, E. *Der Menschensohn im Äthiopischen Henochbuch.* Lund: Gleerup, 1946.

Skehan, P. W. "A Fragment of the 'Song of Moses' (Deut 32) from Qumran." *BASOR* 136 (1954) 12-15.

Skjaervø, Prods Oktor. "Zoroastrian Dualism" with an appendix on "The Sources of Zoroastrianism." In *Light against Darkness: Dualism in Ancient Mediterranean Religion and the Contemporary World*, edited by Armin Lange, Eric M. Meyers, Bennie H. Reynolds III, and Randall Styers, 55-91. JAJSup 2. Göttingen: Vandenhoeck & Ruprecht, 2011.

Slater, T. B. "One Like a Son of Man in First-Century CE Judaism." *NTS* 41 (1995) 183-98.

Slingerland, H. D. *The Testaments of the Twelve Patriarchs: A Critical History of Research.* SBLMS 21. Missoula, MT: Scholars Press, 1977.

Smith, J. Z. "Native Cults in the Hellenistic Period." *HR* 11 (1971) 236-49.

———. "Prayer of Joseph." In *The Old Testament Pseudepigrapha*. Volume 2: *Expansions of the "Old Testament" and Legends, Wisdom and Philosophical Literature, Prayers, Psalms, and Odes, Fragments of Lost Judeo-Hellenistic Works*, edited by J. H. Charlesworth, 699-714. Garden City, NY: Doubleday, 1985.

———. "Wisdom and Apocalyptic." In *Religious Syncretism in Antiquity*, edited by B. Pearson, 131-56. Missoula, MT: Scholars Press, 1975.

Smith, M. "The Description of the Essenes in Josephus and the Philosophoumena." *HUCA* 29 (1958) 273-313.

———. "Helios in Palestine." *Eretz Israel* 16 (1982) 199*-224*.

———. "On the History of *Apokalyptō* and *Apokalypsis*." In *Apocalypticism in the Mediterranean World and the Near East: Proceedings of the International Colloquium on Apocalypticism, Uppsala, August 12-17, 1979*, edited by D. Hellholm, 9-20. Tübingen: Mohr Siebeck, 1983.

———. "What Is Implied by the Variety of Messianic Figures?" *JBL* 78 (1959) 66-72.

Smith-Christopher, D. "The Book of Daniel." In *The New Interpreter's Bible*. Nashville: Abingdon, 1996, 17-152.

Soden, W. von. "Die Unterweltsvision eines assyrischen Kronprinzen." In *Aus Sprache, Geschichte, und Religion Babyloniens: Gesammelte Aufsätze*, 29-67. Naples: Istituto universitario orientale, 1989.

Speyer, W. "Fälschung, pseudepigraphische freie Erfindung, und 'echte religiöse Pseudepigraphie.' " In *Frühes Christentum im antiken Strahlungsfeld*, 100-33. Tübingen: Mohr Siebeck, 1989.

———. "Religiöse Pseudepigraphie und literarische Fälschung im Altertum." In *Frühes Christentum im antiken Strahlungsfeld*, 21-58. Tübingen: Mohr Siebeck, 1989.

Starcky, J. "Les Maitres de Justice et la chronologie de Qumrân." In *Qumrân*, edited by M. Delcor. Leuven: Leuven University Press, 1978.

———. "Les quatres étapes du messianisme à Qumrân." *RB* 70 (1963) 481-505.

Steck, O. H. *Israel und das gewaltsame Geschick der Propheten*. Neukirchen–Vluyn: Erziehungsverein, 1967.

Stegemann, H. "Die Bedeutung der Qumranfunde für die Erforschung der Apokalyptik." In *Apocalypticism in the Mediterranean World and the Near East: Proceedings of the International Colloquium on Apocalypticism, Uppsala, August 12-17, 1979*, edited by D. Hellholm, 495-530. Tübingen: Mohr Siebeck, 1983.

———. *Die Entstehung der Qumrangemeinde*. Bonn, published privately, 1971.

————. *Die Essener, Qumran, Johannes der Täufer, und Jesus.* Freiburg im Breisgau: Herder, 1993. English translation, *The Library of Qumran: On the Essenes, Qumran, John the Baptist, and Jesus.* Grand Rapids: Eerdmans, 1998.

————. "The Qumran Essenes — Local Members of the Main Jewish Union of Late Second Temple Times." In *The Madrid Qumran Congress: Proceedings of the International Congress on the Dead Sea Scrolls, Madrid 18-21 March, 1991,* edited by J. Trebolle Barrera and L. Vegas Montaner, 1:83-175. 2 vols. Leiden: Brill, 1992.

————. "Some Remarks to 1QSa, to 1QSb, and to Qumran Messianism." *RevQ* 17 (1996) 479-506.

Steindorff, G. *Die Apokalypse des Elias, eine unbekannte Apokalypse und Bruchstücke der Sophonias-Apokalypse.* Leipzig: Hinrichs, 1899.

Stern, Sacha. *Calendar and Community: A History of the Jewish Calendar, 2nd cent.* BCE – *10th cent.* CE. Oxford: Oxford University Press, 2001.

————. "Qumran Calendars and Sectarianism." *The Oxford Handbook of the Dead Sea Scrolls,* edited by Lim and Collins, 232-53.

————. *Sects and Sectarianism in Jewish History.* Leiden: Brill, 2011.

Steudel, A. "'aḥarît hayyāmîm in the Texts from Qumran." *RevQ* 16 (1993) 225-46.

————. *Der Midrasch zur Eschatologie aus der Qumrangemeinde (4QMidr Eschat a,b).* Leiden: Brill, 1994.

Stokes, Ryan E. "The Throne Visions of Daniel 7, *1 Enoch* 14, and the Qumran *Book of Giants* (4Q530): An Analysis of Their Literary Relationship." *DSD* 15 (2008) 340-58.

Stökl Ben Ezra, Daniel. "Halakha, Calendars, and the Provenances of 2 Enoch." In *New Perspectives on 2 Enoch,* edited by Orlov and Boccaccini, 229-42.

Stone, M. E. *Ancient Judaism: New Visions and Views.* Grand Rapids: Eerdmans, 2011.

————. "Apocalyptic Literature." In *Jewish Writings of the Second Temple Period,* edited by M. E. Stone, 383-441. CRINT 2/2. Assen: Van Gorcum; Philadelphia: Fortress, 1984.

————. "Apocalyptic — Vision or Hallucination?" *Milla wa-Milla* 14 (1974) 47-56.

————. *The Armenian Version of IV Ezra.* Missoula, MT: Scholars Press, 1979.

————. "The Book of Enoch and Judaism in the Third Century BCE." *CBQ* 40 (1978) 479-92.

————. "Coherence and Inconsistency in the Apocalypses: The Case of 'The End' in 4 Ezra." *JBL* 102 (1983) 229-43.

————. "The Concept of the Messiah in IV Ezra." In *Religions in Antiquity: Essays in Memory of E. R. Goodenough,* edited by J. Neusner, 295-312. Leiden: Brill, 1968.

————. "The Fall of Satan and Adam's Penance: Three Notes on the Books of Adam and Eve." *JTS* 44 (1993) 143-56.

————. *Features of the Eschatology of 4 Ezra.* Atlanta: Scholars Press, 1989.

————. *Fourth Ezra: A Commentary on the Book of Fourth Ezra.* Hermeneia. Minneapolis: Fortress, 1990.

————. "Lists of Revealed Things in the Apocalyptic Literature." In *Magnalia Dei: The Mighty Acts of God,* edited by F. M. Cross, W. E. Lemke, and P. D. Miller, 414-54. Garden City, NY: Doubleday, 1976.

————. "On Reading an Apocalypse." In *Mysteries and Revelations: Apocalyptic Studies*

*Since the Uppsala Colloquium*, edited by J. J. Collins and J. H. Charlesworth, 65-78. JSPSup 9. Sheffield: JSOT Press, 1991.

―――. "Reactions to Destructions of the Second Temple: Theology, Perception, and Conversion." *JSJ* 12 (1981) 195-204.

―――. "A Reconsideration of Apocalyptic Visions." *HTR* 96 (2003) 167-80.

―――. *Scriptures, Sects, and Visions: A Profile of Judaism from Ezra to the Jewish Revolts*. Philadelphia: Fortress, 1980.

―――. *The Testament of Abraham*. Missoula, MT: Scholars Press, 1972.

―――. "Testament of Naphtali." In *Qumran Cave 4–XVII: Parabiblical Texts, Part 3*, edited by G. Brooke et al., 73-82. DJD 22. Oxford: Clarendon, 1996.

Stone, M. E., and J. C. Greenfield. "Aramaic Levi Document." In *Qumran Cave 4–XVII*, edited by Brooke et al., 1-72.

Stone, M. E., J. C. Greenfield, and E. Eshel. *The Aramaic Levi Document: Edition, Translation, Commentary*. SVTP 19. Leiden: Brill, 2004.

Strain, C. H. "Ideology and Alienation: Theses on the Interpretation and Evaluation of Theologies of Liberation." *JAAR* 45 (1977) 473-90.

Streete, Gail Corrington. "Paul's Apocalyptic Asceticism in 1 Corinthians." In *Vision and Persuasion*, edited by Carey and Bloomquist, 81-94.

Strugnell, J. "An Angelic Liturgy at Qumran — 4QSerek Šîrôt Haššabbat." In *Congress Volume: Oxford 1959*, 318-45. VTSup 7. Leiden: Brill, 1960.

Strugnell, John, and Devorah Dimant. "4Q Second Ezekiel." *Revue de Qumrân* 13 (1988) 45-56.

Strum, R. E. "Defining the Word 'Apocalyptic': A Problem in Biblical Criticism." In *Apocalyptic and the New Testament*, edited by J. Marcus and M. L. Soards. JSNTSup 24. Sheffield: JSOT Press, 1989.

Stuckenbruck, L. T. *1 Enoch 91-108: Commentaries on Early Jewish Literature*. Berlin: de Gruyter, 2007.

―――. *Angel Veneration and Christology: A Study in Early Judaism and in the Christology of the Apocalypse of John*. WUNT 2/70. Tübingen: Mohr Siebeck, 1995.

―――. *The Book of Giants from Qumran*. Tübingen: Mohr Siebeck, 1997.

―――. "The Book of Jubilees and the Origin of Evil." In *Enoch and the Mosaic Torah*, edited by Boccaccini and Ibba, 294-308.

―――. "Daniel and Early Enoch Traditions in the Dead Sea Scrolls." In *The Book of Daniel: Composition and Reception*, edited by Collins and Flint, 2:368-86.

―――. "Ezra's Vision of the Lady. The Form and Function of a Turning Point." In *Fourth Ezra and Second Baruch*, edited by Henze and Boccaccini, 137-50.

―――. "Messianic Ideas in the Apocalyptic and Related Literature of Early Judaism." In *The Messiah in the Old and New Testaments*, edited by Porter, 90-113.

―――. "The Origins of Evil in Jewish Apocalyptic Tradition: The Interpretation of Genesis 6:1-4 in the Second and Third Centuries BCE." In *The Fall of the Angels*, edited by Christoph Auffarth and Loren T. Stuckenbruck, 99-104. Leiden: Brill, 2004.

Suter, D. W. "Fallen Angel, Fallen Priest: The Problem of Family Purity in 1 Enoch 6–16." *HUCA* 50 (1979) 115-35.

―――. "Mašal in the Similitudes of Enoch." *JBL* 100 (1981) 193-212.

————. *Tradition and Composition in the Parables of Enoch.* SBLDS 47. Missoula, MT: Scholars Press, 1979.

————. "Weighed in the Balance: The Similitudes of Enoch in Recent Discussion." *RelStudRev* 7 (1981) 217-21.

Swain, J. W. "The Theory of the Four Monarchies: Opposition History under the Roman Empire." *Classical Philology* 35 (1940) 1-21.

Tabor, J. D. *Things Unutterable: Paul's Ascent to Paradise in Its Greco-Roman, Judaic, and Early Christian Contexts.* Lanham, MD: University Press of America, 1986.

Talmon, S. "Typen der Messiaserwartung um die Zeitenwende." In *Probleme biblischer Theologie,* edited by H. H. Wolff, 571-88. Munich: Kaiser, 1971.

————. "Waiting for the Messiah at Qumran." In *The World of Qumran from Within,* 273-300. Leiden: Brill, 1989.

Talmon, Y. "Millenarianism." In *International Encyclopedia of the Social Sciences,* edited by D. L. Sills, 10:349-62. New York: Free Press, 1968.

Tarn, W. W. "Alexander Helios and the Golden Age." *JRS* 22 (1932) 135-48.

Tavadia, J. *Die Mittelpersische Sprache und Literatur der Zarathustrier.* Leipzig: Harrassowitz, 1956.

Taylor, J. E. *The Immerser: John the Baptist within Second Temple Judaism.* Grand Rapids: Eerdmans, 1997.

Tcherikover, V. *Hellenistic Civilization and the Jews.* New York: Atheneum, 1970. Reprint: Peabody, MA: Hendrickson, 1999.

Testuz, M. *Les Idées Religieuses du Livre des Jubilés.* Paris: Menard, 1960.

Theisohn, J. *Der auserwählte Richter.* Göttingen: Vandenhoeck & Ruprecht, 1975.

Theissen, G. *Sociology of Early Palestinian Christianity.* Philadelphia: Fortress, 1978.

Thomas, J. *Le Mouvement Baptiste en Palestine et Syrie.* Gembloux: Duculot, 1935.

Thomas, Samuel I. *The "Mysteries" of Qumran: Mystery, Secrecy, and Esotericism in the Dead Sea Scrolls.* SBLEJL 25. Atlanta: SBL / Leiden: Brill, 2009.

Thompson, A. L. *Responsibility for Evil in the Theodicy of IV Ezra.* SBLDS 29. Missoula, MT: Scholars Press, 1977.

Thompson, L. L. *The Book of Revelation: Apocalypse and Empire.* New York: Oxford University Press, 1990.

Thorndike, J. P. "The Apocalypse of Weeks and the Qumran Sect." *RevQ* 3 (1961) 163-84.

Tigchelaar, E. J. C. "Classifications of the Collection of Dead Sea Scrolls and the Case of Apocryphon of Jeremiah C." *JSJ* 43 (2012) 449-50.

————. *Prophets of Old and the Day of the End: Zechariah, the Book of the Watchers, and Apocalyptic.* OTS 35. Leiden: Brill, 1996.

Tigchelaar, E. J. C., ed. *Old Testament Pseudepigrapha and the Scriptures.* BETL 270. Leuven: Peeters, 2014.

Tigchelaar, E. J. C., and Florentino García Martínez. "4QAstronomical Enoch[a-b] ar: Introduction." In *Qumran Cave 4 XXVI: Cryptic Texts and Miscellanea,* Part 1, 95-172. DJD 36. Oxford: Clarendon, 2000.

Tiller, P. A. *A Commentary on the Animal Apocalypse of 1 Enoch.* Atlanta: Scholars Press, 1993.

Tomasino, Anthony J. "Oracles of Insurrection: The Prophetic Catalyst of the Great Revolt." *JJS* 5 (2008) 86-111.

Triplet-Hitoto, Valérie. *Mystères et connaissances caches à Qumrân.* Paris: Cerf, 2011.

Tromp, J. *The Assumption of Moses: A Critical Edition with Commentary.* SVTP 10. Leiden: Brill, 1992.

Tromp, N. J. *Primitive Conceptions on Death and the Nether World.* Rome: Biblical Institute Press, 1969.

Trotter, Jonathan R. "The Tradition of the Throne Vision in the Second Temple Period. Daniel 7:9-10; 1 Enoch 14:18-23 and the Book of Giants (4Q530)." *RevQ* 25 (2012) 451-66.

Turdeanu, E. *Apocryphes Slaves et Roumains de l'Ancien Testament.* Leiden: Brill, 1981.

Turner, N. "The Testament of Abraham: A Study of the Original Language, Place of Origin, and Relevance." Diss., University of London, 1953.

Ullendorff, E. "An Aramaic 'Vorlage' of the Ethiopic Text of Enoch?" In *Ethiopia and the Bible,* 31-62. Oxford: Oxford University Press, 1968.

Ulrichsen, J. H. *Die Grundschrift der Testamente der Zwölf Patriarchen: Eine Untersuchung zu Umfang, Inhalt, und Eigenart der ursprünglichen Schrift.* Stockholm: Almqvist & Wiksell, 1991.

Urbach, E. E. "The Rabbinical Law of Idolatry in the Second and Third Centuries in the Light of Archaeological and Historical Facts." *IEJ* 9 (1959) 156-58, 229-33.

————. *The Sages.* 2 vols. Jerusalem: Magnes, 1975.

Vaillant, A. *Le Livre des Secrets d'Hénoch: Texte Slave et Traduction Française.* Paris: Institut d'Etudes Slaves, 1952.

VanderKam, J. C. "2 Maccabees 6, 7a and Calendrical Change in Jerusalem." *JSJ* 12 (1981) 52-74.

————. "The 364-Day Calendar in the Enochic Literature." In *Society of Biblical Literature 1983 Seminar Papers,* edited by K. H. Richards, 157-65. Chico, CA: Scholars Press, 1983.

————. "The Angel of the Presence in the Book of *Jubilees.*" *DSD* 7 (2000) 378-93.

————. "The Angel Story in the Book of Jubilees." In *Pseudepigraphic Perspectives: The Apocrypha and Pseudepigrapha in Light of the Dead Sea Scrolls,* edited by E. G. Chazon and M. E. Stone, 151-70. STDJ 31. Leiden: Brill, 1999.

————. "The Book of Enoch and the Qumran Scrolls." In *The Oxford Handbook of the Dead Sea Scrolls,* edited by Lim and Collins, 254-77.

————. *The Book of Jubilees.* Guides to Apocrypha and Pseudepigrapha. Sheffield: Sheffield Academic Press, 2001.

————. *The Book of Jubilees: A Critical Text.* Leuven: Peeters, 1989.

————. *Calendars in the Dead Sea Scrolls: Measuring Time.* London: Routledge, 1998.

————. *The Dead Sea Scrolls Today.* Grand Rapids: Eerdmans, 1994.

————. *Enoch: A Man for All Generations.* Columbia, SC: University of South Carolina Press, 1995.

————. *Enoch and the Growth of an Apocalyptic Tradition.* CBQMS 16. Washington, DC: Catholic Biblical Association of America, 1984.

————. "Enoch Traditions in Jubilees and Other Second-Century Sources." In *Society of Biblical Literature 1978 Seminar Papers,* edited by P. J. Achtemeier, 1:229-51. Missoula, MT: Scholars Press, 1978.

————. "Genesis 6:1-4 and the Angel Stories in the Book of the Watchers (1 Enoch 1-36)." In *The Fallen Angels Traditions,* edited by Harkins, Bautch, and Endres, 1-7.

————. "The Interpretation of Genesis in 1 Enoch." In *The Bible at Qumran: Text,*

*Shape, and Interpretation,* edited by Peter W. Flint, 129-48. Grand Rapids: Eerdmans, 2001.

————. "Jubilees and the Priestly Messiah of Qumran." *RevQ* 13 (1988) 353-66.

————. "Messianism in the Scrolls." In *The Community of the Renewed Covenant: The Notre Dame Symposium on the Dead Sea Scrolls,* edited by E. Ulrich and J. VanderKam, 211-34. Notre Dame, IN: University of Notre Dame Press, 1994.

————. "Moses Trumping Moses: Making the Book of Jubilees." In *The Dead Sea Scrolls: Transmission of Traditions and Production of Texts,* edited by Metso, Najman, and Schuller, 25-44. STDJ 92. Leiden: Brill, 2010.

————. "The Origin, Character, and Early History of the 364-Day Calendar: A Reassessment of Jaubert's Hypotheses." *CBQ* 41 (1979) 390-411.

————. "The Putative Author of the Book of Jubilees." *JSS* 26 (1981) 209-17.

————. "Righteous One, Messiah, Chosen One, and Son of Man in 1 Enoch 37–71." In *The Messiah: Developments in Earliest Judaism and Christianity,* edited by J. H. Charlesworth, 169-91. Minneapolis: Fortress, 1992.

————. *Textual and Historical Studies in the Book of Jubilees.* HSM 14. Missoula, MT: Scholars Press, 1977.

————. "The Wicked Priest Revisited." In *The "Other" in Second Temple Judaism,* edited by Harlow et al., 350-67.

VanderKam, J. C., and W. Adler, eds. *The Jewish Apocalyptic Heritage in Early Christianity.* CRINT 3/4. Assen: Van Gorcum; Minneapolis: Fortress, 1996.

VanderKam, J. C., and J. T. Milik. "Jubilees." In *Qumran Cave 4–VIII: Parabiblical Texts,* edited by H. Attridge et al., 1-185. DJD 13. Oxford: Clarendon, 1994.

Vaux, R. de. *Archaeology and the Dead Sea Scrolls.* London: Oxford University Press, 1973.

Vermes, G. *The Dead Sea Scrolls in English.* Rev. ed. London: Penguin, 2004.

————. *The Dead Sea Scrolls: Qumran in Perspective.* Philadelphia: Fortress, 1981.

————. *Jesus the Jew: A Historian's Reading of the Gospels.* Philadelphia: Fortress, 1981.

————. "The Qumran Messiahs and Messianism." In E. Schürer, *The History of the Jewish People in the Age of Jesus Christ (175 B.C.–A.D. 135),* revised and edited by G. Vermes, F. Millar, and M. Black, 2:550-54. Edinburgh: T & T Clark, 1986.

————. "The Son of Man Debate." *JSNT* 1 (1978) 19-32.

Vermes, G., and M. D. Goodman, eds. *The Essenes according to the Classical Sources.* Sheffield: JSOT Press, 1989.

Vermeylen, J. *Du prophète Isaïe à l'Apocalyptique.* Paris: Gabalda, 1977.

Vielhauer, P. "Gottesreich und Menschensohn in der Verkündigung Jesu." In *Festschrift für Günther Dehn,* 51-79. Neukirchen: Kreis Moers, 1957.

Vielhauer, P., and G. Strecker. "Apocalypses and Related Subjects." In *New Testament Apocrypha,* edited by E. Hennecke, W. Schneemelcher, and R. McWilson, 2:542-68. Louisville: Westminster John Knox, 1991.

Villiers, P. G. R. de. "Understanding the Way of God: Form, Function, and Message of the Historical Review in 4 Ezra 3:4-27." In *Society of Biblical Literature 1981 Seminar Papers,* edited by K. H. Richards, 351-78. Chico, CA: Scholars Press, 1981.

Violet, B. *Die Apokalypsen des Esra und des Baruch in deutscher Gestalt.* Leipzig: Hinrichs, 1924.

————. *Die Esra-Apokalypse I: Die Überlieferung.* Leipzig: Hinrichs, 1910.

Viviano, Benedict T. "Eschatology and the Quest for the Historical Jesus." In *The Oxford Handbook of Eschatology*, edited by Jerry L. Walls, 73-90. Oxford: Oxford University Press, 2008.

Vogel, Winfried. *The Cultic Motif in the Book of Daniel*. New York: Lang, 2010.

Volkmar, G. *Das vierte Buch Esra*. Tübingen: Fues, 1863.

Wacker, M.-T. *Weltordnung and Gericht: Studien zu 1 Henoch 22*. Würzburg: Echter, 1982.

Waddell, James A. *The Messiah: A Comparative Study of the Enochic Son of Man and the Pauline Kyrios*. London: T & T Clark, 2011.

Wahman, F. *Ardā Wirāz Nāmag: The Iranian 'Divina Commedia.'* Copenhagen: Curzon, 1986.

Walck, Leslie W. "The Son of Man in the Parables of Enoch and the Gospels." In *Enoch and the Messiah Son of Man*, edited by Boccaccini, 299-337.

Wasserman, Emma. *Apocalypse as Holy War: Religious Polemic and Violence in the World of Paul*. AYBRL. New Haven: Yale University Press, forthcoming.

Wassmuth, Olaf. *Sibyllinische Orakel 1-2. Studien und Kommentar*. Leiden: Brill, 2011.

Watley, Gordon Lyn. "Sibylline Identities: The Jewish and Christian Editions of Sibylline Oracles 1-2." Diss. University of Virginia, 2010.

Watson, Duane F. "Paul's Appropriation of Apocalyptic Discourse. The Rhetorical Strategy of 1 Thessalonians." In *Rhetorical Dimensions of Apocalyptic Discourse*, edited by Carey and Bloomquist, 61-80.

Webb, R. L. *John the Baptizer and Prophet: A Socio-Historical Study*. Sheffield: JSOT Press, 1991.

Weiss, J. *Jesus' Proclamation of the Kingdom of God*. Philadelphia: Fortress, 1971; German original, 1892.

Weitzman, Steven. "The Song of Abraham." *HUCA* 65 (1994) 21-33.

Werman, Cana. "Epochs and End-Time: The 490-Year Scheme in Second Temple Literature." *DSD* 13 (2006) 229-55.

————. "The *Torah* and the *Teudah* Engraved on the Tablets." *DSD* 9 (2002) 75-103.

Wernberg-Møller, P. "A Reconsideration of the Two Spirits in the Rule of the Community (1QSerek III,13–IV,26)." *RevQ* 3 (1961) 413-41.

Wessinger, Catherine. "Apocalypse and Violence." In *The Oxford Handbook of Apocalyptic Literature*, edited by Collins, 422-40. Oxford: Oxford University Press, 2014.

White, S. A. "A Comparison of the 'A' and 'B' Manuscripts of the Damascus Document." *RevQ* 12 (1987) 537-53.

Whitters, Mark F. *The Epistle of Second Baruch: A Study in Form and Message*. JSPSup 42. Sheffield: Sheffield Academic Press, 2003.

Widengren, G. *The Ascension of the Apostle and the Heavenly Book*. Uppsala: Almqvist & Wiksell, 1950.

————. "Leitende Ideen und Quellen der iranischen Apokalyptik." In *Apocalypticism in the Mediterranean World and the Near East: Proceedings of the International Colloquium on Apocalypticism, Uppsala, August 12-17, 1979*, edited by D. Hellholm, 77-162. Tübingen: Mohr Siebeck, 1983.

Widengren, G., A. Hultgård, and M. Philonenko, eds. *Apocalyptique Iranienne et Dualisme Qoumrânien*. Paris: Maisonneuve, 1995.

Wilder, Amos. "The Rhetoric of Ancient and Modern Apocalyptic." *Int* 25 (1971) 436-53.

Wildgruber, Regina. *Daniel 10-12 als Schlüssel zum Buch.* FAT 2/58. Tübingen: Mohr Siebeck, 2013.

Willis, Amy C. Merrill. *Dissonance and the Drama of Divine Sovereignty in the Book of Daniel.* New York and London: T & T Clark, 2010.

Willis, W., ed. *The Kingdom of God in Twentieth-Century Interpretation.* Peabody, MA: Hendrickson, 1987.

Wills, L. M. *The Jew in the Court of the Foreign King.* HDR 26. Minneapolis: Fortress, 1990.

Wilson, B. R. *Magic and the Millennium.* New York: Harper & Row, 1973.

Wilson, R. R. "From Prophecy to Apocalyptic: Reflections on the Shape of Israelite Religion." *Semeia* 21 (1981) 79-95.

————. *Prophecy and Society in Ancient Israel.* Philadelphia: Fortress, 1980.

————. "This World — and the World to Come." *Encounter* 38 (1977) 117-24.

Windisch, H. *Die Orakel des Hystaspes.* Amsterdam: Akademie, 1929.

Winninge, M. *Sinners and the Righteous: A Comparative Study of the Psalms of Solomon and Paul's Letters.* Stockholm: Almqvist & Wiksell, 1995.

Wintermute, O. S. "Apocalypse of Zephaniah." In *The Old Testament Pseudepigrapha.* Volume 1: *Apocalyptic Literature and Testaments,* edited by J. H. Charlesworth, 497-515. Garden City, NY: Doubleday, 1983.

Wise, M. O. "Dating the Teacher of Righteousness and the Floruit of His Movement." *JBL* 122 (2003) 53-87.

————. "The Eschatological Vision of the Temple Scroll." *JNES* 49 (1990) 155-72.

————. "The Origin and History of the Teacher's Movement." In *The Oxford Handbook of the Dead Sea Scrolls,* edited by Lim and Collins, 92-122.

Wise, M. O., and J. Tabor. "The Messiah at Qumran." *Biblical Archaeology Review* (Nov.–Dec. 1992) 60-65.

Witetschek, Stefan. "Ein weit geöffnetes Zeitfenster? Überlegungen zur Datierung der Johannesapokalypse." In *Die Johannesapokalypse,* edited by Frey, Kelhoffer and Tóth, 117-48.

Witulski, Thomas. *Die Johannesoffenbarung und Kaiser Hadrian. Studien zur Datierung der neutestamentlichen Apokalypse.* FRLANT 221. Göttingen: Vandenhoeck & Ruprecht, 2007.

Worsley, P. *The Trumpet Shall Sound.* London: Macgibbon & Kee, 1957.

Woude, A. S. van der, ed. *The Book of Daniel.* BETL 106. Leuven: Peeters, 1993.

————. "Die Doppelsprachigkeit des Buches Daniel." In *The Book of Daniel,* edited by van der Woude, 3-12.

————. "Melchizedek als himmlische Erlösergestalt in den neugefundenen eschatologischen Midraschim aus Qumran Höhle XI." *OTS* 14 (1965) 354-73.

————. *Die messianischen Vorstellungen der Gemeinde von Qumran.* Assen: van Gorcum, 1957.

Wright, Archie T. *The Origin of Evil Spirits. The Reception of Genesis 6.1-4 in Early Jewish Literature.* WUNT 2/198. Tübingen: Mohr Siebeck, 2005.

Wright, J. E. *Baruch Ben Neriah: From Biblical Scribe to Apocalyptic Seer.* Columbia, SC: University of South Carolina, 2003.

————. "The Cosmography of the Greek Apocalypse of Baruch and Its Affinities." Dissertation, Brandeis University, 1992.

————. *The Early History of Heaven*. Oxford: Oxford University Press, 2000.

Wright, N. T. "Paul and Caesar: A New Reading of Romans." In *Royal Priesthood: The Use of the Bible Ethically and Politically,* edited by C. Bartholomew, 173-93. Carlisle: Paternoster, 2002.

Xeravits, Géza G., ed. *Dualism in Qumran*. Library of Second Temple Studies 76. London: T & T Clark, 2010.

Yadin, Y. "Le Rouleau du Temple." In *Qumrân,* edited by M. Delcor, 115-19. Leuven: Leuven University Press, 1978.

————. *The Scroll of the War of the Sons of Light against the Sons of Darkness*. Oxford: Oxford University Press, 1962.

————. *The Temple Scroll*. 3 vols. Jerusalem: Shrine of the Book, 1977.

Yarbro Collins, A. *The Apocalypse*. Wilmington, DE: Glazier, 1979.

————. "Apocalypticism and Christian Origins." In *The Oxford Handbook of Apocalyptic Literature*, edited by Collins, 326-39.

————. "The Book of Revelation." In *The Encyclopedia of Apocalypticism* 1:384-414.

————. "Christian Messianism and the First Jewish War with Rome." In *Biblical Traditions in Transmission: Essays in Honour of Michael A. Knibb*, edited by Charlotte Hempel and Judith M. Lieu, 333-43. JSJSup 111. Leiden: Brill, 2006.

————. *The Combat Myth in the Book of Revelation*. HDR 9. Missoula, MT: Scholars Press, 1976.

————. "Composition and Redaction of the Testament of Moses 10." *HTR* 69 (1976) 179-86.

————. *Cosmology and Eschatology in Jewish and Christian Apocalypticism*. Leiden: Brill, 1996.

————. *Crisis and Catharsis: The Power of the Apocalypse*. Philadelphia: Westminster, 1984.

————. "The Dream of a New Jerusalem at Qumran." In *The Bible and the Dead Sea Scrolls*. 3 vols., edited by J. H. Charlesworth, 3:231-54. Waco, TX: Baylor University Press, 2006.

————. "The Early Christian Apocalypses." *Semeia* 14 (1979) 61-121.

————. "Early Christian Apocalyptic Literature." In *Aufstieg und Niedergang der römischen Welt,* II.25:4665-4711.

————. "Eschatology in the Book of Revelation." *Ex Auditu* 6 (1990) 63-72.

————. "The Influence of Daniel on the New Testament." In *Daniel: A Commentary on the Book of Daniel,* by J. J. Collins, 90-123. Hermeneia. Minneapolis: Fortress, 1993.

————. "Introduction: Early Christian Apocalypticism." In *Early Christian Apocalypticism: Genre and Social Setting,* edited by A. Yarbro Collins, 1-12. *Semeia* 36. Decatur, GA: Scholars Press, 1986.

————. "Mark 13: An Apocalyptic Discourse." In eadem, *The Beginning of the Gospel: Probings of Mark in Context,* 73-91. Minneapolis: Fortress, 1992.

————. "Numerical Symbolism in Jewish and Early Christian Apocalyptic Literature." In *Cosmology and Eschatology in Jewish and Christian Apocalypticism,* 55-138. Leiden: Brill, 1996.

————. "The Origin of Christian Baptism." In *Cosmology and Eschatology in Jewish and Christian Apocalypticism,* 218-38. Leiden: Brill, 1996.

―――. "The Origin of the Designation of Jesus as 'Son of Man.' " In *Cosmology and Eschatology in Jewish and Christian Apocalypticism,* 139-58. Leiden: Brill, 1996.

―――. "The Political Perspective of the Revelation to John." In *Cosmology and Eschatology in Jewish and Christian Apocalypticism,* 198-217. Leiden: Brill, 1996.

―――. "The Seven Heavens in Jewish and Christian Apocalypses." In *Cosmology and Eschatology in Jewish and Christian Apocalypticism,* 21-54. Leiden: Brill, 1996.

―――. "The Son of Man Sayings in the Sayings Source." In *To Touch the Text: Biblical and Related Studies in Honor of Joseph A. Fitzmyer, S.J.,* edited by M. P. Horgan and P. J. Kobelski, 369-89. New York: Crossroad, 1989.

―――. "The 'Son of Man' Tradition and the Book of Revelation." In *Cosmology and Eschatology in Jewish and Christian Apocalypticism,* 159-97. Leiden: Brill, 1996.

Yarbro Collins, A., ed. *Early Christian Apocalypticism: Genre and Social Setting. Semeia* 36. Decatur, GA: Scholars Press, 1986.

Yarbro Collins, A., and John J. Collins. *King and Messiah as Son of God.* Grand Rapids: Eerdmans, 2008.

Zetterholm, Magnus. "Paul and the Missing Messiah." In *The Messiah in Early Judaism and Christianity,* edited by idem, 33-55. Minneapolis: Fortress, 2007.

Zimmermann, Johannes. *Messianische Texte aus Qumran.* WUNT 2/104. Tübingen: Mohr Siebeck, 1998.

Zurawski, Jason M. "The Two Worlds and Adam's Sin: The Problem of *4 Ezra* 7:10-14." In *Interpreting 4 Ezra and 2 Baruch,* edited by Boccaccini and Zurawski, 97-106.

# Index of Authors

# Index of Subjects

Aaron, messiahs of, 174, 175, 196, 200-201, 203-4, 218

Adam: in the Animal Apocalypse, 86; apocalypse of, 4; in the *Apocalypse of Abraham*, 282; dialogues of *4 Ezra*, 248-54; and Enoch, 55, 81, 305-6; and Eve, 70, 105; in lament of *2 Baruch*, 273, 278; in the *Testament of Abraham*, 318

Aemilius Sura, 116

Afterlife, 43, 78, 90, 102, 123, 175, 176; and Qumran, 212-17

Ahikar, 113

Ahriman, 38-39

Ahura Mazdā, 37-39, 117, 123

Akiba, Rabbi, 198, 276, 289

Akkadian dream visions, 34-35

Akkadian prophecies, 33-34

Alcimus, 95-96

Alexander Jannaeus, 184, 186, 210

Alexander the Great, 62, 119, 145, 209

Alexandria, 44, 54, 294, 296

Animal Apocalypse, 7, 51, 85-89

*Apocalypse of Abraham*, 280-89; the underlying questions, 283-89

Apocalypse of Weeks, 7, 53, 79-83; schematization of history, 80-83

Apocalyptic eschatology, 14-15; and millenarianism, 1, 46, 352-54; Qumran War of Light and Darkness, 206-

12; typology/typological implications for, 27, 64, 152, 268

Apocalyptic language, 17-26; the influence of Charles, 18-20; the influence of Gunkel, 20-21; the quest for traditional sources, 24-26; traditional imagery, 22-24

Apocalyptic literature, 1-52; Babylonian matrix, 32-36; compositional setting, 47-50; definitions, 2-3, 4-7, 9-11, 13-15, 51; device of pseudonymity, 6, 33, 48-50, 75, 138-39, 155, 163, 169, 248, 340-42; Diaspora, 300-320; the earliest apocalypses, 31-32; early Christianity, 321-51; as genre, 3-14, 279-80; Hellenistic milieu, 41-46; language of, 17-26; literary function of, 50-52; Persian, 36-41; postexilic prophecy, 28-31; the settings of the genre, 26-27; social settings, 46-47

Apocalypticism, 15-17, 337; Christian, 321-51; conventicle theory of, 27, 47, 51, 155; modern, 354-58; Persian, 36-41; quest for traditional sources of, 24-26

Aqhat, 109

Arda Viraf, 41

Astronomical Book, 53-54, 75-79

Atrahasis, 56

Augustus, 145, 292

# Index of Scripture and Other Ancient Sources

# MICHAEL MOORCOCK

Winner of the Nebula and World Fantasy awards
August Derleth Fantasy Award
British Fantasy Award
Guardian Fiction Award
Prix Utopiales
Bram Stoker Award
John W. Campbell Award
SFWA Grand Master
Member, Science Fiction and Fantasy Hall of Fame

'A major novelist of enormous ambition.'

— *Washington Post*

'Moorcock's writing is top-notch.'

— *Publishers Weekly*

'He casts a heady, enslaving spell.'

— *Daily Telegraph*

'He is . . . [in his nonfiction] scathing about "the anaemic, phallocentric self-advertisements of Notting Hill colons or East Anglian clones", but full of affectionate enthusiasm for such friends as JG Ballard, Angela Carter, Iain Sinclair, Peter Ackroyd and Andrea Dworkin. He writes movingly and at length about Jack Trevor Story . . . and about Mervyn Peake . . . "who made me realise it was possible to confront real human issues through the medium of fantasy". He writes wittily and perceptively about such elective literary forefathers as Aldous Huxley, HG Wells, George Meredith and W Pett Ridge, author of *Mord Em'ly* . . .

'These days he lives with his American wife in Lost Pines, a liberal enclave of Texas, and deplores the way in which England seems to be shedding her virtues as fast as she can, celebrating her vices . . . as class-bound as ever, and in some ways far more repressive than similar Oriental cultures . . .

'Moorcock is elegant and aggressive ("badly educated people are suspicious of ambiguity"), consistently entertaining, and frequently wise and generous. One applauds the louder when he adds: "Our scientific advances will be merely obscene unless they help the large part of our world's population emerge from miserable uncertainty and debilitating terror".'

— *Spectator*

'Moorcock's . . . book is an astounding compilation, displaying a panorama of sympathy and engagement over a lifetime's reading and writing. The Monument Valley which is Moorcock's mighty imagination here provides us with the background reading to his career. Many of these encounters are not merely intellectual engagements, but personal ones too. In a poignant account of the life and times of Jack Trevor Story we learn that on the Christmas night which became the hinge of that troubled writer's existence, he had been spending the evening with Moorcock before setting off home with his girlfriend. The forces of law and order banged him up, unjustly, and effectively drained him of hope for many years to come. In his account of Philip K Dick we learn how Moorcock intervened to try to help that author make more money, though it came to nothing. He then looked on at a slight distance as Dick became famously loopy. Moorcock does not merely befriend Mervyn Peake's highly distinctive imagination; he befriends the Peake family too. He writes of Iain Sinclair, a writer he admires, who is also a personal friend. And so it goes on. This isn't name-dropping, because Moorcock is as big a name as any of the ones he mentions . . .

One of the most striking things about this prodigiously gifted and productive writer . . . is the unexpectedness of some of his liaisons and alliances. Like *New Worlds* under his editorship, he seems to exist to demolish boundaries. I had the constant sensation of being accompanied through the metropolis of modern culture by the most engaging companion I could hope to meet.'

—Alan Wall, ReadySteadyBook.com

'Moorcock is a throwback to such outsized 19th-century novelistic talents as Dickens and Tolstoy.'

—*Locus*

'No one . . . is doing more to break down the artificial divisions that have grown up in novel writing—realism, surrealism, science fiction, historical fiction, social satire, the poetic novel—than Michael Moorcock.'

—Angus Wilson

'He is the master storyteller of our time.'

—Angela Carter, author of *Nights at the Circus*

# London Peculiar and
# Other Nonfiction

# London Peculiar and
# Other Nonfiction

## By Michael Moorcock

Edited by Michael Moorcock and Allan Kausch

With an Introduction by Iain Sinclair

For Jean-Luc Fromental and Lili Sztajn

London Peculiar and Other Nonfiction
Michael Moorcock
© 2012 by Michael Moorcock
This edition © 2012 PM Press

Bibliography reprinted with the kind permission of Moorcock's Miscellany (www.multiverse.org)

ISBN: 978–1-60486–490–8
Library of Congress Control Number: 2011927964

Cover by John Yates / www.stealworks.com
Interior design by briandesign
Cover photo by Linda Steele

10 9 8 7 6 5 4 3 2 1

PM Press
PO Box 23912
Oakland, CA 94623
www.pmpress.org

Printed in the USA on recycled paper, by the Employee Owners of Thomson-Shore in Dexter, Michigan.
www.thomsonshore.com

Published in the UK by Green Print, an imprint of The Merlin Press Ltd.,
6 Crane Street Chambers, Crane Street, Pontypool NP4 6ND, Wales
ISBN: 978–1–85425–106–0

# ◼ Contents

## ▌ ABSENT FRIENDS

## ▌ MUSIC

## ▌ POLITICS

## ▌ INTRODUCTIONS AND REVIEWS

# The Man on the Stairs

**An Introduction to Michael Moorcock**

I could never quite persuade myself that there was any such human entity as Michael Moorcock. I mean in the sense that you could touch him, or talk to him, or sit down with him for a meal at which the seamless stories, the astonishing anecdotes, the myths and memories, would ravel and unravel, lap and overlap like swirling, contradictory, sediment-heavy Thames tides. The man was too fecund, too prolific, in too many places, high and low culture, for me to believe that he was one person and not a Warholite factory or a nest of Edgar Wallace typists. Comics, sombre periodicals, political pamphlets, rock shows, numerous TV and fanzine interviews: Mike was a shape-shifter, a character actor in the labyrinth of his own fictions. He was Sydney Greenstreet, Robert Morley, Akim Tamiroff. And the always reliably untrustworthy Colonel Pyat. He played so many parts in this complex, many-chaptered, cliff-hanging serial of a life that readers, panting to keep up, were left dizzy and breathless by the rush of language. But somewhere beyond the Casablanca cafés, the arms dealers in the lifts of Cairo hotels, somewhere behind the smoked glasses, the Bedouin headgear, is a well-set-up Englishman with a proper pen in his shirt pocket and a sturdy notebook tucked into his linen jacket. A person quite capable of writing with the precision and clarity of a coin-per-word professional. Nobody knows better than Moorcock how to manipulate the white spaces, how to compose pages so slick with narrative devices that they do the turning for you. Our trust has been won by the confident and breezy tone of the author's address; very soon, we are walking in his sleep, navigating by the architectural markers of a fantastic city much like London. Moorcockian prose is discovered, not prescribed or advertised. You will come across it like a monument in a park you thought you knew. His books seem to have been there for generations, waiting on readers with the right password: affection. Affection for self, for a remembered and ever-present past, for place. For people. The bruised and the blustering mob of individuals.

The trappings of style are just part of a magician's kit, like the conjuring tricks of Orson Welles, the pass of a scarlet cloak disguising the authorship of *Citizen Kane* and an afterlife of sherry commercials. That Moorcock beard has a genealogy of its own: Rasputin, James Robertson Justice, Robert Newton, Richard Hughes, Augustus John. The beard's cultivator is revealed as pirate, clubman detective, Russian prince, Crowleyite magus, desert prophet. But, underneath those curling barbs, is a handsome, seductive presence: Michael Moorcock, the absolute storyteller of our time. An author whose genius lies in the range of his sympathies, the depth of his affections (and his piques). Mike is intensely local, and loyal to the ground of his upbringing in South London, and also comfortable in the world at large, in Texas, Finland, Istanbul, Majorca. All those fabulous harbours and Circle Squared ranches. The Kensington apartments from the Arts and Crafts era. And the hidden Holborn yards of a customised geography. The *London Peculiar* of Moorcock initiates. Those strange creatures able to step out of literature and into the streets. Psychic detectives healing the wound in society, taking on the eternal battle with the forces of darkness, politicians, developers, undying vampires.

Moorcock is the essential conduit between Beowulf songs and sagas of mead-hall poets and the banjo-plucking, cattle-drive yarns at campfires of the American West. He shifts, effortlessly, from the established forms of the Victorian and Edwardian masters of narrative to the fragmentation of high modernism. I am stopped by the quiddity of voice, that point of recognition for any good writer. You know, from the confident rhythms of the first sentence, you can trust the person who is spinning this tale. Trust him to trick you, lead you astray, excite you, carry you right back to that good place where there is a suspension of disbelief and the closing down of critical faculties for the pure pleasure of wanting to know what happens next. Both author and actor, Moorcock is the designer of a complex Word City in the last era when readers have the stamina and wit to undertake a journey through such a vast and unknowable concourse. A voyage during which they understand that they must allow themselves to be swept away by oceanic surges of inspired prose.

*London Peculiar* is the chart of a writer's odyssey through time and space, from the fertile dreams of childhood, through encounters with teachers and fellow visionaries, to heartfelt polemics and tender tributes to the immortals with whom Mike has shared tea and sympathy. All dues paid, the labyrinth of this imagined city is illuminated in every ditch and twitten, from hard-drinking journalists' pub to some enclosed religious order, where high walls mask the entry to a subterranean world so improbable that it has to be true. Readers coming to the anthology *London, City of Disappearances* (2007) were as inclined to believe the mythical gazetteer of Michael Moorcock as the authentic research undertaken by the historian Sarah Wise. I'm sure there are folk out there now, tapping at bricks, poring over ancient maps, trying to find their way into the Hearst Castle of Ladbroke Grove or the tunnel beneath the Convent of the Poor Clares. Moorcock's London is a multiverse, curled back on itself, traumatised by war, papered with shilling-shockers and odd-volume three-deckers, enlivened and animated by collisions between the real and the fabulous.

Angela Carter, another magnificent writer from the wrong side of the river, presented Mike's literary terrain as 'a vast, uncorseted, sentimental, comic, elegiac salmagundy'. The scale, richness and diversity, does that to commentators; adjectives spill promiscuously as we struggle to hint at the boundless energy of the original. Carter saw the work as coming from a zone 'so deeply within a certain tradition of English popular culture, that it feels foreign, just as Diana Dors, say, scarcely seems to come from the same country as Deborah Kerr.' And this too is on the money, no one was better placed than Carter, the white witch of Streatham, a celebrant of rouge and gin and talcum powder, and the best kind of bad behaviour, to equate Moorcock with an actress who could live a life of tabloid sensation and, at the same time, deliver the broadest of lowlife comedy and the scrubbed-down realism of *Yield to the Night*. Moorcock's sprawling, sharp-tongued old ladies, Mrs Cornelius and the rest, are worthy of Angela Carter. He has been, for many years, a champion of his friend Andrea Dworkin and a promoter of W Pett Ridge's wild child of the streets, Mord Em'ly. (Both find their place in the pantheon of *London Peculiar*. Along with a tribute to hardboiled novelist, screenwriter, and author of influential works of science fiction, Leigh Brackett. Only Moorcock could discuss Brackett by way of a 'Spanish-speaking Swede', encountered while hitchhiking through Germany. A person who recommends the stories of Borges, before the Argentinean has been published in England. Moorcock, of course, met both Brackett and Borges.)

I was in the process of deprogramming myself, after emerging from school and university, when Jerry Cornelius began his seductive dance across my London consciousness. I was a dim provincial, originally from Wales and, more recently, from a Dublin still unravished by the Celtic Tiger, when I noticed Mike's dandified, Carnaby Street assassin in the comic strip drawn by Mal Dean for *IT*, the underground newspaper. As much countercultural impresario as author, Moorcock would appear in the strip, offering jocular asides and winking at the audience. Dean, who drew on Tenniel and Heath Robinson, as well as jazz and movie lore, and the German satirists of the twenties, was married to the poet Libby Houston. Houston sometimes performed with the travelling poetry circus of Michael Horovitz and Pete Brown. It seemed, from where I was sitting out on the eastern fringes, that Notting Hill was the only show in town. It was, among other things, a famous street market drawing in tourists and outsiders. The district held on to echoes of the novels of Colin MacInnes. And, behind these, the vegetal stink of *Rotting Hill* by Wyndham Lewis. And faint whispers of *The Napoleon of Notting Hill* by GK Chesterton. William Burroughs, in his brief, hallucinated English exile, lived in a small hotel on the edge of this area. Moorcock brought JG Ballard, his *New Worlds* collaborator, along to see him. The children of the Raj, the private income gypsies, the psychedelic hustlers, and the indigenous traders, working folk and layabouts who had been there all along, rubbed shoulders with rock musicians and, occasionally, with Michael Moorcock, in pubs where legends of place cooked and simmered. The end of the era was signalled by the Nicolas Roeg/Donald Cammell film, *Performance*—which was, among other things, an unconscious salute to the Jerry Cornelius template. (Even if those teasingly titled Cornelius books, *A Cure for Cancer*, *The English Assassin* and *The Condition of Muzak*, were still to be published.) It wasn't that Mick Jagger, the sequestered rock star of *Performance*, was the inspiration for Jerry Cornelius, but, rather, the other way round. Dartford's Sir Michael was a gaunt Xerox spectre, his stellar career anticipated and resolved in Moorcock's dazzling fictions. Which are always intercut with melting news, headlines of the moment sliced like Cubist cut-ups.

It seemed, in the mid-sixties, that Moorcock had the keys to the kingdom. He swayed and drifted through temporal vortices, channelling postwar bohemians, Dylan Thomas and Mervyn Peake, recognising Burroughs and Borges as mentors and peers (good sources to steal from), nodding to Angus Wilson in the British Museum, sitting in with skiffle groups in Soho, anticipating new waves of hopeful and ambitious authors, a friend and supporter to China Miéville and Tony White. And in all of this activity, with all these avatars and off-cuts, the fundamental reality was a man in a room with a typewriter. A man who has now assembled, like a market trader, a spread of objects, startling or familiar, as a form of refracted auto-biography. 'Here I began, look at my fleet of miniature battleships. Step out into Christmas suburbs that do not fade or change their season. Follow me into bazaars that never close. Come closer and I'll tell you about Arthur C Clarke's curious birthday party in Tottenham. About adventures in the Hollywood night. And cruises on Russian liners.'

*London Peculiar* is a lovely record of the evolving tastes and fancies of the most sure-footed and generous author of his era. This book, like the block-buster marvel *Into the Media Web*, edited by John Davey for Savoy Books, is an index of numerous careers, starts and detours, unlikely connections. Document morphs into fiction, fiction into legend. Moorcock is the only contemporary who could have rubbed shoulders with George Meredith, PG Wodehouse, Jack Trevor Story, Edgar Rice Burroughs and William Burroughs. And yarned with them on equal terms. He is a genuinely popu-lar writer, in several genres, who has also produced such literary masterworks such as *Gloriana*, *Mother London* and the criminally undervalued Pyat quartet.

Towards the end of my active phase as a used-book dealer, I remember carrying out boxes of stock from the offices of a publisher who had decided to 'rationalise' the archive by dumping file copies going back generations, in a gesture of mindless cultural erasure (by which I was happy to profit). And as I staggered down the stairs, Michael Moorcock, in his fancy waist-coat, fingers flashing with rings, ascended, to become at once the centre of an excited buzz at a launch party. Literary London paid homage to a man who, little did they know, would soon be away on his travels. Never to return. As other than a passing rumour, a presence on stage or in some favoured Indian restaurant or fish bar.

Before this, I had seen Charing Cross Road brought to a standstill by a queue snaking out of the Forbidden Planet shop, which was then on Denmark Street, and right back, almost to Cambridge Circus. Furtive figures stooped under the weight of carrier bags filled with Moorcock multiples. Dealers. Ghosts. Hardcore fans up from Surbiton or Pinner. All of them soliciting the validation of that lavish, free-flowing signature. Mike was a dedicated defacer of title pages. I knew collectors who built up libraries of his playful (and clearly admitted) forgeries, when he livened up first editions of science-fiction worthies of the old school by offering presentation inscrip-tions on their behalf. Mike also kept street dealers such as myself awake by handing out many-sheeted wants lists of the lost volumes required to inspire and inform any one of the half-dozen books he'd be working on at the time.

It was a great moment for me when I met the Moorcocks, Mike and Linda, at the home of my Paladin editor, Nick Austin. Like all the other shuffling penitents on Charing Cross Road, I had my copy of *Mother London* personally inscribed. Soon after that, I began to meet Mike, and his friend Peter Ackroyd too, for lunches at which we rambled across the subject of London: as topography, gossip, memoir. Ackroyd, I felt, had an astonishing ability to absorb what he needed for the project in hand and then to brush aside matters of detail, names, dates. Not his concern. His sense of the city was of eternal recurrence, certain qualities assigned to favoured areas, such as Clerkenwell, Limehouse, Southwark. A conservative prospectus highly attractive to those who dealt with riverine heritage. We were being sold a consoling version of the past, gothic and occulted, to dress sets where new towers were mushrooming. The Ackroydian library, curated by 'Cockney visionaries' (from Blake to Moorcock), made London into a glorious theme park of approved history. Moorcock's sets and characters were quite different, animated by something that happened, an incident, a rumour. London was held in affectionate exasperation as she tried to live up to her own legends: the fire-storms of German WWII bombers bringing together a tribe of sleepwalkers, ranters, spivs, and damaged urban poets, who stitch a memory blanket for survivors.

*London Peculiar* is a personal audience with Moorcock. He tells stories, terse or at length. He reminds us of people we used to know. And he encourages us to take a look at those we might have missed on their first appearance in print. Journalism sits agreeably alongside fiction, diary with essay, obituary tribute with informed analysis. There is even a bibliography offering a glimpse at a fraction of what Moorcock has produced in the regular days of work that he describes, a routine that allows time for hairy escapades, travel, and meals with friends and loved ones. If there is such a person as Michael Moorcock, this might be a good place to search him out. Here is a magical staircase on which you can pass the same person, coming down, at every turn.

**Iain Sinclair**

# Editor's Foreword

**by Allan Kausch**

In the seventies and eighties there were half a dozen living artists who stood far above the rest in my esteem: Joe Strummer, John Lydon, Siouxsie, Philip K Dick, JG Ballard and Michael Moorcock. The inspired work of these six people (and encounters with them in person) showed me that compassion and anger can be used against the bastards who enslave us, that the only art that matters is the truth. Of these six, Mike's work has always been the most varied, the most entertaining, the most surprising, the most complex. Eternal Champion of what is best in our nature, his example compels us to reciprocate: to embrace life in all its ambiguity, in all its beauty and all its ugliness, with courage, dignity and hope. Thanks, Mike, for being you. It's been an honour to share the multiverse with you, pard.

Not surprisingly given Mike's incredible output, this project has been a fair amount of work. It would have been considerably more work without the help of John Davey, the editor of the previous UK collection of nonfiction, *Into the Media Web*, who provided the raw files for most of the pre-2006 pieces, along with his expert advice. I'd also like to thank Ramsey Kanaan, publisher, for his patience and guidance, Terry Bisson for recommending me to edit the book and for his help on the back cover copy, Gregory Nipper for copyediting, John Yates for the cover design, Brian Layng for the interior layouts, Andrea Gibbons, Tina Mills and Alan Wall for their timely assistance, Iain Sinclair for his superb introduction and Linda Moorcock for her astute art direction on the cover and for providing the strigine cover photo.

The Bibliography included in this volume is the result—one small part—of the ongoing dedicated work of Ian Covell, John Davey and David Mosley, with the assistance of Berry Sizemore, other bibliographers (past and present), and various members of 'Sporting Club Square'.

If you'd like to comment on, or ask questions about this book, go to the 'London Peculiar' thread on the official Michael Moorcock website: Moorcock's Miscellany at www.multiverse.org

*Sauf pour délivrer camarade capturé, ne donnez jamais à l'ennemi signe d'existence.*

—René Char

# ■ Scratching a Living

**From *Punch*, 17th April 1985**

It once occurred to me that if Henry Luce II, having axed *Life* in the interest of economic efficiency, had taken over this particular journal, its staff might now be clocking in at Time-Punch Inc. I thought of this because a couple of weeks ago I was described by *Time* as 'a British writing machine'. Flattered though I was to be condensed and, as it were, cleaned up for mass-market presentation, I was also a little stunned to be so characterised by one who as far as I know never met me, let alone spent a few days at my home.

If I'm any sort of machine, then I'm more on the lines of the engine which took the *African Queen* up-river than the astonishing device which gave lift-off to *Jupiter One*. I'm far better at sighing, wheezing, clanking, covering myself with warm grease and mysteriously losing pressure in midstream than I am at purring unostentatiously into sophisticated drive mode and carrying a mighty creative tonnage to safe harbour on the other side of some imaginative universe.

It's not a fact I'm particularly proud of, but I feel obliged to record—not only am I baffled by the very notion of word processors, I have been known to write whole novels with the aid of nothing more than a couple of exercise books, a leaking Osmiroid and a bottle of Quink.

When interviewed about my working day I generally say I do a regular nine-to-five shift, take an hour off for lunch and keep weekends free. Actually, when everything's going particularly well I manage a routine which approximates to this. I believe an author has no special right to temperamental fits or an erratic lifestyle which discommodes family and friends.

My image of a really grown-up writer is someone I'd guess George Meredith or Thomas Mann to have been. After a light but nourishing breakfast you disappear discreetly to your study. Emerging for lunch you glance through papers and mail, exchanging a polite word or two with spouse and whatever children are knocking about, returning to work until six or so, when you appear again ready to relax with friends and loved ones.

In the early stages of a book perhaps you rise around dawn. Disturbing no-one, you take your setters for a long stroll. Your keen eye misses nothing of the world around you. With one of those thin gold propelling pencils and neat leather-bound notebooks you record your thoughts and observations before returning home. While consuming your yoghurt and orange juice, you write, in a clear yet idiosyncratic hand, a few pages of your journal. It's true you might be a trifle abstracted. You apologise for this; you make a little joke about it. Your affectionate family, respectful of your creative processes, goes about its business with the minimum of noise or bustle.

In other words a thoroughly humane, well-balanced, civilised sort of working day. All one really needs, I'd guess, if one wants to start aiming for it, is a house roughly the size of Tara, a bunch of servants as cheerful and loyal as the cast of *Upstairs, Downstairs*, a soul mate who is a cross between Albert Schweitzer and St Thérèse, an agent who is to you what Joan of Arc was to the Dauphin, and offspring combining the decency and virtue of *Little Women*'s Jo and Beth with the resourcefulness of *The Railway Children*. Not much to ask for, all in all, one thinks as one sits blearily picking one's feet and watching the IBA Test Card at 11:45 a.m. while, elsewhere in the house someone, with the ruthless self-absorption of Caligula, clatters dishes in the sink and demands your attention in the matter of your preferences for that evening's supper. Is it any wonder you haven't got further than typing *Chapter One: I am born*, and it's now three weeks since your contract stipulated you had to turn in an 'acceptably finished manuscript'? Who would not feel profoundly wounded?

The fact is that like most people I have several sorts of working day. When all's well it's up at seven, feed the cats, make the tea, check the news, get into the shower, and by 8:30 sit down to the previous day's output before rolling another sheet into the typewriter. A break for lunch—soup, some crackers—and by six I'm ready to unwind. That's when I'm fairly well into a book, with a good idea who the characters are and what they're doing. Although sometimes scarcely aware of my surroundings I'm otherwise cheerful, a reasonably tolerable companion. If there's a domestic crisis, I spring to meet it. With loved ones I'm solicitous. These are the days most closely approaching my sense of what is proper.

There are other days, however, when I rise determinedly at seven, feed the cats, etc., etc. By 8:30, having arranged notebooks and pens to hand, I switch on breakfast TV for the news. By 9:30, when all news is over, I catch the weather and headlines on Teletext. This done I look up my Stars on Oracle, road conditions in England and Wales, the value of the zloty against the yen, air-traffic movements at Heathrow, by which time I'm ready for *Advanced Urdu*, *A-Level Mathematics* or *Scandinavian Reindeer Breeding*. As an example of my iron discipline I must say I draw the line at *Cartoon Time*, *Postman Pat*, *Playschool* and, by and large, *Pebble Mill At One*. If questioned on the matter ('I thought you said you had a lot of work to do') I explain as patiently as possible when dealing with philistine simpletons that this is, of course, research.

When Schools programmes finish I switch off the TV (I can honestly claim never to have seen a full episode of *Grange Hill*) and go out for a breather before beginning work. I might do a little crucial shopping (five old picture frames, a full set of plastic funnels, a *Roy Rogers Annual* for 1954) or visit the library for essential reference (*Do It Yourself Winegrowing*; *That Most Urgent Agony: The Creative Process in Crisis 1975–79*; *First Steps in Urdu*; *More About Reindeer Breeding*). Naturally when I get home I note the living-room floor needs hoovering and that I've forgotten to clean the paint brushes I used just before Christmas. These tasks done I pick up my notebook and retire to bed, saying I'll work as soon as I'm refreshed. By the time I rise again it's close to dinner, so I decide to start after I've eaten. When I've washed up and put the dishes away it's far too late to do much so I watch TV until bedtime. At bedtime I begin to work furiously for fifteen minutes until I fall into an exhausted slumber. At 3:30 a.m. I wake in a sweat of anxious confusion wondering at my weakness of character and the plight of my finances. I resolve to get up earlier tomorrow for a proper start. Let the reader's cynicism determine how long they think this cycle lasts.

At least such working days don't much involve anyone else in my private horror. There are some days, however, when reason and humanity desert me completely. I become a monster of egomania, self-pity, psychosomnia, vicious complaint and paranoia. There was a time, long ago, when the local glazier used to estimate his annual budget based on my regular custom (we had glass doors then). It's still fair to admit that the occasional cup or lighter item of furniture is not altogether safe during such working days as these. I'm not greatly given to physical violence but whatever creative gift I possess becomes wholly devoted to the art of accusatory rhetoric. Stalin condemning counter-revolutionaries in the Comintern or Hitler on the subject of International Zionism are as nothing when I take on, for instance, *The Shocking Discovery of Saboteurs and Traitors in My Own Home*.

Perhaps this is why I've become fascinated with the private lives of the great dictators. There's a familiar echo both in their technique and the general drift of their subject matter. I suppose we should all be grateful I never seriously considered going into conventional politics and that sustaining a singular line of argument is not my strong point. I think on the whole I prefer a working day involving a *blitzkrieg* on a ream of A4 while issuing belligerent communiqués to the cats, rather than one devoted to dividing up Poland or invading Abyssinia. However, on such days it's admittedly a fine difference for those in my immediate vicinity whether I'm getting on with *Chapter Two: My Schooling*, or invading the Sudetenland.

When it comes right down to it the only important distinction between your war machine and your average writing machine is that the latter is marginally more interested in other people's points of view.

# ■ A Child's Christmas in the Blitz

**From *Dodgem Logic* #8, April 2011**

Dear Jean-Luc,

Because you said that you were curious about my memories of growing up and celebrating Christmas during the Second World War, I'll tell you. Well, Christmas at that time had a special luminosity, a particular atmosphere which I have never been able to recapture, perhaps because I was born into a world darkened, of necessity, by conflict in which one dull day would be followed by a black, black night sometimes suddenly filled with noise and brilliant explosions.

I remember a tree whose tinsel glowed faintly in the light of a dying fire, standing in one corner of the room where I also slept. Out beyond the blackout curtains, occasionally visible as a momentary glare of yellow light or heard as a screaming drone when some plane spiralled to earth under fire, or the steady thump of the ack-ack, the war in the air pursued its course. I hardly knew why or what was happening. Bombs fell, landscapes changed, and occasionally I was even allowed to watch from a darkened room as the searchlights roamed across clouds and silvery barrage balloons, seeking targets.

I'm sure you feel little nostalgia for those times which are marked for most post-war generations by the war films which followed, whether they were stories of the Resistance or epics like *Von Ryan's Express*, but for me the war years are marked by a sense of domestic warmth and a deep, attractive melancholy which I suspect I am forever attempting to reproduce in my fiction; feelings allied to those that come from what Rose Macaulay describes as 'the Pleasure of Ruins', a romanticism not so much for the vanished splendours of the past as marked by a sense of human aspiration thwarted, of beauty destroyed, of surviving memory, which is the enemy of death.

I might have been able to tell you that Germany was attacking England, but more likely I would have said something about 'dog-fights' and 'us' or 'them'. I was absorbed with my Britain's toy soldiers, miniature hollow-cast models of English Tommies, French poilus and American doughboys locked in conflict with the ultra-masculine Germans, in their pointed helmets, whom I imagined flying the planes that I passed through the beams of my battery-powered searchlights, re-enacting under our steel-strengthened dining room table the conflict which would very much decide my family's fate.

Actually, I always liked the French infantry best, perhaps for the colour of the uniforms, then the English, then the Americans. I must have learned enough not to admire the Germans, who, of course, wore grey, for me never an attractive colour. Even my fleet of tiny battleships seemed dull and though they were distinguished by name and type on the cigarette cards I had inherited from my father's neatly collected sets ('Modern British Warships', 'Our Modern Navy', or 'Our Maritime Heritage') I never could summon much interest in them. The planes at least had brown and green camouflage and could be given thrilling noises as they closed in on their targets.

Of course my army wasn't exactly up to date, any more than our real armies had been in 1939. It consisted chiefly of my father's boyhood collection added to by what had been presented to me at birthdays and Christmas. I had rather more cavalry than was currently in action, a lot of auxiliaries dressed as cowboys or red Indians and rather a preponderance of French zouaves, whose uniforms were considerably more romantic. There were a bunch of rather crudely cast solid metal 1914 machine-gunners. A couple of motorcycle dispatch riders. And a bunch of farm and zoo workers, who were ready, I suppose, as the final line of defence. There was a certain egalitarianism amongst them, I will admit. Sets of British soldiers, usually six to the box, consisted of two running men, two kneeling and firing men, two standing and firing men. More elaborate sets would include perhaps two machine gunners, an officer with a sword, two men lying down and firing. They had identical opposite numbers in the German, American and French armies, in identical poses. The cowboys were often armed only with pistols and the Indians with tomahawks.

Before the war began, there had been a natural tendency for manufacturers, mostly Britain's (though there were some inferior makers who tended to supply the bulk of the cannon fodder), to match both infantry, cavalry and artillery exactly one for one. There were, to be sure, no anti-aircraft gun-crews other than British. They came with each gun or searchlight, specially modelled to operate their machines. They sat in little bucket seats to wind their range-fingers, or stretched their tiny arms to operate firing mechanisms. There was something of a dearth of airmen, too, all of whom were either English or American and far too big to enter the cockpits of the planes I sailed over their heads.

The dull thump of guns was echoed by my own childish imitations: '*Bam! Bam! Kerrrump!*'

The red boxes that the tiny materiel had arrived in became houses, aircraft hangars, barricades. The dark floral carpet was fields and cushions were hills. As the bombs outside whined down, I would crawl into a world bounded on four sides by heavy wire mesh into which had been let a small door. The mattress and pillows were a haven for my other comforts, the soft toys—patchwork rabbits, curly furred dogs, Mickey and Minnie. Even then I was identifying with the Mouse. Not the middle-class, long-trousered Mouse of sanitized 1950s Disneyland, but the original, aggressive, trickster Mouse whose ancestors were Brer Rabbit and Tom Sawyer. That Mouse sported an evil grin and took cunning revenge on his enemies, mostly muscular cats and dogs in baggy pants supported by a single strap.

Christmas 1944. Homemade bunting, red, green, gold, silver, hanging in every room of the house. The candles flickering to life on the tree, wax dripping over the holders. You had to be careful. Many a house was destroyed by its Christmas candles. First a trip to Kennard's, the big, grey Portland Stone department store in Croydon. They had made the most of little, as we had done at home. And suddenly I am looking in awe at an intense colour. I can't take my eyes off it. A colour I have never seen before. If it spelled a word, I wasn't aware of it. Besides, I couldn't read. It is the sign over Santa Claus's grotto. Neon, rescued from some prewar hoard. A gorgeous, unworldly colour. A heavenly colour. I focussed on it as others might have focussed on gold nuggets or streaks of silver in a mine. I was looking at indigo. Glowing, pulsing indigo. Even as I passed under the sign into Santa's grotto, all scarlet and white, with a big green tree festooned with the square fruit of brightly wrapped packages, I could not take my eyes off it. Indigo. Not until I saw *Fantasia*, the following Christmas, would I ever witness such intense colour again. Indigo. And then the enveloping scarlet, soft as my mother's furs, of Santa as I sat on his knee and demanded ponies and—and something else. What is it, young man? What do you want?

I wanted indigo. I wanted to swallow or be swallowed by that colour. With Mickey Mouse and Santa Claus and a long-legged homemade Teddy Bear indigo will always mean Christmas to me. My birthstone, according to some, is Blue Zircon, Blue Topaz or Lapis Lazuli. Blue for a boy, the blues and birthdays, for a memory more vivid than flame shuddering up from a ruined house, of thick, black smoke coiling across a blue, late summer sky. Blue for mother's eyes. Blue for peace. Infinite indigo.

That Christmas, haunted by the memory of indigo, Mickey Mouse would be the first movie I ever saw. I woke up on Christmas Day, just after dawn, unable to sleep for the excitement. The smoke of heavy coke and what little wood we had left. Distant voices. Busy voices. Savoury smells from the kitchen. My mother was up already and my father was doing something outside. I had been dimly aware of activity. Within me built a rising chord of anticipation. I pushed back the covers. The fire in my room was no more than a glow, a few rubies glittering amongst the pale ashes. I crawled out from under the steel-strengthened table and was getting into my dressing gown and slippers just as the door opened and my mother came in. My mother. Dark eyed, loving beauty. My constant.

'It's a white Christmas,' she said. 'We're having a white Christmas.' It's the first I remember. She went to the big French windows and pulled back the heavy curtains so that I could see into our garden. Mrs White, our next-door neighbour, came in. She was holding a red-wrapped parcel. She was laughing. Big, heavy flakes were coming down so thick you could hardly see through them. But outside there was a shape. A dim figure moving about on the lawn, under the bare apple trees. Santa? No, it was too late for him. He would have come and gone with his sleigh and his reindeer when it was night, his passage muffled by the already settling snow. Who was it?

My mother laughed. 'It's your daddy,' she said. 'He's gone mad.'

My father was out there rolling the snow into huge balls. One for a body, one for a head. He had made a Christmas snowman. As I watched he put pieces of anthracite in for eyes, a stick of dowel for a nose and another for a cigar sticking out of his lopsided mouth. A snowman. What else? I knew what to expect from Christmas. There was no such thing as disappointment. Not then. I watched wide-eyed as my mother got me out of my pyjamas and into my little boiler suit, a miniature of the kind Mr Churchill wore (though I heard later his were silk). And then she led me into the next room, the sitting room, where the tree rose so tall to the ceiling, topped by a tinsel fairy, the branches covered with crimson balls and little, pale tinkling bells. With red, green and white candles, each in its own little tin holder, clipped to a branch.

But this I had already seen. What was new were the green, red and silver wrapped boxes. The strangely shaped thing lying on the floor beneath them. And in the grate was a fire so lively and bright, sending its light skipping

from golden globe to silver bell, so that the whole room seemed full of movement, full of a warmth and a merriment, a completeness which denied everything in the world outside, where grey reality reared up through the thicken-
ing snow doing its best to hide the ruins, the anti-aircraft guns, the craters
and the dull, dull blackouts, the eye sockets of houses that would never live
again. White as icing on a poisoned cake, it grew thicker and thicker while
inside my father came stamping in, laughing as he did more rarely these
days, his white breath rising around his head like a halo, slapping his gloved
hands together, stamping his feet on the thick, wheat-coloured doormat
to knock the already melting snow from his clothes, eagerly taking off his
overcoat and hat as he shouted 'Merry Christmas' to Mrs White. 'Merry
Christmas! Merry Christmas!'

My father, smelling of soap and brilliantine and cologne sat down
on the floor with me between his legs and helped me unwrap presents as
our black and white Welsh collie, Pat, came running in, half-dried by my
mother, to sit panting by the fire and watch, half an ear cocked to the radio
playing carols and dance music. 'There'll be bluebirds over, the white cliffs
of Dover . . . I'm going to get lit up when the lights come on in London . . .
Silent night, holy night . . .'

Of course, there was a box of soldiers. Red-coated ones this time, in
the formal uniforms of the Scots Guards, in bearskins, marching with their
shouldered guns. Not the most useful troops, but welcome nonetheless.
A field gun, complete with tiny shells, fired by means of a spring-lever. A
Rupert Annual from Mrs White, with that little bear always running towards
some far horizon over perfect downs and welcoming woods, towards some
wonderful adventure from which he would always return to the security of
Mr and Mrs Bear and their beautiful cottage. Some Quality Street choco-
lates, wrapped in gold, silver and coloured cellophane, a picture of a dashing 18th century soldier and his lady on the box, bought with carefully
hoarded ration-coupons, some bullseyes, bigger than my mouth, all brown
and black and white stripes. And then the piece-de-resistance—the mysteriously wrapped monster in red paper and tied with silver string—a scooter! A
big, solid, wooden scooter, painted dark green and post-office red. A scooter
like no other child I knew had ever owned. A huge, solid machine, with
beautifully running rubber-tyred wheels. A scooter I could only run up and
down the hall, unable to go out with it until the snow had melted. My father
had made it, of course, as he made everything. It was meticulously finished,
perfectly painted, aerodynamically designed as he made everything. You
could smell the fresh paint on it, mingling with the smell of burning wood

and coke from the fire, the cooking smells to which my mother dashed every so often to supervise the lunchtime turkey.

Those are the colours of that first Christmas I remember in detail. Indigo, deep green, scarlet, gold and the blanketing white snow. I'm sure I enjoyed our Christmas lunch and was happy to show off my presents to my uncles and aunts and their American friends from the airfields who began to arrive through the afternoon. There was the smell of tobacco, of beer and whisky, gin and sherry, the loud, happy laughter of my uncles, telling mysterious jokes which made my mother and her sisters squeal with mock outrage, the radio playing Bing Crosby and Carol Gibbons's Royal Canadians, comic patter and crooning, the upbeat tempo of Harry James and Benny Goodman, of Glenn Miller. Coming in on a wing and a prayer—I'm dreaming of a White Christmas—Jingle-bells—and the carpet and furniture rolled back against the walls so that my mother and father, uncles and aunts could foxtrot until the evening when one of our American guests would start to set up the movie projector and there would be Mickey Mouse again, the first movies I had ever seen, in flickering black and white projected against a slightly crumpled bedsheet. I have never since enjoyed a cartoon as much. The projector and movies were borrowed from the American base. Everyone loved them. Silently Mickey flew planes in amazing patterns, captained a steamboat, serenaded Minnie.

Only the Americans weren't in civilian clothes. They were glamorous, attractive men whose uniforms were smarter than our own, who produced chewing gum and candy at will from their infinite pockets. They had brought me Captain Marvel comics. Unlike the black and white English comics, these were in full colour. Captain Marvel, with his white hussar's cloak trimmed with gold, in his red suit with the yellow flash across his chest, looking exactly like Fred MacMurray, whom I would later see in *Double Indemnity*, as powerful and benign an image as Santa, able to fly, to knock the evil scientist Sivana for six, given his powers by someone who actually looked a bit like Santa, the kindly old scientist Shazam. Captain Marvel was part of the Christmas pantheon. I loved Captain Marvel, who seemed pleasantly, even stupidly human, and I hated the rather pious, humourless Superman whom I had never seen, as I had seen Captain Marvel, handing out presents from the Christmas tree.

My family had opened their homes to the American flyers, some of them friends of my RAF uncle who had disappeared while ferrying a Spitfire in Rhodesia and was disappointed to be found in the Bush by rescuers. He hadn't wanted to be rescued, he admitted to me many years later, he had enjoyed his African Christmases and had several African wives, extraordinary status in the village, and no chance of being shot at. He was already burned across his face and body, from where his Spitfire had been shot down in flames and he had had to bale out. And his wife, one of my mother's many powerful sisters, he confided, was a bit of a harridan, though she had seemed very friendly, I thought, to our American visitors. He remained the most handsome man I ever knew, the living exemplar of the modestly heroic flying ace.

My father wasn't a combatant. Like most of the other men in my family he was excused military service. Some were too old, or unfit or, as in his case, were doing necessary war work. I grew up in what was essentially a matriarchy. One of the first fictitious characters I ever identified with was Jo March of *Little Women*. Jo March had known how to celebrate Christmas. She's introduced to us discussing the subject. 'Christmas isn't really Christmas without presents . . .' I would later see Judy Garland play her. Or was it my heart-throb June Allyson? Those girls also had an absent father, away fighting for the Union in the American Civil War. Mine, of course, wasn't fighting. I think he was already involved in one of the several affairs he enjoyed as the only good-looking young man at Phillips, the electrical firm where he worked on the radar which was helping us beat the apparently overwhelming Nazi forces. (A couple of Christmases later, his presents to me consisted of sheets of linen taken from his drawing offices, a box of pencils and a ruler. Looking back, I can assume he had missed the shops. It was, after all, on a Christmas Day that he had told my mother he was spending the holiday with his mistress; that he was leaving her).

I would never see my father on Christmas Day again.

I have to admit I mostly remember my father in terms of the Christmas presents he gave me—his own collection of cigarette cards, his own toy soldiers, his beautiful, multicoloured marbles, his watercolour box, the tricycle and the full size Norton motorbike frame and untyred wheels which he told me he was working on for me. He had also given me a Hornby clockwork train set which he took back in order to trade it for the bike frame. I remember one sharp December afternoon standing beside him in his workshop at the end of our garden, near the underground shelter we hardly ever used.

'This is going to be yours,' he assured me, as I held the oilcan for him. 'You can have it for Christmas when you're sixteen.' My birthday was a week before Jesus's, I knew. But I also understood his promise to be an abstraction. I knew the bike was really his and that, even if I was old enough to ride it at that time so far, far into the distant future, I probably wouldn't.

He hadn't been able to resist it. 'Your father loved bikes more than he loved us,' my mother would tell me.

Even dressed as Santa, my father would reveal himself by his neatly pressed flannels, his fastidiously clipped fingernails. In spite of my uncle, the RAF hero, my father was the embodiment of elegant masculinity for me from his neatly cut fair hair to his smartly polished brogues.

At some point in time between Christmas and New Year's, I got the train back again. I don't remember what happened to the Norton. A busy trade would often occur between the children of the neighbourhood. Some time after Boxing Day, when I swapped my tricycle with a neighbour's child for a different clockwork Hornby locomotive, my mother had stepped in and stopped the deal. After the train set was returned, I never saw the Norton again. It disappeared with the melting snow. I later wondered if this was one of the issues which had led to his leaving us on Christmas Day 1945. I had little affection for him at that time. I felt no pain at his departure, probably because he lacked the nerve to tell me he was leaving. Besides, all boys of my age had absent fathers. Many of them, like me, would grow up in mother-run homes.

But that first Christmas I remember, the bombs grew infrequent. The decorations were still up when my mother and I mounted the electric tram, whose brass rails sliced through the remains of the slushy snow, to go up to the centre of the city, to visit my Uncle Jack at 10 Downing Street. He hadn't been able to spend Christmas with us, so we went to lunch with him and and my Aunt Ivy, a rather pious Christian who didn't believe in too much pleasure. Uncle Jack had been on duty. He worked for Churchill. 'Happy New Year, my boy!' beamed the old warrior-drunk, puffing avuncularly on his vast cigar and smelling strongly of tobacco and brandy. I think he would have offered me a glass of brandy if my mother hadn't been with me. He did, however, give me the benefit of his wisdom that afternoon. 'Never be tempted to vote Liberal,' he said.

After tea with my uncle we went to Oxford Street and Regent Street, where the big toy shop was and where I could spend the money I had been given for birthday and Christmas. My Uncle Jack always gave me a ten shilling note. With this and my other cash I could replenish my miniature armies. This was the equivalent of an FDR loan to the British military. My mother couldn't afford to buy me more than a box at a time, mostly restricted to infantry, though she might add the occasional tank. But with my Christmas wealth I could add to my cavalry, to my Indians and my cowboys, perhaps to my anti-aircraft batteries.

Then, as we left Hamley's or Gamages or one of the other emporia supplying my reinforcements, my heart would leap with pleasure at the sound of the aircraft siren, warning us of an attack. I knew what this meant. One of the rarest of pleasures. To my enormous delight, we were forced to descend into the underground, to the depths of the Central Line, and join our fellow Londoners, some of whom lived there almost permanently. It would mean I could sleep on a platform with all the other people who would rather risk being buried alive or drowned than remain overhead in the dangerous, blacked out streets. I used to hope for a bombing raid so that we could enjoy the adventure, the subterranean camaraderie and what didn't seem like a false security.

Back at home, the Christmas holidays were still in force. My father disappeared again. From Boxing Day to the first full week in January we were free not only to play with our new planes, Roy Rogers cap pistols or other treasures, we were let out, wrapped tightly in little coats and scarves and mittens, to explore the surrounding destruction, a wonderland. There was only one condition. If we heard an air-raid siren, we were to come straight home. I followed older friends over ruins which became defensives, Nevada hills, the Sheriff of Nottingham's castle. We climbed through the piled snow-topped rubble filled doorways, found staircases still intact, mounted them with practised balance as they swayed beneath our feet, reaching the second storey where whole rooms remained, sliced as if with a knife, everything in perfect condition—bathrooms, bedrooms, store-rooms— and if we were lucky we found unlooted booty, including toys, saucepans, kettles and books. Christmas made us greedy for more and more wealth.

We became adept as high-wire artists at crossing the beams, all that remained of destroyed floors and roofs, glancing insouciantly down at the broken rooms some of which were still decorated for Christmas, with trees and tinsel. But these did not interest us. We learned to unroll lead from roofs and gutters, which the older kids hoarded or sold to scrap metal dealers. The dealers made us put the lead into shopping bags or baskets so that our trade went unnoted. Churches were by far the richest source of lead, especially those which had stained-glass windows. The coloured glass was sometimes picked up before Christmas to make decorations. But we searched constantly for the Holy Grail of any boy's collection—a piece of shrapnel which was more than tortured metal twisted like barley sugar sticks, but recognisable as part of a plane. What we longed to find were whole pilots, whose goggles and parachutes, flying suits, helmets and perhaps even pistols we could scavenge.

We grew up instinctive scavengers. Vulture chicks hunting for choice tidbits, for treasures we could carry home and show off to our parents and friends. We worked with busy efficiency and concentration, desperate to get the most we could before the Christmas holidays were over.

The snow never lasted for long in the city. For a while it gave a pristine, pseudo-virginity to our wrecked landscapes. As it melted, the old reminders of our situation, all the symbols of destruction, began to re-emerge. And, as school loomed, we became all the more frantic. How we longed for an unexploded anti-aircraft shell or a bomb or other ammunition to complete our Christmas collections. Shell cases were common currency and generally disdained. We had learned how to clamp the live shells and then set off the firing pins by putting a nail against them and striking them with a hammer. We tried to dig out the graphite, the powder, to make our own guns. Nobody seemed to think there was anything unwholesome in our warlike pursuits. Or perhaps their imaginations didn't stretch to how we were entertaining ourselves. Presumably, they had no idea how long the war would last. We might need those skills when we were adults.

I don't remember too many dogfights around Christmas, however. I somehow had the impression that the Nazis and the Allies broke for Christmas, much as we did for school. But I had seen some of the fiercest airfighting. For years I thought that watching the Battle of Britain through the windows of our house as the Spitfires and Messerschmitts wheeled and flared in a darkness speared by shafts of yellow light, had been nothing but a false memory, something inspired by watching movies. I put this to my mother a few years ago. 'Oh, no,' she said, 'you saw the Battle of Britain. We were between three airfields, Biggin Hill, Croydon and another one whose name I forget. I used to hold you up to the window to watch the dogfights. They were amazing. And they kept you quiet when you were teething or whatever.' Perhaps that's why I've never sought the distraction of war movies. The real thing was so much more exciting. And, in an almost mythical fight, we actually won command of the skies.

During those quiet Christmas times, when it seemed Hitler's Luftwaffe was permanently beaten, we enjoyed incredible freedom which would be unknown to our own children. In our little grey suits of flannel windjammers and shorts, shirts and jerseys, twice-tied black Oxfords, ties askew and hair sticking up like the wire which jutted dangerously from the blasted remnants of reinforced concrete, we were forever dusty.

That this was the dust of the doomed and the dead never occurred to us. That bodies might still lie undiscovered in those cellars or that the rust on exposed pipes might be blood was never mentioned by our elders and therefore never considered by us. We were told it was dangerous to climb the ruined houses, but we knew anyone could learn that skill. We were told to watch for 'bad men' lurking in the wreckage or in the bushes and copses of the nearby Common and golf-links, so we kept our distance from adults. But the rest of the world was ours as it never would be again. The world was unbordered. All its walls had been smashed down. We came upon large, abandoned houses with stables and outhouses. We ranged through glass-roofed conservatories. We found tools and glue in the work-shops. We learned to walk on roofs. The movie *Hope and Glory* catches some of this atmosphere but seemed bland to me compared to the rich-ness of the reality.

When the flying bombs came back the next Christmas we returned to the shelters, the reinforced tables, the dugouts. My grandmother was Jewish, my father unmistakably Anglo-Saxon. She would sit across from him in the big communal shelter, which nobody really trusted. She would hug her ther-mos flask and her packet of sandwiches as we heard the drone of the V1s overhead, then the sudden silence as their engines cut out, then the shriek of their passage earthwards as they hit Dahlia Gardens and Northborough Road and Mitcham Lane and all the other suburban streets laid out by planners in the twenties, following the course of the railways to build bijou Tudor-style mansions for the upwardly mobile professional classes repre-sented by my father and mother, the first of their families not to live by trade or the work of their hands.

My grandmother knew what would happen to her and presumably her children and grandchildren if the Nazis won. Facing my father in the cramped shelter stinking of sweat and urine she would rock back and forth as if in prayer as we listened to the dull drone of the V1 engines. She had a conceit which she was too intelligent a woman to believe, but she knew it annoyed my father. Her conceit was that if the Germans won the war, then all the Jews would be rounded up, put in concentration camps and killed. But if the English won the war, she insisted, then all the Anglo-Saxons would be rounded up, put in concentration camps and killed.

So she would sit rocking, her finger wagging, grinning into my father's infuriated face. 'Better hope the Germans win, Arthur,' she would say. 'Better hope the Germans win.'

It seemed the rockets, when they came, would never stop. British pilots had discovered ways of flying close to the V1s, which were essentially drone aircraft, and nudging them out of the way, but tracing the course of the V2s was almost impossible. And it seemed we were getting more than our fair share of both.

We didn't know at the time that Churchill was deliberately misdirecting those flying bombs, that his departments would report strikes on crucial factories and aeroplane fields when actually all they were hitting were the civilians of South London. As a result of this inspired misdirection, South London received by far the greatest number of strikes. One day the house across the road was a living entity, containing people you knew, who lived much as you did, who tended little rose gardens and wisteria plants and kept their paintwork up to scratch; the next day it would be something else entirely. Something ruined and already in the process of being forgotten. Somewhere to explore, to loot, to roll the lead from. Mrs Archer and the little Archer girls, whom I still miss and dream about—removed. Their blonde pageboy haircuts and pleated grey skirts, their crisp white blouses and school hats are the originals of images I continue to find attractive. But they had gone before I noticed the intimations of sex. That would come a couple of years later when the war was over and we had moved to a timber-yard. The smell of sawdust is almost as erotic for me as the smell of garlic or Mitsouku. Mr and Mrs Wall, their pebble-dashed miniature chateau a heap of rubble scarcely worth sifting through, forgotten. 'Auntie' Pat, who had run the corner newsagents and lent me all those wonderful books from her stock—Scott, Stevenson, Ballantine—gone one bright Sunday morning as she laid out the papers ready for delivery.

With my friends, and perhaps with my adult family, I learned never to mourn. To move on. To keep going. To act as if your number was never going to come up. Yet in all other respects we were far from stoical. We always knew, for instance, that we were luckier than the Russians, for instance. 'Mustn't grumble' became a familiar refrain. 'How are you?' *'Mustn't grumble.'—'Are your in-laws still living with you?'* 'Yes. Mustn't grumble . . .' It would be a refrain that outlasted the war and allowed restaurateurs, in particular, to get away with horror.

I was sent to infant school in Robin Hood Road, part of the estate planned in that corrupted arts and crafts style which is so characteristic of early 20th century London, a style it shares on a larger scale with Hollywood, where I always feel immediately at home. I was at school long enough to know what boredom meant, because I could already read and write. The headmistress said she would have to have a word with my mother, because I could not concentrate on the primers. I had in fact ruined one by putting it, open, on my brilliantined little head. When she asked what I read at home I said Edgar Rice Burroughs and George Bernard Shaw, which was true. For years I believed that to be taken seriously as a writer one had to have three names.

The headmistress seemed to get even angrier at my answer but she never got to have that word. Over the weekend a V2 dropped out of a pale and silent sky and eliminated the school. I was free. Hitler had saved me. The school was a leadmine and, what was more, not even the headmistress had died. Within a day, little that was valuable remained of its site.

The V2s were worse than anything we had suffered. Morale, which had remained almost hysterically high during the Blitz, began to fray. Hitler knew the power of those massive rockets which could come out of nowhere and kill you before you had time to say a word. They were a cruel weapon. Today, when I hear about the bombardments of Baghdad or other cities, I know just how cruel those weapons are. No time to compose yourself for death. No time to say 'I love you' or 'Look after yourself' and no time to find the inadequate safety of those shelters. The only warning you ever had was a few seconds when the yelling tube of explosives was streaking down on your head.

My imagination, however, was informed by those early years, just as my life felt dull after the war's end. I had become used to metamorphosis, of almost constantly changing landscapes, of being able to see for miles. I had become used to the adrenaline rush of the bombing raids and the exploration of tottering ruins, of squeezing up through chimneys, of clambering walls whose only handholds were pits in the brick.

On VE Day, as if he had waited for Hitler to be defeated, my father announced that he was in love with the woman who would remain his companion for the rest of his life.

'I couldn't have loved him much,' my mother said, 'because I didn't really mind. My pride was hurt, of course, but I had what I wanted. I had you.' That was how she saw it. She never questioned her own emotions, she never wondered if her sexuality was repressed. She always vehemently defended her own father, whom some thought had 'interfered' with her and had been thus thrown out of the house by her mother. She was visibly happy throughout my childhood and would only grow miserable when the time came for me to leave home. She had what she wanted. Her brother and sister-in-law, who had come to live in our house when their own was blitzed, took advantage of my father's leaving. In those days it was not easy for a single woman with a child to rent such a house for herself. So they took over the rent as soon she had left. She went to find a job and in doing so changed my life all the more for the better. Her job was in a timber-yard as a bookkeeper.

Earlier, when my father had gone for good, I found a pair of those brown brogues of his and put my feet into them, feeling as masculine as I ever had, then I went outside in my Wellington boots and joined the people jumping over the fire on which effigies of Hitler and Goering burned in the half-hearted rain. I loved those shoes. I loved the smell of the polish. I found the Cherry Blossom 'Oxblood' boot cleaner and I shone them up as proudly as he ever had. I looked forward to the day when they would fit. I suppose Oedipus could not have enjoyed greater satisfaction than I had with those captured shoes.

But my mother must have discovered them, no doubt, because she presented them to him on the first birthday I had after the Blitz when he came to take me off to the toyshop on the back of his BSA. He had forgotten to get me Christmas or birthday presents, of course. Happily my nativity was only a week before the Saviour's, so he could get me both sets of presents at the same time.

I climbed onto his pillion. He gunned the engine. He kicked up the stand. There was a stink of 'mixture' as the engine fired. He told me to hold on tight to the belt of his leather jacket and then we were off, roaring through the darkening December streets to the big, usually unattainable toyshop in Streatham, close to the ice-rink, which was usually far too expensive for me, even when I could get there. I don't think he ever felt so guilty again, because he let me have the pick of the store. I bought infantry. I bought imperial Indian cavalry. I bought cowboys and Indians. I bought a ranch house. I bought long-range guns and I bought light cannon. I bought another searchlight, more glorious, more powerful than any I had ever owned before. I bought planes and battleships. And I bought Mickey and Minnie Mouse, who shared my initials and for whom I had developed a profound affection.

We came back with his saddle bags loaded with treasure. My mother insisted that much of it be wrapped for Christmas Day, even though I knew what most of it was. I think it was then that she gave him the shoes. I caught a whiff of Cherry Blossom as she handed him a bag.

The yard was in the grounds of a ruined mansion. There was a small two-room cottage made of corrugated iron, heated by an old-fashioned cooking range. We moved into that. By the winter of 1947 we were still there. I remember the snow being so deep that the path cleared to the outside toilet was actually higher than my head. We made the trip to the toilet as rarely as possible. I still remember the chamber pots and the smell of them.

By the time the war ended, Britain was massively in debt to America, who had only loaned her the money to fight a war they had advised her against pursuing. She was, like the rest of the European powers, in the process of losing her empire. Her returning soldiers, determined to overturn the old order, which they blamed for their troubles, voted in vast numbers for the Labour government and nationalisation of major industries, the implementation of our National Health Service and a whole programme of reform which it would take Margaret Thatcher to dismantle some thirty years later. We could not afford immediate rebuilding and so London remained in ruins far longer than Germany, by then benefitting from the Marshall plan.

When I was fifteen I left school, determined to become a journalist (I had not yet set my sights on being a novelist) and worked for a shipping company in the city. From there I would go down to the countless miles of docks, filled with ships, with loading cranes and warehouses for as far as the eye could see. My way back would take me through a devastated landscape only slowly recovering from the intensity of the Blitz. I could walk from the river into the depths of the city using as my points of reference the same buildings used by my 18th century ancestors. It was possible to stand outside the old Billingsgate fish market, whose porters carried up to fifteen baskets of fish on their heads and were famous for their foul language, and look over to the Customs House. As you climbed the hill up towards St Paul's, you could see the Royal Mint, the Monument (to the Great Fire of London) and all the other buildings which had miraculously survived the Blitz while more recent structures, from the 19th century, had been totally blasted into rubble. On the artificial hills, like Celtic burial mounds, grew Rosebay Willowherb, imported from the slopes of Vesuvius by 19th century botanists, escaped from Oxford nurseries and now growing wherever there was the ash it loved. You can still see it, blossoming beside the railway tracks which originally carried it from Oxford to London.

You didn't need to make an effort of the imagination to feel the psychogeography of the place. I have often wondered if the Frenchman who created psychogeography and the wonderful philosophy of *dérive*, Guy Debord, had witnessed what I had witnessed in London. The very bones of the city, all her history, from Roman times to the present, were exposed and clearly visible. Here was Defoe's city and Johnson's city and Smollett's city, while the city of Dickens, who had turned London into a character, a monstrous entity, was in ruins. Where great warehouses had loomed over black water, now there were green hillocks where, at weekends, Londoners enjoyed their picnics. Where diseased warrens of slums had existed, an indictment to all civilised beings, Hitler's incendiaries had allowed the new socialist government to build attractive estates, designed by idealistic architects, not all of whom, as they later admitted, were misguided followers of Le Corbusier. Some built curving terraces, echoing the half-timbered lines of Tudor streets though without the chi-chi ersatz nostalgia which had characterised South London. Others erected monuments to the people, intended to bring sunlight and sanitation to all.

Even at their most brutal, the new estates were an improvement on the rat-runs thrown up in the 19th century to house the wage-slaves servicing Britain's imperial commerce. And in those noir-ish times, when every young man desired nothing much more than a trenchcoat and a battered fedora, Graham Greene, John Lodwick and the bitter-sweet romantics of the London literary scene came into their own. They were hard times. Poor times. It always seemed to be raining. Even in the Ealing comedies you felt that the rain had only stopped for about ninety minutes and would continue again the moment *Hue and Cry* and *Passport to Pimlico* began to roll their credits. Disenchanted men, old before their time, smoked moody cigarettes and lounged unhappily on the Thames embankment, brooding on lost love and forgotten ideals. Colour seemed almost obscene, an outrage. The late forties and the fifties were black and white years of *Odd Man Out* and *It Always Rains on Sunday*. All my girlfriends wore black and thought a lot about suicide. The novelists and playwrights, the so-called Angry Young Men, people like Kingsley Amis and John Osborne, expressed themselves with bitter laughter. They were still old enough to have swallowed the imperial myth which had betrayed them. By my generation, we had never accepted such myths in the first place and had no particular argument with our fathers, no inclination to shake our fists and yell 'Damn you, England!'. And the poets—Betjeman, Larkin and the rest—wallowed in nostalgia, in melancholy, equally disenchanted, seeking the certainties of their boyhood. Larkin in particular could not bear the idea of being rescued from the black and white world and when it threatened to explode into colour, as it did in the sixties, going from monochrome to Technicolor like Dorothy's transportation from Kansas to Oz, he resisted, he grumbled and he sought out the pockets of gloom which even today can be found in the remoter parts of the British provinces.

The Angries were probably not the only ones to yearn for the camaraderie of hopelessness. Many missed the years of anxiety and austerity. For my own part I was delighted to escape the grey years, when one's only choice of trousers was grey flannel or green corduroy. I embraced the sixties. From 1963 to 1976 was my (rough) decade. I knew we had discovered ourselves in a golden age and that it would not last. I became determined to enjoy that age while it did continue.

The metamorphosis of Blitzed London became the Chaotic landscapes of Elric the Albino. As in need of his soul-drinking sword as Chet Baker was in need of his junk, he witnessed the death of his Empire, even conspired in it. The adrenaline rushes of aerial bombardment and imminent death informed the Jerry Cornelius stories where London's ruins were recreated and disaster had a celebratory face. And the Holocaust became the background for the black comedies of my Colonel Pyat books. We tried to create a new literature which expressed our own experience—Ballard of his years in the Japanese civilian camp, Aldiss of the terrors of being a boy-soldier in Malaya—all the great writers who contributed to my journal *New Worlds* were rejecting modernism not from any academic attempt to discover novelty but in order to find forms which actually described what they had witnessed, what they had felt. By 1945, Proust and Joyce and even Eliot felt as if they belonged to the 19th century, even if they were indeed that century's greatest products. By 1945, we knew what had happened in Auschwitz and Dachau. We did not mourn the passing of liberal humanism or indeed of our humanity. We sought new ways of expressing them. We found humour in the H-Bomb, we made jokes about Vietnam, we sought our models not in the great moderns like Mann or Faulkner, but in earlier centuries, in the work of Grimmelshausen, Smollett, even Balzac. I myself unearthed a hero in George Meredith, marginalised by the modernist literary critics because he looked back to the 18th century for his models and in so doing spoke to those of us who found ourselves at last in the 21st.

All this experience, all this fiction, all this philosophy had its origins in what for me were the Blitz years, my years of childhood, when I was as unaware of any impeding doom as a new-born lamb in a field knows nothing of the slaughterhouse. Circumstances made me something of an autodidact, unable to settle at any school for very long, expelled from a couple. The schools were always glad to see me go. I learned from reading and not knowing what was respectable literature and what was not. I read everything. I became an enthusiast for the blues, in common with many of my generation, and learned some of Woody Guthrie's licks from Jack Elliott. I met Big Bill Broonzy and Muddy Waters and Howlin' Wolf. Their music was the music of hard times and though I don't pretend a white Londoner shared the same experience as that of a black Clarksdale share-cropper, that music did find an echo in my soul so that I was also privileged to enjoy the enthusiasms and pleasures of Rock and Roll from its earliest years. I am decidedly a child of my times. And I did inherit some enthusiasms from my father, though we saw so little of each other. It was my father, after all, who left behind the Edgar Rice Burroughs and George Bernard Shaw books, which were amongst the first I read. And he left some jazz records which ultimately led me to the blues. He then did me a great favour by leaving me to the love of my egalitarian mother and the man who fell in love with her (though I suspect never shared her bed) whose name was Jellinek.

Ernst Jellinek had helped Jews escape from Germany and Austria, going in and out of those countries to save as many as he could. Two of my friends, she a Jewish poet, he a Jamaican sculptor, were trapped in France when the Germans arrived and, I learned from them, it had been the man who had become my unofficial guardian, Ernst Jellinek, who had helped them get across the Pyrenees and from there eventually into Portugal and back to England. If my father had been faithful, I would never have had such a model of quiet, philosophical heroism as Ernst Jellinek. I would never have understood that there is nothing wrong with sticking to one's ideals, to following one's altruistic instincts while remaining, in his case, a practical business man. I have never ceased to be grateful to my father for finding love outside the home . . .

I don't remember my parents ever quarrelling, though I think I remember a few intense, whispered exchanges. One day when I opened the newspaper I found a piece cut out of it. I believe my mother must have done that. Probably a report of the separation proceedings. People avoided divorce in those days, because it was so hard to obtain.

When I was eighteen, my father came to see me on my birthday, as usual. He gave me an LP record of T-Bone Walker and we went out for a Christmas drink. Back in his car, he cleared his throat with some embarrassment and told me that he had taken out an endowment policy for me to help with my education or perhaps marriage when I was twenty-one. I told him that I was earning good money (I was already a successful journalist) and to keep it for himself. Without another word, that's exactly what he did. My own children's birthdays he was always a bit hazy about and it never occurred to him to transfer the policy for their benefit. He remained an emotionally lazy, rather likeable man, who tended to change jobs whenever he was promoted to management, because he could not take the responsibility. But he was an obsessive record keeper.

My father and mother never divorced. It would have involved too much trauma in those days. My father set up home with his mistress and in time she changed her name to his by deed poll. Many years later, when both were in their seventies, my father decided to apply for a divorce. He was afraid of my mother. The first I heard of it was when my mother phoned me, sobbing, to ask if I had spoken to my father recently. Although I saw more of him than she knew, I had not, as it happened, seen him for a while.

'What's the trouble, mum?'

'He wants a divorce,' she said. 'I got the papers from his solicitor this morning. Why would he want a divorce after all this time?'

Not long afterwards came the expected call from my father. 'Um—does your mother live in Gratwicke Road?'

He had discovered what I had known for over a decade, that by chance they were living about quarter of a mile apart in the same seaside town of Worthing. I had often wondered what would happen if they met. His solicitor, it emerged, was at the bottom of her road. And he was terrified.

They were both so emotionally overwrought by this event that I found myself acting as the mediator in my own elderly parents' divorce, calming both of them down, assuring that neither had sinister or greedy motives.

'If he thinks he's not going to give me that two pounds a week, he'll have to fight me for it,' she declared. She had settled, out of pride, for the minimum support which he had always sent late, but never missed a payment.

And so the knot was severed at last. This time I did not receive a visit to the toyshop, but he did offer to give me the family bible. I said that he should hang on to it. That I would have it when he died. I had it expensively rebound for him as a Christmas present.

As it happened, he gave the bible to my cousin, forgetting that he had promised it to me. When he died, I found photographs of all my family except my mother and myself and discovered that his father had remembered everyone in the neighbourhood in his will, but not me. I had been 'vanished'. My mother and I had been an embarrassment, evidence that he and his mistress had been living a lie. I also found every driving license he had ever owned and, neatly stored in cardboard boxes, the stub of every postal order he had ever bought to send to the court for my mother's and my support. I also discovered that in his youth he had been a passable artist and while I had always assumed that I got my own taste for the arts from the Jewish side of the family, I also discovered, thanks to another friend, that my great-great-great aunt Rachel Moorcock had been a passable poet who had published a book of memoirs and a book of poems in her lifetime.

Outside, the all-clear sirens begin to blast through the early morning light. It's Christmas Day. I get up and find that my mother is already building a fire in the grate. She kisses me and wishes me a Merry Christmas. There are all my presents arranged around the bushy little tree with the candles burning on it.

'Which one shall I open first?' I ask her.

She smiles and shakes her head. 'You choose.'

I know what I want. The large box. I rip the paper off it and see the familiar maroon red beneath. Slowly I take the top from the box and stare down at the camouflage green of the long-barrelled anti-aircraft gun. I remove it from the box and begin to set it up, settling it on its stand. Soon it is pointing menacingly towards the ceiling. Once again, Londoners will be able to rest easily in their beds tonight.

# LONDON

# ◼ Heart and Soul of the City

**From the _Observer_ magazine, 4th March 1990**

The stretch of the Thames from Teddington to the sea, the old Port of London, covered some seventy miles. For me, the Port's heart and soul was the Pool, between London Bridge and Limehouse Reach and once the origin of the country's greatest wealth.

Both a dramatic and visual inspiration, a source of characters and images, a profoundly potent symbol of London's psyche, the river is the reason for the city's existence. A trip from Greenwich to Hampton Court remains one of our easiest and cheapest forms of time travel and, if some of the old working river has become unrecognisably genteel, many of those miles have hardly altered in a century.

The Thames is impossible to separate from our national history. Celts, Romans, Saxons and Normans built along its banks. Vikings raided it up at least as far as Fulham, where they sacked the Bishop's Palace. William the Conqueror built the Tower to the protests of citizens. At the Tabard Inn in Southwark, Chaucer's pilgrims remembered Thomas à Becket, to whom the first stone on London Bridge was dedicated. From that same bridge Queen Eleanor was pelted with mud and offal as she fled to Windsor from a mob enraged by her husband's profligacy. Edward III's London fleet was created at Rotherhithe to back up his claim to France.

A crude, incoherent kind of democracy came up the river out of Kent and Essex. Jack Straw and Jack Cade brought their rebellions to London and incidentally helped strengthen the power of those commoners whose wealth derived from the Thames and the sea. Falconbridge, the pirate, took Southwark in 1471 and was repulsed by Londoners who pursued his men as far as Blackwall, Stratford and Rotherhithe. Elizabeth I's reign was crowded with references to the river—Shadwell and Purfleet and Tilbury, Greenwich and Deptford where Sir Francis Drake was knighted aboard the *Golden Hind* and where Sir Walter Raleigh spread his cloak.

By 1665, to escape the Plague, Londoners took to living on boats and barges moored off-shore, while no ships came up further than Gravesend. In 1666 they again found the river a useful refuge as the Great Fire engulfed the city. In 1701 Captain Kidd was hanged at Execution Dock, actually Middleton's Wharf, off Wapping High Street. In 1778, the Thames was frozen over for nine weeks and oxen were roasted for the Frost Fair, and in 1797, inspired by the spirit of the French Revolution, sailors of the fleet anchored in the Thames Estuary mutinied until their demands were met.

By 1799 a group of merchants, threatened by the level of plundering and smuggling going on at the old wharves, obtained Parliamentary powers to build the first dock on the Isle of Dogs. The West India Docks were surrounded by high walls and a message in their foundations called them "an undertaking which, under the favour of God, shall contribute Stability, Increase and Ornament to British Commerce". It was only in 1805, however, that the docks were ready for ships. Thomas Telford built the St Katherine Docks and destroyed whole streets in the process. When they were opened in 1828, the first ships to lock in were the *Elizabeth* (at seven hundred tons) and the *Mary*, whose rigging was crowded with fifty men who had fought at the Battle of Trafalgar.

By the nineteenth century, the Thames was so thoroughly identified with the city in all its ambitious variety, its commerce and pleasures, that it had become perhaps our most complex icon. It brought us a more cosmopolitan population than the world had ever known and it brought us confirmation of our mighty imperial security. It also brought us our worst examples of urban misery, crime and social injustice, especially in Stepney, Whitechapel and Limehouse—an East End of alien rituals, sweatshops, secret societies, fanatic radicalism, white slavery, drugs and every form of illicit pleasure.

At Wapping Old Stairs the dark-eyed Jews arrived, having been duped into thinking they had reached America; in Lavender Dock a corpse, pulled into their boat by watermen, had the contents of its pockets emptied before being passed along to the authorities; up closer to Aldgate, armed police constables shot it out with anarchists, one of whom, legend has it, was the young Stalin, who escaped down the river. Victorian and Edwardian novelists made the river into a myth at least as powerful as Ned Buntline's Wild West: a myth that still affects Londoners and tourists alike.

As a boy I wandered across vast acreages of docks, still full of the world's ships. I climbed piles of bombed brick bright with Rosebay Willowherb, the 'fireweed' brought from the slopes of Vesuvius and which took so happily to our ruins. I frequently became thoroughly lost for hours. There were still a few of the old Thames barges with terracotta-red sails and lots of grimy little tugs (one mysteriously called *The Moorcock*). There were dredgers and floating cranes and grain-ships for the flour mills of the Royal Victoria Dock, and all the ferries and barges and paddle-wheelers hooting and screaming and jostling, almost as busy as they had been before so many of them set out to bring the BEF back from Dunkirk. There was the smell of every spice-island, every jungle, every navigable river, every ocean, every tea, coffee or rubber plantation, every rice-paddy, every banana grove, desert, factory, orchard, every filthy port or oily quayside built since the Phœnicians (or maybe the Trojans) founded their first trading colony where the Thames was both fordable and navigable.

All sorts of inspiration came to me via the river. Anywhere I went in the cities of London or Westminster, in any pub or café or crowded cellar drinking-club, some sailor would turn up with bits of personal contraband, or a girl I knew would fall tragically for a Danish naval lieutenant. A Eurasian whore from Hong Kong might befriend me or an Australian stevedore offer to introduce me to the pleasures of opium. Many of my friends earned their livings from the docks, not always legally. The smuggling of firearms and drugs is not new.

By the time I was fifteen, I knew people whose ships flew virtually every known flag. By the time I was seventeen, I had lost two friends in the river, victims of gangland differences. Commerce still thrived in the docks and crime thrived with it. Frequently the two worlds were so thoroughly intertwined that many of us failed to grasp their fundamental character, even as that grand pivot of world trade began to decay, its monstrous body starved by the advent of carriers flying goods more swiftly, more cheaply, to the newly wealthy consumers of the 1950s. Soon only crime was left.

As the cranes rusted and the old sheds were stripped and vandalised, as the empty warehouses began to smell only of mould and rot, the Pool rapidly declined into a desolate waste of drifting garbage, scuffling rats and stinking, slimy lagoons. But what happened next is for me a bizarre illusion . . .

. . . Dinky 'villages' of a genre until then only existing on Los Angeles or Marbella beach fronts began to grow out of the bleak ruins, together with 'Olde Englishe' eating houses and mock Victorian taverns previously only provided on the Champs-Elysées or Fifth Avenue for foreigners nostalgic for Sherlock Holmes and Mrs Miniver. In Paris or New York these places represented a kind of quaint flattery. At Disneyworld, in the Florida sunshine, pubs and fish 'n' chip shops are like something from Oz, sea-changed and magical. But in London, where it is still raining, I prefer the Barbican's lazy brutalism to these glimpses of some Home Counties heaven.

From what was predominantly a working river, the Thames has become a profitable scenic resource. Not very long ago the GLC built fairly imaginative blocks of flats looking over the water. World's End, always well-named, was transformed to give many residents a chance to live with a view instead of a damp problem. Now the idea of local government wasting such important real estate on its ordinary citizens is received by many pretty much as *The Satanic Verses* was received in Bradford. Battersea Power Station aims to become Battersea Leisure Centre—a potent symbol of what is happening. There is more profit in leisure than there is in product. The river is now a facility, no longer the reason for London's existence.

There is no fog, no yellow naphtha glow, no black movement caught by a flickering beam, no gleam of something terrible just below the surface, no groaning horns sounding out of Greenland, Albion or Lady docks. No typhus or cholera or any of the other diseases the river helped spread; nothing to stir the anthropological conscience quite like the Thameside poor, the shanty-dwellers, the mudlarks and riverhounds. In place is a singularity, a tidiness, an uncertain smugness and a neat conformity of 'design'. A river view is something most of us can no longer afford. Only the very rich or the hopelessly destitute who crowd the walkways of Cardboard City on the old Festival site, which was supposed to show us a better future, can these days go to bed looking at the Thames.

If, for me, the river has lost some of its romance, it has admittedly lost most of its danger. The dark mysteries of Dickens's Thames have gone but the benevolent Thames of Jerome K Jerome still exists. I would guess we are still only beginning to discover appropriate commercial uses which could bring back fresh life and variety, and realise the promise, the optimism, of the South Bank's Festival Exhibition of 1951. The Dream of Property Development and the Dream of Leisure Industries cannot be enough.

If the little fœtid canals and waterways under the rotting jetties have given way to dainty fountains and ornamental streams, at least we are no longer as likely to die from some nameless toxin as we were when Steam was king. For better and for worse, the times, as well as the Thames, are changing.

# ◼ A Place of Perpetual Rehearsal and Audition

**From the *Daily Telegraph*, 18th August 1990**

I doubt if any modern Londoner is willing to die for a literary cause like John Scott, editor of the *London Magazine* (who published Cockneys and *The Opium Eater* in the 1820s), killed in a duel with a representative of his bitter rival, Edinburgh's *Blackwood's*. Indeed, few nowadays seem to see their city as anything but a symbol of moral decay, something to endure, and hardly anyone celebrates the virtues of an extraordinarily ordered and complex organism offering so much security, so many options to its umpteen-million residents, workers and visitors.

Our cities are civilisation's most concrete expression. The capital city must therefore always represent the conscience of its country. How we run it is surely the most rigorous test of our collective ingenuity and humanity. Why tell tourists that the capital is not the 'real' England when London, like Washington or Berlin, is the quintessence of her nation's history and the measure of its morality? As in the Blitz, London is where you will find dramatic and enduring examples of our virtues and our vices.

In spite of Defoe, Johnson, Hogarth, Smollett, Fielding and the curiously attractive worlds of Ravenscroft's *London Cuckolds* or O'Crook's *London Rakehell*, for me the city's most potent images are, with the majority of her architecture, from the nineteenth and twentieth centuries. Even her history is the invention of Ainsworth and his followers who, as did Gay, filled the town with a gaudy collection of rogues and gallants, plots and mysteries, creating enduring legends from Richard the Third's Tower to Dick Turpin's taverns, and I must admit that my own sense of the past owes more to *The Knight of the Road* and Conan Doyle than it does, say, to Mayhew.

I have enjoyed Tomlinson, Orwell, Fletcher or Pevsner, the admirably thorough and revealing LCC/GLC-commissioned 'Survey of London' (which might never be completed now), but in recent years Nicholas Shakespeare's *Londoners*, recording with graphic accuracy the lives, speech and observations of a wide spectrum of citizens, is the nonfiction book that has most impressed me. It is a masterly piece of good reportage, with the reporter for once only discreetly in evidence. With Jonathan Raban's *Soft City*, Shakespeare's is the best contemporary book on London I know. *Soft City* remains Raban's finest book. His city is a place of perpetual rehearsal and audition. It represents a central contradiction of the human condition, an entity striving for stability and survival in the face of an inevitably diffusing universe. As 'social entropy' increases, the city must shift rapidly to maintain equilibrium and her favoured citizens, instinctively learning with her, are thoroughly prepared to make the best of an inconstant future. Perpetual disintegration and reformation, perpetually altering rules. What a roller coaster! What a trip!

A city like London is the ideal place for a writer to observe, chart and examine rapid changes in manners and vocabularies. He must live, sometimes, at the core of the social hurricane if he is to turn up the odd fresh insight.

Dickens lived most of his life near that core and his novels, especially *Bleak House*, remain the finest London fiction we have. When *Oliver Twist* was published it caused enormous outrage from critics who complained that Dickens was fascinated by filth and poverty and went to thoroughly unnecessary and unpleasant lengths to dwell on those aspects of life we knew existed but did not need to have shoved under our noses! Nothing much changes. Although Dickens gave us the most durable images of Victorian London, he had some excellent contemporaries. Thackeray's London is a very different place and only Marryat's *Jacob Faithful*, about barge life on the Thames, has a spontaneous combustion scene to rival Mr Krook's.

Inspired by Dickens (and Gissing and Zola), a number of realists flourished around the turn of the century and most are now largely forgotten. All deserve to have their work revived. My favourite is W Pett Ridge. His best-known novel was *Mord Em'ly*, its early chapters vividly recreating a Whitechapel where all-female gangs terrorised the East End. Mord Em'ly's career, from her early life of crime to the humiliation of charitable institutions and 'service', all of which she spiritedly resists, is told with an authority, a lack of sentimentality which makes the book for me a minor classic. Many Pett Ridges make good reading, though. His contemporary (and contemporary of that other ignored realist, Leonard Merrick) was Arthur Morrison, who is still enjoyed for *The Hole in the Wall* and *Martin Hewitt*, but his finest books are *Tales of Mean Streets* and *A Child of the Jago*, displaying a genuine liking for his East End families, anger at their conditions, respect for their constant struggle to improve their lot. They evoke a London of cobbles, knockers-up and blanket-funds which even then was beginning to disappear—thanks to the efforts of such writers, who frequently took an active part in social reform. These contemporaries of Wells—himself an affectionate observer of suburban London—lacked his political formulæ as well as his originality, but they made up for it with accurate detail. With Zangwill, Whiteing and Bennett they are valuable for their pictures of a vanished London a couple of decades before the First World War.

Later came Galsworthy, Compton Mackenzie's *Our Street*, about West Kensington, the Westminster of Virginia Woolf's *Mrs Dalloway*, Michael Arlen's languid Mayfair, Wodehouse's fantasy clubland, Waugh's demimonde. Then we had the menaced Fitzrovia of Bowen's *Heat of the Day* merging with the surrealistic *Ministry of Fear*, fog-diffused images of Allingham's convincing parables *Tiger in the Smoke* and *Hide My Eyes*, the social comedy of *The Music of Time* together with the shifting fabric of space *and* time in Ackroyd's *Hawksmoor* and *Chatterton*. There was the seedy, exciting Soho and Notting Hill of MacInnes's *City of Spades*, the shabby-genteel Kensington of Angus Wilson's *Such Darling Dodos* and, his masterpiece, *No Laughing Matter*.

Jack Trevor Story's suburban comedies of *Live Now, Pay Later*, *The Urban District Lover* and the exhilarating *One Last Mad Embrace* are only matched by my other lasting favourite, Gerald Kersh's *Fowlers End*. Both authors are bewilderingly neglected now. Kersh wrote at least a dozen good novels of London life, full of superb characters and atmosphere, and his brother wrote three, beginning with *The Revelations of Minnie Ashe*, a classic of London Jewish humour. The unspeakably terrible slum Fowlers End has a mephitic cinema owned by Sam Yudenow, who requires a manager with the diplomatic skills of Talleyrand and the punch-power of Joe Louis. He hires the amiable but horrifyingly ugly Daniel Laverock. Laverock's encounters with Yudenow and his struggles with the disgusting inhabitants make this the funniest novel I have ever read.

London has also inspired some wonderful poetry, much of it written during the Blitz. I think the most moving narrative poem to emerge from this period is Mervyn Peake's *Rhyme of the Flying Bomb*, with its hallucinatory vision of the city as a living creature, tortured and ruined, but still, in the character of the sailor who finds the baby in the rubble, full of hope, and a will not merely to survive but to triumph with humane dignity.

Peake's illustrations, Gillray's, Leach's, Browne's, Phil May's—all these Londons, in all their variety, cannot quite match the marvellous daily experience of the city itself.

London, said Disraeli in *Lothair*, is a nation, not a city. It is perhaps best represented in George Meredith's vivid glimpses, best addressed with Meredith's moral exactness, best celebrated in Meredith's precise, quirky, elegant prose. For Meredith is the greatest of all the neglected writers who ever lived in or described his sturdy capital, and his *The Amazing Marriage* would, if ever reprinted, surely prove it. Curious that, with almost all the publishers based in London, not one of them has thought of reviving the work of so many fine London writers. Maybe, in this decade, someone will decide it is time some of them, at least, were put back in the bookshops. Meanwhile, they will continue to reward anyone who manages to find them second-hand—or who joins the London Library.

# ▌Building the New Jerusalem

**From *Time Out*, 12th October 1988**

Prediction has never been my strong point. My vision of London, since my first unpublished novel in 1957 and the first Jerry Cornelius novel, *The Final Programme*, in 1965, has tended to be somewhat on the apocalyptic and fanciful side, rather than the realistic. I'm inclined to regard *2001*, for instance, as one of the dullest films ever made. Much predictive SF has always seemed to me to be about little utopias and written by littler Hitlers.

My attitude might have more to do with my past, with its rockets and bombed sites, than with any immediately likely future. I thoroughly enjoyed the landscapes of my early childhood and felt a deep resentment when, after the War, people began to build on the ruins I had made my own.

What they built, by and large, was ugly, unimaginative and inhumane. The rejection of all forms of romantic flourish characterised a country recovering from the insane, tacky romanticism of Nazi grandiosity but it allowed architects and planners to justify the 'clean' lines of their concrete blocks, those machines-for-existing-in given authority by misusing the theories of Le Corbusier who was never, himself, very happy with urban environments.

Because of the Blitz, further destruction was justified in the spirit of spartan exigency conditioned by wartime thinking. By the end of the '50s London was filled with some of the cruellest living accommodation to be found outside of the penal system and some of the most miserably uninspired public buildings, providing us, in places with a skyline owing more to Stalin than to Wren or Norman Shaw, all raised in the name of 'the Future', all reflecting a vision of a sleek, easily-run and uncomplicated city.

But cities are complicated.

Cities can be neither simplified nor easily defined. They are hard to interpret. They are the ultimate and natural expression of human evolution, of human dreams and needs; they are as complex as the people who build them, as the planet itself; they have a sensitive ecology. In their architecture and their social organization they are capable of reflecting the very best in us.

What's more, cities traditionally have liberal, even radical, governments responding to an infinite variety of demands. They tend to oppose conservative and reactionary governments and as a result always come under attack from the Right. The Nazis' hatred of Berlin is well known and was convincingly documented by Speer, their own architect.

Clearly Thatcherites have the same animosity towards London. Simpleminded authoritarians always fear the city's complexity. But when you bring rural remedies to the city they have disastrous results. The Arab insurgents in 1918 and the Ukrainian and Spanish anarchists rapidly discovered this, while Soviet zoning policies helped turn the Russian capital into the bleak non-place travellers found so depressing. Ironically, as opponents of the poll tax have pointed out, such simplifications actually require an ever-increasing bureaucracy to sustain them.

Repressive governments hate cities because their populations are hard to control and frequently impossible to brainwash. The South East Asian communist remedy of driving citizens piecemeal into the countryside is a clear example of this. As in Savonarola's Florence a hatred of ordinary human ambiguity always characterises the authoritarian. Those who love cities are also inclined to celebrate such ambiguity and subtlety.

While the city represents the best in human nature, the worst is not inevitably represented.

Crime and violence are not necessarily a consequence of large numbers of people coming together. Crime and violence can just as readily be the result of our failure to recognize the city for the organic, living expression of human evolution that it is. If the city fails to provide the best education, the best moral and social experience, the best in humane legislation, it is not the city itself which has failed; any failure could as easily be a failure of vision and understanding on the part of the citizens, their legislators and educators.

Ultimately the best answer to crime is to spend more on improving the quality of life in the city, to reduce tensions resulting from the politics of polarity, to emphasise equality in every possible aspect, to provide real hope, a moral education based on a profound belief in liberty and egalitarianism.

As a great supporter of autonomy in all things, I've often wondered whether there's an ideal population to a city, beyond which it becomes unwieldy, even unworkable. I was once attracted to the idea of independent cities or city-states of no more than a million or so, yet finally this seemed unrealistic. Now I'd like to see London of 200 million or more functioning at its peak. The greater the population, the greater the variety of people and the more stimulus to art and ideas there can be. Possibly, too, more wealth would be generated which could be used to fund all kinds of enlightened social experiment. Recent studies also show that cities are more economical and eco-friendly than rural communities.

This, needless to say, is unlikely to happen to London in another few years. Certain predictions can easily be made for the near future; there will be more traffic, there will probably be more crime and increasingly youthful criminals, there will be, given present trends, a greater division than ever between the poor and the rich and, unless there is better and more funding, our social services are likely to be eroded even further.

On one hand the bizarre ruralisation of the city will continue, with Home Counties yuppie colonists confidently moving in to take over traditional working-class and lower middle-class strongholds; on the other we'll see an increase in the brutalisation resulting from short-sighted unintelligent Thatcherite capitalism.

These policies are not accidental. Just as powerful South Kensington helped polarise and ghettoise North Kensington in the '60s and '70s, so will certain Tories continue with schemes which will produce self-fulfilling prophecies of doom and decay. It's not difficult to achieve when you control the funding.

In spite of all that, I remain optimistic for London, particularly if enough Londoners grow tired of divide-and-rule reactionary policies from both major parties and begin organizing their own local groups to represent their real interests, to resist the erosion of their traditional liberties, the attack on their dignity as citizens, and the greed of the speculators and developers.

Old-fashioned socialism won't do any better than Toryism. It is too bound up with imposed ideological notions, too given to over-simplification and bureaucratic solutions to be able to feel the real pulse of London and find the means of remedying her ills.

Perhaps the reactionary threat will stimulate us to find new ways of resisting those devolutionary tendencies and build street-level organizations actually representing our needs as Londoners. That is the hope of one who loves London and would like to see her grow bigger and better, pushing out her boundaries beyond the Green Belt, possibly even swallowing redundant parts of it, ultimately absorbing Dorking and Guildford and all the smug little stock-brokers who have not yet moved to Stepney or Wapping.

We must repossess our city.

With good modern architecture echoing and amplifying the best of London's existing character and reflecting the return to a more imaginative, flexible and creative phase in our history, by extending the real city into the suburbs, we could, in the twenty-first century, have become a magnificent model for great cities.

Instead of retreating from the notion of the megametropolis we should have embraced it, celebrated it, grown comfortable with it, equipped it with hospitals, crèches, schools, houses set among imaginatively laid-out parks and 'wild gardens', with low-rise asymmetrical buildings designed to blend with and reflect the organic world around them. We should acknowledge and revel in the natural complexity of the London we can create for ourselves.

We should consider the best, most optimistic, possibilities our future offers. To romanticize the worst aspects of the city is to provide ourselves with a formula for doing nothing, solving none of our problems. By accepting the logic and aesthetic of the true city we can produce for ourselves an environment at once civilised, stimulating and secure, a city of equals, sharing equal liberties, equal rights of speech and expression. We should have to work for it, take positive action, determine what we really want for ourselves.

For me London's future could be one representing the true harmony of a highly complex but healthy organism, providing the best social services and transportation, with education and creative life at a peak of excellence, ultimately benefiting Londoners and non-Londoners alike.

Again, this vision can't be imposed on London. It has to be developed from what already exists, what Londoners actually want. It would mean some disruption, if the existing bleak barracks are to be destroyed and better accommodation built to replace them. Some of the money for this could be levied from those who put virtually nothing back into the city they exploit—those who live in Surrey, for instance, but derive their wealth from London, could pay an extra non-resident's tax, just as people who don't live in countries from which they derive their wealth must pay appropriately higher rates.

This move to increase London's power would not go unresisted. Also we should have to make sure that non-city-dwellers would not be disenfranchised in the way they have helped disenfranchise Londoners. As we reclaim our city, our identity, our power, we should show tolerance to those who prefer the dormitory towns and suburbs, or even the rural life, while remembering our responsibility, which will be to take our civilisation into the next great phase of its evolution.

For Londoners to retrieve control of our city would not be difficult. All it requires is the will to use existing legislation—some of which was actually designed to erode our power—to our advantage. By dismantling a party political structure which has nothing to do with our needs, by using the resources we still have, by supporting those who genuinely represent Londoners' interests, we could see a massive improvement—even by the year 2000!

There's no point in passively bemoaning the dissolution of the GLC and ILEA and blaming all our ills on those awful but not very bright people in Downing Street and Whitehall when we can take advantage of the chances we now have to make positive and optimistic plans for a better, not to say Utopian, London!

We can repossess our city. And in doing so we could recover an important power-base from which to build a brighter and better future for all.

# ■ City of Wonderful Night

A Review of *Night Haunts* by Sukhdev Sandhu

**From the *Daily Telegraph*, 22nd September 2007**

Clinical technicians observing on screens London's wired-up sleepless—sufferers from apnoea, insomnia and night anxieties—are sometimes shocked at the level of terror or rage they find. Samaritans, trying to offer comfort and reassurance to suicidal widowers or desperate immigrants, live in dread of sudden silence at the other end of the line.

The Tyburn Benedictine nuns whose convent lies where Bayswater Road meets Marble Arch pray in shifts for the souls of overstretched, noise-bombarded Londoners, while a Camden friar grows anxious that he is failing the homeless and wretched who occupy the streets around St Michael's church. Elsewhere, professional marksmen pride themselves on the skill with which they dispatch urban foxes, commenting on the condition of pelts that in their heyday fetched top prices from the fur trade.

Overhead fly the 'avian police', Hawkman and Hawkgirl with thrumming rotors, their equipment, like something from a Philip K Dick movie, imaging every street and moving object as they zoom down to scare off some potential housebreaker or bank to follow the glaring wonder of the river out towards the sea.

They grow lyrical to the reporter seated beside them. They would have no other job, for no other job offers them the chance to witness such beauty. The neon city. Dawn breaking over St Paul's, the Gherkin, Canary Wharf. Yet, in spite of the hi-tech kit they share with patrolling soldiers in Iraq, in the end they are more PC 49 than Judge Dredd, relying on experience, street wisdom, human instinct to do a job which at base scarcely differs from that of the bobby on his night-beat whom they have largely supplanted.

In the sewers, kitted up in waders, goggles, breathing equipment and paper overalls, flushers make their way through measureless rivers of filth, alert for the legendary glowing fatberg, like "a huge packet of lard", which, they insist, a large food chain offered to buy back for recycling to the customers who contributed to its existence. They admire the workmanship of bricklayers who built the sewers a century or more ago, never expecting their skills to be seen.

The few remaining Thames bargees tell of porpoises in the Fulham reaches; exorcists, like characters from some bleak Alan Moore novel, cancer-suffering ex-military blingers with bottles of holy water, seek to drive out powerful demons, emigrated from Surrey, haunting the old House of Detention in Clerkenwell.

Minicab drivers, legal immigrants without the right qualifications to practise their professions, hoping to save enough to open a shop or move on to more hospitable climes, take payment in kind from prostitutes, help pregnant women give birth and pray they won't be mugged.

At nightfall buses offload gangs of illegal office cleaners and before dawn take them back to bleak dormitories while graffiti artists snap their latest train job, knowing they'll be lucky if their work lasts a day as London cleans up for the Olympics and security guards hunt them with renewed vigour.

Sukhdev Sandhu goes with all these and others, seeing with a film-maker's eye and reporting in sharp language laden with pithy metaphors. Not since Nicholas Shakespeare's outstanding *Londoners* has anyone offered so many insights into the varied lives of the capital's workers.

Sandhu uses as his model HV Morton's *The Nights of London* (1926), one of my favourites, but writes with considerably greater flair than Morton, a journeyman who turned out a string of books on the city. Where Peter Ackroyd uses his own fascination as a key to the past and Iain Sinclair brings his idiosyncratic poet's brilliance to his observations, Sandhu offers high-end documentary.

Indeed, he is rather dismissive of what he understands as psychogeography, perhaps in reaction to all those who have used the term in imitation of Sinclair without understanding that the one response he isn't offering is romantic nostalgia.

Indeed Sandhu's fascination with the fringes of society and its myths closely echoes Sinclair's and I would add his work to the likes of *Lights Out for the Territory* or *Sorry Meniscus* as offering some of the greatest insights we have into rarely described aspects of contemporary London. The two authors together offer about as complete an urban portrait as it's possible to read.

If Sinclair is a day person, striding around the city from dawn until dusk, stopping to observe some obscure landmark whose narrative perhaps illuminates the life of an eccentric street dweller he encounters, Sandhu is a night person, examining the aspects Sinclair might miss after he returns to Hackney and hangs up his walking boots.

But whereas the night-haunting journalist of the 1920s and earlier might have drawn a picture of Limehouse opium dens, river police, music halls and soup kitchens, Sandhu goes up with the police in their helicopters or down into waste tunnels kept flowing by the unseen flushers, the sewermen whose black humour has something in common with the nurses of the casualty wards, and other men and women whose jobs bring them into contact with the least palatable aspects of London life.

This laconic, beautifully produced little book is an enduring portrait of a city that manufactures fresh narratives as rapidly as they are revealed. Sandhu joins a small group of outstanding investigators into what remains in so many ways the world's richest city.

# ■ London Peculiar

**From the *Financial Times*, 27th June 2009**

There aren't many pictures of my childhood London. To get a glimpse of the world I grew up in, I have to give microscopic attention to the backgrounds of English movies made between 1945 and 1955 in the hope of seeing the ruined South Bank in *Hue and Cry* or the remains of Wapping in *Night and the City*. If I'm willing to sit through hours of cockney stereotypes, I might occasionally catch a few metres of library footage shot through the windows of a tram with Sid James's head in the way. My London is fleeting, mysterious, torn down or buried.

London was different up to 1940. In illustrated books, it often seems tranquil and quaint, full of lost churchyards and hidden courts. There were always places where the traffic noise dropped away and you could enjoy a bit of peace. That was before the firestorms blasted the East End into blazing fragments of people and buildings, when so much of that quaint tranquillity became heaps of rubble, tottering walls, fire-blasted windows, cutaways of people's private lives, their bathrooms and bedrooms, everything they'd valued, exposed to the hasty curiosity of the survivors.

Wartime London had been a malleable place in which you could leave home in the morning and find your street utterly transformed by the evening; where the house next door could become a pile of junk or your best friend could disappear forever. By 1945, when the bodies and the worst of the rubble had been cleared away, I see from those pathetic scraps of newsreels and old magazine pictures the London I loved and grew up in. It was in some ways a more innocent place. We hadn't quite taken in the Nazi Holocaust, let alone the A-bomb. We were a bit bewildered by how, having won, we were somehow poorer than when we were losing. The London in which Orwell wrote *1984* was my first peacetime London.

I wouldn't much want to live through that period again. Most of those films I give so much attention to were terrible, about keeping a stiff upper lip and knowing your place while facing down the chaos. We kept replaying that trauma for years. What had gone wrong?

Our general entertainment in that postwar decade was mostly dreadful and, like our styles, shrunken cheap imitations of what boom-time America was offering. It was a world with no representation in the physical world around me. My ruins have vanished, unfamiliar, often beautiful, buildings erected in their place, offering me few co-ordinates to calibrate my memories.

By the early 1950s, when I had my first job as a messenger for a shipping company in the City, I could take a bus or a train down to the docks and then walk for miles looking for the appropriate ship or customs office: grey cranes, redbrick warehouses, endless rust-grimed ships. I never had any idea of where docklands ended. Apart from the great shipping lines, banks and insurance companies, the City was still an area of small businesses. There were scrap-yards, independent stationers, booksellers, printers, chop houses, eel and pie shops, tea shops: a London whose variety and complexity you didn't have to guess at.

Then there were the places where London was simply *not*—a few irregular mounds of grass and weeds with rusted wire sticking through concrete, like broken bones, exposed nerves. These parts of London could very easily be identified because almost nothing survived except the larger 17th- and 18th-century buildings such as Tower Hill, the Customs House, the Mint, the Monument. And, of course, St Paul's, her dome visible from the river as you came up out of the delicious stink of fresh fish from Billingsgate Market, a snap of cold in the bright morning, and walked between high banks of overgrown debris along lanes trodden to the contour of the land. You had made those paths by choosing the simplest routes through the ruins. Grass and moss and blazing purple fireweed grew in every chink. Sun glinted on Portland stone, and to the west, foggy sunsets turned the river crimson. You never got lost. The surviving buildings themselves were the landmarks you used, like your 18th-century ancestors, to navigate from one place to the other.

Slowly the big brutal blocks of concrete and fake Le Corbusier flats began to dwarf St Paul's and the Royal Mint, and the familiar trails disappeared, along with the alleys and yards, the little coffee shops and printers. Like an animal driven from its natural environment, I'd turn a corner and run into a newly made cliff. The docks disappeared with astonishing speed. One day the ships were shadows honking out of the smog and the next they were gone. Air freight and containers were replacing the old systems.

Without our heavy exports we didn't need ships; without the ships we didn't need the docks.

The west London where I got my next job—in 1956 as a sixteen-year-old 'junior consultant' at Harold Whitehead's management consultants—is a lot easier to identify from 1950s Rex Harrison comedies. Almost everything was dark green and brass: motor cars, front doors, porters' uniforms. Everything else was bright yellow (driving caps, cars, frocks). Smart young voices imitated Noël Coward or Gertie Lawrence and their owners buzzed about in MGs and Mayflowers. I worked for people rather like them.

For some reason, Jim Sandford Smith, the boss, liked the cut of my jib and made it my main job to go the *Times* library twice a week to pick out books for myself and for him. The staff there were extraordinarily generous. They completed my education. They gave me my taste for good food and wine and introduced me to TS Eliot and Proust. I went through a *fin-de-siècle* phase, reading Oscar Wilde and a literary journal called the *Yellow Book*, and affected what I hoped was a pale and interesting look. I was regarded as a bit of an *enfant terrible* and they encouraged me to write. I hardly had to work at all. For a while it was always Maytime in Mayfair and spring in Park Lane. By the time I was seventeen, I was in Holborn, in the City again, editing *Tarzan Adventures*, a juvenile weekly where I'd sold most of my early work. But I'd added a lot to my social and literary education.

In Soho I had discovered jazz and skiffle and had played substitute washboard on the radio with the Vipers, who later became The Shadows. I'd cut a demo (which set my musical career back years) and hung out with writers and musicians such as Alexis Korner, Cyril Davies, Long John Baldry and Graham Bond, who introduced me to Howlin' Wolf and Sonny Terry. I learned Woody Guthrie licks from Ramblin' Jack Elliott and corresponded with Guthrie and Pete Seeger, who were effectively under house arrest as they were investigated by the House Un-American Activities committee.

Soho was coffee bars and formica signs, formica table-tops. Formica hid all the old shop signs and looked at least superficially modern. Rock and roll, sex and drugs. Trad jazz became skiffle, and skiffle became blues or R&B. I augmented my living by playing guitar for a while in a whores' hotel. There were no clothes in the shops. Just grey suits, tweed jackets and corduroys. We took old stiff detachable collars and wore them with thin black ties, a car coat, white shirt, trousers stitched tight to our legs. My children say I was a Mod. I say those were the only clothes we had.

In the early 1960s my digs were in North Kensington and Fulham, which had sustained a bit more of the Blitz and were full of poor immigrants.

They were grey, dirty, hopeless and often violent. I did wonder why the posh bits of London were only what you might call lightly bombed and why the working-class suburbs were piles of ashy rubble. When Churchill, as he later explained, was sending back false intelligence about the Nazi strikes, suggesting that Streatham was the centre of our steelyards, he didn't seem too eager to give the impression that Belgravia was an industrial beehive. But I don't hate him for it. He did, after all, give me a lot to write about and a strong sense that nothing is permanent.

Around 1963 my wife and I moved to Colville Terrace in Notting Hill, where our next-door neighbour, a big knife-fighting whore called Marie, was regularly noisily arrested at about 2 am, and where we had our two daughters in swift succession. One of my best friends was another young father, JG Ballard, who shared my frustration with the state of English fiction. We met often and our wives became good friends, too. I took over *New Worlds* magazine, determined to bring some fresh conventions that Ballard, Barrington Bayley and I felt were needed to reinvigorate English fiction.

My main contribution to this period of experiment was Jerry Cornelius, whose name was pinched from a greengrocer's sign in Notting Hill. Like me, Jerry relished ruins. Unlike me, he enjoyed making more of them. Throughout that era we called 'the 1960s'—which really ran from about 1963, with the Beatles first No 1 to around 1978 with Stiff's second tour—we continued to experiment in almost every field and genre; and through the 1970s I frequently performed with Hawkwind and my own band the Deep Fix.

We moved to a wonderful flat with a big leafy square behind it.

It was a good time to have kids. I took them to music festivals and to little parks and museums, my secret boltholes like the Derry & Toms' roof garden, where only old ladies met for tea after doing their shopping. None of these places had yet become self-conscious or been persuaded to exploit their 'features'.

I knew we enjoyed a golden age that couldn't last but I was determined we should get the most out of it. Even with strikes and hard economic times we had the first Notting Hill Carnivals, local open-air gigs and a general improvement in local morale, but we could already see the end coming. One afternoon I was in my garden when a liberal solicitor asked me if I was coming to a newly formed 'gardens committee'. When I told him I wasn't, he cheerfully informed me that that was my right. I knew what my rights were. I also sensed that this was definitely the beginning of the end.

By 1980 the roof garden had become a private club. While it was still possible to lunch there, its casual nature had changed. Slowly, I began to

feel like a stranger in my own city. I had, of course, been part of the gentrification process but I didn't like the way people from the country and the
suburbs were beginning to displace the locals. I like my classes mixed. We
sold up and moved to Texas.

In all those years I lived around the Portobello Road I learned that what
people want more than authenticity is a provenance, a narrative. It wasn't
enough to sell a modern flowery chamber pot as 'Victorian', it had to be GK
Chesterton's chamber pot. The developers and remodellers soon learned
this lesson. The formica signs were stripped away and now old buildings
were made to look older.

By the 1980s good, innovative writers such as Iain Sinclair and Peter
Ackroyd, all too aware of our need for authentic as well as virtual memory—
and sharing my deep fascination for London—would meet in Clerkenwell
and Earls Court to discuss our mutual sense that the city was being disman-
tled into a kind of Disneyland before our eyes. The media, particularly television, picked up on the idea and soon had created 'London', the character: golden-hearted London, whose dark spine was the Thames, whose
dark soul was the Thames. This character appeared again and again, in all
those sequels to famous Victorian novels or pastiches that spoke fruitily of
Limehouse and Wapping.

By the new millennium, when the giant circus tent was erected on
the Isle of Dogs, Ackroyd's reaction was to play to this dark image, he was
filmed for TV, lit from below, with a bearded Dickens impersonator trotting
in his wake. Sinclair, however, was having none of it. The first of London's
psychogeographers, he headed for the M25, daring anyone who followed
him to make something romantic out of the motorway cafés and discarded
Big Mac boxes. While Ballard reflected on the curve of the Westway flyover
mirrored in suburban reservoirs, Sinclair peered into the bays underneath,
searching for the remains of the population.

The rise of psychogeography was in some ways an impulse to rediscover those old natural paths that I and others like me had trodden through
the ruins, to find ways of rediscovering serious memory, something which
Peter Ackroyd (with *Chatterton*), Alan Moore (*From Hell*) and Will Self (*The
Book of Dave*) were searching out among the virtual ruins of a London that
was becoming a shadow played out on the newly tarted-up walls of Notting
Hill and Shadwell.

As well as the friends and relatives who have also become memories,
we are equally dependent on the geography of our cities for the myths and
rituals by which we live. Without conscious ritual, all we have left are buried

tram tracks, some vague ideas of what still lies under the steel-and-concrete cladding and a few bits of film footage.

I have nothing against virtuality. We create virtual identities for London. We create them for ourselves. We seek options allowing us to survive and, with luck, be happy. Jerry Cornelius knows, as he strolls—in clothes that have just recently come back into fashion—through virtual ruins, virtual futures, that it's the only way we'll survive, *as long as we're fully conscious*, so that when fashions such as Dickens World cease to satisfy the tourists, we'll have another city standing by. I'm hoping for a London that neither swings nor sags, is neither grim nor gay, but rises defiantly, a fresh guarantee against the dying of our memories.

# ■ Introduction to Gerald Kersh's *Fowlers End*

**From the Harvill Press edition, April 2001**

It's always dangerous to proclaim your favourite comic novel as the funniest anyone will ever read. You more or less guarantee the kiss of death, for you and the book.

And don't even hint it's a neglected masterwork by an overlooked genius. Human nature dictates that the less well-known the object of your admiration, the greater the resistance you receive and the wilder your claims for them. You can't help yourself. I once insisted Kingsize Taylor was bigger than the Beatles, which is probably only physically true. Bang went Kingsize's rock career. He's now running a successful butcher's in Bury. I had an agent who annually claimed a client had produced the greatest book since *Ulysses.* He claimed it for me twice. He's still claiming it for new clients, who really are pretty good. But when your trusting (or mentally bludgeoned) audience spends good money on your much-praised hero only to discover he isn't actually the greatest since Dickens (or Joyce), you lose a certain credibility. If you've recommended him to your unimpressed spouse, you lose credibility for the rest of your life. So that's why I'm not saying what I really think about *Fowlers End.*

I won't note how Anthony Burgess rated it one of the funniest books of the 20th century or how he was in the company of Kersh fans like Iain Sinclair, Chris Petit, Nancy Spain, Maurice Richardson, Ian Fleming, Hilary Bailey, Simon Raven, Robin Cook, Angela Carter, Harlan Ellison, Jack Trevor Story and a thousand more. I'd warn readers to avoid *Fowlers End* and its denizens at all costs, not to listen to a word Laverock says and not to treat Sam Yudenow like a die. He's a corkscrew. I would sneer at claims that Yudenow is amongst the great comic grotesques of English fiction. I'd especially warn you to take no interest in the Pantheon kinema and its predatory customers. They will not amuse you.

Of course I have a grudge. I'm still blaming Kersh for the bad back I got in 1964 after finding this in Ace Book form at Mrs Miller's bookstall, Portobello Road. Uncontrollable laughing soon shook off the garish cover. Anyone who borrowed it loved it. Later, I lent it, the way you do, to a trusted wife. And I never saw either again. That was the last I knew of *Fowlers End* in print, until now.

Until *Fowlers End* I had not knowingly read Kersh. I must have read him unknowingly, of course, because during the forties and fifties, if you visited the dentist, you could scarcely avoid him. *John O' London's*, *Lilliput*, *Argosy*, *Everybody's*, *Illustrated*, even *The Strand* still ran excellent fiction. People tell stories of Kersh's extraordinary powers. He could produce features or fiction more or less to order. Newspapers employed boys in those days to go from The George to El Vino to The Punch and round up any talent that could still stand. They'd fetch him in to *The News Chronicle* for two columns of topical rhyming couplets or a piece for *The Daily Mirror* on one of the many crises that keep papers in business. The papers certainly kept Kersh in business.

Kersh left a nice middle class family and a leafy London suburb. His family was Jewish. Kersh was not religious but he never rejected or senti-mentalised his origins. His first novel, *Jews Without Jehovah* (1932), so offended members of his family that it had to be withdrawn and I don't think has ever been reprinted. It was Gerald's brother Cyril Kersh, managing editor of *The Daily Mirror* before he retired, who wrote a more affectionate and perhaps accurate picture of Kersh's family. Cyril's *The Aggravations of Minnie Ashe* (1971) and his other West London Jewish novels also deserve reprinting.

Kersh originally came from Ballard country. Twickenham was never the hottest crucible of the city. But Kersh did what all suburban young men of spirit and lust did. He got the bus into Soho. As a later Fleet Street prod-igy drinking in Soho, I staggered in and out of the same pubs and clubs and met the remains of Kersh's contemporaries. As a teenager I discovered the pleasures of Old Compton Street, Dean Street and Meard Street. I met Henry (*Salar the Salmon*) Williamson in a Soho club with a blonde. I mixed with like-minded musicians, painters, writers; toking reefers, playing chess with glaring Bolsheviks at The Partisan Coffee Bar, listening to intellectual crooks and crooked intellectuals. Working women confided in me, perhaps because I was innocent. That's where Kersh got his material all right. That's the easy bit. But where did his genius come from? Nobody has told more or better Soho tales or described the place and its people so well.

Born in 1909, he started writing as a small boy. By twenty-three he had published his first novel and in 1936 a bit of Poland Street Zola, *Men Are So Ardent*, a novel of wounded, doomed, dreaming Londoners.

Before the Second World War Kersh joined the Coldstream Guards and produced *They Die With Their Boots Clean* (1942), *The Nine Lives of Bill Nelson* (1942) and a popular poem of the day *A Soldier: His Prayer*. As a war correspondent he was buried alive three times in the bombing and shelling. *Brain and Ten Fingers* (1943) is about his time with the Yugoslav guerillas. Even before the end of the war he had returned to Soho/Fitzrovia, to *Faces in a Dusty Picture* (1944), Jules Dassin's *Night and the City* (1946), and *The Song of the Flea* (1948). I have described only a portion of his output at this time. There were hundreds and hundreds of short stories, scores of novellas. He listened as well as he talked. He was quick, clever and very funny. He learned fast. He took his own athletics seriously and had no fear of violence. He wrote quite a bit about London sporting life. His Soho stories remain probably his best, after *Fowlers End*. In 1950 *Night and the City* became a moody movie. The backgrounds were depressed post-war London, all ruins. Richard Widmark was oddly convincing in the leading role. Critic Richard Roud thought it a 'brilliantly photographed example of neo-expressionism at its most potent'. Unlike a more recent remake, it's still worth watching.

His journalistic speed and eclecticism might have kept him slightly on the margins of the English lit biz, but Kersh's graceful ability to move from stark realism to wildest invention, often in the same short story, kept him an admiring readership scarcely aware of his comic social fiction. He told beautiful little horror tales, one of which was filmed with Michael Redgrave as *The Horrible Dummy*. For years copyright problems meant that only now is his work being republished in the UK and USA.

Kersh offered everything best in that post-war ambience, that bitter-sweet sense of defeat in victory which gave us movies where it always rained on Sunday's mean streets, handsome odd men out last-gasped eloquently in bombsite black and white, sinister war profiteers philosophised from the tops of Viennese ferris wheels, passionate lovers parted in impossible circumstances, and the crowd endured.

Of course, Kersh's comedy has the same ironic humanity of those years when master actors played their own murder victims, mild-mannered gangsters practised the cello and music hall comedians declared Pimlico a Free State or tried to smuggle gold Eiffel Towers into France. Again, the Ealing protagonists are never really alone. The crowd is always present. It frequently features in the plot. The War had bonded us. In fiction at least we were still a people. Still an amiable mob. When, in a new era, that same master actor came to the small screen, George Smiley was isolated, melancholy, adrift.

Kersh had a sharp eye for a face or a gesture and a drinker's acceptance of human failings—at least where they mirrored his own. I started working as a journalist in the 1950s. My territory was pretty much the same as Kersh's. It didn't extend much further than Ludgate Circus at one end and Wardour Street at the other, bounded on the South by the River and on the North by Goodge Street. I occasionally travelled the same bleak stretches of suburbs that he knew, where bomb craters were more common than carparks.

By then Kersh was a vanishing legend. I saw his elegant, bearded figure at a bar or two. He had style. He had bearing. Maybe a drunkard's discipline? Maybe his Guardsman years? Your eye was drawn to him. He was still witty, you could tell by peoples' responses. I stood near him when a mutual acquaintance was enjoying a word, but I didn't really know who he was and then he returned to America and never came back. The last years weren't his golden years. He paid the price of fluency, that habit of working which can always turn out another book for another advance but needs stronger and stronger fuel, anxiety, adrenalin, stress. Like many a performer before him Kersh drank himself to a disappointed death.

For me *Fowlers End* (1957) is his best memorial. His touch was sure, his material was securely his own and his territory was just waiting to be settled. Welcome, then, to the most cancerous spot on the pelt of old London, to the domain of Sam Yudenow, Daniel Laverock, Copper Baldwin, Miss Noel, Kyra Costas and Mr Godbolt. Welcome to what the author considered his modern *Beggar's Opera*. Welcome to the best and funniest bunch of grotesques ever likely to stumble, hobble or sidle your way. They're starting to settle around you now. Behind you a chattering projector casts a grubby shadow on a screen while the tinny, out-of-tune piano begins a lugubrious movement. The audience stirs. A strange miasma lifts from the stalls. A barely human ululation begins . . .

Mr Kersh—if you please . . .

# ■ A Child of Her Times

## A Review of W Pett Ridge's *Mord Em'ly*

**From *Waterstone's Guide to London Writing*, February 1999**

London S.E. Winter '98. Resisting all efforts to cheer it up, the New Kent Road grimly meets the Old. Warrens of dejected streets surround tenement rookeries where shifty crooks prey off the hooked, the fearful, the sick, the ruined and the unemployed. Young girls with babies are hopeless addicts, going for the easy money of casual prostitution. Truant youths savour the streets, on the lookout for unguarded vehicles, houses, shops, or vulnerable individuals. The police can't catch them. Most crimes go unreported. But ordinary people manage to survive and even improve their lives. The media urgently demand solutions to welfare dependency, health and education problems, teenage crime, child abuse and domestic violence. Can the public or the private sector provide the best cure? Meanwhile—

> The members of the Gilliken Gang, who, in the slow, thick stream of traffic in Walworth Road, had been noticeable only for the peculiar whistle given when one happened to be out of sight of her colleagues, turned into Trafalgar Street. The leader, a round, white-faced young woman of fifteen, upset a sieve of Brussels sprouts from a stall with a calm, methodical air, as though performing a State duty. Some of her followers had less than her years; all wore black, braided jackets (pinned), maroon skirts, hats with plush decorations and smart boots. It was near to being a uniform.
>
> "Mord Em'ly! Seen anything of them Bermondsey bahnders?"
>
> "Not yet I ain't." Mord Em'ly was a short girl, with a green plush bird in her hat that nodded as she hurried up to the leader of the Gilliken Gang. She seemed pleased at being singled out . . .

Things haven't changed much. The date, of course, is 1898. The novel is *Mord Em'ly*. Its author W Pett Ridge was the most famous literary Londoner of his day. He walked everywhere. He knew the city from suburbs to centre. He knew everyone. An energetic social reformer, he was a good friend of HG Wells, JM Barrie, WS Gilbert, Jerome K Jerome, E Nesbit and many contributors to the *Pall Mall Gazette, The Idler, Westminster Gazette*, journals of what we'd call today the moderate Left. All testified to his experience and talent. 'There is nobody else in London,' said JM Barrie, 'with his unique literary ear.'

*Mord Em'ly* was his best-loved book. Reprinted regularly, it became a major silent film and last appeared in paperback in 1992. Mord Em'ly herself is spirited, witty and pugnaciously charming. Living wretchedly with her drunken mother in Pandora Buildings, Walworth, she's caught stealing a meringue. The reform school's repressive methods fail to break her so she's put into service as a housemaid. She proudly resists. Returning to her old territory, she finds Gilliken in the Salvation Army. Other friends are now whores. She's not attracted to either prospect. Getting a job as a waitress, she's courted by a socialist soap-box orator and a wholesome young liberal-minded boxer. She begins a better life, determining her own destiny.

Born in Kent in 1860, 'Pett' wrote down, for fifty years, an unmatched record of lower-class London life. He heard the subtleties of Cockney and could repeat the conversations of charwomen, costers, vanmen, railwaymen, telephonists, shopgirls and petty crooks. His books, such as *Nearly Five Million* (1907), often combined fact and fiction. *A Storyteller, Forty Years in London* (1926) gives us a revealing picture of the rewards and frustrations of a still familiar London literary life. Train buffs seek out the work he based on his railway years—*Love at Paddington, Top Speed, London Only, Lost Property, The Bustling Years*. His stories of *Thomas 'Enry* (1910), from Kings Cross delivery boy to parcels clerk, are autobiographical.

Like so many of his contemporaries from poor backgrounds, he educated himself at the Birkbeck Institute's evening classes. With his clever sketches of London life, he soon gained a name. For all his huge literary output—much of which was never collected—he was actively involved in the life of the city, rigorously helping underprivileged Londoners help themselves. He married late, fathered a daughter and a son (whom I knew) and had a heart attack in September 1930, leaving his family all but penniless. Friends rallied round but failed to get his widow and school-age children a civil-list pension.

In its warm obituary, the *Daily Telegraph* remarked on his philanthropic work, his brilliance as an after-dinner speaker, the lasting value of his novels which, 'besides being good reading in themselves, have the further value of being a record of the impressions of a man of humour, veracious, and entirely unsentimental, as to the conditions of life among the London poor.'

An exemplary Londoner, his public reputation soon faded. His kindly books live on.

# ■ Mysteries of London

## A Review of *Vale Royal* by Aidan Dun

**From *New Statesman and Society*, 25th August 1995**

> Near wonderful anvils, through openings of true cycles,
> he navigates the legends of London Stone,
> the legends of the Trojan race in the Silver Islands.

Over the past decade or so, perhaps in response to the failures of rationalism, romanticism has returned to dominate English literature. Disguised as SF, magic realism, allegory, neo-Gothicism and even post-modernism, romantic themes and methods characterise most of our bestselling literary and popular fiction. Vampires, visions and ghostly visitations are once again useful devices.

This new mainstream, largely unacknowledged, is represented in its purest form by writers such as Iain Sinclair and Peter Ackroyd, whose fascination with London obscurities and antiquities informs everything they write.

Both are champions of Aidan Dun's great epic, *Vale Royal*. Some impressive London verse has been published since the War, including Peake's *The Rhyme of the Flying Bomb* (especially in its musical setting by Langdon Jones) and Sinclair's own recently re-issued *Lud Heat*. But until now, no ambitious poet has chronicled the mystical and mythical history of the city.

*Vale Royal* itself has a heroic tale attached: there were twenty-one years between its conception in a King's Cross squat and publication. Perhaps this long genesis has helped give the poem that moral authority of a literature won from experience, which JG Ballard once demanded of imaginative writers in *New Worlds*.

In these ninety-two pages of vivid, unrhymed triplets, its author reveals himself as a genuine visionary, a Celtic Christian mystic whose symbols can be as powerful and memorable as Bunyan's, whose faith in his own understanding of the world is as strong as Blake's, whose anger at social inequity is as passionate as Shelley's.

It is dark down here. The light is bad.
It is London in the olden days. Take care.
But nothing here is real without belief.

In two cycles, chiefly through the persona of a poet hero identified variously as Blake, Chatterton/Rowley or Thomas the Rhymer, Dun retails a
profoundly personal, supernatural history of London. His is a spiritual and
symbolic view of the world's most complex city, from her fabled Atlantean
foundation by Brut the Trojan—millennia ago on the site of King's Cross—
to her dark, desanctified modernity.

Trynovant, great forerunner of London on the Thames!
Over ten-thousand rooftops the green-headed Penton rises
with other high skylines of the ten-mile ridge . . .

Magical forces struggle over London's ancient burial sites and battlefields,
her holy monuments and her places of shame and power. Demigods search
among her ruins for stolen talismans. Her great myths, which we are forever
rediscovering, redefining and reworking, sustain our souls and keep us sane
in the face of Chaos and Old Night.

In an epic both deeply idiosyncratic and inescapably public, Dun
reminds us of our golden potential, of our spiritual hunger for justice, of our
forgotten archetypes—King Lud, Gog and Magog, Boadicea, Constantine
the Great, Arthur, the Grail, Old St Pancras Church and the foundations of
our Christian Celtic glory.

Perhaps I would have made some connections more readily if I had first
read Dun's illuminating thirty-five-page appendix, but the poem's symbolism is always coherent and never falls into obscurity. In spite of the mystic
grandeur of its themes, *Vale Royal* sustains a human perspective: an identification with what, in his 1872 book on London, Blanchard Jerrold called
'that most miserable of human creatures, the unskilled, dependent, roof-
less man'. Dun equates him with Christ, the Lord of the Dance, the Mighty
Youth, the Sunchild.

In the wind-labyrinths of early May he goes hunting.
His verse-satires hang like vultures of conscience
in hot skies above the rottenness of the Tories.

False Druids, malevolent Masons, fallen angels and literary predators
pursue the poet through all the disasters that ever consumed the capital. He
is tormented by timeless visions, by the mass murder of children, the brutal

disempowerment of women, the sacrifice of the Wicker Man. Through thousands of years he experiences every form of suffering, but like Blake he is always an optimist, fiercely refusing the possibility of the soul's destruction.

The final part of *Vale Royal* offers a brief glimpse of the future, with London as the New Jerusalem and the promise of the coming millennium. The poem rewards many readings. An enduring mystical epic has been added to our literature.

# ▪ Benglish for Beginners

## A Review of Tony White's *Foxy-T*

**From the *Guardian*, 27th September 2003**

Constantly invigorated by successive waves of immigrants, London produces a literature unrivalled by any other great city; she's a powerhouse of fiction, using whole cultures for fuel. London erupts with street language to match the tenor of the times, drawing vitality from the word-hoards of the powerless and disenfranchised. Working novelists, usually too poor to live anywhere but the ghettos, listen and take notes.

Spontaneously created, the new language soon becomes a strategy against authority, ultimately responding to general experience and achieving a level of expression useful to all. Rapid, exact, poetic, its cadences are as persuasive as those of Shakespeare's taverns, so subtle that, by the time words make it to the glossaries, they've already altered, even reversed, their meanings.

Gaelic, French, Spanish and Italian have all done their part to broaden our vocabulary. In the 17th century Romany was one of the richest veins writers tapped. That became vagabonds' cant, the slang of theatre and gay night-life, before entering our common speech. Yiddish, which I grew up using, in common with every Londoner of my age and background, informed 20th-century metropolitan English as thoroughly as it did German. Then American black idiom, itself borrowing from other immigrant dialects, came to us via the movies, jazz, R&B and rap. Nowadays West Indian and Bengali set the dominant rhythms of the city. In the East End, cockney is replaced by another dialect some already call Benglish.

East-Ender Tony White has always had his finger on the vulgar pulse. He edited a seminal anthology, *Britpulp!*, gave us the lively *Road Rage* and *Charlieunclenorfolktango*, and, as literary editor of the *Idler*, did much to promote his talented contemporaries. In *Foxy-T* he excels himself. His skilfully sustained use of Bangladeshi idiom combines with a surprising plot and wholly believable characters. White becomes the nearest thing to a fly on the wall in today's urban society, and you don't even guess how until his final pages.

White gives us the English heard every day in a street I once knew, whose parade of greasy spoons, betting shops and minicab businesses has mutated into video renters, sweet centres and computer cafes. Good friends Foxy-T and Ruji Babes (their old spraycan tags) are two young women running E-Z Telephone And Internet, coping with local predators and mutually maintaining their morale. They share a flat over the shop and work for Ruji's uncle, who is away in Bangladesh.

Zafar Iqbal, just freed from juvenile detention, accepts the chance to sleep on their couch for a while. Within days he has conceived a passion for a dazed Foxy-T, proposed marriage, fallen in with his old druggy mates, got up the nose of Ruji's Beemer-owning gangster cousin, and seems to have broken the women's friendship while heading rapidly for disaster.

Here he is on his first night out after four years, trying to find his feet in the world again: '. . . aint take long till them reach at the Glass House is it and by the time them inside the place ram up believe me. Couple a well fit girl make straight over where Shabbaz and Ranky is wait at the bar. Them two was dress up init and Zafar find him cant take him eye off them behind and how them G-strings show through them white trousers. Them G-string is disappear right up there arse. Easy now Zafar. Shit man them two girl was lean over and say something in him spar ear and touch them arm and laugh init but Zafar just watch them behind like he never seen a girl before. . . . Him no figure how some fit woman like Foxy-T aint make the most of herself is it and just wear them trackie bottom and polo shirt.'

With vivid economy White describes young Bangladeshis' domestic, business and street life in intelligent, beautifully sustained prose. Coherent and compelling, the novel has a wonderful, if slightly tricky, denouement which made me grin with surprised admiration. Rejecting familiar influences of the past twenty years, White joins a handful of contemporary writers who are proving that the novel has never been more alive. He is a serious, engaging voice of the modern city.

# ◼ Cockney in Translation

A Review of Roberta Taylor's *Too Many Mothers: A Memoir of an East End Childhood* and *The New East End: Kinship, Race and Conflict* by Geoff Dench, Kate Gavron and Michael Young

**From the *Guardian*, 18th March 2006**

Anyone expecting London's contemporary East End to be like the TV soap opera would have a surprise strolling down today's Brick Lane. The soap is peopled by cockney stereotypes from the last century. Oldsters talk fondly of the Blitz to crooks with hearts of gold. Who can believe that inhabitants of Walford, living in terraced houses worth half a million, should ever know a moment's financial worry? We watch the series much as we read W Pett Ridge or Arthur Morrison, whose Edwardian London is actually much closer to the TV series. The only family from the Indian sub-continent was phased out of Albert Square; the only regular black faces belong to two loveable old West Indian immigrants and a couple of essentially white stereotypes (Gus the Crossing Sweeper and Jules the wide-boy). My familiar Cockney-Jewish East End has given way either to Bangladeshi working poor, speaking an English as rich and strange to the suburban ear as Cockney used to be, monied City types or, most recently, Russian mafiosi, whose global operations make the Krays look like provincial amateurs.

I have children living in the new East End. One daughter had to learn Bengali in order to teach effectively in Tower Hamlets. My son, married to a middle-class professional of Jamaican origin, runs a culturally diverse pre-school nursery. Their friends are drawn from every social and racial group in London and their experience, profoundly multicultural though definably English middle class, is considerably different from mine, though I lived in Notting Hill when it was still considered a dangerous area full of poor immigrants.

While I celebrate this transition in my fiction, my own roots remain in London's white, lower middle-class culture, celebrated in *The Likes of Us*, Michael Collins's recent book about his Southwark family, which referenced Dunn's *Up The Junction*. That old world can also be found in actress Roberta

Taylor's engrossing memoir *Too Many Mothers*, though even she had an Uncle Korim who taught her to say *salaam alaikum*. She must have felt odd appearing on a time-warped *East Enders*. In her memoir people dine regularly off pie and mash and are scandalised when their sisters have brown babies, yet the frustrations, warmth and continuity shared by generations of mothers, sisters and daughters is pretty much the same as Monica Ali describes in *Brick Lane*, while the 'Benglish' used by East Ender Tony White for his marvellous *Foxy-T* is as vividly expressive as the Yiddish-flavoured cockney of my own generation.

The East End of 17th century merchants still exists where it escaped Hitler's bombs and Thatcher's developers. Houses of Jewish shopkeepers remain off Brick Lane. In *Rodinsky's Room*, Sinclair and Lichtenstein found Princelet Street and a small synagogue behind a house originally used by Huguenot weavers. Sinclair, of course, remains the area's greatest living recorder, celebrating its revivifying immigration while urgently warning against conglomerate developers. The tsunami of exploitation accelerated horribly once London won the Olympics site. Even as fresh groups of immigrants bring their own cultural identity to East London, the developers threaten it in a way no well-meaning blanket funders or Mosleyite fascists ever could.

That said, *The New East End* is a wonderfully readable study of its subject, carrying some of the approachable flavour of the best Mass Observation Penguins of the thirties and forties and intended to chart social change as it occurred. The authors discuss the difference between old and new Bethnal Green and Spitalfields, using Michael Young's and Peter Willmot's *Family and Kinship in East London* as their main comparison. That was the first major study from the Institute of Community Studies in 1957 and remains a classic, though later sociologists found it distorted and sentimental. Nonetheless, the study survived sociological fashions as thoroughly as the East End itself. While *The New East End* has a similar emotional investment, it flags a new kind of change involving gentrification and property development and tensions between Pakistani and white neighbours which its predecessor could not anticipate.

Even though I'd happily see a London stretching from Oxford to Folkstone, I share this anxiety, not from conservative nostalgia, but because the threatened sub-culture, enduring and benefitting from many transitions, represents a currency of memory, identity and political power. Its loss to London would attack the depth and balance of our national narrative. Our rich inheritance would be replaced by a commercial heritage industry substituting a sentimentalised and corrupted version of what it destroys. The layered memory of the East End, which so profoundly moves Peter Ackroyd, might soon only be accessed through valuable semi-academic accounts like this one.

*Family and Kinship* mourned the death of an old cockney chirpiness, yet it's easy to detect similar qualities in the defiant cadences of Benglish. Traditional trades still flourish in Bethnal Green and Spitalfields. Livings are still made from food and clothing as well as electronics and therefore the new communications industry. Ambitious parents still seek to educate their children through public educational institutions which, by 1900, had already produced one generation of professionals, artists and intellectuals.

But this new East End is now seriously threatened by the vestiges of a colonial logic encouraging xenophobia and racialism, still useful to the new imperialists, the developers with a financial interest in disempowering existing cultures. The enemy is identified by its characteristic impatience with history. Where government serves such forces, it has a common aim in denying or sentimentalising history and cultivating a self-interested amnesia.

If it is the responsibility of our nation's representatives to preserve our memory and dignity as well as our material wealth, then government is clearly failing in its duty. One understands from *The New East End*'s descriptions of Bengali families and their clashes with earlier cultures how neighbours too frequently turn against one another rather than against the common threat. Left to themselves Londoners intermarry and mix sturdy bloodlines as thoroughly as they mix culture and religion. Stronger, they are able to promote change which benefits them and resist that which attacks them. The East End does not need to stay poor, but these days it certainly can't afford not to be proud.

Since this was written, Rachel Lichtenstein's superb *On Brick Lane* has been published.

# OTHER PLACES

# ■ Diary: 13th October 2001

*Lost Pines, Texas*

Home after two months. Linda and I drove to northern California and back with our two cats. Some 4,000 miles. A surprisingly smooth journey. The cats behaved considerably better than I did. We vacationed directly over the abyss in San Andreas Bay, near where Drake careened the *Golden Hind* on his way round the world. Good days with grey whales, water-birds, sea lions, elk and deer. Great food, company, wine. Tuscany, USA. Lucky Texans tend to summer in the liberal North. In Marin County we read how a crime victim called the sheriff's office to report the theft of six marijuana plants. I remarked on this to a local officer. He shook his head in disgust. Such thieves were beneath contempt. Not much chance of finding the evidence now, though.

British TV gives the impression of the entire country weeping into flags or waving M-16s and swearing bloody revenge. Texans, it is assumed, must be weeping and waving the most vigorously. In fact, under the 'x' in Texas we're mostly doing outreach stuff. Books on Islam sell steadily now that Nostradamus's popularity has subsided. People discuss all sides in the conflict with painstaking care; not a single Arab hassled. The relatively few flags waving were, until recently, at half-mast.

Lost Pines's Lebanese restaurant is the only place displaying an inordinate number of Old Glories, but the local cowboys still wash down their hummus and pitta with mint tea and wish the owner a nice day as they leave. One pick-up truck has Confederate flag and Stars and Stripes decals, but no gun-rack and no hound dog; not even a 'Nuke bin Laden' bumper sticker. There are public debates, and interfaith picnics and barbecues. Jews, Muslims and Christians assert their commonality on local TV. There is a fair amount of told-you-so-ing and mea-culpa-ing among liberal academics on PBS, but so far the Republic of Texas hasn't sent a single son to the crusade. In fact, after spending thousands on provisions, the local militia-men have disappeared into somewhere uncomfortable ready to withstand the first wave of 'terris'. The E-Z Pawn on the highway hardly has a gun left. Real patriots, they've done their bit for the local economy and withdrawn discreetly to the wilderness. What more could they do at a time of crisis?

Our house, the Circle Squared, was built of local timber in 1865 by the only Confederate governor of Texas. We live among old trees. Until December we enjoy dreamy, extended autumns. Pecans and walnuts become plentiful, the light grows mistier, and in the woods you experi-ence the extraordinary sound of the Houston toad. There is always some casual bloodshed going on outside. Recently, a large hawk stooped on our cat. Bill was meditating on the lawn, minding his own business. Almost too late the hawk realised that Bill was slightly too big for him, and performed an impressive mid-air brake. As the days narrow down to a precious few, I prefer to forget the buzzards amiably circling over the old spread.

Our best friend in Lost Pines is black, an ex-Washington insider now doing AJ Cronin-type projects to bring cheap medical attention to the (mostly white) rural poor. Linda is impressed by Colin Powell's deft handling of the terrorist situation. Many Democrats I know are saying that they'd vote Republican if he stood for president. Linda thought that Powell would have a good chance of winning. With a shake of the head, our friend laughed. 'He's a black man, Linda. No way.' Powell would make an ideal modern president, Linda insisted. But our friend was adamant. 'He hasn't got a chance. He's black, Linda!' 'OK.' Linda dropped her voice. 'Here's the deal. If you don't tell them, I won't tell them.'

An ad on local TV: 'If your child has been introduced to Satanism by Harry Potter books, call this number . . .' As far as I can make out, the ad has been placed by a commercial exorcism outfit. See what happens when you deregulate?

I'm getting ready for the Royal Festival Hall on 11 October when I'll be appearing there with Hawkwind. Thanks to satellites, I'll be performing with the band in London while remaining at home with two startled cats. Of course I lose their respect, but I save a fortune in travel expenses, and there's absolutely no danger of my teeth flying into the audience. Austin rightly prides itself on its broad variety of live popular music. We also have a decent ballet and an improving symphony orchestra. Visiting the local Gilbert and Sullivan Society was, however, a disappointment. Great costumes, enthusiastic attack. Yet the splendid singers didn't know their drolleries from their parodies. We slipped away as the English tea was served by ladies in blazers.

It was a relief to drop in at the Gin-U-Wine Oyster Bar in Lost Pines, where gents who never take their hats off stand up to drink while playing Willie Nelson on the jukebox. I have some good friends there now. Initially, it was a bit touch and go. I felt obliged to inform my drinking compadres that I had last voted socialist, (i.e. NuLabor). The bar fell silent. Somewhere a piano stopped playing. Then a cowboy in a black ten-gallon Stetson rose over me, clapped his massive hand on my shoulder and growled, 'Mahchael, ah gotta tell yuh. Yore a true Texan.'

I've done my share of dirty jobs, but never thought I'd be Tony Blair's speech-writer. It was Kipling or me. In my *Warlord of the Air*, Cpt. Bastable, a decent, idealistic British officer, NW Frontier, 1903, plunges into a future whose benign Pax Britannica is subtly maintained by armed paternalism and limited civil rights. Bastable offers 'enlightened' reasons for taking up the White Man's Burden, and I'll swear PM Blurr pinched that bit for his Brighton speech. Have I at last accurately predicted the future? I think so. This means that by Christmas the editor of this paper will declare the Henley Commune; Zeppelin stocks will be hot; Imperial Chinese flying iron-clads will liberate Balham; the Stuart flag will fly over free Southwark; France will apply to rejoin the United Kingdom; and England will win the World Cup. That's right, dear reader. The end of civilisation as we know it.

From the *Spectator*

# ■ Diary: 30th August 2003

*San Andreas Bay*

Back from a flying visit to friendly, overheated Britain, we begin the annual migration north. Like thousands of other Texans, we are escaping our terrible weather. Some of us go to Maine, others to Oregon. My wife, Linda, and I go to northern California. It's a radical change of political climate, too, and we have to cross a desert or two to get there. The drive from Texas to California can still stir romantic chords: hundreds of miles of semi-desert relieved by an occasional distant butte. This *She Wore a Yellow Ribbon* territory was once commanded by fierce Apache tribes, like the Chiricahua, who gave us Cochise and Geronimo. It's easy to understand the terror in which those masters of strategy were held as they became pretty much the last fighting nation to go down before encroaching settlers and a cavalry consisting largely of Irish conscripts enforcing American rule with a genocidal ferocity which the Apache respected. The Apache and Kiowa combined deep spiritual beliefs with a philosophical understanding that total war was the only way to survive in an unforgiving land.

Hundreds of grey spindly-legged tripod windmills, rotors slowly turning, march over barren hills into the distance. Martian invaders from HG Wells's *War of the Worlds*. Welcome to California. They are de-electing a governor. Just as important is news that *Pirates of the Caribbean*, a movie based on a Disneyland ride, sweeps the box-offices with the campest naval performance (by Johnny Depp) since Charles Hawtrey. A few lacy bosoms being chased around the mainmast and Disney will have a great series to carry on through the new century. The desert behind us, our spirits lift. We are thoroughly exhausted. As you grow older, driving hours have to be adjusted to allow for a certain diminishment of stamina. I have a wounded foot, so must sit in the back seat with my legs stretched out on the folded-down front seats. Beside me are our amiable cats, disdaining cages. The inside of the car resembles a mixture of first world war field hospital and mobile menagerie. Clean and considerate, the cats love travelling, investigating every new motel with relish. Beds are swiftly selected as territory. Having been confined all day, they spend the night at play, which adds to our exhaustion. One night we take an adjoining room for them. Our tempers improve. The Promised Land of peace and plenty lies only a matter of hours away.

Leave the Bible Belt behind and the number of evangelical Christian radio stations actually increases. Maybe they aren't needed in Texas, where even the most politically liberal people tend to be regular churchgoers. In California it's hard to find a station that isn't preaching at you. We settle for National Public Radio when we can receive it. Until times like this, you tend to forget what a cultural treasure the BBC is. Much talk of lies and deception over the invasion of Iraq. On the motel's television I watch White House advisers being questioned by Congress. They resemble the old commies and Trots one argued with in the 1950s and '60s. They have learned the power of the dialectic. They can do the Q&A. Anything you ask they have heard before. Anything which opposes their rote logic is sentimental or naive. It makes you wonder if those old sf stories about the authoritarian takeover of the US are actually coming true. Of course, that's where I've read it all before! In Dick and Bradbury, in warning fables published in 1950s American magazines with titles like *Amazing*, *Astounding* and *Startling*. Sadly, not so amazing or startling these days.

Here in liberal northern California, as in Hampstead, a lot of people think they've found the moral high ground just because they can afford to live on top of the hill. My first long dinner subject here was crop circles. My second was consumerism. Most people up here own houses worth at least a million dollars and aren't expecting wolves at the door come winter. Chain stores, such as WalMart, are disdainfully excluded from the county. You have to travel almost to San Francisco to find a Toys 'R' Us. My friends sneer at consumerism, which they identify with a mall culture which has seen shopping become America's only leisure activity. Straight-faced, Linda complains that this year the boutiques don't have any clothes she wants. Immediately, our friends begin telling her about the best places to buy shoes and frocks. Sometimes you wonder which brand of hypocrisy is the most preferable, Southern Baptist or Secular Liberal?

Of course, we've travelled from a world where George Bush is a popular hero to one where he might as well be the Antichrist incarnate. We go from being the only ones in town with an 'Americans for Peace' sign in our front yard to the only ones in town who believe that there is anything to be said for the old anti-imperialist Republican tradition, as represented, for example, by Ron Paul, the Texas congressman who has spoken out against the administration's policies in Iraq and Afghanistan. Not that I could vote Republican (if I had the vote, which, as an Englishman, I do not). As far as Democratic presidential candidates go, my money's on Howard Dean, because he talks a good, realistic game. I believe that even if he doesn't get to be president—and I think his chances are slim—there will be a large enough vote for him to show that millions of Americans still hold American democratic values and share a growing repugnance for ugly and violent rhetoric which has no place in this wonderful country's politics.

I'm here mainly to retreat, to work on the last book in the sequence I've been writing for almost thirty years, beginning with *Byzantium Endures*. It's taken four volumes to show how many millions of individuals conspired in the Nazi Holocaust. My disagreeable and paranoid narrator, Colonel Pyat, is now experiencing some of the realities which led to Hitler and what followed. He's getting chummy with the likes of Mussolini and Röhm.

On Tuesday we arrived at the pale, balmy beaches of San Andreas Bay, where the shore is smooth and virtually deserted, the surf is gentle, the sea is blue. There are no touts, no commercial pressures of any kind—unless you count the squawk of the seabirds—and all I have to think about for the next couple of months is the random movement of a few tectonic plates.

From the *Spectator*

# ■ Diary: 7th January 2006

Thanks to the wonderful French health service—specifically, beautiful Dr Jeanne at Salpêtrière Hospital, Paris—I'm now much more mobile again, my wounded foot only short of a couple of toes and no further mumbling from US medics about amputation. I spent some months in a wheelchair being pushed to the Bon Marché or the Jardins du Luxembourg by Ashley, a pleasant Mauritian student. In my ice-cream suit and panama, I was tempted to insist on being called 'Colonel' but was nevertheless surprised by how many tourists took my picture as I sat working in the park. Lunching outside at the Brasserie Luxembourg, Boulevard St-Michel, with my dandy friend, the ace rock guitarist turned antiquarian book dealer, Martin Stone, we were disturbed by flashes from Japanese tourists' cameras. As we sipped our coffee, a pleasant American and his daughter approached us. In simple French they politely asked permission to snap us. Amiably we agreed, whereupon the American thanked us warmly. It was a pleasure, he said, to come across two real Parisians at last. We realised that as long as we kept our mouths shut an easy career opportunity had opened up for us in our remaining years. Les deux Parisiens vrais. T-shirts? Posters? Mugs?

Back in Texas, via my dentist in liberal northern California (all pixilated and un-PC, flattered over the Prince of Wales's interest in local organics), we scarcely unpacked before setting off to visit my wife's mother in Mississippi for Christmas. Neither recent hurricane did much damage to my wife Linda's hometown, but the devastation between Beaumont, Texas, and Lafayette, Louisiana, was terrible. Huge trees down, houses turned to matchwood, bright blue plastic replacing roofs of churches, stores and homes. Massive, tottering piles of fallen trees lining the roadside. Some houses abandoned, the crushing trunks of trees still lying on their remains. Metal signboards twisted like discarded beer cans. Roads full of trucks hauling lumber and prefab houses: 160,000 homes in New Orleans were ruined. 'God ain't helping us,' said one refugee, 'so I hope the Devil will.'

Born in Clarksdale, Linda was raised in West Point, Mississippi where the great bluesman Chester 'Howlin' Wolf' Burnett also grew up. (Martin Stone backed Wolf on two of his British tours.) With desegregation, the whites decided swiftly to fill in the town swimming pool and turn it into a park. Today Wolf's three-quarter-size monument (he was a huge man) stands looking no doubt rather sardonically over the flower beds. There's now a museum dedicated to him: West Point's most famous rejected son is the town's only profitable tourist attraction.

Heading back to Texas, we eat at Prejean's Cajun restaurant in Lafayette where the waitress recommends the Croc de Jacques, but neither of us enjoys alligator. You can, however, hear great music and see some of the most graceful dancing in Acadiana. While we eat the best catfish in the world, Woody Daigle, Ray Lavergne, Yves Thibodeaux and Vincent Romero play triangle, accordion, fiddle and guitar. Voices rich as filet gumbo, performing two-steps, waltzes and polkas which, these days, only the old people seem to know, moving with such straightbacked grace they might be on castors. Woody's wife Thelma stops by our table. Cajun French is her native language, but she also uses that disappearing old, precise Dixie English. You can hear it on recordings of Faulkner and Welty. There are dozens of Cajun dialects across Acadiana, all of them, she says, going back to the 18th century and different French regions. Where she will say *J'ai allé*, others just a parish away will say *J'ai couri*. We mourn how few dancers there are left these days. You might be lucky to see some on the restaurant's live webcam if you go to www.Prejeans.com.

Houston bypassed, it's back up towards Austin beside the Southern Pacific, 100 cars pulled by three locos. You can hear the whistle blow, lonesome and low, just the way Howlin' Wolf sang. New estates full of identical 'McMansions', now called villages in realtor's jargon, surround strip malls with identical clothing outlets, identical burger and Tex-Mex chains, Starbucks; brand-names found from Anchorage to Abilene. You can identify the newest by their Olde Englishe place-names. I half expect to spot Ambridge-in-the-Wold. They make Milton Keynes look positively picturesque.

At last we're back. Lost Pines and the Old Circle Squared, our Graeco-Southern house, built in 1865 by Texas's only Confederate governor. I hardly have time to read the mail and write this before we leave for London to promote my final Colonel Pyat novel, about the events and attitudes which permitted the Nazi Holocaust. I think I have a new persona. Having been the sci-fi guy when the media needed one, I became the counter-culture guy for a while, then, for a brief, enjoyable time, the Arab literature guy, then the London guy (Sinclair and Ackroyd now share that role). I hope I won't be the Nazi Holocaust guy for long.

I take a breather before hitting the keyboard. It's a cool 65°F under our pecan, walnut and oak trees. Our patient, much-travelled cats follow me out to the back porch. I pick up my guitar. Now I remember why I chose Texas as my American home. In the distance the freight train moans long and slow and I can't resist playing a few bars of 'Smokestack Lightnin' ' in homage to Howlin' Wolf who brought the blues to London, inspiring the Rolling Stones and the rest of us. Whoo-eee. It won't be long before I'm on the road again.

From the *Financial Times*

# ■ Diary: 26th October 2007

**Suture Imperfect**

House-hunting is at the best of times an experience rivalling divorce and map-reading as one of the most hellish the average European can go through; house-hunting in a foreign language is that much harder. We're looking for an apartment in Paris. In spite of reports informing us that the price of property has dropped or, at least, frozen, prices here seem to rise every few seconds. Hideous, dark, minuscule basement hovels in Montmartre might even inspire a romantic response, as you imagine a thrice-ruined character from Balzac spending his dying months picking at the thin coverlet on his bug-infested mattress, as he waits hopelessly for some uncaring offspring to knock on the rotting wood of the door. But for this, they're asking €400,000. Why is it that these days the apartment you want, whether you're in London, Paris or central Texas (where we also live) always costs just that much more than you want to pay? Mind you, given the real fall in property prices and the exchange rate, for the same money in Texas we could probably buy ourselves a good-sized ranch, stocked with a mature herd of longhorns for about half what a two-bedroom apartment in the 15th would cost us.

In our part of rural Texas, many skilled people still can't afford to look after their families on a day-to-day basis and pay for decent health insurance. Recently, the man who maintains our house cut his hand with his chainsaw. He couldn't afford a doctor so he went to the local WalMart and bought himself something commonly sold there—a kit for sewing up your own wounds. He was very proud of the neat job he had done, though admitting that he almost fainted a couple of times in the process. What astonished us was that such kits, looking a bit like bicycle puncture repair ones, should be on sale at all. After recently benefiting so much from the

French health system and understanding that there are funding problems that have to be addressed, I'm still worried that the somewhat distracted Nicolas Sarkozy will try to privatise along US lines. We complain a lot about the NHS but, after everything I've witnessed in America, where brilliant treatments are available only to those who can afford them, I would still rather take my chances in a 'socialised' system. If I had to choose between spending my last years in the US or France, there's absolutely no question where I'd rather be. And that thought spurs me on to further, rather more optimistic home-hunting.

The Parisian transport strike made searching a bit harder last week. It would have helped if I'd been in a position to ride a bike. My agent's car is garaged some distance from where he lives so he decided to keep his appointments by motorbike. Then his motorbike broke down. Undaunted, he went to his nearest Vélib station and got himself a bicycle for the day. This system of municipal bikes that can be picked up at one station and left at another has been a brilliant success in Paris and is a lot more popular than the bus and taxi-lanes that now create, in certain parts of the city, almost unblockable jams, especially on Fridays. The other positive thing about Vélib is that it's stimulated the sale of bikes enormously, as people discover the pleasures and ease of cycling in what is, after all, a very small city compared to London. I wonder if Ken Livingstone or his successor could ensure his popularity by installing a similar system. I'm sure Boris Johnson would back it.

The chief reason for buying a place in Paris is because Eurostar gets us to London, my children and grandchildren faster than the average train from, say, Manchester. And most of Paris still retains its old, local character. Although I still love London, I don't like what heritage developers have made of her. Every small town in the US nowadays has to have some 'historic' monument to attract tourist money, in order to support the kind of civic infrastructure people used to take pride in paying for. It saddens me that so much of London now runs on the same economic logic, resulting in the heritaging up of every obscure nook and idiosyncratic cranny Londoners used to think of as their own.

On Friday night I shall make a quick dash to the Bishopsgate Institute, near Liverpool Street station, at 6:30 sharp to take part in London Lip, a celebration of *London: City of Disappearances*—Iain Sinclair's latest compendium of writing about the capital. Alan Moore, me and Sinclair himself will discuss changing times and mythologies while Kirsten Norrie and Brian Catlin liven things up with their performances. Then it's back to Paris to do a nostalgic reading at Shakespeare and Co, where I used to busk outside to get money for books when I was a lad.

Another good reason for not wanting to live permanently in England was illustrated last Saturday night by the spectacle of English rugger fans on the loose. Why they decided to stock up on booze in our local shops I've no idea. They shove past queuing, purse-lipped old ladies, shouting over their heads to one another. 'Better get another couple of six packs! Oh, and a bottle of wine for the girls.' You immediately see the function of the women. It's to carry the beer. With red crosses all over their faces, on their hats, on their shirts, they threaten to put the *entente cordiale* back to the time of Agincourt. I do my best to shrink. I think of feigning muteness. Thankfully, my wife Linda's accent is American. Mine is so clearly English there's no escape for me even when I'm buying bread at my favourite *boulangerie*. Years of goodwill fly away as the fans stand yelling outside the door: 'They haven't *got* any *proper* sandwiches!' Next morning, when we take our Sunday stroll beside the Seine, little pockets of them wander dazedly along the Quai d'Orsay. Now, at least, they resemble a defeated army, their uniforms hidden in their packs, hoping to sneak home undetected.

From the *Financial Times*

# ■ Diary: 12th April 2008

**In the Oxygen Chamber with a Spacey Fan**

Possibly as a result of time spent pounding Parisian pavements last year while flat-hunting, I have had to have an infected toe amputated. Now I'm having hyperbaric treatment, which helps your super-oxygenated blood get busy healing the wound. Hyperbarics has already saved my foot once and I'm convinced it will save it again. However, it once had a bad reputation. Stories that Michael Jackson slept every night in a hyperbaric chamber didn't help. Had he actually done so, he'd now be dead as more than three or four hours of pure oxygen can poison you. What's more, the chamber requires a gradual rise and fall in pressure to ensure patients don't get what divers call 'the bends'.

The chamber in Austin holds compressed air at around three times sea-level pressure. It is rather like a mini-sub, with portholes through which you can, if you wish, watch the operators watching you. For the pure compressed oxygen, you wear a clear plastic helmet, which makes you look like an actor in a 1960s episode of *The Twilight Zone*. In a communal chamber (there are other kinds), you can read, write or watch TV. The other advantage to this system is that I'm brought in daily contact with my fellow Texans, some of whom are studying, reading Tocqueville for pleasure, or watching reruns of teen comedies.

Though crammed with brainy people, Austin also has its share of paranoid know-nothings, who are ignorant of the world, including the US. One woman told my wife Linda how scared her Baptist missionary son had been in Calcutta, where 'all those people really hate Americans'. Trying to make friends, her son had approached 'some of those Muslims' but they showed considerable anti-American sentiments. Linda gently suggested that maybe they were a bit over-familiar with Christian missionaries, especially those who confused Hindus with Muslims. Someone else chimed in to say how terrified of being knifed they had felt in such anti-American strongholds as Brussels and Amsterdam. They shared strong views on the United Nations, the federal government 'giving away' money to Africa and John McCain's unnerving liberalism. Reflecting sentiments that run the length of the nation's spine, they are in no doubt that 9/11 was the result of a plot between al-Qaeda, Iran and Iraq. They're also anti-immigrant and antisemitic but absolutely love Brits.

Nevertheless, Austin doesn't conform to European stereotypes of Texas. Newcomers are always surprised by its parks, lakes, hills and woods. Once west of here you get into country more readily associated with Larry McMurtry and Cormac McCarthy—hundreds of miles of desert and scrubland. At the moment, though, unusual rainfall has perked up the badlands a treat. Vivid carpets of wildflowers are everywhere. A friend is desperately trying to sell his land to some unsuspecting Yankee speculator while the desert blooms. Another couple of days and it could again become the kind of vastness John Wayne might contemplate as he weighs up the choice between surviving the terrain ahead or the pursuing posse.

As you go east towards Louisiana, the landscape, though greener, can be even more depressing than the desert. Katrina's damage to the settlements along Interstate 10 resembles that done by the Blitz. Bright blue plastic still covers what's left of roofs. We sympathise with the resentment of people making the best they can of living there while a growing recession further reduces their quality of life. Despite the money and physical help sent by churches and charities, very little seems to improve. A presidential candidate who could guarantee real help to our disaster spots would do well. But while it seems Obama has sewn up the black vote, many black friends of our age or older are firm Clinton supporters. They detect a line from FDR through LBJ to HRC and see certain other members of the Washington establishment as mistaken in allowing the 'untried' Obama to run.

As I recovered from my treatments, I decided to return to my literary roots. Not HG Wells, as some might guess, but PG Wodehouse, especially his pre-1925 fiction. I start with his school stories in *The Captain*, the adventures of Psmith, the Ukridge stories and the likes of *Piccadilly Jim*, all of which are distinguished by observation, rather than formula. PGW was well into his career before hitting on the Commedia dell'arte approach of using brilliantly conceived stock characters in clever farces. Fine as these later novels are, I prefer him before the real world finally faded around him and he became the man capable of making those infamous Second World

War Berlin broadcasts that you can find on the internet. He was no traitor but it is noticeable how he heaps all calumny on our defeated allies, the French and Belgians, and lets the Nazis off.

There's a downside to hyperbarics that I haven't mentioned: it might impair your hearing. At the insistence of a couple of fellow divers watching TV in the communal tank, I suffered through two hours of *Beyond the Sea*, Kevin Spacey's 2004 biopic of the third-rate pop singer Bobby Darin, who died in his mid-thirties after attempting to sound like, among others, Presley, Sinatra, Dylan and even Ella Fitzgerald. Much as I admire Spacey's revivification of the Old Vic, I am heartfelt in my prayers that he keep his dosh firmly in his pocket next time he develops a similar musical enthusiasm. Otherwise, I won't be able to trust myself. Some dark night, as he locks the stage door behind him, Spacey had better watch the shadows for a man on crutches, with a small black cat on his shoulder, clacking remorselessly in pursuit. There will be no escape.

From the *Financial Times*

# ■ Diary: 4th October 2008

I'm becoming a bit of an expert at low-tech global performance. Last weekend, at an event honouring my friend and colleague Robert Calvert, who died of a heart attack twenty years ago, I attempted to bellow a few lyrics down the blower from Texas while, in Kent, Nik Turner, who was a bandmate of mine and Calvert's in the prog-rock band Hawkwind, held the phone up to a microphone. To picture the effect, think *Spinal Tap*.

This transatlantic tribute was to celebrate the under-appreciated work of a witty and inventive singer/songwriter. Calvert's first solo album, 1974's *Captain Lockheed and the Starfighters* was followed, a year later, by my favourite, *Lucky Leif and the Longships*, produced by Brian Eno, on which I—as an occasional Calvert collaborator—had a lot of fun doing banjo and background vocals. I later graduated to a 12-string Rickenbacker on his 1981 album *Hype*, which accompanied Calvert's novel of the same name, and, with my wife Linda, sang backgrounds on his fine single 'The Greenfly and the Rose'. Happy days.

Calvert was a brilliant performer but psychologically unsuited to the rock and roll life. He was bipolar and his friendship could be rewarding and exhausting. His ambition was to be a poet and playwright. His other work included a play about Jimi Hendrix, *The Stars That Play with Laughing Sam's Dice*. I suspect he would have gone on to do great things.

As Iggy Pop said recently, contemporary rock and roll often rocks and frequently rolls but it rarely does both. This was demonstrated to a degree last Saturday night at the annual Austin City Limits festival in Texas, when Robert Plant and Alison Krauss performed. I love them together but have to admit the music is high-end easy-listening. Beck, in a cowboy hat, closed the festival in what was almost lullaby mode. Favourites of mine, such as David Byrne, John Fogerty and the Raconteurs, were also on the bill but I'd like to have seen more local bands, since so many of America's best musicians make their homes in Austin.

Someone who certainly rocks and rolls is my friend and neighbour Ian 'Mac' McLagan (the former Faces keyboardist) and I was sorry to see that he wasn't performing at the festival. At the moment he's in England with his Bump Band, so check him out if you get the chance. Mac has toured with the Stones, Dylan, Bonnie Raitt and is a member of Billy Bragg's band. He is also the author of *All the Rage*, one of the best rock autobiographies. In it you'll find a picture of Howlin' Wolf, whom Mac's first band, the Muleskinners, backed on an English tour. Wolf sits in the front of a Roller, full of his famous gravitas, while Mac's teenage face beams ecstatically from the back seat.

Wolf is arguably the greatest bluesman ever—he and Woody Guthrie were my first musical heroes. I'm reminded of him whenever I visit West Point, Mississippi, which is both Wolf's and my wife's home town. When I first went there thirty years ago, almost nobody, black or white, had heard of him. Then they discovered he was famous, a tourist attraction, and now they hold a blues festival in his name every year. He was a huge man and a three-quarter life-size monument to him now looks over the town park created after the swimming pool was filled in following desegregation. The other remarkable feature of West Point is the massive concrete cross erected outside the high school and painted red, white and blue with the stars and stripes. That's the Bible Belt for you.

The evangelical Christian sign of the fish appears everywhere in the Bible Belt, on all kinds of businesses, from car dealerships to druggists. But the strangest to set up in our Texan town recently is the Christian Fitness Center. Muscular Christianity indeed!

The fish is a powerful brand and nobody underestimates its effect in trade or politics. In the past decade, the deep south has not only seen a revival of dispensationalism—a theology that emphasises the imminent return of Christ—but of overt racialism. Many white southerners are openly declaring they won't vote for a black man, although they're not too sure about McCain/Palin either. For some Republican friends, the selection of Palin was the last straw and they'll be voting Democrat.

Because of a recent trip to Mississippi, we never made it to our local rodeo this year. During the parade down Main Street, a bored longhorn apparently broke away from the others, pursued by a young cowboy. Spurring his bronc and whirling his lariat, he cast the noose neatly over the animal's horns and, to the town's great delight, was promptly pulled from his saddle. The steer was soon discovered a couple of hundred yards away, placidly cropping the grass outside the courthouse. The young cowboy was found in a nearby bar, his hat pulled well down over his face.

Meanwhile, we returned expecting to have to deal with Hurricane Ike and felt a bit foolish when it skimmed past us, hardly bringing a drop of the rain we need. Now we're looking at the piles of bottled water, gas cylinders, batteries and canned food that we'd been advised to stock. At our first opportunity, we plan to take it down to Galveston, which was hit hard. A friend there e-mailed to warn us to prepare for the one thing TV news coverage never quite leads you to expect: the smell. I remember how my car stank after vandals had driven it into a river but I'm sure that's nothing to how the Gulf coast must smell to our friends picking through the remains of their damaged homes.

At the time of writing, we still don't know the exact nature of the Wall Street bail-out but the irony of Republicans pressing for what amounts to nationalisation, while Democrats resist the idea, hasn't gone unremarked by Texan satirists such as Jim Hightower. We hear rumours about migrant settlements being sighted in the back country further west—semi-mobile tent towns of the newly homeless, resembling the 'Hoovervilles' of the Great Depression. Meanwhile, along our interstates are whole ghost towns of new homes thrown up in anticipation of a never-ending lending boom. I'm wondering how long it will be before local authorities requisition the abandoned McMansions in order to shelter the homeless and avoid events familiar to those of us who grew up watching *The Grapes of Wrath*, though it will be a shame we won't have Woody Guthrie to write the soundtrack.

From the *Financial Times*

# ■ Diary: 28th March 2009

Unable to make it to Paris this spring, my wife Linda and I, along with our cats Bill and Betty, are heading towards the Mississippi Delta, via a science fiction convention in Biloxi.

With its tall Greek-columned houses, the holiday homes of southern aristocrats, Biloxi was once a rather genteel resort: Hove to New Orleans' Brighton. But, after Hurricane Katrina, she is taking longer to restore herself than New Orleans and, sadly, might never come back as she was.

Flat, gleaming white sands again stretch down to the water of the Gulf of Mexico; the occasional hotel stands where there used to be a 'steamboat gothic' mansion. But a few yards from our hotel, all that remains of a family and its memories are the foundations of a house, a weathered For Sale sign, and huge heaps of newly delivered sand giving an alpine contour to the landscape. Bulldozers stand ready to lay the beach down as soon as a viable property has been erected on the other side of the promenade. But there are more lots for sale than have been sold.

I rarely attend SF conventions. Sentiment got me involved in this one. Biloxi is in my wife's home state and my old friend and illustrator, John Picacio, was a guest of honour. The people running it were courteously southern. But I haven't really been to a regular SF convention for years, so was unprepared for the changes I found. Now, such conventions are frequently supported by role-playing gamers. They play for hours, rolling dice and muttering as they perform mysterious strategies and move tiny figures in what HG Wells called 'little wars'. Frequently, the participants dress as elaborately as the characters they represent. If so much of what I see strikes me as vaguely familiar it's because, along with Tolkien, I've been a main influence on gaming ever since the publication in the late 1970s of the first Dungeons and Dragons rulebook, which contained my fantasy 'pantheon' of characters, demons, deities, magical concepts, symbols and other stuff drawn from my stories.

Having created so much of the fundamental elements found in fantasy games and fiction, it's weird for me to observe my own private tools passing into common ownership. For instance, the kid wearing that 'Chaos' sign on his T-shirt has no idea that, circa 1963, I was trying to think of a symbol for entropy and drew the thing on a piece of scrap paper in our kitchen. Arthur C Clarke used to complain he never got a penny for predicting the communications satellite. Now I know what it's like to be old.

As a group of us discuss the work of Balzac in relation to French imaginative fiction, I say that these days it is impossible for anyone to tell you they don't like science fiction. SF is so diverse it would be like someone telling you they don't like poetry. While I've read almost no SF or fantasy for decades, I still believe that a reader merely reveals their lack of education by dismissing such an extraordinarily broad field out of hand. Readers of PD James might not consider her novel *Children of Men* (1992) to be science fiction, for example, but if it isn't SF, then there is no such thing as SF. Several of us agree on this, if nothing else.

We pass Hattiesburg, where a few years ago my son Max got his degree, and travel on to Laurel. Here, we once shared a great southern experience. Taking Max up to see his Mississippi grandmother, we spotted a sign for the local county fair. One of its chief attractions was all-day pig racing. Linda has never been able to resist the prospect of a really good pig race. Like most old-fashioned fairs of its kind, this one was a mixture of carnival, freak show, travelling zoo and church fête.

We were enjoying an evangelical Punch and Judy show, when Beau attached himself to us. Beau was about the size and shape of Ratso Rizzo, Dustin Hoffman's character in *Midnight Cowboy*. He wore a filthy white cowboy hat, cracked, worn-out western boots and a greasy red, white and blue shirt. He was grotesquely ugly, stank and was clearly simple. Fixing us with a friendly eye, he elected to be our tour guide. 'That's the carousel, this here's the bearded lady. Over there's your two-headed man. And here's the zoo!'

He brightened. The zoo was horrible: a stinking tent filled with rows of various sizes of pet cages containing mostly common forms of local wildlife. 'He's a alligator. He'd bite y'all's arm off soon as look at y'all. Thet there's a raccoon. Make good eating if y'all kin ketch yerself one. See the bobcat? Hey!' The dying animal looked up through tired, uncaring eyes. Beau produced a stick and began inserting it through the wire. 'He'll liven up if ya poke him!' The cat uttered a half-hearted snarl; the nearby alligator tried to sink into its too-shallow water.

We fled from Beau into a tent where, to our astonishment, a cheerleading contest was being held. In the deepest heart of the Baptist Bible Belt, these cheerleaders were aged between four and nine, and heavy with make-up (mascara, blusher, lipstick) and perms. They looked like downmarket Tokyo whores. The creators of these creatures, good Baptist pimp-moms to a woman, urged their offspring on to greater deeds of hip-jutting, chest-thrusting, bottom-pushing cheerleading prowess.

We slipped out and were just able to catch the start of the pig race—black ones running against white. The prize? An Oreo cookie. Those pigs were as hooked on Oreos as some of their human equivalents were on steroids. Just as well there was no betting or I'd have felt obliged to complain to the pig racing authorities.

The road from Laurel to West Point grows more and more beautiful. Red clover rises from the lush grass; redbud trees are in bloody bloom, dogwoods are bursts of white against evergreens dripping with wild blue or white wisteria. The air is warm and smells dry. The sun sets, a ruby blaze against gold, hiding sad recent histories. Clarksdale in the spring. Only a bit of a change from Paris.

From the *Financial Times*

# ■ Diary: 31st October 2009

Paris in October tends to be my favourite place and time—though there are specific dangers to someone still on crutches, as I am, not least the special bike lanes. I approve of these but it can be hard trying to hop for safety at the sound of a tinkling bell as a pious two-wheeler comes zooming out of the sun. Golden leaves, picturesque as they are, can cause me a nasty skid. Even pregnant women have apparently less right to the pavement than a stern youngster on a *Vélib'*.

Nonetheless, coming from Texas—where I live for much of the year—to Paris, I think anyone in the US who believes they have the 'best healthcare in the world' should sample the French system. You can see a specialist here in the blink of an eye, appointments are arranged in an instant, doctors still visit and the rate of medical error is considerably lower.

The chances of real healthcare reform in the US do not look good. A Parisian banker friend observes, sadly: 'My heart is conservative, but in the States I know I'd be called a communist.' He supports France's health system but not its current president (the principled right here also despairs of Sarko's nepotism and empire building). Like so many European conservatives, he is rooting for Obama.

The TGV speeds us to Switzerland and the pretty old spa town of Yverdon-les-Bains. On the station I'm met by a cheery wheelchair attendant who gets me into a car, and before long we're at the science fiction museum Maison d'Ailleurs (House of Elsewhere). I'm to speak at the opening of the most spectacular exhibition of Mervyn Peake drawings to be shown on the continent, brought together by curator Patrick Gyger.

Peake, who died in 1968, is now best known for his Titus Groan series— *Titus Groan, Gormenghast* and *Titus Alone*—perhaps the greatest work of imagination in English of the 20th century, following in the tradition of

Laurence Sterne, Thomas Love Peacock or Lewis Carroll. But early in his career he was perceived as a brilliant draughtsman and portraitist who wrote prose chiefly for children and poetry for adults. The drawings on display remind us of this earlier reputation—illustrations for Carroll's Alice books and Peake's own children's books such as *Captain Slaughterboard Drops Anchor* or *A Book of Nonsense*, but also pictures for his novels, including the gentle parable *Mr Pye*, are present.

His Alice drawings remain, in my view, superior to all others, including Tenniel's original wood engravings for the first edition of *Alice in Wonderland*, and his illustrations for *Treasure Island*, *Strange Case of Dr Jekyll and Mr Hyde* and other classics are also arguably the best ever done. While I was familiar with many of the drawings I had never seen them so superbly displayed. NC Wyeth, Howard Pyle, Arthur Rackham and Heath Robinson have produced memorable illustrations for many of those books but none, I think, as stunning or as authoritative as Peake's. My favourite single drawing is probably of Israel Hands's fall from the topmast, which perfectly matches the power of Robert Louis Stevenson's prose.

I was lucky enough to have been befriended by Peake and his wife Maeve but later witnessed his terrible collapse into Parkinsonism. His children and many of his grandchildren were present at the opening, some faces at once identifiable as his models, and even characters in *Titus Groan* are recognisable as versions of his nearest and dearest. Too often seen as a rather doomed figure, Peake is best remembered by friends and family for his ebullient drollery, present here at every turn. His Long John Silver is powerful but subtly sinister, in contrast to the comical crew Slaughterboard commands.

The book accompanying the exhibition is exquisitely produced with a long introduction in French and English by Peake's biographer G Peter Winnington, and its reproductions are the closest to the originals I have seen. They rival those in the recent *Mervyn Peake: The Man and His Art* (Peter Owen) compiled by Sebastian Peake and Alison Eldred and edited by Winnington. There's nothing better, however, than seeing the originals, and our pleasure was increased by spending so much time in the company of the Peake family, which did me quite as much good as any amount of even the very best French doctoring.

The trip back to Paris wasn't quite as comfortable, vis-à-vis two large ladies returning from a communism conference in Dijon who weren't strong on the equal distribution of space. But again, as we joined a depressingly long line for taxis at Gare de Lyon, I was gently hooked out of the queue by a station official who summoned a taxi and popped us in it without a murmur of complaint from any fellow travellers. Such an action might have caused a minor riot at an Amtrak terminus. A dozen voices would have risen to assert their rights to our cab.

Back to our place on Rue des Vinaigriers, near Canal St-Martin in a pleasant area convenient to the Eurostar terminal. The neighbourhood is still *populaire*—that is, mixed and cosmopolitan—arrested in its climb towards *bobo* gentrification by the crunch. We're rather glad it has kept its character, adding only a couple of posh shops and an internet café to its mix of north African grocers and Vietnamese takeaways. Senegalese, Chinese, Indians and some Italians make up much of the population, resulting in an astonishing variety of great, relatively cheap restaurants.

In a couple of weeks I'll be speaking at a private celebration of my friend JG Ballard's life. Another unique talent. I've been privileged to know some of the most imaginative artists of our time. Like Peake, Ballard's childhood was spent in China and his apparently dark vision was also full of perceptive wit. It will feel a bit hard to leave this sophisticated, cosmopolitan environment and return to Texas which, for all its many virtues, is not generally familiar with the rest of the world. Too frequently one has to explain, for instance, who Sarkozy is before continuing a conversation. President Obama would no doubt be enjoying an easier time should a larger proportion of his electorate be as casually well-educated as the French middle class.

I'll be returning to an intellectual environment marked by its provincialism, preferring hearsay to information. I hope, however, that I won't display the arrogance of most Europeans who think they know America mostly from her on-screen entertainment and who tend to mock American ignorance of the world. Everyone thinks they know 'America' but few foreigners really do understand her in all her unique complexity. Obama is not only fighting powerful international vested interests spending billions to protect themselves from his reforms, he is trying to address that profoundly felt individualism that informs the mythology, if not the reality, of modern America.

From the *Financial Times*

# ■ Diary: 15th May 2010

I'm just completing my 'Doctor Who' novel. It's been fun and also harder work than I expected. I've no idea how it will be received. Humour and wild science fiction ideas are the series' hallmark, so I decided to write it as if PG Wodehouse and Arthur C Clarke had collaborated. I hope it comes up to the high standards the existing TV writers have set. To get myself in the mood I read Barry Pain, the Edwardian writer who was Wodehouse's main inspiration. I knew I wasn't up to rivalling the master. Wodehouse and Clarke had more in common than I at first supposed. Wodehouse wrote the odd fantasy story and Clarke could be amusing, if not exactly a rib-tickler. Both writers were quintessentially English, yet both spent most of their lives out of the country, survived a scandal and received knighthoods late in life.

I never met Wodehouse, who was my favourite writer as a boy, but Clarke was a friend whom I liked a great deal. When I wrote to sympathise with him about the *Sunday Mirror*'s allegations regarding his sex life in 1998 he took the whole thing with his usual Wodehousian sunniness. He told me it was obviously a plot to embarrass his pal Prince Charles and not to worry, his friend Rupert Murdoch would sort it out for him. He and 'Plum' [Wodehouse] had the same way of dealing with trouble, were not altogether of this world and lived long, productive, athletic and rather enviable lives.

Although I'm often referred to as a science fiction writer, I've written comparatively few SF novels, most of them in the 1960s when I was lucky enough to think of a few ideas which turned out to be fairly accurate. In 1961 I came up with the 'multiverse'—the notion of a near-infinite number of parallel universes nesting inside the other—and also predicted what we now call black holes and miniaturised computers (this was in the days when computers took up whole buildings and, logically, a better one was always a bigger one) but they weren't based on any profound knowledge of astrophysics. If anything the ideas had more in common with metaphysics. Still, I'm proud of my predictions. Whether I'll be so lucky with this new story remains to be seen.

The Doctor's job done, I'd hoped to borrow the Tardis and leave Texas, where I live for much of the year, for Europe. The BBC haven't yet responded to my request. If they do I suppose it will be the usual red tape about time paradoxes and all that. Even if we're forced on to more conventional transport, I'll be glad to get out of Texas, where the temperature is over 90°F most days now.

That said, we have a great time in Austin. During the recent SXSW music festival a huge variety of music was heard across the city. You could walk less than a block and hear western swing, salsa, hardcore rock, reggae, bluegrass, indie or zydeco—everything but commercial pop. The festival blends scores of influences. Even traditional country music has a far greater range than many realise, as heard on Willie Nelson's latest album, *Country Music*. Willie, of course, is pretty much on a level with God in this bible belt state. A few years ago a rookie cop inspected a truck on the side of the road. There he found Willie asleep, a strong smell of top-quality skunk wafting from his glove compartment. So he arrested Willie. As Texans anticipated, when the case came to court, Willie walked. The cop was fired. Willie represents the progressive individualistic style you find in Texas, always ready to support a good cause. He's seventy-three now and still touring. A city couldn't have a better ambassador.

A major advantage to living in the Texas hill country is, especially after a wet winter, the gorgeously varied wealth of wild flowers that stretches for miles. Lady Bird Johnson, former first lady, established a wildflower centre near Austin and made city authorities stop cutting highway verges willy-nilly. Some farmers let fields lie fallow so when we drive the backroads we see a tapestry of astonishing colour and richness, second only, in my experience, to the high meadows of Morocco's Atlas mountains. Newcomers expect dust and cactus so it's always a pleasure to show off the flowers and the city's civilised attention to green spaces, trees and waterside walks.

Another of Austin's treasures is the huge collection of modernist manuscripts, visual art and rare books kept at the University of Texas's Harry Ransom Center. This is largely the work of the literary scholar Tom Staley, who used the university's wealth to put together an unrivalled resource. They have Charlotte Brontë's earliest notebooks written in a tiny but decipherable hand, Norman Mailer's office reproduced in its entirety and collections from living writers. I was delighted when they purchased my friend Iain Sinclair's papers, inviting him to help with their cataloguing.

Sinclair, who is London's leading psychogeographer and author of *Downriver, Lights Out for the Territory* and *Hackney, That Rose-Red Empire*, was asked to give some poetry readings, a talk and appear with me for a public conversation. We discussed the modern mythology that draws writers to London or Texas. I was attracted to the state because you can witness myths being made and embellished almost by the day. In our little town, a few miles from Austin, the Tractor Store still sells working chaps, hats, saddles, boots and lariats. Working cowboys still sometimes ride down Main Street to tie their horses up outside the local saloon, some packing long-barrelled .38s. A friend who writes fine books about the Wild West insists on sporting black-powder Colt revolvers.

I have one or two myself that I keep unloaded and often imagine catching a burglar in the living room, then asking him to wait a few minutes while I ram gunpowder into the chambers and fix my firing caps. Mainly I just like to practice my quick draws, border rolls, Mexican switches and other fancy tricks learned as a boy when the local common stood in for the prairie and I was the only law west of the Circle Line. My tricks are pretty impressive but my wife still insists I practise my yodelling in the garage.

Explaining the English elections to American friends has proven a bit tricky recently. Personally, I suspect more Brits are now enfranchised. We might just get some decent moderate rational progress, for which we're often admired. I'm only worried by 'Atlanticists' who think that borrowing US solutions to our problems is all that's needed. Home-grown methods are always the sturdiest. I'm embarrassed by British politicians' US-style campaigning. There's material for a good comic novel about MPs desperately looking for a black candidate to become Britain's prime minister. I suspect all Obama needs to do to ensure his next job is establish his British dual nationality. He could probably lead a consensual coalition as Britain's next prime minister. I'd applaud that—so long as he leaves the NHS alone!

From the *Financial Times*

# ■ A Review of *Another Fool in the Balkans: In the Footsteps of Rebecca West* by Tony White

**From the *Telegraph*, 9th May 2006**

Tony White is an outstanding novelist (his *Foxy-T*, written in East End Benglish, remains one of my favourite London books). Editor of dynamic anthologies (*Britpulp!* and *Croatian Nights*), literary editor of *The Idler* and publisher (Piece of Paper Press), his passion for all the creative arts makes him the best kind of Arts Council staffer.

When he was curating the Yugoslav performance artist Gordana Stanisic's Walk to Belgrade from London on a Treadmill (1994), he decided he might as well read Rebecca West's detailed account of her journey through Yugoslavia a few years after the nation was formed, just before the Nazi invasion.

*Black Lamb, Grey Falcon* (1941) appeared in two volumes and, for all its Serbian bias, is a masterpiece, an essay on the nature of power and on history, evoking a world before Europe looked west to the US, but looked east to the Ottoman empire, when the region loosely called 'the Balkans' was central to our perspective.

Since her book, we have known Tito's post-war communist state (amiably, but not uncritically evoked in Brian Aldiss's *Cities and Stones*) and the 'ethnic cleansing', refragmented, often savagely warring states of the old republic. With an awkward peace at last established, White made several trips to the former Yugoslavia.

Old bitternesses still prevailed. Writers who once travelled freely to one another's cities could no longer do so. Arriving in Zagreb, immediately whisked off to a public interview and asked what he intended to see while there, White mentioned how he planned to go to Belgrade. Only by some nifty strategies did the organisers defuse the baffled rage of the audience. Far from expressing liberal humanism, many artists remain nostalgic nationalists.

Authoritarianism stops time. It corrupts history. The best artists working under dictatorships either escape time altogether, into fabulism, or move into an imaginary future or an idealised past. The past is the most dangerous place, luring vulnerable artists into narrow folkic nationalism, turning myth and legend into propaganda and xenophobia.

Under communism, reality was suppressed, exacerbating regional rivalries already exploited by divisive Nazi policies. Those of us who travelled in the East before the Wall fell found ourselves amazed at the prevalence of 19th-century racialism. A friendly KGB officer with a passion for Pushkin once explained to me how the poet's volatile personality was the result of 'his Negro blood'. Sadly, it was no surprise when vicious war broke out between peoples whom the victors of two world wars had only artificially united.

Through all the region's terrible times, a few local heroes resisted attempts to co-opt their work and fame in the interests of their political bosses. Under Tito, the sculptor Ivan Mestrovic refused to serve the dictator's interest, while Mate Parlov, the Olympic boxer, was equally unwilling to give legitimacy to Milosevic. Many other journalists, artists and public personalities found clever strategies to retain their integrity. Their bravery and intelligence, whether they came from Istrea or Kosovo, Belgrade or Dubrovnik, was exemplary.

It is their stories that form the backbone of White's book as he travels from Belgrade to Split, reporting the words of a people confused by shame, pride and hope, trying to make sense of brutal murder and hatred, managing to create something universally valuable from their lives and their history.

The enormity of crimes and lies committed in their names might have struck a less-resilient people dumb, at least for a generation or two, but many continue to remain positive, hopeful, humane.

White's profoundly fascinating, highly idiosyncratic book celebrates the region and its culture. Knowing many of the artists and writers working in Serbia, Croatia, Bosnia and elsewhere, he understands their specific problems. This is no conventional travel book, though he does have a way of making you yearn to taste the region's food and wine, and his novelist's sense of character brings even the simplest taxi-driver to life.

To his great credit, White not only makes you want to pack a bag and leave immediately for Belgrade or Istrea, he has captured the confusion and courage of those who have survived with their souls and their idealism intact, who represent that universal yearning for peace and individual dignity that, in the end, is what most of us desire and which the greatest of Balkan artists still express in so many varied and extraordinary ways.

# ■ A Construction Site of the Mind

A Review of *In Europe: Travels through the Twentieth Century* by Geert Mak

**From the *Telegraph*, 18th March 2007**

From 1999, the Dutch journalist Geert Mak determined to travel through European time as well as space, visiting key sites where recent history was experienced most intensely. Describing the prevailing psychic atmosphere of places where, in 1914, pacifist socialists voted enthusiastically for war or, in 1939, patriotic imperialists desperately opposed it, Mak explores the myths and legends which continue to cloud our judgment as Europeans.

*In Europe* argues that almost any year of the 20th and early 21st centuries is fully alive in some part of Europe, with the earliest decades found mainly in the East, and the future mainly in the West. For many, joining the EU means the chance to enter modern times, though few understand the subtle price they must pay, the comforting traditions and folklore they must sacrifice in order to share Europe's wealth.

The cultural spasms which shook advanced industrial countries must be even more marked elsewhere. The flow of wealth from capital to labour fired the optimism and reforms we now take for granted, but the reversal of that flow since 1970 also created the disturbing incoherence we discover in present-day Britain and the collapse of institutions we value in France, say, or Ireland.

The bloody, rebellious 1960s in Germany or Italy and the civil strife in former Yugoslavia were probably caused as much by confrontation with modern economics as by frustrated bourgeois youth or the unaddressed tensions Tito swept under the Communist carpet.

Moving from one key historic site to another, Mak argues that we do not always correctly identify the real threats to our social stability or, indeed, our sovereignty; and, of course, in the worst scenarios we turn on minorities and newcomers when in fact we have ourselves encouraged these imagined threats by embracing economic liberalism without understanding its high psychic and social price.

This idea is not that hard to understand, but Mak relentlessly forces us to give it our serious attention, to consider the kind of informed action we need to take if we are to make the best of European modern times.

Moving across a vivid historical landscape, his portrait of Europe, in all her bloody barbarism and civilised glory, helps us confront exactly what we need to know. The great capitals, no matter how perfect their glossy modern facades and citywide heritage-dioramas, are major symbols in his narrative, but so are Ypres, Guernica and Riga. So are Nuremberg, Auschwitz and Bielefeld. Babi'yar. Odessa. Sarajevo and Srebrenica. Lisbon. Istanbul. Vichy. How could cultivated Europe allow the horror of racist fascism? And then let that horror happen all over again?

For those of us whose idealism embraces our own culture within a unified Europe, Mak offers a profoundly informative map of our past and a practical plan for our potential future. He challenges some of our most sentimental myths, showing how America deliberately bankrupted Britain through Lend-Lease; how the Allies bombed non-strategic civilian targets as policy; how France managed to preserve three quarters of her Jewish population during the (originally popular) Vichy regime; how Europe's economic revival began long before the Marshall Plan was implemented. More than 40 million people died violently between 1940 and 1945, cities were flattened, infrastructure destroyed, yet by 1955 we were already on the road to our present economic power.

The contemporary chapters are presented with an authoritative urgency rejecting any form of messianism. Those who try to understand and experience the modern world's realities, rather than retreat into the same nostalgia and complacency which led the last century down so many disastrously wrong turnings, must welcome Mak's brave, clear-eyed exploration.

Page after page presents us with profoundly vivid images: Berlin, battered into a frenetic new identity; Vienna, the cradle of Nazism, frozen without a future; Rome, crowded with complex contradictions, confronting her fascist past and a conflicted Vatican; London, ruthlessly recreating herself by eating her own soul; Paris, pensively facing the fact that the Republic needs a serious fix; Stockholm, shocked by threats to her perhaps too easily earned liberalism; Moscow, a confused giant hamstrung by authoritarian habits; Istanbul, a smoggy backwater; the veneer of American wealth—McDonald's, Gap—failing to cover quaint but unmodernised Baltic cities, some still openly anti-semitic. Yet Europe's capital and know-how are abundant. Maintaining their national sovereignty, as practical democracy demands, Europeans still yearn for a common vision, a passionate parliament to make that vision a reality.

On the 50th anniversary of the Treaty of Rome, Europe is one vast construction site of the mind, and we still have no coherent vision of what we intend to build there. As well as a mirror to our past delusions, *In Europe* offers us an image of the present which just might bring us the secure, humane and generous future our ancestors imagined to be inevitable 100 years ago. Mak's implications are plain: if we wish to survive and prosper, we really have no choice but to see sense, start working and do some serious business together.

'For let us not forget,' he warns in his final sentence, 'Europe has only one chance to succeed.' This is a timely book, and one we can't afford to ignore.

# ABSENT FRIENDS

# ■ The Patsy

## A Review of *I Sit in Hanger Lane* by Jack Trevor Story

**From *New Worlds*, January 1969**

Our most talented living English comic novelist, Jack Trevor Story is the author of *The Trouble with Harry* (made into a Hitchcock film) and the *Live Now, Pay Later* series about the adventures of Albert Argyll, ace conman of the '60s. He has written the best comedy thrillers ever published, film scripts and TV scripts for series like *No Hiding Place* that were minor achievements in that his laconic style was immediately recognisable from the moment the story began. His novels of suburbia and the New Towns, written with superb observation, sympathy and wit (Angus Wilson is the only other author capable of writing with such sympathetic consideration for the very ordinary person) have not received sufficient serious attention.

It is the hardest thing in the world to write a good novel about outwardly mundane events and characters and if it is achieved there are few critics who can understand the extent of that achievement. Story is a much better writer than, say, Amis or Powell, but he refuses to be precious, 'significant' or even 'satirical' and he does not do what so many lesser and better-received novelists do, which is to make the reader feel superior in some way to the characters he reads about. Like Wilson, Jack Trevor Story is a writer without arrogance, a writer of fiction which has as its starting point the intention of offering the public a 'good read', but a good read that offers its catharsis through humour, not through a simple-minded distortion of the realities of the human condition.

The hero sits in the bath with the high-society prostitute who has adopted him:

> "Your only true allegiance is to your talent," she said.
>
> Horace Spurgeon Fenton, writer, artist and year-book, I thought.
>
> She said: "You have the arrogance which comes from that. Whatever their sufferings—be it wife, mistress, child, girlfriend, brother or

whatever—you feel that they are privileged to be part of your life because it gives them, in return for this pure accident, a place in English letters. Forever."

"Yes-no!" I said. Nobody could be as conceited as that. It didn't sound conceited the way she said it. It sounded very nice.

Story's talent for capturing the speech, frustrations, ambitions and individuality of the shop assistant, the office worker, the local librarian and the housewife is apparent in everything he writes. His style is unpretentious (though extremely personal) and sometimes shows marks of haste, but it is always vigorous and almost invariably has the quality of Dickens at his least ponderous best.

His latest novel, *I Sit in Hanger Lane*, is perhaps a more melancholy book than his previous ones and it is quite evidently autobiographical. It describes the final desperate efforts of a film writer to stay ahead of the rat race, even though he knows in his bones that the crunch has finally come. It is not, however, a novel of a man whose ambitions have led him to the brink of disaster—it is a rarer book than that, for it is about someone whose lack of ambition brings him down; he is caught up in a world whose rules he cannot understand. Horace Spurgeon Fenton has been 'withering through the summer, working on a film that seemed fated not to go through. I had two wives, eight children, seventeen cats, dozens of rats and mice, a hedgehog, a squirrel, a hundred or so creditors, my bank manager, all waiting for it to go through.'

His final attempts to save himself from complete ruin place him even more firmly in the hands of those who have been exploiting him and, indeed, attract new exploiters such as Albert Harris, his milkman friend, whose greedy imagination is captured by the supposed glamour of the film-writer's life. The humour is still there, but it is the grim humour of the arrested man who knows suddenly that he's the patsy, the bitter humour of the last section of *Catch-22*.

The opening and closing sequences of the novel, which are quietly bizarre, give force and structure to the book so that it finally adds up to something considerably greater than the sum of its parts.

Story's inventiveness has always been exceptional, but this novel seems to be based very firmly on his own experiences and its first-person retrospective narrative gives it a note of sardonic self-appraisal. It is, perhaps because of this, a more awkwardly written book than we usually expect from him, as if he is attempting to come to grips with something he has managed to avoid thinking about up to now. It has a traumatic quality which perhaps only another writer recognises, with its record of unpaid debts, threatened lawsuits, irrational loyalties, ambitious friends who wind up betraying him when he's served as an introduction to the more powerful, wistful and fleeting relationships with girls met at clubs and parties—a familiar enough piece of literary autobiography, a rake's progress, the record of a fucked-up life, of a writer who has been so interested in other people's lives and problems that he has not had time to consider his own.

This novel has the atmosphere of a confession, a self-purgative, and seems to indicate that Story has reached a watershed in his own career. The slightly more sober mood of the book makes one feel that in a year or two we should see a new book from him which will be the major novel he is so well-equipped to write.

# ■ Jack's Unforgettable Christmas

**From *New Statesman and Society*, Christmas Supplement 1991**

On Thursday, 5th December, 1991, Jack Trevor Story, one of my oldest and best friends, died suddenly of a heart attack. He was at his typewriter and had completed the revisions to his new novel *Shabby Weddings*, which he knew was his best since *One Last Mad Embrace*, that I considered to be his masterpiece. After twenty years, he said, he had found his bearings again.

I knew what he meant. Although he published some wonderful, quirky books during those years, including *Letters to an Intimate Stranger*, a collection of his *Guardian* columns, some of the most honest, funniest non-fiction a novelist ever wrote, he had never entirely recovered from what happened at Christmas 1969, when, after leaving my Ladbroke Grove flat, he and his friend Maggie MacDonald were arrested by the Notting Hill police.

Jack's work contains many references to that terrifying night. He frequently relived it. He had discovered at first hand what most black youths already knew, that the 'basic decency' of the English police was little more than a reassuring myth. It was a singular irony of which Jack, the master of irony, was thoroughly aware.

He had always produced his novels from a considerable fund of working-class and lower middle-class experience. Yet he had been content in his comedy thrillers and TV series (distinctive, clever scripts for *Budgie*, *No Hiding Place* and his own *You're Only Young Twice*) to portray the police as, at worst, bumbling incompetents. Since policemen were human beings, he reasoned, and since they were usually from similar backgrounds to his own (at fourteen, having failed to get a job as potboy at the big house, his first job was delivering meat for a Cambridge butcher), and since they spoke the same language, used the same pubs, had the same interests as most of his people, they must be as reasonable and ordinary as himself.

Jack's early work abounds with likeable coppers (his Spike Milligan film *Postman's Knock*, for instance, or *Live Now, Pay Later*), some of whom are almost as nice as his villains.

Though he never had any money, went bankrupt twice, lived mostly in bedsitters and was ambitious only for his craft, Jack described an England that was fundamentally benign. Socially, he took people on their own terms. He relished simple pleasures. He said true love wasn't actually about grand passions but about how you went round the supermarket together. He celebrated characters who were as amiably baffled in the corridors of power as he was (even though CP Snow had been an early mentor). His attitude towards authority was tolerantly amused. Courts, judges, tax inspectors, bailiffs and repo-men were, he had discovered, as inconsistent as everyone else and, though their reprimands, threats and exhortations puzzled and occasionally irritated him, he found they could do him no real harm and could be ignored like bad weather. He went on his way in spite of them, writing whatever was needed to pay his rent arrears or meet the payments on his car.

He never needed much nor expected much and he was frequently exploited. Hitchcock exploited him, paying him for film rights of *The Trouble with Harry*; Bill Howard Baker exploited him, getting perfectly crafted gems of comedies for *Sexton Blake Library* at a discount; his publishers, especially the infamous Allison & Busby, ripped him off. Only the Manchester publisher Savoy stood by him through the hard times, recognising both his talent and his generosity.

I never blamed any of the women when they left him, for while Jack swam cheerfully at the centre of the mælstrom and had in those days a profound optimism, a sublime lack of anxiety about the future, for most his way of life was too uncertain. But nobody ever gave up on Jack easily. It was almost impossible not to like him. Radical feminists, determined to hate him, rarely failed to be charmed by him, for he had a way of taking everyone as equals. He never understood why people wanted power over others. He was proud of his vocation, dedicated to his art, selfish in its pursuit, but, of all the human beings I ever loved, he was one of the few almost entirely without malice or guile. In private or in the pages of the *Guardian*, his agonies when Maggie left him were intense and he knew that his crazed efforts to win her back were driving her further away, yet I never heard a bad word about her or, indeed, any lover, any woman. Not a few, including daughters and ex-wives, continued to care for him, but he remained determinedly independent as a cat. He respected others' humanity, privacy and freedom as thoroughly as he protected his own. He had a singular delicacy, a courtesy that manifested itself in a rather old-fashioned reticence. To him the human spirit was sacred. He saw it manifested in the most unlikely places.

The minutiæ of ordinary life provided for Jack the real clues to the mystery of the human condition. 'Life,' he wrote, 'runs on such tiny points, like fat overstuffed sofas run on tiny castors.' Abstractions, no matter how elegant, left him cold.

Jack's priorities were the same as his characters'—World War Three might be starting or the biosphere about to collapse, but you had to make sure you got the tea on the table before your spouse came home from work. He observed, he recorded, he was naturally unjudgemental, and this led some to detect in him a weak social conscience. Yet one of his greatest heroes was the Orwell of *Keep the Aspidistra Flying* and *Coming Up for Air*. Another was Arnold Bennett. Another was William Saroyan. He admired authors who dignified the common, the vulgar and the mundane and could make of it something extraordinary.

I never knew a writer more willing to take on any job—pulp-thriller, movie, TV soap, newspaper column or experimental novel—and bring the same sense of integrity, of accuracy and truth to whatever he did. He never sold out. He gave every job his own stamp. You could turn on the TV and always recognise Jack Story dialogue. Sometimes his commercial work was so thoroughly and beautifully his own that those who commissioned it didn't quite know what to do with it. Frequently it was simply filed away and forgotten. His sporadic attempts at self-publicity, which were intended to improve his fortunes, were so blatantly inept, so impossibly bizarre and uncompromising, that they almost always failed. His TV appearances showed an affectionate eccentric with an almost infinite number of enthusiasms—for people, places, food, music, animals, literature. He always went too far in his own direction. He never got his contracts renewed.

Jack never blamed anyone else for his failures. To his friends and to him they were never failures. They were just something else he'd tried. He was incapable of sustained anger or even resentment. He envied no-one their success, was always cheered when a good writer found a wider audience than his own. He had a strong sense of commonality and naturally identified his interests with society's. He was a genuine, unselfconscious egalitarian, as cheerfully tolerant of the Great and Pompous as he was of the Small and Meek.

After leaving my flat that Christmas, where we'd enjoyed a noisy orgy of guitar-playing—Jack was an ex-danceband musician—and cocoa-drinking, interspersed with some serious draughts games, Jack and Maggie got into their battered old American car and, as far as I knew, set off home to their Hampstead bedsit. But the traffic lights were stuck on red at the Elgin Crescent intersection and, after waiting for some time, Jack decided to creep across. It was 1:00 a.m. Ladbroke Grove was deserted. As he moved slowly over the intersection, a police car appeared and stopped him. He explained the trouble. The policemen ignored him. Instead they asked him if the car was his. 'Of course it's mine,' said Jack, amiable as always.

'And that's your girlfriend, is it?' said one policeman, staring in. Taken aback, Jack asked what that had to do with them. 'Isn't she a bit young for you?' he said. They told him they wanted him to take a Breathalyser. This was ridiculous, Jack said. He'd hardly had a drink all day. They became increasingly aggressive. Jack pointed out that they could now see for themselves that the light wasn't working. They asked him for his driving licence. They asked again what an old man like him was doing with such a young girlfriend (Jack was around fifty, Maggie still in her twenties). Jack said it was none of their business. Maggie, furious at their rudeness and innuendo, told them to bugger off. But then, Jack told me, things began to get increasingly surreal. The police informed Jack and Maggie they were under arrest and took them to Ladbroke Grove police station.

Jack, seriously asthmatic and suffering from claustrophobia, still couldn't take it very seriously but, as an asthma attack was developing, said he was leaving. They had his name and address. The police promptly grabbed him and began to push him around. Jack panicked. Then they performed the well-known local trick of stepping on his foot and pushing him heavily backwards, permanently damaging the tendons of his right foot. Maggie shouted at them to take their hands off him. She was also manhandled and dragged off to a cell. Jack was put in another cell. By now the asthma was worse. Jack begged the policeman on duty to have his inhaler brought in from his car. The policeman told him to fucking stop whining and threw a bowl of water in his face. After several hours, Jack and Maggie were charged with assault and Jack with drunk driving. They had not been allowed to make a phone call. Still confident that a court must surely set things straight, Jack was shocked when on perjured police evidence, he was found guilty. Later, on appeal, with a better prepared case and a good witness, the verdict was reversed. However, Jack was advised that prosecuting the police would waste his time and cost money he didn't have.

It's a familiar case, unremarkable to most of us raised in big cities, especially if we're black. I wrote to Jim Callaghan, then Home Secretary, to Leo

Abse, then generally considered to be the conscience of the Labour Party, to other police officers at Ladbroke Grove, to the local papers, to the national papers and to Sir Robert Mark when he told us he was going to clean up the Met. In Notting Hill at that time we were familiar with this kind of behaviour and worse. Certain officers blatantly pursued vendettas against West Indians, and did more to polarise our community than even the invading gentry. Jack's misfortune was to seem working class, to have a woman friend younger than himself and a face which has been described as "lived in". He had assumed the police to be ordinary, reasonable people. It was probably his most serious mistake, for by then the police were learning techniques of civilian control. They had new rôle models derived from TV cop-shows. They were heavy lads. PC Plod was assigned to school crossings and a Santa suit at the annual charity do. Jack had been misguided enough to believe that the police were more or less on the side of the angels.

Jack had a living to earn. After the appeal, he tried to get it out of his system in a political fantasy, *The Wind in the Snottygobble Tree*, which was serialised in *New Worlds* with dedications to the police in question. But the experience had profoundly changed Jack. His books—*Morag's Flying Fortress*, *Little Dog's Day*—were no longer about the ordinary vicissitudes of working-class tally-men and pissed-off housewives—they were about corporate plots, international conspiracies, worlds where nothing was what it seemed.

Trying to get to grips with the trauma, Jack wrote a dozen novels, still unpublished. He had lost his old certainty in the fundamental decency of human nature and could not quite find anything to replace it. His working-class and lower middle-class protagonists still interested themselves in life's minutiæ, but they now existed in a world of threat. The majority of these books, though full of brilliant insights, wonderful language and extraordinary scenes, never fully came into focus. People thought Jack was being self-indulgent. He wasn't. He was trying for a technique which would help him make sense of his experience and it was still hard for him to stay angry. *Hitler Needs You*, the sequel to *One Last Mad Embrace*, was completed in the aftermath of his arrest.

Jack kept working. His *Guardian* column was axed. He published articles, reviews, did some TV work. For twenty years he went on producing novels, most of which are still unpublished: Thatcher's yuppies scared him. He couldn't begin to understand their priorities. He had grown up at a time when there was no shame in being poor. From somewhere he always managed to find hope. He knew that something in him had died and whatever was being born had not gestated completely. Then, at last, in August

1990, Jack had a serious psychological breakdown. Pathetically terrified of authority, convinced that almost all his old friends and family were against him, he eventually escaped from Stoke Mandeville (where he should never have been) and for a short while lived rough. But he had a heart condition and carried no medicine. Eventually, in his own words, he gave himself up. Almost as soon as he took himself off the psychiatric drugs, he recovered. He never quite understood what had happened to him, but it seemed he had finally rid himself of that twenty-year trauma. He began re-examining his literary and social roots, considering his old techniques, developing new ones and at last making clear sense of his experience.

*Shabby Weddings*, he said, was the best thing he'd written. But the memory of his Notting Hill Christmas remained and he continued to hold a deep suspicion of authority, fearful of any attempt to check his liberty. He told me that he felt if he made too much of his heart condition it would give the authorities another excuse to lock him up. I promised I would never let it happen to him.

I miss him deeply. My only consolation for his loss is that he died knowing he had written a masterpiece, that he had finally shaken off the ghosts of Christmas Past.

And that, Jack, is what I intend to celebrate this year.

# ■ When the Political Gets Too Personal

**From *New Statesman*, 27th May 1988**

Until the publication of *Intercourse* (Arrow, £3.50) last year, most of the Left considered Andrea Dworkin a respectably radical feminist; sometimes a little extreme in certain areas, solidly on the side of reform, her books accepted cornerstones of modern feminism. *Our Blood*, *Right-Wing Women* and *Pornography* continued the work of Millett, Firestone and Mitchell, providing us with fresh political ideas, deeper understanding of the fundamental issues, a new hope for sexual equality.

*Intercourse*, it seems, went too far. Dworkin suggested the political might be altogether too personal. 'Traditional' sexuality might have something to do with sexual inequality, she thought.

And there was an outcry, not just from the predictable sources: the plummy El Vino socialists and nervous Chestertonoids, the right-wing women journalists whom one suspects of having been rugger groupies in their youth, the hearties of the *Literary Review*, which seems to be the book world's answer to *The Sun*. The Left joined in too, devoting, in this country and in the USA, enormous amounts of space condemning Dworkin's proposal that the politics of inequality were reflected in, and maintained by, the way we approach the sexual act itself.

In Minneapolis, the Dworkin/MacKinnon Bill had been passed and for a short while a city law accepted that pornography, as defined by the Bill, could be a direct as well as indirect cause of sexual crime and sex discrimination. Had not the mayor vetoed it twice, the Bill would have allowed anyone harmed by pornography to bring a case against the pornographer on the basis that pornography contravened their civil rights as citizens. This legislation would have taken the debate away from an obscenity issue to a sex equality issue and made redundant repressive legislation like our own Obscene Publications Act, thus dismantling at least some of the machinery of state censorship.

This radical and clear-sighted approach to pornography as a civil-rights issue was attacked by many organisations, including the well-known '*Playboy* lobby', employing ACLU lawyers. The city of Indianapolis was actually sued for passing the Bill. As Dworkin remarks in *Letters from a War Zone*:

> [Feminists] are the ones with different ideas, political ideas, subversive ideas. Yet the energy of the civil liberties lawyers as well as the pornographers . . . has gone into shutting us up. Their argument is that when we address male sexual hegemony as expressed in and perpetuated by pornography . . . we are endangering the speech of others.

The attacks continued, especially from *Playboy*, *Penthouse* and *Hustler*, who began to spend fortunes in attempts to discredit radical feminists in general and Dworkin in particular. This at least was understandable. What's presently baffling me is hearing the Left condemn Dworkin as a right-wing pro-censorship activist and criticising her works from that perspective. It is from the Left and her traditional allies that she has begun to receive her most savage attacks. Few have read the Dworkin/MacKinnon Bill; few have read the published evidence of the Minneapolis Hearings, *Pornography and Sexual Violence* (Everywoman, £4.95); few have read Dworkin herself on the subject. Reports, frequently from people describing themselves as feminists, referred to her efforts to 'ban' porn and represented her as a misanthropic 'anti-obscenity' biological determinist when the truth is very much the opposite.

'With pornography we're talking about the Left defending commodity capitalism in all of its forms so that when you defend free speech, what it means in this country is that you're defending the right of people who have money, who have been able to buy speech, over the rights of people who have been disenfranchised from the system', Dworkin said in a recent interview in *On The Issues*.

Dworkin says her books are not prescriptive but descriptive. While continuing to expand the boundaries of feminist dialectic, she argues from a humanistic and idealistic perspective both intellectually stunning and stylistically eloquent. In her reluctance to remain within the defensive walls of accepted liberal wisdom she shares something with Orwell, who so angered the Left with his own refusal to repeat the comforting reassurances of conventional socialist thinking. She attacks male supremacy, male injustice, male cruelty, but she has no belief in any biologically inherited wickedness. Her own father was loving and tender and it shocked her to find that not all men were like him. She still believes that most men could be both just and sensitive, that men and women are socialised into their rôles and that legal reform and enlightened education together can change society, ridding us of inequality, providing genuine liberation for women and, incidentally, for men. All her arguments are founded in this belief.

In *Intercourse*, she devotes much of the book to discussions of male writers she admires. In *Letters from a War Zone*, she says where she has benefited from identifying with male writers. What she fights against, in everything she writes and does, is male refusal to acknowledge sexual inequality, male hatred of women, male contempt of women, male power. And it is when she addresses these issues that she is impressive in her anger, her articulation, her perceptions. Gloria Steinem has referred to Dworkin as the women's movement's Old Testament prophet. But Dworkin is more than a visionary; she is an analyst, a polemicist, a political force whose influence on the politics of liberation many radicals already acknowledge as seminal. Moreover, Dworkin is not an ivory-tower feminist; she remains an active speaker and organiser throughout the West and a powerful voice for working-class women:

> Pornography is an issue that has mobilised poor women; the kind of women who have been in pornography or prostitution, the women who have been incest victims or homeless. Women . . . who make the $60,000 a year also control the media in the Women's Movement. They are the ones who are saying "Shut up, we really don't want the stigma of this issue on us." Whereas the poor women are saying, we have no escape from the impact of what pornography means in our lives. It's a real rich/poor issue.

Perhaps this is why Dworkin has lately become such an object of hatred to the middle-class Left. Certainly it continues to misrepresent her to an astonishing degree, discussing her anti-pornography campaigning as an issue of censorship rather than an issue of civil rights and seeing her as attacking female sexuality, when in fact she is passionate in her vision of a world in which human sexuality is not only heightened but qualitatively improved by changes in the way we perceive and experience it:

> It's amazing to me how little attraction the word "equality" really has for people. How they so deeply get their pleasure from forms of inequality of all kinds. It seems to me that if a society had real equality, the forms of sensuality that would exist between people would be deeper and richer and more various, less fetishised and alienated.

Scarcely the words of a puritan. But then Dworkin is only puritanical in the zeal with which she is currently keeping the flame of radical feminism alive.

These are bad times for social reform. In the present economical and social climate, allies are deserting the Left on almost every issue. Surely the few of us with the courage and capacity to fight on should be supported, not condemned? It would seem that the least we could do is to read and understand such writers, before allowing ourselves to be talked into passivity by interests currently using the debased slogans of an earlier liberalism to ensure their own commercial security. Dworkin is not the first genuine radical to be pilloried by the Left. Neither would she be the first free spirit to be silenced in the name of free speech.

# ■ Andrea Dworkin: Memorial

**From: Memorial service for Andrea Dworkin, September 2005**

Even now when I see her picture I can't emotionally come to terms with her death. In her most despairing, painful moments her vitality informed all she did and thought. She died so suddenly, so unexpectedly, that I had no time to prepare myself for it. I suspect there are many others who feel as I do.

Quite simply Andrea was the sister I never had. I loved her. We had a huge amount in common. She loved me unconditionally, if never uncritically, and she helped me through some of my hardest times. When I was overly self-pitying (especially if relations with women were involved) she would laugh at me and tell me to live with it, but if things went badly for me she was the first to give me her active support and her sympathy, her hard, honest common sense. Under terrible conditions, in extremely poor health, she came all the way from New York to Austin just to attend my sixtieth birthday party, the day after my mother had died. In spite of her illness, she again was able to offer me comfort.

I was constantly aware at how lucky I was to have two such strong women as Andrea and Linda, my wife, as friends, as intellectual company, as models of integrity and social behaviour, as observers, as people fired above all with a sense of social justice. With John Stoltenberg, I think we constituted a pretty formidable foursome, but it has to be said that Andrea's extraordinary original powers of political analysis were an inspiration to the rest of us and can now only be revisited in books which I know will continue to speak to more and more people in future generations. She was an astonishing public presence, and it is that which will remain such a special loss to those of us involved in gender politics.

For someone who could hold the attention and fire the emotions of a large audience so well from the platform, she was, as many here know I'm sure, both extremely shy and retiring, always terrified of making public appearances and needing as much support as she could get both before and after she spoke. Linda, whom she often described as 'a warrior', was initially astonished at how hard it was for Andrea sometimes just to get from her hotel to her speaking engagement and how so many people seemed to be in awe of her—such awe that it often never occurred to them that she might need a little help, a little reassurance, even a cup of tea or a sandwich. She rarely, of course, asked for anything. She saw her rôle as the helper, the reassurer, the supporter and, as many strong people discover, did not know easily how to ask for what *she* sometimes needed, especially in later years, when her knees weakened and she had such a hard time getting from her kitchen to her office, let alone from an airport to a venue.

Andrea was courteous to those who disagreed with her, who insulted her, who felt threatened by her. She could argue levelly and logically with people who raved at her in their anger, as I discovered the first time we met, at a public meeting where we were both to read and speak from the same platform. She experienced antagonism from the stage, let alone the audience, and she took it incredibly well. That night, her speech moved me so much I was almost incapable of speaking my own piece.

I knew already from her work that she was an extraordinarily conscientious reviewer and debater. Unlike many who spend so much of their time in public with politics she was also the warmest most steadfast friend.

The world is greatly impoverished by her loss. I am immeasurably impoverished by it. She died far too soon and in the middle of writing a book which would have done still more to light up the world. She was working with enormous difficulty in considerable pain much of the time. Yet she remained that same loving friend to me.

As far as her work is concerned, I can't imagine who will continue with her unfinished business. I suppose it is up to all of us to shoulder part of her burden as best we can.

I will never know a person I loved in quite the same way. We have lost an orator, a politician, a campaigner, a writer, a genius.

I have lost my sister.

# ■ JG Ballard Introduction

**From *Arthur*, March 2005**

Born in 1930, JG Ballard spent his formative years in a Shanghai civilian prison camp, experiences which form the basis of his autobiographical novel *Empire of the Sun*, filmed by Steven Spielberg. In England he abandoned his medicine degree at Cambridge to become a technical journalist. His first stories in *New Worlds*, *Science Fantasy* and *Science Fiction Adventures* from 1956 including 'The Voices of Time', 'Vermilion Sands' and 'Chronopolis' are in *The Complete Short Stories of JG Ballard* (2002). Three novels, *The Drowned World* (predicting climate change), *The Crystal World* and *The Drought* increasingly reflected his interest in surrealist painting. 'The Terminal Beach' in *New Worlds* (1964) marked a new phase, dispensing altogether with the conventions of science fiction.

Appearing in *New Worlds*, which by then I was editing, 'The Assassination Weapon' (1966) was the first of Ballard's 'condensed novels' where iconographic personalities and events became the basis of narrative. Other stories included 'The Atrocity Exhibition', 'You: Coma: Marilyn Monroe' and 'Plan For The Assassination of Jacqueline Kennedy' in *New Worlds* and, increasingly, in literary magazines such as *Ambit* and *Transatlantic Review*. His work encountered considerable hostility in the United States, where its irony went largely undetected. Doubleday, the publisher of *The Atrocity Exhibition*, ordered all copies pulped after it was printed. It eventually appeared from Grove Press in 1970. Meanwhile, 'Why I Want to Fuck Ronald Reagan' became the basis of a UK court case, while his 'Assassination of John Fitzgerald Kennedy Considered as a Downhill Motor Race', 'lost' by his US agent, eventually appeared in *New Worlds* and *Evergreen Review*.

He remains a seminally controversial writer hugely admired by the likes of Martin Amis, Salman Rushdie, Fay Weldon, Angela Carter, Iain Sinclair and most of the best science fiction writers. Described as pornographic and psychotic when first reviewed, *Crash* (1973) was filmed by David Cronenberg starring James Spader in 1996. *Concrete Island* (1974) and *High-Rise* (1975) continued similar themes of our psychological and sexual relationship with contemporary phenomena and iconography. *The Unlimited Dream Company* (1979) and *Hello America* (1981) are enjoyable satires; his autobiographical *The Kindness of Women* (1991) was a sequel to *Empire of the Sun*. Recent novels like *Cocaine Nights* (1996), *Super-Cannes* (2000) and *Millennium People* (2003) continue to develop techniques describing his unique experience and his notion that contemporary bourgeoisie have become the new slave class. Today he lives in the same London suburb where he settled some forty-five years ago and, as a widower, raised three children, eschewing electronics and working at his typewriter. Combining the creative insight and originality of a modern William Blake, Ballard is our greatest living visionary writer.

# ■ Time Made Concrete

## A Review of *The Crystal World* by JG Ballard

**From *Delap's F&SF Review*, May 1977**

Since this novel, in slightly shorter form, was the first I commissioned as a serial when I took over *New Worlds* in 1964, I can't pretend lack of bias in reviewing it.[1] Ballard was one of the imaginative authors I most admired then and he is one of the few I still admire. Although *The Crystal World* is marketed as SF and can legitimately be described as SF it is to my mind the work of a symbolist who by this time had discarded the pseudo-physical rationales of the two earlier SF novels, *The Drowned World* and *The Burning World*, with which it forms an obvious and thematically interlinked trilogy. In it, as in most symbolist work of this kind, the images are made to reflect the inner conflicts and passions of the characters who occupy landscapes which have come increasingly to represent certain elementary needs and fears.

Ballard's images—crystallised forests, jewelled men and animals, dying lepers, isolated and strangely empty hotels—are the substance of *The Crystal World*. Characters, plot and theme are of secondary interest in this kind of fiction which upends the usual methods of structuring a novel rather as the subject matter itself shows the psychic landscape externalised and the external world gradually becoming (as in almost all Ballard's protagonists) little more than a subconscious notion. The dramatic tensions are maintained by a conflict between those who will not accept the supra-reality (or surreality) of the psychic world and those who accept it but are checked either by the others or by their own 'normal' impulses to cling to the logic of the

---

1 There was also a short story version, 'The Illuminated Man' in *F&SF*, which preceded the serial, called 'Equinox' in *NW*. The book's divisions into two parts as 'Equinox' and 'The Illuminated Man' do not relate to chronological publication. These sections are substantially the same as the two parts of the serial in *NW* 142 & 143. The expansion is chiefly amplification of characterisation, to the book version's considerable improvement. None of this information is given in the current edition. US History: Farrar, Straus & Giroux, 1966; SF Book Club, 1966; Berkley Medallion paperback 1967; Equinox 'SF Rediscovery Series No. 25', 1976.

external world. This is the so-called 'pessimistic' aspect of Ballard's work, for in his book the villains are those who are trying to save the world from 'disaster' which, to Ballard's heroes, is no disaster at all, but the very reverse. Ballard claims the surrealist painters and writers of the twentieth century as his chief influences and there is little doubt that in *The Crystal World* he is writing directly in their tradition—with the additional virtue that he is writing better and with considerably greater control of his materials than most of those he admires. Ballard's prose has often been called 'poetic' by critics who are, in fact, actually describing his images, but he shares one thing with a good poet—his work aims for concentration of image and language. This was the essence of the *New Worlds* movement in the '60s (directly in contrast to the American 'new wave' which aimed increasingly towards a sentimental rhetoric). But if Max Ernst and Dalí are the strongest influences on Ballard's subject matter, his main stylistic influence here is Greene while the whole fable is a deliberate homage to Conrad's *Heart of Darkness*. If one wished to one could make out a good case for an imagist 'tradition' from Conrad to Ballard, but there is little evidence of any direct influence of Conrad on Ballard's main work.

Ballard's central character (it might as well be Traven, or Ballard, but in this book he's called Dr Sanders) arrives at the 'straggle of warehouses and small hotels that constituted Port Matarre' in a remote part of the Cameroon Republic. His travelling companions are a mysterious European, Ventress, wearing a white tropical suit, and an apostate chain-smoking priest, Father Balthus. Sanders and the others have taken the small steamer from the capital. A river boat normally serves the interior where Sanders has been invited by Suzanne and Max Clair (a microbiologist) to join them in the running of a leper colony. Peculiar relationships and secret goals are hinted at in the first few pages; we receive a variety of presentiments, including a letter from Suzanne in which she describes the forest as 'a house of jewels'. Sanders discovers it is impossible to get upriver to Mont Royal (primarily a diamond mining area) but no-one will tell him what is going on there. With Louise Peret, a journalist, he plans to overcome attempts to dissuade him from going in (official stories are inconsistent—they speak of plant diseases and yet a physicist has been summoned to inspect the jungle). An 'immense crystalline orchid' is displayed for sale in the local bazaar ('As Dr Sanders moved his head, a continuous font of light poured from the jewel'); the priest discovers a jewelled cross with similar properties and brandishes it, muttering that it is 'obscene'. Sanders can't understand what the priest finds obscene in a jewelled cross. Balthus denies that the cross was *jewelled*. He seems to be trying to confirm his doubts rather than allay them. The Echo satellite is seen passing overhead, its luminosity increased by at least tenfold—'a vast aerial lantern fired by the same light he had seen in the jewelled flowers'. Ventress is spotted, also behaving strangely, maniacally, and is attacked 'perhaps trying to steal some jewellery from the boats', suggests the girl. They find the body of a drowned man, a European, whose body is unnaturally malleable and warm, though he must have been in the river for days. From elbow to fingers his right arm has turned into 'a mass of translucent crystals, through which the prismatic outlines of the hand and fingers could be seen in a dozen multi-coloured reflections. This huge jewelled gauntlet, like the coronation armour of a Spanish conquistador, was drying in the sun, its crystals beginning to emit a hard vivid light.'

Sanders and Louise hire a speedboat and begin the journey into the interior. There are many signs that the country has been deserted—fled from, perhaps. They reach Mont Royal to discover that it is controlled by the military and that Balthus has arrived ahead of them. The forest is crystallising. No-one knows why. Two other sites exist, in the Florida Everglades and the Pripet Marshes in the USSR. At Mount Hubble Observatory they have seen distant galaxies efflorescing. There is a theory that the effect is like an incurable cancer—'an actual proliferation of the sub-atomic identity of all matter. It's as if a sequence of displaced but identical images of the same object were being produced by refraction through a prism, but with the element of time replacing the role of light.' Into the magical forest they go, to witness a helicopter trying to take off:

> The soldiers and the visiting party stopped to watch the vivid discharges of light that radiated from the blades like St Elmo's fire. Then, with a harsh roar like the bellow of a stricken animal, it slid backwards through the air and plunged tail-first towards the forest canopy a hundred feet below.

The party tries to go to the assistance of the pilots:

> The process of crystallization was more advanced. The fences along the road were so heavily encrusted that they had formed a continuous palisade, a white frost at least six inches thick on either side of the palings. The few houses between the trees glistened like wedding cakes, their white roofs and chimneys transformed into exotic minarets and baroque domes. On the lawn of green glass spurs a child's tricycle glittered like a Fabergé gem, the wheels starred into brilliant jasper crowns.

They come upon a jewelled crocodile, still able to move a little. 'Its blind eyes had been transformed into immense crystalline rubies. . . . Dr Sanders kicked its snout, scattering the wet jewels that choked its mouth.' Ventress watches them from a building, a gun levelled at Sanders.

The second part of the book begins with a straightforward rationale for all this. And yet the rationale also provides us with the metaphysical themes of the book. Time ('with the Midas touch') is responsible for the transformation.

> As more and more time "leaks" away, the process of super-saturation continues, the original atoms and molecules producing spatial replicas of themselves, substance without mass, in an attempt to increase their foot-hold upon existence. . . . It may be possible eventually for a single atom to produce an infinite number of duplicates of itself and so fill the entire universe, from which simultaneously all time has expired, an ultimate macrocosmic zero beyond the wildest dreams of Plato and Democritus.

The main characters are now confronted by their own psyches (the images of leprosy increase), by this terrifying many-sided metaphor. Does Man seek to order his universe by means of elaborate art imposed upon the fact of death? 'For a moment he seemed twenty years younger, the ruddy over-lay of colours on his cheeks more skilful than the palette of any Rubens or Titian.' Men appear to fight for jewels in a world becoming one vast jewel, but actually, like the priest, like Radek, the physician, they are fighting against death itself, denying the inevitability of the human condition—this is not my interpretation, Ballard is absolutely clear as he reveals, step by step, the motives of his characters. And towards the end Ballard gives us this familiar but deceptively simple message—that immortality can indeed be ours—'a direct consequence of the surrender by each of us of our own physical and temporal identities'. The message of an old-fashioned Romantic, a true surrealist, but not, as some would have it, a hopeless pessimist.

In *The Crystal World* Ballard had not completely rejected the trappings of the naturalistic novel (trappings which were once used to give verisimilitude to an earlier kind of British SF, derived from Wells, exemplified by the 'disaster' novels of Wyndham and Christopher) but he used them almost as if he intended to show how such devices confused the effect of the central symbolic images, for the book is as much about Ballard's own art—in its rejection of the exotic romance—as it is about our experiences of the world. Shortly after completing *The Crystal World* Ballard began (with

'The Assassination Weapon') to publish his ironic 'condensed novels' in *New Worlds* and to lose an audience which, particularly in the United States, seems willing only to reward those writers who embellish bar-room philosophising with the vulgar imagery of, as it were, an expensive whorehouse. He's doing all right in France, these days, where those effete intellectuals don't seem to mind a bit of uncompromising irony now and again. And Doubleday found themselves forced to pulp their entire edition of his last published collection *before* publication, they found it so unpleasant.[2] Or was 'pessimistic' the word they used?

---

2 Grove subsequently published it under the title *Love & Napalm: Export U.S.A.* Since then Ballard has published *Crash* (Farrar, Straus & Giroux, 1973; Pinnacle, 1974), *Concrete Island* (FS&G, 1974), *High-Rise* (Holt, Rinehart & Winston, 1977), and a collection, *Low-Flying Aircraft* (British publication, 1976).

# ■ The Voice

From *New Worlds*, October 1966

Whether JG Ballard realises it as yet or not, there is no doubt that he is the first clear voice of a movement destined to consolidate the literary ideas—surrealism, stream of consciousness, symbolism, science fiction, etc., etc.—of the twentieth century, forming them into something that is prose, but no longer fiction (as the term is generally understood) and that is a new instrument for dealing with the world of the future contained, observable, in the world of the present. Ballard does not reject the past—but he refuses to see why it should be allowed to influence the present. Most modern fiction, he says, is retrospective in its objectives. He wants a form—and is single-handedly moulding one—that is genuinely speculative and introspective in its objectives. Lacking a sufficiently precise instrument for his purposes, he has built one (an enormous achievement in itself). The instrument has no name, it has still to be refined and developed, but it exists in the shape of a group of stories that have caused impassioned controversy both in this country and the United States (though they have been accepted with general enthusiasm, it appears, in the Latin countries). The titles of these stories are: 'You and Me and the Continuum' (*Impulse* No. 1), 'The Assassination Weapon' (*New Worlds* 161), 'You: Coma: Marilyn Monroe' (*New Worlds* 163), and 'The Atrocity Exhibition' (*New Worlds* 166).

Critics may be forgiven for failing to see the significance of these stories as yet. The form is new, the obsessions are personal; but they cannot be identified with any one particular writer or literary movement of the past or the present, and those who have tried to identify them in this way have failed. To identify Ballard with Burroughs is impossible, in spite of Ballard's own enthusiasm for Burroughs's language and obsessions (it is probably fair to say that Ballard has interpreted Burroughs in terms of Ballard, but one cannot interpret Ballard in terms of Burroughs). Ballard's enthusiasm for Herman Melville and Joseph Conrad, as well as the surrealists, Joyce, Kafka and Borges, is quite as marked (if rarely expressed in print) as his enthusiasm for Burroughs, and while he sees Burroughs in a different light from these other writers, he clearly owes far more to them than to Burroughs.

As with music, as with painting, as with poetry, prose is metamorphosing to meet the demands of its time. The most unwieldy, least formal form of art, prose is always the last to change. James attempted to give it rules of structure that resembled those of music or painting, and his success was superb, but James was still adapting the form as it existed, tending to limit the form rather than expand it, whereas writers like Joyce and Burroughs— and now Ballard—were attempting to expand their range and produce something new. Ballard is not advocating a general overthrow of the prose form as we know it, he is saying that we need a new tool in the workshop—preferably a whole range of new tools—and he has invented one such tool.

In the past, composers have had to sit down to develop new musical instruments to express what they are doing (or have had to wait until those instruments were invented), painters have had to produce new pigments and radically new techniques, just as scientists, through the centuries, have had to make or wait for instruments to enable them to pursue their particular lines of enquiry.

Perhaps this is why so many scientists appreciate and sympathise with the work Ballard is doing and why literary critics, with a few outstanding exceptions, have failed (whether they like the work or not) in their interpretation of his recent prose.

In this country there now exists, centred around this magazine, a group of writers and critics who understand and enthusiastically support the work Ballard is doing. This does not mean they intend to follow Ballard—his is his own direction—but that they realise the need Ballard is fulfilling, and hope, in future, to play some part in fulfilling that need themselves. Their object is to write for an audience, to sell in the marketplace, to produce prose that, given a sympathetic reading, will be explicit, precise, directed, and operating on the levels of emotion, intellect and myth, as all good prose has done. Their object, if you like, is to tell stories—but to tell them in a form that is *not necessarily* conventional in construction or use of language. These writers are not all British. As well as JG Ballard, Langdon Jones, Michael Butterworth and several others, supporters of this movement include the Americans Judith Merril, Thomas M Disch and more, as well as editors and writers in France, Italy, Spain, and the Argentine who have written to this magazine or published comments about it in their own countries. The need has been with us for fifty years. It could take another ten to produce a large body of work which can meet this need. But we are now at last marshalling our forces. Watch this space.

# ■ *The Atrocity Exhibition*

**From the *Telegraph*, 28th August 1999**

Some thirty years ago, my magazine *New Worlds* enthusiastically commissioned much of *The Atrocity Exhibition*. I'm still inclined to think it's the book that best reflects our times.

You could argue that William Burroughs's *Naked Lunch* (1959) or Kate Millett's *Sexual Politics* (1970) had more influence on the century and while I'll admit to the greatness of, say, *Ulysses* or *Remembrance of Things Past*, they're really late 19th century books—a sort of culmination.

Ballard showed an intense, creative interest in the second half of the 20th century. I admire many of his later novels, including *Empire of the Sun*, but it seems to me that most of them, from *Crash* to *Cocaine Nights*, have been extended riffs on the themes he encapsulated so successfully in *The Atrocity Exhibition*.

In 1969 Ballard ran into American prurience when the whole first edition was pulped on the orders of the publisher Doubleday, largely because of two short pieces that are not especially typical, 'Why I Want To Fuck Ronald Reagan' and 'The Assassination of John Fitzgerald Kennedy Considered As A Downhill Motor Race'.

Together with such stories as 'You: Coma: Marilyn Monroe', 'The Assassination Weapon' and 'Plan for the Assassination of Jacqueline Kennedy', the book contains the original three-page version of *Crash*. It's largely free of the dodgy, sentimentalized sadism permeating Cronenberg's *Crash*. Ballard's wonderful elegiac tone, vaguely reminiscent of *nouvelle vague* voice-overs, saves this litany of destroyed celebrity and annihilated emotion from the coldness of its technique—pseudo-clinical, non-linear, fragmented, apparently plot-less. Ballard shared the engagement of many of his best sf contemporaries with issues only now in the public mind, but whereas writers like Dick were content to frame their parables in conventional narratives,

Ballard felt that the narrative itself distorted what he was trying to examine. His technique has been much imitated since. Without his intentions and concerns, his profoundly original imagination, it rarely succeeds.

While Burroughs demonstrated how to use modern language and metaphor, it was Ballard who focussed on those mythic images of the 20th century, fusing personalities and events, the public with the personal, fashioning the bombing of Hiroshima, the tragic legend of Princess Margaret, the assassination of Kennedy, the sexualized automobile, into enduring symbols of the human dilemma.

# ■ JG Ballard: In Memoriam

**From the *Times*, 25th April 2009**

'Jimmy' to early generations of friends and family, JG Ballard was typically stoical in dealing with his painful cancer, seeming to belong to the world of stiff upper-lip colonial hands into which he was apparently born. Actually he could not have been more different in outlook, turning down a CBE in protest at what he saw as a neocolonial war in Iraq and devoting much of his fiction to attacks on nostalgic atavism in the English character.

Although we were on nodding terms when we met occasionally at the offices of *New Worlds*, the science-fiction magazine, in the late 1950s, we did not become close friends until 1960, after we attended a conference of SF writers and discovered that the rest of our colleagues were interested merely in seeking new markets. From then on, together with the late Barrington Bayley, we met regularly, discussing our determination to make use of some of science fiction's generic conventions to write a form of fiction which, in our view, would address the specific conditions of post–Second World War society. Though he was nine years older, we had both emerged from that war with intense childhood memories. Most fiction we read had little to do with our generation's experience and was fundamentally backward-looking. While Jimmy admired Ray Bradbury and I liked Alfred Bester, our real heroes were a handful of absurdists and surrealists.

Perhaps as important to our friendship were the family visits to each others' homes soon after he moved to Shepperton in 1960. His wife Mary and my then wife Hilary were young mothers. Mary would cheerfully contradict him in the middle of one of his rhetorical flights, just as Hilary would remind me of my own exaggerations.

We began as journalists and were soon supporting our families by our fiction, finding our first publisher in EJ Carnell's science-fantasy magazines. Gradually we produced more idiosyncratic stories. When Carnell was reluctant to publish Jimmy's 'The Terminal Beach', Bayley and I persuaded him. We often discussed founding a magazine which was imaginative but ran fiction with, in Ballard's succinct phrase, 'the moral authority of a literature won from experience'. When, in 1964, I became editor of *New Worlds*, Jimmy contributed a guest editorial about William Burroughs, one of our inspirations ('A New Literature for the Space Age'), as well as a serial, 'Equinox', which became *The Crystal World*, where the Earth suffers a kind of crystalline contagion, a thematic sequel to *The Drowned World*, set in an inundated London, a work that some believe to be one of the first warnings of global warming.

That same year, he took his family on holiday to Alicante after Mary's operation for appendicitis. Not long after they left, we received a telegram telling us that Mary had died. He would be returning with the children by road. Mary had been buried in the Protestant cemetery. Jimmy had been unable to afford to bring her home.

On his arrival he told me how he had been forced to pull his old Armstrong Siddeley to the side of the road whenever tears made it impossible to continue. At the time he blamed himself for Mary's death. He never mentioned this to me again. He devoted himself to raising 'Little Jimmy', Bea and Fay on his own, claiming convincingly that the baked bean, the staple gun and a pot of fabric glue were the cornerstones of successful childcare.

Like many great visionaries, Jimmy had an enormous store of common sense and ordinary wisdom, which enabled him to raise the children and, as they said, have the sheets washed on time. But the stress of earning a living and raising his family told on him. He drank far too much Johnnie Walker and, when friends tried to find him girlfriends, did not always treat them well. In fact, the first time we fell out was over his treatment of women. But I did manage to introduce him eventually to Claire Walsh, who became his long-time companion.

I don't think he changed anything about the Shepperton house after Mary died. For a while his back garden served as a pit in which he burnt review copies (he phoned me to complain bitterly that Fahrenheit 451 was *not* the temperature at which book paper burned) or as a jungle of sunflowers, which he had seeded. For years Mary's clothes remained in her closets, his typewriter sat on the same living room table, commissioned copies of lost Delvaux paintings hung on the opposite wall and a unicycle stood in his hallway.

Although unreliable sources claimed he regularly took LSD, the only tab he ever dropped he obtained from me. I gave him some important advice about how best to take it which, typically, he completely ignored. The subsequent trip was so horrific that he never took another. The title of his book *Cocaine Nights* was actually chosen by his publisher. By 1966 he was writing arguably his best short work, including 'The Assassination Weapon', offering all the factors resulting in Kennedy's murder, and most of the stories which appeared in his 1969 collection *The Atrocity Exhibition*. Published without incident in the UK, when the book appeared in the US it was pulped before publication by Doubleday, the publishing firm, who objected to his sardonic 'Plan for the Assassination of Jacqueline Kennedy'. 'The Assassination Weapon' helped to define the character of the fiction we were to run increasingly, making a clear break with generic science fiction. These 'condensed novels' demonstrated a theory we had developed whereby iconographic figures, with their own dense stories, functioned as narratives, enabling us to tell many stories at once.

Our friend Bill Butler, publisher of Unicorn Books, ran 'Why I Want to Fuck Ronald Reagan', famously prosecuted under the Obscene Publications Act. Jimmy did not appear at the trial because he was asked to defend himself against obscenity charges. He claimed that the story was intentionally obscene and, if called, would have to say so. In my view *The Atrocity Exhibition* contains Ballard's finest and most innovative work. Together with *Empire of the Sun*, his autobiographical novel set around a Second World War Japanese civilian prison camp, it remains perhaps his best book.

Jimmy had quickly shown himself to be a true original with a distinctive style and subject matter. His obsessions with suburbia, drained swimming pools, abandoned hotels, deserted motorways and mysterious beaches littered with mid-20th-century technology, his poetic, retrospective harmonies, rich with original metaphors, became trademarks of his exotic, erotic stories. His characters were solitary, sleepwalking through landscapes that might have been painted by Dalí or Ernst, and if his gift for dialogue was limited, he compensated by offering utterly fresh observations of the contemporary world, resonating on levels understood by Freud or Jung. Ironically, his late novels are closer to the conventions of SF satire than the earlier ones.

Although literary critics were quick to minimise his years as an SF writer, Jimmy made no effort to divorce himself from his SF roots, though preferring to call himself first a 'speculative' and later an 'apocalyptic' writer. His influence was seen in the work of his admirers including Angela Carter, Martin Amis, Will Self, Iain Sinclair, Alan Moore, M John Harrison and Christopher Priest. Tending, in the early years, to rely on me to introduce him to fellow spirits, like Burroughs, Chris Evans (*New Worlds*' science editor), the artist Eduardo Paolozzi (our 'aeronautics adviser') and others, Jimmy remained a modest and rather shy man, a loyal friend who avoided what he called 'the literary crowd' even more assiduously than SF conventions, living quietly at home and only rarely going out. He was a working writer, leading the rather dull life the job usually entails.

After *The Atrocity Exhibition* the equally controversial *Crash* followed, describing the characters' obsession with sexually fetishised car crashes that some say anticipated the death of Diana, Princess of Wales. First of a loose trilogy including *Concrete Island* (in which a man finds himself stranded on a traffic island) and *High-Rise* (occupants of a posh apartment block revert to primitivism), published between 1973 and 1975, the books were produced during what was arguably the time when his life and fiction were at their closest. I found it hard not to feel ambivalent about his famous exhibition of crashed cars. There were hair-raising rides and the occasional smash. I recall going with him to collect his almost completely totalled Ford Granada from the wrecker's yard. He insisted on driving the thing home, creaking and stinking of mildew, at a top speed of 20mph.

By the time his children were grown he began work on the book I had hoped he would write. *Empire of the Sun* appeared in 1984. In my view this book revealed, with its images of a Shanghai deserted by its former residents, its empty buildings and swimming pools, its crashed plane and wrecked machines, its solitary, introspective protagonist, the realities of his supposedly invented images. It grounded many of his early traumas as well as his previously unexamined behaviour, including his understandable expectations of betrayal, his suspicion of kindness and, together with the security its success as a bestseller and movie brought him, allowed him to relax and become again the generous, affable human being he had been when we first met.

Soon after his sale to Spielberg we went out to eat together. 'Have you noticed, Mike, how rude customers in restaurants have become?' he asked. 'I'm not sure it's that, Jimmy,' I said. 'I think we can now afford to eat in the rude people's restaurants.' The cash simply went into his current account. Until then he had never owned a credit card, taking a sum of money from the bank on a Monday and making it last the week. This had not prevented him offering me his last £200 when he heard I was broke. Nor did wealth change him. He remained one of the least materialistic people I knew.

# ■ Introduction to *The Secret of Sinharat* by Leigh Brackett

**From the Planet Stories edition, December 2007**

### Stark Rides Again

They all came out of Edgar Rice Burroughs, of course—Brackett, Bradbury, even Ballard—and Burroughs came out of the Western desert lands as obviously as Hammett and Chandler came out of the Western cities—San Francisco and Los Angeles. Those ochre vistas of Nevada, New Mexico, Arizona and California, broken by old, eroded mountains and inhabited by a mysterious people, who left cities and monuments behind them before vanishing forever, were Burroughs's inspiration just as they inspired native Californians Leigh Brackett and her protégé Ray Bradbury. In both cases the original inspiration of Burroughs was modified by later Californians. In Leigh Brackett's case it was Sam Spade and Philip Marlowe who clearly gave something to Eric John Stark and her other lone adventurers. In Bradbury's it was Steinbeck's characters, especially those who lived on Tortilla Flats or Cannery Row. There's a strong argument for claiming that the majority of the best and most influential fiction of the 20th century (at least the first half) came out of California, from Jack London to Philip K Dick.

Leigh Brackett is probably best known now for her involvement in movies from *The Big Sleep* to *The Empire Strikes Back* but it was as a writer of 'sword and planet' fiction that I first knew her. As a boy I would scour the second-hand bookshops of South London for copies of *Planet Stories*, *Startling Stories* or *Thrilling Wonder Stories*, eager for more tales of Eric John Stark, whose adventures I had first come across in the rather thin UK versions of those magazines. I'm not sure if the titles were Leigh's or the choice of the editors but they had a great resonance for me—*Queen of the Martian Catacombs*, *Black Amazon of Mars*, *The Temptress of Venus* and others. For me, Stark was even more of a hero than John Carter and, of course, he was much more in tune with my own times when the screen was filled with movies like *The Maltese Falcon*, *The Killers* and *Pick Up on South Street*, what Leigh's husband Edmond Hamilton called 'urban adventure tales' and what we these days call simply 'noir'—movies full of grim-eyed men and taunting, beautiful, exotic women united against the system and frequently put, through no fault of their own, on the wrong side of the Law. Even the westerns of those days, like *Shane*, took on that same romantic quality. Later, in the movies of Clint Eastwood, for instance, those qualities would emerge again and again, for these were men a bored woman could love and an adventurous man emulate.

For half my youth I yearned to be riding some strange, complaining reptilian steed across the dead sea bottoms of Mars while for the other half I longed to be wearing a trench coat, a snap-brim fedora and walking the rain-sodden streets of the big city. Even when I could afford the trench coat and the fedora (I was already in the rain-sodden big city) I was still wondering if it would ever be possible to find a Mars whose vast red deserts were interrupted by low, broken bluffs and the ruins of cities that were ancient before Man first emerged on Earth. If my very earliest teenage stories were influenced by Burroughs, there was no doubt that my first published adult fantasy stories were influenced by Brackett. And I wasn't the only one. Half the British sf writers I knew could quote Brackett verbatim and had written their own versions of Stark, the best known of which today is Edward C Tubb's *Dumarest of Terra*, perhaps the longest running single-character series in UK sf.

Edmond Hamilton, whose reputation in science fiction preceded Leigh's, was one of her first mentors, as was the great Henry Kuttner. Kuttner's own fantasy hero Elak of Atlantis was never as convincing as any Leigh gave us. Like Hamilton, he was at heart a true science fiction man. But both recognised the originality of Leigh's imagination and encouraged her to write the stories which are best described as science fantasy, incorporating elements of both science fiction and fantasy, as well as the old-fashioned scientific romance. Of course, she could write straight science fiction and often did. She could also write hard-boiled detective thrillers in the manner of Carroll John Daly, Lester Dent and the more sophisticated *Black Mask* writers who followed them. She published several including her first, *No Place for a Corpse*, and one ghosted for the actor George Sanders, as *Stranger at Home*, which showed that she could have pursued a perfectly lucrative career as a full-time crime novelist had she wished. But interplanetary adventure fiction remained her first love and by the time she was encouraging the young Ray Bradbury (who co-wrote *Lorelie of the Red Mist* with her) she had become a star of *Planet Stories* and the other pulps.

I considered those pulps far superior to the more respectable sf magazines like *Astounding* (later *Analog*) and *The Magazine of Fantasy & Science Fiction*. I think my preference was mostly to do with the unchecked vividness of the writing. Astounding was too wooden, too evidently written by enthusiastic engineers. *F&SF* struck me as too pretentious.

I have often argued that the language and music of *Black Mask* came out of California, along with the imagery. James M Cain, originally from Maryland, used to say that 'Californian' was what made him write as he did. The author of *Double Indemnity* and *Mildred Pierce* claimed that his noir stories were inspired by hearing the language of the California streets. He would become irritable when people suggested he copied Chandler. His stories, he said, sounded like Chandler's because both writers (along with Hammett) were subject to the same daily, casual influences. They heard 'Californian' all around them and the language of the West Coast cities was as vivid and as vital as anything you could hear in 20th century New York. Brackett's experiences, of course, were the same. She grew up with that language. She didn't live too far from where Burroughs settled (on land he christened 'Tarzana'). And she grew up admiring, along with Douglas Fairbanks, characters who weren't a million miles from Sam Spade. Burroughs could never, for instance, have made John Carter smoke a cigarette and grind it out in the sand of a dead sea bottom as Stark does in the opening pages of *The Secret of Sinharat*, for all the world like some character out of *Casablanca*.

A few years passed before I realized that Leigh was a woman, just as I didn't know that CL Moore, creator of Northwest Smith (also something of an ancestor of Stark's) was of the opposite sex to my own. They became known as the 'Queens of the SF Pulps' and both certainly knew how to write a great embittered romantic man as well as any Brontë. Stark was a role model for me long before I had read *Wuthering Heights* and discovered Heathcliff or Mr Rochester. Stark was Humphrey Bogart playing Douglas Fairbanks parts. Leigh had a photograph of herself as a little girl with Fairbanks. She grew up loving those dashing sword-wielding adventurers, as I did. Later, she would get to know Bogart, too. While decades and thousands of miles apart, we developed the same enthusiasms and when together could be like a couple of kids recollecting our favourite scenes from *The Thief of Baghdad* or *The Warlord of Mars*. We loved westerns, too, and you'll find resonances of Max Brand in her stories, while some of my first fiction was about Kit Carson and other heroes of the borderlands.

The story of how Howard Hawks sent for 'this guy Brackett', wanting to work with him on *The Big Sleep*, is today very well-known. To his credit (and somewhat typically—for in Hawks's world women divided into strong ones he could work with and weak ones he could romance) he went on to get her to do the lion's share of that script and she would later write some of his finest later films with John Wayne, beginning with the magnificent *Rio Bravo*. She was in some ways a typical Hawks heroine. She had a big, steady voice and a way of looking at you directly which made you decide to cut out the bullshit, should you be thinking of offering her any. You could easily imagine her staring down an Apache war-chief while she forked a cartridge into her Winchester.

She and I became very close friends, in spite of our considerable political differences (she tended to share Wayne's views) and we frequently met, often visiting one another's houses when I was in the US or she and Ed were in England, which they loved. We would swap favourite food—I'd send her English tea (then hard to get) and she'd send me maple syrup from their own farm. During the years of the Vietnam War we had quite distinctly opposing views, but somehow they never got in the way of a deepening friendship which was fuelled by all the many things we did have in common, including a powerful respect for the individual. This respect coloured all Leigh's fiction, whether it was about lone sword-wielding outlaws like Stark or black frontiersmen like the hero of her historical novel *Follow the Free Wind*.

Whatever her powers of synthesis, Leigh emerged as a great original almost from the moment she started publishing. Her name on the cover of *Planet* would put sales up in a moment. And if it was an Eric John Stark story, people would go to enormous trouble to seek a copy out. I remember some sf writers at a convention quoting whole passages aloud and competing together to produce a pastiche on a typewriter borrowed from somewhere. Stark was one of the most influential characters to come out of the sf pulps and Brackett's style influenced more than one generation: you can, of course, hear echoes of it in Ray Bradbury who in turn influenced the likes of Harlan Ellison and JG Ballard.

As already noted, Leigh was a screen writer of the first rank and her script for *The Long Goodbye* with Elliott Gould was more than a faithful adaptation of Chandler. She took Chandler's original into areas he might have taken it himself if he had been working in Brackett's age. It is a movie whose reputation has continued to grow, at once an homage and an interpretation of Philip Marlowe very different to the one she did for Bogart. When Leigh was asked to write the script of *The Empire Strikes Back* for George Lucas, she saw a version of Stark in Han Solo and might have done something very interesting with the character had she not died prematurely a year after her husband, Ed. As it is, there was always an element of Stark in Solo, just as there is in every other planet-hopping outlaw who rides the space-lanes and is as handy with a sword (or lightsabre) as he is with a ray-gun.

Stark's planetary system was one in which most worlds were just about inhabitable, but the majority of his adventures took place on Mars (the desert world) or Venus (by common consent of the times a world of seas and swamps). This is a system which was largely sketched out by Burroughs and Kline and their followers and developed through the 1930s and '40s in the romantic sf pulps. For me, it remains the actuality no rational astronomer will ever challenge. And Brackett gave us memorable heroines and villain- esses worthy of her great heroes, the greatest of whom is Eric John Stark. Not until the cyberpunks of the 1980s did anyone combine the definitive style of '40s noir with the wilder reaches of sf romanticism and in this, as in so many ways, Leigh was an innovator and an inspiration.

Her work lives precisely because of her ability to combine full-strength technicolour imagery with all-out power prose that was written at top speed, rarely revised, and had a clarity and punch few of her pulp peers ever mastered, let alone bettered. What she did in these stories, expanded from their original *Planet Stories* appearance and all the better for that, was to offer a generation of writers and readers a gold standard for the production of uninhibited imaginative adventure fiction which has yet to be improved upon. If you're reading her for the first time, I envy you.

# ■ James Cawthorn: 1928–2008

**From *Locus*, January 2009, and in part from *Relapse*, May 2009**

It's impossible to measure how important Jim Cawthorn's friendship was to me. Apart from one childhood pal he was my oldest surviving friend. I feel I knew Jim all my life.

Visiting me one afternoon at my place in Ladbroke Grove, the eminent artist Eduardo Paolozzi, whose work is found in most major galleries worldwide, paused in front of a drawing and began to enthuse about it in a way I'd rarely seen him do before. 'Who is this guy? Why don't I know him?' It was a portrait of Elric that Jim had drawn for the dust-wrapper of *Stormbringer*. Eduardo demanded that I introduce him. Similarly Burne Hogarth, whom many believe the best Tarzan comic illustrator, wrote his only introduction to a living artist about Jim. His admirers were from everywhere, yet until he started to draw for fanzines, his work had been seen by very few. His incredibly detailed and delicate stencil technique (a lost art today like steel engraving) immediately made him a hit.

A keen Edgar Rice Burroughs fan, he illustrated *Erbania* and went on to work for local fanzines before improving the appearance of *Camber*, *Eldritch Dream Quest, AMRA* and my own fanzines, including my book, SF and music fanzines (including *Burroughsania*). We had been friends since 1955 and his early professional work—illustrations, comic strips and fiction— first appeared in *Tarzan Adventures* when I took over as editor in 1957. He moved to London at this time and illustrated *Sexton Blake Library* when I moved to Amalgamated (now Fleetway) Press and we wrote *Caribbean Crisis* together. By then Jim was writing and drawing mostly educational material for a variety of publications, including the prestigious *Look and Learn* weekly. With Pauline Baynes, he was the first Tolkien artist (apart from Tolkien).

When I took over *New Worlds* in 1964, Jim did our first covers, illustrating 'Equinox' (later *The Crystal World*) by Ballard. He became a mainstay of

*New Worlds* magazine, illustrating many Ballard stories, in particular, and also my own Dancers at the End of Time novellas. He remained associated with the magazine until 1978. He also illustrated many books by me in US, UK and German editions. Savoy had commissioned his large-size graphic novel of *Stormbringer* in 1976 and he became their resident artist until his death, illustrating books by me, Henry Treece, Maurice Richardson and others, as well as doing stunning graphic versions of my Hawkmoon books. In 1975 we co-wrote the script, intended to be faithful to the ERB novel, of *The Land that Time Forgot* and Jim then wrote a version of *The People that Time Forgot* which was largely distorted by the producers and from which he disassociated himself.

In 1988 he wrote *Fantasy: The 100 Best Books* which, though credited to both of us, was almost wholly by Jim. A brilliant series of encapsulating essays, the book remains an outstanding work of witty scholarship. He continued as an illustrator and journalist until relatively recently when poor health stopped his professional work. His last commission was for Savoy's website, showing himself drawing some favourite characters. A gentle, unaggressive, slightly reclusive man, Jim was a good, funny friend, the last survivor to share a house in Princedale Road, Notting Hill, with Judy Merril, Tom Disch, Barry Bayley, John Sladek and others during the '60s. He had illustrated them all and written some hilarious parodies of their work. He introduced me to ER Eddison, W Hope Hodgson, Leiber, Peake, Richardson, Poul Anderson and some of the less well-known writers and illustrators of the twentieth century. Widely read in all fields, able to illustrate anything he was asked to do from fiction to technical manuals, Jim remained modest and generous. He made many friends and no enemies. He was admitted to the Queen Elizabeth Hospital in Gateshead, Co. Durham, UK, on Friday, 28th November, for routine tests, and died there unexpectedly on 2nd December, 2008. An autopsy revealed the cause as pancreatic cancer. Those to whom he regularly sent personal, funny birthday and Christmas cards will miss him. His death remains a tremendous blow to all his friends.

Even now, when I come across something I know would give him pleasure, it's my impulse to phone him or write to him and then I remember, as with Barry Bayley, that he isn't there and I realise how very much I miss him, how completely a part of my life he was.

# ■ Fascination with Mortality: The Late Thomas M Disch

A Review of *The Wall of America*

**From the *Telegraph*, 26th November 2008**

A few writers—Bradbury, Vonnegut and Ballard among them—possess such coherent, idiosyncratic talent that, in spite of their visionary imaginations, the reader becomes engaged chiefly with their style or characters. The invention, superb as it is, becomes almost secondary. Thomas M Disch, who shot himself in Manhattan on July 4 this year, was such a writer.

An ironist and a satirist, he published his final novel in June, the hilarious *The Word of God*, in which Satan sends Philip K Dick back to Minnesota in 1939 to ensure that he, Disch (or God), will not be conceived as a result of Thomas Mann's affair with Disch's mother in a Minneapolis hotel room.

Disch knew Dick and had a low opinion of him, certain he had conned the public. Dick, not the most mentally stable of writers, and frequently jealous of his talented contemporaries, had attempted to turn Disch in to the FBI as a spy. Disch himself did not easily forgive a bad turn; *The Word of God* was his comical revenge.

*The Wall of America* is a collection of short stories compiled before he died. Disch's fascination with mortality permeated his fiction and poetry. His first novel was called *The Genocides* (1965) and his second story collection *Getting into Death* (1971). Some readers found his work pessimistic; others regarded his fascination with mortality as a romantic posture. His blog gave a taste of what an original, funny and clever companion and poet he was and the stories in this collection offer an idea of his extraordinary range.

The title story mocks the thinking that leads to the construction of a vast, high wall across the US-Canadian border. The wall is soon used by artists as an informal gallery space and we are drawn into the life of one not especially good painter. 'The White Man' is a delicately complex tale set against a New York City of the near future where global warming gradually breaks down the familiar life of the city. Rising tides, changing weather patterns and the erosion of the social infrastructure make life less comfortable for those unable to move away.

A black schoolgirl, coping with collapsing public services, comes under the influence of a church leader not unlike President-Elect Obama's own Reverend Wright, who blames all ills on 'the white man'. She strikes up a relationship with a quirky shopkeeper whose raison d'être is to bring a little light-hearted fantasy into the lives of those who pass his window. Her misunderstanding of her pastor and the white store owner's motives result in a tragically ironic development with as many moral surprises as the best of Annie Proulx.

Not all these stories are so ambitious, but all are every bit as good as Ballard or Vonnegut. 'Ringtime' amusingly suggests how people of the future learn to make a living as surrogates for more jaded citizens. 'The Owl and the Pussycat' looks at the relationship between human beings and the creatures we anthropomorphise, while 'The Abduction of Bunny Steiner, or A Shameless Lie' comments slyly on the modern penchant for publishers and agents to persuade writers to tell outright lies to their readers.

Given that Disch, who regretted joining the military in the late fifties, and finessed an honourable psychiatric discharge by telling as his own the story of Oedipus (transformed to a Minnesota farm house), 'In Praise of Older Women' is a sharply knowing version of the Jocasta myth. 'Painting Eggplants' again riffs on Disch's belief that much conceptual art is, like science fiction, a kind of children's art, a conspiracy between a public yearning to be bamboozled and con-artists only too willing to comply.

Since Disch held several gallery exhibitions of his paintings (many conceptual), the story is somewhat self-mocking. 'Three Chronicles of Xglotl and Rwang' is another commentary on the use of science fiction for witty and sardonic ends.

Disch thought a lot about his calling. 'In Xanadu' is about the relation between art and commerce. Indeed, most of these stories deal with Disch's thoughts on the relation between the worlds of creativity and venality, whether it is 'One Night, or Scheherazade's Bare Minimum', 'The Man Who Read a Book' or 'The First Annual Performance Art Festival at the Slaughter Rock Battlefield'.

Disch was a working writer, producing a substantial body of poetry, criticism and fiction, including his classic homage to Mann, *Camp Concentration*. If there is a sense of finality about these stories, all his work can probably be seen as a progress towards death, for he talked often of suicide when not entertaining us. These stories are usually humorous, thoughtful and in no way pessimistic. They are as good as any you will find this year, whether published as 'science fiction' or 'literature'.

If you enjoy the work of JG Ballard, you will, I guarantee, get as much from his contemporary, Thomas M Disch.

# ■ Tom Disch Tribute

**From *Locus*, August 2008**

Tom was one of my most valued friends. When he arrived in Europe, with John Sladek, in the early '60s, I thought they were the funniest pair I had ever met. Tom got to London in time to alternate with Ballard as *New Worlds'* resident genius. He was a huge asset and over the years gave the magazine some superb fiction including 'The Squirrel Cage', *Camp Concentration* and *334.* I was also privileged to publish his first story collection *102 H-Bombs (*Compact 1966*).* Literate, quick-witted, clever, he was something of a catalyst. His friends Pam Zoline, already in London, and John Clute, freshly there from Crete, were recruited to our pages and we all became great pals. At one point the rooming house around the corner from me in Ladbroke Grove was exclusively occupied by sf people—Barry Bayley, John Sladek, Jim Cawthorn, Judy Merril and Tom—while another group shared Zoline's flat in Camden Town. Our lives became as intertwined as characters in a Disch masterpiece, with a lot more good times than bad. We were soon travelling or hiking together on the Continent, in Britain and across America.

In 1967, on a poetry reading tour, Tom had formed an unhappy attachment for his first lover, the promiscuous poet Lee Harwood. Always emotionally vulnerable, Tom had a hard time coming to terms with his sexuality until, back in Manhattan, he met translator and poet Charlie Naylor and entered a stable relationship, which ended three decades later with Charlie's tragic death from cancer.

Tom was a true, old-fashioned man of letters, an enormously gifted all-rounder, a wit and ironist of the highest order, a kindly teacher, perceptive critic and essayist, generous with his gifts but quick as a dagger if he felt under attack. He suffered fools perhaps less readily than some, but valued, encouraged and praised intelligence. Though popular fame generally evaded him, Tom knew considerable *succès d'estime* in almost everything he did. Pretty much to the last, rallying again and again, he continued to find humour in his life and his art but, under the weight of circumstances, he also began talking undramatically of suicide. His friends did everything possible to divert him as the world loaded further misfortune on him. Shortly before he died he had begun a new novel. 'This is one I *have* to finish,' he said, 'it starts so well.' And it did and I wish he had gone on with it. But, much as I loved his work, it will be his affectionate, jovial friendship I shall miss the most.

# ■ A Constant Curiosity

**From a Barrington Bayley website: previously unavailable in print**

I have said it before and he proves it almost every time he publishes a story—Barry Bayley is unique. He has a mind like no-one else's. He has written stories so strange, so oddly logical, that you wonder if he isn't, after all, a changeling of some kind. I seem to remember he used to think that he might be. He told me that his parents used to promise to take him to a movie, an event he anticipated with much pleasure. He thought his father was some kind of wizard. He imagined that when he got to the cinema there would be three seats, two for his parents, and one for him. They would sit there and watch the movie rather like Stalin and his daughter, Svetlana, would visit the private underground theatre in the Kremlin and sit there together watching Charlie Chaplin and Mickey Mouse. He must have wondered at the number of his parents' friends and relations when he finally did get to go to the pictures.

I met Barry Bayley in the mid-1950s. I made a number of friends through those weekly meetings of The Globe, Hatton Garden, but the late Pete Taylor and Barry, both recently emerged from their Air Force National Service, were the best. If I have science fiction fandom to thank for anything, it is those long lasting friendships. Pete died young many years ago. Barry and I remained good friends (with a few ups and downs) for close to fifty years. Through all that time, he continued to inspire me, both as a person and as a writer.

I used to stay with Barry at his Chelsea flat when I had no home of my own. We were an oddly mismatched pair. When we walked along Kings Road together (in those days Chelsea was still a slightly rundown bohemian neighbourhood) people used to smile at us. I never knew quite why until one day I glimpsed the two of us in a shop mirror and couldn't stop laughing. Talk about Fafhrd and the Gray Mouser! It was clear that we were not actually of the same species or, if of the same species, of very different types. I was 6' 2" and Barry was about a foot shorter. I was burly and bearded. He was delicate and clean-shaven. He had a ready intelligence, able to absorb scientific ideas with extraordinary speed. I didn't know one end of an equation from the other.

Barry never did grow a beard, but thanks to him I did become a little bit smarter. Or better informed, at any rate. He turned me on to all kinds of ideas, strange books, odd phenomena. And, of course, there was the ultimate introduction, for which I shall remain forever grateful. He turned me on to the Beatles. We used to hang out at the Duke of York (I think it was) at the top of Charlotte Street, West London. A short passage ran from Charlotte up into Goodge Street. The little area had everything we needed—a pub, a betting shop and a café. Very occasionally we would back a horse, though more often would be persuaded to part with a few bob on a cert by one of the local ladies of the night, whose off-duty company we frequently found ourselves in. The café was run by a Greek and maybe it had dolmades (it certainly had tasty kebabs), but I remember it mostly as a fairly standard greasy spoon, except that it had a very good juke box. Coming home from one of my trips abroad, I met Barry there and he told me about this great record he'd heard. It was the Beatles' first single. After that, there was no looking back. (Ironically I'd missed my chance to see them a few years earlier at the Cavern, Liverpool, when my friend Bill Harry failed to persuade me that this group wasn't the usual imitation of US rockers and I'd refused to leave the pub to go across the street to hear them).

That wasn't all Barry introduced me to. His enthusiasm for fiction led me to a lifelong relish for the best of what the pulps could offer, including the work of Charles Harness, which I was later to have the privilege of reprinting, and Herman Hesse, then very hard to find in translation. He introduced me to John Cowper Powys, Ouspenski and many other idiosyncratic writers and thinkers. He introduced me to composers. We were both great fans of Mozart, but Barry also liked certain jazz musicians, especially Duke Ellington. It's fair to say that from about the age of sixteen, Barry Bayley provided me with a great deal of my cultural education. He also had the kind of brain which could spot the flaws in arguments. When John W Campbell went nuts and started trying to save the world with such things as Dianetics and the Dean Drive (perpetual motion) Barry would demonstrate what my instincts already told me were flawed arguments. Barry even anticipated the Dean Drive with an idea of his own, which is why he could see the logical gaps in that particular invention. Because of his abundant curiosity, he would make friends with people, like the guy who had been an auditor at an early Hubbard operation in East Grinstead, who had pinched an e-meter and was able to show us how it worked (it was an old ex-army lie-detector with a different gauge stuck over the original). He told good stories, too, and provided me with many anecdotes which I still repeat to any willing audience.

Like me, Barry had started writing early. I had become editor of *Tarzan Adventures* at sixteen. He had published his first story in the Vargo Statten sf magazine at fifteen. His career was nipped in the bud because he was a little older than me. Which meant that he had been snapped up by the Draft to do National Service whereas I had missed it by what seemed seconds (though I had done basic training in the ATS, much to my chagrin when I learned I didn't have to go in). The RAF had not done Barry any favours. It really had been an unpleasant experience for someone of such a quietly strange, independent mind. Some people argue that National Service made 'men' of their boys (whatever that means). Few discuss the thoughtful, intelligent young men whose lives were occasionally ruined and very often curtailed because of those two years. Any momentum Barry had achieved before he went in was largely dissipated by the time he came out. Many of his short story markets vanished during that period and we saw most of the British sf magazines go under before I was twenty. All we had left, after a while, were the Carnell-edited magazines, *New Worlds*, *Science Fantasy* and *Science Fiction Adventures*. Try as he might, Barry could not get Ted Carnell to take one of his stories. Eventually, when so many excellent pieces of short fiction had been rejected by Ted, I decided to ask him what he disliked about them. Ted told me frankly that he just didn't like Barry's work. It was a blind spot, he said. A prejudice. He couldn't help it.

I went straight to Barry, of course, and told him this, suggesting he get a friend to agree to let Barry use his name (it was the only way we knew of getting paid in those days when few of us had bank accounts) to submit stories and pass the money on to him if they should be accepted. Sure enough, the first 'PF Woods' story which Carnell received he bought and thereafter 'PF Woods' became a bit of a new star in the sf firmament. Carnell was delighted with his find. Meanwhile the actual Mr Woods got a bit tempted by the cash and eventually Barry, though getting published, was no longer getting paid. I went to Carnell again. 'All those PF Woods stories you published,' I told him, 'were by Barry Bayley. Now will you look at his stories on their own merits?' Carnell could be an obstinate man (Kyril Bonfiglioli, who took over *Science Fantasy* when I took over *New Worlds*, said

Carnell had the ability to see straight to the heart of your story and tell you to cut it out). 'Well, I still don't like Barry Bayley stories,' he insisted.

So PF Woods's career continued for a little while longer and then Carnell retired, naming me as his successor. The first chance I got, I began to publish Barry under his own name. And I do mean the first chance. The initial issue of *New Worlds* I edited carried his new long novella, 'The Star Virus'. I sent a copy of the magazine to an acquaintance of mine, then living in Paris. His name was William Burroughs.

Bill Burroughs was so struck by 'The Star Virus' that he sent me an enthusiastic note back. He had decided, he said, to lift the idea. Would Barry mind? Barry didn't. Thereafter, the idea of human beings as a kind of virus, spreading through the cosmos, became one of Bill's useful metaphors. Barry was to return the compliment some ten years later when he wrote 'The Four Colour Problem'. Much of his other work was reprinted in the outstanding short story collection *The Knights of the Limits*.

Thereafter Barry really did become a star of the magazine, along with the likes of JG Ballard, Brian Aldiss, Thomas M Disch and Roger Zelazny. M John Harrison, who would later become a welcome regular to the pages of *New Worlds*, was knocked out by the next stories Barry contributed to the magazine. 'All the King's Men' and 'The Ship of Disaster' had the same weird quality of mind, the same strange angle of attack, which made a Bayley story like none other. Harrison was unstinting in his enthusiasm for Bayley who inspired short stories like 'The Machine in Shaft Ten' as well such novels as *The Centauri Device* and whose influence can be found even in Harrison's late work, such as the much-admired *Light*. 'The Ship of Disaster' also helped Harrison to formulate his own outstanding fantasy stories found in such collections as *Viriconium Nights*.

Barry's enormous influence on my work, especially my early science fiction (to which he contributed, sometimes anonymously!), shouldn't go unremarked. He encouraged me to think for myself and, indeed, feel for myself, though I must admit I never had his mental discipline, nor his capacity for meditation, which was one of the other things that in those days set him apart from most of us. Here was the first contemporary I knew who was capable of just sitting all day and *thinking.*

Of course, we used to rib him about it a lot, congratulating him on finding a way to do nothing all day, but the strange thing was that stuff actually came out of those sessions. Extraordinary stories. By that time Don Wollheim had taken the novelised version of *The Star Virus*. Wollheim began to publish Barry with considerable enthusiasm. Don had always had the capacity to find and encourage people with 'different' mind sets and while he might be best remembered now as the man who started the Hobbit cult in America (by producing a pirate edition of *Lord of the Rings* after he discovered it was in the public domain in the US) he and Damon Knight were probably the two editors in their day to publish most of the outstanding science fiction and fantasy writers.

A little earlier than this, Barry and I had formed a partnership. The rubber stamp still exists somewhere. Moorcock & Bayley, it reads, 8 Colville Terrace, London W11. We would write in collaboration or as individuals but all our work would be submitted under both names. This led to some confusion in later years, when both Barry and I discovered we couldn't tell each other's work apart. Occasionally a short story would appear with Barry's name on it and it would be by me. Sometimes a story of Barry's would be credited to me. We had enjoyed the anonymity of writing for weekly magazines. We had done a vast amount of educational material for such periodicals as *Look and Learn*, *Knowledge* and *Boys' World*. We wrote comic strips for *Lion*, *Tiger*, *Thriller Picture Library* and most of the other Fleetway juveniles. We filled the best part of entire 'annuals' (the hardcover albums associated with the weeklies, which appeared every Christmas in the UK) and we collaborated on stories, though rarely publishing them under both our names. Our first joint sale to *New Worlds* was with a story called 'Going Home'. Barry also collaborated with my then wife, Hilary Bailey, though again he wasn't credited.

By the late 1960s Barry was living in a boarding house in Portland Road, Notting Dale, whose landlord gave him the responsibility of looking after the apartments and renting them out. Within a very short time the entire boarding house was crammed with sf writers. At the top lived John Sladek. Next door to him lived Thomas M Disch. On the floor below were Jim Cawthorn and in the basement was Judith Merril. All these writers were attracted to the UK because at the time the arts scene was considerably livelier and the so-called 'new wave' (never a term we used ourselves—it was Jim Linwood's description of a kind of fanzine, originally) with *New Worlds* as its flagship was doing the most interesting literary work around. It was at this time that Barry and I had our only falling out, caused by the demon drink, by Barry's reaction to my wishing to break up our partnership and my over-kill response. He had, I must admit, stopped me from setting fire to a tube train and had, in my eyes, abandoned me on the platform when he tricked me into getting out. Looking back, I see this more sympathetically from his point of view than my own. I forgave him for bringing a drunken

Greek to my party, who was promptly sick in my bed, and he forgave me for the tube incident. There was more, but since it shows me in a much poorer light than it does Barry, I'll draw a veil over the rest of it.

Barry and I have kept our affection for each other for almost half a century. He's the kind of modest guy who doesn't push himself forward, and I'm the kind of immodest guy who not only pushes himself forward but also likes to try to push his friends forward. Sometimes I wish I was still publishing *New Worlds*, just so I could keep publishing Barry Bayley. Not that he hasn't had a willing editor in the likes of David Pringle who, thank goodness, inherited my enthusiasm when he and a few others started *Interzone* all those years ago. Barry, like me, is still inclined to write stories for people who ask, rather than write a story and make it do the rounds. It was always to *New Worlds*'s advantage that he and Ballard didn't care about 'better paying markets'.

I've written elsewhere about how Barry, Ballard and I used to meet a couple of times a week at The Swan, Knightsbridge and plot the death of science fiction as we knew it. Mostly, of course, we discussed ideas, talked about our frustrations with the powers that be, but for me they were a golden time when I felt in the company of two of the smartest, weirdest men I had ever known. Such friendships endure. They even mature, sometimes. I like to think that I must have had something which Barry enjoyed, or our friendship couldn't have lasted so long. Whatever it is, I'm sure much of it was influenced by him in the first place. Nothing can substitute for his kind of constant curiosity about the world, its constituents and ideas. Nothing can compare to his stories. They are the work of a unique mind, the kind of person I've heard, on occasions, described as a genius. Don't let that last bit put you off. Bayley knew how to tell a tale and though his characters might sometimes be out to lunch in left field, his feet are usually firmly on the ground. I think these qualities transfer themselves to his fiction. Give yourself a chance to find out.

# ■ Introduction to *Expletives Deleted* by Angela Carter

**From the Vintage edition, 2006**

Although we were near contemporaries, born a few months and few miles apart, and were acquainted for some twenty-five years, Angela Carter and I did not become good friends until after my wife and I returned to London from Yorkshire in the early 1980s. Angie was especially kind to Linda, who, as an American, felt a bit excluded by many English people. The two women were natural sisters; they shared political views, were both outspoken, forthright, untricky, could swear like Tommy Atkins and were dramatically good-looking.

With Angie's companion, Mark Pearce, we got on easily and well. Neither Mark nor Linda had much time for the literary demimonde and they helped Angie and me keep our feet on the ground. We all had strong likes and dislikes (not always the same). We relished many of the same activities. Mark was an archer, as I had been when younger, and taught their son Alex to shoot. Mark never wasted words and like Linda could say a great deal with a glance. Not making many literary friends at the best of times, I valued Angie's friendship a lot.

Her instincts for special occasions were always exactly right. I'm looking now at the photograph of a seaside pierrot she gave me for my fiftieth birthday. It is one of the most fruitful images I have. She was very generous with her time in aid of a good cause. Her insights were always original and witty. She was one of the easiest companions to relax with. She could be a discreet and sensitive friend. Her gossip was never, ever treacherous, rarely malicious. If she attacked someone, it was almost always directly and, like Linda, if she didn't like you, you knew it pretty quickly. She had taught in the USA and had good stories about it. She also knew Japan well. She and Linda exchanged anecdotes of their experiences there.

As South Londoners we had a great deal in common. We had enjoyed the same enthusiasms as teenagers when folk music, blues, early rock-and-roll and science fiction all seemed to offer possibilities which the more conventional forms lacked. Because we were so frequently abroad, our early meetings had been intermittent, but it was comfortable to share the same memories of South London and recall childhood frustrations and hopes. She didn't tell me she was writing one, but when I read her review of my novel *Mother London* in the *Guardian* I burst into tears, not because she had praised me but because it was another example of her generosity. We had in common a love of popular English culture—Dan Leno, Marie Lloyd and other stars of the music hall; Arthur Askey, Max Miller and Max Wall; Ealing comedies and those writers of working-class and lower middle-class comedies such as Gerald Kersh and Jack Trevor Story, whose talents and observations were rarely recognised by the literary world.

I especially liked Angie's fiction of the 1980s as it moved from the fantastic to the extraordinary, still conveying the uniqueness of individuals and their experience. It seemed to me that she was entering an incredibly fruitful period in which she transferred her attention from, as it were, the alienated to the marginalised.

We were part of a small group of people who, for one reason or another, considered ourselves a bit outside the mainstream. Her other friends included Salman Rushdie, Tariq Ali, JG Ballard, Lorna Sage and, of course, Carmen Callil, publisher and co-founder of Virago, mostly people who, for various reasons, did not identify readily with the English establishment and, indeed, did not always make easy relationships. All, however, were united in their friendship and concern for her.

In early 1991, while in California, I asked her if she'd like to contribute to an anthology version of *New Worlds* which was at that time being revived by my friend David Garnett. She had regretted not appearing in the original, so it struck me she would be a great addition to Garnett's contents page. He was extremely enthusiastic. But after I wrote to her and asked her, I heard nothing. I was surprised, since she wasn't normally given to embarrassed silences, but I assumed in this case that she hadn't wanted to say no. The anthology went ahead without her.

After California, Linda and I had continued on to Spain and did not return to England until August. The first issue of *New Worlds* was due to come out in the autumn. Amongst the letters waiting for me was one from Angie which I opened hoping she had decided to do something for the second number.

I still have the letter:

> August Bank Holiday
> The Chase,
> London SW4

Dear Mike,

Seeing the ad. for 'New Worlds' prompted me to write and apologise for not replying to your letters, earlier this year. I am sorry, and even sorrier that I won't be able to contribute a story to 'New Worlds'—though honoured to be asked . . .

Why beat about the bush. I had a diagnosis of cancer shortly before Easter, and the entire summer has been taken up with tests, and treatments, and now more tests. (It's in the lung.) As a result, this house has been at sixes and sevens, somewhat, and most things not connected with daily living have gone by the board. It's very difficult not to sound melodramatic, under the circumstances, but there we are. I'm not one of those people who can work through anything, unfortunately—I've been doing a little book reviewing, and stuff, and catching up on my reading. (All those books, you understand, that one always meant to read . . .)

What the hell. I feel reasonably chipper, in myself, as they say, and contrary to rumour, nothing hurts. If I think of a 'New Worlds'-type idea, then I'll be in touch, soonest. But, at the moment, I am bereft of any ideas at all—except, and plentifully, theories about current events in Russia, but those I share with my own paranoia, not with this type-writer, even.

We still have a plan to take you and Linda down the canal. Or, up the canal. Or, since the canal does not flow, I suppose I should say, along the canal, because it goes neither up nor down, like the Grand Old Duke of York.

Lots of love and to Linda. Your Angie.

I'm not sure any of us realised how little life she had left, but we began to see quite a lot of each other for the rest of that year. Linda and I had settled down in London. Linda would prepare easily transported food and we would take it over to Clapham to save Angie and Mark the trouble of cooking. I found her some hash, which could be eaten rather than smoked, since we had heard that cannabis helped off-set the effects of chemotherapy. She thought it worked.

We didn't dwell on the details of her treatments. Apart from the odd reference to hospitals and doctors, our friendship went on pretty much as

it had done. We discussed issues of the day, our hatreds and our enthusiasms. I don't think we were pretending that anything was normal. She was
straightforward about her symptoms ('Don't worry,' she'd say if she started
coughing, 'I'm not bringing up bits of lung.'). We never avoided the fact, but
we didn't tend to brood about it either. Soon she knew there was very little
chance of her recovering from the cancer which was advanced before her
diagnosis. She began to hope for enough time to see friends and relatives
and became primarily concerned for Mark and Alex.

Angie was confident that Mark would provide for them but she was
worried about leaving some sort of inheritance for Alex. She found she
could not easily take on new work once she knew she was going to die, so
she concentrated on the material that was already published or about to be
published. Carmen Callil was a great help and this collection of previously
published literary journalism was one way in which Carmen was able to do
something positive for her.

She had an eager curiosity about the world and a deep knowledge and
understanding of the traditional English literary canon. She was, in my
view, profoundly well-educated, like my other great friend, her acquaintance
Andrea Dworkin, who also died far too soon, in her fifties. She and Angie
had much in common, though the two were sometimes at odds, frequently
interpreting feminism very differently, especially where the Marquis de
Sade was concerned. As Andrea and other American radicals had done,
Angie adopted the German spelling of Amerika to describe the imperialist,
bullying, unjust aspects of a nation which she felt had let her down.

The USA, as she happily admitted, had an enormous cultural influence on her. She admired the vigour and willingness to engage with important subjects which characterised American novelists. She had, in the main,
enjoyed her time teaching in Austin, which remains one of the centres of US
radicalism, but she could not condone the cynicism of the country's foreign
policy, its gunboat politics, its willingness to support dictatorships and to
interfere, sometimes violently, with the governance of other sovereign states.
Equally, she was highly critical of the policies of the Thatcher government.

She loved novels, as she says, especially unusual novels like those of
William Burroughs, JG Ballard, Iain Sinclair or the unfairly sidelined Walter
de la Mare. Her reviews of John Berger, Milorad Pavić, Grace Paley and
others all led to a better understanding and relish for their work. Angie was
always a political animal. Even her literary enthusiasms were coloured by
her strongly held principles and beliefs. She loved experiment as much as
she loved traditional stories and as such was part of a movement which often

instinctively rejected modernism. She created new models and conventions of narrative and subject matter as enthusiastically as she looked to old methods in folklore and legend. As what came to be called an early 'magic realist', she loved Eastern European, South American, Pakistani and other writers who emerged from national traditions rather than Western modernism.

For perhaps the same reasons, she was attracted to romantics and surrealists, to visionaries, though in some ways she was too down-to-earth to be a fully-fledged romantic herself. Her work grew increasingly realistic as it matured and, in my view, was all the better for it. Those of us who had experienced an intensified childhood, as Ballard had in wartime Shanghai or, as she and I had, in blitzed London, found even those writers we admired lacking certain techniques which could readily describe that experience. Like me, she was born into a dangerous world, knowing the permanent possibility of sudden death. This was not easily dealt with in the tradition of Joyce, Woolf, Bowen or even Angus Wilson. The finer sensibilities cultivated and admired by the likes of FR Leavis seemed, if anything, rather inappropriate given the monumental events of her early life, including the Second World War, the Nazi Holocaust and the dropping of the atomic bomb on Hiroshima. She didn't seek sensation—far from it—but she did prefer work which described extremes, however calmly. She looked to writers who were either fascinated by intense experience or who sought to provide that experience with a fresh lexicon, and you will find in these pieces a tendency to be drawn to writers like Jarry, Kafka and Primo Levi, who remained, for a variety of reasons, on the outskirts looking in. She felt most comfortable in their company, even though her own career as a novelist, an academic and a journalist had been relatively conventional.

Angie had never cared about literary prizes or being fashionable but when her last and best novel, *Wise Children*, was shortlisted for the *Daily Mail* fiction prize she was told that she would only stand a chance of winning the fairly substantial cash award if she agreed to turn up for the ceremony, so she endured the smoke of the presentation dinner only to learn that she had not, after all, won. My agent, the late Giles Gordon, told me that at the last minute one of the judges voted against her merely because he didn't like John Mortimer's assumption that her book was certain to win. Like other disappointments, Angie took that one well, but the rest of us were furious at the people who had so thoughtlessly taxed her resources. That Christmas she went north to visit her organist brother and in February Linda and I went to Mexico. Angie spent the rest of the time left to her with close friends and relatives, enjoying their company, preparing this book. I heard about her death on the BBC World Service a short time later. It happened too suddenly. I wished that I had stayed in London and seen just a little more of her.

I never wanted to admit that Angie was gone. She was one of the few people whose good opinion I valued and I could scarcely grasp the idea that such a fount of energy, enthusiasm, generous friendship and fierce political passions was mortal, let alone that she was dead. Of course, she's very much alive in her work and revisiting her essays is rather like hearing her speak again—funny, opinionated, passionate, full of original insights. Those qualities of enthusiasm and generosity (except perhaps towards food journalists) radiates from this book.

As in her later novels, Angie made it her business to represent the outsider. She had a particular sympathy for writers who were in some way pushed to the margins by fashion, which is as powerful in the literary world as anywhere. Perhaps the best essay in her book is about Christina Stead, an Australian writer whose unique genius remained largely unacknowledged in her lifetime. Stead's reputation has continued to grow since her death, thanks at least in part to Angie's championing of her. In writing about Stead, Angie also reveals her own considerable understanding of her craft, her eclecticism, her own willingness to tackle unusual subjects in new and distinctive ways. Her work speaks for itself, and it remains a monument to a great woman, as well as a great writer, a fine artist with a brilliant, disciplined mind.

In her piece on Danilo Kis's *The Encyclopedia of the Dead* she says: 'Truth is always stranger than fiction because the human imagination is finite while the truth is not. . . . Books don't really have lives of their own. They are only as important as the ideas inside them. [Kis] is wise, grave, clever and complex. His is a book on the side of the angels.' Though far too dismissive of her own insights, she might again be talking about her work which reveals without doubt a woman decidedly on the side of the angels.

# ■ Ted Carnell

**From the *Bulletin of the Science Fiction Writers of America*, July 1972**

Ted Carnell was not exactly the father of the British 'New Wave'—he was, in fact, rather surprised when my wife Hilary suggested to him, a few weeks before he died, that he was. But it was Ted's readiness to publish unusual work by people like Aldiss, Ballard and myself which gave us a certain encouragement to press on with our individual experiments in SF. There was certainly for us no American magazine editor at that time who showed the willingness to accept experiment (if sometimes a little wryly) that Ted showed. Ted was more of a father figure to writers like myself—kindly, tolerant, a bit old-fashioned but willing to believe that there might be some virtue in newfangled notions. We loved him. Only a few months before his sudden death, we were planning—Aldiss, Ballard and I—to organise a dinner at which Ted would be the guest of honour. I, certainly, owed a good deal to Ted. He encouraged me to write my first successful fantasy stories for the adult magazines, he recommended me as editor of *New Worlds* when he decided to retire and, as an agent, he sold my first ever novel for me. However different our professional ideas became and even when I decided to change to another agent, we remained extremely good friends, often passing on to each other stories which we felt unable to use for our respective publications. I know many other writers who shared this affection for Ted—Ken Bulmer, Chris Priest, Keith Roberts, Mike Harrison among them—and he was also regarded with great respect and fondness by the publishers with whom he dealt as an agent. It is a cliché—but there really are few people as much loved as Ted. There are few British (and some American) SF writers who do not owe him a debt. My own problems with *New Worlds* have been much publicised (perhaps over-publicised) but most people do not know that Ted kept the three magazines, *New Worlds*, *Science Fantasy* and *SF Adventures*, going often purely by virtue of his own willpower and was able to convince publishers to give them time to build up when their circulations would, periodically, go down. Ted recalled to me a year or so ago that there was only one short period of two years, in the late '50s, when the magazines did not give him anxiety. Ted kept the magazines alive for eighteen years, most of which were difficult. He might not have had very high rates but in this country he was the only editor who paid promptly on acceptance. Many of us, on many occasions, would have been in very bad straits if it hadn't been for Ted. He was an honest man and a kindly one. For all his modest manner, he had considerable strength of character and hardly anyone knew how much he suffered from crippling arthritis in the last eighteen months or so of his life. He still continued to edit *New Writings in SF* on schedule (and read manuscripts in good time, too) and to run his agency smoothly.

Nobody expected his death. For most of the present generation of writers Ted had always been there. We took him for granted. I wish he was still alive.

# ■ A Review of *No Laughing Matter* by Angus Wilson

**Previously unpublished**

Although he made his reputation as a sardonic observer of the self-decep-
tions and prejudices of the English middle-class in collections of stories
like *The Wrong Set* and *Such Darling Dodos*, Angus Wilson's literary ambitions grew with every book he published. *Hemlock and After* and *Anglo-
Saxon Attitudes* dissected the literary and academic worlds of the 1950s with
their rivalries and jealousies, while *The Old Men at the Zoo* satirised the
English civil service, with which he was so familiar, having had a career
at the British Museum and been at Bletchley during the Second World
War. As Margaret Drabble points out in her perceptive and detailed biography (1995) Wilson wrote critically of what he considered the prevailing
misogyny in most English fiction of his day. Perhaps the two books which
cemented his reputation were *The Middle Age of Mrs Eliot* and *Late Call*,
both of which were sympathetic, though not uncritical, portraits of women
who had arrived at a crisis in their lives. Having won the trust of his readers he felt he could begin a more ambitious novel, with a larger number of
social and geographical elements, which he hoped would unify the disparate
genres into which the modern novel had fallen. The result was *No Laughing
Matter*, his masterpiece.

   Growing up the youngest of a large, somewhat eccentric family, Wilson
came to hate what he saw as his parents' refusal to confront the real evil
which manifested itself in the years following 1914 and the sardonic hypocrisy enabling their class to lead a blinkered existence. He often drew on his
own family and friends for models but never so much as in *No Laughing
Matter*, which covers the 20th century from its Edwardian beginnings to the
mid-1960s, seen through the eyes of the Matthews family: cruel-tongued
fantasising mother, 'The Countess'; no-longer-published writer father 'Billy
Pop'; Quentin, a passionate socialist Lothario who becomes a cynical media

personality; dumpy, self-mocking Gladys, who longs to find a man, eventually winding up with Mr Wrong; Rupert, a glamorous, successful actor ultimately facing life as a has-been; Margaret, the popular highbrow novelist and wit, and her twin Sukey, who, without the family's gift for making light of serious matters, opts for a sheltered existence as a mum and schoolmaster's wife, her illusions ultimately shattered by war; the youngest, Marcus, clearly based on Wilson himself, a graceful, clever, homosexual rent-boy turned art-dealer; while Regan, their cook-housekeeper acts as the family's working class chorus.

Wilson's complex but always engaging plot looks at the relationships of the children with their parents, partners, offspring and one another as the world moves into and out of the Second World War. The family's qualities combine to offer a detailed picture of England and the English. Wilson offers a moral lesson without otherwise judging the characters as exceptional products of their class and age, the class which dominated English politics until the 1960s and helped accomplish most of its failures as well as its successes. Wilson, whose own slogan to himself was always 'Not Good Enough Wilson' when he was slipping into easy self-deception or hypochondria, was at his best when observing the obfuscations and moral avoidances of the English, their habits of escape into ideology, irony, jokes, philistinism, nostalgia, children's books or comfy notions of rural retreat which still form much of the consolation offered us by *The Daily Mail*, *The Spectator* or Radio Four.

Incorporating elements of the modernist novel, dropping into play form, using various distancing devices such as the description of a Family Game, he shows how Quentin's utopian predictions, founded in little but wish-fulfilment, result in the brutalism and authoritarianism of the 1950s, how Robert's ideas about the theatre develop into trivial movie conventions, how Sukey's attempts to hide herself in the rural past at her husband's West Country pre-school can't save her from a world growing more complex and more savage as Europe slides towards war and the Nazi Holocaust. The tensions within the family reflect the social and political tensions around them. Through their eyes Wilson shows up the Edwardian myth which enabled us to go so blithely into the First World War, the glamour of the 1920s hiding poverty and deep injustice, the chic of the 1930s which took attention away from the looming terror of fascism, even the lack of realism with which so many of us passed through the Second World War. The failures, idealism and austerity of the 1950s led us at last into the 1960s with their own particular delusions which Wilson, while welcoming signs of a more genuinely equable society, saw clearly.

The story goes rapidly from London to the English suburbs, to the Soviet Union and North Africa and back again, but everywhere the same inescapable elements prevail upon Marcus's fantasies and Margaret's relationships, however much they try to avoid them through ironic laughter and self-mockery. Their attempts to construct fantasy worlds, marked by myths inherited from Edwardian times, are inexorably attacked and defeated by reality. Even poor, innocent, bewildered, unglamorous Gladys, who has also used laughter to hide the truth of her life, finds herself going to prison in an act of self-sacrifice which only further enables the man who has used her so cynically. Yet at no time does Wilson show anything but sympathy for their self-deception, their urgent need to make true what is manifestly false. Neither is he convinced that this state of mind will prevail. As the optimistic 1960s began to make advances in social justice and sexual liberation, as the students he taught in England and America rose up in thousands to demonstrate for peace, he welcomed many changes for the better while anticipating the attendant materialism and corrupted individualism.

*No Laughing Matter* was published in 1967 to extensive and generous reviews, yet Wilson confided to me that he was a little disappointed so few critics had seen what he was driving at and chose to read the book as a kind of Galsworthian family saga. Julien Mitchell, quoted in the Drabble biography, told Wilson he thought the book was like Virginia Woolf at her best, and even Martin Amis, impatient with most of Wilson's contemporaries but an admirer of much of his work, believed that it was 'the foundation of everything he had done'. Amis probably had the clearest eye for the book's merits, even though he found Wilson's next novel, *As If By Magic*, concerned with emerging GM technology, sexual abuse and other issues remarkable for their prescience, less successful.

The novel's reputation is bound to grow. With Elizabeth Bowen's *Death of the Heart*, Henry Green's *Living*, John Cowper Powys's *Wolf Solent*, Iris Murdoch's early books, and with Woolf, Mansfield, Lawrence and Joyce, *No Laughing Matter* is one of the finest English novels published between 1920 and 1970.

Sir Angus Wilson died in a Suffolk nursing home on May 31st, 1991. With Malcolm Bradbury he started the MA creative writing programme at UEA. A Chairman of the Arts Council Literature Panel, he gave generous encouragement to younger writers. A campaigner for homosexual law reform, he was also a key activist in achieving the Public Lending Right, which pays authors for books borrowed from libraries.

# ■ Mal Dean

**From *New Worlds 8: The Science Fiction Quarterly*, March 1975**

Mal Dean was born in Widnes, near Liverpool, in 1941 and between 1959 and 1961 studied at Liverpool Art School. He was part of that renaissance which, for a variety of reasons, seemed to stem from Liverpool in the '60s. He was associated with many of the Liverpool poets and, a musician himself, with jazz and rock performers. In many ways, however, Mal's inspiration as an artist came from his nostalgia for the recent past—he preferred jazz to rock; his idols were the great American jazzmen—the images in his paintings and cartoons were often drawn from World War Two and he was influenced by graphic artists of the late Victorian and Edwardian periods—Tenniel, Heath Robinson and others. He was not merely talented, he was one of the most individual talents to come out of his time and, perhaps because of that, did not share the success which came to many of his contemporaries. He wasn't much good at compromising and almost everything he did was done on his own terms—illustration, record sleeves, painting, record reviews, cartoons and music—and, as a result, it was almost always vital, complex, sardonic, highly personal. He drew a regular cartoon each week for *Melody Maker* and those who knew about such things said that he had a great gift for bringing out the essence of the performers who were often satirised but never cruelly—Mal was too subtle for that.

As an illustrator Mal could complement an author's work better than the majority of his rivals. He first came to New Worlds as an illustrator in 1967 and among the best drawings he did were those for my own 'The Tank Trapeze' and *A Cure for Cancer*. He illustrated the first British and US editions of *The Final Programme* and would have illustrated several other Jerry Cornelius books if he had lived.

From 1967 we were very grateful to have Mal working on *New Worlds*. It was a happy coming together; he gave something to the magazine which, up to that time, it had lacked. We needed a skilful black-and-white artist who felt at ease with the kind of fiction we were publishing and who had the same respect for craftsmanship which we hoped we encouraged in our authors. There was intelligence, vitality and irony in Mal's work, but it was also highly disciplined. At his best his sense of black-and-white values equalled that of his masters, who included Mervyn Peake. When tired and overworked Mal could, occasionally, become self-indulgent, his pictures become too crowded, sensational, but this was because he had the special problems of any illustrator forced to produce work in someone else's time, to a deadline not his own, and glancing through the pages of *New Worlds* it is surprising how rarely he produced unsatisfying work.

Mal also produced posters (an excellent one for the early Edgar Broughton Band), record sleeves (notably for Pete Brown's Battered Ornaments) and comic strips (chiefly published in *IT*). He illustrated two books of poems by his wife, Libby Houston, *A Stained Glass Raree Show* and *Plain Clothes*. His own book of cartoons, *Black Dog*, appeared in 1969. His chief interest as a painter in recent years was in painting life-size pictures of World War Two aeroplanes—often taking only a detail and producing a strange, spare, splendid result. These were shown in 1972 in the *War Machine* exhibition as part of the Islington Festival.

Sardonic, anecdotal, almost sentimental on subjects dear to his heart (Spitfires, for instance, or certain highlands and fells, Liverpool), he was fine company. His wit could be caustic, but he was not above telling a very bad joke for the fun of it, and his stories were hilarious, particularly when they came from his own experience and observations.

Mal discovered he had cancer in 1973. His sister had just died from the same kind of cancer a few months previously. His courage in coping with the knowledge was extraordinary; he fought self-pity as hard as he fought to stay alive. Treatments were tried and failed. Gradually he became worse, but he would not give up. His bravery, cheerfulness and kindness at this time were astonishing and spoke of a strength of character which was remarkable. In February 1974 he contracted pneumonia as a result of treatments which had weakened him. He was sent home from the hospital. The pneumonia grew worse. He died on 24th February, leaving his wife, Libby, and his two small children, Sam and Alice. His personality lives on in the memories of his many friends. His talent, his generosity, his wit, are preserved for ever in his work.

# ■ The Ego Endures

**From the *Guardian*, 22nd March 2008**

I was a very young journalist of seventeen or so when Arthur C Clarke invited me to celebrate his birthday before he returned to Ceylon, where he had recently settled. The party was scheduled for November 5 in north London. Flattered to be asked, I gave up plans to get drunk and do exciting things with explosives and set off into the terra incognita of Tottenham where Arthur's brother Fred lived a modest and respectable life. A bottle in my pocket, I knocked at the door to be greeted by Fred. 'It's round the corner,' he said. 'I'm just off there myself.' He turned a thoughtful eye on the bottle. 'I don't think you'll need that.'

Promising, I thought. Ego (Arthur's nickname since youth) has laid everything on. I let Fred place the bottle on the hallstand and followed him for a few hundred yards through misty streets, determinedly reenacting the Blitz with Roman Candles and Catherine Wheels, until we arrived at a church and one of those featureless halls of the kind where the Scouts held their regular meetings. Sure enough, inside was a group of mostly stunned friends and acquaintances holding what appeared to be teacups, one of which was shoved into my hand as I was greeted by Arthur in that Somerset-American accent that was all his own. 'Welcome,' he said. 'Got everything you want?'

'Um,' I stammered. 'Is there only tea?'

'Of course not!' beamed the mighty intelligence, who had already published the whole concept of satellite communications on which our modern world is based. 'There's orange juice, too.' He indicated a serving hatch. 'But you'd better hurry, Mike. The film show's starting soon.' I saw that ladies of the kind who help out at church socials were organising chairs. I strolled up to Ted Carnell who, in the 1930s, had founded *New Worlds* with Arthur and John Wyndham when it was still a mimeographed fanzine.

Ted had the air of melancholy satisfaction I'd spotted on the faces of boys at school as they saw you turn up beside them on the headmaster's carpet. It read 'Caught you, too, did he?'

Once we were seated, Fred downed the lights and the real ordeal began. Arthur's early home movies of the Great Barrier Reef. The projector breaking down was the high point. When it did, the relief was tangible.

In spite of it all, my liking for Arthur continued. Everyone knew he was gay. In the 1950s I'd go out drinking with his boyfriend. We met his proteges, western and eastern, and their families: people who had only the most generous praise for his kindness. Self-absorbed he might be, and a teetotaller, but an impeccable gent through and through.

He had absolutely unshakeable (and why not?) faith in his own visions. After all, SatCom was by no means his only accurate prediction. He retained a faith in the power of reason and science to cure our ills. At one point, when the Tamil Tigers emerged on the Sri Lankan political scene, I asked if he wasn't worried. He assured me that it was all a misunderstanding and that the Tigers, who subsequently became expert terrorists, were basically sound chaps who'd soon give up their wild ideas.

His view of our world, rather like PG Wodehouse's (whom he resembled physically) didn't include much room for the Four Horsemen galloping through his rhododendrons. His preferred future was extremely Wellsian, full of brainy people sitting about in togas swapping theorems.

And he was unflappably The Ego. After we watched the preview of 2001, Brian Aldiss, JG Ballard and I all admitted it had left us a bit cold in the visionary department. He took our poor response with his usual amused forgiveness reserved for lesser mortals and told us how many millions the movie had already made in America.

Around that time, I was able to introduce Arthur to William Burroughs. Everyone invited to my party expected the master of optimistic hard SF and the master of satirical inner space to get on about as well as Attila the Hun and Pope Leo. In fact, they spent the entire evening deep in animated conversation, pausing only to sip their OJ and complain about the rock 'n' roll music on the hi-fi. At the end of the evening both were warm in their gratitude for the introduction.

I scarcely read a word of his, apart from a few classic short stories, though I came to publish him occasionally in New Worlds, and he knew I was broadly unfamiliar with his work.

He understood this to be my loss. And, as he became a massive bestseller, partly because of 2001 but perhaps even more because of his TV series investigating the paranormal, he didn't change. He would still turn up in the pub to show us brochures for his latest ventures and mention casually all the famous people who admired him, including Rupert Murdoch and Richard Nixon, showing us 8 × 10 glossies of himself with the world's movers and shakers.

He still understood that we would rather watch his home movies than enjoy a drunken evening playing with rockets whose only technical secrets lay in the length of their blue touch-paper. But, I have to admit, I became much warier of accepting his 'party' invitations.

Angus Wilson once returned from Sri Lanka exasperatedly describing Arthur as the most egocentric person he had ever met. Yet somehow, in spite of everything, Arthur remained a beloved friend of whom I retain only the fondest memories. He was a sweet-natured optimist in a world of grief. I'm really going to miss him.

# MUSIC

# ■ Adding to the Legend

**From *Casablanca*, 1989**

*Gold Diggers of 1977* was originally written and published in about two weeks to coincide with the release of *The Great Rock 'n' Roll Swindle*, a reasonably competent film featuring the Sex Pistols, a rock-and-roll band which revived a number of fashions in the late '70s, rode high (though maybe not very happily) on a variety of publicity stunts (most of which were banal and most of which, of course, worked) and eventually broke up. A fairly typical set of recriminations and antagonisms between band-members, management, record-companies, culminated in a miserable tragedy in Greenwich Village, New York, when Sid Vicious, accused of knifing his girlfriend to death in The Chelsea Hotel, died of a drug overdose.

A great deal of sentimental publicity followed Sid's death—as it seems to follow the death of any rock figure—and another young martyr was added to contemporary popular mythology.

The music press, feeding on its own fictions, characteristically compounded the myth while at the same time appearing to deny it. Like all mass-circulation periodicals, they first inflate someone to larger-than-life proportions and then attempt, often by the cheapest kind of mockery, to deflate the idols they have helped to create. Their ugly criticisms of Elvis Presley just before he died were matched in intensity only by the exaggerated tributes following his death. People seem to need heroes desperately and resent any signs of ordinary humanity in them—to the point, on occasions, of assassinating them if they refuse to conform or respond to the dreams of their loonier fans.

When Virgin asked me to write a book to go with the film I agreed (after I'd watched the film) because it fitted in with one of my own obsessions (see for instance 'A Dead Singer') and because I'd always seen Irene Handl as Mrs Cornelius. The third reason was that 'Anarchy in the UK' introduced a lot of people to the idea of anarchism and presumably led at least a few to Kropotkin and other anarchist theorists whose work is gaining increasing attention. For me, Nestor Makhno is the spirit of romantic, active anarchism, and although he might have been a trifle naïve in some of his hopes, I have a considerable soft spot for him. He, too, died young, of consumption, in poverty and some despair, in Paris in 1936. This story is as much dedicated to his memory as it is to the memory of Sid Vicious and all those others who have, in one way or another, been destroyed by their own simple dreams.

# ■ Phil Ochs

**From *Into the Media Web*, 2010**

'If it wasn't for me,' the British skiffle singer Lonnie Donegan once famously remarked, 'Guthrie's songs would be on the scrapheap.' Well Lonnie's in Spain and Woody got on a stamp and Donegan's abominably commercialised travesties of Leadbelly and Guthrie arouse a kind of nostalgia for the second-rate that we all have for some aspect of our childhood. Van Morrison gets all sentimental about the man who introduced a whole generation of teenagers, it says here, to the music of the great American populist singers, though that isn't how I remember it. I remember my correspondence with Pete Seeger and Woody who reported that they were under virtual house arrest, harassed by McCarthy's zealots, bent on eradicating the history of the American working class as aggressively as they had tried to eradicate Indian history and black history.

In London, as a boy, hating the commercial music of the day, I remember getting blues discs from the jazz shop and then listening to Ramblin' Jack Elliott playing in damp cellars that made the Cavern seem spacious. Elliott in his own right and as a kind of John the Baptist to Woody really does have a huge place in English musical history. A true catalyst. He made his first LPs in England, with Topic, the worthy Workers' Music Association, and one of them was his version of Woody doing Woody's songs. He showed us Woody's licks and explained how he couldn't imitate that picking style. He had to use a flat pick.

Meanwhile in the Hit Parade Lonnie was doing upbeat versions of 'Railroad Bill' and 'The Battle of New Orleans' (only he sang 'we fired our guns and the rebels started running') and everyone jumped on the bandwagon. My own group was aptly called The Greenhorns and we were proud of our genuine John B Stetsons. We looked a bit like Woody doing one of those cowboy radio shows in the late '30s. We sang 'Ludlow Massacre' and

'Pretty Boy Floyd' and 'Goodnight Irene' and 'Red River Valley' and Chicago blues and gradually we became the British rock revival which gave us the Stones, Yardbirds and, from a slightly different Liverpool tradition, The Beatles. More cross-fertilisation came a little later with the likes of Paul Simon and Bob Dylan playing a well-established British folk circuit (in some cases doing exactly what Donegan had done with US songs and copyrighting the traditional material they picked up in the UK).

Generally speaking, with Dylan and Co., the righteous anger, the identification with the underdog, became increasingly abstract as the comforts and problems of millionaires gave them more in common with scientologist superstars and NRA-fronting hams. The psychic infrastructure can't take that sort of assault.

There were other singer-songwriters who were lucky enough not to have to cope with the extraordinary adulation afforded Dylan and who actively avoided his route. Phil Ochs was one of those and he paid, as others have, a high price for keeping the faith, of wishing not only to sing the songs of his great predecessors but of nurturing the rough and ready integrity they managed to maintain through temperament and idealism. Of writing songs not only in the idiom of their heroes but out of the same despairing fury, the same contempt for corrupted power.

It isn't just nobility of mind that stops an artist taking the road to Hit Parade Heaven, it's an attitude, a habit of behaviour that they can't do anything about. Woody had his chances, Jack had his and Billy Bragg has had his. There are a lot of seminal, world-respected musicians around Austin, Texas, who are living fairly contentedly in trailer homes, selling their CDs off the Internet. Their talent has inspired young songwriters in dozens of countries. They care more for freedom than they do for social approval. As I once said to my wife who was worried about us being invited to dinner by the cream of local society—don't worry, we only ever get invited once. Some of us aren't even offered the chance to compromise. A very few, like Dylan, don't have to.

Phil Ochs, like Woody and Jack before him, made sure he only got invited once. He was no more able to compromise, even when he tried, than they were. It wasn't booze or drugs or mental problems. It wasn't bad manners or envy or narrow self-interest. It was a streak of egalitarianism which in some of us is as impossible to remove from our make-up as any other part of our DNA. My grandmother had it. My mother had it. I celebrate it. It is the hope of the human race. It's angry and it's often aggressive but it is rooted in empathy with the weak and the victimised, with those who struggle for freedom against all odds. It's rooted in love. It's willing to die for freedom. It's as American as Hammett, Malcolm X and César Chávez and it lets the world know that the mass of American people are not only represented by thieves, rogues and bloody-handed murderers in the pay of the commercial gun business and the crime business and the oil business and all the other business which provides the only language for a morally bankrupt parliament. Despite the conservatism of its rhetoric, the American public is at heart tolerant and wants a just society. That public finds a voice in the musicians and performers from folk to rap who provide real evidence to the international community that maybe one day America really will walk the democratic walk as well as talk the democratic talk. It is the voice I heard as a kid when we were worried that US belligerence would get us into World War Three, when John Wayne was fighting communism and black people were denied the vote. It is the voice of the best America can be. It can't be silenced. It is the voice of Phil Ochs.

# ■ The Deep Fix

**From *New World's Fair* by Michael Moorcock & The Deep Fix, CD boxed set, Griffin, 1994**

In the early 1970s, Ladbroke Grove was and still is crammed with rock-and-roll people and it was almost impossible not to know at least half a dozen musicians who were either already famous or would soon become famous. In this atmosphere, with Island's amazing studio ten minutes from my house and almost everyone you knew working in some capacity for the music business, it felt a little weird if you didn't have a recording contract. I was doing a lot of stuff with Hawkwind at the time, both writing and performing, and it revived my interest in music. I had begun in the mid-1950s, doing rock-and-roll and bluegrass as well as R&B and what was known as 'skiffle'—an American white and black folk music played up-tempo for dancing and made commercially successful by the likes of Lonnie Donegan, Chas McDevitt and The Vipers. Those early years in the clubs of Soho, where British rock first began, were fairly similar to the '60s in Ladbroke Grove—everybody knew everybody and it was quite often possible to be involved in a session with someone like Charlie Watts on drums, Long John Baldry doing vocals and Pete Green playing guitar. I cut my first demo with EMI in 1957 and it was, even by the standards of the day, considered too dreadful to release. So it was perfectly natural, living as I did in Ladbroke Grove, to slide back into music. Also I was helping Jon Trux and others put on concerts under the motorway in Portobello Road—my first performance with Hawkwind was at one of these gigs, and at that first performance I did 'Sonic Attack'. I think it was Dave Brock who encouraged me to do a demo of two songs I'd written, 'Dodgem Dude' and 'Starcruiser', and I somehow found myself having lunch with an A&R man from Liberty records who casually asked me when I intended to schedule my first LP. Almost without realising it, I had a record contract and *The New Worlds Fair* was the result. I was already doing some stuff with Steve Gilmore, who was performing solo, and Graham Charnock, although gigging with an R&B band while helping edit *New Worlds* magazine, agreed to play bass. Knowing that both Steve and Graham drew more of their living from music, I insisted that they be represented on the album, which is why you'll hear several of their songs here. Steve was at the time working with Sam Shepard (now more famous as a film star, but then a writer who had scripted *Zabriskie Point* and whose first collection of poems was called *Hawk Moon*) and it's Sam's lyrics you'll hear on 'Song for Marlene'. It was a very small world, in many ways. The idea was mine and 'Dodgem Dude', in particular, set the theme for *NWF*. Ironically, Liberty never showed any great interest in taking it beyond the demo stage and the record wasn't released until some seven years after the album. The Deep Fix was formed in 1972. By the time we made the album it consisted of myself, Steve, Graham, Pete Pavli (late of the Third Ear Band and High Tide), with Simon House (also of the Third Ear Band and High Tide), Snowy White and Kumo. Terry Ollis was our first drummer (ex-Hawkwind) but Simon King is on most of the tracks you'll hear here.

The original album was musically a bit more ambitious than it turned out, partly because some of the people weren't happy with doing eccentric rhythms and bar lines, while some tracks were abandoned altogether. One of those, which you'll hear for the first time on this album, was 'Candy Floss Cowboy', which I dropped off the album because I was disappointed in it, but which doesn't sound too bad to me now! If you listen to 'The Brothel in Rosenstrasse' or even 'Time Centre' you'll have a better idea of the flavour I was aiming for. 'The Brothel in Rosenstrasse' is in many ways more typical of the Deep Fix, who gave their final live performance (with Adrian Shaw on bass) at Nik Turner's Bohemian Love-In, the Roundhouse, Chalk Farm, in 1978—in many ways the Grand Finale of the alternative music scene as we had experienced and enjoyed it. After that, our music got less and less commercial and times had changed so radically that nobody, except occasionally Flicknife, actually wanted to produce it. The work Pete Pavli and I did on *Gloriana* and *The Entropy Tango*[1], two ambitious projects, scarcely got beyond demo stage before we grew tired of the record industry's increasing orthodoxy. Like many of our contemporaries who were not quite young enough to feel immortal and not old enough to have grown cynical, we gradually dropped out of doing music. The Deep Fix did a few numbers on Flicknife and then we went our different ways. Since then, of course, there has been a lot of interest in this album and some of the other stuff

1 Since released from Noh Poetry Records

we did, which is why there are some extra tracks included here as a kind of epilogue! I hope you enjoy it. If I had my time over again, I think I'd have done it a bit differently, but there's enough stuff on this album for everyone to find something they like. And maybe, who knows, we'll find enough tracks knocking around to do a follow-up album sometime. I hope you enjoy this. Keep on rocking!

# ■ Death by Hero Worship

A review of *The Life and Death of Elvis Presley* by WA Harbinson and *My Life with Elvis* by Becky Yancey & Cliff Linedecker

**From the *Irish Press*, 26th January 1978**

Elvis Presley was born to Gladys and Vernon Presley in Tupelo, Mississippi, 1935. The shotgun house, built by his poor-white father just before his birth is now a museum close to Elvis Presley Park. He died at his Graceland mansion, Memphis, Tennessee, 1977. The main street outside his estate has been renamed by the city Elvis Presley Boulevard. He had become the South's greatest hero, its biggest business. During his childhood he was asthmatic, sensitive. In his last years he had become increasingly self-conscious, bored and introverted. Many of the journalists who had called him 'King' had begun to attack him as he showed signs of age. Investors in new religions can be even more vicious than defenders of the old ones when it comes to prosecuting men and women who fail, or refuse, to be the supernatural beings they crave.

From Ms Yancey's account, Presley was a conventional Southern boy, not outstandingly intelligent, of average good humour, generous to friends and charities, relieving his boredom by taking over fairgrounds for the pleasure of himself and his entourage, by driving flashy cars and motor-boats, by playing practical jokes on his employees. He was surrounded by sycophants not from choice but because it is in the nature of things that normal people find it hard to stay with someone who is worshipped as an emblem. People who like the man can't bear to see him being eaten alive and so they leave the field clear for the kind of fans who, as in this case, helped to kill the object of their admiration. Those who worship the famous for their 'vitality', their apparent superhuman qualities, are the very ones who drain them dry. Later—and brighter—rock stars were to learn this. Some soon broke with the sycophants. Many of those who did not are now dead, mad or tragically addicted to drink or drugs. And it is the fans who drive them to it: flattering bewildered egos, offering glamorous shape and pseudo-dignity to confused lives, driving them further away from the common realities which can save them. Close friends and lovers vanish. Only fools remain.

These two books confirm that Presley's tragedy was the familiar one and that as a result of it he died a familiar death. When his death was reported there seemed to be an appalling note of satisfaction—even glee— in the voices of the journalists. Could envy be so gross? Could people be so blind as not to see the person dying on stage before them? Must they always see only the image they themselves invent? It seemed to me at that moment that their cynicism had made a strong contribution to Presley's death.

The cynicism continues, of course. These books are a witness to it. A dozen or more books were rushed out to cash in on Presley's death. One of the best, Harbinson's, was originally called 'Elvis Presley: An Illustrated Biography' (retitled now thanks to a two-page tacked-on 'afterword'). Cliff Linedecker is a journalist, author of *Professional Spy* and *The Man Who Became a Woman*. In his introduction he writes:

> I realized finally that Elvis Presley was truly a legend in his time. No entertainer alive or dead, not Frank Sinatra, nor Tom Jones, nor the late Rudolph Valentino nor Marilyn Monroe nor all the Beatles and Rolling Stones put together generated and maintained over a period of two decades the epic appeal of Elvis. Elvis fans, I learned, were unquestion-ably the most numerous, fanatic and devoted in the world. That fact was dramatically illustrated when a national tabloid printed a story about Elvis which gave the erroneous impression that he was a Gemini, with a May or June birthday. Elvis was born on January 8, 1935 . . . a Capricorn. This was pointed out in an angry torrent of letters-to-the-editor. Many were abusive. Some were threatening. The message was clear. Elvis was a Capricorn and anyone who did not know his birthday or his astrologi-cal sign was about the same kind of American who wouldn't know that Independence Day was observed on the Fourth of July.

Ms Yancey's story of Presley from her first chance meeting with him in 1954, to her further acquaintance on a roller coaster, to her going to work for him as a secretary in 1962, is more interesting than most. Although she hero-worshipped her subject she does provide a naïve and honest account of his private life. If private is the word, for Graceland teemed with relatives, friends, bodyguards, secretaries. Presley was never alone. The group of young men with whom he consorted most of the time came to be called the 'Memphis Mafia' and they guarded him jealously as they would guard a legendary treasure. His father kept the accounts. The mysterious

Svengali-figure (nothing much about him here) 'Colonel' Tom Parker, Elvis's manager, who received twenty-five percent of all his earnings, made occasional visits (it was Parker who always sought the lowest common denominator for his protégé). A wife, Priscilla, came and went (with added daughter). A step-mother and mother-in-law came and went. The estate became a Never-Never-Land populated by Elvis and other lost children. Outside the walls wept the girls denied his presence. Ms Yancey's book gives us plenty of clues as to why Elvis (fascinated and repelled by the intensity of his worshippers) would have become so thoroughly miserable over the years, but either it never occurred to her to question the set-up or else she was tactfully reluctant to say anything untoward about the people who were, like her, too dazzled by the star's fame, his extraordinary sex-appeal, to wonder for an instant if they were genuinely serving his interests.

Mr Harbinson's book concentrates on Presley's public life. The 'processing' of the rocker into a willing 'all-round entertainer'. It describes (in pictures) his musical career from the early beginnings with Sun Studios, 1956, when they were looking for 'a white man who had the Negro sound, the Negro feel' to the last, sad days in Las Vegas singing to an audience of simpering matrons, looking about him (it always seemed) for the 'kids' whom he still thought were his 'real' audience. His film career declined naturally from soft-core Brando-esque 'rebel-with-a-heart-of-gold' movies to 'all-American-boy' pictures. Harbinson bemoans this, but for those who were brought up on the original black music, Presley always seemed a commercially 'acceptable' wild boy, diluting the songs of Jimmy Reed and Arthur Crudup the way Whiteman diluted the blues. Similarly the Rolling Stones became the acceptable sinners from London's suburbs, though the great advantage of groups was to be that 'nice' and 'nasty' sides could be represented by different people and failings could be explained in terms of individuals. Presley's fans had to reconcile his 'meanness' with his 'wholesomeness'. Most of the girls did it by turning him into a child. Presley responded happily to this image. It was safe, easily confirmed. His infantile 'hell-raising' then equated perfectly with his 'charm' ('bashful, brash, boyish'). It could be said that, like so many heroes, he was never given the chance to become a man, which is doubtless why his romances so frequently failed. Childish self-indulgence becomes addictive, particularly when everyone around you— and millions of fans—are encouraging you in your habit. In the end Presley, unable to discipline even his waistline, resorting to amphetamines, suffering the consequent depressions, drowned in his own 'charm'. And all those who worshipped him as an emblem conspired to some degree in his death.

Elvis Presley was forty-two when he died on 16th August, 1977, of 'acute respiratory difficulty'. Had he, like Hendrix, choked on his own vomit? His career had lasted twenty-one years. He had become a mythic hero, bound to maintain the faith of his followers by disguising all signs of ordinary mortality. When those signs could not be disguised he was jeered at, mocked and attacked by the popular press which had—in its voracious need for fictive simplification—originally created the myth. Presley was an entertainer. Lacking a sophisticated ego he sought self-gratification in an effort to please his audience and so destroyed himself. He was killed by the acceptance of a hero-myth which has killed many other artists and performers before him and until we all learn to see people in human rather than emblematic terms, will certainly kill more.

# ■ Living with Music: A Playlist
**From the *New York Times*, 10th March 2010**

I write such diverse books that my regular readers probably won't be surprised that I play everything from BB King to Bartok when writing, but I do have some regulars I play over and over, depending on the kind of book I'm writing. I've also written and performed music from straight rock 'n' roll to fairly progressive contemporary stuff, but the last thing I ever want to do of course is play my own records. Here are ten favourites I enjoy while working:

1) *Working Man's Dead/American Beauty*, Grateful Dead. I use this to quell anxieties about starting work. The steady, driving rhythms, solid, well-crafted lyrics and recollection of good times on the road before we learned that there were a few more pitfalls ahead than we anticipated all serve to put me in an easy frame of mind. For me this is the very best of ambitious West Coast music from a band who put their money where their ideals were and, through the Rex Foundation, have financed some of the best modern composers worldwide.

2) Mozart String Quartets, Amadeus String Quartet. I've had these for years. I'm inclined to play lots of Mozart, particularly when working on a book's structure. For me, these are among the most sublime examples of form. There was a time I was such a snob I believed the string quartet was the only form worth listening to, whether from Mozart, Ravel, Bartok, R Strauss or Schoenberg. Since then I've broadened my taste to include even certain Italian operas (though I've written too many melodramas of my own either to need their input or, indeed, to scorn them).

3) *Are You Experienced*, Jimi Hendrix. Years ago I was in the Flamingo, hangout for most British R&B musicians and fans in London's Wardour Street, when I saw Hendrix walk in with Chas Chandler, who would help him make his UK debut with 'Hey Joe' on Jack Good's influential show *Top*

*of the Pops.* Hendrix already had a style about him that was the epitome of 1967 cool. I play this album when I need to remember how stimulating and extraordinary those few years were when the Beatles and the Who were changing our expectations of what popular music could do. When Hendrix died about a block from where I lived in Ladbroke Grove, the hub of Britain's 'alternative' culture, it symbolized the beginning of the end. Every great rock band has an inspired drummer. Mitch Mitchell and Noel Redding perfectly augmented Hendrix's guitar. They supplied the discipline he needed to soar and produce what must surely be the greatest debut rock album ever.

4) *American Folk Legend,* Woody Guthrie. I learned some of Woody's licks from Jack Elliott when he was living and working in England. For years Guthrie was, with Robert Johnson, the greatest of my American heroes. At the time I started listening to him he embodied the finest elements of American idealism and had become a victim of McCarthyism, perhaps an example of the worst political cynicism. His songs continue to inform my own faith in the best of what the United States means to the world.

5) *The Complete Symphonies,* Vaughan Williams, conducted by Adrian Boult. With Elgar, Williams is the most accessible of British composers, and even more than Elgar he embodies a sense of the variety and quiet beauty of our landscapes. When I was younger I was wary of his sentimentality, but as I've mellowed over the years I've learned to appreciate his genius. He's a great antidote for homesickness, too, as my work grows increasingly autobiographical.

6) *Quatuor pour la fin du temps/Turangalila Symphonie,* by Olivier Messiaen. Performed by Yvonne Loriod with Pierre Boulez conducting. I haven't heard more recent recordings, but Messiaen's wife, Yvonne Loriod, was piano soloist on the versions I first heard (also the first time I heard the ondes martenot, an early electronic instrument), which changed my whole experience of modern music. Messiaen's work provided me with my most significant notions on the nature of time, which slipped into my experimental stories. His extraordinary spirituality informed his work, as did his sophisticated association of colour and sound, producing some of the most intense and stimulating music I know.

7) *Holidays Symphony,* Charles Ives. Some of the most joyous and wittiest music ever composed. I'm continually revived by Ives, who for me embodies the best of American modernism, at once combining a gravitas and humour of a kind rarely found in his European contemporaries. I couldn't readily tell you why, but for me he is the Twain of American music,

encompassing that distinctive mixture of fun and melancholy found in so much great art from the United States.

8) *Pierrot Lunaire*, Arnold Schoenberg. While 'Moses und Aron' remains perhaps Schoenberg's most moving work for me, this is the first record of his that I bought and it's that to which I most frequently return. From it came my interest in the Commedia dell'arte, its imagery and techniques, which I used extensively in my fiction, especially my Jerry Cornelius stories.

9) *String Quartet in F*, Maurice Ravel. Whenever I'm trying to get a story's structure right I return to the F string quartet, one of the most beautiful examples I know of 20th-century musical structure. Purity compounded?

10) Bob Dylan. Pretty much anything by Dylan, from his first Guthriesque album to the recent Christmas album, does something good for me. His lyrics are, of course, frequently brilliant but I don't think Dylan, in all his complex wit and invention, would have kept such a large international audience if it weren't for his extraordinary musicality. For me Dylan and the Beatles bridged any perceived gulf between popular and highbrow music and set a benchmark to which all of us interested in returning the arts to a level of seriousness and popularity aspire.

# ■ Signs of the Times

**From the *Daily Telegraph*, 17th December 2005**

During the mid-1950s, I corresponded with one of the seminal forces in modern popular music. Originating principally in Oklahoma, Texas, Louisiana and Mississippi, this music was forged from an extraordinary meeting of black and white folk music, adapted by a number of conscious artists including Leadbelly, Louis Armstrong and Woody Guthrie.

Bob Dylan was only one of the young men of my generation to serve an apprenticeship with Guthrie who, by the time I was writing to him, was under investigation by Senator Joe McCarthy and in hospital suffering from Huntington's Disease, a neurological condition which had already killed his mother.

One of the pleasures of receiving Woody's brief letters, written in a slightly shaky but educated hand, usually on the same yellow legal stationery, were the little cartoons he sometimes drew in the margins. The drawings for his autobiography, *Bound for Glory*, and his designs for Folkways' record sleeves showed that he was a talented illustrator—but only recently have we discovered the extraordinary variety and power of his visual art.

In the 1990s, Woody's daughter began opening her father's boxes, which had been stored for years. First Nora approached Billy Bragg, proposing that he put music to Woody's newly discovered words. The result was the record *Mermaid Avenue*. Next she found an incredible treasure-trove of drawing blocks and writing pads, which gave her an unexpected insight into her father's work, confirming, as in songs like 'This Land is My Land', his mastery of apparent simplicity.

In 1937, Woody left his first family in Oklahoma, setting off for California down the Okie trail, not with a guitar on his back but with his paintbrushes in his hip pocket and plans to earn his living as a sign painter.

On his way to Sonora he met many of the working poor, victims of the killing dust he wrote about in 'So Long, It's Been Good to Know You'.

Guthrie, typically, was not really the product of the working class he celebrated, but the son of a land speculator fallen on hard times. Tragedy came in Greek proportions. His mother was sent to a mental home. His sister died in a fire. His father was almost killed in another fire. Farmed out to various friends and relatives, and largely self-educated, he read widely—and he listened to the rich music you can still hear casually played on the front porches of the region's small towns.

Soon he began writing his own songs, celebrating the resourcefulness of exploited Americans, the wonders of his nation's landscape, and the engineering miracles of the New Deal era. On the radio, he sang songs reflecting common experience, and at last discovered his vocation.

When Woody got to New York in 1940 and began mixing with intellectual radicals, he saw the metropolis as a city of signs, where he could find work to support himself. But he was soon earning a living from his music, recording with Folkways, the small, influential company run by Moses Asch, son of Sholom Asch, the Yiddish writer. His own illustrations, mostly produced for the pleasure of his friends, became increasingly sophisticated, until he could paint beautifully erotic, modernist figures as readily as he drew clever, simple political cartoons.

Woody gave his work away to whoever admired it, and much was irretrievably lost. Until this year his pictures, at last well reproduced and often at their original size, were appreciated only by a few contemporaries, including his second wife Marjorie, a Martha Graham dancer, whom he drew constantly. This beautiful, substantial book is confirmation of his extraordinary graphic talent.

He was a complex, sometimes self-mythologising man. It would not have suited him for people to suspect he took at least some correspondence courses in art, but there is evidence that he began consciously to learn to paint. He remained determinedly American, a populist left-libertarian. Just as he preserved the vital character of the music he had grown up with, his visual work always had the same immediacy and emotional directness.

*Art Works* is a celebration of working people, of erotic and romantic passion, of children. There are expressions of outrage at racism, social injustice and corrupted power. There are self-portraits showing a keen, knowing eye. There are illustrated letters to his family and intricately decorated typescripts of songs; a record of his naval wartime service; passionate, confused notes reflecting the contradictions of his love of family and his almost constant adultery. And there are musical instruments, always.

While Marjorie worked, Woody drew for the entertainment of his children. His illness worsened. He drank heavily, attempting to offset his symptoms. He and Marjorie separated. In 1954, at last properly diagnosed, he went into hospital. Marjorie returned to care for him. He continued to write and draw ('Paper and pencil is my only little dose of relief . . .') though his line grew heavier and his colours stronger. He died in 1967 at the age of fifty-five, to the end remaining an optimist, a generous correspondent, a seminal artist who devoted his life to celebrating ordinary human dignity in words, music and pictures.

# ■ Rewriting the Blues

A Review of *In Search of the Blues: Black Voices, White Visions* by Marybeth Hamilton

**From the *Guardian*, 20th January 2007**

The generally accepted creation narrative about blues music, which most of us take, as it were, as gospel, is that it came out of the fields around cotton-rich Clarksdale in the Mississippi delta and the whorehouse bands of Storyville, New Orleans. The earliest 'race' recordings, produced for a black audience in the 1920s, and the prison recordings of John Lomax and his son Alan, give the best idea of what this music was like to listen to in the juke joints of the south. Records by country players such as Charlie Patton and Robert Johnson illustrate how delta blues first sounded—raw, irregular and hugely inventive. The first commercial blues recordings were almost all by women such as Mamie Smith, Ma Rainey and Victoria Spivey.

By the time the Illinois central railroad took the blues up to Chicago it had gained, in the hands of masters such as Jimmy Rogers or Otis Spann, a far more regular bar structure, forming the base of R&B and rock 'n' roll. Classical pianist and blues enthusiast Joanna MacGregor believes early blues can only be learned by copying the records of geniuses such as Skip James and Jelly Roll Morton, not from annotation. Each performance of the same number would be very different, as friends of mine, who backed those great surviving country bluesmen, discovered.

The early collectors, hardly ever musicians themselves, translated their aesthetic response into what was essentially a political view. Traditionalists have long used the now-familiar narrative to fuel revivals of their favourite music, to justify its preservation and to give ownership to primarily leftwing versions of black history. Alan Lomax, in England escaping McCarthyism, told me he copyrighted traditional music to himself to keep it from being 'corrupted' by the likes of skiffle-king Lonnie Donegan—an argument that, as a performer, I found disingenuous. Donegan's skiffle records took kids of my generation to the authentic originals, helping fuel the British blues revival of which Alexis Korner was the best-known exponent. Korner's followers—among them Eric Clapton, Paul Jones and Bill Wyman—later sold R&B back to white Americans. Today most blues performers and audiences are white.

While not questioning this immeasurable cultural contribution of black Americans to the US and the world, Marybeth Hamilton challenges the authority of the origin story. Based mostly on the Lomaxes' accounts, she tells how Huddie Ledbetter or Leadbelly, their most famous protégé, swiftly lost his 'purity' when he got to Harlem and met the great jazz entertainer Cab Calloway. While Hamilton relies heavily on John Lomax's accounts of his relationship with Leadbelly, she hasn't interviewed any of the surviving Ledbetter relatives and has done little new research to support her claim that the narrative was constructed by 'commercialisers' such as WC Handy and white, mostly north-eastern, enthusiasts. As it is, she makes no mention of Martin Scorsese's monumental series *The Blues*, televised a year or so ago, and seems not to have heard of living bluesmen such as Honeyboy Edwards, who knew Robert Johnson in the Mississippi delta. Nor does she make any reference to BB King, who feels somewhat bitter about the 'skinny white boys' who came along just as he was starting to make decent money. King knew such people as Howlin' Wolf. Wolf learned directly from Patton and, like Edwards, also told the origin story Hamilton challenges. In the end I was left rather confused by a book which argues, reasonably, that the blues was hijacked by white visionaries but which offers no living black voices to support it.

# POLITICS

# ■ To Kill a King

## A Review of Geoffrey Robertson's *The Tyrannicide Brief*

**From the *Guardian*, 17th December 2005**

I owe Geoffrey Robertson an apology. As a witness in a Savoy Books obscenity trial, where Robertson appeared for the defence, I became so absorbed in his *Media Law* that I lost his page markers for what proved an eloquent and persuasive argument. I left the trial feeling a trifle guilty but with considerable respect for Robertson's quick wits, legal logic, intelligence and passionate social conscience.

This extraordinarily good book refreshes that respect. *The Tyrannicide Brief* is about John Cooke, a heroic, conscientious, reforming lawyer, selected by parliament to prosecute the trial of Charles I. Until now royalists have tended to have the last word on Cooke, presenting him as an arriviste regicide, but Robertson, one of our very best contemporary QCs, restores his reputation and gives him his central place in English history.

In the 1640s, tensions between the king and parliament over taxation led to invocations of Magna Carta and the freedom of the individual under the law. A puritan farmer's son, Cooke was among the vanguard, arguing the principle of no taxation without representation. When Charles effectively declared war on his own people, causing the deaths of one in ten Englishmen, everyone involved was a monarchist. The only agnostic parliamentarian, Henry Marten, was sent to the Tower when he proposed a republic.

As presbyterians and others sought to impose their views on the nation, Cooke argued: 'To force men to come to church is but to make them hypocrites' and 'the sword has no capacity to settle religion'. Cooke thought justice a moral rather than a religious virtue. He proposed a form of social security and NHS, as well as a national land registry so the condition of estates could be immediately checked, a right of silence, prison reform, poverty relief, liquor licensing, commercial law, labelling of medicines and much more.

After parliament's defeat of the royalists, a general disgust for corrupt legal institutions led Cooke to write his first full-length book, demanding law reform to serve the interests of common justice, established by parliament, not the legal profession itself, and based on the best foundations of English law: 'One of the saddest spectacles in peace is to see might overcome right—a poor man's righteous cause lost for want of money to follow it.' Extensive law reform, he felt, would make an honest lawyer 'a necessary member of the kingdom'. He argued for legal aid, for uncorrupt judges, for use of plain English in court rather than Latin and French.

Cooke was, Robertson claims, writing the first real work on legal ethics, asking for a fair system of fees, demanding that lawyers let clients know the chances of a suit's success. Much was original; some was imported 'proto-socialism', such as capping lawyers' earnings, thus encouraging the profession to take pro bono cases. Cooke was especially concerned that England's slow legal process worked against common justice. 'Law is a labyrinth, the entry very easy but the exit very difficult.' Cases involving life and liberty, he believed, should always be heard first.

In 1648 Cooke was still a monarchist. All he and parliament required was a constitutional settlement before allowing Charles back on the throne. But, as in most revolutions, events rolled rapidly, uncontrollably forward. The army, levellers, parliament and others were all in flux, and a pressing need for stability grew, even as the Scottish covenantors 'sold' Charles to London where, confident in his case, reneging on his promises, he rejected all terms and instead began secretly raising another army, effectively hastening his own end.

Conscious of the magnitude of its burden, parliament found it all but impossible to appoint a prosecutor and, while others feigned illness or faded into the country, Cooke, known for his originality of thought, allowed himself to be selected, assuming Charles would formulate a case in his own defence. But no such case was proposed. Like so many tyrants after him, Charles arrogantly refused to recognise the legality of the court. So Cooke had to argue that Charles, by continuing to plot war against his subjects, was a traitor to his nation and his avowed duty to protect his kingdom. Thus, writes Robertson, Charles effectively signed his own death warrant for, with troubled mind, Cooke successfully proved Charles guilty. In his case against the king Cooke established a precedent, that tyranny was not a right of rulers but a crime against the ruled. This precedent was used in 18th-century France and 20th-century Germany continuously to the present day.

Under English law, the punishment for aristocratic treason was beheading. In due course, the punishment was carried out. Charles died.

The kingdom became in essence a republic. Events in England now gained their familiar historical momentum. Parliaments came and went. Cromwell became lord protector. Careerists followed the direction of the wind while Cooke kept his own principled course, including frustrated service as chief justice in Ireland and a dogged pursuit of legal reform.

His conscience, rooted in his faith, was to prove his downfall. In 1660, those who had supported Cromwell were swift to shift allegiance to Charles II on his restoration, turning against Cooke and in some cases appearing as prosecution witnesses at what Robertson shows to have been an unjust, vengeful trial that led to Cooke's conviction as a traitor and a regicide. Again under existing English law, being a commoner, his fate was to be hanged, drawn and quartered (which Robertson describes in suitably gruesome detail). Nonetheless he made a death at least as brave as Charles's and met his maker with a clear conscience, perhaps reconciled in the knowledge that he had made tyranny a crime and forever changed the course of our legal and constitutional history.

# ■ Before Armageddon

**From *Before Armageddon: An Anthology of Victorian and Edwardian Imaginative Fiction Published Before 1914*, 1975**

I am almost unendurably lonely and miserable. I've got tired. I've done no end of work and good work. I've really changed British policy about Russia and when I sit in judgement on myself I smother myself with wreaths. *The Outline of History* is going to change History. I've done good things and big things. It doesn't matter a damn so far as my wretchedness is concerned. Righteous self applause is not happiness.

—HG Wells, in a letter to Rebecca West,
from *HG Wells and Rebecca West*, 1974

A glance through the pages of any of the English popular magazines of the last quarter of the nineteenth century (*Blackwood's, The Windsor, The Strand* or *Pall Mall*) shows that the 'scientific romance' existed in a distinct form some years before 1895, when HG Wells's serial 'The Time Traveller' (later, in book form, *The Time Machine*) was running in the pages of the *New Review*. The 'marvel tale' (astonishing journeys on incredible vehicles over and beyond the Earth, and with minimal human interest) was also thoroughly established, with Jules Verne as its best known (though by no means sole) exponent.

It would take a more careful reading of these magazines, however, to discover that the stories were by no means alike, either in quality, technique or intention. If the traditional 'marvel tale' is set aside altogether, the remaining stories seem to me to fall into three more or less distinct types. The chief examples of these types are 'The Battle of Dorking', by GT Chesney (from *Blackwood's*, 1871) and 'The Great War in England in 1897', by William Le Queux (originally 'The Poisoned Bullet' in *Answers*, 1893). *When William Came*, by HH Munro ('Saki'), published by John Lane in 1913, is a fine example of the third type. These stories have basic premises and subject-matter in common (the conquest of England by a foreign power) but are markedly different in emphasis and literary intention.

Most critics of prophetic and imaginative literature (loosely described nowadays as 'science fiction') have tended to discuss stories entirely in terms of their basic subject-matter, which enables them to yoke together books otherwise quite dissimilar. For example, two bizarre bedfellows might be EM Forster and Vargo Statten (the pseudonymous writer of scores of shilling novelettes published in the years immediately after World War Two), sharing a chapter because they both wrote 'future city stories'—and it's true that plot comparison of *The Machine Stops* and one of Mr Statten's (they had titles like *The Cosmic Conqueror!*) would make them seem virtually identical. Because they have all written 'interplanetary fiction' we find Jules Verne, John Cowper Powys, Doris Lessing, Edgar Wallace and Isaac Asimov blithely lumped together, although their literary intentions and methods have nothing in common. Critics might just as well be comparing RS Surtees, Thomas Hardy, George Borrow, Dorothy Sayers and PG Wodehouse because they all wrote novels with English rural backgrounds.

Such critics—and unfortunately they are often the ones to whom the confused reader turns for help in selecting the best books published today as 'science fiction'—only perpetuate confusion. I suggest that they, like Kingsley Amis, receive little pleasure from the novel of character. Neither do they seem intelligent enough to distinguish easily between social satire, the moral novel or the good, old-fashioned allegory. This sort of muddy thinking seems to permeate all English criticism nowadays; the critic's response is almost entirely to an author's subject-matter, not his manner of writing. The more familiar the subject-matter, the more at ease the critic feels, and so the more he praises the author. This state of affairs has accelerated the current decadence of English prose and led to the astonishing elevation of extremely poor writers.

In the sort of criticism I have described, it is rare to find any discussion, however naïve, of the quality of an author's writing, and I have seen quite well-known critics unthinkingly quoting excruciating prose in an attempt to make a case for a writer they admire.

## 1. The Visionary Tract

One of the reasons why the work of HG Wells has survived, while that of many writers who inspired him has been forgotten, is that his prose, though often very spare and apparently simple, is capable of carrying the strength of his vision. Very often an original and intense vision is best served by a very direct style (what one modern imaginative writer has described as 'hot' material and 'cool' technique, or, as Sir Walter Raleigh put it in *Romance*,

1916: 'The Classical school taught simplicity, directness, and modesty of speech. They are right: it is the way to tell a ghost story. The Romantic school taught a wider imaginative outlook and a more curious analysis of the human mind. They also are right: it is the way to investigate a case in the police courts.'). The young writer wishing to harness his riotous visions could hardly do better than study Wells at his best, or, perhaps, Rudyard Kipling. It is worth reading 'The Battle of Dorking' with Wells in mind. The author, TG Chesney, used phrases that we have come to regard as characteristic of Wells, particularly when he wished to point up his message a little. In the second paragraph of Chesney's story, for example, there is a sentence with a very familiar Wellsian ring: 'We thought we could go on building and multiplying for ever.' And elsewhere, where Chesney becomes hortatory, we hear Wells at his most intense—'Fools that we were!'

There is no question but that Wells was strongly influenced by 'The Battle of Dorking' (his Martians gave Chesney's blighted territory an even more thorough going-over in *The War of the Worlds*, 1898), nor that he borrowed much of his technique from Chesney. The use of a retrospective tone for telling a tale of the future was probably Chesney's masterstroke. His story, first published in magazine form, later in pamphlet form, went through several large editions and aroused the interest not only of the soldiers and politicians already involved in the army debate, but of eminent writers as well. George Meredith, for instance, at the height of his fame, but crippled and deaf, approached Wells (whose work he admired) and offered him the notes for a story he had conceived after reading Chesney's tale. Meredith, whose admirable but highly complex, individualistic style was the very antithesis of Wells's, thought that Wells could handle the idea better than himself. I've always regretted Wells's decision not to collaborate.

The political and military situation (the Prussian defeat of the French, the urgent need for reforms within the British army, and so on) that gave rise to Chesney's story is explained by Professor Asa Briggs in his introduction to *The Battle of Dorking Controversy* (Cornmarket Reprints, 1972) and by Professor IF Clarke in his bibliographically useful *Voices Prophesying War* (OUP, 1966), this latter emphasising the social, rather than literary, aspects of the 'future war' story. In common with many other officers of his day, Chesney, then a captain in the Royal Engineers, was concerned by the ramshackle state of Britain's military preparedness and the decadence of the army system, underlined a few years earlier by the blunders of the Crimean War. His decision to use fiction as the vehicle for his warnings probably came about as a result of his own and others' failure to make any real impact by journalism and letters on the public consciousness. Chesney's motives, therefore, were not literary but messianic, inspired by almost the same impulses that had led Bunyan to write *The Pilgrim's Progress*, whose direct, spare, unselfconscious prose had such an excellent effect on English fiction.

If Chesney's motives were not literary, neither were they mercenary. He wrote 'The Battle of Dorking' because he believed that England was in urgent need of 'waking up' from her self-congratulatory stupor, her greedy materialism, her easy and lazy assumptions of natural superiority, her mindless (and baseless) jingoism. Doubtless, had *Blackwood's* rejected his story he would have tried to publish it elsewhere and, if necessary, might well have published it at his own expense. It is this messianic impulse that gives the story its authority. It is naïve, perhaps, as a piece of literary fiction, but at least it avoids most of the affectations favoured by popular writers of the day. Chesney would undoubtedly have regarded himself as one of the few sane men in a nation of fools and madmen. He had a vision of his country destroyed by complacency and materialism, and, where Milton would have seen a solution in spiritual regeneration (associated in his case with republicanism), or Morris would have proposed his brand of socialism, Chesney saw the answer in the simpler terms of a professional soldier: in military reform, in increased defence spending. To strengthen his message he presented his warning as a *fait accompli*—the battle is over, the enemy is triumphant, and 'A nation too selfish to defend its liberty, could not have been fit to retain it.' The message is driven home with familiar messianic glee. 'I told you so,' cries the somewhat vindictive voice from the wilderness. However naïve or sophisticated the political beliefs of the prophet (and the majority are all too often frighteningly simple-minded, witness Ayn Rand or Robert Heinlein in the USA), the message remains the same: 'Wake up—or perish!' Reinterpreted, this usually means 'See things my way—or else!' (Artists, fortunately, rarely gain political power, though I have sometimes seen World War Two as a squabble between two mediocre painters, extended to terrifying proportions.) For Chesney, the fictional method was effective—his story started a full-scale controversy that, by giving ammunition and inspiration to the politicians who supported his views, eventually led to the reforms he sought.

It's hard to decide how important a political influence 'The Battle of Dorking' really was. Its literary influence, however, was considerable. Yet, perhaps through Wells, whose influence on popular radical thought remains very strong, its impact was very different from that which Chesney had intended. Whether the prophet (or anxiety-neurotic) is heard in his own country or time must depend to some extent on how close his particular private nightmare approaches existing political realities. Chesney, I would imagine, had a more satisfactory feeling about the worth of his having written the story than, say, Bertrand Russell had some years later after the publication of *Nightmares of Eminent Persons*.

## 2. The Genre Novel

Professor Clarke, in *Voices Prophesying War*, gives a detailed account of the vast number of imitations which 'The Battle of Dorking' inspired in America, France, Germany, Italy and elsewhere, as well as in England. While they doubtless lacked the force of the original, these pamphlets were written by people whose concerns were urgently patriotic. During the following twenty years a number of 'answers' to Chesney's story appeared (see the pamphlets cited in *The Battle of Dorking Controversy*), while a variety of Verne-influenced 'marvel tales' proliferated in the monthly and weekly magazines that were emerging to serve a growing middle- and working-class readership. During these years, too, appeared various satires and allegories, much less readable for the most part than Chesney's tale, but clearly influenced by him. Among them were Bulwer Lytton's *The Coming Race*, Samuel Butler's *Erewhon*, and William Morris's *News from Nowhere*.

The straightforward 'warning' book continued to appear—Hay's *Three Hundred Years Hence* was one of many to warn our forefathers of the dangers of "racial contamination". (It is not really remarkable, I suppose, that so much of this kind of fiction is, to this day, both authoritarian and racialistic in its assumptions.) But it was not until the newspaper and magazine circulation wars of the late 1880s and '90s, when Harmsworth, Pearson, and Newnes were making increasingly grandiose 'special offers' to the public in an effort to boost circulations, that this kind of fiction could be adapted so as to exploit public anxieties while at the same time bringing reassurance by inverting the Chesney method: despite having a tough time of it at the hands of a variety of vile foreign foes (sometimes the Germans, sometimes the French, sometimes the Russians and, occasionally, all three), Britain finally emerges the victor, stronger than ever thanks to her national virtues of manliness, pluck, and bulldog tenacity—besides which, it's all happened in 'the future', so it hasn't *really* happened: it's just been a nasty dream—a description, incidentally, that fits most modern genres.

If Chesney saw these publications at all (he died, a general, KCB and Conservative MP for Oxford city, in the year that *The Time Machine* was published) it is likely that he would have identified the stories with the very aspects of social and spiritual decadence he had set out to expose in 1871.

In January 1891 the first issue of George Newnes's illustrated monthly *The Strand*, was published. It was by no means the first monthly magazine aimed at the middle classes, but it was the first in England (inspired, I would guess, by *Harper's* in the USA) to base its appeal as much on its visual appearance as on its articles and fiction. In its first year, *The Strand* began *The Adventures of Sherlock Holmes* by Conan Doyle (Holmes had originally appeared, unremarked, in *Beeton's Christmas Annual* for 1888, in 'A Study in Scarlet') and discovered the considerable demand not only for Holmes but for the detective story in general. As a result there came the first 'boom' in detective fiction; writers were specifically commissioned to write detective series for *The Strand* (and its competitors). Right up to its death (having been published in revived form by John Creasey) in the early 1960s, it continued to specialise in tales of crime and detection. Hugh Greene's *Rivals of Sherlock Holmes* books have shown just how good many of these popular writers were, and it would be worthwhile to revive other work, like the working-class stories of Arthur Morrison and W Pett Ridge, to reveal the excellence of many 'second-rank' writers of this era.

*The Strand's* lesson (that a particular *kind* of fiction could boost circulation) was quickly learned by other magazines. The press barons had, as well as their newspapers, a variety of other publications aimed at different classes of readers. Of the popular, middle-class monthlies the strand was undeniably the best and most successful, but Newnes's empire was founded firmly on a weekly designed to appeal to "the office-boy and the shop-girl". It was called *Tit-Bits*, and was a kind of digest of various extraordinary news items, tips on getting stains out of moleskin trousers, jokes and short, sensational stories sometimes disguised as fact. Its nearest rival was Harmsworth's *Answers* (whose items were almost identical but pretended to be answers to readers' inquiries), and after that, almost as successful as *Answers*, was *Pearson's Weekly*. All were tabloid, contained very little pictorial matter, and the tiny, packed type in three dense columns makes them virtually unreadable today.

One of the journalists working on *Pearson's* in the 1890s was George Griffith, a vicar's son who had led a rather desultory life until his late twenties, when he became a schoolmaster. He wrote freelance articles in his spare time, then he joined a small newspaper. But after becoming involved in some sort of political crusade, he left the paper and began to write secular pamphlets, one of which was called *Ananias, The Atheist's God: For the Attention of Charles Bradlaugh.* There was, without doubt, a streak of messianism in Griffith and he held, at one time, strong political beliefs. But after he had been working for a while for Pearson he had, in common with most journalists of his kind, probably left most ideals behind him, and his work was dictated entirely by the demands of his publishers.

Another weekly, illustrated and selling for a higher price, was *Black and White*. It was more pointedly imperialistic than the other weeklies. Doubtless it was for political as well as commercial reasons that it decided to publish, from the beginning of 1892, Admiral Philip H Colomb's own version of 'The Battle of Dorking', in which he sought this time to alert Britain to the weaknesses of her navy. Called 'The Great War of 1892', it was, in fact, a collaboration between Colomb and various experienced journalists. Rather like Orson Welles's famous *War of the Worlds* broadcast in the 1930s, it used journalistic techniques to report, 'as it was happening', the progress of this fictitious war—there were transcripts of cables, interviews, reports from the front, and so on—and it proved a great success. Pearson was among those impressed by the success of the serial. He brought the matter up at a staff discussion and asked whether any staff member could produce something along the same lines for his own weekly. Griffith had written no fiction until then, but thought he would like to try. Next day he brought in a synopsis for a story to be called 'The Angel of the Revolution'. The synopsis was approved and Griffith began work. 'The Angel of the Revolution' was perhaps the first full-scale marriage between the 'marvel tale' of Verne, with its flying machines, compressed-air guns and spectacular aerial combat, the 'future war' tale of Chesney and his imitators, and, to some degree, the political utopianism of *News from Nowhere* and the like. Griffith described a society of anarchists who acquire the secret of powered flight. Under the leadership of a crippled, highly intelligent Russian Jew and his beautiful daughter (Natasha, the Angel of the Revolution) these Terrorists, as they are called, succeed in emerging victorious in a world conflict and establishing what later writers were to term a 'pax aeronautica' throughout the world. The story is remarkable for its controlled imaginative flight, its essentially socialist message, and for a strong dose of the romanticism normally associated with the kind of historical fiction derived from Scott. But it lacks the conviction of Chesney's story: the prose is often high-flown and self-conscious, the dialogue sometimes wooden and the characters derived from popular fiction rather than experience, as it had in Chesney's case.

Griffith was to become the first 'professional' science fiction writer, working primarily for money and for the magazines, anxious to please his public, to serve his editorial masters. He came to depend on the scientific romance for his chief source of income (though he later wrote some detective tales and thrillers, as well as speculative articles) and found that he had to increase the sensational aspects of his work to keep his public. Consequently, as he racked his imagination for bigger and better marvels with which to earn next week's money, any integrity that his earlier fiction had possessed was soon lost. Griffith had become a genre-writer and the scientific romance, thanks to him and several of his contemporaries, had become an acceptable commercial form. He followed 'The Angel of the Revolution' with a sequel, 'The Syren of the Skies' (published in book form as *Olga Romanoff*), and he was to write many more scientific romances, chiefly for Pearson, few of them possessing the merits of his first two, before he died of cirrhosis of the liver, aged forty-eight, in 1906.

'The Angel of the Revolution' proved itself a circulation booster. Harmsworth answered by commissioning another journalist, William Le Queux, to produce a rival tale for *Answers*. This was 'The Poisoned Bullet', and it used straight reportage techniques, after the Colomb method but without the variety of devices used by Colomb and his team. Part of that novel, published by Tower Publishing (a firm specialising in a list of scientific romances) as *The Great War in England in 1897* is included in this volume of the anthology. The final episodes, which are the ones we reprint, are enough to show what had happened to the visionary story between 1871 and 1893. The basic story and, to some extent, the method is identical to Chesney's; but whereas Chesney was fired by messianic urgency, moral outrage, a sense of duty, which gave his prose its dignity and its conviction, Le Queux, competent though he is, is writing only for money and using a form which has already become established, so that the form itself lacks the power to spark the author's imagination (for the author must first be struck by the originality of his vision before he can convey any genuine feeling to his audience). Le Queux was a journalist of the Harmsworth school, able to exploit any popular fad or anxiety at a moment's notice; his inspiration was Harmsworth, who knew better than any of his rivals how to play on the terrors and delusions of the public. Le Queux certainly had some talent for writing sensational thrillers, as his later career showed, but his work is cynical in essence, pretending to a social purpose it does not believe in and is devoid of any moral or literary purpose whatsoever. It is therefore far more 'dated', far more obviously of its own time, than Chesney's earlier tale.

It seems to me that in the genre science fiction of the present day we see pretty much the same pattern. Inspired by the urgently conceived, somewhat messianic, but tightly controlled imaginative tales of Wells (who in his day was quickly sought out by Pearson, who serialised his work *as genre fiction* to capitalise on the market discovered by Griffith), which overcame or made personal use of the conventions of genre, many writers, particularly in the USA, began to write what, by the 1920s, had received the generic title of 'science fiction'. As a result, the form was established by the 1960s as a highly commercial category, selling better (as a category) than westerns, historicals, romances or thrillers. A body of commercial writers, chiefly British and American, supplied a popular market with sensational material that drew its inspiration from exactly the same kinds of source as Le Queux (who doubtless thought of himself as a 'serious' writer). Publishers, finding the category lucrative, displayed as much cynicism and lack of taste as the press barons of the 1890s, whose main concern was with making money and 'keeping up' with the public's fancies. Bound by their established conventions, these writers produce tales virtually indistinguishable one from the other, using the same technical devices, the same vocabulary, the same characters and the same plots, but introducing a new 'marvel' from time to time. Changes are rung on a few ideas against a few basic, prepared backdrops (overcrowded future cities, space war/exploration, virgin planet) and it seems to me that the title of one of these books, recently published, neatly summed the whole process up—it was called *Inverted World*.

Most of these writers, of course, are not literary writers—their interest is in the invention of fresh marvels and they do not feel bound to do anything else but present them as they occur to their readers. It is essentially the marvel school of Verne in a modern guise. The concentration is chiefly on the wonders of science, from Verne's air-ships to Blish's 'spindizzies' (space-going cities); and American magazine and paperback SF continues to emphasise these aspects of imaginative fiction as it has done, with a varying degree of sophistication, since the nineteenth century. It is a sort of technological pornography—ritualised, sterile—having neither social nor literary pretensions and becoming quickly stale. Its readership is chiefly juvenile and its authors, where they attempt characterisation and social commentary at all, reveal themselves as immature. This is what makes up the bulk of modern genre SF as it made up the bulk in the '90s. Chiefly American in origin, though there are several British practitioners, it is quickly outgrown by the majority of those who, as teenagers, are attracted to it. As a result it is able to continue repeating itself on the same basis as juvenile magazines, which can reprint or revamp old stories and features every five years.

Naturally, like Marie Corelli, who was convinced of her own profundity, there are writers like Robert Heinlein who have pretensions to social criticism. This is embarrassingly unintelligent, but, for their fans, who are usually of a naïvely messianic disposition themselves (Heinlein's most notable fan must be Charles Manson), it puts their work somewhere 'above' mere commercial fiction. As a further aside, I have often wondered how much Marie Corelli, perhaps the greatest bestseller of her day, is to blame for the popularity of that particularly obnoxious brand of sentimental spiritualism still so prevalent in our seaside towns and spas, our suburbs and stockbroker villages of the Home Counties.

But there are signs of the circle beginning to turn full, with a number of sophisticated and clever writers kicking themselves free of the encumbering corpse of genre fiction and taking from it only what they need in order to write individual and genuinely imaginative books in the spirit, if not the tradition, of Wells.

## 3. The Literary Novel

> Good books describe the world, and teach whole generations to interpret the world. Because they throw light on the life of man, they enjoy a vast esteem, and are set up in a position of authority. Then they generate other books; and literature, receding further and further from the source of truth, becomes bookish and conventional, until those who have been taught to see nature through the spectacles of books grow uneasy, and throw away the distorting glasses, to look at nature afresh with the naked eye. They also write books, it may be, and attract a crowd of imitators, who produce a literature no less servile than the literature it supplants.
>
> —Sir Walter Raleigh, *Romance*, 1916

HH Munro was as convinced a British patriot as was Chesney, and the complacent materialism of Edwardian England disturbed him as much as Chesney had been disturbed by the state of society forty years earlier. As 'Saki', Munro satirised that society, and society was amused by him.

Munro came from a military family but was not himself a soldier (he was to join up in the ranks in 1914 and be killed in action in 1916 at the age of forty-six). He had, however, served a short term with the military police in Burma before being invalided out, due to recurrent bouts of fever. Until the age of twenty-seven he lived at his family home in Devon. Then he made up his mind to become a writer. He moved to London and, in 1899, published his first book, a work of history, *The Rise of the Russian Empire*. In his excellent introduction to the Bodley Head 'Saki', JW Lambert describes Munro's career in as much detail as possible (a sister destroyed most of the relevant papers). His first work of fiction was a satire on the politics and politicians of his day, parodying Carroll, called *The Westminster Alice*, published every week in the *Westminster Gazette*; this was followed with a less successful series of *Not-So Stories*, after Kipling. In 1903 he became foreign correspondent of the *Morning Post*, travelling to Germany, Russia and the Balkans, and was abroad when his first volume of epigrammatic sketches, *Reginald*, was published in book form in 1904. Returning to England, a firmer patriot and a sterner critic of his country than when he left, 'Saki' settled in London again in 1908 and began to write his characteristic stories for the magazines, publishing *Reginald in Russia* in 1910 and *The Chronicles of Clovis* in 1911. In 1912 *The Unbearable Bassington* appeared, his only other novel, and much less satisfying than *When William Came* which was published the following year and which will be included in Volume II of this anthology. A further collection, *Beasts and Super-Beasts*, came out in 1914 and a posthumous collection, *The Toys of Peace*, in 1919.

While 'Saki' was concerned throughout his career with social criticism, satire and comedy, and while his horror stories are among the most chilling, precisely because they are written in the same light, sardonic style as his other pieces, *When William Came* was his only real attempt at a full-scale moral novel. In it he is holding a mirror to the face of the English upper class, and showing how individuals and whole societies can be destroyed by complacency. Like Chesney, he is trying to warn against the dangers of complacency and materialism, but the difference is that 'Saki' is a sophisticated, humane and literary writer; he is able to describe the process in terms of what happens to human beings, not in the broad generalised terms of battles and defeats. Like Chesney, he writes from conviction; like Le Queux he is a professional, but the difference is that 'Saki' is more talented, more intelligent and more perceptive than either of them; he can earn his living and maintain his integrity by virtue of his superior gifts and character. He is not merely writing a warning to the country to arm itself against a threat of German invasion, he is also telling a story of intelligent, sophisticated people destroying themselves by making easy assumptions about their virtues, by their casual pride and a very subtle form of self-deception which cheerfully admits to almost any vice but that of anxiety. In *When William Came* I am reminded not nearly so much of Angus Wilson's *The Old Men at the Zoo* (which, superficially, it could be said most to resemble) as I am of *The Middle Age of Mrs Eliot*.

'Saki's' story of Cicely Yeovil and Murrey Yeovil involves us much more deeply than the clever and likely descriptions of how a conquered Britain is gradually brought to heel by her German victor. For 'Saki' the theme of 'The Battle of Dorking' provided a useful metaphorical ambience in which to write his story, and I believe it to be far superior to anything else he produced. That the book is generally held to be his least successful I attribute to the tendency of critics to praise only that which is safely familiar and to reject that which is comparatively unfamiliar. The fact that this opinion has been held for so long I attribute to another marked tendency of critics: to read only what a previous generation has recommended to them, and to pass on, for the rest, the opinions they have received. Particularly good examples can be seen in almost all the Wells criticism published in the last forty years, and in the majority of Meredith criticism.

During the period between the turn of the century and the start of the Great War, a number of novels were published which set out to describe the moral decline of a nation whose people had become spiritually weakened by comfort and complacency and therefore, according to the authors, had put themselves at the mercy of powerful financiers (often satanically Jewish), capable of deciding the course of history with a few key telegrams. At their best, these novels had a certain crude power. At their worst, they were poorly written, pandering to every kind of mystical sentimentality about the 'real' virtues of the British nation. The solutions they offered to the ills they described were simplistic, sometimes savage, often to do with the 'rediscovery' of whatever brand of Christianity the authors subscribed to. Although they contained sensational, sometimes imaginative, elements, theirs was a sugar-coated messianism, and because of this many of the books became bestsellers. Marie Corelli was the most successful of these writers. Her stock in trade was to show how the 'spiritual' person always, eventually, triumphed over the materialist. The only lasting literary influence she appears to have had is on PG Wodehouse, many of whose comic sentimental lady characters have plainly had a strong dose of Corelli. Another great pre-1914 bestseller (again warning of German infamy, but by means of a mystery story) was *The Riddle of the Sands* (1903) by Erskine Childers. Few of these books survive because they were directed at a contemporary audience, using a vocabulary of terms and ideas to which their public could respond. They have their modern equivalents, however, in some of the authors already mentioned and, I suppose, in those strange hodgepodge books of Erich von Däniken (*Chariots of the Gods*, etc.), Lyall Watson and their like.

Books like *The Riddle of the Sands* certainly reflected a growing disquiet and an increasing tension which might well have led to the comparative relief of war-hysteria in 1914. There is a case to be made for the existence of a literature of paranoia that echoes the disquiet of a public that can 'feel something going wrong' but can't identify the source. Perhaps imaginative literature, like science fiction, does best during such periods—the Gothic, after all, flourished while the most sudden effects of the Industrial Revolution were being felt in England.

One of the strangest examples, published in 1901, was *The Inheritors*, a collaboration between Joseph Conrad and Ford Madox Ford. It deals with a sinister plot by people from "the Fourth Dimension" to take over the world and populate it with their own passionless kind by manipulating the world's money. The theme owes more to Conrad than to Ford, though much of the writing and characterisation is typical of Ford at this time (waspish rather than witty), and overall it has a certain power. It is well worth comparing with *When William Came*, for it deals with much the same theme of moral decline through pride, complacency and unthinking materialism, showing decent people destroyed by their old-fashioned virtues. The novel deserves republication, for it is highly readable and has a remarkable atmosphere, and is not available, as far as I can discover, in a modern edition. The imaginative element is even more muted than in 'Saki's' book, but it has an excellent ambience and helps point up the main themes very well.

As for the other stories and features in this anthology, drawn chiefly from late Victorian and Edwardian magazines, they will serve, I hope, to show that imaginative and speculative writing was as familiar to our great-grandparents as to us, that a variety of talent and opinion existed and that all it did not have, at that time, was the burden of category definition.

# ■ A Million Betrayals

**From the *Telegraph*, 7th January 2006**

During the Second World War my grandmother, who was of Jewish ancestry, enjoyed winding up my Anglo-Saxon father. If the Germans won, she insisted, then all the Jews would be taken to camps; but if the British won, then obviously all the Anglo-Saxons would be arrested instead. Sitting across from my father in the air-raid shelter as the bombs thumped down outside, she would wag a mocking finger. 'Better hope the Germans win, Arthur,' she'd say. 'Better hope the Germans win.'

At that time my Uncle Jack worked for Churchill and lived in Downing Street. Whenever I visited him he would take me up the staircase to where a big portrait of Benjamin Disraeli hung and we'd stand looking at it together. 'One day,' he'd say, 'your portrait might be hanging here, too.' He was proud of our family's relationship to the great Tory through his father, Isaac D'Israeli. I grew up wondering if I would go into politics or journalism first. I disappointed Uncle Jack by taking a job with the Liberal Party's press office, yet none the less Disraeli remained my model for some years. When I met my first wife I was still considering trying to get experience by standing for some unwinnable seat. She felt cheated by my decision to become a novelist though I did base one of my first sf books on Coningsby.

A working journalist by the age of sixteen, I started my career in fiction earlier than most. By the mid-1970s I was riding pretty high. My books were selling well. I had won some prizes. I had a film out. Hawkwind, the prog-rock band I appeared with, had a platinum disc and we were playing major venues. I edited a magazine, *New Worlds*, which had received notoriety and praise. I was something of a hero of the counter-culture. I was the subject of TV programmes and my activities interested gossip columnists. Fame had come easily to me. The attention didn't do much for my character and ultimately led to the breakdown of my first marriage. I was disgustingly self-involved. By the mid-1970s, however, I began to realise that most of my old friends wanted little to do with me and I was worried about my unpaid dues. After repairing my friendships and completing the satirical Jerry Cornelius quartet set mostly in Notting Hill (which would win the Guardian Fiction Prize) I felt I needed to take on something demanding, that would be both substantial and serious.

The first book I ever bought myself was John Bunyan's *Pilgrim's Progress*, and I grew up believing that a book should have at least one other implied narrative beyond its surface plot. As I had often insisted in *New Worlds* editorials, I thought that good escapism should confront real issues, and that confrontational fiction should always contain a fair amount of escapism, no matter how experimental the form. One reason I never wrote fantasy and sf under a pseudonym was because I thought it important to reunite popular and literary forms. That was why I had been attracted to visionary fiction in the first place, along with other writers of what came to be called the sf 'new wave', because good sf so frequently dealt with moral issues.

Since the 1950s writers such as Dick, Sheckley, Aldiss and Ballard had engaged themselves less with futuristic invention than with problems of the present. After my teens I was not, however, a great reader of imaginative fiction. My main enthusiasm was for novels in what is generally called the European moral tradition. I was also a fan of Grimmelshausen's ironic picaresque *Simplicissimus*, and felt that my next ambitious project should somehow model itself on that book and deal with events of the 20th century leading up to the Nazi Holocaust. I had become dissatisfied with all the fiction at that time written about the Holocaust and wondered how best to tackle the subject in a way which would, as I saw it, properly honour the dead.

Though the Cornelius books had raised a number of serious questions, they were perhaps just a little too pyrotechnical, their points lost in the fun I had running riffs on popular fiction and contemporary obsessions. They offered a good technique, which I was to develop in shorter stories of the same kind, dealing with everything from apartheid to militant Islam, but they could not, I felt, give due respect to the Holocaust's victims. Though a number of fine factual books had appeared, there was still very little fiction which satisfactorily explained for me how such a crime could have been committed. I became obsessed with finding explanations, but I still had no key to the method. So I started to sketch out an idea for a comic novel, which would touch on the subject, involving Jerry's terrible old mum, Honoria Cornelius, on a Zeppelin journey around the world of the 1930s.

In those days, I preferred to cross the Atlantic on Russian passenger ships sailing between Leningrad and New York. They took twice as long to reach America but you could get a huge stateroom for the cost of steerage on the QE2, and you met a more interesting class of passenger.

In 1976 I decided to make a road trip across the US from New York to San Francisco to celebrate the bicentennial of the American Revolution. I booked passage on the recently renamed SS *Mikhail Lermontov*. She carried the usual mix of seasoned travellers and, as usual, I was soon enjoying a glass or two of vodka in the bar. I found myself talking to some recent German immigrants who had made Wisconsin their home and were delighted that they had encountered no prejudice there. The Russians were always good company as long as you avoided talking politics, whereupon they would clam up and look shifty.

Ending that trip, as I had done before, I got up early one morning in order to see the Statue of Liberty when we sailed into New York harbour. The statue and the skyline still aroused strong sentimental feelings in me. The bar was filled mainly with Germans and Russians already in a celebratory mood. New York came in sight. One of the Germans raised his glass. 'Aha' he said. 'Here we are in Synagogue City!' There was general laughter, a decided atmosphere of antisemitism. Instead of confronting it I quietly put down my drink and left. I had lacked the courage to object. And I knew I had betrayed something within myself as well as all the suffering millions of the recent past.

I had discovered how easy it was to betray not only one's principles but one's history merely by avoiding minor social discomfort. It was that realisation which gave me the way of writing, over the next quarter of a century, the four novels which make up the Pyat sequence. Already familiar with Holocaust guilt, I now felt a more specific guilt. The Nazi Holocaust had been permitted not just by cynical government decisions in London, Moscow, Paris and Washington, but by thousands, perhaps millions, of minor refusals to confront intolerance and to permit, even promote, prevailing prejudices.

By the time I returned to England I was planning the sequence which I called provisionally Between the Wars. Without any conscious imitation of Balzac, I had a habit of developing characters from book to book, often in entirely different settings. A minor character in a fantasy novel, for instance, might become a major character in a realistic story and vice versa. I did this mostly to carry certain themes from book to book. Colonel Pyatnitski, based on a neighbour of mine in Ladbroke Grove who collected mechanical junk and shared his hatred of Jews and Arabs, first appeared as one of Mrs Cornelius's lovers and seemed the ideal narrator. The story had to lack the pitfalls and portentousness of most other 'Holocaust fiction' I had read. It had to confront the deep roots of prejudice. I had to get inside the mind of 'the enemy'.

Pyat could not just be my model for the victim. He also had to represent the perpetrator, the betrayer. He had to embody and speak for what I considered to be all the follies and distractions of humanity; he had to be the century's apologist as well as the target of its most infamous villainies and, of course, he had to be an entertainer, someone the reader could remain interested in, even identify with, for the length (as it turned out some 2,000 pages) needed to tell his story from 1900 to the near-present. I was inclined to agree with a former mother-in-law that, no matter how serious a book's intention, it wasn't worth reading unless it had some humour in it. Therefore, as I had done with Cornelius, where I found myself weeping over pictures of burning children yet only an hour later writing a comic scene about the 'Vietnamisation' of Ladbroke Grove, I realised I could only contain my anger and grief by giving the story a strong element of grotesque comedy borrowed in part from my enthusiasm for the Commedia dell'arte.

So I've written a comic novel sequence about the inevitable road not, in this case, to Auschwitz but to Dachau. I chose Dachau because it was closest to Munich, where Nazism was born. Pyat the Jew, unreliable narrator, forever proclaiming his Slav soul, mourning the death of what he calls Christendom, constantly getting things wrong, wanders across a landscape of prejudice, illusion and delusion, from Odessa to Istanbul, from Rome to Paris, New York, Hollywood, Venice and Munich. He claims to be an Orthodox Christian, an engineer of genius, a film-star and a visionary who almost achieved victory for the Whites in the Russian Civil War, was forced into Ataturk's service in Constantinople, built a giant airship for the French, helped formulate race laws in the US, was enslaved in Egypt, built an airforce for the Caid of Marrakesh and by the final book is co-opted as an inventor by Mussolini and then the Nazis. The titles of the books form a couplet: Byzantium Endures The Laughter of Carthage; Jerusalem Commands The Vengeance of Rome, hopefully rooting the books in our ancient common history pointing to the road to Auschwitz. His distorted idealism, his belief in mechanistic salvation, leads him deeper and deeper into the heart of the nightmare, experiencing antisemitism in Turkey, the Ku Klux Klan in Dixie, racialism in Cairo and Marrakesh. A con-man in love with his own lies, Pyat is a small-time movie actor whose faith in his ability to invent monster airships, dynamite-driven cars and super-fast aeroplanes leads him to Mussolini's Rome, then to Hitler's Munich and finally to Franco's Barcelona. Caught up in the Spanish Civil War, he is mistakenly 'repatriated' to London and the scenes of his ultimate and perhaps most contemptible betrayal in the 1960s. Meanwhile, he has enjoyed the confidence of some of history's other great opportunists and his engineering miracles have turned to nothing but wreckage.

Although I enjoyed flying in airships and seaplanes, for instance, the intensity and variety of the research more than once made me half-crazy. Entering the personality of a monster became so exhausting I took longer and longer breaks between novels. The bulk of my initial work was with survivors or personal, often naïve, accounts of ordinary people trapped in monumental events. Some survivors were unregenerate Nazis who had escaped Hitler after the Night of the Long Knives, some were Jews who had known persecution. I talked to Leah Feldmann, who worked on the education train organised by the much misrepresented Ukrainian anarchist Nestor Makhno and to my own benefactor, Ernst Jellinek, who immediately before the war ventured in and out of Germany and Austria 'buying' Jews with money raised in England. I talked to people in Mississippi who had been Klan members, to ex-mercenaries working for El Glaoui in Morocco. I heard more stories than I could possibly use, many of them offered in confidence.

In the end it seemed to me that, with a few exceptions, all Christendom and Islam played a part in the betrayal of the victims. I could not exonerate those English and American Jews who might have said and done more but turned a blind eye to the fate of their people overseas. By the time the Second World War was under way, of course, there was far less that could be done to save the Jews of Eastern Europe when, under the cloak of war, the Nazis began to implement the Final Solution.

Could we have stopped the rise of Hitler? From all the newspapers and magazine articles I read, from the people I talked to and the accounts I absorbed, I am certain that we could, though I understand how sick and tired of struggling we all were. Did we learn anything from Nazism's rise and fall? I hope we did. My fear now, of course, is that we have not only forgotten that lesson but have, for ignoble, self-serving ends, consciously or unconsciously distorted the history of the Holocaust.

I have tried to demonstrate, through the comic antics of my Ukrainian Falstaff, that neither belligerent rhetoric and lachrymose sentimentality, nor nostalgia for vanished power will stop something like the Holocaust happening but rather will add fuel to existing fires. By reproducing what is familiar to us, rather than taking intellectual and political risks, by dismissing liberal humanism or, if you like, traditional spiritual values, as an unrealistic basis for our actions, we could well create the conditions for another holocaust even more terrible than the last.

# INTRODUCTIONS
# AND REVIEWS

# ■ The Cosmic Satirist

## A review of *Naked Lunch* by William Burroughs

**From *New Worlds*, February 1965**

Mary McCarthy has said of Burroughs and *Naked Lunch* 'This must be the first space novel, the first serious piece of science fiction—the others are entertainment . . . In him, as in Swift, there is a kind of soured Utopianism.' Although this suggests that she is not all that familiar with modern SF, she has a good point and Burroughs's genius of course towers over the talents of the majority of our SF writers. Even those who object to his subject matter and literary innovations must admit that his ability to handle the English language is greater than any of his contemporaries.

Not since Joyce has there been a writer of such power and richness, and never before has there been purely imaginative writing of such wildness and intelligence. Burroughs is a satirist—his most obvious talents lie in this direction. More savage and puritanical than Swift or Eliot, more sweeping in his attacks, he is a cosmic satirist, taking a rise not only out of the human race but also out of Time and Space. He lets no-one and nothing—physical or metaphysical—off lightly. Although often compared with Rabelais, he is much closer to Swift in that he lacks the magnanimity of Rabelais—there is no gentle fun in *Naked Lunch*. If Swift wrote the first SF tale, then Burroughs has produced the ultimate one—choosing a wider selection of targets, dealing with them with a fierceness of attack, an intensity of vision, a mastery of language that inspires horror at a picture of life which is at once distorted and more truthful than anything else in literature.

The book covers such a wide range of subjects and ideas that it can be interpreted on dozens of different levels. JG Ballard sees Burroughs as fashioning from 'our dreams and nightmares the first authentic mythology of the age of Cape Canaveral, Hiroshima and Belsen. His novels are the terminal documents of the mid-twentieth century, scabrous, scarifying, a progress report from an inmate in the cosmic madhouse' (*New Worlds* 142). On the other hand Irving Wardle (*The Observer*, 22nd November, '64) thinks that 'the essence of the book is in its record of the addict's life—the daily pursuit of dope, the voluptuously savoured moment of the fix, and the apocalyptic fantasies it releases for which Burroughs draws on a large medical vocabulary as a brilliant extension of emotional language'. Anthony Burgess does not agree—'Burroughs is demonstrating that his difficult subject can only be expressed through the static (that is neither didactic nor pornographic) shaping of the imagination' (*The Guardian*, 20th November, '64)—and so on and so on. Those who admire Burroughs cannot always agree on *why* they like him—he has so much to offer that *Naked Lunch* can be read many times before all its levels and implications become clear. This is partially its appeal for me—to know that I can enjoy it once, begin it again immediately I have finished it and find more to enjoy.

The reader who likes a book with a 'beginning, a middle and an end' need not be in the least alarmed by *Naked Lunch*. I am much more inclined towards the conventional novel myself. I certainly do not welcome novelty for novelty's sake, nor obscenity for obscenity's sake—I find most of the fiction produced under the label of 'avant-garde' boring and pretentious, disguising bad, undisciplined writing under a superficial cloak of equally bad and undisciplined 'experimental' styles. Just as the Buck Rogers brigade of SF writers bring SF into disrepute, so do these so-called experimental writers bring the handful of genuine innovators into disrepute. The simple fact with Burroughs is that he can *write*. He can write better than anyone else at work today. He has an ear for dialogue, an eye for reality, an ability to conjure up phantasmagoric visions that immediately capture the imagination, a powerful, uncompromising style that rips away our comforting delusions and displays the warts and the sores that can fester in the human mind. Not a pleasant vision at first, yet we are soon captured by Burroughs's deadpan style which aids us to look upon the horrors without revulsion, and take, instead, a cool, objective look at perversion in all its states and forms—mental, physical and spiritual.

Burroughs's Black Utopias are more horrifying, more relevant and more convincing than any that have appeared to date in SF. His State of Interzone, dominated by the coolly grotesque figure of Doctor 'Cancer is my first love' Benway makes the worlds of Huxley and Orwell seem like paradise in comparison. Its nearest equivalent is the world of *Limbo '90*.

> Dr Benway had been called in as an advisor to the Freeland Republic, a place given over to free love and continual bathing. The citizens are

well adjusted, co-operative, honest, tolerant and above all clean. But the invoking of Benway indicates all is not well behind that hygienic façade: Benway is a manipulator and co-ordinator of symbol systems, an expert on all phases of interrogation, brainwashing and control. I have not seen Benway since his precipitate departure from Annexia, where his assignment had been TD—Total Demoralisation. Benway's first act was to abolish concentration camps, mass arrest and, except under certain limited and special circumstance, the use of torture. "I deplore brutality," he said. "It's not efficient. On the other hand, prolonged mistreatment, short of physical violence, gives rise, when skilfully applied, to anxiety and a feeling of special guilt. A few rules or rather guiding principles are to be borne in mind. The subject must not realise that the mistreatment is a deliberate attack of an anti-human enemy on his personal identity. He must be made to feel he deserves *any* treatment he receives because there is something (never specified) horribly wrong with him. The naked need of the control addicts must be decently covered by an arbitrary and intricate bureaucracy so that the subject cannot contact his enemy direct."

Annexia is somewhat like the world of *The Trial*—though Burroughs tends to be rather more explicit and specific than ever Kafka was. Interzone is not only a State, it is a state of time and mind:

Panorama of the City of Interzone. Opening bars of East St Louis Toodleoo . . . at times loud and clear then faint and intermittent like music down a windy street. . . . The room seems to shake and vibrate with motion. The blood and substance of many races, Negro, Polynesian, Mountain Mongol, Desert Nomad, Polyglot Near East, Indian—races as yet unconceived and unborn, combinations not yet realised pass through your body. Migrations, incredible journeys through deserts and jungles and mountains (stasis and death in closed mountain valleys where plants grow out of genitals, vast crustaceans hatch inside and break the shell of the body) across the Pacific in outrigger canoe to Easter Island. The Composite City where all human potentials are spread out in a vast silent market.

Minarets, palms, mountains, jungle. . . . A sluggish river jumping with vicious fish, vast weed-grown parks where boys lie in the grass, play cryptic games. Not a locked door in the City. Anyone comes into your room at any time. The Chief of Police is a Chinese who picks his teeth and listens to denunciations presented by a lunatic. Every now and then the Chinese takes the tooth-pick out of his mouth and looks at the end of it. Hipsters with smooth copper-coloured faces lounge in doorways twisting shrunken heads on gold chains, their faces blank with an insect's unseeing calm. . . . High mountain flutes, jazz and bebop, one-stringed Mongol instruments, gypsy xylophones, African drums, Arab bagpipes. . . . The City is visited by epidemics of violence, and the untended dead are eaten by vultures in the streets. Albinos blink in the sun. . . . People eaten by unknown diseases watch the passerby with evil, knowing eyes.

Other inhabitants of Interzone are 'servers of fragmentary warrants taken down in hebephrenic shorthand charging unspeakable mutilations of the spirit, bureaucrats of spectral departments, officials of unconstituted police states . . .', etc., etc. These descriptions of Interzone are amongst the most powerful in the book.

Benway's sidekick is Dr Schafer 'The Lobotomy Kid':

SCHAFER: "I tell you I can't escape a feeling . . . well, of *evil* about this."
BENWAY: "Balderdash, my boy . . . We're scientists . . . Pure scientists. Disinterested research and damned be him who cries, 'Hold, *too much!*' Such people are no better than party poops."

In *Naked Lunch* we have left for ever the mythological worlds of Winston Churchill, Mickey Mouse and Ernest Hemingway, have gone past the worlds of The Beatles and James Bond, and have entered the world of the present, seen an indication of Things To Come for, whereas most SF is speculation, *Naked Lunch* is visionary—and this contributes to its fascination. Anyone attracted to SF by its more serious elements will find *Naked Lunch* rewarding. The novel costs 42s. and is published by John Calder.

# ■ Dark Continents, Dying Planets

**Foreword to *Master of Adventure: The Worlds of Edgar Rice Burroughs* by Richard A Lupoff, 2005**

It's probably fair to say that I owe my career to Edgar Rice Burroughs. From the age of fourteen I produced an ERB fanzine, *Burroughsania*, before I really knew what fanzines were. Through it I discovered the world of science fiction fandom and began to exchange letters with Richard Lupoff!

When I was sixteen I interviewed the editor of *Tarzan Adventures* in London. He didn't much like my interview, but his assistant liked it a lot. Before I knew it I was writing a series of articles about Burroughs for that magazine. *Tarzan Adventures* published reprints of the Sunday newspaper strips as well as original text features and fiction. Soon the assistant editor, the new editor, had commissioned a serial, an ERB pastiche, for *Tarzan Adventures*. This was 'Sojan the Swordsman', my first fantasy hero. The new editor offered me the job of assistant. My career in journalism and fiction had begun.

In the late 1950s, by the time I was seventeen, I was editing the magazine and filling it with all kinds of Burroughs-derived science fiction and fantasy as well as more features about Edgar Rice Burroughs himself. By the 1960s, when my magazine *New Worlds* needed financing, I wrote a series of Burroughs-type novels to support it (more of this later). My last close association with Burroughs was writing *The Land that Time Forgot* for Amicus Films in the early 1970s. As Lupoff does, I regard that novel as probably Burroughs's finest, with an intriguing idea that puts it firmly in the realm of science fiction, even though the form of the story is more of a fantasy adventure. I worked with Jim Cawthorn, a long-time friend and Burroughs illustrator, who had also drawn strips and written stories for *Tarzan Adventures*. Cawthorn broke the book down into scenes. I then did the finished script, turning the stereotypical German U-boat commander into, I hope, a subtler character who became the intellectual 'voice' for the story's fascinating central idea, which Lupoff describes in detail here. Cawthorn and I also wrote an outline for the sequel, *The People that Time Forgot*, but after seeing the final shots of the first film, we pulled out from any further involvement. We had hoped to bring 'authentic' Burroughs to the screen. We didn't want any part of producing further bastardisations.

We had been attracted to doing the film for the same reasons Richard Lupoff liked the book—it is perhaps one of the two best science fiction ideas Burroughs ever had. In the hands of its producer, John Dark, *The Land that Time Forgot* (with Doug McClure and Susan Penhaligon) rather obscured its central idea and came dangerously close to being just another dinosaur picture with a volcanic explosion as the cliché dénouement, robbing the movie of much of its special atmosphere, although some, I think, was retained.

The same company corrupted Burroughs's novel *At the Earth's Core*, another of his best works, but luckily box office receipts began to drop, as they deserved to, so that the producers gave up any further attempts to bastardise the work of a writer who, for all his faults of repetition and sometimes hasty writing, deserved far better treatment. What was more, as I understood it, Edgar Rice Burroughs, Inc., the company which looks after Burroughs's copyrights, couldn't stand the bastardisation any better than we could. Aside from some decent versions of Tarzan made in recent years, ours was more or less the last attempt to make a movie worthy of Burroughs's originals. He has never been served well by movies, which, considering that he lived within driving distance of most of the Hollywood studios, has always seemed ironic to me.

It makes me wonder whether, for instance, John Carter's Martian adventures will ever successfully be brought to the screen. I would love to see the moody landscapes of the Red Planet populated with baroquely armoured Tharks and their noble human foes, the ancient towers of gorgeous Helium rising into the thin air, the horrors of the River Iss, the lazy curve of fliers as they stream across the skies beneath the twin moons of Mars. It would need the same sort of loving attention as that which brought *The Lord of the Rings* to the screen, but it would definitely beat anything *Star Wars* has yet been able to offer. If they ever do decide to make the movies, I hope the writers, director and producers will read Lupoff's excellent account of the stories and their merits before they begin.

Lupoff has an intelligent, sensitive taste for the virtues of Burroughs's books. Not only can he explain the merits of Burroughs's best work, he can say what's wrong with the fiction that doesn't measure up to the best.

I was surprised to learn from this book how poorly served American readers were with Burroughs during the years I was most enjoying him. Unlike American readers of the 1950s I had plenty of Burroughs available to me in the United Kingdom. The Methuen hardbacks with their wonderful J Allen St John dust-wrappers were still cramming our library shelves while the Pinnacle paperbacks could be bought at any bookstore or railway news-stand. Not only the Tarzan stories, but the Martian, Venusian, Pellucidarian and other novels could be found everywhere. It was even possible to get rela-tively obscure titles, such as *The Outlaw of Torn* and, as I recall, *The Bandit of Hell's Bend*, *The Eternal Lover* and *Apache Devil*. Why this should have been so, I have no idea, except that perhaps Burroughs's popularity remained high in Britain, where we did not have quite so many rival fantasy publica-tions in the years immediately following the Second World War.

The paperback covers weren't always the best, but I spent many a summer vacation acquiring and reading most of what ERB had published in book form before his death. When I bought second-hand hardbacks I could even write to Methuen and ask for fresh jackets, which they were happy to send entirely free of charge! A different and happier era!

Contrary to George Orwell's predictions about the bad influence of popular fiction on young minds, I did not grow up to become a fascist, racist or casual killer of beasts and men from reading Burroughs. Indeed I some-how managed to be a left-winger, a committed anti-racist and a preserver of animal life firmly opposed to the death penalty! If I now blanch at some of the disgusting racial language which so infects Burroughs's work, as it does that of John Buchan, Edgar Wallace, Ernest Hemingway and a mass of lesser writers, I can always listen to the BBC serialisation of, say, *Tarzan of the Apes*, which was cleansed of its racist comments and stereotypes yet lost none of the pace and pleasure of the original. A talking book can get rid of a multitude of sins.

Burroughs was indeed a master tale-spinner. The serial devices he used keep readers turning pages as fast as you would in Dickens. His influence on the likes of Robert E Howard, Leigh Brackett, Philip Farmer and Fritz Leiber continues to be felt in the work of writers *they* influenced. He is without a doubt a key figure in the history of science fiction, fantasy and adventure fiction.

In the mid-1960s, as I said, I paid direct homage to Burroughs. Writing as Edward Powys Bradbury I produced, in nine days, three books still in print as *Kane of Old Mars*. In them I tried to make my hero behave not like John Carter of Mars but according to Burroughs's stated moral views. Rather than respond violently to aggression, as they usually do in his books, I have my heroes and heroines incline, as much as they can, to negotiate their way out of trouble. I never read the Kane books myself (I sent them directly to the publisher as I finished them), but the act of writing them at such speed had induced in me a kind of trance-state, where I began to understand Burroughs as a true visionary!

I eventually calmed down and my mind readjusted to the business of real life, but I never entirely lost a sense of the genuine quality of that rather crude genius whose books were not always served by the best prose.

Burroughs's vision of Mars has lasted almost as long as Dickens's vision of London. The place has become a character. It is so pervasive it has continued through the work of Leigh Brackett, Ray Bradbury and PK Dick, and even to the sophisticated stories of JG Ballard. Burroughs's Mars, all scientific and historical evidence aside, *is* Mars. The collective unconscious being the powerful thing it is, my guess is that by the time we get a proper chance to explore the Red Planet we'll find the wondrous city of Helium, various tribes of four-armed Tharks riding their *thoats*, and somewhere we'll interrupt a pair of red-skinned men sitting outside an atmosphere plant profoundly engaged in a game of *jetan* (Martian chess).

As Lupoff so convincingly tells us here, Burroughs was more than a popular writer. With Tarzan's fantastic Africa, John Carter's ancient Mars and David Innes's hidden world of Pellucidar, he created an enduring and powerful mythology.

Constantly reprinted, forever being rediscovered, Burroughs, for all his extraordinary visionary gifts, continued to think of himself throughout his own life as 'a normal bean'. Sometimes he seemed almost ashamed of his original imagination and tended to minimise his gifts.

But along with Lupoff and millions of readers I believe that Burroughs was a master, an original. As you will discover when you read this study (which I found as absorbing as one of Burroughs's own books), the creator of Tarzan may have written a few too many sequels, but the core of his work remains powerful and influential. Lupoff's study is a fascinating account of a seminal American writer, as influential in his own way as James Fenimore Cooper or Mark Twain. He is a writer whose best work is quite as readable now as on the day it was published almost a century ago. Few more respected writers have lasted as well. I suspect few writers today will continue to be as successful as Edgar Rice Burroughs, Master of Adventure. He deserves this book. I am glad Richard Lupoff has revised and reprinted it. I hope you'll find it as illuminating as I do.

# ■ A Fiercer Hen

A Review of *Again, Dangerous Visions* and *The Beast that Shouted Love at the Heart of the World*

**From *New Society*, 29th July 1976**

Even more than the world of publishers, the world of professional SF writers and fans is notoriously timid and conservative. In the last ten years, as the popularity of this genre has grown, the number of writers supplying it has risen accordingly. Now, like battery hens, they produce regularly and reliably and what they produce is virtually without flavour or value of any kind. The label on these eggs is a bald lie: this 'imaginative fiction' is a series of well-established tropes and commercial fiction conventions designed not to frighten off a public now established in publishers' minds as a 'market'.

In the United States (where the logic of category publishing flourishes even more than in Europe) since the mid-sixties Harlan Ellison has adopted the rôle of fox in the SF hen-coop, and while many of the inmates believe he is merely after their blood and flesh and the ultimate destruction of the coop, others argue that his activities will produce a brighter, fiercer hen, with improved survival characteristics, laying a tastier, more nourishing egg. Ellison has been stirring things up with a series of speeches, television appearances, personal confrontations, letters, stories and anthologies designed to provoke the complacent and to stimulate the despondent into producing genuinely radical stories in a popular genre whose practitioners range from a majority like Heinlein turning out naïve and reactionary 'mechaporn' to a minority who, like Disch or Ballard, have created their own sophisticated, highly idiosyncratic styles.

A little ironically, the latter writers are represented in *Again, Dangerous Visions* by rather tame stuff, whereas some of the old hardliners have been goaded into producing lively and untypical stories. There are to be three volumes (each about 450,000 words long) in the series of anthologies which began with *Dangerous Visions*, itself published here in a mutilated edition, and will end with *Last Dangerous Visions*, yet to go to press.[1] The second book is much better than the first and the signs are that the third will be the best of all, for there are now many more promising writers in SF, due partly to Ellison's own efforts (*Dangerous Visions* is an SF bestseller in paperback in the US and is widely used as a teaching text). The quality of contents varies greatly. Some of the voices often seem to be shouting too loudly—but it could be argued that a few of the quieter voices are far too quiet, mumbling self-consciously because they don't want people to confuse them with the rowdy, rather embarrassing crowd with whom they're forced to associate. But individual quality isn't important. A good anthology should be, as this is, a work of synthesis in which the contributions form parts of a mosaic of the editor's creation.

*Again, Dangerous Visions* is vulgar, brash, sometimes silly; but it is alive and optimistic in a way we can expect from few books of any kind these days. There is no point here in attempting to deal with individual stories (there are forty-six, each with a foreword by Ellison and an afterword by the author). I can, however, recommend the collection. Ellison's enthusiasm is infectious, his involvement is admirable, his own judgement eccentric and his taste questionable. In an introduction, he admits that he turned down a Disch submission out of personal dislike for the author; he berates himself for his foolishness, relates how he came to like and respect Disch, how they became friends, and how he insisted Disch be included in this volume.

He leaves himself open to every sort of cynical response from his critics—and this is his real strength both as a writer and as an anthologist. He reports private conversations, describes the characters of his contributors, sometimes with sentimentality, sometimes with contempt, and gives us a book which, for all that it was published in the US four years ago, retains an energy, a liveliness which refuses to fade. More cautious rivals might cultivate a well-bred tone, select their contents with cooler judgement and better taste, but none of them will contribute as much to the genre or last as long. This monster stands as a monument to the SF genre at a time when it is in a state of metamorphosis, when writers are excited about what they are doing. No other popular genre has such a monument, possibly because messianism is an integral part of the SF writer's temperament.

Reflecting this temperament, a collection of Harlan Ellison's own stories is also published in what I gather is a planned uniform edition of his work (which includes documentary novels from the time he joined a New

---

1 Still due in 2012!

York street gang and the incisive articles on the visual media written for the *Los Angeles Free Press*—Ellison's main income is from script-writing). This collection includes stories originally published between 1957 and 1969 and show far less development in technique than they do in subject matter. The many Ellison enthusiasts will be glad to have these stories available at last. The collection includes a longer, revised version of the Nebula-winning 'A Boy and His Dog', first published in England. All the stories are written with an almost maniacal energy, but if they have a drawback for me it is probably because they still contain far too much SF and not nearly enough Ellison. He is a brave and lively little beast, who makes a great show of himself to the hounds, but remains far too wary ever to lead them to his real lair.

# ■ An Introduction to *The Babylonian Trilogy* by Sébastien Doubinsky

**From the PS Publishing edition, March 2009**

The French have a sense of and a talent for the absurd which only rarely manifests itself in English—Sterne, Peacock, Firbank, William Burroughs, David Britton, Steve Aylett—and is perhaps at its most inventive when combined with a Jewish or Russian sensibility: Vvedensky comes to mind. Sébastien Doubinsky, who has already established himself in France, who has lived in America and England and now in Denmark, has an enthusiasm for the ridiculous and a talent for ridicule reminiscent of Cendrars and Vian, yet, like all Frenchmen, longs to be a Beatle or a Pistol, preferably, but not necessarily a living one. For me, he is, therefore, a personification of the best modern French literature and living proof that French culture is alive and well and living in Tours or Nantes, even if it thinks it would rather be living in Liverpool or San Francisco.

Doubinsky is impressively, superbly multilingual, well educated in America and France. He shames the average Anglo-Saxon (or even Anglo-Jewish) writer with his fluency and his cultural reference. Steeped in Balzac and Flaubert, he loves Dashiell Hammett and Robert Sheckley; familiar since birth with Ravel and Messiaen, he listens to Robert Johnson and The Clash, investing them with a meaning and subtlety which might escape the average Englishman who, in turn, venerates Django or *Les Triplettes de Belleville*. He engages, in other words, in that eternal love affair, frequently unadmitted, denied or denigrated, between the Anglophone and the Francophone.

None of this, of course, would be worth remarking if Doubinsky didn't have an original talent, if he wasn't astonishingly entertaining. That, of course, is his main attraction.

'The world was much better when you looked at it from underneath . . .' An observation which informs the work of every thieving poet since time began. Some would say it's the only way to see the world, that the moment the writer ceases to be the underdog he relinquishes his authority—that he substitutes an authoritative tone, like Eliot, for the authority of experience. By experience I don't mean the author has to steal church silver or suffer in a garret (though I've long held that a writer who hasn't been bankrupted or gone to prison at least once has to make greater efforts to convince us of their credentials) but has to retain that sense of marginalization at any price, if their work is to resonate on as many possible levels.

The *Babylonian Trilogy* certainly works on many levels, sniffing its way through an imaginary city that is all cities; lifting its leg where it feels like it, loyal only to itself. A loyalty, perhaps, which not all of us have yet discovered. Out of the noise.

Babylon, as Bob Marley knew, is noise first. And then colour, of course, and scent. And sex. The home of Lilith and hiding place of the Other. Heaven and Hell. Order and Chaos. Angels and devils. Fame and obscurity. Chips and fish. And, of course, mystery. As Georg Ratner knows, studying *The Book of Gates*, reading the Tarot, looking for answers. Beasts and women. Gods and men. Crime and justice. Blindness and vision. Sleep and wakefulness. Peace. Noiseless peace. Death. And is that Bill Burroughs or Raymond Chandler whispering in the void? Maybe only Jimmy can hear him above the Babylonian babble, the rise and fall of the music of all the cities of the world? Or is it a child's scream? Pain or pleasure? Maybe only good-natured Sheryl knows.

The assassin goes about his work and dogs run free. They fly back to the godhead, they embrace death. Everything must die. Everything lives eternally. Grim men with soft hearts. Soft women with good, grim heads. Their actions are their secrets. Cassandra spikes up. Life goes on. The dragon dreams he's a machine, a ticket to ride. Louise is a breeze. We walk through a hanging garden; Eden's a biochemical lake; spiders crawl under your skirt. Sailor Jack's staggering home again. Time for one last cup of coffee in the Luxembourg, the Jardin Americain where Doubinsky and I first shared a few hours, thanks to that willing catalyst, book sniffer, first rate guitarist, mighty baby Martin Stone. Since I can't remember much of that conversation I was probably talking about me. But his story must have been interesting enough for me to ask to read something he'd written. And this was it. Then we met Sophie, his talented wife, with Theo and Selma, their children. Then we became friends. But it's fair to say, as is often the case, that the book came first.

What else can I say. Do what I did.

Enjoy.

# ■ Like a Fox

A Review of *I Am Alive and You Are Dead: A Journey into the Mind of Philip K Dick* by Emmanuel Carrère

**From the *Guardian*, 4th June 2005**

Like Hammett, Chandler, Faulkner and Eudora Welty, US writer Philip K Dick was first taken seriously in England and France. *New Worlds* magazine serialised his 'breakthrough' novel *Time Out of Joint* in 1959, and I believe mine was the first published essay on Dick[1] to suggest that he was something more than a good genre writer. People such as Maxim Jakubowski began to publicise him in France. *New Worlds* commissioned the late John Brunner to write the first appreciation of Dick to run in a national magazine.

In 1965, after *The Man in the High Castle* won Dick his only Hugo award, I contacted his agent on behalf of the publisher I was advising. The agent said we could have any four Dick titles for £600, and an option to buy the next four at the same price. The publisher, perhaps believing books that cheap couldn't be any good, passed. I wrote to Dick saying he was being undersold. Dick, notoriously his own worst enemy, did not, as I suggested, change his agent. Had it not been for Tom Maschler, impressed by the enthusiasm of other writers, Dick might have been as indistinguishably published in the UK as he was in the US. At Cape, Maschler presented Dick, like Ballard, as non-generic, bringing him to a wider if not more lucrative audience. Younger writers such as Fay Weldon and Martin Amis became fans. And Dick's legend as the Acid Sage of Berkeley (though he only ever took one trip, a bad one) was established. Initially, he did nothing to dispel it. Already a mythomane to rival SF writer L Ron Hubbard, founder of Scientology, he discovered the reputation passingly useful as he enjoyed guru-status with the Berkeley young.

In 1952, Anthony Boucher, founding editor of *Fantasy & SF*, serial mentor and customer of the classical record store where Dick worked, had

---

1 'The Real Life Philip K Dick', in *Vector*, No. 39, ed. Rog Peyton, April 1966.

published his first story. After that, Dick's chief inspiration, when he began turning out fiction for the dwindling magazine market, was his need to pay the rent. He wasn't the only SF writer of his generation to make whole-hearted use of dexedrine and valium but for a while he allowed readers to think inspiration came from acid, far more chic in the '60s. Mostly, he was running, as prolific writers generally do, on adrenaline and caffeine.

Emmanuel Carrère thinks the posthumously published social novels Dick produced were done to please snobbish friends and lovers. However, Dick was continually looking for the form which would best suit his ideas. No great stylist, his problem was that he had a hard time putting a story together without the conventions of genre fiction. His best work uses the methods developed in the pages of *Galaxy* by a group of writers including Pohl, Kornbluth, Bester, Sheckley and Harlan Ellison. What we today recognise as the 'PKD future' is actually a collaboration between these socially conscious writers responding to Eisenhower's and J Edgar Hoover's America and specifically to McCarthyism. Unlike the conservative techno-SF writers, they actually predicted the world we know today.

Dick began to produce twists on conventional dystopias. He lacked Bester's sophistication, Pohl's Marxism, Sheckley's irony or Ellison's eloquence, but he captured the readers' imagination as previously only HP Lovecraft (Carrère's other literary hero) had done. Educated by Quakers, raised in radical Berkeley, a born-again Episcopalian by 1964, he accepted the malignity of the consumer state, but questioned the nature of its reality.

By the early '60s he had written *The Man in the High Castle*, *Dr Bloodmoney* and *The Three Stigmata of Palmer Eldritch*, and was consistently exploring the themes which would make his wider reputation. Not all his contemporaries found his obsessions stimulating; they saw, in fact, the ruination of a talent. Ellison expressed it with his usual laconicism: 'Took drugs, saw God. BFD.' But Dick was on a roll, helped by God and the I-Ching. *Do Androids Dream of Electric Sheep?* (on which the film *Blade Runner* was based), *Ubik* and *A Maze of Death* led steadily away from his generic roots. Meanwhile he divorced his third wife, left the relative isolation of Marin County, returned to the city and married again, increasingly losing his grip on reality, eventually coming to believe that a spirit guide had saved him and his newborn son from madness and death. After a short spell in a Canadian rehab clinic, he left admirers and hangers-on behind, and wound up in Fullerton, outside LA.

When Dick finally began to make money from foreign sales and film rights, he credited his spirit guide with helping release a secret store of cash.

Living off this money, struggling with mental instability and an imagination no longer reined by genre demands, Dick produced little publishable work in the last years of his life. He devoted himself to a kind of sequel to *The Man in the High Castle*, called *Exegesis*, in which he tried to develop the notion that his world where Hitler and Hirohito had won the Second World War was no more the real world than was this one. He became so strange that when I was living in Southern California in 1979/'80 I felt no desire to visit him. Some paranoiacs seem touched by divinity but equally they can be touched by banality. As with William Burroughs, listening to conspiracy theories could be exhausting.

Never leaving his home for weeks, sitting in the dark, playing Dowland and the Grateful Dead, he became increasingly absorbed in his own myth, fed back to him by fans who, like Tolkien's crankier readers, could fairly be called disciples. Yet at an SF convention in Metz, he seriously disappointed fans who had expected a divine junkie and got a Christian missionary. He died in 1982, leaving hundreds of thousands of unpublished words, many of which have yet to see the light.

It's a shame this book contains no index and does not refer to the half a dozen or so other critiques and biographies of PKD, nor to interviews, such as Charles Platt's, which was done towards the end of Dick's life and is a rather better journey into his mind. In his excellent *Who Writes Science Fiction?* Platt spoke respectfully of his subject, revealing a courteous, self-mocking man and recording a classic piece of monologue. Off-tape, Platt wanted to know if Dick was discussing his fiction or whether he really believed all he had talked about in his interview. Fairly typically, Dick switched to ironic mode: 'Why, no, of course not. You'd have to be crazy to believe in something like that.'

Another friend, Tom Disch, had his own interview terminated by the intervention of Dick's spirit guide who said it was time for Disch to leave. A courteous soul, he complied.

'Do you think he's crazy?' I asked later.

Disch smiled tolerantly. 'Like a fox,' he said.

# ■ Button-Holed by Erudition

## A Review of the Complete Centenary Edition of Aldous Huxley

**From the *Daily Telegraph*, 22nd January 1994**

On re-reading Aldous Huxley in Flamingo's centenary edition, my first response was of affectionate respect for a generous and enthusiastic writer who, if not the 'god of my adolescence' as he was of Angus Wilson's, was certainly among my boyhood pantheon. I believe I owe more of my real education to Huxley and to a few other popular intellectuals than to any formal schooling.

Refusing to be drawn by political cant, Huxley, in common with Orwell, came to be viewed as suspiciously by the orthodox Left as by the orthodox Right. John Clute recently pointed out how the horror central to all our great English visionary dystopias is not of social change but of imposed orthodoxy, the consequent social stasis and its dreadful effect on the human spirit. After a quasi-fascistic flirtation in the '30s with ideas not dissimilar to Wells's notions of society run by a kind of benign intellectual samurai, Huxley (like Wells) was soon able to see where such ideas led, as a frustrated petite bourgeoisie put élitist leaders into power across Europe.

But unlike Wells—or Orwell—Huxley ultimately refused to discount or condemn the past's spiritual wisdom. For years he sought to bridge the rifts he perceived between science and religion and the arts, reflecting his own struggles between the rationalist ideals of his family and contemporaries, and his pursuit of a relationship with God.

Refusing to trade one orthodoxy for another, as Evelyn Waugh did, Huxley spent his life trying to escape the elegant straight-waistcoat of a privileged inheritance which gave him scientific method, intellectual rigour, Eton, Balliol, and an entry into the literary world of Ottoline Morrell's Garsington where Lawrence became his friend and where he met his future wife.

Huxley's first big success was in 1921 with *Crome Yellow*, that mixture of parody, satire and social irony owing something to Peacock and Meredith, set in a house not dissimilar to Garsington and peopled by characters readily recognisable as part of the Morrell clique. It was a wonderfully entertaining expression of Huxley's awkward fury with a generation he believed had allowed the obscenity of the Great War and the resultant social instability. Further novels—*Antic Hay, Those Barren Leaves*—have much in common with the early work of Waugh (who admired them). Together with his essays and poetry, they established Huxley's reputation.

To a degree he escaped further constricting approval by choosing to live and work abroad. His travel books, like *Jesting Pilate*, have remarkable contemporary relevance. For years, in wide-ranging, influential essays like 'Do What You Will' and 'Music at Night', Huxley was understood to be carrying the torch of scientific humanism lit by his famous grandfather. On principle he was often prepared to repress his artist's instincts to produce journalism addressing the great moral and political debates of our century, but his scepticism was never as strong as his faith.

If *Brave New World* was the visionary culmination of Huxley's first period, *Point Counter Point* must be its literary masterpiece. The novel's ambition and technical sophistication confirmed the respect many other writers, from Faulkner to Powell, had for him. His next, *Eyeless in Gaza*, displayed a new interest in Christian mysticism. Huxley's powers were as considerable as ever, but changing their emphasis. This was the last novel he published before leaving, he thought temporarily, for the United States.

There is a myth that Huxley went a bit daft in California, yet it was during this period that he produced another masterpiece, *The Perennial Philosophy*, with its urgent argument that by studying and synthesising our common ideals and spiritual wisdom we could arrive at a Highest Common Factor, a moral code to help unify mankind. The novels *After Many a Summer* and *Time Must Have a Stop* showed no diminishing of his talent, only of his ambition, and when in the mid-1950s he published *The Doors of Perception* and *Heaven and Hell*, accounts of his experiments with the hallucinogen LSD, he showed as keen a curiosity and as much intellectual courage as ever. The books are exemplary, wonderfully eloquent descriptions of what, because of society's incoherent attitude towards drugs, remains an area of human experience seldom properly examined.

Only towards the end, as in *The Human Condition*, a collection of lectures, did some of Huxley's writing grow a little woolly, but his desperate need to educate and improve others still informed everything. He died of cancer in 1963, a few hours after Kennedy's assassination.

In some ways Huxley, again like Wells, produced so much that was merely brilliant we are inclined to forget that from time to time he gave us authentic masterpieces. I never much liked *Brave New World*, but cannot deny its relevance to our recurring failure to achieve that just social order of which almost everyone dreamed when the century began. Huxley tells us in his later introduction that he did not rewrite the novel, as he had considered doing, to include a third strand of argument which he came to see as our only political hope: a kind of sophisticated Proudhonism drawing on the ideas of that kindly anarchist, Prince Kropotkin.

If Huxley could never be a wild, gutter visionary, could never experience the powerlessness and frustration of Bunyan or Blake, nor rise to their sublime heights, he could present a convincingly rational case for what some Europeans now call 'A Federation of the Regions', a world of small, autonomous states recognising a common law and interest, a common spiritual heritage, and operating a decentralised form of self-government with real power at every level of the community. He continues to persuade me it is better to seek that Highest Common Factor than pursue, as modern politicians do, the Lowest Common Denominator as if it were a moral quality.

Aldous Huxley still offers realistic and positive solutions to our terrible twentieth-century cycle of catastrophically repeated mistakes, where centralism, aggressive nationalism, unthinking fundamentalism and demagoguery have led inevitably to disaster. And he still engages the reader with that charming, enthusiastic, button-holing urgency of a marvellously witty and erudite English visionary who believed that human virtue, in spite of all the obstacles, must ultimately triumph.

# ■ Cricket by Moonlight

An Introduction to *The Hopkins Manuscript* by R.C. Sheriff

**From the *New York Review of Science Fiction*, September 2005**

SF is predefined in the minds of the general reading public as something they know they aren't going to like. When Margaret Atwood won the Arthur C Clarke Award for the year's best science fiction book there was a general feeling amongst her regular readers that the prize had been a mistake. *The Handmaid's Tale* couldn't be SF because it 'was about real life' and referred to historical and contemporary experience. Similarly, her *Oryx and Crake* has a *mise en scène* perhaps overfamiliar to most SF readers. Atwood has sometimes rejected the definition, as if a science fiction book couldn't possibly be taken seriously. Vonnegut, Ballard and even Philip K Dick are frequently refused the description of SF author they have claimed for themselves! Critics insist they are "too good" to be SF. Of course, most grownup visionary SF, while not being primarily interested in character, has always touched on serious subjects, whether in *The Space Merchants* by Pohl and Kornbluth, *The Man in the High Castle* by Philip K Dick, *Ice* by Anna Kavan, *The Atrocity Exhibition* by JG Ballard, *The Female Man* by Joanna Russ, *The Left Hand of Darkness* by Ursula K Le Guin, *Light* by M John Harrison or *Iron Council* by China Miéville. The writing is frequently highly ambitious. The marvel tale, of the kind written by Verne and Flammarion in the nineteenth century, is an altogether different kind of story, which concerns itself primarily with predicting scientific inventions, and has little to do with moral vision. America has, of course, produced a considerable number of visionary and literary moral fantasies, including stories by Mark Twain, Jack London, James Branch Cabell, Ray Bradbury, Frederick Pohl, Cyril Kornbluth, Philip K Dick, Robert Sheckley (whose work Douglas Adams looted rather lavishly for his *Hitchhiker's Guide to the Galaxy*), Harlan Ellison, Norman Spinrad, Jeffrey Ford and many others.

*After London; or, Wild England* (1885) by Richard Jeffries became a Victorian bestseller. It is perhaps the first elegiac romance about humanity destroying its own civilisation through greed, ignorance and folly, and ten years later HG Wells adopted a similar tone—what became, in fact, the characteristic tone of the English disaster story. Wells, fired by his own scientific and political visions, remains one of the greatest English writers of what is usually called SF. His *The Time Machine* (1895) not only proposed the notion that time was an element that could be negotiated by means of human invention (until then all time travel stories had used supernatural elements), but offered a commentary on British society as well as a stark vision of the end of everything, where the world, either through natural means or by our abuse of her resources, was an exhausted planet circling a dying star. His space invaders in *The War of the Worlds* were, by happy coincidence, cephalopods, perhaps the intellectuals of our seas, and he predicted many of the machines that would be used in 1914 with such stories as 'A Dream of Armageddon' (1903) and *The War in the Air* (1908). Though not the first scientific visionary (his predecessor Grant Allen anticipated many of his themes), Wells was the most important writer to employ modern literary skills and ideas to tell a traditional moral tale. Kipling had also offered us his brilliantly imagined but somewhat authoritarian stories of aerial power, 'With the Night Mail' (1905) and 'As Easy as ABC' (1912). EM Forster's 'The Machine Stops' (1909) proves that almost every major English writer of the twentieth century had at least one good visionary tale in them.

The first story I know about an interplanetary body crashing into the Earth is HG Wells's 'The Star' (1897). MP Shiel's *The Purple Cloud* (1901), very popular in its day, describes how civilisation is wiped out as the result of a mysterious gas killing everyone but one woman and one man, who are clearly seen as the new Adam and Eve. Conan Doyle's *The Poison Belt* (1913) doesn't have quite such disastrous consequences. JJ Connington's *Nordenholt's Million* (1923) shows a world severely harmed by a mutated bacterium that destroys our crops and could be seen as anticipating the current genetic experiments being introduced into our world. Floods and earthquakes destroyed civilisation in S Fowler Wright's *Deluge* (1928) and *Dawn* (1929), and in *The Strange Invaders* (1934) by Alun Llewellyn, his characters cope with surviving a new Ice Age (where Marx and Lenin have become legendary saints in a new, barbaric religion). No doubt Sherriff read some of these stories, especially the Kipling and the Wells, and expressed his own urge to give the world his ideas of where mankind's small-minded greed and lack of foresight were leading us.

Clearly a profound ignorance exists about science fiction amongst those who believe they won't enjoy it. It has been a category notoriously difficult to define because it is not really one genre, but several. In the bookshops great visionary tales and literary fiction share space with commercial pulp adventures. By that predefinition, readers understand SF to be the kind of thing their children read or watch—*Star Wars*, *Star Trek* or the rafts of bulky young adult space and fantasy adventure stories that have nowadays come to dominate our bookshops and bestseller lists. This is rather like defining *Jane Eyre* in terms of a Mills and Boon 'Gothic' romance or *The Turn of the Screw* in terms of *The Exorcist*, and reminds us how Conrad was marginalised for years as a 'sea story writer'.

I'm not a great reader of most genre fiction. I usually prefer stories written before they could be identified as genre—Bret Harte's 'The Outcasts of Poker Flat', for instance, rather than *Riders of the Purple Sage*, or Wilkie Collins rather than Ian Rankin. There is something stimulating about exploring unknown literary territory, whether it be that of Defoe, Swift, Austen or Woolf. By the time the generic process has taken place, there seems to me to be a falling off of originality, of intensely imagined metaphor and of narrative inspiration. No matter how good the writing, one begins to hear a chorus rather than an individual voice. That's why I can read and re-read HG Wells but have enjoyed only one space story (*Tiger! Tiger!* by Alfred Bester). I still get something out of *Beowulf*, but *The Lord of the Rings* is a defeating struggle. If Harry Potter leaves me cold, it's probably because I was exposed as a lad to too much Wrykin and Greyfriars. This isn't to say that the great originals don't have their roots in earlier books or that we aren't inclined to prefer the example of genre we first read, when we brought our own sense of novelty to a work (I remember being stunned, for instance, by the originality of *No Orchids for Miss Blandish*!), but a writer who is either unaware of genre, or rejects genre, or even one who assumes that certain generic conventions are their own invention, will often bring something to their fiction which gives it distinction. That is why it's possible for Margaret Atwood to say she isn't writing SF (because she thinks she isn't) or that RC Sherriff's *The Hopkins Manuscript* (1939) has little to do with Sinclair Lewis's *It Can't Happen Here*, Angus Wilson's *The Old Men at the Zoo* or Philip Roth's *The Plot Against America*.

When I was growing up, I understood that Sherriff had written an important book in the English SF canon. He was thought to be, if you like, the missing link between Wells and Wyndham, both of whom were inclined to use ordinary, modest, unimaginative men to record the wonders and cataclysmic horrors visited on our planet.

The disaster story is a peculiarly English form refined in recent years by the likes of Ballard and Aldiss. Indeed, when they first appeared, critics attempted, to the consternation of Tolkien and Peake, to fit both *The Lord of the Rings* and *Titus Groan* into this genre! Rachel Carson's *Silent Spring* set many writers to thinking about the problems of our effect on our environment, and some of the finest predictions about coming climate change came in the early 1960s. Perhaps the most lyrical and moving is JG Ballard's extraordinary *The Drowned World* (1962), first published as a novella in *Science Fiction Adventures* (which, somewhat at odds with its title, published some of the most thoughtful British SF), where the melting ice caps produce a planet that is reverting to the Triassic, and that contains some extraordinarily lyrical scenes of an inundated London. The elegiac tone of work written after the First World War found a clear echo in earlier books like John Christopher's *The Death of Grass* (1956) or John Bowen's *After the Rain* (1958), written since the Second. It's certainly characteristic of *The Hopkins Manuscript* and I think it's fair to say that only this novel really expressed Sherriff's yearning that the follies and cruelties he had experienced in the Great War should never be repeated again.

The author of *The Hopkins Manuscript* was born in Surrey in 1896 and attended Kingston Grammar School where he was a keen rower. RC 'Bob' Sherriff wanted to become a games master at a public school, couldn't afford to attend university and felt he wasn't bright enough to get a scholarship; so he followed his father and grandfather into a job with Sun Insurance. At the outbreak of the First World War he joined the East Surrey Regiment, serving as a captain. Wounded at Ypres by flying concrete from an exploding pillbox, he returned to Sun in 1918 as a claims adjuster, with ambitions to write. His earliest professional success appears to have been a script for a film version of *Toilers of the Sea* (1919), Richmond-born Ronald Colman's first important screen appearance.

For years Sherriff's work was only performed on the amateur stage, to raise funds for his beloved Kingston Rowing Club. Then, using letters he had sent home from the trenches, he wrote his seventh play, *Journey's End*, and submitted it to the agent Curtis Brown who liked it, suggesting he see what George Bernard Shaw thought of it. Shaw responded positively (the notoriously tight-fisted playwright even returned the stamps Sherriff had included). Nonetheless, the play was turned down by all West End theatres until, thanks to a single supporter on the board of the Incorporated Stage Society, founded to put on works unlikely to reach a wide public, it was given a private Sunday night/Monday afternoon production (featuring Laurence Olivier as Stanhope) at the Apollo Theatre in December 1928. For a fiver, an obscure set designer and bit-part actor called Jimmy Whale (another war veteran and ex-POW) agreed to direct it.

Contrary to all expectations, *Journey's End* received wonderful reviews. 'The Greatest of All War Plays' was Hannan Swaffer's headline in the *Daily Express*. James Agee devoted the whole of his weekly radio review to praising the play. Other influential critics thundered its virtues. Sadly, none of this impressed West End managements. If anything, they were even more suspicious of a play that found such popularity with highbrow critics. Curtis Brown continued to support the play, showing it to an unsuccessful producer, Maurice Browne, just back from trying to introduce Americans to Greek drama. Browne loved *Journey's End*. By good fortune he'd just received private backing to put on a West End production of his choice.

When Jimmy Whale finally presented it to the general public, with Colin Clive in the Stanhope rôle (Olivier having accepted a good part in *Beau Geste* at His Majesty's), it became an instant and worldwide success, quickly transferring to the larger Prince of Wales theatre. Soon it was earning Sherriff over £1,000 a week. He became a celebrity, meeting his heroes Kipling and Barrie. He went to New York with Whale to do the play there. Film rights were sold to Hollywood, and he bought a house, Rosebriars in Esher, near the Thames, for himself and his mother. Realising the play must eventually come off, Sherriff wrote his cricketing comedy *Badger's Green* as a follow-up. Put on at the Prince of Wales immediately after *Journey's End*, it bombed. Realising he couldn't maintain Rosebriars on the success of one play, he knew he might have to go back to regular work, but now he needed better pay. A friend helped him get into New College, Oxford, for a history degree. With that he could get a post as a sports master at a public school. He began rowing for his College Eight, anticipating a chance at the Boat Race, which would have improved his chances of a well-paid position, and meanwhile wrote his first novel, about a lower middle-class family on holiday in Bognor, *The Fortnight in September*, which became a bestseller in England and America, recalling his success with *Journey's End* and reviving his optimism.

Having returned briefly to do *Badger's Green*, Jimmy Whale was back in Hollywood. He'd been dialogue director on *Hell's Angels*, made a successful movie of *Journey's End*, and become a golden boy at Universal, who, after the success of *Waterloo Bridge*, contracted him for several pictures. *Frankenstein*, staring Colin Clive and other friends of Whale's, was an enormous hit (bit-part actor Karloff had been suggested by Jimmy's lover David Lewes). Whale's next production was *The Old Dark House* based on JB Priestley's novel and play. The third film was to be HG Wells's *The Invisible Man*, by then in the doldrums at the script department. Whale convinced Carl Laemmle, the studio head, that Bob Sherriff would produce the best script. Bob was torn between Hollywood and Oxford until an injury scotched his rowing chances and he was warned he wasn't likely to get a decent degree. Universal offered him an unusually large fee for his services, and he returned to Hollywood. His mother came too. She set up house for them in Santa Monica.

Bob worked first on *The Old Dark House*, then produced a tremendous script for *The Invisible Man* by the simple expedient of going back to the original book. Not having read Wells's novel, the studio heads were highly impressed (as indeed was Wells himself). Starring Claude Rains (another debuting rôle), the film was a worldwide hit. Sherriff had begun a successful career as screenwriter.

Though avoiding the 'wild' side of Hollywood, Sherriff mixed with many talented English people introduced to the screen by Whale, including Charles Laughton, Elsa Lanchester, Ernest Thesiger and Una O'Connor. Other Sherriff collaborations with Whale included *One More River*, based on Galsworthy's novel; *Dracula's Daughter*, adapted from Stoker's story; and *The Road Back*, originally an Erich Maria Remarque novel. Sadly, *The Road Back* was their last collaboration, a famous disaster. After Sherriff, Scott Fitzgerald worked on the doomed script, putting back all the anti-Nazi material which was again removed at the insistence of the German distributors. Whale disassociated himself from the film and Sherriff and his mother went home.

Happily, Alex Korda arrived in the nick of time and Sherriff's fortunes again improved. He scripted *The Four Feathers* with Ralph Richardson and *Goodbye, Mr Chips* with Robert Donat. At the outbreak of the Second World War he went to Hollywood to work on Korda's *That Hamilton Woman* and various morale-raising movies. Then the Japanese attacked Pearl Harbour, Santa Monica got the blackout and Bob returned to England where he and his mother weathered the rest of the war at Rosebriars.

During a successful career, which by his own account never again gave him quite the 'high' of *Journey's End*, Sherriff was associated with many memorable films of three decades: *Mrs Miniver*, *Cargo of Innocents*, *Forever and a Day*, *Odd Man Out*, *The Night My Number Came Up*, *Quartet* and *Trio* (based on Maugham stories), *No Highway*, *Home at Seven* (based on his own popular play) and *The Dam Busters*, many of which bore his distinctive, rather elegiac style, featuring modest, decent men caught up in extraordinary events. *Aces High*, a remake of *Journey's End* with airmen rather than soldiers, directed by Jack Gold and starring Christopher Plummer, Trevor Howard, John Gielgud and Malcolm McDowell, came out in 1976, shortly after Sherriff's death.

With Wells and Priestley, Sherriff helped create a characteristic English tone in the American cinema which frequently made a hero of the common man. Some of his plays eventually did well and were frequently revived and filmed. From pre-war days into the '60s they appeared frequently on radio and on TV. They included *Badger's Green*, filmed in 1934 with Valerie Hobson; *Windfall*; *St Helena*, about Napoleon, written with Jeanne de Casalis and produced for the Old Vic by Lilian Bayliss; *Miss Mabel*; *Home at Seven* (televised with Peter Cushing and filmed with Michael Redgrave); and *The White Carnation*. He became a keen amateur archæologist and his last play to be staged, *The Long Sunset*, one of my own favourites about the end of Roman rule in Britain, was produced by Bernard Miles for The Mermaid. In his rather unrevealing autobiography, *No Leading Lady* (1966), Sherriff says:

> I rang the changes to keep from getting in a rut. First a stage play; then a novel; after that a screenplay; then something new for television. Always something different: a boy's adventure story called *King John's Treasure*, a play about the East End called *The Telescope*, and a thriller called *Cards with Uncle Tom*. I had got the old *Journey's End* label off my neck at last, and saw to it that I didn't get another label in its place.

After *The Fortnight in September*, Sherriff's novels never had quite the same success and his autobiography says nothing about them, including *The Hopkins Manuscript. Greengates, Chedworth, Another Year* and *The Wells of St Mary's* were mostly published after 1940. Vernon Bartlett wrote the novel version of *Journey's End* in 1930. *The Siege of Swayne Castle* (1975), Sherriff's last novel, was completed by Graham Humphreys. He died a bachelor, leaving Rosebriars to Elmbridge Borough Council for social and cultural purposes, and his copyrights to the Scouts Association and Kingston Grammar.

For all their Hollywood success with supernatural subjects, neither Sherriff nor Whale had any special interest in 'horror' fiction. The director's struggle to get away from this association was recorded in *Gods and Monsters* (1998) in which Ian McKellen played Whale. Though some of his best films had elements of fantasy, *The Hopkins Manuscript* was Sherriff's only SF novel.

The book might have done better if it hadn't been published on the eve of Britain's declaration of war on Germany in 1939. It is ironic that it appeared at the time when the Nazis were putting their horrific policies in place and the next war was about to begin. Sherriff makes little reference to contemporary European politics, and his demagogues are invented from whole cloth. There is no hint of racialism being used in the furtherance of fascist banditry (indeed Sherriff's predictions of Eastern menace mildly reflect the racialism of his day), yet he understands how reactionary nationalism and an unthinking greed for control of the world's wealth will drag us almost automatically into bloody conflict. In this he could be said to have anticipated our current concerns with climate change as a result of a continual reliance on fossil fuels. These are the resources his various dictators are fighting over by the end of the book. Just as today, no lessons have been learned. Rather than looking to new methods of fuelling our industries and various forms of transport, Europe and America would rather squabble over the old methods, prepared to send their people to self-destructive wars when they could as easily be seeking alternatives. It was the American satirist and moralist Philip Wylie, in *Generation of Vipers* (1942), who pointed out that the cost of war and the costs of peace were pretty much the same—it was just easier to stick in a familiar rut and go to war than devote the same amount of time and energy to finding new, peaceful solutions to our problems.

Sherriff's politics were quietly conservative and he took the *Daily Telegraph* all his life. He had no axes to grind. Yet his observations in *The Hopkins Manuscript* reflect the disappointment and observations of a man who has seen too many repetitions of attitudes which he hoped had ended with the war to end wars, to which he had devoted his idealism and for which he'd risked his life.

Of course Sherriff didn't believe that there was any real likelihood of the moon crashing into Earth, though when writing the script of *The Invisible Man* he had worked with Philip Wylie, who had predicted a similar catastrophe in *When Worlds Collide* (1933). We write such books not because we are convinced they describe the future, but because we hope they do not. As warnings, they seek to avert disaster, especially disasters which we, as voters and citizens, can perhaps avoid. Sherriff's warnings came a little too late, reminding us how 'Saki's' predictive tale of England's upper classes living under the conquering Germans in *When William Came* didn't appear until 1914, just before the war which killed him and which left such a profound impression on Sherriff.

In 1942, in his contribution to *Mrs Miniver*, Sherriff once again celebrated the inherent decency of ordinary people caught up in events that they neither wanted nor, except by the remotest kind of omission, contributed to. Unlike Wells, he never let himself be taken over by Big Ideas. He didn't set out to abolish human vice but to show what effect vice could have on virtue. That said, he never quite lost his optimistic belief in human decency. Perhaps the most memorable scene in *The Hopkins Manuscript* is where the defiant villagers play a game of cricket in the light of the vast, looming moon.

The fictitious introduction to the story (from the point of view of the Royal Society of Addis Ababa, which provides a cunning glimpse into the culture of those who find the manuscript in the ruins of London) sets poor Mr Hopkins up, as well as allowing Sherriff to make it plain that he is not Hopkins, the small-minded exemplar of everything that later goes wrong in the world. While we're irritated with Hopkins—his petty, dull life, his obsessions with chickens and stamp collecting, his clinging to his secret knowledge, which gives him, in his imagination, power over his fellow villagers—it's clear the author doesn't want us to like him very much; yet we find ourselves increasingly identifying with him, even sympathising with him. He's not so different from the rest of us. He's an Everyman for a century that had already given us the horror of the Belgian Congo, No-man's-land, Mussolini, Stalin and Hitler, and he has never engaged with these events, nor involved himself with their implications, nor believed himself in any way concerned with them.

Sherriff created a creature only too typical of his time—a man who distracts himself with minutiæ while life grows daily more abnormal and horrific. He's not Bert Smallways or Mr Chips, those brave, sensible 'little men' who were ultimately heroes of sorts. Hopkins is in fact closer to another near-contemporary, Soames Forsyte, who, in the early volumes of the saga at least, knows the value of everything, including honour, but not its quality. Yet by the time the book finishes, Mr Hopkins has shown some almost heroic instincts and though moved by snobbery at first, feels genuine affection for the Squire's surviving relatives after the disaster has occurred.

The unscientific qualities of the story can be safely ignored (though I suspect John Wyndham would have given us a more realistic rationale) because they are not the point of the book any more than the Malaysian shipping news is the point of *Victory*. Like most of the best science fiction, the story is not 'about' the moon striking our planet. It is about human behaviour, and as such it has more in common with *The Pilgrim's Progress* than it does with *A Journey to the Centre of the Earth*. Perhaps a little more verisimilitude could have been offered—after all, although the British weather might be able to disguise developments in outer space from Hopkins and his fellow citizens, it's unlikely the residents of California or even the South of France would notice nothing! The business of this kind of fiction is to suspend disbelief, not make us believe, though I'm not entirely sure the English newspapers wouldn't have speculated on a phenomenon noted, say, in the Mediterranean. I'm prepared to let Sherriff off where Hoyle or Asimov might not. I would rather be offered an unlikely marvel than an unlikely character.

By the time Hopkins has learned the awful truth and indulged in various petty jealousies, Sherriff's prose takes on an atypical visionary quality as his imagination catches fire. There is the surreal pre-disaster village 'gala' as they watch the "immense, incredible golden scimitar rise slowly behind the trees.... I just sat there admiring it. I do not think that I should have been surprised if a pierrot and pierette had danced across the hillside, climbed the cedars and sat in the crescent of the moon to sing a love-song to us."

He waits in his garden for the moonlight cricket match to begin:

> I have never been fond of cricket. It is a game too slow for my restless temperament, and after our hectic 'gala week' I would have preferred an early bed. But as I sat in my garden that afternoon ... as I heard the familiar 'chock' of bat against ball.... I knew that I must go—if only to be with the village upon its last defiant night of gaiety....
>
> Gradually, along the hillcrest of Burgin Park, there came a golden glow as if all the cities of Eastern England were on fire.... The breathless glory of that rising moon robbed all terror from it and left me humbled and speechless: a blazing, golden mountain range that seemed to press the dark earth from it: clear rays of amber that caught the hills beyond the Manor House and crept down to drink the jet-black darkness of the valley—that flowed over the church and onwards to the cricket ground, emblazoning that shabby marquee and the threadbare bowling screens into a Field of the Cloth of Gold.

Sherriff's understanding of the power of nature reminds us of the 2004 tsunami in the Indian Ocean. The first intimation of what is to come is in the hurricane which springs up apparently out of nowhere:

> Somebody laughed—and then the marquee was hit by a resounding buffet. Every peg upon one side was wrenched from the ground, and for a moment the marquee was like a giantess standing grotesquely upon her head with skirts flying upwards, hanging to the ground by a few surviving pegs. I only saw it for a second because suddenly the hurricane seemed to rise from the very pores of the earth ...

If our narrator finds solace in children's fiction, in *The Wind in the Willows*, *Treasure Island* and *Huckleberry Finn*, this again is perhaps a criticism of the British tendency to return to the nursery at the first sign of trouble (it's fair, however, to recall that Hitler found similar solace in the westerns of Karl May or that Stalin comforted himself by watching Mickey Mouse movies). In the end he chooses not to join the rest of the village in the great shelter that has been built to withstand the impact of the Moon hitting the Earth. Some inner voice tells him to remain on the surface to witness the catastrophe. The first hint is the repetition of the hurricane, but much worse:

> My house no longer lay beneath the storm: as the tempest rose it lashed away the darkness. Light returned—but not the steady, golden light of yesterday: it came in a dirty brown, diseased glow that pulsated with the morbid rhythm of a totem drum. For the space of a second I saw the light in the Manor House across the valley—then suddenly it was gone. . . . The wind no longer came in scattered, thudding blows: it came in a torrent—one shrieking, ceaseless torrent of maniacal fury. . . . I saw the giant elms brace themselves—quiver and fall like corn before a scythe . . .

When the vast tsunami is over, Sherriff offers us a telling image of the disaster's strength:

> Sprawled in my meadow, almost covering the whole five acres of it, lay a huge black shape . . . as I drew nearer I saw to my amazement that it was an enormous ship . . . towering above me—its three immense funnels stuck out upon the other side, their tops resting upon the gentle slope that rose towards the downs. . . . It was the *King Lear*.

Hopkins's first response to this is to phone a complaint to the North Star Shipping Company and insist they remove the offending ship. Of course the telephone is dead 'as dead as my Bantam hens and Wyandotte pullets . . . I collapsed onto the sofa and burst into tears.'

Gradually, however, the survivors begin to restore their familiar civilisation. Hopkins's skill with chickens provides a local boost to 'the Epoch of Recovery', which begins around 1948 (there is no hint here, of course, of the Second World War). They talk of forming a United States of Europe, of sharing the new resources of the Moon, now embedded in the Atlantic and linking Britain to the Continent (thanks to the rather cavalier extinction of Portugal). Gradually honest, brave men (women don't feature much in the political picture Sherriff paints) restore civilisation. Then, as the mineral wealth of the crashed satellite is disputed, follow the Years of Decline. Britain's severed routes to her great empire threaten 'the abandonment of our people'. Demagogues arise to turn ordinary people against one another. This is where Sherriff, who hated the idea of a second Great War, imagines not the Nazi war we actually fought, but a terrible repetition of the first:

> Unfortunately the northern part of the moon had so far proved more fruitful than the south, and the north had been assigned by the British Plan (before the wealth was known) to the Scandinavian countries. Naturally this led to uproar. Italy demanded the coalfields in Denmark's area. France clamoured for the oil-wells in Sweden's territory and all without exception shouted for the goldfields reported in the strip assigned to Holland. . . . When I speak of "France clamouring" or "Italy clamouring", or any other nation "clamouring", I mean that the leaders "clamoured". The poor, bewildered people knew little and cared less about their "rights" upon the moon. All they desired was leave to rebuild their houses, to grow their corn and to graze their cattle . . . and to sit in the evening sunlight when the day's work was done. All that they desired was peace, and the dignity of quietness.

Needless to say this isn't what happens. Europe now faces a man-made threat. America is next to claim Lunar territory. Nationalist parties whip up familiar fascistic rhetoric. Major Jagger, clearly based on Oswald Mosley, becomes the British leader. To Sherriff he is the antithesis of the decent Englishman whom Hopkins, rather ennobled by his experience, now represents. Denigrating the honest, rational ex-Premier John Rawlings, Jagger addresses the nation over the radio:

> Rawlings, with his spineless compromise—his ignominious retreats—his futile arguments—has made our country the laughing stock of Europe! He disguised his terror of his opponents under such words as "reason" and "sanity"! To reason with these men is insanity itself! A few more weeks of Rawlings's "reasoning" and the British Empire would have been wrecked beyond repair!

Sherriff supported Chamberlain. Like so many, he thought there was only one thing worse than European dictators and that was another European war. He wasn't alone in wanting to avoid one. He dreamed of a union of European states, preferably with America as an ally, to avoid a repetition of the trench warfare he had described so well in *Journey's End*. Yet, reluctantly, he saw the necessity of a Churchill. Hopkins doesn't stand up and resist heroically the new British dictator, Jagger. Instead Hopkins accepts that: 'The only way to stamp out the pest of "Leaders" in Europe was to produce one ourselves, worse than any of them, and stronger . . .'

If in earlier chapters Sherriff anticipated the spirit of the Blitz, with everyone united against a common threat, he shared the conviction of those in government (see also Charles Williams's *Shadows of Ecstasy*, 1933) that London would react in panic and mass hysteria to a serious threat. Of course, the majority did not, and we knew surprisingly high public morale from 1941. Perhaps this is why Sherriff's tale actually seems more relevant to a post-9/11 generation than to those who suffered through the Second World War, and in some ways his book has more in common with the rash of H-bomb fiction exemplified by *Dr Strangelove* and *On the Beach* in the late 1950s and early '60s. Nationalistic leaders effectively destroy the civilisation they claim to defend, leaving us open to the Eastern invaders under 'Selim the Liberator', a native of Tehran, a revolutionary and an anarchist, 'preaching against the exploitation and oppression of the Eastern peoples by the white nations of the West'. But Selim, it appears, need hardly have bothered. In our greed, according to Sherriff, we destroy ourselves.

His friends and relatives all gone, Hopkins leaves the countryside, feeling he will survive better in the wretched remains of London, in Notting Hill. He makes a daily trip with his bucket to draw water from the Round Pond, he hunts amongst the ruins for canned food, he nurses his regrets. 'It need not have happened. If Europe had remained united we could have scattered them to the winds. . . . It need never have happened.' Finally Hopkins completes his manuscript and hides it, the only history to survive the desolation, to be discovered centuries later by Abyssinian explorers who find his evident barbarism and self-involvement somewhat distasteful.

And so Bob Sherriff joined the ranks of all those other English visionaries, from Bunyan to Wells, whose warnings failed to save us from ourselves. Unlike Wells, however, he did live to know a better world and write nostalgically of British heroes whose actions actually saved us from the threat of a monster rather closer to our shores than Selim the Liberator. Before his death in 1975 he witnessed Britain's joining the European Union. Though it came true a little later than he hoped, the vision he had defended in the trenches seemed realised and his own journey ended with a glimpse of that secure, decent future for which, half a century earlier, he had risked his life.

**From the Vintage Classics edition, December 2007**

The publication in English of Kafka's fiction in the early 1930s had an impact on the literary world only equalled by that of Borges or William Burroughs on my own generation. Like them, Kafka did not so much produce converts to his method as show writers how it was possible effectively to break the existing conventions. The 1920s and '30s saw a crop of idiosyncratic novels including Green's *Blindness* (1926) and *Living* (1929), Wyndham Lewis's *The Childermass* (1928), Williams's *War in Heaven* (1930) Garnett's *The Grasshopper's Come* (1931), Gibbons's *Cold Comfort Farm* (1931), Gerhardi's *Memoirs of Satan* (1932), Powys's *A Glastonbury Romance* and Read's *The Green Child* (1935) among them. Earlier, there had been Ronald Firbank, whose influence on Evelyn Waugh has never been fully recognised, but his work, brilliant as it was, bore the taint of *The Yellow Book* and the worst posturings of the *fin-de-siècle*.

Firbank was an absurdist rather than a surrealist or an expressionist. Kafka made the world of dreams manifest, borrowing from universal anxieties to produce his mysterious allegories, and this, with the paintings of such as Ernst and Dalí, affected the imagination of certain English writers resisting a fashionable Modernism and the late-Victorian sentimentality which characterised so much English fiction after the First World War. Imaginative writers tended to call on Kafka as many do Borges, these days, especially when they wanted their work to be taken with critical seriousness.

The likes of Bennett and Wells were decidedly out of fashion, dismissed as mere 'materialists' by Virginia Woolf. The novel was no longer considered a 'public instrument'. Warnings of coming social or natural disasters, therefore, were not in keeping with the need to address, in Forster's terms, 'the little society'. One addressed one's class rather than one's world. This put the aspiring writer in a bit of a spot, especially if they were, like Rex Warner, of a messianic disposition. 'The great society' is what modern artists opposed.

They had to search for individual worth, as Lawrence's characters do, rather than broad common remedies.

The Oxford Marxists, like Warner and his friends, were in some conflict concerning the personal and the political and resolved their problems in their various different ways. Kafka, driven by his personal nightmares and tortured by his understanding of a world which could never be just, came along as a bit of a godsend as a reference.

Rex Warner was born in 1905, the son of an Anglican vicar, and brought up mostly in Gloucestershire. From St George's School in Harpenden he went to Wadham College, Oxford. His messianism might in earlier days have turned to Methodism rather than Marxism and he retained an enthusiasm for Milton all his life. He was also keen supporter of EM Forster, whose 'The Machine Stops' (1909) directly challenged the benign totalitarianism envisaged by the likes of HG Wells in favour of the rights and dignity of the individual. Warner retained a lifelong fondness for Jane Austen and shared her love of temperate nature. At Oxford his friends included Auden, Day Lewis and Spender. Auden dedicated one of his 'Odes' in *The Orators* (1932) to Warner's son John. After leaving Oxford he wrote for the *Left Review* and taught for a while in Egypt and England, publishing his first book, *Poems* (1937) shortly before his novel, *The Wild Goose Chase* (1937). The latter concerned three brothers on a cycling holiday who become involved in a chase for the goose, which leads them into a mysterious country ruled by an authoritarian government which they are helpful in overthrowing. This was followed by *The Professor* (1938), another dystopian fantasy referring to Nazi Germany, about an academic whose accommodation with a Hitler-style regime eventually leads to his humiliating death. The books were well received critically but were not great commercial successes. Warner's acknowledgement of Kafka was noted. *The Aerodrome* (1941) would be his final and best dystopia, but not his final excursion into visionary fiction, which was *Why Was I Killed* (1943), an after-death fantasy on a pacifist theme.

Warner served in the Home Guard during the Second World War, headed the British Institute in Athens from 1945 and came to translate the work of George Seferis, contributing to the Greek poet's being awarded the Nobel Prize for Literature. He became well known as classical translator and broadcast regularly on literary and historical subjects. His translation of Thucydides's *History of the Peloponnesian War* (1954) was a massive success, selling a million copies. He wrote other popular books, including one about English Public Schools in the pictorial Discovering Britain series, and various introductions to Greek and Roman history and mythology, some of which he regarded as a form of high-brow hack work. In 1961 he went to America, becoming an English professor at the University of Connecticut in 1962. His fiction followed a rather familiar course from dystopia, to fantasy to comedy and ultimately the historical novel. After his comic novel *Escapade* (1953) also failed to be a commercial success he devoted himself to writing fiction only with a background in the ancient world. Including *Young Caesar* (1960) and *Pericles the Athenian* (1963) these books reflected his growing disenchantment with prescriptive politics. He turned his imagination to recreating the glories of Greece and Rome. Troubled by alcoholism and a sense of personal failure as a writer, Warner married four times and had four children. He confided to one interviewer that he felt he had 'bolloxsed up my life.' He enjoyed a strong, sometimes bitter rivalry, with some contemporaries, Robert Graves in particular, and felt he had failed to fulfill the promise he had at Oxford, when he, Auden and Day Lewis were young together. In 1973 he retired from teaching and returned to Wallingford, where he died at the age of eighty-one in 1986.

Warner never became a public figure like Auden or Spender but there is not much evidence he had the same drive as a poet. His messianism and his enthusiasms led him naturally into teaching and didactic fiction. There is no doubting his continuing admiration for Kafka, but *The Aerodrome* has more in common with prewar dystopian fiction such as Huxley's *Brave New World* (1932), or even RC Sherriff's *The Hopkins Manuscript* (1939), a rather strange book with an unlikely premise for disaster, when the moon crashes into earth, leading to war and the establishment of an authoritarian, militaristic dictatorship in England. Two other novels which have some of the same atmosphere are David Lindsay's *A Voyage to Arcturus* (1920), an enormous influence on CS Lewis's 'Perelandra' trilogy, and *Many Dimensions* (1931) by that under-admired Oxford 'Inkling' Charles Williams. In fact Warner's interest in metaphysics is often reminiscent of Williams, though he had turned his back on religion as his commitment to Marxism grew. While his politics were clearly opposed to those of Sherriff, the resemblance in theme and atmosphere is noticeable. Both books show English village life as a model of feudalism (rather more benign in Sherriff) and both offer a vision of a very English kind of fascism not unlike that offered years later by Angus Wilson's accurately predictive *The Old Men at the Zoo* (1961).

Although he was writing in the context of an existing tradition, I am not suggesting that Warner read all those other books, but I would be very surprised if he had not been to see Cameron Menzies's impressive Korda film *Things to Come* (1936) from a script by HG Wells. It was the *2001: A*

*Space Odyssey* of its day and predicted a great universal war destroying civilisation. The world's only saviours are the 'airmen' who not only restore civilisation but, after the fashion of the airshipmen in Kipling's *With the Night Mail* (1905), maintain a benign autocracy through the power of their planes. Warner, of course, chose, like Forster, to argue with this idea. *The Aerodrome* is the other voice in a dialogue between prescriptive totalitarianism and individualism. By the time of the Molotov-Ribbentrop Pact in 1939, Warner had lost considerable faith in communism.

There is no question that, in spite of his claims, Warner was far more in the English tradition than he was in Kafka's. Nothing Warner wrote had the obsessive drive, the pure genius, of Kafka. A far more obvious influence seems to be Bunyan's *Pilgrim's Progress*. The village is a modern version of the Pilgrim's. Roy's journey, though more a psychological journey than Christian's, resembles his. Warner's work was didactic rather than visionary. By no means alone in understanding that the greater the sentimentality, the greater the vice it hides, he was far too English and well bred to offer his readers the nightmarish images of *In der Strafkolonie* (1919) or *Das Schloss* (1926) which have so much more in common with pre-Nazi German expressionist films. For all that, of course, *The Aerodrome* is very much about Nazism and Warner is at his most intense when he describes sudden violence or has his Air Marshall lecturing his men about how to keep themselves aloof from common sentiment and to maintain a Machiaevellian sense of *realpolitik*.

From the first pages, it is obvious that Warner is examining his own familiar culture in the light of militaristic fascism in spite of his author's note at the beginning of this novel. By the time it was published, Britain was fighting for her life against a very real Nazism from beyond its shores.

One can't help, of course, being reminded of the actions of the SS or SA both in the 1930s Germany and in the occupied countries of the 1940s when, for instance, the Flight Lieutenant behaves completely at odds with conventional good manners on the understanding from both sides, that he acts with impunity. Very clearly, he echoes attitudes which Hitler, Goering and the rest failed to hide from the general public. The killing of one of the community's pillars and his replacement by his murderer, the general sense of gang rule, the uncomplaining acceptance of the village which seems too dazed to demur, the 'folkish' sentiments with which they console themselves as the power of the Aerodrome grows, all mirror what had already happened in Germany. In some ways the lack of airforce sentimentality is shown as more acceptable than its opposite, yet both are horrible in their coldness and mawkishness respectively.

On a dramatic level, the novel engages us from the beginning. One revelation follows another as in a good Victorian melodrama. People are shocked to death or die of grief. Anyone who receives bad news isn't long for the village. Sometimes the moral message is so clear that the book resembles an exemplary mural painted on the wall of an Oxfordshire church. After the Air Marshall's lecture to new recruits concerning 'the weaker sex' (hinting at another mutely stated theme in this novel, the extra-marital affair of Warner's wife Frances) it is almost a shock to be presented with a femme fatale so obviously designed to counter the Air Marshall's remarks, reflecting the unexpected subtleties Warner offers, so much at odds with the direct terror of *1984* (1949), which Orwell wrote immediately after the war as a warning that totalitarianism was by no means overcome. Warner displays no despair in this book, not a hint of cynicism. Indeed, there is considerable evidence that he was at heart an optimist. His concern is to reveal the loss of human virtue which comes with blackshirt fascism. In this, his penultimate essay into visionary fable, Warner clearly states his own hope, his own fierce belief in humanity, in a world, at 'its most intricate, fiercer than tigers, wonderful and infinitely forgiving'.

*The Aerodrome* is expertly structured and Warner's characters, if not subtly delineated, are credible and familiar. His writing, capable and robust, has the same sense of considered craftsmanship, that hint of retrospective melancholy colouring the work of so many young Englishmen of the time. Valuing the peace and sense of perpetual renewal of the Gloucestershire countryside, he no doubt felt a combination of excitement and resentment as the big RAF airfields were established in the wide, flat valleys of the counties he knew well. They represented the modernity he embraced as an intellectual and a poet and which alarmed him as a countryman. This conflict can certainly be seen in his progress from dystopian expressionism to classical imagery and subject.

This terrible note of loss runs through a great deal of 20th century English writing in contrast to the almost bumptious tone of the likes of Bennett and Priestley. Warner's prose is wistful, but has consistently careful structuring, a steadfast refusal to take an easy or flashy way out. It convinces the reader by its simplicity and rejection of received language which clothes the majority of contemporary literary prose and makes it comfortably non-confrontational. There is in fact something quietly, stubbornly confrontational in Warner which helps explain why he must periodically be rediscovered. If his characters sometimes seem to be stereotypes it is perhaps to challenge our perceptions of what those stereotypes stand for. He is frequently at his most intense when he has his airmen lectured on the need to keep themselves above common sentiment. The cool rhetoric of the SS, detached and 'realistic' when Himmler told them that running death camps was a filthy job which only the pure and unemotional could rise above to achieve what was needed. Familiar echoes of Goebbels are heard here, in the voice of the First Lieutenant, a certain tone of swaggering certainty which one hears in recordings from the Reichstag after it was taken over by the Nazis. That slightly slangy, mocking tone was perceived as young, vital, self-confident impatience with an old, decadent order. One has heard recent versions of it in our own politics. It offers certainties in troubled times and of course its simple solutions rarely bring us anything but more trouble. Sometimes it takes the colour of the right, sometimes of the left, but it is almost always dangerous. Fiction which opposes it, as *The Aerodrome* does so convincingly, is rarely welcomed by a large audience, particularly in its day.

In 1913 HH Monroe or 'Saki', the well-loved humorist, wrote a novel about England being conquered by Germany. *When William Came*, showed how readily the English upper and middle classes accommodated the Kaiser. It was published a little too close to August 1914 for comfort and Saki, joining up though over age, was killed soon after in the trenches. While his other fiction remained in print, that novel was left out of all 'complete Saki' volumes until relatively recently. Apparently we don't like to be reminded of our own eagerness to embrace authority in times of unrest. Warner was received equally uncomfortably when he reminded us of our capacity for giving up freedom and social justice in return for perceived security and went similarly unread, whereas Orwell, less than a decade later could have a massive success with *1984* precisely because he did not challenge our complacency. Orwell's dystopia is almost reassuring, its noirish atmosphere almost romantic, its backgrounds sufficiently removed from common experience. Only Golding's *Lord of the Flies* (1954), holding a mirror up to Britain's imperial self-image, seems to me to have the power of *The Aerodrome*. Golding's commercial success might have something to do with the fact that his novel, too, was set apart from contemporary England.

Down to the intensity of its sexual triangle which plays such an important part in the plot *The Aerodrome* never allows itself that abstraction, however dreamlike it sometimes seems. Warner, quite as thoroughly a patrician lefty as Orwell, actually raises some serious and enduring questions about our nostalgia for the surviving trappings of feudalism, our capacity for profound betrayal of ourselves and others. And that is why this book endures.

# ▮ *Les Livres Dimanches*

An Introduction to *The Sunday Books*
Pictures by Peake
Words by Moorcock

**From the Editions Denoël edition, 2010**

Mervyn Peake's earliest memories were a mixture of the exotic and the mundane, both of which could be discovered in the European compound in China where he was born. There, the privileged but good-hearted missionaries, living in detailed reproductions of their familiar homes, did their best to relieve the miseries of desperate people who in many ways found themselves impoverished as a result of Western imperial ambitions.

This social, psychological and moral ambiguity would inform Peake's writings and paintings from the beginning, finding its apotheosis in the three superb and wholly original Titus Groan books which remain unique in all literature. These books are impossible to classify, standing outside genre, idiosyncratic works of genius as original in English literature as Swift, Sterne or Peacock, worthy many critics believe, to stand beside Cervantes, Rabelais or Grimmelshausen. Peake's stories reflect an unconscious understanding of imperial injustice and inherited privilege, blending images from oriental baroque, the English Gothic and Dickens, their compelling narrative and grotesque but credible characters guaranteeing Peake his place in the English literary canon (he now regularly appears in the list of our first fifty authors when polls are taken to establish the Anglo-Saxon public's favourite writers).

While sometimes described as 'fantasy' fiction, actually Peake's stories are grotesque, sardonic, macabre but have few magical elements and are sui generis. Apart from his one novel set on Sark, *Mr Pye*, Peake rarely included the supernatural in his work. Rather he was influenced by his favourite boyhood reading, including, with Dickens, Robert Louis Stevenson, Christopher Marlowe, Shakespeare and John Bunyan. In common with other lads of his generation he also read GA Henty, Morton Pike and S Clarke Hook whose work appeared regularly in the periodical literature of his day and were frequently illustrated by the great Stanley L Wood, who had spent years in the American West, had accumulated an enormous amount of cowboy and Indian costumes and paraphernalia, as well as costumes enabling him to draw 18th century pirates and highwaymen, Indian army lancers, laskars or Chinese coolies. Peake's favourite boyhood artist, Wood illustrated both adult and juvenile magazines, including *The Strand*, *Pearson's Magazine*, *The Captain*, *Chums* and *Boys' Own Paper*. Peake was not the only one to admire him. Wood's sense of movement, his understanding of anatomy and his ability to show all forms of action made him a favourite of many illustrators of the day. In a radio talk given in the 1950s Peake recalled the deep impression made by Wood's illustrations for a serial called 'Under the Serpent's Fang'. It is fair to say that Wood's drawings and paintings were frequently more memorable than the stories they illustrated and his portrait of the proto–Fu Manchu evil genius, Guy Boothby's infamous 'Dr Nikola' (from *Pearson's*) remains one of my own favourites. I have Wood's Nikola's portrait on my study wall to this day. From Wood in particular Peake learned to draw horses, which impressed his schoolmasters when he returned to England to be educated.

While at boarding school, in Surrey and South London, Peake's talents as an artist eventually encouraged his parents to send him to art school first in Croydon and then in London. In an early self-portrait, he painted himself as a pirate and by the 1920s was dressing very much in the romantic, Byronic tradition of many of Wood's heroes. By the time he was training at the Royal Academy Schools, Peake had adopted a dashing appearance, with a broad-brimmed hat and, sometimes, a cloak. As a student he also began writing fiction. Little of that early work survives but some of it was published in an anthology of short pieces called *Peake's Progress* (1978).

In 1930 Peake even planned to write an opera set in China with a hero who woos an Emperor's daughter but is forced to become an outlaw and which owed a little to Gilbert and Sullivan. From the beginning his ambitions were as involved with narrative as they were with images and, together with the opera, he outlined a story to be called *The Three Principalities*, about a marooned sailor. The book was rejected by publisher Chapman and Hall and abandoned.

By the 1930s Mervyn had become a strikingly handsome figure, with a wicked sense of humour, highly gregarious and full of fun. Many women remembered him from this period and not a few admitted to falling in love with him. Unusually, for his rather conservative era, he wore a gold earring. He had wonderful hands, one of which sported an enormous, almost vulgar green malachite in a silver ring which emphasised his odd way of holding his pencil, a habit he retained all his life (together with his taste in rings!). At this stage he was still signing his work in echo of Stanley L Wood as Mervyn L Peake and he would go 'head-hunting' in London, drifting from cafés to pubs to the tops of buses, drawing mostly faces. He spent a great deal of time in Soho, London's main bohemian quarter. He joined a school of young artists grouped around a café known as *Au Chat Noir* and calling themselves the Soho Group, later the Twenties Group, because they were all under thirty. He planned a book to be called *Head-Hunting in London*, based on pictures he began to have reproduced in the journals of the day. He started to exhibit his paintings.

As Peake's reputation grew a friend persuaded him to visit the Channel Island of Sark where another acquaintance had permission from the local authorities to set up an artists' colony. In 1932 he got his first sight of the island. Sark is about twenty-five miles from Normandy and only about three-and-a-half miles long by one-and-a-half miles wide. Yet in that small space it has some wonderful scenery, superb cliffs overlooking deep bays, some fine beaches and, in those days, the further advantage of very cheap accommodation. Sark is a semi-independent state, though acknowledging the sovereignty of the English royal family, and in its day sheltered Victor Hugo, Swinburne and Turner as well as a host of less famous artists and writers.

Peake did not immediately settle in Sark. He had begun to do well in London. Among other commissions he designed the costumes for the Capeks' famous *The Insect Play* and perhaps he didn't study hard enough as a result, because he failed his exams in 1933 and soon afterwards left for Sark where Eric Drake was building a gallery which would exhibit their group's work. His paintings were generally considered the best of those shown, including landscapes and local portraits and he, with the others, soon began to get publicity in the British national press. At this time, too, Peake began to show a strong interest in circus subjects, perhaps after Chapman's Circus had visited the nearby island of Guernsey. By 1935, however, he had left Sark. He claimed that the local ruler, the famous Dame of Sark, had ordered him to leave after he had been discovered drawing the corpse of an old man who had been laid out in the chapel.

Back in England, Peake first lived with his parents, in Surrey, sharing a studio with a friend, returning to his old haunts like *Au Chat Noir* and beginning work on a children's story which would become his first published book, *Captain Slaughterboard Drops Anchor*, bearing some similarities with other work of the 1940s such as his illustrated book of children's nonsense verse *Rhymes Without Reasons* and *Letters from a Lost Uncle* as well as his far more ambitious *Titus Groan*. He was still unable to make a living from his painting and began to teach life-drawing at the Westminster School of Art. He began to see a fair amount of a group of poets who included Roy Campbell and Dylan Thomas. Thomas chose to consider Mervyn (whose dark looks were extremely Celtic) as a fellow Welshman and they became friends, though temperamentally had little in common. Thomas talked about doing a travel book together but tended to forget appointments and as often as not turned up unannounced in Mervyn's studio, throwing up on his couch and borrowing his clothes.

Both Thomas's and Peake's fame continued to grow. It was while teaching at Westminster that Peake met Maeve Gilmore, a fellow South Londoner, who was exquisitely beautiful and extraordinarily shy. She was studying sculpture. They fell in love. They made a remarkable couple. Although often tongue-tied and self-conscious she struck all who knew her as having, in the words of one friend, 'a Madonna-like composure'. She also had a powerful and surprisingly down-to-earth sense of humour, which was one of the things I most enjoyed about her when we met years later. Peake certainly appreciated it. Her beauty and her grace, as well as her humour, inspired him. He began to write some of his best poetry and became regularly published. 'I am too rich already,' he wrote, 'for my eyes mint gold'. The daughter of an Irish surgeon, a rather strict Catholic, she was not at all sure what her family would think of the son of 'low church' general practitioners and indeed their romance was not to get much of a Gilmore blessing. Eventually, however, they were married in December 1937 at St James's, Spanish Place, a fashionable West London church.

In 1939, when *Captain Slaughterboard* was published, Peake's fortunes were improving. He was becoming well-known and increasingly sought after. But by January 1940 when his first son, Sebastian, was born, the war had begun to colour his future and he had to make plans about how best to serve his country. At one point he returned home in the Blitz to find Sebastian missing and eventually discovered him sitting on Dylan Thomas's knee enjoying, with the poet, the 'fireworks' of the Blitz. While he waited to be commissioned as a war artist, Peake began work on *Titus Groan*, the first of his great trilogy, a tale of stultifying privilege and class anger full of grotesque but highly credible characters and wonderful, original language. He began to compile his first book of poetry which would be *Shapes and Sounds, 1941*. That same month his illustrated *The Hunting of the Snark* appeared and was very well received. Thomas introduced him to the influential Kaye Webb, an editor of *Lilliput* magazine, which published a vast amount of both British and émigré talent and had been founded by a Hungarian, Stephan Lorentz, recently escaped from Hitler's prisons. Kaye Webb not only commissioned illustrations from Peake, she also published his writing, even when he was recruited into the army. Through these harrowing years he completed *Titus Groan* which was published in 1946, after he had been sent to Belsen as the first war artist into the camps. The experience was to have an enormous influence on future work. By the end of the war, Peake's reputation was high, both as a poet, novelist, illustrator and painter. The joke was frequently made that it was just as well he didn't play the violin, too. By the end of the war, with money coming in, he and Maeve felt they could afford to 'retreat' from blitzed London and Peake suggested they look again at Sark, which she had visited briefly with him.

Renting a large, rather primitive, house on Sark, Peake began *Gormenghast* and completed his *The Rhyme of the Flying Bomb*, which was to become lost and not published until 1962. In homage to his great love, RL Stevenson, he illustrated *Dr Jekyll and Mr Hyde* and *Treasure Island* as well as *The Swiss Family Robinson* and others. He also wrote a children's book *Letters from a Lost Uncle*.

In lots of ways the Sark years were the Peake family's happiest. Peake was something of an ideal father. He knew how to entertain his boys with conjuring tricks, bizarre games and practical jokes. Although, like all artists, he had anxiety spells and claimed to be desperately in need of peace and quiet, he loved to be part of his family and rather than be hampered by their presence was actually inspired by them. The boys went to the local school and in 1949 a little girl, Clare, was born. Their pets included a cat, some ducks and a donkey who more or less had the run of the household and frequently turned up in illustrations. Every so often Peake would return to London, to make some well-received radio broadcasts, to obtain further commissions and to discuss ideas for books. He published a superb book on technique, *The Craft of the Lead Pencil*.

When he was away he was homesick and when he was home he quickly resumed his habit of drawing for his boys every Sunday. It was a delightful time for them and for Peake. There was little cinema, no television, precious little else to do on Sark, especially on Sundays, especially in the winter, with the wind howling outside a house with no mains electricity. The boys would sit on the arms of his chair, watching as he called on his own boyhood memories and enthusiasms to create pirates, cowboys, weird monsters and weirder characters, making up stories and sometimes nonsense rhymes to accompany the pictures. Clowns, trains, forest outlaws, jungle animals were

produced out of the whole cloth of his imagination, frequently at the immediate demands of his sons, who might want him to draw a plane, a ship, a
lion. The drawings contained private jokes (as in some of his published
work) and homages to his own heroes. An astonishing number of them
were in full colour. Until the boys were ready to go to school (and the Peakes
were beginning to find it impractical to remain on Sark) he filled page after
page with drawings, a great many of them in full colour. Though Stanley L
Wood's style had never influenced him, the earlier artist's subject matter had.
Peake's own childhood revisited, he offered his children private versions of
*Chums* and *Boys' Own Paper*. Only because it was Peake drawing them is the
phenomenon especially remarkable, of course. Many less talented parents
do the same for their children. But Peake was a very special talent and he
was an artistic powerhouse. The work produced then for his children is as
vivid today. Sadly, any stories or rhymes which Peake invented to go with
the drawings were never written down, though some similar ideas might
turn up in later books, including the Titus novels.

Circumstances brought the family back to the mainland by 1949 but
for Peake the following decade was to be one of growing ill-health and ill-
fortune. *Mr Pye*, a fable set on Sark, won the prestigious Hawthornden Prize
in 1953 but his plays, many of them idiosyncratic and surrealistic, rarely ran
for long and failed to make him the money he needed. In spite of continuing
to accept commissions to illustrate many classics, Peake found his painting, poetry and fiction going briefly out of fashion at exactly the time he
began to experience the early symptoms of what has since been diagnosed
as Parkinson's Disease. It became harder for him to earn money.

By 1957, after completing the first draft of the third Titus book, *Titus
Alone*, which drew considerably on his own experience, including the War
and Belsen, he began to feel the typical tremors and loss of attention which
were to worsen. He received radical and, by modern standards, rather brutal
treatment in a desperate effort to help him, but this did nothing to improve
his condition, even as a new generation began to discover him and celebrate him. He continued to work until only a few years before his death in
1968 and his reputation in the Anglo-Saxon world grew rapidly until he was
recognised as the creator of a modern classic. Today he is regarded as one
of the 20th century's great imaginative artists, showing regular exhibitions
around the world, while his fiction and poetry is consistently reprinted and
his *Rhyme of the Flying Bomb* set very successfully to music by Langdon Jones,
yet he was never to become conscious of his own remarkable success. He died
in 1968, at a small nursing home run by Maeve's brother. Almost as soon as

he died his reputation began to grow and now everything he produced in his lifetime has been reprinted many times over, apart from the 'Sunday books' done for his boys. It has been my ambition for some time to put at least some of these drawings before the public and give perhaps a taste of the narratives and verses with which he would have embellished them at the time.

As you look at this work, it is worth bearing in mind an extraordinary fact. No matter how spontaneous his public work was, Peake did not generally produce drawings for people 'on the spot'. Although he was a generous-spirited artist and writer, who gave much of his work away, he was very rarely able spontaneously to draw on request. Yet every weekend, for several years, he produced these drawings for his own children. Therefore I think we are perhaps doubly privileged at last to enjoy the pleasure which Sebastian and Fabian experienced more than half a century ago on Sark. We must be thankful they have survived. Later, in London, Maeve Peake would paint wonderful murals for the benefit of her own grandchildren. They filled entire rooms of their house in Drayton Gardens, London. Hardly an inch of wall space was not filled with her work or Peake's paintings. Sadly, when the house was sold on Maeve's death, the new owners whitewashed over them all. We are lucky, therefore, to have so many of these illustrations to remind us of those remarkable parents. Few of us, loving mothers and fathers though we may be, have such a wealth of talent and are able to entertain our children so thoroughly. Now many of those drawings can be reproduced for the benefit of people outside the privileged Peake family circle which today, of course, also consists of Sebastian's, Fabian's and Clare's children.

Mervyn Peake's last years were filled with despair and misery in which his friends and family vainly sought to save his health and his reputation. We lived in frustrating times, when so much less was known about conditions of the brain, and we could not make his health any better. We had to watch him decline and experience that great, creative intelligence slowly slip away from us while ironically his reputation continued to grow around the world with every passing year. Yet Peake's humour remained with him almost to the end and continued to inspire us. Until quite late in the progress of his illness he was able to make a joke and draw a small, humorous drawing. I think these illustrations will serve to show that other, even more personal side, of a great artist at home and I can only hope that Mervyn Peake, who became such an inspiring, wonderful friend to me and my own family, would forgive any liberties I have taken here to supply his pictures with the narratives which, sadly, he never wrote down.

# ■ Echoes of Peake

A Review of *Titus Awakes* by Maeve Gilmore, Based on a Fragment by Mervyn Peake

**From the *Los Angeles Times*, 28th August 2011**

An outstanding painter, illustrator, poet, novelist and playwright, Mervyn Peake is now solidly part of the British literary canon; voted in a recent London *Times* critics' poll one of the best fifty UK writers since 1945. His centenary, celebrated this year, includes an exhibition at the British Library, an academic conference, the publication of new material such as *The Sunday Books* and republication of several of his very best works including *The Illustrated Gormenghast*.

In the US Peake tends to be mentioned in the same breath as Tolkien simply because he wrote three books set in a world 'parallel' to our own. But his Gormenghast sequence was never intended to be a trilogy, has little or no supernatural content and lacks Tolkien's sentimentality. Before his descent into the debilitating illness which eventually killed him Peake planned further novels which would bring his protagonist Titus Groan into worlds more specifically like our own. *Titus Alone* drew more directly on what he had seen in Belsen and Europe in the aftermath of WW2.

Planning *Titus Awakes*, the fourth book, Peake sketched out where he would take Titus. Scenes were headed 'Titus in the mountains; among the snows' and so on. He would take his naïve protagonist into the contemporary world, returning him to Gormenghast to suit a narrative blending fantasy and reality. He discussed these ideas with his wife, the painter Maeve Gilmore, his close collaborator in the preparation of his novels, with whom he was probably happiest on the island of Sark.

Maeve Gilmore loved Peake passionately and selflessly. His illness and death devastated her. In an effort to ground her grief she decided to write the novel he had planned, using his notes and remembered conversation. She used four notebooks and when she had finished she set them aside, making no real effort to publish. She died in 1983 and last year, her daughter rediscovered the manuscript, an ideal work for this year's centenary.

A fascinating, intensely personal homage, *Titus Awakes*, with its themes of baffled love and loss, becomes a testament of Maeve Gilmore's devotion as Titus wanders into a world even more dreamlike than the original. Accompanied only by his faithful Dog, Titus is soon on a quest for place and identity in a succession of increasingly uncomfortable landscapes. Frequently a passive participant in the ambitions of others Titus reflects the increasing bewilderment of Peake as his hold on reality weakened. The protagonist is really more Peake or Gilmore than he is Titus. Finding a way successfully to echo the music of the originals if not the eloquent precision of her husband's baroque style, she sends Titus first on Peake's proscribed adventures and then, as her confidence grows, into situations of her own devising.

Ultimately Titus finds friends in a painter's colony whose backgrounds and characters have the authority of observed reality. There are chilling scenes in a hospital reminiscent of Peake's own experience as his condition worsened. One character—the artist—might even be Peake.

Death is present everywhere, even in the lyrical passages. Close to the novel's end, Titus is captured by a nihilistic political gang and begins to grow into a substantial character, no longer merely reacting to others. Gilmore's talent, as in her paintings, was for intensified reality and gradually she reveals herself as perhaps the ideal person to take Titus into Peake's intended world. 'He knew he was at last determining his own life.' Ultimately Titus crosses the sea and arrives at an island very much like Sark, where the Peakes were so happy. Before he disembarks he sees a tall man watching the ship. To us it is evidently Peake, surrounded by his children, who joins Titus as he walks from the ferry. 'Titus no longer felt alone but part of someone who would shape his life to come. There's not a road, not a track, but will lead him home.'

Thus Maeve Gilmore as well as Titus finds resolution, affirming the deep love of life, the fundamental optimism she always shared with the man she loved.

# ■ Breaking Free

## An Introduction to Mervyn Peake's *Titus Alone*

**From the Klett-Cotta (German) edition, February 2011**

In many ways *Titus Alone* is for me the most interesting of the three books Mervyn Peake wrote concerning the young Lord of Gormenghast, even if it lacks the compelling plot of the first two. For a number of years *Titus Alone* was considered the weakest because an uncomprehending copy editor cut it to pieces while Peake was in the first stages of the Parkinsonism which would take his life. In its restored form the novel proved far better than critics originally supposed.

If Langdon Jones, the composer, then assistant editor of *New Worlds*, had not been leafing through Peake's original manuscript and noticed serious discrepancies between it and the published version, we might never have had the far more complete version. It took Jones the best part of a year, making line by line, page by page examinations of text and manuscripts, to restore the novel as closely as possible to Peake's original version. The editor had made a bewildering number of unnecessary changes and few would have been capable of the intellectual intensity and powers of concentration displayed by Jones in his great labour of love. Happily, he finished in time for his version to be published in the definitive Penguin 'Modern Classics' edition and it is the translation of that which you have here.

*Titus Alone* was Peake's attempt to take his character and method out of the hermetic world he had created in *Gormenghast* and *Titus Groan* and make it confront not only issues of identity, time and human interaction but the problems of modernity and even post-modernity—the world as it emerged from terrible, unprecedented conflict, confronting the Cold War, nuclear weapons and new forms of authoritarian dictatorship springing up like weeds from the ruins of the old world. In following this path Peake recognized the limitations of the form he had developed with such genius and was consciously seeking a means by which he could expand it to expose his protagonist to the 20th century in general and the second half in particular.

Peake's instincts were, as always, towards actuality if not towards realism as it was then understood. In this, he was perhaps the very first English 'magic realist' and an inspiration to the so-called *New Worlds* group which saw him, Vian, Kafka, Borges and William Burroughs as models to emulate in steering imaginative fiction away from nostalgic escapism and obsession with the supernatural towards examination of our common psyche and shared experience.

When I first met Peake he was in the last stages of completing *Titus Alone*. Both he and his wife Maeve were distracted by the mysterious symptoms which would be properly identified only after his death. He had already written his play *The Cave*, tackling the subject of nuclear war, and discovered that the majority of people at that time did not want to examine the issues, certainly in the form he chose. He was depressed and disappointed in a large public's lack of interest in his work but at that point I had no idea what he was going through. On that afternoon and in the course of many others he gave me far too much of his time and I fully appreciated his charming generosity. That generosity was to be his most enduring characteristic. I think it was what also sustained him through the writing of his great Titus Groan sequence, that wish to give his readers everything he could imagine and describe.

As the earlier books were dominated by Steerpike, that embodiment of rage against the establishment who, even at his most wicked, still keeps our empathy if not our sympathy, so *Titus Alone* is dominated by Muzzlehatch, Titus's mysterious half-mad mentor and guide to the world beyond Gormenghast's walls. We don't have quite the same range of comic and grotesque characters here but we do have another cast of gorgeously different women—Juno, who elects to become a kind of guardian, the Black Rose and Cheetah, femme fatale daughter of a wealthy industrialist. But Titus, who scarcely featured in the earlier plots, here begins to come into his own, an innocent, a *naïf* in comparison to Steerpike. This is far more Titus's book.

Some readers were originally disappointed not to be given another *Gormenghast* in *Titus Alone* and missed the castle's claustrophobic atmosphere. Muzzlehatch's vibrant beast of a car, the references to helicopters and other modern inventions, the obvious images reminding us of Bergen-Belsen concentration camp which Peake observed at first hand when sent there as a war artist to record, were not at all what they were hoping for. Some of us welcomed these developments, however, as well as the continuation of the absurdism which is perhaps at its best in the court scene where Titus reveals his father's fate. This shows Peake working in that great tradition of Sterne, Peacock, Carroll, Lear and Firbank, the same tradition which infuses his nonsense verse and informs so many of his drawings in his Grimm, for instance, and in the most recently published *The Sunday Books*.

Peake was incapable of resting on his laurels and it is a mark of his genius that he continued to expand his range as a poet, draughtsman and novelist even as that terrible illness, exacerbated by doctors ignorant of the advances we have since made in diseases affecting the brain and nervous system, consumed him.

I saw Peake regularly during those years and was astonished by how rarely his wit deserted him, even when his memory failed. I remember taking the cover proofs of this book to show him at the hospital, knowing that his understanding had almost entirely deserted him. He did not recognise his own work but he did sense that his wife Maeve was distressed. Obviously in an effort to cheer her up, he rose shakily and tried to embrace her. That was the clearest memory I have of his final days, reaching towards his beloved wife and attempting to comfort her, his own work ignored. It remains one of the most moving and significant moments of my life and was typical of his generous nature. His mind had almost completely deserted him, but his humane heart beat as steadily as always.

As it will beat forever, here and through the rest of his magnificently varied work.

# ■ The Time of *The Time Machine*

## An Introduction to HG Wells's *The Time Machine*

**From the Everyman edition, 1993**

> The idea of it seemed to be his "one idea". He had saved it up so far in the hope that he would one day make a much longer book of it than *The Time Machine*, but the urgent need for something marketable obliged him to exploit it forthwith. As the discerning reader will perceive, it is a very unequal book: the early discussion is much more carefully planned and written than the later chapters. A slender story springs from a very profound root. The early part, the explanation of the idea, had already seen the light in 1893 in Henley's *National Observer*, it was the latter half that was written in 1894.
>
> —HG Wells, Introduction to *The Time Machine*, 1931.

### I

The *New Review*, number 68, for January 1895 was now a monthly. Edited by that legendary model for Long John Silver, the exuberant and influential man of letters WE Henley, it contained poetry by a recently dead Stevenson and a memoir of him; pieces on the Navy and the new Ibsen, impressions of India, the Armenian Question, 'Les Sentiments de la France pour l'Angleterre' by Émile Ollivier, the dangers of forming new European alliances, and the socialist threat to sexual purity. There was poetry by George Wyndham, a fashionably sentimental story by George Fleming and the first instalment of a serial by HG Wells whose opening chapter began: "The man who made the Time Machine—the man I shall call the Time Traveller—was well known in scientific circles a few years since, and the fact of his disappearance is also well known."

As he was to note in *Experiment in Autobiography*, 1934, Wells got his real start in national journalism from the flamboyant Frank Harris who, with enormous enthusiasm, published his 'The Rediscovery of the Unique' in the July 1891 issue of the *Fortnightly Review* and then rejected the next article (about a four-dimensional space-time universe) in such a devastating way that Wells was horribly disheartened, set aside works like *Lady Frankland's Secret* and considered giving up writing altogether until on holiday at Eastbourne he read JM Barrie's new *When a Man's Single* in which young authors are convincingly advised to write about the commonplace.

Inspired by this, Wells wrote 'On Staying at the Seaside' and sent it to his cousin Bertha at Windsor for her to type. He then posted the manuscript to the *Pall Mall Gazette*, a new evening paper financed by the American millionaire Astor. With a liberal, sometimes radical bias and a relatively small but highly influential readership it was not unlike a daily version of a 1990s *New Statesman*.

The '*PMG*' was edited by Harry Cust, another eccentric star of that literary firmament, a close friend of Henley's and, thanks to Astor's munificence, paying top rates. 'Henley's Men', happy to work for both editors, included W Pett Ridge (who would become a friend and introduce Wells to the others), JM Barrie, Yeats, Verlaine, George Wyndham, Walter Sickert, Kipling and Arthur Morrison. *PMG* regulars were dismissed by 'Yellow Dwarf' in the *Yellow Book* for July 1895 as 'Mr WE Henley's truculent fifth form'.

Wells could imagine no better company. When a proof came back by way of acceptance, he was working on a second article, also accepted. Next he dug up an old piece he had written for *Science Schools Journal* when he had edited it, and rewrote this as 'The Man of the Year Million' which appeared, well illustrated, in the *PMG*'s new stablemate *Pall Mall Budget*. Soon Wells was in demand. He became a regular, inventing his first self-deluding bombast—a knowing and somewhat unjust self-portrait—the 'Uncle' with whom he had smart little conversations in the paper's columns. He also became identified as a man who could write entertainingly on scientific and speculative subjects, who could produce science fiction short stories to equal Verne, Flammarion or Griffith. 'The first of the single sitting stories I ground out was "The Stolen Bacillus" and after a time I became quite dextrous in evolving incidents and anecdotes from little possibilities of a scientific or a quasi-scientific sort. I presently broadened my market and found higher prices were to be got from the *Strand Magazine* and the *Pall Mall Magazine*.'

Recommended by Cust, Henley himself began to take an interest in Wells, who was summoned to riverside Putney (a stone's throw from the Pines where Swinburne lived, an industrious recluse, with Watts-Dunton). There the 'old giant' awaited him, 'a magnificent torso set on shrunken withered legs'. A High Tory arch-imperialist, Henley gladly encouraged the socialist Wells. He was particularly curious about the idea of time-travel and asked Wells to write some articles on the subject for his *National Observer*. These were based on an awkward early piece done for *Science Schools Journal* in 1888 with the mad scientist Dr Nebogufek as protagonist of 'The Chronic Argonauts'.

Wells's literary reputation continued to grow. 'Rediscovery of the Unique' had already been praised by Oscar Wilde. Frank Harris remembered him chiefly for his strikingly intelligent, contemplative blue eyes. He was now very much part of Henley's truculent fifth form, with its strong interest in social issues, but he still felt a new boy. Intimates knew him as the talkative, bumptious, jokey, boisterous 'Bertie' while Jerome K Jerome, already a grand figure and editor of *The Idler*, remembered HG initially as 'a shy, diffident young man' and Wells himself recalled an early literary dinner attended by the likes of Sickert, Morrison, Barrie and Kipling, helping himself to a huge amount of caviar not knowing what it was or how to eat it and, disliking the taste, pretending to relish it as he forked it all down.

Wells's fortunes did not immediately rise with his reputation. By 1894, with an estranged wife, a mistress, her mother, his mother, father, brother to support and his tubercular condition recurring sometimes dramatically, his earnings from writing had risen from £1. 0s. 0d. in 1888 to £380. 13s. 7d. in 1893 to £583. 12s. 7d. which, towards the end of the Great Depression of 1873–96, was a good income for a young man of twenty-eight without dependants.

Then inexplicably the *PMG* stopped taking his pieces, several regular markets were over-inventoried with his work, the deepening recession caused the collapse of other journals and he had a severe TB attack. His wife to be, 'Jane', was also unwell and required a change of air. Wells decided to move them out of London to healthier Kent where they could live more economically. Meanwhile Henley, who had lost the *National Observer* with a change of proprietor, had wind of a new job. He asked Wells to write up his time-travel ideas as a novel he could serialise. With little else to do, Wells began *The Time Machine*. He wrote it on the kitchen table of Tusculum Villas, 23 Eardley Road, Sevenoaks while his landlady, hysterically critical of him, his relationship, and his profligate use of her lamp oil, berated him loudly to neighbours in his hearing as he worked by the open window one warm August night on the scene where the horrified Time Traveller discovers his machine is stolen and his retreat cut off.

By now they also had Jane's disapproving mother staying with them, but he still managed to send his chapters for Bertha to type and for Henley to read. His luck was already changing. His best *Select Conversations with an Uncle* from the *PMG* were accepted by John Lane, publisher of the *Yellow*

*Book* and closely associated with the æsthetes. Lane paid Wells a £10. 0s. 0d. advance. Henley replied. He was delighted with *The Time Machine* and was taking over the *New Review* to start it as a monthly. He would run the first part in the January issue ("the invention is so wonderful, so running over . . . it must certainly make your reputation"). He paid Wells a relatively modest £100 for magazine rights but got him another £50 advance from Heinemann, publishers of the *New Review*.

The story Wells had described as his top card seemed about to pay off. But he was not sanguine. When offered a job as theatre critic for the *PMG* (he discovered that a Wells-hating locum had taken the opportunity to sack him temporarily) he ordered himself the appropriate evening dress. Admitting his previous experience was nothing but panto and Gilbert and Sullivan, he began his new job in January 1895 and meanwhile carried home armfuls of books for himself and Jane to review. He was revising his serial as it appeared, responding to Henley's acutely perceptive suggestions respectfully conveyed ('You might very well give your fancy play and at the same time oblige your editor').

In 1895 England, especially in the major cities, was a disgrace to her own ideas of civilisation and social justice. Her streets were full of homeless beggars and the health of the vast class of unemployed or casually employed was actually worse than the previous decade. There were concerns about German expansionism and Wells would write to his brother in South Africa: 'Here things have been of the liveliest, war rumours, all the Music Halls busy with songs insulting the German Emperor, fleets being manned and nobody free to attend to the works of a poor struggling author from Lands End to John O'Groats.'

1895 was indeed a bad year for a new author trying to get noticed. It was an extraordinary literary year in an extraordinary decade. Apart from *The Time Machine* and *Select Conversations*, Wells published *The Wonderful Visit* and the story collection *The Stolen Bacillus* while writing the bulk of *The Wheels of Chance* and *The Island of Dr Moreau*, composing at the familiar pace of a newspaper journalist used to working sometimes to hourly deadlines. He continued to produce for the *PMG* and others, but the world at large had not yet noticed him much.

The middlebrow, conventional *Chamber's Journal* best reflected the broadly educated taste of the time. In its April 27th number it carried a new Anthony Hope serial, *Chronicles of Count Antonio* ('Countless are the stories told of the sayings Count Antonio spoke . . .'), somewhat disappointing after *The Prisoner of Zenda*, while an article on the Modern Novel offered the opinion that the increase in 'Sexmania' novels was a passing disease in fiction which would doubtless yield to healthier influences. The anonymous writer described the huge print runs and earnings of popular novelists Lew Wallace, Hall Caine, Du Maurier, Stanley J Weyman, SR Crockett, Mrs Hodgson Burnett, Marie Corelli, Rider Haggard and Mary E Wilkins. He discussed the extraordinary successes of Anthony Hope, F Anstey, Mrs Oliphant, Miss Braddon, Edna Lyall, Ouida, W Clark Russell, Rhoda Broughton, Grant Allen, Anthony Trollope and Lord Lytton. There were other modern bestsellers not easy to account for such as Mrs Henry Wood's ('the novelist of the commonplace respectables, of whom there are thousands around us . . . exactly as she describes them'). Enduring writers not subject to the vagaries of public taste included William Black and Walter Besant who, it was implied, were guaranteed immortality.

Meanwhile the queen of the illustrated magazines *The Strand* began a new Conan Doyle serial, *The Exploits of Brigadier Gerard* and continued its popular detective series by LT Meade and Clifford Halifax MD with *The Hooded Death*. Rather daringly, *Harper's* ran Hardy's serial *Hearts Insurgent*! Sexton Blake first appeared in the *Union Jack*. The *Westminster Gazette*, *Black and White*, *The Idler* and *Punch* offered their readers the humour of Anstey, Jerome, WW Jacobs and Barry Pain, sharp sketches of ordinary life by Pett Ridge, Arthur Morrison, Israel Zangwill and others who made it their business to describe, often with telling sentiment, the world of working-class and immigrant London. Fiction was by Stephen Crane, Henry James, E Nesbit, John Oliver Hobbes, Arnold Bennett, Grant Allen, Mark Twain, George Gissing, WD Howells, Ella D'Arcy, JM Barrie, Joseph Conrad, Mrs Leverson and Richard Le Gallienne, illustrated by Sickert, Stanley L Wood, Rothenstein, Burne Jones, Sidney Paget, Beardsley, Phil May or Heath Robinson. These journals were in frequent rivalry, representing a wide variety of taste and opinion in the fashion of good modern TV, reflecting sometimes a bias towards the arts, sometimes towards political and social issues or popular fiction but trying to address the whole of society and entertain as wide a public as possible. Their best contributors and series were enjoyed by large readerships. Authors were often heroes. Intellectual life was profoundly stimulated and informed by the Press. For every editorial demanding Wilde's blood there was another expressing horror at the brutality and backwardness of our society.

In 1895 Wilde's trial was not the only scandal in Bohemia. As a reviewer Wells gave enthusiastic notices to Meredith's masterpiece *The Amazing Marriage*, Conrad's first novel *Almayer's Folly*, Crane's *Red Badge of Courage*,

Gissing's *Sleeping Fires* and Arthur Morrison's *Child of the Jago*, perceptively recognising the intentions and artistry of these brilliant but frequently misread authors. But in common with Mrs Fawcett and other feminists, he roundly attacked a book by a man with whom he shared much, for both had studied under TH Huxley and remained disciples. Grant Allen's *The Woman Who Did* was intended to be a pro-feminist book. It disgusted and alarmed the popular press. In it a free woman chooses to live unmarried publicly with the father of her child and suffers terribly for her decision. Wells was contemptuous. 'In these problem novels at least, truth is absolutely essential. But to handle the relation of the sexes truly needs a Jean Paul Richter, or a George Meredith. It is not done by desiring . . .' *The Amazing Marriage* remains as vital as the day it was written while *The Woman Who Did* seems very artificial, but it went to some thirty editions and Grant Allen (who generously accepted Wells's criticism) was the toast of liberal society.

Wells might have preferred Allen's other novel of that year, recalling Ruskin's observation that an angel visiting our modern age would immediately be shot. Allen's first time-travel story 'Pausodyne' had appeared in 1884. His *The British Barbarians* was a charming satirical fable in which an alien from the twenty-fifth century returns to 1895 and is shocked by the crude tribalism and violence of the English. When an enlightened woman befriends him he is shot by her jealous husband. Wells was to use a similar notion in *The Wonderful Visit*.

The Wilde revelations were dividing literary London. Fired by John Lane from the *Yellow Book*, Aubrey Beardsley went to Arthur Symons's *Savoy*. Lane vigorously declared his horrified ignorance of all perverse erotomania while continuing to exploit the sexy *frisson* of his press's image, marked by his distinctive green, Beardsley-decorated bindings on books which became increasingly wholesome, hearty and heterosexual. As a theatre critic Wells praised *An Ideal Husband* and attended the infamous first night of James's *Guy Domville* when the author suffered the appalling humiliation of being booed off the stage. Wells saw the play's failures in the gulf between its subtle writing and the crude acting ('Be key-und to her! Be key-und to her!' he reports an actor proclaiming). That night he fell in with George Bernard Shaw, critic for Harris's *Saturday Review* and began a lifelong friendship.

The new Ibsen was *Little Eyot*. Tom Browne created *Weary Willie and Tired Tim* to become stars of Harmsworth's money-spinning *Comic Cuts* companion, *Chips*. Wells's other publisher, Heinemann, panicked at the Wilde scandals and withdrew Robert Hichens's amiable *The Green Carnation*, which would not reappear in England until 1949. *Hearts Insurgent* in a somewhat different form became *Jude the Obscure* and was so savagely attacked that Hardy would never write ambitious prose again, but Wells chose it as his book of the year and would choose it again the following year. Mark Twain, in desperate financial straits, crept into England with his family. Kenneth Grahame's *The Golden Age* and Kipling's *Second Jungle Book* appeared. Pater's *Greek Studies*, Vernon Lee's *Renaissance Fancies and Studies*, Arthur Symons's *London Nights*, and Fiona Macleod's *The Sin Eater* were noticed; GA Henty's *Life of a Special Correspondent* was running in the *Boys' Own Paper* and MR James's first ghost story, 'Canon Alberic's Scrapbook' appeared in the *National Review*.

1895 was a good year for imaginative fiction, including Arthur Machen's *The Three Impostors*, MP Sheil's *Prince Zaleski* and George Griffith's *Outlaws of the Air*. Griffith had already anticipated radar, atomic energy and aerial warfare in his successful 'Angel of the Revolution', with its anarchist anti-hero, considered by many superior to Lytton's *The Coming Race*, Fawcett's *Hartmann the Anarchist* or even William Morris's *News from Nowhere*. William Le Queux, like Griffith a professional scientific romancer, had in 1893 published 'The Great War in England of 1897', using journalistic techniques anticipating Orson Welles's version of *The War of the Worlds*, but in 1895 he published *Zoraida: A Romance of the Harem and the Great Sahara*, while that hugely popular favourite of Kipling's, Guy Boothby, brought out *The Beautiful White Devil*.

Wells was not the only writer filling the media with speculative pieces. *The Strand* for December offered 'An Express of the Future' by Jules Verne and Fred C Jane (famous for his *Fighting Ships*) published a future war adventure, *Blake of the Rattlesnake*. More exotically the æsthetes, baroque Victorians, embraced the *fin de siècle* with languid relish, celebrating a civilisation in its last stages of decadent refinement, but Wells had the practical instincts of the trained scientist and was on his way up. Like many others, he was seeking solutions for social ills, wanting to turn the coming century into an earthly paradise. While a general acceptance of the logic of entropy meant that everyone was resigned to the Earth's ultimate doom, opinion was divided about the nature and moment of her death. In 1895 Dumas the Younger died and inspired a eulogy from Henry James on *La Dame aux Camelias*, which had fascinated him as a child when he first saw it staged. Henry Harland, editor of the *Yellow Book*, produced a quintessential *Grey Roses*, Ernest Dowson, his decadent superior, published *Dilemmas, Stories and Studies in Sentiment*. Lane issued E Nesbit's *A Pomander of Verse*, Rhys's *A London Rose* and Ella D'Arcy's *Monochromes*.

Big sellers included *The Sorrows of Satan* by Marie Corelli, *The Manxman* by Hall Caine and *Trilby* by George Du Maurier. John Buchan's mannered first novel *Sir Quixote of the Moors* appeared. Max Beerbohm's satirical drawings and verse attacked the mood of piety which had overwhelmed the popular papers in the wake of the Wilde trials. Wilde went to Reading.

## II

That one idea is now everybody's idea. It was never the writer's own peculiar idea . . . It is the idea that Time is a fourth dimension and that the normal present is a three-dimensional section of a four-dimensional universe.

(Ibid.)

Time-travel stories, like all kinds of speculative romance, were popular with late Victorian readers. Edwin Lester Arnold's *Phra the Phoenician* had proceeded through Time by a process of reincarnation and Mark Twain's Yankee had gone back to the Court of King Arthur via a blow on the head. Like F Anstey's *Tormalin's Time Cheques*, 1891, such stories were often used to examine human society and find it wanting. Most travellers had merely to fall asleep, a Rip Van Winkle, to wake up a century or millennia hence, while Bellamy's *Looking Backward* had employed the original notion of placing the narrator in the future and reviewing our coming history as his past. In spite of all this and his own modest claims, Wells's *The Time Machine* stands out immediately as something different. It is about the *mastery* of Time itself, and all that it implies. As it appeared, month by month, through the first half of 1895, it became a talking point. WT Stead's influential *Review of Reviews* called Wells 'a man of genius'. James, Meredith, Conrad and Hardy all recognised a peer. Publishers and editors began to court him and humourists begin to satirise him. He could write to his parents that he had 'arrived'.

While improving Wells's fortunes radically, *The Time Machine* was to have an effect on the popular imagination not unlike the film *2001: A Space Odyssey* some seventy years later. It established a public vision of the future, a powerful myth in which human beings evolved into something alien. As he would from now until his film *Things to Come* in 1935, he issued a clear warning: Go on as we are now and we are doomed to devolve to the level of brutes and from brutes back to the mud from which we came. In scenes left out of the book version he emphasised this point, describing the process of devolution following the time of the Morlocks. If his motives were Dante's, to show us Hell so that we might avoid it, and his methods were consciously borrowed from Swift, the author's natural optimism is implicit in his decision to write the story. There is no misanthropy in Wells, only distress. It is his characters who despair of dissuading us from our cruel follies.

That issue of the *New Review* for January is full of excellent journalism. Henley was an impeccable editor, offering his readers only the best. And yet one is immediately struck by the economy, the modernity of Wells's writing and it is not at all surprising that so many recognised his unique gifts. Admirers have pointed out the skill with which he allows us to use our own imagination, describing the Time Traveller's laboratory in precise detail but giving only the vaguest description of the machine; conjuring up other people's visions of the future in order to dismiss those detailed pictures as unlikely—and certainly nothing *he* has observed; offering powerful images of the planet in its decadent and dying years, evoking all the Gothic *frisson* of ruins and loss. He combines the unique personal vision of a Bunyan or a Blake with vivid, economical prose and a driving urgency to alert the world to its moral and physical danger! His language is given further authority by its use of scientific terms. His methods are novel but his instincts have much in common with Jeremiah. He is an authentic original and *The Time Machine* continues to define and influence all those stories that came after it, which have never equalled it.

## III

One must err to grow and the writer feels no remorse for his youthful effort. Indeed he hugs his vanity very pleasantly at times when his dear old Time Machine crops up once more in essays and speeches, still a practical and convenient way to retrospect or prophecy. . . . So the Time Machine has lasted as long as the diamond-framed safety bicycle, which came in at about the date of its first publication. And now it is going to be printed and published so admirably that its author is assured it will outlive him. He has long since given up the practise of writing prefaces for books, but this is an exceptional occasion and he is very proud and happy to say a word or so of reminiscence and friendly commendation for that needy and cheerful namesake of his, who lived back along the time dimension, six and thirty years ago.

(Ibid.)

By December 1895, inspired chiefly by the urgent need for money, Wells had published *Select Conversations with an Uncle* and *The Time Machine* in June, *The Wonderful Visit* in September and *The Stolen Bacillus and Other*

*Incidents* in November. He was also at work on *The Wheels of Chance*, his 'holiday romance' of cycling (he and Jane were keen long-distance cyclists). Read individually (and preferably with some experience of his contemporaries) these books not only make it clear how superior Wells was to most of the substantial writers of his day but why the public took so readily to him. Read together the books are a stunning display of youthful genius, offering an example of almost every kind of book Wells would write in the future.

The angel has grown human with time, brutalised by exposure to English society, and by the end of *The Wonderful Visit* turns on an aggressor:

> "You bestial thing of pride and lies! You who have overshadowed the souls of other men. You shallow fool with your horses and dogs! To lift your face against any living thing! Learn! Learn! Learn!"
>
> Gotch began screaming for help. Twice he tried to clamber to his feet, got to his knees and went headlong under the ferocious anger of the Angel . . .
>
> "Truly this is no world for an Angel," said the Angel. "It is a World of War, a World of Pain, a World of Death. Anger comes upon one . . ."

Wells's anger never left him and informs so much of his best work, giving it lasting resonances. What makes *The Wonderful Visit* a better book than *The British Barbarians* is precisely its lack of well-bred urbanity, the directness and vulgarity of its attack.

In 1895 Bertie Wells was a touchy, eager, socially awkward, aggressive, well-educated representative of a petite bourgeoisie which had emerged in the boom years, found its hopes for improvement threatened by politically bankrupt government and increasingly turned to socialism for its promise of a better world. He was recognised as the voice of this new class and he continued to see himself as a representative of 'the Common Man'. But he was also a man of science, a campaigner for change. Warren Wagar's portrait of him in *HG Wells, Journalism and Prophecy*, 1964, is the familiar one:

> He was a short, fattish, broad-shouldered man, his voice high and thin, his eyes blue and dreaming. He walked with a vulgar little bounce. He was the everlasting Cockney never quite able to forget years of hunger and ill health in a *fin-de-siècle* adolescence . . . he was the resentful ex-counter-jumper of the Southsea Drapery Emporium, the ex-student of that lugubrious pagan TH Huxley, the erstwhile consumptive London journalist eager to *épater le bourgeois*, and beyond all this, the tireless propagandist of a great unified world order he never lived to see.

Quixotic, emotionally never quite as sophisticated as he proclaimed but willing to drop everything one Christmas Eve to speed from London to the Spanish border to attend a dying Gissing ('What a brick Wells is', said James), throwing out all kinds of opinions, often simply to hear what came back, forever modifying, enthusing, losing heart, trying again to fix the human condition, to ensure the rule of love and rationality, Wells was not only sensitive to others, but almost always listening, almost always generous, always loved, even by those he had betrayed or offended, refusing to discuss a Jewish Question because he resisted the whole notion of Zionism (which he saw as nationalistic and reactionary) and failing to understand why some might feel the need to have the power of a nation state on their side if they were to survive; shocked by the Nazi bestiality which seemed the culmination of everything he had tried to stop since he had written *The Time Machine*, horrified by the revelations of the Holocaust, he wrote his last book, *Mind at the End of Its Tether* in which he desperately sought to find some cause for optimism in the evidence. He grieved rather infrequently for himself but often for others and remained a good-hearted inspiration, a practical friend. In *The Wheels of Chance*, that charming taster for *Kipps* or *Mr Polly*, he gives us a description of Mr Hoopdriver, the draper, his reminder to himself of what he had escaped:

> If you had gone into the Drapery Emporium—which is really only magnificent for shop—of Messrs Antrobus and Co.—a perfectly fictitious "Co.", by-the-by—of Putney, on the 14th of August 1895, had turned to the right-hand side, where the blocks of white linen and piles of blankets rise up to the rail from which the pink and blue prints depend, you might have been served by the central figure of this story that is now beginning. He would have come forward, bowing and swaying: and he would have asked you, protruding a pointed chin and without the slightest anticipation of pleasure in his manner, what he might have the pleasure of showing you . . .

In his preface to *Select Conversations* Wells describes himself as 'short, but by no means conspicuously short, and of a bright, almost juvenile, complexion, very active in his movements and garrulous—or at least very talkative. His judgements were copious and frequent in the old days, and some at least I found entertaining. At times his fluency was really remarkable. He had a low opinion of eminent people—a thing I have been careful to suppress, and his dissertations had ever an irresponsible gaiety of manner that may have blinded me to their true want of merit. That, I say, was in the old days, before his abrupt extinction, before the cares of the world suddenly sprang upon him, and choked him.'

*Conversations* established HG Wells in Henley's fifth form but it was *The Time Machine* that got him into the upper sixth. He is irresistible. There are many descriptions of him as he grew self-confident and ambitious through the 1890s. One of my favourites is from Jerome K Jerome's amiably accurate *My Life and Times*:

> I mentioned once in a letter to him that I was a bit run down. He invited me to spend a day or two with him at Folkestone: get some sea air in my lungs and a rest. To 'rest' in the neighbourhood of Wells is like curling yourself up and trying to go to sleep in the centre of a cyclone. When he wasn't explaining the universe, he was teaching me new games— complicated things that he had invented himself, and under stress of which my brain would reel. There are steepish hills on the South Downs. We went up them at four miles an hour, talking all the time. On the Sunday evening a hurricane was raging with a driving sleet. Wells was sure a walk would do us good—wake us up. While Mrs Wells was not watching, we tucked the two little boys into their mackintoshes and took them with us.
>
> "We'll all have a blow," said Wells.

(In preparing this introduction I referred to my own library and to Wells's *Experiment in Autobiography*, 1934, Norman and Jeanne Mackenzie's definitive *The Time Traveller*, 1974, and David C Smith's *Desperately Mortal*, 1986.)

# ■ Ubu C'est Moi?

A review of *Alfred Jarry; A Pataphysical Life* by Alastair Brotchie

**From the *Guardian*, forthcoming**

Alfred Jarry is perhaps the least known important writer of his generation, with a profound influence on the British authors around *New Worlds* and the likes of Boris Vian, Maurice Richardson and David Britton, that mysterious, twice-jailed creator of Lord Horror, surely Père Ubu's favourite son. Both Burroughs and Ballard were inspired by him. He was admired by artists from Duchamp to Paolozzi and any number of playwrights including Artaud, Beckett and Ionesco. His posthumous *Gestes et Opinions de Docteur Faustroll, Pataphysicien* (*Exploits and Opinions of Dr Faustroll, Pataphysician*) was a major influence on several of today's most innovative authors. This fine biography, written with loving honesty by Alastair Brotchie, is the best about Jarry to date.

Relying on a considerable amount of original research, Brotchie refuses to speculate except in specifics and will then indicate where Jarry himself, say, has not been clear. He gives us an unmatched and vivid picture of the *Belle Époque's* avant-garde of which Jarry was an important, original part. At a time when we are beginning to re-examine and even redefine modernism, Jarry is seen increasingly as a major influence on contemporary writing as well as the most important precursor of the Dadaists, the Surrealists and the British pop art movement.

Born in 1873 to a somewhat impoverished Breton bourgeois family, the precocious Jarry nonetheless received a first-class education in Rennes and became as familiar with advanced physics as he was with Greek and Latin. Lord Kelvin was amongst the theoretical physicists whom he read. Although a little bookish, writing poetry and fiction from the age of twelve, Jarry enjoyed fishing, fencing and cycling, sports to which he remained attached all his short life.

The Lycée at Rennes had many excellent teachers but one became the butt of all the boys: a rather pompous, cowardly master, Hébert, whom

Jarry and his young pals nicknamed 'Père Ubu'. Over time Ubu became his own terrible creature, no longer a mockery of one individual. The bombastic, scatological sayings and doings of this increasingly fantastic grotesque were probably mostly written by Jarry. When he left the school his friends were perfectly happy to let him take Ubu, too. Jarry went to Paris to study for his *bac* and Ubu went with him.

A conscientious student, soft-spoken and courteous, the tiny (he sometimes wore women's shoes) and fey Jarry appears to have been just as popular at the Lycée Henri IV crammer for the École Normale Supérieure, perhaps because he found it hard to check his wit when addressing masters and lecturers, one of whom was Bergson, who was for a while a strong influence. Soon he was impressing other students with his talent, his charm and his eccentricity. Now, however, he was among peers appreciative of Ubu when he assumed the role which he increasingly did, doubtless to disguise his shyness or, perhaps, his homosexuality. At this time he formed a close friendship with Fargue, who would become a well-known poet. Fargue introduced him to the work of the Symbolists, then France's acknowledged avant-garde.

For a while Lautréamont was Jarry's chief inspiration. I agree with Brotchie who thinks the influence malign, but the innovations in *Les Chants de Maldoror* impressed Jarry and encouraged him to continue with his own. Gradually he and Fargue found themselves moving in bohemian society. Jarry's first work appeared anonymously in *L'Écho de Paris*. Soon he was writing regularly for some of the most interesting journals in Paris, the majority of which held regular gatherings of contributors. Here Jarry, often adopting the Ubu persona so that friends began to call him 'Pa Ubu', began to meet other ambitious writers.

In 1896, after publishing several books in small, independent editions, Jarry was at last able to get *Ubu* staged by Lugné-Poe at the Théâtre de l'Oeuvre, originally created to promote Symbolist works (except nobody was altogether sure what these were). Earlier productions of Maeterlinck and Ibsen had their philistine detractors but none as violent as *Ubu*'s audiences. *Ubu* was uncompromising. Indeed with its opening neologism spouted by the vulgar, obscene grotesque Père Ubu—*Merdre!!!!*—it immediately announced its intentions. "It was," says Brotchie, "as though a modernist play from the middle of the next century had been dropped on the stage without all the intervening theatrical developments that might have acclimatized the audience to its conventions." Since Jarry had been in the thick of the riot, encouraging the response, he clearly wasn't disappointed. He had a very good eye for publicity and laboured hard behind the scenes to get it.

Jarry published regularly in some of the most prestigious journals of his day, including the leading one, *Mercure de France*, and quickly joined their inner circles. For a few years he enjoyed a relatively regular, if small, income from the *Mercure* and a few others, spending much of his time in the company of Gide, Lautrec, Rousseau, Gourmont, Mallarmé and other exceptional writers and artists of his day (there is some question whether he ever knew Picasso through their mutual friend Apollinaire).

In 1899 *Mercure* serialized Wells's *The Time Machine.* This gave Jarry the idea of writing a pseudo-scientific paper on the machine, as if one really existed, an idea perfectly in keeping with his notions of 'pataphysics', in part sardonic combination of metaphysics and theoretical physics described in some of his earliest work. At the beginning of his piece Jarry refers to the difference between physical time and duration. His description of the machine is not surprising, since both authors were enthusiastic cyclists. The last section of the piece 'Time as Seen from the Machine' offers a new definition of duration, 'The Becoming of Memory'. This connects, Brotchie points out, what is an apparently theoretical text with notions of nostalgia and the erotic in Jarry's short novel *Days and Nights* and suggests, convincingly, that it was probably the first time scientific and technical language had been used entirely to produce a work of fiction. *On the Construction of a Time-Exploring Machine* was a straight-faced piece of exposition so well done that it had a number of eminent British scientists almost convinced. Wells himself would have been a bit puzzled by Pataphysics. As Jarry had Ubu explain elsewhere: "Pataphysics is a science which we have invented and for which a crying need is generally expressed." As usual, Jarry was at least half a century ahead of his time.

Jarry's life became increasingly difficult as his health failed, the magazines folded and he was pursued by creditors. While the avant-garde journals existed, Jarry was able to scrape a small living. He fished for most of his food. He had his bicycle for transport, his revolver for security and ultimately his own little house, built on land he bought beside the Seine. He lived for and by his art, caring very little for material things. Over the years he learned to discard most comforts except alcohol. He died in 1907, aged thirty-four, inspiring a cycle of myth almost as rich as that surrounding his own monstrous Pa Ubu. Subsequent biographies were all informed by these myths, the most prevalent being that Ubu, the fiction, destroyed Jarry, the man, that, like some comics or actors, he 'became' Ubu, incapable of distinguishing between himself and his horrible invention.

Perhaps the greatest single thing Brotchie has done in his magnificent biography is to dispel those myths. He shows how Jarry was perfectly capable of telling truth from reality. He did not die 'of drink' but of complications from undiagnosed TB affecting his brain. He was a genius, certainly, but a rather sweet-natured, obstinate and luckless genius, who charmed not only his friends but occasionally the entire populations of small towns.

Quasi-romantics, actually sensationalists and sentimentalists, prefer to gild the lily and turn a talented person into a simplified fiction. A real romantic, like Jarry, had to fight or drug himself in order to rein in his imagination and control his invention. Alastair Brotchie has done his subject and us a considerable service in presenting this exhaustive, realistic picture of a man still not properly recognized as one of the most influential writers of modern times.

# ■ What to Buy for the Grown-Up Boy

A Review of *Grandville Mon Amour* by Bryan Talbot

**From the *Guardian*, 11th December 2010**

Bryan Talbot has always specialised in that brand of nostalgic satire known as 'steampunk'. His *Luther Arkwright* stories were set against the background of a British Empire where uniformed airshipmen fought for queen and country until discovering their idealism to be a little misplaced whereupon their adventures continued apace, only with somewhat altered objectives.

In those books Talbot drew heavily on a wide range of English iconography depicting an 'Albion' ruled by a monarchy and church which came in for some stern thrashings as he continued his relentless prosecution of authoritarian power through the 1990s until he came up with what still remains my own favourite *The Tale of One Bad Rat*. This moving story of child abuse set pretty much in the here and now referenced of course Beatrix Potter.

Talbot's story-telling as well as his draughtsmanship has grown steadily more assured and subtle. With his superb graphic novel *Grandville*, published last year, he extended his range to include references to the French artist JJ Grandville who worked in the mid-19th century and was also best known for his anthropomorphic representations of animals. That said, Talbot's animal characters owe more to British artists like Tourtel and Bestell, who drew the Rupert stories for many years. Their inhabitants of Nutwood included characters like Percy the Pug, Bill the Badger and Edward the Elephant, all drawn to the same human scale. It's a tradition dating at least from ancient Egypt and gave us such 20th century favourites as Tiger Tim, Korky the Cat and, of course, the enduring characters from *The Wind in the Willows* and *Winnie the Pooh*. These very British creations don't have quite the same place in our collective psyche, or hearts, as Mickey Mouse or Bugs Bunny but Talbot knowingly chooses to work in a European, predominantly English, tradition. While his narrative clearly invokes pre-*entente* rivalries and prejudices, referencing Grandville, *Fantomas* and the incredibly bloody French sixty *centimes* dreadfuls like *Le Charcutier Parfumé* or *Agathe La-Goule*, Talbot achieves ironic counterpoint using our old nursery favourites grown-up.

Rather than quaint rural fantasies, Talbot tells a violent mystery story set in a world where Britain only recently freed herself from a France in which Napoleon won and we still use French as our first language. In this sequel, *Grandville Mon Amour*, Talbot develops ideas explored in his first story, again employing Detective Inspector LeBrock (a badger) and Detective Ratzi (a rat), a pair of relentless coppers.

Although Talbot's narratives lack the complexity or originality of Alan Moore's, he brings a rare subtlety, even beauty to his medium. His drawing is first class and his dialogue is superb, adding credibility to his characterisation while moving his narrative along at a laconic lick. The story is set a few years after Britain has won her independence from France which retains a contempt for her uncouth former colony. In turn the British carry chips on their collective shoulder, having won independence through a mixture of terrorism and political bargaining. Our terrorists, known as The Angry Brigade, were the usual collection of idealists and psychopaths, most of whom are dead, mysteriously betrayed, LeBrock's dad amongst them.

One ex-terrorist, Mad-Dog Mastock (you guessed it, a dog) about to be guillotined for the serial murder of women, escapes, killing a jail-full of guards. Brock is horrified and vows to bring in Mastock, whom he arrested for the original crimes. Mastock, needless to say, has sworn to slay Brock and meanwhile turns up in Paris murdering whores apparently at random. Brock and Ratzi entrain for the French capital, doing their best to keep a step ahead of the killer and stop the slaughter while trying to solve the larger mystery behind his escape. This involves various French and British friends and enemies in high places, several of whom are not at all what they seem.

Talbot's elaborate brass-and-mahogany steampunk paraphernalia constantly add to the visual delights of the tale, demonstrating his mastery of the graphic narrative. If some revelations are a bit too easily anticipated his sophisticated draughtsmanship more than makes up for any simplifications of story.

For over a century children have loved getting a *Rupert* or *Beano* annual as part of the season's largesse. This year a lot of grown-ups should feel similar delight when *Grandville Mon Amour* is discovered, suitably wrapped, under their Christmas tree.

# ■ Yesterday's Tomorrow

## A Review of *Against the Day* by Thomas Pynchon

**From the *Telegraph*, 25th November 2006**

I have been familiar with Thomas Pynchon's work since the 1960s, when I ran his story 'Entropy' in *New Worlds*, the magazine I edited. The *New Worlds* authors shared Pynchon's interest in urban mythology, entropy as a metaphor and mathematics. They celebrated his forays into earlier fictions via pastiche, but many argued that he lacked William Burroughs's laconic virtues.

Though he can fairly be considered sui generis like Ronald Firbank or Boris Vian, Pynchon was co-opted by some critics into the steampunk movement. The opening of *Against the Day* reminded me of Alan Moore's Tom Strong graphic novels which drew on late-19th-century 'science hero' dime novels to examine Edwardian mechanical optimism exemplified by the real Nikola Tesla.

The first half of this romance recaptures the prevalent mood of pre-1914 America, when 'wizards' such as Thomas Edison and Tesla were public legends, but, like Mark Twain before him, Pynchon introduces a questioning, deeply elegiac note into his story of Yankee 'can-do' optimism, producing a tall tale entirely serious in intention, if only rarely in tone.

A massive engine, depending on its size for its aesthetic the way some rock bands depend on loudness, *Against the Day* takes a while to build momentum and requires patience while its inventor unrolls blueprints, explains the maths, polishes a bit of brass here, makes a modest joke there, showing off his machine cog by cog, then introducing his passengers and their histories.

Representing every 20th-century concern, most of his protagonists are connected to the aptly named Traverse family and its murdered anarchist patriarch, as well as the skyshipmen 'Chums of Chance', who drift across the world, in and out of relationships, meeting strange customers with Marx Bros names and resolving differences.

With eerie echoes of Sinclair Lewis's *It Can't Happen Here* and similar pre–Second World War moral fables, Pynchon creates a visionary tapestry covering the years after the Chicago World's Fair of 1893. Embracing the narrative methods of popular fiction, his tales are designed to deceive as well as to create expectations. As a parodist, he can slip smoothly from Nick Carter to Black Mask and then into 1950s movies.

Having in *Mason and Dixon* examined the American Enlightenment, Pynchon, perhaps the greatest intellectual showman of our time, turns his attention to post–Civil War idealism and the apparently unstoppable way it warped into the Crash.

There are more talking dogs, daft songs, and a whole slew of nutty professors, working on time machines, deathrays and beamable electromagnetic power, some opposing big business, others in its employ. Pinkertons, Wall Street grafters, Robber Barons, frontier whores, anarchist dynamiters, gun-fighters, angels, gamblers, mad prophets, time-travellers, Theosophists, spies, magicians, painters, beautiful adventuresses and secret societies are all involved in an increasingly metaphysical Great Game across the multiverse, from Kathmandu to Colorado to Cambridge, Contra-Earth to Contra-Earth.

Marvel by marvel, pathetic fallacy becomes art beyond Ruskin's wildest dreams, and you wonder if you aren't reading the smartest stoner in the universe.

By page 550, when he brings you to the novel's melancholy heart, Pynchon has you firmly in the palm of his Barnum-like fist. It's no accident that we are now in Belgium, narrowly missing being drowned in mayonnaise, or that a half-mad time-traveller warns a fellow ukulelist 'Chum of Chance' of future trench war: 'This world you take to be "the" world will die, and descend into Hell, and all history after that will belong properly to the history of Hell.'

Soon string theory is used to rationalise time travel and we're hurtling through a collection of slightly different realities, threatened by phantoms of past, present and future, power-mongers of every kind moving the worlds towards versions of the destructive events that have threatened our humanity since 1914.

Noting how memories fade into folklore before our eyes, Pynchon finds self-similarity contradicting the logic of entropy. He travels not imaginary universes but universes of the imagination. One alternative shifts into another, one reality makes space for the next. The best visionary fiction reflects shared realities. Once his barker-persona has lured us in, Pynchon holds before us a whole hall full of mirrors.

Some of those reflected images are comic, a few almost flattering. We're laughing and crying. Yet what's the point? Be assured. The great Ludlow strike looms. Resolutions are offered through Pynchon's clever use of triplets and his brief finale in the future tense. We stagger out of this one man World's Fair with our hearts and our sides splitting. *Against the Day* is a fine example of a successful marriage between the popular and the intellectual, between fiction and science. Many modern writers are rediscovering or taking over science fiction tropes, as PD James did in *Children of Men*, though its subject had already been treated rather more subtly in Brian Aldiss's *Greybeard* (1964). Aldiss, Burroughs, JG Ballard and Kurt Vonnegut predicted long ago that the arts and sciences would be reunited in speculative fiction, that the novel would not die if it could rediscover vulgarity.

Gloriously, demandingly, daringly, Pynchon has rediscovered vulgarity and continues to prove that the novel has never been more vibrant, more various or better able to represent our complex world. Give this book your time—you'll agree it's worth it.

# ■ A Review of *Mythago Wood* by Robert Holdstock

**Modified from *Horror: The 100 Best Books*, 1988**

There is a type of English fantasy story which for me holds a special fascination. It can loosely be described, I suppose, as the 'haunted wood' fantasy. The haunted wood is that place where England's most ancient history impinges upon the modern world, where prehistoric spirits still live, sometimes yearning for their old power in the world, sometimes merely content to be left alone to hide from the new creatures, the human creatures, whose religions and realities have overwhelmed their own. In the haunted wood magic still persists. Sometimes it is little more than a faint aura, a hint of what it once was. Sometimes it is concentrated, merely awaiting the right catalyst to set it loose, to wreak revenge upon those who opposed it, imprisoned it or sent it into hiding.

Various authors have produced fine examples of this kind of story. Machen, Blackwood and Buchan spring immediately to mind, as well as EF Benson, MR James and several other outstanding English horror writers. For me, Barrie's *Dear Brutus* has much of the atmosphere I have described. In recent years, however, only Robert Holdstock was able to recreate this special *frisson* for me, in his marvellous fantasy *Mythago Wood* (1984).

Inspired as much by the music of Vaughan Williams as by earlier fiction, *Mythago Wood* has the feel of a classic horror story, both in its elegant style and in its choice of form. Holdstock uses traditional devices to draw us into his tale—mysterious activities, leaves torn from a journal, cryptic letters, discovered objects—until slowly we are as hooked, as obsessed with curiosity, as the protagonists themselves. By the time we begin our expedition into the magic wood we share the same compulsions to search for the truth.

Again, as in the very best stories of this kind, the truth is not immediately definable. Indeed Holdstock employs all these traditional devices to his own ends, to discuss the nature of our perceptions, of our understanding of what truth actually is. While with one hand he offers us an answer to a mystery, an explanation for certain events, identification of shadowy characters, with the other he compounds the mysteries. With every revelation comes a fresh doubt until by the end of the novel we know a great deal about Mythago Wood but are left with an entirely new set of questions. Some of these are answered in the author's follow-up, *Lavondyss* and further sequels.

The story concerns two generations of the Huxley family, who live at Oak Lodge, an old country house situated at the edge of three square miles of post–Ice Age forest known as Ryhope Wood and which, by chance, has been left uncleared, undeveloped and largely unexplored for centuries. The sons, somewhat embittered with their father, who tended to ignore them and their mother in favour of his obsession with the wood and its 'mythago' inhabitants, are gradually also hooked on the wood's mysteries. Their father's journals and letters provide some of the narrative, while the younger brother Steven's first-person story provides most of the rest.

The wood has a cryptic geography. Its boundaries expand the deeper one goes into it; it seems impossible ever to reach the far side. Within it dwell the 'mythagos'—whole tribes, whole civilisations, as well as individuals, representing the British national unconscious, all the races which have gone to create it. Familiar figures of myth and legend exist here, frequently in their purest or most primitive personæ—Herne the Hunter, King Arthur, Robin Hood and many others—while the explorer is apt to come upon the ruins of a Tudor manor farm, a Celtic stone fort or an eleventh-century castle. And meanwhile, wandering the trails of this infinite place, are men and women, some 'real' and some little more than memories, following desires and urges which even they are scarcely able to describe or define. It is a dangerous place, the mythago wood, where it is perfectly possible for an explorer to be cut down by a Stone Age axe or a Bronze Age sword, to be killed by warriors brought into reality by his own racial memory. These archetypes as described by Holdstock have all the power that genuine archetypes should possess. Even the woman whom Steven falls in love with and who, it seems, falls in love with him, probably has only as much substance as his longings can provide.

The genuine pathos of Holdstock's love story again has similarities with the theme of *Dear Brutus* and its heroine's desperate final cry that she does not want to be a 'might have been'. Holdstock avoids the sentimentality which some detect in Barrie by offering us tougher questions, moral dilemmas, an imagined world far more complex than anything found in the wood's precursors. For me, this is one of the outstanding fantasy books of recent decades and an essential addition to any library, to be read several times and to rediscover the same delight with each new reading.

Postscript: We ran 'Pauper's Plot,' Rob's first published story in *New Worlds*, in 1968 and it was evident we had discovered a fine new writer. A medical zoologist by training, Rob brought a strong physical sense of the English countryside to his Ryhope Wood series, which included *Lavondyss*, *The Bone Forest*, *The Hollowing*, *Merlin's Wood*, *Gate of Ivory*, *Gate of Horn* and *Avilion* the last book he published before his tragically early death from E.coli in 2009 at the age of sixty-one. A good friend, a great gentleman and an outstanding writer, frequently compared to Tolkien for his ability to evoke the ancient English countryside and its mysteries, he was one of the best-liked fantasts of his generation and deeply missed by his many friends.

# ■ North Pole Ghetto

A Review of *The Yiddish Policemen's Union* by
Michael Chabon

**From the *Telegraph*, 23rd June 2007**

Michael Chabon's fascination with popular culture was evident in his first
books, as was his outstanding command of contemporary prose, but it was
not until his Pulitzer prize-winning masterpiece, *The Amazing Adventures
of Kavalier and Clay* (2000), that he displayed a sophisticated technical
command, enabling him to manipulate the iconography and historical
substance of superhero comics to tell the American story as successfully
as his best contemporaries, from Don DeLillo and Philip Roth to Thomas
Pynchon and Cormac McCarthy.

In common with British writers such as JG Ballard or Iain Sinclair,
Chabon is obsessed with finding ways of uniting the highest ambitions
of modernism with popular fiction, especially science fiction, to produce a
literature which engages the reader on the most serious level, while creating
a medium capable of addressing the urgent issues of our times.

At the same time, without resort to irony, he offers the intelligent reader
an engaging and entertaining narrative.

Chabon's stories never become intrusively experimental or arch. Like
Pynchon, he has taken what might be called the anti-modern novel well
beyond pastiche or parody. This novel marks a further development in his
talents, placing him in the top rank of living American writers.

Superficially, *The Yiddish Policemen's Union* employs the form of
a 1940s noir urban mystery story, paying specific homage to Dashiell
Hammett.

Written entirely in the present tense, rich with the wisdom and experience as well as the sardonic rhythms of Yiddish, reminiscent of Isaac
Bashevis Singer at his best, this is an alternative history novel, like Philip
K Dick's *The Man in the High Castle* (1962), Kingsley Amis's *The Alteration*
(1976) or Roth's *The Plot Against America* (2004).

Chabon sets up his alternate world with considerably more subtlety and economy than these predecessors. We learn, for instance, that the Second World War was ended by the dropping of the Atomic Bomb on Berlin only in a passing reference to a clock that somehow survived.

In this world, very close to our own, the US, in the wake of the Nazi Holocaust and the 1948 destruction of the State of Israel, has leased a large stretch of Alaska to Jews.

This sixty-year lease is almost up and Washington is about to take back the land known as the Federal District of Sitka. This means that some two and a half million Yiddish-speaking Jews, who have created a kind of ghetto far too near the North Pole for comfort, will shortly be looking for a new homeland or, at least, new homes.

The novel's protagonist, Meyer Landsman, is a cop who, when control of the Federal District returns to the US, will probably be out of a job.

Divorced from his wife, now his boss, drinking heavily, sunk in self-loathing, Landsman is more or less reconciled to treading water for the last few months of his time in Sitka when, in the cheap flophouse where he has washed up, a middle-aged junkie is murdered.

True to the best noir conventions, Landsman takes the murder personally and proceeds, against various warnings from on high, to investigate, learning that the murdered man has used dozens of pseudonyms (mostly of chess masters) and not only was a genius at chess but was also considered by many, including the father who has turned his back on him, to be the Messiah.

In the course of tracking down the killer, which he does ultimately by working out the clue hidden in the victim's last, unfinished, chess game, Landsman begins to uncover an almost impossibly complex and ambitious plot that becomes increasingly relevant to present conflicts over politics and religion.

Apart from his level-headed and disapproving ex-wife, Meyer cares most for his partner, the half-Tlingit Berko Shemets, who reluctantly allows himself to be dragged into the morass of crazed messianic visionaries, organised crime and Washington intrigue.

Shemets is the only cop who has enough respect in the Verbover district to go in and come out alive.

The Verbover is a fundamentalist, orthodox community ruled over by one of Chabon's best characters, the grotesquely overweight Rabbi Heskel Shpilman, who makes Sydney Greenstreet seem skinny.

Not only is Shpilman the highly respected religious leader of the community, he is also the boss of all Sitka's rackets. Sensitive and intelligent, he is ruthless enough to have them wiped out in an instant should they prove an inconvenience.

Chabon's plot grows increasingly terrifying and complex, yet is resolved with the technical mastery we have come to expect from this astonishingly disciplined and inventive writer.

If *Kavalier and Clay* was a meditation on Jewish mythology and history, then *The Yiddish Policemen's Union* is an absorbing meditation on Jewish faith and the future of its people. It is also an outstandingly good read.

# ■ Wagner and Wodehouse, Together at Last

## A Review of *Expecting Someone Taller* by Tom Holt

**From the *Los Angeles Times*, 17th June 1988**

Fantasy and comedy are cousins. Together they produced some of the happiest entertainments in a tradition going back at least to Mark Twain's *Connecticut Yankee*, through Thorne Smith and John Collier, and became almost an independent genre during the great days of *Unknown Worlds*, fantasy fiction's equivalent of *Black Mask*.

Writers like Anthony Boucher ('The Compleat Werewolf'), L Sprague de Camp and Fletcher Pratt (the 'Harold Shea' stories), Fritz Leiber, Henry Kuttner and even L Ron Hubbard (before his sense of the ridiculous gave way to a sense of holy pomposity) cheered up our war- and post-war years with a series of spoofs and satires on what had previously been the province of more portentously morbid writers like Edgar Allan Poe, Bram Stoker and HP Lovecraft. Unwitting and deeply embarrassed werewolves, vampires unable to stand the taste of blood, heroes who abhorred violence, and hideous monsters who wanted only to open small grocery stores in Ohio were *Unknown*'s stock in trade in the days before humour was banished from our shelves by the relentless Universal Ironies and Common Room Wit of JRR Tolkien and his even more sober followers.

In those dark times, we needed Boucher or De Camp, but publishers, being the timid creatures they are, preferred to perpetuate a trend celebrating the depressive comforts of quasi-religion in implacably second-rate prose produced by the mediocre prophets of an all-too-easily-imagined future. Their monstrous catalogues of reactionary conservatism, misogyny and high school philosophising became, as with Ayn Rand a decade earlier, the pseudo-radical bibles of a generation that soon readily returned to a fold it had only pretended to leave.

In fantastic comedy, the Gods very rarely have a sense of humour, and indeed the Wagnerian seriousness of magicians, demigods and the other supernaturals is what frequently provides a foil for writers whose skeptical heroes and heroines, like so many latter-day Alices, can't help perceive the fundamental ridiculousness of those who blithely hold the power of life and death over the universe.

This kind of humour is the ideal antidote to all pseudo-literary Tolkienoid pomposities and makes me optimistic for a more fun-filled, if not a better, world. Not only is the best humour back in print, but new authors like M John Harrison, Terry Pratchett and now Tom Holt are expanding on the tradition, doing rather more for fantasy than Douglas Adams has done for sci-fi. Publishers with the voices of lions and the hearts of rabbits are at last convinced that not all of us require the consolations of religiosity in our light reading.

Intelligent, original and solidly entertaining, Holt is a very good comic fantast and *Expecting Someone Taller* is a superb debut, introducing us to perhaps the nicest of reluctant heroes, Malcolm Fisher.

All his life Malcolm has been conditioned to believe himself a failure, existing only to offer contrast to his altogether more favoured sister. But when he accidentally runs over a Frost Giant, disguised as a badger, he finds himself the inheritor of the Tarnhelm, a magic cap, and also the actual Ring of the Nibelungs. The Tarnhelm lets him change shape at will. The Ring quite simply makes him Master of the World. Meanwhile, the surviving cast of *Götterdämmerung*, all eager to acquire these items, are waiting in the wings.

For the first time in its history, the Ring has a really pleasant owner, with the result that simply by being his ordinary, decent self, Malcolm creates a Golden Age on Earth. However, he soon realizes he has a terrible responsibility to remain even-tempered at all times, because, if he doesn't, earthquakes are felt in California; typhoons threaten the Malay Archipelago; diplomatic relations break down between the United States and the Soviet Union, and the English cricket team looks to lose a crucial match. By and large, Malcolm controls himself and the age of peace and plenty continues.

This situation doesn't suit the more apocalyptic and romantic sensibilities of Wotan, Alberich, the Rhine Maidens and a variety of Volsungs, Valkyries, Trolls and Norns whose various vested interests seem likely to bring about positively the last Twilight of the Gods, this time written not by Wagner but by Gilbert and Sullivan.

All this is thoroughly and satisfactorily resolved in the best traditions of comedy. Holt's delightful, readable, cheerfully intelligent book offers first-class comic relief to fantasy fans and to readers who simply mourn the passing of SJ Perelman, Gerald Kersh or (dare I say?) even PG Wodehouse.

# ■ Homage to Cornucopia

**From *Alan Moore: Portrait of an Extraordinary Gentleman*, 2003**

Although we have been in a movie together (Iain Sinclair's *The Cardinal and the Corpse; or, A Funny Night Out*) I have as far as I recall only met Alan Moore once at a party given for a Jerry Cornelius book by my crooked but idiosyncratic publisher Allison & Busby. We got on well and I was impressed enough to start following his work. He hadn't at that time made a big name in the popular arena, but I couldn't fail to be impressed by someone who sported an even wilder crop of hair than my own and whose eye carried the same sort of mad, uncompromising glint. Here, it seemed to me, was a genuine visionary, a generous risk-taker, someone barmy and bolshy enough to follow his own dream no matter what.

As someone who started his career as a teenager editing *Tarzan Adventures* and writing dialogue and text for old Hal Foster 'Tarzan' strips (because I preferred to reprint Foster and Hogarth over the less interesting artists who followed them and because the pages came without English versions), and who earned the bulk of his early living writing *Cowboy Picture Library*, *Thriller Picture Library*, 'Karl the Viking' and 'Olac the Gladiator' strips for Fleetway, I have to admit that I never saw what Alan saw in comics. My generation, who included some excellent writers and brilliant artists, like Hampson, Bellamy, the Embletons and Don Lawrence, simply saw comics as a way of earning a decent living. We did our best to make the strips as good as possible, within their terms, but we understood the medium to be about as permanent and respected as the daily newspapers we also worked for. We had no idea that there were people out there who were actually beginning to take note of the best of us. Our ambition was to get out of comics and into something more satisfying, whether it be novels or film-work. Our employers gave us limited scope for any ambition and the idea of using our work to say something substantial about the world was simply beyond our capacity to imagine!

My own idealism did, indeed, focus on popular art-forms, but I saw science fantasy as the way to go. In common with writers like Ballard, Disch, Sladek and a few others, I was trying to produce a form robust enough to carry the most sophisticated and furious ideas of my generation and carry them to a popular audience. Others chose film, music or broadcasting. We were all part of the same movement, whatever medium we chose.

As soon as I could I put comic work behind me and while 'Danny and his Time Machine' and 'Zip Nolan of the Highway Patrol' funded some early issues of *New Worlds*, I began to try to produce engaged and angry experimental fiction which reflected the modern world and appealed to an audience tired of the failures of contemporary modernism. For a while I saw 'intellectual' comic strips as an affectation of the French and while I enjoyed Moebius and Druillet (with whom I also worked), I wasn't at all sure that this wasn't a reverse of what I envisioned—that is, work using popular forms to get across traditionally 'serious' ideas to a popular audience. The French adoption of comics, at that time, I saw more as a sort of cultural raiding. These aren't opinions I've retained and I tell you all this to describe my own prejudices and biases of those days. In short, I simply couldn't see the possibilities of the graphic novel.

I think many of us would have remained as sceptical if it hadn't been for the work of one man, who began to come into his own with a series of DC comics questioning the nature of charismatic power and asking us who was watching 'The Watchmen'. While there had been attempts to humanise and, indeed, sentimentalise super-heroes (*Spider-Man*, for instance), no American, as far as I know, had ever questioned the actual nature of the super-hero and his relationship to the fascism we had recently defeated as well as the neo-fascism which began to spring up almost as soon as Hitler lay, a messy suicide, in his bunker or Mussolini was hoisted upside down at the hands of Italian partisans. What was especially substantial about Moore's work was not the innovations, the new riffs on the super-hero theme, but the fundamental questioning of the nature of power and those we invest with power. What British musicians did for American rock-and-roll, Moore began to do consistently for American comics. Without affectation or loss of impact, he used the graphic novel to confront the serious issues of his day. In this tradition he followed such popular cartoonists as Gillray and Hogarth, of course. Few genuine innovators are not moralists, from Bunyan and Blake to the present, but the trick is to entertain a broad audience while getting those moral points across.

It is maybe an irony that the angry moralist is generally an innovator—they have to be, since the old forms have, for their purposes, become corrupted or stale. It is equally ironic that they are usually followed by enthusiastic admirers who take their innovations and produce sophisticated riffs without understanding the sense of social outrage which inspired them. I have seen many come after Moore, but only one or two (Bryan Talbot, for instance) have understood what drives him and what his innovations are actually able to do. As others take up his notions and milk them to death, Moore leaves them his carrion and, showing the stuff of a genuine trail-blazer, moves on to fresh, new territories.

So it's fair to say that Moore changed the comics field for ever. Almost everything produced these days is produced in the climate he created. Any work of ambition, which seeks to confront social issues, must refer to him. And it's also fair to repeat as often as possible that Moore, unlike some innovators, has remained uncomfortably original, temperamentally unable to rest on his laurels or to exploit his early dynamic. While the movie version of *From Hell* might have brought in the Johnny Depp fans, it's clear that it ripped the heart out of the Moore original, as such movies often do. Moore was not producing another crossword puzzle speculation on the identity of the Whitechapel monster, he was writing another parable about power and its uses and abuses.

And that, of course, is also the background to his wonderfully entertaining new series *The League of Extraordinary Gentlemen*, which inhabits the world of late Victorian and Edwardian imperialism only to examine it, confront it, subvert it and so cast a cold eye on contemporary imperialism, manifested in the deeds and actions of George W Bush and his yapping dancing papillon Tony Blair.

Moore has produced a series which at its most popular level calls on our nostalgia for a world in which unselfconscious white men defended and expanded European and US empires, putting down rebellious 'natives', whether in the Middle East, India, Africa or the American homeland, giving their lives to preserve the expansionist values of the nation states they served. While he never labours his metaphors and allegories, they are always present, always speaking to the concerns and sensibilities of the modern reader.

Alan Moore has a generous soul, a cornucopian talent, an inventive mind, a fine social eye and a righteous political anger. He is also an outstanding entertainer. In his recent series, he has offered his readers all kinds of extra fun and adventure, as well as some delightful parodies, but at all times, frequently with sparing subtlety, he never ceases to confront the moral, political and social issues which continuously concern him. This is why he is still the best, why he has commanded so much respect for so many years and why, I am sure, he will continue to command respect for many years to come.

# ■ Forever Dying, Forever Alive

Thomas Mallory's *Le Morte d'Arthur*

**A foreword to the Cassell edition, 2000**

It's appropriate, I think, that Malory's great elegy for a mythical age of chivalry draws together the works of Welsh, French, German, Arab, Italian and other romancers to produce a national story whose resonances are universal. Celts, Saxons and Normans have all, in some form, claimed Arthur and his story for their own. The Matter of Britain itself attracts some hefty interpreters, from Spenser to Sinclair. Composers from Purcell onwards have given us musical interpretations. Tennyson was inspired by Malory's eloquent prose to offer Victorians an ideal past to emulate. Pre-Raphaelite, genre painting and symbolist work abounds with Arthurian imagery. Malory has had a thousand illustrators, including the Wyeths and Robinsons. Twain and White drew very different comedies from him. *A Yankee at the Court of King Arthur*, even as a musical interpreted by Bing Crosby, echoes the tragic heart of Malory, as does *Camelot*.

By all accounts, White himself, who inspired my idealism and whose personal kindness helped me become a writer, was lucky not to be jailed for buggery. He kept out of trouble by staying in Alderney. White's moving *The Once and Future King* sequence grows darker as it marches towards its tragic end with the relentless inevitability of Malory. Even in Disney's *The Sword in the Stone*, with its appalling cuteness, the myth itself shines through.

Henry Treece, one of the founders of the Apocalypse school of poetry, turned the story into a pure Celtic historical epic in his wonderful novel *The Great Captains* (1956), part of his sequence about the early settlement of Britain. In his version, Arthur is Artos the Bear, Count of the Saxon Shore, defender of Romano-Celtic culture against the invading Saxons and Guinevere is 'Golden Hair', almost a demigoddess. Morgana, Merlin and the rest all make appearances. There are dark sins of blood. There are no dramatic marvels in the book, just an extraordinary sense of brooding mystery, of a pagan mind-set, a way of personifying the forces of nature and understanding their real, often random, effect on human destiny. Using powerful, simple language, the novel depends upon character for its tensions. Treece preceded Mary Stewart, Nikolai Tolstoy and others who have since given Malory's Arthur a fresh and interesting literary twist. Treece treats the myth with reverence, but without mysticism and with only a hint of the supernatural. He remains one of the most substantial of Malory's successors.

It's a very robust myth. The Knights of the Round Table can survive anything, including being represented by Roger Moore, Tony Curtis, a slick-haired Alan Ladd and a boozed-up Richard Burton. It can occasionally surpass expectations as in Cornell Wilde's *Lancelot and Guinevere*. It can be knowingly debunked in a film like *Monty Python and the Holy Grail* (Terry Jones's first published work was, after all, on Sir Gawaine and the Green Knight!) and cloned for those fantasy trilogies which pop up like toadstools these days. It can even give a bit of class to a light beer commercial while remaining as uncorrupted as the Grail itself.

The Grail, by the time Malory came to write of it, had turned from a Celtic magic cauldron into a jewelled cup, a profound symbol of purity, holding the blood which had flowed from Christ as he hung on the cross. Only a knight of the purest chivalry was permitted its grace.

It hasn't always been a goblet. Wolfram von Eschenbach, in an early version of the Parsival story, describes the Holy Grail as a granite block (or emerald green stone), owing more to Mecca than Jerusalem. Did the Grail go West via the first Crusaders who had absorbed, almost unknowingly, the wisdom of Islam? An addition to a cultural fusion giving our national story the endurance of woven steel?

I agree with John Matthews that the idealism in Malory goes deeper than mere chivalric convention. I would not necessarily agree, however, that Sir Thomas Malory of Newbold Revel was too much of a villain to be the author. Marlowe might have done a bit of murdering before being murdered himself; rape is, alas, scarcely an uncommon crime; and Robert Nye (whose *Merlin* is one of the great versions of the myth) reminds us in his *Gilles de Rais* that Bluebeard himself, the tormentor and murderer of innumerable children, was a devout Christian, believing absolutely in the divinity and purity of Joan of Arc and risking his own life to defend her. Eloquence, intelligence and creative gifts, even idealism, as we've learned from Morgan-le-Fay, aren't the privilege of virtue. You can read irony into Malory pretty easily. Sometimes there's a foreshadowing of Cervantes, even

Jonson, and it's possible to believe one's hearing the echoes of a sardonic, knowing, educated language before Shakespeare transformed the voices of Elizabethan London into public poetry. I once planned a novel about Thomas Malory, condemned brute anticipating a painful death, veering between repentance and recidivism, hoping Caxton's *Le Morte D'Arthur* brings him enough cash to buy a release.

This great book contains robust, resonating myths and legends. Both are wonderful, but they are not the same things. Myths are the stories on which we base our lives. Legends are a colourful distraction from the grim realities the myths reveal. Professor Tolkien offers us, by his own prescription, the comfort of a fairy tale. Beneath the conventional pieties and train-spotter lists of the smiting and the smote, Malory presents real life in all its terrible comedy, its familiar tragedy, its unlikely hope. He gives us flawed, self-betraying, brutal, noble, greedy humanity. I like to think he is also giving us himself, on his back, a betraying sword fallen from his hand, a sardonic prayer on his lips, his repentant eyes defying oblivion, his bloody fingers grasping for the Grail.

# Introduction to *Lud Heat* and *Suicide Bridge* by Iain Sinclair

**From the Vintage edition, 1995**

No mere pasquinader, Iain Sinclair, larking, drags from London's amniotic silt the trove of centuries and presents it to us, still dripping, still stinking, still caked and frequently still defiantly kicking. In a series of ever more ambitious raree shows, ring-mastered with a mixture of relish and horror, with sly Celtic magic, with almost supernatural control, he has established himself as London's most original celebrant and one of her great creative voices. Peter Ackroyd, another subtle London visionary who has much in common with Sinclair, enthusiastically points to *Lud Heat* as an inspirer of his time-travelling *Hawksmoor*. Sinclair always leads my own imagination back to its true territory.

At its best London fiction has, in the past twenty years, become characteristically a visionary medium. In contrast to the rational, neatly written disappointments of Old Sir Kingsley, we have a Gillrayish Young Martin, as unenlightened as they come, sifting the Sunday morning Portobello gutters for revelations and gagging like Swift. We have the unfortunate Rushdie, not quite suffering almost the noblest fate of any visionary, and Fay Weldon and, these days, even AS Byatt. To those of us who have been exploring the territory for some time, it looked like everyone started knocking back the laudanum and investigating the paranormal pretty much as soon as a handy tourist trail had been blazed to the high ground where angels live. Territory penetrated and mapped long since by Sinclair and other extra-mural romantics like Angela Carter, Philip K Dick and JG Ballard in largely unpublicised expeditions since the mid-1960s.

It could be argued that the Occult has in the nick of time come to the aid of a threatened Orthodoxy. Talismans and omens are eagerly snapped up by a technologically challenged middle class. Some days, any old bone will do. Little visionary peels are slipped into Professor Lodge's jellies. The modern English novel contains almost as many ghosts and visitations as a Radcliffe three-decker. Spontaneous combustion should soon become an acceptable literary convention. A larger measure of supernatural melodrama is allowed to English domestic fiction than at any time since *Northanger Abbey* put a welcome lid on the Gothic's groaning trick coffin. Fifty-year-old notions of pulp SF writers become novel and exciting elements to spice the traditional mix. No wonder all these people are obsessed with vampires and rejuvenation formulæ.

Most of the recycling undertaken by English fiction's best-known careerists is about as effective as a Hampstead green bin in evading the inevitability of decay and death or even disguising that familiar, rather unpleasant sweetish smell. A bit of genre-borrowing isn't really the same thing as owning an original vision, but at least those grave-robbers and wine-waterers, those croppers and *colons*, helped produce the climatic shift which now allows a writer as original as Iain Sinclair to find the larger audience he has deserved for years.

He started showing up in high-street bookshops with a tangle of bombsite brambles and gaudy fireweed, the contents of long-buried basements, the muttering bones and whispering rags of his book-dealer's trawls through a city largely unexplored by her own inhabitants and thus insufficiently respected or feared, which he called *White Chappell, Scarlet Tracings*. He followed this with a structurally more sophisticated *Downriver* and then gave his widening readership *Radon Daughters* as glorious proof of his ever-increasing powers. A manipulative harlequin slipping through the alleys and twitters between one world and another, one supernatural realm and another, one age and another, weaving what at close perspective sometimes seems a chaotic course. Sinclair is an authentic visionary. Only at the end of a book, however, do we realise we've also been in the power of a genuine wizard, someone capable of tracing patterns and designs only barely perceptible to most people and, more to the point, able to reveal them to us.

Iain Sinclair's rich enthusiasms, his relish for the idiosyncratic, the original and profoundly grotesque gives his work a certain Dickensian flavour, but Sinclair's never as desperate as Dickens to discover hope. His literary heroes are Hodgson, Burroughs, the beats, the best pulp writers—all people madly in love with their own powers of language, their own massive turbulences, their own impossible paradoxes, their own perceptions of non-linear Time, of coexistent past, present and future, forever seeking to communicate the ecstasy of their unguarded souls to an average reader who has come to look to books for consolation, not inspiration.

Sinclair works as a revenant, a publicist, an archivist of the marginal, the unfashionable and the self-doomed, against the general tenor of Litbiz power politics whose vested interests permit no real assault on the status quo, where the established canon is forcefully promoted because lazy convention also acts to employ academics, critics and literary editors at good wages for small effort. The old catholics like Walter Raleigh or Quiller-Couch, who founded our English schools, were soon replaced in the early twentieth century by ambitious puritans, low Tories or worse.

It's against a tide hazardous with rotting driftwood, snapping predators and the not-quite-dead, queer lights reflecting from his benign dome, his terrifying glasses, that Sinclair poles his stately punt. He has a book-dealer's eye for obscurity and rarity, a way of spotting something which, until he fishes it out and polishes it up a bit, we hadn't ourselves noticed among the ordinary, the disgusting or even alarming flotsam of London's endless flux. Sinclair's people are no more bizarre or grotesque than most real people. That is to say, they are often, like Dickens's, larger than fiction, but in no way larger than life. Sinclair celebrates what is idiosyncratic in men and women, yet no character is stranger or more quirkily obsessed than half the people you'd meet on a long train trip. You always leave Sinclair, as you leave Rembrandt or Hals, looking at the familiar world with freshly informed eyes.

Sinclair's relish for language, for lost words and forgotten notions, his lust for metaphor, links him with earlier London visionaries like Blake or Eliot, just as the breadth of his enthusiasms allows the inspiration of Ginsberg and De Quincey, but it's neither his eclecticism nor his influences which define his work—it's his curiosity, his sense of justice, his bardic instincts, his generosity, and above all his original vision of what remains in spite of everything the greatest and most complex of all cities. He proves to us why London is still the best and most rewarding place for a poet or a novelist to live.

He proves it through celebrations like this.

# Norton Goes to the Seaside

## A Review of *Dining on Stones* by Iain Sinclair

**From the *Guardian*, 1st May 2004**

Norton is back. Iain Sinclair's culture-stocked avatar is at the seaside, giving it the treatment, turning the commonplace magical; his world freshly observed by a super-vigilant poet who makes the language his own and the world his oyster bar.

Norton, his body strapped with literary dynamite, undertakes a potential suicide mission from the capital to the coast. Kurtz, or someone pretending to be him, waits on the edge of reality in a rundown resort, at Cunard Court, a Ballardian neo-deco hotel gone to seed and infused with the kind of low-level despair you wouldn't know unless you'd actually done time amongst those peeling sea-fronts. Cheap renderings and patched stucco are moulded by a natural graffiti spelling out the dreams of failed novelists who come to escape, to set down their stories before it dawns on their horrified minds that the bungalows and boarding houses are as hungry as the sea. Stay too long and you inevitably drown in a quicksand of disappointment, seedy nostalgia and self-deception. Here, on the shingle of Kent and Sussex, East Enders habitually come to die, just as South and West Londoners choose Worthing or Bournemouth as their final resting places, no longer able to attain the dormitory heavens of Brighton and Hove.

Sidling around the Estuary, Sinclair, via Norton, has learned the secret of the English seaside: It was designed only to be visited. This is where desperate immigrants, former showbiz stars, ancient juvenile delinquents seek asylum. To live here for more than a few weeks is to be caught in a 1950s time-trap where all the prejudices, loyalties, hatreds, myths and desires of immediate post-WW2 England constantly recycle.

As sentiment and pastiche replace London's original identity to facilitate the appetites of heritage investors, it is to these museums of our deepest social history that Sinclair is drawn, his nonfiction and fiction offering an existential black-and-white version of Ackroyd's technicolour or Ballard's glamorous geometries. Where Ballard looks at the motorways as aesthetic markers of our group pathology, Sinclair peers under them, investigates the margins, wondering where the exits lead and who is buried in the foundations. Ballard takes the fastest route to Super Cannes and the middle-class nightmare; Sinclair checks out B-roads winding down to abandoned Butlin's holiday camps, undemolished tank-traps, Edwardian fun-palaces and concrete sea-forts, their layered paint recording the geology of English commonplace dreams that never made it into the 21st century and never will. He samples the pulp fiction, old movies, forgotten TV series which created lower middle-class fantasies, treads forgotten promenades and bleak beaches psychically mined against foreign invasion.

If you enjoyed *London Orbital*, Sinclair's last nonfiction, you'll find the transition to *Dining on Stones* seamless. Even some of the myth figures are the same. His writing restores any imagination grown tired of a standard English fiction which merely changes the nationality, gender or colour of its characters, never its conflicts or concerns, rarely its prosacked prose or plots.

Indeed it's fair to say that Sinclair is pretty free of plot altogether (though not story). The page-turning momentum of *Dining on Stones* is carried on language, character, curiosity. The rhythms and images form a dream-narrative, a super-accurate picture of time and place seen through a benignly glinting viewfinder as the author employs all he learned at that seminal South London academy, the London School of Film Technique. Without the options he offers, we could easily become punchy, but the book allows us the decision at which speed to take him, to reflect on a particular scene, storyline or observation.

Sinclair lets his characters make use of the maps he drew so thoroughly in previous nonfiction, to embark on journeys both sinister and hilarious (check out the vicar's severed head or the kidnappers who snatch the wrong Max Bygraves from Bexhill). Their accounts of explorations to the perimeter paradoxically lead deeper and deeper into the centre. They discover and lose clues to one another's visions and plans. Escapees from a *Carry On* movie shot by Godard in the style of Hitchcock, they leave their novels, postcards and sketches in roadside cafes for others to puzzle, offering pointers to further adventures like some piece of insane reality TV: *I'm a Novelist: Get me out of here.*

*Dining on Stones* is vivid and sardonic, describing a world as idiosyncratic and recognisable as Greene's or Ballard's; not exactly effortless, but as natural as walking, offering layers under layers, delicately digging through the archaeology of dreams and desires, resolving towards the condition of music, making you wonder if Sinclair's is the last possible form of literary writing before the CD takes over from the printed word.

# ■ How to Poach Magpie Eggs

## A Review of Iain Sinclair's *The Falconer* and *Slow Chocolate Autopsy*

**Previously unpublished**

*The Falconer.* A documentary investigation into the lives and careers of Peter Lorrimer Whitehead. A film in which nothing is true and everything is permitted. Directed and written by Iain Sinclair and Chris Petit. Graphics by Dave McKean. Stills Marc Atkins. Researched by and featuring Françoise Lacroix. Edited by and featuring Emma Matthews, with Olga Utetchenya, Howard Marks, Francis Stuart, Kathy Acker and others. Including samples from Whitehead's own films. Illuminations Films for Channel 4.

*Slow Chocolate Autopsy:* Incidents from the notorious career of Norton, Prisoner of London. by Iain Sinclair and Dave McKean. Orion Books, London.

### 1. The Owl of the Remove

'. . . treating this man's life as
*more* of a fiction than he's
treated his own . . .'

—Chris Petit, *The Falconer*

'. . . I've never felt that anything
*is* true . . .'

—Peter Whitehead, *The Falconer*

'. . . he's a vampire!'

—Iain Sinclair, *The Falconer*

'. . . he's a dangerous man . . .'

—Kathy Acker, *The Falconer*

*The Falconer* is the movie. *Slow Chocolate Autopsy* is the book. They are both by Iain Sinclair with collaborators Mark Atkins, Chris Petit and Dave McKean. Together they've forged a highly successful media mix, far more substantial and ambitious than anything else around. With a soundtrack by Martin Bennett, Olivier Messiaen, Graham Parker or some other musical force, it would be perfect. They've made something bigger than all of them.

Iain Sinclair by the consent of many peers is our finest modern English writer. His style is hammered and fashioned to match the realities of his very considerable subject matter, his mighty loyalties, his authentic junk.

A respected poet for many years, only in the last ten has Sinclair had any popular success. His *Lud Heat* inspired his friend Ackroyd's *Hawksmoor*. His novels have become increasingly assured and ambitious and have won him prizes. His modern tapestry, *Lights Out for the Territory*, a series of visionary essays on contemporary London, continues to be a best-seller.

Dave McKean is one of our great graphic artists. He's worked with writers like Moore and Gaiman expanding the possibilities of the mass-market comic book to extraordinary effect, making it the equal, as a potent medium for social criticism, to the best rock music. He comes fully into his own as an animator. His work includes the phenomenally successful DC series *Mr Punch* and *Black Orchid* with Neil Gaiman. With The Rolling Stones he produced *Voodoo Lounge*.

Chris Petit is an expert Londonista, critic, once a mainstay of *Time Out*, a cool thriller writer (*The Psalm Killer*, *The Packer)* who makes movies like *Radio On* and *Chinese Boxes*, novels like *Robinson.* He directed Sinclair's last documix, *The Cardinal and the Corpse: or, A Funny Night Out* (Channel 4).

Petit and Sinclair were originally approached by Peter Whitehead ('60s glam-*verité* band movies, *The Fall, Daddy,* a novel, *North End,* some stories, once-potent connections) to do an autobiographical documentary on Whitehead himself. A self-styled aeromancer and an inexpert conjure-husband, he is interested in falcony, claims to have been an egg-thief, a murderer, a woman, an *oiseauphile*, a corpse, and to have had incestuous relations with his amorphous young daughter. Whatever pulls your focus.

A self-starred pop extravaganza, Whitehead wanted this pair, of all people, to be his backing band, to amplify his stories for him and bring him out of obscurity to his due place amongst the gorgeous old names he evokes like spells. But this is the local witch-doctor offering Merlin a job as his assistant. Merlin, the great Welsh wizard, who can turn you into anything he pleases.

## 2. Old Mother Riley and Her Daughter Kitty Meet the Lancashire Witches

'The falcon is my myth . . .'

—Peter Whitehead

'Salome, the daughter. That is my myth . . .'

—Peter Whitehead

'What I believe is that when I take photographs of a woman, I *become* a woman.'

—Peter Whitehead

I felt Sinclair's power when I became a minor character in *The Cardinal and the Corpse*. The person you see on the screen doesn't even dress or talk like me. I have never worn a beret. I know nothing of Flann O'Brien. I found myself with a past, personality and a circle of friends I had never heard of until then. All real. Robin Cook. Jack Trevor Story. Gerald Kersh. Martin Stone. Alexander Barron. Driffield. Gerry and Pat Goldstein. Suddenly they'd been there my entire life. Nothing I'd complain about. You get used to it. But in a Phil Dick novel it would take surgery, an implant or at least a pill to achieve that degree of identity change.

Under Sinclair's power coincidence upon coincidence worked to compound my legendary Other. I felt it absorbing me. Replacing him. I was at last able to break for it, going West, the Docklands Light Railway squeal-ing and shuddering with an energy which either pursued or escaped me. I'm not sure I ever did get free. Is that you, Sinclair? Who is really writing this?

Whitehead wouldn't have had a chance. He's too far gone already. He's like Norton, prisoner of London, trapped in the book, who grows insubstantial the further he gets from the city's centre. His mysterious Olga already has him in a wheelchair. Whitehead's *ka* is in his cans of gyrated footage. Without them he has no earned ground, nothing to prove he ever lived and died or made his mark. The public never knew him. They can't place him. He's a substance-abuser. He'll take yours if you let him. Olga's pale in her painful new shoes. Hear Kathy Acker on the subject. He's not the first to demand the concrete-ness and meaning from us that the generality refuse him. He's got references. Antecedents. Corvo. Pursuing the hole. Born to make Symons's name. Yours, too, if you'll let him. The Falcon. Gerhardi. Copouts. George Sanders, smooth Hollywood demi-hero, as Horus. Angel of death. Carrion for the crow houses. *Hippolais polyglotta.* Infamous forgeries. Mocking birds. Ossian. The shadow of wings. A forgotten feather. A distant dove. A shrike. A whiff of snuff.

Here's Whitehead in the movie, haunting the hospital he calls Alphaville, where he claims to have died and been resurrected, frowning over entrails, spinning his totems, making claims of kinship with old stones. Here he is in the book, changing names and roles, sketched by McKean, ghosted by Sinclair, his lures emptying into the air as he chants his over-rehearsed mantras, displays his primitive *tilsamim*, his desert charms. The mummified falcons, petrified apes, familiar *bijouterie* of backstreet Cairo, the stock of desert *souks* pitched beside the tourist routes, are buried, resurrected, reburied, re-resurrected, forever preserved. Popular pre-war grotesques before Dachau ruined the trade. The Arabs are natural taxidermists.

The lost and stolen treasures of Bedouin are made ageless by dust. Deserts hide time even better than oceans. Deserts preserve and perpetuate the past. Urban deserts are best. Mad and isolated the live falcons travel on the arms of nomad retainers in the elevators of the Saudi Hilton. You come face to face with them. Glaring from furious bondage.

What makes them the object of those needy blue eyes shifting from under the bone-white, gene-bleached hair, on a skeleton that walked into the Yorkshire Dales fifteen hundred years ago and only walked out again when Appalachia called? Those people were white headed like that before they ever left England. And longed for deliverance.

Whitehead's recent ancestors might not have been at all shocked at his goings on. There's much more of it about than you think. When I lived in the northern dales I was contacted by different sorcerers—all blacksmiths—all very bluff—and asked for my formula for putting souls into iron. Once, in the Hill Inn, Chapel-le-Dale, someone else offered to show me how. There were days you'd have thought The Damned and every Goth band in the world were flapping and squawking like ravens all over the fells. During the Falklands adventure magnificent RAF Vulcans, the size of towns, sliced the air just below my feet, but the slab I hung on had known blood sacrifice until the 19th century at least. Every name was romantic largely because romantics had named everything. That's how the waters come down from Lodore. Whitehead's not even unusual up there.

The team gives him more identities than he bargained for. Three at least from Sinclair. He's McKean's. He's Petit's. Atkins'. He might belong to Olga Utetchenya. And conclusively he's Françoise Lacroix's and Emma Matthews'. Their faces tell other stories. For in the film the power, the attention, the curiosity, the sense of investigation is increasingly focused on the female characters who begin as choruses, narrative devices, and end as the real mysteries. Flapping like a pantomime dame, Whitehead desperately tries to upstage them. Woman? You need a woman? Whitehead the pornographer, patroned by both Howard and Harrison Marks, becomes their subject. First they note the absences. Then they begin to fill him in. Singing like a charm of blackbirds.

And where's the real black bird? Who's that trading in the wings? Some shifty Anglo-Saxon. Archer? Chandler? Thatcher? Spade. Houston's round robin ace? Or just Eddie Constantine pretending to be Marlowe? Robed as a bride? Or stripped bare by his bachelors even. Slipping over the surfaces until he finally slides off at an unexpected tangent. Look for him in McKean's hawk-woman, his bat-mobiles, his fluttering depths.

Unlike the boy writers with whom he is sometimes compared, Sinclair seems to demonstrate a genuine liking for women, a proper respect. Which is further informed by his deep sense of outrage, at the casual, common injustices of the ordinary world. Rather than turning women into romantic ikons who can then be killed in exciting ways with a bit of sonorous retrospective VO, Sinclair and Petit let the women carry the work. Typically, Sinclair casts the potent ikons back into real people. He gets as good as he gives. It's what marks this writing. It has depth. It has humanity. Rather than the noirish sentimentalities which usually substitute for a heart and soul in those confections, Sinclair's work has considerable feeling. Which reminds you that for all his vast visionary gifts, his wonderful bardic flair. Sinclair is also a seasoned husband, a father, an earner, a working stiff.

## 3. Meet the Scarecrow

'I did it physically. I copulated with falcons.
I was in love with those falcons and they were in love with me.'
—Peter Whitehead

However respectable Sinclair's home life, however reassuring his looks (he really should have been a liberal archbishop), his neighbours know that he departs frequently on mysterious trips. Leaving at night. Returning before dawn. With blanketed hooves, he rustles across the border, slips unseen through the cultural mist, sticking to the margins, smuggling spirits from where the mix is richest and official attention is off.

Concentrated information. Low interference. Language so dense with meaning almost every word has a thousand specific contexts and every analogy tells a hundred stories.

It's in the margins that natural language is at its most poetic. The closer it gets to the middle, the less complex, the more it becomes a specific pidgin suitable for street signs, newspapers, low politics, trade and simple debate. Okay for peacepipes and campfires, for the less complex forms of negotiation. But not much good for orientation. Or fine definitions. Or tuning up for the new century.

By and large it's in this simple pidgin, with some modifications, that most Englit fiction and criticism is now written. It mourns the loss of an educated public. As usual, of course, the public's cheerfully educating itself elsewhere.

Sinclair lives in East London, in the Hackney marches, the borderline marked by fake Le Corbusier towers, where the language is made, where context is defined. These days everyone sings in English. It's the language of power. Of public magic. Naturally, it's Sinclair's chief instrument.

As Sinclair knows, for he was raised in Wales where they're connoisseurs of language, London is the root of our common tongue. London English retains the authority of age and experience while adapting constantly to changing contexts. It's efficient and rapid. It requires no preservation, no formal rules. The city provides authentic definitions, the first and last words. It's a poet's best stock. Gorgeous alleys stuffed with secret voices.

Sinclair navigates these amniotic gutters. In hidden synagogues he studies forgotten texts by lost London writers like Zangwill, Pett Ridge and Kersh. He sits in obscure pubs and listens. He watches. He absorbs the elements. Here no common medium feels safe and only well adapted magicians can trawl with confidence. *The Daily Mail* fears this world. But *The Times* can prove it doesn't exist. Others dismiss reports as mere *nostalgie de la boue*. TV channels occasionally let some of the news out at 4 a.m., when cult movies air and only speed-crazed insomniacs get a hint of what's happening in the real world, on the psychic mainland. The world beyond the screens.

Off-duty, Sinclair hangs out with magicians—people like Alan Moore the writer; the poets Brian Catling and Aidan Andrew Dunn, with sculptor Rachel Whiteread who makes memory concrete and Mike Goldmark, the barefoot quixote, who blew his entire inheritance on the fantasy of the Royal Albert Hall *Return of the Reforgotten* poetry night. With divine bull-shitters like Cook and Marks. People who, in the course of an hour, can retell your anecdote as their own and make you think it was never yours to start with. He sits down with the talkative dead, Jewish East End writers, rappers and revenants. With the undiscovered and the self-invented. People who long for public authority, who think they can change the world through the alchemy of their art. The insistence of their golden tongues. Their improved versions of the other. They hint of better realities for all.

They don't turn up much in the commoner denominations, in the regular media we all casually regard as an analogue of actuality. But they're not unheard. They often make a good living. Not from university literary magazines, rarely from municipal art projects or local television, but as often as not in mass-selling comic books called *Swamp Thing* or *Transmetropolitan*. Like the notorious Savoy productions from Manchester (*Lord Horror* and *ReverbStorm* comics plus PJ Proby records that growl with anti-authoritarian fury, bizarre readings of *The Waste Land*), these comics are now as consistently angry and suspicious and coherent and profoundly subversive as Gillray or Grosse. As sf once was in the hands of Dick, Bester and Ballard.

All this in the margins, if you like, where high culture can't walk alone or in any degree of safety, but not in the margins of the real world where real literature is made. The graphic story can sometimes do what sf sometimes did in the sixties. For the same reasons. When Ballard was first publishing his 'concentrated novels' like *The Atrocity Exhibition* in *New Worlds* no established critic would take them seriously. We knew we were safe when both Kingsley and Martin Amis bemoaned and dismissed his Frenchified nonsense. Clare Tomalin suggested he seek psychiatric help. And so it went.

It meant you could work unselfconsciously, unobserved by the establishment. As happens with comics today.

### 4. I, Said the Sparrow

'It's all about addressing verticality,
rather than linear narrative.'

—Peter Whitehead, *The Falconer*

In comics the respected names include Talbot, Gaiman, Gibbons, Simonson, Moore, Goodwin, Chaykin, McKean and a handful of others, all experts at non-linear narrative, all of whom have large followings and who have, like some of the musicians identified with Stiff Records, quietly carried the matured values of the '60s into the pragmatic nineties. What attracted WS Burroughs to sf in the '50s and '60s is what attracts Iain Sinclair to certain comics. It's a medium heavy with metaphor and symbolism, much of it sophisticated, conscious.

Here are creative intelligences as good, if not better, than anything you'll find in academia, but speaking a living language, with a specific attitude and sensibility, an instinct which keeps them out of the universities and the art magazines and in the streets and pubs. Where their own experience began and their own stories are still being told. To keep their judgement perfect, they address an audience drawn from the same backgrounds, with the same attitudes. Who can follow the idiom, understand the vocabularies. People who still take authenticity for granted. Who recognise it and pay for it and won't buy anything else. Just the way an earlier generation sought out the authentic voices of Leadbelly, Hank Williams, Bessie Smith or Woody Guthrie and created Kerouac and Dylan, Don DeLillo, Andrea Dworkin, Hunter S Thompson and other eloquent devils.

Iain Sinclair has been writing stories and making films for decades. Only in the relatively recent past, with the mainstream publication of his first novel *White Chappell, Scarlet Tracings* and the showing of his and Chris Petit's movie *The Cardinal and the Corpse*, has he started to creep into our living rooms.

With his happily placed *Lights Out for the Territory* which has become one of those icons you never have to read as long as its firmly at your side, he even made it into the dim consciousness of Bookerland, the world of primitive Englitspik, whose pharisees think Fay 'n' Martin must be the meat of the great tradition and wonder why they're starving. Who grasp at Sinclair's language like manna. They know it's nourishing but don't much like the gamey taste. They're addicted to blancmange. Like that schoolmasterly James Wood, carefully pronouncing from some provincial sinecure, how the flavour is rich and fresh but the unfamiliar ingredients are definitely wrong.

Kyril Bonfiglioli, our nasty old charmer, long-since dropped into the black well, fencing ex-Balliol self-tuner, once took Whitehead's home town in an afternoon. Flying kites. He knew all about englitsmen. Lifting his poor fat head from the carpet he'd say, these people can go right to the heart of your story, dear, and tell you to cut it out.

Sinclair has been too long getting it down to listen to politicians. He has the same dogged determination to stay where the action is that you find reflected in McKean's drawings.

Others may offer buzzing highways, charming Scotch junkies, the chittering self-approving English, misted Janeites and the stripping unemployed, but only Mike Leigh and Iain Sinclair deal in the real matters of Britain. Without the machinery of sentiment, they celebrate our recognisable heroic selves. They judge but they understand what they judge. They see what our privileges frequently make invisible. They have a fair idea whose side they're on.

I know they're on mine. Most of that other stuff could have been written by Wolf Mankowitz. The kids are alright, governor. Local honey. Guaranteed pasteurized.

Sinclair finds authenticity in the daily life and thoughts of second-string London mobsmen, glorious weirdoes and his invisible walker, in William Burroughs, speedfreaks and mad Poles. Observations from life. Fact and fiction grown sublimely coherent.

Whitehead comes and goes through the book. He's Wolfehead. He's Pytchley. Sometimes he might even be Norton himself. All aggressive ghosts. Dybuks and the undead. Needing us much more than we need them. Back and forth, the book's a shuttle, weaving a thousand tapestries, a million stories. Each re-read, each new look at the film, provides a fresh insight, another plot.

Like the climbing egg-thieves, Sinclair and his team blaze their trails through desert and up rock, finding routes which are dangerous, new, circuitous. They cross barriers via cave systems, underground conduits and rivers, elbowing along gutters, chimneying between walls, jamming in the cracks, traversing across, absailing down. Filching the ingredients of the perfect omelette.

Amplifying, complementing, shedding new light, revealing new angles, new information, this fusion of first class literary writing, avant-garde filming, state-of-the-edge graphics blurring and blending high and popular art until the distinctions become only irritating, does what we were all fearing wasn't being done.

You couldn't ask for a better beginning. Call it computer-literate Conrad for the Age of Virtuality if you need the plummy bloom of yesterday's laurels, but, while Thackerayan sympathy and Eliotian moral perception can easily be found here, those comparisons tend to be useless, even confusing. This is the start of something new. And I think big.

Nothing's now stopping us from packing this lot digitally on a fifteen coin CD and there we'll have it—authentic narrative art for the 21st century. Easily accessed on your home screen. Sounds and pictures. Something we can all understand, even if we don't always know what's going on. Sit back and let it consume us.

Meanwhile this package—almost quaint in its massivity, like a classic motor—is the only one to get. See the book. Read the movie.

They'll change your mind.

# ■ The Triumph of Time

## A Review of R Crumb's *Genesis*

### From (French) *Libération*, 5th November 2009

> The stuff off the main road was where the force of reality was.
>
> —Bob Dylan

Some artists are so thoroughly copied they are constantly changing their style to dodge their imitators, some doggedly pursue their own star, seeing in others only the same influences as theirs. The effect, it has to be said, is often the same. The work follows certain impulses, sometimes of experience, sometimes of style, sometimes of technique but frequently, of course, of all three.

Arguably, the fifteen-year period of iconoclasm and innovation we call 'the '60s' began in 1963 with the release of the Beatles' first single and the assassination of JFK, ending with the final Stiff tour of 1978. Those of us who tried to face certain realities in the beginning are still trying to face them now or have settled for comfortable repetition. That repetition pays dividends is why there are so many tribute bands making a decent living. Albums are played note for note on stage with exactly the same amount of time between each number. Bruce Springsteen, the great hope of rock and roll, takes *Born to Run* on the road for a lot more gigs and a lot more money than his first tour. Brian Wilson reproduces the whole of *Pet Sounds* to big audiences. The Beatles albums are remastered to sound exactly as you might have heard them had you been privileged to share a set of cans with George Martin at Abbey Road. Frankly it reeks to me of nostalgia rather than re-examination. All great fun, but for those who somehow managed to maintain that spark of questioning, attacking integrity originally firing their work, it really hasn't been enough. Such artists feel compelled to keep on their own paths, irrespective of audience expectation. What they do and who they are remain inextricably bound together. You could argue that Ray Davies redoing 'Waterloo Sunset' as a choral piece is moved at least partly by a commercial instinct to resell former hits, but in no way can Bob Dylan be accused of exploiting his fans by putting out *Christmas in the Heart* or, indeed, any of his records. His journey remains as internal, as personal as it ever was. And the same can be said for Robert Crumb.

If Dylan was the soundtrack to the '60s, then Crumb was the illustrator who best represented the spirit of the times. Both were unregenerate outsiders, both identified with the marginalized, the eccentric and the idiosyncratic. With roots in the Midwest they questioned everything they had grown up being taught. As soon as they could they left home and headed for the nearest urban complex which suited them. In Dylan's case it was to New York and the coffee-houses, Jack Elliott and Woody Guthrie. In Crumb's it was ultimately to San Francisco, underground comics and 'alternative' rock bands. Both attracted controversy from liberal America almost as much as from conservatives. Dylan when he returned to the electric guitar (he had originally been in a rock band called The Golden Chords) and Crumb for his use of stereotypical 'lolitas' and Afro-Americans which were greeted literally with howls of outrage. Both, as it happened, drew considerable musical inspiration from blues and bluegrass music and Crumb soon became associated, for his posters and album covers, with Bay Area bands. If Dylan's 'Blowin' in the Wind' and *The Times They Are A-Changin'* were the theme tunes of my generation, Fritz the Cat, Mr Natural and 'Keep on Truckin' were our thematic images.

Both artists have kept faith with themselves to a degree that is extraordinary for people subject to so much adulation and commercial success. Both have also been accused of failing to keep faith with their fans who, of course, have imposed an astonishing weight of interpretation onto their work. Crumb's career has followed a curve from *Zap Comix* to *The New Yorker* but, like Dylan, he has never modified his work to court a publisher's good will. Those who objected to Dylan's various changes of style were frequently the same people to object to Crumb's *Kafka*. They wanted Mr Natural to keep on truckin' forever.

Crumb was always a satirist, making fun of underground culture as much as he employed racial and sexual stereotypes to take a hard look at the American people. We became used to reading irony into his work, just as we read it into Dylan, when it often wasn't intended.

When the buzz began to go around four or five years ago that Crumb was planning a graphic version of *Genesis*, it was generally thought that he would be offering some kind of irreverent parody intended to strike out at the Bible-bashing fundamentalists who grew powerful in the US during the '80s. But, like Dylan, Crumb admits to a strong sense of mysticism.

In an interview with Steve Bell, the *Guardian* cartoonist, in 2005 he was asked about *Genesis*. Was it intended to offend Christians. He replied 'I don't have to offend them. I just want to make them see, like, the scene where Abraham is having sex with his daughter-in-law, who is faking being a temple priestess. That's in the Bible. How will they take that, I don't know. I'm just going to do what's in there. It tends to get glossed over. It's surprising what's actually in there, when you read it closely.' He not only resisted his audience's interpretation of his work but planned to do the graphic as straight as possible, consulting only Biblical scholars (specifically the Californian Robert Alter) and historical reference to ensure his architecture, landscapes and costumes were as faithful as possible to the appropriate periods. His characters have a generally Mediterranean look except for God, who looks pretty much the way he has been represented in European biblical illustrations (his God bears a resemblance to Charlton Heston, while his Adam looks a bit like Johnny Weissmuller, the most famous of a long line of screen Tarzans). If Crumb's publishers around the world were expecting a controversy from Church spokesmen, they appear to have been largely disappointed. The book's scholarship has been acknowledged at least in the Protestant world. Even a French cleric was heard recently praising it on radio. My guess is that Crumb has yet to receive his routine supply of death-threats from Texas and the American Bible Belt where most of my own (for *Behold the Man*) came from in the 1960s and '70s. Of course, the caution of American publishers, who added to the book's cover a warning that 'Adult supervision is recommended for minors', has done a little to cut down on the criticism. The fact is Crumb's *Genesis* is a great page-turner, especially for one who really never read the original. There's an awful lot of smiting, adultery and fornicating going on and the God character seems to take credit for a lot of stuff after the event, but apparently it's all there in the original, because I checked. Even Crumb's faithful listing of the begats carries an almost lunatic rhythm. The blood, sex and supernatural elements of the story offer an illumination of modern Middle Eastern politics which, I have to say, made me at once despair and hope for peace in the region.

Like Dylan, Crumb has lasted so long not by adapting to passing taste but on the contrary steering his own ship firmly in the direction his instincts take him. The result is that the world is inclined to catch up with him, rather than the other way around, and the insights in Crumb's *Genesis* are as sharp and smart as they are idiosyncratic.

Many Americans, at least, have not quite known how to respond to something which is clearly both respectful, honest (Crumb has no religion) and yet which gives such a fresh account of itself. For that is the true success of Crumb's *Genesis* and why he has no intention of doing further work of the kind: While he employs no tricks of novelty, no special change of perspective, no evident ironies or mordant commentary, he brings his original artist's eye to a powerful slice of our common mythology. He achieves this with the same sense which makes so many great artists return again and again to our folklore and legends for subjects to which we respond on sometimes unfamiliar levels but which have come to represent, in profound ways, every one of our fears and aspirations.

# ■ Conan: American Phenomenon

**Foreword to *Conan the Phenomenon* by Paul Sammon, 2007**

For all his roots in our earliest fables, Conan the Cimmerian is a thoroughly American creation. Like Natty Bumppo, Ahab, Tarzan, Hopalong Cassidy, Sam Spade or Superman, he is as much a product of his culture and landscape as Gandalf or Maigret are of theirs. Some writers reacted to the Depression by creating worldly-wise high verbals investigating human courage and villainy in mean streets. Others reacted with glorious escapism—with historical melodramas like *Captain Blood*, musicals like *Gold Diggers of Broadway* and westerns which routinely used the landscapes of California and Arizona the way Brontë used the Yorkshire moors, as an essential part of the narrative. Take those a short step further and you are in the brutal, glamorous, Gothic-inspired world of Robert E Howard's Conan.

There's no record of Howard learning the ukulele as a result of seeing a Busby Berkeley musical (if he ever did see one) but it's clear he was affected by the Depression and by the wild, endless landscapes of Texas where the weather changes so suddenly and frequently that natives tell you, if you don't like it, you just have to wait a few minutes and you'll get something more to your taste. It operates on a Biblical scale. Famed as they are for their boasting, Texans are only stating the truth when they claim something to be bigger, wilder or more terrifying than almost anything the rest of us are more familiar with. I'm an Englishman, trained in English understatement, but when someone in France tells me how terrible their storm is, I have to bite my tongue to stop from murmuring 'Storm? That's not a storm. That's a light shower where I come from.' Although I have been trapped by frightening tornados in, of all places, Majorca, I had never known what it was to be on the edge of a Texas twister until one went past, taking one of our huge elm trees down and demolishing the local filling station in a matter of moments. I survived the Blitz and the V-bombing of London and know how a place can be metamorphosed by violence, how familiar landscapes can become suddenly utterly transformed, but I was still shocked by the sights I came upon in East Texas and Louisiana after Katrina hit or by TV footage of tsunami damage. Americans, considered a little jumpy about terrorism by Europeans who have lived with it over a longer time, casually accept natural realities on a scale which would scare the pants of the average Dane or Scot. But that is one of the many mysteries of America, which the US never stops debating and which brought me to settle in what many still consider one of the least progressive parts of the Union.

Another of those mysteries has to be the dichotomy of an unshakeably republican and democratic nation's love affair with the notion of Royalty, especially British royalty; even (as when Errol Flynn's Robin Hood defies the wicked Prince John) slightly sinister royalty. Early in his written career, as opposed to the fictitious chronology later imposed upon him, the smart, suspicious Cimmerian, barbarian-and-proud-of-it, became King Conan, ideally demonstrating that dichotomy. Indeed, his creator's stories often considered the will to egalitarianism as opposed to the glory of kingship, just as his contemporary (in the pulps) Philip Marlow was both fascinated and repelled by Californian high society. Somewhat in denial, Conan couldn't resist the top job and property bonanza (feudalistic cultures, after all, give ownership of the country to the king) when it was offered. He felt awkward with the responsibilities and problems of power and never could identify himself with his nation, the way the better-respected European monarchs did. Even in Europe foreign usurpers generally have a hard time of it, as the Hanovers did until they achieved the biggest and best rebrand ever in turning their early aristocratic indiscretions and leadership failures of the 18th and new 19th centuries into the security and acceptability of 'La Roie Bourgeoise', the Victorian Empire, becoming role models not only for the British middle class but also for the newly rich industrialists of their former American colonies. Not the most comfortable identity for those who had inherited a genuinely egalitarian tradition which had made their forbears move constantly west in the search for a place where they could be free and where social pretension, sophistry and guile could be dealt with swiftly, often in a straightforwardly violent manner.

The defeated and disappointed survivors of Cromwell's Revolution, knowing what not to do, as well as what they still yearned to do, began to settle in the Americas soon after Charles II was restored to the British throne. Their mixture of puritan conservatism and rebellious anti-authoritarianism came to characterise American rhetoric long before it led to a full-scale uprising against the Crown. Their Puritanism looked back to Eden as much as it looked forward to the New Jerusalem but it also brought with it the ills as well as the cure to the Promised Land. That dichotomy between paternalistic fundamentalism and individualistic egalitarianism was established in those pioneers long before they arrived. Their some-what self-contradictory celebration of the simple, honest, nature-loving Pure Man, suspicious of over-civilised ways, together with the judgemen-tal, law-loving Tamer of the Wild, found its expression in Fenimore Cooper, Longfellow and the Transcendentalists. The differences between democrat and dictator, intellectual orator and practical soldier, fiery preacher and phlegmatic law-maker, thanks to the muscularity of the Constitution and the Bill of Rights, continue to be part of that great American conversation, symbolised in fiction down the generations in forms which reflect or even sometimes change the taste of their times.

Landscape has played an important part in American fiction since *The Last of the Mohicans*, becoming a personification of a prevailing mood, whether it be in the once endless forests of the North, the lush rivers and bayous of the South, the rich plains and mountains of the West or the dark, urban jungles of the East. All continue to attract writers and some, like Robert E Howard, found a way to combine most of them in stories which allowed their heroes to be city thieves or threatened kings in one story and self-sufficient frontiersmen in another. Howard also added the supernatu-ral element, the terror of the unknown, which had characterised a strand in American fiction at least since Poe. To a boy like me, therefore, he offered pretty much everything I liked to read in one vivid package.

I loved Leigh Brackett's stories of Eric John Stark and the Sea Kings of Mars before I ever read *Conan the Conqueror*, the retitled half of an Ace Double which had Brackett's *Sword of Rhiannon* as the other half—the half which first attracted me. I next found Conan in the second-hand shops of London, where it was still possible, if you were lucky, to buy cheap pre-war copies of *Weird Tales*. I looked for issues containing Howard and for Seabury Quinn, who were my favourite contributors. It would be years before I learned that these two were also the favourites of most *Weird Tales* readers. By then I had become rich enough to buy Arkham House's *Skullface and Others* and the Gnome Press Conan editions. Soon, and I was still in my mid-teens, I was corresponding with L Sprague de Camp, then Howard's greatest publicist and supporter, and before long I was discussing writ-ing a new Conan tale for Hans Stefan Santesson's idiosyncratic magazine *Fantastic Universe* where a few of the pastiches were beginning to appear.

As it happened, the story which I started writing, in collaboration with my fellow enthusiast Jim Cawthorn was never completed (at least as a Conan story) because the magazine folded as so many idealistic ventures of the kind have folded before and since. I would not return to Conan or Howard for a number of years, when Jim and I produced an Elric outline for Roy Thomas to write in one of the early Conan comics. I have said elsewhere (in my study of epic fantasy, *Wizardry and Wild Romance*) how bad I think those pastiches were, so I'm rather glad we never had the chance to write some of them. The republication of the original stories in their original order helped me recall how good Howard really was.

Some years after I had made my name with my own epic fantasy characters, I moved to central Texas, a few hours drive from Cross Plains, where Howard spent most of his life. It was a surprise to my friends that I chose to leave the sophistication of London for rural Texas, but I was determined to find out for myself, as best I could, what that part of America was really like. I had no interest in substituting one large city for another, much as I loved New York, Chicago and Los Angeles, and I wanted to avoid, as much as possible, running into fellow countrymen who gathered in the enclaves of New England and Hollywood to reassure themselves in the way that Christopher Lee reassured me when I met him in Hollywood that the secret of survival in America was 'never to forget that you're British'. If I still have no theories about why Howard decided to end his life, at least I feel I have a better understanding of the world which shaped him and inspired him.

That gloriously all-American hero Conan the Cimmerian came out of the remote northwest the way his creator came out of the remote southwest. Howard would have known people, both red and white, who recalled the great wars between the Americans and the indigenous tribes, the Kiowa, Comanche, Apache and Navajo—names which made the invaders forever careful to save their last shots for themselves and their loved ones. In common with many of his contemporaries, Howard saw the old virtues fading as the Depression and the Dustbowl separated the weakened individuals from predatory banks and loan-companies until folk-heroes like John Wesley Harding and Bonnie and Clyde began to symbolise people who at least had the nerve to take fate in their own hands and stand against the wealthy industrialists and resource-owners who ensured their own security at the expense of the rest of us.

Like all his great American predecessors, Conan judged men not by their status or their words, but by their actions. I suspect Howard had much the same way as Conan of looking at body language at least as much as he listened, of measuring his words before he replied to a question, of testing the motives of those he encountered. This might have been why certain others in Cross Plains were made uncomfortable by him. I'm not suggesting that Howard was especially conscious of the lessons he had learned and it's clear he tended to romanticise the world around him. He was, however, creating heroes whose characters and experience resonated with his own. If he hadn't actually visited, say, the great Chaco site where New Mexican natives had established the most sophisticated 'Indian' civilisation in what is now the US, only to see the whole thing destroyed in less than a century by the forces of nature and human lack of foresight, he must have read about it. The Southwest was full of men like Narbona, Mangas Coloradas, Geronimo and Cochise who made their stand against those who sought to 'civilise' them and fought often to their last breath against the 'death-bringers', of hunters and trail-blazers like Jim Bridger, Jedediah Smith, Bowie, Houston and Carson, who took up local ways both from preference and practicality in order to survive in those unforgiving landscapes and whose published words made it clear that they had no faith in government promises or the ignorant soldiers sent to break them.

All those characters had become fodder for the Eastern dime novelists long before Howard was born. Kit Carson remembered coming upon one of his fictitious adventures in the camp of a band of Navajo he had trailed, trying to rescue a captured white woman who was killed moments before he could reach her. It troubled him that the woman might have kept a false hope alive by reading the novel, which echoed her own experiences but in which, of course, Kit was able to save the kidnapped beauty. Jesse James and his gang used to pass around fictionalised versions of their own lives while Buffalo Bill, it seemed, came to believe his own legend. No doubt Howard read these tales, or something of the kind, and longed to emulate those heroes. I know that I did, in South London, where there was a lot less chance of it happening.

This isn't the place to ask if real 'barbarians' actually turn their noses up at the often empty attractions of civilisation, though it's worth remembering that the best way to break the ice with an Iroquois was to offer him a nice cup of tea and a decent blanket (which, among other things, dried a lot faster than fur or leather) and that you did him no courtesy by admiring his noble savagery, given that his sophisticated federal system is today considered the original of our own. Conan, like Uncas and Umslopogaas, is an ideal rather than a reality. A symbol of a certain kind of perfection and all the more enduring as a result. The mistake of Howard's literary contemporaries, even into the 1960s, was to judge fantasy and fantastic characters according to the tenets of a realism which had come to dominate our literature at most levels. I'm a huge fan of the realists and the best modernists and tend, these days, to read Balzac, Zola and Proust in preference to Edgar Rice Burroughs or even the magic realists, but when I want to read fantasy, I want it full strength and that's how Howard supplies it. What attracted the symbolists of the 19th century to pulp tales like *The Mysteries of Paris* was the fact that Eugene Sue's penny dreadful *feuilleton* serials did find an echo in the unliterary tastes of most people and that those tastes, far from being unsophisticated, reflected a reality far more powerful than most of the bourgeois novels whose function was to reassure respectable society rather than reveal horrors often all-too familiar to the semi-literate masses. In the 20th century the surrealists and their heirs developed a similar liking for pulp thrillers and science fiction.

It was in this populist tradition, borrowing elements from French, German and British sources, that the American dime novels came to entertain people. Frequently, like *Frankenstein* and the Gothic, this kind of fiction showed a deep suspicion of all authority figures, whether they represented church or state. They tended to be sentimental in support of the dispossessed and the unenfranchised. Often, the shadowy villain would turn out to be a cleric or an aristocrat and the hero, for a variety of reasons, would be drawn from an underclass. Voicing the aspirations of the real underclass, the author could still suggest that the reason some privileged aristo was corrupt, unstable, selfish and so on was because they had failed to rise to the noble demands of the institution, just as the noble savage (or poor working girl) might eventually be revealed as a person of aristocratic blood. The murals on our 15th century parish church, when I lived in Oxfordshire, took great relish in showing bishops and kings falling out of the dipping scales of justice and into the maws of the horrid beasts of hell, while simple commoners were in the opposite scale, rising to heaven. That identification with powerlessness and martyrdom was always a strong part of the early church's appeal.

Conan's dark mistrust of priests and politicians was in the same tradition. He would not have continued to attract an audience if he hadn't found strong resonances in people like me. As representative politics goes through one of its periodic crises, where it seems so many of us are again disenfranchised, the attraction of the independent hero begins to increase again and I don't think it's any coincidence that Conan and his ilk have begun to enjoy renewed popularity as we struggle to restore the balance of public life. When our world gets this complicated and we feel helpless to affect its big problems, we turn with relief to heroes and heroines whose troubles, when they have them, are on an heroic, life-or-death scale, whose dreams are equally heroic and who inhabit landscapes reflecting our deepest, most archetypical emotions.

Conan, like Tarzan and others before him, has also had the good fortune, from the very beginning, of attracting a number of brilliant illustrators and narrative artists. Tarzan had J Allen St John, Foster, Hogarth, Marsh, Krenkel and others. Conan had Brundage, Frazetta, Windsor-Smith, Kuluta, Mignola and half a dozen other giants of their craft. The fantastic landscapes, the swift translation of emotion into weather, scenery and violent action, the bizarre supernatural images, the vivid quality of the writing, have always attracted the best artists. The great Golden Age of book illustration which gave us a vast range of artists from Pyle to Heath Robinson to Nielsen now has its equivalent in the Golden Age of narrative art. Not for nothing are artists attracted to The Lord of the Rings and Conan as they were attracted to *The Arabian Nights* and *Grimms' Fairy Tales*. Out of the Romantic revival of the 1960s, which was when other 'forgotten' fantasts came into their own, emerged many good things, not least a generation of artists who influenced other generations in their admiration for writers creating images which were neither prosaic nor familiar, which allowed them the full reign of their own invention, when it came to interpreting those stories—so long as they made sure that the human figures were credible, for it is on that familiar form that so many good supernatural narratives are carried.

Fritz Leiber, that extraordinary American prose stylist and ironist, author of the Fafhrd and Gray Mouser stories (perhaps the finest fantasy adventures to follow Howard's) came up with the term 'sword and sorcery' to describe the kind of fiction which he loved by no means uncritically, of whom Conan was perhaps the best example. In 1960/61 I was also part of this naming debate in *Amra*, the Howard fanzine, and preferred, like Karl Wagner, the term 'epic fantasy' to describe what might be more prosaically described as a supernatural adventure story, itself a genre which has grown out of the continuing tradition of historical Gothic stories by the likes of Ann Radcliffe or even Sir Walter Scott, but it's worth remembering that in Howard's day there was no such term available. Indeed, similar stories not by him were generally called 'Howard-type stories'. It was in Conan's gigantic shadow that the rest of us worked, even before an Oxford academic published a trilogy which his earliest critics tried, to Tolkien's dismay, to see as some sort of post-nuclear-holocaust allegory. True, we also admired the likes of Lord Dunsany or James Branch Cabell, but it was Howard who brought a robust, direct and wholly American quality to the form and it is to this vitality, both in prose and imagery, that many of us continue to be most attracted. Conan is about story first and rationalisation second. His landscapes unroll before him, reflecting his emotions as his adventures race along at breakneck speed. One doesn't need a complicated alphabet of Late Hyrkanian or Middle Aquilonian or especially detailed maps of his world to enjoy his stories and feel the blood race in one's veins as Conan (or Kull or Solomon Kane) plunges, sword in hand, into a maelstrom of wild invention and dark goings on, any more than in Raymond Chandler's urban thrillers we care who actually did the murder and how.

Conan has become, from his beginnings in *Weird Tales* (that fantasy equivalent of *Black Mask*) a national icon as identifiable to members of the public as Davy Crockett or Zorro. That is why he has translated naturally into every possible medium. Like Zorro, he's far better known than his creator, a sure sign of iconic status. I was made aware of this a few years ago when I was coming into the US at a major international airport and was questioned briefly by a friendly immigration officer. He read my name in my passport and frowned, clicking his fingers as he tried to work something out. I became a little alarmed as I stood there, wondering if there was some crime a person with my name was wanted for. Then the officer's brow cleared and he handed me back my passport. 'I know who you are,' he said triumphantly. 'You're the guy who writes Conan, yeah?'

So, said Kurt Vonnegut in another iconic novel of our times, it goes . . .

# ■ Learning to Be a Jew

A Review of *Letters to Auntie Fori: The 5,000-Year History of the Jewish People and Their Faith* by Martin Gilbert

**From *London Magazine*, February/March 2004**

> "*We thank Thee, O Lord our God, because Thou didst give us an heritage unto our fathers a desirable, good, and ample land, and because Thou didst bring us forth, O Lord our God, from the land of Egypt, and didst deliver us from the house of bondage—*"
>
> Barstein heard no more for the moment; the paradox of this retrospective gratitude was too absorbing. What! Sir Asher was thankful because over three thousand years ago his ancestors had obtained—not without hard fighting for it—a land which had already been lost again for eighteen centuries. What a marvellous long memory for a race to have!
>
> —Israel Zangwill, *Ghetto Comedies*, 1907

Growing up in South London, attending an Anglican church on the few occasions school demanded it, knowing only a version of Christianity implicit in Rudolf Steiner's methods, I never had any reason to conceal my Jewish roots. My Austrian godfather was part of an organisation which helped many Jews escape from Hitler, but he rarely talked about it. Children and adults of Jewish and Christian origin mixed together and intermarried, and our world at least was free of any stereotypes. Culturally we were secular Londoners. The Yiddish words we used were part of our common slang. We were as ignorant of synagogues as we were of Roman Catholic churches, and Jesus was a figure sentimentally invoked by school teachers at Easter and Christmas; otherwise he rarely came into our lives.

My mother and grandmother made no secret of their Jewish origins. Both told anecdotes about such things as my great grandmother's being mourned as dead because she didn't marry an Orthodox Jew, of the claustrophobic strictness of those times, synonymous as they saw it with the general puritanism of a vanished Victorian age. My grandmother and my mother were both Liberal voters admiring Lloyd George and cultivating a fierce hatred of intolerance which I inherited. My Uncle Jack, who lived and worked in 10 Downing Street, would always pause before the portrait of Disraeli as we went up the stairs and remind me of our connection with the great Tory in the hope that I would follow in his footsteps. So ingrained was this idea that it was not until I was twenty-five or so that I gave up ambitions for a political career.

If my father's family entertained reservations about his marrying my mother (as I now suspect they had), I never knew it. My father disappeared when I was five, and his family found me an embarrassment after he settled down with a lady of his own heritage. His great-aunt had been of stern Lutheran Methodist principles who published some pretty good poetry with a distinctly radical but sometimes antisemitic bent.

When hitch-hiking in Germany in the late 1950s, I first encountered antisemitism in its most virulent forms, confided to me unselfconsciously on account of my blue eyes and fair complexion. I was horrified. Only then did I begin seriously to consider my Jewish background, though my natural secularism, which came out of a non-religious postwar culture, never led me to consider identifying with any organised religion.

After the German experience, however, I increasingly identified with my Jewish family. Realising what a relatively narrow escape from Hitler I'd had, I found myself experiencing what has come to be known as 'survival guilt'. I studied accounts of the Holocaust and read about Jewish history and culture. Then, on a ship coming in to New York harbour one day, I was again shocked by the blatant antisemitic remarks of the German and Russian passengers from which I fled without protest. That cowardice led me to conceive and write, in the course of the past twenty-five years, a sequence of novels in which I hope to explain how the Nazi Holocaust drew strength from many such acts as mine. My work became a form of atonement in which I took on the burden of guilt, not only of the gentile but also of the antisemitic Jew, the 'assimilator'. I still feel discomfort with organised religion and ritual, but my respect for Jewish traditions and culture has steadily grown. In the course of my self-education I read books about the Holocaust as well as Jewish history and culture, many of them by Martin Gilbert, but it would have helped me considerably if, when younger, I had been able to consult a book as accessible, humane and engaging as *Letters to Auntie Fori*.

This is Gilbert's most idiosyncratic book and probably the best to give to a non-Jew who wants to learn more about Jewish history and customs without reading a formal account and who doesn't want to turn up with a date at Bloom's, as I once did, to find it closed for Yom Kippur. Eloquent and readable as Gilbert usually is, his choice of form is attractive and clever. Auntie Fori befriended him when as a youth he was travelling in India. Only much later did he learn that she was not a native Indian at all, but a woman of Hungarian Jewish origin whose family was called Friedmann. In 1928 she went to university in England where she met her husband, BK, a Hindu whom she had married in 1935, returning to Delhi with him and working for Indian independence as part of the highly political Nehru family and later devoting herself to her adopted people. She knew nothing of the culture she had left behind and, in her nineties, asked Gilbert if he could provide her with a brief account of her people's history. Astonished to learn of her origins, Gilbert agreed to 'educate' her in her Jewish past and traditions by writing her a letter every week for two and a half years. Long used to describing Jewish tragedy in his best known works about the Nazi Holocaust, he decided here to emphasise the positive and celebratory aspects of Jewish life. This splendid book is that collection of letters.

'According to Jewish mystical tradition—the Kabbalah—Cain's soul belongs to the demonic aspect of mankind, while Abel's soul came down to earth again as the soul of Moses,' he writes early on. 'Was this not a type of Hindu-style reincarnation?' Respectfully, and with remarkable delicacy, Gilbert leads Aunti Fori through the origins of the Jewish people.

The history of the Jews, especially after Moses led them out of Egypt, was often cruel and bloody. Pity the poor Melianites who had their male children slaughtered and only their virgin girls spared. The first three thousand years is in fact a familiar Old Testament account of slaughter and counter-slaughter in which the Jews behaved no worse than their various rivals whom they conquered and by whom they were in turn conquered. The Persians and Romans and particularly the Greeks who settled around Bethlehem seem positively benign in comparison, especially when it came to the wholesale slaughter of first-born or tainted women. Monotheism appears to have no special virtues; only the astonishing longevity of the Jewish people, their greatness of language and complexity and firmness of belief continues to impress as you read.

Roman imperialism ultimately became viciously repressive, of course, and as rival monotheistic faiths grew in ascendancy it was especially bad news for the Jews. After the diaspora they were persecuted in almost every region they settled, even in Goa when it was conquered by the Portuguese. Only the Hindus, Chinese and a few other pantheists appear to have tolerated them, but there they assimilated so thoroughly that little of their heritage remained. Why the Jews became the focus of such extraordinary fury remains a constant question asked by gentile and Jewish scholars to this day.

Gilbert's letters describe the rise of Zionism, explaining why the state of Israel is so important and why its boundaries are disputed and why it has been so fiercely defended. In particular Israel's current policies towards Palestinians are more easily understood.

Without question those policies have led to a revival of antisemitism, or at any rate have allowed the buried anti-Jewish sentiments of, say, Midwestern Lutherans to re-emerge. That is why an American can easily link criticism of Israel with the kind of antisemitism which let Hitler reign unchecked by America until 1941 when, in solidarity with Japan, he declared war on the US. That action at last gave FDR the popular support he needed to fight the Nazis but it should be remembered how FDR and others studiously ignored the plight of European Jewry in spite of repeated representations from American Jews and gentiles.

The Holocaust remains recent history's dominant landmark as well as the measure of our political morality, and if some Israelis employ something close to ruthless blood feuding, inarguably in self-defence, it must be remembered that this country, for all it effectively represents the USA in the region, is surrounded by traditional enemies, millions of whom are still determined to destroy them, who still praise Hitler's policies and repeat casual sayings such as 'Let a Jew into your house and you will have a month's bad luck'.

The confidences offered my blue eyes and fair skin in Germany have more recently been repeated in Arab countries, as well as in America and even Britain. Only with this understanding can any debate concerning Palestine and the Arabs begin, and *Letters to Auntie Fori* helps establish that background. Almost half the Israelis disagree with current policies towards Palestine, and Israel's press and parliamentarians continue to protest, perhaps more effectively than those gentiles and Jews who condemn Israel from the relative safety of Europe and America. If Gilbert's book does nothing else, it makes such issues and responses clear while also explaining the Torah and the Talmud, the Maccabean martyrs, the meaning of the ritual candlestick's branches, the Kabbalah, the Kaddish, Hanukkah, Hebrew prayers and traditions, all rooted in Jewish history.

I have one small quarrel with the book: it deals only sketchily with the role of Jews in the arts and does not draw enough on some of the great Jewish writers of the past hundred years or so. Gilbert seems positively unaware of them. Singer gets a passing mention, but he says little of Disraeli, the novelist, or of Kafka, and nothing at all of Israel Zangwill, the Londoner whose very readable books included *Children of the Ghetto* and *Ghetto Tragedies*, who coined a famous phrase in his play *The Melting Pot* and whose criticisms of imperial Britain were as apt to Edwardians as they are to us. Without sentimentality, stereotyping or proselytising Zangwill did an enormous amount to help English speakers understand and sympathise with Jews, especially with the immigrant Jews. His *Mantle of Elijah* not only deals with the subtleties of antisemitism but also confronts the way in which politicians 'sell' wars of colonial expansion to the public. Babel's brilliant Odessa stories, about Jewish gangsters, go unmentioned. Nor do we hear of Gerald Kersh, author of *Jews Without Jehovah*, *Fowlers End* and *Night and the City*, which told of assimilated London Jews, Jewish crooks and entrepreneurs. Nothing is said of Mandelstam, Mankowitz, Baron, Pinter, Edna Ferber, Hecht, Dorothy Parker, Olsen, Bellow, Andrea Dworkin or any of the great modern Israeli writers.

I would dearly love to see in the next edition of this useful and humane book an appendix recommending the work of other Jews whose writings help understand the living culture. Perhaps from necessity of space Martin Gilbert has narrowed his parameters a little too much for me, and it seems unfair to carp. This is a wonderful introduction to the meaning, history and heritage of being Jewish. No doubt Aunti Fori treasured her letters and reread them quite as much as I shall in years to come.

# ■ Introduction to *The Hooligan* by Rudolf Nassauer

**From the Ashgrove edition, forthcoming**

The philosophical novel was never especially attractive to English writers or readers. Of the existing examples not many compared well to those in German, French or Russian. Until the 1960s Hesse or Camus had relatively few admirers and were even met with the aggressive discomfort of the Anglophone middlebrow mainstream. Apart from the likes of Angus Wilson or Iris Murdoch few recognised the merit and intention of these novels. Most British and American novelists were unfamiliar with the form and were not prepared to interpret, let alone enjoy them.

When in 1960 Rudolf Nassauer published this, his first novel, it was handicapped not only by its then unfamiliar form but also by its original title. *The Hooligan* summoned up an image of an Irish bully boy rather than a Nazi careerist psychopath. No writer of fiction had as yet begun trying to get into the head of a character quite like this, trying to understand what it was like to be a Nazi, what would drive you to become one. At that stage it was probably too much to ask many readers to see things from the point of view of 'the other'—in this case the quintessential Nazi—not the SA brute but the educated SS man, who had usually known a Christian moral code yet chose to serve Hitler in full knowledge of what was involved. It would take the likes of Hannah Arendt to interview surviving high-ranking Nazis and develop a deep familiarity with the language as well as the banality of evil.

Rudolf Nassauer came to England in 1939. Born 1924 in Frankfurt into a family of assimilated Jews in 1924 he experienced the rise of the Nazis at first hand and after 'Kristallnacht' in November 1938 his father and sister fled to England leaving Rudi and his mother to do their best to wind up the family business. They followed in 1939. Speaking fairly good English, Rudi was enrolled at St Paul's School in London. The Nassauers were wine merchants and eventually Rudi worked in the family business while writing in his spare time. His first volume of poetry was published in 1947, the year he married Bernice Rubens, who would eventually publish many novels of her own, winning the Booker in 1969. The couple rented rooms in their London house and made many friends amongst English artists and intellectuals. His first novel took ten years to write, being turned down by a number of publishers who found its subject matter too harrowing or its method too difficult. Eventually it was published by Peter Owen in 1960, the same year as his wife's debut (with *Set on Edge*). His novel had been extremely hard to write, given its subject matter and method, but it remained in the eyes of many his best work. It was never reprinted after its second edition which appeared in the same year of publication.

Although highly praised by fellow writers including Elias Canetti, Peter Vansittart, Iris Murdoch and Angus Wilson, the book was forgotten by all but its fans and eventually, though he wrote a number of other novels, Nassauer's career was eclipsed by his wife's. The novel, however, remains one of the great pieces of fiction attempting to make some kind of sense of the Holocaust.

The questions most frequently asked about the rise and rule of the Nazis is how sophisticated, civilized nations can permit such barbarism. The fact is of course that the 'barbarians' are always with us. It is hard to know how to stop them emerging. They are integral to our society. They are simply awaiting their chance. In times of crisis they emerge to exploit our fears and weaknesses to their own benefit. From time to time such people are given the chance to fulfill their desires without fear of consequence, even acting in the name of the law.

The SA and SS controlled by Röhm and Himmler represented society at its most brutal. The notion of common rights under the law was abandoned where 'non-Aryans', lefties and others were concerned. Brutality towards minorities was not merely tolerated; it was encapsulated by reactionary decree, encouraged by those who came to represent the State. Arbitrary arrests, deportations, torturing, executions became the norm while the majority went about their daily lives either refusing to accept the truth or murmuring mild puzzlement or slightly shocked protestations as liberals do in most sophisticated societies. It was this phenomenon which focused the attention of artists, most of whom could only at first deal with it in symbolic terms. Some of the best of these were produced as films like *High Noon* or novels like *1984*. To find a more direct way of writing about Nazism was a challenge and Nassauer rose to it.

Perhaps the hardest thing for the imaginative person to imagine is the unimaginative person. Nassauer succeeded in getting into the head of just such a person and that, I think, is what makes this novel such an important achievement. The unimaginative person rarely has what most of us understand as an inner life. In a sense they can be said to live what the rest of us dream. Fantasies, as such, are mostly unknown to them. It seems they can only feel through extreme actions, frequently nightmare actions. They are fascinating to those of us whose lives are led to quite a large degree in the imagination. And a certain animosity, even hatred, can exist between the two kinds of people. It can be the novelist's or film-maker's hardest job to try to get inside the psyche of the kind of person who is often their natural enemy.

As a boy Rudi Nassauer saw life change rapidly with Hitler's grab for power. During his formative years plodding paternal officers of the law, still wearing the trappings of the old German regime, representing common justice, became monsters. Increasingly the law presented itself in the sharp, 'modern' uniforms of Nazism. Children grew up speaking the aggressive, slangy, cynical language of those they admired, the 'new men', the men who were going to get things done. There are recordings available of their early speeches in the Reichstag. They chill your blood not because you have heard such tones in old documentaries but because these days you can still hear them in the streets, in the media, in parliament, wherever you live. You are depressed that so little was learned from the horrors which occurred in your own lifetime and which the majority are already forgetting. You want to know how such terrible times can be stopped from occurring again. If you are a survivor, like Rudi Nassauer, you no doubt devote much of your life to thinking about such matters, you hope that by analysing the phenomenon you can somehow prevent it from happening again.

The horror of that barbarism is made worse when, escaping it, you begin to understand its extent and power. You learn more and more what happened to the relatives and friends you left behind. You try to imagine the kind of creature which could commit such evil deeds and what kept those creatures ruling over us. If Rudolf Nassauer was like many people, he tried to imagine not only how we might have behaved if he had stayed to be engulfed by Hitler's Holocaust but how he might have resisted. And what should we do to stop another terrible descent into barbarism? Although he could hardly know what would happen in the Balkans in the 1990s, Nassauer was already seeing what was happening in the 1950s. Certainly he heard of the Japanese atrocities against the defeated Chinese of Manchukuo and learned what was going on in the Soviet Union. It would have become clear to him that Nazi antisemitism was only one (albeit especially horrifying) expression of the rule of the brute.

Maybe the first question which comes to us is 'am I like that?' Is there a part of oneself which could turn into a cruel monster relishing the pain of others? Can we be made into such people? How close to the edge would we have to be pushed to be an efficient SS man or a capo in a camp? Or is there actually a type of human being which simply waits its opportunity? I suspect these questions were frequently asked by Rudi Nassauer as he came to grips with the ideas at the heart of this novel.

My mother recalls singing popular songs as the bombs came down all around and the anti-aircraft guns went off. Everything banging and flashing and hissing and roaring. And I remembered it, too. It had to be a false memory, I said. But when I asked her she said that she remembered holding me up to the window to watch the dogfights which were the cheapest firework display London ever knew. They were almost a distraction. She said that the thought of Nazi conquest was at the back of their minds all the time, especially those with of Jewish identity. And it was true that, for all the adults knew, German tanks would soon come rolling up Farringdon Street over Blackfriars and Southwark bridges into our High Streets. What then? Mass 'round-ups'? Concentration camps on Jersey and the Isle of Man? Few had any coherent explanation of what exactly it was could turn people into degenerate savages who could in turn make many of us also behave like degenerate savages, through the cruelly relished application of pain and terror. Some of us tried to imagine what the minds of such brutes could be like, especially the intelligent, educated ones. What might make us behave like them? How would we have survived? Perhaps we knew what it was like to be threatened with a bayonet or feel one's bowels turn to water at the sight of a knife some psycho was threatening us with.

We shored up our hopes with declarations that it could never happen here, that the British were somehow sturdier than all those others conquered by Nazism. But there had already been books anticipating that it *could* happen in England and America. In our bones we must have known the truth, that the decent elements in any society could be crushed and the cruel ones elevated, turning our lives into the nightmares Nassauer had already witnessed. But it was not a message we welcomed and the more sophisticated message of Nassauer's book was even less acceptable to the general reader. While other good novelists and a few critics recognized the truth of this novel most did not. Kurt Vonnegut's *Mother Night*, describing the career of American Nazi Howard W Campbell Jnr, would not be published until a year after Nassauer's novel and would be received with a similar silence from a public not then interested in discussing how such people might be living amongst them.

What would you do? Were brutes made or born? These questions began to be asked increasingly as we found ourselves able to gain some distance and understand why so few survivors wanted to discuss their experiences. Detailed accounts of death camps were published. The first crop of writers in English to try to deal with the Holocaust had been people whose triumphalism, taste for melodrama and vengeance neither explained nor analysed satisfactorily. In Europe there were Levi, Wiesel, Kosinksi and a few others getting to grips with the subject as best they could. Camus and French existentialists, who had fought Nazism, also had ideas on the subject. Another generation would give us increasingly sophisticated attempts at understanding. Meanwhile there were also more generalised accounts by European writers—a few of them British—concerning the new belief that evil was not as easily conquered as in our arrogance we had thought it was. These were the most urgent debates amongst those of us who survived.

As a miserable sufferer from 'Holocaust guilt' I am relieved I did not suffer as so many suffered but I also understood how it felt. In my early years which I spent in that besieged London, never knowing when our island might be occupied, we saw country after country fall to Hitler's thugs. In those occupied nations the law worked against us and we saw swaggering, needy, horrible, power-junkies morphing out of the faces of friendly neighbours, even relatives, and the world was suddenly divided into the victims and the perpetrators. That was what threatened.

Happily we in Britain escaped the pogroms and round-ups. Then, slowly, the prejudice also went away for the most part and it didn't matter whether we were Sephardim, Ashkenazim, half-bloods, assimilated, Orthodox or anything in between. Meanwhile, the authority of a nation state gave identity and authority to many more and the anger at the horrors done by the Nazis at last began to enter the unconsciousness of decent people. A new sensibility developed, a culture in which it was unacceptable to make racist jokes or treat other races badly. Human rights increased and grew in Europe in spite of the ghastly horrors of the Balkan wars. The practical uses of a Universal Charter of Human Rights became clear to many more people. Possibly, we began to see, the martyrs didn't die for nothing. Many swaggering predators will be detected and curbed before they can come to power again.

Rudolf Nassauer, already a published poet, wrote this book before most of the dreadful events in Europe and Africa. In a sense he anticipated them. At the heart of his parable, Nassauer describes people who cannot love. His main characters are hobbled by their inability to find love and hold on to it in a world which sees love only as a weakness. Early on he has a brothel-keeper tell a story about another brothel-keeper and blackmailer: 'He is somehow convinced that the men and women of Europe have ceased to love one another. . . . He says that love is held in shame and therefore causes fear which kills love . . .'

Andreas, Nassauer's malevolent Everyman, neither understands nor loves the world. It baffles him even as he learns to manipulate it. The more power he acquires the more contempt he has for those who give it to him. The ultimate cynic, the man without a soul, he reminds me not so much of Hesse's Harry Haller or Knulp as of Camus' Caligula. This novel is almost the antithesis of Hesse's themes, though it has some of the same qualities and asks some of the same questions. Nassauer is what Hesse might have been had he early on experienced the horrors and consequences of Nazism. In comparison, Hesse is almost innocent in his understanding of the world.

Who could have anticipated the Nazis or for that matter the Serbian Black Hand and its offspring? Nassauer is writing what many believed impossible after 1946, because it was thought that the evil of the Holocaust wiped out the possibility of any creative artist being able to write a novel again. He struggled to find a form which would give him the necessary distance any novelist needs when tackling such an appalling subject and he found it in what some would call early magic realism, a kind of fairy tale or allegory which allows him distance and reminds us most, I think, of Kosinksi's *The Painted Bird* (1959).

Although he bears comparison with the writers I have mentioned, Rudolf Nassauer reveals himself as a genuine original. He was one of the first to tackle the 'impossible' themes involving the rise and establishment of Nazism. He tried to understand how so many apparently civilized people could become monsters and what kind of monster might have led them to this transformation. Like others, he also came to understand the banality of evil as well as its exotic attractions, how Goering or Himmler might present evil as a spiritual ideal, how it inspires men and women to love its exponents as persons of great nobility, wisdom and self-sacrifice, just as Andreas is loved.

When Andreas is finally brought to book he resorts to the familiar end of the megalomaniac psychopath who cannot bear to give up control of the world. Cornered he does what so many Nazis did when faced with the consequences of their actions. Yet, again, one is reminded of Camus and Caligula's final mocking, triumphant shout when the assassins' swords enter his body:

"I'm still alive!" he cries, as the curtain drops.

As, perhaps ironically, this fine novel will live, to teach us something of those predators who would destroy us and our values.

# ■ When Worlds Collide

A Review of *Fortunate Son* by Walter Mosley

**From the *Guardian*, 12th August 2006**

More than any other contemporary novelist, Walter Mosley's work affects the reader on an immediate, visceral level. His anger is as infectious as his humanity. In his urban adventure stories featuring the unwilling sleuth Easy Rawlins and his friend Mouse, Mosley has plotted the history of black life in Los Angeles from shortly after the Second World War (*Devil in a Blue Dress*) to the present. His metaphysical fantasies, such as *The Wave*, are strongly reminiscent of Charles Williams, while in literary novels such as *RL's Dream* and *The Man in My Basement* and nonfiction such as *Workin' on the Chain Gang* he writes relentlessly on the subject of race, individual conscience and the American dichotomy.

With the possible exception of Don DeLillo, Mosley offers a depth and seriousness which shames the efforts of more fashionable novelists like Roth or Updike. Mosley chiefly identifies with the black underclass which moved from Louisiana and Texas in the 1940s to take manufacturing jobs in Los Angeles as white men were called to the War. They came to inhabit the suburbs of Watts and Compton which, to those of us not familiar with the pointers of wealth and privilege in America, seem considerably more attractive than the ghettoes of Houston and New Orleans but where, in the 1960s, riots occurred advertising an anger most recently expressed in the vertical slums on the outskirts of Paris and are the background of his urban adventure *Little Scarlet*.

Mosley's latest literary novel develops an earlier American tradition represented by the likes of Sinclair Lewis, with its emphasis on social injustice and the great gulf between the American dream and American actuality. In prose echoing the rich warmth of an East Texas bayou, he tells a story as gripping as Dickens, instantly drawing us into contrasted worlds. Like Dickens, Mosley stands confidently on the social borderline. His lucid style resists sentimentality while constantly offering fresh insights into the mind-set of complex characters, drawn from a wide spectrum of American race and class. Moving between worlds, gathering information, testing ideas, he presents a wealthy, emotionally bewildered white doctor as convincingly as a poor, angry black mechanic. Apparent stereotypes, such as his high-school campus queen, become complete individuals. Both furious and forgiving, he assumes our common awareness of social injustice and concentrates instead on what we might have missed. And on the strength of this remarkable book alone, his best to date, Mosley must be considered one of our great novelists.

*Fortunate Son* has a plot worthy of any great Victorian novel: it involves two boys who early on bond as loving brothers, one a sickly black kid with his roots in the ghetto and the other a sturdy white boy from a distinctly upper-class background. Tommy is a 'bubble' baby, unlikely to survive, watched over in the hospital by his single mother Branwyn. Understanding her to be alone, Minas Nolan, a recently widowed doctor at the hospital, offers her a lift home one night. The relationship between the black working-class woman and the white upper-class doctor deepens and they become lovers. In the face of criticism from her own people, knowing this to be Tommy's best chance of gaining health, Branwyn moves in with the doctor. Owing her son's life to Nolan, she loves him but can't bring herself to marry him; the chemistry between herself and Tommy's father, which she resists, underlines the fact that she does not feel the same passion for the white man whose own young son, Eric, is a lusty, bawling, brawling golden boy.

What the adults bring to their relationship is reflected in the qualities the two sons bring to theirs. Tommy is sensitive, observant and imaginative; Eric is athletic, aggressive, extrovert. Both receive the benefits of the doctor's wealth and social position until catastrophe throws Tommy back into the ghetto in the uncertain keeping of his father. From then on the two boys, while continuing to recall and even yearn for each other, are separated and experience utterly different lives. Imaginative, artistic Tommy sustains himself on the street as a drug-dealer before he is ten years old, while extrovert Eric shines as a high-school hero, admired by his friends, lusted after by the prom queen.

Bullied, shot up, imprisoned, raped, the visionary Tommy barely survives a brutal, horribly violent childhood, becoming a street bum. Eric's career is smooth, brilliant, mundane, conventional, with problems of conscience rather than survival, his ride on the golden escalator only interrupted when he has to marry his pregnant girlfriend. Yet both boys are complicated, motherless, somehow certain that they bring bad luck, even death, to those they love. They carry psychic and spiritual burdens which they cannot easily express and keep to themselves, as if airing them will bring worse disaster to those close to them. In avoiding familiar temptations, they fall prey to less obvious ones. How their lives move apart and eventually come together is the substance of a beautifully engineered story constantly asking which of the boys is actually the 'fortunate son'.

# ■ Kit Carson Rides Again

A Review of Hampton Sides's *Blood and Thunder*

**From the *Guardian*, 10th March 2007**

As a young hack I wrote dozens of stories featuring the heroic adventures of Robin Hood, Dick Turpin, Billy the Kid, Kit Carson and Buffalo Bill. To my disappointment, I swiftly discovered that Robin Hood was a legend, Dick Turpin had been a brutal butcher who never rode to York and Billy the Kid was a teenage psychopath. It was therefore natural to assume that the redman's friend Kit Carson, in his fringed finery, was a self-invented opportunist like Buffalo Bill.

Remarkably, Hampton Sides confirms that Carson wore fancy buckskins, was an expert scout profoundly familiar with the southwest, spoke all local languages, was respected by Utes, Apache, Navajo and Comanche, and generally succeeded in keeping the peace between natives and newcomers.

*Blood and Thunder* tells its story chiefly through Carson and the Navajo leader Narbona, but offers considerable new research and understanding of the unlikable President Polk's mission to expand US dominion over Mexican territories from Texas to California in a colonising push to the Pacific. He had heavy resistance from the British, also anxious to control oriental trade routes and, of course, Mexico. Eventually, once most of the tribes had been defeated, these ambitions culminated in the Mexican-American war beginning in 1846, largely manufactured by the US.

Carson was born on Christmas Eve, 1809, and at the age of sixteen headed down the Santa Fe Trail into largely unknown territory, an innocent catalyst with an exaggerated respect for federal authority and its representatives. A trapper and wagon-train guide, he worked as a scout and Indian fighter over a forty-year period and was inducted into the Union army during the Civil War (winding up a brevet general), fighting slave-owning Texans and Indians but rigorously opposing massacres and accounting for himself bravely on his own terms. Famous for his integrity, he was everything, in fact, the pulps claimed for him (except our Kit was taller, with a better hat).

Indeed, he married successively two Indian wives, whom he loved faithfully, and was a dutiful, playful father who ensured that his children would be better educated than he was. Carson was from Missouri, then the southwestern outpost of the American empire, and while he spoke fluent French, Spanish and various Indian languages, was completely illiterate. His memoirs, dictated to a journalist who embellished them against Carson's wishes, were the basis for all the dime novels, films and comics that succeeded them. Long before he died, he was a legendary hero in the east, deeply embarrassed by his fame.

Like many frontiersmen, he was an honest friend to the Indians, showed them considerable respect, yet wound up being the instrument of their defeat. Unlike William Johnson, Boone, Houston and the rest, he was at least able to help some tribes reclaim their traditional homelands, while serving Washington's interest, admittedly largely because the semi-desert revealed no gold. When he died, the Pacific territories were all firmly within the Union.

Narbona was a war chief, a master strategist and negotiator, who did all he could to ensure his way of life, first fighting Mexican settlers, then their soldiers and, eventually, the Americans. In a typically mishandled meeting, he was killed. Eventually bowing to the inevitable, his people accepted removal to Bosque Redondo, an apparently idyllic desert oasis which quickly became overpopulated, subject to drought and disease, killing huge numbers. Thanks partly to Carson's intervention, shortly before his death in 1868, Narbona's tribe were eventually able to return to their familiar world, and Navajoland, a vast area the size of Ohio, exists to this day, growing wealthier, like so many tribal territories, through gambling concessions.

There are other major characters in this absorbing and well-written popular history offering the real background politics to the myths and legends of the region, including the glory-hunting Lieutenant Fremont and the idealistic but inept General Carleton. Anyone who has read Cormac McCarthy's *Blood Meridian* or grew up on John Ford westerns will be enlightened. Those yet to read that novel or see the movies will find that this book adds deep resonances to their pleasure.

# ■ The Undertaker and the Actress

## A Review of Zoran Živković's *Hidden Camera*

**From the *Guardian*, 4 February 2006**

It's conventional to mourn the dearth of good idiosyncratic publishers, but smaller presses are still turning out excellent work. In England these include Savoy Books, Menard Press, Persephone Books and PS Publishing, while Dalkey Archive, based in the US but publishing internationally, has one of the most impressive lists in the world, including Céline, Fuentes, Henry Green, Harry Mathews, Queneau, Gertrude Stein, Boris Vian and now Zoran Živković.

Živković's family narrowly missed being killed by the US rocket that blasted the Chinese embassy in Belgrade. Opposed to Milosevic, like their father, Živković's twin sons were in the vanguard storming the parliament building. Through all that terrible time, Živković kept up his good-hearted, sardonic correspondence with Europe and America, maintaining a steady, angry eye on the Milosevic regime. First translated into English some twelve years ago, with *The Fourth Circle*, he attracted a wide audience in the online Fantastic Metropolis as well as in *Leviathan*, *Interzone* and *Postscripts*, where readers compared him to the best European ironists.

He generally writes in an imaginative tradition largely untouched by western modernism and derived from that literature which emerged from rediscovered folk roots during the 19th and 20th centuries, when nationalism was a crucial cultural obsession. Usually identified by dreamlike traits associated with the subconscious, the tradition embraces the convention of nameless, often grotesque, protagonists, anonymous cities and vaguely contemporary times. Echoing habits established under authoritarian regimes, it freed writers from distracting specificity, keeping moral and metaphysical focus for reasons not unlike those of a good pulp story.

Otherwise, such writers worked in code, hiding their real subjects under layers of irony and faux naïveté. Their fiction achieved a painterly quality, which comes from the application of so many layers of narrative, refracting, defracting and reflecting, depending on the angle from which you view the work. While this technique, poorly applied, can be irritating or over-vague to the anglophone used to a more realistic convention, Živković employs it to distinct effect, developing character and story from what at first seems to be a simple portrait or still life.

*Hidden Camera*'s narrator is a prissy undertaker who lives by himself in an anally ordered apartment in which only his exotic fish demand his responsibility. When he receives an invitation to a local art cinema, his initial impulse is to ignore it. Then, with uncharacteristic spontaneity, he decides to go. Although he's late arriving, there is only one other person in the cinema, a behatted young woman with an alluring perfume. Attracted to her, he self-consciously tries to indicate with body language that he means her no threat. The movie starts. He realises that someone has filmed him eating his lunch in a park and that this woman was there at the same time. It dawns on him that he's become the subject of a *Candid Camera* reality TV show. Furiously maintaining his dignity, he finds himself alone in the theatre; he can find no one in authority with whom to remonstrate. All he gets is another envelope: an invitation to a bookshop. And we're in the world of the best Slav fabulists, hooked into a parable of death and rebirth involving the undertaker, an actress, a musician and an obstetrician playing out a series of mysterious cameos which the narrator swears will soon be featured on a TV show. Convinced that he is being scrutinised, our undertaker finds himself drawn deeper into the atmosphere of a dream.

Živković suggests modern narcissism is increasingly turning us into one another's entertainment fodder; that our objective experience is nothing more than a series of realities broadcast for the world's pleasures. Our pain is their gain. But what if it's our civic duty to put on the best possible show?

A short, meaty book, this is a parable heavy enough for you to know you've absorbed real substance, yet ironic enough to ensure you don't want to kill yourself when it's over. I'm looking forward to next year, when PS Publishing do Živković's *Twelve Collections and the Teashop* and a massive omnibus *Impossible Stories*, books which are likely to give new readers a fair sense of the spectrum covered by this wonderfully sardonic writer whose idiosyncratic vision so thoroughly serves his bleak, absurdist sense of fun.

# ■ The Spaces in Between

## A Review of China Miéville's *The City & the City*

**From the *Guardian*, 30th May 2009**

China Miéville is perhaps the current generation's finest writer of science fantasy, that beguiling genre for which JG Ballard and M John Harrison have produced so much of their fiction. Miéville's first novel, *King Rat*, was a grim urban horror story about contemporary London. His later work is primarily set in the alternative world of Bas-Lag—ambitious novels such as *Perdido Street Station* and *Iron Council*, packed with grotesque characters, gorgeous imagery, amazing monsters, political parables and intricate plotting.

The City & the City is very different. It takes place in our familiar world, a post-Soviet locale which draws on string theory for its ideas and conventional experience for its story. Apart from one exceptional detail, this book could be a clever mystery story told from the point of view of a Balkan policeman struggling to cope with the problems of a society burdened by traditions and attitudes from its recent authoritarian past. Featureless concrete, rattling trams and antiquated office equipment invoke Greene's *The Third Man* and Vienna's zones of occupation. You can almost hear a zither twanging somewhere in an echoing sewer.

Playing off the current theoretical physicists' notion that more than one object can occupy the same physical space, Miéville demonstrates a disciplined intelligence reminiscent of the late Barrington Bayley (who specialised brilliantly in scientific implausibilities), helping us to hang on to the idea that the city of Beszel exists in the same space as the city of Ul Qoma. Citizens of each city can dimly make out the other, but are forbidden on pain of severe penalties (administered by a supreme authority known simply as Breach) to notice it. They have learned by habit to 'unsee'. The cities have different airports, international dialling codes, internet links. Cars navigate instinctively around one another; police officers cooperate but are not allowed to stop or investigate crimes committed in the other city.

Subtly, almost casually, Miéville constructs a metaphor for modern life in which our habits of 'unseeing' allow us to ignore that which does not directly affect our familiar lives. Yet he doesn't encourage us to understand his novel as a parable, rather as a police mystery dealing with extraordinary circumstances. The book is a fine, page-turning murder investigation in the tradition of Philip K Dick, gradually opening up to become something bigger and more significant than we originally suspected.

Though Kafka is predictably invoked by the publisher, this is in no way an absurdist or surrealist narrative. All mysteries and events are either explained or open to explanation; the protagonist, Inspector Borlú of the Beszian Extreme Crime Squad, is a dogged discoverer of the truth, frustrated by but accepting Breach's rules, which we see early on demonstrated in all their stern inflexibility.

A young woman's body is found on a rundown housing estate and Borlú is assigned to the case. Pretty much from the beginning he realises there's something unusual about the murder; he's convinced that it involved illegal passage between the two cities and is thus a matter for Breach. Someone with power, maybe a politician, is keeping it as an ordinary police case. But why? Soon Borlú's investigations lead him to request official permission to follow up inquiries in co-existent Ul Qoma; after considerable bureaucratic rigmarole, he meets his rather condescending opposite number, who escorts him across the border from one reality to the other.

The wealthier city has succeeded in getting better foreign investment. North American archaeologists have been discovering mysterious remains there for some years. The murdered girl had been participating in a dig which clearly plays a crucial part in the mystery. Under the influence of her team's senior archaeologist (who now strenuously denies any such belief) she became convinced that a third city, Orciny, exists in the interstices between one city and another, unseen by occupants of both and guarding its secret by means of cynical violence, perhaps in direct opposition to Breach or even identical to it.

Steadily, Miéville thickens his plot with exceptional mastery. Next, evidently terrified of something, the senior archaeologist disappears, maybe taken by those mysterious Orcinians whose artefacts he's helped to uncover. A friend of the murder victim is next to vanish. Against their wills, Borlú and his partner begin to believe in Orciny, and ultimately events force Borlú into contemplating an act of Breach. But Breach severely punishes all transgressions, no matter what their motives or status. Those who defy Breach usually disappear for good. Even those who commit Breach accidentally are found with their memories wiped. Why does it have to be so unforgiving?

Despite the violent deaths of those he seeks to help or interrogate, and a growing fear for his own life, Inspector Borlú slogs on in pursuit of the truth as the book moves remorselessly towards its extraordinary denouement. As in no previous novel, the author celebrates and enhances the genre he loves and has never rejected. On many levels this novel is a testament to his admirable integrity. Keeping his grip firmly on an idea which would quickly slip from the hands of a less skilled writer, Miéville again proves himself as intelligent as he is original.

# ■ Bites at the Red Apple

A Review of John Julius Norwich's *Byzantium: The Decline and Fall* and Philip Mansel's *Constantinople: City of the World's Desire 1453–1924*

**From the *Times Literary Supplement*, 17th November 1995**

No sophisticated understanding of modern European politics is possible without some knowledge of late Byzantium and its Ottoman successor. 'Meanwhile in Serbia . . .' is almost a refrain in John Julius Norwich's admirable third volume of his history of Byzantium, while Serbia turns up just as regularly in Philip Mansel's entertaining recreation of life in Constantinople from its conquest in 1453 to its demotion in 1924 to the status of Turkey's 'second city'.

In Constantinople's last Christian centuries, whenever things looked like settling down a bit, the Serbs would take another bite at the Red Apple (as the Ottomans called the city). The Serbs, seasoned by one conquest and defeat after another, had an invulnerable national identity. Their legendary heroes had reached the very gates of 'Tsargrad' to claim the imperial crown. They knew they had a destiny. Byzantium figures very little in our own local epics. It was dismissed by Gibbon and his Victorian successors as a decadent, dark oriental culture given up to intrigue, forbidden pleasure and refined cruelty. While most schoolboys of my generation knew the key figures in republican or imperial Rome, we would have a hard time saying much about Byzantium other than that Constantine, its founder, was half-British and had a vision which inspired him to make Christianity the Empire's official religion.

Norwich demonstrates how the Christian rulers of Byzantium, though turning up the odd spectacular tyrant, were on the whole actively more pious than almost any Pope or Holy Roman Emperor. They left a wealth of literature and art, much of it unfamiliar. They were often of a mystical disposition, which makes Anglo-Saxons uncomfortable, while English-speaking readers have also found their titles confusing: sebastocrators, despots, domestics and caesars. Norwich's singular achievement is to enable us to distinguish clearly between the characters and ambitions of successive emperors and their families, bringing their dark formal portraits to vivid life.

*Byzantium: The Decline and Fall* shows one scholarly far-sighted public servant after another reluctantly assuming the burden of empire and working tirelessly at consolidation and progress until someone's short-sighted avarice or maybe just a storm at sea, conspires in a few hours to destroy the gains of years. As a rule, the unfortunate visionary is then blinded and incarcerated. Frequently it is not the Serbs or the Bulgars or the various waves of Turks and Asiatic nomads—all of whom successfully tore chunks off the old Empire—who emerge as Byzantium's greatest threat, but the Normans, with their characteristic mixture of arrogance, ignorance, self-righteous philistinism, ruthless greed and false piety.

After the defeat at Manzikert by the Seljuk Turks in 1071, Byzantium was cut off from its main sources of manpower. When the Norman Robert Guiscard threatened Constantinople in 1081, the Emperor Alexius took the field against him supported mostly by mercenaries and his Varangian guard, Saxons who had survived the Battle of Hastings and wanted a crack at their old conquerors (unfortunately they were wiped out). The consummate politician John Comnenus was able to steer the knights of the First Crusade through his territories, avoiding the bloody fate of so many of the Crusaders' co-religionists, but at the height of his successes he received a small wound while hunting and died of it.

Despite appeals to the Pope and attempts to heal the schism between the Roman and Greek Churches, successive emperors failed to stop the waves of barbarians and adventurers who invaded on the pretext of rescuing Christianity from the infidel. On the other hand, the later Byzantines got on better with the Turks, who shared much of their tolerance and intellectual spirit. They noted how Islam was generally kinder to Christians than Christians were to one another.

Thus Byzantines were characterized in the West as little better than Muslims, given up to luxury and tyranny, hand in glove with the enemies of Christ. Their coolness towards the various Crusades opened them to accusations of aiding the Turks, especially when the Turks proved capable of out-fighting the astonished Norman knights on every level. Someone had to be blamed for defeat, and Byzantium was a natural candidate. Future Crusaders, as well as the Venetians and Genoese, came increasingly to regard Constantinople as an obstacle, quite as important as the Turks, to their expanding ambitions.

Constantinople's real defeat came at the hands of the Christians. In April 1204, an unholy alliance of Franks and Venetians conquered the city. The consequent bloodshed, rapine, pillage and desecration were greater than anything perpetrated by the Turks before or since leaving Byzantium under sixty years of Latin rule, from which she would never recover. Thereafter the story is one of gradual decline with very few redeeming moments save for episodes of individual heroism. The Byzantine crown jewels were pawned to Venice, and Byzantium became dependent on increasingly unstable alliances. When Manuel II and John VIII asked for a Western crusade to save Byzantium from the infidel, none was forthcoming. Christ, said the Serbs, was betrayed twice: once by Judas and once by the Pope.

By 1453, when the well-disciplined Turks, armed with superior German siege guns and under the inspired generalship of Mehmet II, attacked the city, it was little more than a few villages, separated by grassy hills on which sheep grazed, surrounded by vast and no longer impregnable walls. In his last days, the Emperor Constantine XI Dragases witnessed a phenomenon— 'St Sophia seemed suffused with an unearthly red glow that crept slowly up from the base to the summit and then went out. . . . For the Byzantines there could be only one explanation; the Spirit of God had departed from their city.'

Later on the walls the Emperor flung off his royal vestments and died sword in hand, leading the last Byzantines in the final defence of Christendom's mother city. After the traditional pillage was over, cut short on the orders of the Sultan, Mehmet entered on a white horse appalled at the poverty he saw and profoundly conscious of everything he inherited. Within days, Mehmet began the task of securing his empire and moving its capital to the city the Turks continued to call after its Christian founder.

The Ottoman centuries brought fresh wealth, magnificent public art and one of the world's greatest cuisines. In *Constantinople: City of the World's Desire, 1453–1924*, Philip Mansel describes the gorgeous emergence from the medieval world, where they systematically strangled their closest relatives, to the modern, to which they were sublimely unsuited, of the House of Osman, which gradually relinquished the power of life and death over its subjects in favour of egalitarian reforms, then quietly vanished from the city, by train, in 1924. Not until then would nationalists anxious to dissociate themselves from the sins of the Ottoman capital, refuse to deliver letters addressed to Constantinople. From now on it was Istanbul or nothing.

With the shameful genocide of the Armenians, followed by the expulsion of the Jews, Greeks and Kurds, the city ended the tolerant, cosmopolitan tradition which had made it the most glamorous pivot of East and West, ancient and modern. It became just another sprawling provincial port. And yet, smog-corroded, covered in urban blight, its noblest traditions forgotten, Constantinople still has a soul. Its beauty is inextinguishable, its accomplishments an inspiration, and its potential is as romantic as ever.

# ■ The Water Maze

## A Review of *Sylvie's Riddle* by Alan Wall

**From the *Telegraph*, 27th October 2008**

Alan Wall is unique amongst literary novelists and living poets in his fascination for and understanding of physics. In earlier novels, such as *The
Lightning Cage*, he showed an informed interest in the origins of modern
science. His last novel *China* concerned itself with our confusion between
aesthetics and the morality of acquisition. This new novel was written with
the help of an Arts Council/AHRB fellowship to promote understanding of
the arts and sciences and while it is not involved with the sciences, as much
as the arts (there have been other projects involving Wall and particle physicist Goronwy Tudor Jones which have addressed specific scientific ideas)
it displays an understanding of Einstein quite as subtle as that of Picasso.
*Sylvie's Riddle* is about image, identity, memory and betrayal and has, in its
intellectualism, something in common with the best work of Aldous Huxley.

Owen Treadle, prize-winning script-writer with film director John
Tamworth, suffers from bouts of amnesia for which he is periodically insti-
tutionalised. His wife Sylvie, to whom he is regularly unfaithful, suspects
him of escaping into this condition in order to avoid confronting the consequences of his artistic ruthlessness and his failures as a husband. She is
an arts lecturer studying how we use images to create the narratives by
which we live. Her own sometime lover, riverside gallery owner Humphrey
Allardyce, enjoys a comfortable rather than passionate relationship with her.
He is not entirely sure what she finds most attractive about him, but he's
pretty sure it's his wonderful set of Picasso's Vollard Suite Minotaur prints,
which he keeps separate from the work he sells. These images of the man-
beast engage Humphrey quite as much as they do Sylvie.

Meanwhile, in a filthy Highland bothy, Alex, a young woman convinced
by the 'Delta Foundation' cult that she can live on air alone, is dying a
wretched death. By contrast, cult leader 'Lady Pneuma' lives in an hotel

suite off the fat of the land. We will not know the connection between these and other characters until close to the novel's end. We do understand, however, that pretty much the whole cast is in some way involved with the study, production and exploitation of images, whether drawings, photographs or films. And together with the symbols of the Minotaur in his maze, the novel offers a series of water images, of rising rivers and terrifying seas threatening to drown everyone and everything civilized people value.

Wall seems to suggest that at some point in our development as a sentient race, we turned from drawing on cave walls the things we had seen to painting the things we wished to see: from the purely descriptive to the prescriptive. When does description become imposition and when are they the same? Which comes first in innovative science and art, imagination or experience? How are memory, identity and ideas intertwined? To what degree have we become obsessed with creating the appropriate lenses through which to examine images of ourselves and the surrounding universe before we can even hope to identify and understand human relationships and the natural world.

'Picasso,' writes Wall in this relatively short, highly readable, yet extremely substantial novel, 'became the emblematic figure of artistic genius for our time, as Einstein became the image of the scientific variety. A simple vignette of their faces is enough to signify their meaning: their physiognomies are so potent, words are not required. Their appearances have become signs.'

Wall's curiosity about the purposes, personal, psychic and political, to which we put our pictures focuses itself through his cast's complicated, sometimes surprising relationships and a plot which develops a whole set of inter-related ideas.

Within the context of an emotionally engaging, fast-paced and absorbing story of character, Wall has succeeded in exploring many of the most interesting ideas of the late 20th and early 21st centuries, yet he never strays into mere abstraction and all his observations are anchored in the maze-like relationships of a well-drawn cast of characters. The book's dramatic and very moving denouement cleverly brings together all his themes and reveals the truth behind the mysteries which make *Sylvie's Riddle* such a thoroughly satisfying page-turner.

# ■ Sexton Blake, Detective

An Introduction to George Mann's *Sexton Blake, Detective*

**From the Snowbooks edition, 2009**

Does Sexton Blake still exist? Almost every day I receive letters from my chums asking me this question. It serves to show the great enthusiasm which the great detective has aroused in the minds of the readers of our new serial, *Sexton Blake in the Congo*, as well as of our weekly complete novels which appear in *The Union Jack*. Well, then, the great detective does exist, and very much so, as members of the criminal profession know to their cost. He is occasionally to be seen in his office, the whereabouts of which I am not permitted to disclose, other than to say that it is situated less than five miles from Charing Cross. Another thing I am not permitted to state is his name, for obvious reasons, he does not practice professionally under the name of Sexton Blake.

—*The Boys' Friend*, New series, Vol. 6, Issue 301, 3 December 1907

Sexton Blake still exists, of course. In fact, it's impossible for him to die from natural causes, as readers will discover, if not from this collection, then from the next book of Blake stories, written by George Mann, Mark Hodder and myself, which hopes to offer readers a few more cases pinched from the famous Index and given a touch of extra melodrama. He and several of his contemporaries, among them Tinker, Inspector Coutts, Mrs Bardell and Pedro the Bloodhound, are as incapable of fading away as the likes of Biggles, Just William, Tarzan, Nancy Drew or Doctor Who. Blake's longevity is considerably greater than Bond's, though there are people I know who can prove conclusively from the records that not only is Bond merely Blake with a few minor details changed but that Blake is evidently a direct descendant of Sir Percy Blakeney (otherwise the infamous 'Scarlet Pimpernel') as Wold Newton followers will know. Moreover, there's plenty of evidence that since the 1970s, and in spite of his disrespectful 'resurrection' via recent wireless broadcasts, Blake has been living quietly in legal wedlock with a well-known retired adventuress whose feelings for him were often hinted at in the fictional versions of his adventures, also culled from the Index, which appeared in a host of publications including, of course, *The Union Jack* and *Sexton Blake Library* which ran most of the stories collected here. How his editors have presented him and the way in which his chroniclers depicted him has depended as much on his anticipated audience as the fashion of his day. George Mann has done a superb job in showing how Blake matured, in fiction at least, over the years.

The first author to be commissioned to write Blake's memoirs, once Amalgamated Press had secured the rights to publish his adventures in fictional form, was Harry Blythe. Blythe received nine guineas for his trouble but my guess is that his work was found unsatisfactory by the real 'Blake' (who had received a considerable fee and signed a complicated contract with AP) and it would take a while before a good team of writers was assembled who could be relied upon to present him as something at least close to the truth, even if the long, boring aspects of detective work were often cut out in favour of an unlikely piece of action.

This early history can be read either online on Mark Hodder's Blakiana website (www.sextonblake.co.uk) or in the previous compilation published by Wordsworth (2009). On the website you will not only find information about all the main characters and authors but there is even a layout of Blake's house.

As well as the pleasure of reading these stories, many of which are superior to better known thrillers of their day, we also have our curiosity satisfied about the earliest years of popular modernism. Editors', authors' and readers' tastes were all reflected in those stories which help act as a barometer of the tastes, attitudes and popular feelings through the British Empire from the late 19th century to the late 20th and into our present period. They offer a flavour of the times and form a record of how public attitudes changed quite radically in some ways and scarcely changed at all in others and especially how attitudes of writers and public alike were transformed on many levels as the idea of Empire faded into the idea of Commonwealth and we became a very different people.

George Orwell predicted that everyone who grew up reading the 'story papers' would be a ripe candidate for fascism. As it happened, I was one of those candidates (perhaps a little later than most) and, while they might have called me a woolly-minded liberal (because I supported the Race Relations Act) or a pie-in-the-sky idealist (because I like being a European), nobody has yet to accuse me of being a ranting member of the BNP. It's always hard to know what to do with the language one finds in popular fiction republished for the pleasure of the reader. It's true the language in some of those early Blakes makes them subject to modern editing without losing the flavour of the stories. To leave such language out altogether would be to give a distorted view of how Blake stories reflected their era. Popular fiction offers an unselfconscious record of public tastes and when it disappears, the barometer itself is lost.

That through the 1890s and early 1900s the editorial staff of Amalgamated Press (now IPC) took quite a long time to decide how to present Blake and to what kind of public is evident from the early stories reprinted here. George Mann has done a superb job in selecting work which is not only a good reflection of what was being published but which was good in its own right. All so-called pulp fiction suffers from the speed at which it is written. You will sometimes find repeated words in sentences; slightly contradictory statements being made; a tendency to finish the plot in haste at breakneck speed. Yet pulp fiction's very rate of production, the work of editors and writers able to think (and write) literally on their feet is what gives it enduring vitality and remains an inspiration to those of us who believe that fiction should not only take chances and catch the mood of its time, it should also never be frightened of seeming (or indeed being) vulgar. Vulgarity is inclined to endure, especially when there other sturdy elements in the mix. That is why we continue to find the adventures of Sexton Blake entertaining, invigorating and, I have to say it, educational to those of us who want an insight into the popular thinking of the past.

In those years before AP were sure where to aim their Blake stories we saw him go from one of the many stiff-collared detecting gents aimed at audiences hungry for more Holmes-like cases and presented as they might appear in such respectable magazines as *The Strand, Pearson's* or *The London*, bought very much for fiction by the likes of Arthur Morrison, Baroness Orczy, Joseph Conrad, HG Wells, GK Chesterton or Jack London, accompanied by solid wash drawings of the protagonists. In Blake's case, his clash with the evil Marston Hume, first of his enemies with a notable personality, by the excellent and mysterious Michael Storm, were amongst the earliest to be presented in this way, but clearly he was found to be popular with the boys who bought the massive bedsheet size weeklies AP published, including *Boys' Herald, Boys' Realm* and *Boys' Friend*, which ran long serials containing most of the hallmarks of the boys adventure fiction of the day, including a great deal of jocular badinage and slapstick between characters (much of it borrowed from Talbot Baines Reed, Kipling's Stalky stories and

Wodehouse's Wrykyn tales) and a set of recurring stereotypes, such as brave captains of the cricket team, fat boys, evil bullies and various members of racial minorities who usually turned out to be 'white through and through' at the end of their story. Tinker, Blake's young assistant, frequently found himself at these schools in the early days as did poor Nipper, assistant to Nelson Lee (Blake's closest successful clone), who found himself and his boss pretty much permanently at St Frank's, (Greyfriars' closest rival) written by perhaps the greatest survivor of the pre-war Blake era, Edwy Searles Brooks, whose revamped Blakes (with Waldo the Wonderman transformed into Norman Conquest) were still appearing in hardcover into the 1960s.

Authors who turned out probably as many school stories as Blake adventures were William Murray Graydon and Cecil Hayter. They belonged to what was essentially a different age. There is something deliciously crazed about their stories if you can get over the racialism. Hayter's Africa is populated by alligators, emus and the fauna and flora of at least two continents. There's a surreal atmosphere to his landscapes, while his 'natives' appear to come from similar territory. I'm sure I'm not the first to note that the Inari, whose treasure is sought in the story reprinted here[1], seem to have a lot more in common with a lost tribe of Incas than Lobangu's Zulus.

After *Union Jack* became 'Sexton Blake's Own Paper' the juvenile aspects of the stories gradually disappeared, although a few of the characters who had hung over from the early days with cut-price copies of the likes of Quatermain and Umslopogaas (Losely and Lobangu) continued to stay on in somewhat more sophisticated versions. Andrew Murray's Hon. John Lawless[2] (the spelling changed after the first few stories) was one of the best of a long line of gentleman crooks/adventurers to pit their wits against Blake. Hornung's cricketing cracksman Raffles, taken over by Barry Perowne, would be one of the last to be written for the SBL in the late '30s, reprinted in the 1950s. But the imperial bluebloods would gradually give way to more plebian characters. Again, the pleasure of reading the stories is increased by the way in which they act as a literary barometer, giving us an excellent idea of changing patterns not only in entertainment but also in popular thinking. I find it fascinating to trace the change in public taste as Blake moves into more familiar versions of our times. The writers fall into roughly two groups—those who wrote in the manner of wholesome periodicals for healthy (imperial) boys and those who brought a modern sensibility to the likes of *Union Jack* as the First World War loomed. We can see

---

1 *The Mystery of the Inari Treasure*
2 Originally 'Lawliss'. See *The Boundary Raiders*

the end of the old and the beginning of the new in these stories as a breed of younger writers began to emerge.

Andrew Murray had a knack for creating series characters and another of his best villains was the malevolent Professor Kew who, in *Tinker's Terrible Test*, plotted a dastardly revenge on Blake's assistant. One of Murray's few superiors as a writer was Edwy Searles Brooks (whom I knew and admired as a boy). Brooks also created a group of superb villains and adventuresses who populated Blake's golden age, which had its beginnings around 1910 and had faded away by the early 1940s. Michael Storm, who created George Marsden Plummer, a villain with extraordinary longevity, passed the character on to George Hamilton Teed, a Canadian writer who allegedly met Storm's widow on a boat. She suggested he 'ghost' her dead husband's stories. *The Great Bank Fraud*, however, is by neither writer, but by Lewis Carlton, who wrote a good number of Blake stories featuring Plummer.[3]

Teed is represented here by two stories, the first of which is the splendid full length novel *The Sacred Sphere*, featuring, together with Wu Ling and Dr Huxton Rymer, perhaps his finest adventuress Mademoiselle Yvonne Cartier. These stories were written, as the title pages announced, to 'Appeal to All Tastes, All Ages—Either Sex'.

Better than any of the Blake regulars Teed could suggest sexual attraction and tension in a few lines and there's no doubt that readers of these stories understood exactly what was happening between Yvonne Cartier and Sexton Blake. This steamy stuff had little in common with the wholesome stories of manly comradeship written for clean-living young chaps advertised and serialised in *The Boys' Friend*. I wonder how many readers of, say, *The Boys' Friend Library* retired blushing to their beds with, instead of a Hayter *BFL*, a Teed *Sexton Blake Library*.

It was not long before Teed's real identity was revealed.[4] He worked as a Blake regular for several years and then did a long spell of war service. He had become one of the most prolific (and arguably the best) Blake authors,

---

3 After the mysterious disappearance of Michael Storm (aka Ernest Sempill), a number of Blake's chroniclers continued to write tales of George Marsden Plummer, the corrupt ex-Scotland Yard man, including Lewis Carlton and JW Bobin, before Teed eventually reinvented the character in the 1920s after returning from his service during the war.

4 Legend has it that after a period 'ghosting' stories for the late Michael Storm, Teed fell out with Mrs Storm and approached the editors at Amalgamated Press to declare himself as the true author of the works in question. The editor at the time did not believe Teed's apparently wild claims, and challenged him to prove his case. Teed then seated himself at a nearby typewriter and hammered out the first few chapters of a new Blake tale. The editor was astonished and consequently bought the piece, and Teed went on to become a staple writer for the press.

giving us Prince Wu Ling, the intellectual blue blood with whose ambitions to reunite China Teed was clearly sympathetic, Huxton Rymer, the brilliant doctor who had set aside his work on cancer to pursue a life of crime, often in the company of the likes of Marie Galante, the Voodoo Queen, or Vali Mata Vali, the French songstress turned crook, and many more, including perhaps the finest, sexiest, bravest and most beautiful bunch of adventuresses in all of popular fiction, among them Yvonne Cartier, Roxane Harcourt and June Severance.

Already, in 1915, Teed was considered the best of the Blake chroniclers, chosen to write a Wu Ling adventure, *The Yellow Tiger*, for the very first issue of *Sexton Blake Library*. Wu Ling appeared in the same year as Fu Manchu and in my opinion is a far better, subtler and more interesting character than Rohmer's. What's more, Teed did far more with Wu Ling over the years than Rohmer, perhaps because Teed had sympathy for the Chinese cause. After Yvonne had sided so thoroughly with Blake that it might be suspected they were secretly married, another great femme fatale was required of him and Roxane Harcourt's determination to be avenged on those who had destroyed her father and mother might have seemed like a rerun of the Yvonne series in shorter skirts, but there are subtle differences between the women which reflect the times when they came into being.

Although not exactly a lefty, Teed wrote stories often in marked contrast, say, to Gwyn Evans's. Reading Evans sometimes makes me think of Rex Warner's *The Aerodrome*, for the undoubted sense of Merrie Englande he could conjure up. Equally, his racial views could be nasty. He spent some time as a reporter in Palestine, and I think revealed how the usual awful British tendency to partition caused quite a few of the conflicts still concerning us. I find that reading Evans in context gives me a strong idea of what it must have been like to have overheard the average British official after his fifth gin sling at almost every officer's bar around the Empire in, say, 1935. On the other hand, Evans was without doubt one of Blake's best story-tellers and his Christmas stories were much looked forward to. *Suspended from Duty!* is another of the stories reprinted here which shows that fraudulent financiers and bent coppers are by no means new to our own day. At his best Evans did much to humanise both Inspector Jim Coutts and Mrs Martha Bardell and knew how to use the Blake regulars to their greatest advantage.

In the eyes of a number of Blake enthusiasts, neither Evans nor Teed wrote Blake's greatest adventures but Anthony Skene[5], a government

---

5  The pseudonym of George N Phillips

surveyor who travelled the country dictating his stories to his secretary (also rumored to be his mistress). Skene's great character was one of the few to have an original hardback novel (sans Blake) devoted to him. The novel was reprinted relatively recently in a superb edition by the enthusiastic non-profit house of Savoy, who only publish books that are obscure and which they love to read. The novel, originally published in 1936, was called simply *Monsieur Zenith* and recorded the adventures of a character I borrowed for my Elric stories, written when I still worked for SBL, who became one of the most influential of them all.

Skene based Zenith on a somewhat less glamorous, rather slovenly character he'd spotted in an ABC Tea Rooms some time during the First World War. Adding several Demon Lover/Byronic extras to the man he'd seen, making him wear full evening dress on all occasions (when not say disguised as Mrs Bardell), making him play the fiddle like Paganini and giving him an anti-social attitude and a drug habit to rival Holmes's or James Dean's, Skene produced an enduring anti-hero in Monsieur Zenith when the Albino debuted in *Union Jack* with *A Duel to the Death*. Like Tinker and occasionally Blake, Zenith occasionally told his stories in first person, as, in part he does in *A Mystery in Motley*, revealing a tortured, courageous, existential soul. In *A Mystery in Motley* Skene, as he often did, somehow picks a title offering a clue into character as much as plot. Perhaps that's why this is one of my favourite Zenith adventures, where he also flirts wonderfully with Julia Fortune.

Zenith is at his best when there is clearly sexual attraction between himself and a member of the opposite sex, whether she be a poor crippled girl, an ethereal princess or a resourceful secret service agent. These Zenith stories remain perhaps the most popular of all and the first edition of *Monsieur Zenith* is almost impossible to find. I believe there are only four known copies, two in private hands. I'm glad incidentally to see in the first Zenith story, *A Duel to the Death*, that Blake's Grey Panther is still an aeroplane, no doubt close to making its transition into Blake's Rolls-Royce, which takes part in so many of Blake's great car chases. Zenith was one of the first real moderns to appear in Sexton Blake stories and his fascination for all types of inventions, including TV, often has the exhilaration of a Futurist.

Another popular writer, creator of The Criminals' Confederation, The Bat (perhaps the first of many precursors to the 'Dark Knight'), Professor Reece, and several other major characters, was Robert Murray whose *Lord of the Ape Men* is actually a lot less like an Edgar Rice Burroughs Tarzan story than it sounds, though Dr Satira has more of the qualities of an American horror pulp than most Blake villains. The *UJ* or *SBL* contained a few jungle lords raised by various mammals, showing first Kipling's influence and later Burroughs's, but Murray's isn't one of them. The story has the Gothic atmosphere which ran in an unbroken direct line from the earliest penny dreadfuls to so many AP/Fleetway publications well into the '60s and, if you count *2000 AD*, beyond! Stories of macabre terror were reprinted as the only text pages in IPC comics. This brooding atmosphere also haunts *The Gnomid*, the story announced originally as Gilbert Chester's[6] masterpiece.

Chester wrote Blakes into the 1950s and saw all the story papers turned into comics. Blake himself appeared in comic form more than once and for a long time was a regular in *Knockout*, drawn by Eric Parker, whose distinctive style, influenced perhaps by Fred Bennett, an earlier Blake artist and AP regular, came to be associated with all readers of *UJ*, *SBL* and *Detective Weekly* and whose last Blake covers appeared in the early 1960s. I had suggested commissioning them and sat in awe as I watched Parker order up artboard, poster colours and inks from the Fleetway stationery department and proceed to paint the covers directly onto the boards without even preparing a sketch! His depictions of M. Zenith remain for me the only true portraits ever made of the great albino.

I find it depressing that attempts to introduce Blake to a more recent public via radio have reduced the character to a risible cipher, without humour or character. It's the easiest thing in the world to make fun of attitudes and manners which have gone out of common currency and presenting characters like Blake in broad parody demeans, it seems to me, everyone concerned. If any reader believes that the great Blake writers were unaware of the humorous aspects of their thrillers, *The Next Move* should dispel that impression. Four of the top authors—Evans, Robert Murray, Teed and Skene—were asked to write a 'round robin' story. Teed set up the first episode, challenging his fellow writers to explain, for instance, the mystery of a London underground river, the prisoner in the punt, the brightly dressed organ grinder's monkey (deceased) and Roxane's presence all in the same opening. Gwyn Evans's next episode has lines which might have come from a *Carry On* or *Monty Python* script.

There's little doubt that tongues were firmly in cheeks by the time we were reading lines like *'Anastasia's gone!' he burst out wildly. 'She's gone, and with her my combinations!'* nor that Evans was not exactly serious when

6  The pseudonym of HH Clifford Gibbons

he introduced in his second chapter a dead parrot (a close relative to the Norwegian Blue).

As well as being a very enjoyable and well told story, *The Next Move* gives us an idea what it might have been like to spend an evening in The George or The Punch or any of a score of Fleet Street pubs with a bunch of Blake regulars who, while probably not being quite the Jacobean characters Blakian apocrypha makes them out to be, were clearly great company who enjoyed their work, respected their readers and at the same time had a lot of fun earning what were for their day very substantial fees (most of which went over the counters of the Fleet Street drinkers).

I was lucky to be a teenage journalist at the very end of that era when certain writers, especially the great Jack Trevor Story (*The Trouble With Harry*, *Live Now, Pay Later*), had to be watched fairly carefully to see what they tried to slip into their stories, but the tales told about them (and which they told, too) were never quite as good as the reality. I was there when Story explained to an editor who accused him of exaggeration that it was the prosaic stuff which had to be invented and the stuff which seemed impossibly unlikely which was the flat truth. He was right. In his case at least.

How many times Gwyn Evans smuggled his tiny girl-friend in a suitcase past the suspicious eyes of hotel managers we don't know, any more than we know how often editors were fooled into paying for stories by manuscripts whose first top few pages were typed while the rest were blank, but we can be sure all the tricks you hear about were tried once. I know, because I tried several of them myself.

As a boy I would send off a weekly postal order to 'story paper' dealers for copies of magazines like *Union Jack*, which I would buy in the order they had originally appeared. My original interest had been in PG Wodehouse and then in the library I found Brooks, whose style and often his characters had much of Wodehouse's flair. From Brooks's hardbacks it was on to his Blakes. His best writing was crisp and snappy, and travelled well through the 20th century, as I'm sure it would travel now. Then I discovered Zenith and my loyalties wavered a little as I sent off for stories with titles like *Marked By The Leopard Men*, which depicted the activities of the Tyneside Leopard men, whose leader Zenith was, and had Blake and the Albino duelling with rapiers in a Gateshead pit.

Throughout my boyhood I did my best to collect all the Waldo and Zenith stories I could come by. Then I extended my loyalties to include Teed's characters. I have yet to find some, in particular those offering the adventures of Mlle Yvonne and Huxton Rymer, and I dream of the day when all the great Blake characters are made available in their own reprinted anthologies of stories. Meanwhile we have this enthusiastically and carefully made collection to offer a taste of what helped influence writers like myself and others from Ian Fleming to Alan Moore. We chose to tap in to a mythological cycle Dorothy Sayers believed to be the nearest thing to a national epic we could ever hope to find.

I know I shall probably never read them all as they grow scarcer and scarcer. Some of those I own are already close to turning to dust as fast as enthusiasts can create electronic files of their copies. With luck there are still complete sets in some libraries or even private collections. Meanwhile, the best most of us can hope for are enlightened publishers and editors who will put as many of the stories back into print as possible.

I am sure there will be readers like me who develop a taste if not for Blake himself, then at least for certain series by the best writers. It's true that tastes have changed and attitudes improved but at their best these stories are great escapism. I'm sure, too, they'll continue to inform and influence those like me who take pleasure in learning how our immediate ancestors thought and what, instead of a good TV thriller (which so many of these stories resemble) would send them to bed happy.

George Mann has done us all a great service in assembling this collection. I have a feeling there are already a few more keen Blake fans out there. I wish you hours of enjoyable reading. And if you like this book, why not ask a chum to order a copy for themselves? If Sexton Blake is making a comeback, then the very least we can do is cheer him on!

# ■ A Review of *The Manual of Detection* by Jedediah Berry

**From the *Guardian*, 22nd August 2009**

If rural nostalgia fuels the continuing appeal of Trollope or Tolkien, then its urban equivalent is most commonly found in Dickens pastiches such as Philip Pullman's *Ruby in the Smoke*, in Holly Black's gritty fairy stories and in the steampunk genre. These days, you can barely pick up a speculative fantasy without finding a zeppelin or a steam-robot on the cover. Containing few punks and a good many posh ladies and gents, most of these stories are better described as steam operas. *The Manual of Detection* formalises many of the genre's themes and includes a dash of cyberpunk noir.

Cyberpunks were what the likes of Bruce Sterling and William Gibson called themselves when first signalling their break with conventional SF. What identified cyberpunk was a sophisticated interest in current events, a guess that the Pacific Rim might soon become the centre of world politics, a keen curiosity about the possibilities of post-PC international culture and a love of noir detective fiction. Characteristically, cyberpunk revived the noir thriller and might as easily be considered a development of the mystery as of science fiction. Sterling and Gibson's *The Difference Engine* was an early example of cyberpunk merging into steampunk, proposing a Victorian world with Babbage computers and airships. Airships also appear in *The Golden Compass* and *Watchmen*, among other recent movies: they signify you are in an alternate reality.

Steampunk reached its final burst of brilliant deliquescence with Pynchon's *Against the Day* and his Airship Boys. Once the wide world gets hold of an idea, however, it can only survive through knowing irony. Its tools, its icons, its angle of attack are absorbed into the cultural mainstream. The genre has started to write about itself, the way *Cat Ballou* or *Blazing Saddles* addressed the western. Steampunk no longer examines context and history but now looks ironically at its own roots, tropes and cliches.

Thankfully, it does it in a book as good as *The Manual of Detection*. Jedediah Berry has an ear well tuned to the styles of the detective story, and can reproduce atmosphere with loving skill.

The city in which this mystery is set is never named. There are brooding skyscrapers. It's always raining. And there appears to be no public authority save the monumental, stratified Detective Agency where Charles Unwin works as a clerk, filing reports for the sleuth to whom he's assigned, in this case the legendary Travis Sivart, famous for solving cases such as 'The Oldest Murdered Man' and 'The Man Who Stole November Twelfth'. Unwin is fascinated by a woman he sees at Central Terminal station, where he is recruited by a detective. Someone is murdered. A brooding sense of doom dogs him as he reluctantly uncovers not only a new and terrifying case but realises many earlier famous cases were not properly solved. In a world suddenly populated by somnambulists, everyone has their alarm clock stolen. The whole city is dreaming or falling asleep at odd times. Even the hallowed Agency Manual, as Unwin discovers, contains mysteries. He encounters a femme fatale who might be on his side; a nightclub singer; two sinister former conjoined twins who drive a gaudy steam-truck; a malevolent carnival proprietor; a thieves' kitchen. Larger threats and mysteries increase.

Helped by an old museum guard and his own plucky girl assistant (every detective is issued with one), and taking his life and sanity in his hands, Unwin proves a dogged investigator. Soon, he is forced to question the truth of the Manual itself. Despite the grim, unnamed city where Unwin constantly receives contradictory or absurd instructions, this engrossing book isn't at all like Kafka. By the end, almost too many mysteries are explained. And then, at last, it stops raining and, with the novel's final brilliant revelation, the sun comes out.

# ■ *Paraxis* Introduction

From *Paraxis* 01, April 2011

For far too many years, as human consciousness modified to process the products of its own restless invention, academia and literary circles argued about what to call certain developments in modern fiction. Karl Marx proposed that in the future we would all be reading what he called 'contemporary fairy tales', produced to pass the time for people who no longer looked to fiction for anything but insubstantial entertainment. He suggested that we wouldn't need realists like Balzac, Dickens, Flaubert, Tolstoy, Zola or others to look into human society or the hearts of individuals and would prefer to be entertained by what Hugo Gernsback called the 'marvel tale', a sort of roller-coaster ride of the mind, not unlike the mediaeval Peninsula Romance.

I think Marx was anticipating the kind of fantasy fiction which developed almost completely without content of any kind and which these days crowds our media, deriving more from board games and e-games than it does from individual imagination. Much science fiction merely seeks to suspend disbelief and enable an individual to achieve maximum escape, yet pretends to a higher intention. A great deal of this is found in the deeply nostalgic form of steampunk, a form deriving to some degree from the earlier 'cyberpunk' which looked at the impact of computers, in particular, on the human psyche.

Steampunk, produced early on by cyberpunkers Sterling and Gibson, could examine the kind of culture imagined by our ancestors and, in *The Difference Engine*, understand the thinking which shaped our present. I specifically addressed our continuing nostalgia for empire, especially the British, in my own *Warlord of the Air*, attacking the sentimentality at the root of Fabian thinking. I hoped to show how we were still not rid of dreams of a world-dominating Anglo-Saxon alliance and how those dreams so swiftly turned into nightmares.

When it sometimes challenged interpretations of root industrial cultures and historical events, steampunk acted as a kind of intervention into the attitudes and ideas of early 20th century speculative writers. Its continuing social and historical interpretations of the world can still produce the odd novel of great merit and skill but generally reveals itself as being on a par with the least robust forms of commercial entertainment: nostalgic fashion. At its worst it produces a wretched kind of popular fiction, typically pretending to tackle serious subjects while actually supporting the notion that a simplified past, reduced to a superficial style, offers an interpretation of contemporary society more valid than our day-to-day experience. I think it tells some fundamental lies by confirming that the reader's own primitive analysis reflects reality. This sort of fiction is a form of anti-art in which, rather than examine apparent truth in order to separate it from reality, the author constructs methods of verifying the often complex lies we are told by those who would commodify us for their own profit and power.

Nostalgia for a vanished innocence is one of the chief manipulative tools used in all societies whether for selling bread or electing presidents. It is invoked by most quasi-political movements from the Taliban to US Tea Partiers, from neoliberal to right libertarian demagogues. This yearning for a vanished Eden, while it can be satisfied easily with faux-history and the like, is probably at near-saturation in the multi-volumed xeroxes I once referred to as phat phantasy and has artistic or intellectual substance almost in direct contrast to the width of its spines.

There seems to me to be even less good fantasy and science fiction than there was when Ballard and I, for instance, took our inspiration from the form. In those days the likes of Bradbury, Pohl/Kornbluth, Dick, Bester and Sheckley filled the pages of *Galaxy* magazine with speculation about mainly cultural developments in a world whose economies and strategies were becoming increasingly alarming. We are now living in an authentic version of the world they identified.

The *Galaxy* writers understood themselves to be writing about their present—the abandonment of the inner cities, the building of protected suburbs, the psychopathology of a species increasingly deprived of direct experience or access to verifiable information. Of course, that wasn't all they wrote about, sometimes employing a language as thoroughly coded as that used by their Soviet contemporaries.

In the 1950s we had to be afraid of McCarthy as well as Stalin and Khrushchev. That was why so many of us around the world, rejecting the generic literary fiction of our day, looked towards science fiction (as magic realists looked to myth and folklore) as the most authentic fiction reflecting our experience. I have spoken to Nobel laureates who drew their inspiration from the SF/fantasy of the 1960s and '70s, whose admiration for its writers was as enthusiastic and sincere as for any modernist in the canon. One friend envies my early pulp paperbacks as I envy his Pulitzer. I am today by no means the only contemporary writer to have both literary and genre awards. Literary visionary fiction is now the form of fiction best positioned to take us into the next decades of the century. As in the rest of the world, we are at a threshold when we can determine which way we, as readers and writers, go.

Perhaps because we no longer work in ciphers but can write pretty much as freely as we like, there has been what seems to me a lack of focus in younger writers' approach to their subject matter; anger at perceived injustice seems to be lacking, sentimental or unfocussed. A fiction which was initially attractive precisely because it responded rapidly to events as they were happening, now frequently seems to have inherited the worst traits of internalised modernist fiction. Perhaps it has imitated the methods of the 'mainstream' so thoroughly it has become the poison rather than the antidote. That is why, I think, we need as many short fiction platforms as possible, to rediscover the attraction of imaginative fiction and why it offered such a robust alternative to the majority of other kinds of fiction— why Sartre and Vian, De Beauvoir and Algren, DeLillo, Vonnegut, Pynchon and Chabon, among others, read it and liked it, why William Burroughs, one of the great innovative visionary talents of his age, chose to borrow extensively from what he read in *Galaxy* and *New Worlds*.

Happily, a revival seems to be in the offing with editors like Massie and Hedgecock encouraging authors to move away from what was in danger of becoming a kind of third-rate modernism and return the human imagination to the apex of the arts.

The stories collected here should show some of the directions in which imaginative fiction can go as we begin again to search out some good ways of meeting reality head on.

# ■ Frances Bret Harte

**From *Book Collectors' News*, September 1956**

Francis Bret Harte usually known as Bret Harte, was born at Albany in the State of New York, on 25th August, 1839.[1] He was of Dutch descent.

His father, a professor of Greek at the Albany College, died during Harte's boyhood.

Mrs Harte was left penniless and as soon as young Frank was able to work he set out to earn his keep in a big New York store. When seventeen he left the city for California, taking his mother with him. From San Francisco he trudged on foot to the mines of Sonora, and there, falling back upon his father's calling when alive, became a teacher.

Here Bret Harte was thrown in contact with the mining community of the Far West which had provided so much material for his pen. Abandoning the attempt to train their offspring, Bret consorted with the parents and tried his luck in the mines—no luck so he had a go at a variety of jobs until he found his true calling—printer, express-messenger, Secretary of the San Francisco Mint and finally—Editor.

In the newspaper office of Eureka he followed the craft of compositor and his earliest familiarity with type was acquired in setting up articles and essays of his own, contributed to the pages of the 'Eureka' newspapers. Here was the first gleam of coming success. Bret Harte must have risen rapidly in the confidence of the proprietor of the *Eureka Journal* for during the absence of its editor he was left in charge. After writing an article denouncing the citizens of Eureka for their massacre of the Pimas Indians in a recent uprising, Bret Harte thought it wise to leave for other parts. Such mistaken sympathies as he exhibited rendered him offensive to the citizens and patriots of Eureka; so he retraced his steps to San Francisco to become

---

1  One writer of an essay on Harte stated that Harte was born 1837.

editor of the *Golden Era* in which articles and essays by him frequently appeared—but nothing, as yet, fiction. What had become of his mother by this time I do not know.

Harte soon left the *Era* to start his own paper and he became founder/editor of *The Californian*. He began his career as a writer of fiction with a series of "Condensed Novels"—travesties on well-known works of fiction. The best in my opinion is his *The Haunted Man* after Charles Dickens's *The Christmas Carol*. Other writers' styles and books he imitated were Charlotte Brontë, Fenimore Cooper, Belle Boyd (an American writer popular at the time) Frenchmen: Hugo, Michelet and Dumas, Captain Marryat, Wilkie Collins, Charles Reade and many other American and European writers. These were published weekly in *The Californian* and were—to use a well-worn cliché—an instant success. The stories were accompanied, in some cases at least, with cartoons of the period and published in book form a year later in 1867 under the collective title of *Sensation Novels, Condensed*.

In 1868 *The Californian*, its sales dropping considerably, folded. Luckily in the same year the earliest considerable literary magazine of the Pacific Coast was launched and Mr FB Harte was asked to edit it. He accepted and all of his work for the period he acted as editor was published in the *Overland Monthly*. The tales, sketches and poems which he contributed during the following years attracted attention not only in the United States but in Great Britain and Europe.

Harte was one of the earliest masters of the short story. His Californian tales were found to be something quite different from the ordinary run of short stories, in fact they were to start an entirely new trend in fiction.

Like Mark Twain (Samuel L Clemens), Harte was way ahead of his time in many phases of his writing, and his stories can be read today without dating the slightest.

In 'The Luck of Roaring Camp', written in 1868, 'The Outcasts of Poker Flat' (1869) and later 'How Santa Claus Came to Simpson's Bar', 'Barker's Luck', 'Mliss', 'The Yellow Dog', 'A Passage in the Life of Mr John Oakhurst' and the verses 'Plain Language from Truthful James' he combined humour, pathos, and powerful character drawing. It is impossible to list all of his stories here, it is sufficient to say that every story had this amazing gift of characterisation, this insight into human nature, threaded through it. Although some are better than others, they are, without doubt, all fine stories. Harte never had his 'off moments' as many popular authors have.

Only a small fraction of the English public has ever heard of Bret Harte but he is recognised among literary circles as America's Dickens, and rightly so. In Bret Harte, that new land of mining gulches, gamblers, unassimilated Asiatics, and picturesque and novel landscapes, had at last found its true delineator.

A number of films and stage plays have been made of Harte's stories. Most of them, alas, were mere 'second features'—the sponsors having the clay in the shape of a Harte story but failing to mould it as it should be moulded.

The film classic *Stagecoach*, starring John Wayne and shown recently on BBC television, was based on some of Harte's characters. Most of them were taken from 'The Outcasts of Poker Flat'.